OREGON
REVISED STATUTES 2017

VOLUME 1

COURTS
OREGON RULES OF CIVIL PROCEDURE

Revised August 20, 2018

OREGON LAW LIBRARY

Table of Contents

TITLE 1 COURTS OF RECORD; COURT OFFICERS; JURIES 3

Chapter 1 — Courts and Judicial Officers Generally 3
Chapter 2 — Supreme Court; Court of Appeals 23
Chapter 3 — Circuit Courts Generally 26
Chapter 4 (Former Provisions) 37
Chapter 5 — County Courts (Judicial Functions) 38
CHAPTER 6 [Reserved for expansion]_____ 39
Chapter 7 — Records and Files of Courts 39
Chapter 8 — Court Officers and District Attorneys 42
Chapter 9 — Attorneys; Law Libraries 50
Chapter 10 — Juries 66
Chapter 11 (Former Provisions) 72

TITLE 2 PROCEDURE IN CIVIL PROCEEDINGS 73

Chapter 12 — Limitations of Actions and Suits 73
Chapter 13 (Former Provisions) Parties; Class Actions 80
Chapter 14 — Jurisdiction; Venue; Change of Judge 81
Chapter 15 — Choice of Laws 84
Chapter 16 (Former Provisions) Pleadings; Motions; Orders; Process; Notices; Papers .. 88
Chapter 17 — Compromise; Settlement 90
Chapter 18 — Judgments 93
Chapter 19 — Appeals 159
Chapter 20 — Attorney Fees; Costs and Disbursements 170
Chapter 21 — State Court Fees 175
Chapter 22 — Bonds and Other Security Deposits 185
Chapter 23 (Former Provisions) 186
Chapter 24 — Enforcement and Recognition of Foreign Judgments; Foreign-Money Claims .. 189
Chapter 25 — Support Enforcement 195
Chapter 26 (Former Provisions) 222
Chapter 27 (Former Provisions) 223

TITLE 3 REMEDIES AND SPECIAL ACTIONS AND PROCEEDINGS 223

Chapter 28 — Declaratory Judgments; Certification of Questions of Law 223
Chapter 29 (Former Provisions) 226
Chapter 30 — Actions and Suits in Particular Cases 229
Chapter 32 (Former Provisions) 278
Chapter 33 — Special Proceedings and Procedures 279
Chapter 34 — Writs 288
Chapter 35 — Eminent Domain; Public Acquisition of Property 297
Chapter 36 — Mediation and Arbitration 307
Chapter 37 — Receivership 330

TITLE 4 EVIDENCE AND WITNESSES 339

Chapter 40 — Evidence Code 339
Chapter 41 — Evidence Generally 357
Chapter 42 — Execution, Formalities and Interpretation of Writings 362
Chapter 43 — Public Writings 363
Chapter 44 — Witnesses 365
Chapter 45 — Testimony Generally 369

TITLE 5 SMALL CLAIMS DEPARTMENT OF CIRCUIT COURT 376

    CHAPTER 46 — SMALL CLAIMS DEPARTMENT OF CIRCUIT COURT 376

TITLE 6 JUSTICE COURTS 382

    CHAPTER 51 — JUSTICE COURTS; JURISDICTION 382
    CHAPTER 52 — CIVIL ACTIONS 387
    CHAPTER 53 — APPEALS IN CIVIL ACTIONS 392
    CHAPTER 54 — JURIES 394
    CHAPTER 55 — SMALL CLAIMS 395

TITLE 1 COURTS OF RECORD; COURT OFFICERS; JURIES

Chapter   1.   Courts and Judicial Officers Generally
           2.   Supreme Court; Court of Appeals
           3.   Circuit Courts Generally
           5.   County Courts (Judicial Functions)
           7.   Records and Files of Courts
           8.   Court Officers and District Attorneys
           9.   Attorneys; Law Libraries
          10.   Juries

Chapter 1 — Courts and Judicial Officers Generally

2017 EDITION

COURTS AND JUDICIAL OFFICERS GENERALLY

COURTS OF RECORD; COURT OFFICERS; JURIES

COURTS

1.001   State policy for courts

1.002   Supreme Court; Chief Justice as administrative head of judicial department; rules; presiding judges as administrative heads of courts

1.003   Chief Justice's powers to appoint Chief Judge and presiding judges; terms; disapproval of appointment

1.004   Supreme Court rules governing coordination of class actions

1.005   Credit card transactions for fees, security deposits, fines and other court-imposed obligations; rules

1.006   Supreme Court rules

1.007   Judicial Department Revolving Account; uses; sources

1.008   Personnel plan, fiscal plan and property plan

1.009   Judicial Department Operating Account

1.010   Powers of courts in administration of court business and proceedings

1.012   State Court Technology Fund

1.020   Contempt punishment

1.025   Duty of court and court officers to require performance of duties relating to administration of justice; enforcement of duty by mandamus

1.030   Seal; form; custody; affixing

1.040   Sittings of court to be public; when may be private

1.050   Time for decision on submitted questions; certificate of compliance with requirement; penalty for false certificate

1.060   Days for transaction of judicial business; exceptions

1.070   When court deemed appointed for next judicial day

1.080   Place of holding court

1.085   Chief Justice to designate principal location for sitting of courts; alternative sites

1.090   Trial elsewhere than at usual location on agreement of parties

1.110   Adjournment when judge does not attend

1.120   Proceedings unaffected by vacancy in office

1.130   Power to adjourn proceedings

1.140   Manner of addressing application or proceeding to court or judge

1.150   Proceedings to be in English; foreign language translation; rules and procedures

1.160   Means to carry jurisdiction into effect; adoption of suitable process or mode of proceeding

1.171   Powers and duties of presiding judge for judicial district

1.175   Docket priorities

COURT FACILITIES

1.176   Capital improvements to county courthouses; plan; report

1.177   State plan for security, emergency preparedness and business continuity for court facilities; Chief Judicial Marshal; deputy judicial marshals

1.178   State Court Facilities and Security Account

1.180   Advisory committees on court security and emergency preparedness; plans

1.182   Court facilities security accounts; funding; expenditures; reports

OPERATION OF COURTHOUSES

1.185   County to provide courtrooms, offices and jury rooms

1.187   State to provide supplies and personal property for courts

1.188   Surcharge on fines for courthouse

1.189   Courthouse surcharge accounts

(Temporary provisions relating to courthouse capital construction and improvement are compiled as notes following ORS 1.189)

COLLECTION OF COURT ACCOUNTS

1.194   Definitions for ORS 1.194 to 1.200

1.195   Reports on liquidated and delinquent accounts of state courts

1.196   Agreement for reciprocal offsets

1.197   Assignment of liquidated and delinquent accounts to collection agencies; relinquishment of accounts by collection agencies; collections by Department of Revenue

1.198   Exemptions from requirements of ORS 1.197

1.199   Policies and procedures for exempting accounts from requirements of ORS 1.197 and for ceasing collection efforts

1.200   Effect of ORS 1.194 to 1.200 on authority of judge

1.202   Fee for establishing and administering account for judgment that includes monetary obligation; fee for judgment referred for collection

JUDICIAL OFFICERS GENERALLY

1.210   Judicial officer defined

1.212   Oath of office for judges

1.220   Judicial officer or partner acting as attorney

1.230   Powers of a judge out of court

1.240   Powers of judicial officers

1.250   Punishment for contempt

1.260   Powers of judges of Supreme Court, Court of Appeals, Oregon Tax Court and circuit courts; where powers may be exercised

1.270   Powers of other judicial officers; where powers may be exercised

1.290   Leaves of absence

1.300   Senior judge; assignment; duties and powers; compensation and expenses

1.303   Disability of judge; procedures upon receipt by Chief Justice of complaint or information

1.305   Commencement of judicial term of office

INVOLUNTARY RETIREMENT OF JUDGES

1.310   Involuntary retirement of judges for disability; rules

COMMISSION ON JUDICIAL FITNESS AND DISABILITY

1.410   Commission on Judicial Fitness and Disability; term; Senate confirmation

1.415   Powers and duties of commission; rules

1.420   Investigation; hearings; consent to discipline; recommendation; temporary suspension

1.425   Commission proceedings upon receipt of complaint of disability; hearing; physical examination; disposition

1.430   Supreme Court review; censure; order of suspension or removal

1.440   Status of records of proceedings under ORS 1.420 or 1.425

1.450   Status of testimony in proceedings under ORS 1.420 or 1.425

1.460   Judge not to participate in proceedings involving self except in defense

1.470   Service of process; proof; return; witness fees

1.475   Procedure when process not obeyed

1.480   Officers; quorum; compensation and expenses

CITATION AND PETITION FORMS

1.525   Uniform citation and petition forms for certain offenses

REPRESENTATION OF JUDGES BY PRIVATE COUNSEL

1.550   Private counsel for judges

1.560   Procedure for employment of private counsel; terms and conditions

1.570   Claims for compensation of private counsel; approval by State Court Administrator

JUDGES PRO TEMPORE

1.600   Appointment pro tempore to Supreme Court or Court of Appeals; powers and duties

1.605   Compensation and expenses for judges under ORS 1.600

1.615   Appointment pro tempore to tax court or circuit court; powers and duties

1.625   Compensation and expenses for judges under ORS 1.615

1.635   Appointment pro tempore of eligible person to tax court or circuit court

1.645   Transfer, challenge, disqualification, supervision of person appointed under ORS 1.635

1.655   Extension and termination of appointment under ORS 1.635; eligibility to appear as attorney

1.665   Compensation and expenses of persons appointed under ORS 1.635

1.675   Judge pro tempore ineligible to participate in selection or removal of Chief Justice, Chief Judge or presiding judge

COUNCIL ON COURT PROCEDURES

1.725   Legislative findings

1.730   Council on Court Procedures; membership; terms; rules; meetings; expenses of members

1.735   Rules of procedure; limitation on scope and substance; submission of rules to members of bar and Legislative Assembly

1.740   Employment of staff; public hearings

1.745   Laws on civil pleading, practice and procedure deemed rules of court until changed

1.750   Legislative Counsel to publish rules

1.755   Gifts, grants and donations; Council on Court Procedures Account

1.760   Legislative advisory committee

JUDICIAL CONFERENCE

1.810   Judicial conference; membership; officers

1.820   Function of conference

1.830   Meetings

1.840   Annual report

ADVISORY COUNCILS

1.851   Local criminal justice advisory councils

JUSTICE AND MUNICIPAL COURT REGISTRY AND REPORTS

1.855   State Court Administrator to establish registry of justice and municipal courts

1.860   Reports relating to municipal courts and justice courts

COURTS

1.001 State policy for courts. The Legislative Assembly hereby declares that, as a matter of statewide concern, it is in the best interests of the people of this state that the judicial branch of state government, including the appellate, tax and circuit courts, be funded and operated at the state level. The Legislative Assembly finds that state funding and operation of the judicial branch can provide for best statewide allocation of governmental resources according to the actual needs of the people and of the judicial branch by establishing an accountable, equitably funded and uniformly administered system of justice for all the people of this state. [1981 s.s. c.3 §1]

1.002 Supreme Court; Chief Justice as administrative head of judicial department; rules; presiding judges as administrative heads of courts. (1) The Supreme Court is the highest judicial tribunal of the judicial department of government in this state. The Chief Justice of the Supreme Court is the presiding judge of the court and the administrative head of the judicial department of government in this state. The Chief Justice shall exercise administrative authority and supervision over the courts of this state consistent with applicable provisions of law and the Oregon Rules of Civil Procedure. The Chief Justice, to facilitate exercise of that administrative authority and supervision, may:
(a) Make rules and issue orders appropriate to that exercise.
(b) Require appropriate reports from the judges, other officers and employees of the courts of this state and municipal courts.
(c) Pursuant to policies approved by the Judicial Conference of the State of Oregon, assign or reassign on a temporary basis all judges of the courts of this state to serve in designated locations within or without the county or judicial district for which the judge was elected.
(d) Set staffing levels for all courts of the state operating under the Judicial Department and for all operations in the Judicial Department.
(e) Establish time standards for disposition of cases.
(f) Establish budgets for the Judicial Department and all courts operating under the Judicial Department.
(g) Assign or reassign all court staff of courts operating under the Judicial Department.
(h) Pursuant to policies approved by the Judicial Conference of the State of Oregon, establish personnel rules and policies for judges of courts operating under the Judicial Department.
(i) Establish procedures for closing courts in emergencies.
(j) Establish standards for determining when courts are closed for purposes of ORCP 10, ORS 174.120 and other rules and laws that refer to periods of time when courts are closed.
(k) Take any other action appropriate to the exercise of the powers specified in this section and other law, and appropriate to the exercise of administrative authority and supervision by the Chief Justice over the courts of this state.
(2) The Chief Justice may make rules for the use of electronic applications in the courts, including but not limited to rules relating to any of the following:
(a) Applications based on the use of the Internet and other similar technologies.
(b) The use of an electronic document, or use of an electronic image of a paper document in lieu of the original paper copy, for any record of the courts maintained under ORS 7.095 and for any document, process or paper that is served, delivered, received, filed, entered or retained in any action or proceeding.
(c) The use of electronic signatures or another form of identification for any document, process or paper that is required by any law or rule to be signed and that is:
(A) Served, delivered, received, filed, entered or retained in any action or proceeding; or
(B) Maintained under ORS 7.095.
(d) The use of electronic transmission for:
(A) Serving documents in an action or proceeding, other than a summons or an initial complaint or petition;
(B) Filing documents with a court; and
(C) Providing certified electronic copies of court documents and other Judicial Department records to another person or public body.
(e) Payment of statutory or court-ordered monetary obligations through electronic media.
(f) Electronic storage of court documents.
(g) Use of electronic citations in lieu of the paper citation forms as allowed under ORS 153.770, including use of electronic citations for parking ordinance violations that are subject to ORS 221.333 or 810.425.
(h) Public access through electronic means to court documents that are required or authorized to be made available to the public by law.
(i) Transmission of open court proceedings through electronic media.
(j) Electronic transmission and electronic signature on documents relating to circuit court jurors under ORS 10.025.
(3) The Chief Justice may make rules relating to the data that state courts may require parties and other persons to submit for the purpose of distinguishing particular persons from other persons. If the rules require the submission of data that state or federal law does not require that the courts make public, the rules may also require courts to keep the data confidential and not release the data except pursuant to a court order issued for good cause shown. Data that is made confidential under the rules is not subject to disclosure under ORS 192.311 to 192.478.

(4) Rules adopted by the Chief Justice under subsection (2) of this section must be consistent with the laws governing courts and court procedures, but any person who serves, delivers, receives, files, enters or retains an electronic document, or an electronic image of a paper document in lieu of the original paper copy, in the manner provided by a rule of the Chief Justice under subsection (2) of this section shall be considered to have complied with any rule or law governing service, delivery, reception, filing, entry or retention of a paper document.

(5) Rules made and orders issued by the Chief Justice under this section shall permit as much variation and flexibility in the administration of the courts of this state as are appropriate to the most efficient manner of administering each court, considering the particular needs and circumstances of the court, and consistent with the sound and efficient administration of the judicial department of government in this state.

(6)(a) The Chief Justice may establish reasonable fees for the use of the Oregon Judicial Case Information Network, including fees for electronic access to documents.

(b)(A) Before permanently adopting or increasing fees under this subsection, the Chief Justice shall provide notice to interested persons and allow a reasonable opportunity for comment.

(B) Before temporarily adopting or increasing fees under this subsection, the Chief Justice shall provide notice to interested persons.

(C) The Chief Justice shall by order establish a process for notice and comment under this paragraph.

(c) Fees adopted under this subsection must be reasonably calculated to recover or offset costs of developing, maintaining, supporting or providing access to or use of state court electronic applications and systems.

(7) The judges, other officers and employees of the courts of this state shall comply with rules made and orders issued by the Chief Justice. Rules and orders of a court of this state, or a judge thereof, relating to the conduct of the business of the court shall be consistent with applicable rules made and orders issued by the Chief Justice.

(8) The Chief Judge of the Court of Appeals and the presiding judge of each judicial district of this state are the administrative heads of their respective courts. They are responsible and accountable to the Chief Justice of the Supreme Court in the exercise of their administrative authority and supervision over their respective courts. Other judges of the Court of Appeals or court under a presiding judge are responsible and accountable to the Chief Judge or presiding judge, and to the Chief Justice, in respect to exercise by the Chief Justice, Chief Judge or presiding judge of administrative authority and supervision.

(9) The Chief Justice may delegate the exercise of any of the powers specified by this section to the presiding judge of a court, and may delegate the exercise of any of the administrative powers specified by this section to the State Court Administrator, as may be appropriate.

(10) This section applies to justices of the peace and the justice courts of this state solely for the purpose of disciplining of justices of the peace and for the purpose of continuing legal education of justices of the peace. [1959 c.552 §1; 1973 c.484 §1; 1981 s.s. c.1 §3; 1995 c.221 §1; 1995 c.781 §2; 1999 c.787 §1; 2001 c.911 §1; 2007 c.129 §1; 2009 c.47 §1; 2009 c.484 §1; 2009 c.885 §37a; 2013 c.2 §3; 2013 c.685 §1; 2014 c.76 §1]

1.003 Chief Justice's powers to appoint Chief Judge and presiding judges; terms; disapproval of appointment. (1) The Chief Justice of the Supreme Court shall appoint after conferring with and seeking the advice of the Supreme Court, and may remove at pleasure:

(a) The Chief Judge of the Court of Appeals.

(b) The presiding judge for each judicial district.

(2) Except as provided in subsection (3) of this section, the term of office of the Chief Judge or presiding judge is two years, commencing on January 1 of each even-numbered year. A judge is eligible for reappointment as Chief Judge or presiding judge.

(3) If there is a vacancy for any cause in the office of Chief Judge or presiding judge:

(a) When the vacancy occurs after January 1 of an even-numbered year and before July 1 of the following odd-numbered year, the Chief Justice shall make an appointment for a term expiring December 31 of that odd-numbered year.

(b) When the vacancy occurs after June 30 of an odd-numbered year and before January 1 of the following even-numbered year, the Chief Justice shall make an appointment for a term expiring December 31 of the odd-numbered year following that even-numbered year.

(c) The Chief Justice may designate a judge of the Court of Appeals to serve as acting Chief Judge until an appointment is made as provided in this section. The Chief Justice may designate any circuit court judge to serve as acting presiding judge until an appointment is made as provided in this section.

(4) Before appointing a Chief Judge or presiding judge the Chief Justice shall confer with and seek the advice of the judges of the courts concerned in respect to the appointment.

(5) The Chief Justice shall give written notice of the judge appointed as Chief Judge or presiding judge to each judge of the court concerned not later than 10 days before the effective date of the appointment. A majority of the judges of the courts concerned may disapprove the appointment by a written resolution signed by each judge disapproving the appointment and submitted to the Chief Justice before the effective date of the appointment. If the appointment is so disapproved, the Chief Justice shall appoint another judge as Chief Judge or presiding judge, and shall notify each judge of the courts concerned as provided in this subsection. If the courts concerned have five or more judges, a second appointment is subject to disapproval, as provided in this subsection, by a majority of the judges of the courts concerned. A third appointment is not subject to disapproval under this subsection. [1981 s.s. c.1 §4; 1995 c.658 §7; 1995 c.781 §3; 2013 c.155 §2]

1.004 Supreme Court rules governing coordination of class actions. Notwithstanding any other provision of law or the Oregon Rules of Civil Procedure, the Supreme Court shall provide by rule the practice and procedure for coordination of class actions under ORCP 32 in convenient courts, including provision for giving notice and presenting evidence. [Formerly 13.370]

1.005 Credit card transactions for fees, security deposits, fines and other court-imposed obligations; rules. The Chief Justice of the Supreme Court or the presiding judge of any judicial district of this state may establish by rule a program to permit the use of credit card transactions as security deposits, fines, assessments, restitution or any other court-imposed monetary obligation arising out of an offense. The program may also provide for the use of credit card transactions to pay for filing fees, response fees, certification fees and any other fees charged by the court. Any rules adopted pursuant to this section may provide for recovery from the person using the credit card of an additional amount reasonably calculated to recover any charge to the court by a credit card company resulting from use of the credit card. [1983 c.763 §54; 1989 c.1008 §2; 1993 c.531 §2; 1995 c.781 §4; 1997 c.801 §112; 1999 c.1051 §234]

1.006 Supreme Court rules. (1) The Supreme Court may prescribe by rule the form of written process, notices, motions and pleadings used or submitted in civil proceedings and criminal proceedings in the courts of this state. The rules shall be designed to prescribe standardized forms of those writings for use throughout the state. The forms so prescribed shall be consistent with applicable provisions of law and the Oregon Rules of Civil Procedure. The form of written process, notices, motions and pleadings submitted to or used in the courts of this state shall comply with rules made under this section.

(2) The Supreme Court may prescribe by rule the manner of filing of pleadings and other papers submitted in civil proceedings with the courts of this state by means of a telephonic facsimile communication device. The manner so prescribed shall be consistent with applicable provisions of law and the Oregon Rules of Civil Procedure. [1959 c.552 §3; 1973 c.630 §1; 1981 s.s. c.1 §19; 1989 c.295 §2]

1.007 Judicial Department Revolving Account; uses; sources. (1) There is established in the State Treasury an account to be known as the Judicial Department Revolving Account. Upon the written request of the Chief Justice of the Supreme Court, the Oregon Department of Administrative Services shall draw warrants in favor of the Supreme Court and charged against appropriations to the Supreme Court for court expenses. The warrants shall be deposited in the revolving account. The revolving account shall not exceed the aggregate sum of $1 million, including unreimbursed disbursements.

(2) Moneys in the revolving account may be used for the payment of court expenses for which appropriations are made to the Supreme Court and for which immediate cash payment is necessary or desirable. Moneys in the revolving account may be disbursed by checks issued by or under the authority of the Chief Justice.

(3) All claims for reimbursement of disbursements from the revolving account shall be approved by the Chief Justice or, as directed by the Chief Justice, the State Court Administrator, and by the Oregon Department of Administrative Services. When claims have been approved, a warrant covering them shall

be drawn in favor of the Supreme Court, charged against appropriations to the Supreme Court for court expenses, and used to reimburse the revolving account.

(4) This section does not authorize the drawing of a warrant against or the disbursement of any appropriation to the Supreme Court for court expenses in excess of the amount, or for a purpose other than, established by or pursuant to law therefor.

(5) As used in this section, "court expenses" includes expenses of the Supreme Court, Court of Appeals, Oregon Tax Court and State Court Administrator and expenses of the circuit courts required to be paid by the state. [1983 c.737 §1; 1985 c.502 §14]

1.008 Personnel plan, fiscal plan and property plan. The Chief Justice of the Supreme Court shall establish and maintain, consistent with applicable provisions of law:

(1) A personnel plan for officers, other than judges, and employees of the courts of this state who are state officers or employees, governing the appointment, promotion, classification, minimum qualifications, compensation, expenses, leave, transfer, layoff, removal, discipline and other incidents of employment of those officers and employees.

(2) A plan for budgeting, accounting and other fiscal management and control applicable to expenditures made and revenues received by the state in respect to the courts of this state.

(3) A plan for acquisition, use and disposition of supplies, materials, equipment and other property provided by the state for the use of the courts of this state. [1981 s.s. c.3 §4]

1.009 Judicial Department Operating Account. (1) The Judicial Department Operating Account is established in the State Treasury, separate and distinct from the General Fund. Interest earned by the account shall be credited to the account. All moneys in the account are continuously appropriated to the Judicial Department and may be used only to pay the operating expenses of the department.

(2) All moneys received by the department pursuant to ORS 151.216 (1)(i) shall be deposited in the Judicial Department Operating Account.

(3) The department may accept gifts, grants or contributions from any source, whether public or private, for deposit in the Judicial Department Operating Account. [2003 c.737 §83]

1.010 Powers of courts in administration of court business and proceedings. Every court of justice has power:

(1) To preserve and enforce order in its immediate presence.

(2) To enforce order in the proceedings before it, or before a person or body empowered to conduct a judicial investigation under its authority.

(3) To provide for the orderly conduct of proceedings before it or its officers.

(4) To compel obedience to its judgments, orders and process, and to the orders of a judge out of court, in an action, suit or proceeding pending therein.

(5) To control, in furtherance of justice, the conduct of its ministerial officers, and of all other persons in any manner connected with a judicial proceeding before it, in every matter appertaining thereto.

(6) To compel the attendance of persons to testify in an action, suit or proceeding pending therein, in the cases and manner provided by statute.

(7) To administer oaths in an action, suit or proceeding pending therein, and in all other cases where it may be necessary in the exercise of its powers or the performance of its duties. [Amended by 2003 c.576 §267]

1.012 State Court Technology Fund. (1) The State Court Technology Fund is established in the State Treasury, separate and distinct from the General Fund. Interest earned by the State Court Technology Fund shall be credited to the fund.

(2) All fees received on and after July 1, 2013, for the use of the Oregon Judicial Case Information Network under ORS 1.002 (6) and for the use of other state court electronic applications and systems shall be deposited into the fund.

(3) The fund consists of the moneys deposited into the fund under subsection (2) of this section, the moneys deposited into the fund under ORS 21.006 and the moneys allocated to the fund under ORS 137.300.

(4) Moneys in the fund are continuously appropriated to the Judicial Department for the purposes of:

(a) Developing, maintaining and supporting state court electronic applications, services and systems and for providing access to and use of those applications, services and systems; and

(b) Providing electronic service and filing services. [2013 c.685 §46; 2014 c.76 §14; 2017 c.712 §6]

1.020 Contempt punishment. For the effectual exercise of the powers specified in ORS 1.010, the court may punish for contempt in the cases and the manner provided by statute.

1.025 Duty of court and court officers to require performance of duties relating to administration of justice; enforcement of duty by mandamus. (1) Where a duty is imposed by law or the Oregon Rules of Civil Procedure upon a court, or upon a judicial officer, clerk, bailiff, sheriff, constable or other officer, which requires or prohibits the performance of an act or series of acts in matters relating to the administration of justice in a court, it is the duty of the judicial officer or officers of the court, and each of them, to require the officer upon whom the duty is imposed to perform or refrain from performing the act or series of acts.

(2) Matters relating to the administration of justice include, but are not limited to, the selection and impaneling of juries, the conduct of trials, the entry and docketing of judgments and all other matters touching the conduct of proceedings in courts of this state.

(3) The duty imposed by subsection (1) of this section may be enforced by writ of mandamus. [1957 c.565 §1; 1979 c.284 §40]

1.030 Seal; form; custody; affixing. (1) Each of the following courts, and no other, has a seal:

(a) The Supreme Court and the Court of Appeals.

(b) Each circuit court and the Oregon Tax Court.

(c) Each county court.

(2) The seals shall have the arms of the state engraved in the center, with the following inscription surrounding the same:

(a) For the Supreme Court, "Supreme Court, State of Oregon."

(b) For the Court of Appeals, "Court of Appeals, State of Oregon."

(c) For the circuit court, "Circuit Court, _____County, State of Oregon," inserting the name of the particular county.

(d) For the Oregon Tax Court, "Oregon Tax Court, State of Oregon."

(e) For the county court, "County Court, _____County, State of Oregon," inserting the name of the particular county.

(3) The clerk of the court shall keep the seal, and affix it to any process, transcript, certificate or other paper required by statute. [Amended by 1957 c.246 §1; 1961 c.533 §35; 1969 c.198 §16; 1991 c.790 §1; 1995 c.658 §9]

1.040 Sittings of court to be public; when may be private. The sittings of every court of justice are public, except that upon the agreement of the parties to a civil action, suit or proceeding, filed with the clerk or entered in the appropriate record, the court may direct the trial, or any other proceeding therein, to be private; upon such order being made, all persons shall be excluded, except the officers of the court, the parties, their witnesses and counsel. [Amended by 1985 c.540 §18]

1.050 Time for decision on submitted questions; certificate of compliance with requirement; penalty for false certificate. Any question submitted to any judge of any court of, or any justice of the peace in, any of the courts of this state, excepting the Supreme Court and the Court of Appeals and the judges thereof, must be decided and the decision rendered within three months after submission, unless prevented by sickness or unavoidable casualty, or the time be extended by stipulation in writing signed by the counsel for the respective parties and filed with the judge before the expiration of said three months. This section is mandatory, and no officer shall sign or issue any warrant for the payment of the salary or any installment of the salary of any such judge or justice of the peace unless the voucher for such warrant shall contain or be accompanied by a certificate of such judge or justice of the peace that all matters submitted to the judge or justice of the peace for decision three months or more prior to the filing of said voucher have been decided as required herein; and, in case the time has been extended by stipulation in writing, or a decision has been prevented by sickness or unavoidable casualty, said certificate shall state the facts excusing the delay. The making and filing of a false certificate shall be just cause for complaint to the legislature and removal of said judge or justice of the peace. [Amended by 1969 c.198 §17]

1.055 [1959 c.638 §1; repealed by 2015 c.212 §2]

1.060 Days for transaction of judicial business; exceptions. (1) Except as provided in subsection (2) of this section, the courts of justice may be held and judicial business transacted on any day.

(2) On any legal holiday in this state no court may be open or transact any judicial business for any purpose except:

(a) To give instructions to a jury then deliberating upon its verdict;

(b) To receive the verdict of a jury, or to discharge a jury in case of its inability to agree upon a verdict; or

(c) For the exercise of the powers of a magistrate in criminal actions or proceedings of a criminal nature.

(3) Except to the extent provided by the order, a court may not be open or transact judicial business for any purpose when the court is closed by an order of the Chief Justice. [Amended by 1971 c.240 §1; 1973 c.512 §1; 1981 s.s. c.3 §21; 2002 s.s.1 c.10 §7]

1.070 When court deemed appointed for next judicial day. If a day appointed for holding a court, or to which it is adjourned, is a legal holiday, the court is deemed appointed for or adjourned to the next judicial day.

1.080 Place of holding court. Every court of justice shall sit at the location designated by or pursuant to law for that purpose. [Amended by 1983 c.763 §1]

1.085 Chief Justice to designate principal location for sitting of courts; alternative sites. (1) Except to the extent otherwise specifically provided by law, the Chief Justice of the Supreme Court shall designate the principal location for the sitting of the Supreme Court, Court of Appeals, Oregon Tax Court and each circuit court. For each circuit court there shall be a principal location in each county in the judicial district.

(2) The Chief Justice may designate locations for the sitting of the Supreme Court, Court of Appeals, Oregon Tax Court and each circuit court other than those designated under subsection (1) of this section. Except as provided in subsection (3) of this section, locations designated under this subsection for a circuit court must be in the circuit court's judicial district.

(3) The Chief Justice may designate locations in the state for the sitting of circuit courts in the event of an emergency. Locations designated under this subsection need not be in the circuit court's judicial district. [1983 c.763 §2; 1995 c.658 §10; 2007 c.547 §8]

1.090 Trial elsewhere than at usual location on agreement of parties. Upon agreement of the parties to a civil action, suit or proceeding in a circuit or county court, filed with the clerk or entered in the register, the court may direct that the trial or any other proceeding therein be had elsewhere within the county than at a location otherwise designated by or pursuant to law for the sitting of the court. [Amended by 1983 c.763 §3; 1985 c.540 §19]

1.100 [Repealed by 1983 c.763 §9]

1.110 Adjournment when judge does not attend. If no judge attend on the day appointed for holding a court, before 4 p.m., the court shall stand adjourned until the next day at 9 a.m. [Amended by 1959 c.638 §2; 2015 c.212 §9]

1.120 Proceedings unaffected by vacancy in office. No action, suit or proceeding pending in a court of justice is affected by a vacancy in the office of any or all of the judges. [Amended by 2015 c.212 §10]

1.130 Power to adjourn proceedings. A court or judicial officer has power to adjourn any proceedings before the court or the judicial officer, from time to time, as may be necessary, unless otherwise expressly provided by statute.

1.140 Manner of addressing application or proceeding to court or judge. An application or other proceeding addressed to a court shall be addressed to it by its style as given by statute; an application or other proceeding addressed to a judicial officer shall be addressed to the judicial officer by name, without any other title than the style of office.

1.150 Proceedings to be in English; foreign language translation; rules and procedures. (1) Except as provided in this section, every writing in any action, suit or proceeding in a court of justice of this state, or before a judicial officer, shall be in English.

(2) A writing in an action, suit or proceeding in a court of justice of this state, or before a judicial officer, may be submitted in English and accompanied by a translation into a foreign language that is certified by the translator to be an accurate and true translation of the English writing. If the writing requires a signature, either the English or the foreign language writing may be signed.

(3) If a writing is submitted in English and accompanied by a translation under subsection (2) of this section, a copy of the writing and the translation must be provided to the other parties in the proceeding in the manner provided by the statutes and rules relating to service, notice and discovery of writings in civil and criminal proceedings in courts of justice of this state and before judicial officers.

(4) The State Court Administrator may establish policies and procedures governing the implementation of subsection (2) of this section.

(5) Subsection (1) of this section does not prohibit the use of common abbreviations. [Amended by 1995 c.273 §1; 2003 c.14 §2]

1.160 Means to carry jurisdiction into effect; adoption of suitable process or mode of proceeding. When jurisdiction is, by the Constitution or by statute, conferred on a court or judicial officer, all the means to carry it into effect are also given; and in the exercise of the jurisdiction, if the course of proceeding is not specifically pointed out by the procedural statutes, any suitable process or mode of proceeding may be adopted which may appear most conformable to the spirit of the procedural statutes.

1.165 [1981 s.s. c.3 §7; renumbered 1.185 in 1999]

1.167 [1981 s.s. c.3 §18; renumbered 1.187 in 1999]

1.169 [1987 c.559 §2; 1989 c.1008 §1; 1995 c.781 §5; repealed by 1995 c.658 §127]

1.170 [Repealed by 1981 s.s. c.3 §141]

1.171 Powers and duties of presiding judge for judicial district. (1) A presiding judge appointed under ORS 1.003 is presiding judge for the circuit court of a judicial district established under ORS 3.012.

(2) The presiding judge, to facilitate exercise of administrative authority and supervision over the circuit court of the district and consistent with applicable provisions of law and the Oregon Rules of Civil Procedure, may:

(a) Apportion and otherwise regulate the disposition of the judicial business of the circuit court of the judicial district; and

(b) Make rules, issue orders and take other action appropriate to that exercise.

(3) The presiding judge may assign actions and proceedings pending before a court to other judges of the judicial district for hearing and disposition. A judge who is assigned an action or proceeding under this subsection shall hear and dispose of the assigned action or proceeding unless the presiding judge withdraws the assignment for good cause shown.

(4) The presiding judge may delegate the exercise of any of the administrative powers of the presiding judge to another judge of the court or to the trial court administrator for the judicial district. [1995 c.781 §1; 1997 c.801 §146; 2009 c.484 §2]

1.175 Docket priorities. Any time a court of this state is directed by a provision of Oregon Revised Statutes to accord priority on its docket for a particular action or proceeding, and the priority to be accorded is unclear in light of other provisions of Oregon Revised Statutes, the court may accord such priorities as are consistent with:

(1) Specific statutory time limits; and

(2) The court's efficient administration of its caseload, giving due consideration to the interests sought to be furthered by according docket priorities to certain actions or proceedings before the court. [1989 c.322 §2]

COURT FACILITIES

1.176 Capital improvements to county courthouses; plan; report. (1) The Chief Justice of the Supreme Court shall develop a biennial plan for capital improvements to county courthouses. The plan shall prioritize the need for capital improvements in the counties and establish budgets for capital improvement projects. The list of projects and costs of those projects shall be submitted to the Legislative Assembly with the Judicial Department's request for an allocation from the Criminal Fine Account for the purpose of funding the State Court Facilities and Security Account established under ORS 1.178.

(2) The Chief Justice of the Supreme Court shall prepare a biennial report to the Legislative Assembly that reflects the original budget of projects funded in whole or part with amounts from the State Court Facilities and Security Account, any revisions to those budgets, and the amounts from the account actually expended on those projects. [2011 c.689 §2; 2011 c.597 §312]

1.177 State plan for security, emergency preparedness and business continuity for court facilities; Chief Judicial Marshal; deputy judicial marshals. (1) The Chief Justice of the Supreme Court may adopt state standards, and a state plan, for:

(a) State court security, emergency preparedness and business continuity for facilities used by the judges or staff of a court operating under the Judicial Department or the staff of the office of the State Court Administrator; and

(b) The physical security of the judges or staff of a court operating under the Judicial Department or the staff of the office of the State Court Administrator.

(2)(a) The Chief Justice may appoint a Chief Judicial Marshal and other deputy judicial marshals charged with:

(A) Implementing a state plan adopted under subsection (1) of this section;

(B) Ensuring the physical security and safety of judges of a court operating under the Judicial Department;

(C) Ensuring the physical security and safety of the staff of a court operating under the Judicial Department, the staff of the office of the State Court Administrator and the public in and around court facilities as defined in ORS 166.360; and

(D) Ensuring the security of the real and personal property owned, controlled, occupied or used by the Judicial Department.

(b) Persons appointed as judicial marshals under this section are subject to the personnel rules and policies established by the Chief Justice under ORS 1.002.

(c) When appointed and duly sworn by the Chief Justice, judicial marshals appointed under this section who are trained pursuant to ORS 181A.540 have the authority given to peace officers of this state for the purposes of carrying out the duties of their employment.

(d) The Chief Justice may define the duties of judicial marshals appointed under this section.

(e) Judicial marshals granted the authority of a peace officer under this section who detain any person in accordance with the marshal's duties retain the authority until the law enforcement agency having general jurisdiction over the area in which the person is detained assumes responsibility for the person.

(f) Persons appointed as judicial marshals under this section are not police officers for purposes of the Public Employees Retirement System.

(3) Except as provided in this subsection, a plan adopted under this section and all documents related to development of the plan are confidential and need not be disclosed under the provisions of ORS 192.311 to 192.478. The Chief Justice may authorize the disclosure of all or part of a plan prepared under this section if the Chief Justice determines that the interest of the public would be served by the disclosure and that the disclosure will not impair the integrity of the plan. Records of expenditures for a plan adopted under this section and records of equipment purchased under the plan are not confidential under the provisions of this subsection, and are subject to disclosure as public records under the provisions of ORS 192.311 to 192.478. [2005 c.804 §3; 2012 c.88 §1; 2012 c.107 §104; 2013 c.154 §1]

1.178 State Court Facilities and Security Account. (1) The State Court Facilities and Security Account is established separate and distinct from the General Fund. The account consists of moneys allocated to the account under the provisions of ORS 137.300. Moneys in the account are continuously appropriated to the State Court Administrator for the purposes described in subsection (2) of this section.

(2) Expenditures by the State Court Administrator from the State Court Facilities and Security Account shall be made only for the following purposes:

(a) Developing or implementing the plan for state court security, emergency preparedness, business continuity and physical security adopted under ORS 1.177.

(b) Statewide training on state court security.

(c) Distributions to court facilities security accounts maintained under ORS 1.182.

(d) Capital improvements for courthouses and other state court facilities. [2005 c.804 §4; 2011 c.597 §61; 2012 c.107 §76; 2013 c.154 §§2,3]

1.180 Advisory committees on court security and emergency preparedness; plans. (1) As used in this section, "court facility" means a state court or justice court other than the Supreme Court, Court of Appeals, Oregon Tax Court or office of the State Court Administrator.

(2) The presiding judge for a judicial district may appoint an Advisory Committee on Court Security and Emergency Preparedness for the judicial district. A committee appointed under this section shall consist of:

(a) The sheriff of each county in which a court facility is located;

(b) The district attorney of each county in which a court facility is located;

(c) A member of the local governing body of each county in which a court facility is located, or the member's representative;

(d) The president of the county bar association, if any, for each county in which a court facility is located, or the president's representative;

(e) A justice of the peace from each county in the district in which a justice court is located; and

(f) The following persons as designated by the presiding judge:

(A) The trial court administrator for each county in which a court facility is located; and

(B) A judge from each county in which a court facility is located.

(3) A committee appointed under this section shall meet at the call of the presiding judge that appointed the committee.

(4) A committee appointed under this section shall submit to the presiding judge of the judicial district a plan for court security improvement, emergency preparedness and business continuity for each building containing a court facility in the county. The plan shall include capital outlay needs and may include recommendations concerning:

(a) Security procedures for the transportation and supervision of prisoners for court appearances including, as otherwise allowed by law, the use of video transmission equipment for the appearance of defendants who are in custody;

(b) Procedures for the secure handling, transportation and disposal of hazardous substances and contraband in court proceedings;

(c) Emergency alarm systems accessible to all court employees;

(d) Physical security for judges, justices of the peace, staff and the public;

(e) Procedures for emergency evacuation of buildings containing court facilities;

(f) Procedures for identifying court security personnel, including a court security officer to be appointed by the presiding judge, who shall be responsible for:

(A) The management of the plan;

(B) A regular security inspection of each building containing a court facility; and

(C) Regular security training of sheriff department, judicial department and district attorney personnel; and

(g) Priorities for available court facilities within the building based on the level of security needed.

(5) The plan may also include:

(a) An evaluation of how each of the items listed in subsection (4) of this section is being addressed and should be addressed;

(b) How practices, facilities and equipment falling below appropriate levels are to be improved;

(c) The anticipated cost of improving practices, facilities and equipment that fall below appropriate levels;

(d) The funding source for each improvement; and

(e) The time schedule for implementation of improvements.

(6) Adoption of a plan under this section is subject to the approval of the presiding judge that appointed the committee. The plan may conclude that court facility security is adequate.

(7) Implementation of the elements of a plan that have a significant fiscal impact are subject to availability of funding.

(8) As soon as a plan, revision or amendment is adopted, the presiding judge shall provide the Chief Justice of the Supreme Court with a copy of the plan adopted under this section and any revisions or amendments to the plan. Each plan shall be reviewed and revised or amended as needed, not later than June 30 of each odd-numbered year.

(9) Except as provided in this subsection, plans prepared under this section are confidential and need not be disclosed under the provisions of ORS 192.311 to 192.478. The presiding judge of a judicial district, with the concurrence of all sheriffs for the counties of the district, may authorize the disclosure of all or part of a plan prepared under this section if the judge determines that the interest of the public would be served by the disclosure and that the disclosure will not impair the integrity of the plan. Records of expenditures for a court security plan and records of equipment purchased under the plan are not confidential under the provisions of this subsection, and are subject to disclosure as public records under the provisions of ORS 192.311 to 192.478. [1993 c.637 §15; 1995 c.658 §124; 1997 c.513 §§1,2; 1997 c.801 §113; 2005 c.804 §1]

1.182 Court facilities security accounts; funding; expenditures; reports. (1) The county treasurer shall deposit moneys received from distributions under ORS 1.178 into a court facilities security account maintained by the county treasurer. The following apply to the account:

(a) The moneys in the account and interest upon the account are reserved for the purpose of providing security in buildings that contain state court or justice court facilities other than the Supreme Court, Court of Appeals, Oregon Tax Court or office of the State Court Administrator located within the county.

(b) Expenditures by the county governing body from the court facilities security account shall be made only for developing or implementing a plan for court security improvement, emergency preparedness and business continuity under ORS 1.180.

(c) Moneys deposited in the account from distributions under ORS 1.178 and expended under the provisions of this section shall be in addition to any other moneys expended by the county on court facilities security programs and personnel. A county shall not reduce other expenditures on court facilities security programs and personnel by reason of the additional moneys provided from distributions under ORS 1.178.

(d) The county treasurer may charge against the court facilities security account an administrative fee for the actual costs associated with maintaining the account. The total administrative fees charged each year may not exceed five percent of the moneys received from distributions under ORS 1.178 for that year.

(e) The county treasurer shall provide to the county governing body, the Advisory Committee on Court Security and Emergency Preparedness and the presiding judge of the judicial district at least quarterly a financial report showing all revenues, deposits and expenditures from the court facilities security account maintained by the county treasurer. The county treasurer may charge against the court facilities security account the actual costs associated with providing financial reports under this paragraph.

(f) The presiding judge of the judicial district shall provide to the Chief Justice of the Supreme Court a financial report showing all revenues, deposits and expenditures from the court facilities security account for each fiscal year. The report shall be submitted to the Chief Justice not later than August 30 of each year.

(2) Except as otherwise provided in subsection (3) of this section, a county may not reduce its actual operating expenditures on court facilities security programs and personnel, including funds from all local sources, exclusive of state and federal funds and other short term special funding, below the level of such expenditures in the preceding fiscal year beginning with the 1992-1993 fiscal year.

(3) A county may reduce the operating expenditures described in subsection (2) of this section if the reduction is in an amount no greater than the average reduction in general fund commitment to all county agencies during the fiscal period. [1993 c.637 §16; 2005 c.804 §2; 2011 c.597 §60]

OPERATION OF COURTHOUSES

1.185 County to provide courtrooms, offices and jury rooms. (1) The county in which a circuit court is located or holds court shall:

(a) Provide suitable and sufficient courtrooms, offices and jury rooms for the court, the judges, other officers and employees of the court and juries in attendance upon the court, and provide maintenance and utilities for those courtrooms, offices and jury rooms.

(b) Pay expenses of the court in the county other than those expenses required by law to be paid by the state.

(2) Except as provided in subsection (1) of this section, all supplies, materials, equipment and other property necessary for the operation of the circuit courts shall be provided by the state under ORS 1.187. [Formerly 1.165]

1.187 State to provide supplies and personal property for courts. Except as provided in ORS 1.185 (1) and subject to applicable provisions of a plan established by the Chief Justice of the Supreme Court, the state shall provide the supplies, materials, equipment and other personal property necessary for the operation of the circuit courts. The cost of property provided by the state shall be paid by the state from funds available for the purpose. [Formerly 1.167]

1.188 Surcharge on fines for courthouse. (1) As used in this section, "offense" means:

(a) A violation of a parking ordinance; or

(b) A traffic offense as defined in ORS 801.555 (2).

(2) Notwithstanding ORS 137.143, the presiding judge of the judicial district in which a county is located may order that the circuit court for the county impose a surcharge in the amount of $5 on each fine assessed for an offense in the county if:

(a) The county has received funds, or has legislative authorization to receive funds, for a county courthouse from the proceeds of bonds issued pursuant to Article XI-Q of the Oregon Constitution deposited in the Oregon Courthouse Capital Construction and Improvement Fund established in section 64, chapter 723, Oregon Laws 2013;

(b) Debt service is owed on any Article XI-Q bonds issued related to the county courthouse;

(c) Debt service is owed on any bonds issued under ORS 271.390 or ORS chapter 287A to finance capital costs of the courthouse project for which bonds are or will be issued under section 8, chapter 705, Oregon Laws 2013, in the county imposing the surcharge;

(d) The board of county commissioners has requested that the presiding judge of the judicial district in which the county is located order the imposition of a surcharge and has identified the purposes for which the surcharge funds would be used; and

(e) The Chief Justice of the Supreme Court has approved the surcharge.

(3) The circuit court for the county may not impose a surcharge under this section unless, before July 1 of the calendar year preceding the imposition of the surcharge, the court submits to the State Court Administrator a copy of the order imposing the surcharge. The court may begin imposing the surcharge on fines for offenses occurring on and after January 1 of the calendar year following submission of the order to the State Court Administrator.

(4) Except as provided in ORS 153.640 and 221.315, the surcharge shall be levied fully if any fine is imposed.

(5) The surcharge shall be collected by the circuit court for the county and paid to the county for deposit in the account established under ORS 1.189 and used solely for:

(a) Payment of capital costs of the courthouse project for which bonds are or will be issued under section 8, chapter 705, Oregon Laws 2013, in the county imposing the surcharge; or

(b) Payment of debt service and related expenses and funding of debt service reserves, if any, for bonds issued under ORS 271.390 or ORS chapter 287A to finance capital costs of the courthouse project for which bonds are or will be issued under section 8, chapter 705, Oregon Laws 2013, in the county imposing the surcharge. [2016 c.78 §1]

1.189 Courthouse surcharge accounts. (1) The county treasurer shall deposit moneys received from surcharges imposed under ORS 1.188 in a courthouse surcharge account maintained by the county treasurer.

(2) The moneys in the courthouse surcharge account and interest upon the account are reserved for the purposes of:

(a) Payment of capital costs of the courthouse project for which bonds are or will be issued under section 8, chapter 705, Oregon Laws 2013, in the county imposing the surcharge; or

(b) Payment of debt service and related expenses and funding of debt service reserves, if any, for bonds issued under ORS 271.390 or ORS chapter 287A to finance capital costs of the courthouse project for which bonds are or will be issued under section 8, chapter 705, Oregon Laws 2013, in the county imposing the surcharge.

(3) The county treasurer may charge against the courthouse surcharge account an administrative fee for the actual costs associated with maintaining the account. The total administrative fees charged each year may not exceed five percent of the moneys received from surcharges imposed under ORS 1.188 for that year. [2016 c.78 §2]

(Temporary provisions relating to courthouse capital construction and improvement)

Note: Sections 8 and 9, chapter 705, Oregon Laws 2013, provide:

Sec. 8. (1) Out of the amount specified in section 1 (6), chapter 705, Oregon Laws 2013, the State Treasurer may issue Article XI-Q bonds in an amount not to exceed $19 million of net proceeds for the purposes specified in subsection (3) of this section, plus an amount estimated by the State Treasurer to pay estimated bond-related costs.

(2)(a) Bonds may not be issued pursuant to this section or section 10, chapter 685, Oregon Laws 2015, unless:

(A) The Chief Justice of the Supreme Court has determined that:

(i) The courthouse with respect to which the bonds will be issued has significant structural defects, including seismic defects, that present actual or potential threats to human health and safety;

(ii) Replacing the courthouse, whether by acquiring and remodeling or repairing an existing building or by constructing a new building, is more cost-effective than remodeling or repairing the courthouse; and

(iii) Replacing the courthouse creates an opportunity for colocation of the court with other state offices; and

(B) The Oregon Department of Administrative Services has approved the project for which the bonds will be issued.

(b) The Oregon Department of Administrative Services, after consultation with the Judicial Department, shall determine when net proceeds are needed for the purposes described in subsection (3) of this section and shall consult with the Judicial Department regarding the sale of bonds to be issued pursuant to this section.

(3) The State Treasurer shall deposit the net proceeds of bonds issued pursuant to this section and section 10, chapter 685, Oregon Laws 2015, in the Oregon Courthouse Capital Construction and Improvement Fund. The net proceeds and any interest earnings may be used solely to finance costs related to acquiring, constructing, remodeling, repairing, equipping or furnishing land, improvements, courthouses or portions of courthouses that are, or that upon completion of a project funded under this section will be, owned or operated by the State of Oregon.

(4) As used in ORS 286A.816 to 286A.826 with respect to this section:

(a) "Project agency" means the Judicial Department.

(b) "Project fund" means the Oregon Courthouse Capital Construction and Improvement Fund. [2013 c.705 §8; 2014 c.121 §6; 2016 c.118 §2]

Sec. 9. (1)(a) Notwithstanding ORS 1.185, a county and the state, acting by and through the Oregon Department of Administrative Services on behalf of the Judicial Department, may enter into interim agreements that provide for the funding, acquisition, development and construction of a courthouse and require the parties to negotiate in good faith and execute a long-term lease agreement or a long-term intergovernmental agreement with respect to the ownership or operation of a courthouse or portions of a courthouse that the county is required to provide under ORS 1.185, pursuant to which the state agrees to provide the property and services described in ORS 1.185 (1)(a).

(b)(A) An agreement entered into pursuant to this subsection may include a requirement that the county transfer to the Oregon Courthouse Capital Construction and Improvement Fund an amount not less than 50 percent of the total estimated costs of a project funded with bonds issued pursuant to section 8, chapter 705, Oregon Laws 2013, or section 10, chapter 685, Oregon Laws 2015, with respect to the courthouse or portions of a courthouse that are the subject of the agreement.

(B) The amount transferred by a county pursuant to this paragraph may comprise, singly or in any combination and proportion:

(i) Property tax revenues, bond proceeds or any other county moneys; and

(ii) A credit equal to the higher of the appraised value or the actual purchase price of land purchased by the county for the courthouse if the state approves of the land as the site for the courthouse.

(C) The amount required to be transferred by the county under this subsection may not be less than 75 percent of the total estimated costs unless the project includes colocation in the courthouse of state offices in addition to the state circuit court facilities.

(2) For purposes of section 8, chapter 705, Oregon Laws 2013, and section 10, chapter 685, Oregon Laws 2015, the state shall be considered to operate a courthouse or portions of a courthouse that are the subject of an agreement entered into pursuant to subsection (1) of this section if, as applicable:

(a) The lease agreement conveys to the state a full leasehold interest, including exclusive rights to control and use the courthouse or portions of the courthouse that are typical of a long-term lease, for a term that is at least equal to the term during which the bonds issued pursuant to section 8, chapter 705, Oregon Laws 2013, and section 10, chapter 685, Oregon Laws 2015, will remain outstanding.

(b) The intergovernmental agreement grants the state the exclusive right to control and use the courthouse or portions of the courthouse for a term that is at least equal to the term during which the bonds issued pursuant to section 8, chapter 705, Oregon Laws 2013, and section 10, chapter 685, Oregon Laws 2015, will remain outstanding. [2013 c.705 §9; 2014 c.121 §7; 2016 c.118 §3]

Note: Section 64, chapter 723, Oregon Laws 2013, provides:

Sec. 64. (1) The Oregon Courthouse Capital Construction and Improvement Fund is established in the State Treasury, separate and distinct from the General Fund. Interest earned on moneys in the Oregon Courthouse Capital Construction and Improvement Fund shall be credited to the fund.

(2) The fund consists of moneys deposited in the fund pursuant to section 8, chapter 705, Oregon Laws 2013, and section 10, chapter 685, Oregon Laws 2015, and moneys transferred to the fund by a county pursuant to section 9 (1)(b), chapter 705, Oregon Laws 2013, and may include fees, revenues and other moneys appropriated by the Legislative Assembly for deposit in the fund.

(3) Moneys in the fund are continuously appropriated to the Judicial Department for:

(a) The purposes described in section 8 (3), chapter 705, Oregon Laws 2013;

(b) Payment of the costs incurred by the department to administer the fund; and
(c) Payment of bond-related costs, as defined in ORS 286A.816. [2013 c.723 §64; 2016 c.118 §4]

1.190 [1999 c.1064 §3; repealed by 2007 c.626 §3]

1.192 [1999 c.1064 §4; repealed by 2007 c.626 §3]

COLLECTION OF COURT ACCOUNTS

1.194 Definitions for ORS 1.194 to 1.200. As used in ORS 1.194 to 1.200:
(1) "Payment" means an amount of money voluntarily paid by a debtor or an amount of money involuntarily paid by a debtor through offset or garnishment.
(2) "State court" means a circuit court, the Oregon Tax Court, the Court of Appeals or the Supreme Court. [2001 c.823 §11; 2003 c.14 §3]

1.195 Reports on liquidated and delinquent accounts of state courts. (1) Not later than October 1 of each fiscal year, all state courts and all commissions, departments and divisions in the judicial branch of state government shall submit reports to the Legislative Fiscal Office that describe the status of the liquidated and delinquent accounts of the judicial branch of state government, and the efforts made to collect those liquidated and delinquent accounts during the immediately preceding fiscal year. The reports required under this subsection shall be in a form prescribed by the Legislative Fiscal Office and shall include but not be limited to:
(a) The total number of all liquidated and delinquent accounts, and the balance for those accounts, at the beginning of the fiscal year;
(b) The total number of all liquidated and delinquent accounts, and the balance for those accounts, at the end of the fiscal year;
(c) The liquidated and delinquent accounts that have been added during the immediately preceding fiscal year;
(d) The total amount collected on liquidated and delinquent accounts during the immediately preceding fiscal year;
(e) The total amount and total number of liquidated and delinquent accounts that have been written off during the immediately preceding fiscal year;
(f) The total amount and total number of liquidated and delinquent accounts that have been assigned for collection, and the collection efforts made for those accounts, during the immediately preceding fiscal year;
(g) The total amount and total number of liquidated and delinquent accounts that have been turned over to private collection agencies under ORS 1.197 and the total amount that has been collected by those agencies during the immediately preceding fiscal year;
(h) The total amount and total number of accounts that have ceased to be liquidated and delinquent during the fiscal year for reasons other than having been collected or written off;
(i) The total number and total amount of all liquidated and delinquent accounts that have been exempted under ORS 1.199;
(j) A statement indicating whether the reporting state court, commission, department or division in the judicial branch of state government has liquidated and delinquent accounts that are not exempt under ORS 1.198 or 1.199, or are otherwise prohibited or exempted by law from assignment, for which no payment has been received for more than 90 days and that have not been assigned to a private collection agency or to the Department of Revenue under ORS 1.197; and
(k) Any other information necessary to inform the Legislative Fiscal Office of the status of the liquidated and delinquent accounts of the judicial branch of state government.
(2) The Legislative Fiscal Office shall include information on the status of the liquidated and delinquent accounts of the judicial branch of state government in the annual report required under ORS 293.229. The information shall be based on the reports submitted under subsection (1) of this section.
(3) The reports required under subsection (1) of this section may be made by the State Court Administrator on behalf of some or all of the state courts and on behalf of some or all of the commissions, departments and divisions in the judicial branch of state government. [2001 c.823 §12; 2015 c.766 §2a]

1.196 Agreement for reciprocal offsets. The State Court Administrator may enter into an intergovernmental agreement with the United States Financial Management Service and the Internal Revenue Service for the purpose of the reciprocal offsetting of the following amounts:
(1) Federal tax refunds of debtors, to be offset against liquidated and delinquent accounts of those debtors resulting from unpaid financial obligations imposed by state courts; and
(2) Overpayments to state courts, to be offset against federal tax obligations. [2009 c.791 §2]

1.197 Assignment of liquidated and delinquent accounts to collection agencies; relinquishment of accounts by collection agencies; collections by Department of Revenue. (1) Except as otherwise provided by law, all state courts and all commissions, departments and divisions in the judicial branch of state government shall offer to assign the liquidated and delinquent accounts of the state court, commission, department or division to a private collection agency, or to the Department of Revenue under the provisions of ORS 293.250, not later than:
(a) One year from the date the account was liquidated if no payment has been received on the account within that year; or
(b) One year from the date of receipt of the most recent payment on the account.
(2) Nothing in subsection (1) of this section prohibits a state court or a commission, department or division in the judicial branch of state government from assigning a liquidated and delinquent account to a private collection agency at any time within the one-year period, or from assigning a liquidated and delinquent account to the Department of Revenue during the one-year period, if that assignment is otherwise allowed by law.
(3) Nothing in this section prevents a state court or a commission, department or division in the judicial branch of state government from assigning an account to the Department of Revenue for the purpose of seeking an offset against tax refunds or other amounts due the debtor at the time the account is assigned to a private collection agency. A state court and any commission, department or division in the judicial branch of state government that assigns the same account to both the Department of Revenue and a private collection agency shall ensure that both the Department of Revenue and the private collection agency are kept informed of the status of all collections made on the account.
(4) If a private collection agency is unable to collect on an account assigned under this section, the private collection agency shall notify the state court, commission, department or division that assigned the account that the private collection agency is unable to collect on the account and that the private collection agency will relinquish the account. The private collection agency shall relinquish the account within a reasonable time or within such time as may be set by agreement. A private collection agency that is assigned an account under this section shall be held to the same standard of confidentiality, service and courtesy imposed on a state court in collecting on liquidated and delinquent accounts.
(5) If a liquidated and delinquent account is assigned to the Department of Revenue as provided in ORS 293.250, the Department of Revenue shall have one year from the date of liquidation, or from the date of receipt of the most recent payment on the account, to collect a payment. If the Department of Revenue does not collect a payment within the one-year period or if one year has elapsed since the date of receipt of the most recent payment on the account, the Department of Revenue shall notify the state court, commission, department or division that assigned the account. The state court, commission, department or division shall then immediately offer assignment of the account to a private collection agency.
(6) For the purposes of this section, a state court or a commission, department or division in the judicial branch of state government shall be considered to have offered an account for assignment to a private collection agency if:
(a) The terms of the offer are of a type generally accepted by the collections industry for the type of account to be assigned; and
(b) The offer is made to a private collection agency that engages in the business of collecting the type of account to be assigned or made generally to private collection agencies through a bid or request for proposal process.
(7) The offer of assignment of accounts required under this section may be made by the State Court Administrator on behalf of some or all of the state courts and on behalf of some or all of the commissions, departments and divisions in the judicial branch of state government. [2001 c.823 §13]

13

1.198 Exemptions from requirements of ORS 1.197. (1) ORS 1.197 does not apply to liquidated and delinquent accounts that are:

(a) Prohibited by state or federal law or regulation from assignment or collection; or

(b) Subject to collection through an offset of federal tax refunds pursuant to an agreement entered into under ORS 1.196.

(2) Notwithstanding ORS 1.197, a state court or a commission, department or division in the judicial branch of state government, acting in its sole discretion, may choose not to offer a liquidated and delinquent account to a private collection agency or to the Department of Revenue if the account:

(a) Is secured by a consensual security interest in real or personal property;

(b) Is based on that part of a judgment that requires payment of restitution or a payment to the Crime Victims' Assistance section of the Criminal Justice Division of the Department of Justice;

(c) Is in litigation, mediation or arbitration or is subject to a stay in bankruptcy proceedings;

(d) Is owed by a local or state government or by the federal government;

(e) Is owed by a debtor who is hospitalized in a state hospital as defined in ORS 162.135 or who receives public assistance as defined in ORS 411.010 or medical assistance as defined in ORS 414.025;

(f) Consists of moneys for which a district attorney has assumed collection responsibility under ORS 8.680;

(g) Consists of moneys owed by a person who is incarcerated;

(h) Is an account that was previously offered to a private collection agency and was refused, or that was previously assigned to a private collection agency and the agency thereafter relinquished the account;

(i) Is less than $100, including penalties; or

(j) Would result in loss of federal funding if assigned. [2001 c.823 §14; 2009 c.791 §3; 2013 c.688 §3]

1.199 Policies and procedures for exempting accounts from requirements of ORS 1.197 and for ceasing collection efforts. (1) The State Court Administrator may establish policies and procedures for exempting accounts from the requirements of ORS 1.197. All policies establishing exemptions under this section must be documented and justified by the State Court Administrator.

(2) The State Court Administrator may establish criteria and standards by which state courts and commissions, departments and divisions in the judicial branch of state government may cease to make collection efforts for specified types of accounts. [2001 c.823 §15]

1.200 Effect of ORS 1.194 to 1.200 on authority of judge. Nothing in ORS 1.194 to 1.200 limits or affects the ability of a judge of a state court to enforce, modify, set aside, suspend, delay, condition, schedule or take any other action authorized by law with respect to a debt or money obligation owed to this state. [2001 c.823 §16]

1.202 Fee for establishing and administering account for judgment that includes monetary obligation; fee for judgment referred for collection. (1) All circuit courts and appellate courts of this state, and all commissions, departments and divisions in the judicial branch of state government, shall add a fee of not less than $50 and not more than $200 to any judgment that includes a monetary obligation that the court or judicial branch is charged with collecting. The fee shall cover the cost of establishing and administering an account for the debtor and shall be added without further notice to the debtor or further order of the court. The fee shall be added only if the court gives the defendant a period of time in which to pay the obligation after the financial obligation is imposed. Fees under this subsection shall be deposited in the General Fund.

(2) All circuit courts and appellate courts of this state, and all commissions, departments and divisions in the judicial branch of state government, that use private collection agencies, the Department of Revenue or an offset of federal tax refunds pursuant to an agreement entered into under ORS 1.196 shall add a fee to any judgment referred for collection that includes a monetary obligation that the state court or the commission, department or division is charged with collecting. A fee to cover the costs of collecting judgments referred to the private collection agency, the Department of Revenue, the United States Financial Management Service or the Internal Revenue Service shall be added to the monetary obligation without further notice to the debtor or further order of the court. The fee may not exceed the actual costs of collecting the judgment.

(3) The Chief Justice of the Supreme Court may authorize courts to waive or suspend the fees required to be added to judgments under this section. Except to the extent authorized by the Chief Justice, a court may not waive or suspend the fees required to be added to judgments under this section. [2001 c.823 §20; 2007 c.860 §32; 2009 c.484 §3; 2009 c.659 §§34,36; 2009 c.791 §4a; 2011 c.595 §§92,92a]

1.204 [2001 c.823 §25 (enacted in lieu of 8.172); 2003 c.518 §11; repealed by 2011 c.595 §173]

JUDICIAL OFFICERS GENERALLY

1.210 Judicial officer defined. A judicial officer is a person authorized to act as a judge in a court of justice.

1.212 Oath of office for judges. (1) Before entering upon the duties of a judge of the Supreme Court, whether upon election or appointment as a judge of the Supreme Court or upon appointment as a senior judge or a judge pro tempore, a person must take and subscribe, and submit to the Secretary of State, an oath in the form provided by section 7, Article VII (Amended) of the Oregon Constitution.

(2) Except as provided in subsection (3) of this section, before entering upon the duties of a judge of the Court of Appeals, the Oregon Tax Court or a circuit court, a person who is appointed or elected to the office must take and subscribe, and submit to the Secretary of State, an oath in the following form:

_____

I, _____, do solemnly swear (or affirm) that I will support the Constitution of the United States, and the Constitution of the State of Oregon, and that I will faithfully and impartially discharge the duties of a judge of the _____ (court), according to the best of my ability, and that I will not accept any other office, except judicial offices, during the term for which I have been _____ (elected or appointed).

_____

(3) Before entering upon the duties of a judge pro tempore of the Court of Appeals, the Oregon Tax Court or a circuit court, a person must take and subscribe, and submit to the Secretary of State, an oath in the following form:

_____

I, _____, do solemnly swear (or affirm) that I will support the Constitution of the United States, and the Constitution of the State of Oregon, and that I will faithfully and impartially discharge the duties of a judge of the _____ (court), according to the best of my ability.

_____

(4) Before entering upon the duties of a senior judge of the State of Oregon, a person must take and subscribe, and submit to the Secretary of State, an oath in the following form:

_____

I, _____, do solemnly swear (or affirm) that I will support the Constitution of the United States, and the Constitution of the State of Oregon, and that I will faithfully and impartially discharge the duties of a senior judge of the State of Oregon, according to the best of my ability.

_____

(5) Subsections (3) and (4) of this section do not require that any person take an oath more than once during the term that the person is approved to serve as a senior judge or judge pro tempore, or that a person serving as a senior judge or judge pro tempore take the prescribed oath before each assignment as a judge of the Court of Appeals, Oregon Tax Court or circuit court. Subsection (3) of this section does not require that a judge assigned to serve as judge pro tempore under ORS 1.615 take any additional oath of office. [2003 c.518 §6]

1.220 Judicial officer or partner acting as attorney. (1) Except as provided in this section, a judicial officer appointed or elected to a full-time position may not act as an attorney in an action or proceeding.

(2) A judicial officer appointed or elected to a full-time position may act as an attorney in an action or proceeding if the judicial officer is an active member of the Oregon State Bar and is either a party to the action or proceeding or the judicial officer has a direct interest in the action or proceeding.

(3) A judge of a county court or justice court who is an active member of the Oregon State Bar:

(a) May act as an attorney in a court other than the court in which the judge presides; and

(b) May not be engaged in the practice of law with an attorney who appears in the court in which the judge presides.

(4) A judge pro tempore may not preside in an action or proceeding if an attorney who is engaged in the practice of law with the judge appears in the action or proceeding. [Amended by 2007 c.547 §4]

1.230 Powers of a judge out of court. A judge may exercise, out of court, all the powers expressly conferred upon a judge as distinguished from a court, and not otherwise.

1.240 Powers of judicial officers. Every judicial officer has power:

(1) To preserve and enforce order in the immediate presence of the judicial officer, and in the proceedings before the judicial officer, when the judicial officer is performing a duty imposed by statute.

(2) To compel obedience to the lawful orders of the judicial officer, as provided by statute.

(3) To compel the attendance of persons to testify in a proceeding pending before the judicial officer in the cases and manner provided by statute.

(4) To administer oaths in a proceeding pending before the judicial officer, and in all other cases where it may be necessary, in the exercise of the powers and the performance of the duties of the judicial officer.

1.250 Punishment for contempt. For the effectual exercise of the powers specified in ORS 1.240, a judicial officer may punish for contempt, in the cases and manner provided by statute.

1.260 Powers of judges of Supreme Court, Court of Appeals, Oregon Tax Court and circuit courts; where powers may be exercised. The judges of the Supreme Court, the Court of Appeals, the Oregon Tax Court and the circuit courts have power in any part of the state:

(1) To take and certify:

(a) The proof and acknowledgment of a conveyance of real property, or any other written instrument authorized or required to be proved or acknowledged.

(b) The acknowledgment of satisfaction of a judgment in any court.

(c) An affidavit or deposition to be used in any court of justice or other tribunal of this state.

(2) To exercise any other power and perform any other duty conferred or imposed upon them by statute. [Amended by 1963 c.423 §1; 1969 c.198 §18]

1.270 Powers of other judicial officers; where powers may be exercised. Every other judicial officer may, within the county, city, district or precinct in which the judicial officer is chosen:

(1) Exercise the powers mentioned in ORS 1.260 (1).

(2) Exercise any other power and perform any other duty conferred or imposed upon the judicial officer by statute.

1.280 [1959 c.552 §4; repealed by 1981 s.s. c.1 §25]

1.290 Leaves of absence. (1) As used in this section, unless the context requires otherwise, "judge" means any judge of the Supreme Court, the Court of Appeals, the Oregon Tax Court or any circuit court, but does not include any person appointed by the Supreme Court as judge pro tempore of any of those courts who does not hold the elective office of judge of any of those courts.

(2) Upon receipt of the written application of any judge, the Supreme Court may grant the judge a leave of absence without salary for a period of not more than one year. The Supreme Court may grant a leave of absence only if the court is satisfied that the administration of justice in Oregon will be enhanced by granting the leave. Application for a leave of absence is considered a waiver of salary by the applicant for the period of time the applicant is absent under the leave granted by the court.

(3) A leave of absence shall be granted by order of the Supreme Court. The order shall state the maximum period of time for which the leave is granted. Promptly after the granting of the leave, the State Court Administrator shall cause a certified copy of the order granting the leave to be sent to the Secretary of State and the Public Employees Retirement Board.

(4) At the termination of leave of absence under this section, unless the judge sooner dies or resigns, a judge shall resume the duties of office and cause written notice of the resumption to be sent to the Supreme Court, the Secretary of State and the Public Employees Retirement Board. The resumption and sending notice thereof constitutes a termination of the leave whether or not the full maximum period of time granted has expired.

(5) Absence on leave by a judge under this section does not create a vacancy in the office to which the judge was elected or appointed, nor is the judge subject to removal as a consequence thereof.

(6) Absence on leave under this section by a judge who is a member of the Public Employees Retirement System under ORS chapter 238 does not break the continuity of the membership of the judge in the system. [1965 c.12 §1; 1969 c.198 §19; 1971 c.193 §8; 1991 c.815 §2]

1.300 Senior judge; assignment; duties and powers; compensation and expenses. (1) A judge who retires from the circuit court, Oregon Tax Court, Court of Appeals or Supreme Court, except a judge retired under the provisions of ORS 1.310, may be designated a senior judge of the State of Oregon by the Supreme Court and, if so designated, shall be so certified by the Secretary of State.

(2) Upon filing with the Secretary of State an oath of office as a senior judge as prescribed in ORS 1.212, a senior judge is eligible for temporary assignment, with the consent of the senior judge, by the Supreme Court to a state court as provided in this subsection, whenever the Supreme Court determines that the assignment is reasonably necessary and will promote the more efficient administration of justice. A senior judge who retired from the Supreme Court may be assigned to any state court. A senior judge who retired from a court other than the Supreme Court may be assigned to any state court other than the Supreme Court.

(3) The assignment of a senior judge shall be made by an order which shall designate the court to which the judge is assigned and the duration of the assignment. Promptly after assignment of a senior judge under this section, the Supreme Court shall cause a certified copy of the order to be sent to the senior judge and another certified copy to the court to which the judge is assigned.

(4) Each senior judge assigned as provided in this section has all the judicial powers and duties, while serving under the assignment, of a regularly elected and qualified judge of the court to which the senior judge is assigned. The powers, jurisdiction and judicial authority of the senior judge in respect to any case or matter tried or heard by the senior judge while serving under the assignment shall continue beyond the expiration of the assignment so far as may be necessary to:

(a) Decide and dispose of any case or matter on trial or held under advisement.

(b) Hear and decide any motion for a new trial or for a judgment notwithstanding a verdict, or objections to any cost bill, that may be filed in the case.

(c) Settle a transcript for appeal and grant extensions of time therefor.

(5) A senior judge assigned as provided in this section shall receive as compensation for each day the senior judge is actually engaged in the performance of duties under the assignment an amount equal to five percent of the gross monthly salary of a regularly elected and qualified judge of the court to which the senior judge is assigned, or one-half of that daily compensation for services of one-half day or less. However, a retired judge shall not receive for services as a senior judge during any calendar year a sum of money which when added to the amount of any judicial retirement pay received by the senior judge for the year exceeds the annual salary of a judge of the court from which the senior judge retired. The compensation shall be paid upon the certificate of the senior judge that the services were performed for the number of days shown in the certificate. Services by a senior judge under an

assignment and receipt of compensation for services shall not reduce or otherwise affect the amount of any retirement pay to which the senior judge otherwise would be entitled.

(6) A senior judge assigned to a court located outside the county in Oregon in which the senior judge regularly resides shall receive, in addition to daily compensation, reimbursement for hotel bills and traveling expenses necessarily incurred in the performance of duties under the assignment. The expenses shall be paid upon presentation of an itemized statement of the expenses, certified by the senior judge to be correct. [1973 c.452 §2; 1975 c.706 §9; 1979 c.56 §1; 1983 c.628 §1; 1987 c.762 §2; 2003 c.518 §7]

1.303 Disability of judge; procedures upon receipt by Chief Justice of complaint or information. (1) As used in this section and ORS 1.425:

(a) "Judge" means a judge of any court of this state.

(b) "Subject judge" means a judge whose alleged disability is involved in proceedings under this section or ORS 1.425.

(c) "Disability" means a physical or mental condition of a judge, including but not limited to impairment derived in whole or in part from habitual or excessive use of intoxicants, drugs or controlled substances, that significantly interferes with the capacity of the judge to perform judicial duties. A disability may be permanent or temporary.

(2) When the Chief Justice of the Supreme Court receives a complaint as provided in ORS 1.420 (2) or has reliable information that would lead a reasonable person to believe that a judge has a disability, the Chief Justice may:

(a) Confer with the subject judge in respect to the alleged disability.

(b) Consult with other judges of the court in which the subject judge serves and other persons who may have knowledge concerning the alleged disability.

(c) Conduct other inquiry in respect to the alleged disability as the Chief Justice considers appropriate.

(3) If, after inquiry, and on clear and convincing evidence, the Chief Justice determines that the subject judge has a temporary disability, that informal disposition is appropriate and that the subject judge agrees to informal disposition, the Chief Justice may enter into an informal disposition of the matter with the subject judge. The informal disposition may include agreement by the subject judge to obtain professional counseling, medical treatment or other assistance or to comply with other conditions in respect to the future conduct of the judge. If an informal disposition is entered into, the Chief Justice may grant the subject judge a leave of absence with salary for a period of not more than one year.

(4) If, after inquiry, and on clear and convincing evidence, the Chief Justice determines that the subject judge has a permanent disability, or that the subject judge has a temporary disability and informal disposition is not appropriate or the subject judge does not agree to informal disposition, the Chief Justice may file a written request for an investigation under ORS 1.310 (2) or a complaint under ORS 1.425, as the Chief Justice considers appropriate.

(5) When the Chief Justice enters into an informal disposition with a subject judge under subsection (3) of this section, or files a written request or complaint in respect to a subject judge under subsection (4) of this section, or determines that a subject judge does not have a disability, the Chief Justice shall prepare a written summary of the nature of the complaint or information received, the inquiry conducted and the basis for the determination. The Chief Justice shall immediately send a copy of the summary to the Commission on Judicial Fitness and Disability, which shall retain the copy in a file for the subject judge.

(6) Documents filed with or prepared by the Chief Justice under subsections (2), (3) and (5) of this section shall not be public records unless received as competent evidence in the course of a hearing pursuant to ORS 1.310 (4) or 1.420. [1987 c.520 §1]

1.305 Commencement of judicial term of office. The term of office of a judge of the Supreme Court, the Court of Appeals, the Oregon Tax Court, or of any circuit court shall begin on the first Monday in January following the election of the judge. [1979 c.451 §7]

INVOLUNTARY RETIREMENT OF JUDGES

1.310 Involuntary retirement of judges for disability; rules. (1) As used in this section:

(a) "Chief Justice" means the Chief Justice of the Supreme Court of Oregon, except that, if the Chief Justice is the subject judge, then the term "Chief Justice" means the one of the remaining judges of the Supreme Court who has served the longest period of time as a judge of that court.

(b) "Disability" means physical or mental incapacitation of such a degree as to cause a judge to be unable to discharge the duties of judicial office.

(c) "Judge" includes any judge of the Supreme Court, the Court of Appeals, the Oregon Tax Court, or any circuit court, of the State of Oregon.

(d) "Subject judge" means any judge whose alleged disability is involved in proceedings under this section.

(2) Any judge who becomes disabled may be retired in the manner provided in this section. The Governor, the Chief Justice, the Judicial Conference or the Board of Governors of the Oregon State Bar may file at any time with the Secretary of State a written request for an investigation to determine whether a judge named in the request has a disability. Upon receipt of a request, the Secretary of State shall transmit to the subject judge a certified copy of the request, with a notice to the effect that, unless the judge files a resignation within 45 days after the date of the notice, an investigation will be made to determine whether the judge has a disability. The certified copy and notice shall be served on the subject judge, either by delivering them to the judge in person or by transmitting them by registered mail or by certified mail with return receipt to the judge at the last residence address of the judge as shown in the records of the Secretary of State.

(3) If the subject judge fails to file a resignation within 45 days after the date of the notice, the Secretary of State, within 10 days after the expiration of that period, shall transmit to the Commission on Judicial Fitness and Disability certified copies of the request and notice, with a certificate to the effect:

(a) That the Secretary of State served the notice and copy of the request on the subject judge as provided in subsection (2) of this section; and

(b) That the judge did not file a resignation.

(4) Upon receipt of the certified copies and certificate referred to in subsection (3) of this section, the commission shall make the requested investigation and, after hearing, determine whether the subject judge has a disability. The commission shall prepare an official record that shall include the testimony taken and the exhibits considered. If the subject judge refuses or is unable to attend, the commission may proceed with the hearing in the absence of the judge.

(5) If a majority of the members of the commission determines that the subject judge in fact has a disability, the members shall make and sign written findings of fact upon which the determination is made and transmit the findings to the Secretary of State. If no appeal is filed, the office of the judge shall become vacant 10 days after the filing of the findings, and thereupon the Secretary of State shall certify to the Governor the existence of the vacancy. If a majority of the members of the commission does not find that the subject judge has a disability, the members shall sign and file with the Secretary of State a written report to that effect, and thereupon the proceeding shall terminate.

(6) The commission may prescribe rules of procedure for the conduct of the investigation and fix the time and place of the hearing, giving the subject judge due notice thereof. The fees and mileage allowance of witnesses, including experts, shall be fixed by the commission.

(7) A judge retired under the provisions of this section may not be appointed as judge pro tempore to serve upon any court of the State of Oregon.

(8) The subject judge may appeal to the Supreme Court from a determination by the commission that the judge has a disability, by filing a notice with the Secretary of State within 10 days after the date of filing of the written findings of fact by the commission. The Secretary of State shall thereupon notify the commission and the Chief Justice. The commission shall forthwith transmit the official record to the Supreme Court, which upon receipt of the record shall have full jurisdiction of the proceeding.

(9) The Supreme Court shall review the proceeding de novo on the record with authority to affirm, reverse or annul the determination. Prior to a final determination, remand may also be made to the commission for additional findings of fact. In the event that the Supreme Court reverses or annuls the determination of the commission, the proceeding shall thereupon terminate and notice to that effect shall be filed with the Secretary of State. If the determination of the commission is affirmed, a decision to that effect shall be filed with the Secretary of State and the office of the subject judge shall forthwith become vacant. Thereupon, the Secretary of State shall certify to the Governor the existence of the vacancy. [Amended by 1963 c.488 §1; 1965 c.394 §1; 1969 c.332 §2; 1983 c.740 §2; 1987 c.520 §11; 1991 c.249 §1; 1991 c.815 §3; 2007 c.70 §1; 2009 c.11 §2]

1.312 [1969 c.332 §1; repealed by 1991 c.815 §21]

1.314 [1959 c.551 §2 (1.314, 1.318, 1.322 and 1.326 enacted in lieu of 1.320); 1961 c.568 §1; 1963 c.592 §1; 1965 c.394 §2; 1969 c.332 §3; repealed by 1991 c.815 §21]

1.316 [1971 c.101 §2; repealed by 1991 c.815 §21]

1.318 [1959 c.551 §3 (1.314, 1.318, 1.322 and 1.326 enacted in lieu of 1.320); 1961 c.568 §2; 1963 c.464 §3; 1965 c.394 §3; 1969 c.332 §4; 1983 c.770 §13; repealed by 1991 c.815 §21]

1.320 [Amended by 1955 c.496 §1; repealed by 1959 c.551 §1 (1.314, 1.318, 1.322 and 1.326 enacted in lieu of 1.320)]

1.322 [1959 c.551 §4 (1.314, 1.318, 1.322 and 1.326 enacted in lieu of 1.320); 1965 c.394 §4; 1969 c.332 §5; repealed by 1991 c.815 §21]

1.326 [1959 c.551 §5 (1.314, 1.318, 1.322 and 1.326 enacted in lieu of 1.320); 1963 c.464 §4; repealed by 1991 c.815 §21]

1.328 [1959 c.551 §§10,11; repealed by 1961 c.568 §5]

1.330 [Amended by 1961 c.568 §3; 1963 c.464 §5; 1965 c.394 §5; 1969 c.332 §6; 1971 c.101 §3; repealed by 1991 c.815 §21]

1.340 [Amended by 1953 c.529 §5; 1955 c.496 §2; 1955 c.511 §1; 1959 c.551 §6; 1961 c.568 §4; 1963 c.464 §6; 1965 c.394 §6; 1969 c.332 §7; 1971 c.101 §4; 1983 c.770 §14; repealed by 1991 c.815 §21]

1.343 [1979 c.609 §2; 1983 c.770 §15; 1989 c.757 §2; 1991 c.796 §8; repealed by 1991 c.815 §21]

1.345 [1961 c.702 §5; repealed by 1963 c.464 §10]

1.346 [1977 c.84 §2; repealed by 1991 c.815 §21]

1.350 [Amended by 1959 c.551 §7; 1963 c.464 §7; 1969 c.332 §8; 1989 c.966 §1; repealed by 1991 c.815 §21]

1.355 [1963 c.464 §2; 1973 c.704 §1; 1975 c.614 §1; repealed by 1991 c.815 §21]

1.360 [Amended by 1953 c.529 §5; 1959 c.551 §8; 1961 c.702 §1; 1963 c.464 §8; 1965 c.394 §7; 1969 c.332 §9; 1975 c.125 §3; 1975 c.614 §2; repealed by 1991 c.815 §21]

1.365 [1987 c.625 §6; repealed by 1991 c.815 §21]

1.370 [Repealed by 1963 c.464 §10]

1.380 [Amended by 1963 c.464 §9; subsection (7) enacted as 1969 c.332 §11; subsection (8) enacted as 1969 c.332 §17; repealed by 1991 c.815 §21]

1.385 [1969 c.332 §15; repealed by 1991 c.815 §21]

1.387 [1979 c.727 §1; 1981 c.684 §1; repealed by 1991 c.815 §21]

1.390 [1969 c.332 §10; repealed by 1991 c.815 §21]

COMMISSION ON JUDICIAL FITNESS AND DISABILITY

1.410 Commission on Judicial Fitness and Disability; term; Senate confirmation. (1) There is created the Commission on Judicial Fitness and Disability consisting of:
(a) Three judges appointed by the Supreme Court;
(b) Three persons appointed by the Board of Governors of the Oregon State Bar from among persons admitted to practice law in this state; and
(c) Three persons appointed by the Governor who are not qualified under either paragraph (a) or (b) of this subsection.
(2) The term of a member is four years, but whenever a member ceases to meet the qualifications under which the member was appointed, membership shall end. Before the expiration of the term of a member, a successor shall be appointed to perform the functions of a member on the day next following expiration of the term of the member. In case of a vacancy for any cause, the appointing authority shall make an appointment to become immediately effective for a four-year term.
(3) Appointments by the Governor are subject to confirmation by the Senate in the manner provided in ORS 171.562 and 171.565. [1967 c.294 §2; 1969 c.695 §16; 1971 c.511 §1; 1985 c.565 §2]

1.415 Powers and duties of commission; rules. (1) The Commission on Judicial Fitness and Disability may:
(a) Subject to the State Personnel Relations Law, appoint such subordinates and employees as the commission considers necessary to carry out the duties and powers vested in the commission.
(b) Request the assistance of and compensate physicians, expert witnesses and special counsel.
(c) By its chairperson or vice chairperson, take and preserve testimony and administer oaths to witnesses on any matter within its jurisdiction.
(2) Upon majority vote of the members of the commission or upon request of a judge whose conduct is subject to a hearing under ORS 1.420 or a judge whose alleged disability is subject to a hearing under ORS 1.425, the chairperson or vice chairperson of the commission shall issue any processes necessary to compel the attendance of witnesses and the production of any books, papers, records or documents as may be required.
(3) The commission shall adopt rules of procedure governing proceedings under ORS 1.420 and 1.425. [1967 c.294 §10; 1987 c.520 §4]

1.420 Investigation; hearings; consent to discipline; recommendation; temporary suspension. (1) Upon complaint from any person concerning the conduct of a judge or upon request of the Supreme Court, and after such investigation as the Commission on Judicial Fitness and Disability considers necessary, the commission may do any of the following:
(a) The commission may hold a hearing pursuant to subsection (3) of this section to inquire into the conduct of the judge.
(b) The commission may request the Supreme Court to appoint three qualified persons to act as masters, to hold a hearing pursuant to subsection (3) of this section and maintain a record on the matter referred to them and to report to the commission on the conduct of the judge.
(c) The commission may allow the judge to execute a consent to censure, suspension or removal. If a consent is entered into under this paragraph, the judge and the commission must enter into a written stipulation of facts. The consent and stipulation of facts shall be submitted by the commission to the Supreme Court.

(2) If the commission receives a complaint that appears to indicate that a judge has a disability as defined in ORS 1.303, the commission may refer the complaint to the Chief Justice of the Supreme Court for appropriate proceedings under ORS 1.303.

(3) When a hearing is held by the commission or by masters as authorized in subsection (1) of this section, the hearing shall be public and all the testimony and evidence given and received in the hearing shall be public records. The judge shall have the right to be present at such hearing, to be represented by counsel, to present testimony and evidence and to cross-examine witnesses.

(4) If, after hearing or after considering the record and report of the masters, the commission finds that the conduct of the judge justifies censure, suspension or removal from office, the commission shall recommend to the Supreme Court the censure or suspension or removal of the judge.

(5) The Supreme Court by order may temporarily suspend a judge whose conduct is the subject of proceedings under this section from exercising any judicial functions during the pendency of those proceedings. [1967 c.294 §7; 1971 c.511 §3; 1987 c.520 §5; 1997 c.720 §1]

1.425 Commission proceedings upon receipt of complaint of disability; hearing; physical examination; disposition. (1) Upon complaint from the Chief Justice of the Supreme Court as provided in ORS 1.303, and after such investigation as the Commission on Judicial Fitness and Disability considers necessary, the commission may:

(a) Proceed as provided in ORS 1.420; or

(b) If the investigation under this subsection indicates that the subject judge may have a temporary disability, hold a hearing pursuant to subsection (2) of this section to inquire into the alleged disability, or request the Supreme Court to appoint three qualified persons to act as masters, to hold a hearing pursuant to subsection (2) of this section and maintain a record on the matter referred to them and to report to the commission on the alleged disability.

(2) When a hearing is held by the commission or by masters as authorized in subsection (1)(b) of this section, the hearing shall not be open to the public unless the subject judge requests a public hearing. The testimony and evidence given and received in the hearing shall not be public records. The subject judge shall have the right to be present at such hearing, to be represented by counsel, to present testimony and evidence and to cross-examine witnesses.

(3)(a) The commission may direct that a subject judge, prior to a hearing, submit to a physical examination by one, two or three physicians licensed to practice in this state and appointed by the commission to conduct the examination, or submit to a mental evaluation by one, two or three physicians, psychologists or other mental health professionals licensed to practice in this state and appointed by the commission to conduct the evaluation, or submit to both that examination and evaluation. The persons appointed to conduct the examination or evaluation shall report thereon to the commission. A copy of any report to the commission shall be provided by the commission to the subject judge. The costs of the examination, evaluation and reporting shall be paid by the commission.

(b) If a subject judge directed to submit to an examination or evaluation fails to do so, the judge may not present as evidence in the proceeding the results of any medical examination of the judge done at the instance of the judge, and the commission or masters may consider the failure of the judge to submit to examination or evaluation as evidence that the judge has a disability.

(4) If, after hearing or after considering the record and report of the masters, the commission finds that the subject judge has a temporary disability, the commission may:

(a) Enter into a disposition of the matter with the subject judge, which may include agreement by the judge to obtain professional counseling, medical treatment or other assistance or to comply with other conditions in respect to the future conduct of the judge and provide for supervision of compliance by the judge and for investigation, hearing as provided in subsection (2) of this section and, if appropriate, action by the commission as provided in paragraph (b) of this subsection if the judge fails to comply; or

(b) If the commission also finds that the conduct of the subject judge justifies suspension, recommend to the Supreme Court that the judge be suspended without loss of salary for a period not exceeding one year.

(5) The Supreme Court, on its own motion or on recommendation by the commission, by order may temporarily suspend a judge whose alleged disability is involved in proceedings under this section from exercising any judicial functions during the pendency of those proceedings.

(6) If the commission recommends suspension under subsection (4)(b) of this section, the Supreme Court shall review the record of the proceedings under this section on the law and facts and may receive additional evidence and permit argument. The Supreme Court may order the judge suspended without loss of salary for a period not exceeding one year. Upon an order of suspension, the judge shall be suspended from office for the period specified in the order. Suspension does not create a vacancy in the office of judge during the period of suspension. In addition to or in lieu of an order of suspension, the Supreme Court may require that the judge obtain professional counseling, medical treatment or other assistance or comply with other conditions in respect to the future conduct of the judge. [1987 c.520 §3]

1.430 Supreme Court review; censure; order of suspension or removal. (1) If a hearing has been held under ORS 1.420, the Supreme Court shall review the record of the proceedings on the law and facts and may receive additional evidence. The Supreme Court may censure the judge or it may order the judge suspended or removed from office.

(2) If the commission has agreed to allow the judge to submit a consent to censure, suspension or removal, the Supreme Court shall review the stipulation of facts and the disciplinary action to which the judge has consented. If the Supreme Court approves the consent, the court shall censure the judge or order the judge suspended or removed from office pursuant to the terms of the consent. If the Supreme Court rejects the consent and stipulation in full, the court shall remand the matter to the commission for a hearing under ORS 1.420. The hearing shall be conducted as though the consent and stipulation had never been entered into, and the stipulations made by the judge may not be considered as evidence by the commission in the hearing. If the Supreme Court accepts the stipulation of facts but rejects the disciplinary action agreed to by the judge and the commission, the court may remand the matter to the commission for such further fact-finding as the court may direct on the issue of the appropriate discipline for the conduct, and may request that the matter be briefed and argued before the court. The Supreme Court may thereafter censure the judge, or enter an order suspending or removing the judge, as the court finds appropriate under the law and the facts.

(3) Upon an order for removal, the judge shall be removed from office and the salary of the judge shall cease and the office of the judge is vacant on the date of such order.

(4) Upon an order of suspension, the judge shall be suspended from office for the period specified in the order and the salary of the judge shall cease, if so ordered, from the date of the order until the end of the specified period. Suspension does not create a vacancy in the office of judge during the period of suspension. [1967 c.294 §7; 1971 c.511 §3; 1997 c.720 §2]

1.440 Status of records of proceedings under ORS 1.420 or 1.425. (1) Documents filed with the Commission on Judicial Fitness and Disability and the investigation conducted by the commission prior to a hearing pursuant to ORS 1.420 or 1.425 shall not be public records unless received as competent evidence in the course of a hearing pursuant to ORS 1.420. The decision of the commission after hearing or upon review of the record and report of masters under ORS 1.420 shall be a public record, together with the recommendations, if any, of the commission to the Supreme Court. The decision of the commission after hearing or upon review of the record and report of masters under ORS 1.425 shall not be a public record, except for a decision and recommendation to the Supreme Court under ORS 1.425 (4)(b). A consent to censure, suspension or removal executed by a judge under ORS 1.420 (1)(c), and a stipulation of facts entered into between the commission and a judge under ORS 1.420 (1)(c), shall not be a public record until the consent and stipulation are submitted to the Supreme Court.

(2) Documents filed and testimony given in proceedings under ORS 1.420 or 1.425 are privileged communications which may not be received in evidence in any judicial proceedings other than those directly connected with the administration of ORS 1.410 to 1.480 unless expressly or impliedly waived by the person tendering the document to or testifying in such proceedings or except in a criminal prosecution for perjury or false swearing before the commission.

(3) Members of the commission, masters appointed pursuant to ORS 1.420 or 1.425 and staff of the commission shall not disclose or use any investigation, testimony or documents which are not public records as defined in ORS 1.410 to 1.480 for any purpose other than in connection with their official duties in the administration of ORS 1.410 to 1.480. The commission may, upon the request of a judge who has been the subject of a complaint and proceedings thereon that are not public records, state the disposition of the complaint and proceedings and the reasons for its decision when the

commission finds that the complaint or proceedings have been publicized and fairness requires such comment. [1967 c.294 §8; 1981 c.354 §2; 1987 c.520 §6; 1997 c.720 §3]

1.450 Status of testimony in proceedings under ORS 1.420 or 1.425. Any testimony given by a witness compelled to appear before the Commission on Judicial Fitness and Disability or the masters appointed pursuant to ORS 1.420 or 1.425 shall not be used against the witness in any criminal action or proceeding, nor shall any criminal action or proceeding be brought against such witness on account of any testimony so given by the witness, except for perjury or false swearing committed before the commission or the masters. [1967 c.294 §14; 1987 c.520 §7]

1.460 Judge not to participate in proceedings involving self except in defense. A judge who is a member of the Commission on Judicial Fitness and Disability or of the Supreme Court or who acts as a master under ORS 1.420 or 1.425 shall not participate in any proceedings involving the conduct or alleged disability of the judge except in the defense of the judge. [1967 c.294 §9; 1987 c.520 §8]

1.470 Service of process; proof; return; witness fees. (1) Process issued by the commission or by the chairperson and vice chairperson of the commission shall be served by a person authorized to serve summons and in the manner prescribed for the service of a summons upon a defendant in a civil action in a circuit court. The process shall be returned to the authority issuing it within 10 days after its delivery to the person for service, with proof of service as for summons or that the person cannot be found. When served outside the county in which the process originated, the process may be returned by mail. The person to whom the process is delivered shall indorse thereon the date of delivery.
(2) Each witness compelled to attend any proceedings under ORS 1.420 or 1.425, other than an officer or employee of the state, a public corporation, or a political subdivision, shall receive for attendance the same fees and mileage allowance allowed by law to a witness in a civil case, payable from funds appropriated to the commission. [1967 c.294 §§11,12; 1973 c.827 §1; 1977 c.877 §1; 1979 c.284 §41; 1987 c.520 §9]

1.475 Procedure when process not obeyed. (1) Whenever a person summoned by the Commission on Judicial Fitness and Disability fails to appear to testify or fails to produce any books, papers, records or documents as required, or whenever any person so summoned refuses to answer any question pertinent to the subject under inquiry before the commission, or the masters appointed pursuant to ORS 1.420 or 1.425, the commission may apply to the circuit court for the county in which the failure occurred for an order to the person to attend and testify, or otherwise to comply with the demand or request of the commission or the masters.
(2) The application to the court shall be by ex parte motion upon which the court shall make an order requiring the person against whom it is directed to comply with the demand or request of the commission within three days after service of the order, or within such further time as the court may grant, or to justify the failure within that time.
(3) The order shall be served upon the person to whom it is directed in the manner required by this state for the service of process, which service is required to confer jurisdiction upon the court. Failure to obey an order issued by the court under this section is contempt of court. [1967 c.294 §13; 1987 c.520 §10]

1.480 Officers; quorum; compensation and expenses. (1) The Commission on Judicial Fitness and Disability shall select one of its members as chairperson, and another as vice chairperson, for such terms and to perform such functions as the commission shall determine.
(2) A majority of the commission constitutes a quorum for the transaction of business. Every recommendation on matters relating to the removal of a judge to the Supreme Court must be concurred in by a majority of the members of the commission.
(3) A member of the Commission on Judicial Fitness and Disability is entitled to compensation and expenses as provided in ORS 292.495. [1967 c.294 §§4,5; 1969 c.314 §2]

1.510 [Formerly 484.420; 1969 c.314 §3; 1971 c.404 §3; 1973 c.43 §1; 1973 c.374 §1; 1975 c.304 §2; 1979 c.477 §1; 1983 c.740 §3; repealed by 1985 c.725 §17]

1.520 [Formerly 484.410; 1971 c.404 §4; 1973 c.374 §2; 1977 c.132 §7; 1981 c.692 §4; 1981 s.s. c.3 §4; 1985 c.396 §5; 1985 c.725 §8a; 1993 c.531 §3; 1995 c.383 §120; 1995 c.545 §1a; 1995 c.781 §52; repealed by 1999 c.1051 §74]

CITATION AND PETITION FORMS

1.525 Uniform citation and petition forms for certain offenses. (1) The Supreme Court shall adopt one or more forms for the following purposes:
(a) A form of uniform violation citation for the purposes of ORS 153.045;
(b) A form of uniform criminal citation without complaint for the purposes of ORS 133.068;
(c) A form of uniform criminal citation with complaint for the purposes of ORS 133.069;
(d) Any form of uniform citation for categories of offenses as the court finds necessary or convenient; and
(e) A uniform petition for a driving while under the influence of intoxicants diversion agreement for the purposes of ORS 813.210.
(2) If changes are made to a uniform citation form under this section, the Supreme Court shall make a reasonable effort to minimize the financial impact of the changes on the state agencies and political subdivisions of this state that use the uniform citation form. Where possible, the effort to minimize the financial impact shall include a reasonable time for the state agencies and political subdivisions to exhaust their existing supplies of the citation form before the changes become effective.
(3) Except as provided in subsection (4) of this section, the uniform citation forms adopted by the Supreme Court under this section must be used by all enforcement officers, as defined in ORS 153.005, when issuing a violation citation or criminal citation.
(4) The uniform citation forms adopted by the Supreme Court under this section need not be used for:
(a) Offenses created by ordinance or agency rule governing parking of vehicles; or
(b) Offenses created by the ordinances of political subdivisions. [1979 c.477 §3; 1981 c.692 §5; 1981 c.803 §1; 1983 c.338 §879; 1985 c.725 §9; 1999 c.1051 §73]

1.530 [Formerly 484.430; repealed by 1973 c.43 §2]

REPRESENTATION OF JUDGES BY PRIVATE COUNSEL

1.550 Private counsel for judges. Whenever, pursuant to ORS chapter 180, the Attorney General is requested to represent a judge of the Supreme Court, Court of Appeals, Oregon Tax Court or circuit court and declines to do so, the judge may, subject to the provisions of ORS 30.260 to 30.300 and 30.310 to 30.400, employ private counsel as provided under ORS 1.560. [1977 c.79 §2]

1.560 Procedure for employment of private counsel; terms and conditions. In any case in which the judge desires the appointment of private counsel, the judge shall so notify the State Court Administrator. The State Court Administrator, under the direction of the Supreme Court, may authorize the judge to employ private counsel under the following circumstances:
(1) When the judge is a defendant in an action, suit or proceeding and there is no other party directly interested in the outcome of the action, suit or proceeding who should fairly bear the cost of representation;
(2) When the judge is a defendant in an action, suit or proceeding and the State Court Administrator concludes that no party interested in the outcome of the action, suit or proceeding will provide adequate representation for the judge; or

(3) In any action, suit or proceeding, when the State Court Administrator finds that employing private counsel is necessary to protect the public interest, the integrity of the judicial system, or the interests of the judge in performing duties as a state officer. [1977 c.79 §3; 2007 c.71 §2]

1.570 Claims for compensation of private counsel; approval by State Court Administrator. If private counsel is employed under ORS 1.560, such counsel shall submit to the State Court Administrator a verified and detailed claim for compensation, which claim shall include a statement of reimbursable expense incurred and the amount of time devoted to the matter on behalf of the judge. The State Court Administrator, under the direction of the Supreme Court, shall examine the claim and shall approve payment thereof in a reasonable amount. [1977 c.79 §4]

JUDGES PRO TEMPORE

1.600 Appointment pro tempore to Supreme Court or Court of Appeals; powers and duties. (1) The Supreme Court may appoint any regularly elected and qualified, or appointed and qualified, judge of the Court of Appeals, Oregon Tax Court or circuit court to serve as judge pro tempore of the Supreme Court, or any regularly elected and qualified, or appointed and qualified, judge of the Supreme Court, Oregon Tax Court or circuit court to serve as judge pro tempore of the Court of Appeals, whenever the Supreme Court determines that the appointment is reasonably necessary and will promote the more efficient administration of justice.
(2) An appointment under this section shall be made by order of the Supreme Court. The order shall designate the court to which the judge is appointed and the duration of the appointment. The Supreme Court shall cause a certified copy of the order to be sent to the judge appointed and another certified copy to be filed in the records of the court to which the judge is appointed.
(3) Each judge serving as judge pro tempore as provided in this section has all the judicial powers and duties, while so serving, of a regularly elected and qualified judge of the court to which the judge is appointed. However, a judge pro tempore shall not participate in the review of any case in which the judge pro tempore participated while serving on a lower court. Every decision, order or determination made by the Supreme Court or Court of Appeals while one or more judges pro tempore are serving as judges of the court shall be as binding and effective in every respect as if all of the judges participating were regularly elected and qualified judges of the court. [1975 c.706 §1; 1995 c.781 §5a; 2003 c.518 §8]

1.605 Compensation and expenses for judges under ORS 1.600. (1) A judge of the Supreme Court serving as judge pro tempore of the Court of Appeals as provided in ORS 1.600 shall receive the regular salary and expenses of a judge of the Supreme Court, including reimbursement for hotel bills and traveling expenses necessarily incurred by the judge pro tempore in the performance of duties as judge pro tempore.
(2) A judge of the Court of Appeals serving as judge pro tempore of the Supreme Court or a judge of the Oregon Tax Court or circuit court serving as judge pro tempore of the Supreme Court or Court of Appeals as provided in ORS 1.600 shall receive during the period of service as judge pro tempore, in addition to regular salary and expenses, the following compensation and expenses:
(a) An amount equal to the salary for the period of a regularly elected and qualified judge of the court to which the judge is appointed diminished by the amount received by the judge for the period in payment of regular salary as a judge; and
(b) If the judge is required to travel outside the county where the court of the judge is located, reimbursement for hotel bills and traveling expenses necessarily incurred by the judge in the performance of duties as judge pro tempore.
(3) The additional compensation and expenses payable under this section shall be paid by the state upon an itemized statement of the compensation and expenses, certified by the judge pro tempore that the services were performed and the expenses were necessarily and actually incurred. [1975 c.706 §2]

1.610 [1965 c.494 §1; 1967 c.270 §1; 1969 c.198 §27; 1969 c.577 §1; repealed by 1971 c.311 §2]

1.615 Appointment pro tempore to tax court or circuit court; powers and duties. (1) The Supreme Court may assign any regularly elected and qualified, or appointed and qualified, judge of the Supreme Court, Court of Appeals, Oregon Tax Court or circuit court to serve as judge pro tempore of the tax court or any circuit court, whenever the Supreme Court determines that the assignment is reasonably necessary and will promote the more efficient administration of justice.
(2) It is the duty of a judge assigned under this section to comply with the assignment. A judge assigned under this section is not required to take, subscribe or file any additional oath of office.
(3) Each judge assigned as provided in this section has all the judicial powers and duties, while serving under the assignment, of a regularly elected and qualified judge of the court to which the judge is assigned. The powers, jurisdiction and judicial authority of the judges in respect to any case or matter tried or heard by the judge while serving under the assignment shall continue beyond the expiration of the assignment so far as may be necessary to:
(a) Decide and dispose of any case or matter on trial or held under advisement.
(b) Hear and decide any motion for a new trial or for a judgment notwithstanding a verdict, or objections to any cost bill, that may be filed in the case.
(c) Settle a transcript for appeal and grant extensions of time therefor. [1975 c.706 §3; 1979 c.56 §2; 1989 c.124 §1; 1995 c.781 §5b]

1.620 [1965 c.494 §8; repealed by 1971 c.311 §2]

1.625 Compensation and expenses for judges under ORS 1.615. (1) A judge assigned as provided in ORS 1.615 shall receive the regular salary of the judge and expenses as a judge of the court of the judge.
(2) A judge assigned as provided in ORS 1.615 outside the county in which the judge regularly serves shall receive reimbursement for hotel bills and traveling expenses necessarily incurred by the judge in the performance of the duties of the judge under the assignment.
(3) The additional compensation and expenses payable under this section shall be paid by the state upon an itemized statement of the compensation and expenses, certified by the judge pro tempore that the services were performed and the expenses were necessarily and actually incurred. [1975 c.706 §4; 1995 c.658 §11]

1.630 [1965 c.494 §2; 1969 c.577 §2; repealed by 1971 c.311 §2]

1.635 Appointment pro tempore of eligible person to tax court or circuit court. The Supreme Court may appoint any eligible person to serve as judge pro tempore of the Oregon Tax Court or as judge pro tempore of the circuit court in any county or judicial district, whenever the Supreme Court determines that the appointment is reasonably necessary and will promote the more efficient administration of justice. A person is eligible for appointment if the person is a resident of this state and has been a member in good standing of the Oregon State Bar for a period of at least three years next preceding the appointment. [1975 c.706 §5; 1987 c.762 §1; 1989 c.124 §2; 2003 c.518 §9]

1.640 [1965 c.494 §3; 1967 c.270 §2; 1969 c.198 §28; repealed by 1971 c.311 §2]

1.645 Transfer, challenge, disqualification, supervision of person appointed under ORS 1.635. (1) A judge pro tempore of a circuit court appointed to serve in any county or judicial district as provided in ORS 1.635 may, at any time while serving under the appointment, be transferred and assigned by the Supreme Court to serve as judge pro tempore in any one or more other counties or judicial districts during the term of the appointment.
(2) Each judge pro tempore appointed and qualified as provided in ORS 1.635 has all the judicial powers, duties, jurisdiction and authority, while serving under the appointment, of a regularly elected and qualified judge of the court to which the judge pro tempore is appointed or assigned.
(3) The eligibility, appointment or qualification of an appointee under ORS 1.635, or the right of the appointee to hold the position of judge pro tempore in any particular county or judicial district while serving under the appointment, is subject to challenge only in a direct proceeding instituted for that purpose as provided in ORS 30.510 to 30.640. The proceeding may be instituted in the Supreme Court if it consents to take original jurisdiction thereof.

20

(4) A judge pro tempore appointed as provided in ORS 1.635 is subject to disqualification to sit in any case for any of the causes specified in ORS 14.210 or 14.250.

(5) A judge pro tempore appointed as provided in ORS 1.635 or assigned as provided in subsection (1) of this section to a court with one or more regularly elected and qualified judges on active duty shall be subject to the directions of the regular presiding judge of the court in respect to the assignment of cases and the general administration of the business of the court. [1975 c.706 §6]

1.650 [1965 c.494 §4; repealed by 1971 c.311 §2]

1.655 Extension and termination of appointment under ORS 1.635; eligibility to appear as attorney. (1) It is the duty of a judge pro tempore appointed as provided in ORS 1.635 to hear, decide and dispose of all cases and matters submitted to the judge pro tempore as promptly as the nature of the questions involved will permit. The powers, jurisdiction and judicial authority of the judge pro tempore in respect to any case or matter tried or heard by the judge pro tempore while serving under the appointment shall continue beyond the expiration of the appointment so far as may be necessary to:

(a) Decide and dispose of any case or matter on trial or held under advisement.

(b) Hear and decide any motion for a new trial or for a judgment notwithstanding a verdict, or objections to any cost bill, that may be filed in the case.

(c) Settle a transcript for appeal and grant extensions of time therefor.

(2) The Supreme Court at any time by order may:

(a) Extend the term of appointment of a judge pro tempore appointed as provided in ORS 1.635.

(b) Terminate the term of appointment of a judge pro tempore appointed as provided in ORS 1.635 as of a date specified in the order; but termination does not affect the validity of any judgment, order or other action of the judge pro tempore prior to the effective date of the termination.

(3) A judge pro tempore of a circuit court appointed as provided in ORS 1.635 is not eligible to appear as attorney in that court in any case tried by a jury during the time the judge pro tempore served as judge pro tempore. [1975 c.706 §7; 2003 c.576 §268; 2015 c.212 §11]

1.660 [1965 c.494 §5; 1967 c.270 §3; 1969 c.706 §64b; repealed by 1971 c.311 §2]

1.665 Compensation and expenses of persons appointed under ORS 1.635. (1) A judge pro tempore appointed as provided in ORS 1.635 shall be entitled to receive upon application therefor as compensation for each day the judge pro tempore is actually engaged in the performance of duties under the appointment an amount equal to five percent of the gross monthly salary of a regularly elected and qualified judge of the court to which the judge is appointed, or one-half of that daily compensation for services of one-half day or less. The compensation shall be paid upon the certificate of the judge pro tempore that the services were performed for the number of days shown in the certificate, and in the same manner as the salaries of the regularly elected and qualified judges are paid. A person who wishes or is willing to serve without compensation may do so.

(2) A judge pro tempore appointed as provided in ORS 1.635 or assigned as provided in ORS 1.645 to serve outside the county in which the judge pro tempore resides or maintains an office shall receive, in addition to daily compensation, if any, reimbursement for hotel bills and traveling expenses necessarily incurred by the judge pro tempore in the performance of duties as judge pro tempore. The expenses shall be paid upon an itemized statement of the expenses, certified by the judge pro tempore that the expenses were necessarily and actually incurred, in the same manner as like expenses of regularly elected and qualified judges are paid. [1975 c.706 §8; 1981 c.65 §1]

1.670 [1965 c.494 §6; repealed by 1971 c.311 §2]

1.675 Judge pro tempore ineligible to participate in selection or removal of Chief Justice, Chief Judge or presiding judge. A person appointed or assigned to serve and serving as judge pro tempore of a court under ORS 1.600, 1.615 or 1.635 is not eligible to be, or to participate in the selection or removal of, the Chief Justice, Chief Judge or presiding judge of the court to which the person is appointed or assigned. [1981 s.s. c.1 §6]

1.680 [1965 c.494 §7; 1969 c.314 §4; repealed by 1971 c.311 §2]

1.690 [1965 c.494 §9; repealed by 1971 c.311 §2]

1.700 [1965 c.494 §10; repealed by 1971 c.311 §2]

1.710 [1965 c.494 §11; 1967 c.270 §4; repealed by 1971 c.311 §2]

COUNCIL ON COURT PROCEDURES

1.725 Legislative findings. The Legislative Assembly finds that:

(1) Oregon laws relating to civil procedure designed for the benefit of litigants which meet the needs of the court system and the bar are necessary to assure prompt and efficient administration of justice in the courts of the state.

(2) No coordinated system of continuing review of the Oregon laws relating to civil procedure now exists.

(3) Development of a system of continuing review of the Oregon laws relating to civil procedure requires the creation of a Council on Court Procedures.

(4) A Council on Court Procedures will be able to review the Oregon laws relating to civil procedure and coordinate and study proposals concerning the Oregon laws relating to civil procedure advanced by all interested persons. [1977 c.890 §1]

1.730 Council on Court Procedures; membership; terms; rules; meetings; expenses of members. (1) There is created a Council on Court Procedures consisting of:

(a) One judge of the Supreme Court, chosen by the Supreme Court.

(b) One judge of the Court of Appeals, chosen by the Court of Appeals.

(c) Eight judges of the circuit court, chosen by the Executive Committee of the Circuit Judges Association.

(d) Twelve members of the Oregon State Bar, appointed by the Board of Governors of the Oregon State Bar. The Board of Governors, in making the appointments referred to in this paragraph, shall include but not be limited to appointments from members of the bar active in civil trial practice, to the end that the lawyer members of the council shall be broadly representative of the trial bar and the regions of the state.

(e) One public member, chosen by the Supreme Court.

(2)(a) A quorum of the council shall be constituted by a majority of the members of the council. If a quorum is present, an affirmative vote by a majority of the members of the council who are present is required for action by the council on all matters other than promulgation of rules under ORS 1.735. An affirmative vote of fifteen members of the council shall be required to promulgate rules pursuant to ORS 1.735.

(b) The council shall adopt rules of procedure and shall choose, from among its membership, annually, a chairperson to preside over the meetings of the council.

(3)(a) All meetings of the council shall be held in compliance with the provisions of ORS 192.610 to 192.690.

(b) In addition to the requirements imposed by paragraph (a) of this subsection, with respect to the public hearings required by ORS 1.740 and with respect to any meeting at which final action will be taken on the promulgation, amendment or repeal of a rule under ORS 1.735, the council shall cause to be published or distributed to all members of the bar, at least two weeks before such hearing or meeting, a notice which shall include the time and place and a description of the substance of the agenda of the hearing or meeting.

(c) The council shall make available upon request a copy of any rule which it proposes to promulgate, amend or repeal.

(4) Members of the Council on Court Procedures shall serve for terms of four years and shall be eligible for reappointment to one additional term, provided that, where an appointing authority has more than one vacancy to fill, the length of the initial term shall be fixed at either two or four years by that authority to accomplish staggered expiration dates of the terms to be filled. Vacancies occurring shall be filled by the appointing authority for the unexpired term.

(5) Members of the Council on Court Procedures shall not receive compensation for their services but may receive actual and necessary travel or other expenses incurred in the performance of their official duties as members of the council, as provided in ORS 292.210 to 292.288. [1977 c.890 §2; 1981 c.545 §1; 1993 c.772 §1; 1995 c.658 §12; 1997 c.137 §§1,2; 2003 c.110 §2; 2007 c.65 §1]

1.735 Rules of procedure; limitation on scope and substance; submission of rules to members of bar and Legislative Assembly. (1) The Council on Court Procedures shall promulgate rules governing pleading, practice and procedure, including rules governing form and service of summons and process and personal and in rem jurisdiction, in all civil proceedings in all courts of the state which shall not abridge, enlarge or modify the substantive rights of any litigant. The rules authorized by this section do not include rules of evidence and rules of appellate procedure. The rules thus adopted and any amendments which may be adopted from time to time, together with a list of statutory sections superseded thereby, shall be submitted to the Legislative Assembly at the beginning of each odd-numbered year regular session and shall go into effect on January 1 following the close of that session unless the Legislative Assembly shall provide an earlier effective date. The Legislative Assembly may, by statute, amend, repeal or supplement any of the rules.

(2) A promulgation, amendment or repeal of a rule by the council is invalid and does not become effective unless the exact language of the proposed promulgation, amendment or repeal is published or distributed to all members of the bar at least 30 days before the meeting at which the council plans to take final action on the promulgation, amendment or repeal. If the language of the proposed promulgation, amendment or repeal is changed by the council after consideration of the language at the meeting, the council must publish or distribute notification of the change to all members of the bar within 60 days after the meeting. All changes made to proposed promulgations, amendments or repeals of rules pursuant to the provisions of this subsection must be clearly identified when the promulgation, amendment or repeal is submitted to the Legislative Assembly under subsection (1) of this section. [1977 c.890 §3; 1979 c.284 §1; 1983 c.751 §6; 1993 c.772 §2; 2003 c.110 §1; 2011 c.545 §27]

1.740 Employment of staff; public hearings. In the exercise of its power under ORS 1.735, the council:
(1) May employ or contract with any person or persons, as the council considers necessary, to assist the council; and
(2) Shall endeavor to hold at least one public hearing in each of the congressional districts of the state during the period between odd-numbered year regular sessions of the Legislative Assembly. [1977 c.890 §4; 1993 c.772 §3; 2011 c.545 §69]

1.742 [1993 c.634 §3; repealed by 2001 c.716 §30]

1.745 Laws on civil pleading, practice and procedure deemed rules of court until changed. All provisions of law relating to pleading, practice and procedure, including provisions relating to form and service of summons and process and personal and in rem jurisdiction, in all civil proceedings in courts of this state are deemed to be rules of court and remain in effect as such until and except to the extent they are modified, superseded or repealed by rules which become effective under ORS 1.735. [1977 c.890 §5; 1979 c.284 §2]

1.750 Legislative Counsel to publish rules. The Legislative Counsel shall cause the rules which have become effective under ORS 1.735, as they may be amended, repealed or supplemented by the Legislative Assembly, to be arranged, indexed, printed, published and annotated in the Oregon Revised Statutes. [1977 c.890 §6]

1.755 Gifts, grants and donations; Council on Court Procedures Account. (1) The Council on Court Procedures is authorized to accept gifts, grants and donations from any source for expenditure to carry out the duties, functions and powers of the council.
(2) The Council on Court Procedures Account is established separate and distinct from the General Fund. All moneys received by the council, other than appropriations from the General Fund, shall be deposited into the account and are continuously appropriated to the council to carry out the duties, functions and powers of the council. [1995 c.61 §3; reenacted by 1997 c.196 §3; 2001 c.716 §20]

1.760 Legislative advisory committee. (1) The Council on Court Procedures shall elect five persons from among its members to serve as a legislative advisory committee. Two members of the committee shall be judges. Two members shall be members of the Oregon State Bar who are not judges. One member shall be the public member designated under ORS 1.730 (1)(e). The committee shall elect one of its members to serve as chairperson of the committee.
(2) Upon the request of the chairperson of a legislative committee considering legislation that proposes changes to the Oregon Rules of Civil Procedure, the legislative advisory committee established under this section shall provide technical analysis and advice to the legislative committee. Analysis and advice shall be by a majority vote of the legislative advisory committee. The committee shall consult with and consider comments from the full Council on Court Procedures to the extent possible. Analysis and advice under this subsection must be provided within 10 days after the request from the chairperson of a legislative committee.
(3) The legislative advisory committee established under this section may vote to take a position on behalf of the Council on Court Procedures on proposed legislation. If the legislative advisory committee has voted to take a position on behalf of the council, the committee shall so indicate to the legislative committee.
(4) Members of the legislative advisory committee established under this section may meet by telephone and may vote by telephone. Meetings of the committee are not subject to ORS 192.610 to 192.690.
(5) Members of the legislative advisory committee established under this section may appear before legislative committees for the purpose of testifying on legislation that proposes changes to the Oregon Rules of Civil Procedure. [1995 c.455 §8]

JUDICIAL CONFERENCE

1.810 Judicial conference; membership; officers. There hereby is created and established a Judicial Conference of the State of Oregon. The conference shall consist of all the judges of the Supreme Court, the Court of Appeals, the Oregon Tax Court and the circuit courts and all senior judges certified under ORS 1.300. The Chief Justice of the Supreme Court shall be chairperson of the conference and shall have power to invite any persons not members of the conference to attend the meetings of the conference and consult with it in the performance of its duties. The State Court Administrator shall act as executive secretary of the conference. [1955 c.470 §1; 1959 c.552 §12; 1963 c.423 §2; 1965 c.494 §13; 1969 c.198 §29; 1971 c.95 §1; 1983 c.465 §1; 1995 c.658 §5; 2013 c.155 §8]

1.820 Function of conference. The conference may make a continuous survey and study of the organization, jurisdiction, procedure, practice and methods of administration and operation of the various courts within the state. [1955 c.470 §2; 1965 c.494 §14; 1995 c.273 §2]

1.830 Meetings. The Judicial Conference of the State of Oregon shall meet annually or at such other times as the Chief Justice of the Supreme Court directs. [1955 c.470 §3; 1965 c.494 §15; 2013 c.155 §9]

1.840 Annual report. The conference shall report annually to the Governor with respect to such matters, including recommendations for legislation, as it may wish to bring to the attention of the Governor or of the legislature. [1955 c.470 §4; 1959 c.552 §13; 1965 c.494 §16]

1.850 [1985 c.725 §5; repealed by 1993 c.742 §38]

ADVISORY COUNCILS

1.851 Local criminal justice advisory councils. (1) The presiding judge of each judicial district shall establish a local criminal justice advisory council, unless one already exists, in each county in the judicial district. Membership of the council shall include, but is not limited to, representatives of the following:

(a) The presiding judge;

(b) The district attorney;

(c) The local correctional administrator;

(d) Public defense service providers;

(e) The county bar association;

(f) Local law enforcement; and

(g) State law enforcement.

(2) In addition to the persons listed in subsection (1) of this section, the judge may invite the participation of any other persons involved in the criminal justice system whose participation would be of benefit.

(3) The local criminal justice advisory council shall meet regularly to consider and address methods of coordinating court, public defense and related services and resources in the most efficient and cost-effective manner that complies with the constitutional and statutory mandates and responsibilities of all participants.

(4) To assist the council in these efforts, council participants shall provide the council with proposed budget information and caseload and workload projections. [1993 c.481 §1; 2001 c.962 §100]

JUSTICE AND MUNICIPAL COURT REGISTRY AND REPORTS

1.855 State Court Administrator to establish registry of justice and municipal courts. (1) The State Court Administrator shall establish a registry of municipal courts and justice courts of this state. The registry shall include all information required to be provided by counties and cities to the State Court Administrator under this section.

(2) Upon creation of a justice court, the county in which the justice court is established shall give notice to the State Court Administrator of the boundaries of the justice court district. The county shall also provide to the State Court Administrator the name of each justice of the peace, the term of each justice of the peace and the mailing address for the justice court. Upon modification or dissolution of a justice court district, the county shall promptly notify the State Court Administrator of the modification or dissolution.

(3) Upon creation of a municipal court, the city establishing the municipal court shall give notice to the State Court Administrator that the court has been created. The city shall also provide to the State Court Administrator the name of each municipal judge elected or appointed to the court, the term of each municipal judge elected or appointed and the mailing address for the municipal court. Upon ceasing to operate a municipal court, the city shall promptly notify the State Court Administrator that the municipal court is no longer in operation. [2001 c.761 §1]

1.860 Reports relating to municipal courts and justice courts. (1) Once every two years, the League of Oregon Cities and the Association of Oregon Counties shall report to the Legislative Fiscal Officer information identified by the Legislative Fiscal Officer relating to the caseload, revenues and expenditures of municipal courts and justice courts. Before establishing the list of information to be provided, the Legislative Fiscal Officer shall consult with the League of Oregon Cities and the Association of Oregon Counties. The Legislative Fiscal Officer may not request information that requires additional data gathering by municipal courts, justice courts, cities and counties. The reported information shall be based on the fiscal year used by each municipal court and justice court.

(2) The reports required by this section must be made not later than October 1 of each even-numbered year. The Legislative Fiscal Officer may specify the manner in which the reports are made. The Legislative Fiscal Officer shall provide a summary of the information provided under this section to the Joint Committee on Ways and Means upon the convening of the next odd-numbered year regular session of the Legislative Assembly. Copies of the summary shall be provided to the League of Oregon Cities and the Association of Oregon Counties. [2012 c.107 §86]

Chapter 2 — Supreme Court; Court of Appeals

SUPREME COURT; COURT OF APPEALS

COURTS OF RECORD; COURT OFFICERS; JURIES

SUPREME COURT

2.010   Number of judges of Supreme Court

2.020   Qualifications of judges

2.040   Position number of judges

2.045   Chief Justice

2.100   Quorum

2.111   Departments of court; sitting in departments or en banc; participation in decision of matter

2.120   Rules, generally

2.130   Rules governing original jurisdiction

PUBLICATION OF COURT DECISIONS

2.141   Filing of court decisions

2.150   Publication and distribution of court decisions and other official documents

2.165   Court Publications Account

COURT OF APPEALS

2.510   Court of Appeals

2.516   Jurisdiction of all appeals exclusive; exceptions

2.520   Procedure for review of decisions of Court of Appeals

2.540   Number of judges of Court of Appeals; qualifications; term

2.550   Chief Judge

2.560   Rules; where court sits; appellate settlement program; fees

2.570   Departments of court; sitting in departments or en banc; participation in decision of matter

2.590   Expenses for judges when away from state capital

ALTERNATIVE DISPUTE RESOLUTION

2.700   Liability of persons providing dispute resolution services

SUPREME COURT

2.010 Number of judges of Supreme Court. The Supreme Court shall consist of seven judges.

2.020 Qualifications of judges. (1) The judges of the Supreme Court shall be citizens of the United States, and shall have resided in this state at least three years next preceding their election or appointment.
(2) All persons elected judges of the Supreme Court must, at time of their election, have been admitted to practice in the Supreme Court of Oregon.

2.040 Position number of judges. The positions of the members of the Supreme Court shall be designated by the numbers 1 to 7, following the designation made by section 1, chapter 241, Laws of Oregon 1929, and each incumbent shall be designated by the same position number as the judge whom the incumbent succeeds in office.

2.045 Chief Justice. (1) The Chief Justice of the Supreme Court shall be a judge of the court selected by vote of a majority of the judges of the court. The judges of the court shall endeavor to select a judge who is well qualified to act as the administrative head of the judicial department of government in this state.
(2) The Chief Justice may be removed from the office of Chief Justice by vote of a majority of the judges of the court when the Chief Justice fails to perform adequately the functions of the office.
(3) The term of office of the Chief Justice is six years, commencing on the date of selection. The term of office of the Chief Justice is not interrupted by expiration of the term of the Chief Justice as a judge of the court if the judge is elected judge of the court for a succeeding term. A judge may be selected as Chief Justice for successive terms of the office of Chief Justice.
(4) If there is a vacancy for any cause in the office of Chief Justice, a successor Chief Justice shall be selected by vote of a majority of the judges of the court.
(5) The Chief Justice may designate another judge of the court to perform the functions of the office of Chief Justice when the Chief Justice is temporarily unable to perform those functions. [1959 c.384 §2 (enacted in lieu of 2.050); 1981 s.s. c.1 §1]
  2.050 [Repealed by 1959 c.384 §1 (2.045 enacted in lieu of 2.050)]
  2.052 [1959 c.44 §1; 1969 c.198 §31; repealed by 1975 c.706 §10]
  2.055 [1959 c.44 §2; repealed by 1975 c.706 §10]
  2.058 [1959 c.44 §3; 1961 c.387 §1; 1969 c.198 §32; repealed by 1975 c.706 §10]
  2.060 [Amended by 1955 c.127 §1; repealed by 1959 c.44 §7]
  2.070 [Repealed by 1983 c.763 §9]
  2.080 [Repealed by 1979 c.55 §1]
  2.090 [Repealed by 1979 c.55 §1]

2.100 Quorum. Subject to ORS 2.111, the presence of a majority of all the judges of the Supreme Court is necessary for the transaction of any business, except that less than a majority of the judges may meet and adjourn from day to day, or for the term, with the same effect as if all the judges were present. [Amended by 1959 c.44 §6; 2003 c.14 §4]
  2.110 [Repealed by 1959 c.44 §4 (2.111 enacted in lieu of 2.110)]

2.111 Departments of court; sitting in departments or en banc; participation in decision of matter. (1) In hearing and determining causes, the Supreme Court may sit all together or in departments.
(2) A department shall consist of not less than three nor more than five judges. For convenience of administration, each department may be numbered. The Chief Justice shall from time to time designate the number of departments and make assignments of the judges among the departments. The Chief Justice may sit in one or more of the departments and when so sitting may preside. The Chief Justice shall designate a judge to preside in each department.
(3) The majority of any department shall consist of regularly elected and qualified judges of the Supreme Court.
(4) The Chief Justice shall apportion the business to the departments. Each department shall have power to hear and determine causes and all questions which may arise therein, subject to subsection (5) of this section. The presence of three judges is necessary to transact business in any department, except such as may be done in chambers by any judge. The concurrence of three judges is necessary to pronounce a judgment.
(5) The Chief Justice or a majority of the regularly elected and qualified judges of the Supreme Court at any time may refer a cause to be considered en banc. When sitting en banc, the court may include not more than two judges pro tempore of the Supreme Court. When the court sits en banc, the concurrence of a majority of the judges participating is necessary to pronounce a judgment, but if the judges participating are equally divided in their views as to the judgment to be given, the decision being reviewed shall be affirmed.
(6) The Chief Justice may rule on motions and issue orders in procedural matters in the Supreme Court.
(7) A judge or judge pro tempore of the Supreme Court may participate in the decision of the matter without resubmission of the cause even though the judge is not present for oral argument on the matter.
(8) A judge or judge pro tempore of the Supreme Court may participate in the decision of a matter without resubmission of the cause in the following circumstances:

(a) The judge was appointed or elected to the Supreme Court after submission of the cause.

(b) The judge is participating in the decision of a cause that was submitted to a department, and the judge is participating in lieu of a judge of the department who died, became disabled, was disqualified or was otherwise unable to participate in the decision of a cause submitted to the department.

(c) The judge is considering a cause en banc, but the judge was not part of the department that originally considered the cause. [1959 c.44 §5 (enacted in lieu of 2.110); 1995 c.273 §24; 1999 c.659 §1]

2.120 Rules, generally. The Supreme Court shall have power to make and enforce all rules necessary for the prompt and orderly dispatch of the business of the court, and the remanding of causes to the court below.

2.130 Rules governing original jurisdiction. The Supreme Court is empowered to prescribe and make rules governing the conduct in that court of all causes of original jurisdiction therein.

2.140 [Repealed by 1953 c.345 §3]
PUBLICATION OF COURT DECISIONS

2.141 Filing of court decisions. The judges of the Supreme Court and Court of Appeals shall cause their decisions to be prepared, in such number and manner as they may determine, and delivered to the State Court Administrator. The administrator shall file a copy of each decision in the office of the administrator and cause other copies to be distributed as determined by the Supreme Court. [1953 c.345 §1; 1965 c.233 §2; 1967 c.398 §1; 1971 c.193 §9; 1971 c.348 §2; 1971 c.526 §1; 1973 c.781 §1; 1975 c.69 §4; 1979 c.876 §1]

2.145 [Formerly 2.580; repealed by 1975 c.69 §8]

2.150 Publication and distribution of court decisions and other official documents. (1) The Supreme Court shall arrange for the publication and distribution of bound volumes of reports of decisions of the Supreme Court and Court of Appeals, of bound volumes of reports of decisions of the Oregon Tax Court determined to be of general public interest under ORS 305.450, of unbound copies of those decisions to be used as advance sheets and press summaries, rules and other official judicial department publications. The bound volumes of reports or advance sheets shall contain additional material as the Supreme Court may direct.

(2) The bound volumes of reports or advance sheets or both may be printed and bound, as the Supreme Court shall determine, by:

(a) The Oregon Department of Administrative Services in the same manner as other state printing; or

(b) A private printer pursuant to a contract entered into by the Supreme Court with the printer and not subject to ORS 282.020.

(3) The bound volumes of reports or advance sheets or both may be distributed, as the Supreme Court shall determine, by:

(a) The State Court Administrator; or

(b) A private distributor pursuant to a contract entered into by the Supreme Court with the distributor.

(4) The bound volumes of reports and advance sheets shall be distributed without charge as determined by the Supreme Court or sold by the distributor. Except as otherwise provided in a contract entered into under subsection (3)(b) of this section, the State Court Administrator shall determine sale prices and all moneys collected or received from sales shall be paid into the Court Publications Account established by ORS 2.165.

(5) In addition to bound volumes of reports or advance sheets under the provisions of this section, the Supreme Court may make any of the decisions of courts or other court publications available in electronic format. Access to the electronic publications may be without charge or subject to such charge as may be established by the Supreme Court. All moneys collected or received from sales shall be paid into the Court Publications Account established by ORS 2.165. [Amended by 1961 c.103 §1; 1973 c.781 §2; 1975 c.69 §5; 1979 c.876 §2; 1982 s.s.1 c.7 §1; 1987 c.328 §1; 1993 c.98 §10; 1995 c.79 §2; 1997 c.801 §111]

2.160 [Amended by 1961 c.103 §2; 1971 c.193 §10; 1973 c.781 §3; 1975 c.69 §6; repealed by 1979 c.976 §4]

2.165 Court Publications Account. There is established in the General Fund an account to be known as the Court Publications Account. All moneys in the account are appropriated continuously to the Supreme Court for the purpose of paying expenses incurred by the court under ORS 2.150 and for the purpose of paying all or part of the expenses of providing electronic access to State of Oregon Law Library materials and other official Judicial Department publications. Disbursements of moneys from the account shall be approved by the Chief Justice of the Supreme Court or, as directed by the Chief Justice, the State Court Administrator. [1982 s.s.1 c.7 §3; 2001 c.779 §4]

2.170 [1967 c.398 §9(1),(2); 1971 c.193 §11; 1975 c.69 §7; repealed by 1979 c.976 §4]

2.310 [1953 c.34 §1; repealed by 1959 c.552 §16]

2.320 [1953 c.34 §4; 1955 c.437 §1; repealed by 1959 c.552 §16]

2.330 [1953 c.34 §§2,3,7; repealed by 1959 c.552 §16]

2.340 [1953 c.34 §5; repealed by 1959 c.552 §16]

2.350 [1959 c.552 §2; renumbered 8.060]

COURT OF APPEALS

2.510 Court of Appeals. As part of the judicial branch of state government, there is created a court of justice to be known as the Court of Appeals. [1969 c.198 §1; 1969 c.591 §262a; 1971 c.567 §1; 1971 c.734 §33; 1975 c.611 §22; 1977 c.158 §4]

2.515 [1969 c.198 §77; repealed by 1977 c.158 §5]

2.516 Jurisdiction of all appeals exclusive; exceptions. Except where original jurisdiction is conferred on the Supreme Court by the Oregon Constitution or by statute and except as provided in ORS 19.405 and 138.255, the Court of Appeals shall have exclusive jurisdiction of all appeals. [1977 c.158 §2; 1981 c.550 §5]

2.520 Procedure for review of decisions of Court of Appeals. Any party aggrieved by a decision of the Court of Appeals may petition the Supreme Court for review within 35 days after the date of the decision, in such manner as provided by rules of the Supreme Court. [1969 c.198 §2; 1973 c.516 §1; 1983 c.774 §2]

2.530 [1969 c.198 §3; repealed by 1977 c.158 §5]

2.540 Number of judges of Court of Appeals; qualifications; term. (1) The Court of Appeals shall consist of 13 judges.

(2) A judge of the Court of Appeals shall be an elector of the county of the residence of the judge and be admitted to the practice of law in this state.

(3) Each judge of the Court of Appeals shall hold office for a term of six years and until a successor is elected and qualified. [1969 c.198 §4; 1973 c.377 §1; 1977 c.451 §1; 2012 c.87 §1]

2.550 Chief Judge. (1) The Chief Judge of the Court of Appeals shall be a judge of the court appointed as provided in ORS 1.003.

(2) The Chief Judge may designate another judge of the court to perform the functions of the office of Chief Judge when the Chief Judge is temporarily unable to perform those functions.

(3) The Chief Judge, to facilitate exercise of administrative authority and supervision over the court and consistent with applicable provisions of law, may make rules, issue orders and take other action appropriate to that exercise. [1969 c.198 §5; 1981 s.s. c.1 §7]

2.560 Rules; where court sits; appellate settlement program; fees. (1) The Court of Appeals shall sit primarily in Salem, but also may sit in other locations designated under ORS 1.085 (2).

(2) The Court of Appeals may make and enforce all rules necessary for the prompt and orderly dispatch of the business of the court, and the remanding of causes to the lower courts, and not inconsistent with applicable rules made or orders issued by the Chief Justice of the Supreme Court or the Chief Judge of the Court of Appeals.

(3) The Court of Appeals shall establish an appellate settlement program and adopt and enforce all rules necessary for the prompt and orderly dispatch of the business of the program.

(4) Rules adopted by the Court of Appeals under subsection (3) of this section shall establish fees payable for services provided under the program. [1969 c.198 §7; 1971 c.193 §7; 1973 c.484 §2; 1981 s.s. c.1 §20; 1983 c.763 §4; 1997 c.801 §87; 2011 c.595 §85; 2012 c.48 §5]

2.565 [1997 c.801 §88; repealed by 2011 c.595 §68a]

2.570 Departments of court; sitting in departments or en banc; participation in decision of matter. (1) In hearing and determining causes, the judges of the Court of Appeals may sit together or in departments.

(2)(a) Except as provided in paragraph (b) of this subsection, a department shall consist of three judges. For convenience of administration, each department may be numbered. The Chief Judge shall from time to time designate the number of departments and make assignments of the judges among the departments. The Chief Judge may sit in one or more departments and when so sitting may preside. The Chief Judge shall designate a judge to preside in each department.

(b) The Chief Judge may order that a department consist of two judges unless a third judge is necessary to break a tie vote by the department.

(3) Except as provided in this subsection, the majority of any department shall consist of regularly elected or appointed judges of the Court of Appeals. If disqualifications, recusals or other events reduce the number of available judges to fewer than the necessary number of judges, the Supreme Court may appoint such number of qualified persons as may be necessary as pro tempore members of the Court of Appeals.

(4) The Chief Judge shall apportion the business of the court between the departments. Each department shall have power to hear and determine causes, and all questions that may arise therein, subject to subsection (5) of this section. The presence of two judges is necessary to transact business in any department, except such business as may be transacted in chambers by any judge. The concurrence of two judges is necessary to pronounce judgment.

(5) The Chief Judge or a majority of the regularly elected or appointed judges of the Court of Appeals at any time may refer a cause to be considered en banc. When sitting en banc, the court may include not more than two judges pro tempore of the Court of Appeals. When the court sits en banc, the concurrence of a majority of the judges participating is necessary to pronounce judgment, but if the judges participating are equally divided in their view as to the judgment to be given, the judgment appealed from shall be affirmed.

(6) The Chief Judge may rule on motions and issue orders in procedural matters in the Court of Appeals or may delegate the authority to rule on motions and issue orders in procedural matters to an appellate commissioner as provided for in the court's rules of appellate procedure.

(7) A judge or judge pro tempore of the Court of Appeals may participate in the decision of the matter without resubmission of the cause even though the judge is not present for oral argument on the matter.

(8) A judge or judge pro tempore of the Court of Appeals may participate in the decision of a matter without resubmission of the cause in the following circumstances:

(a) The judge was appointed or elected to the Court of Appeals after submission of the cause.

(b) The judge is participating in the decision of a cause that was submitted to a department, and the judge is participating in lieu of a judge of the department who has died, become disabled, is disqualified or is otherwise unable to participate in the decision of a cause submitted to the department.

(c) The judge is considering a cause en banc, but the judge was not part of the department that originally considered the cause. [1969 c.198 §6; 1973 c.108 §1; 1985 c.734 §1; 1989 c.124 §3; 1999 c.59 §2; 1999 c.659 §2; 2003 c.14 §5; 2007 c.547 §13; 2009 c.231 §1]

2.580 [1969 c.198 §8; renumbered 2.145]

2.590 Expenses for judges when away from state capital. When a judge of the Court of Appeals holds court or performs any other official function away from the state capital, hotel bills and traveling expenses necessarily incurred by the judge in the performance of that duty shall be paid by the state. Such expenses are to be paid upon the certificate of the judge to the truth of an itemized statement of the expenses in the manner provided by law. [1969 c.198 §10]

2.600 [1969 c.198 §30; repealed by 1975 c.706 §10]

ALTERNATIVE DISPUTE RESOLUTION

2.700 Liability of persons providing dispute resolution services. In any program established by the Oregon appellate courts to promote settlement of cases that have been filed with that court, persons assigned to a case through the program to assist and facilitate in working toward a settlement for the case are immune from civil liability for or resulting from any act or omission done or made while engaged in efforts to assist or facilitate a settlement, unless the act or omission was made or done in bad faith, with malicious intent or in a manner exhibiting a willful, wanton disregard of the rights, safety or property of another. [1995 c.678 §3]

Chapter 3 — Circuit Courts Generally

New sections of law were enacted by the Legislative Assembly during its 2018 regular session and pertain to or are likely to be compiled in this ORS chapter. See sections in the following 2018 Oregon Laws chapters: 2018 Session Laws 0029

2017 EDITION

CIRCUIT COURTS GENERALLY

COURTS OF RECORD; COURT OFFICERS; JURIES

JUDICIAL DISTRICTS, JUDGES AND JURISDICTION

3.012   Judicial districts

3.013   State as single judicial district

3.014   Special provisions for fourth judicial district (Multnomah County)

3.016   Special provisions for sixth judicial district (Morrow and Umatilla Counties)

3.030   Election of circuit judges

3.041   Qualifications of circuit judges; residence

3.050   Circuit judges to be members of bar

3.060   Salary of judges; expenses

3.070   Powers of judges in chambers; filing and entering of decisions not signed in open court

3.075   Powers of judges to act in joint or separate session; testing process

3.130   Transfer of judicial jurisdiction of certain county courts to circuit courts

3.132   Concurrent jurisdiction with justice and municipal courts

3.134   Application of state statutes to municipal ordinance

3.136   Jurisdiction over violations of Portland charter and ordinances; disposition of moneys; hearings officers

3.185   Habeas corpus hearings by Circuit Court for Marion County

3.220   Rules; procedure when judges disagree

3.225   Establishing specialized subject-matter departments; approval by Chief Justice; eligibility and assignment of judges

JURISDICTION OVER JUVENILE AND FAMILY-RELATED MATTERS

3.250   Definitions for ORS 3.250 to 3.280

3.255   Policy and intent

3.260   Juvenile jurisdiction vested in circuit courts; authority for transfer of jurisdiction over family-related matters to circuit courts

3.265   Limits on transfer of juvenile jurisdiction

3.270   Transfer of juvenile jurisdiction and jurisdiction over family-related matters to circuit courts

3.275   Procedure for transfer of jurisdiction over certain family-related matters

3.280   Court services for circuit courts

PANEL OF REFERENCE JUDGES

3.300   Establishment and termination of panel for disposition of civil actions in circuit court; eligibility for panel; limitation on powers

3.305   Request for referral of action to reference judge; selection of reference judge; revocation of referral

3.311   Delivery of order to reference judge; notice of time and place of trial; procedure; witnesses

3.315   Proposed report of reference judge; objections; final report; filings with clerk; entry of report as judgment of court

3.321   Compensation of reference judge; payment procedure

FAMILY LAW
(Family Court Departments)

3.405   Application to establish family court department; assignment of judges; authority of judges

3.408   Matters assignable to family court department

3.412   Chief family court judge

3.414   Assignment of matters relating to same child

3.417   Coordination of services

3.420   Abolishment of family court department

3.423   Family court department rules

3.425   Family law education programs

(Family Law Facilitation Programs)

3.428   Family law facilitation programs

(Family Court Advocate Programs)

3.430   Family court advocate programs; goals; duties

3.432   Judicial education program on establishment and management of family court departments

(Coordination of Services to Families in Family Law Cases)

3.434   Adoption of coordination plan for services; local family law advisory committees; plan contents

3.436   Appointment of statewide family law advisory committee

3.438   Duties of State Court Administrator

3.440   Family Law Account

DRUG COURT PROGRAMS
3.450   Drug court programs; fees; records

COURTCARE PILOT PROGRAMS

(Temporary provisions relating to CourtCare pilot programs are compiled as notes following ORS 3.450)

3.010 [Amended by 1957 c.713 §3; repealed by 1961 c.724 §34]

    3.011 [1961 c.724 §1; 1963 c.491 §1; 1965 c.510 §1; 1965 c.618 §1; 1967 c.532 §1; 1967 c.533 §1; 1969 c.370 §1; 1971 c.640 §1; 1971 c.777 §1; 1973 c.572 §1; 1975 c.629 §1; 1977 c.386 §1; 1979 c.568 §14; 1981 c.215 §2; 1981 c.759 §1; 1985 c.65 §1; 1985 c.274 §1; 1985 c.311 §1; 1987 c.359 §1; 1989 c.1021 §1; 1991 c.298 §1; 1995 c.658 §§6,142,143a,144; repealed by 1997 c.801 §1 (3.012 enacted in lieu of 3.011)]

JUDICIAL DISTRICTS, JUDGES AND JURISDICTION

    3.012 Judicial districts. (1) The judicial districts, the counties constituting the judicial districts and the number of circuit court judges for each judicial district are as follows:
    (a) The first judicial district consists of Jackson County and has nine judges.
    (b) The second judicial district consists of Lane County and has 15 judges.
    (c) The third judicial district consists of Marion County and has 14 judges.
    (d) The fourth judicial district consists of Multnomah County and has 38 judges.
    (e) The fifth judicial district consists of Clackamas County and has 11 judges.
    (f) The sixth judicial district consists of the counties of Morrow and Umatilla and has five judges.
    (g) The seventh judicial district consists of the counties of Gilliam, Hood River, Sherman, Wasco and Wheeler and has four judges.
    (h) The eighth judicial district consists of Baker County and has one judge.
    (i) The ninth judicial district consists of Malheur County and has two judges.
    (j) The tenth judicial district consists of the counties of Union and Wallowa and has two judges.
    (k) The eleventh judicial district consists of Deschutes County and has seven judges.
    (L) The twelfth judicial district consists of Polk County and has three judges.
    (m) The thirteenth judicial district consists of Klamath County and has five judges.
    (n) The fourteenth judicial district consists of Josephine County and has four judges.
    (o) The fifteenth judicial district consists of the counties of Coos and Curry and has six judges.
    (p) The sixteenth judicial district consists of Douglas County and has five judges.
    (q) The seventeenth judicial district consists of Lincoln County and has three judges.
    (r) The eighteenth judicial district consists of Clatsop County and has three judges.
    (s) The nineteenth judicial district consists of Columbia County and has three judges.
    (t) The twentieth judicial district consists of Washington County and has 14 judges.
    (u) The twenty-first judicial district consists of Benton County and has three judges.
    (v) The twenty-second judicial district consists of the counties of Crook and Jefferson and has three judges.
    (w) The twenty-third judicial district consists of Linn County and has five judges.
    (x) The twenty-fourth judicial district consists of the counties of Grant and Harney and has one judge.
    (y) The twenty-fifth judicial district consists of Yamhill County and has four judges.
    (z) The twenty-sixth judicial district consists of Lake County and has one judge.
    (aa) The twenty-seventh judicial district consists of Tillamook County and has two judges.
    (2) The Secretary of State shall designate position numbers equal to the number of judges in each of the judicial districts established by this section. The positions shall reflect any qualifications established by ORS 3.041. [1997 c.801 §2 (enacted in lieu of 3.011); 1997 c.801 §2a; 2001 c.779 §1; 2001 c.823 §1; 2005 c.800 §1]

    Note: The amendments to 3.012 by section 1, chapter 631, Oregon Laws 2017, become operative on January 7, 2019, except that the provisions for new circuit court judges are operative on August 2, 2017, for the purposes of nominating and electing new judges in 2017 and 2018 to assume the duties of the office on January 7, 2019. See section 2, chapter 631, Oregon Laws 2017. The text that is operative on and after January 7, 2019, is set forth for the user's convenience.
    3.012. (1) The judicial districts, the counties constituting the judicial districts and the number of circuit court judges for each judicial district are as follows:
    (a) The first judicial district consists of Jackson County and has nine judges.
    (b) The second judicial district consists of Lane County and has 15 judges.
    (c) The third judicial district consists of Marion County and has 14 judges.
    (d) The fourth judicial district consists of Multnomah County and has 38 judges.
    (e) The fifth judicial district consists of Clackamas County and has 11 judges.
    (f) The sixth judicial district consists of the counties of Morrow and Umatilla and has five judges.
    (g) The seventh judicial district consists of the counties of Gilliam, Hood River, Sherman, Wasco and Wheeler and has four judges.
    (h) The eighth judicial district consists of Baker County and has one judge.
    (i) The ninth judicial district consists of Malheur County and has two judges.
    (j) The tenth judicial district consists of the counties of Union and Wallowa and has two judges.
    (k) The eleventh judicial district consists of Deschutes County and has seven judges.
    (L) The twelfth judicial district consists of Polk County and has three judges.
    (m) The thirteenth judicial district consists of Klamath County and has five judges.
    (n) The fourteenth judicial district consists of Josephine County and has five judges.

(o) The fifteenth judicial district consists of the counties of Coos and Curry and has six judges.
(p) The sixteenth judicial district consists of Douglas County and has five judges.
(q) The seventeenth judicial district consists of Lincoln County and has three judges.
(r) The eighteenth judicial district consists of Clatsop County and has three judges.
(s) The nineteenth judicial district consists of Columbia County and has three judges.
(t) The twentieth judicial district consists of Washington County and has 15 judges.
(u) The twenty-first judicial district consists of Benton County and has three judges.
(v) The twenty-second judicial district consists of the counties of Crook and Jefferson and has three judges.
(w) The twenty-third judicial district consists of Linn County and has five judges.
(x) The twenty-fourth judicial district consists of the counties of Grant and Harney and has one judge.
(y) The twenty-fifth judicial district consists of Yamhill County and has four judges.
(z) The twenty-sixth judicial district consists of Lake County and has one judge.
(aa) The twenty-seventh judicial district consists of Tillamook County and has two judges.
(2) The Secretary of State shall designate position numbers equal to the number of judges in each of the judicial districts established by this section. The positions shall reflect any qualifications established by ORS 3.041.

3.013 State as single judicial district. For the purposes of 15 U.S.C. 1692i, the state shall be considered a single judicial district. [1997 c.340 §7]

3.014 Special provisions for fourth judicial district (Multnomah County). (1) One of the judges of the fourth judicial district shall hold court in the City of Gresham, Multnomah County, as directed by the Chief Justice of the Supreme Court but in no event less than one day a week. All proceedings resulting from alleged state traffic offenses or misdemeanors occurring east of 122nd Avenue extended to the north and south boundaries of Multnomah County shall be conducted in the court in Gresham unless the accused at first appearance in each action requests trial in Portland.
(2) A proceeding to be conducted in Gresham as provided in subsection (1) of this section shall be transferred without further order of the court to a court facility in Portland for all purposes if:
(a) The accused person is in the custody of a county sheriff or the Department of Corrections at the time set for any scheduled proceeding; or
(b) A circuit court in the fourth judicial district issues a bench warrant or a warrant of arrest against the accused for any criminal action pending before the court.
(3) Multnomah County shall provide facilities in the City of Gresham for a court judge to hold court as described under subsection (1) of this section. [Formerly 46.010; 2005 c.275 §1]

3.015 [1961 c.724 §32; repealed by 1965 c.510 §24 and 1965 c.618 §11]

3.016 Special provisions for sixth judicial district (Morrow and Umatilla Counties). In the sixth judicial district, the judges of the district shall hold court in Pendleton, Hermiston, Milton-Freewater and Heppner as required by caseload. [1995 c.658 §6c; 2005 c.800 §2]

3.020 [Amended by 1955 c.677 §2; 1957 c.665 §2; 1957 c.713 §4; repealed by 1959 c.557 §1 (3.022 enacted in lieu of 3.020)]

3.021 [1953 c.52 §§1,2,3; repealed by 1955 c.677 §6]

3.022 [1959 c.557 §2 (enacted in lieu of 3.020); repealed by 1961 c.724 §34]

3.030 Election of circuit judges. Each circuit judge shall hold office for the term for which the circuit judge was elected; and at the general election or, if applicable, at the election specified in ORS 249.088 next prior to the expiration of the term of office there shall be elected a circuit judge to succeed the circuit judge. [Amended by 1991 c.719 §1]

3.040 [Amended by 1955 c.677 §3; 1957 c.665 §4; 1957 c.713 §5; repealed by 1961 c.724 §34]

3.041 Qualifications of circuit judges; residence. (1) Each judge of the circuit court shall be a citizen of the United States and a resident of this state.
(2) Each judge of the circuit court shall be a resident of or have principal office in the judicial district for which the judge is elected or appointed, except that in any judicial district having a population of 500,000 or more, according to the latest federal decennial census, any judge of the circuit court may reside within 10 miles of the boundary of the judicial district.
(3) In the seventh judicial district, two of the judges of the circuit court shall be residents of or have principal offices in Wasco County, Sherman County, Gilliam County or Wheeler County and two shall be residents of or have principal offices in Hood River County, Sherman County, Gilliam County or Wheeler County.
(4) In the fifteenth judicial district, four of the judges of the circuit court shall be residents of or have principal offices in Coos County and two shall be residents of or have principal offices in Curry County.
(5) The residence within this state required by subsection (1) of this section shall have been maintained for at least three years, and the residence or principal office required by subsections (2) to (4) of this section shall have been maintained for at least one year, immediately prior to appointment or becoming a candidate for election to the office of circuit court judge. [1961 c.724 §2; 1963 c.491 §6; 1965 c.510 §2; 1965 c.618 §4; 1967 c.532 §3; 1967 c.533 §7; 1971 c.777 §2; 1973 c.572 §2; 1977 c.386 §4; 1979 c.568 §15; 1981 c.759 §8; 1985 c.65 §2; 1985 c.311 §3; 1995 c.79 §3; 1995 c.658 §6a; 1997 c.801 §6; 2001 c.779 §2]

3.050 Circuit judges to be members of bar. No person is eligible to the office of judge of the circuit court unless the person is a member of the Oregon State Bar. [Amended by 1961 c.724 §3]

3.060 Salary of judges; expenses. Each of the judges of the circuit court shall receive such salary as is provided by law. When any judicial district is composed of more than one county a judge thereof is entitled to reimbursement for hotel bills and traveling expenses necessarily incurred by the judge in the performance of duties outside the county of residence. When any circuit judge holds court in any county outside of the judicial district for which the circuit judge was elected or appointed, hotel bills and traveling expenses necessarily incurred by the judge in the performance of that duty shall be paid by the state. Such hotel bills and traveling expenses are to be paid by the state upon the certificate of the judge to the truth of an itemized statement of such hotel bills and traveling expenses. The certificate of expenses is a sufficient voucher upon which the Oregon Department of Administrative Services shall review the claim as required by ORS 293.295 and draw its warrant upon the State Treasurer for the amount thereof in favor of such circuit judge. [Amended by 1953 c.516 §3; 1955 c.531 §1; 1957 c.646 §1; 1959 c.552 §14; 1961 c.702 §2; 1965 c.171 §1; 1965 c.619 §1; 1967 c.38 §1; 1967 c.111 §1; 1969 c.365 §1; 1971 c.95 §2; 1971 c.642 §1]

3.065 [1967 c.531 §1; 1981 s.s. c.1 §8; repealed by 1995 c.781 §51]

3.070 Powers of judges in chambers; filing and entering of decisions not signed in open court. Any judge of a circuit court in any judicial district may, in chambers, grant and sign defaults, judgments, interlocutory orders and provisional remedies, make findings and decide motions, demurrers and other like matters relating to any judicial business coming before the judge from any judicial district in which the judge has presided in such matters. The judge may hear, in chambers, contested motions, demurrers and other similar matters pending within the judicial district, at any location designated under ORS 1.085.

Upon stipulation of counsel, the judge may try and determine any issue in equity or in law where a jury has been waived and hear and decide motions, demurrers and other like matters, in chambers, at any location in the state where the judge may happen to be, relating to any judicial business coming before the judge from any judicial district in which the judge has presided in such matters. The judge may exercise these powers as fully and effectively as though the motions, demurrers, matters or issues were granted, ordered, decided, heard and determined in open court in the county where they may be pending. If signed other than in open court, all such orders, findings and judgments issued, granted or rendered, other than orders not required to be filed and entered with the clerk before becoming effective, shall be transmitted by the judge to the clerk of the court within the county where the matters are pending. They shall be filed and entered upon receipt thereof and shall become effective from the date of entry in the register. [Amended by 1983 c.763 §5; 1991 c.111 §1; 2003 c.576 §269; 2007 c.547 §9]

3.075 Powers of judges to act in joint or separate session; testing process. If two or more persons are sitting as judges of the circuit court in a judicial district:

(1) Any two or more of them may act in joint session for the trial or determination of any cause, matter or proceeding before the court in the judicial district, including jury cases. If the judges acting in joint session are equally divided in opinion, the opinion of the presiding judge prevails; otherwise the decision of the majority prevails.

(2) Each of them may proceed separately with and try, simultaneously in the judicial district, all causes, matters and proceedings brought before the court.

(3) Process may be tested in the name of any of them. [1959 c.552 §9; 1995 c.781 §6; 2015 c.212 §12]

3.080 [Repealed by 1959 c.552 §16]

3.081 [1959 c.552 §5; repealed by 1975 c.706 §10]

3.090 [Repealed by 1959 c.552 §16]

3.091 [1959 c.552 §6; repealed by 1975 c.706 §10]

3.096 [1959 c.552 §7; repealed by 1975 c.706 §10]

3.100 [Repealed by 1959 c.552 §16]

3.101 [1961 c.405 §1; 1969 c.591 §263; repealed by 1995 c.658 §127]

3.102 [Formerly 3.110; 1959 c.576 §1; renumbered 3.570]

3.105 [1953 c.35 §1; repealed by 1959 c.549 §7]

3.106 [1953 c.35 §2; repealed by 1959 c.549 §7]

3.107 [1953 c.35 §3; repealed by 1959 c.549 §7]

3.108 [1953 c.35 §4; repealed by 1959 c.549 §7]

3.109 [1953 c.35 §5; repealed by 1959 c.549 §7]

3.110 [Renumbered 3.102 and then 3.570]

3.111 [1953 c.35 §6; repealed by 1959 c.549 §7]

3.112 [1953 c.35 §9; repealed by 1959 c.549 §7]

3.113 [1953 c.35 §7; repealed by 1959 c.549 §7]

3.114 [1953 c.35 §8; repealed by 1959 c.549 §7]

3.115 [1953 c.35 §10; repealed by 1959 c.549 §7]

3.120 [Repealed by 1959 c.552 §16]

3.130 Transfer of judicial jurisdiction of certain county courts to circuit courts. (1) All judicial jurisdiction, authority, powers, functions and duties of the county courts and the judges thereof, except the jurisdiction, authority, powers, functions and duties exercisable in the transaction of county business, are transferred to the circuit courts and the judges thereof:

(a) In Baker, Clackamas, Columbia, Coos, Douglas, Jackson, Josephine, Klamath, Lake, Lane, Marion and Tillamook Counties.

(b) In any county for which a county charter providing for such transfer is adopted under ORS 203.710 to 203.770, to the extent that the judicial jurisdiction, authority, powers, functions and duties were not previously transferred as provided by law.

(2) All matters, causes and proceedings relating to judicial jurisdiction, authority, powers, functions and duties transferred to the circuit courts and the judges thereof under this section, and pending in a county court on the effective date of the transfer, are transferred to the circuit court for the county. [Amended by 1955 c.677 §4; 1957 c.275 §1; 1957 c.713 §6; 1961 c.724 §4; 1963 c.512 §1; 1965 c.247 §1; 1965 c.510 §3; 1965 c.618 §5; 1967 c.268 §1; 1967 c.533 §8; 1967 c.534 §9; 1969 c.286 §1; 1969 c.591 §264]

3.132 Concurrent jurisdiction with justice and municipal courts. In addition to other cases over which they have jurisdiction, circuit courts shall have the same criminal and quasi-criminal jurisdiction as justice courts and shall have concurrent jurisdiction with municipal courts of all violations of the charter and ordinances of any city wholly or in part within their respective judicial districts committed or triable within the counties in the judicial district. [Formerly 46.040]

3.134 Application of state statutes to municipal ordinance. When an offense defined by municipal ordinance is tried in circuit court, it shall be subject to the same statutes and procedures that govern the trial and appeal of a like offense defined by a statute of this state. [Formerly 46.047]

3.135 [1961 c.724 §5; repealed by 1965 c.510 §24]

3.136 Jurisdiction over violations of Portland charter and ordinances; disposition of moneys; hearings officers. (1) The circuit court for a county within the boundaries of which there is situated the largest part of a city having a population of more than 300,000 shall have all judicial jurisdiction, authority, powers, functions and duties of the municipal court of each such city and the judges thereof with respect to all violations of the charter and ordinances of each such city.

(2) All fees, fines, security deposit forfeitures and other moneys collected and received by a circuit court in matters, causes and proceedings with respect to all violations over which such circuit court is granted judicial jurisdiction by subsection (1) of this section shall be collected, handled and disposed of by the clerk of such circuit court as otherwise provided by law for moneys collected and received by such circuit court.

(3) Subsection (1) of this section does not preclude the city from employing one or more quasi-judicial hearings officers empowered to hold hearings concerning violations of the charter, ordinances, rules and regulations of the city, to adopt rules and regulations relating to the conduct of the hearings process and to impose civil penalties and grant other relief as may be necessary to enforce and obtain compliance with the charter, ordinances, rules and regulations of the city. The jurisdiction and authority of a hearings officer shall not include any traffic or parking offense. The city may enforce any order of a hearings officer by a civil action in a court of appropriate jurisdiction. [Formerly 46.045; 1999 c.1051 §235]

3.140 [Amended by 1965 c.510 §4; repealed by 1969 c.591 §305]

3.150 [Amended by 1957 s.s. c.8 §1; 1961 c.724 §6; 1965 c.510 §5; 1979 c.77 §1; repealed by 1983 c.673 §26]

3.160 [Amended by 1957 s.s. c.8 §2; 1959 c.557 §3; 1961 c.724 §7; 1965 c.510 §6; repealed by 1981 c.215 §8]

3.165 [1961 c.724 §8; repealed by 1965 c.510 §24]

3.170 [Amended by 1965 c.510 §7; repealed by 1981 c.215 §8]

3.180 [1965 c.618 §7; 1967 c.533 §9; repealed by 1969 c.591 §305]

3.185 Habeas corpus hearings by Circuit Court for Marion County. (1) Notwithstanding ORS 1.040, a judge of the Circuit Court for Marion County when hearing matters relating to writs of habeas corpus as provided in ORS 34.310 to 34.730 may direct that the court be held or continued at any location designated under ORS 1.085 and under such conditions as may be ordered.

(2) When a court is held at a location directed as provided by subsection (1) of this section, every person held or required to appear at the court shall appear at the location so directed. [1975 c.236 §1; 1983 c.763 §6; 2007 c.547 §10]

3.210 [Amended by 1955 c.677 §5; 1957 c.665 §3; 1957 c.713 §8; 1959 c.557 §4; repealed by 1961 c.724 §34]

3.220 Rules; procedure when judges disagree. (1) A circuit court may make and enforce all rules necessary for the prompt and orderly dispatch of the business of the court and not inconsistent with applicable provisions of law, the Oregon Rules of Civil Procedure or rules made or orders issued by the Chief Justice of the Supreme Court or the presiding judge for the judicial district. If a majority of the judges of the court in a judicial district having two or more circuit court judges do not agree in respect to the making of rules under this subsection, the decision of the presiding judge shall control.

(2)(a) A certified copy of a rule referred to in subsection (1) of this section made or in effect before January 1, 1984, shall be filed in the office of the State Court Administrator not later than January 1, 1984. If a copy of a rule is not so filed, the rule is void.

(b) A certified copy of a rule referred to in subsection (1) of this section made or amended on or after January 1, 1984, shall be filed in the office of the State Court Administrator. No rule or amendment shall be effective unless so filed, and no rule or amendment so filed shall become effective before the 30th day after the date of filing.

(c) The State Court Administrator shall maintain the copies of all rules filed pursuant to this subsection, and shall keep a record of the date of filing thereof. The administrator shall, upon request, supply copies of the rules, and may charge a reasonable fee for such copies in order to recover the cost of compilation, copying and distribution of the rules. [Subsection (2) of 1955 part derived from 1953 c.52 §§6,7; 1957 c.713 §9; 1961 c.724 §9; 1967 c.531 §2; 1973 c.484 §3; 1981 c.215 §4; 1981 s.s. c.1 §9; 1983 c.763 §31; 1995 c.781 §7]

3.225 Establishing specialized subject-matter departments; approval by Chief Justice; eligibility and assignment of judges. Subject to the approval of the Chief Justice of the Supreme Court, a circuit court, by rule under ORS 3.220, may establish specialized subject-matter departments of the court, and may modify or abolish departments so established. Any judge of the court may act in any department so established or modified by rule. The presiding judge for the judicial district may assign any judge of the court to act in any department so established or modified by rule. [1981 c.215 §1; 1995 c.781 §8]

3.227 [1987 c.714 §4; repealed by 1995 c.658 §127]

3.229 [1987 c.714 §5; 1995 c.781 §9; repealed by 1995 c.658 §127]

3.230 [Subsection (3) of 1957 part derived from 1953 c.52 §6; 1957 c.713 §10; 1957 s.s. c.8 §3; repealed by 1959 c.552 §16]

3.232 [Formerly 4.010; repealed by 2015 c.212 §3]

3.235 [Formerly 4.105; 2015 c.119 §3; repealed by 2015 c.212 §3]

3.238 [Formerly 4.410; 1985 c.540 §20; repealed by 2013 c.155 §12]

3.240 [Amended by 1957 c.713 §11; repealed by 1961 c.724 §34]

JURISDICTION OVER JUVENILE AND FAMILY-RELATED MATTERS

3.250 Definitions for ORS 3.250 to 3.280. As used in ORS 3.250 to 3.280, unless the context requires otherwise:

(1) "Child" means a person under 18 years of age.

(2) "Court services" includes but is not limited to services and facilities relating to intake screening, juvenile detention, shelter care, investigations, study and recommendations on disposition of cases, probation on matters within the jurisdiction of the court under ORS 3.260, family counseling, conciliation in domestic relations, group homes, and psychological or psychiatric or medical consultation and services provided at the request of or under the direction of the court, whether performed by employees of the court, by other government agencies or by contract or other arrangement. [1967 c.534 §1; 1987 c.158 §2; 1987 c.320 §12; 2001 c.904 §10; 2001 c.905 §10]

3.255 Policy and intent. It is declared to be the policy and intent of the Legislative Assembly:

(1) Notwithstanding concurrent jurisdiction, that family and family-related matters before the courts be concentrated in a single judicial jurisdiction, the circuit court.

(2) The judges of the circuit court need adequate court services to assist them in exercising jurisdiction over the family and family-related matters. [1967 c.534 §2]

3.260 Juvenile jurisdiction vested in circuit courts; authority for transfer of jurisdiction over family-related matters to circuit courts. (1) The circuit courts and the judges thereof shall exercise all juvenile court jurisdiction, authority, powers, functions and duties.

(2) Pursuant to ORS 3.275, in addition to any other jurisdiction vested in it by law, the circuit court shall exercise exclusive and original judicial jurisdiction, authority, powers, functions, and duties in the judicial district in any or all of the following matters that on the date specified in the order entered under ORS 3.275 are not within the jurisdiction of the circuit court:

(a) Adoption.

(b) Change of name under ORS 33.410.

(c) Filiation.

(d) Commitment of persons with mental illness or mental retardation.

(e) Any suit or civil proceeding involving custody or other disposition of a child or the support thereof or the support of a spouse, including enforcement of the Uniform Reciprocal Enforcement of Support Act and enforcement of out-of-state or foreign judgments and decrees on domestic relations.

(f) Waivers of the three-day waiting period before a marriage license becomes effective under ORS 106.077.

(g) Issuance of delayed reports of live birth. [1967 c.534 §3; 1979 c.724 §1; 2003 c.576 §270; 2007 c.70 §2; 2013 c.366 §47]

3.265 Limits on transfer of juvenile jurisdiction. (1) Notwithstanding ORS 3.260, no transfer of jurisdiction required by ORS 3.260 (1) shall occur in the following counties until the county court approves such transfer either as of July 1, 1968, or thereafter:

(a) Gilliam, Sherman, Wheeler, Harney or Morrow County.

(b) Any county that as of July 1, 1968, has a population of less than 11,000 and in which the judge of the circuit court does not reside.

(2) Notwithstanding the limitation on transfer of juvenile jurisdiction in subsection (1) of this section, the circuit court in the judicial district shall exercise exclusive and original judicial jurisdiction, authority, powers, functions and duties in all proceedings under ORS 419B.500 to 419B.508 filed after October 3, 1989. [1967 c.534 §3a; 1989 c.531 §1; 1993 c.33 §272; 1995 c.658 §13]

3.270 Transfer of juvenile jurisdiction and jurisdiction over family-related matters to circuit courts. (1) All judicial jurisdiction, authority, powers and duties of the county courts and the judges thereof over matters described in ORS 3.260 (1), are transferred to the circuit courts and the judges thereof.

(2) All judicial jurisdiction, authority, powers and duties of the county courts and justice courts and the judges thereof over matters described in ORS 3.260 (2) or so much thereof as may be ordered under ORS 3.275, in so far as such jurisdiction, authority, powers, functions and duties are exercised by such courts and the judges thereof on the date specified in the order entered under ORS 3.275, are transferred to the circuit courts and the judges thereof by which the order was entered.

(3) All matters, causes and proceedings relating to jurisdiction, authority, powers, functions and duties transferred to the circuit court and the judges thereof under either subsection (1) or (2) of this section and pending in the county or justice court on the effective date of the transfer, are transferred to the circuit court for the county.

(4) Appeals pending in a circuit court under ORS 179.650 (1987 Replacement Part), 419.561 (1991 Edition) or 419.A.200 immediately before the date specified in the order entered under ORS 3.275 shall be conducted and completed pursuant to the provisions of law in effect immediately before that date, except that the circuit court shall be considered to be the court appealed from in so far as further disposition of the case is concerned. [1967 c.534 §4; 1989 c.348 §13; 1993 c.33 §273; 1993 c.717 §3; 1995 c.658 §14]

3.275 Procedure for transfer of jurisdiction over certain family-related matters. (1) After making a determination that conditions in the judicial district make it desirable to concentrate jurisdiction over all or part of family and family-related matters in the circuit court, the circuit court by its own order shall exercise jurisdiction over any or all of the matters described in ORS 3.260 (2) on and after July 1 next following entry of the order.

(2) Any circuit court that enters an order pursuant to this section shall cause copies of the order to be filed with the Oregon Supreme Court and with the county or justice court whose jurisdiction is affected by the order. [1967 c.534 §5; 1995 c.658 §16]

3.280 Court services for circuit courts. (1) The circuit court may obtain court services by using services available without charge or, with the prior approval of the governing body of each county in the judicial district, by:

(a) Employing or contracting for personnel or services; or

(b) Contracting or entering into agreements with public or private agencies or with private firms or individuals, or any of them.

(2) Court services obtained under subsection (1) of this section shall be subject to the supervision of the circuit court.

(3) The compensation and expenses of personnel performing or providing court services and the expenses of providing court services shall be determined by the circuit court and shall be subject to the approval of and be paid by the county or counties making up the judicial district, subject to the Local Budget Law. For purposes of retirement benefits, personnel employed by the court may be considered county employees. Personnel performing or providing court services are not state employees, and their compensation and expenses shall not be paid by the state. [1967 c.534 §6; 1981 s.s. c.3 §22]

PANEL OF REFERENCE JUDGES

3.300 Establishment and termination of panel for disposition of civil actions in circuit court; eligibility for panel; limitation on powers. (1) Subject to the approval of the Chief Justice of the Supreme Court, the presiding judge for a judicial district may establish, and may terminate, the use of a panel of reference judges for the trial and disposition of civil actions in the circuit court under ORS 3.300 to 3.321.

(2) The Supreme Court, upon motion of the Chief Justice and the presiding judge may appoint any eligible person as a reference judge on the panel established under this section. A person is eligible for appointment as a reference judge if the person is a member in good standing of the Oregon State Bar. An eligible person need not reside within the judicial district for which use of the panel is established.

(3) A person appointed as a reference judge on a panel may be removed from the panel by the Chief Justice or the presiding judge for the judicial district, in the sole discretion of the Chief Justice or presiding judge.

(4) A person appointed as a reference judge on a panel is subject to the jurisdiction of the Commission on Judicial Fitness and Disability and the Supreme Court under ORS 1.420 and 1.430 in the same manner as a judge of the circuit court.

(5) A person appointed as a reference judge on a panel shall not be considered to be, or to have the judicial powers, duties, jurisdiction and authority of, a judge of the circuit court except to the extent provided in ORS 3.300 to 3.321. [1983 c.704 §1; 1995 c.781 §10]

3.305 Request for referral of action to reference judge; selection of reference judge; revocation of referral. (1) At any time before trial of a civil action in a circuit court for which use of a panel of reference judges is established under ORS 3.300, the parties to the action may file with the presiding judge for the judicial district a written request for referral of the action to a reference judge on the panel. Upon receipt of the request, the presiding judge, by order, shall refer the action to a reference judge.

(2) The parties, in their request for referral, may specify a particular reference judge, and the presiding judge shall refer the action to the reference judge so specified.

(3) If the parties do not specify a particular reference judge, the presiding judge shall select a reference judge and notify the parties of the selection. Within 10 days after selection of a reference judge by the presiding judge, the parties may file with the presiding judge a written rejection of the reference judge so selected and request that the presiding judge make another selection.

(4) A reference judge may decline to accept a referral of an action by the presiding judge. If a reference judge declines to accept a referral, the parties may file with the presiding judge a written specification of, or the presiding judge may select, another reference judge.

(5) The request by parties for referral of an action shall include a stipulation by the parties to the entry of the judgment arising from the reference as the judgment of the court. If the action is triable by right to a jury, the request shall constitute a waiver of the right of trial by jury by any party having that right.

(6) The presiding judge may revoke a referral of an action when, in the opinion of the presiding judge, the trial of the action on reference is being unduly delayed. If the referral is revoked, the presiding judge may require the person or persons responsible for the undue delay to bear all or part of the expense of the trial incurred before the revocation. [1983 c.704 §2; 1995 c.781 §11]

3.310 [Amended by 1955 c.715 §2; 1959 c.557 §5; 1961 c.724 §10; 1965 c.510 §8; repealed by 1981 c.215 §8]

3.311 Delivery of order to reference judge; notice of time and place of trial; procedure; witnesses. (1) Upon entry of an order of the presiding judge for a judicial district referring an action under ORS 3.305, the clerk of the court shall cause a copy of the order to be delivered to the reference judge. Upon receipt of the copy of the order, the reference judge shall set the action for trial on reference at a time and in a place agreeable to the parties.

(2) At least five days before the date set for a trial on reference, the reference judge shall notify the clerk of the court of the time and place of the trial. The clerk shall post a notice of the time and place of the trial in a conspicuous place for trial notices at the principal location for the sitting of the court in the county in which the action is commenced.

(3) Any person interested in attending a trial on reference is entitled to do so as in a trial of a civil action in the court. Upon receipt of written request by any person, the reference judge shall give the person written notice of the time and place set for a trial on reference.

(4) Except as otherwise provided in ORS 3.300 to 3.321, the reference judge has all the judicial powers and duties of a judge of the circuit court to regulate all proceedings in the trial and disposition of the action on reference.

(5) The reference judge shall provide clerical personnel necessary for the conduct of the proceedings in the trial on reference, including a trial court reporter unless waived by the parties. If use of a trial court reporter is waived by the parties, the proceedings in the trial shall be reported by an audio record reporting device.

(6) The trial on reference shall be conducted in the same manner as a trial by the circuit court without a jury. The reference judge shall apply the substantive law used in the courts of this state in deciding the issues submitted by the parties. Unless waived in whole or part by the parties, the reference judge shall apply the rules of pleading, practice, procedure and evidence used in the circuit courts of this state.

(7) The parties may procure the attendance of witnesses before the reference judge by the issuance and service of subpoenas as provided in ORCP 55. If, without adequate excuse, a witness fails to appear or give evidence, that witness may be punished as for a contempt by the reference judge and be subjected to the consequences, penalties and remedies provided in ORCP 55 G.

(8) Reference judges may conduct proceedings for the imposition of remedial sanctions under ORS 33.055, but may not conduct proceedings for the imposition of punitive sanctions under ORS 33.065. [1983 c.704 §3; 1991 c.724 §15a; 1995 c.781 §12]

3.312 [1961 c.724 §12; repealed by 1965 c.510 §24]

3.314 [1961 c.724 §13; repealed by 1981 c.215 §8]

3.315 Proposed report of reference judge; objections; final report; filings with clerk; entry of report as judgment of court. (1) Within 20 days after the close of all evidence offered in a trial on reference conducted under ORS 3.311, unless a later time is agreed upon by the parties, the reference judge shall mail to each party a copy of the proposed written report of the reference judge. The proposed report shall contain the findings of fact and conclusions of law by the reference judge, and the judgment thereon of the reference judge.

(2) Within 10 days after receipt of the copy of the proposed report, any party may serve written objections and suggested modifications or corrections to the proposed report upon the reference judge and the other parties. The reference judge without delay shall consider the objections and suggestions and prepare a final written report. If requested by any party, the reference judge shall conduct a hearing on the proposed written report and any objections or suggested modifications or corrections thereto before preparing the final written report.

(3) Upon completion of the final written report, the reference judge shall file with the clerk of the circuit court:
(a) Copies of all original papers in the action filed with the reference judge;
(b) The exhibits offered and received or rejected in the trial on reference;
(c) The transcript of the proceedings in the trial, if a trial court reporter was used in the trial;
(d) The audio record of the proceedings in the trial, if a trial court reporter was not used in the trial; and
(e) The final written report containing the findings of fact and conclusions of law by the reference judge, and the judgment thereon of the reference judge.

(4) In the interest of economy, the presiding judge for a judicial district may allow the reference judge to file the final written report under subsection (3) of this section without any of the items listed in subsection (3)(a) to (d) of this section. However, the presiding judge shall require the reference judge to file the items listed in subsection (3)(a) to (d) of this section if timely notice of appeal of the judgment is filed.

(5) At the time the reference judge files the final written report under subsection (3) of this section, the reference judge shall mail to each party a copy of the report.

(6) Upon receipt of the final written report by the clerk of the court, the referral of the action shall terminate and the presiding judge shall order the judgment contained in the report entered as the judgment of the court in the action. Subsequent motions and other related post-trial proceedings in the action may be conducted and disposed of by the reference judge upon the order of the presiding judge, in the sole discretion of the presiding judge, or may otherwise be assigned by the presiding judge.

(7) The judgment of the reference judge entered as provided in subsection (6) of this section may be appealed in the same manner as a judgment of the circuit court in a civil action. [1983 c.704 §4; 1995 c.781 §13; 2003 c.576 §231]

3.320 [Repealed by 1981 c.215 §8]

3.321 Compensation of reference judge; payment procedure. (1) Unless otherwise agreed by the parties, the compensation of a reference judge to whom an action is referred under ORS 3.305 shall be an amount for each day actually engaged in the performance of duties under the referral and in the conduct and disposition of post-trial proceedings under ORS 3.315 (6) equal to five percent of the gross monthly salary of a regularly elected and qualified judge of the circuit court, or one-half of that daily compensation for services of one-half day or less.

(2) Payment of the compensation of a reference judge and the expense of the trial on reference before the reference judge shall be the obligation of the parties. The obligation shall be borne equally by the parties unless the parties agree to a different allocation.

(3) The presiding judge for the judicial district shall estimate the compensation of the reference judge and the expense of the trial on reference in advance of the trial, and shall notify the parties of the estimate. The parties shall deposit with the clerk of the court the amount estimated by the presiding judge. The presiding judge may order the clerk to pay a portion of the deposited amount to the reference judge during the trial on reference. Upon termination of the referral of the action, the reference judge shall cause to be delivered to the presiding judge and each party a written statement of any remaining unpaid compensation and expense. The presiding judge shall hear and decide any objection to the written statement, and thereafter shall order payment to the reference judge or refund of any remainder of the deposited amount accordingly. [1983 c.704 §5; 1995 c.781 §14]

3.330 [Amended by 1971 c.108 §1; 1979 c.77 §2; repealed by 1981 c.215 §8]

3.340 [Repealed by 1969 c.591 §305]

3.350 [Repealed by 1981 c.215 §8]

3.360 [Repealed by 1981 c.215 §8]

3.370 [Repealed by 1959 c.552 §16]

3.380 [Amended by 1961 c.724 §14; 1973 c.484 §4; repealed by 1981 c.215 §8]

3.390 [Repealed by 1981 c.215 §8]

3.400 [Repealed by 1981 c.215 §8]

FAMILY LAW

(Family Court Departments)

3.405 Application to establish family court department; assignment of judges; authority of judges. (1) A family court department may be established in the circuit court of a judicial district upon the written application of the presiding judge. The written application must be made to the Chief Justice of the Supreme Court. Upon receipt and approval of a written application, the Chief Justice shall designate a date for commencing operation of the family court department in the judicial district. The provisions of this section do not affect the ability of a circuit court to establish specialized subject-matter departments in the manner provided by ORS 3.225.
(2) In every judicial district in which a family court department is established under this section, the presiding judge of the judicial district may assign one or more judges to serve in the family court department.
(3) Judges serving in the family court department have the same jurisdiction, authority, powers, functions and duties as any other circuit court judge and shall be elected and qualified in the same manner as any other circuit court judge.
(4) For the purposes of this section, "judicial district" means a judicial district enumerated under the provisions of ORS 3.012. [1993 c.165 §1; 1995 c.658 §125]

3.408 Matters assignable to family court department. (1) The presiding judge of the judicial district may assign to a family court department established under ORS 3.405 all of the following matters:
(a) Proceedings under the provisions of ORS chapters 107, 108, 109 and 110;
(b) Proceedings under the provisions of ORS chapter 25;
(c) Guardianship proceedings for minors under the provisions of ORS chapter 125;
(d) Juvenile court proceedings under ORS chapters 419A, 419B and 419C;
(e) Proceedings to commit a person with a mental illness under the provisions of ORS chapter 426;
(f) Probate proceedings under ORS chapters 111, 112, 113, 114, 115, 116 and 117; and
(g) Any other proceeding in which a family is involved.
(2) In addition to the matters specified in subsection (1) of this section, the presiding judge of the judicial district may assign to a family court department any criminal proceeding that involves domestic violence or other crime between family members. [1993 c.165 §2; 1995 c.608 §19; 1995 c.664 §67; 1995 c.781 §15; 1995 c.800 §7; 1999 c.1081 §1; 2007 c.70 §3; 2011 c.720 §51]

3.410 [Amended by 1955 c.715 §3; 1959 c.557 §6; repealed by 1961 c.724 §34]

3.411 [1961 c.724 §15; 1965 c.618 §9; 1967 c.531 §3; 1967 c.533 §11; 1971 c.640 §2; repealed by 1981 c.215 §8]

3.412 Chief family court judge. If there is more than one judge assigned to a family court department for the judicial district, the presiding judge of the judicial district may designate one of the judges as the chief family court judge. [1993 c.165 §3]

3.414 Assignment of matters relating to same child. Upon assignment to the family court department of the cases specified in ORS 3.408, the presiding judge of the judicial district shall insure, when reasonable and appropriate, that all cases that involve the same minor child be assigned to the same judge. [1993 c.165 §4]

3.417 Coordination of services. The presiding judge of the judicial district may establish procedures for coordinating all services that may be available to persons who are or who may become parties in the proceedings specified in ORS 3.408. [1993 c.165 §5]

3.420 Abolishment of family court department. At any time after the establishment of a family court department under ORS 3.405, the family court department shall be abolished if the presiding judge of the judicial district makes written application to the Chief Justice of the Supreme Court requesting that the family court department for that judicial district be abolished. [1993 c.165 §6; 1995 c.658 §126]

3.423 Family court department rules. The Chief Justice of the Supreme Court may promulgate court rules for family court departments established under ORS 3.405. [1993 c.165 §7]

3.425 Family law education programs. (1) The family court department or, if there is no family court department, the presiding judge or designee of each circuit court may establish an education program designed to inform parents about the impact of family restructuring on children when the parent is a named party in any of the following proceedings:
(a) An annulment or dissolution of marriage action.
(b) A legal separation action.
(c) A petition to establish custody or parenting time.
(d) Post-judgment litigation involving custody or parenting time.
(2) An education program established under subsection (1) of this section must include, but need not be limited to, information about:
(a) The emotional impact of a dissolution of marriage or a separation on children at different developmental stages.
(b) Parenting during and after a dissolution of marriage or a separation.
(c) Custody, parenting time and shared parenting plans.
(d) The effect on children of parental conduct including, but not limited to, long distance parenting.
(e) Mediation and conflict resolution.
(3) The family court department or, if there is no family court department, the presiding judge or designee of each circuit court may establish an education program designed to provide information about dissolution law and legal procedures, mediation and other dispute resolution alternatives to persons seeking to annul or dissolve a marriage or to separate from each other. The program must include, but need not be limited to, information about:
(a) Shared parenting plans.
(b) Division of marital property.
(c) Spousal and child support.

(d) Court procedures and time requirements.
(e) Litigation, mediation and conflict resolution.
(f) The role of attorneys in mediation.
(4) The court may order the parties in any action listed in subsection (1) of this section to participate in education programs described in this section unless:
(a) Subject to the approval of the court, the parties agree not to participate;
(b) On motion of either party or on its own motion, the court determines that participation is unnecessary; or
(c) With prior approval of the court, the parties select and participate in comparable education programs.
(5) The court may not require both parties to attend an education program established under this section at the same time.
(6)(a) The family court department or, if there is no family court department, the presiding judge or designee of each circuit court shall designate the program providers for the education programs.
(b) A program provider may charge a person a reasonable fee to attend education programs. A program provider may not exclude a person from attending education programs due to an inability to pay the fee if the court has indicated that the person is indigent or otherwise unable to pay the fee.
(c) A program provider shall issue a certificate of completion to a participant when the participant has satisfactorily completed the education programs. A certificate of completion must be filed with the court prior to the entry of the judgment in the action. [1995 c.800 §10(1),(2),(3); 1997 c.249 §2; 1997 c.707 §4; 1999 c.59 §3; 2003 c.576 §271]

(Family Law Facilitation Programs)

3.428 Family law facilitation programs. (1) A family law facilitation program may be established by the judges of the family court department of a circuit court. If there is no family court department for the court, a family law facilitation program may be established for a circuit court by the presiding judge for the judicial district. A family law facilitation program shall be designed to assist litigants in domestic relations or other family court proceedings described in ORS 3.408. The program shall be developed in consultation with the local family law advisory committee established for the judicial district under ORS 3.434. The program shall operate under the supervision of the family court department or, if there is no family court department, under the supervision of the presiding judge for the judicial district. Services under the program shall be provided by court personnel in facilities under the supervision and control of the family court department or, if there is no family court department, under the supervision and control of the presiding judge for the judicial district. The program may provide:
(a) Educational materials.
(b) Court forms.
(c) Assistance in completing forms.
(d) Information about court procedures.
(e) Referrals to agencies and resources that provide legal and other services to parents or children.
(2) All materials, forms, instructions and referral lists provided through the program must be approved by the family court department or, if there is no family court department, by the presiding judge for the judicial district.
(3) Except for those fees authorized for forms under ORS 21.245, services provided through the program shall be provided without charge.
(4) An employee or other person providing services to litigants through a family law facilitation program as provided in this section is not engaged in the practice of law in this state for the purposes of ORS 9.160.
(5) Except as provided in subsection (6) of this section, an employee or other person who assisted litigants through a family law facilitation program may not, for a period of one year after leaving the program, charge or collect any fee from a litigant for services relating to a matter that was the subject of assistance under the program.
(6) The prohibition of subsection (5) of this section does not apply to persons admitted to the practice of law in this state. [1999 c.1095 §1; 2009 c.218 §5]

(Family Court Advocate Programs)

3.430 Family court advocate programs; goals; duties. (1) The Judicial Department shall establish family court advocate programs in counties specified in subsection (4) of this section. The programs shall be designed to develop an efficient system for providing integrated, family-focused prevention and intervention services to at-risk families identified by the family courts in those counties, and to coordinate available human services and community resources with the family courts in those counties, both for the purpose of court proceedings and for the purpose of preventing the types of problems that eventually lead to involvement with the judicial system.
(2) The family court advocate programs implemented under this section shall emphasize the following goals:
(a) Protection of children.
(b) Successful completion of family plans designed by the programs.
(c) Improved linkage between the family court and community services.
(d) Improvements in the functioning of each family that is provided services by the programs.
(e) Decreased caseload in the courts of this state in matters relating to families.
(f) Integration of family services.
(g) Identification of and referral to alternatives to court proceedings.
(3) The family court advocate programs shall:
(a) Coordinate services that are available to persons who are parties in proceedings before the family court, or who may become parties in proceedings before the family court.
(b) Assist human services agencies in efforts made by those agencies to collaborate with the family court.
(c) Assist circuit court judges in viewing litigation involving families with a focus on the family instead of viewing the parties as individual litigants.
(d) Intervene with at-risk families who do not receive governmental assistance.
(e) Research, identify and advocate new programs that will improve the use of family courts.
(4) Family court advocate programs shall be established in Jackson County, Deschutes County and such other counties as may be designated by the Chief Justice of the Supreme Court. [1997 c.801 §85; 1999 c.1081 §4]

3.432 Judicial education program on establishment and management of family court departments. The State Court Administrator shall implement an education program for state judges that emphasizes issues and problems encountered in the establishment and management of family court departments. The program shall provide education on the manner in which family court departments may be established, and shall identify means of removing obstacles to the establishment of family court departments. The program shall provide recommendations for improving the quality of service provided by family court departments. The program may provide specific instruction in issues arising under the different proceedings conducted in family court departments. [1997 c.593 §2]

(Coordination of Services to Families in Family Law Cases)

3.434 Adoption of coordination plan for services; local family law advisory committees; plan contents. (1) No later than January 1, 1999, the presiding judge of each judicial district shall adopt a plan to coordinate the provision of services to families involved in domestic relations or other family court proceedings.
(2) The presiding judge of the judicial district shall establish a local family law advisory committee for the judicial district. The committee will prepare the plan required by subsection (1) of this section. The membership of the local advisory committee must reflect the diversity of the judicial district and must

include, in addition to the presiding judge or a judge designated by the presiding judge, the trial court administrator and business, social service, community and government representatives who must be knowledgeable in family and family law issues. In judicial districts composed of more than one county, the presiding judge may establish a local advisory committee in each county or establish one or more committees to serve multiple counties.

(3)(a) At a minimum, the local family law advisory committee shall address the following in the plan:

(A) Mandates for mediation of child custody or parenting time disputes, requiring each party to attend either a group or private mediation orientation session;

(B) Methods of coordinating cases when the same child or family is involved in multiple cases; and

(C) The need for, and provision of, conciliation services, mediation services, child custody evaluations, parent education and visitation services.

(b) The local advisory committee may include other elements in the plan, including but not limited to:

(A) The need for, and provision of, services relating to prevention and early intervention; and

(B) The use of settlement options such as mediation, conciliation, arbitration and settlement conferences.

(c) The local advisory committee shall include in the plan a list of mediators qualified to provide mediation in cases involving spousal support and division of property issues. Once the list is developed, the judicial district shall maintain the list.

(4) The local family law advisory committee shall present the plan to the county governing body of each county within the judicial district and to the presiding judge of the judicial district for their approval. The local advisory committee shall send copies of the plan to the Chief Justice of the Supreme Court and those members of the Oregon House of Representatives and the Oregon Senate who represent the areas within the judicial district.

(5) The local family law advisory committee may assist in implementing, monitoring and revising the plan. The local advisory committee, working in conjunction with legal service providers, may coordinate access to family law resources, including family law facilitation and other services. [1997 c.801 §135; 1999 c.1081 §8; 2007 c.71 §3]

3.436 Appointment of statewide family law advisory committee. (1) The Chief Justice of the Supreme Court may appoint a statewide family law advisory committee to assist the State Court Administrator in carrying out the administrator's responsibilities under ORS 3.438 (2) and (4)(a) and in identifying family law issues that need to be addressed in the future. The Chief Justice shall consider the diversity of this state in appointing the members of the statewide advisory committee.

(2) The Chief Justice shall determine the terms and organization of the statewide advisory committee.

(3) Members of the statewide advisory committee are not entitled to compensation, but may be reimbursed from funds available to the State Court Administrator from the Family Law Account for actual and necessary travel expenses incurred by them in the performance of their official duties. [1997 c.801 §136; 2001 c.779 §18]

3.438 Duties of State Court Administrator. To the extent that adequate funds are available from the Family Law Account established under ORS 3.440, the State Court Administrator:

(1) Shall hire a director of family court services and sufficient staff, whose compensation must come solely from the Family Law Account, and may delegate to the director of family court services any of the duties listed in subsections (2) to (6) of this section.

(2) Shall administer the Family Law Account demonstration grant program for funding implementation of new, innovative family court services within this state. The State Court Administrator may not fund services under the demonstration grant program for a period exceeding 24 months. The statewide family law advisory committee shall review all applicant programs and shall recommend programs for approval to the Chief Justice of the Supreme Court.

(3) Shall compensate the per diem expenses of the members of the statewide family law advisory committee from the Family Law Account.

(4)(a) Shall plan and implement an annual statewide conference to:

(A) Review legislation relating to family law issues;

(B) Provide family law training;

(C) Review elements of successful family law programs; and

(D) Foster the development of enhanced services to families involved in proceedings before the court.

(b) May pay the expenses of program development and production for program sessions and materials for the statewide conference from the Family Law Account. The State Court Administrator shall credit any receipts from registration or materials fees charged to the Family Law Account.

(5) Shall pay the expenses of the Family Law Legal Services Commission.

(6) Shall carry out other activities in support of the statewide and local family law advisory committees determined by the State Court Administrator to be necessary to achieve the purposes of ORS 3.434 to 3.440. [1997 c.801 §137]

3.440 Family Law Account. The Family Law Account is established as an account in the General Fund. All moneys in the account are appropriated and constitute a continuous appropriation out of the General Fund to the State Court Administrator for the purposes of ORS 3.436 and 3.438. The State Court Administrator may accept and deposit into the account contributions of funds and assistance from the United States or its agencies or from any other source, public or private, and agree to conditions thereon not inconsistent with the purposes of ORS 3.438. [1997 c.801 §138]

DRUG COURT PROGRAMS

3.450 Drug court programs; fees; records. (1) As used in this section:

(a) "Drug court program" means a program in which:

(A) Individuals who are before the court obtain treatment for substance abuse issues and report regularly to the court on the progress of their treatment; and

(B) A local drug court team, consisting of the court, agency personnel and treatment and service providers, monitors the individuals' participation in treatment.

(b) "Individual-provider relationship" includes a relationship between an individual and a physician, a physician assistant or nurse practitioner.

(2)(a) The governing body of a county or a treatment provider may establish fees that individuals participating in a drug court program may be required to pay for treatment and other services provided as part of the drug court program.

(b) A court may order an individual participating in a drug court program to pay fees to participate in the program. Fees imposed under this subsection may not be paid to the court.

(3) Records that are maintained by the circuit court specifically for the purpose of a drug court program must be maintained separately from other court records. Records maintained by a circuit court specifically for the purpose of a drug court program are confidential and may not be disclosed except in accordance with regulations adopted under 42 U.S.C. 290dd-2, including under the circumstances described in subsections (4) to (7) of this section.

(4) If the individual who is the subject of the record gives written consent, a record described in subsection (3) of this section may be disclosed to members of the local drug court team in order to develop treatment plans, monitor progress in treatment and determine outcomes of participation in the drug court program.

(5) A record described in subsection (3) of this section may not be introduced into evidence in any legal proceeding other than the drug court program unless:

(a) The individual who is the subject of the record gives written consent for introduction of the record; or

(b) The court finds good cause for introduction. In determining whether good cause exists for purposes of this paragraph, the court shall weigh the public interest and the need for disclosure against the potential injury caused by the disclosure to:

(A) The individual who is the subject of the record;

(B) The individual-provider relationship; and

(C) The treatment services being provided to the individual who is the subject of the record.

(6) A court, the State Court Administrator, the Alcohol and Drug Policy Commission or the Oregon Criminal Justice Commission:

(a) May use records described in subsection (3) of this section and other drug court program information to track and develop statistics about the effectiveness, costs and other areas of public interest concerning drug court programs.

(b) May release statistics developed under paragraph (a) of this subsection and analyses based on the statistics to the public.

(7) Statistics and analyses released under subsection (6) of this section may not contain any information that identifies an individual participant in a drug court program. [2003 c.385 §1; 2005 c.706 §25; 2011 c.673 §3; 2014 c.45 §1]

COURTCARE PILOT PROGRAMS

Note: Sections 1 to 4, chapter 672, Oregon Laws 2017, provide:

Sec. 1. Legislative findings. The Legislative Assembly finds that:

(1) Many individuals and families experience life circumstances that necessitate court involvement and visits to local governmental offices, including but not limited to juvenile dependency and delinquency proceedings, domestic relations cases, protective proceedings related to domestic abuse or violence, child protection proceedings, meetings with probation officers and visits to local governmental offices to transact governmental business.

(2) Often individuals and families in such matters are responsible for the care of young children and obtaining child care can distract from, if not present obstacles or barriers to, effective and complete participation in court proceedings or dealing with important governmental matters.

(3) Individuals and families in court-related matters also need and would benefit from the availability of a clearinghouse for information and resource referrals relating to family support services within the local community.

(4) The availability of programs to provide quality child care and serve as a clearinghouse for information and resource referrals in facilities located in or near courthouses and governmental offices would benefit individuals and families with court-related matters and governmental business to transact and would ensure that individuals and families with children are able to participate fully in court and governmental processes in this state. [2017 c.672 §1]

Sec. 2. Pilot programs to provide child care for families involved in court proceedings or governmental business. (1) As used in this section:

(a) "Child care" means care and supervision provided to a child between six weeks and 10 years of age on behalf of a person with responsibility for the child.

(b) "CourtCare program" means a program that provides child care and serves as a clearinghouse for information and resource referrals for individuals and families with court-related matters or governmental business in or near a county courthouse or courthouse complex.

(2) Marion and Polk Counties may establish one or more CourtCare programs as pilot programs to provide quality child care to individuals and families who are:

(a) Participating in or serving as jurors in court proceedings at the local courthouse; or

(b) Transacting business at a local governmental office in or near a county courthouse or courthouse complex.

(3) A CourtCare program established under subsection (2) of this section must also serve as a clearinghouse for information and resource referrals relating to family support services that are available to individuals and families in the local community, including but not limited to housing, emergency services, early learning programs, parent education, public health, relief nurseries, health insurance, behavioral health services, legal assistance, screening and referral services for developmental health and referrals to community organization as appropriate.

(4) A CourtCare program established under subsection (2) of this section must ensure that:

(a) Children receive quality child care and are in a safe and nurturing environment while their caretakers are participating in court proceedings or transacting local governmental business;

(b) Staff at the CourtCare program site are able to provide information and make referrals to appropriate local area resources; and

(c) Court and local governmental business continues without interruption or distraction from children cared for in the CourtCare program.

(5) If Marion or Polk County establishes a CourtCare program under this section, the county shall ensure that:

(a) Volunteers, employees and staff at the CourtCare program are enrolled in the Central Background Registry under ORS 329A.030; and

(b) The CourtCare program is either certified under ORS 329A.280 or registered under ORS 329A.330 by the Office of Child Care or is exempt from the requirements for certification or registration under ORS 329A.250.

(6) If Marion or Polk County establishes a CourtCare program under this section, the county shall enter into an agreement with a nonprofit or nongovernmental entity to implement and administer the CourtCare program. At a minimum, the contract must require that the nonprofit or nongovernmental entity report to the county on an annual basis regarding outcomes and objectives that include, but are not limited to:

(a) The number of individuals and families utilizing the CourtCare program;

(b) The type of services provided to individuals and families that utilized the CourtCare program;

(c) Unmet needs and barriers to the provision of services in the CourtCare program;

(d) The effect of the CourtCare program on courtroom, judicial and local government efficiency; and

(e) The types of information and resource referrals provided by the CourtCare program. [2017 c.672 §2]

Sec. 3. Report on pilot programs. The governing bodies of Marion and Polk Counties shall report on the progress of CourtCare pilot programs implemented under section 2 of this 2017 Act, in the manner provided in ORS 192.245, to the interim committees of the Legislative Assembly related to child welfare no later than September 15, 2019. [2017 c.672 §3]

Sec. 4. Repeal of pilot programs. Sections 1 to 3 of this 2017 Act are repealed on January 2, 2021. [2017 c.672 §4]

3.510 [1959 c.549 §1; 1961 c.465 §1; repealed by 1975 c.706 §10]

3.520 [1959 c.549 §2; repealed by 1975 c.706 §10]

3.530 [1959 c.549 §3; repealed by 1975 c.706 §10]

3.540 [1959 c.549 §4; repealed by 1975 c.706 §10]

3.550 [1959 c.549 §5; repealed by 1975 c.706 §10]

3.560 [1959 c.549 §6; 1961 c.465 §2; 1965 c.521 §1; 1969 c.198 §33; 1969 c.269 §1; 1971 c.213 §1; repealed by 1975 c.706 §10]

3.570 [Formerly 3.110 and then 3.102; 1965 c.521 §2; 1969 c.269 §2; 1971 c.213 §2; repealed by 1975 c.706 §10]

Chapter 4 (Former Provisions)

Circuit Court Terms

CIRCUIT COURT TERMS

COURTS OF RECORD; COURT OFFICERS; JURIES

4.010 [Renumbered 3.232]

4.105 [Formerly 4.120; 1979 c.474 §1; renumbered 3.235]

4.110 [Amended by 1975 c.95 §1; repealed by 1979 c.474 §2]

4.120 [Amended by 1955 c.175 §1; 1957 c.713 §12; 1961 c.81 §1; 1977 c.631 §1; renumbered 4.105]

4.130 [Repealed by 1979 c.474 §2]

4.140 [Amended by 1967 c.376 §1; 1975 c.301 §1; repealed by 1979 c.474 §2]

4.150 [Amended by 1955 c.68 §1; repealed by 1979 c.474 §2]

4.160 [Amended by 1961 c.724 §15a; repealed by 1979 c.474 §2]

4.170 [Amended by 1967 c.533 §13; repealed by 1979 c.474 §2]

4.180 [Repealed by 1979 c.474 §2]

4.190 [Repealed by 1979 c.474 §2]

4.200 [Repealed by 1979 c.474 §2]

4.210 [Amended by 1967 c.532 §4; 1967 c.533 §14; repealed by 1979 c.474 §2]

4.220 [Amended by 1953 c.88 §3; repealed by 1979 c.474 §2]

4.230 [Amended by 1965 c.176 §1; repealed by 1979 c.474 §2]

4.240 [Repealed by 1979 c.474 §2]

4.242 [1957 c.713 §13; 1969 c.163 §1; repealed by 1979 c.474 §2]

4.244 [1957 c.713 §14; 1975 c.95 §2; repealed by 1979 c.474 §2]

4.248 [1971 c.777 §3; repealed by 1979 c.474 §2]

4.250 [Repealed by 1967 c.532 §8 and 1967 c.533 §20]

4.260 [Amended by 1963 c.491 §4; 1969 c.163 §2; repealed by 1979 c.474 §2]

4.265 [1963 c.491 §5; 1969 c.163 §3; repealed by 1979 c.474 §2]

4.270 [Amended by 1969 c.163 §4; 1971 c.777 §4; repealed by 1979 c.474 §2]

4.410 [Amended by 1967 c.532 §5; 1967 c.533 §15; 1971 c.777 §5; renumbered 3.238]

Chapter 5 — County Courts (Judicial Functions)

2017 EDITION

COUNTY COURTS (JUDICIAL FUNCTIONS)

COURTS OF RECORD; COURT OFFICERS; JURIES

5.010   Who holds court

5.020   Juvenile court jurisdiction in certain counties

5.030   Power of county judge to grant injunctions and orders in suits in circuit court

5.060   Times of holding court

5.080   County judge as interested party

5.090   Absence of county judge, or vacancy; authority of circuit judge; pro tem county judge

5.100   Order of docketing and disposal of business; records of proceedings

5.105   Records of county court

5.110   Jury

5.120   Appeals

5.125   County court fees

5.010 Who holds court. The county court is held by the county judge, except when county business is being transacted therein.

5.020 Juvenile court jurisdiction in certain counties. The county court of counties from which no transfer of jurisdiction is made under ORS 3.260 or 3.265 or other provisions of law shall have all juvenile court jurisdiction, authority, powers, functions and duties. [Amended by 1959 c.432 §61; 1963 c.512 §3; 1965 c.247 §2; 1965 c.618 §10; 1967 c.268 §2; 1967 c.533 §12; 1967 c.534 §3b]

5.030 Power of county judge to grant injunctions and orders in suits in circuit court. The judge of any county court having judicial functions shall grant preliminary injunctions or orders in any suit in the circuit court commenced in the county, upon application made in the manner prescribed by ORCP 79. The order or injunction shall be made returnable to the circuit court of such county, to be there heard and determined. [Amended by 1981 c.898 §15]

5.040 [Amended by 1961 c.344 §95; repealed by 1969 c.591 §305]

5.050 [Repealed by 1969 c.591 §305]

5.060 Times of holding court. There shall be a term of the county court in each county for the transaction of judicial business on the first Monday of each month, and at such other times as the court in term or the judge in vacation may appoint. The court shall be open at 10 a.m. [Amended by 2013 c.155 §13]

5.070 [Repealed by 1969 c.591 §305]

5.080 County judge as interested party. Except as otherwise provided in ORS 111.115, any judicial proceedings commenced in the county court in which the county judge is a party or directly interested, may be certified to the circuit court for the county in which the proceedings are pending, and the matter shall be proceeded with in the circuit court as upon appeal from the county court to the circuit court. [Amended by 1969 c.591 §265]

5.090 Absence of county judge, or vacancy; authority of circuit judge; pro tem county judge. (1) When the county judge is incapacitated, or absent from the county, or whenever there is a vacancy in the office of county judge, any circuit judge for or assigned to the county may perform the judicial functions of the county judge, hear proceedings, and enter any judgment or order necessary to carry into effect the judicial jurisdiction of the county court in all matters with the same force and effect as if done by the county judge when present in the county.
(2) A county judge that exercises judicial functions may exercise judicial powers and functions in another county court as a pro tem county judge:
(a) In the event of a vacancy in the office of county judge in another county, until the vacancy is filled as provided by law; or
(b) In the event of the absence, incapacity or disqualification of a county judge in another county, during the period of the absence, incapacity or disqualification. [Amended by 1997 c.650 §1; 2003 c.576 §272]

5.100 Order of docketing and disposal of business; records of proceedings. (1) The business of the county court at each term shall be docketed and disposed of in the following order:
(a) Judicial business.
(b) County business.
(2) The proceedings and records of the court pertaining to the respective classifications of business specified in this section shall be kept in separate books. [Amended by 1969 c.591 §266]

5.105 Records of county court. The records of the county courts include a register and a judgment docket. [2003 c.576 §174a]

5.110 Jury. A county court trial jury shall consist of six persons drawn by lot from the jurors in attendance upon the court at a particular term and sworn to try and determine a question of fact.

5.120 Appeals. (1) A party to a judicial proceeding in a county court may appeal from a judgment or other final determinative order given therein. The appeal shall be taken at the time and in the manner prescribed by law for the taking of an appeal from a judgment or other appealable order of the justice court. The appeal shall lie to the circuit court for the county in which the county court is located and be prosecuted, heard and determined in the manner prescribed by law for the prosecution, hearing and determination of appeals from the justice court.
(2) An appeal shall lie to the Court of Appeals from the whole or a specified part of the judgment or other final determinative order of the circuit court given upon such appeal to it, in like manner and with like effect as though it were from a judgment or other appealable determinative order of such circuit court given in a suit in equity therein. [Amended by 1959 c.558 §50; 1977 c.290 §1; 2003 c.576 §273]

5.125 County court fees. In the county court there shall be charged and collected in advance by the county clerk as clerk of the court, for the benefit of the county, the following fees, and no more, for the following purposes and services:
(1) Making transcription from the judgment docket, $4.
(2) Filing and entering transcript of judgment, $4.
(3) Filing and docketing copy of foreign judgment and affidavit filed as provided in ORS 24.115 and 24.125, $25.
(4) Issuing writs of execution or writs of garnishment, $3 for each writ.
(5) Preparing clerk's certificate of satisfaction of judgment, $3.75.
(6) For any service not enumerated in this section, the fees provided or established under ORS 205.320. [Formerly 21.375; 2003 c.576 §166]

CHAPTER 6 [Reserved for expansion]_____

Chapter 7 — Records and Files of Courts

RECORDS AND FILES OF COURTS

COURTS OF RECORD; COURT OFFICERS; JURIES

COURT RECORDS GENERALLY

7.010   Records of court; minimum record retention schedules

7.015   Consolidation of records

7.020   Register

7.070   Jury register

7.090   Files of court

7.095   Electronic data processing for court records; standards for preservation and security

CUSTODY AND EXAMINATION OF RECORDS AND FILES, AND THEIR DISPOSITION, SUBSTITUTION OR RESTORATION

7.110   Custody of records and files

7.120   Disposition of exhibits, notes and audio records of circuit court cases

7.124   Procedures for destruction of documents; photographic and electronic copies

7.130   Search and examination of records and files; certified copies

7.132   Access to case information not otherwise open to public

7.140   Substitution of copy of lost record

7.150   Order of restoration when no copy available

7.160   Restoration of destroyed probate records

7.170   When copy of higher court record may be filed in lower court; effect when original is lost or destroyed

RECORDS IN PROBATE AND JUVENILE PROCEEDINGS

7.230   Probate and juvenile court records to be kept separate

7.240   Records in probate matters

USE OF RECYCLED PAPER AND PAPER PRINTED ON BOTH SIDES

7.250   Use of paper printed on both sides; use of recycled paper

COURT RECORDS GENERALLY

7.010 Records of court; minimum record retention schedules. (1) The records of the circuit courts include a register and jury register.
(2) The record of the Supreme Court and the Court of Appeals is a register.
(3) All references in this chapter to the clerk or court administrator relate to the office of the clerk or court administrator of the appropriate trial or appellate court.
(4) Minimum record retention schedules and standards for all records of the state courts and the administrative offices of the state courts may be prescribed by the State Court Administrator pursuant to ORS 8.125. The State Court Administrator shall ensure that the minimum record retention schedules and standards prescribed under ORS 8.125 conform with policies and standards established by the State Archivist under ORS 192.105, 357.825 and 357.835 (1) for public records valued for legal, administrative or research purposes. [Amended by 1969 c.198 §34; 1975 c.588 §3; 1985 c.540 §1; 1989 c.768 §2; 1995 c.244 §9; 2003 c.576 §174]

7.015 Consolidation of records. Any of the records of the court required under ORS 7.010 may be consolidated, as the court may deem appropriate, so long as the essential elements of information and the inherent purpose of those records are maintained. [1975 c.588 §2]

7.020 Register. The register is a record wherein the clerk or court administrator shall enter, by its title, every action, suit or proceeding commenced in, or transferred or appealed to, the court, according to the date of its commencement, transfer or appeal. Thereafter, the clerk or court administrator shall note therein all the following:
(1) The date of any filing of any document.
(2) The date of making, filing and entry of any order, judgment, ruling or other direction of the court in or concerning such action, suit or proceeding.
(3) Any other information required by statute, court order or rule. [Amended by 1971 c.193 §12; 1975 c.588 §4; 1985 c.540 §2; 1989 c.768 §3; 2007 c.129 §3]

7.030 [Amended by 1971 c.193 §13; 1975 c.588 §5; repealed by 1985 c.540 §47]

7.040 [Amended by 1975 c.588 §6; 1977 c.591 §1; 1985 c.540 §3; 1989 c.768 §4; 1993 c.763 §5; repealed by 2003 c.576 §580]

7.050 [Amended by 1975 c.588 §7; 1977 c.592 §1; repealed by 1989 c.768 §11]

7.060 [Amended by 1971 c.193 §14; 1975 c.588 §8; repealed by 1985 c.540 §47]

7.070 Jury register. The jury register is a record wherein the clerk or court administrator shall enter the names of the persons attending upon the court at a particular term as grand or trial jurors, the time of the attendance of each, and when discharged or excused, and the amount of fees and mileage earned by each. [Amended by 1975 c.588 §9]

7.080 [Amended by 1975 c.588 §10; repealed by 1985 c.540 §47]

7.090 Files of court. The files of the court are all documents filed with or by the clerk of the court or court administrator, in any action, suit or proceeding therein, or before the judge. [Amended by 1975 c.588 §11; 2007 c.129 §4]

7.095 Electronic data processing for court records; standards for preservation and security. (1) Where the application of electronic data processing techniques is determined to be feasible and expedient in maintaining records of the courts of this state, the Chief Justice of the Supreme Court may authorize records to be kept by use of electronic data processing equipment. Court records maintained as provided by this section shall contain the information otherwise required by law for the records of courts in this state.
(2) The State Court Administrator may prescribe standards governing the use of such techniques, the preservation of the records so maintained, and controls to prevent unauthorized access to records maintained through the use of electronic data processing equipment. [1971 c.499 §1; 1985 c.540 §4; 1995 c.244 §2]

7.110 Custody of records and files. (1) The records and files of the court shall be maintained by the clerk or court administrator of the respective trial or appellate court, and the clerk or court administrator is the custodian of and responsible for those records and files. Paper records and files may not be taken out of the office, and electronic records may not be removed from any file or electronic database, by any person except when allowed by special order of the court or a judge or general rule made by the court.

(2) Custody of and responsibility for records and files of the court relating to an action, suit or proceeding may be transferred to the clerk or court administrator of another court, for the purposes of storage and servicing, after the expiration of 25 years after the entry of final judgment in the action, suit or proceeding. [Amended by 1971 c.193 §15; 1975 c.588 §12; 1985 c.540 §5; 2007 c.129 §5]

7.120 Disposition of exhibits, notes and audio records of circuit court cases. (1) The presiding judge for a judicial district may authorize destruction of any court record or document at any time after the expiration of the minimum retention period established by the State Court Administrator under ORS 8.125. Records and documents that may be destroyed under this section include registers, dockets, indexes, files, citations, notes, audio records, video records, stenographic records, exhibits, jury records and fiscal and administrative documents.

(2) The presiding judge for a judicial district may order the return, destruction or other disposition of exhibits offered or received in any case in circuit court at any time after the case becomes final and not subject to further appeal. This subsection does not apply to exhibits in a case involving the determination of water rights, which exhibits shall be permanently retained. [Amended by 1955 c.497 §1; 1975 c.481 §1; 1979 c.58 §1; 1985 c.540 §6; 1993 c.33 §274; 1993 c.546 §116; 1995 c.781 §§16,16a; 1997 c.872 §13]

7.124 Procedures for destruction of documents; photographic and electronic copies. (1) Pursuant to ORS 8.125 (11), the State Court Administrator may establish procedures that provide for the destruction of records, instruments, books, papers, transcripts and other documents filed in a state court after making a photographic film, microphotographic film, electronic image or other photographic or electronic copy of each document that is destroyed.

(2) A state court may use procedures established under subsection (1) of this section only if at the time of making the copy of the document or group of documents, the court administrator attaches to the copy, attaches to the sealed container in which the copy is placed or incorporates or causes to be incorporated into the copy:

(a) A statement that the copy is a correct copy of the original, or of a specified part of the original document or group of documents; and

(b) The date on which the copy of the document or group of documents was made.

(3) A court administrator using film for copies under this section must promptly seal and store at least one original or negative copy of the film in a manner and place that will ensure that the film will not be lost, stolen or destroyed.

(4) A court administrator using electronic images for copies under procedures established under subsection (1) of this section must ensure that the electronic images are continuously updated into commonly used formats and, if necessary, transferred to media necessary to ensure that the electronic images are accessible through commonly used electronic or computerized systems.

(5) If a copy of a document created under this section is retained in lieu of the original document, the copy is the official court record for all purposes and must be retained for the period established by the schedule prescribed in ORS 8.125 (11). [2007 c.129 §2; 2013 c.685 §3]

Note: 7.124 was enacted into law by the Legislative Assembly but was not added to or made a part of ORS chapter 7 or any series therein by legislative action. See Preface to Oregon Revised Statutes for further explanation.

7.125 [1985 c.540 §8; 1995 c.781 §§17,17a; repealed by 1995 c.658 §127]

7.130 Search and examination of records and files; certified copies. Whenever requested, the clerk or court administrator shall furnish to any person a certified copy of any portion of the records or files in the custody of the clerk or court administrator. No person other than the clerk or court administrator or a representative designated by the clerk or court administrator is entitled to make such copy, or to have the use of the records or files for such purpose. Whenever requested, the clerk or court administrator shall search the records and files, and give a certificate thereof according to the nature of the inquiry. [Amended by 1971 c.193 §16; 1979 c.833 §2; 1985 c.540 §9]

7.132 Access to case information not otherwise open to public. Notwithstanding any other provision of law, the State Court Administrator may authorize access to case calendars, case registers and other case information that is kept in electronic form and that is otherwise not open to public inspection, including information on cases under ORS chapters 419A, 419B, 419C, 426 and 427. Any person granted access to records under this section must preserve the confidentiality of the records. The State Court Administrator shall prescribe standards and procedures for access to case information under this section for persons who need access to the information in order to perform duties with respect to the case. [2007 c.331 §2]

Note: 7.132 was enacted into law by the Legislative Assembly but was not added to or made a part of ORS chapter 7 or any series therein by legislative action. See Preface to Oregon Revised Statutes for further explanation.

7.140 Substitution of copy of lost record. If the record of any judgment or other proceeding of any judicial court of this state, or any part of the record of any judicial proceeding, is lost or destroyed, any party or person interested may, on application, by petition in writing under oath to the court and on showing to its satisfaction that the record has been lost or destroyed without fault or neglect of the applicant, obtain an order from the court authorizing the defect to be supplied by a certified copy of the original record when it can be obtained. The certified copy shall have the same effect as the original record. [Amended by 2003 c.576 §274]

7.150 Order of restoration when no copy available. If the loss or destruction of any record or part thereof as mentioned in ORS 7.140 has happened and the defect cannot be supplied as therein provided, any party or person interested may make a written application to the court, to which the record belonged, verified by affidavit showing its loss or destruction and that certified copies cannot be obtained by the applicant. It shall also show the substance of the record and that its loss or destruction occurred without the fault or neglect of the applicant. Thereupon the court shall cause the application to be entered of record in the court, and due notice of it shall be given as in actions at law, that it may be heard by the court. If, upon the hearing, the court shall be satisfied that the statements contained in the written application are true, it shall make an order reciting what was the substance and effect of the lost or destroyed record. This order shall be entered of record in the court, and have the same effect which the original record would have had so far as concerns the applicant and the persons who shall have been notified as herein provided. The record in all cases when the proceeding was in rem, and no personal service was had, may be supplied upon like notice as nearly as may be as in the original proceeding. The court in which the application is pending may in all cases in which publication is required direct, by order, to be entered of record, the form of the notice, and designate the newspaper or newspapers in which it shall be published.

7.160 Restoration of destroyed probate records. In case of the destruction of the records or any part thereof of any court having probate jurisdiction, the judge of the court may proceed, upon the motion of the judge or upon application in writing of any party in interest, to restore the records, papers and proceedings of the court relating to the estate of a deceased person, including recorded wills and wills probated or filed for probate in the court. For this purpose the judge may cause citations to be issued to any parties designated by the judge, and the judge may compel the attendance in court of witnesses whose testimony may be necessary to the establishment of the record or part thereof. The judge may also compel the production of written or documentary evidence which the judge deems necessary in determining the true import and effect of the original record, will, paper or other document belonging to the files of the court. The judge may also make orders and judgments establishing the original record, will, paper, document or proceeding, or its substance, as to the judge shall seem just and proper. The judge may make all rules and regulations governing the proceedings for the restoration as in the judgment of the judge will best secure the rights and protect the interest of all parties concerned. [Amended by 2003 c.576 §275]

7.170 When copy of higher court record may be filed in lower court; effect when original is lost or destroyed. In case of the loss or destruction of the original record of any cause removed to the Supreme Court or to the Court of Appeals, a certified copy of the record of the cause remaining in the Supreme Court or the Court of Appeals may be filed in the court from which the cause was removed, on motion of any interested party or person. The copy filed shall have the same effect as the original record would have had if it had not been lost or destroyed. [Amended by 1969 c.198 §35]

7.210 [Repealed by 1957 c.412 §1]

7.211 [1957 c.412 §3 (enacted in lieu of 109.340); 1975 c.588 §14; 1979 c.58 §5; 1983 c.672 §17; 1985 c.540 §10; 1995 c.79 §4; 1995 c.730 §6; 1997 c.873 §25; 1999 c.859 §25; 2003 c.576 §276; repealed by 2013 c.346 §7]

7.215 [1969 c.619 §8; 1975 c.588 §15; 1979 c.58 §6; 1985 c.540 §11; repealed by 1993 c.138 §1]

7.220 [Amended by 1965 c.510 §9; 1975 c.588 §16; repealed by 1981 c.215 §8]

7.225 [Amended by 1965 c.510 §10; repealed by 1981 c.215 §8]

RECORDS IN PROBATE AND JUVENILE PROCEEDINGS

7.230 Probate and juvenile court records to be kept separate. Insofar as may be practicable and convenient the records and proceedings pertaining to probate and juvenile matters shall be kept separate from the other records and proceedings of the circuit courts. [Amended by 1969 c.591 §267]

7.240 Records in probate matters. (1) For probate matters in state courts, the clerk or court administrator shall enter and record the proceedings in the register described in ORS 7.020.
(2) For probate matters in courts other than state courts, the clerk or court administrator shall enter and record the proceedings in the following records:
(a) A register, in which shall be entered a memorandum of all official business transacted by the court or judge thereof pertaining to the estate of each decedent, under the name of the decedent, and that pertaining to each protective proceeding under ORS chapter 125, under the name of the protected person.
(b) A probate index, in which shall be kept an index of all the entries in the register under the names of the persons to whose estate, person or business the entries relate, which names shall be arranged chronologically in alphabetical order. [Amended by 1973 c.823 §84; 1975 c.588 §17; 1985 c.540 §12; 1995 c.664 §68; 2013 c.685 §2]

USE OF RECYCLED PAPER AND PAPER PRINTED ON BOTH SIDES

7.250 Use of paper printed on both sides; use of recycled paper. (1) The State Court Administrator and the courts of this state shall encourage persons who make paper filings in the courts, including all pleadings, motions, copies and other documents, to use paper that has been printed on both sides of each sheet. The courts of this state may not decline to accept any paper filing because the filing is printed on both sides of each sheet of paper.
(2) All paper filings in the courts of this state, including all pleadings, motions, copies and other documents, shall be printed on recycled paper if recycled paper is readily available at a reasonable price. The State Court Administrator and the courts of this state shall encourage persons who make paper filings in the courts to use recycled paper that has the highest available content of post-consumer waste, as defined in ORS 279A.010, and that is recyclable in office paper recycling programs in the community in which the filing is made. A court of this state may not decline to accept any paper filing because the paper does not comply with the requirements of this subsection. [1997 c.762 §2; 2003 c.794 §193; 2007 c.129 §6]

_____

Chapter 8 — Court Officers and District Attorneys

2017 EDITION

COURT OFFICERS AND DISTRICT ATTORNEYS

COURTS OF RECORD; COURT OFFICERS; JURIES

JUDICIAL DEPARTMENT STAFF

8.100   Authority of Judicial Department to require fingerprints; rules

JUDICIAL DEPARTMENT COMPENSATION CHANGES

8.105   Submission of proposed change to legislative committee

STATE COURT ADMINISTRATOR; COURT STAFF

8.110   State Court Administrator; appointment; term; duties

8.120   Duties as court administrator for Supreme Court and Court of Appeals; delegation

8.125   Duties to assist Chief Justice and other courts

8.130   Fees payable to State Treasurer

8.150   Appointment and compensation of employees

8.155   Bailiffs of higher courts

8.160   Administrator and staff not to engage in private practice of law

8.170   Status of court officers and employees

TRIAL COURT ADMINISTRATORS AND STAFF

8.185   Trial court administrator for judicial district

8.195   Appointment of trial court administrators; removal

8.225   Duties of trial court administrator; delegation; transcript coordinator

8.235   Trial court administrators as state employees

8.245   Trial court administrators and other personnel not to engage in private practice of law

8.255   Agreement between state and county to provide services with county employees; payment to county; supervision of employees

COLLECTIVE BARGAINING

8.270   Collective bargaining rights of court administrators and staff

REPORTERS AND REPORTS

8.340   Reporter's duties

8.350   Transcript of testimony

8.360   Certified report as prima facie correct; reading as deposition; proceedings where reporter has ceased to be official reporter

CERTIFIED SHORTHAND REPORTERS

8.415   Definitions for ORS 8.415 to 8.455

8.420   Qualifications and certification of shorthand reporters

8.435   Certificate of certified shorthand reporter; prohibition on use of title "certified shorthand reporter" unless certified

8.440   Grounds for revocation, suspension or refusal to issue certificate

8.445   Fees

8.450   Disposition of fees and other revenues

8.455   Advisory committee, membership; terms

DISTRICT ATTORNEYS

8.610   Election and term of office

8.620   Filing certificate of election

8.630   Qualifications; general powers and duties

8.640   Filling vacancies in office

8.650   District attorney as public prosecutor

8.660   Attending court and prosecuting offenses

8.665   Prosecuting violations

8.670   Proceedings before magistrates and grand jury

8.675   Priority given to administration of laws relating to public assistance and enforcement of support

8.680   Prosecuting and collecting penalties and forfeitures; prosecuting and defending for state

8.685   Assisting juvenile court; right to appear

8.690   Advising and representing county officers and employees

8.700   Register to be kept

8.710   Disqualification; appointment of special district attorney

8.720   Receiving private fee in criminal action; acting as attorney in civil action involving same controversy

8.726   District attorneys and deputies prohibited from engaging in private practice of law; exception

8.730   Partner prosecuting or defending certain cases

8.760   Deputies may be authorized and paid by county

8.780   Appointment of deputies; qualifications; duties

8.790   Compensation of district attorney and deputies limited to salaries

8.830   Additional compensation from county for district attorney and deputies paid by state

8.850   Offices, supplies and stenographic assistance for district attorneys and deputies

8.852   Salary plan for district attorneys

8.010 [Amended by 1953 c.382 §4; 1969 c.198 §36; 1983 c.763 §28; renumbered 8.155]

8.020 [Amended by 1965 c.225 §1; 1981 c.126 §1; 1981 s.s.1 c.3 §23; repealed by 1983 c.77 §1]

8.030 [Repealed by 1983 c.77 §1]

8.060 [Formerly 2.350; repealed by 1971 c.193 §30]

8.070 [1965 c.328 §1; 1975 c.260 §1; 1977 c.594 §1; repealed by 1981 s.s.1 c.3 §141]

8.075 [1977 c.594 §3; repealed by 1981 s.s.1 c.3 §141]

JUDICIAL DEPARTMENT STAFF

8.100 Authority of Judicial Department to require fingerprints; rules. (1) For the purpose of requesting a state or nationwide criminal records check under ORS 181A.195, the Judicial Department may require the fingerprints of a person who:
(a) Is employed or applying for employment by the department; or
(b) Provides services or seeks to provide services to the department as a contractor, vendor or volunteer.
(2) After considering the rules adopted by the Oregon Department of Administrative Services under ORS 181A.215, the Chief Justice of the Supreme Court may, by order, adopt rules used to determine whether a person described in subsection (1) of this section is fit to be employed by, or provide services to, the Judicial Department. The order may incorporate, in whole or in part, the rules adopted by the Oregon Department of Administrative Services under ORS 181A.215. [2005 c.730 §51; 2015 c.758 §3]

JUDICIAL DEPARTMENT COMPENSATION CHANGES

8.105 Submission of proposed change to legislative committee. (1) Before making any change to a compensation plan, an administrative division of the judicial department must submit the proposed change to the Joint Committee on Ways and Means during the period when the Legislative Assembly is in session, or to the Emergency Board or the Joint Interim Committee on Ways and Means during the interim period between sessions.
(2) This section applies to all boards, commissions, committees and departments of the judicial department, as defined in ORS 174.113, including but not limited to the Public Defense Services Commission and the Commission on Judicial Fitness and Disability. [2012 c.107 §79]

STATE COURT ADMINISTRATOR; COURT STAFF

8.110 State Court Administrator; appointment; term; duties. (1) The office of State Court Administrator is established.
(2) The Chief Justice of the Supreme Court shall appoint after conferring with and seeking the advice of the Supreme Court, may remove at pleasure and shall fix the compensation of the State Court Administrator.
(3) The State Court Administrator shall perform the duties, powers and functions of the office under the supervision and subject to the direction of the Chief Justice of the Supreme Court. [Amended by 1953 c.382 §4; 1971 c.193 §1; 1981 s.s. c.1 §12]

8.120 Duties as court administrator for Supreme Court and Court of Appeals; delegation. (1) The State Court Administrator shall, for the Supreme Court and Court of Appeals:
(a) Act as court administrator for the court.
(b) Keep the seal of the court, and affix it in all cases required by law.
(c) Record the proceedings of the court.
(d) Keep the records, files, books and documents pertaining to the court.
(e) File all documents delivered to the administrator for that purpose in any action or proceeding in the court.
(f) Attend the terms of the court, unless excused by the court, and administer oaths.
(g) Under the direction of the court enter its orders and judgments.
(h) Authenticate, by certificate or transcript, as may be required, the records, files or proceedings of the court, or any document pertaining thereto, and filed with the administrator.
(i) In the performance of duties pertaining to the court, conform to the direction of the court.
(2) The State Court Administrator may delegate powers of the office of State Court Administrator to officers and employees of the Judicial Department designated by the State Court Administrator in writing. [Amended by 1971 c.193 §2; 1981 s.s. c.1 §13; 1985 c.540 §21; 1995 c.273 §3; 2003 c.518 §4; 2007 c.129 §7]

8.125 Duties to assist Chief Justice and other courts. The State Court Administrator shall, to the extent directed by the Chief Justice of the Supreme Court:
(1) Assist the Chief Justice in exercising administrative authority and supervision under ORS 1.002.
(2) Consistent with applicable provisions of law and rules made thereunder:
(a) Supervise the personnel plan for officers, other than judges, and employees of the courts of this state who are state officers or employees.
(b) Prescribe the form and content and supervise the preparation of consolidated budgets, for submission to the Legislative Assembly, applicable to expenditures made and revenues received by the state in respect to the courts of this state.
(c) Supervise an accounting system for the recording, monitoring and auditing of expenditures made and revenues received by the state in respect to the courts of this state.
(d) Establish and maintain inventory records of property of the state in the custody or control of the courts of this state or any judge, other officer or employee thereof.
(3) Conduct a continuing survey of the administrative methods and activities, records, business and facilities of the courts of this state and make recommendations to the Chief Justice based on the survey.
(4) Collect and compile statistical and other data relating to the courts of this state and municipal courts, including the caseload, workload, performance, status, management, expenses and revenues of those courts, and make reports on the business and condition of those courts.

(5) Establish and supervise a statewide public information service concerning the courts of this state.

(6) Establish and supervise education programs for judges, other officers and employees of the courts of this state and municipal courts pertinent to the performance of the functions of those judges, other officers and employees.

(7) Provide to the judges, other officers and employees of the courts of this state, to attorneys and to the public appropriate assistance services relating to the administration and management of the courts of this state.

(8) Prepare and maintain a continuing long-range plan for improvement and future needs of the courts of this state.

(9) Supervise and maintain the law libraries of the judicial department of government of this state, including the State of Oregon Law Library, and excluding county law libraries except as provided in ORS 9.825.

(10) Enter into contracts on behalf of the Judicial Department, including but not limited to financing agreements entered into pursuant to ORS 283.087.

(11) Prescribe minimum retention schedules and standards for all records of the state courts and the administrative offices of the state courts, including but not limited to minimum retention schedules and standards for registers, dockets, indexes, files, citations, notes, audio records, video records, stenographic records, exhibits, jury records and fiscal and administrative documents, whether maintained in paper, micrographic, electronic or other storage form. The State Court Administrator shall ensure that the minimum record retention schedules and standards prescribed under this subsection conform with policies and standards established by the State Archivist under ORS 192.105, 357.825 and 357.835 (1) for public records valued for legal, administrative or research purposes. [1981 s.s. c.1 §15; 1985 c.308 §1; 1991 c.790 §19; 1995 c.244 §1; 1999 c.787 §2; 2001 c.779 §5; 2011 c.224 §6; 2011 c.595 §106]

8.130 Fees payable to State Treasurer. Unless otherwise provided by law, all fees and other moneys collected by the State Court Administrator shall be paid to the State Treasurer promptly, and shall be deposited in the General Fund available for general governmental expenses. [Amended by 1971 c.193 §3; 1981 s.s. c.1 §16]

8.140 [Amended by 1971 c.193 §4; repealed by 1981 s.s. c.1 §25]

8.150 Appointment and compensation of employees. The State Court Administrator, with the approval of the Chief Justice of the Supreme Court, may appoint and shall fix the compensation of employees to perform or assist in the performance of duties, powers and functions of the administrator. [Amended by 1971 c.193 §5; 1981 s.s. c.1 §17]

8.155 Bailiffs of higher courts. (1) Bailiffs for the Supreme Court and the Court of Appeals shall be appointed under a personnel plan established by the Chief Justice of the Supreme Court. The bailiffs shall be executive officers of the respective courts.

(2) Process in cases of original jurisdiction in the Supreme Court may be executed by the bailiff or any sheriff of the state as directed by the court. [Formerly 8.010]

8.160 Administrator and staff not to engage in private practice of law. The State Court Administrator and employees of the administrator shall not engage in the private practice of law. [Amended by 1953 c.382 §4; 1971 c.193 §6; 1981 s.s. c.1 §18]

8.170 Status of court officers and employees. Officers and employees of the Supreme Court, Court of Appeals and Oregon Tax Court, and employees of the State Court Administrator, who are appointed under a personnel plan established by the Chief Justice of the Supreme Court are state officers or employees in the exempt service and not subject to ORS chapter 240. However, such personnel shall have the right to be dismissed only for just cause after hearing and appeal. [1983 c.763 §27]

8.172 [1995 c.658 §146; repealed by 2001 c.823 §24 (1.204 enacted in lieu of 8.172)]
TRIAL COURT ADMINISTRATORS AND STAFF

8.185 Trial court administrator for judicial district. Unless otherwise ordered by the Chief Justice of the Supreme Court, there shall be a trial court administrator for each judicial district described in ORS 3.012. The Chief Justice may order that one trial court administrator serve for two or more adjoining judicial districts. [1981 s.s. c.3 §8; 1995 c.658 §17; 1997 c.801 §115]

8.195 Appointment of trial court administrators; removal. (1) Subject to applicable provisions of a personnel plan established by the Chief Justice of the Supreme Court, a person to serve as trial court administrator for:

(a) One judicial district shall be appointed by the presiding judge for the judicial district, with the approval of a majority of the circuit court judges in the district.

(b) The circuit court in a judicial district shall be appointed by the presiding judge for the judicial district, with the approval of a majority of the circuit court judges.

(c) Two or more adjoining judicial districts shall be appointed by the presiding judges for the judicial districts, with the approval of a majority of the circuit court judges in the districts.

(2) A trial court administrator may be removed from the office by the appointing presiding judge as provided in a personnel plan established by the Chief Justice of the Supreme Court. [1981 s.s. c.3 §9; 1995 c.658 §18; 1995 c.781 §18]

8.205 [1981 s.s. c.3 §10; 1995 c.658 §19; repealed by 1997 c.801 §131]

8.210 [Repealed by 1973 c.781 §4]

8.215 [1981 s.s. c.3 §11; 1995 c.658 §20a; 1995 c.781 §19; repealed by 1997 c.801 §131]

8.220 [Repealed by 1973 c.781 §4]

8.225 Duties of trial court administrator; delegation; transcript coordinator. (1) The trial court administrator for a judicial district has the duties, powers and functions prescribed by law or by rules of the circuit courts in the district.

(2) A trial court administrator shall, for each court served by the officer:

(a) Keep the seal of the court, and affix it in all cases required by law.

(b) Record the proceedings of the court.

(c) Maintain the records, files, books and other documents pertaining to the court.

(d) File all documents delivered to the trial court administrator in any action or proceeding in the court.

(e) Attend the court, administer oaths and receive the verdict of a jury in any action or proceeding therein, in the presence and under the direction of the court.

(f) Under the direction of the court enter its orders and judgments.

(g) Authenticate, by certificate or transcript, as may be required, the records, files or proceedings of the court, or any document pertaining thereto, and filed with the officer.

(h) In the performance of duties pertaining to the court, conform to the direction of the court.

(3) A trial court administrator may take and certify the proof and acknowledgment of a conveyance of real property or any other written instrument authorized or required to be proved or acknowledged.

(4) A trial court administrator may delegate powers of the office of trial court administrator to employees of the trial court administrator.

(5) A trial court administrator shall designate a person to act as transcript coordinator for the court. [1981 s.s. c.3 §12; 1985 c.540 §22; 1993 c.223 §1; 1995 c.273 §4; 1997 c.801 §§117,117a; 2007 c.129 §8; 2015 c.212 §13]

8.235 Trial court administrators as state employees. Trial court administrators appointed under ORS 8.195 and other nonjudicial officers and employees of the circuit courts who are appointed under a personnel plan established by the Chief Justice of the Supreme Court are state officers or employees in the exempt service and not subject to ORS chapter 240. However, such personnel shall retain the right to be dismissed only for just cause after hearing and appeal. [1981 s.s. c.3 §13; 1997 c.801 §118]

8.245 Trial court administrators and other personnel not to engage in private practice of law. Trial court administrators appointed under ORS 8.195 and other nonjudicial officers and employees of the circuit courts who are appointed under a personnel plan established by the Chief Justice of the Supreme Court shall not engage in the private practice of law. [1981 s.s. c.3 §15; 1997 c.801 §119]

8.255 Agreement between state and county to provide services with county employees; payment to county; supervision of employees. (1) The State Court Administrator, on behalf of the state, and the governing body of a county, on behalf of the county, may enter into an agreement whereby services required to be provided by the state for the circuit court for the county are provided by employees of the county, instead of by state officers and employees, and the expenses of the county in providing those services are paid to the county by the state from funds available for the purpose.

(2) County employees providing services under an agreement shall be under the supervision and control of the trial court administrator appointed under ORS 8.195. County employees providing services under an agreement are not thereby state employees. County employees providing services under an agreement shall not engage in the private practice of law.

(3) With the prior approval of the State Court Administrator, a trial court administrator appointed under ORS 8.195, on behalf of the state, and the governing body of a county, on behalf of the county, may enter into an agreement under this section in respect to services for a circuit court for the county served by the trial court administrator. [1981 s.s. c.3 §16; 1995 c.781 §20; 1997 c.801 §120]

8.260 [1953 c.34 §6; repealed by 1959 c.552 §16]

COLLECTIVE BARGAINING

8.270 Collective bargaining rights of court administrators and staff. All officers and employees of the courts of this state who are referred to in ORS 8.170 and 8.235 are subject to collective bargaining to the extent provided in ORS 243.650 to 243.782, and ORS 8.170 and 8.235 shall not be construed to reduce or eliminate any collective bargaining rights those officers and employees may have under ORS 243.650 to 243.782. [1983 c.763 §27a]

8.310 [Amended by 1965 c.369 §1; 1967 c.229 §1; 1971 c.565 §2; 1981 c.126 §2; repealed by 1981 s.s. c.3 §141]

8.320 [Amended by 1971 c.565 §3; repealed by 1981 s.s. c.3 §141]

8.330 [Repealed by 1981 s.s. c.3 §141]

REPORTERS AND REPORTS

8.340 Reporter's duties. (1) It is the duty of each official reporter of the circuit court, justice court or municipal court to attend the court for which the reporter is appointed at such times as the judge or justice of the peace may direct.

(2) A circuit court reporter shall be appointed under a personnel plan established by the Chief Justice of the Supreme Court. Reporters for a justice or municipal court are not subject to this subsection.

(3) A reporter is an officer of the court in which the reporter serves and of any court to which an appeal is made whenever the reporter has recorded the proceedings that are the subject of the appeal.

(4) Upon the trial or hearing of any cause, the judge or justice of the peace upon the motion of the judge or justice of the peace may, and upon the request of either party shall, order a report of the proceedings. The reporter shall, in the manner provided in subsection (5) of this section, make a report of the oral testimony and other proceedings of the trial or hearing to the extent required by the court or by the requesting party.

(5) When a report is required, the reporter shall:

(a) Take accurate notes by shorthand or by means of a mechanical or electronic typing device; or

(b) Make audio records pursuant to policies and procedures established by the State Court Administrator.

(6) The notes or audio records of the official reporter or a reporter providing services under subsection (7) of this section shall be filed in the office of the clerk of the court subject to the provisions of ORS 7.120 and except as provided in ORS 19.385.

(7)(a) In any circuit court proceeding in which the court uses audio recording or video recording, any party may, with reasonable notice to the trial court, arrange for the reporting of the proceeding by stenographic means. A reporter providing stenographic reporting services under this paragraph shall be certified in shorthand reporting under ORS 8.415 to 8.455 or by a nationally recognized certification program. The party arranging for reporting of the proceeding by stenographic means must provide the court with the name of the reporter and an address and telephone number where the reporter may be contacted.

(b) If all parties to the proceedings agree, the stenographic reporting of the proceedings by a reporter arranged for by a party may be used by the parties during the proceedings.

(c) If all parties to the proceedings agree, the stenographic reporting of the proceedings by a reporter arranged for by a party is the official record of the proceedings for the purpose of a transcript on appeal. For all other purposes, the official record of the proceedings shall be the record produced by the reporting technique used by the court, unless otherwise ordered by the court.

(d) Unless other parties agree to pay all or part of the cost of the reporter, the party arranging for the reporting of the proceeding by stenographic means under this subsection must pay all costs of the reporter and the cost of providing copies of the transcript to the court. [Amended by 1955 c.497 §2; 1971 c.565 §4; 1975 c.481 §2; 1981 s.s. c.3 §24; 1985 c.496 §9; 1985 c.540 §42; 1989 c.1009 §1; 1995 c.244 §5; 1999 c.682 §9; 2007 c.394 §1]

8.350 Transcript of testimony. When a report of the proceedings, or any part thereof, has been made in any case as provided in ORS 8.340, if the court or either party to the suit or action or the party's attorney requests transcription of the notes or audio records into longhand, the official reporter shall cause full and accurate typewritten transcripts to be made of the testimony or other proceedings, which shall, when certified to as provided in ORS 8.360, be filed with the clerk of the court where the cause was tried or heard, for the use of the court or parties. [Amended by 1955 c.497 §3; 1985 c.496 §10; 1985 c.540 §43; 2009 c.11 §3]

8.360 Certified report as prima facie correct; reading as deposition; proceedings where reporter has ceased to be official reporter. (1) The report of the official reporter, when transcribed and certified to as being a correct transcript of the notes or audio records of the testimony, exceptions taken, charge of the judge, and other proceedings in the matter, shall be prima facie a correct statement thereof, and may thereafter be read in evidence as the deposition of a witness.

(2) When the official reporter in any cause has ceased to be the official reporter of that court, any transcript made from the notes or audio records by the former official reporter, or made by a competent person under direction of the court, and duly certified to by the maker, under oath, as a full, true and

complete transcript of the notes or audio records, shall have the same force and effect as though certified in the same manner by the official reporter. [Amended by 1955 c.497 §4; 1979 c.284 §42; 1985 c.540 §44]

8.370 [Amended by 1953 c.566 §2; repealed by 1959 c.445 §1]

8.372 [Formerly part of 8.381; repealed by 1981 s.s. c.3 §141]

8.375 [Formerly part of 8.381; repealed by 1981 s.s. c.3 §141]

8.377 [Formerly part of 8.381; 1981 c.759 §9; repealed by 1981 s.s. c.3 §141]

8.379 [Formerly part of 8.381; 1971 c.144 §1; 1971 c.390 §1; repealed by 1981 s.s. c.3 §141]

8.380 [Amended by 1953 c.550 §22; 1957 c.666 §1; 1957 c.713 §15; 1959 c.509 §1; repealed by 1961 c.447 §1]

8.381 [1961 c.447 §3; 1965 c.369 §2; 1967 c.532 §6; 1967 c.533 §16; parts renumbered 8.372, 8.375, 8.377, 8.379, 8.383, 8.385 and 8.387]

8.383 [Formerly part of 8.381; 1981 c.759 §10; repealed by 1981 s.s. c.3 §141]

8.385 [Formerly part of 8.381; repealed by 1981 s.s. c.3 §141]

8.387 [Formerly part of 8.381; 1971 c.777 §6; 1975 c.430 §1; repealed by 1981 s.s. c.3 §141]

8.390 [Amended by 1953 c.550 §22; 1961 c.447 §2; repealed by 1981 s.s. c.3 §141]

8.395 [1967 c.273 §1; repealed by 1981 s.s. c.3 §141]

8.400 [Amended by 1953 c.550 §22; repealed by 1981 s.s. c.3 §141]

8.410 [Repealed by 1981 s.s. c.3 §141]

CERTIFIED SHORTHAND REPORTERS

8.415 Definitions for ORS 8.415 to 8.455. As used in ORS 8.415 to 8.455, unless the context requires otherwise:
(1) "Administrator" means the State Court Administrator.
(2) "Advisory committee" means the Certified Shorthand Reporters Advisory Committee created in ORS 8.455.
(3) "Certified shorthand reporter" means an individual who has been certified to engage in the practice of stenographic reporting or voicewriting reporting under ORS 8.415 to 8.455.
(4) "Stenographic reporting" means the making and transcribing of a verbatim record of any court proceeding, deposition, hearing or other proceeding by means of a written system of either manual or machine shorthand procedures.
(5) "Voicewriting reporting" means the making and transcribing of a verbatim record of any court proceeding, deposition, hearing or other proceeding by:
(a) Recording the words in the proceeding using a voice silencer for subsequent transcription; or
(b) Using a computerized speech-recognition transcription program. [Formerly 703.400; 1997 c.249 §3; 2003 c.14 §6; 2013 c.470 §1]

8.420 Qualifications and certification of shorthand reporters. (1) The State Court Administrator shall verify the qualifications of shorthand reporters to be certified and shall issue the certificate of shorthand reporter to qualified applicants.
(2) The administrator shall adopt policies necessary to administer ORS 8.415 to 8.455 and may appoint any committees necessary to function in accordance with ORS 8.415 to 8.455.
(3) The administrator shall:
(a) Adopt policies establishing the qualifications necessary for the issuance of a certificate of certified shorthand reporter. A shorthand reporter may be certified to perform stenographic reporting, voicewriting reporting, or both.
(b) Determine the qualifications of persons applying for certificates under ORS 8.415 to 8.455.
(c) Adopt policies for the examination of applicants and the issuing of certificates under ORS 8.415 to 8.455.
(d) Grant certificates to qualified applicants upon compliance with ORS 8.415 to 8.455 and policies of the administrator.
(e) Establish continuing education requirements for renewal of certificates.
(f) Collect fees as set by the administrator.
(g) Require the regular renewal of all certificates.
(h) Establish a code of conduct and grounds for disciplinary action.
(i) Investigate complaints regarding court reporters.
(4) The Certified Shorthand Reporters Advisory Committee shall recommend:
(a) Standards establishing the qualifications necessary for the issuance of a certificate of certified shorthand reporter;
(b) Qualifications required of persons applying for certificates under ORS 8.415 to 8.455;
(c) Procedures for the examination of applicants and the issuing of certificates under ORS 8.415 to 8.455;
(d) Certificates be granted by the administrator to qualified applicants upon compliance with ORS 8.415 to 8.455 and policies of the administrator;
(e) Continuing education requirements for renewal of certificates;
(f) A code of conduct and grounds for suspension or revocation of certificates or other disciplinary action to the administrator;
(g) Investigation of complaints regarding court reporters at the direction of the administrator; and
(h) Any corrective action that may be required. [Formerly 703.402; 1997 c.249 §4; 2005 c.22 §2; 2013 c.155 §4; 2013 c.470 §2]

8.430 [Formerly 703.404; repealed by 2013 c.470 §7]

8.435 Certificate of certified shorthand reporter; prohibition on use of title "certified shorthand reporter" unless certified. (1) The certificate of certified shorthand reporter shall be granted to any person who meets the requirements of ORS 8.415 to 8.455 and policies of the State Court Administrator.
(2) Any person who has received from the administrator a certificate of "certified shorthand reporter" shall be styled and known as a "certified shorthand reporter" and may also use the abbreviation of "C.S.R."
(3) A certificate shall be renewed regularly as provided by policies of the administrator.
(4) Certificates issued by the administrator may be renewed upon payment of the fee established under ORS 8.445, completion of established continuing education requirements and compliance with the code of conduct policy as established by the administrator.
(5) A person may not assume or use the title or designation "certified shorthand reporter" or the abbreviation "C.S.R." or any other title, designation, words, letters, abbreviation, sign or device tending to indicate that the person is a certified shorthand reporter unless the person has received a certificate

as a certified shorthand reporter under ORS 8.415 to 8.455 and policies of the administrator that is not revoked, suspended or lapsed. [Formerly 703.406; 2013 c.155 §5; 2013 c.470 §3]

8.440 Grounds for revocation, suspension or refusal to issue certificate. (1) The State Court Administrator may:
(a) Revoke, suspend or refuse to issue any certificate described in ORS 8.415 to 8.455 or policies of the administrator.
(b) Require additional education or training.
(2) The administrator may revoke, suspend or refuse to issue any certificate described in ORS 8.415 to 8.455 or policies of the administrator in the case of a violation of any provision of ORS 8.415 to 8.455 or policies of the administrator.
(3) The administrator may require additional education or training if the administrator finds the person engages in or has engaged in conduct that evidences a lack of knowledge or ability to apply skills of stenographic reporting or voicewriting reporting. [Formerly 703.408; 2013 c.470 §4]

8.445 Fees. (1) The State Court Administrator shall establish and collect reasonable fees for applications, examinations, certifications and renewals of certification authorized by ORS 8.415 to 8.455.
(2) Fees collected under this section are nonrefundable.
(3) The fees established under this section may not exceed the cost of administering and enforcing ORS 8.415 to 8.455. [Formerly 703.410; 2003 c.737 §99; 2013 c.155 §6; 2013 c.470 §5]

8.450 Disposition of fees and other revenues. All fees, moneys and other revenues received or collected under ORS 8.415 to 8.455 shall be paid into the account established in ORS 45.294, and such moneys are continuously appropriated to the State Court Administrator for the administration and enforcement of ORS 8.415 to 8.455. [Formerly 703.412]

8.455 Advisory committee, membership; terms. (1) There is created a Certified Shorthand Reporters Advisory Committee consisting of no more than seven members appointed by the State Court Administrator. At least four members of the advisory committee shall be persons skilled in the practice of stenographic reporting or voicewriting reporting and shall have been engaged continuously in the practice of stenographic reporting or voicewriting reporting for a period of not less than five years prior to the date of appointment as a member of the advisory committee. Appointees must be certified under ORS 8.415 to 8.455.
(2) The term of a member of the advisory committee shall be three years. A member is eligible for reappointment to the advisory committee. Vacancies occurring shall be filled by appointment for the unexpired term.
(3) The advisory committee shall organize by the election of one of its members as president and one as secretary.
(4) A majority of the advisory committee shall constitute a quorum for all purposes. [Formerly 703.414; 2013 c.155 §7; 2013 c.470 §6]

8.510 [Amended by 1953 c.566 §2; 1957 c.706 §1; 1963 c.494 §1; 1981 c.215 §9; repealed by 1981 s.s c.3 §141]

DISTRICT ATTORNEYS

8.610 Election and term of office. A district attorney for each county shall be elected by the electors of the county, at the general election or, if applicable, at the election specified in ORS 249.088 next preceding the expiration of the term of the then incumbent. The district attorney shall hold office for the term of four years and until a successor is elected and qualified. [Amended by 1991 c.719 §2]

8.620 Filing certificate of election. A person elected to the office of district attorney must, before entering upon the office, qualify by filing with the Secretary of State the certificate of election of the person. [Amended by 1987 c.158 §3; 2005 c.22 §3; 2005 c.797 §27]

8.630 Qualifications; general powers and duties. A person elected district attorney must, at the time of election, have been admitted to practice in the Supreme Court of Oregon. District attorneys shall possess the qualifications, have the powers, perform the duties and be subject to the restrictions provided by the Constitution for prosecuting attorneys, and by the laws of this state.

8.640 Filling vacancies in office. When a vacancy occurs in the office of district attorney, the Governor must appoint some suitable person to fill the vacancy until the next election and qualification of a successor at the next general election. A person appointed to fill a vacancy in the office must qualify in the same manner as a person elected thereto, and shall have like power and compensation, and perform the same duties.

8.650 District attorney as public prosecutor. The district attorney in each county is the public prosecutor therein and has the authority to appear and prosecute violations of the charter and ordinances of any city provided the circuit court for the county has jurisdiction with respect to violations of the charter and ordinances of each such city. In cities of a population of more than 300,000 the district attorney shall be responsible for the prosecution of all city ordinance violations. [Amended by 1971 c.633 §14; 1995 c.658 §21]

8.660 Attending court and prosecuting offenses. (1) The district attorney shall attend the terms of all courts having jurisdiction of public offenses within the district attorney's county, and, except as otherwise provided in this section, conduct, on behalf of the state, all prosecutions for such offenses therein.
(2) A district attorney shall not conduct prosecutions under this section when:
(a) A city attorney is prosecuting a violation under ORS chapter 153; or
(b) The district attorney is prohibited from appearing in a violation proceeding under the provisions of ORS 153.076. [Amended by 1975 c.451 §170; 1981 c.626 §1; 1981 c.692 §6a; 1999 c.1051 §116]

8.665 Prosecuting violations. Upon the issuance of a citation by any person authorized to issue citations for violations, a district attorney shall prosecute the case if it appears that a violation has occurred. [1981 c.692 §10; 1999 c.1051 §117]

8.670 Proceedings before magistrates and grand jury. The district attorney shall institute proceedings before magistrates for the arrest of persons charged with or reasonably suspected of public offenses, when the district attorney has information that any such offense has been committed, and attend upon and advise the grand jury when required.

8.675 Priority given to administration of laws relating to public assistance and enforcement of support. In the performance of official duties, unless otherwise specifically required by law and except for criminal and juvenile proceedings, the district attorney shall give priority to the performance of those duties involving the administration of the laws relating to public assistance and reciprocal enforcement of support. [1959 c.539 §5]

8.680 Prosecuting and collecting penalties and forfeitures; prosecuting and defending for state. The district attorney shall prosecute for all penalties and forfeitures to the state that may be incurred in the county of the district attorney, and for which no other mode of prosecution and collection is expressly provided by statute, and in like case, prosecute or defend all actions, suits and proceedings in the county to which the state is a party.

8.685 Assisting juvenile court; right to appear. (1) The district attorney shall, upon request of the juvenile court, appear in the juvenile court to assist the court in any matter within its jurisdiction.
(2) In counties having a population of more than 150,000, according to the latest federal decennial census, the district attorney shall designate a deputy to assist the juvenile court as provided in subsection (1) of this section.

(3) The district attorney is entitled to appear on behalf of the state in the juvenile court in any matter within the jurisdiction of the court. [1959 c.432 §63 (enacted in lieu of 8.750); 1991 c.681 §4]

8.690 Advising and representing county officers and employees. Upon request of a county officer, the district attorney and deputies of the district attorney shall advise the county court and other county officers on all legal questions that may arise. When any action is instituted against any county officer or county employee for damages for an alleged wrongful act or omission in the performance of official duty, the district attorney shall defend such action. The district attorney shall also prosecute and defend all actions, suits, and proceedings to which the county may be a party. For such services the district attorney shall receive no compensation other than salary. [Amended by 1957 c.151 §1; 1965 c.419 §1]

8.700 Register to be kept. The district attorney must keep a register of official business, in which the district attorney shall make a note of every action, suit or proceeding commenced or defended by the district attorney in official capacity, and the proceedings therein. The register shall, at the expiration of the term of office of the district attorney, be delivered by the district attorney to the successor in office.

8.710 Disqualification; appointment of special district attorney. If a district attorney fails to attend any court at which the district attorney is required to be, or is related to the accused by consanguinity or affinity, or, prior to the district attorney's election as district attorney, represented the accused in the matter to be investigated by the grand jury or the crime charged in the indictment, or is associated with the accused in business, or is interested financially in the matter or property out of which the alleged crime or criminal action arose, or is a stockholder in any corporation, any officer or stockholder of which is charged with the commission of any crime, or declines to prosecute or participate in proceedings for the imposition of sanctions for a contempt of court under ORS 33.065, or because of any other conflict cannot ethically serve as district attorney in a particular case, and such facts appear to the satisfaction of the court by affidavit or otherwise, the court shall appoint a regularly licensed and practicing attorney of this state who is not counsel for an interested party to perform the duties of district attorney during the district attorney's absence or inability to serve, or the trial or investigation of such accused. When the district attorney is disqualified as provided in this section, the person so appointed by the court shall receive reasonable compensation for that person's attendance, to be allowed by the court. The court in such case shall order compensation to be paid by the county, except that when the person so appointed performs the district attorney's responsibilities under ORS 25.080, the court shall order compensation to be paid by the Oregon Department of Administrative Services of the state from funds available for that purpose. [Amended by 1985 c.611 §1; 1991 c.724 §16]

8.720 Receiving private fee in criminal action; acting as attorney in civil action involving same controversy. A district attorney shall not receive any fee or reward from any private person for services in any criminal action, nor during the pendency of such prosecution can the district attorney act as attorney for either party in any civil action, suit or proceeding involving substantially the same controversy.

8.725 [1957 c.645 §2; 1959 c.539 §1; 1961 c.586 §3; repealed by 1965 c.633 §4]

8.726 District attorneys and deputies prohibited from engaging in private practice of law; exception. (1) Except as authorized by subsection (2) of this section, district attorneys and deputy district attorneys may not engage in the private practice of law.
(2) A district attorney or deputy district attorney may engage in volunteer or pro bono legal work. [1965 c.633 §2; 1971 c.583 §1; 1975 c.378 §7; 1977 c.834 §5; 1979 c.418 §8; 1981 c.908 §2; 2007 c.658 §1]

8.730 Partner prosecuting or defending certain cases. It is not lawful for any district attorney who has a law partner to allow that partner to prosecute or defend divorce cases or to defend cases in which the state is plaintiff and the district attorney is the public prosecutor. It is the duty of the judicial officers of this state to prohibit such practice in all cases coming before them. [Amended by 2003 c.14 §7]

8.740 [Amended by 1953 c.652 §6; 1957 c.490 §1; 1959 c.539 §2; 1961 c.586 §2; repealed by 1967 c.556 §5]

8.750 [Repealed by 1959 c.432 §62 (8.685 enacted in lieu of 8.750)]

8.760 Deputies may be authorized and paid by county. The county court or board of county commissioners may empower the district attorney to appoint one or more deputy district attorneys whose compensation shall be fixed by the county court or board of county commissioners and paid out of the county funds in the same manner as county officers are paid. [Amended by 1961 c.586 §4]

8.770 [Repealed by 1961 c.586 §6]

8.780 Appointment of deputies; qualifications; duties. A district attorney shall appoint deputies. A deputy district attorney shall have the same qualifications as the district attorney, and subject to the direction of the district attorney, has the same functions as the district attorney. [Amended by 1961 c.586 §5]

8.790 Compensation of district attorney and deputies limited to salaries. No salary, fees, percentage or compensation of any kind shall be allowed, paid to or received by any district attorney or deputy district attorney except as provided in ORS 8.110 to 8.150, 8.160 and 8.670 to 8.852.

8.795 [1957 c.645 §3; 1959 c.539 §3; 1961 c.586 §6a; repealed by 1965 c.633 §4]

8.800 [1953 c.652 §6; 1957 c.645 §1; 1959 c.539 §4; 1961 c.586 §1; repealed by 1965 c.633 §4]

8.801 [1965 c.633 §1; 1967 c.597 §1; 1969 c.320 §1; repealed by 1971 c.711 §6]

8.810 [Repealed by 1967 c.111 §7]

8.820 [Repealed by 1967 c.111 §7]

8.830 Additional compensation from county for district attorney and deputies paid by state. Whenever, in the judgment of any county court or board of county commissioners, the salaries paid by the state to the district attorney, or to any deputy district attorney, are not commensurate with the character of the service performed, the county court or board of county commissioners may pay out of the funds of the county such additional amounts as will properly compensate said officers for the service performed. [Amended by 1955 c.220 §1]

8.840 [Repealed by 1953 c.652 §6]

8.850 Offices, supplies and stenographic assistance for district attorneys and deputies. Each county shall provide the district attorney and any deputies for such county with such office space, facilities, supplies and stenographic assistance as is necessary to perform efficiently the duties of such office. [1953 c.652 §3]

8.852 Salary plan for district attorneys. The district attorneys of the various counties shall be paid monthly salaries as adopted in the salary plan provided for in ORS 240.240 (2), to include salary adjustments awarded management service employees. [1991 c.432 §2; reenacted by 1993 c.290 §2; reenacted by 1995 c.9 §2; reenacted by 1997 c.75 §2]

Chapter 9 — Attorneys; Law Libraries

ORS sections in this chapter were amended or repealed by the Legislative Assembly during its 2018 regular session. See the table of ORS sections amended or repealed during the 2018 regular session: 2018 A&R Tables

ATTORNEYS; LAW LIBRARIES

COURTS OF RECORD; COURT OFFICERS; JURIES

OREGON STATE BAR

9.005   Definitions for ORS 9.005 to 9.757

9.010   Status of attorney and Oregon State Bar; applicability of statutes

9.025   Board of governors; number; eligibility; term

9.030   Voting rights; eligibility of members for board of governors and house of delegates

9.040   Election of governors; rules; vacancies

9.042   Determination of eligibility of candidate for board of governors; procedure; review by Supreme Court

9.050   Recall of governors

9.055   Chief executive officer

9.060   President, president-elect and immediate past president

9.070   Duties of president and president-elect; deposit and disbursement of fees

9.080   Duties of board of governors; professional liability fund; quorum; status of employees of bar

9.090   Appropriation and disbursement of funds

9.100   Statement of financial condition

9.110   Board of governors to formulate rules

9.112   Board of governors to establish minimum continuing legal education requirements

9.114   Mandatory training on duties relating to reporting child abuse and abuse of elderly persons; rules

HOUSE OF DELEGATES

9.136   House of delegates created; membership; terms

9.139   Powers of house of delegates

9.142   Rules for conduct of business; meetings

9.145   Public members

9.148   Participation by nondelegates; referral of question for vote; petition for consideration or vote

9.150   Termination of delegate's term

9.152   Election of delegates; rules

9.155   Recall of delegate

PRACTICE OF LAW; MEMBERSHIP IN THE BAR

9.160   Bar membership required to practice law; exceptions

9.162   Definitions for ORS 9.160 to 9.166

9.164   Investigation of alleged violation of ORS 9.160

9.166   Enjoining practicing law without a license; restitution to victim

9.180	Classes of membership
9.191	Annual membership fees; professional liability assessments
9.200	Effect of failure to pay membership fees; reinstatement
9.210	Board of bar examiners; fees of applicants for admission to bar
9.220	General requirements for admission
9.241	Practice of law by attorneys licensed in other jurisdictions; rules; fee
9.242	Advice on law of foreign jurisdiction; rules
9.250	Order for admission; oath of qualified applicant
9.261	Resignation of attorney
9.280	Prohibition on acting as immigration consultant; definitions; exception

ATTORNEY AND CLIENT RELATIONSHIP

9.310	Attorney defined; counsel
9.320	Necessity for employment of attorney; effect of employment
9.330	Authority of attorney
9.340	Challenge by party of attorney's authority to appear for party
9.350	Challenge of attorney's authority to appear for adverse party
9.360	Compelling delivery by attorney of money or papers
9.370	Compelling delivery when attorney claims lien
9.380	Changing attorneys and terminating attorney-client relationship
9.390	Notice of change or termination

PROFESSIONAL CONDUCT

9.460	Duties of attorneys
9.490	Formulation of rules of professional conduct; prohibition on certain sanctions for violation of rule

PROHIBITED CONDUCT

9.500	Solicitation of personal injury business by nonlawyer
9.505	Payment for referring claims resulting from personal injury or death
9.510	Solicitation by attorneys
9.515	Referral of claims, suits or actions between attorneys; division of fees
9.520	Acceptance and prosecution of solicited claims

BAR DISCIPLINARY PROCEEDINGS

9.527	Grounds for disbarment, suspension or reprimand
9.528	Advice on conducting covert operations; participation in covert operations
9.529	Status of proceedings relating to discipline, admission or reinstatement
9.532	State professional responsibility board
9.534	Disciplinary board; procedure before board; oaths; subpoenas; hearing; record
9.536	Disciplinary board decision; appeal to Supreme Court; review; costs
9.537	Civil immunity of witnesses, bar officials and employees
9.539	Application to admission and reinstatement proceedings
9.542	Rules for investigation of attorneys and applicants; authority of board of governors to require fingerprints
9.555	Copy of complaint or notice to Attorney General when bar is plaintiff or defendant; exceptions
9.565	Tax return information from Department of Revenue; use

ATTORNEY ASSISTANCE

9.568   State lawyers assistance committee; personal and practice management assistance committees; rules; confidentiality; civil immunity

LEGAL SERVICES PROGRAM

9.572   Bar to establish Legal Services Program; director; advisory and technical committees

9.576   Review of providers; mediation; hearing; suspension of funding

9.577   Legal Aid Account
9.578   Other funding sources

9.582   Use of amounts not paid to class members in class action lawsuits

CLIENT SECURITY FUND

9.615   Definition for ORS 9.615 to 9.665

9.625   Plan to relieve client losses; rules

9.635   Sources of client security fund

9.645   Annual payment by state bar members

9.655   Investigation of claim of loss; subpoena

9.657   Immunity from civil liability

9.665   Authority for reimbursement of client; waiver of conditions; subrogation for amount paid

LAWYER TRUST ACCOUNTS

9.675   Mandatory certification and disclosures for lawyer trust accounts

9.685   Trust account overdraft notification program

SEARCH OR SEIZURE OF LAWYER FILES OR PREMISES

9.695   Status of files or work premises of lawyer; inadmissibility of evidence subject to search or seizure

ASSUMING PRACTICE OF NONPERFORMING ATTORNEY

9.705   Definitions for ORS 9.705 to 9.757

9.710   Jurisdiction of circuit court over law practice of nonperforming attorney

9.715   Petition to take jurisdiction over law practice

9.720   Court taking jurisdiction over law practice

9.725   Appointment of bar as custodian of law practice; duties of custodian, court and financial institution

9.727   Service of order of custodianship

9.730   Assistance by professional liability fund and other attorneys

9.735   Compensation of custodian

9.740   Court orders appealable; stay

9.745   Statutes of limitation suspended

9.750   Confidentiality of files and records; attorney-client privilege

9.755   Final report of custodian; petition for compensation; court approval

9.757   Retention of client materials

LAW LIBRARIES

9.760   Judicial department library services; fees

9.780   Exchange of legal publications

9.790   Legislative Counsel furnishing copies of codes and session laws for exchange

9.800   Sale of surplus codes and session laws

9.815   County law libraries and law library services

9.820   Law libraries in Multnomah County

9.825   Law library surveys; reports

9.829   Use of moneys distributed to counties

PENALTIES

9.990   Penalties

OREGON STATE BAR

9.005 Definitions for ORS 9.005 to 9.757. As used in ORS 9.005 to 9.757, unless the context or subject matter requires otherwise:
(1) "Attorney" and "member" mean a member of the bar.
(2) "Board" and "board of governors" mean the board of governors of the bar.
(3) "Delegate" means a delegate of the house of delegates of the Oregon State Bar.
(4) "Governor" means a member of the board of governors of the bar.
(5) "House" and "house of delegates" mean the house of delegates of the Oregon State Bar.
(6) "Oregon State Bar," "state bar" and "bar" mean the Oregon State Bar created by the State Bar Act set forth in ORS 9.005 to 9.757.
(7) "Rules of procedure" means the rules of procedure relative to admission, discipline, resignation and reinstatement of members of the bar adopted by the board and approved by the Supreme Court. [1975 c.641 §2; 1979 c.252 §14; 1995 c.302 §15; 1997 c.249 §5; 2017 c.94 §3]

9.010 Status of attorney and Oregon State Bar; applicability of statutes. (1) An attorney, admitted to practice in this state, is an officer of the court.
(2) The Oregon State Bar is a public corporation and an instrumentality of the Judicial Department of the government of the State of Oregon. The bar is authorized to carry out the provisions of ORS 9.005 to 9.757.
(3) The bar is subject to the following statutes applicable to public bodies:
(a) ORS 30.210 to 30.250.
(b) ORS 30.260 to 30.300.
(c) ORS 30.310, 30.312, 30.390 and 30.400.
(d) The Oregon Rules of Civil Procedure.
(e) ORS 192.311 to 192.478.
(f) ORS 192.610 to 192.690.
(g) ORS 243.401 to 243.507.
(h) ORS 244.010 to 244.040.
(i) ORS 297.110 to 297.230.
(j) ORS chapters 307, 308 and 311.
(k) ORS 731.036 and 737.600.
(4) Except as provided in subsection (3) of this section, the bar is not subject to any statute applicable to a state agency, department, board or commission or public body unless the statute expressly provides that it is applicable to the Oregon State Bar.
(5) The Oregon State Bar has perpetual succession and a seal, and may sue and be sued. Notwithstanding the provisions of ORS 270.020 and 279.835 to 279.855 and ORS chapters 278, 279A, 279B and 279C, the bar may, in its own name, for the purpose of carrying into effect and promoting its objectives, enter into contracts and lease, acquire, hold, own, encumber, insure, sell, replace, deal in and with and dispose of real and personal property.
(6) No obligation of any kind incurred or created under this section shall be, or be considered, an indebtedness or obligation of the State of Oregon. [Amended by 1955 c.463 §1; 1965 c.461 §1; 1985 c.446 §1; 1997 c.249 §6; 2003 c.794 §194; 2007 c.60 §1]

9.020 [Amended by 1971 c.103 §1; repealed by 1973 c.114 §5]

9.025 Board of governors; number; eligibility; term. (1)(a) The Oregon State Bar shall be governed by a board of governors consisting of 19 members:
(A) Fourteen of the members shall be active members of the Oregon State Bar elected from the regions established under subsection (2)(a) of this section. A member elected under this subparagraph must maintain the member's principal office in the region for which the member seeks election throughout the member's candidacy and term of office.
(B) One member shall be an active member of the Oregon State Bar elected from the region established under subsection (2)(b) of this section. The member elected under this subparagraph must maintain the member's principal office in the region established under subsection (2)(b) of this section throughout the member's candidacy and term of office.
(C) Four of the members shall be appointed by the board of governors from among the public. The public members must be residents of this state throughout their terms of office and may not be active or inactive members of the Oregon State Bar.
(b) A person charged with official duties under the executive and legislative departments of state government, including but not limited to elected officers of state government, may not serve on the board of governors. Any other person in the executive or legislative department of state government who is otherwise qualified may serve on the board of governors.
(2) The board of governors shall establish regions for the purpose of electing board members as follows:
(a) The board shall divide the State of Oregon into regions for the purpose of electing board members described in subsection (1)(a)(A) of this section. Regions established under this paragraph must be based on the number of attorneys who have their principal offices in the region. To the extent that it is reasonably possible, regions established under this paragraph must be configured by the board so that the representation of board members to attorney population in each region is equal to the representation provided in other regions. At least once every 10 years the board shall review the number of attorneys in the regions and shall alter or add regions as the board determines is appropriate in seeking to attain the goal of equal representation.
(b) The board shall establish one region composed of all areas not located in the State of Oregon for the purpose of electing the board member described in subsection (1)(a)(B) of this section.
(3) Members of the board of governors may be elected only by the active members of the Oregon State Bar who maintain their principal offices in the regions established by the board under subsection (2) of this section. The regular term of a member of the board is four years. The board may establish special terms for positions that are shorter than four years for the purpose of staggering the terms of members of the board. The board must identify a position with a special term before accepting statements of candidacy for the region in which the position is located. The board shall establish rules for determining which of the elected members for a region is assigned to the position with a special term.
(4) A judge of a municipal, state or federal court or any other full-time judicial officer is not eligible for appointment or election to the board of governors.
(5) The term of any member of the board of governors terminates on the date of the death or resignation of the member or, if the member of the board is required to be a member of the Oregon State Bar, the term terminates on the date:
(a) Of the termination of active membership in the Oregon State Bar for any reason;

(b) When the member discontinues to maintain the principal office of law practice in the region in which it was maintained at the time of the appointment or election of the member; or

(c) When the member assumes office as a judge of a municipal, state or federal court, or fills a full-time judicial office.

(6) A member of the board of governors is not eligible during the member's term of office for service pro tempore as a judge of any municipal, state or federal court. [1973 c.114 §1; 1981 c.193 §3; 1993 c.307 §1; 1995 c.302 §1; 2009 c.218 §1; 2011 c.303 §1; 2015 c.122 §1]

9.030 Voting rights; eligibility of members for board of governors and house of delegates. (1) An active member of the Oregon State Bar shall vote for members of the board of governors and house of delegates representing the region in which the bar member maintains the member's principal office.

(2) An active member of the Oregon State Bar is eligible to be a candidate for, and to be appointed or elected to, the board of governors or house of delegates to represent the region in which the bar member maintains the member's principal office. [Amended by 1971 c.103 §2; 1973 c.114 §2; 1995 c.302 §16; 2011 c.303 §2]

9.040 Election of governors; rules; vacancies. (1) The election of governors shall be held annually on a date set by the board of governors. Any member of the Oregon State Bar who is eligible to serve as a governor for a region may file a signed statement of candidacy for the region. Statements of candidacy must be filed with the chief executive officer of the bar. The board shall establish a deadline for filing statements of candidacy.

(2)(a) The bar shall distribute ballots containing the names of the candidates for the office of governor in each region to every active member in the region. Voting must be completed on or before the day of the election. The chief executive officer shall canvass the votes and record the results of the election.

(b) The board by rule may provide for electronic elections under paragraph (a) of this subsection. Rules adopted under this paragraph may provide for electronic distribution of election materials and electronic tabulation of votes.

(3) In a region in which only one position is to be filled, the candidate receiving the highest vote shall be declared elected. If a region has more than one position to be filled, the candidate with the most votes received shall be declared elected, the candidate with the next highest number of votes received shall then be declared elected, and so on until all positions are filled. The balloting shall be conducted so that only eligible active members can vote, and the secrecy of the ballot shall be preserved.

(4) Notwithstanding subsection (1) of this section, the board may not conduct an election for a region if the number of candidates for the region is equal to or less than the number of open positions for the region. If the number of candidates for the region is equal to or less than the number of open positions for the region, the board shall declare the candidate or candidates elected on a date specified by the board.

(5) A vacancy in the office of elective member of the board of governors that occurs more than 24 months before the expiration of the term shall be filled for the remainder of the term by a governor elected at a special election held in the manner provided in this section as soon as possible after the occurrence of the vacancy, or as provided in subsection (4) of this section if there is only one candidate. The vacancy may be filled for the period between the occurrence of the vacancy and the election of a new governor by a person appointed by the board. A vacancy in the office of elective member that occurs 24 months or less before the expiration of the term shall be filled for the remainder of the term by a person appointed by the board.

(6) A vacancy in the office of public member of the board of governors shall be filled for the remainder of the term by a governor appointed by the board. [Amended by 1973 c.114 §3; 1979 c.252 §15; 1985 c.512 §1; 1995 c.302 §2; 2001 c.297 §1; 2003 c.192 §1; 2005 c.347 §1; 2011 c.303 §3; 2017 c.94 §4]

9.042 Determination of eligibility of candidate for board of governors; procedure; review by Supreme Court. (1) Upon the written request of any member of the Oregon State Bar, or upon the board's own motion, the board of governors shall determine the eligibility of a candidate for the board. A request under this section must be filed with the chief executive officer of the bar within 30 days after the final day on which statements of candidacy are required to be filed. The board shall give written notice of the request to the candidate whose eligibility will be determined. The board shall provide an opportunity to the candidate to respond on the issue of the candidate's eligibility.

(2) The board shall give written notice to the candidate, and to any member of the bar who has requested a determination on the eligibility of the candidate under the provisions of this section, of the board's determination on the candidate's eligibility. The notice must be given not later than 75 days after the final day on which statements of candidacy are required to be filed. The notice shall state the specific grounds for the board's determination.

(3) A candidate, or a member of the bar who has requested a determination on the eligibility of a candidate under the provisions of this section, may file a petition for review of the board's determination with the Supreme Court. The petition for review must be filed within 15 days only after notice is given to a candidate or member under subsection (2) of this section.

(4) Upon the timely filing of a petition for review under subsection (3) of this section, the Supreme Court has jurisdiction to resolve all issues arising under the Oregon Constitution, state statutes, rules of the court and rules of the board that are related to the eligibility of candidates for the board.

(5) The board of governors shall establish procedures for the implementation of subsections (1) and (2) of this section. The procedures shall be designed to ensure that there will be a final determination on the eligibility of a candidate for the board no later than 10 days before the distribution of the ballots to members of the bar in the election that is affected by the determination.

(6) This section provides the exclusive procedure for challenging the eligibility of a candidate for the board. No other administrative or judicial proceeding may be brought to challenge the eligibility of a candidate for the board. [1993 c.307 §3; 2011 c.303 §4; 2017 c.94 §5]

9.050 Recall of governors. (1) On petition signed by 25 percent of the members in any region for the recall of any governor elected from that region, the chief executive officer of the Oregon State Bar shall serve notice as soon as possible on the governor informing the governor that the petition has been filed. If the governor does not resign within 10 days after the date the notice is served, the chief executive officer shall distribute ballots to each active member of the bar within the region eligible to vote, submitting the question whether the governor shall be recalled. If a majority of the members voting at the election vote in favor of the recall, the governor is recalled.

(2) On the affirmative vote of two-thirds of the entire membership of the board of governors, the board shall refer the question of the recall of any governor from any region to a vote of the members of that region. The chief executive officer shall serve notice as soon as possible on the governor informing the governor that the board has approved a recall election. If the governor does not resign within 10 days after the notice is served, the chief executive officer shall distribute ballots to each active member of the bar within the region eligible to vote, submitting the question whether the governor shall be recalled. If a majority of the members voting at the election vote in favor of the recall, the governor is recalled.

(3) The board of governors shall approve the ballot and any information submitted to the members in connection with a recall vote. [Amended by 1973 c.114 §4; 1979 c.252 §16; 2003 c.14 §8; 2005 c.347 §2; 2017 c.94 §6]

9.055 Chief executive officer. The board of governors shall appoint a chief executive officer of the Oregon State Bar. The chief executive officer is the chief administrative employee of the bar. The chief executive officer may, but need not, be a member of the bar. The chief executive officer serves at the board's discretion and shall perform such duties as the board prescribes. [2017 c.94 §2]

9.060 President, president-elect and immediate past president. A president and president-elect shall be elected by the governors each year immediately following the annual election of governors and before the newly elected governors have qualified. The president and president-elect shall be elected from among the attorney board members. All officers shall continue in office until their successors are elected and qualify. Vacancies in any of the offices shall be filled by the board by appointment for the remainder of the term. Upon completion of the term for which the president is elected or appointed, the president becomes the immediate past president and shall serve as a nonvoting, ex officio member of the board for one year. All officers shall take office as provided by the bar bylaws. [Amended by 1985 c.512 §2; 1991 c.726 §1; 1995 c.302 §3; 2017 c.94 §13]

9.070 Duties of president and president-elect; deposit and disbursement of fees. (1) The president shall preside at all meetings of the house of delegates and of the board of governors, and in the president's absence or inability to act, the president shall designate another officer to preside. The board of governors may prescribe other duties of the president and president-elect.

(2) All fees shall be paid into the treasury of the Oregon State Bar, and when so paid shall become part of its funds and shall be disbursed only on order of the board of governors. [Amended by 1981 c.193 §4; 1991 c.331 §1; 1995 c.302 §4; 2017 c.94 §14]

9.080 Duties of board of governors; professional liability fund; quorum; status of employees of bar. (1) The state bar shall be governed by the board of governors, except as provided in ORS 9.136 to 9.155. The board is charged with the executive functions of the state bar and shall at all times direct its power to the advancement of the science of jurisprudence and the improvement of the administration of justice. It has the authority to adopt, alter, amend and repeal bylaws and to adopt new bylaws containing provisions for the regulation and management of the affairs of the state bar not inconsistent with law.

(2)(a)(A) The board has the authority to require all active members of the state bar engaged in the private practice of law whose principal offices are in Oregon to carry professional liability insurance and is empowered, either by itself or in conjunction with other bar organizations, to do whatever is necessary and convenient to implement this provision, including the authority to own, organize and sponsor any insurance organization authorized under the laws of the State of Oregon and to establish a lawyer's professional liability fund. This fund shall pay, on behalf of active members of the state bar engaged in the private practice of law whose principal offices are in Oregon, all sums as may be provided under such plan which any such member shall become legally obligated to pay as money damages because of any claim made against such member as a result of any act or omission of such member in rendering or failing to render professional services for others in the member's capacity as an attorney or caused by any other person for whose acts or omissions the member is legally responsible.

(B) The board has the authority to assess each active member of the state bar engaged in the private practice of law whose principal office is in Oregon for contributions to the professional liability fund and to establish the date by which contributions must be made.

(C) The board has the authority to establish definitions of coverage to be provided by the professional liability fund and to retain or employ legal counsel to represent the fund and defend and control the defense against any covered claim made against the member.

(D) The board has the authority to offer optional professional liability coverage on an underwritten basis above the minimum required coverage limits provided under the professional liability fund, either through the fund, through a separate fund or through any insurance organization authorized under the laws of the State of Oregon, and may do whatever is necessary and convenient to implement this provision. Any fund so established shall not be subject to the Insurance Code of the State of Oregon.

(E) Records of a claim against the professional liability fund are exempt from disclosure under ORS 192.311 to 192.478.

(b) For purposes of paragraph (a) of this subsection, an attorney is not engaged in the private practice of law if the attorney is a full-time employee of a corporation other than a corporation incorporated under ORS chapter 58, the state, an agency or department thereof, a county, city, special district or any other public or municipal corporation or any instrumentality thereof. However, an attorney who practices law outside of the attorney's full-time employment is engaged in the private practice of law.

(c) For the purposes of paragraph (a) of this subsection, the principal office of an attorney is considered to be the location where the attorney engages in the private practice of law more than 50 percent of the time engaged in that practice. In the case of an attorney in a branch office outside Oregon and the main office to which the branch office is connected is in Oregon, the principal office of the attorney is not considered to be in Oregon unless the attorney engages in the private practice of law in Oregon more than 50 percent of the time engaged in the private practice of law.

(3) The board may appoint such committees, officers and employees as it deems necessary or proper and fix and pay their compensation and necessary expenses. At any meeting of the board, two-thirds of the total number of members then in office shall constitute a quorum. It shall promote and encourage voluntary county or other local bar associations.

(4) Except as provided in this subsection, an employee of the state bar shall not be considered an "employee" as the term is defined in the public employees' retirement laws. However, an employee of the state bar may, at the option of the employee, for the purpose of becoming a member of the Public Employees Retirement System, be considered an "employee" as the term is defined in the public employees' retirement laws. The option, once exercised by written notification directed to the Public Employees Retirement Board, may not be revoked subsequently, except as may otherwise be provided by law. Upon receipt of such notification by the Public Employees Retirement Board, an employee of the state bar who would otherwise, but for the exemption provided in this subsection, be considered an "employee," as the term is defined in the public employees' retirement laws, shall be so considered. The state bar and its employees shall be exempt from the provisions of the State Personnel Relations Law. No member of the state bar shall be considered an "employee" as the term is defined in the public employees' retirement laws, the unemployment compensation laws and the State Personnel Relations Law solely by reason of membership in the state bar. [Amended by 1955 c.463 §2; 1975 c.641 §3; 1977 c.527 §1; 1979 c.508 §1; 1983 c.128 §2; 1985 c.486 §1; 1989 c.1052 §5; 1995 c.302 §17; 2015 c.122 §4]

9.090 Appropriation and disbursement of funds. The board may make appropriations and disbursements from the funds of the bar and pay all necessary expenses. [Amended by 1969 c.314 §5; 1979 c.252 §17]

9.100 Statement of financial condition. The board shall have prepared annually a statement explaining the financial condition of the Oregon State Bar for the 12 months preceding. The chief executive officer of the bar shall promptly submit the statement to the Chief Justice of the Supreme Court. [Amended by 1991 c.726 §2; 2017 c.94 §7]

9.110 Board of governors to formulate rules. The board of governors may formulate and declare rules for carrying out the functions of the state bar. [Amended by 1975 c.641 §4; 1981 c.193 §5; 1995 c.302 §5]

9.112 Board of governors to establish minimum continuing legal education requirements. The board of governors shall by rule establish minimum continuing legal education requirements for all active members of the Oregon State Bar. Rules adopted by the board of governors are subject to review by the Supreme Court. [1999 c.953 §3]

9.114 Mandatory training on duties relating to reporting child abuse and abuse of elderly persons; rules. The Oregon State Bar shall adopt rules to establish minimum training requirements for all active members of the bar relating to the duties of attorneys under ORS 124.060 and 419B.010. Rules adopted under this section are subject to review and approval by the Supreme Court. [1999 c.953 §2; 2013 c.352 §7]

9.120 [Repealed by 1995 c.302 §23]

9.130 [Amended by 1979 c.508 §2; 1981 c.193 §2; 1983 c.373 §1; repealed by 1995 c.302 §23]

9.132 [1993 c.131 §2; renumbered 9.685 in 2011]

HOUSE OF DELEGATES

9.136 House of delegates created; membership; terms. (1) The house of delegates of the Oregon State Bar is created. The house consists of elected and ex officio voting delegates. All delegates must be active members of the state bar except for the public members of the board of governors and the public members appointed by the board pursuant to ORS 9.145.

(2) The members of the board of governors of the Oregon State Bar are ex officio voting delegates.

(3) The chairperson of each Oregon State Bar section is an ex officio voting delegate.

(4) The elected president of each county bar association is an ex officio voting delegate. Not more than one county bar association from each county may be represented by a delegate under this subsection.

(5) Elected delegates shall be elected from the regions established by ORS 9.025. Only active members of the bar may vote for delegates. A member may vote for delegates from the region in which the member maintains the member's principal office.

(6) Each region shall elect at least five delegates. If more than 550 active members maintain their principal offices in the region, the members shall elect delegates as follows:

(a) The members shall elect one delegate for each 100 members who maintain their principal offices in the region.

(b) The members shall elect one additional delegate if more than 50 members who maintain their principal offices in the region are not accounted for after the allocation provided for in paragraph (a) of this subsection.

(7) Elected delegates shall serve for terms of three years. A vacancy in the office of an elected delegate shall be filled for the remainder of the term by a delegate appointed by the board of governors.

(8) An elected delegate may not serve as a member of the board of governors, as a section chairperson or as a county bar association president during the delegate's term.

(9) For the purposes of this section, "county bar association" means a general purpose bar association established by the lawyers of one or more counties for the purpose of maintaining good professional relations between members of the bench and of the bar in the county or counties, and for the purpose of improving the administration of justice in the county or counties. [1995 c.302 §7; 2001 c.297 §2; 2015 c.122 §2]

9.139 Powers of house of delegates. (1) The delegates at a meeting of the house of delegates may, by a vote of the majority of the delegates attending the meeting, do either of the following:

(a) Modify or rescind an action or decision of the board of governors.

(b) Direct the board of governors as to future action.

(2) The board of governors is bound by a decision of the house of delegates made in the manner prescribed by subsection (1) of this section.

(3) The power of the house of delegates to direct, modify or rescind an action or decision of the board of governors under subsection (1) of this section does not include the power:

(a) To invalidate payments previously made at the direction of the board;

(b) To direct, modify or rescind any assessment by the board for contributions to a professional liability fund established under ORS 9.080; or

(c) To direct, modify or rescind any other action or decision by the board that is subject to control, approval or review by the Supreme Court.

(4) Subsection (3)(c) of this section does not affect the ability of the house of delegates to formulate disciplinary rules under ORS 9.490. [1995 c.302 §8]

9.142 Rules for conduct of business; meetings. (1) The board of governors shall formulate rules for the conduct of the business of the house of delegates. Rules adopted by the board become effective upon the adoption of the rules by the house of delegates. The president of the Oregon State Bar may call special meetings of the house. The president shall call a special meeting of the house if 25 or more delegates make a written request for a special meeting. A majority of the total number of delegates constitutes a quorum for any regular or special meeting of the house.

(2) The board of governors shall set a time and place for the annual meeting of the house of delegates. At the annual meeting, the board of governors shall submit to the house of delegates reports of the proceedings by the board since the last meeting of the house, reports of the officers and committees of the state bar and recommendations of the board. [1995 c.302 §9]

9.145 Public members. The board of governors shall appoint a public member delegate for each region in the State of Oregon established by ORS 9.025 (2)(a). A public member delegate shall serve a three-year term. A vacant public member delegate position shall be filled for the remainder of the term by a delegate appointed by the board of governors. The appointment of public member delegates shall be made by the board before the time set for the election of delegates under ORS 9.152. The term of a public member delegate shall commence on the same date that the term of an elected delegate commences. [1995 c.302 §10; 2001 c.297 §3; 2015 c.122 §3]

9.148 Participation by nondelegates; referral of question for vote; petition for consideration or vote. (1) Active members of the Oregon State Bar may participate in the discussion of matters before the house of delegates, but only delegates may vote. The house of delegates may by rule impose restrictions on participation by members of the state bar who are not delegates.

(2) The board of governors or the house of delegates, acting on its own motion, may refer to the members of the bar by ballot any question or measure considered by the board or house to be appropriate for submission to a vote of the members. Referral may be made under this subsection at any time.

(3) Active members of the state bar, by written petition signed by at least two percent of all active members, may have placed on the agenda of a meeting of the house of delegates any question or measure appropriate for a vote of the house. The petition shall contain the full text of the question or measure proposed. The petition must be filed with the chief executive officer of the bar at least 45 days before the annual or special meeting of the house specified in the petition at the meeting when the petitioners seek to have the question or measure considered.

(4) Active members of the state bar, by written petition signed by no fewer than five percent of all active members, may request that the board of governors submit to a vote of the members any question or measure. The board of governors shall submit the question or measure to a vote of the members of the bar if the question or measure is appropriate for a vote of the members. The initiative petition must contain the full text of the question or measure proposed. [1995 c.302 §11; 2017 c.94 §8]

9.150 Termination of delegate's term. The term of service of any delegate shall end upon the death or resignation of the delegate. If the delegate is an attorney delegate, the term of service shall end on the date that the delegate:

(1) Terminates the delegate's active membership in the Oregon State Bar for any reason;

(2) Ceases to maintain the delegate's principal office in the region the delegate was appointed or elected to represent;

(3) Takes office as a member of the board of governors, as a chairperson of a state bar section or as a county bar association president; or

(4) Is recalled pursuant to ORS 9.155. [1995 c.302 §12; 2001 c.297 §4]

9.152 Election of delegates; rules. (1) The election of delegates to the house of delegates shall be held annually on a date set by the board of governors. The election shall be by ballot. Any member of the Oregon State Bar who is eligible to serve as a member for a region may file a signed statement of candidacy for the region. Statements of candidacy must be filed with the bar at least 30 days before the election.

(2)(a) The bar shall distribute ballots containing the names of the candidates for the office of delegate in each region to every active member in the region. Voting must be completed on or before the day of the election. The chief executive officer shall canvass the votes and record the results of the election.

(b) The board by rule may provide for electronic elections under paragraph (a) of this subsection. Rules adopted under this paragraph may provide for electronic distribution of election materials and electronic tabulation of votes.

(3) In a region in which only one position is to be filled, the candidate receiving the highest vote shall be declared elected. If a region has more than one position to be filled, the candidate with the most votes received shall be declared elected, the candidate with the next highest number of votes received shall then be declared elected, and so on until all positions are filled. The balloting shall be conducted so that only eligible active members can vote, and the secrecy of the ballot shall be preserved.

(4) Notwithstanding subsection (1) of this section, the board may not conduct an election for a region if the number of candidates for the region is equal to or less than the number of open positions for the region. If the number of candidates for the region is equal to or less than the number of open positions for the region, the board shall declare the candidate or candidates elected on a date specified by the board. [1995 c.302 §13; 2001 c.297 §5; 2003 c.192 §2; 2011 c.303 §5; 2017 c.94 §9]

9.155 Recall of delegate. Upon the filing of a petition with the Oregon State Bar signed by 25 percent of the members of the bar from a region for the recall of a delegate elected from that region, the chief executive officer of the bar shall serve notice on the delegate of the filing of the petition. If the delegate does not resign within 15 days after the date that the notice is served, the chief executive officer shall distribute ballots to each member of the bar within the region. The ballots shall submit the question of whether the delegate should be recalled. If a majority of the members voting in the election vote in favor of the recall, the delegate is recalled and the position held by the delegate becomes vacant upon the chief executive officer's declaration of the results of the election. [1995 c.302 §14; 2001 c.297 §6; 2017 c.94 §10]

PRACTICE OF LAW; MEMBERSHIP IN THE BAR

9.160 Bar membership required to practice law; exceptions. (1) Except as provided in this section, a person may not practice law in this state, or represent that the person is qualified to practice law in this state, unless the person is an active member of the Oregon State Bar.

(2) Subsection (1) of this section does not affect the right to prosecute or defend a cause in person as provided in ORS 9.320.

(3) An individual licensed under ORS 696.022 acting in the scope of the individual's license to arrange a real estate transaction, including the sale, purchase, exchange, option or lease coupled with an option to purchase, lease for a term of one year or longer or rental of real property, is not engaged in the practice of law in this state in violation of subsection (1) of this section.

(4) A title insurer authorized to do business in this state, a title insurance agent licensed under the laws of this state or an escrow agent licensed under the laws of this state is not engaged in the practice of law in this state in violation of subsection (1) of this section if, for the purposes of a transaction in which the insurer or agent provides title insurance or escrow services, the insurer or agent:

(a) Prepares any satisfaction, reconveyance, release, discharge, termination or cancellation of a lien, encumbrance or obligation;

(b) Acts pursuant to the instructions of the principals to the transaction as scrivener to fill in blanks in any document selected by the principals;

(c) Presents to the principals to the transaction for their selection any blank form prescribed by statute, rule, ordinance or other law; or

(d) Presents to the principals to the transaction for their selection a blank form prepared or approved by a lawyer licensed to practice law in this state for one or more of the following:

(A) A mortgage.

(B) A trust deed.

(C) A promissory note.

(D) An assignment of a mortgagee's interest under a mortgage.

(E) An assignment of a beneficial interest under a trust deed.

(F) An assignment of a seller's or buyer's interest under a land sale contract.

(G) A power of attorney.

(H) A subordination agreement.

(I) A memorandum of an instrument that is to be recorded in place of the instrument that is the subject of the memorandum.

(5) In performing the services permitted in subsection (4) of this section, a title insurer, a title insurance agent or an escrow agent may not draft, select or give advice regarding any real estate document if those activities require the exercise of informed or trained discretion.

(6) The exemption provided by subsection (4) of this section does not apply to any acts relating to a document or form that are performed by an escrow agent under subsection (4)(b), (c) or (d) of this section unless the escrow agent provides to the principals to the transaction a notice in at least 12-point type as follows:

YOU WILL BE REVIEWING, APPROVING AND SIGNING IMPORTANT DOCUMENTS AT CLOSING. LEGAL CONSEQUENCES FOLLOW FROM THE SELECTION AND USE OF THESE DOCUMENTS. THESE CONSEQUENCES AFFECT YOUR RIGHTS AND OBLIGATIONS. YOU MAY CONSULT AN ATTORNEY ABOUT THESE DOCUMENTS. YOU SHOULD CONSULT AN ATTORNEY IF YOU HAVE QUESTIONS OR CONCERNS ABOUT THE TRANSACTION OR ABOUT THE DOCUMENTS. IF YOU WISH TO REVIEW TRANSACTION DOCUMENTS THAT YOU HAVE NOT YET SEEN, PLEASE CONTACT THE ESCROW AGENT.

---

(7) The exemption provided by subsection (4) of this section does not apply to any acts relating to a document or form that are performed by an escrow agent under subsection (4)(b), (c) or (d) of this section for a real estate sale and purchase transaction in which all or part of the purchase price consists of deferred payments by the buyer to the seller unless the escrow agent provides to the principals to the transaction:

(a) A copy of any proposed instrument of conveyance between the buyer and seller to be used in the transaction;

(b) A copy of any proposed deferred payment security instrument between the buyer and seller to be used in the transaction; and

(c) A copy of any proposed promissory note or other evidence of indebtedness between the buyer and seller to be used in the transaction.

(8) The notice and copies of documents that must be provided under subsections (6) and (7) of this section must be delivered in the manner most likely to ensure receipt by the principals to the transaction at least three days before completion of the transaction. If copies of documents have been provided under subsection (7) of this section and are subsequently amended, copies of the amended documents must be provided before completion of the transaction.

(9) Failure of any person to comply with the requirements of subsections (3) to (8) of this section does not affect the validity of any transaction and may not be used as a basis to challenge any transaction. [Amended by 2003 c.260 §1; 2007 c.319 §24; 2009 c.218 §4]

9.162 Definitions for ORS 9.160 to 9.166. As used in ORS 9.160 to 9.166 and 9.280, unless the context or subject matter requires otherwise:

(1) "Person" means a human being, a public body as defined by ORS 174.109, a public or private corporation, an unincorporated association, a partnership, a limited liability company or any other business entity created under law.

(2) "Restitution" means full, partial or nominal payment of pecuniary damages to a victim.

(3) "Victim" means any person who the court determines has suffered pecuniary damages as a result of any other person's violation of ORS 9.160. [1987 c.860 §2; 2009 c.218 §3]

9.164 Investigation of alleged violation of ORS 9.160. Upon written complaint of any person or upon its own initiative, the Board of Governors of the Oregon State Bar shall investigate any alleged violation of ORS 9.160. [1987 c.860 §3]

9.166 Enjoining practicing law without a license; restitution to victim. If the board has reason to believe that a person is practicing law without a license, the board may maintain a suit for injunctive relief in the name of the Oregon State Bar against any person violating ORS 9.160. The court shall enjoin any person violating ORS 9.160 from practicing law without a license. Any person who has been so enjoined may be punished for contempt by the court issuing the injunction. An injunction may be issued without proof of actual damage sustained by any person. The court shall order restitution to any victim of any person violating ORS 9.160. The prevailing party may recover its costs and attorney fees in any suit for injunctive relief brought under this section in which the board is the plaintiff. [1987 c.860 §4; 2001 c.300 §57; 2003 c.260 §3; 2003 c.670 §6]

9.180 Classes of membership. All persons admitted to practice law in this state thereby shall become active members of the bar. Every member shall be an active member unless, at the member's request, or for reasons prescribed by statute, the rules of the Supreme Court, or the rules of procedure, the member is enrolled as an inactive member. An inactive member may, on compliance with the rules of the Supreme Court and the rules of procedure and payment of all required fees, again become an active member. Inactive members shall not hold office or vote, but they shall have such other privileges as the board may provide. [Amended by 1961 c.499 §1; 1979 c.252 §18]

9.190 [Amended by 1957 c.271 §1; 1961 c.138 §1; part renumbered 9.200 (2); repealed by 1969 c.602 §1 (9.191 enacted in lieu of 9.190)]

9.191 Annual membership fees; professional liability assessments. (1) Except as provided in subsection (2) of this section, the annual membership fees to be paid by members of the Oregon State Bar shall be established by the Board of Governors of the Oregon State Bar, and each year notice of the proposed fees for the coming year shall be published and distributed to the membership not later than 20 days before the annual meeting of the house of delegates. Any increase in annual membership fees over the amount established for the preceding year must be approved by a majority of delegates of the house of delegates voting thereon at the annual meeting of the house of delegates. The board shall establish the date by which annual membership fees must be paid.

(2) The board shall establish prorated membership fees payable for the year that a member is admitted to the practice of law in this state. If the new member is admitted on or before the date established by the board for the payment of annual membership fees under subsection (1) of this section, the new member must pay the full annual membership fees established under subsection (1) of this section.

(3) In establishing annual membership fees, the board shall consider and be guided by the anticipated financial needs of the state bar for the year for which the fees are established, time periods of membership and active or inactive status of members. Annual membership fees may include any amount assessed under any plan for professional liability insurance for active members engaged in the private practice of law whose principal offices are in Oregon as provided in ORS 9.080 (2). The board may not require that a member who has been admitted to practice law in Oregon for 50 years or more pay membership fees, assessments or any amount under ORS 9.645, except that the member shall be required to pay any amount assessed under any plan for professional liability insurance if the member is engaged in the private practice of law and the member's principal office is in Oregon. [1969 c.602 §2 (enacted in lieu of 9.190); 1973 c.21 §1; 1975 c.641 §5; 1977 c.527 §2; 1979 c.508 §3; 1985 c.486 §2; 1985 c.512 §3; 1995 c.302 §18; 1999 c.171 §7; 2001 c.104 §2; 2003 c.192 §3]

9.200 Effect of failure to pay membership fees; reinstatement. (1) Any member in default in payment of membership fees established under ORS 9.191 (1) or any member in default in payment of assessed contributions to a professional liability fund established under ORS 9.080 (2) shall be given written notice of delinquency and a reasonable time to cure the default. The chief executive officer of the Oregon State Bar shall send the notice of delinquency to the member at the member's electronic mail address on file with the bar on the date of the notice. The chief executive officer shall send the notice by mail to any member who is not required to have an electronic mail address on file with the bar under the rules of procedure. If a member fails to pay the fees or contributions within the time allowed to cure the default as stated in the notice, the member is automatically suspended. The chief executive officer shall provide the names of all members suspended under this section to the State Court Administrator and to each of the judges of the Court of Appeals, circuit and tax courts of the state.

(2) An active member delinquent in the payment of fees or contributions is not entitled to vote.

(3) A member delinquent in the payment of fees or contributions may be assessed a late payment penalty determined by the board of governors.

(4) A member suspended for delinquency under this section may be reinstated only on compliance with the rules of the Supreme Court and the rules of procedure and payment of all required fees or contributions. [Amended by 1957 c.271 §1; 1961 c.499 §2; subsection (2) formerly part of 9.190; 1979 c.508 §4a; 2013 c.3 §2; 2015 c.122 §5; 2017 c.94 §11]

9.210 Board of bar examiners; fees of applicants for admission to bar. (1) The Supreme Court shall appoint a board of bar examiners to carry out the admissions functions of the Oregon State Bar as set forth in the bar bylaws and the rules of the Supreme Court. The composition of the board of bar examiners shall be as provided in the rules of the Supreme Court, but the board must include at least two public members.

(2) The board shall examine applicants, investigate applicants' character and fitness and recommend to the Supreme Court for admission to practice law those who fulfill the requirements prescribed by law and the rules of the Supreme Court.

(3) With the approval of the Supreme Court, the board may fix and collect fees to be paid by applicants for admission, which fees shall be paid into the treasury of the bar.

(4) Applications for admission and any other material pertaining to individual applicants are confidential and may be disclosed only as provided in the rules of the Supreme Court. The board's consideration of an individual applicant's qualifications is a judicial proceeding for purposes of ORS 192.610 to 192.690. [Amended by 1979 c.252 §20; 1981 c.193 §6; 2015 c.122 §6]

9.220 General requirements for admission. An applicant for admission as attorney must apply to the Supreme Court and show that the applicant:

(1) Is at least 18 years old, which proof may be made by the applicant's affidavit.

(2)(a) Is a person of good moral character and fit to practice law.

(b) For purposes of this section and ORS 9.025, 9.070, 9.110, 9.210, 9.250 and 9.527, the lack of "good moral character" may be established by reference to acts or conduct that reflect moral turpitude or to acts or conduct which would cause a reasonable person to have substantial doubts about the individual's honesty, fairness and respect for the rights of others and for the laws of the state and the nation. The conduct or acts in question should be rationally connected to the applicant's fitness to practice law.

(3) Has the requisite learning and ability, which must be shown by the examination of the applicant, by the judges or under their direction. However, no rule shall establish any maximum on the number of times an applicant may apply for and take the bar examination whenever presented if the reason for refusing admission to practice law is failure to pass the bar examination. [Amended by 1973 c.827 §2; 1981 c.193 §7; 1983 c.373 §2; 1985 c.599 §1; 1991 c.726 §3; 1995 c.302 §21; 1999 c.171 §3]

9.230 [Repealed by 1981 c.193 §12]

9.240 [Amended by 1961 c.499 §3; repealed by 1993 c.213 §2]

9.241 Practice of law by attorneys licensed in other jurisdictions; rules; fee. (1) Notwithstanding ORS 9.160, the Supreme Court may adopt rules to govern the appearance in judicial and administrative proceedings by attorneys who have not been admitted to practice law in this state. Subject to those rules, an attorney who has not been admitted to practice law in this state may appear as counsel for a party in an action or proceeding before a court, or may appear as counsel for a party in an administrative proceeding, if the attorney is associated with an active member of the Oregon State Bar.

(2) Notwithstanding ORS 9.160, the Supreme Court may adopt rules pursuant to the procedures established by ORS 9.490 that allow attorneys who have not been admitted to practice law in this state to practice law in Oregon on a temporary basis, including performing transactional or prelitigation work.

(3) The Supreme Court may by rule require the payment of a fee by an attorney appearing as counsel for a party in an action or proceeding before a court under the provisions of subsection (1) of this section. All amounts collected from any fee imposed by the Supreme Court under the provisions of this subsection shall be deposited with the Oregon State Bar and are continuously appropriated to the Oregon State Bar. Amounts appropriated to the Oregon State Bar under this subsection may be used only for the funding of legal services provided through the Legal Services Program established under ORS 9.572 and for expenses incurred by the Oregon State Bar in the administration of the Legal Services Program and in collecting fees imposed under this subsection. [1993 c.213 §1; 2001 c.223 §1; 2003 c.260 §5]

9.242 Advice on law of foreign jurisdiction; rules. (1) The Supreme Court may adopt rules permitting a person licensed to practice law in a foreign jurisdiction to advise on the law of that foreign jurisdiction in Oregon without the necessity of compliance with ORS 9.160.

(2) As used in this section, "foreign jurisdiction" means any nation, country, state, political or other entity other than any state of the United States, the District of Columbia, Puerto Rico or a United States Territory or possession. [1989 c.1052 §2]

9.250 Order for admission; oath of qualified applicant. (1) If the Supreme Court finds that an applicant for admission as an attorney is 18 years of age or more, is of good moral character and fit to practice law, and possesses the requisite learning and ability to practice as an attorney in all the courts of this state, the court shall enter an order that the applicant be admitted to practice as an attorney. The order shall specify that admission take effect upon the applicant taking the oath required by subsection (2) of this section.

(2) The applicant shall execute a written oath that in the practice of law the applicant will support the Constitution and laws of the United States and of this state, and be of faithful and honest demeanor in office. The applicant is entitled to practice as an attorney after the State Court Administrator has received the oath executed under this subsection. [Amended by 1973 c.827 §3; 1981 c.193 §8; 1989 c.1052 §6; 1991 c.726 §4; 1997 c.388 §3]

9.260 [Amended by 1953 c.604 §1; 1979 c.252 §21; repealed by 1989 c.1052 §7 (9.261 enacted in lieu of 9.260)]

9.261 Resignation of attorney. (1) An attorney may resign from membership in the bar pursuant to rules adopted by the board under ORS 9.542. After acceptance of the resignation by the Supreme Court, the attorney shall not be entitled to the rights nor subject to the disabilities or prohibitions incident to membership, except that the attorney is still subject to the power of the court in respect to matters arising prior to the resignation.
(2) An attorney who has resigned may be readmitted to practice only in compliance with rules adopted pursuant to ORS 9.542. [1989 c.1052 §8 (enacted in lieu of 9.260)]

9.270 [Amended by 1953 c.604 §1; 1961 c.499 §4; 1971 c.193 §17; 1979 c.252 §22; repealed by 1989 c.1052 §26]

9.280 Prohibition on acting as immigration consultant; definitions; exception. (1) It shall be a violation of ORS 9.160 for any person to engage in the business or act in the capacity of an immigration consultant in this state, for compensation, unless the person is an active member of the Oregon State Bar.
(2) As used in this section, unless the context or subject matter requires otherwise:
(a) "Immigration consultant" means any person who gives advice on an immigration matter, including but not limited to drafting an application, brief, document, petition or other paper or completing a form provided by a federal or state agency in an immigration matter.
(b) "Immigration matter" means any proceeding, filing or action affecting the immigration or citizenship status of any person which arises under immigration and naturalization law, executive order or presidential proclamation, or action of the United States Department of Homeland Security, the United States Department of Justice, the United States Department of State or the United States Department of Labor.
(3) This section does not apply to any person or qualified designated entity authorized by federal law to represent persons before the United States Department of Homeland Security or the United States Department of Justice. [1987 c.860 §5; 2007 c.61 §1]

ATTORNEY AND CLIENT RELATIONSHIP

9.310 Attorney defined; counsel. An attorney is a person authorized to represent a party in the written proceedings in any action, suit or proceeding, in any stage thereof. An attorney, other than the one who represents the party in the written proceedings, may also represent a party in court, or before a judicial officer, in which case the attorney is known as counsel, and the authority of the attorney is limited to the matters that transpire in the court or before such officer at the time.

9.320 Necessity for employment of attorney; effect of employment. Any action, suit, or proceeding may be prosecuted or defended by a party in person, or by attorney, except that the state or a party that is not a natural person appears by attorney in all cases, unless otherwise specifically provided by law. Where a party appears by attorney, the written proceedings must be in the name of the attorney, who is the sole representative of the client of the attorney as between the client and the adverse party, except as provided in ORS 9.310. [Amended by 1975 c.451 §171; 2015 c.7 §1]

9.330 Authority of attorney. An attorney has authority to bind the attorney's client in any of the proceedings in an action, suit or proceeding, by the attorney and client agreement, filed with the clerk or entered in the appropriate record of the court. The attorney also has authority to receive money or property claimed by the client in an action, suit or proceeding, during the pendency thereof, or within three years after judgment, and upon the payment or delivery thereof to discharge the claim or acknowledge satisfaction of the judgment. This section does not prevent a party from employing a new attorney to issue execution upon a judgment or to take other proceedings prescribed by law for its enforcement, and when the party does so, the authority of the former attorney ceases. [Amended by 1985 c.540 §23; 2003 c.576 §277]

9.340 Challenge by party of attorney's authority to appear for party. If it is alleged by a party for whom an attorney appears that the attorney does so without authority, and the allegation is verified by the affidavit of the party, the court may, if it finds the allegation true, at any stage of the proceedings relieve the party for whom the attorney has assumed to appear from the consequences of the attorney's acts.

9.350 Challenge of attorney's authority to appear for adverse party. The court or judge thereof may, on motion of either party and on showing reasonable grounds therefor, require the attorney for an adverse party to prove the authority under which the attorney appears, and until the attorney does so, may stay all proceedings by the attorney on behalf of the party for whom the attorney assumes to appear.

9.360 Compelling delivery by attorney of money or papers. When an attorney refuses to deliver over money or papers to a person from whom or for whom the attorney has received them in the course of professional employment, the attorney may be required by an order of the court in which a judicial proceeding was prosecuted or defended, or if none were prosecuted or defended, then by an order of the circuit court or judge thereof for the county where such attorney resides or may be found, to do so within a specified time, or show cause why the attorney should not be punished for a contempt.

9.370 Compelling delivery when attorney claims lien. If an attorney claims a lien, under the provisions of ORS 87.430, upon the money or papers subject to delivery under ORS 9.360, the court shall:
(1) Impose, as a condition of making the order, the requirement that the client give security, in form and amount to be directed, to satisfy the lien when determined in an action or suit;
(2) Summarily inquire into the facts on which the claim of a lien is founded, and determine the same; or
(3) Direct the trial of the controversy by a jury, or refer it, and upon the verdict or report, determine the same as in other cases. [Amended by 1975 c.648 §70; 1991 c.67 §2; 2003 c.14 §9]

9.380 Changing attorneys and terminating attorney-client relationship. (1) The attorney in an action or proceeding may be changed, or the relationship of attorney and client terminated, as follows:
(a) Before judgment or final determination, upon the consent of the attorney filed with the clerk or entered in the appropriate record of the court; or
(b) At any time, upon the order of the court, based on the application of the client or the attorney, for good and sufficient cause.
(2) The relationship of attorney and client may be terminated after the entry of a judgment or other final determination in an action or proceeding by the filing of a notice of termination of the relationship in the action or proceeding. The notice must be signed by the attorney and must state that all services required of the attorney under the agreement between the attorney and the client have been provided. [Amended by 1985 c.540 §24; 2003 c.576 §278; 2011 c.60 §1]

9.390 Notice of change or termination. When an attorney is changed, or the relationship of attorney and client is terminated, as provided in ORS 9.380, written notice of the change or termination shall be given to the adverse party. Until the notice is given, the adverse party is bound to recognize the former attorney. [Amended by 2011 c.60 §2]
9.400 [1987 c.774 §8; renumbered 20.340 in 1997]

PROFESSIONAL CONDUCT

9.460 Duties of attorneys. An attorney shall:

(1) Support the Constitution and laws of the United States and of this state;

(2) Employ, for the purpose of maintaining the causes confided to the attorney, such means only as are consistent with truth, and never seek to mislead the court or jury by any artifice or false statement of law or fact;

(3) Maintain the confidences and secrets of the attorney's clients consistent with the rules of professional conduct established pursuant to ORS 9.490; and

(4) Never reject, for any personal consideration, the cause of the defenseless or the oppressed. [Amended by 1989 c.1052 §9; 1991 c.726 §5]

9.470 [Repealed by 1965 c.353 §2]

9.480 [Amended by 1965 c.353 §1; 1981 c.193 §9; renumbered 9.527]

9.490 Formulation of rules of professional conduct; prohibition on certain sanctions for violation of rule. (1) The board of governors, with the approval of the house of delegates given at any regular or special meeting, shall formulate rules of professional conduct, and when such rules are adopted by the Supreme Court, shall have power to enforce the same. Such rules shall be binding upon all members of the bar.

(2) A court of this state may not order that evidence be suppressed or excluded in any criminal trial, grand jury proceeding or other criminal proceeding, or order that any criminal prosecution be dismissed, solely as a sanction or remedy for violation of a rule of professional conduct adopted by the Supreme Court. [Amended by 1995 c.302 §19; 1995 c.708 §2]

PROHIBITED CONDUCT

9.500 Solicitation of personal injury business by nonlawyer. No person shall solicit within the state any business on account of a claim for personal injuries to any person, or solicit any litigation on account of personal injuries to any person within the state, and any contract wherein any person not an attorney agrees to recover, either through litigation or otherwise, any damages for personal injuries to any person shall be void.

9.505 Payment for referring claims resulting from personal injury or death. No person shall offer or promise payment of money or other consideration, or accept any offer or promise of payment of money or other consideration, nor shall any person pay or accept money or other consideration, for referring to an attorney any claim for damage resulting from personal injury or death. [1961 c.561 §1]

9.510 Solicitation by attorneys. No attorney shall solicit business at factories, mills, hospitals or other places, or retain members of a firm or runners or solicitors for the purpose of obtaining business on account of personal injuries to any person, or for the purpose of bringing damage suits on account of personal injuries.

9.515 Referral of claims, suits or actions between attorneys; division of fees. (1) Nothing contained in ORS 9.505 shall prevent referral of claims, suits or actions between attorneys.

(2) The provisions of ORS 9.505 shall not prohibit the referral of claims, suits or actions between attorneys or the dividing of fees for legal services with another lawyer consistent with the rules of professional conduct adopted pursuant to ORS 9.490. [1961 c.561 §§2,3; 1989 c.1052 §10]

9.520 Acceptance and prosecution of solicited claims. No attorney shall accept from a solicitor described in ORS 9.500 any claim for damages, or bring an action for damages on account of any claim obtained from such solicitor. Any agreement between an attorney and such solicitor regarding compensation to be paid to the attorney or solicitor is void.

9.525 [1975 c.641 §8; repealed by 1983 c.618 §1]

BAR DISCIPLINARY PROCEEDINGS

9.527 Grounds for disbarment, suspension or reprimand. The Supreme Court may disbar, suspend or reprimand a member of the bar whenever, upon proper proceedings for that purpose, it appears to the court that:

(1) The member has committed an act or carried on a course of conduct of such nature that, if the member were applying for admission to the bar, the application should be denied;

(2) The member has been convicted in any jurisdiction of an offense which is a misdemeanor involving moral turpitude or a felony under the laws of this state, or is punishable by death or imprisonment under the laws of the United States, in any of which cases the record of the conviction shall be conclusive evidence;

(3) The member has willfully disobeyed an order of a court requiring the member to do or forbear an act connected with the legal profession;

(4) The member is guilty of willful deceit or misconduct in the legal profession;

(5) The member is guilty of willful violation of any of the provisions of ORS 9.460 or 9.510;

(6) The member is guilty of gross or repeated negligence or incompetence in the practice of law; or

(7) The member has violated any of the provisions of the rules of professional conduct adopted pursuant to ORS 9.490. [Formerly 9.480; 1989 c.1052 §11]

9.528 Advice on conducting covert operations; participation in covert operations. (1) Notwithstanding ORS 9.527 (4), the attorneys listed in subsection (2) of this section:

(a) May provide legal advice and direction to the officers and employees of a public body, as defined in ORS 192.311, or to the officers and employees of the federal government, on conducting covert activities for the purpose of enforcing laws, even though the activities may require the use of deceit or misrepresentation; and

(b) May participate in covert activities that are conducted by public bodies, as defined in ORS 192.311, for the purpose of enforcing laws, or in covert activities that are conducted by the federal government for the purpose of enforcing laws, even though the participation may require the use of deceit or misrepresentation.

(2) The provisions of this section apply to the Attorney General, the Deputy Attorney General, assistant attorneys general, district attorneys, deputy district attorneys and any other attorney employed by, or working on behalf of, a public body, as defined in ORS 192.311, or the federal government. [2001 c.667 §2]

9.529 Status of proceedings relating to discipline, admission or reinstatement. Bar proceedings relating to discipline, admission and reinstatement are neither civil nor criminal in nature. They are sui generis and within the inherent power of the Supreme Court to control. The grounds for denying any applicant admission or reinstatement or for the discipline of attorneys set forth in ORS 9.005 to 9.757 are not intended to limit or alter the inherent power of the Supreme Court to deny any applicant admission or reinstatement to the bar or to discipline a member of the bar. [1983 c.618 §3; 1997 c.249 §9]

9.530 [Repealed by 1965 c.353 §2]

9.532 State professional responsibility board. The Supreme Court shall appoint a state professional responsibility board to institute disciplinary proceedings of the Oregon State Bar against members of the bar, as provided in the bar bylaws and the rules of the Supreme Court. [1983 c.618 §4; 2017 c.524 §1]

9.534 Disciplinary board; procedure before board; oaths; subpoenas; hearing; record. (1) The Supreme Court shall appoint a disciplinary board, which may include one or more professional adjudicators as set forth in the rules of the Supreme Court and the Oregon State Bar bylaws, to adjudicate disciplinary proceedings of the bar.

(2) A member, formally accused of misconduct by the bar, shall be given reasonable written notice of the charges against the member, a reasonable opportunity to defend against the charges, the right to be represented by counsel, and the right to examine and cross-examine witnesses. The member has the right to appear and testify, and the right to the issuance of subpoenas for attendance of witnesses and the production of books, papers or documents in the defense of the member.

(3) Rules of evidence and discovery in disciplinary proceedings shall be as provided in the rules of procedure.

(4)(a) The disciplinary board has the authority to take evidence, administer oaths or affirmations, and issue subpoenas to compel the attendance of witnesses, including the accused member, and the production of books, papers and documents pertaining to the matter before the disciplinary board.

(b) A witness in a disciplinary proceeding who testifies falsely, fails to appear when subpoenaed, or fails to produce any books, papers or documents pursuant to subpoena, is subject to the same orders and penalties to which a witness before a circuit court is subject. Subpoenas issued pursuant to paragraph (a) of this subsection may be enforced by application to any circuit court.

(c) Any member of the disciplinary board may administer oaths or affirmations and issue any subpoena provided for in paragraph (a) of this subsection.

(5) The hearing before the disciplinary board shall be held in the county in which the member charged maintains an office for the practice of law, the county in which the member resides, or the county in which the offense is alleged to have been committed. With the consent of the member, the hearing may be held elsewhere in the state.

(6) A record of all hearings shall be made and preserved by the disciplinary board. [1983 c.618 §5; 2017 c.524 §2]

9.535 [1975 c.641 §9; 1979 c.450 §1; repealed by 1983 c.618 §1]

9.536 Disciplinary board decision; appeal to Supreme Court; review; costs. (1) Upon the conclusion of a hearing, the disciplinary board shall file with the State Court Administrator a written decision in the matter. The Oregon State Bar or the accused may seek review of the decision by the Supreme Court. Such review shall be a matter of right upon the request of either party. Otherwise, the decision of the disciplinary board shall be final. The procedure for seeking discretionary review and on review shall be as provided in the rules of procedure.

(2) When a matter is before the Supreme Court for review, the court shall consider the matter de novo and may adopt, modify or reject the decision of the disciplinary board in whole or in part and thereupon enter an appropriate order.

(3) The Supreme Court, or the disciplinary board in cases where its decision has become final, may award judgment in any bar proceeding for all or part of a party's actual and necessary costs and disbursements incurred. The procedures for recovery of such costs and disbursements shall be the same as in civil cases.

(4) The State Court Administrator shall enter any judgment for costs and disbursements in the records of the Supreme Court and shall forward a certified copy of the judgment to the clerk of the circuit court of the county in which the member or applicant resides or maintains an office for the practice of law or other business. If a judgment for costs and disbursements is entered against the bar, the State Court Administrator shall forward a certified copy of the judgment to the clerk of the circuit court of the county in which the bar maintains its principal place of business. On receipt of a certified copy of the judgment, the clerk of the circuit court shall file it and cause it to be entered in the circuit court register. Such judgment shall thereafter have the same force and effect, may be enforced by execution in the same manner, may be extended in the same manner and, upon payment, shall be satisfied in the same manner as other judgments entered in circuit court. [1983 c.618 §6; 1985 c.540 §25; 1991 c.790 §2; 1997 c.149 §1; 2003 c.192 §4; 2003 c.576 §175]

9.537 Civil immunity of witnesses, bar officials and employees. (1) Any person who has made a complaint to the bar concerning the conduct of an attorney, or who has given information or testimony in or relative to a proposed or pending admission, reinstatement or disciplinary proceeding is absolutely immune from civil liability for any such acts.

(2) The Oregon State Bar and its officers, the members of the state professional responsibility board, the board of bar examiners, the board of governors and the disciplinary board, bar counsel, investigators, disciplinary monitors, mentors and employees of the bar are absolutely immune from civil liability in the performance of their duties relative to proposed or pending admission, professional licensing requirements, reinstatement or disciplinary proceedings. [1983 c.618 §7; 2017 c.524 §3]

9.539 Application to admission and reinstatement proceedings. ORS 9.534 and 9.536 apply to admission and reinstatement proceedings to the extent provided in the rules of procedure. However, the Supreme Court shall review the decisions of the disciplinary board in all such matters. [1983 c.618 §8]

9.540 [Amended by 1961 c.499 §5; 1971 c.193 §18; repealed by 1973 c.490 §1 (9.541 enacted in lieu of 9.540)]

9.541 [1973 c.490 §2 (enacted in lieu of 9.540); repealed by 1975 c.641 §13]

9.542 Rules for investigation of attorneys and applicants; authority of board of governors to require fingerprints. (1) The board of governors, subject to the approval of the Supreme Court, may adopt rules of procedure relating to the investigation of the conduct of attorneys and applicants for admission and reinstatement to the bar, and relating to the conduct of admission, reinstatement and disciplinary proceedings.

(2) For the purpose of requesting a state or nationwide criminal records check under ORS 181A.195, the board of governors may require the fingerprints of a person who is applying for admission or reinstatement to the bar or for renewal of a license issued by the bar. [1983 c.618 §9; 2005 c.730 §56]

9.545 [1983 c.617 §2 (enacted in lieu of 9.595); 1999 c.171 §1; renumbered 9.568 in 1999]

9.550 [Amended by 1961 c.499 §6; 1973 c.490 §3; 1975 c.641 §6; 1979 c.252 §23; repealed by 1983 c.618 §1]

9.555 Copy of complaint or notice to Attorney General when bar is plaintiff or defendant; exceptions. (1) Upon commencement of any action in which the bar is a plaintiff, the bar shall mail a copy of the complaint by certified or registered mail, return receipt requested, to the Attorney General and shall file proof of such mailing with the court.

(2) When the bar is served with summons and complaint in an action in which the bar is named as a defendant, the bar shall give notice to the Attorney General by mailing a copy of the summons and complaint to the Attorney General by certified or registered mail, return receipt requested, within five working days of the date of service on the bar.

(3) The notice provisions of subsections (1) and (2) of this section shall not apply to matters involving admission of any applicant to the bar, discipline or reinstatement of a member of the bar or claims made against a member of the bar for which the professional liability fund of the bar may be obligated to pay money damages under ORS 9.080 (2). [1985 c.446 §3]

9.560 [Amended by 1963 c.106 §1; 1973 c.490 §4; 1975 c.641 §7; 1979 c.252 §24; repealed by 1983 c.618 §1]

9.565 Tax return information from Department of Revenue; use. The Department of Revenue may furnish to the Oregon State Bar the name and address, if known, of any person admitted to practice law in this state who prepares a return or report permitted or required to be filed with the department for another, and may also furnish to the bar the name and address of the taxpayer, in instances where the department has reasonable grounds to believe the person preparing the return or report prepared it in violation of any provision of ORS 9.460 to 9.542 or 9.705 to 9.757 or the disciplinary rules adopted thereunder. The department shall provide a statement of the basis for its belief that a violation may have occurred. The bar and any person or board described in ORS 9.537 (2), shall use the names, addresses and information furnished under this section solely in the enforcement of ORS 9.460 to 9.542 or 9.705 to 9.757 or the disciplinary rules adopted thereunder. Any information disclosed by the department pursuant to this section may be used in any bar proceeding relating to the discipline, admission or reinstatement of the person preparing the return or report. [1985 c.602 §10; 1999 c.171 §2; 2017 c.524 §4]

ATTORNEY ASSISTANCE

9.568 State lawyers assistance committee; personal and practice management assistance committees; rules; confidentiality; civil immunity. (1)(a) The board of governors of the Oregon State Bar may create a state lawyers assistance committee for the purpose of implementing a lawyers assistance program and, pursuant thereto, authorize the state lawyers assistance committee to investigate and resolve complaints or referrals regarding lawyers whose performance or conduct may impair their ability to practice law or their professional competence.

(b) The board may adopt rules for the operation of the state lawyers assistance committee.

(c) The purpose of the state lawyers assistance committee is the provision of supervision and assistance to those lawyers whose performance or conduct may impair their ability to practice law or their professional competence.

(2)(a) In addition to the state lawyers assistance committee created under subsection (1) of this section, the board may create personal and practice management assistance committees to provide assistance to lawyers who are suffering from impairment or other circumstances that may adversely affect professional competence or conduct. Personal and practice management assistance committees may also provide advice and training to lawyers in practice management.

(b) The board may adopt rules governing the provision of assistance to lawyers by personal and practice management assistance committees.

(c) The purpose of a personal and practice management assistance committee is the provision of completely confidential assistance, advice and training to lawyers in a manner that fosters maximum openness in communications between a lawyer and the committee and that encourages a lawyer to seek assistance from the committee.

(3) Any information provided to or obtained by the state lawyers assistance committee or any personal and practice management assistance committee, or provided to or obtained by any agent of those committees, is:

(a) Confidential;

(b) Exempt from the provisions of ORS 192.311 to 192.478;

(c) Not discoverable or admissible in any civil proceeding without the written consent of the lawyer to whom the information pertains; and

(d) Not discoverable or admissible in any disciplinary proceeding except to the extent provided by rules of procedure adopted pursuant to ORS 9.542.

(4) The limitations placed on the disclosure and admissibility of information in this section shall not apply to information relating to a lawyer's noncooperation with the state lawyers assistance committee or any agent of the committee, or to information otherwise obtained by the bar from any other source.

(5) The board may authorize the state lawyers assistance committee to act as the monitor or supervisor for lawyers placed on probation or in diversion in connection with a disciplinary investigation or proceeding, or who have been conditionally admitted or reinstated to the practice of law. Any information provided to or obtained by the state lawyers assistance committee when the committee acts as a monitor or supervisor under the provisions of this subsection is not subject to subsection (3) of this section.

(6) All meetings of the state lawyers assistance committee and the personal and practice management assistance committees are exempt from the provisions of ORS 192.610 to 192.690.

(7) Any person who makes a complaint or referral to the bar as to the competence of an attorney or provides information or testimony in connection with the state lawyers assistance committee or any personal and practice management assistance committee is not subject to an action for civil damages as a result thereof.

(8) With respect to their acts in connection with the state lawyers assistance committee or any personal and practice management assistance committee, the same privileges and immunities from civil and criminal proceedings that apply to prosecuting and judicial officers of the state shall apply to the board, all officers and employees of the bar, and the members of the committees and their agents.

(9) For the purposes of this section, agents of the state lawyers assistance committee or a personal and practice management assistance committee include investigators, attorneys, counselors, staff personnel and any other individual or entity acting on behalf of or at the request of the committees. [Formerly 9.545; 2005 c.347 §3]

9.570 [Repealed by 1983 c.618 §1]

LEGAL SERVICES PROGRAM

9.572 Bar to establish Legal Services Program; director; advisory and technical committees. (1) The Oregon State Bar shall by rule establish a Legal Services Program. The program shall provide standards and guidelines for legal service providers receiving funding from the program. The rules shall also provide methods for evaluating legal service providers. Funding received under the program may be used only for the provision of legal services to the poor without charge and for expenses incurred by the Oregon State Bar in the administration of the Legal Services Program.

(2) The Oregon State Bar shall appoint a director of the Legal Services Program established under this section. The bar shall prescribe the duties of the director and fix the salary of the director.

(3) The Oregon State Bar may establish any advisory or technical committees it deems necessary to advise the bar in establishing and operating the Legal Services Program. [1997 c.801 §73; 2011 c.595 §99]

9.574 [1997 c.801 §72; 2003 c.737 §98; repealed by 2011 c.595 §97a]

9.576 Review of providers; mediation; hearing; suspension of funding. (1) The director of the Legal Services Program appointed under ORS 9.572 shall periodically review legal service providers who receive funding from the program. If the director determines that there are reasonable grounds to believe that a provider is not in substantial compliance with the standards and guidelines adopted under ORS 9.572, the director shall negotiate with the provider in an attempt to bring the program into compliance.

(2) If the director of the Legal Services Program is unable to negotiate satisfactory compliance with the standards and guidelines of the program established by the Oregon State Bar under ORS 9.572, the director shall give the provider 30 days in which to bring the program into compliance. If the director concludes that the program is not in compliance at the end of the 30-day period, the matter shall be submitted to mediation. The director and the provider shall jointly select a mediator. If the director and provider are unable to select a mediator within 15 days after the expiration of the 30-day period, any presiding judge for a judicial district may appoint a mediator upon the petition of the director.

(3) If mediation under subsection (2) of this section fails to produce a resolution of the matter, the director shall give the provider notice that a hearing will be held not sooner than 30 days after the date the notice is given. If, after hearing, the director determines that the provider is not in compliance with the standards and guidelines of the program and that the provider has failed to show satisfactory progress toward achieving compliance, the director shall suspend further funding of the program until such time as the provider makes a showing of compliance. [1997 c.801 §74; 2011 c.595 §100]

9.577 Legal Aid Account. (1) The Legal Aid Account is established in the General Fund of the State Treasury. All moneys in the account are continuously appropriated to the State Court Administrator for the purpose of the distributions required by this section. Interest earned by the account shall be credited to the General Fund.

(2) Each month, the State Court Administrator shall transfer to the Legal Aid Account, from amounts collected by the State Court Administrator as fees and charges in the circuit courts, the amounts necessary to make the distributions required by subsection (3) of this section.

(3) Each biennium, the State Court Administrator shall distribute to the Oregon State Bar $11.9 million from the Legal Aid Account. Distributions under this section shall be made by the State Court Administrator in eight quarterly installments of equal amounts, with the first distribution to be made as soon as possible after July 1, 2011. Amounts distributed to the Oregon State Bar under this subsection may be used only for the funding of the Legal Services Program established under ORS 9.572. [2011 c.595 §3a]

Note: 9.577 was enacted into law by the Legislative Assembly but was not added to or made a part of ORS chapter 9 or any series therein by legislative action. See Preface to Oregon Revised Statutes for further explanation.

9.578 Other funding sources. The Oregon State Bar may apply for, accept and expend moneys from any public or private source, including the federal government, made available for the purpose of establishing or funding legal service programs in Oregon. [1997 c.801 §75]

9.580 [Repealed by 1983 c.618 §1]

9.582 Use of amounts not paid to class members in class action lawsuits. All amounts paid or delivered to the Oregon State Bar under ORCP 32O are continuously appropriated to the Oregon State Bar, and may be used only for the funding of legal services provided through the Legal Services Program established under ORS 9.572. [2015 c.2 §4]

Note: 9.582 was enacted into law by the Legislative Assembly but was not added to or made a part of ORS chapter 9 or any series therein by legislative action. See Preface to Oregon Revised Statutes for further explanation.

9.590 [Repealed by 1953 c.609 §2]

9.595 [1981 c.193 §11; repealed by 1983 c.617 §1 (9.545 enacted in lieu of 9.595)]

9.600 [Repealed by 1953 c.609 §2]

9.610 [Repealed by 1953 c.609 §2]

CLIENT SECURITY FUND

9.615 Definition for ORS 9.615 to 9.665. As used in ORS 9.615 to 9.665, "client security fund" means a fund created under ORS 9.625. [1967 c.546 §2]

9.620 [Repealed by 1953 c.609 §2]

9.625 Plan to relieve client losses; rules. The board of governors may adopt a plan to relieve or mitigate pecuniary losses to the clients of active members caused by dishonest conduct of those members in their practice of law. The plan may provide for establishing, administering and dissolving a separate fund and for payments from that fund to reimburse losses and costs and expenses of administering the fund. The board may adopt rules of procedure to carry out the plan. The insurance laws of the state shall not apply to this fund. [1967 c.546 §3; 1975 c.641 §10; 1989 c.1052 §12]

9.630 [Repealed by 1953 c.609 §2]

9.635 Sources of client security fund. A client security fund may include:
(1) Transfers by the board of governors from other funds of the state bar;
(2) Voluntary contributions and payments by members under ORS 9.645;
(3) Claims recovered under ORS 9.665; and
(4) Income from investments of the fund. [1967 c.546 §4]

9.640 [Repealed by 1953 c.609 §2]

9.645 Annual payment by state bar members. To establish and maintain a client security fund, the board of governors may require an annual payment by each active member of the state bar. The payment authorized by this section shall be due at the same time, and enforced in the same manner, as payment of the annual membership fee. [1967 c.546 §5; 1975 c.641 §11; 1979 c.314 §1; 1983 c.122 §1; 1989 c.1052 §25; 1991 c.726 §6]

9.650 [Repealed by 1953 c.609 §2]

9.655 Investigation of claim of loss; subpoena. (1) Upon the filing of a claim, verified under oath, by a client claiming a pecuniary loss payable from the client security fund, the board of governors or its designated representative shall determine if the person named in the claim as the attorney whose dishonest conduct caused the loss was an active member of the Oregon State Bar engaged in the practice of law in Oregon at the time of the transaction out of which the claim arose and whether the transaction arose out of the person's practice of law in Oregon. The board or designated representative shall then determine whether the loss was caused by the person's dishonest conduct and if the person:
(a) Has been found guilty of a crime arising out of the dishonest conduct;
(b) In the case of a claim of loss of $5,000 or less, has been disbarred, suspended or reprimanded in disciplinary proceedings or has resigned from the bar due to circumstances arising out of the dishonest conduct; or
(c) Is a judgment debtor under the money award portion of a judgment entered in favor of the client in a proceeding arising out of the dishonest conduct, and execution issued on the judgment has been returned uncollected or issuance of execution would be a useless act.

(2) At any time after a claim is filed by a client claiming a pecuniary loss payable from the client security fund, the board or the board's representative may compel by subpoena the person named in the claim as the attorney whose dishonest conduct caused the loss, or any other person having knowledge of the matter, to appear for the purpose of giving testimony, and may compel by subpoena the production of records and documents pertinent to the claim. The subpoena shall have the same force and effect as in a civil action in the circuit court, and may be enforced by order of the circuit court for the county in which the person was served. [1967 c.546 §6; 1975 c.641 §12; 1979 c.383 §1; 1989 c.1052 §13; 2003 c.576 §279; 2005 c.347 §4; 2007 c.59 §1]

9.657 Immunity from civil liability. (1) Any person who has made a claim with the client security fund committee of the bar concerning a loss allegedly caused by the intentional dishonest conduct of the person's lawyer, or who has given information to the bar relative to a proposed or pending client security fund claim shall be absolutely immune from civil liability for such acts.

(2) The Oregon State Bar, its officers, the members of the client security fund committee, the board of governors, bar counsel, investigators and employees of the bar shall be absolutely immune from civil liability in the performance of their duties relative to proposed or pending client security fund claims. [1989 c.1052 §4]

9.660 [Repealed by 1953 c.609 §2]

9.665 Authority for reimbursement of client; waiver of conditions; subrogation for amount paid. (1) Except as provided in this section, reimbursement from the client security fund is discretionary with the board of governors.

(2) The board shall not authorize payment unless the conditions of ORS 9.655 (1) have been found to exist. However, the board may, in its sole discretion, waive one or more of the conditions of ORS 9.655 (1) in cases of extreme hardship or special and unusual circumstances. The state bar is subrogated, in the amount that a client's claim is reimbursed from the client security fund, to all rights and remedies of that client against the attorney whose dishonest conduct caused the loss, against the estate of the attorney or against any other person liable for the loss. [1967 c.546 §7; 1989 c.1052 §14; 1991 c.726 §7; 2003 c.14 §10]

9.670 [Repealed by 1953 c.609 §2]

LAWYER TRUST ACCOUNTS

9.675 Mandatory certification and disclosures for lawyer trust accounts. (1) An active member of the Oregon State Bar shall certify annually to the bar whether the member maintains any lawyer trust accounts in Oregon. If a member maintains one or more lawyer trust accounts, the member must disclose the financial institution in which each account is held and the account number for each account. The chief executive officer of the bar shall prescribe a form and due date for the certification and disclosures required by this section.

(2) If a member does not file the certificate and disclosures required by this section within 30 days after the due date prescribed under subsection (1) of this section, the chief executive officer shall send written notice of the default to the member at the member's electronic mail address on file with the bar on the date of the notice. The chief executive officer shall send the notice by mail to any member who is not required to have an electronic mail address on file with the bar under the rules of procedure. If a member does not file the certificate and disclosures required by this section within 60 days after the date of the notice, the person's membership in the bar is automatically suspended. The chief executive officer shall provide the names of all persons suspended under this section to the judges of the circuit courts, the Court of Appeals and the Oregon Tax Court.

(3) A person suspended under this section may be reinstated to membership in the bar only if the person pays all required fees and contributions and complies with all rules of procedure and rules of the Supreme Court relating to reinstatement. [2011 c.304 §2; 2013 c.3 §3; 2017 c.94 §12]

9.680 [Repealed by 1953 c.609 §2]

9.685 Trust account overdraft notification program. (1) Subject to the requirements of ORS 9.490, the Supreme Court may establish a trust account overdraft notification program for attorneys.

(2) The board of governors may adopt regulations for the administration of a trust account overdraft notification program established under this section. Regulations adopted under this subsection are binding upon all members of the bar only after those regulations are approved by the Supreme Court. [Formerly 9.132]

9.690 [Repealed by 1953 c.609 §2]

SEARCH OR SEIZURE OF LAWYER FILES OR PREMISES

9.695 Status of files or work premises of lawyer; inadmissibility of evidence subject to search or seizure. (1) Notwithstanding ORS 133.535, the files, papers, effects or work premises of a lawyer relating to the provision of legal service by the lawyer shall not be subject to search or seizure by any law enforcement officer, either by search warrant or otherwise.

(2) The provisions of subsection (1) of this section do not apply where there is probable cause to believe that the lawyer has committed, is committing or is about to commit a crime.

(3) As used in this section, "lawyer" means a member of the Oregon State Bar or a person licensed to practice law in any court of this state or any court of record of the United States or of any state, territory or other jurisdiction of the United States.

(4) Evidence or the fruits thereof obtained in violation of this section shall be inadmissible in any criminal or civil action or proceeding, except for an action or suit brought for violation of this section or the rights protected thereby. [1981 c.908 §1]

9.700 [Repealed by 1953 c.609 §2]

ASSUMING PRACTICE OF NONPERFORMING ATTORNEY

9.705 Definitions for ORS 9.705 to 9.757. As used in ORS 9.705 to 9.757:

(1) "Affected attorney" means a member or former member of the Oregon State Bar whose law practice is placed within the jurisdiction of the court under ORS 9.720 or as to whom a petition has been filed to place such law practice within the jurisdiction of the court under ORS 9.715.

(2) "Law practice" means a practice conducted by an individual, a partnership or a professional corporation. [1979 c.252 §2; 1985 c.512 §4; 1989 c.1052 §15; 2015 c.6 §1]

9.710 Jurisdiction of circuit court over law practice of nonperforming attorney. The circuit court of the county in which an attorney engaged in the practice of law in this state maintains or has maintained a principal office has jurisdiction as provided in ORS 9.705 to 9.757 whenever the attorney has died, is disbarred or suspended from the active practice of law, is incarcerated or has abandoned the practice and:

(1) The attorney failed to make arrangements for the orderly suspension or termination of the law practice of the attorney; or

(2) A duly appointed personal representative or other person assisting with the suspension or termination of the law practice is unable to adequately protect the interests of the attorney's clients. [1979 c.252 §3; 1985 c.512 §5; 1989 c.1052 §16; 2015 c.6 §2]

9.715 Petition to take jurisdiction over law practice. When the Oregon State Bar determines that one of the circumstances listed in ORS 9.710 exists, the bar may petition the court ex parte to take immediate jurisdiction over the affected attorney's law practice as provided in ORS 9.705 to 9.757. [1979 c.252 §4; 1985 c.512 §6; 1989 c.1052 §17; 1991 c.249 §2; 2015 c.6 §3]

9.720 Court taking jurisdiction over law practice. If the court finds that it has jurisdiction and finds that the assumption of such jurisdiction is necessary in order to protect the interest of the clients of the affected attorney or to protect the public interest, the court may, by appropriate order, immediately take jurisdiction over the law practice of the affected attorney to the extent the court determines is necessary. The exercise of jurisdiction may extend only to the affected attorney's lawyer trust account or may include all legal files, clients' trust funds, clients' property and all books, records, funds and property used in the law practice of the affected attorney. [1979 c.252 §5; 2015 c.6 §4]

9.722 [1997 c.135 §2; repealed by 2015 c.6 §5]

9.725 Appointment of bar as custodian of law practice; duties of custodian, court and financial institution. (1) If the court assumes jurisdiction under ORS 9.705 to 9.757, it shall appoint the Oregon State Bar to act as custodian of the law practice of the affected attorney. Immediately upon appointment, the bar shall take possession and control of all property over which the court assumed jurisdiction. The court may order the bar to do one or more of the following:

(a) Examine the files and records of the law practice and obtain information as to any pending matters which may require attention;

(b) Notify persons and entities who appear to be clients of the affected attorney that the court has assumed jurisdiction and inform such persons that it may be in their best interest to obtain other legal counsel;

(c) Apply for extensions of time pending employment of other counsel by the client;

(d) File notices, motions and pleadings on behalf of the client where jurisdictional time limits are involved and other legal counsel has not yet been obtained;

(e) Give notice to appropriate persons and entities who may be affected, other than clients, that the court has assumed jurisdiction;

(f) Arrange for the surrender or delivery of clients' papers or property; and

(g) Do such other acts as the court may direct to carry out the purposes of ORS 9.705 to 9.757.

(2) The court has jurisdiction over that portion of the files, records and property of the affected attorney for the purposes of ORS 9.705 to 9.757 as established in the order, and may make all orders necessary or appropriate to protect the interest of the affected attorney, the clients of the affected attorney and the public.

(3) Any financial institution holding funds in a lawyer trust account of the affected lawyer shall release the funds to the bar upon presentment of a copy of the order appointing the bar as custodian. The bar shall determine the ownership of the funds in the lawyer trust account and distribute the funds as directed by the interested client. Any funds for which ownership cannot be determined or for whom the owner cannot be located shall be turned over to the bar as provided in ORS 98.302 to 98.436.

(4) The bar may not be required to pay a filing fee for filing a petition under ORS 9.715. [1979 c.252 §6; 1985 c.512 §7; 1989 c.1052 §18; 2015 c.6 §6]

9.727 Service of order of custodianship. The Oregon State Bar shall serve a copy of an order appointing the bar as custodian of a law practice under ORS 9.725 on the affected attorney or any person assisting in the suspension or termination of the affected attorney's practice. The bar shall serve the copy of the order by regular mail to the last-known address of the affected attorney in the records of the bar or to a duly appointed fiduciary at the address provided in an official filing. The affected attorney or assisting person may, within 10 days of the service, request a hearing to challenge the order. After the hearing, the court may vacate or modify the custodianship order as the court finds appropriate. [2015 c.6 §9]

9.730 Assistance by professional liability fund and other attorneys. After appointment as custodian of a law practice under ORS 9.725, the Oregon State Bar may engage the services of the Oregon State Bar Professional Liability Fund created under ORS 9.005 to 9.757 or any active member of the bar to assist in the performance of the bar's duties as custodian. Acts performed by a member of the bar in assisting the custodian do not constitute acceptance of employment by any client of the affected attorney. [1979 c.252 §9; 1985 c.512 §8; 1989 c.1052 §19; 2015 c.6 §7]

9.735 Compensation of custodian. The court shall enter a judgment awarding reasonable compensation and expenses to the Oregon State Bar for acting as custodian under ORS 9.705 to 9.757. The judgment shall be against the affected attorney or the estate of the affected attorney. The judgment is a lien upon all nontrust funds, office furnishings, supplies, equipment, library and other personal property used in the law practice of the affected attorney retroactive to the date of filing of the petition for jurisdiction under ORS 9.705 to 9.757. The judgment lien takes priority over all general unsecured creditors, nonpossessory liens and security interests that were unperfected on the date the court assumed jurisdiction, and may be foreclosed as provided in ORS chapter 87. [1979 c.252 §11; 1985 c.512 §9; 1989 c.1052 §20; 2003 c.576 §225; 2013 c.3 §1; 2015 c.6 §11]

9.740 Court orders appealable; stay. Jurisdictional and final orders of the circuit court pursuant to ORS 9.705 to 9.757 are appealable but may not be stayed except as ordered by the circuit court or any appellate court. [1979 c.252 §7; 1985 c.512 §10; 1989 c.1052 §21]

9.745 Statutes of limitation suspended. Any applicable statute of limitations or time limit for the filing set by statute or rule of court as it relates to the affected attorney's clients shall be suspended automatically by the filing of a petition for jurisdiction under ORS 9.705 to 9.757 for a period of 120 days following the date of filing of such petition. [1979 c.252 §8; 1985 c.512 §11; 1989 c.1052 §22]

9.750 Confidentiality of files and records; attorney-client privilege. Persons examining the files and records of the law practice of an affected attorney pursuant to ORS 9.705 to 9.757 shall preserve the confidentiality of the information relating to the affected attorney's representation of a client and shall make disclosure only to the extent necessary to carry out the purposes of ORS 9.705 to 9.757. Such disclosure is a disclosure which is reasonably necessary for the accomplishment of the purpose for which the affected attorney was consulted. Communications between the Oregon State Bar or its designees and a client of the affected attorney are subject to the attorney-client privilege to the same extent as it would have applied to communications by or to the affected attorney. [1979 c.252 §10; 1985 c.512 §12; 1989 c.1052 §23; 2015 c.6 §12]

9.755 Final report of custodian; petition for compensation; court approval. Whenever the purposes of ORS 9.705 to 9.757 have been accomplished with respect to the law practice of an affected attorney for which the Oregon State Bar has been appointed as custodian under ORS 9.725, the bar shall file with the court a final report and accounting of all funds and property coming into the possession or control of the bar as custodian and a petition for compensation and expenses of the bar for acting as custodian. The bar shall mail a copy of the report and accounting and a copy of the petition of the bar for compensation and expenses to all persons upon whom service was made pursuant to ORS 9.727. Upon approval by the court, an order shall be entered approving the final report and accounting, fixing the amount of compensation and expenses to be allowed to the bar, and discharging the bar from further duties. [1979 c.252 §12; 1985 c.512 §13; 1989 c.1052 §24; 2015 c.6 §13]

9.757 Retention of client materials. (1) Except as provided in subsection (2) of this section or by court order, the Oregon State Bar may dispose of client papers and files that have not been claimed by a client of an affected attorney within six months after written notice to the client from the bar. The bar must dispose of the papers and files in a manner reasonably calculated to protect the confidentiality of the information contained in the papers and files.

(2) The bar may dispose of an unclaimed original will as provided in ORS 112.815 and 112.820.

(3) The bar shall maintain a log of all retained wills that is accessible to the public.

(4) Upon receipt of satisfactory proof of identity, the bar shall release a will belonging to a client to the client or to a duly appointed personal representative or conservator of the client.

(5) The bar may retain wills in digitized form, and a digitized copy, certified by the bar as a true copy of the digital document retained by the bar, shall be admissible in evidence to the same extent as the original. [2015 c.6 §10]

LAW LIBRARIES

9.760 Judicial department library services; fees. The State Court Administrator may authorize any library of the judicial department of government to provide photographic or other copies of any of its materials, and to make reasonable charges for such copies or services. [Amended by 1959 c.655 §1; 1985 c.308 §2]

9.770 [Amended by 1959 c.655 §2; repealed by 1985 c.308 §6]

9.780 Exchange of legal publications. The State Court Administrator may send, free of charge, one copy of the codes, session laws and Supreme Court, Court of Appeals and Oregon Tax Court reports of this state as the same may be published, to each state and foreign country that exchanges, free of charge, its codes, session laws and equivalent reports with this state. All legal books and publications received in exchange by the state shall be added to the collection of the State of Oregon Law Library. [Amended by 1985 c.308 §3; 2001 c.779 §6]

9.790 Legislative Counsel furnishing copies of codes and session laws for exchange. The Legislative Counsel shall, upon requisition of the State Court Administrator, supply a sufficient number of copies of the codes and session laws of this state, as the same may be published, to carry out the provisions of ORS 9.780. [Amended by 1985 c.308 §4]

9.800 Sale of surplus codes and session laws. The State Court Administrator may sell the unused sets of Oregon codes and session laws which are not needed for the purpose of exchanging for the codes and session laws of other states and for other books. The sales shall be for cash and the proceeds deposited as provided by ORS 8.130. [Amended by 1985 c.308 §5]

9.810 [Repealed by 1985 c.308 §6]

9.815 County law libraries and law library services. (1) Each county shall:
(a) Operate a free law library at a location that is convenient and available at reasonable hours; or
(b) Provide free law library services at one or more locations that are convenient and available at reasonable hours.
(2) A county governing body may enter into a contract with a law library association or other organization for the operation of the law library, or the provision of law library services, required by this section. [2011 c.224 §1; 2011 c.595 §176]

9.820 Law libraries in Multnomah County. In all counties containing more than 400,000 inhabitants, according to the latest federal decennial census, the governing body of the county may contract with any law library association or corporation owning and maintaining a law library in the county at or convenient to the courthouse, for the use of the library by the judges of the circuit and county courts, county commissioners, district attorney and all members of the bar. [Amended by 1963 c.519 §1; 1965 c.619 §3; 2011 c.595 §105]

9.825 Law library surveys; reports. (1) The State Court Administrator shall conduct every two years an electronic survey of all county law libraries and the law library services provided by counties. The survey must request information on:
(a) The extent to which counties provide access to statutes, rules, cases and other legal information, whether through printed materials or electronic access;
(b) Staffing in county law libraries;
(c) The number and types of persons who use county law libraries and other law library services;
(d) The hours that county law libraries are open, or access to law library services is available;
(e) The hours that law library staff assistance is available, either in person, by telephone or through the Internet; and
(f) The extent to which persons who use county law libraries and law library services have free or low-cost public, on-site access to computers, printers, copiers and other electronic devices provided by the counties.
(2) The State Court Administrator shall submit a report to the Legislative Assembly in the manner provided by ORS 192.245 based on each survey conducted under this section. The report must be delivered to the Legislative Assembly not later than February 1 of each odd-numbered year. [2011 c.224 §5]

9.829 Use of moneys distributed to counties. Notwithstanding any other law, the governing body of a county may, after consulting with the presiding judge of the circuit court, use up to one-half of the moneys distributed to the county by the Chief Justice of the Supreme Court from moneys appropriated to the Judicial Department for the purpose of operating law libraries or providing law library services, for the purpose of providing conciliation and mediation services in circuit courts. [2017 c.725 §19]

9.830 [Amended by 1965 c.619 §4; 1981 s.s. c.3 §78; 1983 c.763 §36; repealed by 2011 c.595 §104]

9.840 [Amended by 1963 c.519 §2; 1965 c.619 §5; 1981 s.s. c.3 §79; 1983 c.763 §37; 1997 c.801 §147; 2011 c.224 §2; repealed by 2011 c.595 §104]

9.850 [Amended by 1963 c.519 §3; 1965 c.619 §6; 2003 c.14 §11; 2011 c.224 §3; repealed by 2011 c.595 §104]

PENALTIES

9.990 Penalties. (1) Any person who violates ORS 9.160 shall be fined not more than $500 or imprisoned in the county jail for a period not to exceed six months, or both.
(2) Any person who violates any of the provisions of ORS 9.500 or 9.520 commits a Class A violation.
(3) Any person violating any of the provisions of ORS 9.505 shall, upon conviction, be fined not more than $1,000 or imprisoned in the county jail for a period not to exceed one year, or both. [Subsection (3) enacted as 1961 c.561 §4; 1999 c.1051 §143]

———————————

Chapter 10 — Juries

2017 EDITION

JURIES

COURTS OF RECORD; COURT OFFICERS; JURIES

GENERAL PROVISIONS

10.010   Definitions

10.020   Kinds of juries

10.025   Rules for use of electronic transmission and electronic signature on documents

10.030   Eligibility for jury service; discrimination prohibited

10.050   Excuse from jury duty

10.055   Deferment of jury service

10.061   Fees payable to jurors; required waiver

10.065   Mileage fee and reimbursement of other expenses

10.075   Payment of per diem and mileage fees by state; payment of other expenses

10.080   Seeking or offering to procure place on jury or list of jurors and selection of juror pursuant to request prohibited

10.090   Prohibited acts by employers against jurors; notice to jurors; remedy for violations

10.092   Insurance coverage for employee during jury service; unlawful employment practice

10.095   Duty of jury; instructions

10.100   View of premises by jury

10.105   Jury service term

10.107   Implementation of "one day, one trial" jury service

10.115   Jurors with disabilities

10.125   Security for jury sequestered or kept overnight

SELECTION AND SUMMONING OF GRAND JURORS AND TRIAL JURORS IN CIRCUIT COURTS

10.205   Selection and summoning of jurors; identification numbers

10.215   Master jury list; sources; contents

10.235   Additional jurors; selection; notice

10.245   Determining eligibility of jurors; eligibility form; effect of false statements or failure to respond

10.255   Record of persons summoned to serve as jurors

10.265   Preservation of jury orders, records and papers

10.275   Jury challenges; request for access to confidential jury records; order allowing disclosure; exclusive procedure

JURY OF INQUEST

10.810   Definition

10.820   Number of jurors required to concur

PENALTIES

10.990   Penalties

GENERAL PROVISIONS

10.010 Definitions. As used in this chapter, unless the context requires otherwise:
(1) "Clerk of court" means the trial court administrator or any other nonjudicial officer or employee of the circuit court for a county authorized by the presiding judge for the judicial district.
(2) "Juror" means any juror or prospective juror.
(3) "Jury" means a body of persons temporarily selected from persons who live in a particular county or district, and invested with power to present or indict in respect to a crime or to try a question of fact. [Amended by 1985 c.703 §1; 1995 c.658 §22; 1995 c.781 §21; 1997 c.801 §121]

10.020 Kinds of juries. A jury is of three kinds:
(1) A grand jury.
(2) A trial jury.
(3) A jury of inquest.

10.025 Rules for use of electronic transmission and electronic signature on documents. (1) The Chief Justice of the Supreme Court may make rules for the use of electronic transmission and electronic signature on documents transmitted to or from a circuit court under this chapter.
(2) ORS 84.072 does not apply to rules adopted under this section. [2013 c.2 §2]

10.030 Eligibility for jury service; discrimination prohibited. (1) Except as otherwise specifically provided by statute, the opportunity for jury service may not be denied or limited on the basis of race, religion, sex, sexual orientation, national origin, age, income, occupation or any other factor that discriminates against a cognizable group in this state.
(2) Any person is eligible to act as a juror in a civil trial unless the person:
(a) Is not a citizen of the United States;
(b) Does not live in the county in which summoned for jury service;
(c) Is less than 18 years of age; or

(d) Has had rights and privileges withdrawn and not restored under ORS 137.281.

(3)(a) Any person is eligible to act as a grand juror, or as a juror in a criminal trial, unless the person:

(A) Is not a citizen of the United States;

(B) Does not live in the county in which summoned for jury service;

(C) Is less than 18 years of age;

(D) Has had rights and privileges withdrawn and not restored under ORS 137.281;

(E) Has been convicted of a felony or served a felony sentence within the 15 years immediately preceding the date the person is required to report for jury service; or

(F) Has been convicted of a misdemeanor involving violence or dishonesty, or has served a misdemeanor sentence based on a misdemeanor involving violence or dishonesty, within the five years immediately preceding the date the person is required to report for jury service.

(b) As used in this subsection:

(A) "Felony sentence" includes any incarceration, post-prison supervision, parole or probation imposed upon conviction of a felony or served as a result of conviction of a felony.

(B) "Has been convicted of a felony" has the meaning given that term in ORS 166.270.

(C) "Misdemeanor sentence" includes any incarceration or probation imposed upon conviction of a misdemeanor or served as a result of conviction of a misdemeanor.

(4) A person who is blind, hard of hearing or speech impaired or who has a physical disability is not ineligible to act as a juror and may not be excluded from a jury list or jury service on the basis of blindness, hearing or speech impairment or physical disability alone.

(5) A person is ineligible to act as a juror in any circuit court of this state within 24 months after being discharged from jury service in a federal court in this state or circuit court of this state unless that person's service as a juror is required because of a need for additional jurors. [Amended by 1971 c.630 §1; 1975 c.781 §4; 1977 c.262 §1; 1985 c.703 §2; 1989 c.224 §3; 1997 c.313 §8; 1997 c.736 §1; 2007 c.70 §4; 2007 c.100 §13; 2009 c.484 §13]

10.040 [Amended by 1961 c.454 §208; 1975 c.84 §1; repealed by 1979 c.728 §1]

10.050 Excuse from jury duty. (1) A judge of the court or clerk of court shall excuse a person from acting as a juror upon a showing of undue hardship or extreme inconvenience to the person, the person's family, the person's employer or the public served by the person. In applying this subsection the judge or clerk of court shall carefully consider and weigh both the public need for juries which are representative of the full community and the individual circumstances offered as a justification for excuse from jury service. A person may request and be granted excuse from jury service under this subsection by means of telephone communication or mail.

(2) Notwithstanding ORS 10.030 (4), a judge may, by own motion, excuse a juror whose presence on the jury would substantially impair the progress of the action on trial or prejudice the parties thereto.

(3) A judge of the court or clerk of court shall excuse a person from acting as a juror upon the request of that person if the person is 70 years of age or older. A person may request and be granted excuse from jury service under this subsection by means of telephone communication or mail.

(4) A judge of the court or clerk of court shall excuse a woman from acting as a juror upon the request of the woman if the woman is breast-feeding a child. A request for excuse from jury service under this subsection must be made in writing.

(5) Unless the public need for juries in the court outweighs the individual circumstances of the person summoned, a judge of the court or clerk of court shall excuse a person from acting as a juror upon the request of that person if the person is the sole caregiver for a child or other dependent during the court's normal hours of operation, the person is unable to afford day care or make other arrangements for the care of the dependent, and the person personally attends to the dependent during the court's normal hours of operation. [Amended by 1967 c.389 §1; 1975 c.160 §3; 1977 c.262 §2; 1977 c.631 §2; 1979 c.728 §2; 1985 c.703 §5; 1995 c.808 §1; 1997 c.313 §35; 1999 c.1085 §1]

10.055 Deferment of jury service. (1) A judge of the court or clerk of court may allow, for good cause shown, a person summoned to serve as a juror for a particular jury service term to defer jury service to any other term beginning within one year after the end of the term for which the person was summoned. Except as provided in this section, a judge or clerk may not allow more than one deferral to a person under this section. The name of a person allowed to defer jury service shall be included with the names of persons to be summoned as jurors for the subsequent term to which jury service is deferred.

(2) A judge or clerk may allow more than one deferral of jury duty under this section only for good cause. A person requesting a deferral under this subsection must provide a list of not less than 10 dates within the six-month period following the date of the request on which the person would be able to commence jury duty. [1967 c.473 §2; 1969 c.176 §1; 1971 c.207 §1; 1975 c.342 §13; 1985 c.703 §6; 2011 c.377 §1]

10.060 [Amended by 1955 c.296 §1; 1971 c.358 §1; 1981 c.509 §1; 1985 c.703 §7; repealed by 1999 c.1085 §3 (10.061 enacted in lieu of 10.060)]

10.061 Fees payable to jurors; required waiver. (1) The fee of jurors in courts other than circuit courts is $10 for each day that a juror is required to attend.

(2)(a) The fee of jurors for the first two days of required attendance in circuit court during a term of service is $10 for each day that a juror is required to attend.

(b) The fee of jurors for the third and subsequent days of required attendance in circuit court during a term of service is $25 for each day that a juror is required to attend.

(3) Unless otherwise provided by the terms of an employment agreement, a juror must waive the juror's fee provided for in subsection (1), (2) or (4) of this section if the juror is paid a wage or salary by the juror's employer for the days that the juror is required to attend a court, including a municipal or justice court. The provisions of this subsection do not affect any claim a juror may have for mileage reimbursement under ORS 10.065.

(4) In addition to the fees and mileage prescribed in subsection (1) of this section and ORS 10.065 for service in a court other than a circuit court, the governing body of a city or county may provide by ordinance for an additional juror fee and for city or county reimbursement of jurors for mileage and other expenses incurred in serving as jurors in courts other than circuit courts. [1999 c.1085 §4 (enacted in lieu of 10.060); 2001 c.761 §3; 2001 c.779 §13; 2002 s.s.1 c.10 §3]

10.065 Mileage fee and reimbursement of other expenses. (1) In addition to the fees prescribed in ORS 10.061, a juror who is required to travel from the juror's usual place of abode in order to execute or perform service as a juror in a court other than a circuit court shall be paid mileage at the rate of eight cents a mile for travel in going to and returning from the place where the service is performed.

(2) In addition to the fees prescribed in ORS 10.061, a juror who is required to travel from the juror's usual place of abode in order to execute or perform service as a juror in a circuit court shall be paid mileage at the rate of 20 cents a mile for travel in going to and returning from the place where the service is performed. Mileage paid to a juror shall be based on the shortest practicable route between the juror's residence and the place where court is held.

(3) In addition to the fees prescribed in ORS 10.061, the State Court Administrator may reimburse a juror who uses public transportation to travel from the juror's usual place of abode in order to execute or perform service as a juror in a circuit court, without regard to the distance traveled by the juror.

(4) In addition to the fees prescribed in ORS 10.061, a juror serving in circuit court may be paid for lodging expenses, dependent care expenses and other reasonable expenses that arise by reason of jury service. Expenses under this subsection may be paid only upon written request of the juror, made in such form and containing such information as may be required by the State Court Administrator. The State Court Administrator shall establish policies and procedures on eligibility, authorization and payment of expenses under this subsection. Payment of expenses under this subsection is subject to availability of funds for the payment.

(5) A juror shall be paid the mileage and other expenses provided for in this section for each day's attendance at court.

(6) The State Court Administrator shall establish policies and procedures on eligibility, authorization and payment of mileage and expenses under subsections (2) to (4) of this section. [1957 c.676 §1; 1971 c.358 §2; 1981 c.509 §2; 1999 c.1085 §5; 2002 s.s.1 c.10 §4]

10.070 [Repealed by 1957 c.676 §2]

10.075 Payment of per diem and mileage fees by state; payment of other expenses. (1) The per diem fees, mileage and expenses due to each juror in the circuit court shall be paid by the state from funds available for the purpose. Payment shall be made upon a certified statement, prepared by the clerk of court, showing the number of days each juror has served and the amount due each juror for mileage and other expenses.

(2) If a jury in the circuit court is provided food, drink, lodging or transportation by order of the circuit court, the cost thereof shall be paid by the state from funds available for the purpose.

(3) Each circuit court shall offer each juror the opportunity to waive receipt of the per diem and mileage expenses otherwise payable to the juror for the purpose of funding Judicial Department programs and activities identified by the Chief Justice of the Supreme Court. All amounts waived by a juror under the provisions of this subsection are continuously appropriated to the Judicial Department programs and activities that are identified by the Chief Justice for receipt of the waived amounts, and may be used only for the purposes of those programs and activities.

(4) This section does not apply to mileage and other expenses of jurors reimbursed by a county as provided in ORS 10.061 (4). [1981 s.s. c.3 §43; 1985 c.703 §8; 1999 c.1085 §6]

10.077 [Formerly 17.315; 1981 s.s. c.30 §60; repealed by 1985 c.703 §28]

10.080 Seeking or offering to procure place on jury or list of jurors and selection of juror pursuant to request prohibited. (1) A person may not ask or request any sheriff, constable or any other person, whose duty it is under the law to select or summon any jury or juror, to select or put the person upon the jury. A person may not procure or offer to procure for the person or for another person a place upon any jury or seek to have the person or another placed upon the list of jurors that is required by law to be made.

(2) A sheriff, constable or other person who has a duty under the law to select or summon a jury may not select, summon or place upon any jury any person whom the sheriff, constable or other person has been asked or requested to select or summon. [Amended by 2003 c.14 §12]

10.090 Prohibited acts by employers against jurors; notice to jurors; remedy for violations. (1) An employer commits an unlawful employment practice under ORS chapter 659A if the employer discharges, threatens to discharge, intimidates or coerces any employee by reason of the employee's service or scheduled service as a juror on a grand jury, trial jury or jury of inquest.`

(2) An employer may not require that an employee use vacation leave, sick leave or annual leave for time spent by the employee in responding to a summons for jury duty, and the employer shall allow the employee to take leave without pay for time spent by the employee in responding to a summons for jury duty.

(3) This section may not be construed to alter or affect an employer's policies or agreements with employees concerning employees' wages during times when an employee serves or is scheduled to serve as a juror.

(4) When summoning jurors, the person whose duty it is under the law to summon shall notify each juror of the juror's rights under this section.

(5) An employee who alleges a violation of subsection (1) of this section may bring a civil action under ORS 659A.885 or may file a complaint with the Commissioner of the Bureau of Labor and Industries in the manner provided by ORS 659A.820. [1975 c.160 §1; 1985 c.703 §11; 2011 c.118 §3; 2011 c.377 §3]

10.092 Insurance coverage for employee during jury service; unlawful employment practice. (1) An employer who employs 10 or more persons commits an unlawful employment practice under ORS chapter 659A if:

(a) The employer ceases to provide health, disability, life or other insurance coverage for an employee during times when the employee serves or is scheduled to serve as a juror; and

(b) The employee elected to have coverage continued while the employee served or was scheduled to serve as a juror, and the employee provided notice of that election to the employer in compliance with the employer's policy for notification.

(2) Notwithstanding ORS 652.610 (3), if, following an election described in subsection (1) of this section, an employer is required or elects to pay any part of the costs of providing health, disability, life or other insurance coverage for the employee that should have been paid by the employee, the employer may deduct from the employee's pay such amounts upon the employee's return to work until the amount the employer advanced toward the payments is paid. The total amount deducted for insurance under this subsection may not exceed 10 percent of the employee's gross pay each pay period.

(3) Notwithstanding ORS 652.610 (3), if the employer pays any part of the costs of providing health, disability, life or other insurance coverage for an employee under subsection (2) of this section, and the employee ceases to work for the employer before the total amount the employer advanced toward the payments is paid, the employer may deduct the remaining amounts from any amounts owed by the employer to the employee or may seek to recover those amounts by any other legal means.

(4) An employee who alleges a violation of this section may bring a civil action under ORS 659A.885 or may file a complaint with the Commissioner of the Bureau of Labor and Industries in the manner provided by ORS 659A.820. [2011 c.118 §2]

10.095 Duty of jury; instructions. The jury, subject to the control of the court, in the cases specified by statute, are the judges of the effect or value of evidence addressed to them, except when it is thereby declared to be conclusive. They are, however, to be instructed by the court on all proper occasions:

(1) That their power of judging of the effect of evidence is not arbitrary, but to be exercised with legal discretion, and in subordination to the rules of evidence;

(2) That they are not bound to find in conformity with the declarations of any number of witnesses, which do not produce conviction in their minds, against a less number, or against a presumption or other evidence satisfying their minds;

(3) That a witness false in one part of the testimony of the witness may be distrusted in others;

(4) That the testimony of an accomplice ought to be viewed with distrust, and the oral admissions of a party with caution;

(5) That in civil cases the affirmative of the issue shall be proved, and when the evidence is contradictory, the finding shall be according to the preponderance of evidence;

(6) That in criminal cases a person is innocent of a crime or wrong until the prosecution proves otherwise, and guilt shall be established beyond reasonable doubt;

(7) That evidence is to be estimated, not only by its own intrinsic weight, but also according to the evidence which it is in the power of one side to produce and of the other to contradict; and, therefore,

(8) That if weaker and less satisfactory evidence is offered when it appears that stronger and more satisfactory was within the power of the party, the evidence offered should be viewed with distrust. [Formerly 17.250; 2013 c.25 §1]

10.100 View of premises by jury. Whenever, in the opinion of the court, it is proper that the jury should have a view of real property which is the subject of the litigation, or of the place in which any material fact occurred, it may order the jury to be conducted in a body, in the custody of a proper officer, to the place, which shall be shown to them by the judge or by a person appointed by the court for that purpose. While the jury are thus absent, no person, other than the judge or person so appointed, shall speak to them on any subject connected with the trial. [Formerly 17.230]

10.105 Jury service term. The length of a jury service term in a county shall be established by the presiding judge for the judicial district, but no trial juror shall be required to serve more than 10 days unless necessary to complete the trial of an action. A day of service is each day during a jury service term on which a juror is required to attend and attends. [1985 c.703 §4; 1995 c.781 §22]

10.107 Implementation of "one day, one trial" jury service. The Chief Justice of the Supreme Court shall take all reasonable actions necessary to expedite implementation of juror service procedures for circuit courts that will allow a person called for jury service to serve for one day, or for one trial if selected to serve on a trial. [1999 c.1085 §10]

10.110 [Amended by 1955 c.717 §1; 1957 c.393 §1; 1973 c.836 §312; 1981 s.s. c.3 §44; repealed by 1985 c.703 §28]

10.115 Jurors with disabilities. (1) As used in this section:
(a) "Assistive communication device" means any equipment designed to facilitate communication by a person with a disability.
(b) "Juror with a disability" means a person who is hard of hearing or speech impaired, who is summoned to serve as a juror and whose name is drawn for grand jury or trial jury service.
(c) "Qualified interpreter" means a person who is readily able to communicate with a juror with a disability, accurately communicate the proceedings to the juror and accurately repeat the statements of the juror.
(2) The court to which a juror with a disability is summoned, upon written request by the juror and upon a finding by the court that the juror requires the services of a qualified interpreter or the use of an assistive communication device in examination of the juror as to the juror's qualifications to act as a juror or in performance by the juror of the functions of a juror, shall appoint a qualified interpreter for the juror and shall fix the compensation and expenses of the interpreter and shall provide an appropriate assistive communication device if needed. The compensation and expenses of an interpreter so appointed and the cost of any assistive communication device shall be paid by the public authority required to pay the fees due to the juror.
(3) An oath or affirmation shall be administered to a qualified interpreter appointed for a juror with a disability, in substance that the interpreter will accurately communicate the proceedings to the juror and accurately repeat the statements of the juror.
(4) A qualified interpreter appointed for a juror with a disability, or a person operating an assistive communication device for a juror with a disability, shall be present during deliberations by the jury on which the juror serves. An interpreter or person operating an assistive communication device may not participate in the jury deliberations in any manner except to facilitate communication between the juror with a disability and the other jurors or other persons with whom the jurors may communicate, and the court shall so instruct the jury and the interpreter.
(5) When a juror with a disability serves on a trial jury, the court shall instruct the jury on the presence of the qualified interpreter or person operating an assistive communication device. [1985 c.703 §9; 1989 c.224 §4; 1991 c.750 §6; 2007 c.70 §6; 2007 c.96 §1]

10.120 [Amended by 1965 c.387 §1; repealed by 1973 c.836 §358]

10.125 Security for jury sequestered or kept overnight. When a jury is kept overnight or otherwise sequestered and the sheriff is ordered to provide security for the jury by a judge or clerk of court of the court to which the jurors were summoned, the sheriff shall provide that security. The cost of providing the security shall be paid by the county. [1985 c.703 §10]

10.130 [Amended by 1979 c.728 §3; repealed by 1985 c.703 §28]

10.135 [1969 c.219 §1; 1973 c.836 §313; repealed by 1985 c.703 §28]

10.140 [Amended by 1955 c.717 §2; repealed by 1969 c.219 §2]

10.150 [Amended by 1955 c.717 §3; 1977 c.465 §1; 1981 s.s. c.3 §45; repealed by 1985 c.703 §28]

10.160 [Amended by 1955 c.717 §4; 1981 s.s. c.3 §46; repealed by 1985 c.703 §28]

SELECTION AND SUMMONING OF GRAND JURORS AND TRIAL JURORS IN CIRCUIT COURTS

10.205 Selection and summoning of jurors; identification numbers. (1) ORS 10.205 to 10.265 govern the selection and summoning of persons for service as grand jurors or trial jurors in the circuit court in a county.
(2) The presiding judge for the judicial district may authorize the use of juror identification numbers in place of juror names in the performance of functions under ORS 10.215 to 10.265, 132.020 and ORCP 57 B for the selection of jurors in the county, except for functions under ORS 10.215 (4), when to do so would promote the efficiency of the selection process, but the selection must be done randomly. [1985 c.703 §12; 1995 c.781 §23; 2005 c.385 §4; 2013 c.2 §7]

10.210 [Amended by 1957 c.594 §1; 1961 c.705 §4; 1965 c.510 §11; 1977 c.519 §1; repealed by 1981 s.s. c.3 §141]

10.215 Master jury list; sources; contents. (1) The State Court Administrator shall cause to be prepared at least once each year a master jury list containing names selected at random from the source lists. The source lists are the most recent list of electors of the county, the records furnished by the Department of Transportation as provided in ORS 802.260 (2) and any other sources approved by the Chief Justice of the Supreme Court that will furnish a fair cross section of the citizens of the county. The State Court Administrator and circuit courts may use source lists obtained from any person or public body, and jury lists containing names selected from a source list, only for purposes consistent with administering the selection and summoning of persons for service as jurors, the drawing of names of jurors, and other tasks necessary to accomplish those functions. Source lists may not contain and the State Court Administrator is not required to obtain information about individuals who are participants in the Address Confidentiality Program under ORS 192.820 to 192.868. Except as specifically provided by law, the State Court Administrator and circuit courts may not disclose source lists obtained from any person or public body, and jury lists containing names selected from a source list, to any other person or public body.
(2) A public body having custody, possession or control of any list that may be used as a source list for preparation of a master jury list, upon written request by the State Court Administrator, shall make its list available at any reasonable time and, except as otherwise provided in ORS 802.260, without charge to the State Court Administrator for inspection or copying. The public body, upon written request by the State Court Administrator, shall provide a copy of its list for the date and in the form requested to the State Court Administrator. Except as otherwise provided in ORS 802.260, the copy shall be provided without charge.
(3) The number of names placed on a master jury list shall be sufficient to meet the projected need for grand jurors and trial jurors in the circuit court in the county, but the total number may not be less than two percent of the population of the county according to the latest federal decennial census.
(4) A master jury list shall contain the first name, the surname, the place of residence and, if assigned, the juror identification number of each person whose name is placed thereon.
(5) A master jury list for a circuit court shall be certified by the State Court Administrator to have been prepared in compliance with the requirements of this section. A certified copy of the master jury list shall be provided to the circuit court for the county as soon as possible after the list is prepared.
(6) A newly filed master jury list shall be maintained separately from the previously filed master jury list. The presiding judge shall designate when a newly filed master jury list becomes effective. After a newly filed master jury list becomes effective, names of persons for a jury list for a panel or term must be selected for a jury list for a panel or term from the newly filed master jury list and from names of any persons from the previously filed master jury list whose service was deferred. When a newly filed master jury list becomes effective, all orders, records and papers prepared in connection with the selection

process based on the previously filed master jury list shall be preserved by the trial court administrator and State Court Administrator for the period prescribed by the State Court Administrator under ORS 8.125.

(7) The State Court Administrator may make adjustments to the master jury list, and may authorize the presiding judge of a judicial district to make adjustments to a jury list for a panel or term, for the purpose of updating the addresses of persons appearing on the lists and removing the names of persons who are deceased, permanently ineligible for jury service or permanently excused from jury service. The State Court Administrator shall ensure that a record is maintained of all adjustments to jury lists made under this subsection.

(8) For the purposes of this section, "public body" has the meaning given that term in ORS 174.109. [1985 c.703 §13; 1987 c.681 §3; 1995 c.273 §6; 1995 c.781 §24a; 1997 c.872 §15; 2001 c.779 §14; 2003 c.803 §18; 2005 c.385 §5; 2007 c.542 §14; 2013 c.2 §4]

10.220 [Amended by 1955 c.717 §5; 1957 c.594 §2; 1959 c.462 §1; 1961 c.705 §5; 1965 c.510 §12; 1977 c.519 §2; 1981 s.s. c.3 §47; repealed by 1985 c.703 §28]

10.225 [1985 c.703 §14; 1995 c.781 §25; repealed by 2013 c.2 §6]

10.230 [Amended by 1981 s.s. c.3 §48; repealed by 1985 c.703 §28]

10.235 Additional jurors; selection; notice. (1) When an additional number of jurors is needed for a jury service term in a county because the jury list for the term becomes exhausted, or in the opinion of the presiding judge for the judicial district is likely to become exhausted, before the end of the term, additional jurors may be selected and summoned as provided in this section.

(2) The presiding judge for the judicial district may order an additional number of names selected from the master jury list and added to the jury list for the panel or term in the same manner as the original jury list is prepared. As directed by the presiding judge of the circuit court, the persons whose names are added to the jury list for the panel or term shall be summoned by the clerk of court giving written notice to each of them by mail or by the sheriff or other officer giving written notice to each of them personally or by leaving written notice at the person's place of residence with some person of suitable age and discretion. The notice need be given only a reasonable time before the day on which the persons summoned are required to attend.

(3) If the master jury list becomes exhausted or in the opinion of the presiding judge is likely to become exhausted, the presiding judge may order that the clerk of court select an additional number of names from the source lists described in ORS 10.215 (1) and that the persons whose names are so selected be summoned as provided in subsection (2) of this section.

(4) If there is an immediate need for additional jurors, a judge of the circuit court for the county may direct the clerk of court, sheriff or other officer to summon a sufficient number of eligible persons to meet that need. Those persons shall be summoned as directed by the judge. [1985 c.703 §15; 1995 c.781 §26; 2013 c.2 §5]

10.240 [Amended by 1981 s.s. c.3 §49; repealed by 1985 c.703 §28]

10.245 Determining eligibility of jurors; eligibility form; effect of false statements or failure to respond. (1) Before or at the time a person summoned to serve as a juror reports for jury service in a county, a judge of the circuit court for the county or clerk of court shall question the person as to the eligibility of the person to act as a juror under ORS 10.030. If a judge or clerk of court determines that a person so questioned is not eligible to act as a juror, the person shall be discharged.

(2) The presiding judge for the judicial district may cause to be mailed or delivered with a juror's summons a juror eligibility form and instructions for completion of the form and return of the completed form by mail or personal delivery to the clerk of court by a specified date. The form shall set forth the eligibility requirements prescribed in ORS 10.030.

(3) A person who knowingly makes a false statement of material fact in response to a question on a juror eligibility form may be punished for contempt.

(4) A completed juror eligibility form shall contain the summoned person's signed declaration that the responses to questions on the form are true to the best of the person's knowledge and an acknowledgment that a knowingly made false statement of material fact may be punished by a fine or imprisonment or both. Notarization of a completed form shall not be required.

(5) If a person summoned is unable to complete a juror eligibility form, another person may do it for the person summoned. Another person completing a form shall indicate on the form that the person did so and the reason therefor.

(6) If a person summoned fails to return a properly completed juror eligibility form as instructed, a judge of the circuit court may direct the person to appear forthwith and properly complete a form. If the person fails to appear as directed, a judge of the circuit court shall order the person to appear and show cause for that failure. If the person fails to appear pursuant to the order or appears and fails to show good cause, the person may be punished for contempt.

(7) Before or at the time a person summoned reports for jury service, a judge of the circuit court or clerk of court may question the person as to responses to questions on a completed jury eligibility form returned by the person and grounds for any ineligibility of the person to act as a juror. Any pertinent information so acquired shall be noted on the form.

(8) Review by a judge of the circuit court or clerk of court of a completed juror eligibility form returned by a person summoned satisfies the requirement prescribed in subsection (1) of this section that a person summoned be questioned. If a judge or clerk of court determines that a person is not eligible to act as a juror based on a completed form, the person shall be discharged. [1985 c.703 §16; 1995 c.781 §27]

10.250 [Amended by 1981 s.s. c.3 §50; repealed by 1985 c.703 §28]

10.255 Record of persons summoned to serve as jurors. The clerk of court shall cause to be prepared a record on all persons summoned to serve as jurors for a jury service term in a county, specifying:

(1) Those who did not attend.
(2) Those who were discharged for ineligibility to act as jurors.
(3) Those who were discharged for any other reason.
(4) Those whose jury service was deferred and the term to which jury service of each was deferred.
(5) Those who attended and were not discharged or deferred.
(6) The per diem fees and mileage due to each entitled thereto. [1985 c.703 §17]

10.260 [Repealed by 1985 c.703 §28]

10.265 Preservation of jury orders, records and papers. After the end of a jury service term in a county, all orders, records and papers prepared in connection with the selection and summoning of persons to serve as jurors for the term as provided in ORS 10.235 to 10.255 shall be preserved by the clerk of court for the period established by the State Court Administrator under ORS 8.125. [1985 c.703 §18; 1995 c.244 §6]

10.270 [Amended by 1967 c.532 §7; 1967 c.533 §17; repealed by 1985 c.703 §28]

10.275 Jury challenges; request for access to confidential jury records; order allowing disclosure; exclusive procedure. (1) A person challenging a jury panel under ORS 136.005 or ORCP 57 A who seeks jury records that are confidential under ORS 10.215 must include a request for access to the confidential records in the motion challenging the jury panel. The motion and supporting affidavit must be served on the trial court administrator and the State Court Administrator. The request must:

(a) Specify the purpose for which the jury records are sought; and

(b) Identify with particularity the relevant jury records sought to be released including the type and time period of the records.

(2) The court may order release of the jury records if the court finds that:

(a) The jury records sought are likely to produce evidence relevant to the motion; and

(b) Production of the jury records is not unduly burdensome.

(3) An order under subsection (2) of this section may include, but need not be limited to:

(a) A requirement that the moving party provide advance payment to the trial court administrator and, if applicable, the State Court Administrator for the reasonable costs of providing copies of the jury records; and

(b) Restrictions on further disclosure of the jury records including, but not limited to:

(A) A requirement that the moving party return all originals and copies to the court at the conclusion of the proceeding;

(B) A requirement that the jury records may be used only for the purpose of supporting the jury panel challenge made in the motion;

(C) A prohibition against distributing the jury records to a person who is not an agent or representative of the moving party; and

(D) A prohibition against contacting or attempting to contact the persons whose names appear on the jury records without specific authorization of the court.

(4) The trial court administrator or the State Court Administrator may intervene at any time as a matter of right as to any issues relating to the release of jury records under this section.

(5) The procedure established by this section is the exclusive means for compelling production of confidential jury records as evidence relevant to a challenge to a jury panel under ORS 136.005 or ORCP 57 A. The procedure established by ORS 138.585 is the exclusive means for compelling production of confidential jury records as evidence in post-conviction relief proceedings under ORS 138.510 to 138.680. [2001 c.779 §16; 2011 c.308 §4]

10.280 [Repealed by 1985 c.703 §28]

10.290 [Amended by 1965 c.387 §2; repealed by 1975 c.342 §1]

10.300 [Amended by 1963 c.519 §4; 1973 c.836 §314; repealed by 1985 c.703 §28]

10.310 [Repealed by 1985 c.703 §28]

10.320 [Amended by 1979 c.728 §4; 1981 s.s. c.3 §51; repealed by 1985 c.703 §28]

10.330 [Amended by 1981 s.s. c.3 §52; repealed by 1985 c.703 §28]

10.340 [Amended by 1963 c.519 §5; repealed by 1975 c.342 §1]

10.350 [Repealed by 1975 c.342 §1]

10.400 [1975 c.342 §3; 1977 c.631 §3; 1981 s.s. c.3 §53; repealed by 1985 c.703 §28]

10.410 [1975 c.342 §4; 1977 c.631 §4; 1981 s.s. c.3 §54; repealed by 1985 c.703 §28]

10.420 [1975 c.342 §5; 1977 c.631 §5; repealed by 1985 c.703 §28]

10.430 [1975 c.342 §6; 1977 c.631 §6; 1981 s.s. c.3 §55; repealed by 1985 c.703 §28]

10.440 [1975 c.342 §7; 1977 c.631 §7; 1981 s.s. c.3 §56; repealed by 1985 c.703 §28]

10.450 [1975 c.342 §8; 1977 c.631 §8; 1981 s.s. c.3 §57; repealed by 1985 c.703 §28]

10.460 [1975 c.342 §9; 1977 c.631 §9; 1981 s.s. c.3 §58; repealed by 1985 c.703 §28]

10.470 [1975 c.342 §10; 1977 c.631 §10; repealed by 1985 c.703 §28]

10.480 [1975 c.342 §11; 1977 c.631 §11; 1981 s.s. c.3 §59; repealed by 1985 c.703 §28]

10.490 [1975 c.342 §12; repealed by 1981 s.s. c.3 §141]

JURY OF INQUEST

10.810 Definition. A jury of inquest is a body of six persons, legally qualified to serve as jurors, summoned from the inhabitants of a particular district before the district attorney, sheriff or other ministerial officer, to inquire of particular facts. [Formerly 146.010; 1965 c.221 §9]

10.820 Number of jurors required to concur. The verdict of a jury of inquest is sufficient if two-thirds of the jurors concur therein. [Formerly 146.020]

PENALTIES

10.990 Penalties. (1) Violation of ORS 10.080 is a Class B violation.

(2) If a person summoned to serve as a juror in a circuit court fails to attend as required, the court shall order the person to appear forthwith and show cause for that failure. If the person fails to appear pursuant to the order or appears and fails to show good cause, the person may be punished for contempt.

(3) A juror summoned to a court who fails to give attention in court, or who leaves without permission while the court is in session or otherwise fails to complete required jury service without permission, may be punished for contempt of the court. [Amended by 1985 c.703 §19; 1999 c.1051 §144]

10.992 [1975 c.160 §2; 1999 c.1051 §145; repealed by 2011 c.118 §5]

_____

Chapter 11 (Former Provisions)

Forms of Actions and Suits

FORMS OF ACTIONS AND SUITS

COURTS OF RECORD; COURT OFFICERS; JURIES

11.010 [Repealed by 1979 c.284 §199]

11.020 [Repealed by 1979 c.284 §199]

11.030 [Renumbered 30.715]

11.040 [Repealed by 1973 c.85 §3]

11.050 [1973 c.85 §1; repealed by 1979 c.284 §199]

11.060 [1973 c.85 §2; repealed by 1979 c.284 §199]

———————————

TITLE 2 PROCEDURE IN CIVIL PROCEEDINGS

Chapter 12. Limitations of Actions and Suits
14. Jurisdiction; Venue; Change of Judge
15. Choice of Laws
17. Compromise; Settlement
18. Judgments
19. Appeals
20. Attorney Fees; Costs and Disbursements
21. State Court Fees
22. Bonds and Other Security Deposits
24. Enforcement and Recognition of Foreign Judgments; Foreign-Money Claims
25. Support Enforcement

———————————

Chapter 12 — Limitations of Actions and Suits

2017 EDITION

LIMITATIONS OF ACTIONS AND SUITS

PROCEDURE IN CIVIL PROCEEDINGS

GENERAL PROVISIONS

12.010 Time of commencing actions

12.020 When action deemed begun

12.040 Limitations of suits generally; land patent suits; defense of possession by equitable title; suit on new promise, fraud or mistake

12.050 Action to recover real property

12.060 Suit or action on land contracts; time when they cease to affect the property

12.070 Action on judgment, decree or sealed instrument

12.080 Action on certain contracts or liabilities

12.085 Action against garnishee

12.090 Accounts; accrual of cause of action

12.100 Action on official act or penalty

12.110 Actions for certain injuries to person not arising on contract; action for overtime or premium pay; action for professional malpractice; effect of fraud or deceit; action for injuries to person arising from nuclear incident

12.115 Action for negligent injury to person or property

12.117 Actions based on child abuse

12.120 Action on escape; action for defamation

12.125 Action arising under rental agreement

12.130 Action for penalty

12.132 Action arising out of real estate appraisal activity

12.135 Action for damages from construction, alteration or repair of improvement to real property; "substantial completion" defined; application

12.137   Action for loss of or damage to property arising from nuclear incident

12.140   Actions not otherwise provided for

12.150   Suspension of running of statute by absence or concealment

12.155   Effect of notice of advance payment on running of period of limitation

12.160   Suspension for minors and persons who have disabling mental condition

12.170   Disability must exist when right of action accrues

12.180   Coexisting disabilities must all be removed

12.190   Effect of death on limitations

12.195   Effect of attorney death on limitations

12.200   Suspension by war as to alien

12.210   Suspension by injunction or prohibition of statute

12.220   Commencement of new action after involuntary dismissal

12.230   Acknowledgment or promise taking contract case out of statute; effect of payment

12.240   Effect of payment after obligation becomes due

12.250   Actions by state, county or public corporations

12.270   Conclusive presumption of validity of governmental subdivision boundary proceedings one year after effective date

12.272   Action based on pesticide application

12.274   Action against trustee of express trust

12.276   Action for death, injury or damage resulting from breast implants

12.278   Action against manufacturer of certain pickup trucks

12.280   Action based on practice of land surveying

12.282   Action against manufacturer of extendable equipment

UNIFORM CONFLICT OF LAWS-LIMITATIONS ACT

12.410   Definitions for ORS 12.410 to 12.480

12.420   Purpose

12.430   Claims based on law of other states; limitation period

12.440   Application of statutes and rules governing conflict of laws

12.450   When limitation period of another state not applicable

12.460   Claims to which statutes apply

12.470   Severability

12.480   Short title

GENERAL PROVISIONS

12.010 Time of commencing actions. Actions shall only be commenced within the periods prescribed in this chapter, after the cause of action shall have accrued, except where a different limitation is prescribed by statute. [Amended by 1979 c.284 §43]

12.020 When action deemed begun. (1) Except as provided in subsection (2) of this section, for the purpose of determining whether an action has been commenced within the time limited, an action shall be deemed commenced as to each defendant, when the complaint is filed, and the summons served on the defendant, or on a codefendant who is a joint contractor, or otherwise united in interest with the defendant.
(2) If the first publication of summons or other service of summons in an action occurs before the expiration of 60 days after the date on which the complaint in the action was filed, the action against each person of whom the court by such service has acquired jurisdiction shall be deemed to have been commenced upon the date on which the complaint in the action was filed. [Amended by 1973 c.731 §1]

12.030 [Repealed by 1973 c.731 §2]

12.040 Limitations of suits generally; land patent suits; defense of possession by equitable title; suit on new promise, fraud or mistake. (1) A suit shall only be commenced within the time limited to commence an action as provided in this chapter; and a suit for the determination of any right or claim to or interest in real property shall be deemed within the limitations provided for actions for the recovery of the possession of real property.

(2) No suit shall be maintained to set aside, cancel, annul or otherwise affect a patent to lands issued by the United States or this state, or to compel any person claiming or holding under such patent to convey the lands described therein, or any portion of them, to the plaintiff in such suit, or to hold the same in trust for, or to the use and benefit of such plaintiff, or on account of any matter, thing or transaction which was had, done, suffered or transpired prior to the date of such patent, unless such suit is commenced within 10 years from the date of such patent.

(3) This section shall not bar an equitable owner in possession of real property from defending possession by means of the equitable title; and in any action for the recovery of any real property, or the possession thereof, by any person or persons claiming or holding the legal title to the same under such patent against any person or persons in possession of such real property under any equitable title, or having in equity the right to the possession thereof as against the plaintiff in such action, such equitable right of possession may be pleaded by answer in such action, or set up by bill in equity to enjoin such action or execution upon any judgment rendered therein; and the right of such equitable owner to defend possession in such action, or by bill for injunction, shall not be barred by lapse of time while an action for the possession of such real property is not barred.

(4) In a suit upon a new promise, fraud or mistake, the limitation shall only be deemed to commence from the making of the new promise or the discovery of the fraud or mistake.

12.050 Action to recover real property. An action for the recovery of real property, or for the recovery of the possession thereof, shall be commenced within 10 years. No action shall be maintained for such recovery unless it appear that the plaintiff, an ancestor, predecessor, or grantor was seized or possessed of the premises in question within 10 years before the commencement of the action.

12.060 Suit or action on land contracts; time when they cease to affect the property. (1) Unless suit or action to enforce a contract for the sale of real property is instituted in the county in which the real property is situated within five years from the date of maturity of the final payment provided for in the contract, or from the date to which the final payment shall have been extended by agreement of record, the contract shall not thereafter be a lien, encumbrance, or cloud on the title of the property.

(2) When the purchase price fixed in the contract is payable in installments, the contract shall be deemed to mature on the date upon which the final payment would be payable if the minimum amount of the principal due on each installment had been paid as provided in the terms of the contract.

12.070 Action on judgment, decree or sealed instrument. (1) An action upon a judgment or decree of any court of the United States, or of any state or territory within the United States; or

(2) An action upon a sealed instrument entered into before August 13, 1965,

shall be commenced within 10 years. [Amended by 1965 c.502 §3]

12.080 Action on certain contracts or liabilities. (1) An action upon a contract or liability, express or implied, excepting those mentioned in ORS 12.070, 12.110 and 12.135 and except as otherwise provided in ORS 72.7250;

(2) An action upon a liability created by statute, other than a penalty or forfeiture, excepting those mentioned in ORS 12.110;

(3) An action for waste or trespass upon or for interference with or injury to any interest of another in real property, excepting those mentioned in ORS 12.050, 12.060, 12.135, 12.137 and 273.241; or

(4) An action for taking, detaining or injuring personal property, including an action for the specific recovery thereof, excepting an action mentioned in ORS 12.137;

shall be commenced within six years. [Amended by 1957 c.374 §3; 1961 c.726 §396; 1973 c.363 §1; 1983 c.437 §2; 1987 c.705 §3; 1991 c.968 §2]

12.085 Action against garnishee. (1) Except as provided in subsection (2) of this section, proceedings against a garnishee under ORS 18.775 to 18.782 must be commenced within one year after the delivery of the writ of garnishment.

(2) If the writ of garnishment is delivered to a person in the person's capacity as a personal representative of an estate, proceedings against the garnishee under ORS 18.775 to 18.782 must be commenced within one year after the entry of a judgment of final distribution for the estate. [1977 c.786 §3; 1981 c.883 §29; 2001 c.249 §66; 2003 c.85 §1; 2003 c.576 §279a]

12.090 Accounts; accrual of cause of action. In an action to recover a balance due upon an account, the cause of action shall be deemed to have accrued from the time of the last charge or payment proved in the account. Interest, financing and carrying charges shall not be deemed such a charge. [Amended by 1973 c.204 §1]

12.100 Action on official act or penalty. (1) An action against a sheriff or constable upon a liability incurred by the doing of an act in an official capacity and in virtue of the office of the sheriff or constable; or by the omission of an official duty, including the nonpayment of money collected upon an execution, but not including an action for an escape, shall be commenced within three years.

(2) An action upon a statute for penalty or forfeiture, where the action is given to the party aggrieved, or to such party and the state, excepting those actions mentioned in ORS 12.110, shall be commenced within three years. [Amended by 1957 c.374 §4; 1965 c.221 §10]

12.110 Actions for certain injuries to person not arising on contract; action for overtime or premium pay; action for professional malpractice; effect of fraud or deceit; action for injuries to person arising from nuclear incident. (1) An action for assault, battery, false imprisonment, or for any injury to the person or rights of another, not arising on contract, and not especially enumerated in this chapter, shall be commenced within two years; provided, that in an action at law based upon fraud or deceit, the limitation shall be deemed to commence only from the discovery of the fraud or deceit.

(2) An action upon a statute for a forfeiture or penalty to the state or county shall be commenced within two years.

(3) An action for overtime or premium pay or for penalties or liquidated damages for failure to pay overtime or premium pay shall be commenced within two years.

(4) An action to recover damages for injuries to the person arising from any medical, surgical or dental treatment, omission or operation shall be commenced within two years from the date when the injury is first discovered or in the exercise of reasonable care should have been discovered. However, notwithstanding the provisions of ORS 12.160, every such action shall be commenced within five years from the date of the treatment, omission or operation upon which the action is based or, if there has been no action commenced within five years because of fraud, deceit or misleading representation, then within two years from the date such fraud, deceit or misleading representation is discovered or in the exercise of reasonable care should have been discovered.

(5) An action, arising from a nuclear incident, as defined in 42 U.S.C. 2014(q), that involves the release of radioactive material, excluding releases from acts of war, that causes bodily injury, sickness or death, shall be commenced:

(a) Within two years from the time an injured person discovers or reasonably could have discovered the injury and the causal connection between the injury and the nuclear incident; or

(b) Within two years from any substantial change in the degree of injury to the person arising out of a nuclear incident. [Amended by 1957 c.374 §1; 1967 c.406 §1; 1969 c.642 §1; 1971 c.473 §1; 1975 c.796 §10a; 1981 c.149 §1; 1987 c.705 §4]

12.115 Action for negligent injury to person or property. (1) In no event shall any action for negligent injury to person or property of another be commenced more than 10 years from the date of the act or omission complained of.

(2) Nothing in this section shall be construed to extend any period of limitation otherwise established by law, including but not limited to the limitations established by ORS 12.110. [1967 c.406 §2]

12.117 Actions based on child abuse. (1) Notwithstanding ORS 12.110, 12.115 or 12.160, an action based on conduct that constitutes child abuse or conduct knowingly allowing, permitting or encouraging child abuse that occurs while the person is under 18 years of age must be commenced before the person attains 40 years of age, or if the person has not discovered the causal connection between the injury and the child abuse, nor in the exercise of reasonable care should have discovered the causal connection between the injury and the child abuse, not more than five years from the date the person discovers or in the exercise of reasonable care should have discovered the causal connection between the child abuse and the injury, whichever period is longer.

(2) As used in subsection (1) of this section, "child abuse" means any of the following:

(a) Intentional conduct by an adult that results in:

(A) Any physical injury to a child; or

(B) Any mental injury to a child which results in observable and substantial impairment of the child's mental or psychological ability to function caused by cruelty to the child, with due regard to the culture of the child;

(b) Rape of a child, which includes but is not limited to rape, sodomy, unlawful sexual penetration and incest, as those acts are defined in ORS chapter 163;

(c) Sexual abuse, as defined in ORS chapter 163, when the victim is a child; or

(d) Sexual exploitation of a child, including but not limited to:

(A) Conduct constituting violation of ORS 163.435 and any other conduct which allows, employs, authorizes, permits, induces or encourages a child to engage in the performing for people to observe or the photographing, filming, tape recording or other exhibition which, in whole or in part, depicts sexual conduct or contact; and

(B) Allowing, permitting, encouraging or hiring a child to engage in prostitution or commercial sexual solicitation, as defined in ORS chapter 167.

(3) Nothing in this section creates a new cause of action or enlarges any existing cause of action. [1989 c.643 §§2,3; 1991 c.386 §4; 1991 c.932 §1; 1993 c.18 §5; 1993 c.296 §1; 1993 c.622 §2; 2009 c.879 §1; 2011 c.151 §4; 2015 c.98 §2]

12.120 Action on escape; action for defamation. (1) An action against a sheriff or other officer for the escape of a prisoner arrested or imprisoned on civil process; or

(2) An action for libel or slander shall be commenced within one year. [Amended by 1957 c.374 §2]

12.125 Action arising under rental agreement. An action arising under a rental agreement or ORS chapter 90 shall be commenced within one year. [1973 c.559 §39]

12.130 Action for penalty. An action upon a statute for a penalty given in whole or in part to the person who will prosecute for the same, shall be commenced within one year after the commission of the offense; and if the action is not commenced within one year by a private party, it may be commenced within two years thereafter, in behalf of the state, by the district attorney of the county where the offense was committed or is triable.

12.132 Action arising out of real estate appraisal activity. (1) Except as provided in subsection (2) of this section, an action arising out of real estate appraisal activity, as defined in ORS 674.010, must be commenced before the earlier of:

(a) The applicable period of limitation otherwise established by law; or

(b) Six years after the date of the act or omission giving rise to the action.

(2) Subsection (1)(b) of this section does not apply to an action arising out of real estate appraisal activity based on fraud or misrepresentation. [2017 c.143 §1]

Note: 12.132 was enacted into law by the Legislative Assembly but was not added to or made a part of ORS chapter 12 or any series therein by legislative action. See Preface to Oregon Revised Statutes for further explanation.

12.133 [1983 c.589 §2; repealed by 1999 c.130 §1]

12.135 Action for damages from construction, alteration or repair of improvement to real property; "substantial completion" defined; application. (1) An action against a person by a plaintiff who is not a public body, whether in contract, tort or otherwise, arising from the person having performed the construction, alteration or repair of any improvement to real property or the supervision or inspection thereof, or from the person having furnished design, planning, surveying, architectural or engineering services for the improvement, must be commenced before the earliest of:

(a) The applicable period of limitation otherwise established by law;

(b) Ten years after substantial completion or abandonment of the construction, alteration or repair of a small commercial structure, as defined in ORS 701.005, a residential structure, as defined in ORS 701.005, or a large commercial structure, as defined in ORS 701.005, that is owned or maintained by a homeowners association, as defined in ORS 94.550, or that is owned or maintained by an association of unit owners, as defined in ORS 100.005; or

(c) Six years after substantial completion or abandonment of the construction, alteration or repair of a large commercial structure, as defined in ORS 701.005, other than a large commercial structure described in paragraph (b) of this subsection.

(2) An action against a person by a public body, whether in contract, tort or otherwise, arising from the person having performed the construction, alteration or repair of any improvement to real property or the supervision or inspection thereof, or from the person having furnished design, planning, surveying, architectural or engineering services for the improvement, must be commenced not more than 10 years after substantial completion or abandonment of such construction, alteration or repair of the improvement to real property.

(3)(a) Notwithstanding subsections (1) and (2) of this section, an action against a person registered to practice architecture under ORS 671.010 to 671.220, a person registered to practice landscape architecture under ORS 671.310 to 671.459 or a person registered to practice engineering under ORS 672.002 to 672.325 to recover damages for injury to a person, property or to any interest in property, including damages for delay or economic loss, regardless of legal theory, arising out of the construction, alteration or repair of any improvement to real property must be commenced before the earliest of:

(A) Two years after the date the injury or damage is first discovered or in the exercise of reasonable care should have been discovered;

(B) Ten years after substantial completion or abandonment of the construction, alteration or repair of a small commercial structure, as defined in ORS 701.005, a residential structure, as defined in ORS 701.005, or a large commercial structure, as defined in ORS 701.005, that is owned or maintained by a homeowners association, as defined in ORS 94.550, or that is owned or maintained by an association of unit owners, as defined in ORS 100.005; or

(C) Six years after substantial completion or abandonment of the construction, alteration or repair of a large commercial structure, as defined in ORS 701.005, other than a large commercial structure described in subparagraph (B) of this paragraph.

(b) This subsection applies to actions brought by any person or public body.

(4) For purposes of this section:

(a) "Public body" has the meaning given that term in ORS 174.109; and

(b) "Substantial completion" means the date when the contractee accepts in writing the construction, alteration or repair of the improvement to real property or any designated portion thereof as having reached that state of completion when it may be used or occupied for its intended purpose or, if there is no such written acceptance, the date of acceptance of the completed construction, alteration or repair of such improvement by the contractee.

(5) For purposes of this section, an improvement to real property is considered abandoned on the same date that the improvement is considered abandoned under ORS 87.045.

(6) This section:

(a) Applies to an action against a manufacturer, distributor, seller or lessor of a manufactured dwelling, as defined in ORS 446.003, or of a prefabricated structure, as defined in ORS 455.010; and

(b) Does not apply to actions against any person in actual possession and control of the improvement, as owner, tenant or otherwise, at the time such cause of action accrues. [1971 c.664 §§2,3,4; 1983 c.437 §1; 1991 c.968 §1; 2009 c.485 §3; 2009 c.715 §1; 2013 c.469 §1]

Note: Section 2, chapter 469, Oregon Laws 2013, provides:
Sec. 2. The amendments to ORS 12.135 by section 1 of this 2013 Act apply only to causes of action arising on or after the effective date of this 2013 Act [January 1, 2014]. [2013 c.469 §2]

12.137 Action for loss of or damage to property arising from nuclear incident. (1) An action, arising from a nuclear incident that involves the release of radioactive material, excluding releases from acts of war, that causes loss of or damage to property, or loss of use of property shall be commenced:
(a) Within two years from the time an injured person discovers or reasonably could have discovered the injury to property and the causal connection between the injury and the nuclear incident; or
(b) Within two years from any substantial change in the degree of injury to the property arising out of a nuclear incident.
(2) As used in this section, "nuclear incident" has the meaning given that term in 42 U.S.C. 2014(q).
(3) In no event shall any action under subsection (1) of this section or ORS 12.110 (5) be commenced more than 30 years from the date of the nuclear incident. [1987 c.705 §§1,2]

Note: 12.137 was enacted into law by the Legislative Assembly but was not added to or made a part of ORS chapter 12 or any series therein by legislative action. See Preface to Oregon Revised Statutes for further explanation.

12.140 Actions not otherwise provided for. An action for any cause not otherwise provided for shall be commenced within 10 years.

12.150 Suspension of running of statute by absence or concealment. If, when a cause of action accrues against any person, the person is out of the state and service cannot be made within the state or the person is concealed therein, such action may be commenced within the applicable period of limitation in this chapter after the return of the person into the state, or after the termination of the concealment of the person; and if, after a cause of action has accrued against a person, the person shall depart from and reside out of this state, or if the person is concealed therein, the time of the absence or concealment of the person shall not be deemed or taken as any part of the time limited for the commencement of such action. [Amended by 1973 c.206 §1; 1987 c.158 §4]

12.155 Effect of notice of advance payment on running of period of limitation. (1) If the person who makes an advance payment referred to in ORS 31.560 or 31.565 gives to each person entitled to recover damages for the death, injury or destruction, not later than 30 days after the date the first of such advance payments was made, written notice of the date of expiration of the period of limitation for the commencement of an action for damages set by the applicable statute of limitations, then the making of any such advance payment does not suspend the running of such period of limitation. The notice required by this subsection shall be in such form as the Director of the Department of Consumer and Business Services prescribes.
(2) If the notice required by subsection (1) of this section is not given, the time between the date the first advance payment was made and the date a notice is actually given of the date of expiration of the period of limitation for the commencement of an action for damages set by the applicable statute of limitations is not part of the period limited for commencement of the action by the statute of limitations. [1971 c.331 §5; 1981 c.892 §85b]

12.160 Suspension for minors and persons who have disabling mental condition. (1) Subject to subsection (2) of this section, if a person is entitled to bring an action mentioned in ORS 12.010 to 12.050, 12.070 to 12.250 or 12.276, and at the time the cause of action accrues the person is a child who is younger than 18 years of age, the statute of limitation for commencing the action is tolled for so long as the person is younger than 18 years of age.
(2) The time for commencing an action may not be extended under subsection (1) of this section for more than five years, or for more than one year after the person attains 18 years of age, whichever occurs first.
(3) Subject to subsection (4) of this section, if a person is entitled to bring an action mentioned in ORS 12.010 to 12.050, 12.070 to 12.250 or 12.276, and at the time the cause of action accrues the person has a disabling mental condition that bars the person from comprehending rights that the person is otherwise bound to know, the statute of limitation for commencing the action is tolled for so long as the person has a disabling mental condition that bars the person from comprehending rights that the person is otherwise bound to know.
(4) The time for commencing an action may not be extended under subsection (3) of this section for more than five years, or for more than one year after the person no longer has a disabling mental condition that bars the person from comprehending rights that the person is otherwise bound to know, whichever occurs first.
(5) If a child's cause of action is tolled under subsection (1) of this section, a cause of action for recovery of damages for medical expenses incurred by a parent, guardian or conservator of the child is tolled for the same period of time as the child's cause of action if the medical expenses resulted from the same wrongful conduct that is the basis of the child's cause of action. [Amended by 1973 c.827 §4; 1979 c.246 §1; 1983 c.762 §9; 1997 c.339 §1; 2007 c.285 §1; 2015 c.510 §1]

12.170 Disability must exist when right of action accrues. No person shall make use of a disability unless it existed when the right of action of the person accrued.

12.180 Coexisting disabilities must all be removed. When two or more disabilities coexist at the time the right of action accrues, the limitation shall not attach until all are removed.

12.190 Effect of death on limitations. (1) If a person entitled to bring an action dies before the expiration of the time limited for its commencement, an action may be commenced by the personal representative of the person after the expiration of that time, and within one year after the death of the person.
(2) If a person against whom an action may be brought dies before the expiration of the time limited for its commencement, an action may be commenced against the personal representative of the person after the expiration of that time, and within one year after the death of the person. [Amended by 1969 c.591 §268]

12.195 Effect of attorney death on limitations. Notwithstanding the time established by statute for the commencement of an action, a person must commence the action within 180 days after the death of an attorney for the person, or within the time established by statute for the commencement of the action, whichever is later, if:
(1) The attorney has agreed to represent the person in the action;
(2) The attorney-client relationship between the person and the attorney is confirmed in a writing prepared by the attorney or at the direction of the attorney; and
(3) The attorney dies before the expiration of the time allowed by statute for commencement of the action. [2005 c.457 §2]

Note: 12.195 was added to and made a part of ORS chapter 12 by legislative action but was not added to any smaller series therein. See Preface to Oregon Revised Statutes for further explanation.

12.200 Suspension by war as to alien. When a person is an alien subject or citizen of a country at war with the United States, the time of the continuance of the war shall not be a part of the period limited for the commencement of the action.

12.210 Suspension by injunction or prohibition of statute. When the commencement of an action is stayed by injunction or a statutory prohibition, the time of the continuance of the injunction or prohibition shall not be a part of the time limited for the commencement of the action.

12.220 Commencement of new action after involuntary dismissal. (1) Notwithstanding ORS 12.020, if an action is filed with a court within the time allowed by statute, and the action is involuntarily dismissed without prejudice on any ground not adjudicating the merits of the action, or is involuntarily dismissed with prejudice on the ground that the plaintiff failed to properly effect service of summons within the time allowed by ORS 12.020 and the statute of limitations for the action expired, the plaintiff may commence a new action based on the same claim or claims against a defendant in the original action if the defendant had actual notice of the filing of the original action not later than 60 days after the action was filed.

(2) If, pursuant to subsection (1) of this section, a new action is commenced in the manner provided by ORS 12.020 not later than 180 days after the judgment dismissing the original action is entered in the register of the court, the new action is not subject to dismissal by reason of not having been commenced within the time allowed by statute.

(3) A new action may be commenced only once under this section for the same claim or claims.

(4) All defenses that would have been available if the original action had been commenced within the time otherwise allowed by statute shall be available in a new action commenced under this section. [Amended by 1961 c.726 §397; 2003 c.296 §1]

12.230 Acknowledgment or promise taking contract case out of statute; effect of payment. No acknowledgment or promise shall be sufficient evidence of a new or continuing contract, whereby to take the case out of the operation of this chapter, unless the same is contained in some writing, signed by the party to be charged thereby; but this section shall not alter the effect of any payment of principal or interest.

12.240 Effect of payment after obligation becomes due. Whenever any payment of principal or interest is made after it has become due, upon an existing contract, whether it is a bill of exchange, promissory note, bond, or other evidence of indebtedness, the limitation shall commence from the time the last payment was made.

12.250 Actions by state, county or public corporations. Unless otherwise made applicable thereto, the limitations prescribed in this chapter shall not apply to actions brought in the name of the state, or any county, or other public corporation therein, or for its benefit.

12.260 [Repealed by 1987 c.536 §9]

12.270 Conclusive presumption of validity of governmental subdivision boundary proceedings one year after effective date. On September 13, 1975, any proceeding that establishes or alters the boundaries of a governmental subdivision previously or hereafter initiated and purported to be effected in accordance with applicable legal requirements shall be conclusively presumed valid for all purposes one year after the purported effective date of the action. No direct or collateral attack on the action may thereafter be commenced. This statute of limitations includes but is not limited to the following proceedings:

(1) Formations and change of organizations under ORS 198.705 to 198.955.
(2) Boundary changes under ORS 199.410 to 199.519.
(3) Consolidations under ORS 199.705 to 199.795.
(4) Incorporations under ORS 221.010 to 221.090.
(5) Annexations under ORS 222.111 to 222.180, 222.750 and 222.840 to 222.915.
(6) Consolidations under ORS 222.210 to 222.310.
(7) Withdrawals and transfers of territory under ORS 222.510 to 222.580.
(8) Mergers under ORS 222.610 to 222.710.
(9) Formations and changes under ORS chapter 261.
(10) Alterations, changes, mergers and consolidations under ORS 330.080 to 330.123, 330.505 to 330.780 (1989 Edition) and 335.490 to 335.505.
(11) Alterations, changes, mergers and consolidations under ORS chapter 333 commenced before July 1, 2003.
(12) Formations and boundary changes under ORS 341.025 to 341.125 and 341.565 to 341.575.
(13) Organizations and boundary changes under ORS 545.002 and 545.025 to 545.043, 545.051 to 545.105, 545.109, 545.123, 545.126 and 545.131.
(14) Formations and boundary alterations under ORS 547.005 to 547.060 and 547.250 to 547.260.
(15) Formations and organizations under ORS chapter 551. [1975 c.326 §2; 1991 c.167 §1; 1999 c.452 §29; 2003 c.226 §20; 2005 c.209 §1]

Note: 12.270 was enacted into law by the Legislative Assembly but was not added to or made a part of ORS chapter 12 by legislative action. See Preface to Oregon Revised Statutes for further explanation.

12.272 Action based on pesticide application. (1) Notwithstanding any other provision of this chapter, no action against a landowner, person for whom the pesticide was applied or pesticide operator arising out of the use or application of any pesticide shall be commenced unless the person commencing the action, within the time specified by ORS 634.172, files the report required by ORS 634.172 and mails or personally delivers true copies of that report to:

(a) The landowner or pesticide operator who is allegedly responsible for the loss; and
(b) The person for whom the pesticide was applied if that person is not the person commencing the action.
(2) For the purposes of this section:
(a) "Landowner" includes any person, firm, corporation, the state, any county within the state, or municipality, shown by records of the county to be the owner of land or having such land under contract for purchase.
(b) "Pesticide operator" has the meaning given in ORS 634.006. [1991 c.351 §3; 1995 c.96 §1]

12.274 Action against trustee of express trust. Notwithstanding any other provision of this chapter, an action against the trustee of an express trust, whether in contract, tort or otherwise, arising from any act or omission of the trustee constituting a breach of duty shall be commenced within six years from the date the act or omission is discovered or in the exercise of reasonable diligence should have been discovered. However, no such action shall be commenced more than 10 years from the date of the act or omission complained of, or two years from the termination of any fiduciary account established under the trust, whichever date is later. [1991 c.968 §4]

12.276 Action for death, injury or damage resulting from breast implants. (1) Notwithstanding ORS 12.110 (1) or 30.020, an action for death, injury or damage resulting from breast implants containing silicone, silica or silicon as a component must be commenced not later than two years after the date on which the plaintiff first discovered, or in the exercise of reasonable care should have discovered:

(a) The death or specific injury, disease or damage for which the plaintiff seeks recovery;
(b) The tortious nature of the act or omission of the defendant that gives rise to a claim for relief against the defendant; and
(c) All other elements required to establish plaintiff's claim for relief.
(2) Except as provided in subsections (3) and (4) of this section, an action for death, injury or damage resulting from breast implants containing silicone, silica or silicon as a component is not subject to ORS 12.110 (1) or 12.115 or any other statute of limitation or statute of ultimate repose in Oregon Revised Statutes.

(3) An action for death, injury or damage against a physician licensed pursuant to ORS chapter 677, or against a health care facility licensed under ORS chapter 441, resulting from breast implants containing silicone, silica or silicon as a component, remains subject to the limitations imposed by ORS 12.110 (4), 12.115, 30.020 and 30.075.

(4) An action for death, injury or damage against a person that supplied component parts or raw materials to manufacturers of breast implants containing silicone, silica or silicon as a component remains subject to the limitations imposed by ORS 12.110 (1), 12.115, 30.020 and 30.075 if:

(a) The person did not manufacture breast implants containing silicone, silica or silicon as a component at any time; and

(b) The person was not owned by and did not own a business that manufactured breast implants containing silicone, silica or silicon as a component at any time.

(5) For the purposes of subsection (1) of this section, an action for wrongful death must be commenced not later than two years after the earliest date that the discoveries required by subsection (1) of this section are made by any of the following persons:

(a) The decedent;

(b) The personal representative for the decedent; or

(c) Any person for whose benefit the action could be brought. [1993 c.259 §2; 2009 c.485 §4; 2011 c.9 §2]

12.278 Action against manufacturer of certain pickup trucks. (1) A civil action against a manufacturer of pickup trucks for injury or damage resulting from a fire caused by rupture of a sidesaddle gas tank in a vehicle collision, including any product liability action under ORS 30.900 to 30.920 and any action based on negligence, must be commenced not later than two years after the injury or damage occurs. A civil action against a manufacturer of pickup trucks for death resulting from a fire caused by rupture of a sidesaddle gas tank in a vehicle collision, including any product liability action under ORS 30.900 to 30.920 and any action based on negligence, must be commenced not later than three years after the death.

(2) A civil action against a manufacturer of pickup trucks for death, injury or damage resulting from a fire caused by rupture of a sidesaddle gas tank in a vehicle collision is not subject to ORS 12.115, 30.020, 30.905 or any other statute of limitation or statute of ultimate repose in Oregon Revised Statutes.

(3) For the purposes of this section, "sidesaddle gas tank" means a gas tank mounted outside of the side rails of the frame of a pickup truck. [1995 c.55 §2; 2009 c.485 §5]

12.280 Action based on practice of land surveying. Notwithstanding ORS 12.135 or any other statute of limitation, an action against a person for the practice of land surveying, as defined in ORS 672.005, to recover damages for injury to a person, property or to any interest in property, including damages for delay or economic loss, regardless of legal theory, arising out of the survey of real property must be commenced within two years after the date the injury or damage is first discovered or in the exercise of reasonable care should have been discovered. In no event may an action arising out of a survey be commenced more than 10 years after the date on which any map prepared by the land surveyor is filed under the provisions of ORS 209.250, or, if no map is filed, more than 10 years after the completion of work on the survey. [1995 c.310 §2; 2009 c.715 §2]

12.282 Action against manufacturer of extendable equipment. (1) A civil action against a manufacturer of extendable equipment for injury or other damage arising out of contact with power lines, including any product liability action under ORS 30.900 to 30.920 and any action based on negligence, must be commenced not later than two years after the injury or damage occurs. A civil action against a manufacturer of extendable equipment for death arising out of contact with power lines, including any product liability action under ORS 30.900 to 30.920 and any action based on negligence, must be commenced not later than three years after the death.

(2) A civil action against a manufacturer of extendable equipment for injury, death or other damage arising out of contact with power lines is not subject to ORS 12.115, 30.020 or 30.905 or any other statute of limitation or statute of ultimate repose in Oregon Revised Statutes.

(3) For purposes of this section, "extendable equipment" means cranes, truck-mounted cranes, truck-mounted booms, and any self-powered vehicle with booms or other extensions that can reach power lines from the ground. [1999 c.514 §1; 2009 c.485 §6]

Note: 12.282 was enacted into law by the Legislative Assembly but was not added to or made a part of ORS chapter 12 or any series therein by legislative action. See Preface to Oregon Revised Statutes for further explanation.

UNIFORM CONFLICT OF LAWS-LIMITATIONS ACT

12.410 Definitions for ORS 12.410 to 12.480. As used in ORS 12.410 to 12.480:

(1) "Claim" means a right of action that may be asserted in a civil action or proceeding and includes a right of action created by statute.

(2) "State" means a state, commonwealth, territory or possession of the United States, the District of Columbia, the Commonwealth of Puerto Rico, a foreign country or a political subdivision of any of them. [1987 c.536 §1]

Note: 12.410 to 12.480 were enacted into law by the Legislative Assembly but were not added to or made a part of ORS chapter 12 or any series therein by legislative action. See Preface to Oregon Revised Statutes for further explanation.

12.420 Purpose. ORS 12.410 to 12.480 shall be applied and construed to effectuate its general purpose to make uniform the law with respect to the subject of ORS 12.410 to 12.480 among states enacting it. [1987 c.536 §6]

Note: See note under 12.410.

12.430 Claims based on law of other states; limitation period. (1) Except as provided by ORS 12.450, if a claim is substantively based:

(a) Upon the law of one other state, the limitation period of that state applies; or

(b) Upon the law of more than one state, the limitation period of one of those states, chosen by the law of conflict of laws of this state, applies.

(2) The limitation period of this state applies to all other claims. [1987 c.536 §2]

Note: See note under 12.410.

12.440 Application of statutes and rules governing conflict of laws. If the statute of limitations of another state applies to the assertion of a claim in this state, the other state's relevant statutes and other rules of law governing tolling and accrual apply in computing the limitation period, but its statutes and other rules of law governing conflict of laws do not apply. [1987 c.536 §3]
Note: See note under 12.410.

12.450 When limitation period of another state not applicable. If the court determines that the limitation period of another state applicable under ORS 12.430 and 12.440 is substantially different from the limitation period of this state and has not afforded a fair opportunity to sue upon, or imposes an unfair burden in defending against the claim, the limitation period of this state applies. [1987 c.536 §4]

Note: See note under 12.410.

12.460 Claims to which statutes apply. ORS 12.410 to 12.480 apply to claims:

(1) Accruing after January 1, 1988; or

(2) Asserted in a civil action or proceeding more than one year after January 1, 1988, but it does not revive a claim barred before January 1, 1988. [1987 c.536 §5]

Note: See note under 12.410.

12.470 Severability. If any provision of ORS 12.410 to 12.480 or the application thereof to any person or circumstance is held invalid, the invalidity does not affect other provisions or applications of ORS 12.410 to 12.480 which can be given effect without the invalid provision or application, and to this end the provisions of ORS 12.410 to 12.480 are severable. [1987 c.536 §8]

Note: See note under 12.410.

12.480 Short title. ORS 12.410 to 12.480 may be cited as the Uniform Conflict of Laws-Limitations Act. [1987 c.536 §7]

Note: See note under 12.410.

————————————

Chapter 13 (Former Provisions) Parties; Class Actions

PARTIES; CLASS ACTIONS

PROCEDURE IN CIVIL PROCEEDINGS

13.010 [Repealed by 1979 c.284 §199]

13.020 [Amended by 1975 c.457 §1; repealed by 1979 c.284 §199]

13.030 [Repealed by 1979 c.284 §199]

13.040 [Repealed by 1961 c.344 §109]

13.041 [1961 c.344 §96; 1973 c.823 §85; repealed by 1979 c.284 §199]

13.050 [Repealed by 1961 c.344 §109]

13.051 [1961 c.344 §97; 1973 c.823 §86; repealed by 1979 c.284 §199]

13.060 [Repealed by 1979 c.284 §199]

13.070 [Repealed by 1979 c.284 §199]

13.080 [Amended by 1969 c.591 §269; 1975 c.108 §1; repealed by 1979 c.284 §199]

13.090 [Repealed by 1979 c.284 §199]

13.110 [Repealed by 1979 c.284 §199]

13.120 [Repealed by 1979 c.284 §199]

13.130 [Repealed by 1979 c.284 §199]

13.140 [Repealed by 1979 c.284 §199]

13.150 [Repealed by 1979 c.284 §199]

13.160 [Amended by 1975 c.158 §4; repealed by 1977 c.154 §1 (13.161 enacted in lieu of 13.160)]

13.161 [1977 c.154 §2 (enacted in lieu of 13.160); repealed by 1979 c.284 §199]

13.170 [Amended by 1973 c.349 §11; 1975 c.158 §5; repealed by 1979 c.284 §199]

13.180 [1975 c.623 §5; repealed by 1979 c.284 §199]

13.190 [1975 c.623 §13; repealed by 1979 c.284 §199]

13.210 [1973 c.349 §1; repealed by 1979 c.284 §199]

13.220 [1973 c.349 §2; repealed by 1979 c.284 §199]

13.230 [1973 c.349 §3; repealed by 1979 c.284 §199]

13.240 [1973 c.349 §8; repealed by 1979 c.284 §199]

13.250 [1973 c.349 §7; repealed by 1979 c.284 §199]

13.260 [1973 c.349 §4; repealed by 1979 c.284 §199]

13.270 [1973 c.349 §6; repealed by 1979 c.284 §199]

13.280 [1973 c.349 §12; repealed by 1979 c.284 §199]

13.290 [1973 c.349 §13; repealed by 1979 c.284 §199]

13.300 [1973 c.349 §14; repealed by 1979 c.284 §199]

13.310 [1973 c.349 §15; 1979 c.284 §44; renumbered 41.815]

13.320 [1973 c.349 §9; repealed by 1979 c.284 §199]

13.330 [1973 c.349 §§16, 17; 1974 s.s. c.29 §1; repealed by 1979 c.284 §199]

13.340 [1973 c.349 §18; repealed by 1979 c.284 §199]

13.350 [1973 c.349 §19; repealed by 1979 c.284 §199]

13.360 [1973 c.349 §20; repealed by 1979 c.284 §199]

13.370 [1973 c.349 §21; 1974 s.s. c.29 §2; 1979 c.284 §45; renumbered 1.004]

13.380 [1973 c.349 §5; repealed by 1979 c.284 §199]

13.390 [1973 c.349 §10; repealed by 1979 c.284 §199]

13.400 [1973 c.349 §22; 1979 c.284 §46; renumbered 19.015]

13.410 [1973 c.349 §23; 1979 c.284 §47; renumbered 19.013]

Chapter 14 —— Jurisdiction; Venue; Change of Judge

2017 EDITION

JURISDICTION; VENUE; CHANGE OF JUDGE

PROCEDURE IN CIVIL PROCEEDINGS

JURISDICTION AND VENUE

14.030   Jurisdiction as affected by place where cause of action or suit arises

14.040   Actions and suits that are to be brought where subject is situated

14.050   Actions that are to be brought where cause arose

14.060   Venue of suits against state departments and officials

14.080   Venue for other actions; residence of corporations and partnerships

CHANGE OF VENUE

14.110   When place of trial may be changed

14.120   Time of motion; to what county changed; number of changes

14.130   Notice to proper or more convenient court

14.160   When change of venue complete

TRANSFER OF PROCEEDING AGAINST PUBLIC BODY

14.165   Transfer of proceeding against public body; effect of transfer on statute of limitations; adoption of rules by Court of Appeals; filing fees

MOOTNESS

14.175   Acts, policies or practices of public body capable of repetition and likely to evade judicial review

DISQUALIFICATION OF JUDGE

14.210   Disqualification of judge for cause; application of section; waiver

14.250   Disqualification of judge; transfer of cause; making up issues

14.260   Affidavit and motion for change of judge; time for making; limit of two changes of judge

14.270   Time of making motion for change of judge in certain circumstances; limit of two changes of judge

14.275   Disqualification of appellate judge

14.010 [Amended by 1975 c.628 §1; repealed by 1979 c.284 §199]

14.020 [Repealed by 1979 c.284 §199]

14.030 Jurisdiction as affected by place where cause of action or suit arises. When the court has jurisdiction of the parties, it may exercise it in respect to any cause of action or suit wherever arising, except for the specific recovery of real property situated without this state, or for an injury thereto.

14.035 [1963 c.352 §1; 1975 c.628 §2; 1979 c.246 §2; repealed by 1979 c.246 §7]

14.040 Actions and suits that are to be brought where subject is situated. Actions and suits for the following causes shall be commenced and tried in the county in which the subject of the action or suit, or some part thereof, is situated:
(1) Actions for the recovery of real property, or an estate or interest therein, or for injuries to real property.
(2) Actions for the recovery of any personal property distrained for any cause.
(3) Suits for the partition of real property.
(4) Suits for the foreclosure of a lien or mortgage upon real property.
(5) Suits for the determination of an adverse claim, estate, or interest in real property, or the specific performance of an agreement in relation thereto. [Amended by 1997 c.249 §12]

14.050 Actions that are to be brought where cause arose. Actions for the following causes shall be commenced and tried in the county where the cause, or some part thereof, arose:
(1) For the recovery of a penalty or forfeiture imposed by statute, except that when it is imposed for an offense committed on a lake, river or other stream of water, situated in two or more counties, the action may be commenced and tried in any county bordering on such lake, river or stream, and opposite the place where the offense was committed;
(2) Against a public officer or person specially appointed to execute the duties of the public officer for an act done by the officer or person in virtue of the office of the public officer; or against a person who, by the command of the public officer, or in aid of the public officer, shall do anything touching the duties of such officer.

14.060 Venue of suits against state departments and officials. Any suit against any department, official, officer, commissioner, commission or board of the state, as such, or in virtue of such status, other than a suit for the causes enumerated in ORS 14.040, may be brought in the county wherein the cause of suit, or some part thereof, arose.

14.070 [Amended by 1987 c.331 §1; 1995 c.637 §10; 1995 c.666 §10; 1999 c.738 §5; 2003 c.264 §5; repealed by 2003 c.289 §§8,8a]

14.080 Venue for other actions; residence of corporations and partnerships. (1) All other actions shall be commenced in the county in which the defendants, or one of them, reside at the commencement of the action or in the county where the cause of action arose. A party resident of more than one county shall be deemed a resident of each such county. If none of the defendants reside in this state the action may be commenced in any county.
(2) For purposes of this section, a corporation incorporated under the laws of this state, a limited partnership or a foreign corporation authorized to do business in this state shall be deemed to be a resident of any county where the corporation or limited partnership conducts regular, sustained business activity or has an office for the transaction of business or where any agent authorized to receive process resides. A foreign corporation or foreign limited partnership not authorized to transact business in this state shall be deemed not to be a resident of any county in this state.
(3) For purposes of this section, a partnership or other unincorporated association subject to being sued in its own name shall be deemed a resident of any county where any person resides upon whom summons could be served for service upon the partnership or unincorporated association. [Amended by 1983 c.163 §1]

CHANGE OF VENUE

14.110 When place of trial may be changed. (1) The court or judge thereof may change the place of trial, on the motion of either party to an action or suit, when it appears from the affidavit of such party that the motion is not made for the purpose of delay and:
(a) That the action or suit has not been commenced in the proper county;
(b) That the judge is a party to, or directly interested in the event of the action or suit, or connected by consanguinity or affinity within the third degree, with the adverse party or those for whom the adverse party prosecutes or defends;
(c) That the convenience of witnesses and the parties would be promoted by such change; or
(d) In an action, that the judge or the inhabitants of the county are so prejudiced against the party making the motion that the party cannot expect an impartial trial before the judge or in the county, as the case may be.
(2) When the moving party in an action is a nonresident of the county, the affidavit required under this section may be made by anyone on behalf of the moving party. [Amended by 2003 c.14 §15]

14.120 Time of motion; to what county changed; number of changes. The motion for a change of the place of trial may be made and allowed any time after the commencement of the action or suit and before the beginning of trial, except that, if the change sought is pursuant to the provisions of ORS 14.110 (1)(a), the motion must be made before filing of the answer. If the motion is allowed, the change shall be made to the county where the action or suit ought to have been commenced, if it is for the cause mentioned in ORS 14.110 (1)(a), and in other cases to the most convenient county where the cause assigned as the reason for the change does not exist. Neither party shall be entitled to more than one change of the place of trial, except for causes not in existence when the first change was allowed. [Amended by 1963 c.339 §1]

14.130 Notice to proper or more convenient court. When the place of trial has been changed as provided in ORS 14.110, the clerk shall promptly notify the clerk of the proper or more convenient court of the change. [Amended by 2017 c.252 §8]

14.140 [Amended by 1963 c.339 §2; repealed by 2017 c.252 §10]

14.150 [Repealed by 2017 c.252 §10]

14.160 When change of venue complete. A change of venue is complete upon entry of an order changing the place of trial, and thereafter the action shall proceed as though it had been commenced in the proper or more convenient court. [Amended by 2017 c.252 §9]

TRANSFER OF PROCEEDING AGAINST PUBLIC BODY

14.165 Transfer of proceeding against public body; effect of transfer on statute of limitations; adoption of rules by Court of Appeals; filing fees. (1) If an action or other proceeding against a public body is filed in circuit court and the circuit court does not have authority to decide the case, the circuit court shall:
(a) Transfer the case to the court or tribunal authorized by law to decide the case if the circuit court determines that another court or tribunal is authorized by law to decide the case;
(b) Refer the question to the Court of Appeals if the circuit court is in doubt whether there is another court or tribunal authorized by law to decide the case; or

(c) Dismiss the action or proceeding if the circuit court determines that no other court or tribunal is authorized by law to decide the case.

(2) If an action or other proceeding against a public body is filed in the Court of Appeals and the Court of Appeals does not have authority to decide the case, the Court of Appeals shall:

(a) Transfer the case to the court or tribunal authorized by law to decide the case if the Court of Appeals determines that another court or tribunal is authorized by law to decide the case; or

(b) Dismiss the action or proceeding if the Court of Appeals determines that no other court or tribunal is authorized by law to decide the case.

(3) If a case is transferred by the circuit court under this section to a court or tribunal other than the Court of Appeals, and the court or tribunal determines, on its own motion or on the motion of a party, that the court or tribunal is not authorized by law to decide the case, the court or tribunal shall refer the question to the Court of Appeals.

(4) The Court of Appeals shall adopt rules for the referral of questions to the Court of Appeals under this section. The rules shall provide opportunity for the parties to address the question, but shall provide the Court of Appeals with the means to reach an expeditious and summary determination of the question.

(5) Upon referral of a question to the Court of Appeals under this section, the Court of Appeals shall:

(a) Transfer the case to the court or tribunal that the Court of Appeals determines to be authorized by law to decide the case;

(b) Decide the case if the Court of Appeals is the appropriate court; or

(c) Dismiss the action or proceeding if the Court of Appeals determines that no court or tribunal is authorized by law to decide the case.

(6) If an action or proceeding against a public body is transferred under this section, and the action or proceeding was filed in the transferring court within the time allowed by law for filing the action or proceeding in the receiving court or tribunal, the case may not be dismissed as not being filed within the time allowed by law.

(7) If an action or proceeding against a public body is filed in circuit court or the Court of Appeals based on a reasonable interpretation of law, and the circuit court or the Court of Appeals determines that the case should be transferred under this section, the case shall be transferred to the appropriate court or tribunal in the manner provided by this section and may not be dismissed as not being filed within the time allowed by law if:

(a) Under the interpretation of law made by the person filing the action or proceeding, the action or proceeding was filed in the proper court;

(b) Under the interpretation of law made by the person filing the action or proceeding, the action or proceeding was timely filed in the transferring court; and

(c) Any delay caused by the failure to file the action or proceeding within the time allowed for filing in the receiving court or tribunal does not substantially prejudice an adverse interest or public interest.

(8) If an order to transfer is entered under this section, the transferring court shall send a copy of the order to each party to the action or proceeding. Within 10 days after the entry of the transfer order, the person who filed the action or proceeding must file a copy of the transfer order in the receiving court or tribunal and, subject to any provision for waiver or deferral of fees, pay to the receiving court or tribunal any filing fees charged by that court or tribunal. Within such time as may be allowed by the receiving court or tribunal, the person must then comply with such additional pleading and service requirements as may be imposed by the receiving court or tribunal. The person filing the action or proceeding is not entitled to a refund of any filing fees paid to the transferring court.

(9) The provisions of this section do not apply to any action or proceeding that is subject to the provisions of ORS 34.102.

(10) As used in this section:

(a) "Public body" has the meaning given in ORS 192.311.

(b) "Tribunal" means a public body authorized by law to review decisions of another public body. [2001 c.561 §1]

14.170 [Amended by 1971 c.298 §1; repealed by 1981 s.s. c.3 §141]

MOOTNESS

14.175 Acts, policies or practices of public body capable of repetition and likely to evade judicial review. In any action in which a party alleges that an act, policy or practice of a public body, as defined in ORS 174.109, or of any officer, employee or agent of a public body, as defined in ORS 174.109, is unconstitutional or is otherwise contrary to law, the party may continue to prosecute the action and the court may issue a judgment on the validity of the challenged act, policy or practice even though the specific act, policy or practice giving rise to the action no longer has a practical effect on the party if the court determines that:

(1) The party had standing to commence the action;

(2) The act challenged by the party is capable of repetition, or the policy or practice challenged by the party continues in effect; and

(3) The challenged policy or practice, or similar acts, are likely to evade judicial review in the future. [2007 c.770 §1]

DISQUALIFICATION OF JUDGE

14.210 Disqualification of judge for cause; application of section; waiver. (1) A judge shall not act as such in a court of which the judge is a member in any of the following circumstances:

(a) The judge shall not act as judge if the judge is a party to or directly interested in the action, suit or proceeding, except that the judge shall not be disqualified from acting as such in a case in which the judge is added as a party after taking any official action as a judge in the action, suit or proceeding, and in that case the judge shall be dismissed as a party without prejudice.

(b) Except as provided in ORS 2.111 and 2.570, a judge shall not act as judge if the judge was not present and sitting as a member of the court at the hearing of a matter submitted for its decision. A judge may sign an order or judgment reflecting a decision made by another judge if, for good cause, the judge who made the decision is not available.

(c) A judge shall not act as judge if the judge is related to any party, or to the attorney for any party, or to the partner or office associate of any such attorney, by consanguinity or affinity within the third degree.

(d) A judge shall not act as judge if the judge has been attorney in the action, suit or proceeding for any party.

(e) If appeal is made from a decision of another court, or judicial review of a decision of an administrative agency is sought, a judge shall not act as judge on appeal if the judge participated in making the decision that is subject to review.

(2) This section does not apply to an application to change the place of trial, or the regulation of the order of business in court. In the circumstances specified in subsection (1)(c) and (d) of this section, the disqualification shall be deemed waived by the parties unless a motion for disqualification of the judge is made as provided by statute or court rule. [Amended by 1983 c.763 §59; 1999 c.659 §3]

14.220 [Repealed by 1955 c.408 §2]

14.230 [Repealed by 1955 c.408 §2]

14.240 [Repealed by 1955 c.408 §2]

14.250 Disqualification of judge; transfer of cause; making up issues. No judge of a circuit court shall sit to hear or try any suit, action, matter or proceeding when it is established, as provided in ORS 14.250 to 14.270, that any party or attorney believes that such party or attorney cannot have a fair and impartial trial or hearing before such judge. In such case the presiding judge for the judicial district shall forthwith transfer the cause, matter or proceeding to another judge of the court, or apply to the Chief Justice of the Supreme Court to send a judge to try it; or, if the convenience of witnesses or the ends of justice will not be interfered with by such course, and the action or suit is of such a character that a change of venue thereof may be ordered, the presiding judge may send the case for trial to the most convenient court; except that the issues in such cause may, upon the written stipulation of the attorneys in the cause agreeing thereto, be made up in the district of the judge to whom the cause has been assigned. [1955 c.408 §1(1); 1981 c.215 §5; 1987 c.338 §1; 1995 c.781 §28]

14.260 Affidavit and motion for change of judge; time for making; limit of two changes of judge. (1) Any party to or any attorney appearing in any cause, matter or proceeding in a circuit court may establish the belief described in ORS 14.250 by motion supported by affidavit that the party or attorney believes that the party or attorney cannot have a fair and impartial trial or hearing before the judge, and that it is made in good faith and not for the purpose of delay. No specific grounds for the belief need be alleged. The motion shall be allowed unless the judge moved against, or the presiding judge for the judicial district, challenges the good faith of the affiant and sets forth the basis of the challenge. In the event of a challenge, a hearing shall be held before a disinterested judge. The burden of proof is on the challenging judge to establish that the motion was made in bad faith or for the purposes of delay.

(2) The affidavit shall be filed with the motion at any time prior to final determination of the cause, matter or proceedings in uncontested cases, and in contested cases before or within five days after the cause, matter or proceeding is at issue upon a question of fact or within 10 days after the assignment, appointment and qualification or election and assumption of office of another judge to preside over the cause, matter or proceeding.

(3) A motion to disqualify a judge may not be made after the judge has ruled upon any petition, demurrer or motion other than a motion to extend time in the cause, matter or proceeding. A motion to disqualify a judge or a judge pro tem, assigned by the Chief Justice of the Supreme Court to serve in a county other than the county in which the judge or judge pro tem resides may not be filed more than five days after the party or attorney appearing in the cause receives notice of the assignment.

(4) In judicial districts having a population of 200,000 or more, the affidavit and motion for change of judge shall be made at the time and in the manner prescribed in ORS 14.270.

(5) In judicial districts having a population of 100,000 or more, but less than 200,000, the affidavit and motion for change of judge shall be made at the time and in the manner prescribed in ORS 14.270 unless the circuit court makes local rules under ORS 3.220 adopting the procedure described in this section.

(6) A party or attorney may not make more than two applications in any cause, matter or proceeding under this section. [1955 c.408 §1(2); 1959 c.667 §1; 1981 c.215 §6; 1987 c.338 §2; 1995 c.781 §29; 2015 c.272 §1]

14.270 Time of making motion for change of judge in certain circumstances; limit of two changes of judge. An affidavit and motion for change of judge to hear the motions and demurrers or to try the case shall be made at the time of the assignment of the case to a judge for trial or for hearing upon a motion or demurrer. Oral notice of the intention to file the motion and affidavit shall be sufficient compliance with this section providing that the motion and affidavit are filed not later than the close of the next judicial day. No motion to disqualify a judge to whom a case has been assigned for trial shall be made after the judge has ruled upon any petition, demurrer or motion other than a motion to extend time in the cause, matter or proceeding; except that when a presiding judge assigns to the presiding judge any cause, matter or proceeding in which the presiding judge has previously ruled upon such petition, motion or demurrer, any party or attorney appearing in the cause, matter or proceeding may move to disqualify the judge after assignment of the case and prior to any ruling on any such petition, motion or demurrer heard after such assignment. No party or attorney shall be permitted to make more than two applications in any action or proceeding under this section. [1955 c.408 §1(3); 1959 c.667 §2; 1969 c.144 §1; 1981 c.215 §7; 1995 c.781 §30]

14.275 Disqualification of appellate judge. A party or an attorney for a party in a cause before the Supreme Court or Court of Appeals may move to disqualify a judge of the Supreme Court or of the Court of Appeals for one or more of the grounds specified in ORS 14.210, or upon the ground that the judge's participation in the cause would violate the Oregon Code of Judicial Conduct. [1999 c.659 §4]

————————

Chapter 15 — Choice of Laws

2017 EDITION

CHOICE OF LAWS

PROCEDURE IN CIVIL PROCEEDINGS

CHOICE OF LAW FOR CONTRACTS

(Generally)

15.300   Definitions for ORS 15.300 to 15.380

15.305   Applicability

(Contracts Governed by Oregon Law)

15.320   Specific types of contracts governed by Oregon law

15.325   Validity of form

15.330   Capacity to contract

15.335   Consent

(Choice of Law Made by Parties)

15.350   Choice of law made by parties

15.355   Limitations on choice of law by parties

15.360   General rule

(Presumptive Rules)

15.380   Presumptive rules for specific types of contracts

CHOICE OF LAW FOR TORTS AND OTHER NONCONTRACTUAL CLAIMS

(Generally)

15.400   Definitions for ORS 15.400 to 15.460

15.405   Applicability

(Preliminary Issues)

15.410   Characterization

15.415   Localization and other factual determinations

15.420   Determining domicile

(Claims Governed by Oregon Law)

15.430   Claims governed by Oregon law

15.435   Product liability civil actions

(Choice of Law)

15.440   General rules

15.445   General and residual approach

15.450   Joint tortfeasors and third parties

15.455   Agreements on applicable foreign law

15.460   Commentary

15.010 [Repealed by 1979 c.284 §199]

15.020 [Amended by 1977 c.877 §2; repealed by 1979 c.284 §199]

15.030 [Repealed by 1979 c.284 §199]

15.040 [Amended by 1963 c.310 §1; 1967 c.297 §1; 1969 c.181 §1; 1971 c.192 §1; 1977 c.877 §3; repealed by 1979 c.284 §199]

15.050 [Repealed by 1969 c.181 §2]

15.060 [Amended by 1955 c.165 §1; 1973 c.827 §5; 1977 c.877 §4; repealed by 1979 c.284 §199]

15.070 [Repealed by 1979 c.284 §199]

15.080 [Amended by 1961 c.344 §98; 1963 c.310 §2; 1967 c.581 §1; 1973 c.823 §87; 1975 c.604 §1; 1977 c.877 §5; repealed by 1979 c.284 §199]

15.085 [1963 c.445 §2; 1969 c.597 §257; 1971 c.779 §1; repealed by 1979 c.284 §199]

15.090 [Repealed by 1979 c.284 §199]

15.100 [Renumbered 18.135]

15.110 [Amended by 1955 c.293 §1; 1973 c.827 §6; 1977 c.877 §6; repealed by 1979 c.284 §199]

15.120 [Repealed by 1979 c.284 §199]

15.130 [Amended by 1955 c.70 §1; 1965 c.329 §1; 1973 c.529 §1; repealed by 1979 c.284 §199]

15.140 [Repealed by 1979 c.284 §199]

15.150 [Repealed by 1979 c.284 §199]

15.160 [Amended by 1961 c.353 §1; 1977 c.877 §7; repealed by 1979 c.284 §199]

15.170 [Repealed by 1979 c.284 §199]

15.180 [Repealed by 1979 c.284 §199]

15.190 [Amended by 1955 c.287 §15; subsection (5) of 1955 part derived from 1955 c.287 §§33, 34; 1959 c.440 §1; 1967 c.410 §1; 1969 c.389 §1; 1973 c.60 §1; 1977 c.877 §8; repealed by 1979 c.284 §199]

15.200 [Amended by 1955 c.287 §16; subsection (3) of 1955 part derived from 1955 c.287 §§33, 34; 1959 c.440 §2; 1961 c.146 §1; repealed by 1979 c.284 §199]

15.210 [1975 c.623 §7; repealed by 1979 c.284 §199]

15.220 [1975 c.623 §8; repealed by 1979 c.284 §199]

CHOICE OF LAW FOR CONTRACTS

(Generally)

15.300 Definitions for ORS 15.300 to 15.380. For the purposes of ORS 15.300 to 15.380:
(1) "Law" means any rule of general legal applicability adopted by a state, whether that rule is domestic or foreign and whether derived from international law, a constitution, statute, other publicly adopted measure or published judicial precedent. Except for references to the law of Oregon, "law" does not include rules governing choice of law.
(2) "State" means the United States, any state of the United States, any territory, possession or other jurisdiction of the United States, any Indian tribe, other Native American group or Native Hawaiian group that is recognized by federal law or formally acknowledged by a state of the United States, and any foreign country, including any territorial subdivision or other entity with its own system of laws. [Formerly 81.100]

15.305 Applicability. ORS 15.300 to 15.380 govern the choice of law applicable to any contract, or part of a contract, when a choice between the laws of different states is at issue. ORS 15.300 to 15.380 do not apply if another Oregon statute expressly designates the law applicable to the contract or part of a contract. ORS 15.320 does not apply to any contract in which one of the parties is a financial institution, as defined by 15 U.S.C. 6827, as in effect on January 1, 2002. [Formerly 81.102]

(Contracts Governed by Oregon Law)

15.320 Specific types of contracts governed by Oregon law. Notwithstanding any other provision of ORS 15.300 to 15.380, but subject to the limitations on applicability imposed by ORS 15.305, the law of Oregon applies to the following contracts:
(1) A contract for services to be rendered in Oregon, or for goods to be delivered in Oregon, if Oregon or any of its agencies or subdivisions is a party to the contract. The application of Oregon's law pursuant to this subsection may be waived by a person authorized by Oregon's law to make the waiver.
(2) A contract for construction work to be performed primarily in Oregon.
(3) A contract of employment for services to be rendered primarily in Oregon by a resident of Oregon.
(4)(a) A consumer contract, if:
(A) The consumer is a resident of Oregon at the time of contracting; and
(B) The consumer's assent to the contract is obtained in Oregon, or the consumer is induced to enter into the contract in substantial measure by an invitation or advertisement in Oregon.
(b) For the purposes of this subsection, a consumer contract is a contract for the supply of goods or services that are designed primarily for personal, familial or household use. [Formerly 81.105]

15.325 Validity of form. A contract is valid as to form if the contract meets the requirements prescribed either by the law chosen by the parties under ORS 15.350 and 15.355, the law applicable under ORS 15.320, 15.360 or 15.380, or the law of the state from which any party or the party's agent has assented to the contract unless that state has no other connection to the parties or the transaction. [Formerly 81.110]

15.330 Capacity to contract. (1) A party has the capacity to enter into a contract if the party has that capacity under the law of the state in which the party resides or the law applicable to this issue under ORS 15.320, 15.360 or 15.380.
(2) A party that lacks capacity to enter into a contract under the law of the state in which the party resides may assert that incapacity against a party that knew or should have known of the incapacity at the time the parties entered into the contract. If a party establishes lack of capacity in the manner provided by this subsection, the consequences of the party's incapacity are governed by the law of the state in which the incapable party resides. [Formerly 81.112]

15.335 Consent. (1) A party has consented to a contract if the law applicable under ORS 15.320, 15.360 or 15.380 so provides.
(2) In a consumer contract or employment contract, the consumer or employee whose assent to a contract was obtained in the state of the party's residence, or whose conduct leading to the contract was primarily confined to that state, may invoke the law of that state to establish that the party did not consent to the contract or that the consent was not valid by reason of fraud or duress. [Formerly 81.115]

(Choice of Law Made by Parties)

15.350 Choice of law made by parties. (1) Except as specifically provided by ORS 15.320, 15.325, 15.330, 15.335 or 15.355, the contractual rights and duties of the parties are governed by the law or laws that the parties have chosen. The choice of law may extend to the entire contract or to part of a contract.
(2) The choice of law must be express or clearly demonstrated from the terms of the contract. In a standard-form contract drafted primarily by only one of the parties, any choice of law must be express and conspicuous.
(3) The choice of law may be made or modified after the parties enter into the contract. Any choice of law made or modified after the parties enter into the contract must be by express agreement.
(4) Unless the parties provide otherwise, a choice of law or modification of that choice operates retrospectively to the time the parties entered into the contract. Retrospective operation under the provisions of this subsection may not prejudice the rights of third parties. [Formerly 81.120]

15.355 Limitations on choice of law by parties. (1) The law chosen by the parties pursuant to ORS 15.350 does not apply to the extent that its application would:
(a) Require a party to perform an act prohibited by the law of the state where the act is to be performed under the contract;
(b) Prohibit a party from performing an act required by the law of the state where it is to be performed under the contract; or
(c) Contravene an established fundamental policy embodied in the law that would otherwise govern the issue in dispute under ORS 15.360.
(2) For purposes of subsection (1)(c) of this section, an established policy is fundamental only if the policy reflects objectives or gives effect to essential public or societal institutions beyond the allocation of rights and obligations of parties to a contract at issue. [Formerly 81.125]

15.360 General rule. To the extent that an effective choice of law has not been made by the parties pursuant to ORS 15.350 or 15.355, or is not prescribed by ORS 15.320, 15.325, 15.330, 15.335 or 15.380, the rights and duties of the parties with regard to an issue in a contract are governed by the law, in light of the multistate elements of the contract, that is the most appropriate for a resolution of that issue. The most appropriate law is determined by:
(1) Identifying the states that have a relevant connection with the transaction or the parties, such as the place of negotiation, making, performance or subject matter of the contract, or the domicile, habitual residence or pertinent place of business of a party;
(2) Identifying the policies underlying any apparently conflicting laws of these states that are relevant to the issue; and
(3) Evaluating the relative strength and pertinence of these policies in:
(a) Meeting the needs and giving effect to the policies of the interstate and international systems; and
(b) Facilitating the planning of transactions, protecting a party from undue imposition by another party, giving effect to justified expectations of the parties concerning which state's law applies to the issue and minimizing adverse effects on strong legal policies of other states. [Formerly 81.130]

15.380 Presumptive rules for specific types of contracts. (1) To the extent that an effective choice of law has not been made by the parties pursuant to ORS 15.350 or 15.355, or is not prescribed by ORS 15.320, 15.325, 15.330 or 15.335, contracts described in subsection (2) of this section are governed by the law of the state specified in subsection (2) of this section unless a party demonstrates that the application of that law would be clearly inappropriate under the principles of ORS 15.360.

(2)(a) Contracts involving the occupancy of real property, the land use of property or the recording of interests in real property are governed by the law of the state where the property is situated.

(b) Contracts for personal services are governed by the law of the state where the services are to be primarily rendered pursuant to the contract.

(c) Contracts for franchises, as defined in ORS 650.005, except for licensing clauses in such contracts, are governed by the law of the state where the franchise is to operate pursuant to the contract.

(d) Licensing contracts and licensing clauses in contracts for franchises, as defined in ORS 650.005, are governed by the law of the state where the licensor has its place of business or residence with the closest connection to the transactions between the parties. For purposes of this subsection, "licensing" means a grant of a privilege, created by contract, that allows one party, the licensee, to use the property or right of another party, the licensor.

(e) Agency contracts are governed by the law of the state where the agent's duties are to be primarily performed. [Formerly 81.135]

CHOICE OF LAW FOR TORTS AND OTHER NONCONTRACTUAL CLAIMS

(Generally)

15.400 Definitions for ORS 15.400 to 15.460. For the purposes of ORS 15.400 to 15.460:

(1) "Conduct" means an act or omission that has occurred or that may occur in the future.

(2) "Domicile" means the place identified under ORS 15.420.

(3) "Injury" means physical or nonphysical harm to a person or property caused by the conduct of another person.

(4) "Law," when used in reference to the law of another state, does not include that state's choice-of-law rules.

(5) "Noncontractual claim" means a claim, other than a claim for failure to perform a contractual or other consensual obligation, that arises from a tort as defined in ORS 30.260, or any conduct that caused or may cause injury compensable by damages, without regard to whether damages are sought.

(6) "Person" means a person as defined in ORS 174.100 and a public body.

(7) "Public body" means a public body as defined in ORS 174.109, the Oregon Health and Science University, and the Oregon State Bar.

(8) "State" means, unless the context requires otherwise, the United States, any state, territory, possession or other jurisdiction of the United States, any Indian tribe or other Native American, Hawaiian or Alaskan group recognized by federal law or formally acknowledged by a state of the United States, and any foreign country or territorial subdivision of such country that has its own system of laws. [Formerly 31.850]

15.405 Applicability. ORS 15.400 to 15.460 govern the choice of law applicable to noncontractual claims when a choice between or among the laws of more than one state is at issue. ORS 15.400 to 15.460 do not supersede the provisions of other Oregon statutes that expressly designate the law governing a particular noncontractual claim. [Formerly 31.855]

(Preliminary Issues)

15.410 Characterization. (1) Oregon law determines the scope and meaning of terms used in ORS 15.400 to 15.460, including whether a claim is a noncontractual claim.

(2) The law of the state determined to be applicable under ORS 15.400 to 15.460 determines the scope and meaning of terms used in that law. [Formerly 31.860]

15.415 Localization and other factual determinations. For the purposes of ORS 15.400 to 15.460, the following issues are determined under Oregon law:

(1) What conduct caused the injury, and where the conduct occurred. If injurious conduct occurs in more than one state, the state where the conduct occurred that is primarily responsible for the injury is the state where the injurious conduct occurred.

(2) Who caused the injury. If a person is liable for the conduct of another person, both persons are considered to have caused the injury.

(3) Where the injury occurred. If the same conduct causes injury in more than one state, the place of injury is in the state in which most of the injurious effects occurred or may occur. If different persons suffer injury in different states by reason of the same conduct, the place of injury is determined separately for each person. If a person suffers loss by reason of injury or death of another person, the place of injury is determined based on the injury to the other person.

(4) Who suffered the injury. If a claim is made for loss caused by injury or death of another person, both the claimant and the other person are considered to be injured persons. [Formerly 31.862]

15.420 Determining domicile. For the purposes of ORS 15.400 to 15.460:

(1)(a) The domicile of a natural person is in the state in which the person resides with the intent to make it the person's home for an indefinite period of time.

(b) A domicile once established continues until it is superseded by the acquisition of a new domicile. If a person's intent to change domicile is legally ineffective, the previously established domicile continues to be the person's domicile.

(c) If a person's intent to have a domicile in a given state would be legally effective but cannot be ascertained, the state in which the person resides is the person's domicile, and if the person resides in more than one state, the residence state that has the most pertinent connection to the disputed issue is deemed to be the domicile with regard to that issue.

(2) The domicile of a person other than a natural person is located in the state in which the person maintains its principal place of business. If the dispute arises from activities directed from another state in which the person maintains a place of business other than the principal place of business, either state may be considered as the domicile at the choice of the other party.

(3) The domicile of a person is determined as of the date of the injury for which the noncontractual claim is made. [Formerly 31.865]

(Claims Governed by Oregon Law)

15.430 Claims governed by Oregon law. Notwithstanding ORS 15.440, 15.445 and 15.455, Oregon law governs noncontractual claims in the following actions:

(1) Actions in which, after the events giving rise to the dispute, the parties agree to the application of Oregon law.

(2) Actions in which none of the parties raises the issue of applicability of foreign law.

(3) Actions in which the party or parties who rely on foreign law fail to assist the court in establishing the relevant provisions of foreign law after being requested by the court to do so.

(4) Actions filed against a public body of the State of Oregon, unless the application of Oregon law is waived by a person authorized by Oregon law to make the waiver on behalf of the public body.

(5) Actions against an owner, lessor or possessor of land, buildings or other real property situated in Oregon that seek to recover for, or to prevent, injury on that property and arising out of conduct that occurs in Oregon.

(6) Actions between an employer and an employee who is primarily employed in Oregon that arise out of an injury that occurs in Oregon.

(7) Actions for professional malpractice arising from services rendered entirely in Oregon by personnel licensed to perform those services under Oregon law. [Formerly 31.870]

15.435 Product liability civil actions. (1) Notwithstanding ORS 15.440 and 15.445, Oregon law applies to product liability civil actions, as defined in ORS 30.900, if:

(a) The injured person was domiciled in Oregon and the injury occurred in Oregon; or

(b) The injured person was domiciled in Oregon or the injury occurred in Oregon, and the product:

(A) Was manufactured or produced in Oregon; or

(B) Was delivered when new for use or consumption in Oregon.

(2) Subsection (1) of this section does not apply to a product liability civil action if a defendant demonstrates that the use in Oregon of the product that caused the injury could not have been foreseen and that none of the defendant's products of the same type were available in Oregon in the ordinary course of trade at the time of the injury.

(3) If a party demonstrates that the application of the law of a state other than Oregon to a disputed issue is substantially more appropriate under the principles of ORS 15.445, that issue shall be governed by the law of the other state.

(4) All noncontractual claims or issues in product liability civil actions not provided for or not disposed of under this section are governed by the law of the state determined under ORS 15.445. [Formerly 31.872]

(Choice of Law)

15.440 General rules. (1) Noncontractual claims between an injured person and the person whose conduct caused the injury are governed by the law of the state designated in this section.

(2)(a) If the injured person and the person whose conduct caused the injury were domiciled in the same state, the law of that state governs. However, the law of the state in which the injurious conduct occurred determines the standard of care by which the conduct is judged. If the injury occurred in a state other than the one in which the conduct occurred, the provisions of subsection (3)(c) of this section apply.

(b) For the purposes of this section, persons domiciled in different states shall be treated as if domiciled in the same state to the extent that laws of those states on the disputed issues would produce the same outcome.

(3) If the injured person and the person whose conduct caused the injury were domiciled in different states and the laws of those states on the disputed issues would produce a different outcome, the law of the state designated in this subsection governs.

(a) If both the injurious conduct and the resulting injury occurred in the same state, the law of that state governs if either the injured person or the person whose conduct caused the injury was domiciled in that state.

(b) If both the injurious conduct and the resulting injury occurred in a state other than the state in which either the injured person or the person whose conduct caused the injury were domiciled, the law of the state of conduct and injury governs. If a party demonstrates that, under the circumstances of the particular case, the application of that law to a disputed issue will not serve the objectives of that law, that issue will be governed by the law selected under ORS 15.445.

(c) If the injurious conduct occurred in one state and the resulting injury in another state, the law of the state of conduct governs. However, the law of the state of injury governs if:

(A) The activities of the person whose conduct caused the injury were such as to make foreseeable the occurrence of injury in that state; and

(B) The injured person formally requests the application of that state's law by a pleading or amended pleading. The request shall be deemed to encompass all claims and issues against that defendant.

(4) If a party demonstrates that application to a disputed issue of the law of a state other than the state designated by subsection (2) or (3) of this section is substantially more appropriate under the principles of ORS 15.445, that issue is governed by the law of the other state. [Formerly 31.875]

15.445 General and residual approach. Except as provided in ORS 15.430, 15.435, 15.440 and 15.455, the rights and liabilities of the parties with regard to disputed issues in a noncontractual claim are governed by the law of the state whose contacts with the parties and the dispute and whose policies on the disputed issues make application of the state's law the most appropriate for those issues. The most appropriate law is determined by:

(1) Identifying the states that have a relevant contact with the dispute, such as the place of the injurious conduct, the place of the resulting injury, the domicile, habitual residence or pertinent place of business of each person, or the place in which the relationship between the parties was centered;

(2) Identifying the policies embodied in the laws of these states on the disputed issues; and

(3) Evaluating the relative strength and pertinence of these policies with due regard to:

(a) The policies of encouraging responsible conduct, deterring injurious conduct and providing adequate remedies for the conduct; and

(b) The needs and policies of the interstate and international systems, including the policy of minimizing adverse effects on strongly held policies of other states. [Formerly 31.878]

15.450 Joint tortfeasors and third parties. Notwithstanding ORS 15.430, 15.435 and 15.440, if two or more persons are liable for the same claim, the rights and liabilities between those persons are governed by the law determined for the particular issue under ORS 15.445. If a third party pays compensation to a person injured by the conduct of another person, the right of the third party to recoup the amount paid is governed by the law determined for the particular issue under ORS 15.445. [Formerly 31.880]

15.455 Agreements on applicable foreign law. Notwithstanding ORS 15.440, 15.445 and 15.450, but subject to ORS 15.300 to 15.380, an agreement providing that an issue or issues falling within the scope of ORS 15.400 to 15.460 will be governed by the law of a state other than Oregon is enforceable in Oregon if the agreement was entered into after the parties had knowledge of the events giving rise to the dispute. [Formerly 31.885]

15.460 Commentary. The Oregon Law Commission shall make available on the website maintained by the commission a copy of the commentary approved by the commission for the provisions of ORS 15.400 to 15.460. [Formerly 31.890]

———————

Chapter 16 (Former Provisions) Pleadings; Motions; Orders; Process; Notices; Papers

PLEADINGS; PROCESS; NOTICES; PAPERS

PROCEDURE IN CIVIL PROCEEDINGS

16.010 [Repealed by 1979 c.284 §199]

16.020 [Repealed by 1979 c.284 §199]

16.030 [Repealed by 1979 c.284 §199]

16.040 [Repealed by 1979 c.284 §199]

16.050 [Repealed by 1979 c.284 §199]

16.060 [Repealed by 1979 c.284 §199]

16.070 [Repealed by 1979 c.284 §199]

16.080 [Repealed by 1979 c.284 §199]

16.090 [Repealed by 1979 c.284 §199]

16.100 [Repealed by 1979 c.284 §199]

16.110 [Repealed by 1979 c.284 §199]

16.120 [Repealed by 1979 c.284 §199]

16.130 [Repealed by 1979 c.284 §199]

16.140 [Amended by 1975 c.716 §1; repealed by 1979 c.284 §199]

16.150 [Repealed by 1979 c.284 §199]

16.210 [Repealed by 1979 c.284 §199]

16.220 [Amended by 1973 c.59 §1; 1975 c.158 §1; repealed by 1977 c.356 §1 (16.221 enacted in lieu of 16.220)]

16.221 [1977 c.356 §2 (enacted in lieu of 16.220); repealed by 1979 c.284 §199]

16.230 [Repealed by 1975 c.158 §6]

16.240 [Repealed by 1979 c.284 §199]

16.250 [Repealed by 1979 c.284 §199]

16.260 [Repealed by 1979 c.284 §199]

16.270 [Repealed by 1979 c.284 §199]

16.280 [Repealed by 1979 c.284 §199]

16.290 [Amended by 1975 c.623 §9; repealed by 1979 c.284 §199]

16.300 [Repealed by 1975 c.158 §6]

16.305 [1975 c.158 §2; repealed by 1979 c.284 §199]

16.310 [Repealed by 1975 c.158 §6]

16.315 [1971 c.124 §1; 1975 c.158 §3; repealed by 1979 c.284 §199]

16.320 [Repealed by 1979 c.284 §199]

16.325 [1975 c.623 §10; repealed by 1979 c.284 §199]

16.330 [Repealed by 1979 c.284 §199]

16.340 [Repealed by 1979 c.284 §199]

16.360 [Repealed by 1979 c.284 §199]

16.370 [Repealed by 1979 c.284 §199]

16.380 [Repealed by 1979 c.284 §199]

16.390 [Repealed by 1979 c.284 §199]

16.400 [Repealed by 1979 c.284 §199]

16.410 [Repealed by 1979 c.284 §199]

16.420 [Repealed by 1979 c.284 §199]

16.430 [Repealed by 1979 c.284 §199]

16.460 [Repealed by 1979 c.284 §199]

16.470 [Renumbered 17.003]

16.480 [Repealed by 1979 c.284 §199]

16.490 [Repealed by 1979 c.284 §199]

16.500 [Repealed by 1979 c.284 §199]

16.510 [Amended by 1967 c.493 §1; 1975 c.332 §1; repealed by 1979 c.284 §199]

16.530 [Repealed by 1979 c.284 §199]

16.540 [Repealed by 1979 c.284 §199]

16.610 [Repealed by 1979 c.284 §199]

16.620 [Repealed by 1979 c.284 §199]

16.630 [Repealed by 1979 c.284 §199]

16.640 [Repealed by 1979 c.284 §199]

16.650 [Repealed by 1979 c.284 §199]

16.660 [Repealed by 1979 c.284 §199]

16.710 [Repealed by 1979 c.284 §199]

16.720 [Repealed by 1979 c.284 §199]

16.730 [Repealed by 1979 c.284 §199]

16.740 [Repealed by 1979 c.284 §199]

16.760 [Repealed by 1979 c.284 §199]

16.765 [Repealed by 1979 c.284 §199]

16.770 [Repealed by 1979 c.284 §199]

16.780 [Repealed by 1979 c.284 §199]

16.790 [Repealed by 1979 c.284 §199]

16.800 [Repealed by 1979 c.284 §199]

16.810 [Repealed by 1979 c.284 §199]

16.820 [Repealed by 1979 c.284 §199]

16.830 [Repealed by 1979 c.284 §199]

16.840 [Repealed by 1979 c.284 §199]

16.850 [Repealed by 1979 c.284 §199]

16.860 [Amended by 1977 c.607 §1; repealed by 1979 c.284 §199]

16.870 [Repealed by 1979 c.284 §199]

16.880 [Amended by 1959 c.628 §6; 1965 c.221 §11; repealed by 1979 c.284 §199]

————————————

Chapter 17 —— Compromise; Settlement

New sections of law were enacted by the Legislative Assembly during its 2018 regular session and pertain to or are likely to be compiled in this ORS chapter. See sections in the following 2018 Oregon Laws chapters: 2018 Session Laws 0059

2017 EDITION

COMPROMISE; SETTLEMENT

PROCEDURE IN CIVIL PROCEEDINGS

SETTLEMENT OR COMPROMISE WITH INJURED WORKER

17.065   Definitions for ORS 17.065 to 17.085

17.075   When settlement prohibited between employer and employee

17.085   When settlement allowed

SETTLEMENT OR COMPROMISE BY PUBLIC BODY

17.095   Prohibition of confidential settlements and compromises; exceptions

PENALTIES

17.990   Penalties

17.003 [Formerly 16.470; repealed by 1981 c.898 §53]

17.005 [Repealed by 1979 c.284 §199]

17.010 [Repealed by 1979 c.284 §199]

17.015 [Repealed by 1979 c.284 §199]

17.020 [Repealed by 1979 c.284 §199]

17.025 [Repealed by 1979 c.284 §199]

17.030 [Repealed by 1979 c.284 §199]

17.033 [1973 c.812 §5; repealed by 1979 c.284 §199]

17.035 [Repealed by 1979 c.284 §199]

17.040 [Amended by 1957 c.376 §1; repealed by 1979 c.284 §199]

17.045 [Amended by 1955 c.497 §5; 1957 c.376 §2; repealed by 1979 c.284 §199]

17.050 [Amended by 1969 c.388 §1; repealed by 1979 c.284 §199]

17.055 [Amended by 1975 c.512 §4; repealed by 1979 c.284 §199]

SETTLEMENT OR COMPROMISE WITH INJURED WORKER

17.065 Definitions for ORS 17.065 to 17.085. As used in ORS 17.065 to 17.085, unless the context requires otherwise:
(1) "Compromise" means an agreement to allow judgment to be given for a sum or value specified.
(2) "Employer" includes any agent or representative of an employer.
(3) "Release" means an agreement to abandon a claim or right to the person against whom the claim exists.
(4) "Settlement" means an agreement to accept as full and complete compensation for a claim a sum or value specified. [1975 c.512 §1; 1979 c.284 §49]

17.075 When settlement prohibited between employer and employee. (1) An employer whose interest is or may become adverse to that of an injured employee shall not, within 15 days from the date of the occurrence causing the employee's injury:
(a) Negotiate or attempt to negotiate a settlement or compromise with the injured employee;
(b) Obtain or attempt to obtain a general release of liability from the injured employee; or
(c) Obtain or attempt to obtain any statement, either written or oral from the injured employee.
(2) Subsection (1)(c) of this section does not apply to the extent that compliance with statutes or rules of federal or state agencies requiring reports of accidents and injuries necessitates obtaining an employee statement within the 15-day period following the date of the injury.
(3) Any settlement or compromise agreement entered into, any general release of liability or any written or oral statement made by any employee after the employee incurs a personal injury, that is not obtained in accordance with ORS 17.085, requiring notice, may be disavowed by the injured employee within 12 months following the date of the injury and such statement, release, compromise or settlement shall not be admissible evidence in any court action or administrative proceeding relating to the injury. [1975 c.512 §2; 2005 c.22 §5]

17.085 When settlement allowed. ORS 17.075 relating to settlements, compromises, releases and statements obtained by an employer whose interest is or may become adverse to an injured employee shall not apply, if at least five days prior to obtaining the settlement, compromise, release or statement, the injured employee has signified the willingness of the injured employee that a settlement, compromise, release or statement be given. [1975 c.512 §3]

SETTLEMENT OR COMPROMISE BY PUBLIC BODY

17.095 Prohibition of confidential settlements and compromises; exceptions. (1) A public body, or officer, employee or agent of a public body, who is a defendant in an action under ORS 30.260 to 30.300, or who is a defendant in an action under ORS 294.100, may not enter into any settlement or compromise of the action if the settlement or compromise requires that the terms or conditions of the settlement or compromise be confidential.
(2) Notwithstanding subsection (1) of this section:
(a) A public body, or officer, employee or agent of a public body, may enter into a settlement or compromise that requires the terms or conditions to be confidential if federal law requires terms or conditions of that settlement or compromise to be confidential. Only terms and conditions that are required to be confidential under federal law may be confidential in the settlement or compromise.
(b) A court may order that the terms or conditions of a settlement or compromise that reveal the identity of a person be confidential if:
(A) The person whose identity is revealed is a victim of sexual abuse or is under 18 years of age; and
(B) The court determines, by written findings, that the specific privacy interests of the person outweigh the public's interest in the terms or conditions.
(3) Any public body, or officer, employee or agent of a public body, who is a defendant in an action under ORS 30.260 to 30.300, or who is a defendant in an action under ORS 294.100, shall file with the court a full and complete disclosure of the terms and conditions of any settlement or compromise of the claims against the public body, its officers, employees or agents. The disclosure shall be filed prior to the dismissal of the action.
(4) For the purposes of this section:
(a) "Action" means a legal proceeding that has been commenced as provided in ORCP 3; and
(b) "Public body" has that meaning given in ORS 30.260. [Formerly 30.402; 2005 c.352 §1]

17.100 [1989 c.465 §1; renumbered 31.825 in 2003]

17.105 [Repealed by 1979 c.284 §199]

17.110 [Repealed by 1979 c.284 §199]

17.115 [Amended by 1973 c.836 §315; repealed by 1979 c.284 §199]

17.120 [Repealed by 1979 c.284 §199]

17.125 [Repealed by 1979 c.284 §199]

17.130 [Amended by 1975 c.781 §5; 1977 c.262 §3; repealed by 1979 c.284 §199]

17.135 [Repealed by 1979 c.284 §199]

17.140 [Repealed by 1979 c.284 §199]

17.145 [Repealed by 1979 c.284 §199]

17.150 [Repealed by 1979 c.284 §199]

17.155 [Repealed by 1979 c.284 §199]

17.160 [Repealed by 1979 c.284 §199]

17.165 [Repealed by 1979 c.284 §199]

17.170 [Repealed by 1979 c.284 §199]

17.175 [Repealed by 1979 c.284 §199]

17.180 [Repealed by 1979 c.284 §199]

17.185 [Repealed by 1979 c.284 §199]

17.190 [1969 c.222 §1; repealed by 1979 c.284 §199]

17.205 [Repealed by 1979 c.284 §199]

17.210 [Repealed by 1979 c.284 §199]

17.215 [Repealed by 1979 c.284 §199]

17.220 [Repealed by 1979 c.284 §199]

17.225 [Amended by 1969 c.222 §2; repealed by 1979 c.284 §199]

17.230 [Renumbered 10.100]

17.235 [Repealed by 1979 c.284 §199]

17.240 [Repealed by 1979 c.284 §199]

17.245 [Repealed by 1979 c.284 §199]

17.250 [Amended by 1981 c.892 §85a; renumbered 10.095]

17.255 [Amended by 1965 c.534 §1; repealed by 1979 c.284 §199]

17.305 [Repealed by 1979 c.284 §199]

17.310 [Repealed by 1979 c.284 §199]

17.315 [Renumbered 10.077]

17.320 [Amended by 1977 c.357 §1; repealed by 1979 c.284 §199]

17.325 [Repealed by 1979 c.284 §199]

17.330 [Repealed by 1979 c.284 §199]

17.335 [Repealed by 1979 c.284 §199]

17.340 [Amended by 1959 c.638 §3; repealed by 1979 c.284 §199]

17.345 [Repealed by 1979 c.284 §199]

17.350 [Repealed by 1979 c.284 §199]

17.355 [Amended by 1975 c.279 §1; repealed by 1979 c.284 §199]

17.360 [Repealed by 1979 c.284 §199]

17.405 [Repealed by 1979 c.284 §199]

17.410 [Repealed by 1979 c.284 §199]

17.415 [Repealed by 1979 c.284 §199]

17.420 [Repealed by 1979 c.284 §199]

17.425 [Repealed by 1979 c.284 §199]

17.430 [Amended by 1953 c.580 §2; 1959 c.558 §28; 1959 c.638 §4; repealed by 1965 c.177 §1 (17.431 enacted in lieu of 17.430)]

17.431 [1965 c.177 §2 (enacted in lieu of 17.430); repealed by 1979 c.284 §199]

17.435 [Amended by 1965 c.177 §3; repealed by 1979 c.284 §199]

17.440 [Repealed by 1965 c.177 §4 (17.441 enacted in lieu of 17.440)]

17.441 [1965 c.177 §5 (enacted in lieu of 17.440); repealed by 1979 c.284 §199]

17.505 [Amended by 1977 c.357 §2; repealed by 1979 c.284 §199]

17.510 [Amended by 1977 c.357 §3; repealed by 1979 c.284 §199]

17.515 [Amended by 1971 c.565 §5; repealed by 1979 c.284 §199]

17.520 [Repealed by 1955 c.611 §13]

17.525 [Repealed by 1955 c.611 §13]

17.605 [Repealed by 1979 c.284 §199]

17.610 [Repealed by 1979 c.284 §199]

17.615 [Repealed by 1979 c.284 §199]

17.620 [Repealed by 1979 c.284 §199]

17.625 [Repealed by 1979 c.284 §199]

17.630 [Repealed by 1979 c.284 §199]

17.705 [Amended by 1965 c.391 §1; repealed by 1981 c.898 §53]

17.710 [Repealed by 1981 c.898 §53]

17.720 [Repealed by 1981 c.898 §53]

17.725 [Repealed by 1981 c.898 §53]

17.730 [Repealed by 1981 c.898 §53]

17.735 [Repealed by 1981 c.898 §53]

17.740 [Repealed by 1981 c.898 §53]

17.745 [Repealed by 1981 c.898 §53]

17.750 [Repealed by 1981 c.898 §53]

17.755 [Repealed by 1981 c.898 §53]

17.760 [Amended by 1959 c.638 §5; repealed by 1981 c.898 §53]

17.765 [Repealed by 1981 c.898 §53]

PENALTIES

17.990 Penalties. A person violating ORS 17.075 (1) commits a Class A violation. [1975 c.512 §5; 1999 c.1051 §146]

Chapter 18 — Judgments

ORS sections in this chapter were amended or repealed by the Legislative Assembly during its 2018 regular session. See the table of ORS sections amended or repealed during the 2018 regular session: 2018 A&R Tables

2017 EDITION

JUDGMENTS

PROCEDURE IN CIVIL PROCEEDINGS

DEFINITIONS

18.005   Definitions

18.015   Statutory references to decrees and judgments

APPLICATION

18.025   Courts subject to chapter

GENERAL PROVISIONS RELATING TO JUDGMENTS

18.028   Authority of Chief Justice

18.029   Effect of chapter on use of judgment

18.031   Contents of supplemental judgments

FORM OF JUDGMENT DOCUMENT

18.035   Preparation of judgment document

18.038   Form of judgment document generally

18.042   Judgment in civil action that includes money award

18.048   Judgment in criminal action that contains money award

18.049   Adjustments to money awards

18.052   Duty of judge with respect to form of judgment document

18.058   Duty of court administrator with respect to form of judgment document

18.062   Use of electronic judgment forms

ENTRY OF JUDGMENTS IN REGISTER

18.075   Entry of judgments in circuit courts generally

18.078   Notice of entry of judgment in circuit court civil action

18.082   Effect of entry of judgment

CORRECTIONS TO JUDGMENTS

18.107   Corrections to civil judgments

18.112   Correction of designation of judgment as general judgment

JUDGMENT LIENS

18.150   Judgment liens in circuit courts

18.152   Establishing judgment liens in other counties

18.154   Appeal; motion to eliminate lien

18.158   Judgment lien based on judgment for child support or spousal support entered in another state

18.162   Judgment lien based on justice and municipal court judgments; satisfaction filing fee

18.165   Priority of judgment lien over unrecorded conveyance

18.170   Form for lien record abstract; rules

EXPIRATION AND EXTENSION OF JUDGMENT REMEDIES

18.180   Expiration of judgment remedies in circuit court

18.182   Extension of judgment remedies

18.185   Extension of judgment lien of spousal support award

18.190   Spousal support awards in judgments entered before January 1, 2004

18.194   Expiration and extension of judgment remedies for justice and municipal court judgments

RELEASE OF LIEN

18.200   Release of lien

18.202   Reinstatement of lien

ASSIGNMENT OF JUDGMENT

18.205   Assignment of judgment

SATISFACTION OF MONEY AWARDS

18.225   Satisfaction of money awards generally

18.228   Satisfaction of support awards payable to Department of Justice

18.232   Alternate method for satisfaction of support awards payable to Department of Justice

18.235   Motion to satisfy money award

18.238   Proceedings after discharge in bankruptcy

CONTRIBUTION

18.242   Contribution among judgment debtors; subrogation of surety

APPEAL

18.245   Jurisdictional requirements

ENFORCEMENT OF JUDGMENTS

(Generally)

18.252   Execution

18.255   Enforcement of judgment by circuit court for county where debtor resides

(Proceedings in Support of Execution)

18.265   Debtor examination

18.268   Conduct of debtor examination; seizure of property

18.270   Written interrogatories

EXEMPT PROPERTY

(Generally)

18.300   Resident entitled to use federal exemptions or state exemptions in bankruptcy

18.305   Property not exempt from execution for purchase price

18.312   Execution not to issue against property of deceased party; exception

18.318   Execution against property in possession or control of public officer or agency

18.322   Adjudication of claim of exemption

(Personal Property)

18.345   Exempt personal property generally

18.348   Certain funds exempt when deposited in account; limitation

18.352   Proceeds of casualty and indemnity insurance attachable on execution

18.358   Certain retirement plans exempt from execution; exceptions

18.362   Exemption for firearms

18.364   Prohibition on demanding firearms

(Wages)

18.375   Definitions

18.385   Wage exemption

(Homesteads)

18.395   Homestead exemption

18.398   Denial of homestead exemption when judgment is for child support

18.402   Limitations on homestead exemption

18.406   Exemption not applicable to certain liens, mortgages and interests

18.412   Notice of intent to discharge judgment lien against homestead

18.415   Objections to discharge; hearing

18.422   Release of judgment lien

WRITS OF GARNISHMENT

(Definitions)

18.600   Definitions

(Garnishment Generally)

18.602   Garnishment described

18.605   Debts subject to garnishment; when writ may be issued on debt

18.607   Form of writ; single writ for two or more debtors

18.609   Validity of writ after issuance

18.610   Court with authority over writ

(Garnishable Property)

18.615   Garnishable property generally

18.618   Property not subject to garnishment

18.620   Setoff for certain amounts payable to underlying lienholders

(Duration of Writ's Effect)

18.625   Duration of writ's effect

18.627   Multiple writs

(Persons Authorized to Issue Writs)

18.635   Who may issue writs

(Writs Issued by Court Administrators)

18.638   Writs issued by court administrators generally

18.640   Grounds for denying issuance of writ

(Writs Issued by Division of Child Support or District Attorney)

18.645   Writs issued by Division of Child Support or district attorney; rules

(Delivery of Writ)

18.650   Items required to be delivered to garnishee

18.652   Manner of delivery; delivery fee

18.655   Proper person to receive writ

18.658   Documents to be delivered to debtor

(Duties of Garnishee Generally)

18.665   Duties generally

18.668   Immunity by payment to court administrator or delivery to sheriff

18.670   Exceptions to garnishee's duties

18.672   Duties of personal representative who is garnished

(Garnishee Response)

18.680   Response required; time

18.682   When response not required

18.685   Contents of response; manner of making payment

18.688   Response of garnishee who is employer of debtor

18.690   Delivery of garnishee response

18.692   Supplemental garnishee response

(Challenge to Garnishment)

18.700   Manner of making challenge to garnishment

18.702   Notice to garnishor and garnishee of challenge to garnishment

18.705   Duties of garnishor and creditor created by challenge to garnishment

18.708   Duties of garnishee created by challenge to garnishment

18.710   Hearing on challenge to garnishment

18.712   Allowance or denial of challenge

18.715   Sanctions

18.718   Special procedures for writs issued for past due support

(Claim by Person Other Than Debtor)

18.725   Claim by person other than debtor for all or part of garnished property

(Payment of Money Under Writ Generally)

18.730   Payment of money under writ; garnishor's duty to hold payments

18.732   Money owed to debtor that is due within 45 days

(Payment of Nonexempt Wages)

18.735   Payment of wages subject to garnishment

18.736   Processing fee

(Payments Made to Court Administrator)

18.738   Acceptance or rejection of payments by court administrator

18.740   Payments erroneously sent to court

(Crediting of Payments)

18.742   Crediting of payments against debt

18.745   Excess payments

(Property Subject to Sale by Sheriff)

18.750   Application of ORS 18.750 to 18.760
18.752   Garnishee duties

18.755   Request for sale; sheriff's fees

18.758   Sheriff's sale

18.760   Challenge to garnishment

(Release of Garnishment)

18.770   Release of garnishment

(Sanctions Against Noncomplying Garnishee)

18.775   Liability of garnishee

18.778   Order to appear

18.780   Pleadings; default judgment

18.782   Hearing

(Financial Institution as Garnishee)

18.784   Certain financial institution deposits not subject to garnishment; garnishment account review

18.785   Duties of financial institution; notice to account holder

18.787   Liability of financial institution

18.788   Compliance records

18.790   Search fee; garnishment processing fee

18.792   Safe deposit boxes

18.795   Setoff for amounts owing to financial institution

18.798   Effect of garnishment served on financial institution

(Writs Issued to Enforce Agency Orders or Warrants)

18.800   Special procedures for writs issued to enforce agency orders or warrants

(Use of Writ for Provisional Process)

18.810   Use of writ for provisional process

(Forms)

18.830   Writ of garnishment form

18.832   Debt calculation form

18.835   Garnishee response form

18.838   Instructions to garnishee form

18.840   Wage exemption calculation form

18.842   Release of garnishment form

18.845   Notice of exemptions form; instructions for challenge to garnishment

18.847   Notice to debtor of garnishment account review

18.850   Challenge to garnishment form

NOTICES OF GARNISHMENT

18.854   Notices of garnishment generally

18.855   Notices of garnishment issued by state agencies

18.857   Notice of garnishment issued by county tax collector

WRITS OF EXECUTION

(Function and Form of Writ)

18.860   Function of writ

18.862   Form of writ

(Issuance of Writ)

18.865   Court administrator to issue writ

18.867   Issuance of writs for certain judgments awarding child support

18.868   Sheriff to whom writ is issued

18.870   Recording of writ

(Return on Writ)

18.872   Return on writ of execution

(Instructions to Sheriff)

18.875   Instructions to sheriff

(Levy)

18.878   Manner of levying on property

18.880   Alternative procedure for levying on tangible personal property

18.882   Criminal penalty for moving, using or damaging secured property

18.884   Levying on intangible personal property

18.886   Creditor's bond

18.887   Forcible entry for purpose of levying on personal property

18.888   Notice of levy

18.890   Debtor's bond

(Challenge to Writ of Execution)

18.892   Challenge to writ of execution

18.894   Notice of challenge to execution

18.896   Challenge to execution form

18.898   Hearing on challenge to execution

18.899   Sanctions

EXECUTION SALE

(Residential Property)

18.901   Definition of residential property

18.904   Order required for sale of residential property; exceptions

18.906   Motion for order authorizing sale of residential property

18.908   Notice of motion for order authorizing sale of residential property

18.912   Hearing on motion for order authorizing sale of residential property

(Notice of Sale)

18.918   Person entitled to written notice of sale

18.920   Notice of sale of personal property

18.922   Expedited sale of perishable personal property; expedited sale to prevent loss of value

18.924   Notice of sale of real property

18.926   Legal notices website; posting fee

(Conduct of Execution Sale)

18.930   Conduct of sale generally; county fee

18.932   Postponement of sale; rules

18.934   Amount of property to be sold; sheriff and deputies may not purchase

18.936   Bid by judgment creditor

18.938   Manner of payment

18.940   Bill of sale for personal property

18.942   Sheriff's certificate of sale for real property

18.944   Notice of completed sale

18.946   Possession after sale; right to rents or value of use

18.948   Confirmation of sale of real property

18.950   Delivery and distribution of proceeds; satisfaction document

18.952   Effect of sale on judgment debtor's or mortgagor's title; effect of redemption by judgment debtor or mortgagor

18.954   Conduct of sale pursuant to court rule or terms of order or judgment

(Redemption)

18.960   Definitions

18.962   Property that may be redeemed

18.963   Who may redeem

18.964   Time for redemption

18.966   Redemption amount payable to purchaser

18.967   Redemption amount payable to redemptioner

18.968   Setoff for rents, income and profits realized by certificate holder; certificate holder's lien for crops and amounts expended to prevent waste

18.970   Redemption notice

18.971   Objection to redemption notice

18.972   Response to redemption notice

18.973   Objection to response

18.975   Payment of redemption amount

18.978   Court proceedings on objections

18.980   Accounting

18.981   Manner of payment

18.982   Redemptioner must provide sheriff with address

(Waste)

18.983   Court may restrain waste

(Sheriff's Deed)

18.985   Sheriff's deed

SPECIAL RULES FOR SPECIFIC TYPES OF PROPERTY

18.986   Manufactured dwellings and floating homes

18.987   Purchaser's interest in land sale contract; leasehold interest in land with unexpired term of more than two years

18.988   Seller's right to receive payments under land sale contract

18.989   Equitable interests in property

MISCELLANEOUS

18.992   Referral of disputes to court

18.993   Effect of ORS 18.860 to 18.993 on court's ability to direct seizure

18.995   Owner not allowed to neglect foreclosed residential real property; local government to notify owner of violation; lien for unreimbursed costs

18.999   Recovery of expenses incurred in enforcing judgment and certain other monetary obligations

DEFINITIONS

18.005 Definitions. As used in this chapter:
(1) "Action" means any proceeding commenced in a court in which the court may render a judgment.
(2) "Child support award" means a money award or agency order that requires the payment of child support and that is entered under ORS 108.010 to 108.550, 416.310 to 416.340, 416.400 to 416.465, 416.510 to 416.990, 419B.400 or 419C.590 or ORS chapter 25, 107, 109 or 110.
(3) "Civil action" means any action that is not a criminal action.
(4) "Court administrator" means a trial court administrator in a circuit court that has a trial court administrator and the clerk of the court in all other courts.
(5) "Criminal action" has the meaning given in ORS 131.005.

(6) "Execution" means enforcement of the money award portion of a judgment or enforcement of a judgment requiring delivery of the possession or sale of specific real or personal property, by means of writs of execution, writs of garnishment and other statutory or common law writs or remedies that may be available under the law.

(7) "General judgment" means the judgment entered by a court that decides all requests for relief in the action except:

(a) A request for relief previously decided by a limited judgment; and

(b) A request for relief that may be decided by a supplemental judgment.

(8) "Judgment" means the concluding decision of a court on one or more requests for relief in one or more actions, as reflected in a judgment document.

(9) "Judgment document" means a writing in the form provided by ORS 18.038 that incorporates a court's judgment.

(10) "Judgment lien" means:

(a) The effect of a judgment on real property as described in ORS 18.150 (2) and (3) for the county in which the judgment is entered, and as described in ORS 18.152 (2) and (3) for a county in which the judgment is recorded under ORS 18.152; and

(b) A support arrearage lien attaching to real property under ORS 18.150 (3) or 18.152 (3).

(11) "Judgment remedy" means:

(a) The ability of a judgment creditor to enforce a judgment through execution; and

(b) Any judgment lien arising under ORS 18.150 or 18.152.

(12) "Legal authority" means:

(a) A statute;

(b) An Oregon Rule of Civil Procedure;

(c) A rule or order of the Chief Justice of the Supreme Court adopted under ORS 18.028; and

(d) All controlling appellate court decisions in effect December 31, 2003.

(13) "Limited judgment" means:

(a) A judgment entered under ORCP 67 B or 67 G;

(b) A judgment entered before the conclusion of an action in a circuit court for the partition of real property, defining the rights of the parties to the action and directing sale or partition;

(c) An interlocutory judgment foreclosing an interest in real property; and

(d) A judgment rendered before entry of a general judgment in an action that disposes of at least one but fewer than all requests for relief in the action and that is rendered pursuant to a legal authority that specifically authorizes that disposition by limited judgment.

(14) "Money award" means a judgment or portion of a judgment that requires the payment of money.

(15) "Person" includes a public body as defined in ORS 174.109.

(16) "Request for relief" means a claim, a charge in a criminal action or any other request for a determination of the rights and liabilities of one or more parties in an action that a legal authority allows the court to decide by a judgment.

(17) "Supplemental judgment" means a judgment that may be rendered after a general judgment pursuant to a legal authority.

(18) "Support arrearage lien" means a lien that attaches to real property under the provisions of ORS 18.150 (3) or 18.152 (3).

(19) "Support award" means a money award or agency order that requires the payment of child or spousal support. [2003 c.576 §1; 2005 c.542 §§55; 2005 c.568 §4]

Note: Section 7, chapter 568, Oregon Laws 2005, provides:

Sec. 7. Sections 2 [18.245] and 6 [18.029] of this 2005 Act and the amendments to ORS 18.005 by section 4 of this 2005 Act apply to all judgments entered on or after January 1, 2004. [2005 c.568 §7]

Note: Sections 45 and 569 (1) and (2), chapter 576, Oregon Laws 2003, provide:

Sec. 45. (1) Except as provided by this section or by ORS chapter 18, ORS chapter 18 applies only to judgments entered on or after January 1, 2004. Nothing in chapter 576, Oregon Laws 2003, affects the validity, lien effect or enforceability of any judgment or decree entered before January 1, 2004. Nothing in chapter 576, Oregon Laws 2003, affects the validity, lien effect or enforceability of any order or warrant docketed or recorded before January 1, 2004. Except as provided by this section or ORS chapter 18, any judgment or decree entered before January 1, 2004, and any order or warrant docketed or recorded before January 1, 2004, shall continue to be governed by the law in effect on the day immediately preceding January 1, 2004.

(2) ORS 18.107 applies to any corrected judgment entered on or after January 1, 2004, without regard to whether the original judgment is entered before, on or after January 1, 2004.

(3) A judgment creditor may create a judgment lien for a judgment in a county other than the county in which a judgment is entered in the manner provided by ORS 18.152 without regard to whether the judgment is entered before, on or after January 1, 2004.

(4) ORS 18.158 applies to all judgments, whether entered before, on or after January 1, 2004.

(5) Except as provided in ORS 18.190, ORS 18.180 and 18.182 apply to all judgments, whether entered before, on or after January 1, 2004. Notwithstanding ORS 18.182, any order of renewal entered before January 1, 2004, may be recorded in the manner provided by ORS 18.182 (6) with the effect provided by ORS 18.152 (4).

(6) ORS 18.200 applies to the release of any judgment lien after January 1, 2004, without regard to whether the judgment was entered before, on or after January 1, 2004.

(7) ORS 18.205 applies to the assignment of any judgment after January 1, 2004, without regard to whether the judgment was entered before, on or after January 1, 2004.

(8) ORS 18.225 applies to any satisfaction of judgment filed with a court on or after January 1, 2004, without regard to whether the judgment was entered before, on or after January 1, 2004.

(9) ORS 18.228 and 18.232 apply to all judgments, whether entered before, on or after January 1, 2004.

(10) ORS 18.235 applies to any motion for an order declaring that a money award has been satisfied, or to determine the amount necessary to satisfy a money award, filed with a court on or after January 1, 2004, without regard to whether the judgment was entered before, on or after January 1, 2004.

(11) ORS 18.252 and 18.255 apply to execution on any judgment, without regard to whether the judgment was entered before, on or after January 1, 2004.

(12) ORS 18.265 and 18.268 apply to any motion for a debtor examination made on or after January 1, 2004, without regard to whether the judgment was entered before, on or after January 1, 2004.

(13) ORS 18.270 applies to any written interrogatories served on or after January 1, 2004, without regard to whether the judgment was entered before, on or after January 1, 2004.

(14) ORS 18.465 to 18.476 and 18.492 to 18.518 (both 2003 Edition) apply to any writ of execution issued on or after January 1, 2004, without regard to whether the judgment was entered before, on or after January 1, 2004. [2003 c.576 §45; 2015 c.212 §21]

Sec. 569. (1) Except as specifically provided by this 2003 Act, the deletions of statutory references to decrees and the substitutions of references to judgments that are made by the provisions of this 2003 Act do not affect the determination as to whether a person has a right to a jury trial, the scope of review of the court's decision under ORS 19.250, or any other procedural or substantive aspect of the proceedings giving rise to the court's decision in an action.

(2) Except as specifically provided by this 2003 Act, the elimination of statutory references to dockets by this 2003 Act does not affect the validity, lien effect or enforceability of any judgment docketed before the effective date of this 2003 Act [January 1, 2004]. [2003 c.576 §569(1),(2)]

18.010 [Amended by 1977 c.208 §1; 1979 c.284 §50; repealed by 1981 c.898 §53]

18.015 Statutory references to decrees and judgments. (1) References in the statutes of this state to decrees include judgments, and references in the statutes of this state to judgments include decrees.

(2) References in the statutes of this state to judgments of other states include decrees of other states, and references in the statutes of this state to decrees of other states include judgments of other states. [2003 c.576 §1a]

18.020 [Repealed by 1979 c.284 §199]

APPLICATION

18.025 Courts subject to chapter. Except as specifically provided by this chapter, the provisions of this chapter apply to circuit courts, municipal courts and justice courts and to county courts performing judicial functions. [2003 c.576 §2]

GENERAL PROVISIONS RELATING TO JUDGMENTS

18.028 Authority of Chief Justice. The Chief Justice of the Supreme Court by rule or order may:

(1) Authorize or require that specified requests for relief that are not governed by other legal authority be decided by judgment; and

(2) Authorize or require the use of a limited or supplemental judgment for specified requests for relief that are not governed by other legal authority. [2005 c.568 §3]

18.029 Effect of chapter on use of judgment. The provisions of this chapter do not impose any requirement that a court use a judgment for the court's concluding decision on a request for relief if a legal authority allows or requires that the court decide the request for relief by order or other means. [2005 c.568 §6]

Note: See first note under 18.005.

18.030 [Amended by 1973 c.207 §1; 1977 c.616 §1; repealed by 1981 c.898 §53]

18.031 Contents of supplemental judgments. Except as provided in ORS 416.440 (5), a supplemental judgment may only contain provisions that were not included in the general judgment. [2009 c.484 §7; 2013 c.183 §4]

FORM OF JUDGMENT DOCUMENT

18.035 Preparation of judgment document. (1) In a civil action, the court may designate one of the parties to prepare a proposed judgment document. If the court does not designate a party to prepare a proposed judgment document, the prevailing party shall prepare a proposed judgment document. If more than one party has prevailed in the action, the prevailing parties may agree to designate one of the prevailing parties to prepare a proposed judgment document. Nothing in this subsection prevents any party to a civil action from preparing and submitting a proposed judgment document to the court.

(2) In criminal actions and juvenile proceedings under ORS chapters 419A, 419B and 419C, the judge shall ensure that a judgment document complying with ORS 18.038 and 18.048 is created and filed. [2003 c.576 §3; 2005 c.568 §11]

18.038 Form of judgment document generally. (1) A judgment document must be plainly titled as a judgment.

(2) The title of a judgment document must indicate whether the judgment is a limited judgment, a general judgment or a supplemental judgment. This subsection does not apply to:

(a) Justice courts, municipal courts and county courts performing judicial functions.

(b) Judgments in criminal actions.

(c) Judgments in juvenile proceedings under ORS chapters 419A, 419B and 419C.

(3) A judgment document must be separate from any other document in the action. The judgment document may have attached affidavits, certificates, motions, stipulations and exhibits as necessary or proper in support of the judgment.

(4) A judgment document must include:

(a) The name of the court rendering the judgment and the file number or other identifier used by the court for the action or actions decided by the judgment;

(b) The names of any parties in whose favor the judgment is given and the names of any parties against whom the judgment is given; and

(c) The signature of the judge rendering the judgment, or the signature of the court administrator if the court administrator is authorized by law to sign the judgment document, and the date the judgment document is signed.

(5) This section does not apply to any foreign judgment filed with a court under ORS 24.115 or 110.605 to 110.611. [2003 c.576 §4; 2005 c.568 §38; 2015 c.298 §81]

18.040 [Repealed by 1981 c.898 §53]

18.042 Judgment in civil action that includes money award. (1) The judgment document for a judgment in a civil action that includes a money award must contain a separate section clearly labeled as a money award. Any judgment in a civil action that includes a money award, but does not contain a separate section clearly labeled as a money award, does not create a judgment lien but may be enforced by any other judgment remedy.

(2) The separate section required by subsection (1) of this section must include all of the following:

(a) The name and address of each judgment creditor and the name, address and telephone number of any attorney who represents one or more of the judgment creditors.

(b) The name of each judgment debtor and, to the extent known by the judgment creditor:

(A) The address of each judgment debtor;

(B) The year of birth of each judgment debtor;

(C) The final four digits of the tax identification number of each judgment debtor, or the final four digits of the Social Security number of each judgment debtor;

(D) The final four digits of the driver license number of each judgment debtor and the name of the state that issued the license; and

(E) The name of any attorney for each judgment debtor.

(c) The name of any person or public body, as defined in ORS 174.109, other than the judgment creditor's attorney, that is known by the judgment creditor to be entitled to any portion of the money award.

(d) The amount of money awarded in the judgment, exclusive of amounts required to be included in the separate section under paragraphs (e) to (h) of this subsection.

(e) Any interest owed as of the date the judgment is entered in the register, either as a specific amount or as accrual information, including the rate or rates of interest, the balance or balances upon which interest accrues, the date or dates from which interest at each rate on each balance runs, and whether interest is simple or compounded and, if compounded, at what intervals.

(f) Information about interest that accrues on the judgment after entry in the register, including the rate or rates of interest, the balance or balances upon which interest accrues, the date or dates from which interest at each rate on each balance runs, and whether interest is simple or compounded and, if compounded, at what intervals.

(g) For monetary obligations that are payable on a periodic basis, any accrued arrearages, required further payments per period and payment dates.

(h) If the judgment requires the payment of costs and disbursements or attorney fees, a statement indicating that the award is made, any specific amounts awarded, a clear identification of the specific requests for relief for which any attorney fees are awarded and the amount of attorney fees awarded for each request for relief.

(3) The information required by subsection (2) of this section must be set forth in the money award section of the judgment document in the same order as the requirements appear in subsection (2) of this section.

(4) The separate section required by subsection (1) of this section must be placed immediately above the judge's or court administrator's signature. The separate section must be clearly labeled at its beginning as a money award. If the judgment includes a support award, the label of the separate section must so indicate. Except for information described in ORS 24.290, the separate section of the judgment document may not contain any provision except the information required by this section.

(5) The provisions of this section do not apply to foreign judgments that are filed with a court under ORS 24.115 or 110.605 to 110.611. If a foreign judgment is filed with the court under ORS 24.115, the separate statement required by ORS 24.125 must be filed with the foreign judgment. [2003 c.576 §5; 2005 c.568 §12; 2007 c.339 §1; 2009 c.230 §1; 2015 c.197 §1; 2015 c.298 §82]

Note: Section 6 (1), chapter 230, Oregon Laws 2009, provides:
Sec. 6. (1) The amendments to ORS 18.042 by section 1 of this 2009 Act apply only to judgments entered on or after the effective date of this 2009 Act [June 4, 2009]. [2009 c.230 §6(1)]

18.048 Judgment in criminal action that contains money award. (1) Except as provided in this section, the judgment document in a criminal action that contains a money award, whether by reason of a fine, restitution, forfeiture of security under ORS 135.280, a fee, an assessment, costs and disbursements or any other monetary obligation, must contain a separate section clearly labeled at its beginning as a money award. The separate section must be placed immediately above the judge's or court administrator's signature. If the judgment includes an award of restitution, the label of the separate section must so indicate.

(2) The separate money award section described by subsection (1) of this section must contain the following information:

(a) A listing of the specific amounts awarded as fines, assessments, costs, restitution and any other monetary obligations imposed in the sentence as part of the money award. If the court is unable to determine the full amount of restitution at the time of sentencing, the court may include the amount that can be determined or may establish a maximum amount.

(b) If restitution or a compensatory fine is ordered, the name of the person to whom the court should disburse payments, unless the victim requests that this information be exempt from disclosure in the public record.

(c) A statement that, subject to amendment of a judgment under ORS 137.107, money required to be paid as a condition of probation remains payable after revocation of probation only if the amount is included in the money award portion of the judgment document, even if the amount is referred to in other parts of the judgment document.

(d) Unless immediate payment is required, the specific terms of payment imposed or allowed by the court.

(e) If payment of all or part of a monetary obligation is suspended, a statement specifying the nature and amount of the suspended obligations.

(3) The requirements of this section and ORS 18.038 do not apply to a judgment document if the action was commenced by the issuance of a uniform citation adopted under ORS 1.525 and the court has used the space on the citation for the entry of a judgment. The exemption provided by this subsection does not apply if any indictment, information or complaint other than a uniform citation is filed in the action.

(4) If a judgment is for conviction of a violation as described in ORS 153.008, the judgment creates a lien only if the court so orders. If a judgment does not create a lien under this subsection, the judgment document need not contain the separate money award section described by subsection (1) of this section.

(5) A judgment in a criminal action that contains a money award is a judgment in favor of the state and may be enforced only by the state.

(6) A judgment in a criminal action that includes a money award, but does not contain a separate section clearly labeled as a money award, does not create a judgment lien but may be enforced by any other judgment remedy. [2003 c.576 §6; 2005 c.566 §13; 2005 c.568 §13; 2005 c.618 §3a; 2015 c.197 §2]

Note: Section 8 (1), chapter 618, Oregon Laws 2005, provides:
Sec. 8. (1) The amendments to ORS 18.048, 18.075, 18.180 and 18.194 by sections 1 to 4 of this 2005 Act apply to judgments entered on or after the effective date of this 2005 Act [January 1, 2006]. [2005 c.618 §8(1)]

18.049 Adjustments to money awards. After entry of a judgment, the amount owing on the money award portion of a judgment shall be decreased by all payments made by or on behalf of the judgment debtor against the money award and shall be increased by interest accruing on the money award. In addition, the judgment creditor is entitled to recover the expenses specified in ORS 18.999 that are incurred by the judgment creditor in collecting on the judgment, in the manner provided by ORS 18.999. This section does not impose any duty on a court administrator to calculate the amount owing on the money award portion of a judgment. [2007 c.166 §5]

18.050 [Amended by 1959 c.638 §6; repealed by 1981 c.898 §53]

18.052 Duty of judge with respect to form of judgment document. (1) A judge rendering a judgment shall file with the court administrator a judgment document that incorporates the judgment. The judge must sign the judgment document unless the court administrator is authorized by law to sign the judgment document. Before signing a judgment document, the judge shall ensure that all requirements imposed by law for entry of the judgment have been fulfilled, including the making of any written findings of fact or conclusions of law. If a proposed judgment document submitted under ORS 18.035 does not comply with the requirements of ORS 18.038, 18.042 and 18.048, the judge may not sign the judgment document. If a proposed judgment document submitted under ORS 18.035 establishes paternity or includes a provision concerning support, but does not comply with the requirements of ORS 25.020 (8), the judge may not sign the judgment document. Unless the judgment is exempt under ORS 18.038 (2), the judge shall ensure that the title of the judgment document indicates whether the judgment is a limited judgment, general judgment or supplemental judgment. If the judgment is a limited judgment rendered under the provisions of ORCP 67 B, the judge must determine that there is no just reason for delay, but the judgment document need not reflect that determination if the title of the judgment document indicates that the judgment is a limited judgment.

(2) A court administrator who signs a judgment under authority granted by law has the same duties as a judge under the provisions of this section.

(3) This section does not apply to justice courts, municipal courts or county courts performing judicial functions. [2003 c.576 §7; 2005 c.561 §1; 2005 c.568 §14]

18.058 Duty of court administrator with respect to form of judgment document. (1) Except as provided in subsection (2) of this section, the court administrator shall note in the register that a judgment document has been filed if the judgment document is signed by a judge of the court, or by the court administrator if the court administrator is authorized by law to sign the judgment document, and filed with the court administrator, whether or not the judgment document complies with the requirements of ORS 18.038, 18.042 and 18.048.

(2) If the title of a document filed with the court administrator indicates that the document is a decree, or indicates that the document is a judgment but fails to indicate whether the judgment is a limited judgment, general judgment or supplemental judgment, the court administrator may not note in the register that a judgment document has been filed, and shall return the document to the judge, unless the judgment is exempt under ORS 18.038 (2).

(3) The court administrator may rely on a judgment document for entry of information in the register. The court administrator is not liable for entering any information in the register that reflects information contained in a judgment document, whether or not the information in the judgment is correct or properly presented.

(4) The court administrator may rely on the presence or absence of a separate section in the judgment document required by ORS 18.042 or 18.048 in determining whether a judgment contains a money award. The court administrator shall enter information in the register and in the judgment lien record only from the separate section unless otherwise ordered by the court.

(5) This section does not apply to justice courts, municipal courts or county courts performing judicial functions. [2003 c.576 §8; 2007 c.339 §3]

18.060 [Amended by 1979 c.284 §51; repealed by 1981 c.898 §53]

18.062 Use of electronic judgment forms. The provisions of this chapter do not affect the ability of the Chief Justice of the Supreme Court to authorize the use of electronic judgment forms pursuant to rules adopted under ORS 1.002 (2). [2005 c.568 §41]

18.070 [Repealed by 1981 c.898 §53]

ENTRY OF JUDGMENTS IN REGISTER

18.075 Entry of judgments in circuit courts generally. (1) A judgment is entered in circuit court when a court administrator notes in the register that a judgment document has been filed with the court administrator.

(2) Subject to ORS 18.058 (2), when a judge files a judgment document with the court administrator, the court administrator shall note in the register:

(a) That the judgment document has been filed and the day, hour and minute that the judgment is entered.

(b) Whether the judgment is a limited judgment, a general judgment or a supplemental judgment.

(c) Whether the judgment includes a money award.

(d) Whether the judgment creates a judgment lien under ORS 18.150.

(3) If the court administrator notes in the register that a judgment creates a judgment lien, the court administrator shall note in a judgment lien record maintained by the court administrator:

(a) The name of all judgment debtors.

(b) The name of all judgment creditors.

(c) The amount of the money award.

(d) Whether the money award includes a support award or an award of restitution.

(4) If the court administrator makes a notation of judgment in the judgment lien record, the court administrator shall thereafter also note in the judgment lien record:

(a) The date on which any appeal is filed.

(b) Whether a supersedeas undertaking, as defined in ORS 19.005, is filed.

(c) The date of any decision on appeal.

(d) Any execution issued by the court and the return on any execution.

(e) Any satisfaction of the judgment, when entered.

(f) Other such information as may be deemed necessary by court order or court rule.

(5) The court administrator shall enter a judgment in the register within 24 hours after the judgment document is filed with court administrator, excluding Saturdays and legal holidays. If the court administrator is not able to enter the judgment within the time prescribed in this subsection, or fails to do so, the court administrator shall enter the judgment as soon as practicable thereafter.

(6) Except as provided in ORS 18.058, the court administrator shall be subject to the direction of the court in entering judgments in the register.

(7) The court administrator shall not delay entry of judgment under ORCP 68 for taxation of attorney fees or costs and disbursements.

(8) Administrative orders entered in the register under ORS 416.440 have the effect provided for in that section.

(9) The State Court Administrator shall ensure that the register and the judgment lien record be established and maintained in a uniform manner in the circuit courts.

(10) References in Oregon Revised Statutes to docketing of a judgment are equivalent to entry of a judgment as described in subsection (1) of this section.

(11) This section does not apply to justice courts, municipal courts or county courts performing judicial functions. [2003 c.576 §9; 2005 c.568 §15; 2005 c.618 §2; 2007 c.339 §2; 2011 c.398 §1]

Note: Section 9a, chapter 576, Oregon Laws 2003, provides:

Sec. 9a. (1) Notwithstanding any other provision of sections 1 to 44 of this 2003 Act [ORS chapter 18] or any other law, a court administrator need not make any entry in the register or in the separate record maintained under section 9 of this 2003 Act [18.075] that is different from the entries made by the court administrator before the effective date of this 2003 Act [January 1, 2004] until such time as funding is available to make such modifications as may be necessary to accommodate those entries in the computer systems utilized by the circuit courts.

(2) All references to the docket in computer records and documents of the circuit courts shall be construed to be references to the separate record maintained under section 9 of this 2003 Act, without regard to whether those records or documents are created before, on or after the effective date of this 2003 Act. Subject to availability of funding, the circuit courts shall make such changes in their computer systems and other document-generating systems as soon as possible after the effective date of this 2003 Act to eliminate references to the docket.

(3) All references to decrees in computer records and documents of the circuit courts shall be construed to be references to judgments, without regard to whether those records or documents are created before, on or after the effective date of this 2003 Act. Subject to availability of funding, the circuit courts shall make such changes in their computer systems and other document-generating systems as soon as possible after the effective date of this 2003 Act to eliminate references to decrees.

(4) All references to money judgments in computer records and documents of the circuit courts shall be construed to be references to money awards, without regard to whether those records or documents are created before, on or after the effective date of this 2003 Act. Subject to availability of funding, the circuit courts shall make such changes in their computer systems and other document-generating systems as soon as possible after the effective date of this 2003 Act to eliminate references to money judgments. [2003 c.576 §9a]

Note: See note under 18.048.

18.078 Notice of entry of judgment in circuit court civil action. (1) Upon entering a judgment in a civil action, or entry of any corrected judgment under ORS 18.107, the court administrator shall mail the notice described in subsection (2) of this section to the attorneys of record for each party that is not in default for failure to appear. If a party does not have an attorney of record, and is not in default for failure to appear, the court administrator shall mail the notice to the party. The court administrator shall note in the register that the notice required by this section was mailed as required by this section.

(2) The notice required by this section must reflect:

(a) The date the judgment was entered.

(b) Whether the judgment was entered as a limited judgment, a general judgment or a supplemental judgment.

(c) Whether the court administrator noted in the register that the judgment contained a money award.

(d) Whether the court administrator noted in the register that the judgment creates a judgment lien.

(3) This section does not apply to justice courts, municipal courts or county courts performing judicial functions.

(4) This section does not apply to judgments in juvenile proceedings under ORS chapter 419A, 419B or 419C, civil commitment proceedings, probate proceedings, adoptions or guardianship or conservatorship proceedings under ORS chapter 125. [2003 c.576 §10; 2005 c.568 §16]

Note: Section 10a, chapter 576, Oregon Laws 2003, provides:
Sec. 10a. Notwithstanding any other provision of sections 1 to 44 of this 2003 Act [ORS chapter 18] or any other law, a court administrator need not mail notice of judgment in the form provided by section 10 of this 2003 Act [18.078] and may continue to use the form of notice used by the court administrator before the effective date of this 2003 Act [January 1, 2004] until such time as funding is available to allow use of notices of judgments in the form provided by section 10 of this 2003 Act. [2003 c.576 §10a]

18.080 [Amended by 1971 c.365 §1; repealed by 1981 c.898 §53]

18.082 Effect of entry of judgment. (1) Upon entry of a judgment, the judgment:
(a) Becomes the exclusive statement of the court's decision in the case and governs the rights and obligations of the parties that are subject to the judgment;
(b) May be enforced in the manner provided by law;
(c) May be appealed in the manner provided by law;
(d) Acts as official notice of the court's decision; and
(e) May be set aside or modified only by the court rendering the judgment or by another court or tribunal with the same or greater authority than the court rendering the judgment.
(2) A general judgment incorporates a previous written decision of the court that decides one or more requests for relief in the case and that:
(a) Is not a judgment;
(b) Is consistent with the terms of the general judgment and any limited judgments in the case; and
(c) Reflects an express determination by the court that the decision be conclusive as to the requests for relief that are resolved.
(3) Upon entry of a general judgment, any request for relief in the action that is not decided by the general judgment or by a previous limited judgment, that has not been incorporated into the general judgment under subsection (2) of this section, or that cannot be decided by a supplemental judgment, is dismissed with prejudice unless the judgment provides that the dismissal is without prejudice.
(4) Subsection (3) of this section does not affect the right of any party to assign error on appeal to any decision of a court made by order during an action.
(5) Subsection (3) of this section does not apply to a general judgment of dismissal. Except as otherwise provided by law, by the Oregon Rules of Civil Procedure or by the terms of the judgment, a general judgment of dismissal is without prejudice as to any request for relief in the action.
(6) If a document labeled as a decree is filed with the court administrator, or a judgment document is filed with the court administrator that does not indicate whether the judgment is a limited, general or supplemental judgment, and the court administrator fails to comply with ORS 18.058 and makes an entry in the register indicating that a judgment has been filed with court administrator, the document has the effect of a general judgment entered in circuit court. [2003 c.576 §11; 2005 c.568 §17]

18.090 [Amended by 1979 c.284 §52; repealed by 1981 c.898 §53]

18.100 [Repealed by 1981 c.898 §53]

18.105 [1975 c.106 §1; 1977 c.208 §2; repealed by 1979 c.284 §199]

CORRECTIONS TO JUDGMENTS

18.107 Corrections to civil judgments. (1) A court may correct the terms of a civil judgment previously entered as provided in ORCP 71. The court may make the correction by signing a corrected judgment document and filing the document with the court administrator. The title of the judgment document must reflect that the judgment is a corrected limited judgment, corrected general judgment or a corrected supplemental judgment.
(2) Unless a correction to a judgment affects a substantial right of a party, the time for appeal of the judgment commences upon entry of the original judgment.
(3) If the correction of a judgment affects a substantial right of a party, and the corrected judgment is entered before the time for appealing the original judgment has expired, the time for appeal of the judgment commences upon entry of the corrected judgment. If the correction affects a substantial right of a party, and the corrected judgment is entered after the time for appealing the original judgment has expired, the time for appeal of the corrected portions of the judgment and all other portions of the judgment affected by the correction commences upon entry of the corrected judgment.
(4) This section does not apply to justice courts, municipal courts or county courts performing judicial functions.
(5) This section does not apply to juvenile proceedings under ORS chapter 419B. [2003 c.576 §12]

18.110 [Repealed by 1981 c.898 §53]

18.112 Correction of designation of judgment as general judgment. (1) Upon motion of any party, the court may enter a corrected judgment under ORS 18.107 that changes the designation of a judgment from a general judgment to a limited judgment if the moving party establishes that:
(a) Except by operation of ORS 18.082 (3), the judgment does not decide all requests for relief in the action other than requests for relief previously decided by a limited judgment or requests for relief that could be decided by a supplemental judgment; and
(b) The judgment was inadvertently designated as a general judgment under circumstances that indicate that the moving party did not reasonably understand that the requests for relief that were not expressly decided by the judgment would be dismissed.
(2) A motion under subsection (1) of this section must be filed within the time provided by ORCP 71 B.
(3) Upon motion of any party, the court shall enter a corrected judgment under ORS 18.107 that changes to a limited judgment any document that has the effect of a general judgment under the provisions of ORS 18.082 (6) unless all requests for relief in the action are decided by the terms of the document, by previous limited judgments entered in the action or by written decisions of the court that are incorporated in a general judgment under the provisions of ORS 18.082 (2).
(4) Notwithstanding ORS 18.107, the time for appeal of the judgment corrected under this section commences from the entry of the corrected judgment. A motion may be filed under this section while an appeal is pending as provided in ORCP 71 B(2).
(5) This section does not apply to justice courts, municipal courts or county courts performing judicial functions. [2003 c.576 §13; 2005 c.568 §18]

18.115 [1975 c.623 §12; 1979 c.284 §53; repealed by 1981 c.898 §53]

18.120 [Repealed by 1981 c.898 §53]

18.125 [1977 c.208 §3; repealed by 1981 c.898 §53]

18.130 [Repealed by 1977 c.208 §5]

18.135 [Formerly 15.100; repealed by 1981 c.898 §53]

18.140 [Amended by 1957 c.348 §1; 1973 c.207 §2; repealed by 1979 c.284 §199]

JUDGMENT LIENS

18.150 Judgment liens in circuit courts. (1) If a judgment document filed with a court administrator under ORS 18.075 (2) includes a money award and complies with ORS 18.042 (1) or 18.048 (1), the court administrator shall note in the register of a circuit court that the judgment creates a judgment lien unless:

(a) The judgment is entered in the small claims department of a circuit court in an amount of less than $3,000, exclusive of costs, and the judgment creditor has not created a judgment lien for the judgment as provided in ORS 46.488;

(b) The judgment is entered in a criminal action for conviction of a violation, and the court does not order under ORS 18.048 (4) that the judgment creates a judgment lien;

(c) The judgment is entered under ORS 153.820; or

(d) The judgment does not create a lien by operation of other law.

(2) Except as provided in this section, if the court administrator notes in the register that a judgment creates a judgment lien, the judgment has the following effect in the county in which the judgment is entered:

(a) When the judgment is entered, the judgment lien attaches to all real property of the judgment debtor in the county at that time; and

(b) The judgment lien attaches to all real property that the judgment debtor acquires in the county at any time after the judgment is entered and before the judgment lien expires.

(3) Except as provided in this section, if the court administrator notes in the register that a judgment creates a judgment lien and the judgment contains a support award, the support award portion of the judgment has the following effect in the county in which the judgment is entered:

(a) Any lump sum support award existing when the judgment is entered creates a support arrearage lien and has the effect specified by subsection (2) of this section;

(b) When an installment becomes due under the terms of the support award and is not paid, a support arrearage lien for the unpaid installment attaches to all real property of the judgment debtor in the county at that time; and

(c) When an installment becomes due under the terms of the support award and is not paid, a support arrearage lien attaches to all real property that the judgment debtor thereafter acquires in the county for the purpose of enforcing the unpaid installment, and remains attached to that property until satisfaction is made for the installment or the judgment lien arising from support award portion of the judgment expires.

(4) Real property may be conveyed or encumbered free of a judgment lien created by the support award portion of a judgment, but the conveyance or encumbrance is subject to any support arrearage lien that attached to the real property under this section or ORS 18.152.

(5) A judgment lien does not attach to any real property of a judgment debtor acquired after the debt giving rise to the judgment is discharged under federal bankruptcy laws. Debts are presumed to have not been discharged in bankruptcy until the judgment debtor establishes that the debt has been discharged.

(6) A court administrator may rely on the judgment document to determine whether a judgment creates a judgment lien.

(7) This section does not apply to justice courts, municipal courts or county courts performing judicial functions. [2003 c.576 §14; 2005 c.568 §19]

18.152 Establishing judgment liens in other counties. (1) At any time after a judgment that creates a judgment lien is entered under ORS 18.150 and before the expiration of the judgment remedies for the judgment, a judgment creditor may create a judgment lien for the judgment in any other county of this state by recording the judgment in the County Clerk Lien Record for that county. The judgment may be recorded by recording a certified copy of the judgment document or a lien record abstract for the judgment.

(2) Except as provided in this section, a judgment recorded under this section has the following effect in the county in which the judgment is recorded:

(a) When the judgment is recorded, the judgment lien attaches to all real property of the judgment debtor in the county at that time; and

(b) The judgment lien attaches to all real property that the judgment debtor acquires in the county at any time after the judgment is recorded and before the judgment lien expires.

(3) Except as provided in this section, if a judgment recorded under this section contains a support award, the support award portion of the judgment has the following effect in the county in which the judgment is recorded:

(a) When the judgment is recorded, a support arrearage lien attaches to all real property of the judgment debtor in the county at that time for any unpaid lump sum support award contained in the judgment or any unpaid installment that became due under the terms of the support award before the judgment was recorded.

(b) A support arrearage lien for any unpaid lump sum support award contained in the judgment or any unpaid installment that became due under the terms of the support award before the judgment was recorded attaches to all real property that the judgment debtor acquires in the county at any time after the judgment is recorded and before full satisfaction is made for the lump sum or installment or the judgment lien of the support award portion of the judgment expires.

(c) If an installment becomes due under the terms of the support award and is not paid after the judgment is recorded, a support arrearage lien for the installment attaches to all real property of the judgment debtor in the county at the time the installment becomes due and attaches to all real property that the judgment debtor thereafter acquires in the county until full satisfaction is made for the installment or the judgment lien of the support award portion of the judgment expires.

(4)(a) If a certificate of extension is filed under ORS 18.182, and the certificate is filed before the judgment is recorded under this section, a judgment creditor may record a certified copy of the certificate or a lien record abstract for the certificate with the judgment. The recording shall act to extend the judgment lien of a judgment, and any support arrearage lien, in the county for the time provided in ORS 18.180 to 18.190.

(b) If a certificate of extension is filed under ORS 18.182, and the certificate is filed after the judgment is recorded under this section, a judgment creditor may record a certified copy of the certificate or a lien record abstract for the certificate in the County Clerk Lien Record in any county in which the judgment has been recorded under subsection (1) of this section. If the recording is made before the time that the judgment lien for the judgment would otherwise have expired under ORS 18.180 to 18.190, the recording extends the judgment lien of the judgment, without loss of priority, for the time provided in ORS 18.180 to 18.190. If the recording is made after the time that the judgment lien for the judgment would otherwise have expired under ORS 18.180 to 18.190, the recording extends the judgment lien of the judgment for the time provided in ORS 18.180 to 18.190, but the lien is subordinate to all other interests that are of record on the date the certificate or lien record abstract is recorded.

(5) When the judgment lien of a judgment expires in the county in which the judgment was originally entered, the judgment lien and any support arrearage lien created under this section expires in the other county or counties in which the judgment has been recorded.

(6) This section does not apply to justice courts, municipal courts or county courts performing judicial functions. [2003 c.576 §15; 2005 c.568 §20]

18.154 Appeal; motion to eliminate lien. A judgment debtor who appeals a judgment may move the trial court for elimination of the judgment lien created by the judgment. A court may grant a motion under this section if the judgment debtor files a supersedeas undertaking, as defined in ORS 19.005, and provides such additional security as may be required by the court to ensure that adequate amounts will be available to satisfy the judgment if affirmed on appeal. If the court grants the motion, the court administrator shall note in the register and in the judgment lien record that the judgment lien has been eliminated. [2003 c.576 §16; 2007 c.339 §4]

18.158 Judgment lien based on judgment for child support or spousal support entered in another state. (1) At any time after a judgment for unpaid child support or unpaid spousal support becomes effective in another state and before the expiration or satisfaction of that judgment under the other state's law, a judgment creditor under the judgment may record a certified copy of the judgment or a lien record abstract for the judgment in the County Clerk Lien Record for any county in this state.

(2) If a judgment of another state described in subsection (1) of this section is extended or renewed under the laws of the state that rendered the judgment, a judgment creditor under the judgment may record a certified copy of the extension or renewal in the County Clerk Lien Record for any county in this state or may record a lien record abstract for extension or renewal in the County Clerk Lien Record for any county in this state.

(3) Upon recording a judgment, lien record abstract, extension or renewal under this section, the judgment creates a judgment lien as described in ORS 18.152 (3).

(4) When the judgment expires in the state in which the judgment was originally entered, the judgment lien and any support arrearage lien created under this section expire in every county in which the judgment has been recorded under this section.

(5) Liens arising by operation of law in another state against real property for amounts of overdue payments under a support order, as defined in ORS 110.503, shall be accorded full faith and credit if the state agency, party or other entity seeking to enforce the lien follows the applicable procedures for recording and service of notice of claim of lien as required by this section. A state agency, party or other entity may not file an action to enforce a lien described in this section until the underlying judgment has been filed in Oregon as provided in ORS chapter 110.

(6) This section does not apply to justice courts, municipal courts or county courts performing judicial functions. [2003 c.576 §17; 2015 c.298 §83]

18.160 [Repealed by 1981 c.898 §53]

18.162 Judgment lien based on justice and municipal court judgments; satisfaction filing fee. (1) Subject to the requirements of this section and ORS 221.344, from the time that a judgment of a justice or municipal court is transcribed or recorded as provided in ORS 52.635 or 221.351, the judgment creates a judgment lien as described in ORS 18.152.

(2) The judgment lien of a judgment entered in a justice or municipal court may be eliminated as provided in ORS 18.154 if an appeal is taken from the judgment. The clerk of the justice or municipal court shall note the elimination of the lien in the judgment docket.

(3) When the lien of a justice or municipal court judgment ceases in the county in which the judgment was originally recorded or transcribed, the lien shall cease in every other county in which a certified copy of the judgment or a lien record abstract has been recorded. When the judgment has been fully satisfied, it is the responsibility of the judgment creditor to file a full satisfaction in any circuit court to which the judgment has been transcribed under ORS 52.635, and to record the satisfaction in the County Clerk Lien Record for the county in which the court is located if a certified copy of the judgment or a lien record abstract for the judgment was recorded in that County Clerk Lien Record. Upon satisfaction in full of the judgment, the judgment creditor shall deliver to the judgment debtor an executed satisfaction of the judgment for any other county where a certified copy of the judgment or a lien record abstract has been recorded. The county clerk shall charge a fee as provided in ORS 205.320 for filing a satisfaction of judgment. [Formerly 18.355]

18.165 Priority of judgment lien over unrecorded conveyance. (1) If a judgment with lien effect under ORS 18.150, 18.152 or 18.158 is entered or recorded in a county before a conveyance, or a memorandum of a conveyance, of real property of the debtor is recorded in that county, the conveyance of the judgment debtor's interest is void as against the lien of the judgment unless:

(a) The grantee under the conveyance is a purchaser in good faith for a valuable consideration, the conveyance is delivered and accepted before the judgment is entered or recorded in the county where the property is located and the conveyance or memorandum of the conveyance is recorded within 20 days after delivery and acceptance of the conveyance, excluding Saturdays and legal holidays under ORS 187.010 and 187.020;

(b) The judgment creditor has actual notice, record notice or inquiry notice of a conveyance of the debtor's interest to a grantee when the judgment is entered or recorded in the county;

(c) The conveyance by the debtor is a fulfillment deed entitled to priority over the judgment under ORS 93.645; or

(d) The conveyance is a mortgage, trust deed or other security instrument given by the debtor to secure financing for the purchase by the debtor of the real property described in the conveyance.

(2) For the purpose of subsection (1)(a) of this section, a memorandum of conveyance must contain the date of the instrument being memorialized, the names of the parties, a legal description of the real property involved and a description of the nature of the interest created. The memorandum must be signed by the person from whom the interest is intended to pass, and be acknowledged or proved in the manner provided for the acknowledgment or proof of deeds.

(3) As used in this section:

(a) "Conveyance" means a deed, a land sale contract, an assignment of all or any portion of a seller's or purchaser's interest in a land sale contract or any other agreement affecting the title of real property within this state, including a trust deed, a mortgage, an assignment for security purposes or an assignment solely of proceeds, given by a purchaser or seller under a land sale contract or given by a person with title to the real property.

(b) "Grantee" means:

(A) The person deemed to be the mortgagee under a trust deed pursuant to ORS 86.715; and

(B) Any other person to whom the interest that is the subject of a conveyance is intended to pass. [Formerly 18.370; 2005 c.568 §21; 2007 c.166 §1]

18.170 Form for lien record abstract; rules. (1) Unless otherwise prescribed by law, a person recording a lien record abstract shall use substantially the following form:

LIEN RECORD ABSTRACT

The undersigned states:

A. Creditor/Prevailing Party Information:
___ 1.   The creditor/prevailing party is:

_____
and the address of the creditor is:

_____

under judgment, order or petition
entered on _____ (date) in
the _____ Court for
_____ (County) of _____ (State)
under Case No. _____ .
___ 2.   The creditor's attorney's name is

_____
Attorney's Address is:

_____
Attorney's Phone No. is: _____

B. Debtor/Losing Party Information:
___ 1.   The debtor/losing party is:

_____
___ 2.   Debtor's address (if known):

_____

___ 3. The final four digits of the debtor's
Taxpayer Identification No.,
or the final four digits of
the debtor's Social Security No.
(if known):

___ 4. The final four digits of the debtor's
driver license no. and state of
issuance for the license (if known):

___ 5. Name of debtor's attorney
(if known):

C. Judgment Information:
___ 1. The amount of the judgment is:

___ 2. The amount of the costs is:

___ 3. The amount of attorney fees, if any
is: _____

D. The Real or Personal Property to Be
Affected
(Check appropriate box):
___ All real property of the debtor/losing
party, now or hereafter acquired,
in _____ County as provided
under ORS 18.152
___ The following described real or
personal property of debtor (legal
description as set forth or on
attached Exhibit):
_____
_____
_____
_____

IN WITNESS WHEREOF, the
undersigned person or persons have
executed this   abstract this ___ day
of_____, 2____.

_____   _____
_____   _____

State of Oregon   )
)   ss.
County of_____   )

The foregoing instrument was acknowledged before me this ___ day of___, 2___, by_____.

_____
Notary Public for Oregon

My commission expires: _____

State of Oregon   )
)   ss.
County of_____   )

The foregoing instrument was acknowledged before me this ___ day of___, 2___, by _____ and by _____
of_____, a corporation on behalf of the corporation.

_____
Notary Public for Oregon

My commission expires: _____

(2) A lien record abstract that is the result of a judgment for unpaid child or spousal support entered in another state shall be on the form prescribed by rules adopted by the Department of Justice in lieu of the form required by subsection (1) of this section. [Formerly 18.325; 2009 c.230 §2; 2015 c.197 §3]

EXPIRATION AND EXTENSION OF JUDGMENT REMEDIES

18.180 Expiration of judgment remedies in circuit court. (1) Judgment remedies for a judgment expire upon full satisfaction of the money award portion of the judgment.
(2) If a judgment lien arises out of a support award under ORS 18.150 (3) or 18.152 (3), a support arrearage lien attaching to real property under the judgment lien expires upon satisfaction of the unpaid installment that gave rise to the support arrearage lien.
(3) Except as provided in ORS 18.180 to 18.190, judgment remedies for a judgment in a civil action expire 10 years after the entry of the judgment.

(4) Except as provided in this subsection, judgment remedies for a judgment in a criminal action expire 20 years after the entry of the judgment. Judgment remedies for a judgment in a criminal action that includes a money award for restitution expire 50 years after the entry of the judgment.

(5) Judgment remedies for the child support award portion of a judgment, and any lump sum support award for child support, expire 35 years after the entry of the judgment that first establishes the support obligation.

(6)(a) Except as provided by paragraph (b) of this subsection and ORS 18.190, judgment remedies for any unpaid installment under the spousal support award portion of a judgment, including any installment arrearage lien arising under the judgment, expire 25 years after the entry of the judgment that first establishes the support obligation, or 10 years after an installment comes due under the judgment and is not paid, whichever is later.

(b) The judgment lien for the spousal support award portion of a judgment that is entered on or after January 1, 2004, including any installment arrearage lien arising under the judgment, expires 25 years after the entry of the judgment that first establishes the support obligation unless a certificate of extension is filed under ORS 18.185.

(7)(a) If a money award in a judgment under ORS 107.105 (1)(f) provides for a future payment of money, judgment remedies for the portion of the judgment providing for future payment expire 10 years after the date on which the future payment becomes due. At any time before the judgment remedies for a money award described in this subsection expire, judgment remedies for the portion of the judgment providing for a future payment may be extended as provided in ORS 18.182.

(b) This subsection does not apply to support awards.

(8) This section does not apply to justice courts, municipal courts or county courts performing judicial functions. [2003 c.576 §18; 2005 c.568 §22; 2005 c.618 §1; 2007 c.22 §1; 2009 c.354 §1; 2015 c.212 §22]

Note: See note under 18.048.

Note: Section 2, chapter 354, Oregon Laws 2009, provides:
Sec. 2. (1) Except as provided in subsection (2) of this section, the amendments to ORS 18.180 by section 1 of this 2009 Act apply to all judgments, whether entered before, on or after the effective date of this 2009 Act [January 1, 2010].

(2) The amendments to ORS 18.180 by section 1 of this 2009 Act do not operate to revive any judgment remedies that expired before the effective date of this 2009 Act under the provisions of ORS 18.180 as in effect immediately before the effective date of this 2009 Act. [2009 c.354 §2]

18.182 Extension of judgment remedies. (1) Judgment remedies for a judgment may be extended by filing a certificate of extension in the court that entered the judgment. The court administrator shall enter the certificate in the register of the court and in the judgment lien record. Except as provided in ORS 18.180 to 18.190, a judgment creditor may file a certificate of extension only if:
(a) Judgment remedies for the judgment have not expired under ORS 18.180; and
(b) A full satisfaction document for the money award portion of the judgment has not been filed.

(2) Notwithstanding subsection (1) of this section, if the judgment debtor has been discharged from debt under federal bankruptcy laws, a certificate of extension may not be filed except as provided in this subsection. Judgments are presumed to have not been discharged in bankruptcy until the judgment debtor establishes that the judgment has been discharged. If the judgment debtor is discharged from a debt, a certificate of extension may be filed if:
(a) The debtor owned real property and the judgment lien attached to that property before the filing of the bankruptcy petition;
(b) The judgment lien was not avoided by action of the bankruptcy court;
(c) The judgment lien has not been discharged under ORS 18.238; and
(d) The certificate of extension includes a legal description of the real property and a statement that the extension affects only the lien on the real property described in the certificate.

(3) A certificate of extension must be signed by the judgment creditor, or by an attorney who represents the judgment creditor.

(4) Subject to ORS 18.190, if a certificate of extension is filed after the date on which the judgment remedies for the judgment expire under ORS 18.180, the certificate has no effect.

(5) The judgment remedies for a judgment that are extended under the provisions of this section expire 10 years after the certificate of extension is filed. Judgment remedies for a judgment may be extended only once under the provisions of this section.

(6) A certified copy of a certificate of extension, or a lien record abstract for the certificate, may be recorded in any county in which the judgment was recorded under ORS 18.152, with the effect provided by ORS 18.152 (4).

(7) Except as provided in ORS 18.185 and 18.190, the judgment remedies for the support award portion of a judgment, and any lump sum money award for unpaid child support installments, may not be extended under this section.

(8) The judgment remedies for a judgment in a criminal action may not be extended under this section.

(9) This section does not apply to justice courts, municipal courts or county courts performing judicial functions. [2003 c.576 §19; 2007 c.339 §5; 2015 c.212 §23]

18.185 Extension of judgment lien of spousal support award. (1) If a judgment that is entered on or after January 1, 2004, includes a spousal support award, a judgment creditor may file a certificate of extension under ORS 18.182 at any time more than 15 years after the entry of the judgment that first establishes the support obligation and before the judgment lien for the spousal support award portion of a judgment expires under ORS 18.180 (6)(b). If a certificate of extension is filed under this subsection:
(a) The judgment lien for the spousal support award portion of the judgment expires 10 years after the certificate of extension is filed; and
(b) Any installment arrearage lien that arises under the judgment, whether before or after the filing of the certificate, expires 10 years after the installment comes due and is not paid or when the judgment lien for the spousal support award portion of the judgment expires under paragraph (a) of this subsection, whichever is first.

(2) Notwithstanding ORS 18.182 (5), certificates of extension under ORS 18.182 may continue to be filed in the manner provided by subsection (1) of this section and with like effect for as long as the judgment lien for the spousal support award portion of a judgment has not expired and any installments remain to be paid under the judgment. [2003 c.576 §20]

18.190 Spousal support awards in judgments entered before January 1, 2004. (1) The judgment lien for the spousal support award portion of a judgment that is entered before January 1, 2004, including any installment arrearage liens that arise under the judgment, expires 10 years after the entry of the judgment that first establishes the support obligation unless a certificate of extension is filed under ORS 18.182, or the judgment was renewed in the manner provided by the statutes in effect immediately before January 1, 2004, within 10 years after the judgment was entered.

(2) ORS 18.180 (6) does not operate to revive the judgment lien of any judgment that expired before January 1, 2004, under the statutes in effect immediately before January 1, 2004.

(3) This section and ORS 18.180 (6) do not limit the time during which judgment remedies are available for any judgment entered before January 1, 2004, and those judgments may continue to be enforced for the time provided by the law in effect immediately before January 1, 2004, subject to any requirement for renewal of those judgments. [2003 c.576 §21]

18.192 [2003 c.576 §22; repealed by 2015 c.212 §20]

18.194 Expiration and extension of judgment remedies for justice and municipal court judgments. (1) Judgment remedies for a judgment in justice and municipal courts expire upon full satisfaction of the money award portion of the judgment.

(2) Except as provided in this section, judgment remedies for a judgment in a civil action in a justice or municipal court expire 10 years after the entry of the judgment.

(3) Except as provided in this subsection, judgment remedies for a judgment in a criminal action in a justice or municipal court expire 20 years after the entry of the judgment. Judgment remedies for a judgment in a criminal action in a justice or municipal court that includes a money award for restitution expire 50 years after the entry of the judgment.

(4) Judgment remedies for a judgment in justice or municipal court may be extended by filing a certificate of extension in the court that entered the judgment. The clerk shall enter the certificate in the docket of the court. A judgment creditor may file a certificate of extension only if:

(a) Judgment remedies for the judgment have not expired; and

(b) A full satisfaction judgment for the money award portion of the judgment has not been filed.

(5) Notwithstanding subsection (4) of this section, if the judgment debtor has been discharged from debt under federal bankruptcy laws, a certificate of extension may not be filed except as provided in this subsection. Judgments are presumed to have not been discharged in bankruptcy until the judgment debtor establishes that the judgment has been discharged. If the judgment debtor is discharged from a debt, a certificate of extension may be filed if:

(a) The debtor owned real property and the judgment lien attached to that property before the filing of the bankruptcy petition;

(b) The judgment lien was not avoided by action of the bankruptcy court;

(c) The judgment lien has not been discharged under ORS 18.238; and

(d) The certificate of extension includes a legal description of the real property and a statement that the extension affects only the lien on the real property described in the certificate.

(6) If a certificate of extension is filed under this section after the date on which the judgment remedies for the judgment expire, the certificate has no effect.

(7) The judgment remedies for a judgment that are extended under the provisions of this section expire 10 years after the certificate of extension is filed. Judgment remedies for a judgment may be extended only once under the provisions of this section.

(8) A certified copy of a certificate of extension, or a lien record abstract for the certificate, may be recorded in any county in which the judgment was transcribed or recorded as provided in ORS 52.635 or 221.351, with the effect provided by ORS 18.152 (4).

(9) The judgment remedies for a judgment in a criminal action may not be extended under this section. [Formerly 18.365; 2005 c.618 §4]

Note: See note under 18.048.

RELEASE OF LIEN

18.200 Release of lien. (1) A judgment creditor may provide a release of lien document to a judgment debtor or to any other person with an interest in real property to which a judgment lien has attached. The release of lien document may be for all real property in a county or for a single piece of real property in a county. A release of lien document may be signed by the judgment creditor, or by any attorney who represents the creditor. The signature of the judgment creditor or attorney signing a release of lien document must be witnessed by a notary public.

(2) A release of lien document may be filed with the court administrator at any time after a judgment lien attaches under ORS 18.150. The court administrator shall note in the register and in the judgment lien record that the release of lien document has been filed, and also shall note whether the release is for all real property in a county or only for a single piece of real property in a county.

(3) A release of lien document may be recorded in any County Clerk Lien Record in which the judgment was recorded under ORS 18.152.

(4) Upon filing or recording under this section, a release of lien document operates to eliminate any judgment lien arising from the entry or recording of the judgment to the extent reflected in the document. The filing of a release of lien document does not constitute a full or partial satisfaction of the judgment.

(5) The court administrator may not charge a fee for filing a release of lien document.

(6) This section does not apply to justice courts, municipal courts or county courts performing judicial functions. [2003 c.576 §23; 2007 c.339 §6]

18.202 Reinstatement of lien. (1) If the administrator, as defined in ORS 25.010, eliminated a judgment lien document by filing a release of lien document with the court administrator under ORS 18.200, the administrator may reinstate the lien by recording a notice of reinstatement in the County Clerk Lien Record for the county where the judgment was entered.

(2) If the administrator, as defined in ORS 25.010, eliminated a judgment lien by recording a release of lien document in a County Clerk Lien Record under the provisions of ORS 18.200, the administrator may reinstate the lien by recording a notice of reinstatement in the County Clerk Lien Record for the county in which the release was recorded.

(3) The administrator may reinstate a lien under this section only if:

(a) The release was for all real property of a judgment debtor in a county; and

(b) The judgment lien that was eliminated arose out of the support award portion of the judgment.

(4) A certified copy of the judgment document, or a lien record abstract for the judgment, must be attached to the notice of reinstatement and be recorded with the notice. A notice of reinstatement may be recorded at any time after the release of lien document was filed or recorded and before the expiration of the judgment remedies for the judgment that gives rise to the judgment lien.

(5) Upon recording a notice of reinstatement under this section, the reinstated judgment lien has the same force and effect as a judgment lien created under ORS 18.152.

(6) A notice of reinstatement must be signed by the administrator as defined in ORS 25.010, or by an attorney who represents the administrator. The signature must be witnessed by a notary public. [2005 c.568 §9]

ASSIGNMENT OF JUDGMENT

18.205 Assignment of judgment. (1) A judgment creditor may assign all or part of the creditor's rights under a judgment. An assignment of judgment document must be signed by the judgment creditor, by the judgment creditor's agent or by an attorney who represents the judgment creditor. Signature by the judgment creditor's agent is not subject to the requirement of ORS 9.320 that a party that is not a natural person appear by an attorney in all cases. The signature must be acknowledged by a notary public. The document may be:

(a) Filed with the court administrator for the court in which the judgment was entered, and upon such filing shall be entered in the register and in the judgment lien record; or

(b) Recorded in any County Clerk Lien Record in which the judgment was recorded under ORS 18.152.

(2) Upon filing or recording under this section, an assignment of judgment document operates to assign the judgment creditor's rights under the judgment to the extent reflected in the document.

(3) If this or another state is assigned or subrogated to the support rights of a person under ORS 412.024, 418.032, 419B.406 or 419C.597 or similar statutes of another state, an assignment of judgment document bearing the signature of the Administrator of the Division of Child Support of the Department of Justice or the authorized representative of the administrator may be filed or recorded in the same manner as an assignment of judgment document under subsection (1) of this section and shall have the same effect as an assignment of judgment document signed by the judgment creditor.

(4) This section does not apply to justice courts, municipal courts or county courts performing judicial functions. [2003 c.576 §24; 2007 c.339 §7; 2011 c.226 §1; 2015 c.7 §2]

18.210 [Repealed by 1979 c.284 §199]

18.220 [Repealed by 1979 c.284 §199]

SATISFACTION OF MONEY AWARDS

18.225 Satisfaction of money awards generally. (1) A satisfaction document may be for full or partial satisfaction of a money award. The title of the document must indicate whether the money award has been partially or fully satisfied. A satisfaction document must be signed by the judgment creditor or by an attorney who represents the judgment creditor. The signature of the judgment creditor or attorney signing a satisfaction document must be witnessed by a notary public.

(2) When the money award portion of a judgment has been fully satisfied, the judgment creditor must:

(a) File a satisfaction document for the full amount of the money award portion of the judgment in the county in which the judgment was entered; and

(b) Deliver to the judgment debtor a satisfaction document for the full amount of the money award portion of the judgment for every county in which the judgment has been recorded under ORS 18.152.

(3) Upon request by a judgment debtor or any person with an interest in real property subject to a judgment lien, a judgment creditor must provide to the judgment debtor a satisfaction document for all amounts credited against a money award as of the date that the satisfaction document is signed.

(4) A satisfaction document may be filed with the court administrator at any time after entry of a judgment. The court administrator may not charge a fee for filing a satisfaction document. The court administrator shall note in the register and in the judgment lien record that the satisfaction document has been filed, and shall note if the document indicates that the money award has been fully satisfied.

(5) Upon payment of all required fees, the court administrator shall issue a certified copy of any satisfaction document filed with the court administrator and entered in the court register. The certified copy may be recorded in any County Clerk Lien Record in which the judgment was recorded under ORS 18.152.

(6) A satisfaction document for a support award that is paid to the Department of Justice may be filed with the court administrator only as provided in ORS 18.228.

(7) This section does not apply to justice courts, municipal courts or county courts performing judicial functions. [2003 c.576 §25; 2007 c.339 §8]

18.228 Satisfaction of support awards payable to Department of Justice. (1) If a support award is paid to the Department of Justice, the judgment creditor may receive credit for satisfaction of the judgment only in the manner provided by this section. The department may provide judgment creditors with forms and instructions for satisfaction of support awards under this section.

(2) Any satisfaction document for a support award described in subsection (1) of this section must be mailed to or delivered to the Department of Justice, and not to the court administrator. The department shall credit the amounts reflected in the satisfaction document to the support award pay records maintained by the department. Except as provided in subsection (3) of this section, the department shall not credit amounts against the support award pay records to the extent that the judgment is assigned or subrogated to this or another state. The Department of Justice shall thereafter promptly forward the satisfaction document to the court administrator for the court in which the money award was entered, together with a certificate from the department stating the amounts reflected as paid in the support award pay records maintained by the department. The court administrator shall note in the register as paid only the amount stated in the certificate, and not the amount shown on the satisfaction document.

(3) If a support award has been assigned to this state, the Department of Justice may satisfy the support award to the extent of the assignment. The department may credit the amounts reflected in the satisfaction document to the support award pay records maintained by the department and file the satisfaction document with the court administrator for the court in which the money award was entered, together with a certificate from the department stating the amounts reflected as paid in the support award pay records. The court administrator shall note in the register and in the judgment lien record the amount of satisfaction shown on the certificate, and not the amount shown on the satisfaction document.

(4) Unless a judgment requires that payments under a support award be paid to the Department of Justice or enforcement services are provided pursuant to ORS 25.080, all satisfaction documents for a support award must be filed with the court administrator. [2003 c.576 §26; 2007 c.339 §9]

18.230 [Amended by 1967 c.466 §1; 1975 c.134 §1; repealed by 1979 c.284 §199]

18.232 Alternate method for satisfaction of support awards payable to Department of Justice. (1) In addition to or in lieu of the certificate and satisfaction document provided for in ORS 18.228, the Department of Justice may execute and file a satisfaction document for a support award requiring payment to the department if:

(a) The judgment debtor provides a sworn affidavit indicating that the money award has been paid in full;

(b) The department certifies that the department has a complete pay record for the payments under the support award; and

(c) The department certifies that there are no arrearages.

(2) The Department of Justice shall be considered to have a complete pay record for the purposes of subsection (1) of this section if the department has kept the pay record for the support award from the date that the first payment was to be made under the support award, or if the judgment creditor or an entity providing enforcement services under ORS 25.080 establishes arrearages for the time period the pay record was not kept by the department.

(3) The signature of a person signing a satisfaction document filed under this section need not be acknowledged by a notary public.

(4) If a satisfaction document under this section is for any payment made to the Department of Justice for amounts that have not been assigned by the judgment creditor to the state, the department shall give notice to the judgment creditor in the manner provided by ORS 25.085. The notice must inform the judgment creditor that the department will execute and file the satisfaction of judgment unless the department receives a request for a hearing within 30 days after the date the notice was mailed. If a judgment creditor requests a hearing, the Department of Justice shall conduct the hearing as a contested case under ORS chapter 183 before a hearing officer appointed by the department. [2003 c.576 §27]

18.235 Motion to satisfy money award. (1) A judgment debtor, or a person with an interest in real property against which a judgment lien exists, may move the court for an order declaring that a money award has been satisfied or for a determination of the amount necessary to satisfy the money award, when the person making the motion cannot otherwise obtain a satisfaction document from a judgment creditor.

(2) Motions under this section shall be filed in the action in which the judgment was entered. All proceedings on the motion shall be conducted as part of the action in which the judgment was entered. An appearance fee may not be charged for filing a motion under this section.

(3) A motion under this section must include the following information, to the extent known to the person making the motion:

(a) The date of entry and principal amount of the money award.

(b) The rate of interest and the date the interest commenced to accrue.

(c) The date or dates and amounts of any payments on the money award.

(d) Any amount that the person believes remains to be paid on the money award, including any supporting mathematical calculations.

(e) Any other information necessary or helpful to the court in making its determination.

(4) A person making a motion under this section must serve the motion on the judgment creditor. If the person making the motion is not the judgment debtor, the person also must serve the motion and supporting affidavit on the judgment debtor. If an assignment of judgment document has been filed with the court under ORS 18.205, the motion must be served on the person named as the assignee of the judgment. Service on the judgment creditor and judgment debtor under this subsection may be made as provided in ORCP 9 if the motion is filed within one year after entry of the judgment. If the motion is filed more than one year after entry of the judgment, or service is to be made on an assignee of the judgment, the motion may either be personally served as provided in ORCP 7, or be served by certified mail, return receipt requested with signed receipt. The court may waive service on any person under this subsection if the person making the motion files an affidavit with the court stating that the person cannot be found after diligent effort by the person making the motion. The person making the motion shall file proof of service with the court.

(5) A person served with a motion under this section must file a response within 21 days after service is made, or within such time as may be allowed by the court. The response must specifically identify those assertions in the motion that the person contests. The response must contain any information or mathematical calculations necessary to support the contentions of the responding party.

(6) The court shall hear the motion not less than seven days after notice of hearing is given to the person making the motion and to the parties served with the motion. The court shall hear and determine the issues in a summary fashion without a jury. The court shall give the parties a reasonable opportunity to present evidence relevant to any factual issues.

(7) If the court determines that the person making the motion is entitled to relief, the court shall issue an order providing that the money award has been satisfied in full or, if the money award has not been satisfied in full, the specific amount that will satisfy the judgment on a specific date or within a period of time specified in the order.

(8) If the court finds that the judgment creditor willfully failed to provide a satisfaction document under ORS 18.225, the court may render a supplemental judgment awarding reasonable attorney fees to the person making the motion. The supplemental judgment may provide that the person making the motion may satisfy the judgment by paying such amounts the court determines to be necessary to satisfy the judgment less that sum of money the court awards as attorney fees.

(9) If the court finds that the money award has been satisfied, or if the amount specified by the court is paid to the court administrator within the time specified by the court, the court administrator shall note in the register and in the judgment lien record that the money award has been satisfied in full. The court administrator shall deliver any money paid to the court administrator to the party or parties specified in the court's order.

(10) Upon request of the person making the motion, the court administrator shall issue a certificate indicating that the money award has been satisfied. The certificate may be recorded in any County Clerk Lien Record in which the judgment was recorded under ORS 18.152. Recording of the certificate eliminates any judgment lien that was created by the recording of the judgment.

(11) At least five days before filing a motion under this section, the person must serve by personal delivery or first class mail a copy of the motion on the Administrator of the Division of Child Support of the Department of Justice, or on the branch office of the Department of Justice providing support services to the county in which the motion will be made, if:

(a) The motion relates to satisfaction of a support award; and

(b) Child support rights, as defined in ORS 25.010, for the judgment creditor have been assigned to the state.

(12) This section does not apply to justice courts, municipal courts or county courts performing judicial functions. [2003 c.576 §28; 2007 c.166 §3; 2007 c.339 §10]

18.238 Proceedings after discharge in bankruptcy. (1) Any person discharged from debts pursuant to the federal bankruptcy laws may file in any court or tribunal in which a judgment has at any time been rendered against the person, either before or after such discharge, a motion in the suit, action or proceeding for the discharge of the judgment from the record. After notice to the judgment creditor, or to any assignee of the judgment creditor whose assignment has been filed or recorded under ORS 18.205, the court shall enter a final order that the judgment be discharged and satisfied of record if the debtor establishes that:

(a) The debtor has been discharged from the payment of the judgment or the claim upon which the judgment was based; and

(b) Either there was no property to which a judgment lien had attached under ORS 18.150, 18.152, 52.635 or 221.351, as of the date the petition for relief is filed under the federal bankruptcy laws, or if there was such property, the value of the property on the date of the filing of the petition was not more than the outstanding balance of any prior lien or liens upon the property.

(2) If the debtor fails to meet the burden of proof established by subsection (1) of this section, the court shall enter a final order denying the debtor's motion.

(3) For the purposes of this section, when notice was given in connection with bankruptcy proceedings to a creditor retaining a beneficial interest in an assigned judgment or claim, such notice shall provide the basis for the satisfaction of that portion of the judgment in which the creditor retains a beneficial interest. When the bankrupt received notice prior to the adjudication of bankruptcy of the assignment of a judgment or claim, notice to the assignor retaining a beneficial interest may not provide the basis for satisfaction for that portion of the judgment which represents the amount actually paid by the assignee of the judgment for the claim and actual court costs incurred by the assignee in prosecuting the claim. [Formerly 18.420]

18.240 [Repealed by 1979 c.284 §199]

CONTRIBUTION

18.242 Contribution among judgment debtors; subrogation of surety. When property liable to an execution against several persons is sold thereon, and more than a due proportion of the judgment is levied upon the property of one of them, or one of them pays, without a sale, more than that person's proportion, that person may compel contribution from the others; and when a judgment is against several, and is upon an obligation or contract of one of them as security for another, and the surety pays the amount, or any part thereof, either by sale of property or before sale, the surety may compel repayment from the principal. In such cases, the person so paying or contributing shall be entitled to the benefit of the judgment to enforce contribution or repayment, if within 30 days after payment the person files with the clerk of the court where the judgment was rendered, notice of payment and claim to contribution or repayment; upon filing such notice, the clerk shall make an entry thereof in the margin of the docket where the judgment is entered. In any county where the judgment was recorded the person may have the notice of payment and claim to contribution or repayment recorded in the County Clerk Lien Record. [Formerly 18.430]

Note: 18.242 was enacted into law by the Legislative Assembly but was not added to or made a part of ORS chapter 18 or any series therein by legislative action. See Preface to Oregon Revised Statutes for further explanation.

APPEAL

18.245 Jurisdictional requirements. The following requirements are the only requirements of this chapter that are jurisdictional for the purposes of appeal of a judgment:

(1) The judgment document for the judgment must be plainly titled as a judgment as required by ORS 18.038 (1).

(2) The judgment document for the judgment must comply with the requirements of ORS 18.038 (4).

(3) The court administrator for the circuit court rendering the judgment must note in the register of the court that the judgment document has been filed, as required by ORS 18.058 (1). [2005 c.568 §2]

Note: See first note under 18.005.

18.250 [Repealed by 1979 c.284 §199]

ENFORCEMENT OF JUDGMENTS

(Generally)

18.252 Execution. (1) Except as provided in this section, and subject to the terms of the judgment, a judgment may be enforced by execution upon entry of the judgment. The ability to enforce a judgment by execution expires as provided in ORS 18.180 to 18.190.

(2) Any portion of a money award that by the terms of the judgment is to be paid on some date after the date that the judgment is entered may be enforced by execution when payment becomes due under the terms of the money award and is not paid.

(3) Except as provided in ORS 18.255 or by other law, a judgment may be enforced only by the court in which the judgment is entered or, if the judgment is a foreign judgment, the court in which the judgment is first filed under ORS 24.115 or 110.605 to 110.611.

(4) Nothing in ORS 18.252 to 18.993 affects the ability of a judgment creditor to enforce a judgment by means other than execution. [2003 c.576 §29; 2015 c.298 §84]

18.255 Enforcement of judgment by circuit court for county where debtor resides. (1) The circuit court for the county where a judgment debtor resides may enforce a circuit court judgment entered in another circuit court if a transcript of the original judgment is filed with the court. The circuit court for the county where a judgment debtor resides may issue a writ of execution against real property under the provisions of this section only if a certified copy of the original judgment, or a lien record abstract in the form provided by ORS 18.170, is recorded in the County Clerk Lien Record for that county, in addition to the filing of a transcript of the original judgment with the circuit court for that county. In no event shall the court administrator be liable for issuing a writ of execution, writ of garnishment or other execution for a judgment transcribed pursuant to this section.

(2) A judgment creditor who files a transcript of a judgment under subsection (1) of this section must give written notice of the filing to the circuit court in which the judgment was originally entered.

(3) At the time a transcript of a judgment is filed under this section, the judgment creditor or the attorney for the judgment creditor must make and file with the court administrator a statement containing the information required for a money award under ORS 18.042 (2) and an affidavit setting forth:

(a) The name and last-known address of the judgment creditor;

(b) The name and last-known address of the judgment debtor;

(c) A statement that the judgment creditor has a good faith belief that the judgment debtor resides in the county in which the transcript of the judgment is filed;

(d) A statement that the judgment has not been satisfied and that execution on the judgment has not been stayed; and

(e) A statement that written notice of the filing has been given to the circuit court in which the judgment was originally entered.

(4) The circuit court in which a transcript of a judgment is filed under this section is the only court with authority to issue a writ of execution, writ of garnishment or other execution on the transcribed judgment until the judgment creditor files an affidavit with the circuit court certifying that the judgment debtor no longer resides in that county. A copy of the affidavit must be filed by the judgment creditor in the court in which the judgment was originally entered. After the filing of an affidavit under this subsection, only the circuit court in which the judgment was originally entered may issue a writ of execution, writ of garnishment or other execution on the judgment.

(5) When a transcribed judgment is filed with a circuit court under this section, the court administrator shall enter the transcribed judgment in the register but shall not note in the register that the judgment creates a judgment lien. Satisfaction documents under ORS 18.225 and certificates of extension under ORS 18.180 to 18.190 may be filed only in the court in which the judgment was originally entered.

(6) This section does not apply to justice courts, municipal courts or county courts performing judicial functions. [2003 c.576 §30; 2017 c.252 §11]

18.260 [Amended by 1971 c.224 §1; repealed by 1979 c.284 §199]

(Proceedings in Support of Execution)

18.265 Debtor examination. (1) At any time after a judgment is entered, a judgment creditor may upon motion obtain an order requiring the judgment debtor to appear before the court or a referee appointed by the court at the time and place specified in the order, and requiring the judgment debtor to answer under oath questions concerning any property or interest in property that the judgment debtor may have or claim. The motion must be supported by one of the following:

(a) Proof of service of a notice of demand to pay the judgment within 10 days. The notice of demand must be served in the same manner as a summons or by any form of mail addressed to the judgment debtor and requesting a receipt. Service by mail under this paragraph is effective on the date of mailing.

(b) A return of a writ of execution showing that the judgment has not been satisfied.

(c) A garnishee response to a writ of garnishment that does not fully satisfy the judgment.

(2) Only the following courts may issue an order under this section:

(a) The court in which the original judgment was entered.

(b) Any circuit court for the county in which the judgment debtor resides and in which the judgment has been recorded under ORS 18.152.

(c) Any circuit court for the county in which the principal place of employment of the judgment debtor is located and in which the judgment has been recorded under ORS 18.152.

(3) If a motion under this section is filed in the court specified by subsection (2)(b) or (c) of this section, a certified copy of the judgment or a certified copy of the recording made in the County Clerk Lien Record of the county must be filed with the motion unless a transcript of the judgment has been filed with the court under ORS 18.255.

(4) Except as provided in this section, a judgment debtor may not be required to attend in a county other than the county in which the judgment debtor resides or may be found at the time of service of the order requiring the appearance, unless the place where the judgment debtor is to appear is not more than 100 miles from the residence of the judgment debtor.

(5) If the judgment debtor resides more than 100 miles from the place of examination, the judgment debtor shall be required to appear and shall be paid mileage at the time of the hearing as provided for witnesses in ORS 44.415.

(6) Upon motion and good cause shown, the court may order that proceedings under this section be conducted at a time or place other than the time or place specified in the original order.

(7) The court may at any time enter an order restraining the judgment debtor from selling, transferring or in any manner disposing of any property of the judgment debtor that is subject to execution pending an examination under this section. [2003 c.576 §31]

18.268 Conduct of debtor examination; seizure of property. (1) A judgment debtor may be examined on oath concerning the judgment debtor's property in a debtor's examination. Upon request by the judgment creditor, the proceedings shall be reduced to writing and filed with the court administrator. The judgment creditor and judgment debtor may subpoena and examine witnesses.

(2) If it appears that the judgment debtor has any property that may be applied against the judgment, the court may order that the property be seized for application against the judgment. [2003 c.576 §32]

18.270 Written interrogatories. (1) At any time after a judgment is entered, a judgment creditor may serve written interrogatories relating to the judgment debtor's property and financial affairs on a judgment debtor. The interrogatories may be personally served in the manner provided for summons or may be served by any form of mail addressed to the judgment debtor and requesting a receipt. Service by mail under this subsection is effective on the date of mailing. The interrogatories shall notify the judgment debtor that the judgment debtor's failure to answer the interrogatories truthfully shall subject the judgment debtor to the penalties for false swearing as provided in ORS 162.075 and for contempt of court as provided in ORS 33.015 to 33.155.

(2) Within 20 days after receipt of the interrogatories, the judgment debtor must answer all questions under oath and return the original interrogatories to the judgment creditor.

(3) Failure of the judgment debtor to comply with the provisions of this section is contempt of court, and the judgment creditor may commence proceedings under the provisions of ORS 33.015 to 33.155. [2003 c.576 §33; 2005 c.22 §7]

EXEMPT PROPERTY

(Generally)

18.300 Resident entitled to use federal exemptions or state exemptions in bankruptcy. (1) For purposes of a bankruptcy petition, a resident of this state may use the federal exemptions provided in section 522(d) of the Bankruptcy Code of 1978 (11 U.S.C. 522(d)) or the exemptions given to residents of this state under state law, but may not use both.

(2)(a) If a resident of this state uses any of the federal exemptions provided in section 522(d) of the Bankruptcy Code of 1978 (11 U.S.C. 522(d)) for purposes of a bankruptcy petition, the resident may not use any of the exemptions given to residents of this state under state law.

(b) If a resident of this state uses any of the exemptions given to residents of this state under state law for purposes of a bankruptcy petition, the resident may not use any of the federal exemptions provided in section 522(d) of the Bankruptcy Code of 1978 (11 U.S.C. 522(d)).

(3) This section does not apply to executions. [Formerly 23.305; 2013 c.597 §4]

18.305 Property not exempt from execution for purchase price. No article of property, or if the same has been sold or exchanged, then neither the proceeds of such sale nor the articles received in exchange therefor, shall be exempt from execution issued on a judgment recovered for its price. [Formerly 23.220]

18.310 [Amended by 1967 c.471 §1; repealed by 1979 c.284 §199]

18.312 Execution not to issue against property of deceased party; exception. (1) Except as provided in subsection (2) of this section, execution may not be issued against the property of a deceased party. Except as provided in subsection (2) of this section, a judgment against a deceased party may be collected only by making a claim against the estate of the deceased party in the manner prescribed by ORS chapter 115 or ORS 114.505 to 114.560.

(2) This section does not prevent the issuance of execution and sale of property pursuant to a judgment of foreclosure and sale of property of the decedent. If the amount realized from the sale of property is not sufficient to satisfy the judgment and collection of the deficiency is otherwise allowed by law, the amount of the deficiency may be collected by making a claim against the estate in the manner prescribed by ORS chapter 115 or ORS 114.505 to 114.560.

(3) The stay imposed by subsection (1) of this section:

(a) Expires when the property ceases to be property of the estate, including but not limited to upon conveyance of the property by the personal representative to a third party or upon distribution by the personal representative; and

(b) Does not diminish the lien effect of a judgment or bar execution based on a lien when execution commences after the property ceases to be property of the estate. [Formerly 23.105; 2007 c.495 §1; 2017 c.169 §42]

18.315 [1999 c.788 §15; repealed by 2003 c.576 §580]

18.318 Execution against property in possession or control of public officer or agency. Any salary, wages, credits, or other personal property in the possession or under the control of the state or of any county, city, school district or other political subdivision therein, or any board, institution, commission, or officer of the same, belonging or owed to any person, firm or corporation, shall be subject to execution in the same manner and with the same effect as property in the possession of individuals is subject to execution; however, process in such proceedings may be served only on the board, department, institution, commission, agency, or officer charged with the duty of approving a voucher or claim for such salary, wages, credits, or other property. No clerk or officer of any court shall be required to answer as garnishee as to any moneys or property in the possession of the clerk or officer in the custody of the law. [Formerly 23.190]

18.320 [Amended by 1961 c.151 §1; 1983 c.405 §1; 1983 c.696 §3; 1985 c.343 §1; 1987 c.586 §3; 1989 c.768 §5; 1993 c.223 §2; 1997 c.801 §59; 1999 c.80 §31; 1999 c.788 §18; repealed by 2003 c.576 §580]

18.322 Adjudication of claim of exemption. The judgment debtor's claim of exemption shall, upon application of either plaintiff or judgment debtor, be adjudicated in a summary manner at a hearing in the court out of which the execution issues. [Formerly 23.168; 2005 c.542 §56]

18.325 [1987 c.586 §2b; 1989 c.171 §2; 1999 c.59 §6; 1999 c.80 §32; 1999 c.195 §5; 2003 c.73 §13; 2003 c.576 §570; renumbered 18.170 in 2003]

18.330 [Repealed by 1959 c.558 §29 (18.335 enacted in lieu of 18.330)]

18.335 [1959 c.558 §30 (enacted in lieu of 18.330); 1979 c.284 §54; 1983 c.405 §2; 1987 c.873 §21; 1997 c.340 §5; 1997 c.872 §16; 2001 c.249 §67; repealed by 2003 c.576 §580]

18.340 [Repealed by 1959 c.558 §51]

(Personal Property)

18.345 Exempt personal property generally. (1) All property, including franchises, or rights or interest therein, of the judgment debtor, shall be liable to an execution, except as provided in this section and in other statutes granting exemptions from execution. The following property, or rights or interest therein of the judgment debtor, except as provided in ORS 18.305, shall be exempt from execution:

(a) Books, pictures and musical instruments to the value of $600.

(b) Wearing apparel, jewelry and other personal items to the value of $1,800.

(c) The tools, implements, apparatus, team, harness or library, necessary to enable the judgment debtor to carry on the trade, occupation or profession by which the judgment debtor habitually earns a living, to the value of $5,000.

(d) A vehicle to the value of $3,000. As used in this paragraph "vehicle" includes an automobile, truck, trailer, truck and trailer or other motor vehicle.

(e) Domestic animals and poultry kept for family use, to the total value of $1,000 and food sufficient to support such animals and poultry for 60 days.

(f) Household goods, furniture, radios, a television set and utensils all to the total value of $3,000, if the judgment debtor holds the property primarily for the personal, family or household use of the judgment debtor; provisions actually provided for family use and necessary for the support of a householder and family for 60 days and also 60 days' supply of fuel.

(g) All property of the state or any county or incorporated city therein, or of any other public or municipal corporation of like character.

(h) All professionally prescribed health aids for the debtor or a dependent of the debtor.

(i) Spousal support, child support, or separate maintenance to the extent reasonably necessary for the support of the debtor and any dependent of the debtor.

(j) The debtor's right to receive, or property that is traceable to, an award under any crime victim reparation law.

(k) The debtor's right to receive, or property that is traceable to, a payment or payments, not to exceed a total of $10,000, on account of personal bodily injury of the debtor or an individual of whom the debtor is a dependent.

(L) The debtor's right to receive, or property that is traceable to, a payment in compensation of loss of future earnings of the debtor or an individual of whom the debtor is or was a dependent, to the extent reasonably necessary for the support of the debtor and any dependent of the debtor.

(m) Veterans' benefits and loans.

(n) The debtor's right to receive an earned income tax credit under the federal tax laws and any moneys that are traceable to a payment of an earned income tax credit under the federal tax laws.

(o) The debtor's right to the assets held in, or right to receive payments under, a medical savings account or health savings account authorized under section 220 or 223 of the Internal Revenue Code.

(p) The debtor's interest, not to exceed $400 in value, in any personal property. However, this exemption may not be used to increase the amount of any other exemption.

(2) If the property claimed by the judgment debtor as exempt is adjudicated by the court out of which the execution issued to be of a value in excess of that allowed by the appropriate paragraph of subsection (1) of this section, the officer seizing the property shall proceed to sell such property. Out of the proceeds of such sale, the officer shall deduct costs of sale and shall pay to the judgment debtor an amount equivalent to the value declared to be exempt by any of the paragraphs of subsection (1) of this section and shall apply the balance of the proceeds of sale on the execution. A sale may not be made under such execution unless the highest bid made exceeds the appropriate exemption claimed and allowed plus costs of sale. If no bid is received in excess of the value allowed by the appropriate paragraph of subsection (1) of this section, the costs of sale shall be borne by the judgment creditor.

(3) If two or more members of a household are joint judgment debtors, each judgment debtor shall be entitled to claim the exemptions in subsection (1)(a), (b), (c), (d) and (p) of this section in the same or different properties. The exemptions provided by subsection (1)(a), (b), (c), (d), (j), (k) and (p) of this section, when claimed for jointly owned property, may be combined at the option of the debtors.

(4) Notwithstanding any other provision of law except ORS 657.855, if a writ of garnishment or other execution is issued to collect past due support as defined in ORS 18.600, 50 percent of unemployment compensation benefits, workers' compensation benefits and other benefits paid to the debtor by the United States, by the state or by a political subdivision of the state are exempt. The exemption related to unemployment compensation benefits provided by this subsection is subject to ORS 657.855. The exemption provided by this subsection applies without regard to whether the payment is made on a periodic basis or in a lump sum, including any lump sum payable pursuant to a settlement or judgment. Notwithstanding subsection (1)(k) of this section, if a payment is made under a settlement or judgment on account of personal bodily injury and the garnishment or other execution is issued to collect past due support as defined in ORS 18.600, the lesser of 50 percent of the payment or $7,500 is exempt. [Formerly 23.160; 2005 c.456 §1; 2009 c.612 §1; 2011 c.93 §1; 2011 c.317 §4; 2013 c.597 §1]

18.348 Certain funds exempt when deposited in account; limitation. (1) Funds that are exempt from execution under ORS 18.358, 18.385, 178.345, 238.445, 344.580, 407.595, 411.760, 414.095, 655.530, 656.234, 657.855 and 748.207 remain exempt when deposited in an account in a financial institution as long as the exempt funds are reasonably identifiable.

(2) Subsection (1) of this section does not apply to any accumulation of funds greater than $7,500.

(3) All funds that are exempt under federal law remain exempt when deposited in an account in a financial institution as long as the exempt funds are reasonably identifiable.

(4) The application of subsections (1) and (3) of this section is not affected by the commingling of exempt and nonexempt funds in an account. For the purpose of identifying exempt funds in an account, first in, first out accounting principles shall be used.

(5) The provisions of this section do not affect the duties of a garnishee with respect to amounts in accounts that are not subject to garnishment under ORS 18.784. [Formerly 23.166; 2005 c.381 §19; 2009 c.430 §4; 2009 c.718 §37]

18.350 [Amended by 1961 c.151 §2; 1983 c.405 §3; 1983 c.696 §3a; 1985 c.343 §2; 1987 c.586 §4; 1993 c.523 §1; 1997 c.71 §13; 1997 c.801 §66; 1999 c.195 §1; 1999 c.788 §21a; repealed by 2003 c.576 §580]

18.352 Proceeds of casualty and indemnity insurance attachable on execution. Whenever a judgment debtor has a policy of insurance covering liability, or indemnity for any injury or damage to person or property, which injury or damage constituted the cause of action in which the judgment was rendered, the amount covered by the policy of insurance shall be subject to attachment upon the execution issued upon the judgment. [Formerly 23.230]

18.355 [1999 c.788 §16; 2003 c.576 §93; renumbered 18.162 in 2003]

18.358 Certain retirement plans exempt from execution; exceptions. (1) As used in this section:

(a) "Beneficiary" means a person for whom retirement plan benefits are provided or their spouse.

(b) "Internal Revenue Code" means the federal Internal Revenue Code as amended and in effect on December 31, 1998.

(c) "Permitted contribution" means:

(A) A contribution that, at the time of the contribution, is not taxable income to the beneficiary and, if the sponsor is a taxable entity, is tax deductible to the sponsor;

(B) A nondeductible contribution by a beneficiary to a retirement plan to the extent that the contribution is permitted to be made under the Internal Revenue Code;

(C) A deductible or nondeductible contribution to an individual retirement account to the extent the contribution is not subject to federal excise tax as an excess contribution;

(D) A contribution, pursuant to a rollover or transfer, from one retirement plan to another, to the extent the federal tax deferred status is preserved at such time;

(E) A rollover from an individual retirement account described in section 408 of the Internal Revenue Code to an individual retirement account described in section 408A of the Internal Revenue Code; and

(F) Any earnings under a retirement plan which are attributable to a contribution described in subparagraphs (A) to (E) of this paragraph.

(d) "Retirement plan" means:

(A) A pension plan and trust, including a profit sharing plan, that is described in sections 401(a), 401(c), 401(k), 403 and 457 of the Internal Revenue Code, including that portion attributable to contributions made by or attributable to a beneficiary;

(B) An individual retirement account or annuity, including one that is pursuant to a simplified employee pension, as described in section 408 or 408A of the Internal Revenue Code; and

(C) Any pension not described in subparagraphs (A) and (B) of this paragraph granted to any person in recognition or by reason of a period of employment by or service for the Government of the United States or any state or political subdivision of any state, or any municipality, person, partnership, association or corporation.

(e) "Sponsor" means an individual or entity which establishes a retirement plan.

(2) Subject to the limitations set forth in subsection (3) of this section, a retirement plan shall be conclusively presumed to be a valid spendthrift trust under these statutes and the common law of this state, whether or not the retirement plan is self-settled, and a beneficiary's interest in a retirement plan shall be exempt, effective without necessity of claim thereof, from execution and all other process, mesne or final.

(3) Notwithstanding subsection (2) of this section:

(a) A contribution to a retirement plan, other than a permitted contribution, shall be subject to ORS 95.200 to 95.310 concerning fraudulent transfers; and

(b) Unless otherwise ordered by a court under ORS 25.387, 75 percent of a beneficiary's interest in a retirement plan, or 50 percent of a lump sum retirement plan disbursement or withdrawal, shall be exempt from execution or other process arising out of a support obligation or an order or notice entered or issued under ORS chapter 25, 107, 108, 109, 110, 416, 419B or 419C. [Formerly 23.170; 2011 c.317 §5]

18.360 [Amended by 1983 c.405 §4; 1983 c.696 §32a; 1985 c.343 §3; 1987 c.586 §5; 1993 c.716 §1; 1993 c.763 §6; 1995 c.79 §5; 1997 c.801 §103; 1999 c.788 §22; repealed by 2003 c.576 §580]

18.362 Exemption for firearms. Every citizen of this state above the age of 16 years shall be entitled to have, hold and keep, for the own use and defense of the citizen and shall have exempt from execution one rifle or shotgun and one pistol. The combined value of all firearms claimed as exempt under this section may not exceed $1,000. [Formerly 23.200]

18.364 Prohibition on demanding firearms. No officer, civil or military, or other person, shall take from or demand of the owner any firearms mentioned in ORS 18.362, except where the services of the owner are also required to keep the peace or defend the state. [Formerly 23.210]

18.365 [1999 c.788 §17; 2003 c.576 §94; renumbered 18.194 in 2003]

18.370 [Amended by 1987 c.586 §6; 2003 c.576 §45a; renumbered 18.165 in 2003]

(Wages)

18.375 Definitions. As used in this section and ORS 18.385:
(1) "Disposable earnings" means that part of the earnings of an individual remaining after the deduction from those earnings of any amounts required to be withheld by law.
(2) "Earnings" means compensation paid or payable for personal services, whether denominated as wages, salary, commission, bonus or otherwise, and includes periodic payments pursuant to a pension or retirement program.
(3) "Employer" means any entity or individual who engages a person to perform work or services for which compensation is given in periodic payments or otherwise, even though the relationship of the person so engaged to the employer may be as an independent contractor for other purposes.
(4) "Garnishment" means any legal or equitable procedure through which the earnings of an individual are required to be withheld for payment of a debt. "Garnishment" does not include the procedure authorized by ORS 25.372 to 25.427, 419B.408 or 419C.600 or ORS chapter 110. [Formerly 23.175]

18.380 [Repealed by 1985 c.343 §14]

18.385 Wage exemption. (1) Except as provided in this section, 75 percent of the disposable earnings of an individual are exempt from execution.
(2) The disposable earnings of an individual are exempt from execution to the extent that payment under a garnishment would result in net disposable earnings for an individual of less than the following amounts:
(a) $218 for any period of one week or less;
(b) $435 for any two-week period;
(c) $468 for any half-month period;
(d) $936 for any one-month period; and
(e) For any other period longer than one week, $218 multiplied by that fraction produced by dividing the number of days for which the earnings are paid by seven. The amount calculated under this paragraph must be rounded to the nearest dollar.
(3) If an individual is paid for a period shorter than one week, the exemption calculated under subsection (2) of this section may not exceed $218 for any one-week period.
(4) An employer shall deduct from the amount of disposable earnings determined to be nonexempt under subsections (1) to (3) of this section any amounts withheld from the individual's earnings for the same period of time under an order issued pursuant to ORS 25.378, 419B.408 or 419C.600 or ORS chapter 110. The employer shall make payment under a garnishment only of those amounts remaining after the deduction is made.
(5) Subsections (1) to (4) of this section do not apply to:
(a) Any order of a court of bankruptcy.
(b) Any debt due for federal tax.
(6) Subsections (2) to (4) of this section do not apply to any debt due for state tax. Subsection (1) of this section does not apply to a debt due for state tax if a state agency issues a special notice of garnishment under ORS 18.855 (6).
(7) A court may not make, execute or enforce any order or process in violation of this section.
(8) Any waiver by an individual of the provisions of this section is void.
(9) An employer may not discharge any individual because the individual has had earnings garnished. [Formerly 23.186; 2007 c.496 §§9,14; 2011 c.228 §1]

18.390 [Amended by 1961 c.151 §3; 1983 c.696 §4; repealed by 1985 c.343 §14]

(Homesteads)

18.395 Homestead exemption. (1) A homestead shall be exempt from sale on execution, from the lien of every judgment and from liability in any form for the debts of the owner to the amount in value of $40,000, except as otherwise provided by law. The exemption shall be effective without the necessity of a claim thereof by the judgment debtor. When two or more members of a household are debtors whose interests in the homestead are subject to sale on execution, the lien of a judgment or liability in any form, their combined exemptions under this section shall not exceed $50,000. The homestead must be the actual abode of and occupied by the owner, or the owner's spouse, parent or child, but the exemption shall not be impaired by:
(a) Temporary removal or temporary absence with the intention to reoccupy the same as a homestead;
(b) Removal or absence from the property; or
(c) The sale of the property.
(2) The exemption shall extend to the proceeds derived from such sale to an amount not exceeding $40,000 or $50,000, whichever amount is applicable under subsection (1) of this section, if the proceeds are held for a period not exceeding one year and held with the intention to procure another homestead therewith.
(3) The exemption period under subsection (1)(b) and (c) of this section shall be one year from the removal, absence or sale, whichever occurs first.
(4) When the owner of a homestead has been granted a discharge in bankruptcy or has conveyed the homestead property, the value thereof, for the purpose of determining a leviable interest in excess of the homestead exemption, shall be the value on the date of the petition in bankruptcy, whether the value is determined in the bankruptcy proceedings or not, or on the date the conveyance becomes effective, whichever shall first occur. However, with respect to judgments not discharged in the bankruptcy, or entered against the owner after discharge, the value on the effective date of conveyance shall be controlling.
(5) Except as provided in subsection (7) of this section, no homestead that is the actual abode of and occupied by the judgment debtor, or that is the actual abode of and occupied by a spouse, dependent parent or dependent child of the judgment debtor, shall be sold on execution to satisfy a judgment that at the time of entry does not exceed $3,000. However, such judgment shall remain a lien upon the real property, and the property may be sold on execution:
(a) At any time after the sale of the property by the judgment debtor; and
(b) At any time after the property is no longer the actual abode of and occupied by the judgment debtor or the spouse, dependent parent or dependent child of the judgment debtor.
(6) The limitation on execution sales imposed by subsection (5) of this section is not impaired by temporary removal or temporary absence with the intention to reoccupy the property as a homestead.

116

(7) The limitation on execution sales imposed by subsection (5) of this section does not apply if two or more judgments are owing to a single judgment creditor and the total amount owing to the judgment creditor, determined by adding the amount of each individual judgment as of the date the judgment was entered, is greater than $3,000.

(8) Upon the issuance of an order authorizing sale as required by ORS 18.904, and in conformance with subsection (5) of this section, the sheriff may proceed to sell the property. If the homestead exemption applies, the sheriff shall pay the homestead owner out of the proceeds the sum of $40,000 or $50,000, whichever is applicable, and apply the balance of the proceeds on the execution. However, no sale shall be made where the homestead exemption applies unless the sum bid for the homestead is in excess of the sum of the costs of sale and $40,000 or $50,000, whichever is applicable. If no such bid is received, the expense of the sale shall be borne by the petitioner.

(9) The homestead exemption provided by this section applies to a purchaser's interest under a land sale contract, as defined by ORS 18.960.

(10) The homestead exemption provided by this section applies to:

(a) A floating home, as defined by ORS 830.700; and

(b) A manufactured dwelling, as defined by ORS 446.003. [Formerly 23.240; 2005 c.456 §2; 2005 c.542 §57; 2009 c.612 §2]

18.398 Denial of homestead exemption when judgment is for child support. (1) It is the policy of this state:

(a) To afford protection to the debtor and the debtor's family homestead through the homestead exemption;

(b) To maintain dependent children from the financial resources of both parents of those children;

(c) That the homestead exemption should not be permitted to serve as a shield for a debtor's evasion of child support obligations;

(d) That the burden for that support should not be shifted in all cases to the present family of the debtor through the sale of the family residence; and

(e) That to accommodate these policies, the court should have the discretion to decline to allow all or part of a claimed homestead exemption in cases involving child support as provided in this section.

(2) Notwithstanding ORS 18.395 to 18.422, a court in its discretion may decline to allow a homestead exemption in whole or part in any proceeding under ORS 18.912 if the proceeding is based on a judgment for child support that arises out of an order or judgment under ORS 24.115, 107.095, 107.105, 107.135, 108.120, 109.100, 109.103, 109.155, 109.165, 416.400 to 416.465, 419B.400 or 419C.590 or ORS chapter 110 or 125.

(3) In exercising the discretion granted under subsection (1) of this section, the court shall consider:

(a) The financial resources of both parties;

(b) The number of dependents of each of the parties;

(c) The ages, health and conditions of parties and their dependents;

(d) The child support payment history of the judgment debtor on the judgment which is the subject of the petition; and

(e) Other collection attempts by the judgment creditor on the judgment which is the subject of the petition.

(4) This section shall not apply to any proceeding under ORS 18.912 brought by or on the behalf of the state or any agency of the state. [Formerly 23.242; 2005 c.542 §58]

18.400 [Amended by 1965 c.619 §7; 1979 c.694 §1; 1983 c.696 §5; 1985 c.343 §4; 1985 c.496 §18; 1985 c.610 §2; 1987 c.586 §7; 1993 c.33 §275; 1995 c.608 §20; 1997 c.123 §1; 1997 c.704 §12; 1999 c.788 §23; 2001 c.900 §235; 2003 c.73 §14; repealed by 2003 c.576 §580]

18.402 Limitations on homestead exemption. The homestead mentioned in ORS 18.395 shall consist, when not located in any town or city laid off into blocks and lots, of any quantity of land not exceeding 160 acres, and when located in any such town or city, of any quantity of land not exceeding one block. However, a homestead under this section shall not exceed in value the sum of $40,000 or $50,000, whichever amount is applicable under ORS 18.395 (1). [Formerly 23.250; 2005 c.456 §3; 2009 c.612 §3]

18.405 [1979 c.694 §3; 2001 c.334 §1; repealed by 2003 c.576 §580]

18.406 Exemption not applicable to certain liens, mortgages and interests. ORS 18.395 to 18.422 do not apply to construction liens for work, labor or material done or furnished exclusively for the improvement of the homestead property, to purchase money liens, to mortgages lawfully executed, or to the enforcement of a seller's rights under a land sale contract, as defined by ORS 18.960. [Formerly 23.260; 2005 c.542 §58a]

18.410 [Amended by 1985 c.540 §26; 1987 c.586 §8; 1989 c.768 §6; 1999 c.788 §24; repealed by 2003 c.576 §580]

18.412 Notice of intent to discharge judgment lien against homestead. (1) At any time after the date of execution of an agreement to transfer the ownership of property in which a homestead exemption exists pursuant to ORS 18.395, the homestead owner or the owner's transferee may give notice of intent to discharge the property from the judgment lien to a judgment creditor. Each notice shall bear the caption of the action in which the judgment was recovered and shall:

(a) Identify the property and the judgment and state that the judgment debtor is about to transfer, or has transferred, the property and that the transfer is intended to discharge the property from any lien effect of the judgment;

(b) State the fair market value of the property on the date of the notice or of any applicable petition in bankruptcy, whichever is applicable, and list the encumbrances against the property, including the nature and date of each encumbrance, the name of the encumbrancer and the amount presently secured by each encumbrance;

(c) State that the property is claimed by the person giving the notice to be wholly exempt from the lien of the judgment or, if the value of the property exceeds the sum of the encumbrances specified as required under paragraph (b) of this subsection that are senior to the judgment lien and $40,000 or $50,000, whichever amount of the homestead exemption is applicable under ORS 18.395 (1), that the amount of the excess or the amount due on the judgment, whichever is less, will be deposited with the court administrator for the court in which the judgment was entered for the use of the judgment holder; and

(d) Advise the holder of the judgment that the property may be discharged from any lien arising from the judgment, without further notice to the judgment creditor, unless prior to a specified date, which in no case may be earlier than 14 days after the date of mailing of the notice, the judgment creditor files objections and a request for a hearing on the matter as provided in ORS 18.415.

(2) Each notice described by subsection (1) of this section shall be sent by certified mail to the judgment creditor, as shown by the court records, at the judgment creditor's present or last-known address according to the best knowledge of the person sending the notice. A copy of each notice, together with proof of mailing, may be filed with the court administrator for the court in which the judgment was entered and shall be filed by the court administrator with the records and files of the action in which the judgment was recovered. [Formerly 23.280; 2005 c.456 §4; 2007 c.129 §9; 2009 c.612 §4]

18.415 Objections to discharge; hearing. (1) Any holder of an interest in a judgment described in a notice sent pursuant to ORS 18.412 may file objections to the notice and a request for a hearing upon the application for an order made pursuant to ORS 18.422 (4). The objections and the request for a hearing must be filed in the court that entered the judgment. The objections and the request for hearing must be filed prior to the date specified in the notice and must indicate the grounds for the objections and include the address to which notice of any hearing upon request for an order may be sent.

(2)(a) If the holder of a judgment admits the validity of the homestead exemption and objects only that the value placed upon the property in the notice is or was less than the fair market value of the property on the date of the notice or petition in bankruptcy, whichever is applicable, the court shall try the issue of fair market value without formal pleadings. Each party may offer evidence of fair market value, but the holder of the judgment has the burden of proving the fair market value.

(b) If the objection is made to other than the valuation of the property, the court shall try the issues of fact and law in the manner of a quiet title suit and may direct filing of formal pleadings as it considers necessary for definition of issues.

(3) If the court finds that the fair market value of the property specified in the notice reasonably approximates the fair market value of the property on the date of the notice or petition in bankruptcy, whichever is applicable, or, if other issues are raised by the objections and are decided against the holder of the judgment, the court shall make an order that the property is not subject to the lien of the objecting judgment holder. In all other cases, the application for an order shall be dismissed and the lien upon the property shall not be affected by the notice. [Formerly 23.290; 2005 c.568 §23]

18.420 [Amended by 1961 c.538 §1; 1987 c.586 §9; 1991 c.696 §1; 1999 c.788 §25; 2003 c.576 §571; renumbered 18.238 in 2003]

18.422 Release of judgment lien. (1) If a deposit, as required by ORS 18.412 (1)(c), is made by a transferee of any property, the transferee may credit the amount of the deposit against the consideration owed by the transferee for the transfer.

(2) The holder of any judgment described in ORS 18.412 (1) is entitled to receive the full amount of any deposit made with respect to the judgment upon delivery to the court administrator of a release of lien document in the form provided by ORS 18.200 for the property described in the notice. If the real property is located in a county where a certified copy of the judgment or lien record abstract has been recorded, the holder of the judgment, upon receipt of the deposit, shall have a certified copy of the release of lien document recorded in the County Clerk Lien Record.

(3) If a release of lien document for the property is not delivered by the holder of the judgment to the court administrator as required by subsection (2) of this section, the court administrator shall hold the deposit described in ORS 18.412 (1) and the deposit shall be paid by the court administrator to the homestead claimant upon expiration of the judgment remedies for the judgment as provided in ORS 18.180 to 18.190.

(4) At any time after the date specified in a notice, as provided by ORS 18.412 (1)(d), the homestead claimant for the property described in the judgment may apply to the court in which the judgment was entered for an order that the property described in the notice is no longer subject to the judgment lien. If no objections are filed and no hearing is requested in accordance with ORS 18.415, the judge shall issue an ex parte order that the property is no longer subject to the judgment lien if the judge is satisfied that the property has been, or is about to be, transferred and that the notice was prepared and mailed and a deposit was made as required in ORS 18.412. The judge must, in addition, find that the holder of the judgment actually received notice or, if the whereabouts of the holder are unknown, that a reasonably diligent effort has been made to find the holder. If objections and a request for a hearing have been filed by the holder of the judgment, the court shall set a hearing and notify the holder of the judgment of the time and place of the hearing. The homestead claimant may have a certified copy of the ex parte order recorded in the County Clerk Lien Record. [Formerly 23.300]

18.425 [1987 c.774 §29; 1997 c.801 §123; 1999 c.788 §26; repealed by 2001 c.779 §10]

18.428 [Formerly 23.164; 2005 c.542 §59a; 2005 c.568 §24; repealed by 2009 c.612 §9]

18.430 [Amended by 1987 c.586 §10; renumbered 18.242 in 2003]

18.440 [1971 c.665 §1; 1975 c.269 §1; renumbered 31.800 in 2003]

18.445 [1975 c.269 §2; renumbered 31.805 in 2003]

18.450 [1975 c.269 §3; 1995 c.696 §1; renumbered 31.810 in 2003]

18.455 [1975 c.269 §4; 1995 c.696 §2; renumbered 31.815 in 2003]

18.460 [1975 c.269 §5; renumbered 31.820 in 2003]

18.465 [2003 c.576 §34; repealed by 2005 c.542 §73]

18.468 [2003 c.576 §35; 2005 c.568 §24a; repealed by 2005 c.542 §§73,73a]

18.470 [1971 c.668 §1; 1975 c.599 §1; 1995 c.696 §3; renumbered 31.600 in 2003]

18.472 [2003 c.576 §36; 2005 c.542 §60; renumbered 18.867 in 2005]

18.475 [1975 c.599 §4; renumbered 31.620 in 2003]

18.476 [2003 c.576 §37; repealed by 2005 c.542 §73]

18.478 [Formerly 23.410; repealed by 2005 c.542 §73 and 2005 c.568 §42]

18.480 [1975 c.599 §2; 1995 c.79 §6; 1995 c.696 §4; renumbered 31.605 in 2003]

18.482 [Formerly 23.310; repealed by 2005 c.542 §73]

18.485 [1975 c.599 §3; 1987 c.774 §7; 1995 c.696 §5; renumbered 31.610 in 2003]

18.486 [Formerly 23.440; repealed by 2005 c.542 §73]

18.490 [1975 c.599 §5; renumbered 31.615 in 2003]

18.492 [2003 c.576 §38; repealed by 2005 c.542 §73]

18.494 [2003 c.576 §39; repealed by 2005 c.542 §73]

18.500 [Formerly 41.950; renumbered 31.550 in 2003]

18.505 [2003 c.576 §40; 2005 c.542 §61; 2005 c.568 §25; renumbered 18.892 in 2005]

18.508 [2003 c.576 §41; renumbered 18.894 in 2005]

18.510 [1971 c.331 §6; 1975 c.784 §14; 1981 c.892 §85c; 1981 c.898 §17; renumbered 31.555 in 2003]

18.512 [2003 c.576 §42; 2005 c.456 §5; 2005 c.542 §61b; 2005 c.568 §25a; renumbered 18.896 in 2005]

18.515 [2003 c.576 §43; renumbered 18.898 in 2005]

18.518 [2003 c.576 §44; renumbered 18.899 in 2005]

18.520 [Formerly 41.960; renumbered 31.560 in 2003]

18.530 [Formerly 41.970; renumbered 31.565 in 2003]

18.532 [Formerly 23.450; repealed by 2005 c.542 §73]

18.535 [1995 c.688 §3; 2003 c.552 §1; renumbered 31.725 in 2003]

18.536 [Formerly 23.445; repealed by 2005 c.542 §73]

18.537 [1995 c.688 §2; renumbered 31.730 in 2003]

18.538 [Formerly 23.460; repealed by 2005 c.542 §73]

18.540 [1987 c.774 §3; 1991 c.862 §1; 1995 c.688 §1; 1997 c.73 §1; renumbered 31.735 in 2003]

18.542 [Formerly 23.470; repealed by 2005 c.542 §73]

18.545 [Formerly 23.480; repealed by 2005 c.542 §73]

18.548 [Formerly 23.490; repealed by 2005 c.542 §73]

18.550 [1987 c.774 §4; 1989 c.721 §45; 1989 c.782 §34; 1995 c.280 §28; 1999 c.537 §1; renumbered 31.740 in 2003]

18.552 [Formerly 23.515; repealed by 2005 c.542 §73]

18.555 [Formerly 23.500; repealed by 2005 c.542 §73]

18.560 [1987 c.774 §6; renumbered 31.710 in 2003]

18.562 [Formerly 23.510; repealed by 2005 c.542 §73]

18.565 [Formerly 23.520; repealed by 2005 c.542 §73]

18.568 [Formerly 23.530; repealed by 2005 c.542 §73]

18.570 [1987 c.774 §7a; 1995 c.696 §6; renumbered 31.705 in 2003]

18.572 [Formerly 23.540; repealed by 2005 c.542 §73]

18.578 [Formerly 23.550; repealed by 2005 c.542 §73]

18.580 [1987 c.774 §9; 2003 c.576 §232; renumbered 31.580 in 2003]

18.582 [Formerly 23.560; repealed by 2005 c.542 §73]

18.585 [Formerly 23.570; repealed by 2005 c.542 §73]

18.588 [Formerly 23.580; repealed by 2005 c.542 §73]

18.590 [1989 c.1074 §1; renumbered 31.760 in 2003]

18.592 [1999 c.1065 §1; renumbered 31.715 in 2003]

18.594 [Formerly 23.590; repealed by 2005 c.542 §73]

18.598 [Formerly 23.600; repealed by 2005 c.542 §73]

WRITS OF GARNISHMENT

(Definitions)

18.600 Definitions. As used in ORS 18.600 to 18.850:
　(1) "Account" means an account at a financial institution, including a master account or subaccount, to which an electronic payment may be directly routed.
　(2) "Check" has the meaning given that term in ORS 73.0104.
　(3) "Creditor" means a person to whom a debt is owed by a debtor.
　(4) "Debt" means any monetary obligation for which a garnishment may be issued under ORS 18.605.
　(5) "Debtor" means a person whose property is being garnished for the purpose of paying a debt owed to a creditor.
　(6) "Federal benefit payment" means:
　(a) A benefit payment from the United States Social Security Administration that is protected under 42 U.S.C. 407 and 1383(d)(1);
　(b) A benefit payment from the United States Department of Veterans Affairs that is protected under 38 U.S.C. 5301(a);
　(c) A benefit payment from the Railroad Retirement Board that is protected under 45 U.S.C. 231m(a) and 352(e); or
　(d) A benefit payment from the United States Office of Personnel Management that is protected under 5 U.S.C. 8346 and 8470.
　(7) "Financial institution" means a financial institution or trust company as those terms are defined in ORS 706.008.
　(8) "Garnishable property" means all property described in ORS 18.615, but does not include:
　(a) Any property that is not subject to garnishment under ORS 18.618; and
　(b) Any property that is applied as a setoff under ORS 18.620 or 18.795.
　(9) "Garnishee" means a person to whom a writ of garnishment has been delivered.

(10) "Garnishment account review" means the process of examining deposits to an account to determine whether benefit payments described in ORS 18.784 (3) have been deposited in the account during the lookback period.

(11) "Garnishor" means:

(a) The creditor, if the writ is issued by the court administrator on behalf of the creditor under ORS 18.635 (2); or

(b) The issuer, if the writ is issued under ORS 18.635 by any person other than the court administrator.

(12) "Past due support" means the amount of child or spousal support, or both, determined under a court or administrative order in a proceeding under ORS chapter 107, 108, 109, 110, 416, 419B or 419C that has not been paid or is certified to be owed by another state under ORS 25.083.

(13) "Wages" includes all amounts paid for the services of an employee by an employer, including amounts paid as a commission or bonus.

(14) "Writ" means a writ of garnishment. [2001 c.249 §1; 2003 c.85 §2; 2003 c.576 §47; 2005 c.542 §62; 2011 c.733 §1]

(Garnishment Generally)

18.602 Garnishment described. For the purposes of ORS 18.600 to 18.850, garnishment is the procedure by which a creditor invokes the authority of a circuit court, justice court or municipal court to acquire garnishable property of a debtor that is in the possession, control or custody of a person other than the debtor. [2001 c.249 §2]

18.605 Debts subject to garnishment; when writ may be issued on debt. (1) Garnishment may be used to acquire garnishable property for application against the following debts:

(a) A judgment requiring the payment of money that has been entered in the register of a circuit court or docketed in the docket of a justice, county or municipal court.

(b) If the writ of garnishment is issued pursuant to provisional process under ORCP 83 and 84, a claim of one party against another party in a civil action.

(c) Support arrearage shown on the support records of the Department of Justice pursuant to ORS 25.020 and 25.167, even though such records may not constitute a full record of the support arrearage owed.

(d) Monetary obligations imposed under agency orders or warrants recorded pursuant to law in the County Clerk Lien Record.

(2) For the purposes of ORS 18.600 to 18.850:

(a) A writ may be issued for a monetary obligation based on a judgment other than a judgment for support after the judgment is entered in the register of a circuit court or after the judgment is docketed in the docket of a justice, county or municipal court.

(b) A writ may be issued for a monetary obligation based on a judgment for support after the underlying judgment, court order or administrative order that creates the support obligation is entered in the register of the court or after a request for administrative enforcement services is received under ORS 25.083.

(c) A writ may be issued pursuant to provisional process under ORCP 83 and 84 after the court order for provisional process is entered in the docket or register of the court.

(d) A writ may be issued for a monetary obligation based on an agency order or warrant after the order or warrant is recorded in the County Clerk Lien Record. [2001 c.249 §3; 2003 c.576 §176]

18.607 Form of writ; single writ for two or more debtors. (1) Except as otherwise provided by law, a writ of garnishment must be in substantially the form provided by ORS 18.830. Notation on the writ of additional information for purposes of identifying the debtor or the garnishable property believed to be held by the garnishee does not affect the validity or operation of the writ. A debt calculation form, in substantially the form provided by ORS 18.832, must be prepared for each writ of garnishment issued.

(2) A writ of garnishment must contain all of the following information:

(a) The name of the court whose authority is invoked.

(b) The names of the creditor and debtor.

(c) The name of the garnishor.

(d) The date on which judgment was entered against the debtor or the debt otherwise became subject to garnishment under ORS 18.605.

(e) The debtor's employer identification number, or the final four digits of the debtor's Social Security number, if those numbers are known by the garnishor.

(f) The amount subject to garnishment under the writ, as determined by completing the debt calculation form provided in ORS 18.832.

(g) The date on which the writ is issued.

(h) All addresses required in the writ of garnishment form provided by ORS 18.830.

(3) If a writ of garnishment is issued by the court administrator, the creditor must sign the certification in the writ indicating that the creditor has read the writ and that to the best of the knowledge, information and belief of the creditor there is good ground to support issuance of the writ and the amount indicated in the writ as subject to garnishment.

(4) If a writ is issued by any person other than the court administrator, the person issuing the writ must sign the certification described in subsection (3) of this section.

(5) A single writ may be issued for two or more debtors if those debtors are jointly liable on all or part of the debt. [2001 c.249 §4; 2003 c.85 §3; 2003 c.576 §48; 2009 c.230 §3]

18.609 Validity of writ after issuance. (1) A writ of garnishment is valid only if the writ is delivered not more than 60 days after the writ is issued. If the writ is delivered within the time specified in this section, the writ acts to garnish property for the period of time specified by ORS 18.625.

(2) If the court administrator is issuing a writ of garnishment, the date of issuance for the writ is the date the court administrator stamps and signs the writ. If the writ is issued by any other person, the date of issuance for the writ is the date on which the issuer signs the certification described in ORS 18.607 (4). [2001 c.249 §5; 2003 c.576 §49]

18.610 Court with authority over writ. (1) Only the following courts have authority over a writ of garnishment issued for the enforcement of a judgment:

(a) The court in which the judgment to be enforced was originally entered or first registered;

(b) The circuit court for the county in which a judgment debtor resides if the requirements of ORS 18.255 have been met; and

(c) The circuit court for the county in which a debtor has filed a challenge to the garnishment under ORS 18.718.

(2) Only the following courts have authority over a writ of garnishment issued for the enforcement of an agency order or warrant:

(a) The circuit court for the county in which the order or warrant was first recorded; and

(b) The circuit court for the county in which the debtor resides if the order or warrant has also been recorded in that county.

(3) The circuit court for the county in which the order for provisional process is entered has sole authority for issuance of a writ of garnishment issued pursuant to an order for provisional process. [2001 c.249 §6; 2003 c.576 §572]

(Garnishable Property)

18.615 Garnishable property generally. Except as specifically provided in ORS 18.600 to 18.850, a writ of garnishment delivered to a garnishee garnishes all personal property of the debtor, including but not limited to property in safe deposit boxes, stocks, wages, monetary obligations owing to the debtor that are then in existence whether due or to become due, property held on expired and unexpired bailments and leases, and property held by the garnishee pursuant to a security interest granted by the debtor to the garnishee. A writ of garnishment acts to garnish all property of the debtor possessed by the garnishee, all property of the debtor over which the garnishee has control and all property of the debtor that is in the custody of the garnishee. If a person other than the debtor has an interest in the garnished property, the writ of garnishment acts only to garnish the interest of the debtor in the property. [2001 c.249 §7]

18.618 Property not subject to garnishment. (1)(a) Notwithstanding ORS 18.615, the following are not garnishable property:

(A) Equitable interests, except to the extent allowed under ORS chapter 130.

(B) Property in the custody of the law.

(C) Property in the possession of a conservator.

(D) Property in the possession of a personal representative that constitutes the subject matter of a trust contained in a duly probated will of a decedent.

(E) If a residential landlord is the garnishee, property in the possession of a residential landlord that is held as a security deposit or prepaid rent under ORS 90.300.

(F) The right of a seller under a land sale contract, as defined by ORS 18.960, to receive payments that are due more than 45 days after the writ of garnishment is delivered.

(G) Amounts in an account in a financial institution that are not subject to garnishment under ORS 18.784.

(H) An identification document, such as a driver license, passport, certified copy of a record of live birth or Social Security card.

(b) If a garnishee holds any property described in paragraph (a) of this subsection, the garnishee must note in the garnishee response required by ORS 18.680 that the garnishee holds the property, but may not deliver the property to the garnishor.

(2)(a) Notwithstanding ORS 18.615, wages owing by a garnishee to a debtor for a specific pay period are not garnishable property if:

(A) The writ is delivered within two business days before the debtor's normal payday for the pay period;

(B) When the writ is delivered to the garnishee, the debtor's wages are paid by direct deposit to a financial institution, or the garnishee uses the Oregon Department of Administrative Services or an independent contractor as defined in ORS 670.600 as payroll administrator for the garnishee's payroll; and

(C) Before the writ is delivered to the garnishee, the garnishee issued instructions to the financial institution or the payroll administrator to pay the debtor for the pay period.

(b) If a garnishee owes any wages as described in paragraph (a) of this subsection, the garnishee must so note in the garnishee response required by ORS 18.680.

(3) Notwithstanding any other provision of law, if a voluntary or involuntary bankruptcy petition has been filed by or on behalf of the debtor after a writ of garnishment could be issued under ORS 18.605, the garnishment of any property of the debtor in the garnishee's possession, control or custody is stayed pursuant to section 362 of the United States Bankruptcy Code (11 U.S.C. 101 to 1330). [2001 c.249 §8; 2005 c.348 §98a; 2005 c.391 §1; 2005 c.542 §63; 2007 c.496 §1; 2009 c.430 §3; 2011 c.195 §1; 2013 c.366 §48]

18.619 [2009 c.430 §2; 2011 c.733 §2; renumbered 18.784 in 2011]

18.620 Setoff for certain amounts payable to underlying lienholders. (1) Notwithstanding ORS 18.615, a garnishee may apply a setoff against amounts owing to the debtor under the terms of a land sale contract, under the terms of a promissory note or other evidence of indebtedness that is secured by a mortgage or trust deed, or under the terms of a security agreement as defined in ORS 79.0102, to the extent that those amounts are actually paid to another person:

(a) Who is entitled to receive the amounts under the terms of the land sale contract, mortgage, trust deed or security agreement, or under the terms of any other land sale contract, mortgage, trust deed or security agreement that is secured by the same property that is the subject of the land sale contract, mortgage, trust deed or security agreement; and

(b) Who has an interest in the property that is the subject of the land sale contract, mortgage, trust deed or security agreement that is superior to the interest of the creditor under the laws that would govern a foreclosure, trust deed sale, repossession or other action against the property that is the subject of the land sale contract, mortgage, trust deed or security agreement.

(2) A garnishee must deliver in the manner required by ORS 18.600 to 18.850 all amounts in the garnishee's possession, control or custody at the time of delivery of the writ of garnishment that are not actually paid by the garnishee to another person as described in subsection (1) of this section, unless those amounts are exempt from execution under other law.

(3) A garnishee who applies a setoff under this section must disclose that the setoff has been applied, and the amount of the setoff, in the garnishee response required by ORS 18.680. The garnishee must certify in the garnishee response that the amounts specified in the certificate were actually paid by the garnishee to another person entitled to receive those amounts under subsection (1) of this section. [2001 c.249 §9; 2001 c.445 §159a]

(Duration of Writ's Effect)

18.625 Duration of writ's effect. (1) For any property other than wages, a writ of garnishment acts to garnish only garnishable property of the debtor that is in the garnishee's possession, control or custody at the time the writ is delivered, including money that is owed but not yet due.

(2) Except as provided in ORS 18.618 (2), a writ of garnishment acts to garnish all wages owed by the garnishee to the debtor at the time the writ is delivered. Except as provided in subsection (3) of this section, a writ also acts to garnish all wages earned by the debtor by reason of services to the garnishee during the period commencing with the date the writ is delivered and ending on the earlier of:

(a) The expiration of 90 days after the date the writ is delivered; or

(b) The date on which the garnishment is released or satisfied in full.

(3) If a writ of garnishment is issued on behalf of a county or county agency, the writ acts to garnish all wages earned by the debtor by reason of services to the garnishee until the full amount owed to the county or county agency is paid or until the writ of garnishment is released by the county or county agency or by a court order. A writ of garnishment issued on behalf of a county or county agency shall contain language reasonably designed to notify the garnishee of the provisions of this subsection. [2001 c.249 §10; 2007 c.496 §2]

18.627 Multiple writs. (1) Except as otherwise provided by law, the first writ of garnishment delivered to a garnishee has priority over all other writs delivered to the garnishee for the same debtor. A garnishee shall make payments or deliver property under a subsequently delivered writ only if there is garnishable property of the debtor remaining in the garnishee's possession, control or custody after complying with the first writ delivered to the garnishee.

(2) If a debtor earns wages from a garnishee during the period that a writ of garnishment is in effect under ORS 18.625, the garnishee shall make payments under the first writ delivered to the garnishee until the expiration of the period of time specified in ORS 18.625, and shall thereafter make payments on subsequently delivered writs in the order in which they were delivered to the garnishee as long as each writ continues to be effective under ORS 18.625. Any delay in payment under a writ by reason of this subsection does not affect the expiration of the writ's effect at the time specified in ORS 18.625. If the first writ does not garnish all wages of the debtor that are not exempt from execution, the garnishee shall make concurrent payment on a subsequently delivered writ of the balance of the wages that are not exempt from execution.

(3) If a garnishee pays wages to a debtor and the garnishee receives another writ of garnishment during the period that a writ is in effect under ORS 18.625, the garnishee shall note those facts on the garnishee response and indicate the date on which the previous writ will expire.

(4) A subsequent writ of garnishment issued on behalf of the same creditor against the same debtor and delivered to the same garnishee during the period that a previous writ is effective under ORS 18.625 acts only to garnish property of the debtor other than wages. [2001 c.249 §11]

(Persons Authorized to Issue Writs)

18.635 Who may issue writs. (1) A writ of garnishment may be issued only by a person specified in this section.

(2) The court administrator may issue a writ pursuant to ORS 18.638 and 18.640 only:

(a) For the enforcement of a judgment that requires the payment of money and that has been entered in the register of a circuit court or docketed in the docket of a justice or municipal court;

(b) Pursuant to an order for provisional process under ORCP 83 and 84; or

(c) On behalf of a complainant or claimant under an order recorded pursuant to ORS 671.707 or 701.153, if the complainant or claimant has complied with the requirements of ORS 205.126.

(3) An attorney who is an active member of the Oregon State Bar may issue a writ for the purpose of enforcing:

(a) A judgment that requires payment of money and that has been entered in the register of a circuit court of this state or docketed in the docket of a justice or municipal court of this state; and

(b) An order or warrant that an agency has recorded in the County Clerk Lien Record as authorized by law, including any order that has been recorded pursuant to ORS 671.707 or 701.153.

(4) The administrator, as defined in ORS 25.010, may issue writs of garnishment only for the collection of past due support. Writs issued under this subsection are subject to the provisions of ORS 18.645. [2001 c.249 §12; 2003 c.576 §50; 2007 c.793 §1; 2007 c.836 §39]

(Writs Issued by Court Administrators)

18.638 Writs issued by court administrators generally. (1) Unless there are grounds for denying issuance of a writ of garnishment under ORS 18.640, the court administrator shall issue writs of garnishment upon proper application and payment of all required fees. A writ of garnishment issued by the court administrator must be signed by the creditor. The signature constitutes a certificate by the person under ORCP 17 and is subject to the sanctions provided by ORCP 17.

(2) The court administrator may not fill in or complete a writ of garnishment on behalf of a creditor.

(3) The court administrator is not responsible for verifying the amounts set forth in a writ issued by the court administrator and is not liable for errors in the writ made by the creditor. [2001 c.249 §13; 2003 c.576 §51]

18.640 Grounds for denying issuance of writ. (1) The court administrator shall refuse to issue a writ of garnishment that is not substantially in the form required by ORS 18.830.

(2) The court administrator shall refuse to issue a writ of garnishment that is incomplete or contains improper instructions. Grounds for refusing issuance of a writ under this subsection include:

(a) The inability of the court administrator to verify the existence of the debt claimed as the basis for the writ by a review of the register of the court.

(b) A determination by the court administrator, based on a review of the register of the court, that a satisfaction of judgment has been filed with the court.

(3) The court administrator shall refuse to issue a writ of garnishment pursuant to an order for provisional process under ORCP 83 and 84 if the party seeking issuance of the writ has not complied with all requirements of ORCP 82 A(3), A(5) and A(6) and B to G, 83 and 84. [2001 c.249 §14; 2003 c.576 §52]

(Writs Issued by Division of Child Support or District Attorney)

18.645 Writs issued by Division of Child Support or district attorney; rules. (1) The administrator, as defined in ORS 25.010, may issue writs of garnishment for the collection of past due support in the manner provided by this section. Except as otherwise specifically provided in ORS 18.600 to 18.850, the provisions of ORS 18.600 to 18.850 apply to all writs issued under this section.

(2) Notwithstanding ORS 18.607, a writ of garnishment issued under this section need not contain the name of the court whose authority is invoked.

(3) A single writ of garnishment may be issued under this section for two or more judgments for past due support owed by the same judgment debtor. A separate debt calculation form for each of the judgments must be prepared as provided by ORS 18.832. The writ must reflect the captions of all cases for which the writ is issued. The writ also must reflect, as the amount subject to garnishment under the writ, the sum of the amounts due under all of the judgments subject to the writ. Notwithstanding ORS 18.700 (2), the debtor may file a challenge to a writ issued under this subsection with the court administrator for any court in which one of the judgments subject to the writ was entered. Upon receipt of a notice of a challenge to a garnishment under this subsection, the issuer of the writ shall file with the court administrator a response to the challenge, attaching copies of the writ and garnishee response, copies of all judgments for which the writ is issued and the debt calculation forms for those judgments, and any supporting documentation necessary or helpful to the court in making a determination on the challenge. The Department of Justice shall adopt rules governing the distribution to judgment creditors of amounts received by the administrator under a writ issued under this subsection.

(4) Notwithstanding ORS 18.690, a garnishee who receives a writ of garnishment issued under this section need not deliver a copy of the garnishee response to the court administrator.

(5) Notwithstanding ORS 18.730, payments under a writ issued under this section must be delivered to the Department of Justice.

(6) Notwithstanding ORS 18.730, the Department of Justice must hold any payments received from the garnishee under a writ issued pursuant to this section:

(a) For a period of 120 days after delivery of the writ, if the garnishee is making a payment of wages.

(b) For a period of 30 days after delivery of the writ, if the garnishee is making a payment other than wages.

(7) When issuing writs under this section, the Administrator of the Division of Child Support of the Department of Justice shall modify the forms provided in ORS 18.600 to 18.850 to reflect the provisions of this section. [2001 c.249 §15; 2003 c.85 §4; 2003 c.373 §1; 2003 c.576 §53a]

(Delivery of Writ)

18.650 Items required to be delivered to garnishee. (1) All of the following items must be delivered to a garnishee:

(a) The original writ of garnishment in substantially the form provided by ORS 18.830 or a copy of the writ.

(b) A garnishee response form in substantially the form provided by ORS 18.835.

(c) An instructions to garnishee form in substantially the form provided by ORS 18.838.

(d) A wage exemption calculation form in substantially the form provided by ORS 18.840.

(e) Any search fee required by ORS 18.790.

(2) If any of the items described in subsection (1) of this section is not delivered to the garnishee, the garnishment is not effective to garnish any property of the debtor, the garnishee is not required to respond to the garnishment and the garnishee may proceed to deal with any property of the debtor as though the writ of garnishment had not been issued. [2001 c.249 §16; 2003 c.85 §5]

18.652 Manner of delivery; delivery fee. (1) A writ of garnishment may be delivered to the garnishee personally or by certified mail, return receipt requested. Delivery is effective upon receipt of the writ by the garnishee. If the garnishee refuses to accept delivery by certified mail, the garnishor may attempt personal delivery, but the garnishor must have a new writ issued in order to claim additional delivery fees.

(2) Personal delivery of a writ of garnishment may be made only by:

(a) The sheriff of the county where the writ is to be delivered; or

(b) A competent person 18 years of age or older who is a resident of the State of Oregon and who is not a party or attorney in the action.

(3) If personal delivery is made under this section, the person serving the writ must note the date of delivery upon the original writ delivered to the garnishee or upon the copy of the writ delivered to the garnishee.

(4) Notwithstanding subsection (2) of this section, a person other than a sheriff may not deliver a writ of garnishment unless the person has errors and omissions insurance with limits of not less than $100,000 per occurrence from a company authorized to do business in this state.

(5) The delivery fee for a writ of garnishment by a person other than a sheriff shall be in an amount agreed to between the person making the delivery and the garnishor. The delivery fee for a writ by a sheriff under this section is $25. [2001 c.249 §17; 2003 c.85 §6; 2003 c.304 §5; 2009 c.835 §3]

18.655 Proper person to receive writ. (1) Except as otherwise provided in this section, a writ of garnishment may be delivered to any of the following persons:

(a) If the property of the debtor is in the possession, control or custody of an individual, the writ may be delivered to the individual. If the individual is the sole proprietor of a business, the writ may also be delivered to any person designated by the individual to accept service of a writ of garnishment. If the individual maintains an office for the conduct of business, office delivery may be made under subsection (6) of this section.

(b) If the property of the debtor is in the possession, control or custody of a partnership other than a limited partnership, the writ may be delivered to any partner or to any person designated by the partnership to accept service of a writ of garnishment. If the partnership is a limited partnership, the writ of garnishment may be delivered only to a general partner or to a person designated by the partnership to accept service. If the partnership maintains an office for the conduct of business, office delivery may be made under subsection (6) of this section.

(c) If the property of the debtor is in the possession, control or custody of a corporation, the writ may be delivered to any officer or managing agent of the corporation or to any person designated by the corporation to accept service.

(d) If the property of the debtor is in the possession, control or custody of a limited liability company, the writ may be delivered to any member of the company or to any person designated by the company to accept service.

(e) If the property of the debtor is in the possession, control or custody of a financial institution, the writ may be delivered to the manager, assistant manager or other designated person at any office or branch of the financial institution where deposits are received or that has been designated by the institution as a place for receiving writs of garnishment. Delivery of a writ in the manner prescribed in this paragraph is effective to garnish all property of the debtor held at all offices and branches of the financial institution located in this state.

(f) If the property of the debtor is in the possession, control or custody of a public body, as defined in ORS 174.109, the writ may be delivered to the board, department, institution, commission or officer charged with approving a claim for the property, or to such person or place as may be designated by the public body.

(2) Notwithstanding ORS 78.1120 (2), if the property of the debtor is money that is owed to the debtor that is not evidenced by a negotiable instrument, certificate, document or similar instrument, the writ of garnishment must be delivered to the person who owes the money in the manner provided by subsection (1) of this section.

(3) Notwithstanding ORS 78.1120 (2), if the property of the debtor is stock in a corporation, other than stock represented by a negotiable certificate or similar instrument, the writ of garnishment must be delivered to the corporation in the manner provided by subsection (1) of this section.

(4) Notwithstanding ORS 77.6020 and 78.1120, if the property of the debtor is a negotiable instrument, certificate, document or similar instrument, the writ of garnishment must be delivered to the person having possession of the instrument in the manner provided by subsection (1) of this section. The garnishment does not limit the rights of a holder in due course of a negotiable instrument under ORS 73.0302, a holder to whom a negotiable document has been duly negotiated under ORS 77.5010 or a protected purchaser of a security under ORS 78.3030.

(5) If the property of the debtor is an interest of an heir or legatee in an estate of a decedent, the writ of garnishment must be delivered to the personal representative of the estate in the manner provided by subsection (1) of this section.

(6) For the purposes of subsection (1)(a) and (b) of this section, office delivery may be made by leaving all of the items required by ORS 18.650 (1) at the office during normal working hours with the person who is apparently in charge. If office delivery is used, the person delivering the writ, as soon as reasonably possible, shall cause to be mailed by first class mail all of the items required by ORS 18.650 (1) to the garnishee at the garnishee's place of business or such other place under the circumstances that is most reasonably calculated to apprise the garnishee of the garnishment, together with a statement of the date, time and place at which office delivery was made. Office delivery under this subsection is effective upon the receipt of the writ by the person who is apparently in charge of the office. [2001 c.249 §18; 2003 c.85 §7; 2005 c.269 §1]

18.658 Documents to be delivered to debtor. (1) Following delivery of a writ of garnishment to a garnishee, the person who delivered the writ must mail or deliver promptly the following documents to the debtor whose property is being garnished by the writ:

(a) A copy of the writ of garnishment.

(b) The original of the debt calculation form.

(c) A notice of exemptions form in substantially the form provided by ORS 18.845.

(d) A challenge to garnishment form in substantially the form provided by ORS 18.850, with the names and addresses of the garnishor and garnishee entered by the garnishor.

(2) A person serving a writ of garnishment may meet the requirements of subsection (1) of this section by mailing the documents to the address of the debtor that appears in the writ of garnishment. If an address for the debtor does not appear in the writ, the person serving the writ need not comply with subsection (1) of this section. [2001 c.249 §19; 2003 c.85 §8]

(Duties of Garnishee Generally)

18.665 Duties generally. (1) Upon receiving a writ of garnishment, the garnishee shall determine whether a garnishee response is required under ORS 18.680 and 18.682. The garnishee has no duty to determine whether the garnishor, sheriff or other person has complied with the requirements of ORS 18.600 to 18.850, or to otherwise determine whether the writ of garnishment is valid. If a garnishee response is required, the garnishee must make a diligent effort to determine whether the garnishee is the employer of the debtor and whether the garnishee has possession, control or custody of any garnishable property of the debtor as described in ORS 18.615. If the garnishee has possession, control or custody of garnishable property, the garnishee must hold the property, or as much of the property as is necessary to satisfy the garnishment, as required by ORS 18.600 to 18.850, and thereafter make delivery of the property in the manner required by ORS 18.600 to 18.850.

(2) The duty of a garnishee to hold and deliver property is not affected by joint ownership of the property. If a garnishee holds property that is owned, or appears to be owned, by the debtor and one or more other persons, the garnishee must still hold and deliver all of the property, or as much of the property as is necessary to satisfy the garnishment.

(3) If a single writ is issued for two or more joint debtors under ORS 18.607 (5) and the garnishable property in the garnishee's possession, control or custody exceeds the amount necessary to satisfy the garnishment, the garnishee must hold and deliver as much of the property as is necessary to satisfy the garnishment but may select, in the sole discretion of the garnishee, the property to hold and deliver without regard to which of the joint debtors owns the property. [2001 c.249 §20; 2003 c.85 §9; 2009 c.430 §6]

18.668 Immunity by payment to court administrator or delivery to sheriff. (1) Notwithstanding any provision of ORS 18.600 to 18.850, a garnishee may pay to the garnishor or to the court administrator any money that the garnishee reasonably believes may have been garnished and may deliver to the sheriff in the manner provided by ORS 18.600 to 18.850 any property that the garnishee reasonably believes to have been garnished. The garnishee has no duty to determine whether money or property held by the garnishee is exempt from garnishment or to determine whether the money or property is garnishable property.

(2) If the garnishee makes payment of garnished money to the garnishor or to the court administrator under subsection (1) of this section, or delivers garnished property to the sheriff in the manner provided by ORS 18.600 to 18.850, the garnishee is discharged from liability to the creditor for the value of the money paid or property delivered.

(3) If the garnishee requests a receipt, the sheriff or court administrator shall provide the garnishee with a receipt for any property delivered to the sheriff or payment made to the court administrator.

(4) A garnishor or the garnishor's attorney may disclose the full Social Security number for a debtor to a garnishee if the garnishee requests the number for the purpose of identifying the debtor.

(5) A garnishee is not liable to any person by reason of using all or part of a debtor's Social Security number for the purpose of identifying the debtor. [2001 c.249 §21; 2003 c.576 §54; 2009 c.230 §4]

18.670 Exceptions to garnishee's duties. (1) A garnishee has no duty to hold or deliver any property under a writ of garnishment if the property has been released by a court order or a release of garnishment has been delivered to the garnishee under ORS 18.770.

(2) The duty of a garnishee to hold or deliver any property under a writ of garnishment is not breached if the property is removed from the possession, control or custody of the garnishee before the garnishee can act to stop that removal through the exercise of reasonable care. [2001 c.249 §22]

18.672 Duties of personal representative who is garnished. Garnishment does not impair the powers of a personal representative over estate property for the purposes of administration. If a personal representative receives a writ of garnishment, the personal representative must prepare and deliver a garnishee response in the manner provided by ORS 18.600 to 18.850, but no payment of money or delivery of property need be made by the personal representative until such time as specified in this section. The personal representative must note on the response that the property is estate property subject to administration. The personal representative must also file a copy of the writ of garnishment and the garnishee response in the office of the court administrator for the court in which the estate is being administered, and must report the garnishment to the court in any petition for distribution. In a judgment made upon such petition, distribution shall be ordered to the heir or legatee, but delivery shall be ordered to the sheriff or to the garnishor, as required by ORS 18.600 to 18.850. [2001 c.249 §23; 2003 c.576 §55]

(Garnishee Response)

18.680 Response required; time. (1) Except as specifically provided under ORS 18.682, a garnishee must prepare a garnishee response in substantially the form provided by ORS 18.835 and must deliver the response in the manner provided in ORS 18.690.

(2) Except as provided in subsection (3) of this section, a garnishee response must be delivered by the garnishee not later than seven calendar days after the date on which the writ of garnishment was delivered to the garnishee.

(3) If the seventh calendar day after delivery of a writ of garnishment is a Saturday, Sunday or legal holiday, a garnishee response must be delivered by the garnishee on or before the next following day that is not a Saturday, Sunday or legal holiday. [2001 c.249 §24]

18.682 When response not required. A garnishee has no duty to prepare and deliver a garnishee response if:
(1) The writ of garnishment is not delivered to the garnishee within the time provided under ORS 18.609;
(2) The garnishor fails to serve the garnishee with all items required under ORS 18.650;
(3) The garnishee receives a release of garnishment issued under ORS 18.770; or
(4) Any other law or court order directs that the response not be made. [2001 c.249 §25]

18.685 Contents of response; manner of making payment. A garnishee must note upon a garnishee response the date on which the garnishee received the writ of garnishment. The garnishee must also note upon the response the following information and deliver the response in the manner provided by ORS 18.690:
(1) If the garnishee discovers that a voluntary or involuntary bankruptcy petition has been filed by or on behalf of the debtor and the petition was filed after the date shown on the face of the writ as the date on which the judgment was entered or otherwise first became subject to garnishment.

(2) If the garnishee does not employ the debtor and the garnishee does not have any garnishable property of the debtor in the possession, control or custody of the garnishee, the garnishee must so note on the response.

(3) If the garnishee employs the debtor, the garnishee must so state on the response and make all other responses required by this section or ORS 18.688. The garnishee must thereafter make payment under the writ in the manner provided by ORS 18.735.

(4) If the garnishee has any cash belonging to the debtor that is garnishable, or the garnishee owes any money to the debtor other than wages that is due as of the time the response is made, the garnishee must so note on the response. The garnishee must make payment with the response in the manner provided by ORS 18.730 of the amount subject to the garnishment, or of such amount as will satisfy the garnishment, whichever amount is less.

(5) If the garnishee owes any money to the debtor other than wages that is not due as of the time the response is made but that will become due within 45 days after the time the writ is delivered, the garnishee must so note on the response. When the money becomes due, the garnishee must make payment in the manner provided by ORS 18.732 of the amount subject to the garnishment, or of such amount as will satisfy the garnishment, whichever amount is less.

(6) Except as provided in ORS 18.618 (1)(a)(F), if the garnishee owes any money to the debtor other than wages that is not due as of the time the response is made and the money will not become due within 45 days after the time the writ is delivered, the garnishee must so note on the response. The garnishee must thereafter comply with ORS 18.750 to 18.760.

(7) If the garnishee has any garnishable property of the debtor in the possession, control or custody of the garnishee that is not cash or owed money, the garnishee must so note on the response. The garnishee must thereafter comply with ORS 18.750 to 18.760.

(8) If the garnishee can determine from the writ that the garnishee may owe money to or hold garnishable property of the debtor, but is not sure what or how much, the garnishee must so state on the response and must state that the garnishee will file an amended response when the garnishee determines what or how much money or property the garnishee owes or holds.

(9) If the garnishee determines that the writ of garnishment does not comply on its face with ORS 18.600 to 18.850, or if the garnishee is unable to determine the identity of the debtor from the information contained in the writ, the writ of garnishment is ineffective to garnish the property of the debtor. The garnishee must so note on the response and provide an explanation.

(10) If, before delivering the garnishee response, the garnishee receives an order to withhold income issued under ORS chapter 25 that applies to the income of the debtor, the garnishee must so note on the response. The garnishee must provide details of the order to withhold income, including the name of the agency serving the order, the date the order was served on the garnishee and the amount to be withheld. If the garnishee employs the debtor, the garnishee must make the responses required under ORS 18.688.

(11) If the garnishee receives notice of a challenge to the garnishment before delivering the response, the garnishee must so note on the response. The garnishee must thereafter comply with ORS 18.708. [2001 c.249 §26; 2005 c.542 §65; 2007 c.496 §5; 2009 c.430 §7]

18.688 Response of garnishee who is employer of debtor. In addition to the requirements of ORS 18.685, if a garnishee employs the debtor, the garnishee must so note on the garnishee response and indicate the pay period and the next payday for the debtor. [2001 c.249 §27]

18.690 Delivery of garnishee response. (1) Except as provided in subsection (2) of this section, a garnishee who is required to deliver a garnishee response must mail or personally deliver:
(a) The original of the response to the garnishor;
(b) A copy of the response to the debtor; and
(c) A copy of the response to the court administrator for the court specified in the writ of garnishment as having authority over the writ.
(2) The garnishee shall not mail or personally deliver a copy of the garnishee response to the court administrator if:
(a) The garnishee discovers that a voluntary or involuntary bankruptcy petition has been filed by or on behalf of the debtor after the debt was adjudicated as provided in ORS 18.605, and the garnishee will not make payments or deliver property under the writ pursuant to ORS 18.618 (3); or
(b) The garnishee does not employ the debtor and the garnishee has no property of the debtor in the garnishee's possession, control or custody that is garnishable property.

(3) For the purpose of compliance with ORS 18.680, delivery of a garnishee response under this section is accomplished upon mailing or upon personal delivery of the response. [2001 c.249 §28; 2003 c.85 §10; 2003 c.576 §56; 2005 c.391 §5]

18.692 Supplemental garnishee response. (1) The garnishee shall prepare a supplemental garnishee response and deliver the supplemental garnishee response to the garnishor and to the debtor, if either of the following occurs after the garnishee has delivered an initial garnishee response and before the garnishee delivers all property that is subject to garnishment under the writ of garnishment:

(a) The garnishee discovers that a voluntary or involuntary bankruptcy petition has been filed by or on behalf of the debtor under section 301, 302 or 303 of the United States Bankruptcy Code (11 U.S.C. 101 to 1330) after the debt was adjudicated as provided in ORS 18.605; or

(b) The garnishee receives an order to withhold income that is entitled to priority under ORS 25.375.

(2) The supplemental garnishee response required under this section must be in substantially the form provided in the instructions to garnishee form set forth in ORS 18.838. [2001 c.249 §29; 2003 c.85 §11]

(Challenge to Garnishment)

18.700 Manner of making challenge to garnishment. (1) A debtor may use a challenge to a garnishment to claim such exemptions from garnishment as are permitted by law. A challenge to a garnishment may also be used by a debtor:

(a) To assert that the amount specified in the writ of garnishment as being subject to garnishment is greater than the total amount owed by the debtor to the creditor; or

(b) To assert that property is not garnishable property.

(2) A debtor may make a challenge to a garnishment by completing the challenge to garnishment form provided by ORS 18.850, or a substantially similar form, and by delivering, in person or by first class mail, the original of the completed form to the court administrator for the court specified in the writ of garnishment as the court with authority over the writ and a copy of the completed form to the garnishor. A challenge to a garnishment must be delivered:

(a) Within 120 days after a copy of the writ of garnishment is delivered to the debtor, if the garnishee is the employer of the debtor and the challenge is based on an exemption that is claimed for wages earned by the debtor from the garnishee; or

(b) Within 30 days after a copy of the writ of garnishment is delivered to the debtor, if the challenge is made on any other basis.

(3) Upon receiving a challenge to a garnishment under subsection (2) of this section, the court administrator shall retain all payments sent to the court administrator under ORS 18.705 and 18.708 until such time as the court enters a decision on the challenge. The court administrator shall reject any payment that is received after the challenge is made and that is not payable to the court, and the court administrator shall return the payment to the garnishee with instructions to reissue the payment as payable to the court.

(4) A court shall not require the payment of any fee for the filing of a challenge to a garnishment.

(5) A challenge to a garnishment may be used only for the purposes specified in this section and ORS 18.725. [2001 c.249 §30; 2003 c.85 §12; 2003 c.576 §57]

18.702 Notice to garnishor and garnishee of challenge to garnishment. (1) Without unreasonable delay, a court administrator who has received a challenge to a garnishment under ORS 18.700 shall provide written notice of the challenge as provided in this section. The notice must include a statement reflecting the consequences of failure of a garnishor or garnishee to comply with the requirements of ORS 18.705 and 18.708. The notice may include the notice of hearing under ORS 18.710.

(2) The court administrator shall provide the notice of a challenge required by subsection (1) of this section to:

(a) The garnishor.

(b) The garnishee, unless the court administrator knows that the garnishee has already delivered all garnishable property to the garnishor.

(c) The sheriff of the county identified in any notice delivered to the court administrator under ORS 18.755 (5). [2001 c.249 §31; 2003 c.576 §58]

18.705 Duties of garnishor and creditor created by challenge to garnishment. (1) Except as provided in subsection (4) of this section, upon receiving notice of a challenge to a garnishment under ORS 18.702, a garnishor who is a creditor must send to the court specified in the writ of garnishment all amounts received by the garnishor that the debtor has claimed to be exempt or not subject to garnishment, unless the court specifically orders otherwise.

(2) Except as provided in subsection (4) of this section, if the garnishor is not a creditor, upon receiving notice of a challenge to a garnishment under ORS 18.702, the garnishor must promptly send to the court specified in the writ of garnishment all amounts received under the writ that have not been delivered to the creditor and that the debtor has claimed to be exempt or not subject to garnishment. The creditor must promptly send to the court specified in the writ all amounts that the creditor has received under the writ and that the debtor has claimed to be exempt or not subject to garnishment.

(3) Payments made to the court under this section must be in cash or by check made payable to the court. If the payment has not reached the court by the time of the hearing under ORS 18.710, the court administrator shall so notify the judge presiding at the hearing. If the court determines that any of the garnished money should be disbursed to the debtor and the payment has not reached the court by the time of that determination, the court may issue an order requiring that the garnishor or creditor appear and show cause why the garnishor or creditor should not be held in contempt. In addition to contempt proceedings, the court may require the garnishor or creditor to pay attorney fees under ORS 20.105. A court's imposition of sanctions under this subsection does not limit any remedy otherwise available to the debtor.

(4) This section does not apply if the garnishor or creditor is not allowed by law to disburse the payment to the court.

(5) The receipt of a challenge to a garnishment does not affect the requirement under ORS 18.755 (1) that the garnishor mail or deliver a written request for sale of property, and pay the fees determined by the sheriff under ORS 18.755 (3), not later than 20 days after the garnishee delivers the garnishee response to the court administrator for the court specified in the writ of garnishment as having authority over the writ. The garnishor must note upon the request for sale that a challenge to the garnishment has been made by the debtor. [2001 c.249 §32; 2003 c.85 §13; 2003 c.304 §2; 2003 c.576 §59]

18.708 Duties of garnishee created by challenge to garnishment. (1) Upon receiving notice of a challenge to a garnishment under ORS 18.702, a garnishee who would otherwise be required to make a payment to the garnishor shall mail or deliver the payment, by cash or by check made payable to the court, to the court administrator. The garnishee must make the payment to the court within the time that the garnishee would have otherwise been required to mail or deliver the payment to the garnishor. A garnishee who fails to make payment in the manner required by this section is subject to liability under the provisions of ORS 18.775 to 18.782.

(2) Upon receiving notice of a challenge under ORS 18.702, a garnishee who holds any property described in ORS 18.750 must hold the garnished property for the period specified in ORS 18.752 (1). If the sheriff informs the garnishee before the end of the period specified in ORS 18.752 (1) that the property held by the garnishee will be sold, the garnishee shall continue to hold the property until receiving further directions from the court. [2001 c.249 §33; 2003 c.576 §60]

18.710 Hearing on challenge to garnishment. (1) A debtor's challenge to a garnishment shall be adjudicated in a summary manner at a hearing before the court with authority over the writ of garnishment. The court administrator shall immediately set a hearing date and send notice of the hearing to the garnishor, garnishee and debtor at the addresses provided in the challenge to garnishment form. The hearing shall be held as soon as possible. The garnishor shall provide a copy of the writ of garnishment to the court on or before the date set for the hearing.

(2) Hearings on a challenge to a garnishment may be held by telecommunication.

(3) The debtor has the burden to prove timely delivery of a challenge to a garnishment. [2001 c.249 §34; 2003 c.85 §14; 2003 c.576 §61]

125

18.712 Allowance or denial of challenge. (1) Except as provided in subsection (3) of this section, if a challenge to a garnishment is allowed by the court, the court administrator shall mail to the debtor from any payments made to the court administrator all amounts determined to be exempt from or not subject to garnishment within 10 judicial days after the court's order allowing the challenge. If the challenge to a garnishment has been made for property described in ORS 18.750 and a request for sale of the property has been made by the garnishor under ORS 18.755, the court administrator shall give notice of the court's decision to the garnishee and to the sheriff who would conduct the sale.

(2) Except as provided in subsection (3) of this section, any amount determined to be garnishable property that is not exempt after a hearing shall be mailed to the garnishor within 10 judicial days after the court's order denying the challenge as to that amount.

(3) The Judicial Department may by written policy establish time limitations different from the 10-day period provided in subsections (1) and (2) of this section for the delivery of amounts after a judicial determination on a challenge to a garnishment. The time limitations established by the department may be longer or shorter than the 10-day period. The policy may provide for a period longer than 10 days for a category of payments only if the department determines that the category is subject to special circumstances that create substantial difficulties in meeting a requirement of delivery within 10 days. The policy shall provide for delivery in less than 10 days for any category of payments that the department determines can be delivered within a shorter period of time. The department shall consider federal guidelines and rules relating to the timing of transactions in financial institutions in developing a policy under this subsection. Any policy adopted under this subsection applies to all courts of this state, except that municipal courts and justice courts are not bound by any requirement that a category of payments be delivered in less than 10 days. [2001 c.249 §35; 2003 c.576 §62]

18.715 Sanctions. (1) A court may impose sanctions against any person who files a challenge to a garnishment in bad faith. The sanctions a court may impose under this subsection are a penalty of not more than $100 and responsibility for attorney fees under ORS 20.105.

(2) The court shall order a creditor to return any property that is garnished under a writ of garnishment and that was exempt from garnishment or not subject to garnishment, and shall order the creditor to pay a penalty of $200 to the debtor in addition to all costs and reasonable attorney fees incurred by the debtor in recovering the property and penalty, if:

(a) The creditor is the garnishor and fails to provide in the writ any address for the debtor that is known to the creditor; or

(b) The creditor is not the garnishor and fails to provide to the garnishor any address for the debtor that is known to the creditor.

(3) The imposition of sanctions under this section does not limit any remedy otherwise available to the creditor or debtor. [2001 c.249 §36]

18.718 Special procedures for writs issued for past due support. (1) Notwithstanding ORS 18.700 (2), if a writ of garnishment is issued pursuant to ORS 25.083, the debtor may:

(a) Challenge the enforcement of the past due support in the appropriate tribunal of the state upon whose request the writ was issued as indicated in the writ of garnishment; or

(b) File a challenge to the garnishment with the court administrator for the court in the county in which the property was located when the writ was delivered, if the debtor pays the filing fee required for an appearance and files with the court administrator copies of the writ of garnishment, the debt calculation form and the garnishee response delivered to the debtor under ORS 18.658.

(2) When a challenge to a garnishment is filed under this section, the court administrator shall enter the filing in the court register and the court shall decide the challenge in the manner provided by ORS 18.710.

(3) Immediately upon receipt of a notice of a challenge to a garnishment under this section, the issuer of the writ shall file with the court administrator a response to the challenge, attaching copies of the writ of garnishment and garnishee response, and any supporting documentation necessary or helpful to the court in making a determination on the challenge. [2001 c.249 §36a; 2003 c.576 §63; 2007 c.493 §17]

(Claim by Person Other Than Debtor)

18.725 Claim by person other than debtor for all or part of garnished property. Any person other than a debtor who has an interest in any garnished property or in any part of the garnished property may assert that interest by filing with the court administrator for the court specified in the writ of garnishment an application in substantially the form set forth in ORS 18.850 for a challenge to a garnishment. The provisions of ORS 18.700 to 18.715 apply to an application made under this section. [2001 c.249 §37; 2003 c.576 §64]

(Payment of Money Under Writ Generally)

18.730 Payment of money under writ; garnishor's duty to hold payments. (1) Unless the court has directed otherwise or the garnishee has received notice that a challenge to the garnishment has been filed by the debtor, a garnishee shall make payments of money under a writ of garnishment to the garnishor.

(2) Except as provided in ORS 18.645 and 18.745, a garnishor receiving a payment under a writ of garnishment must hold the payment for a period of 10 days after receipt. The payments must be held in this state, must be clearly identifiable and must be held separate and apart from any account used for operating a business or used to pay personal or business expenses. A payment under a writ may be commingled with other garnished money.

(3) If a garnishee receives notice of a challenge to the garnishment from the court administrator under ORS 18.702, the garnishee shall cease making payments to the garnishor and shall make all further payments to the court administrator in the manner provided by ORS 18.708.

(4) Notwithstanding subsection (1) of this section, if a creditor is a state agency as defined by ORS 183.750, the garnishor may require that checks issued for payments under a writ be made payable to the garnishor or to such other person as designated by the garnishor. A state agency may modify the forms provided in ORS 18.600 to 18.850 to reflect the provisions of this subsection. [2001 c.249 §38; 2003 c.85 §15; 2003 c.576 §65]

18.732 Money owed to debtor that is due within 45 days. (1) If the property garnished by a writ of garnishment is money that is owed to the debtor and that is not due to be paid at the time the writ is delivered but that will become due within 45 days after the delivery date, the garnishee is not required to deliver the money until payment is due. Within five days after the payment is due, unless the garnishment has been satisfied or released, the garnishee must mail or deliver to the garnishor the amount of the payment then due or a portion of the payment sufficient to satisfy the garnishment, whichever is less.

(2) If the garnishee receives notice of a challenge to the garnishment at any time before the garnishee mails or delivers the amount due, the garnishee shall comply with ORS 18.708. [2001 c.249 §39]

(Payment of Nonexempt Wages)

18.735 Payment of wages subject to garnishment. Upon delivery of a writ of garnishment, a garnishee that employs the debtor shall pay to the garnishor all wages that are determined to be subject to garnishment, and that are not exempt under ORS 18.385, at the following times:

(1) The garnishee must make an initial payment when the garnishee next pays any wages to the debtor. The payment must be for all wages that were owing to the debtor on the date that the writ was delivered to the garnishee, and all amounts that are being paid to the debtor for work performed after the writ was delivered and before issuance of the paycheck. The garnishee must compute the amount of wages subject to garnishment using the wage exemption calculation form provided by ORS 18.840 and must mail a copy of the completed form along with the first payment under the writ.

(2) Unless the writ of garnishment is satisfied or released, the garnishee must make subsequent payments under the writ whenever the garnishee makes any payment of wages to the debtor during the period specified in ORS 18.625. Each time there is any change in the debtor's pay period or any change in the amount paid to the debtor during the debtor's pay period, the garnishee must complete a new wage exemption calculation form and mail a copy of the completed form along with the payment.

(3) Unless the writ of garnishment is satisfied or released sooner, the garnishee must make a final payment under the writ when the garnishee next makes a payment of wages to the debtor after the writ expires under the provisions of ORS 18.625. The payment must be for all wages that were owing to

the debtor on the date that the writ expires. The garnishee must complete a new wage exemption calculation form and mail a copy of the completed form along with the final payment. [2001 c.249 §40]

18.736 Processing fee. (1) If a garnishee that employs a debtor is required to make any payment under a writ of garnishment by reason of wages payable to the debtor, the garnishee may collect a $2 processing fee for each week of wages, or fraction of a week of wages, for which a payment is made under the provisions of ORS 18.735. The processing fee must be collected after the last payment is made under the writ. The fee shall be withheld from the wages of the debtor, and is in addition to the amounts withheld for payment to the garnishor under the writ or under any other writ delivered to the garnishee.

(2) The fee provided for in this section may not be collected if withholding of the fee would reduce the debtor's net disposable income below the minimum amounts prescribed by ORS 18.385. [2003 c.779 §3; 2009 c.529 §1]

(Payments Made to Court Administrator)

18.738 Acceptance or rejection of payments by court administrator. (1) The court administrator is not liable for accepting any amount of payment under a writ of garnishment, including any payment that is sent to the court administrator in error or any payment that exceeds the amount required to satisfy the garnishment.

(2) The court administrator may return to the garnishee any payment received from the garnishee unless the garnishee has delivered a garnishee response to the court in the manner required by ORS 18.690 or has provided a statement to the court administrator that the payment is a voluntary payment on behalf of the debtor to be applied toward satisfaction of the garnishment or is a payment under another law or court order that requires or allows the garnishee to pay money to the court. [2001 c.249 §41; 2003 c.576 §66]

18.740 Payments erroneously sent to court. (1) If a garnishee erroneously sends a payment to the court that should have been sent to the garnishor, the court administrator shall immediately forward to the garnishor any cash or check made payable to the garnishor. If a garnishee erroneously sends a payment in the form of a check made payable to the court, the court administrator may deposit and hold the check until the check has cleared and then forward the payment to the garnishor.

(2) The court administrator is not liable for interest on money erroneously sent to the court if the court administrator transmits the money to the garnishor in a timely manner. [2001 c.249 §42; 2003 c.576 §67]

(Crediting of Payments)

18.742 Crediting of payments against debt. (1) If a garnishee makes payment to the garnishor, the payment shall be credited against the debt on the date the garnishor receives the payment.

(2) If a garnishee makes payment to the court, the payment shall be credited against the debt on the date the court administrator disburses payment to the garnishor, unless the court otherwise orders. This subsection applies even if the garnishee makes payment to the court in error or when the court administrator holds money pending a decision on a challenge to the garnishment. [2001 c.249 §43; 2003 c.576 §68]

18.745 Excess payments. Within 10 days after receiving a payment under a writ of garnishment, a garnishor or creditor must return to the debtor any amount that exceeds the amount owing on the debt. If payment was made by check, the garnishor or creditor is not required to return the payment until 10 days after the check has cleared. [2001 c.249 §44; 2003 c.85 §16]

(Property Subject to Sale by Sheriff)

18.750 Application of ORS 18.750 to 18.760. (1) A garnishee shall not deliver the property described in this section to the garnishor. If the garnishor seeks to apply the property described in this section against the debt of the debtor, the property must be sold by the sheriff in the manner specified in ORS 18.750 to 18.760.

(2) The provisions of ORS 18.750 to 18.760 apply to:

(a) Except as provided in ORS 18.618 (1)(a)(F), any money owed by a garnishee to a debtor the payment of which is not due at the time the writ of garnishment is delivered to the garnishee and the payment of which does not become due within 45 days after the date of delivery;

(b) Property of the debtor that the garnishee holds under an unexpired bailment or lease;

(c) Property of the debtor in which the garnishee has a security interest that was granted to the garnishee by the debtor before the delivery of the writ; and

(d) Any other garnishable property that is not payable in money.

(3) The property described in subsection (2)(a) to (c) of this section must be delivered by the garnishee to the purchaser in the manner provided by ORS 18.758 (3) if the interest of the debtor in the property is sold by the sheriff under ORS 18.758. Subject to the provisions of ORS 18.755, the garnishee must deliver to the sheriff any other garnishable property that is not payable in money upon receiving notice from the sheriff under ORS 18.755 (4). [2001 c.249 §45; 2005 c.542 §64; 2007 c.496 §6]

18.752 Garnishee duties. (1) If a garnishee indicates in the garnishee response that the garnishee holds any property described in ORS 18.750, the garnishee must hold the garnished property, or a portion of the property sufficient to satisfy the garnishment, for a period of 30 days after the garnishee delivers the garnishee response to the court administrator for the court specified in the writ of garnishment as having authority over the writ, unless the sheriff or the garnishor notifies the garnishee that the garnishment is released or terminated. If the sheriff contacts the garnishee during the 30-day period, the garnishee shall deliver the property to the sheriff or take such other action as may be specified in the notice given to the garnishee under ORS 18.755 (4).

(2) If the garnishee is not contacted by the sheriff before the end of the 30-day period provided for in subsection (1) of this section, the garnishment is of no further force or effect with respect to the property and the garnishee may deal with the garnished property as if the writ had not been delivered to the garnishee. [2001 c.249 §46; 2003 c.304 §3; 2003 c.576 §69a]

18.755 Request for sale; sheriff's fees. (1) If a garnishee indicates in the garnishee response that the garnishee holds any property described in ORS 18.750, the garnishor may require that the property be sold and that the proceeds of the sale be applied against the debt owed to the creditor. A sale of the property shall be conducted by the sheriff only if the garnishor mails or delivers a written request for sale of the property, and pays the fees determined by the sheriff under subsection (3) of this section, not later than 20 days after the garnishee delivers the garnishee response to the court administrator for the court specified in the writ of garnishment as having authority over the writ. A copy of the writ and a copy of the garnishee response must be attached to the request for sale of the property.

(2) A sale of the property described in ORS 18.750 may be conducted under ORS 18.750 to 18.760 only by the sheriff of the county in which the writ was delivered or, if the property is not located within the county in which the writ was delivered, by the sheriff of the county in which the property is located.

(3) A garnishor may request that the sheriff of a county described in subsection (2) of this section provide a statement to the garnishor of the fees that the sheriff will charge for conducting a sale of property that is described in ORS 18.750. The sheriff shall conduct such investigation as may be necessary to determine the difficulty of conducting any sale of the property under ORS 18.758, including any costs that the sheriff may incur in taking into possession any of the property described in ORS 18.750 (3). The sheriff shall determine whether the property described in ORS 18.750 (3) should be taken into possession of the sheriff, or whether the sheriff should enter into an agreement with the garnishee for the garnishee to continue to hold the

property pending sale by the sheriff. The sheriff shall provide the statement of fees to the garnishor not later than five days after the garnishor requests the statement.

(4) If the garnishor mails or delivers a written request for sale of property and pays the sheriff fees determined under subsection (3) of this section within the time allowed by subsection (1) of this section, the sheriff shall promptly mail or deliver a written notice to the garnishee. The notice shall direct the garnishee to:

(a) Hold all property described in ORS 18.750 (2)(a) to (c) until the garnishee receives further instructions with respect to disposition of the property; and

(b) Deliver all property described in ORS 18.750 (2)(d) to the sheriff, unless the sheriff has agreed with the garnishee that the property should continue to be held by the garnishee pending sale.

(5) Upon sending a notice to a garnishee under subsection (4) of this section, the sheriff shall mail or deliver a copy of the notice to the court administrator for the court with authority over the writ.

(6) A sheriff is not liable to the garnishor, the debtor or any other person for loss of, or damage to, property that is not delivered to the sheriff pending sale of the property. [2001 c.249 §47; 2003 c.304 §4; 2003 c.576 §69; 2011 c.195 §3]

18.758 Sheriff's sale. (1) A sheriff shall sell property under ORS 18.750 to 18.760 in the same manner in which property is sold on execution. If the debtor owns only part of the property, the sheriff shall sell the interest of the debtor in the property. The date scheduled by the sheriff for the sale of the property must be:

(a) Within 20 days after notice is sent to the garnishee under ORS 18.755 (4), if the garnishee is directed to continue to hold the property pending sale by the sheriff; or

(b) Within 20 days after the property is delivered to the sheriff, if the garnishee is directed to deliver the property to the sheriff under ORS 18.755 (4).

(2) If the garnishor notifies the sheriff that property should be released to the debtor, the sheriff shall promptly release the property.

(3) If the garnishee continues to hold property of the debtor pending sale of the property under ORS 18.750 to 18.760, within five days after the sale of property under this section the sheriff shall advise the garnishee in writing of the identity of the purchaser and that the purchaser is entitled to possession of the property or to possession of the debtor's interest in the property. If the property is a debt owed to the debtor for which payment is not due or is subject to a bailment, lease or security interest that has not yet expired or been satisfied or released, the garnishee need not deliver the property to the purchaser until five days after payment is due, the bailment or lease has expired, or the indebtedness secured by the property is satisfied or the security interest is released. [2001 c.249 §48; 2007 c.255 §1]

18.760 Challenge to garnishment. If the sheriff receives notice of a challenge to the garnishment pursuant to ORS 18.702 after a request for sale of property has been submitted by the garnishor under ORS 18.755, the sheriff shall not take possession of or sell any property that is subject to the challenge. If the sheriff has taken property into possession before receiving the notice provided for in ORS 18.702, the sheriff shall hold the property pending the court's determination on the challenge. Upon receiving notice of the court's determination under ORS 18.712, the sheriff shall proceed as directed by the court. [2001 c.249 §49]

(Release of Garnishment)

18.770 Release of garnishment. (1) A garnishor may issue a release of garnishment that covers all or any portion of the property held under a writ of garnishment. The release must be in substantially the form provided by ORS 18.842. The garnishor must deliver a copy of the release to the garnishee and the debtor. In addition, the garnishor must deliver a copy of the release to:

(a) The sheriff, if the garnishor has made a request for sale of property under ORS 18.755; and

(b) The court administrator for the court specified in the writ of garnishment as the court with authority over the writ, if the garnishor has made a request for sale of property under ORS 18.755 or if the garnishor has received a challenge to the garnishment.

(2) A person who does not receive a copy of a release under this section is not liable for treating the property as though the writ were still in effect.

(3) Any proceedings for the sale of property under ORS 18.758 shall be terminated immediately upon receipt by the sheriff of a copy of a release of garnishment.

(4) Upon receipt of a copy of a release under this section, the garnishee may proceed to deal with the released property as though the writ of garnishment had not been issued. [2001 c.249 §50; 2003 c.576 §70]

(Sanctions Against Noncomplying Garnishee)

18.775 Liability of garnishee. (1) If a garnishee fails to file a garnishee response within the time required by law, or fails to deliver all garnishable property required to be delivered under the writ of garnishment within the time required by law, the garnishee is liable to the creditor in an amount equal to the lesser of:

(a) The amount required to satisfy the garnishment; or

(b) The value of the debtor's garnishable property held by the garnishee at the time the writ is delivered to the garnishee.

(2) A judgment may be entered against the garnishee for the amounts specified in this section if, after a hearing, the court finds that:

(a) The garnishee at the time of the delivery of the writ of garnishment held garnishable property of the debtor beyond the amount reported in the garnishee response;

(b) The garnishee held any garnishable property of the debtor and the garnishee failed to make a response; or

(c) The garnishee failed to deliver garnishable property required to be delivered under the writ.

(3) A supplemental judgment shall be entered under subsection (2) of this section if the garnishment was issued for a debt described in ORS 18.605 (1)(a) and a general judgment has been entered in the action. A limited judgment shall be entered under subsection (2) of this section if the garnishment was issued for a debt described in ORS 18.605 (1)(a) and a general judgment has not been entered in the action. A limited or general judgment shall be entered under subsection (2) of this section if the garnishment was issued for a debt described in ORS 18.605 (1)(b), (c) or (d).

(4) If a garnishee is liable to a creditor under subsections (1) and (2) of this section, the creditor may also recover costs of the creditor as determined under ORCP 68. If the garnishee fails to file a garnishee response within the time required by law, the costs of the creditor may be recovered from the garnishee even if it is determined that the garnishee held no garnishable property of the debtor at the time the writ was delivered to the garnishee.

(5) Any amounts from a garnishee collected other than costs under a judgment entered pursuant to this section must be credited against the debt owed by the debtor to the creditor. [2001 c.249 §51; 2009 c.484 §8]

18.778 Order to appear. (1) If a garnishee fails to provide a garnishee response within the time required by law, or the response is unsatisfactory to the garnishor, or the garnishee fails to deliver garnishable property under the writ of garnishment within the time required by law, upon application of the garnishor, the garnishee may be ordered by the court to appear at a specified time and place for an examination. In addition to or in lieu of an order to appear for examination, the court may order the garnishee to appear for a hearing under ORS 18.782 to determine whether the garnishee should be held liable for the amount specified in ORS 18.775.

(2) At any time after a garnishor applies for an order under this section, the court may enter an order restraining the garnishee from in any manner disposing of or injuring any of the property of the debtor alleged by the garnishor to be in the garnishee's possession.

(3) Disobedience of any order of the court under this section, or refusal to answer any question upon appearance under an order to appear for examination, may be punished as contempt. [2001 c.249 §52]

18.780 Pleadings; default judgment. (1) If the court orders a garnishee to appear for a hearing under ORS 18.782, the garnishor must serve upon the garnishee written allegations not less than 20 days before the time set for the hearing or within such time as may be specified in the order. The allegations must inform the garnishee that if the garnishee fails to answer the allegations not less than 10 days before the time when the garnishee is required to appear for hearing, default judgment may be given against the garnishee for an amount no greater than the judgment against the debtor, plus any costs awarded by the court in the proceeding. The garnishor may also serve upon the garnishee, not less than 20 days before the time set for the hearing or within such time as may be specified in the order, written interrogatories concerning matters relating to the garnishment.

(2) Unless further time is allowed for good cause, not less than 10 days before the time when the garnishee is required to appear for hearing, the garnishee must file with the court an answer to the allegations and interrogatories of the garnishor and deliver a true copy of the answer to the garnishor. The answer shall be on oath and shall contain a full response to all of the allegations and interrogatories.

(3) The garnishor may except to the answer of the garnishee for insufficiency, within such time as may be allowed by the court. If the answer is adjudged insufficient, the garnishee may be allowed to amend the answer.

(4) If the garnishee fails to answer as required under subsection (2) of this section, the creditor may have judgment against the garnishee for want of answer. In no case shall default judgment be given against the garnishee for an amount greater than the judgment against the debtor, plus any costs awarded by the court in the proceeding. The judgment provided for in this subsection is in lieu of any judgment under ORS 18.775. Any amounts other than costs collected from a garnishee under a judgment entered pursuant to this subsection must be credited against the debt owed by the debtor to the creditor. [2001 c.249 §53]

18.782 Hearing. Witnesses, including the debtor and garnishee, may be required to appear and testify at a hearing held pursuant to an order issued under ORS 18.778. The proceedings against a garnishee shall be tried by the court as upon the trial of an issue of law between a plaintiff and defendant. [2001 c.249 §54]

(Financial Institution as Garnishee)

18.784 Certain financial institution deposits not subject to garnishment; garnishment account review. (1) Except as provided in subsection (6) of this section, if a writ of garnishment is delivered to a financial institution that has an account of the debtor, the financial institution shall conduct a garnishment account review of all accounts in the name of the debtor before taking any other action that may affect funds in those accounts. If the financial institution determines from the garnishment account review that one or more payments described in subsection (3) of this section were deposited in an account of the debtor by direct deposit or electronic payment during the lookback period described in subsection (2) of this section, an amount equal to the lesser of the sum of those payments or the total balance in the debtor's account is not subject to garnishment.

(2) The provisions of this section apply only to payments described in subsection (3) of this section that are deposited during the lookback period that ends on the day before the day on which the garnishment account review is conducted and begins on:

(a) The day in the second calendar month preceding the month in which the garnishment account review is conducted, that has the same number as the day on which the period ends; or

(b) If there is no day as described in paragraph (a) of this subsection, the last day of the second calendar month preceding the month in which the garnishment account review is conducted.

(3) The provisions of this section apply only to:

(a) Federal benefit payments;

(b) Payments from a public or private retirement plan as defined in ORS 18.358;

(c) Public assistance or medical assistance, as defined in ORS 414.025, payments from the State of Oregon or an agency of the State of Oregon;

(d) Unemployment compensation payments from the State of Oregon or an agency of the State of Oregon;

(e) Black lung benefits payments from the United States Department of Labor; and

(f) Workers' compensation payments from a workers' compensation carrier.

(4) The provisions of this section apply only to a payment that a financial institution can identify as being one of the types of payments described in subsection (3) of this section from information transmitted to the financial institution by the payor.

(5) A financial institution shall perform a garnishment account review only one time for a specific garnishment. If the same garnishment is served on a financial institution more than once, the financial institution may not perform a garnishment account review or take any other action relating to the garnishment based on the second and subsequent service of the garnishment.

(6) A financial institution may not conduct a garnishment account review under this section if a Notice of Right to Garnish Federal Benefits from the United States Government or from a state child support enforcement agency is attached to or included in the garnishment as provided in 31 C.F.R. part 212. If a Notice of Right to Garnish Federal Benefits is attached to or included in the garnishment, the financial institution shall proceed on the garnishment as otherwise provided in ORS 18.600 to 18.850.

(7) The provisions of this section do not affect the ability of a debtor to claim any exemption that otherwise may be available to the debtor under law for any amounts in an account in a financial institution. [Formerly 18.619; 2013 c.688 §4]

18.785 Duties of financial institution; notice to account holder. (1) Except as provided in this section, if a financial institution determines from a garnishment account review conducted under ORS 18.784 (1) that one or more payments described in ORS 18.784 (3) have been deposited into the debtor's account by direct deposit or electronic payment during the lookback period described in ORS 18.784 (2), and there is a positive balance in the account at the time the garnishment account review is conducted, the financial institution shall:

(a) Immediately calculate and establish the amount in the debtor's account that is not subject to garnishment and ensure that the debtor has full customary access to that amount; and

(b) Issue a notice to the account holder in substantially the form set forth in ORS 18.847.

(2) A financial institution shall issue the notice required by this section directly to the account holder or to a fiduciary who administers the account and receives communications on behalf of the account holder.

(3) The notice required by this section must be sent separately to the debtor and may not be included with other materials being provided to the debtor by the financial institution that do not relate to the garnishment.

(4) The notice required by this section must be sent to the account holder within three business days after the financial institution completes the garnishment account review required by ORS 18.784 (1).

(5) A financial institution shall perform the calculation described in subsection (1) of this section for each account of the account holder. However, the financial institution may issue a single notice under this section for multiple accounts of the same account holder.

(6) Issuance of a notice under this section does not constitute the giving of legal advice and a financial institution is not obligated to provide legal advice by reason of issuing a notice required by this section. [2011 c.733 §4]

18.787 Liability of financial institution. A financial institution is not liable to any account holder, garnishor or other financial institution, and may not be assessed any penalty, by reason of any action taken by the financial institution in good faith under ORS 18.784 or 18.785, including:

(1) Delivery or refusal to deliver any funds that are not subject to garnishment under ORS 18.784 to a garnishor;

(2) Providing the notice required by this section to an account holder;

(3) Customary clearing and settlement adjustments made to a debtor's account that affect the balance in the debtor's account; and

(4) Any bona fide errors that occur under ORS 18.784 or 18.785 despite reasonable procedures implemented by the financial institution to prevent those errors. [2011 c.733 §5]

18.788 Compliance records. A financial institution shall maintain records of account activity and actions taken by the financial institution in response to a garnishment that are adequate to demonstrate compliance with the requirements of ORS 18.784 and 18.785 for a period of not less than two years after the financial institution receives the writ of garnishment. [2011 c.733 §6]

18.790 Search fee; garnishment processing fee. (1) Except as provided in subsection (4) of this section, at the time of delivery of any writ of garnishment on a financial institution or at the time a notice of garnishment is delivered to the financial institution under ORS 18.854:

(a) A search fee of $10 must be paid to the financial institution if the garnishor is the Department of Revenue.

(b) A search fee of $15 must be paid to the financial institution if the garnishor is a person other than the department.

(2) A separate search fee must be paid under this section to the financial institution for each debtor if the writ is issued for more than one debtor under ORS 18.607 (5).

(3) If the search fee required under this section is not paid:

(a) The garnishment is not effective to garnish any property of the debtor; and

(b) The financial institution need not file a garnishee response.

(4) The search fee required under this section need not be paid to a financial institution if the debtor is an employee of the financial institution.

(5) Notwithstanding subsection (1) of this section, a financial institution may enter into an agreement with any state agency authorized to garnish pursuant to ORS 18.645 or 18.854 for periodic billing and payment of garnishee search fees required under this section.

(6) The right of a financial institution to receive the search fee required under this section does not in any way restrict or impair the right of the financial institution to charge and collect an additional garnishment processing fee from any debtor whose property the financial institution holds, or to whom the financial institution owes money. However, a financial institution may not charge or collect a garnishment processing fee in violation of ORS 652.610. If a financial institution charges a garnishment processing fee, the financial institution may collect the fee by deducting the amount of the fee from any amount that the financial institution owes to the debtor.

(7) If a garnishment account review reveals that a payment was made by direct deposit or electronic payment to the debtor's account during the lookback period described in ORS 18.784 (2), the financial institution may not charge or collect a garnishment processing fee under subsection (6) of this section against the amount that is not subject to garnishment, and may not charge or collect a garnishment processing fee under subsection (6) of this section against any amounts in the account after the date of the garnishment account review. [2001 c.249 §55; 2003 c.85 §16a; 2007 c.356 §1; 2009 c.430 §5; 2011 c.733 §7]

18.792 Safe deposit boxes. (1) Notwithstanding any other provision of ORS 18.600 to 18.850, but subject to the provisions of ORS 18.854, the duty of a financial institution that is a garnishee to deliver any property of the debtor that may be contained in a safe deposit box that is in the garnishee's possession, control or custody at the time the writ of garnishment is delivered is conditioned upon the garnishor first paying to the garnishee, in addition to the search fee provided for in ORS 18.790, all reasonable costs incurred by the garnishee in gaining entry to the safe deposit box. The costs must be paid to the garnishee by the garnishor before access to the safe deposit box is granted. If the garnishor fails to pay such costs to the garnishee within 20 days after the delivery of the garnishee response, the garnishment shall not be effective to garnish any property of the debtor that may be contained in the safe deposit box and the garnishee may proceed to deal with the safe deposit box and its contents as though the writ of garnishment had not been issued. Nothing in this section limits the right of a garnishor to reach the contents of any safe deposit box in any manner otherwise provided by law.

(2) If a sheriff is instructed to seize and sell the contents of a safe deposit box, and the box is found to contain an identification document, such as a driver license, passport, certified copy of a record of live birth or Social Security card, the sheriff shall take possession of the identification document, but the document may not be sold to satisfy the debt. [2001 c.249 §56; 2011 c.195 §5; 2013 c.366 §49]

18.795 Setoff for amounts owing to financial institution. In addition to such rights as the garnishee may have at law or in equity, a garnishee who is a financial institution may, following delivery of a writ of garnishment to the garnishee, set off such sums as are due from the debtor at the time the writ of garnishment is delivered. A garnishee may not set off any amounts that are not otherwise due to be paid but that have been accelerated after the delivery of a writ of garnishment. Notwithstanding any other provision of ORS 18.600 to 18.850, such a garnishee shall have no obligation to remit any sums upon the garnishment that the garnishee has set off pursuant to this section. A garnishee who sets off amounts pursuant to this section shall disclose the fact and the amount of the setoff in the garnishee response required by ORS 18.680, and must certify in the response that the amount set off by the garnishee was due from the debtor to the garnishee at the time the writ was delivered. [2001 c.249 §56a]

18.798 Effect of garnishment served on financial institution. Notwithstanding any other provision of ORS 18.600 to 18.850, if a writ of garnishment is delivered to a financial institution after 4 p.m. and the financial institution has a deposit account held in the name of the debtor, the writ of garnishment only garnishes moneys on deposit in the account at the beginning of the business day next following the day on which the writ is delivered. [2001 c.249 §56b]

(Writs Issued to Enforce Agency Orders or Warrants)

18.800 Special procedures for writs issued to enforce agency orders or warrants. (1) Except as provided in this section, the provisions of ORS 18.600 to 18.850 apply to all writs of garnishment issued on behalf of agencies for the enforcement of agency orders or warrants that are recorded in the County Clerk Lien Record.

(2) Notwithstanding ORS 18.690, a garnishee who receives a writ of garnishment described in subsection (1) of this section need not deliver a copy of the garnishee response to the court administrator for the court identified as having authority over the writ.

(3) Notwithstanding ORS 18.700, a debtor who wishes to make a challenge to a writ of garnishment described in subsection (1) of this section must deliver the challenge in person or by first class mail to the garnishor within the time specified by ORS 18.700 (2).

(4) A person issuing a writ of garnishment described in subsection (1) of this section shall modify the forms provided in ORS 18.600 to 18.850 to reflect that:

(a) The writ of garnishment is issued pursuant to an order or warrant recorded in the County Clerk Lien Record;

(b) A copy of the garnishee response need not be delivered or mailed to the court administrator for the court identified in the writ; and

(c) A challenge to a writ of garnishment described in subsection (1) of this section must be delivered to the garnishor and not to the court.

(5) Within 14 days after receipt of a challenge to a garnishment described in subsection (1) of this section, the garnishor must either:

(a) Release all property claimed as exempt from or not subject to garnishment under the challenge to the garnishment; or

(b) File with the court administrator a response to the challenge attaching copies of the writ and garnishee response and any supporting documentation necessary or helpful to the court in making its determination on the challenge to the garnishment.

(6) The provisions of this section do not apply to writs of garnishment issued by the court administrator, writs issued by an attorney for the enforcement of an order recorded under ORS 671.707 or 701.153 or writs issued by the administrator, as defined in ORS 25.010, under ORS 18.645. [2001 c.249 §57; 2003 c.576 §71; 2007 c.836 §40]

(Use of Writ for Provisional Process)

18.810 Use of writ for provisional process. (1) Notwithstanding any other provision of ORS 18.600 to 18.850, a debt calculation form need not be prepared or delivered for any writ of garnishment issued pursuant to an order for provisional process under ORCP 83 and 84.

(2) Notwithstanding ORS 18.730, if a writ of garnishment is issued pursuant to an order for provisional process under ORCP 83 and 84, all payments of money by the garnishee under the writ shall be made to the court administrator for the court specified in the writ as the court with authority over the writ. The court administrator shall hold the money pending entry of a judgment against the debtor unless the court finds, upon a challenge to the

130

garnishment made by the debtor under ORS 18.700, that all or part of the money is exempt from execution or not subject to garnishment. If judgment is entered in favor of the debtor, the judgment must direct the court administrator to pay the money to the debtor. If judgment is entered in favor of the creditor, the judgment must direct the court administrator to pay to the creditor as much of the money as will satisfy the judgment and to pay the remainder to the debtor.

(3) Notwithstanding ORS 18.750 to 18.760, if a writ of garnishment is issued pursuant to an order for provisional process under ORCP 83 and 84, the sheriff shall not sell any property described in ORS 18.750 before a judgment is entered in the proceedings, unless the court finds, upon a challenge made by the debtor under ORS 18.700, that all or part of the property is exempt from execution or is not subject to garnishment. If judgment is entered in favor of the debtor, the judgment must direct the sheriff to deliver the property to the debtor. If judgment is entered in favor of the creditor, the judgment must direct the sheriff to sell the property in the manner provided by ORS 18.758.

(4) If property taken into the possession of the sheriff under a writ of garnishment issued pursuant to an order for provisional process under ORCP 83 and 84 is perishable, or the cost of storing the property is great, the sheriff shall sell the property in the same manner in which property is sold on execution. The proceeds shall be held and distributed in the same manner as provided in subsection (2) of this section for payments made under the writ.

(5) The court administrator shall attach to any writ of garnishment issued pursuant to an order for provisional process under ORCP 83 and 84 a notice that informs the garnishee of the provisions of subsection (2) of this section. [2001 c.249 §58; 2003 c.576 §72]

(Forms)

18.830 Writ of garnishment form. A writ of garnishment must be in substantially the following form:

_____COURT
COUNTY OF _____

```
_____      )
Plaintiff,    )     WRIT OF
              )       GARNISHMENT
              }
        vs.   }     Case No. _____
              }
_____      )
Defendant.    )
```

TO:_____ .

You are now a Garnishee. AS A GARNISHEE, YOU NEED TO KNOW THE FOLLOWING:

_____(who is called the "Debtor") owes money to _____(who is called the "Creditor"). A judgment was entered against the Debtor for the debt, or the debt otherwise became subject to garnishment, on_____, 2__. The Debtor's employer identification number, or the final four digits of the Debtor's Social Security number, is _____ (insert if known).

The amount subject to garnishment is $_____ .

This writ garnishes all of the following:

- Wages that you owe the Debtor at the time this writ is delivered to you, and all wages that the Debtor earns during the 90-day period following the date on which you receive this writ.

- All property of the Debtor (including money) that is in your possession, control or custody at the time this writ is delivered to you.

- All debts that you owe the Debtor at the time this writ is delivered to you, whether or not payment is due on the debt at the time you receive this writ.

YOU MUST ANSWER THIS WRIT BY COMPLETING THE ATTACHED GARNISHEE RESPONSE WITHIN THE TIME ALLOWED BY LAW, WHETHER OR NOT YOU HOLD ANY OF THE DEBTOR'S PROPERTY OR OWE ANYTHING TO THE DEBTOR. IF YOU DO NOT TRUTHFULLY ANSWER THIS WRIT, OR YOU DO NOT DELIVER MONEY OR PROPERTY WHEN YOU ARE REQUIRED TO DO SO, YOU WILL BE LIABLE TO THE CREDITOR.

If you have questions, you should contact an attorney. Court employees cannot give you legal advice. The Creditor's attorney cannot give you legal advice.

A writ of garnishment may be issued only by the court administrator, by the attorney for the Creditor or by a person who is specifically authorized by law to issue garnishments. This writ is issued by (check one):

___ The court administrator
___ The attorney for the Creditor
___ Other authorized issuer:
     Name and title _____
     Statutory authority to issue writ _____

This writ is valid only if it has been delivered to you within 60 days after the date of issuance. If the court administrator is issuing this writ, the date of issuance is the date the court administrator signs the writ (see "COURT SEAL" below). If this writ is issued by any other person, the date of issuance is the date on which the issuer signs the certification (see "CERTIFICATION" below).

IMPORTANT ADDRESSES
(see Step 2 of Instructions to Garnishee form)

(Court Administrator)

_____Court
Street address _____
City _____ County _____
State _____ Zip Code _____

(Debtor)

131

Name _____
Telephone number (if known) _____

__ Street address _____
City _____ State _____
Zip Code _____

__ Creditor has no knowledge of Debtor's address

(Garnishor; check one)

__ Creditor: (Must be filled in if the court administrator issues writ.)
Name _____
Street address _____
City _____ State _____
Zip Code _____

__ Attorney for Creditor:
Name _____
Street address _____
City _____ State _____
Zip Code _____
Telephone number _____
Oregon State Bar number _____

__ Other authorized issuer of writ:
Name _____
Street address _____
City _____ State _____
Zip Code _____
Telephone number _____

CERTIFICATION

(The following certification must be signed by the Creditor if this writ is issued by the court administrator. In all other cases, the following certification must be signed by the person issuing the writ.)

I certify that I have read this writ of garnishment and to the best of my knowledge, information and belief, there is good ground to support issuance of the writ, and the amount indicated as subject to garnishment is lawfully subject to collection by this writ.

_____ _____, 2__
Signature   Date

_____
Oregon State Bar No. (if attorney)

COURT SEAL

(To be completed only if this writ is issued by the court administrator. The writ must be stamped by the court administrator. The court administrator has not calculated any amounts on the writ and is not liable for errors made in the writ by the Creditor.)

Issued by the court administrator this __ day of_____, 2__.

COURT ADMINISTRATOR

By _____

_____ [2001 c.249 §59; 2003 c.85 §17;
2003 c.576 §73; 2009 c.230 §5]

18.832 Debt calculation form. (1) A debt calculation form shall be prepared for each writ of garnishment issued. A copy of the form need not be served on the garnishee, but a copy must be delivered to the debtor along with a copy of the writ in the manner required by ORS 18.658.
(2) A debt calculation form must be in substantially the following form:

_____ COURT
COUNTY OF _____

_____
Plaintiff,   )
)   DEBT
)   CALCULATION
            vs.   }   Case No. _____
)
_____   )
Defendant.   )

TO: _____(Debtor).

The following amounts have been calculated to be owing from you to _____ (Creditor). The amounts are owed by reason of:

__ A judgment entered against you dated_____, 2__, in Case No._____, _____Court, _____County.

__ Other debt subject to garnishment under the law (provide details):
_____

132

THE COURT ADMINISTRATOR HAS NOT CALCULATED ANY AMOUNTS FOR THE PURPOSE OF THIS FORM AND IS NOT LIABLE FOR ERRORS IN THIS FORM OR IN THE WRIT OF GARNISHMENT MADE BY THE CREDITOR OR GARNISHOR.

Original Debt Amount $_____
+   Pre-adjudication Interest $_____
+   Attorney Fees $_____
+   Cost Bill $_____
+   Post-adjudication Interest $_____
+   Delivery Fee for Writ $_____
+   Sheriff's Fees other
     than Delivery Fees $_____
+   Other (Explain. Attach
     additional sheets
     if necessary.)
     _____ $_____
     _____ $_____
     _____ $_____
     _____ $_____
     Total "Other"
     from additional
     sheets (if used)
+   Past Writ Issuance Fees $_____
+   Past Delivery Fees $_____
+   Transcript and Filing
     Fees for Other Counties $_____

=   Subtotal $_____

LESS Payments Made on Debt $(_____)

=   Total Amount Required to
     Satisfy Debt in Full $_____

NOTE: INSERTING ITEMS AND AMOUNTS NOT LAWFULLY SUBJECT TO COLLECTION BY GARNISHMENT MAY RESULT IN LIABILITY FOR WRONGFUL EXECUTION.

I certify that I have read this Debt Calculation form and to the best of my knowledge, information and belief the amount shown as owing is correct.

_____
Creditor (Creditor must sign if writ issued by court administrator.)

_____
Garnishor (Attorney for Creditor or other person authorized by law to issue writ.)

_____
Address

_____
Telephone Number

_____
Oregon State Bar Number (if attorney)

_____, 2__
Date of Calculation

_____ [2001 c.249 §60; 2003 c.576 §74]

18.835 Garnishee response form. A garnishee response must be in substantially the following form:

_____
                                    _____COURT
                    COUNTY OF _____

_____   )
Plaintiff,   )   GARNISHEE
)   RESPONSE
        vs.   )   Case No. _____
)
)
_____   )
Defendant.   )

The writ of garnishment was delivered to me on the ___ day of_____, 2__. The following responses are accurate and complete as of that date.

_____
PART I: DEBTOR'S PROPERTY
GENERALLY
(ALL GARNISHEES MUST FILL OUT
THIS PORTION OF THE RESPONSE)

Place a check in front of all the following statements that apply. You may need to check more than one statement.

___ I have discovered that a voluntary or involuntary bankruptcy petition has been filed by or on behalf of the Debtor after the date shown on the face of the writ as the date on which the judgment was entered against the Debtor or after the debt otherwise became subject to garnishment. (You need not complete any other part of this response, but you must sign the response and deliver it in the manner specified in Step 2 of the Instructions to Garnishee form.)

133

___ I do not employ the Debtor, I do not have in my possession, control or custody any personal property of the Debtor, and I do not owe any debts or other obligations to the Debtor.

___ I employ the Debtor. (You must complete Part II of this response.)

___ I have in my possession, control or custody garnishable money that belongs to the Debtor (other than wages), or I owe a debt or other obligation to the Debtor (other than wages) that is due as of the time of this response. I am forwarding this money, or enough of it to satisfy the garnishment, to the Garnishor.

___ I owe a debt or other obligation to the Debtor (other than wages) that was not due as of the time of this response but will become due within 45 days after the writ was delivered to me. I will forward the money, or enough of it to satisfy the garnishment, to the Garnishor when the debt or other obligation becomes due.

___ I owe the following debt or other obligation to the Debtor (other than wages) that will not become due within 45 days after the date that the writ was delivered to me. I will not make any payments on the debt or obligation until I receive instructions from the Sheriff or until 30 days have passed from the date on which I deliver this response. (See Instructions to Garnishee form.)
_____
_____
_____
_____

___ I have in my possession, control or custody the following personal property (other than money) that belongs to the Debtor. I will hold all of the property for the Garnishor until I receive instructions from the Sheriff or until 30 days have passed from the date on which I deliver this response. (See Instructions to Garnishee form.)
_____
_____
_____
_____

___ I may owe money to or hold property of the Debtor, but I am not sure what or how much it might be. (You must provide an explanation in the following space and you must deliver an amended response when you find out. You must deliver an amended response even if you find out that you have no property of the Debtor or owe no money to the Debtor.)
_____
_____
_____
_____

___ (FINANCIAL INSTITUTIONS ONLY) We hold one or more accounts for the Debtor, of which $_____ is not subject to garnishment under ORS 18.784. We are forwarding all other garnishable amounts, or enough of it to satisfy the garnishment, to the Garnishor.
_____
_____
_____
_____

___ The writ of garnishment delivered to me, on its face, does not comply with the Oregon laws governing writs of garnishment, or I cannot determine the identity of the Debtor from the information in the writ. (You must provide an explanation in the following space.)
_____
_____
_____
_____

___ I have received an order to withhold income that applies to the income of the Debtor. The order to withhold income has priority over the writ of garnishment, and compliance with the order will reduce or eliminate the money that I would otherwise deliver under the writ. (Provide details, including the name of the agency serving the order to withhold income, the date the order was served on you and the amount to be withheld. If you employ the Debtor, you must still complete Part II of this response.)
_____
_____
_____
_____

___ I have received notice of a challenge to the garnishment. I will deliver to the court administrator all money that I would otherwise deliver to the Garnishor. (See Step 3 of Instructions to Garnishee form.)

___ Other (Explain)
_____
_____
_____
_____

PART II: DEBTOR'S EMPLOYER
(GARNISHEES WHO EMPLOY THE
DEBTOR MUST FILL OUT THIS
PORTION OF THE RESPONSE)

Place a check in front of all the following statements that apply. You may need to check more than one statement.

NOTE: THE LAW PROHIBITS DISCHARGE OF THE DEBTOR FROM EMPLOYMENT BY REASON OF GARNISHMENT.

___ I employ the Debtor. The Debtor is paid on a _____ basis (insert "weekly," "monthly" or other pay period). Wages will next be payable to the Debtor on the ____ day of_____, 2___. I will complete a Wage Exemption Calculation form for each payment of wages that is made during the 90-day period immediately following the date that the writ of garnishment was delivered to me. I will also complete a Wage Exemption

134

Calculation form for the payday immediately following the end of the 90-day period. I will forward to the Garnishor on each of these occasions those wages calculated to be subject to garnishment, or enough of those wages to satisfy the garnishment.

___ I had already received a writ of garnishment from another Garnishor before this writ was delivered to me. Under Oregon law, the previous writ has priority. The previous writ will terminate on the ___ day of_____, 2___.

I hereby certify that I have fully and accurately completed this garnishee response.

Dated_____, 2___

Name of Garnishee

Signature

Telephone number _____

Fax number (if available) _____

Address

[2001 c.249 §61; 2003 c.85 §18; 2003 c.576 §75; 2005 c.542 §66; 2009 c.430 §8]

18.838 Instructions to garnishee form. Instructions to garnishees must be in substantially the following form:

INSTRUCTIONS TO GARNISHEE

Except as specifically provided in these instructions, you must complete and deliver the Garnishee Response within seven calendar days after you receive the writ of garnishment. If the writ does not comply with Oregon law, the writ is not effective to garnish any property of the Debtor, but you still must complete and deliver the Garnishee Response. You must complete and deliver the response even though you cannot determine from the writ whether you hold any property or owe any debt to the Debtor. If the seventh calendar day is a Saturday, Sunday or legal holiday, you must deliver your response on or before the next following day that is not a Saturday, Sunday or legal holiday.

The writ is not effective, and you need not make a Garnishee Response, if:

- You do not receive the writ within 60 days after the date of issuance shown on the face of the writ.

- You do not receive an original writ of garnishment or a copy of the writ.

Statutes that may affect your rights and duties under the writ can be found in ORS 18.600 to 18.850.

NOTE: The Garnishor may be the Creditor, the attorney for the Creditor or some other person who is authorized by law to issue the writ of garnishment. See the writ to determine who the Garnishor is.

STEP 1. FILL OUT THE GARNISHEE RESPONSE.

All garnishees who are required to deliver a garnishee response must fill in Part I of the Garnishee Response. Garnishees who employ the Debtor must also fill in Part II of the response. You should keep a copy of the response for your records.

Completing Part I of the Garnishee Response. If you discover before you deliver your response that a bankruptcy petition has been filed by or on behalf of the Debtor, and the bankruptcy petition was filed after a judgment was entered against the Debtor or after the debt otherwise became subject to garnishment (see the date specified in the writ), you must put a check by the appropriate statement in Part I. If a bankruptcy petition has been filed, you should not make any payments to the Garnishor unless the court orders otherwise. You need not complete any other part of the response, but you still must sign the response and deliver it in the manner described in Step 2 of these instructions.
In all other cases you must list in Part I all money and personal property of the Debtor that is in your possession, control or custody at the time of delivery of the writ. You must also list all debts that you owe to the Debtor, whether or not those debts are currently due (e.g., money loaned to you by the Debtor that is to be repaid at a later time).
If you are the employer of the Debtor at the time the writ is delivered to you, you must put a check by the appropriate statement in Part I. In addition, you must complete Part II of the response.
If you believe that you may hold property of the Debtor or that you owe a debt to the Debtor, but you are not sure, you must put a check by the appropriate statement and provide an explanation. When you find out what property you hold that belongs to the Debtor, or you find out whether you owe money to the Debtor and how much, you must prepare and deliver an amended response. You must do this even if you find out that you have no property of the Debtor or that you do not owe anything to the Debtor.
If you determine that the writ, on its face, does not comply with Oregon laws governing writs of garnishment, or if you are unable to determine the identity of the Debtor from the information in the writ, then the writ is not effective to garnish any property of the Debtor. You must put a check by the appropriate statement in Part I and provide an explanation. You still must complete the response and deliver the response in the manner described in Step 2 of these instructions.
If you have received an order to withhold income that applies to the income of the Debtor and that order has priority over the garnishment, and if compliance with the order will reduce or eliminate the money or property that you would otherwise deliver under the garnishment, you must put a check by the appropriate statement in Part I. You still must fill out the remainder of the response and deliver the response in the manner described in Step 2 of these instructions. If you employ the Debtor, you still must complete Part II of the response.
If you receive notice of a challenge to the garnishment before you send your response, you must complete and deliver your response as otherwise required by these instructions. However, see Step 3 of these instructions regarding payment of money or delivery of property after receipt of notice of a challenge to the garnishment.
If you owe a debt to the Debtor and the Debtor owes a debt to the holder of an underlying lien on your property, you may be able to offset the amount payable to the underlying lienholder. See ORS 18.620. You must note that you have made the offset in Part I of the response (under "Other") and specify the amount that was offset.

Completing Part II of the Garnishee Response (employers only). You must fill in Part II of the response if you employ the Debtor on the date the writ of garnishment is delivered to you, or if you previously employed the Debtor and still owe wages to the Debtor on the date the writ is delivered to you.

Wages affected. Except as provided below, the writ garnishes all wages that you owe to the Debtor for work performed before the date you received the writ, even though the wages will not be paid until a later date. The writ also garnishes all wages that are attributable to services performed during the 90-day period following the date you received the writ, even though you would not pay the Debtor for all or part of those services until after the end of the 90-day period. Wages subject to garnishment under the writ include all amounts paid by you as an employer, whether on an hourly, weekly or monthly basis, and include commission payments and bonuses.

> Example 1: Debtor A is employed by you and is paid a monthly salary on the first day of each month. You receive a writ of garnishment on July 17. The writ garnishes all wages that you owe to Debtor A for work performed on or before July 17. If Debtor A was paid on July 1 for services performed in the month of June, the writ garnishes Debtor A's salary for the period beginning July 1 and ending October 15 (90 days after receipt of the writ).

The writ does not garnish any wages you owe to a Debtor for a specific pay period if:
(a) The writ is delivered to you within two business days before the Debtor's normal payday for the pay period;
(b) When the writ is delivered to you, the Debtor's wages are paid by direct deposit to a financial institution, or you use an independent contractor as payroll administrator for your payroll; and
(c) Before the writ was delivered to you, you issued instructions to the financial institution or the payroll administrator to pay the Debtor for the pay period.

If any wages are not garnishable by reason of the issuance of instructions to a financial institution or a payroll administrator as described above, you must so note in the Garnishee Response. Thereafter, you must pay to the Garnishor all wages that are subject to garnishment that are attributable to services performed by the Debtor during the 90-day period following the date you received the writ.

Calculation of wages subject to garnishment. A Wage Exemption Calculation form is attached to the writ of garnishment. You must use this form to calculate the amount of the Debtor's wages that is subject to garnishment. You should read the instructions printed on the Wage Exemption Calculation form to determine the normal wage exemption and the minimum wage exemption for each payment you make under the writ.

A Wage Exemption Calculation form must be sent with the first payment you make under the writ. For the 90-day period during which the writ is effective, you must also fill out and return a Wage Exemption Calculation form with a subsequent payment any time the initial calculation changes. Finally, you must fill out and return a Wage Exemption Calculation form with the final payment that you make under the writ.

Payment of amount subject to garnishment. Payments under the writ must be made at the following times, unless the amount owing on the judgment or other debt is fully paid before the final payment is made or the writ is released:
(a) You must make a payment to the Garnishor of all wages subject to garnishment at the time you next pay wages to the Debtor. Complete the wage exemption computation, using the Wage Exemption Calculation form, to determine the portion of the Debtor's wages that is subject to garnishment. Be sure to adjust the minimum exemption amount for any payment that covers less than a full pay period. You must include a copy of the Wage Exemption Calculation form with this first payment.

> Example 2: Using the facts given in Example 1, when you next make any payment of wages to Debtor A after you receive the writ on July 17, you must complete the Wage Exemption Calculation form and send the form to the Garnishor along with all amounts determined to be subject to garnishment that are attributable to the period covered by the payment. If you pay Debtor A on August 1, the payment will be for all wages attributable to the period beginning July 1 and ending July 31.

(b) Unless the writ of garnishment is satisfied or released, during the 90-day period following the date you received the writ, you must pay to the Garnishor all wages that are determined to be subject to garnishment whenever you issue a paycheck to the Debtor. If the Debtor is paid on a weekly basis, you must make payment under the writ on a weekly basis. If the Debtor is paid on a monthly basis, you must make payment under the writ on a monthly basis. If the amount paid to the Debtor varies from paycheck to paycheck, or changes at any time from the amount being paid at the time the writ was delivered to you, you must perform a new wage exemption computation to determine the amount of wages subject to garnishment under the writ. You must send a copy of the new Wage Exemption Calculation form with your payment to the Garnishor.

> Example 3: Using the facts given above, as you make each subsequent payment of wages to Debtor A you must make a payment of that portion of the Debtor's wages that are subject to garnishment. If you continue to pay Debtor A on the first of each month, payments must be made on September 1 and October 1.

(c) Upon the expiration of the 90-day period, you must make a final payment to the Garnishor for all wages that were owing to the Debtor for the work performed by the Debtor through the 90th day following your receipt of the writ. This payment may be made at the time of the Debtor's next paycheck. You will need to complete another Wage Exemption Calculation form to determine the amount of the wages subject to garnishment.

> Example 4: Using the facts given above, you must make a final payment for the wages owing to Debtor A for the period beginning October 1 and ending October 15. You may make this payment at the time you issue Debtor A's paycheck on November 1, but you must make the payment at any time you issue a paycheck to Debtor A after October 15. Be sure that in completing the wage exemption computation for the final payment you adjust the minimum exemption amount to take into account the fact that the period covered is only 15 days of the full month (see instructions on Wage Exemption Calculation form).

Processing fee. You may collect a $2 processing fee for each week of wages, or fraction of a week of wages, for which a payment is made under the writ. The fee must be collected after you make the last payment under the writ. The fee must be withheld from the wages of the debtor, and is in addition to the amounts withheld for payment to the garnishor under the writ or under any other writ you have received.

If you receive more than one writ of garnishment. If you receive a second writ of garnishment for the same Debtor from another Garnishor, the first writ will have priority for wages. The priority of the first writ lasts for the 90-day period following delivery of that writ to you, or until the first writ is paid in full, whichever comes first. In your response to the second writ, you must put a check by the appropriate statement in Part II and indicate the date on which the first writ will expire (90 days after the date you received the writ). You should make no payments under the second writ until expiration of the first writ. The expiration date of the second writ is 90 days after the date you received the second writ; the expiration date is not affected by any delay in payment attributable to the priority of the first writ.

STEP 2. DELIVER THE GARNISHEE RESPONSE.

You must deliver your Garnishee Response and copies of the response in the manner provided in this step. The response and copies may be mailed or delivered personally.

You must complete and deliver the Garnishee Response within seven calendar days after you receive the writ of garnishment. If the seventh calendar day is a Saturday, Sunday or legal holiday, you must deliver your response on or before the next following day that is not a Saturday, Sunday or legal holiday.

If you are required to hold any property under the writ or make any payment under the writ, either at the time of making your response or later, you must:

(a) Send the original of your Garnishee Response to the Garnishor at the address indicated on the writ under Important Addresses.
(b) Send a copy of your Garnishee Response to the court administrator at the address indicated on the writ under Important Addresses.
(c) Send a copy of your Garnishee Response to the Debtor if an address is indicated on the writ under Important Addresses.

If you are not required to hold any property under the writ or make any payment under the writ, either at the time of making your response or later, you must:

(a) Send the original of your Garnishee Response to the Garnishor at the address indicated on the writ under Important Addresses.
(b) Send a copy of your Garnishee Response to the Debtor if an address is indicated on the writ under Important Addresses.

STEP 3. DELIVER THE FUNDS OR OTHER PROPERTY.

As long as the writ is in effect, you may be liable to the Creditor if you pay any debt or turn over any property to the Debtor except as specifically allowed by law. If you have any money or property of the Debtor in your possession, control or custody at the time of delivery of the writ, or owe any debt to the Debtor, you must pay the money or hold the property as required by this step. Exceptions to this requirement are listed below.

IF YOU ARE HOLDING MONEY FOR THE DEBTOR OR OWE A DEBT THAT IS CURRENTLY DUE, you must pay the money to the Garnishor with your response. You must send your payment to the Garnishor at the address indicated on the writ under Important Addresses. Make your check payable to the Garnishor.

IF YOU OWE A DEBT TO THE DEBTOR THAT WILL BECOME DUE WITHIN 45 DAYS AFTER THE DATE YOU RECEIVED THE WRIT, you must send your payment directly to the Garnishor at the address provided in the writ when the debt becomes due. Make your check payable to the Garnishor.

IF YOU ARE HOLDING PROPERTY THAT BELONGS TO THE DEBTOR, OR OWE A DEBT TO THE DEBTOR THAT WILL NOT BECOME DUE WITHIN 45 DAYS AFTER THE DATE YOU RECEIVED THE WRIT, you must keep the property or debt in your possession, control or custody until you receive written notice from the Sheriff. The Sheriff's notice will tell you what to do with the property or debt. If you have followed all of the instructions in the writ and you receive no notice from the Sheriff within 30 days after the date on which you delivered your Garnishee Response, you may treat the writ as being of no further force or effect.

EXCEPTIONS:

1. Challenge to garnishment or specific directions from court. If you are making any payments under the garnishment and before making a payment you receive notice of a challenge to the garnishment from the court, or receive a specific direction from the court to make payments to the court, you must send or deliver the payment directly to the court administrator. If the money is currently due when you receive the notice, send the payment promptly to the court. If the payment is for a debt that is payable within 45 days after you receive the writ, make the payment to the court promptly when it becomes due. If you make payment by check, make the check payable to the State of Oregon. Because you may be liable for any payment that does not reach the court, it is better not to send cash by mail.

A challenge to the garnishment does not affect your duty to follow the instructions you receive from the Sheriff for property that belongs to the Debtor and debts that you owe to the Debtor that do not become due within 45 days.

2. Previous writ of garnishment. If you receive a second writ of garnishment for the same Debtor from another Garnishor, the first writ will have priority and you need not make payments or deliver property under the second writ to the extent that compliance with the first writ will reduce or eliminate the payment of money or delivery of property that you would otherwise make under the garnishment. You must still deliver a Garnishee Response to the second writ, and must commence payment under the second writ as soon as the first writ is satisfied or expires.

3. Offset for payment of underlying lien. If you owe a debt to the Debtor and the Debtor owes a debt to the holder of an underlying lien on your property, you may be able to offset the amount payable to the underlying lienholder. See ORS 18.620.

4. Subsequent events:

(a) Bankruptcy. If you make your response and then discover that a voluntary or involuntary bankruptcy petition has been filed by or on behalf of the Debtor after the judgment was entered against the Debtor or after the debt otherwise became subject to garnishment (see date in writ), you may not make any further payments or delivery of property under the writ unless the court orders otherwise. If you have not delivered all property that is subject to garnishment under this writ when you discover that a bankruptcy petition has been filed, you must mail the following notice to the Garnishor and to the Debtor.

(b) Order to withhold income. If you make your response and then receive an order to withhold income that has priority over the writ, you may make payments or deliver property under the writ only after payment of the amounts required under the order to withhold income. If you have not delivered all property that is subject to garnishment under this writ when you receive an order to withhold income that has priority, you must mail the following notice to the Garnishor and to the Debtor.

SUPPLEMENTAL GARNISHEE
RESPONSE

TO: The Garnishor and the Debtor

RE: Writ of garnishment received_____, 2__ (date), in the case of _____ (Plaintiff) vs. _____ (Defendant), Circuit Court of _____County, Oregon, Case No._____.

The undersigned Garnishee furnished a Garnishee Response to this writ of garnishment on_____, 2__ (date). Since that time (check appropriate statement):

___ I have discovered that a voluntary or involuntary bankruptcy petition has been filed by or on behalf of the Debtor after the judgment was entered against the Debtor or after the debt otherwise became subject to garnishment.

___ I have received an order to withhold income of the Debtor by reason of a support obligation. Under ORS 25.375, the order to withhold income has priority over any other legal process under Oregon law against the same income. The withholding of income pursuant to the order to withhold income might reduce or eliminate subsequent payments under the garnishment. (Provide details, including the name of the agency serving the order to withhold, the date the order was served on you and the amounts to be withheld.)

Dated_____, 2___
_____
Name of Garnishee

_____
Signature

_____
Address

Unless a Notice of Right to Garnish Federal Benefits from the United States Government or from a state child support enforcement agency is attached to or included in the garnishment, you must conduct a garnishment account review for each account that you hold for the debtor. If a Notice of Right to Garnish Federal Benefits from the United States Government or from a state child support enforcement agency is attached to or included in the garnishment, you should not conduct a garnishment account review, and should proceed upon the garnishment in the normal manner.

If you hold an account for the debtor, and any of the payments listed below has been deposited in the account by direct deposit or electronic payment during the lookback period described in ORS 18.784 (2) (the period that begins on the date preceding the date of your garnishment account review and that ends on the corresponding date of the month two months earlier, or on the last day of the month two months earlier if the corresponding date does not exist), an amount equal to the lesser of the sum of those payments or the total balance in the debtor's account is not subject to garnishment, and you may not deliver that amount to the garnishor:

(a) Federal benefit payments as defined in ORS 18.600 (payments from the United States Social Security Administration, the United States Department of Veterans Affairs, the United States Office of Personnel Management or the Railroad Retirement Board);
(b) Payments from a public or private retirement plan as defined in ORS 18.358;
(c) Public assistance or medical assistance, as defined in ORS 414.025, payments from the State of Oregon or an agency of the State of Oregon;
(d) Unemployment compensation payments from the State of Oregon or an agency of the State of Oregon;
(e) Black lung benefits payments from the United States Department of Labor; and
(f) Workers' compensation payments from a workers' compensation carrier.

If the Garnishor fails to pay the search fee required by ORS 18.790 and you do not employ the Debtor, you are not required to deliver a Garnishee Response and you may deal with any property of the Debtor as though the garnishment had not been issued.

If the Debtor owes a debt to you that was due at the time you received the writ of garnishment, you may be able to offset the amount of that debt. See ORS 18.795. You must note that you have made the offset in Part I of the Garnishee Response (under "Other") and specify the amount that was offset.

Before making a payment under the writ, you may first deduct any processing fee that you are allowed under ORS 18.790. If you are required to conduct a garnishment account review, you may not charge or collect a processing fee against any amount that is not subject to garnishment, and may not charge or collect a garnishment processing fee against any amounts in the account after the date that you conduct the review.

You need not deliver any property contained in a safe deposit box unless the Garnishor pays you in advance for the costs that will be incurred in gaining entry to the box. See ORS 18.792.

If you are required to conduct a garnishment account review and you determine from the review that one or more of the payments listed in ORS 18.784 (3) have been deposited into the debtor's account by direct deposit or electronic payment during the lookback period described in ORS 18.784 (2), and that there is a positive balance in the account, you must issue a notice to the account holder in substantially the form set forth in ORS 18.847. The notice must be issued directly to the account holder or to a fiduciary who administers the account and receives communications on behalf of the account holder. The notice must be sent separately to the account holder and may not be included with other materials being provided to the account holder that do not relate to the garnishment. You must send the notice to the account holder within three business days after you complete the garnishment account review. You may issue one notice with information related to multiple accounts of a single account holder.

[2001 c.249 §62; 2003 c.85 §19; 2003 c.576 §76; 2003 c.779 §4; 2007 c.496 §3; 2009 c.430 §9; 2009 c.529 §2; 2011 c.733 §8; 2013 c.688 §5]

18.840 Wage exemption calculation form. A wage exemption calculation form must be delivered to the garnishee with each writ of garnishment. A wage exemption calculation form must be in substantially the following form:

WAGE EXEMPTION CALCULATION
(to be filled out by <u>employers only</u>)

1. Debtor's gross wages
   for period covered by this
   payment... $ ____
2. Total amount required to be
   withheld by law for amount in Line 1
   (Federal and state
   withholding, Social
   Security, etc.)..................................... $ ____
3. Debtor's disposable wages
   (Subtract Line 2
   from Line 1).. $ ____
4. Normal exemption
   (Enter 75 percent
   of Line 3)... $ ____
5. Minimum exemption (check one)
   ___ $218 (payment of wages weekly)
   ___ $435 (payment of wages every
       two weeks)
   ___ $468 (payment of wages half-monthly)
   ___ $936 (payment of wages monthly)
   ___ $____ (Any other period longer
       than one week, including partial
       payments for less than full pay
       period) (Multiply $218 by number

of weeks or fraction of a week)
6. Wages exempt from garnishment
(Line 4 or 5,
whichever is greater)...................................... $ _____
7. Nonexempt wages
(Subtract Line 6
from Line 3)... $ _____
8. Amount withheld for this pay period
pursuant to a support order under
support withholding process or under
another writ with priority................................. $ _____
9. Wages subject to garnishment
(Subtract Line 8
from Line 7)... $ _____

INSTRUCTIONS FOR WAGE EXEMPTION CALCULATION FORM

If you employ the Debtor named in the writ of garnishment, you must fill out and return this Wage Exemption Calculation form. A Wage Exemption Calculation form must be sent with the first payment you make under the writ. For the 90-day period during which the writ is effective, you must also fill out and return a Wage Exemption Calculation form with a subsequent payment any time the initial calculation changes. Finally, you must fill out and return a Wage Exemption Calculation form with the final payment that you make under the writ.

Normal wage exemption. The wage exemption calculation is based on the amount of the payment you make under the writ of garnishment. The normal wage exemption in Line 4 is 75 percent of the employee's disposable wages in Line 3.

Minimum wage exemption. The minimum exemption in Line 5 is also based on the amount of the payment you are making. The minimum exemption is designed to ensure that an employee receives at least a certain minimum amount in any one-week period. If the payment is for a one-week period (without regard to whether the period is a calendar week or any other seven-day period), the minimum exemption is $218. The minimum exemption is $435 if the payment is for a two-week period. If the payment is for one-half of one month (i.e., the Debtor is paid twice each month), the minimum exemption is $468. The minimum exemption for a monthly payment is $936.

If the payment you are making is based on some period of time other than one week, two weeks, half month or month, and the payment is for more than one week, you must calculate the minimum exemption by multiplying $218 by the number of weeks covered by the paycheck, including any fraction of a week. You should round the amount calculated to the nearest dollar.

Example 1: You pay Debtor A every 10 days. Each 10-day period is equal to 1.429 weeks (10 divided by 7). The minimum exemption is $312 ($218 ´ 1.429 rounded to the nearest dollar).

You must use this same calculation for computing the minimum exemption when making a payment for less than a full pay period (e.g., for the final payment at the end of the 90-day period covered by the writ).

Example 2: You pay Debtor A on a monthly basis. You are required to make a final payment under a writ of garnishment for the wages owing to Debtor A for the period beginning October 1 and ending October 15. This period is equal to 2.143 weeks (15 divided by 7). The minimum exemption is $467 ($218 ´ 2.143 rounded to the nearest dollar).

The amount of time actually worked by the Debtor during the period covered by the paycheck does not affect the calculation of the minimum exemption.

Example 3: You pay Debtor A on a weekly basis. Debtor A works two days per week. The minimum exemption is $218 for each weekly payment you make for Debtor A.

If the payment you are making is based on a period of time less than one week, the minimum wage exemption may not exceed $218 for any one-week period.

If you receive more than one writ of garnishment. If you receive more than one writ of garnishment for the same debtor, the writs have priority based on the date on which you receive them. If the full amount of wages subject to garnishment for a given pay period is paid on the first writ, you should not make any payment on subsequently received writs until the first writ expires. In some cases, it may be necessary to make payments on two or more writs for the same pay period.

Example 4. You have received two writs of garnishment for Debtor A. You pay Debtor A on a monthly basis. The first writ expires on October 16. The second writ will not expire until November 15. You will need to prepare two wage exemption calculation forms for Debtor A's October wages and make payments under both writs. The wage exemption calculation form for the first writ will be for the wages attributable to October 1 to October 15 as described in Example 2. The wage exemption calculation form for the second writ will be for all wages for the month of October, but the amounts withheld under the first writ must be subtracted on Line 8 to determine the October wages subject to garnishment under the second writ.

_____ [2001 c.249 §63; 2003 c.85 §20;
2007 c.496 §§10,15; 2011 c.228 §2]

18.842 Release of garnishment form. A release of garnishment must be in substantially the following form:

_____

_____COURT
COUNTY OF _____

```
_____          )
Plaintiff,        )    RELEASE OF
                  )       GARNISHMENT
        vs.       )
                  )    Case No. _____
                  )
_____          )
Defendant.        )
```

TO: _____(Garnishee).

A writ of garnishment was delivered to you by the Garnishor named below on the ____ day of_____, 2__. The following money or other property that is subject to the writ is hereby released:

___ All money and property of the Debtor held by you.

___ The following money or property of the Debtor held by you (provide details):
_____
_____

The writ of garnishment has no further force or effect with respect to the specified property.

Dated_____, 2__

_____
Name of Garnishor

_____
Signature

_____
Address
_____ [2001 c.249 §63a]

18.845 Notice of exemptions form; instructions for challenge to garnishment. A notice of exemptions form must be in substantially the form set forth in this section. Nothing in the notice form described in this section is intended to expand or restrict the law relating to exempt property. A determination as to whether property is exempt from execution, attachment and garnishment must be made by reference to other law. The form provided in this section may be modified to provide more information or to update the notice based on subsequent changes in exemption laws.

NOTICE OF EXEMPT PROPERTY
AND INSTRUCTIONS FOR
CHALLENGE TO GARNISHMENT

Property belonging to you may have been taken or held in order to satisfy a debt. The debt may be reflected in a judgment or in a warrant or order issued by a state agency. Important legal papers are enclosed.
YOU MAY BE ABLE TO GET YOUR PROPERTY BACK, SO READ THIS NOTICE CAREFULLY.
State and federal law specify that certain property may not be taken. Some of the property that you may be able to get back is listed below.
(1) Wages or a salary as described in ORS 18.375 and 18.385. Whichever of the following amounts is greater:
(a) 75 percent of your take-home wages; or
(b) $218 per workweek.
(2) Social Security benefits.
(3) Supplemental Security Income (SSI).
(4) Public assistance (welfare).
(5) Unemployment benefits.
(6) Disability benefits (other than SSI benefits).
(7) Workers' compensation benefits.
(8) All Social Security benefits and Supplemental Security Income benefits, and up to $7,500 in exempt wages, retirement benefits, welfare, unemployment benefits and disability benefits, that are held in a bank account. You may attach copies of bank statements to the Challenge to Garnishment form if you claim this exemption.
(9) Spousal support, child support or separate maintenance to the extent reasonably necessary for your support or the support of any of your dependents.
(10) A homestead (house, manufactured dwelling or floating home) occupied by you, or occupied by your spouse, parent or child. Up to $40,000 of the value of the homestead is exempt. If you jointly own the homestead with another person who is also liable on the debt, up to $50,000 of the value of the homestead is exempt.
(11) Proceeds from the sale of a homestead described in item 10, up to the limits described in item 10, if you hold the proceeds for less than one year and intend to use those proceeds to procure another homestead.
(12) Household goods, furniture, radios, a television set and utensils with a combined value not to exceed $3,000.
*(13) An automobile, truck, trailer or other vehicle with a value not to exceed $3,000.
*(14) Tools, implements, apparatus, team, harness or library that are necessary to carry on your occupation, with a combined value not to exceed $5,000.
*(15) Books, pictures and musical instruments with a combined value not to exceed $600.
*(16) Wearing apparel, jewelry and other personal items with a combined value not to exceed $1,800.
(17) Domestic animals and poultry for family use with a combined value not to exceed $1,000 and their food for 60 days.
(18) Provisions and fuel for your family for 60 days.
(19) One rifle or shotgun and one pistol. The combined value of all firearms claimed as exempt may not exceed $1,000.
(20) Public or private pensions.
(21) Veterans' benefits and loans.
(22) Medical assistance benefits.
(23) Health insurance proceeds and disability proceeds of life insurance policies.
(24) Cash surrender value of life insurance policies not payable to your estate.
(25) Federal annuities.
(26) Other annuities to $250 per month (excess over $250 per month is subject to the same exemption as wages).
(27) Professionally prescribed health aids for you or any of your dependents.
*(28) Rental assistance to an elderly person allowed pursuant to ORS 458.375.
(29) Your right to receive, or property traceable to:
(a) An award under any crime victim reparation law.
(b) A payment or payments, not exceeding a total of $10,000, on account of personal bodily injury suffered by you or an individual of whom you are a dependent.
(c) A payment in compensation of loss of future earnings of you or an individual of whom you are or were a dependent, to the extent reasonably necessary for your support and the support of any of your dependents.
(30) Amounts paid to you as an earned income tax credit under federal tax law.

140

(31) Your right to the assets held in, or right to receive payments under, a medical savings account or health savings account authorized under section 220 or 223 of the Internal Revenue Code.

*(32) Interest in personal property to the value of $400, but this cannot be used to increase the amount of any other exemption.

(33) Equitable interests in property.

(34) Security deposits or prepaid rent held by a residential landlord under ORS 90.300.

(35) If the amount shown as owing on the Debt Calculation form exceeds the amount you actually owe to the creditor, the difference between the amount owed and the amount shown on the Debt Calculation form.

Note: If two or more people in your household owe the claim or judgment, each of them may claim the exemptions marked by an asterisk (*).

SPECIAL RULES APPLY FOR DEBTS THAT ARE OWED FOR CHILD SUPPORT AND SPOUSAL SUPPORT. Some property that may not otherwise be taken for payment against the debt may be taken to pay for overdue support. For instance, Social Security benefits, workers' compensation benefits, unemployment benefits, veterans' benefits and pensions are normally exempt, but only 50 percent of a lump sum payment of these benefits is exempt if the debt is owed for a support obligation.

YOU MUST ACT PROMPTLY IF YOU WANT TO GET YOUR MONEY OR PROPERTY BACK. You may seek to reclaim your exempt property by doing the following:

(1) Fill out the Challenge to Garnishment form that you received with this notice.

(2) Mail or deliver the Challenge to Garnishment form to the court administrator at the address shown on the writ of garnishment, and mail or deliver a copy of the form to the Garnishor at the address shown on the writ of garnishment. If you wish to claim wages or salary as exempt, you must mail or deliver the form within 120 days after you receive this notice. If you wish to claim that any other money or property is exempt, or claim that the property is not subject to garnishment, you must mail or deliver the form within 30 days after you receive this notice. You have the burden of showing that your challenge is made on time, so you should keep records showing when the challenge was mailed or delivered.

(3) The law only requires that the Garnishor hold the garnished money or property for 10 days before applying it to the Creditor's use. You may be able to keep the property from being used by the Creditor by promptly following (1) and (2) above.

You should be prepared to explain your exemption in court. If you have any questions about the garnishment or the debt, you should see an attorney. YOU MAY USE THE CHALLENGE TO GARNISHMENT FORM ONLY FOR THE FOLLOWING PURPOSES:

(1) To claim such exemptions from garnishment as are permitted by law.

(2) To assert that property is not garnishable property under ORS 18.618.

(3) To assert that the amount specified in the writ of garnishment as being subject to garnishment is greater than the total amount owed.

YOU MAY NOT USE THE CHALLENGE TO GARNISHMENT FORM TO CHALLENGE THE VALIDITY OF THE DEBT.

IF YOU FILE A CHALLENGE TO A GARNISHMENT IN BAD FAITH, YOU MAY BE SUBJECT TO PENALTIES IMPOSED BY THE COURT THAT COULD INCLUDE A FINE. Penalties that you could be subject to are listed in ORS 18.715.

When you file a Challenge to Garnishment form, the Garnishee may be required to make all payments under the garnishment to the court, and the Garnishor may be required to pay to the court all amounts received by the Garnishor that are subject to the challenge to the garnishment. The Garnishee and Garnishor are subject to penalties if they do not. For a complete explanation of their responsibilities, see ORS 18.705 and 18.708.

[2001 c.249 §64; 2001 c.538 §2a; 2003 c.79 §2; 2003 c.85 §21; 2003 c.576 §77; 2005 c.391 §2; 2005 c.456 §6; 2005 c.568 §25b; 2007 c.71 §6; 2007 c.496 §§11,16; 2009 c.430 §10; 2009 c.612 §6; 2011 c.93 §2; 2011 c.228 §3; 2011 c.317 §6; 2013 c.597 §2; 2015 c.348 §24]

18.847 Notice to debtor of garnishment account review. The notice given by a financial institution to a debtor under ORS 18.785 (1) must be in substantially the following form:

_____

_____

_____

(Name, address of financial institution)

IMPORTANT INFORMATION ABOUT
YOUR ACCOUNT

Date: _____
Notice to: _____
Account Number: _____

Why am I receiving this notice?

On _____ [date on which garnishment order was served], _____ [name of financial institution] received a garnishment order from a court to garnish funds in your account. The amount of the garnishment order was for $_____ [amount of garnishment order]. We are sending you this notice to let you know what we have done in response to the garnishment order.

What is garnishment?

Garnishment is a legal process that allows a creditor to remove funds from your bank/credit union account to satisfy a debt that you have not paid. In other words, if you owe money to a person or company, they can obtain a court order directing your bank/credit union to take money out of your account to pay off your debt. If this happens, you cannot use that money in your account.

What has happened to my account?

On _____ [date of account review], we researched your account and identified that one or more payments identified by ORS 18.784 (1) have been deposited in the last two months (see below for a list of qualifying payments). In most cases, these payments are protected from garnishment. As required by state and federal regulations, therefore, we have established a "protected amount" of funds that will remain available to you and that will not be frozen or removed from your account in response to the garnishment order.

(Conditional paragraph if funds have been frozen)

____ (check if applicable) Your account contained additional money that may not be protected from garnishment. As required by law, we have placed a hold on or removed these funds in the amount of $_____ [amount frozen] and may have to turn these funds over to your creditor as directed by the garnishment order.

The chart below summarizes this information about your account(s):

ACCOUNT SUMMARY AS OF _____ [DATE OF ACCOUNT REVIEW]

Account Number	Amount in Account	Amount Protected
_____	_____	_____
_____	_____	_____

Amount Subject to Garnish-ment (now frozen/ removed)	Garnish-ment Fee Charged
_____	_____
_____	_____

(If the account holder has multiple accounts, use a separate row for each account)

Please note that these amount(s) may be affected by deposits or withdrawals after the protected amount was calculated on _____ (date of garnishment account review).

Do I need to do anything to access my protected funds?

You may use the protected amount of money in your account as you normally would.

There is nothing else you need to do to make sure that the protected amount is safe.

Who garnished my account?

The creditor who obtained a garnishment order against you is _____ (name of creditor).

What types of benefit payments are protected from garnishment?

In most cases, you have protections from garnishment if the funds in your account include one or more of the following benefit payments:

- Social Security benefits
- Supplemental Security Income benefits
- Veterans' benefits
- Railroad retirement benefits
- Railroad Unemployment Insurance benefits
- Civil Service Retirement System benefits
- Federal Employees Retirement System benefits
- Payments from a public or private retirement plan as defined in ORS 18.358
- Public assistance or medical assistance, as defined in ORS 414.025, from the State of Oregon or an agency of the State of Oregon
- Unemployment compensation payments from the State of Oregon or an agency of the State of Oregon
- Black lung benefits payments from the United States Department of Labor
- Workers' compensation payments from a workers' compensation carrier

What should I do if I think that additional funds in my account are from protected benefit payments?

If you believe that funds in your account(s) should not have been frozen or removed, there are several things you can do:

You can fill out a Challenge to Garnishment form and submit it to the court.
You may contact the creditor that garnished your account and explain that funds are from protected benefit payments and should be released to you. The creditor may be contacted at _____ (address of creditor).
You may consult an attorney to help you prove to the creditor that garnished your account that additional funds are from protected benefit payments and cannot be taken. For information about how to find an attorney, contact the Oregon State Bar's Lawyer Referral Service at (800) 452-7636 or go online to www.oregonlawhelp.org.

This notice contains all the information that we have about the garnishment order. However, if you have a question about your account, you may contact us at _____ (telephone number of financial institution).

_____ [2011 c.733 §10; 2013 c.688 §6]

18.850 Challenge to garnishment form. A challenge to garnishment form must be in substantially the following form:

_____COURT
COUNTY OF _____

_____	)	CHALLENGE TO
Plaintiff,	)	GARNISHMENT
	)	
vs.	}	Case No. _____
	)	
_____	)	
Defendant.	)	

THIS FORM MAY BE USED BY THE DEBTOR ONLY FOR THE FOLLOWING PURPOSES:

(1) To claim such exemptions from garnishment as are permitted by law.
(2) To assert that property is not garnishable property under ORS 18.618.
(3) To assert that the amount specified in the writ of garnishment as being subject to garnishment is greater than the total amount owed.

THIS FORM MAY BE USED BY PERSONS OTHER THAN THE DEBTOR ONLY TO CLAIM AN INTEREST IN THE PROPERTY THAT IS GARNISHED.

THIS FORM MAY NOT BE USED TO CHALLENGE THE VALIDITY OF THE DEBT.

I/We claim that the following described property or money is exempt from execution or is not subject to garnishment:
_____
_____

I/We believe this property is exempt from or not subject to garnishment because (the Notice of Exempt Property that you received lists most types of property that you can claim as exempt from or not subject to garnishment):
_____
_____

I/We claim that the total amount owed is:
_____
_____

I am a person other than the Debtor and I have the following interest in the property:
_____
_____

Name_____   Name _____
Signature_____   Signature _____
Address_____   Address _____

_____   _____
Telephone   Telephone
Number_____   Number _____
(Required)   (Required)

TO BE COMPLETED BY GARNISHOR:

Name of Garnishor   _____
Address of Garnishor _____

_____

Name of Garnishee   _____
Address of Garnishee _____

_____ _____ [2001 c.249 §65; 2003 c.85 §22]

NOTICES OF GARNISHMENT

18.854 Notices of garnishment generally. (1) Any state agency authorized to issue warrants to collect taxes and debts owed to the State of Oregon, including but not limited to warrants issued pursuant to ORS 179.655, 184.644, 267.385, 293.250, 314.430, 316.207, 320.080, 321.570, 323.390, 411.703, 651.065, 657.396, 657.642, 657.646, 705.175 and 825.504, or any county tax collector authorized to issue warrants to collect taxes and debts owed to the county pursuant to ORS 311.625, may garnish property of a debtor in the possession, control or custody of a person other than the debtor by delivering to the person all of the following:
    (a) A notice of garnishment;
    (b) A warrant, or a true copy of a warrant;
    (c) The items specified in ORS 18.650 (1)(b) to (d); and
    (d) Any garnishee's search fee payable as provided in ORS 18.790.
    (2) A notice of garnishment may be issued by any person designated by the state agency or by the county tax collector. A warrant need not be recorded in the County Clerk Lien Record as a condition of issuing a notice of garnishment under the provisions of this section. The provisions of ORS 18.800 do not apply to a notice of garnishment.
    (3) If any of the items described in subsection (1) of this section are not delivered to the garnishee, a notice of garnishment shall not be effective to garnish any property of the debtor, and the garnishee shall not be required to respond to the garnishment and may proceed to deal with any property of the debtor as though the notice of garnishment had not been issued.
    (4)(a) Notwithstanding ORS 18.652, but subject to paragraph (c) of this subsection, a notice of garnishment and the other items required by subsection (1) of this section may be delivered in person to the garnishee by any employee of the state agency or of the county tax collector who is authorized by the agency or the county to deliver the notice of garnishment, may be mailed to the garnishee by first class or certified mail or may be sent to the garnishee by other means if the garnishee has agreed to a different delivery method.
    (b) An employee who delivers documents under paragraph (a) of this subsection need not be covered by the errors and omissions insurance required in ORS 18.652.
    (c) A state agency or a county may not seek sanctions against a noncomplying garnishee under ORS 18.775 unless the notice of garnishment and the other items required by subsection (1) of this section are personally delivered to the garnishee under paragraph (a) of this subsection or mailed to the garnishee by certified mail.
    (5) Notwithstanding any provision of ORS 18.600 to 18.850, a debt calculation form need not be prepared or delivered for any notice of garnishment.
    (6) Notwithstanding ORS 18.792, the duty of a garnishee to deliver any property of the debtor that may be contained in a safe deposit box that is in the garnishee's possession, control or custody at the time of delivery of the notice of garnishment to the garnishee is conditioned upon the state agency or the county tax collector first paying to the garnishee, in addition to the search fee provided for in ORS 18.790, all reasonable costs incurred by the garnishee in gaining entry to the safe deposit box. The costs shall be paid to the garnishee by the state agency or the county tax collector at least five days before the date the state agency or the county tax collector takes possession of the property in the safe deposit box. If the state agency or the county tax collector fails to pay such costs to the garnishee within 20 days after the delivery of the garnishee response, the garnishment shall not be effective to garnish any property of the debtor that may be contained in the safe deposit box and the garnishee may proceed to deal with the safe deposit box and its contents as though the notice of garnishment had not been issued. Nothing in this subsection limits the rights of a state agency or county tax collector to reach the contents of any safe deposit box in any manner otherwise provided by law.

(7) Except as provided in this section and ORS 18.855 and 18.857, all provisions of ORS 18.600 to 18.850 apply to notices of garnishment. The state agency or county tax collector shall modify the forms provided in ORS 18.600 to 18.850 as necessary to allow use of those forms for notices of garnishment. The form of the notice of garnishment must clearly indicate that the document is a notice of garnishment and must reflect the date of all warrants on which the notice of garnishment is based.

(8) The Attorney General may adopt model forms for notices of garnishment and other documents issued by state agencies and county tax collectors under this section and ORS 18.855 and 18.857. There is a presumption, as described in ORS 40.120, that any state agency or county tax collector that uses a model form adopted by the Attorney General under this subsection has complied with the requirements of ORS 18.600 to 18.850, and with the provisions of this section and ORS 18.855 and 18.857, with respect to the form of notices of garnishment. [Formerly 18.900; 2007 c.27 §3; 2013 c.472 §1; 2015 c.294 §2]

Note: 18.854 to 18.857 were enacted into law by the Legislative Assembly but were not added to or made a part of ORS chapter 18 or any series therein by legislative action. See Preface to Oregon Revised Statutes for further explanation.

18.855 Notices of garnishment issued by state agencies. (1) Notwithstanding ORS 18.607, a notice of garnishment issued by a state agency need not contain the name of a court whose authority is invoked.

(2) State agencies shall make such modifications as are necessary in the wage exemption calculation form provided by ORS 18.840 if a notice of garnishment is issued for a debt due for a state tax that is subject to the provisions of ORS 18.385 (6).

(3) Notwithstanding ORS 18.625, but subject to ORS 18.618 (2), a notice of garnishment issued by a state agency acts to garnish all wages earned by the debtor by reason of services to the garnishee until the full amount of the debt is paid or until the notice of garnishment is released by the state agency or by court order. A notice of garnishment issued by a state agency must contain language reasonably designed to notify the garnishee of the provisions of this subsection.

(4) Notwithstanding ORS 18.690, a garnishee who receives a notice of garnishment issued by a state agency need not deliver a copy of the garnishee response to the clerk of the court, but must deliver the original of the response to the state agency.

(5) Notwithstanding ORS 18.700, a challenge to a notice of garnishment issued by a state agency must be delivered in person or by first class mail to the state agency within the time specified by ORS 18.700 (2). Upon receiving a challenge, the state agency shall provide notice of the challenge in the manner provided by ORS 18.702. Upon a sheriff receiving notice under ORS 18.702, the sheriff shall proceed as provided by ORS 18.760, except that upon determination of the challenge by an administrative law judge, the sheriff shall proceed as directed by the judge. Within 14 days after receiving the challenge, the state agency must either concede the challenge or give the person making the challenge opportunity for hearing. If the person making the challenge requests a hearing, the agency shall immediately refer the challenge to the Office of Administrative Hearings established under ORS 183.605. The hearing shall be conducted as soon as possible. Notwithstanding ORS 183.315, the hearing shall be conducted as a contested case hearing. An issue that was decided in a previous hearing, or for which the debtor was previously afforded an opportunity for hearing, may not be reconsidered.

(6) If a state agency is issuing a notice of garnishment for collection of a state tax, and the state agency has reason to believe that the debtor intends to leave the state or do any other act that would jeopardize collection of the tax, the state agency may issue a special notice of garnishment. Any earnings, as defined in ORS 18.375, garnished under a special notice of garnishment are not subject to a claim of exemption under ORS 18.385. A special notice of garnishment issued under this subsection garnishes only that property of the debtor that is in the garnishee's possession, control or custody at the time the special notice is delivered, including debts not yet due, and all wages owed by the garnishee to the debtor at the time the special notice is delivered. A special notice of garnishment does not act to garnish wages earned by the debtor by reason of services rendered to the garnishee after the delivery of the special notice of garnishment.

(7) A special notice of garnishment issued under subsection (6) of this section shall contain a statement indicating that it is a special notice of garnishment under subsection (6) of this section and a statement reflecting the provisions of subsection (6) of this section. Notwithstanding ORS 18.854 (1), a wage exemption calculation form shall not be delivered to the garnishee with a special notice of garnishment.

(8) Notwithstanding ORS 18.854 (1)(b), the Department of Revenue is not required to deliver a warrant or true copy of a warrant with the notice of garnishment when garnishing property of a debtor.

(9) Notwithstanding ORS 18.607 (4), a notice of garnishment issued by the Department of Revenue must include the name of the person issuing the notice on behalf of the department, but need not be signed by that person. [Formerly 18.902; 2007 c.496 §4; 2009 c.835 §7; 2013 c.405 §1; 2015 c.294 §2]

Note: See note under 18.854.

18.857 Notice of garnishment issued by county tax collector. (1) A notice of garnishment issued by a county tax collector must name the circuit court for the county that employs the tax collector as the court whose authority is invoked.

(2) At least 15 days before any county tax collector issues a notice of garnishment, the tax collector must mail to the debtor by certified mail, return receipt requested, at the debtor's last-known address, a notification of all amounts owing to the county, a statement that further collection enforcement actions may be taken by the county to collect those amounts, and a statement that those enforcement actions may include seizing any real property owned by the debtor, imposing a lien against any real property owned by the debtor, or garnishing bank accounts, wages and other property owned by the debtor. Only one such notification shall be required and any number of garnishments may be issued after the notification is mailed.

(3) Notwithstanding ORS 18.615, a notice of garnishment issued by a county tax collector acts to garnish only that property of the debtor that is in the garnishee's possession, control or custody at the time the notice is delivered, including debts not yet due, and all wages owed by the garnishee to the debtor at the time the notice is delivered. A notice of garnishment issued by a county tax collector does not act to garnish wages earned by the debtor by reason of services rendered to the garnishee after the delivery of the notice of garnishment.

(4) Notwithstanding ORS 18.690, a garnishee who receives a notice of garnishment issued by a county tax collector need not deliver a copy of the garnishee response to the clerk of the court, but must deliver the original of the response to the county tax collector.

(5) Notwithstanding ORS 18.700, a debtor who wishes to make a challenge to a notice of garnishment issued by a county tax collector must deliver the challenge in person or by first class mail to the county tax collector within the time specified by ORS 18.700 (2). Upon receiving a challenge, the county tax collector shall provide notice of the challenge in the manner provided by ORS 18.702. Upon a sheriff receiving notice under ORS 18.702, the sheriff shall proceed as provided in ORS 18.760.

(6) Within 14 days after receipt of a challenge to a garnishment under subsection (5) of this section, the county tax collector must either:

(a) Release all property claimed as exempt from or not subject to garnishment under the challenge to the garnishment; or

(b) File with the clerk of the court a response to the challenge, attaching copies of the notice of garnishment and the garnishee response, and any supporting documentation necessary or helpful to the court in making its determination on the challenge to the garnishment. [Formerly 18.905; 2009 c.835 §8]

Note: See note under 18.854.

WRITS OF EXECUTION

(Function and Form of Writ)

18.860 Function of writ. (1) A writ of execution may direct a sheriff to:

(a) Levy on and sell real property of the judgment debtor and deliver the proceeds to the court for application against amounts owing on a money award.

(b) Levy on and sell personal property of the judgment debtor in the possession of the judgment debtor, and deliver the proceeds to the court for application against amounts owing on a money award.

(c) Levy on and deliver possession of specific real or personal property pursuant to the terms of the judgment.

(d) Levy on and sell specific real or personal property pursuant to the terms of the judgment.

(e) Levy on currency that is in the possession of the judgment debtor and deliver the currency to the court for application against amounts owing on a money award.

(2) A single writ of execution may be issued for two or more of the purposes specified in this section.

(3) A single writ of execution may be issued for two or more judgments as long as the judgments are against the same judgment debtor or debtors and are entered in the same case.

(4) An identification document, such as a driver license, passport, certified copy of a record of live birth or Social Security card, is not subject to execution and a writ of execution may not direct a sheriff to levy on an identification document except for the purpose of delivering the document pursuant to the terms of a judgment under subsection (1)(c) of this section. [2005 c.542 §1; 2007 c.166 §2; 2011 c.195 §2; 2013 c.366 §50]

18.862 Form of writ. (1) A writ of execution must be directed to a sheriff and must contain the name of the court, the names of the parties to the action and the case number for the action. The writ must contain a mailing address for the judgment creditor. The writ must describe the judgment and, if the writ of execution is issued for application of property of the judgment debtor against a money award or a declaration of the amount of the debt that a lien secures in a foreclosure suit, the writ must state the amount owing on the money award or the amount in the declaration, including interest, as of the date that the request for issuance of the writ is mailed or delivered to the court administrator. The writ must also state the amount of interest accruing on the money award or the debt each day.

(2) If a judgment requires that specific real or personal property of the judgment debtor be sold, the writ must particularly describe the property and direct the sheriff to sell the specified property. The sheriff shall deliver the proceeds of the sale as provided in ORS 18.950.

(3) If a judgment requires delivering possession of real or personal property, the writ must direct the sheriff to deliver the possession of the property. The writ must particularly describe the property and specify the party to whom the property is to be delivered.

(4) Real property identified in accordance with this section must be described using a legal description and a street address, if any. [2005 c.542 §2; 2011 c.195 §6; 2011 c.429 §1; 2015 c.291 §1]

(Issuance of Writ)

18.865 Court administrator to issue writ. (1) Except as otherwise provided by law, upon request of a judgment creditor or other prevailing party under a judgment, a court administrator shall issue a writ of execution for any judgment that includes a money award or that requires the delivery or sale of specific real or personal property. Except as provided by ORS 18.255 and 18.867, writs of execution may be issued only by the court administrator for the court in which the judgment was entered.

(2) A court administrator may rely on the information provided by the person seeking issuance of a writ of execution and is not liable for any errors or omissions in that information. [2005 c.542 §3]

18.867 Issuance of writs for certain judgments awarding child support. (1) If support enforcement services are being provided under ORS 25.080, the administrator as defined in ORS 25.010 may issue a writ of execution for the support award portion of the judgment for which support enforcement services are being provided. A copy of the writ of execution must be filed with the circuit court of the county in which the judgment was entered or recorded. A writ of execution issued under this section must be executed by the sheriff in the same manner as a writ issued by the court administrator.

(2) The Department of Justice shall adopt an appropriate form for writs of execution under this section. The form must be substantially as set forth for writs of execution described in ORS 18.862. [Formerly 18.472]

18.868 Sheriff to whom writ is issued. (1) If a writ of execution directs a sheriff to sell real property or tangible personal property of a judgment debtor and deliver the proceeds to the court for application against amounts owing on a money award, the writ may be issued to the sheriff of any county in this state where property of the judgment debtor to be levied on is located.

(2) If the writ of execution directs the sheriff to sell or deliver possession of specific real or tangible personal property, the writ must be issued to the sheriff of the county where the property is located.

(3) If the writ of execution directs the sheriff to sell intangible personal property and deliver the proceeds to the court for application against amounts owing on a money award, the court administrator shall issue the writ to the sheriff for the county in which the court sits.

(4) More than one writ of execution may be issued at the same time to different sheriffs for the enforcement of a single judgment. If the writ or the instructions to the sheriff direct the sale of a single, contiguous parcel of real property that is located in more than one county, and the judgment creditor has recorded copies of the writ or abstracts of the writ under ORS 18.870 in each county that contains part of the property, the sheriff for any county in which part of the property is located may levy on and sell the entire property. If the sheriff levies on property under this subsection, the sheriff must record a copy of the notice of levy in the County Clerk Lien Record for any county not served by the sheriff. [2005 c.542 §4; 2007 c.166 §6]

18.870 Recording of writ. Upon delivery of a writ of execution to the sheriff of any county, the judgment creditor must record a copy of the writ certified to be true by the court administrator or an abstract of the writ in the County Clerk Lien Record for the county if the writ of execution or the accompanying instructions to the sheriff require the sale of real property. A legal description and a street address, if any, of the real property must be included in, or attached to, the copy of the writ or the abstract. The recording of the writ or abstract in any county in which a judgment lien does not exist under ORS 18.150 or 18.152, or in a county in which a notice of pendency under ORS 93.740 has not been previously recorded for the property to be sold, has the same effect as recording a notice of pendency under ORS 93.740. [2005 c.542 §5; 2011 c.429 §2]

(Return on Writ)

18.872 Return on writ of execution. (1) The sheriff shall make a return on the writ of execution to the court administrator within 60 days after the sheriff receives the writ. The person that requested issuance of the writ may authorize the sheriff to continue execution under the writ and delay making a return on the writ to a date not later than 150 days after the sheriff receives the writ as long as the execution sale occurs no later than 150 days after the sheriff receives the writ. The final date for return on the writ may be extended as provided in ORS 18.932 and 18.938. For good cause shown, the court that issued the writ may extend the time for a return on the writ beyond the time provided by this subsection.

(2) The return on a writ of execution must reflect whether the sheriff levied on any property pursuant to the terms of the writ. If the sheriff did levy on property pursuant to the terms of the writ, the return must reflect the disposition made of the property by the sheriff. If any property was sold, the sheriff shall deliver the net proceeds of the sale to the court administrator with the return as required by ORS 18.950. If currency was levied on, the sheriff shall deliver the currency to the court administrator with the return.

(3) The return on a writ of execution must reflect the amount of costs of sale claimed by the judgment creditor under ORS 18.950 (2). The judgment creditor must provide the sheriff with a statement of the costs claimed on or before the date of the execution sale.

(4) The sheriff shall mail a copy of the return by first class mail to the judgment debtor and to the judgment creditor. [2005 c.542 §6]

(Instructions to Sheriff)

18.875 Instructions to sheriff. (1) The judgment creditor shall provide instructions to the sheriff with a writ of execution. The instructions must be signed by the judgment creditor or the judgment creditor's attorney. The instructions may be delivered to the sheriff after the writ is delivered to the sheriff. The instructions must include:

(a) The names and addresses of the judgment creditor and all debtors to whom notice must be given under ORS 18.888;

(b) The names and addresses of any other persons to whom notice must be given under ORS 18.918;

(c) A description of any personal property to be levied on;

(d) A street address or other description of the place where any tangible personal property may be found;

(e) A legal description for any real property or interest in real property to be levied on;

(f) A statement indicating whether any property to be levied on is residential property as defined by ORS 18.901;

(g) A statement indicating whether any condominium unit, manufactured dwelling or floating home to be levied on is inventory held for sale or lease in the regular course of business; and

(h) A statement identifying any portion of the property to be levied on that is intangible personal property, and any special instructions required to implement an order entered pursuant to ORS 18.884.

(2) If instructions to the sheriff direct the sale of tangible personal property, the judgment creditor may request in the instructions that the property not be seized by the sheriff and that the property be secured in the manner provided by ORS 18.880. The instructions may request that the property be rendered temporarily inoperable, and the manner in which the property should be rendered inoperable.

(3) If a judgment creditor seeks sale of real property under a writ of execution and the real property has a street address, the instructions to the sheriff must include the street address of the real property to be sold. If the real property is residential property that is subject to ORS 18.904, a copy of the court order authorizing the sale, or a copy of the judgment directing sale or foreclosure of the property, must be attached to the instructions.

(4) In addition to the instructions required by this section, a sheriff may require that a judgment creditor provide all other instructions as may be necessary to allow the sheriff to levy on and to sell or deliver property pursuant to a writ of execution. [2005 c.542 §7; 2007 c.580 §1; 2011 c.195 §8]

(Levy)

18.878 Manner of levying on property. (1) Upon receipt of a writ of execution, the sheriff shall indorse upon the writ of execution the time when the sheriff received the writ. The sheriff shall then levy on property pursuant to the writ of execution and the instructions provided to the sheriff under ORS 18.875 by doing all of the following:

(a) Filing a notice of levy with the court if real property is to be sold under the writ, or if residential property as described in ORS 18.901 (2), (3) or (4) is to be sold under the writ.

(b) Seizing any tangible personal property that the sheriff has not been instructed to secure in the manner provided by ORS 18.880.

(c) Securing any tangible personal property in the manner provided by ORS 18.880 if the sheriff has been instructed to secure the property in that manner.

(d) Filing a notice of levy with the court in the manner provided by ORS 18.884 if the sheriff has been instructed to sell intangible personal property.

(e) Securing and delivering possession of property if the writ requires that property be delivered under the writ.

(2) When a sheriff levies on personal property in any manner described in subsection (1) of this section, the interest of the judgment creditor in the personal property is the same as that of a secured creditor with an interest in the property perfected under ORS chapter 79. [2005 c.542 §8; 2007 c.166 §12]

18.880 Alternative procedure for levying on tangible personal property. (1) If a sheriff is instructed to secure tangible personal property under this section, the sheriff shall leave the property in the custody of the judgment debtor.

(2) The sheriff shall attach a notice to the property in substantially the following form:

_____

NOTICE: This property is to be sold by the sheriff pursuant to a writ of execution. Any person who moves this property from this place without authorization from the sheriff, who damages this property or who uses property that the sheriff has rendered inoperable without authorization from the sheriff, commits a crime and is subject to prosecution. If you have any questions, you should contact the Sheriff of _____ County.

[ ] If this box has been checked, the sheriff has rendered the property inoperable and the property may not be used by any person without the authorization of the sheriff.
_____

(3) A sheriff is not liable to the judgment creditor, to the judgment debtor or to any other person for any loss or damage to property that is secured in the manner provided by this section. [2005 c.542 §9]

18.882 Criminal penalty for moving, using or damaging secured property. A judgment debtor or other person commits a Class A misdemeanor if the person knows that a notice has been attached to property secured under ORS 18.880 and the person:

(1) Moves the property without authorization from the sheriff;

(2) Damages the property; or

(3) If the sheriff has rendered the property inoperable, uses the property without authorization from the sheriff. [2005 c.542 §10]

18.884 Levying on intangible personal property. (1) A sheriff shall file a notice of levy on intangible property with the court upon receiving the instructions directing the sale of intangible personal property unless the sheriff is provided with an order entered under subsection (3) of this section. The notice shall identify the nature of the property to be sold.

(2) A judgment creditor may seek an ex parte order from the court for the purpose of determining whether property to be levied on is tangible or intangible.

(3) A judgment creditor may seek an ex parte order from the court directing the manner in which intangible personal property may be secured by the sheriff. The court shall approve the order if the proposed manner of securing the property is reasonable under the circumstances. The judgment creditor must attach a copy of the order to instructions provided to the sheriff under ORS 18.875. The sheriff shall file a notice of levy with the court upon securing the property in the manner directed by the order. [2005 c.542 §11; 2007 c.166 §14]

18.886 Creditor's bond. (1) Before levying on personal property a sheriff may require that the judgment creditor file with the sheriff a good and sufficient bond or irrevocable letter of credit indemnifying the sheriff against any loss to the sheriff by reason of levying on or selling the property if:

(a) The sheriff has identified a specific person other than the judgment debtor who claims an interest in the property to be levied on; or

(b) The property is perishable.

(2) If a sheriff has reasonable doubt as to the ownership of personal property, or if any encumbrances are asserted against the property, the sheriff may require a bond or irrevocable letter of credit as described in subsection (1) of this section before levying on the property unless:

(a) The judgment creditor delivers to the sheriff a copy of a title document or report for the property issued by a state or federal agency that shows that the judgment debtor is the sole owner of the property; or

(b) If there is no title document for the property to be levied on, the judgment creditor delivers to the sheriff a record, prepared under ORS 79.0523 (4) by a filing office described in ORS 79.0501, showing that no financing statement or lien, or certificate or notice affecting a lien, is in effect for the property to be levied on.

(3) The sheriff may not require a bond or irrevocable letter of credit under this section if the writ of execution directs the sale or delivery of specific personal property pursuant to the terms of the judgment.

(4) A bond or irrevocable letter of credit under this section must be for double the amount of the value of the property to be levied on, as estimated by the sheriff. [2005 c.542 §12; 2007 c.166 §18]

18.887 Forcible entry for purpose of levying on personal property. (1) A sheriff may forcibly enter a structure or other enclosure for the purpose of levying on personal property only pursuant to an order issued by the court under this section.

(2) A judgment creditor may at any time file an ex parte motion requesting a court order directed to a sheriff that authorizes the sheriff to use force to enter a structure or other enclosure for the purpose of levying on personal property pursuant to a writ of execution. Except as provided in ORS 18.255, the motion must be filed with the court in which the judgment was entered. The motion must identify the specific structure or other enclosure to be entered and must contain a declaration under penalty of perjury made in the manner described by ORCP 1 E, or an unsworn declaration made in the manner described in ORS 194.800 to 194.835, if the declarant is physically outside the boundaries of the United States, that reflects facts supporting the judgment creditor's good faith belief that personal property subject to a writ of execution is located within the structure or other enclosure.

(3) An order issued under this section shall direct the sheriff to use all force reasonably necessary to enter the structure or other enclosure and levy on personal property pursuant to a writ of execution.

(4) A judgment creditor may deliver a copy of an order issued under this section to a sheriff with a writ of execution, or at any time after a writ of execution is delivered to a sheriff. A sheriff may rely on the copy of the order in entering a structure or other enclosure for the purpose of levying on personal property pursuant to a writ of execution. [2007 c.166 §11; 2013 c.218 §10]

18.888 Notice of levy. (1) After levying on property, a sheriff shall mail or deliver a copy of the writ of execution to each judgment debtor. If the writ is issued pursuant to an in rem judgment against personal property, the sheriff shall mail or deliver a copy of the writ to the person from whom the property was seized. If the writ is issued pursuant to an in rem judgment against real property, the sheriff shall mail or deliver a copy of the writ to the occupants of the property. The sheriff shall mail the copy of the writ to the addresses included in the instructions to the sheriff. If the judgment creditor has not provided an address for a person, the sheriff need not mail a copy of the writ to the person.

(2) If the sheriff has levied on intangible property, in addition to the copy of the writ required under subsection (1) of this section, the sheriff shall mail or deliver to the persons described in subsection (1) of this section a copy of the notice of levy filed with the court pursuant to ORS 18.878 (1)(d).

(3) Unless the writ directs the sheriff to sell or deliver specific real or personal property pursuant to the terms of the judgment, in addition to the copy of the writ required under subsection (1) of this section the sheriff shall mail or deliver to each judgment debtor:

(a) A copy of the notice of levy or a statement of the date and time of the levy; and

(b) A challenge to execution form as provided by ORS 18.896. [2005 c.542 §13; 2007 c.166 §13; 2011 c.195 §10]

18.890 Debtor's bond. If a sheriff is instructed by a judgment creditor to levy on tangible personal property by seizing the property for later sale or by securing the property under ORS 18.880 for later sale, the sheriff may permit the judgment debtor to retain custody and use of all or part of the property until the sale is made if the judgment debtor files with the sheriff a good and sufficient bond or irrevocable letter of credit indemnifying the sheriff against any loss to the sheriff by reason of failure of the judgment debtor to deliver the property at the time and place of sale. The bond or irrevocable letter of credit must be in an amount equal to twice the value of the property, as estimated by the sheriff. A sheriff is not discharged from liability to the judgment creditor for property by reason of the filing of a bond or letter of credit under this section. [2005 c.542 §14]

(Challenge to Writ of Execution)

18.892 Challenge to writ of execution. (1) Except as provided in subsection (2) of this section, a judgment debtor may use a challenge to execution form only:

(a) To claim such exemptions under a writ of execution as are permitted by law; and

(b) To assert that the amount specified in the writ of execution as being subject to execution is greater than the amount owed by the judgment debtor under the money award.

(2) A judgment debtor may not use a challenge to execution form to challenge execution on residential property of the debtor as defined by ORS 18.901 if the judgment creditor has obtained an order under ORS 18.904 authorizing the sale or if the judgment directs the sale or delivery of specific property.

(3) Any person other than a judgment debtor who has an interest in any property levied on by a sheriff may assert that interest by delivering a challenge to execution in the manner provided by subsection (4) of this section.

(4) A person may make a challenge to a writ of execution by completing the challenge to execution form provided in ORS 18.896, or a substantially similar form, and by delivering, in person or by first class mail, the original of the completed form to the court administrator for the court identified in the writ of execution and a copy of the challenge to the judgment creditor. Upon receiving a copy of the challenge, the judgment creditor shall promptly notify the sheriff of the challenge.

(5) A challenge to execution must be delivered in the manner provided by subsection (4) of this section within 30 days after the property is levied on as described in ORS 18.878 or before the property is sold on execution, whichever occurs first. [Formerly 18.505; 2007 c.166 §8]

18.894 Notice of challenge to execution. Without unreasonable delay, a court administrator who has received a challenge to execution under ORS 18.892 shall provide written notice of the challenge to all sheriffs for counties to which writs of execution have been issued and no return made, and to the person that requested issuance of the writ. The notice may include the notice of hearing required by ORS 18.898. [Formerly 18.508]

18.896 Challenge to execution form. (1) The challenge to execution form described in this section does not expand or restrict the law relating to exempt property. A determination as to whether property is exempt from attachment or execution must be made by reference to other law. The form provided in this section may be modified to provide more information or to update the notice based on subsequent changes in exemption laws.

(2) A challenge to execution form must be in substantially the following form:

_____COURT
                    COUNTY OF _____

```
_____        )    CHALLENGE TO
Plaintiff,      )    EXECUTION
                )
                }
          vs.   }    Case No. _____
                }
                )
_____        )
Defendant.      )
```

THIS FORM MAY BE USED BY THE DEBTOR ONLY FOR THE FOLLOWING PURPOSES:
(1) To claim such exemptions from execution as are permitted by law.
(2) To assert that the amount specified in the writ of execution as being subject to execution is greater than the total amount owed.

THIS FORM MAY BE USED BY PERSONS OTHER THAN THE DEBTOR ONLY TO CLAIM AN INTEREST IN THE PROPERTY THAT IS TO BE SOLD ON EXECUTION.

147

THIS FORM MAY <u>NOT</u> BE USED TO CHALLENGE THE VALIDITY OF THE DEBT.

I/We claim that the following described property or money is exempt from execution:

_____
_____

I/We believe this property is exempt from execution because (the Notice of Exempt Property at the end of this form describes most types of property that you can claim as exempt from execution):

_____
_____

I am a person other than the Debtor and I have the following interest in the property:

_____
_____

Name_____   Name _____
Signature_____   Signature _____
Address_____   Address _____
_____   _____
Telephone   Telephone
Number_____   Number _____
(Required)   (Required)

YOU MUST ACT PROMPTLY IF YOU WANT TO GET YOUR MONEY OR PROPERTY BACK. You may seek to reclaim your exempt property by doing the following:
(1) Fill out the Challenge to Execution form that you received with this notice.
(2) Mail or deliver the Challenge to Execution form to the court administrator at the address shown on the writ of execution.
(3) Mail or deliver a copy of the Challenge to Execution form to the judgment creditor at the address shown on the writ of execution.
You should be prepared to explain your exemption in court. If you have any questions about the execution or the debt, you should see an attorney.

YOU MAY USE THE CHALLENGE TO EXECUTION FORM <u>ONLY</u> FOR THE FOLLOWING PURPOSES:
(1) To claim such exemptions from execution as are permitted by law.
(2) To assert that the amount specified in the writ of execution as being subject to execution is greater than the total amount owed.

YOU MAY <u>NOT</u> USE THE CHALLENGE TO EXECUTION FORM TO CHALLENGE THE VALIDITY OF THE DEBT.

IF YOU CLAIM AN EXEMPTION IN BAD FAITH, YOU MAY BE SUBJECT TO PENALTIES IMPOSED BY THE COURT THAT COULD INCLUDE A FINE. Penalties that you could be subject to are listed in ORS 18.899.

NOTICE OF EXEMPT PROPERTY

   Property belonging to you may have been taken or held in order to satisfy a debt. The debt may be reflected in a judgment or in a warrant or order issued by a state agency. Important legal papers are enclosed.
   YOU MAY BE ABLE TO GET YOUR PROPERTY BACK, SO READ THIS NOTICE CAREFULLY.
   State and federal law specify that certain property may not be taken. Some of the property that you may be able to get back is listed below.
   (1) Wages or a salary as described in ORS 18.375 and 18.385. Whichever of the following amounts is greater:
   (a) 75 percent of your take-home wages; or
   (b) $218 per workweek.
   (2) Social Security benefits.
   (3) Supplemental Security Income (SSI).
   (4) Public assistance (welfare).
   (5) Unemployment benefits.
   (6) Disability benefits (other than SSI benefits).
   (7) Workers' compensation benefits.
   (8) All Social Security benefits and Supplemental Security Income benefits, and up to $7,500 in exempt wages, retirement benefits, welfare, unemployment benefits and disability benefits, that are held in a bank account.
   (9) Spousal support, child support or separate maintenance to the extent reasonably necessary for your support or the support of any of your dependents.
   (10) A homestead (house, manufactured dwelling or floating home) occupied by you, or occupied by your spouse, parent or child. Up to $40,000 of the value of the homestead is exempt. If you jointly own the homestead with another person who is also liable on the debt, up to $50,000 of the value of the homestead is exempt.
   (11) Proceeds from the sale of a homestead described in item 10, up to the limits described in item 10, if you hold the proceeds for less than one year and intend to use those proceeds to procure another homestead.
   (12) Household goods, furniture, radios, a television set and utensils with a combined value not to exceed $3,000.
   *(13) An automobile, truck, trailer or other vehicle with a value not to exceed $3,000.
   *(14) Tools, implements, apparatus, team, harness or library that are necessary to carry on your occupation, with a combined value not to exceed $5,000.
   *(15) Books, pictures and musical instruments with a combined value not to exceed $600.
   *(16) Wearing apparel, jewelry and other personal items with a combined value not to exceed $1,800.
   (17) Domestic animals and poultry for family use with a combined value not to exceed $1,000 and their food for 60 days.
   (18) Provisions and fuel for your family for 60 days.
   (19) One rifle or shotgun and one pistol. The combined value of all firearms claimed as exempt may not exceed $1,000.
   (20) Public or private pensions.
   (21) Veterans' benefits and loans.
   (22) Medical assistance benefits.
   (23) Health insurance proceeds and disability proceeds of life insurance policies.
   (24) Cash surrender value of life insurance policies not payable to your estate.
   (25) Federal annuities.
   (26) Other annuities to $250 per month (excess over $250 per month is subject to the same exemption as wages).
   (27) Professionally prescribed health aids for you or any of your dependents.
   *(28) Rental assistance to an elderly person allowed pursuant to ORS 458.375.

*(29) Your right to receive, or property traceable to:
*(a) An award under any crime victim reparation law.
*(b) A payment or payments, not exceeding a total of $10,000, on account of personal bodily injury suffered by you or an individual of whom you are a dependent.
*(c) A payment in compensation of loss of future earnings of you or an individual of whom you are or were a dependent, to the extent reasonably necessary for your support and the support of any of your dependents.
(30) Amounts paid to you as an earned income tax credit under federal tax law.
(31) Your right to the assets held in, or right to receive payments under, a medical savings account or health savings account authorized under section 220 or 223 of the Internal Revenue Code.
(32) Interest in personal property to the value of $400, but this cannot be used to increase the amount of any other exemption.
(33) Equitable interests in property.
Note: If two or more people in your household owe the claim or judgment, each of them may claim the exemptions marked by an asterisk (*).

SPECIAL RULES APPLY FOR DEBTS THAT ARE OWED FOR CHILD SUPPORT AND SPOUSAL SUPPORT. Some property that may not otherwise be taken for payment against the debt may be taken to pay for overdue support. For instance, Social Security benefits, workers' compensation benefits, unemployment benefits, veterans' benefits and pensions are normally exempt, but only 50 percent of a lump sum payment of these benefits is exempt if the debt is owed for a support obligation.

[Formerly 18.512; 2007 c.71 §7; 2007 c.166 §9; 2007 c.496 §§12,17; 2009 c.430 §11; 2009 c.612 §5; 2011 c.93 §3; 2011 c.228 §4; 2011 c.317 §7; 2013 c.597 §3; 2015 c.348 §25]

18.898 Hearing on challenge to execution. (1) A challenge to execution shall be adjudicated in a summary manner at a hearing before the court with authority over the writ of execution. Upon receipt of a challenge to execution, the court administrator shall immediately set a hearing date and send notice of the hearing to the judgment debtor and the judgment creditor. The hearing shall be held as soon as possible. The sheriff may not sell any property that is described in the challenge to execution until the court has issued a decision on the challenge, and the time for making a return on the writ is suspended until the decision is made or the sale completed, whichever is later. The sheriff shall not delay sale if the judgment debtor has filed the challenge to execution in violation of ORS 18.892 (2).
(2) Hearings on a challenge to execution may be held by telecommunication devices.
(3) The judgment debtor has the burden to prove timely delivery of a challenge to execution under ORS 18.892. [Formerly 18.515]

18.899 Sanctions. A court may impose sanctions against any person who files a challenge to execution in bad faith. The sanctions a court may impose under this section are a penalty of not more than $100 and responsibility for attorney fees under ORS 20.105. [Formerly 18.518]

18.900 [2001 c.249 §81; 2003 c.85 §23; 2003 c.578 §3; 2003 c.663 §3; 2005 c.336 §3; renumbered 18.854 in 2005]

EXECUTION SALE

(Residential Property)

18.901 Definition of residential property. For the purposes of this section and ORS 18.904, 18.906, 18.908 and 18.912, "residential property" means any of the following property:
(1) Real property on which no more than four units designed to be used as dwellings are located.
(2) A condominium unit that is designed to be used as a dwelling and that is not being held as inventory for sale or lease in the regular course of business.
(3) A manufactured dwelling as defined by ORS 446.003 that is not being held as inventory for sale or lease in the regular course of business.
(4) A floating home as defined in ORS 830.700 that is not being held as inventory for sale or lease in the regular course of business. [2005 c.542 §15]

18.902 [2001 c.249 §§82,82a; 2002 s.s.3 c.7 §2; 2003 c.75 §22; renumbered 18.855 in 2005]

18.904 Order required for sale of residential property; exceptions. (1) If the judgment debtor is a natural person, residential property may be sold under a writ of execution only after the entry of a court order authorizing the sale.
(2) This section does not apply to writs of execution that direct the sheriff to sell specific property pursuant to the terms of the judgment.
(3) This section does not apply to a writ of execution issued to enforce a judgment foreclosing:
(a) A construction lien for work, labor or material done or furnished exclusively for the improvement of the property to be sold;
(b) A lawfully executed purchase money lien against the property to be sold; or
(c) A lawfully executed mortgage or trust deed on the property to be sold. [2005 c.542 §16]

18.905 [2001 c.249 §83; renumbered 18.857 in 2005]

18.906 Motion for order authorizing sale of residential property. (1) A judgment creditor may file a motion with a court requesting an order authorizing the sheriff to sell residential property. The motion must be filed with a court that has authority to issue a writ of execution for the judgment. The motion must include a statement that does all of the following:
(a) Indicates the amount of the money award or money awards, as reflected in the judgment or judgments.
(b) Indicates the amount owing on the money award or money awards on the date the motion is filed.
(c) Indicates whether any of the money awards arise out of an order or judgment for child support as described in ORS 18.398.
(d) Identifies the residential property to be sold by legal description and by street address, if any.
(e) Indicates whether the property is a homestead. If the property is a homestead, the motion must allege facts showing that the homestead may be sold on execution.
(2) A motion under this section must be accompanied by an affidavit disclosing the basis of the allegations contained in the motion. If the judgment creditor relies on more than one judgment to support the order, the motion must be accompanied by copies of all other judgments on which the judgment creditor relies.
(3) A court shall promptly schedule a hearing on a motion filed under this section. In setting the hearing the court shall allow adequate time to allow service on the judgment debtor under ORS 18.908. [2005 c.542 §17; 2011 c.429 §3]

18.908 Notice of motion for order authorizing sale of residential property. (1) At least 10 days before the hearing on a motion filed under ORS 18.906, the judgment creditor must:
(a) Serve the judgment debtor in the manner provided by ORCP 7 with a copy of the motion and the supporting affidavit, and with a notice of the time and place of the hearing; and
(b) Send a copy of the motion and the notice by first class mail to the property at the mailing address for the property.
(2) The notice required by subsection (1) of this section must be in substantially the following form:

This is to notify you that _____ has asked the court to order the sheriff to sell property located at _____ to satisfy a judgment against_____.

Before deciding whether to order the sale, the court will hold a hearing on_____, 2___, at _____ a.m./p.m., in Room _____,_____.

The law provides that property is your homestead if the property is actually used as a home by you, your spouse, a dependent parent or a dependent child. If you are temporarily absent from the property but intend to move back in, the property is still your homestead.

The law provides that if the property is your homestead, then $_____ of its value may not be taken to satisfy a judgment against you. In addition, a homestead usually may not be sold to satisfy a judgment for $3,000 or less.

The law provides that property may be sold despite the fact that it is your homestead and all of its value may be taken to satisfy a judgment against you if the judgment is for child support.

IF YOU WISH TO PROTECT THIS PROPERTY FROM A SHERIFF'S SALE, YOU SHOULD COME TO THE COURT HEARING.

IF YOU HAVE ANY QUESTIONS, YOU SHOULD SEE A LAWYER AT ONCE.

If you do not own this property, please give this notice and the papers served with it to the owner.

[2005 c.542 §18; 2009 c.612 §7]

18.910 [Formerly 29.367; 2003 c.576 §572a; 2005 c.542 §67; 2005 c.702 §95; renumbered 18.999 in 2005]

18.912 Hearing on motion for order authorizing sale of residential property. (1) Whether or not the judgment debtor appears at the hearing, the court shall inquire as to the facts alleged in a motion filed under ORS 18.906 and make a summary determination on the motion.

(2) The court shall authorize sale of the property pursuant to a motion filed under ORS 18.906 unless the court finds:

(a) That the property is the homestead of the judgment debtor;

(b) That the judgment is subject to the homestead exemption; and

(c) That the amount of the judgment or judgments was $3,000 or less at the time of entry of the judgment or judgments as described in ORS 18.395 (7).

(3) If the court authorizes the sale of residential property, the order must state whether the homestead exemption applies to the property. If the homestead exemption does apply to the property, the order must state the allowed amount of the exemption.

(4) If the court authorizes the sale of residential property, the judgment creditor may recover the costs of service of the motion and notice under ORS 18.908 as part of the costs of the sale. [2005 c.542 §19; 2009 c.612 §8]

(Notice of Sale)

18.918 Person entitled to written notice of sale. (1) A judgment creditor must list in the instructions required by ORS 18.875 the names and addresses of all persons entitled to written notice of the execution sale. For each person listed, the list must include the address last known to the judgment creditor. For all execution sales, the list must include:

(a) The name of the judgment debtor; and

(b) The name of any attorney for a judgment debtor reflected in the judgment document.

(2) If real property is to be sold in the execution sale, the list prepared by the judgment creditor under this section must include the name of each person with one of the following interests in the real property, determined as of a date that is identified by the judgment creditor and that is not more than 10 days before the request for issuance of the writ of execution was filed:

(a) Any person who has a lien of record against the property that attached to the property after the judgment lien attached and before the determination date identified by the judgment creditor.

(b) Any person who has an interest in the property that was acquired from the debtor or any successor to the debtor, and that was recorded after the judgment lien attached and before the determination date identified by the judgment creditor.

(3) Subsection (2) of this section does not apply to a writ of execution requiring the sale of specific real property identified in a judgment of foreclosure or any other judgment directing the sale of specific real property. If a writ of execution is issued pursuant to a judgment in an in rem proceeding, a judgment of foreclosure or another judgment directing the sale of the specific real property, the list prepared by the judgment creditor under this section must contain the names and last known addresses of the persons who were parties to the action at the time of judgment in lieu of the names required under subsection (2) of this section.

(4) Failure to include the name of a person required to be listed under this section does not affect the validity of an execution sale or in any way give that person any right to challenge the sale of the property. By submitting the instructions to the sheriff, a judgment creditor certifies that the list of persons reflected in the instructions complies with this section, and the failure to include the name of any person as required by this section is subject to sanction under ORCP 17. [2005 c.542 §20]

18.920 Notice of sale of personal property. (1) Before conducting an execution sale of personal property, a sheriff shall give written notice of the sale in the manner provided by this section. The notice must identify the property to be sold and the time and place of the sale.

(2) Before any execution sale of personal property, the sheriff shall:

(a) Mail copies of the notice of sale by first class mail and by certified mail, return receipt requested, to the judgment debtor at the address provided in the instructions to the sheriff; and

(b) Mail a copy of the notice of sale by first class mail to any attorney for the judgment debtor identified in the instructions at the address provided in the instructions to the sheriff.

(3) The notices required by subsection (2) of this section must be mailed not less than 10 days before an execution sale is conducted.

(4) The sheriff shall post a notice of the sale in three public places in the county in which the sale is to take place. The notice must be posted not more than 20 days before the date of sale identified in the notice of sale and not less than 10 days before that date.

(5) In lieu of posting notice under subsection (4) of this section, a sheriff shall give notice of an execution sale by Internet posting if the judgment creditor requests that posting in the instructions given to the sheriff under ORS 18.875 and a website has been established under ORS 18.926 for the purpose of giving legal notices under ORS 18.860 to 18.993. Subject to ORS 18.926 (3), the notice must be posted on the Internet not less than 10 days before the date identified in the notice of sale and remain posted until that date. [2005 c.542 §21; 2009 c.835 §5]

18.922 Expedited sale of perishable personal property; expedited sale to prevent loss of value. (1) Notwithstanding ORS 18.920, if perishable personal property is levied on by a sheriff:

(a) The notices required by ORS 18.920 (2) must be mailed by express mail not less than 48 hours before the execution sale is conducted; and

(b) The sheriff shall post notice of the sale in the manner required by ORS 18.920 (4) or (5) not less than 48 hours before the execution sale is conducted.

(2) In lieu of conducting an expedited sale under subsection (1) of this section, a judgment creditor or a sheriff may seek an ex parte order from the court directing the manner of conducting an expedited sale to prevent loss of value. An order issued under this section may modify or eliminate any of the requirements of ORS 18.920. If an ex parte order is entered under this subsection at the request of the judgment creditor, the judgment creditor must provide a copy of the order to the sheriff. [2005 c.542 §22]

18.924 Notice of sale of real property. (1) Before conducting an execution sale of real property, a sheriff shall:

(a) Post notice of the sale on the website established under ORS 18.926 for at least 28 days; and
(b) Publish notice of the sale in a newspaper, as defined in ORS 193.010, in the county where the real property is located once a week for four successive weeks.
(2) The notice posted on the website and published in the newspaper under subsection (1) of this section must include:
(a) The names of the parties subject to the writ of execution;
(b) The street address of the property or, if there is no street address, the tax lot number of the property; and
(c) The date, time and place of the execution sale.
(3) In addition to the information listed in subsection (2) of this section, the notice posted on the website under subsection (1) of this section must include:
(a) The legal description of the property; and
(b) The following notice:

Before bidding at the sale, a prospective bidder should independently investigate:
(a) The priority of the lien or interest of the judgment creditor;
(b) Land use laws and regulations applicable to the property;
(c) Approved uses for the property;
(d) Limits on farming or forest practices on the property;
(e) Rights of neighboring property owners; and
(f) Environmental laws and regulations that affect the property.

---

(4) In addition to the information listed in subsection (2) of this section, a notice published in the newspaper under subsection (1) of this section must include instructions for locating the information posted on the website under subsection (1) of this section.
(5) The sheriff is not required to post or publish the notice of sale of real property under this section until the judgment creditor provides the sheriff with all of the information required under subsections (2) and (3) of this section.
(6) Before any execution sale of real property, the sheriff shall:
(a) Mail copies of the notice of sale posted on the website under subsection (1) of this section by first class mail and by certified mail, return receipt requested, to the judgment debtor at the address provided in the instructions to the sheriff;
(b) Mail a copy of the notice of sale posted on the website under subsection (1) of this section by first class mail to any attorney for the judgment debtor identified in the instructions at the address provided in the instructions; and
(c) Mail a copy of the notice of sale posted on the website under subsection (1) of this section by first class mail to any other person listed in the instructions pursuant to ORS 18.918 at the address provided in the instructions.
(7) The notices required by subsection (6) of this section must be mailed not less than 28 days before an execution sale is conducted.
(8) Before any execution sale of real property for which the judgment creditor has provided a street address under ORS 18.875 (3), the sheriff shall post the notice of the sale posted on the website under subsection (1) of this section in a conspicuous place on the property. The notice must be posted not more than seven days after the sheriff mails notices as required by subsection (6) of this section. [2005 c.542 §23; 2009 c.835 §6; 2011 c.195 §11; 2011 c.429 §4; 2013 c.464 §1]

18.926 Legal notices website; posting fee. (1) The elected sheriffs of this state shall establish and maintain a website where legal notices under ORS 18.860 to 18.993 may be posted. The sheriffs may enter into an intergovernmental agreement for establishing and maintaining the website.
(2) An intergovernmental agreement entered into under this section may establish fees for posting legal notices on a website maintained under this section.
(3) For the purpose of determining whether a legal notice has been posted for the period of time required by law, an interruption of service of a website maintained under this section that does not exceed 48 hours does not affect the continuity of the posting. An interruption of service of a website maintained under this section does not prevent the sheriff from conducting an execution sale unless the court orders otherwise. [2005 c.542 §24; 2009 c.835 §4; 2011 c.195 §13; 2013 c.464 §2]

(Conduct of Execution Sale)

18.930 Conduct of sale generally; county fee. (1) The sheriff shall conduct an execution sale by public oral auction. The sale must be conducted between 9 a.m. and 4 p.m. All property shall be sold by the sheriff in such parcels as are likely to bring the highest price. Any portion of real property belonging to a person other than the judgment debtor must be sold separately if the person requests a separate sale.
(2) At least 10 days before the date first set for an execution sale, a judgment creditor must provide the sheriff with any report for real property to be sold at the execution sale that is in the possession of the judgment creditor and that shows interests of record in the property. The sheriff shall make the report available to bidders who appear at the sale. No civil action may be brought against a title company, the judgment creditor, the sheriff or any other person by reason of omissions or errors in the report, and the validity of the sale is not affected by reason of any omissions or errors in the report.
(3) A judgment creditor that is a public body, as defined in ORS 174.109, may set a minimum bid amount for property to be sold at an execution sale.
(4) Tangible personal property to be sold at an execution sale must be present at the place where the sale is conducted unless the property is not in the possession of the sheriff.
(5) The county may establish a fee to be collected by the sheriff at the time of sale. The amount of the fee shall be established by the governing body of the county and may not be greater than the amount necessary to pay the county for the expenses incurred by the county for giving notice of the sale and conducting the sale and for the anticipated expenses for any notices required to be given after the sale and other post-sale administration of the sale.
(6) A person who purchases real property that is subject to redemption at an execution sale must provide the sheriff with an address to which a redemption notice may be sent and must notify the sheriff of any change in address until the purchaser transfers the purchaser's interest in the property, the property is redeemed or the time allowed for redemption expires, whichever occurs first. Any person who thereafter acquires the purchaser's interest in the property must notify the sheriff of the transfer, provide the sheriff with an address to which a redemption notice may be sent and notify the sheriff of any change in address until there is a another transfer, the property is redeemed or the time allowed for redemption expires, whichever occurs first.
(7) At any time before the sheriff conducts an execution sale for personal property, the judgment debtor may pay to the sheriff the full amount owing on the judgment as of the date the payment is made along with the costs of sale as described in ORS 18.950 (2). The payment must be made in United States currency. If payment is made under this subsection, the sheriff may not sell the property, and shall deliver the property to the debtor. The sheriff shall deliver the amount paid by the judgment debtor to the court administrator with the sheriff's return on the writ. The sheriff is not liable to any person by reason of accepting payment under the provisions of this subsection. [2005 c.542 §25; 2007 c.580 §2; 2011 c.195 §14]

18.932 Postponement of sale; rules. (1) A sheriff may postpone an execution sale to a specified date if:
(a) The sheriff is unable to conduct the sale at the place and time specified in the notice of the sale;
(b) The sheriff considers it appropriate to postpone the sale for want of purchasers; or
(c) For other sufficient cause.
(2) A sheriff shall postpone an execution sale to a specified date upon the request of a judgment creditor. The sheriff may not postpone the execution sale to a date later than the final date for return on the writ of execution under ORS 18.872.
(3) If possible, the sheriff shall make a public announcement of a postponement at the time and place scheduled for the sale.
(4) An execution sale may be postponed more than one time under the provisions of this section. An execution sale may not be postponed beyond the date that a return on the writ is due. If the judgment creditor requests a postponement to a specified date, and the date is more than 60 days after the

sheriff received the writ, the request for a postponement of the sale automatically operates as a request for an extension of the time for a return on the writ of execution under ORS 18.872 (1), and the return on the writ is due three business days after the date specified by the judgment creditor for the sale.

(5) The sheriff need not give additional notice of sale in the manner provided by ORS 18.918, 18.920, 18.922 or 18.924 by reason of a postponement. The State Court Administrator by rule may establish procedures for giving notice of a postponement by a posting on a website maintained under ORS 18.926. [2005 c.542 §26]

18.934 Amount of property to be sold; sheriff and deputies may not purchase. At an execution sale, the sheriff shall sell only the property necessary to satisfy the judgment. A sheriff conducting an execution sale and deputies of the sheriff may not purchase property at the sale or acquire any interest in property by reason of the sale. [2005 c.542 §27]

18.936 Bid by judgment creditor. (1) A judgment creditor that requested issuance of a writ of execution may make oral bids for property to be sold at an execution sale. If the oral bid of the judgment creditor is the highest bid, the judgment creditor need not make any payment to the sheriff other than for:

(a) Any unpaid sheriff's fees for the execution sale;

(b) The amount of an exemption that the debtor claims and that the judgment creditor agrees to or that a court has determined applies to the property; and

(c) Any amount that the judgment creditor bids that:

(A) Exceeds the full amount, calculated as of the date of the execution sale, that is owing on the money award, for a judgment that includes a money award, plus the costs of the sale as described in ORS 18.950 (2) that the judgment creditor paid; or

(B) Exceeds the amount declared in the judgment, calculated as of the date of the execution sale, for a judgment that directs the sale of specific real or personal property, plus the costs of the sale as described in ORS 18.950 (2) that the judgment creditor paid.

(2)(a) A judgment creditor that requested issuance of a writ of execution may submit a written bid for property to be sold in an execution sale before the sale is conducted.

(b) A bid under paragraph (a) of this subsection may not be for more than:

(A) The full amount, calculated as of the date of the execution sale, that is owing on the money award, for a judgment that includes a money award, plus the costs of the sale that the judgment creditor may recover as provided in ORS 18.950 (2); or

(B) The amount declared in the judgment, calculated as of the date of the execution sale, for a judgment that directs the sale of specific real or personal property, plus the costs of the sale that the judgment creditor may recover as provided in ORS 18.950 (2).

(c) The sheriff must receive a bid under this subsection not less than 48 hours before the sale is conducted. The sheriff may rely on the judgment creditor's calculation of the amount due under the money award or the amount declared in the judgment and for the costs of sale. The sheriff is not required to make a separate calculation. If the written bid of the judgment creditor is the highest bid, the judgment creditor need not make any payment to the sheriff other than for:

(A) Any unpaid sheriff's fees for the execution sale; and

(B) The amount of an exemption that the debtor claims and that the judgment creditor agrees to or that a court has determined applies to the property.

(3) A judgment creditor that makes a bid under subsection (2) of this section may instruct the sheriff to accept any bid that matches the amount of the judgment creditor's bid.

(4) A written bid under subsection (2) of this section is irrevocable, but the judgment creditor that submits the written bid may make an oral bid at the time of the sale that is higher than the written bid.

(5) A judgment creditor that makes a bid under this section must notify the sheriff of any amounts included in the bid that are attributable to costs of sale under ORS 18.950 (2). [2005 c.542 §28; 2007 c.166 §7; 2011 c.195 §16; 2015 c.291 §2]

18.938 Manner of payment. (1) Except as provided in this section, a sheriff shall accept as payment from a purchaser of real property at an execution sale a cashier's check or cash. Except as provided in this section, a sheriff shall accept any combination of cashier's checks or cash that is adequate to pay the purchase price.

(2) A sheriff shall accept a cashier's check as payment from a purchaser at an execution sale only if the cashier's check is made payable to the sheriff and is drawn on a financial institution that is authorized to do business under the laws of Oregon or the United States.

(3) If any part of the purchase price at an execution sale is paid with a cashier's check, the sheriff shall give the purchaser a receipt for the funds in lieu of a certificate of sale under ORS 18.942. The receipt must state that the purchaser is the successful bidder and must describe the property sold.

(4) If any part of the purchase price at an execution sale is paid with a cashier's check, the sheriff shall deposit the check in a financial institution not later than the end of the first business day after the day on which the sale is conducted. The check must be deposited in a separate account.

(5) If the sheriff receives verification from a financial institution within 15 days after the date of the execution sale that all cashier's checks delivered to the sheriff for a purchase have received final settlement, the sale is effective as of the date and hour of the sale, and the purchaser has priority over any interest acquired in the real property after that time. The sheriff shall thereafter:

(a) Mail to the purchaser by first class mail a certificate of sale as provided under ORS 18.942 for all real property purchased; and

(b) Deliver the net proceeds of the sale to the court administrator or other official as provided by law.

(6) Subject to subsection (8) of this section, if the sheriff does not receive verification from a financial institution within 15 days after the date of the sale that all cashier's checks delivered to the sheriff for a purchase have received final settlement, the sale is void and the sheriff shall return to the purchaser any cash tendered by the purchaser and any amounts received for cashier's checks for which final settlement was received, less any bank charges incurred for cashier's checks and any other amount allowed by law.

(7) If any part of the purchase price at an execution sale is paid with a cashier's check, and the return date for the writ that is the basis for the sale is less than 18 days after the date of the sale, the return date is automatically extended to 18 days after the date of the sale.

(8) The judgment creditor may extend by a period of not more than 60 days the time for the sheriff to receive verification of a cashier's check provided for in subsections (5) and (6) of this section. If the judgment creditor extends the time for the sheriff to receive verification of a cashier's check, the return date for the writ is automatically extended three business days after the date specified by the judgment creditor.

(9) A judgment creditor may elect to pursue remedies under ORS chapter 73 by reason of the failure of a financial institution to honor a cashier's check tendered under this section, as though the judgment creditor had been the person to whom the check was payable.

(10) As used in this section:

(a) "Cashier's check" has the meaning given that term in ORS 73.0104.

(b) "Financial institution" has the meaning given that term in ORS 706.008. [2005 c.542 §29]

18.940 Bill of sale for personal property. (1) If a sheriff sells personal property at an execution sale, upon receipt of the purchase money the sheriff shall give a bill of sale to the purchaser for any intangible property or other property not in the possession of the sheriff. The sheriff shall deliver personal property in the possession of the sheriff to the purchaser, but shall give the purchaser a bill of sale for that property only if the purchaser requests it.

(2) If the sheriff has secured property in the manner provided by ORS 18.880 and the judgment debtor refuses to make the property available to the purchaser, without further court order the sheriff shall use all reasonable force necessary to allow the purchaser to access the property at the place where the property was located when the sheriff secured the property. [2005 c.542 §30]

18.942 Sheriff's certificate of sale for real property. (1) If a sheriff sells real property at an execution sale, the sheriff shall prepare a certificate of sale containing a particular description of the property sold, the price bid for each distinct lot or parcel and the total amount paid. The certificate must state whether the property is subject to redemption. Except as provided in ORS 18.938 (3), the sheriff shall give the certificate to the purchaser.

(2) A purchaser shall record in the County Clerk Lien Record the sheriff's certificate of sale provided to the purchaser under the provisions of this section. [2005 c.542 §31; 2015 c.168 §6]

18.944 Notice of completed sale. (1) After the execution sale of any residential property as defined in ORS 18.901 that is subject to redemption and not later than 30 days after the purchaser is given the certificate of sale, the sheriff shall:

(a) Securely attach to the main entrance of any dwelling unit upon the property a written notice stating that the property has been sold; and

(b) Send a copy of the notice described in paragraph (a) of this subsection by first class mail and by registered or certified mail to the judgment debtor.

(2) The notice required by subsection (1)(a) of this section shall be in substantially the following form:

YOUR PROPERTY HAS BEEN SOLD

Your property located at _____ has been sold. The property was sold on_____, 2____, to satisfy a court judgment against you. The purchaser's name and address are_____. The purchaser paid _____ for your property.

You may have the right to buy back the property from the purchaser by paying the purchaser the amount paid at the sale plus taxes, expenses and interest. YOU WILL LOSE THE RIGHT TO BUY BACK YOUR PROPERTY ON_____, 2____. If you do not buy back your property, the sheriff will give a deed for your property to the purchaser on that date.

The law on the rights of a person whose property is sold to satisfy a court judgment is found in ORS 18.960 to 18.985. You must follow exactly the instructions provided there.

IF YOU HAVE ANY QUESTIONS, YOU SHOULD SEE A LAWYER AT ONCE.

---

(3) The sheriff shall retain the return receipt for a notice sent by registered or certified mail as provided in subsection (1)(b) of this section and shall make and retain a record of the posting of notice required by subsection (1)(a) of this section.

(4) Failure of the sheriff to comply with any provision of this section does not affect the validity of the sale of residential property. However, this subsection does not limit any other right the judgment debtor may have. [2005 c.542 §32]

18.946 Possession after sale; right to rents or value of use. (1) Subject to subsection (2) of this section, the purchaser of real property at an execution sale is entitled to possession of the property from the date of sale until a redemption of the property, if any. Subject to subsection (2) of this section, the redemptioner of real property is entitled to possession of the property from the date the payment required by ORS 18.966 or 18.967 is made until another redemption, if any.

(2) If property sold on execution or redeemed is in the possession of a tenant who holds the property at the time of the sale under an unexpired lease that has a priority that is inferior to the claim of the judgment creditor, the lessee has the right to remain in possession of the property until expiration of the period allowed for redemption if the lessee makes the lease payments to the purchaser or redemptioner, or pays to the purchaser or redemptioner a monthly payment equal to the value of the use and occupancy of the property, whichever amount is greater. [2005 c.542 §33]

18.948 Confirmation of sale of real property. (1) A sale of real property in an execution sale is conclusively established to have been conducted in the manner required by ORS 18.860 to 18.993 unless the judgment debtor or another person adversely affected by the sale files an objection to the sale no later than 10 days after the filing of the sheriff's return under ORS 18.872.

(2) If an objection to a sale is filed, the court shall schedule a hearing on the objection. The court shall grant an order confirming the sale unless the person objecting to the sale establishes that the sale was not conducted in a manner that substantially conformed with the manner required by law, and that as a result it was probable that the person suffered damage. An order confirming a sale under this subsection conclusively establishes that the sale was conducted in the manner required by ORS 18.860 to 18.993. If the court sustains the objection, the court shall direct that the property be resold. Notwithstanding any other provision of ORS 18.860 to 18.993, the court may establish timelines for the conduct of the second sale and the return by the sheriff upon completion of the second sale.

(3) If the court orders that real property be resold under this section, the sheriff may not accept any bid in the second sale that is less than the amount paid in the first sale. If no higher bid is received in the second sale, the sheriff shall so indicate in the sheriff's return to the court. If a higher bid is received at the second sale, upon receipt of the proceeds the court administrator shall return to the first purchaser the amounts paid by the purchaser. If the original purchaser makes the highest bid in the second sale, the purchaser need pay to the sheriff only the difference between the bid in the second sale and the amounts already paid by the purchaser. [2005 c.542 §34]

18.950 Delivery and distribution of proceeds; satisfaction document. (1) After the deduction of all sheriff's fees and costs allowed by law that have not been paid by the judgment creditor, and deduction of all other amounts required by law, the sheriff shall deliver all net proceeds from an execution sale to the court administrator with the sheriff's return on the writ. The court shall enter an order of distribution for the proceeds. An order directing distribution to the judgment creditor may be entered ex parte.

(2) A judgment creditor is entitled to recover from the proceeds of the sale all of the following costs of sale paid by the judgment creditor:

(a) Sheriff's fees;

(b) The cost of any title report required to determine persons entitled to notice under ORS 18.918 (2);

(c) The cost of any indemnity bond or letter of credit required by ORS 18.886;

(d) Amounts that may be recovered by the judgment creditor under ORS 18.999;

(e) Services fees that may be recovered as costs under ORS 18.912; and

(f) Recording fees incurred pursuant to ORS 18.870.

(3) The court shall order that the costs specified in subsection (2) of this section be paid before application of the remaining proceeds to satisfaction of the judgment.

(4) If any proceeds from an execution sale remain after the payment of costs under subsection (3) of this section and satisfaction of the judgment, the court administrator shall pay the remaining proceeds as directed by the court in the order of distribution.

(5)(a) Upon receipt of the proceeds of the execution sale of real property, the judgment creditor shall file a satisfaction document as provided in ORS 18.225 for the amount credited against any money award portion of a judgment.

(b) The judgment debtor or other person with an interest in the real property may request in writing to the judgment creditor that the judgment creditor file a satisfaction document. If the judgment creditor does not file a satisfaction document within 10 days after receiving the request, the person making the request may file a motion under ORS 18.235.

(c) If the court finds that the judgment creditor failed to file a satisfaction document under ORS 18.225 within 10 days after receiving a written request under paragraph (b) of this subsection, the court may render a supplemental judgment awarding reasonable attorney fees to the person making the motion, unless the judgment creditor establishes that the failure to file the satisfaction document was not the fault of the judgment creditor. [2005 c.542 §35; 2007 c.166 §19; 2017 c.270 §1]

18.952 Effect of sale on judgment debtor's or mortgagor's title; effect of redemption by judgment debtor or mortgagor. (1) The title of a judgment debtor or mortgagor to real property that is subject to redemption under ORS 18.960 to 18.985 is not transferred by the sale of the property at an execution sale. If a judgment debtor or mortgagor, or a successor in interest to a judgment debtor or mortgagor, redeems property sold at an execution sale, the right to possession of the property is restored subject to all liens of record, whether arising before, on or after the sale, as though the sale had never occurred.

(2) If a judgment debtor or mortgagor, or a successor in interest to a judgment debtor or mortgagor, redeems property sold at an execution sale, the property may not be redeemed by any other person. The sheriff shall provide the redemptioner with a certificate of redemption. A certificate of redemption may be recorded in the County Clerk Lien Record for the county in which the property is located. [2005 c.542 §36]

18.954 Conduct of sale pursuant to court rule or terms of order or judgment. A court, by the terms of a judgment or order, may direct that an execution sale under a specific judgment be conducted in a manner different than the manner specified by ORS 18.860 to 18.993. The Chief Justice of the Supreme Court may by court rule provide that execution sales be conducted in a manner different than the manner specified by ORS 18.860 to 18.993. [2005 c.542 §37]

(Redemption)

18.960 Definitions. As used in ORS 18.960 to 18.985:
(1) "Certificate holder" means a person who holds a certificate of sale issued under ORS 18.942 or who holds a certificate of redemption issued under ORS 18.975.
(2) "Claimant" means a person who claims to have a right to redeem under ORS 18.960 to 18.985.
(3) "Land sale contract" means a contract for the transfer or conveyance of an interest in real property. "Land sale contract" does not include earnest money agreements, preliminary sales agreements, options or rights of first refusal.
(4) "Redemptioner" means a person other than a judgment debtor who has redeemed property under ORS 18.960 to 18.985.
(5) "Redemption notice" means a notice described under ORS 18.970. [2005 c.542 §37a]

18.962 Property that may be redeemed. (1) All real property sold at an execution sale may be redeemed except for a leasehold interest with an unexpired term of less than two years.
(2) A manufactured dwelling, as defined by ORS 446.003, may be redeemed only if the manufactured dwelling is sold together with the real property on which the manufactured dwelling is located.
(3) The right of a seller to receive payments under a land sale contract that is sold with the real property may be redeemed.
(4) Except as provided in ORS 18.987 (3), a purchaser's interest in a land sale contract may be redeemed. [2005 c.542 §38]

18.963 Who may redeem. (1) Subject to subsection (3) of this section, property that is described in ORS 18.962 and that is sold at an execution sale may be redeemed by:
(a) The judgment debtor;
(b) A mortgagor whose interest in the property was sold at the execution sale;
(c) Any person with a lien against the property that has a priority that is inferior to the claim of the judgment creditor; or
(d) The successor in interest of any person described in paragraph (a), (b) or (c) of this subsection.
(2) Subject to subsection (3) of this section, for the purposes of ORS 18.960 to 18.985:
(a) All references to a judgment debtor include a mortgagor whose interest in the property that was sold at the execution sale and any successor in interest to such a mortgagor;
(b) All references to a judgment debtor include a successor in interest to a judgment debtor; and
(c) A person described in subsection (1)(c) of this section, and any successor in interest of that person, is a lien claimant.
(3) Any person described in subsection (1) of this section who conveys all of the person's interest in property sold on execution to a successor in interest may not redeem the property. [2005 c.542 §39]

18.964 Time for redemption. (1) Except as otherwise provided in ORS 18.960 to 18.985, the ability of a judgment debtor to redeem property sold at an execution sale expires unless the judgment debtor redeems the property within 180 days after the date of sale.
(2) Except as provided in subsection (3) of this section, the ability of a lien claimant to redeem property sold at an execution sale expires unless the lien claimant redeems the property within 60 days after the date of sale.
(3) If any lien claimant redeems property within the time provided by subsection (2) of this section, any other lien claimant may redeem the property from the redemptioner. The subsequent redemption must be made within 60 days after the redemption amount specified in ORS 18.966 or 18.967 is paid to the sheriff. Other lien claimants may thereafter redeem from a preceding redemptioner, in the same manner, as long as each redemption is made within 60 days after the previous redemption. [2005 c.542 §40]

18.966 Redemption amount payable to purchaser. Subject to ORS 18.968, a claimant may redeem property from the purchaser at an execution sale by paying to the sheriff:
(1) The amount paid by the purchaser at the execution sale, with interest at the rate of nine percent per annum from the date of sale;
(2) The amount of any taxes paid by the purchaser on the property, with interest at the rate of nine percent per annum from the date of payment;
(3) Any amounts necessarily expended by the purchaser to prevent waste, with interest at the rate of nine percent per annum from the date of payment;
(4) Any amounts paid by the purchaser on liens superior to the interest of the purchaser, with interest at the rate of nine percent per annum from the date of payment; and
(5) Any assessments paid by the purchaser to a homeowners association under ORS 94.550 to 94.783, or to an association of unit owners under ORS chapter 100, with interest at the rate of nine percent per annum from the date of payment. [2005 c.542 §41; 2015 c.120 §1]

18.967 Redemption amount payable to redemptioner. Subject to ORS 18.968, a claimant may redeem property from a redemptioner by paying to the sheriff:
(1) The amount paid by the redemptioner, with interest at the rate of nine percent per annum from the date of payment;
(2) The amount owing on the lien of the redemptioner, unless the payment is made by a lien claimant whose lien has a priority that is superior to the lien of the redemptioner;
(3) The amount of any taxes paid by the redemptioner on the property, with interest at the rate of nine percent per annum from the date of payment;
(4) Any amounts necessarily expended by the redemptioner to prevent waste, with interest at the rate of nine percent per annum from the date of payment;
(5) Any amounts paid by the redemptioner on liens superior to the lien of the redemptioner, with interest at the rate of nine percent per annum from the date of payment; and
(6) Any amounts paid by the redemptioner to a homeowners association under ORS 94.550 to 94.783, or to an association of unit owners under ORS chapter 100, with interest at the rate of nine percent per annum from the date of payment. [2005 c.542 §42; 2015 c.120 §2]

18.968 Setoff for rents, income and profits realized by certificate holder; certificate holder's lien for crops and amounts expended to prevent waste. (1) A judgment debtor is entitled to a setoff against the amounts required to redeem property sold at an execution sale for all rents, income and profits realized by the certificate holder from the property.
(2) If the real property sold at an execution sale is farmland, the certificate holder has a lien on the first crops sown or grown after the sale and for all sums reasonably expended by the certificate holder in plowing, cultivating or seeding the property. The lien of the certificate holder is superior to all other liens except the liens provided by law for payment of wages for work in cultivating the land or harvesting the crops grown on the property. If the real

property is not farmland, the certificate holder has a lien on the profits accruing from the property during the period that the certificate holder held the land for sums necessarily expended by the certificate holder to prevent waste. [2005 c.542 §43]

18.970 Redemption notice. (1) A claimant who wishes to redeem property must serve the certificate holder with a redemption notice. The notice must specify a date and approximate time when the claimant will make payment to the sheriff, the redemption amount calculated by the claimant and the manner in which the redemption amount was calculated. The notice must include a mailing address for the claimant. The date of the redemption must be a weekday that is not a legal holiday. The time of the redemption must be between the hours of 9 a.m. and 4 p.m. The notice must inform the certificate holder if an accounting under ORS 18.980 is required.

(2) If the claimant is a lien claimant, the notice must reflect the nature of the lien claimant's interest and the claimant shall attach to the notice copies of any documents necessary to establish that interest. If the claimant is a successor in interest to another person with redemption rights under ORS 18.963, the claimant shall attach to the notice copies of any documents necessary to establish how the person acquired the interest. If the claimant claims to have an interest with a priority that is superior to the interest of the certificate holder, the claimant shall attach to the notice copies of any documents necessary to establish that priority.

(3) A redemption notice must be served by personal service or by first class mail. If the notice is served by first class mail, service is effective on mailing. A copy of the notice may be filed with the sheriff before the notice is given to the certificate holder, but must be filed with the sheriff no later than seven days before the redemption date specified in the notice. The notice must be served on the certificate holder not more than 30 days before the payment date specified in the redemption notice, and:

(a) Not less than 14 days before the payment date specified in the notice, if service is made by first class mail; or

(b) Not less than seven days before the payment date specified in the notice, if personal service is made.

(4) A claimant shall submit proof of service of the notice required by this section at the time the claimant pays the sheriff under ORS 18.975.

(5) If a certificate holder fails to comply with the requirements of ORS 18.930 (6) or 18.982, the certificate holder may not object to a redemption by reason of failure to receive a redemption notice. [2005 c.542 §44a; 2007 c.580 §3]

18.971 Objection to redemption notice. (1) A certificate holder may object to a redemption notice if the certificate holder asserts that the claimant is not eligible to redeem. An objection under this section must be filed with the court administrator, filed with the sheriff and mailed by first class mail to the claimant before the payment date specified in the notice.

(2) The filing of an objection under this section does not affect the requirement of payment of the redemption amount specified in the redemption notice under ORS 18.975. [2005 c.542 §44b]

18.972 Response to redemption notice. (1) A certificate holder shall respond to a redemption notice if:

(a) The notice requests an accounting under ORS 18.980; or

(b) The certificate holder objects to the redemption amount specified in the notice.

(2) A response to a redemption notice must be served by personal service or by first class mail. If the response is served by first class mail, service is effective on mailing. A copy of the response may be filed with the sheriff before the response is given to the claimant, but must be filed with the sheriff before the payment date specified in the notice. The response must be served on the claimant before the payment date specified in the notice.

(3) If the redemption notice requests an accounting, the accounting must be attached to the response given under this section.

(4) If the certificate holder objects to the redemption amount specified in the notice because the certificate holder claims additional amounts are owing under ORS 18.966 or 18.967, the response must include all information specified in ORS 18.980 (1)(a) to (e).

(5) A response filed under this section must include a statement of the amount claimed as the proper redemption amount after deductions or additions by reason of any accounting provided with the response or by reason of additional amounts claimed under subsection (4) of this section. [2005 c.542 §44c; 2015 c.120 §3]

18.973 Objection to response. (1) A claimant may object to the amount claimed in the response as the proper redemption amount. An objection under this section must be filed with the court administrator and mailed by first class mail to the certificate holder within seven days after the response is served under ORS 18.972.

(2) The filing of an objection under this section does not affect the requirement of payment of the redemption amount specified in the redemption notice under ORS 18.975. Payment of the amount claimed in the response waives any objection filed under this section unless the claimant delivers a copy of the objection to the sheriff with the payment. [2005 c.542 §44d]

18.975 Payment of redemption amount. (1) Except as provided in ORS 18.980 (2) and (4), unless a certificate holder has indicated a lower redemption amount in the certificate holder's response under ORS 18.972, a claimant shall pay the sheriff at least the redemption amount specified in the notice on or before the payment date specified in the redemption notice. If the claimant does not make payment as required by this subsection, the redemption notice is of no effect.

(2) The sheriff shall issue to the claimant who makes payment under this section a certificate of redemption on the payment date specified in the redemption notice unless:

(a) Before the payment date specified in the notice, an objection is filed with the sheriff in the manner required by ORS 18.971;

(b) Before the payment date specified in the notice, a response is filed with the sheriff in the manner required by ORS 18.972, and the claimant fails to pay additional amounts claimed in the response on the payment date specified in the notice;

(c) An objection to a response is delivered to the sheriff with the payment in the manner required by ORS 18.973; or

(d) The calculations or other documentation provided to the sheriff appear irregular to the sheriff.

(3) If the calculations or other documentation provided to the sheriff appear irregular to the sheriff, and the claimant objects to the failure of the sheriff to issue a certificate of redemption pursuant to subsection (2)(d) of this section, the sheriff shall give written notice to the court of the objection pursuant to ORS 18.992.

(4) If a claimant pays the sheriff the redemption amount specified in the redemption notice, but the sheriff does not issue a certificate of redemption pursuant to subsection (2) of this section, the sheriff shall give the claimant a receipt for the funds in lieu of a certificate of redemption.

(5) If a response is filed with the sheriff in the manner required by ORS 18.972 before the payment date specified in the notice, and the claimant makes payment as required by subsection (1) of this section but fails to pay additional amounts claimed in the response, the redemption notice is of no effect and the sheriff shall return the payment to the claimant unless:

(a) The claimant objects to the response in the manner provided by ORS 18.973; or

(b) The claimant pays additional amounts claimed in the response, plus interest, in the manner provided by subsection (6) of this section.

(6) If a response is filed with the sheriff in the manner required by ORS 18.972 before the payment date specified in the notice, and the claimant makes payment as required by subsection (1) of this section but fails to pay additional amounts claimed in the response, the sheriff shall issue a certificate of redemption to the claimant dated as of the date that the receipt was issued under subsection (4) of this section if the claimant pays additional amounts claimed in the response, plus interest, within seven days after the date the receipt was issued. [2005 c.542 §44e]

18.978 Court proceedings on objections. (1) If an objection is filed under ORS 18.971 or 18.973, the sheriff shall transmit to the court administrator copies of all records relating to the sale that are within the sheriff's possession.

(2) The court shall schedule a hearing on an objection filed under ORS 18.971 or 18.973 as soon as possible.

(3) If a certificate holder files an objection under ORS 18.971, and the court determines that the claimant is eligible to redeem, the court shall direct the sheriff to issue a certificate of redemption to the claimant, dated as of the date that the receipt was issued under ORS 18.975. If the court determines that the claimant is not eligible to redeem, the court shall direct the sheriff to refund all amounts paid by the claimant to the sheriff.

(4) If an objection is filed by a claimant under ORS 18.973, the court shall determine the proper redemption amount. If the court determines that the proper redemption amount is greater than the amount paid under ORS 18.975, the court shall direct the sheriff to issue a certificate of redemption to the claimant upon payment of the additional amounts plus interest within 10 days after entry of the court's order, dated as of the date that the receipt was issued under ORS 18.975. If the additional amounts and interest are not paid within the time allowed, the redemption is void and the sheriff shall refund to the claimant all amounts paid to the sheriff. If the court determines that the proper redemption amount is less than the amount paid under ORS 18.975, the court shall direct the sheriff to issue a certificate of redemption to the claimant, dated as of the date that the receipt was issued under ORS 18.975, and order a refund to the claimant of the amounts determined by the court to be in excess of the proper redemption amount.

(5) Upon issuance of a certificate of redemption under this section, the sheriff shall deliver to the certificate holder the amount determined to be the proper redemption amount.

(6) If the court determines under subsection (4) of this section that the proper redemption amount is greater than the amount paid under ORS 18.975, and determines that the amount specified in the redemption notice does not represent a good faith attempt to determine the proper redemption amount, the court shall enter judgment against the claimant for all attorney fees incurred by the certificate holder in the proceedings. [2005 c.542 §44f]

18.980 Accounting. (1) A judgment debtor may require that a certificate holder provide an accounting under this section by including a request for an accounting in the redemption notice. If a redemption notice includes a request for an accounting, the certificate holder shall attach an accounting to the response given under ORS 18.972. The accounting must reflect:

(a) The amount of any taxes the certificate holder has paid on the property, with interest at the rate of nine percent per annum from the date of payment.

(b) Any amounts necessarily expended by the certificate holder to prevent waste, with interest at the rate of nine percent per annum from the date of payment.

(c) Any amounts that the certificate holder has paid on liens superior to the lien of the certificate holder, with interest at the rate of nine percent per annum from the date of payment.

(d) The amount of any assessments paid by the certificate holder to a homeowners association under ORS 94.550 to 94.783, or to an association of unit owners under ORS chapter 100, with interest at the rate of nine percent per annum from the date of payment.

(e) The amount owing on the lien of the certificate holder, if the certificate holder is a redemptioner.

(f) The net proceeds of rents, income or profits from the property by the certificate holder while the certificate holder has been in possession of the property.

(2) If a redemption notice includes a request for an accounting and the certificate holder fails to respond as required by ORS 18.972, the time for paying the redemption amount is automatically extended to 30 days after the redemption date specified in the redemption notice or until the time specified by subsection (4) of this section if a claimant files a motion under subsection (3) of this section.

(3) If a redemption notice includes a request for an accounting, and the certificate holder fails to respond as required by ORS 18.972, the claimant may file a motion with the court requesting an order requiring the certificate holder to show cause why the certificate holder should not be held in contempt. A motion under this subsection must be made not more than 28 days after the redemption notice is served on the certificate holder. The claimant must deliver a copy of the motion to the sheriff.

(4) If a motion is filed under subsection (3) of this section:

(a) The time for redemption of the property is automatically extended to 30 days after the accounting is provided by the certificate holder; and

(b) The time for paying the redemption amount is automatically extended to 30 days after the accounting is provided by the certificate holder. [2005 c.542 §45; 2015 c.120 §4]

18.981 Manner of payment. (1) Except as provided in this section, a sheriff shall accept as payment from a claimant a cashier's check or cash. Except as provided in this section, a sheriff shall accept any combination of cashier's checks or cash that is adequate to pay the redemption amount.

(2) A sheriff shall accept a cashier's check as payment only if the cashier's check is made payable to the sheriff and is drawn on a financial institution that is authorized to do business under the laws of Oregon or the United States. If any part of the redemption amount is paid with a cashier's check, the sheriff shall give the purchaser a receipt for the funds in lieu of a certificate of redemption under ORS 18.975.

(3) If any part of the redemption amount is paid with a cashier's check, the sheriff shall deposit the check in a financial institution not later than the end of the first business day after the day on which the check is received. The check must be deposited in a separate account.

(4) If the sheriff receives verification from a financial institution within 15 days after the date of the redemption that all cashier's checks delivered to the sheriff for the redemption have received final settlement, and the sheriff is required to give a certificate of redemption under ORS 18.975, the sheriff shall mail to the claimant by first class mail a certificate of redemption and deliver to the certificate holder all amounts paid to the sheriff. If the sheriff is not required to give a certificate of redemption under ORS 18.975, the sheriff shall give the person tendering the amounts a receipt for the funds in lieu of a certificate of redemption, and shall deliver a certificate of redemption and the amounts paid to the sheriff only as provided in ORS 18.978 after a final decision by the court.

(5) If the sheriff does not receive verification from a financial institution within 15 days after the checks are deposited that all cashier's checks delivered to the sheriff have received final settlement, the redemption is void and the sheriff shall return to the claimant any cash tendered by the claimant and any amounts received for cashier's checks for which final settlement was received, less any bank charges incurred for cashier's checks and any other amount allowed by law.

(6) As used in this section:

(a) "Cashier's check" has the meaning given that term in ORS 73.0104.

(b) "Financial institution" has the meaning given that term in ORS 706.008. [2005 c.542 §46]

18.982 Redemptioner must provide sheriff with address. A redemptioner must provide the sheriff with an address to which a redemption notice may be sent and must notify the sheriff of any change in address until the redemptioner transfers the redemptioner's interest in the property, the property is redeemed or the expiration of the time allowed for another redemption, whichever occurs first. Any person who acquires the redemptioner's interest in the property must notify the sheriff of the transfer, provide the sheriff with an address to which a redemption notice may be sent, and notify the sheriff of any change in address until there is a another transfer, the property is redeemed or the expiration of the time allowed for another redemption, whichever occurs first. [2005 c.542 §46a]

(Waste)

18.983 Court may restrain waste. Upon motion of a claimant, or a certificate holder who is not in possession of the property, the court may restrain waste of the real property sold at an execution sale. A person in possession of the real property does not commit waste of the property by continuing to use the property in the same manner in which the property was used before the execution sale, by engaging in the ordinary course of husbandry on the property or by making necessary repairs to buildings. [2005 c.542 §47]

(Sheriff's Deed)

18.985 Sheriff's deed. (1) Unless the property is redeemed by the judgment debtor, upon request of the certificate holder and payment of the fee required by ORS 21.300 (1)(c), the sheriff shall execute and deliver a deed for real property sold at an execution sale. The deed shall convey the property to the certificate holder. The deed shall be delivered to the certificate holder as soon as possible.

156

(2) Notwithstanding subsection (1) of this section, the court may direct the sheriff to execute a deed to a certificate holder before the expiration of the time allowed for redemption if the certificate holder establishes that the certificate holder has acquired the rights of all persons entitled to redeem. [2005 c.542 §48]

SPECIAL RULES FOR SPECIFIC
TYPES OF PROPERTY

18.986 Manufactured dwellings and floating homes. (1) Except as provided in subsection (2) of this section, a manufactured dwelling or floating home must be levied on and sold in the same manner as provided for real property under ORS 18.860 to 18.993 if the real property upon which the manufactured dwelling or floating home is located is to be sold at the execution sale.

(2) A manufactured dwelling or floating home that is held as inventory for sale or lease in the normal course of business must be levied on and sold in the same manner as provided for tangible personal property under ORS 18.860 to 18.993.

(3) If the real property upon which a manufactured dwelling or floating home is located is not to be sold at the execution sale, and the manufactured dwelling or floating home is not held as inventory for sale or lease in the normal course of business, the manufactured dwelling or floating home must be levied on and sold in the same manner as provided for real property under ORS 18.860 to 18.993 except that:

(a) The legal description required by ORS 18.875 (1)(e) need not be included in the instructions to the sheriff; and

(b) The sheriff shall give the purchaser of a manufactured dwelling or floating home a bill of sale under ORS 18.940 and not a certificate of sale under ORS 18.942.

(4) For the purposes of this section:

(a) "Floating home" has the meaning given that term in ORS 830.700.

(b) "Manufactured dwelling" has the meaning given that term in ORS 446.003. [2005 c.542 §49]

18.987 Purchaser's interest in land sale contract; leasehold interest in land with unexpired term of more than two years. (1) Except as provided in this section, a purchaser's interest in a land sale contract, as defined by ORS 18.960, or a leasehold interest in land with an unexpired term of more than two years must be levied on and sold in the same manner as provided for real property under ORS 18.860 to 18.993.

(2) The legal description required by ORS 18.875 (1)(e) in instructions to a sheriff directing the sale of a purchaser's interest in a land sale contract, as defined by ORS 18.960, or the sale of a leasehold interest in land with an unexpired term of more than two years must be of the property sold under the land sale contract, or of the real property subject to the lease.

(3) There is no right of redemption if a purchaser's interest in a land sale contract, as defined by ORS 18.960, is sold at an execution sale pursuant to a judgment enforcing the seller's rights under the contract and if the judgment directing the sale of the purchaser's interest indicates that the purchaser's interest is sold without redemption rights. [2005 c.542 §50]

18.988 Seller's right to receive payments under land sale contract. (1) Except as provided by this section, the right of a seller to receive payments under a land sale contract, as defined by ORS 18.960:

(a) May not be sold pursuant to a writ of garnishment;

(b) May be sold only under a writ of execution in conjunction with a sale of the seller's interest in the real property; and

(c) Must be levied on and sold in the same manner as provided for real property under ORS 18.860 to 18.993.

(2) This section does not affect the ability of a judgment creditor to garnish payments owed to a seller under a land sale contract, as defined by ORS 18.960, that are due when the writ of garnishment is delivered or within 45 days after the writ of garnishment is delivered, as provided by ORS 18.685 (5). [2005 c.542 §51]

18.989 Equitable interests in property. (1) Except as provided in subsection (3) of this section, an equitable interest in property may be sold pursuant to a writ of execution only if:

(a) An order or judgment specifically authorizes the sale of the equitable interest; and

(b) The writ of execution specifically directs the sale of the equitable interest.

(2) If a writ of execution specifically directs the sale of the equitable interest in property, the judgment creditor must submit a copy of the order or judgment authorizing the sale with the instructions to the sheriff required by ORS 18.875.

(3) If a writ of execution specifically directs the sale of the equitable interest in real property, the equitable interest shall be levied on and sold in the same manner as provided for real property under ORS 18.860 to 18.993.

(4) A purchaser's interest in a land sale contract, as defined by ORS 18.960, or a leasehold interest in land with an unexpired term of more than two years, may be sold pursuant to a writ of execution even though the sale is not specifically authorized by an order or judgment and the writ does not specifically direct the sale of the interest. [2005 c.542 §52]

MISCELLANEOUS

18.992 Referral of disputes to court. If at any time a judgment debtor, judgment creditor, purchaser or lien claimant objects to the performance by a sheriff of any duty imposed on the sheriff under ORS 18.860 to 18.993, the sheriff may give written notice of the objection to the court and request that the court resolve the dispute. If written notice is given to the court under this section, the court shall resolve the dispute and provide such additional instructions to the sheriff as may be necessary. [2005 c.542 §53]

18.993 Effect of ORS 18.860 to 18.993 on court's ability to direct seizure. Nothing in ORS 18.860 to 18.993 affects the ability of a court to direct seizure of property under ORS 18.268 (2). [2005 c.542 §54]

18.995 Owner not allowed to neglect foreclosed residential real property; local government to notify owner of violation; lien for unreimbursed costs. (1) As used in this section:

(a) "Foreclosed residential real property" means residential property, as defined in ORS 18.901, that an owner obtains as a result of:

(A) Foreclosing a trust deed on the residential property; or

(B) Receiving a judgment that forecloses a lien on the residential property.

(b) "Neglect" means:

(A) To fail or a failure to maintain the buildings, grounds or appurtenances of foreclosed residential real property in such a way as to allow:

(i) Excessive growth of foliage that diminishes the value of adjacent property;

(ii) Trespassers or squatters to remain on the foreclosed residential real property or in a structure located on the foreclosed residential real property;

(iii) Mosquito larvae or pupae to grow in standing water on the foreclosed residential real property; or

(iv) Other conditions on the foreclosed residential real property that cause or contribute to causing a public nuisance.

(B) To fail or a failure to monitor the condition of foreclosed residential real property by inspecting the foreclosed residential real property at least once every 30 days with sufficient attention so as to prevent, or to identify and remedy, a condition described in subparagraph (A) of this paragraph.

(c) "Owner" means a person, other than a local government, that forecloses a trust deed by advertisement and sale under ORS 86.752 or by suit under ORS 88.010.

(d) "Reasonable costs" means actual and demonstrable costs that are commensurate with and do not exceed the market rate for services necessary to remedy a condition of neglect, plus the actual and demonstrable costs of administering a contract for services to remedy a condition of neglect or the portion of the costs of a program to remedy conditions of neglect that are attributable to remedying a condition of neglect for specific foreclosed residential real property.

(2)(a) An owner may not neglect the owner's foreclosed residential real property during any period in which the foreclosed residential real property is vacant.

(b) An owner shall provide the owner's name or the name of the owner's agent and a telephone number or other means for contacting the owner or agent to:

(A) The neighborhood association for the neighborhood in which the foreclosed residential real property is located; or

(B) An official that the local government designates to receive the information described in this paragraph.

(c) An owner shall post a durable notice in a conspicuous location on the foreclosed residential real property that lists a telephone number for the owner or for the local government that a person may call to report a condition of neglect. The owner shall replace the notice if the notice is removed from the foreclosed residential real property during a period when the foreclosed residential real property is vacant.

(d) An owner or the agent of an owner shall identify the owner of the foreclosed residential real property to the local government and shall provide to, and maintain with, the local government current contact information during a period when the foreclosed residential real property is vacant.

(3)(a) If a local government finds a violation of subsection (2)(a) of this section, the local government shall notify the owner in writing of the foreclosed residential real property that is the subject of the violation and in accordance with paragraph (b) or (c) of this subsection, as appropriate, shall specify a time within which the owner must remedy the condition of neglect that is the basis for the local government's finding.

(b) The local government shall allow the owner not less than 30 days to remedy the violation unless the local government makes a determination under paragraph (c) of this subsection and shall provide the owner with an opportunity to contest the local government's finding at a hearing. The owner must contest the local government's finding within 10 days after the local government notifies the owner of the violation.

(c) If the local government determines that a specific condition of the foreclosed residential real property constitutes a threat to public health or safety, the local government may require an owner to remedy the specific condition in less than 30 days, provided that the local government specifies in the written notice the date by which the owner must remedy the specific condition. A local government may specify in the written notice different dates by which the owner must remedy separate conditions of neglect on the foreclosed residential real property.

(4)(a) After a local government allows an owner the time specified in subsection (3)(b) of this section or makes a determination under subsection (3)(c) of this section, the local government may remedy or contract with another person to remedy neglect or a specific condition of neglect on foreclosed residential real property and require the owner to reimburse the local government for reasonable costs the local government incurs under this paragraph.

(b) A local government that has incurred costs with respect to foreclosed residential real property under paragraph (a) of this subsection has a lien on the foreclosed residential real property for the sum of the local government's unreimbursed costs. A lien created under this paragraph is prior to all other liens and encumbrances, except that the lien has equal priority with a tax lien. The lien attaches at the time the local government files a claim of lien with the county clerk of the county in which the foreclosed residential real property is located. A local government may bring an action in the circuit court to foreclose the lien in the manner provided for foreclosing other liens on real or personal property. [2013 c.317 §1]

Note: 18.995 was enacted into law by the Legislative Assembly but was not added to or made a part of ORS chapter 18 or any series therein by legislative action. See Preface to Oregon Revised Statutes for further explanation.

18.999 Recovery of expenses incurred in enforcing judgment and certain other monetary obligations. This section establishes the right of a plaintiff to recover certain moneys the plaintiff has expended to recover a debt under ORS 18.854 or to enforce a judgment and establishes procedures for that recovery. The following apply to this section:

(1) When a plaintiff receives moneys under a garnishment, attachment or payment, the plaintiff may proceed as follows:

(a) Before crediting the total amount of moneys received against the judgment or debt, the plaintiff may recover and keep from the total amount received under the garnishment, attachment or payment any moneys allowed to be recovered under this section.

(b) After recovering moneys as allowed under paragraph (a) of this subsection, the plaintiff shall credit the remainder of the moneys received against the judgment or debt as provided by law.

(2) Moneys recovered under subsection (1)(a) of this section shall not be considered moneys paid on and to be credited against the original judgment or debt sought to be enforced. No additional judgment is necessary to recover moneys in the manner provided in subsection (1)(a) of this section.

(3) The only moneys a plaintiff may recover under subsection (1)(a) of this section are those described in subsection (4) of this section that the plaintiff has paid to enforce the existing specific judgment or debt that the specific garnishment or attachment was issued to enforce or upon which the payment was received. Moneys recoverable under subsection (1)(a) of this section remain recoverable and, except as provided under subsection (8) of this section, may be recovered from moneys received by the plaintiff under subsequent garnishments, attachments or payments on the same specific judgment or debt.

(4) This section allows the recovery only of the following:

(a) Statutorily established moneys that meet the requirements under subsection (3) of this section, as follows:

(A) Garnishee's search fees under ORS 18.790.

(B) Fees for delivery of writs of garnishment under ORS 18.652.

(C) Circuit court fees as provided under ORS 21.235 and 21.258.

(D) County court fees as provided under ORS 5.125.

(E) County clerk recording fees as provided in ORS 205.320.

(F) Actual fees or disbursements made under ORS 21.300.

(G) Costs of execution as provided in ORS 105.112.

(H) Fees paid to an attorney for issuing a garnishment in an amount not to exceed $45 for each garnishment.

(I) Costs of an execution sale as described in ORS 18.950 (2).

(J) Fees paid under ORS 21.200 for motions and responses to motions filed after entry of a judgment.

(K) Amounts paid to a sheriff for the fees and expenses of executing a warrant under ORS 105.510.

(L) Fees added to liquidated and delinquent debts under ORS 305.084 (4).

(b) Interest on the amounts specified in paragraph (a) of this subsection at the rate provided for judgments in ORS 82.010 for the period of time beginning with the expenditure of the amount and ending upon recovery of the amount under this section.

(5) The plaintiff shall be responsible for doing all of the following:

(a) Maintaining a precise accounting of moneys recovered under subsection (1)(a) of this section and making the accounting available for any proceeding relating to that judgment or debt.

(b) Providing reasonable notice to the defendant of moneys the plaintiff recovers under subsection (1)(a) of this section.

(6) Moneys recovered under subsection (1)(a) of this section remain subject to all other provisions of law relating to payments, or garnished or attached moneys including, but not limited to, those relating to exemption, claim of exemption, overpayment and holding periods.

(7) Nothing in this section limits the right of a plaintiff to recover moneys described in this section or other moneys in any manner otherwise allowed by law.

(8) A writ of garnishment or attachment is not valid if issued solely to recover moneys recoverable under subsection (1)(a) of this section unless the right to collect the moneys is first reduced to a judgment or to a debt enforceable under ORS 18.854. [Formerly 18.910; 2007 c.860 §§11,31; 2009 c.659 §§5,7; 2011 c.366 §§3,4; 2011 c.595 §115; 2013 c.685 §39; 2017 c.644 §8; 2017 c.663 §19]

Note: The amendments to 18.999 by section 8, chapter 644, Oregon Laws 2017, become operative July 1, 2018. See section 12, chapter 644, Oregon Laws 2017. The text that is operative until July 1, 2018, including amendments by section 19, chapter 663, Oregon Laws 2017, is set forth for the user's convenience.

18.999. This section establishes the right of a plaintiff to recover certain moneys the plaintiff has expended to recover a debt under ORS 18.854 or to enforce a judgment and establishes procedures for that recovery. The following apply to this section:

(1) When a plaintiff receives moneys under a garnishment, attachment or payment, the plaintiff may proceed as follows:

(a) Before crediting the total amount of moneys received against the judgment or debt, the plaintiff may recover and keep from the total amount received under the garnishment, attachment or payment any moneys allowed to be recovered under this section.

(b) After recovering moneys as allowed under paragraph (a) of this subsection, the plaintiff shall credit the remainder of the moneys received against the judgment or debt as provided by law.

(2) Moneys recovered under subsection (1)(a) of this section shall not be considered moneys paid on and to be credited against the original judgment or debt sought to be enforced. No additional judgment is necessary to recover moneys in the manner provided in subsection (1)(a) of this section.

(3) The only moneys a plaintiff may recover under subsection (1)(a) of this section are those described in subsection (4) of this section that the plaintiff has paid to enforce the existing specific judgment or debt that the specific garnishment or attachment was issued to enforce or upon which the payment was received. Moneys recoverable under subsection (1)(a) of this section remain recoverable and, except as provided under subsection (8) of this section, may be recovered from moneys received by the plaintiff under subsequent garnishments, attachments or payments on the same specific judgment or debt.

(4) This section allows the recovery only of the following:

(a) Statutorily established moneys that meet the requirements under subsection (3) of this section, as follows:

(A) Garnishee's search fees under ORS 18.790.

(B) Fees for delivery of writs of garnishment under ORS 18.652.

(C) Circuit court fees as provided under ORS 21.235 and 21.258.

(D) County court fees as provided under ORS 5.125.

(E) County clerk recording fees as provided in ORS 205.320.

(F) Actual fees or disbursements made under ORS 21.300.

(G) Costs of execution as provided in ORS 105.112.

(H) Fees paid to an attorney for issuing a garnishment in an amount not to exceed $45 for each garnishment.

(I) Costs of an execution sale as described in ORS 18.950 (2).

(J) Fees paid under ORS 21.200 for motions and responses to motions filed after entry of a judgment.

(K) Amounts paid to a sheriff for the fees and expenses of executing a warrant under ORS 105.510.

(b) Interest on the amounts specified in paragraph (a) of this subsection at the rate provided for judgments in ORS 82.010 for the period of time beginning with the expenditure of the amount and ending upon recovery of the amount under this section.

(5) The plaintiff shall be responsible for doing all of the following:

(a) Maintaining a precise accounting of moneys recovered under subsection (1)(a) of this section and making the accounting available for any proceeding relating to that judgment or debt.

(b) Providing reasonable notice to the defendant of moneys the plaintiff recovers under subsection (1)(a) of this section.

(6) Moneys recovered under subsection (1)(a) of this section remain subject to all other provisions of law relating to payments, or garnished or attached moneys including, but not limited to, those relating to exemption, claim of exemption, overpayment and holding periods.

(7) Nothing in this section limits the right of a plaintiff to recover moneys described in this section or other moneys in any manner otherwise allowed by law.

(8) A writ of garnishment or attachment is not valid if issued solely to recover moneys recoverable under subsection (1)(a) of this section unless the right to collect the moneys is first reduced to a judgment or to a debt enforceable under ORS 18.854.

Note: Section 21 (1), chapter 663, Oregon Laws 2017, provides:

Sec. 21. (1) The amendments to ORS 18.999 and 21.235 (2) by sections 19 and 20 of this 2017 Act apply to writs of garnishment issued on or after October 1, 2017. [2017 c.663 §21 (1)]

Note: 18.999 was enacted into law by the Legislative Assembly but was not added to or made a part of ORS chapter 18 or any series therein by legislative action. See Preface to Oregon Revised Statutes for further explanation.

———————

Chapter 19 — Appeals

2017 EDITION

APPEALS

PROCEDURE IN CIVIL PROCEEDINGS

GENERAL PROVISIONS

19.005   Definitions

APPEALABLE JUDGMENTS

(Generally)

19.205   Appealable judgments and orders

(Class Actions)

19.215   Determining amount in controversy in class action for purposes of appeal

19.225   Appealability of certain orders in class actions

(Determining Whether Judgment Appealable)

19.235   Jurisdiction for determining whether decision is appealable

COMMENCING AN APPEAL

(Generally)

19.240   How appeal to Court of Appeals taken

19.245   Who may appeal; appeal of default judgments and judgments taken by confession; appeal of stipulated judgments

(Notice of Appeal)

19.250   Contents of notice of appeal

19.255   Time for service and filing of notice of appeal

19.260   Filing by mail or delivery

19.265   Payment of filing fee

(Jurisdiction of Appellate Court and Trial Court)

19.270   Appellate jurisdiction of Supreme Court and Court of Appeals; trial court jurisdiction to enter appealable judgment or order

19.275   Continuing jurisdiction of trial court in certain domestic relations cases

UNDERTAKINGS ON APPEAL AND STAYS OF JUDGMENT

(Undertakings)

19.300   Undertakings on appeal generally; filing and service

19.305   Qualifications of sureties; objections

19.310   Waiver, reduction or limitation of undertaking

19.312   Supersedeas undertaking in certain actions against tobacco product manufacturer

(Letter of Credit in Support of Undertaking)

19.315   Requirements for use of letter of credit

19.320   Expiration and renewal of letter of credit

19.325   Payment on letter of credit

(Stays)

19.330   Stays generally

19.335   Stay by filing of supersedeas undertaking

19.340   Waiver of supersedeas undertaking; sale of perishables

19.345   Enforcement of judgment in contract action notwithstanding appeal

19.350   Discretionary stay by court

19.355   Stay of domestic relations judgment

(Appellate Review of Trial Court Orders
Relating to Undertakings and Stays)

19.360   Appellate review of trial court orders relating to undertakings and stays

RECORD ON APPEAL

19.365   Preparation and transmission of record generally

19.370   Certification and service of transcript; correction of errors; settlement of transcript

19.375   Cost of transcript

19.380   Agreed narrative statement

19.385   Audio records

19.390   Bill of exceptions not required

19.395   Time extensions for preparation of record

HEARINGS ON APPEALS

19.400   Where appeals heard

DISPOSITION OF APPEALS

(Certification of Appeal to Supreme Court)

19.405   Certification of appeal to Supreme Court

(Stipulated Dismissals and Settlements)

19.410   Stipulated dismissals; settlement; effect of settlement on pending appeal

(Disposition on Merits)

19.415   Scope of appellate review

19.420   Action by appellate court on appeal; review of order granting new trial or judgment notwithstanding verdict; reversal upon loss or destruction of reporter's notes or audio records

19.425   Review of intermediate orders; directing restitution

19.430   Review of trial court order granting a new trial on court's own initiative

19.435   Memorandum decisions

(Attorney Fees and Penalties)

19.440   Award of attorney fees authorized by statute

19.445   Damages upon affirmance of judgment

(Appellate Judgment)

19.450   Appellate judgment; when effective; effect of entry in trial court register; effect on judgment lien

MISCELLANEOUS

19.500   Service of documents under provisions of chapter

19.510   Powers of successor trial judge with respect to appeals

GENERAL PROVISIONS

19.005 Definitions. As used in this chapter:
(1) "Exhibits" means exhibits offered and received or rejected in the trial court.
(2) "Judgment" means a judgment or appealable order, as provided in ORS 19.205.
(3) "Notice of appeal" includes a notice of cross-appeal.
(4) "Record" or "record of the case" means the trial court file and any transcript, narrative statement and exhibits.
(5) "Supersedeas undertaking" means an undertaking on appeal that secures performance of a judgment being appealed and operates to stay enforcement of the judgment pending appeal.
(6) "Transcript" means the transcript of the court reporter's report as provided in ORS 8.340, 8.350 and 8.360 and any transcript of an audio record prepared under ORS 19.370.
(7) "Trial court file" means all the original papers filed in the trial court whether before or after judgment, including but not limited to the summons and proof of service thereof, pleadings, motions, affidavits, depositions, stipulations, orders, jury instructions, the judgment, the notice of appeal and the undertaking on appeal.
(8) "Undertaking for costs" means an undertaking on appeal that secures payment of costs and disbursements that may be awarded against an appellant on appeal, and any amounts that may be awarded to the respondent under the provisions of ORS 19.445.
(9) "Undertaking on appeal" means a promise secured by sureties or by money, bond or any other security described in ORS 22.020. "Undertaking on appeal" includes undertakings for costs and supersedeas undertakings. [1959 c.558 §2; 1985 c.734 §2; 1997 c.71 §12; 1997 c.389 §23; 1997 c.801 §124; 1999 c.59 §9; 1999 c.367 §5; 2003 c.576 §280]

19.010 [Amended by 1973 c.197 §1; 1977 c.208 §4; 1979 c.562 §3; 1981 c.898 §18; 1997 c.389 §24; renumbered 19.205 in 1997]

19.013 [Formerly 13.410; renumbered 19.215 in 1997]

19.015 [Formerly 13.400; renumbered 19.225 in 1997]

19.020 [Renumbered 19.245 in 1997]

19.023 [Formerly 19.030; 1969 c.198 §37; 1973 c.207 §3; 1981 c.177 §1; 1997 c.389 §5; renumbered 19.240 in 1997]

19.026 [1959 c.558 §4; 1973 c.207 §4; 1979 c.284 §55; 1987 c.852 §5; renumbered 19.255 in 1997]

19.028 [1979 c.297 §1; 1985 c.734 §3; 1987 c.852 §6; 1989 c.768 §12; 1997 c.389 §6; renumbered 19.260 in 1997]

19.029 [1959 c.558 §5; 1971 c.565 §6; 1973 c.207 §5; 1983 c.621 §1; 1985 c.734 §4; renumbered 19.250 in 1997]

19.030 [Amended by 1959 c.558 §3; renumbered 19.023]

19.033 [1959 c.558 §6; 1969 c.198 §38; 1971 c.565 §7; 1983 c.673 §22; 1983 c.740 §4; 1985 c.734 §5; 1989 c.195 §1; 1995 c.800 §11; 1997 c.71 §14; 1997 c.389 §20; 1997 c.801 §90; renumbered 19.270 in 1997]

19.034 [1987 c.712 §2; renumbered 19.235 in 1997]

19.035 [1959 c.558 §7; 1963 c.27 §1; 1969 c.198 §39; 1971 c.193 §19; 1983 c.774 §6; renumbered 19.265 in 1997]

19.038 [1959 c.558 §8; 1981 c.483 §1; 1983 c.673 §23; 1985 c.734 §6; 1991 c.331 §3; 1995 c.79 §7; repealed by 1997 c.71 §20]

19.040 [Amended by 1977 c.416 §6; 1981 c.483 §2; 1985 c.734 §7; 1991 c.331 §4; repealed by 1997 c.71 §20]

19.045 [1959 c.558 §9; 1977 c.416 §1; 1985 c.734 §8; repealed by 1997 c.71 §20]

19.050 [Amended by 1983 c.763 §60; 1987 c.852 §7; repealed by 1997 c.71 §20]

19.060 [Amended by 1997 c.71 §15; renumbered 19.345 in 1997]

19.065 [1959 c.558 §10; 1969 c.198 §40; 1997 c.389 §21; 1997 c.801 §124a; renumbered 19.365 in 1997]

19.069 [1971 c.565 §10; 1997 c.801 §125; renumbered 19.385 in 1997]

19.070 [Repealed by 1959 c.558 §51]

19.074 [1959 c.558 §11; 1969 c.198 §41; 1971 c.193 §20; 1971 c.565 §8; repealed by 1997 c.389 §22]

19.078 [1959 c.558 §12; 1971 c.193 §21; 1971 c.565 §11; 1981 c.51 §1; 1989 c.1053 §9; 1995 c.273 §7; 1997 c.801 §126; renumbered 19.370 in 1997]

19.080 [Amended by 1959 c.558 §18; renumbered 19.118]

19.084 [1959 c.558 §13; 1985 c.565 §2a; renumbered 19.375 in 1997]

19.088 [1959 c.558 §14; 1969 c.198 §42; 1971 c.193 §22; renumbered 19.380 in 1997]

19.090 [Repealed by 1959 c.558 §51]

19.094 [1959 c.558 §15; 1963 c.372 §1; 1969 c.198 §43; repealed by 1971 c.565 §12 (19.095 enacted in lieu of 19.094)]

19.095 [1971 c.565 §13 (19.095 enacted in lieu of 19.094); renumbered 19.395 in 1997]

19.098 [1959 c.558 §16; 1969 c.198 §44; 1971 c.193 §23; 1971 c.565 §14; repealed by 1997 c.389 §22]

19.100 [Repealed by 1959 c.558 §51]

19.104 [1959 c.558 §27; 1979 c.284 §56; 1997 c.389 §25; 1997 c.801 §128; renumbered 19.500 in 1997]

19.108 [1959 c.558 §20 (enacted in lieu of 19.110); 1969 c.198 §45; 1971 c.193 §24; 1985 c.734 §9; repealed by 1997 c.389 §22]

19.110 [Repealed by 1959 c.558 §19 (19.108 enacted in lieu of 19.110)]

19.111 [1985 c.734 §11; 1997 c.389 §19; 1997 c.801 §89; renumbered 19.410 in 1997]

19.114 [1959 c.558 §22; renumbered 19.390 in 1997]

19.118 [Formerly 19.080; 1969 c.198 §46; 1983 c.763 §7; renumbered 19.400 in 1997]

19.120 [Repealed by 1959 c.558 §51]

19.125 [1959 c.558 §21; 1965 c.177 §6; 1979 c.396 §1; renumbered 19.415 in 1997]

19.130 [Amended by 1955 c.497 §6; 1959 c.558 §24; 1969 c.198 §47; 1985 c.540 §45; renumbered 19.420 in 1997]

19.140 [Renumbered 19.425 in 1997]
19.150 [Amended by 1959 c.33 §1; repealed by 1959 c.558 §25 (19.190 enacted in lieu of 19.150)]

19.160 [Renumbered 19.445 in 1997]

19.170 [1959 c.558 §17; renumbered 19.510 in 1997]

19.180 [1959 c.558 §23; 1969 c.198 §48; renumbered 19.435 in 1997]

19.190 [1959 c.558 §26 (enacted in lieu of 19.150); 1969 c.198 §49; 1981 c.178 §1; 1985 c.540 §27; 1985 c.734 §12; 1987 c.586 §11; 1997 c.71 §16; renumbered 19.450 in 1997]

19.200 [1979 c.284 §58; renumbered 19.430 in 1997]

APPEALABLE JUDGMENTS

(Generally)

19.205 Appealable judgments and orders. (1) Unless otherwise provided by law, a limited judgment, general judgment or supplemental judgment, as those terms are defined by ORS 18.005, may be appealed as provided in this chapter. A judgment corrected under ORCP 71 may be appealed only as provided in ORS 18.107 and 18.112.
(2) An order in an action that affects a substantial right, and that effectively determines the action so as to prevent a judgment in the action, may be appealed in the same manner as provided in this chapter for judgments.

(3) An order that is made in the action after a general judgment is entered and that affects a substantial right, including an order granting a new trial, may be appealed in the same manner as provided in this chapter for judgments.

(4) No appeal to the Court of Appeals shall be taken or allowed in any action for the recovery of money or damages only unless it appears from the pleadings that the amount in controversy exceeds $250.

(5) An appeal may be taken from the circuit court in any special statutory proceeding under the same conditions, in the same manner and with like effect as from a judgment or order entered in an action, unless appeal is expressly prohibited by the law authorizing the special statutory proceeding.

(6) Nothing in ORS chapter 18 affects the authority of an appellate court to dismiss an appeal or to remand a proceeding to the trial court under ORS 19.270 (4) based on the appellate court's determination that the appeal has not been taken from an appealable judgment or order. [Formerly 19.010; 2003 c.576 §85]

19.210 [1981 c.550 §2; 1997 c.389 §3; renumbered 19.405 in 1997]

(Class Actions)

19.215 Determining amount in controversy in class action for purposes of appeal. The aggregate amount of the claims of all potential class members in a class action under ORCP 32 shall determine whether the amount in controversy is sufficient to satisfy the provisions of ORS 19.205 (4) for the purposes of any appeal to the Court of Appeals. [Formerly 19.013; 2003 c.576 §573]

19.220 [1981 c.897 §107; renumbered 19.440 in 1997]

19.225 Appealability of certain orders in class actions. When a circuit court judge, in making in a class action under ORCP 32 an order not otherwise appealable, is of the opinion that such order involves a controlling question of law as to which there is substantial ground for difference of opinion and that an immediate appeal from the order may materially advance the ultimate termination of the litigation, the judge shall so state in writing in such order. The Court of Appeals may thereupon, in its discretion, permit an appeal to be taken from such order to the Court of Appeals if application is made to the court within 10 days after the entry of the order. Application for such an appeal shall not stay proceedings in the circuit court unless the circuit court judge or the Court of Appeals or a judge thereof shall so order. [Formerly 19.015]

19.230 [1987 c.793 §1; 1991 c.817 §17; 1995 c.595 §20; renumbered 34.102 in 1997]

(Determining Whether Judgment Appealable)

19.235 Jurisdiction for determining whether decision is appealable. (1) Notwithstanding ORS 19.270, if any party or the trial court on its own motion, on receiving actual notice of the filing of the notice of appeal, raises the issue whether the decision being appealed is appealable, the trial court shall have jurisdiction to make a summary determination, with or without a hearing, whether the decision is appealable. As used in this section, "decision" means any trial court ruling, either oral or written.

(2) If the trial court determines that the decision is not appealable, the trial court, in its discretion, may proceed through entry of judgment or stay proceedings pending an appellate court determination of the existence of an appealable decision. The trial court may refer the question of the existence of an appealable decision to the court to which the appeal is taken. Neither an order by the trial court to proceed through entry of judgment, an order by the trial court to stay proceedings pending an appellate court determination, nor a trial court referral of the question of the existence of an appealable decision to the appellate court is appealable. However, on motion of any party or on its own motion the appellate court may stay proceedings in the trial court or stay any order or judgment entered by the trial court pending a final determination of appealability.

(3) When a party by motion, the trial court by referral or the appellate court on its own motion raises the issue whether the decision is appealable, the appellate court may make a summary determination of the appealability of the decision. A summary determination of the appealability of a decision under this subsection is subject to review by the Supreme Court as provided in ORS 2.520 except that the petition for review shall be served and filed within 14 days after the date of the court's determination. Either the Court of Appeals or the Supreme Court may shorten the time period within which the petition for review shall be filed. A petition for review of a determination under this subsection shall not be treated as a request for reconsideration by the Court of Appeals. The Supreme Court shall expedite its review of the Court of Appeals' summary determination under this subsection.

(4)(a) The trial court's authority to proceed with a case under subsection (2) of this section shall end when the appellate court has made an express determination that an appeal has been taken from an appealable order or judgment, all means for obtaining review of that determination under subsection (3) of this section have been exhausted, and the State Court Administrator at the direction of the court has mailed copies of the final appellate court determination to the trial court and the parties; otherwise, the trial court's jurisdiction shall continue.

(b) No action by the trial court taken pursuant to subsections (1) and (2) of this section, except for entry of judgment, shall be void solely because an appellate court later determines that a notice of appeal was filed from an appealable decision. [Formerly 19.034]

COMMENCING AN APPEAL

(Generally)

19.240 How appeal to Court of Appeals taken. (1) An appeal to the Court of Appeals shall be taken in the manner prescribed in this chapter.

(2) The appeal shall be taken by causing a notice of appeal, in the form prescribed by ORS 19.250, to be served:

(a) On all parties who have appeared in the action, suit or proceeding;

(b) On the trial court administrator; and

(c) On the trial court transcript coordinator if a transcript is designated in connection with the appeal.

(3) The original of the notice with proof of service indorsed thereon or affixed thereto shall be filed with the Court of Appeals. [Formerly 19.023; 1999 c.367 §2]

19.245 Who may appeal; appeal of default judgments and judgments taken by confession; appeal of stipulated judgments. (1) Except as provided in subsections (2) and (3) of this section, any party to a judgment may appeal from the judgment.

(2) A party to a judgment given by confession or for want of an answer may not appeal from the judgment except as follows:

(a) A plaintiff, third party plaintiff or a party who pleaded a cross-claim or counterclaim may appeal from the judgment if the judgment is not in accord with the relief demanded in the complaint.

(b) A defendant may appeal from the judgment if the trial court has entered a default judgment against the defendant as a sanction or has denied a motion to set aside a default order or judgment.

(c) A defendant may appeal from the judgment if it is void.

(3) A party to a stipulated judgment may appeal from the judgment only if:

(a) The judgment specifically provides that the party has reserved the right to appellate review of a ruling of the trial court in the cause; and

(b) The appeal presents a justiciable controversy. [Formerly 19.020; 1999 c.367 §1; 2001 c.541 §1]

(Notice of Appeal)

19.250 Contents of notice of appeal. (1) The notice of appeal must contain the following:

(a) The title of the cause. The party appealing a judgment must be designated the appellant and the adverse party the respondent, but the title of the action or proceeding is not otherwise changed by reason of the appeal.

(b) The names of the parties and their attorneys.

(c)(A) If an appellant is not represented by an attorney, a postal address for the appellant and either an electronic mail address for the appellant or a statement that the appellant does not have an electronic mail address.

(B) If the appellant is represented by an attorney, a postal address and electronic mail address for the attorney.

(d) A notice to each party that appeared in the action or proceeding, or to the attorney for the party, that an appeal is taken from the judgment or some specified part of the judgment and designating the adverse parties to the appeal. The notice of appeal must contain the postal address and electronic mail address, if known to the appellant, for all other parties designated as parties to the appeal.

(e) A designation of those portions of the proceedings and exhibits to be included in the record in addition to the trial court file. The appellant may amend the designation of record at any time after filing the notice of appeal until 35 days after the filing of a certificate of preparation for the transcript under ORS 19.370 (3). The amendment must be made by filing and serving in the same manner as a notice of appeal a notice of amended designation of record. The amended designation must clearly indicate those portions of the proceedings and exhibits being added to or deleted from the original designation of record. The designation may not be later amended by the appellant unless the appellate court so orders.

(f) A plain and concise statement of the points on which the appellant intends to rely. On appeal, the appellant may rely on no other points than those set forth in such statement. If the appellant has designated for inclusion in the record all the testimony and all the instructions given and requested, no statement of points is necessary. Not later than the 15th day following the filing of the certificate of preparation for the transcript under ORS 19.370 (3), the appellant may serve and file an amended statement of points. Except by approval of the court, the appellant may then rely on no other points than those set forth in such amended statement.

(g) The signature of the appellant or attorney for the appellant.

(2) Within 14 days after the filing of the notice of appeal or amended designation of record, any other party may serve and file a designation of additional parts of the proceedings and exhibits to be included in the record. Such designation must be served and filed as provided for the serving and filing of a notice of appeal under ORS 19.240 and 19.260. If such party also appeals, the designation must be included in the notice of appeal of the party and may not be served and filed separately. [Formerly 19.029; 1999 c.367 §3; 2013 c.685 §4]

19.255 Time for service and filing of notice of appeal. (1) Except as provided in subsections (2) and (3) of this section, a notice of appeal must be served and filed within 30 days after the judgment appealed from is entered in the register.

(2) If a motion for a new trial is filed and served within the time allowed by ORCP 64, or a motion for judgment notwithstanding the verdict is filed and served within the time allowed by ORCP 63, a notice of appeal must be served and filed:

(a) Within 30 days after the order disposing of the motion is entered in the register, or within 30 days after the motion is deemed denied under ORCP 63 D or 64 F, whichever is first; or

(b) Within the time allowed by subsection (1) of this section, if the period of time provided for in subsection (1) of this section expires later than the period of time provided for in paragraph (a) of this subsection.

(3) Any other party who has appeared in the action, suit or proceeding, desiring to appeal against the appellant or any other party to the action, suit or proceeding, may serve and file notice of appeal within 10 days after the expiration of the time allowed by subsections (1) and (2) of this section. Any party not an appellant or respondent, but who becomes an adverse party to a cross appeal, may cross appeal against any party to the appeal by a written statement in the brief.

(4) Except as otherwise ordered by the appellate court, when more than one notice of appeal is filed, the date on which the last such notice was filed shall be used in determining the time for preparation of the transcript, filing briefs and other steps in connection with the appeal. [Formerly 19.026; 2003 c.281 §1]

19.260 Filing by mail or delivery. (1)(a) Filing a notice of appeal in the Court of Appeals or the Supreme Court may be accomplished by mail or delivery. Regardless of the date of actual receipt by the court to which the appeal is taken, the date of filing the notice is the date of mailing or dispatch for delivery, if the notice is:

(A) Mailed by registered or certified mail and the party filing the notice has proof from the United States Postal Service of the mailing date; or

(B) Mailed or dispatched via the United States Postal Service or a commercial delivery service by a class of delivery calculated to achieve delivery within three calendar days, and the party filing the notice has proof from the United States Postal Service or the commercial delivery service of the mailing or dispatch date.

(b) Proof of the date of mailing or dispatch under this subsection must be certified by the party filing the notice and filed thereafter with the court to which the appeal is taken. Any record of mailing or dispatch from the United States Postal Service or the commercial delivery service showing the date that the party initiated mailing or dispatch is sufficient proof of the date of mailing or dispatch. If the notice is received by the court on or before the date by which the notice is required to be filed, the party filing the notice is not required to file proof of mailing or dispatch.

(2)(a) Service of notice of appeal on a party, transcript coordinator or the trial court administrator, or service of a petition for judicial review on a party or administrative agency may be accomplished by:

(A) First class, registered or certified mail; or

(B) Mail or dispatch for delivery via the United States Postal Service or a commercial delivery service by a class of delivery calculated to achieve delivery within three calendar days.

(b) The date of serving the notice under this subsection is the date of mailing or dispatch. The party filing the notice must certify the date and method of service.

(3) Notwithstanding subsections (1) and (2) of this section, if the party filing a notice of appeal is involuntarily confined in a state or local governmental facility, the date of filing of a notice of appeal in the Court of Appeals or the Supreme Court, and the date of service under subsection (2) of this section, is the date on which the party delivers the original notice of appeal, and the appropriate number of copies of the notice for service under subsection (2) of this section, to the person or place designated by the facility for handling outgoing mail.

(4) Except as otherwise provided by law, the provisions of this section are applicable to petitions for judicial review, cross petitions for judicial review and petitions under the original jurisdiction of the Supreme Court or Court of Appeals. [Formerly 19.028; 1999 c.367 §6; 2011 c.310 §1; 2015 c.80 §1]

19.265 Payment of filing fee. At the time the notice of appeal is filed as provided in ORS 19.240, the appellant shall deposit with the State Court Administrator the amount of the appropriate filing fee. The timely deposit of such fee is not jurisdictional, but omission to do so shall be cause for dismissal of the appeal, subject to the provisions of ORS 19.270 (3). [Formerly 19.035]

(Jurisdiction of Appellate Court and Trial Court)

19.270 Appellate jurisdiction of Supreme Court and Court of Appeals; trial court jurisdiction to enter appealable judgment or order. (1) The Supreme Court or the Court of Appeals has jurisdiction of the cause when the notice of appeal has been served and filed as provided in ORS 19.240, 19.250 and 19.255. The trial court may exercise those powers in connection with the appeal as are conferred by law, and retains jurisdiction in the matter for the following purposes:

(a) Deciding requests for attorney fees, costs and disbursements or expenses pursuant to ORCP 68 or other provision of law.

(b) Enforcing the judgment, subject to any stay of the judgment.

(c) Deciding a motion for judgment notwithstanding the verdict under ORCP 63.

(d) Deciding a motion for new trial under ORCP 64.

(e) Deciding a motion for relief from judgment under ORCP 71 B.

(2) The following requirements of ORS 19.240, 19.250 and 19.255 are jurisdictional and may not be waived or extended:

(a) Service of the notice of appeal on all parties identified in the notice of appeal as adverse parties or, if the notice of appeal does not identify adverse parties, on all parties who have appeared in the action, suit or proceeding, as provided in ORS 19.240 (2)(a), within the time limits prescribed by ORS 19.255.

(b) Filing of the original of the notice of appeal with the Court of Appeals as provided in ORS 19.240 (3), within the time limits prescribed by ORS 19.255.

(3) After the Supreme Court or the Court of Appeals has acquired jurisdiction of the cause, the omission of a party to perform any of the acts required in connection with an appeal, or to perform such acts within the time required, shall be cause for dismissal of the appeal. In the event of such omission, the court, on motion of a party or on its own motion may dismiss the appeal. An appeal dismissed on a party's motion or on the court's own motion may be reinstated upon showing of good cause.

(4) Notwithstanding the filing of a notice of appeal, the trial court has jurisdiction, with leave of the appellate court, to enter an appealable judgment or order if the appellate court determines that:

(a) At the time of the filing of the notice of appeal the trial court intended to enter an appealable judgment or order; and

(b) The judgment or order from which the appeal is taken is defective in form or was entered at a time when the trial court did not have jurisdiction of the cause under subsection (1) of this section, or the trial court had not yet entered an appealable judgment or order.

(5) Notwithstanding the filing of a notice of appeal, the trial court has jurisdiction:

(a) To enter in the trial court register a judgment or order that the trial judge signed before the notice of appeal was filed;

(b) To enter an order or supplemental judgment under ORCP 71 or ORS 19.275, 107.105 (4) or 107.452; and

(c) To enter an order or supplemental judgment for the purpose of implementing a settlement as allowed by ORS 19.410 (3).

(6) Jurisdiction of the appellate court over a cause ends when a copy of the appellate judgment is mailed by the State Court Administrator to the court from which the appeal was taken pursuant to ORS 19.450, except that the appellate court may:

(a) Recall the appellate judgment as justice may require;

(b) Stay enforcement of the appellate judgment to allow the filing of a petition for writ of certiorari to the Supreme Court of the United States; and

(c) Stay enforcement of the appellate judgment pending disposition of the matter by the Supreme Court of the United States or for such other time as the Oregon appellate court may deem appropriate.

(7) If a limited or supplemental judgment is appealed, the jurisdiction of the appellate court is limited to the matters decided by the limited or supplemental judgment, and the trial court retains jurisdiction over all other matters in the proceeding.

(8) After jurisdiction of the appellate court ends, all orders which may be necessary to carry the appellate judgment into effect shall be made by the court from which the appeal was taken. [Formerly 19.033; 2003 c.576 §86; 2005 c.568 §25c; 2007 c.66 §1; 2013 c.10 §1]

19.275 Continuing jurisdiction of trial court in certain domestic relations cases. (1) Any motion that requires a showing of a change of circumstances before the court may modify a judgment, including a motion to reconsider the spousal or child support provisions of a judgment pursuant to ORS 107.135, may be filed with the trial court while an appeal from the judgment is pending before an appellate court. The filing of a motion under this subsection does not affect the right of the appellant to pursue the appeal of the judgment.

(2) The trial court in its discretion may proceed to hear and decide a motion under this section or may hold the motion in abeyance pending disposition of the appeal.

(3) Pursuant to the provisions of ORS 19.205, the court's decision on a motion under this section is a supplemental judgment. The appellate court in its discretion may consolidate an appeal from a supplemental judgment under this section with the pending appeal of the general judgment in the case, may direct that both appeals be heard at the same time or may allow the appeals to proceed independently. [1997 c.71 §11; 2003 c.576 §87; 2005 c.568 §26]

UNDERTAKINGS ON APPEAL AND STAYS OF JUDGMENT

(Undertakings)

19.300 Undertakings on appeal generally; filing and service. (1) An appellant must serve and file an undertaking for costs within 14 days after the filing of a notice of appeal. Unless the undertaking is waived, reduced or limited under ORS 19.310, an undertaking for costs must be in the amount of $500.

(2) A supersedeas undertaking may be served and filed by an appellant at any time while a case is pending on appeal.

(3) The original of an undertaking on appeal, with proof of service, must be filed with the trial court administrator. A copy of the undertaking must be served on each adverse party on appeal in the manner prescribed by ORCP 9 B. [1997 c.71 §2; 1999 c.367 §7]

19.305 Qualifications of sureties; objections. (1) Undertakings on appeal are subject to the provisions of ORS 22.020 to 22.070.

(2) A surety for an undertaking on appeal must be qualified as provided in ORCP 82. The amount of liability assumed by a surety or letter of credit issuer must be stated in the undertaking. The liability of a surety or letter of credit issuer is limited to the amount specified in the undertaking.

(3) Objections to the sufficiency of an undertaking on appeal, including the objections to the amount of the undertaking and to the sufficiency of the security for the undertaking, must be filed in and determined by the trial court in the manner provided by ORCP 82. Notwithstanding ORCP 82 F, objections to the undertaking must be filed within 14 days after the date on which a copy of the undertaking is served on the party who objects to the undertaking. [1997 c.71 §3]

19.310 Waiver, reduction or limitation of undertaking. (1) By written stipulation of the parties, an undertaking on appeal may be waived, reduced or limited. The stipulation must be filed with the trial court administrator within 14 days after the filing of the notice of appeal. Unless disapproved or modified by the trial court, the stipulation has the effect specified by the terms of the stipulation.

(2) The trial court may waive, reduce or limit an undertaking on appeal upon a showing of good cause, including indigence, and on such terms as are just and equitable. [1997 c.71 §4; 1999 c.367 §8]

19.312 Supersedeas undertaking in certain actions against tobacco product manufacturer. (1) The provisions of this section apply only to civil actions against a tobacco product manufacturer as defined in ORS 323.800, or against an affiliate or successor of a tobacco product manufacturer, in which:

(a) The tobacco product manufacturer is subject to the requirements of ORS 323.806; and

(b) The state is not a plaintiff.

(2) In any civil action described in subsection (1) of this section, the supersedeas undertaking required of the tobacco product manufacturer, or of an affiliate or successor of the tobacco product manufacturer, as a condition of a stay of judgment throughout all appeals or discretionary appellate review, shall be established in the manner provided by the laws and court rules of this state applicable to supersedeas undertakings, but the amount of the supersedeas undertaking may not exceed $150 million.

(3) If at any time after the posting of the supersedeas undertaking pursuant to the provisions of this section the court determines that a tobacco product manufacturer, affiliate or successor, outside of the ordinary course of its business, is purposely dissipating or diverting assets for the purpose of avoiding payment on final judgment in the action, the court may condition continuance of the stay on an order requiring that the tobacco product manufacturer, affiliate or successor post a supersedeas undertaking in an amount up to the full amount of the judgment.

(4) The provisions of this section apply to any supersedeas undertaking required for a judgment entered by a court of this state and to any security required as a condition of staying enforcement of a foreign judgment under the provisions of ORS 24.135 (2). [2003 c.804 §87; 2005 c.22 §9]

(Letter of Credit in Support of Undertaking)

19.315 Requirements for use of letter of credit. (1) Except as provided in subsection (4) of this section, an irrevocable letter of credit filed in support of an undertaking on appeal must contain:

(a) The name and address of the issuing bank, the date of issuance and the limit of the bank's liability under the letter of credit.

(b) The name of the court that entered the judgment being appealed and the title and file number of the case for which the judgment was entered.

(c) The name and address of the party who is filing the undertaking or, if the party is represented by an attorney, the name and address of the attorney.

(d) The name and address of the beneficiary or, if the beneficiary is represented by an attorney, the name and address of the attorney for the beneficiary.

(e) A statement that the issuing bank will pay to the beneficiary, up to the limit stated in the letter of credit, the amount of any drafts submitted to the issuing bank under ORS 19.325.

(2) An irrevocable letter of credit filed in support of an undertaking on appeal may be issued only by an insured institution, as defined in ORS 706.008, that has an office or other facility in this state or that has a registered agent in this state.

(3) A letter of credit under this section may contain an expiration date. Any letter of credit containing an expiration date must comply with ORS 19.320.

(4) A party filing a letter of credit in support of an undertaking on appeal and the party for whose benefit an undertaking is filed may by agreement waive any of the requirements of subsection (1) of this section. [1997 c.172 §2; 1999 c.59 §10]

19.320 Expiration and renewal of letter of credit. (1) If a letter of credit issued under ORS 19.315 contains an expiration date, the letter of credit must also state an automatic renewal period and contain a statement that the issuing bank will automatically renew the letter of credit on the expiration date and at the end of each automatic renewal period thereafter unless the bank has elected not to renew the letter in the manner provided by subsection (2) of this section.

(2) A bank that issues a letter of credit may elect not to renew a letter of credit by giving written notice to the following persons:

(a) To the party that files the letter of credit, at the address stated in the letter of credit, or, if the attorney for the party is named in the letter of credit, to the attorney at the address stated in the letter of credit.

(b) To the beneficiary, at the address stated in the letter of credit, or, if the attorney for the beneficiary is named in the letter, to the attorney at the address stated in the letter of credit.

(3) Notice of nonrenewal under subsection (2) of this section must be given by certified mail. The notice must be mailed at least 60 days before the expiration date reflected on the letter of credit or 60 days before the end of any subsequent automatic renewal period.

(4) If an issuing bank has given notice of nonrenewal under the provisions of this section, the bank must pay to the trial court administrator who is holding the letter of credit the amount stated in the letter of credit as the limit of the bank's liability unless the beneficiary gives written notice to the bank that the letter of credit has been released. A beneficiary shall promptly notify the issuing bank in writing if the court has entered an order releasing the letter of credit.

(5) Any amount paid by an issuing bank to a trial court administrator under subsection (4) of this section shall be treated as a deposit of money under ORS 22.020. Any amount that is not paid out to the beneficiary pursuant to the appellate judgment shall be refunded to the bank making the deposit. [1997 c.172 §3; 1999 c.367 §9]

19.325 Payment on letter of credit. (1) If an appellate judgment entitles a beneficiary to payment from the issuing bank of a letter of credit, the appellate judgment must direct the trial court administrator to release the letter of credit to the beneficiary. Upon issuance of the appellate judgment, the beneficiary may enforce the letter of credit by submitting a draft to the issuing bank in accordance with the terms of the letter of credit. The amount of the draft must include all amounts determined necessary to cover the interest that will accrue until the date that disbursement will be made to the beneficiary.

(2) Except as provided in this section, a draft submitted by a beneficiary under this section need not be in any particular form. The draft must be dated, must be for a specific sum of money and must contain the following language:

Pay to the order of the undersigned beneficiary the amount of this draft. The undersigned beneficiary hereby certifies that there is now an appellate judgment in this case pursuant to which the amount of the draft stated above is now due and owing to the beneficiary from the party on whose behalf the letter of credit was issued.

(3) In addition to the requirements of subsection (2) of this section, the following items must be attached to a draft submitted by a beneficiary under this section:

(a) The original letter of credit under which the draft is drawn.

(b) A copy of the appellate judgment certified by the State Court Administrator that shows the amount that the beneficiary is entitled to recover under the letter of credit.

(4) If the issuing bank of a letter of credit does not honor a letter of credit, on motion of the beneficiary the trial court shall enter judgment against the issuing bank unless the bank establishes that the bank is not required under the law to honor the letter of credit. [1997 c.172 §4; 1999 c.367 §10]

(Stays)

19.330 Stays generally. The filing of a notice of appeal does not automatically stay the judgment that is the subject of the appeal. A party may seek to stay a judgment in the manner provided by ORS 19.335, 19.340 or 19.350, or as provided by other law. [1997 c.71 §5]

19.335 Stay by filing of supersedeas undertaking. (1) If a judgment is for the recovery of money, a supersedeas undertaking acts to stay the judgment if the undertaking provides that the appellant will pay the judgment to the extent that the judgment is affirmed on appeal.

(2) If a judgment requires the transfer or delivery of possession of real property, a supersedeas undertaking acts to stay the judgment if the undertaking provides that the appellant will not commit waste or allow waste to be committed on the real property while the appellant possesses the property, and the appellant will pay the value of the use and occupation of the property for the period of possession if the judgment is affirmed. The value of the use and occupation during the period of possession must be stated in the undertaking.

(3)(a) If a judgment requires the transfer or delivery of possession of personal property, a supersedeas undertaking acts to stay the judgment if the undertaking provides that the appellant will obey the judgment of the appellate court, and that if the appellant does not obey the judgment, the appellant will pay an amount determined by the trial court and stated in the undertaking.

(b) If a judgment requires the transfer or delivery of possession of personal property, the judgment is stayed without the filing of a supersedeas undertaking if the appellant transfers or delivers the personal property to the court or places the property in the custody of an officer or receiver appointed by the trial court.

(4) If a judgment requires the foreclosure of a mortgage, lien or other encumbrance, and also requires payment of the debt secured by the mortgage, lien or other encumbrance, a supersedeas undertaking acts to stay that portion of the judgment that requires payment of the debt if the undertaking provides that the appellant will pay any portion of the judgment remaining unsatisfied after the sale of the property subject to the mortgage, lien or other encumbrance. The amount of the undertaking must be stated in the undertaking. The requirements of this subsection are in addition to any provisions in a supersedeas undertaking that may be required under subsection (2) or (3) of this section to stay delivery or transfer of property.

(5) If a judgment requires the execution of a conveyance or other instrument, the judgment is stayed without the filing of a supersedeas undertaking if the appellant executes the instrument and deposits the instrument with the trial court administrator. Unless otherwise directed by the appellate court, the instrument must be held by the trial court administrator until issuance of the appellate judgment terminating the appeal.

(6) Except as provided in ORCP 72, a stay of judgment described in this section takes effect only after the party has filed a notice of appeal and filed any supersedeas undertaking required for the stay. [1997 c.71 §6; 1999 c.367 §11; 2007 c.547 §5]

19.340 Waiver of supersedeas undertaking; sale of perishables. (1) The trial court, in its discretion, may stay a judgment without requiring a supersedeas undertaking, or reduce the amount of the supersedeas undertaking required of the appellant, if the appellant is an executor, administrator, trustee or other person acting on behalf of another.

(2) If a judgment that has been stayed requires the sale of perishable property, or if perishable property has been seized to satisfy or secure a judgment that has been stayed, the trial court may order that perishable property be sold and the proceeds of the sale deposited or invested until issuance of the appellate judgment terminating the appeal. [1997 c.71 §7]

19.345 Enforcement of judgment in contract action notwithstanding appeal. If the judgment has been given in an action or suit upon a contract, notwithstanding an appeal and supersedeas undertaking, the respondent may proceed to enforce such judgment, if within 10 days from the time the appeal is perfected the respondent files with the trial court administrator an undertaking to the effect that if the judgment is reversed or modified the respondent will make such restitution as the appellate court may direct. Such undertaking may be excepted to by the appellant in like manner and with like effect as the undertaking of an appellant, and the sureties therein shall have the same qualifications. [Formerly 19.060; 1999 c.367 §12; 2003 c.576 §281]

19.350 Discretionary stay by court. (1) A party may seek a stay of judgment pending a decision on appeal in the manner provided by this section only if the judgment may not be stayed under the provisions of ORS 19.335 or 19.340, or under any other provision of law specifying a procedure or grounds for staying the judgment. A stay of judgment may not be granted under this section if any other provision of law specifies that a stay may not be granted pending a decision on appeal.

(2) Except as provided in subsection (5) of this section, a party seeking a stay under the provisions of this section must first request a stay from the trial court. The trial court may act on a request for a stay before or after a notice of appeal is filed. The time for filing a notice of appeal is not tolled by the making of a request for a stay under this section or by the trial court's action on the request.

(3) The trial court shall consider the following factors in deciding whether to grant a stay under this section, in addition to such other factors as the trial court considers important:

(a) The likelihood of the appellant prevailing on appeal.

(b) Whether the appeal is taken in good faith and not for the purpose of delay.

(c) Whether there is any support in fact or in law for the appeal.

(d) The nature of the harm to the appellant, to other parties, to other persons and to the public that will likely result from the grant or denial of a stay.

(4) The trial court has discretion to impose reasonable conditions on the grant of a stay under the provisions of this section. The court may require that a supersedeas undertaking be filed in a specified amount as a condition of granting a stay under the provisions of this section.

(5) A party may request a stay pending appeal from the appellate court in the first instance, and the appellate court may act on that request without requiring the party to seek a stay from the trial court, if the party establishes that the filing of a request for a stay with the trial court would be futile or that the trial court is unable or unwilling to act on the request within a reasonable time. In considering a request for a stay under this subsection, the appellate court shall consider the factors set out in subsection (3) of this section in addition to any other factors the court considers important. [1997 c.71 §8]

19.355 Stay of domestic relations judgment. (1) The provisions of this chapter relating to stays on appeal apply to a domestic relations judgment.

(2) If an appellant seeks a stay of only specific provisions of a domestic relations judgment, the motion seeking the stay must identify those provisions of the judgment that are to be stayed. If the court allows a stay of only certain provisions of the judgment, the order of the court must specifically indicate those provisions. If a supersedeas undertaking is filed with the court for the purpose of staying specific provisions of the judgment, the undertaking must indicate the specific provisions of the judgment covered by the undertaking. A stay of any specific provision of a domestic relations judgment may be granted only if:

(a) The specific provision is subject to stay under the provisions of this chapter; and

(b) All requirements of this chapter for a stay of the provision are satisfied.

(3) For the purposes of this section, "domestic relations judgment" means a judgment entered in proceedings under ORS chapter 107, 108 or 109. [1997 c.71 §10; 2003 c.576 §282]

(Appellate Review of Trial Court Orders Relating to Undertakings and Stays)

19.360 Appellate review of trial court orders relating to undertakings and stays. (1) Any party aggrieved by the trial court's final order relating to an undertaking on appeal, the trial court's grant or denial of a stay or the terms and conditions imposed by the trial court on the granting of a stay may seek review of the trial court's decision by filing a motion in the appellate court to which the appeal is made. The motion must be filed within 14 days after the entry of the trial court's order. During the 14-day period after the entry of the trial court's order, the judgment shall automatically be stayed unless the trial court orders otherwise. The trial court may impose terms or conditions on the stay or take such other action as may be necessary to prevent prejudice to the parties.

(2) The appellate court may review the decision of the trial court under the provisions of this section at any time after the filing of the notice of appeal. Notwithstanding ORS 19.415 (3), the appellate court shall review the decision de novo upon the record.

(3) On de novo review under subsection (2) of this section, the record shall be restricted to the record made before the trial court unless:

(a) There is additional relevant information relating to the period of time following the decision of the trial court that the appellate court determines to be important to review of the decision; or

(b) The party submitting new information establishes that there was good cause for not submitting the information to the trial court.

(4) On review of a trial court's decision relating to a request for a stay pending appeal, an appellate court may remand the matter to the trial court for reconsideration, may vacate a stay granted by the trial court, may grant a stay, and may impose or modify terms and conditions on a stay. Upon receipt of a request for a stay pending appeal made to the appellate court in the first instance, the appellate court may remand the matter to the trial court for consideration in the first instance, may grant or deny a stay, and may impose terms and conditions on a stay issued by the appellate court. [1997 c.71 §9; 1999 c.294 §1; 2009 c.231 §4]

RECORD ON APPEAL

19.365 Preparation and transmission of record generally. (1) The record of the case must be prepared and transmitted to the court to which the appeal is made in the manner provided in this chapter.

(2) The record on appeal consists of those parts of the trial court file, exhibits and record of oral proceedings in the trial court that are designated under ORS 19.250. The record of oral proceedings is the transcript prepared under ORS 19.370, an agreed narrative statement prepared under ORS 19.380 or the audio record if the appellate court has waived preparation of a transcript under ORS 19.385.

(3) The trial court administrator shall make the trial court record available to the State Court Administrator in the manner specified by rules of the appellate court.

(4) When it appears to the appellate court that the record on appeal is erroneous or that the record does not contain material that should have been part of the trial court file, and the erroneous or incomplete record substantially affects the merits of the appeal, on motion of a party or on its own motion the appellate court may make such order to correct or supplement the record as may be just.

(5) If the record on appeal is not sufficient to allow the appellate court to review an assignment of error, the appellate court may decline to review the assignment of error and may dismiss the appeal if there are no other assignments of error that may be reviewed.

(6) Except as provided by rules of the appellate court, the State Court Administrator shall return the trial court file and the exhibits to the trial court administrator upon issuance of the appellate judgment disposing of the appeal. [Formerly 19.065; 2013 c.685 §5]

19.370 Certification and service of transcript; correction of errors; settlement of transcript. (1) If a transcript is prepared from audio records by a person other than the reporter, the reporter shall certify the records and the transcriber shall certify the transcript. In all other cases, the transcript must be certified by the reporter or the trial judge.

(2) A transcriber shall prepare a transcript in the format prescribed by the court by the later of:

(a) Thirty days after the filing of the notice of appeal; or

(b) Thirty days after the expiration of any abeyance of the appeal imposed by reason of the referral of the appeal to the appellate settlement program established by the Court of Appeals pursuant to ORS 2.560.

(3) Immediately after preparing a transcript, the transcriber shall:

(a) Serve a copy of the transcript on the parties to the appeal in the manner required by subsection (4) of this section; and

(b) File a certificate of preparation for the transcript with the State Court Administrator. The certificate must indicate that the transcript has been served in the manner required by subsection (4) of this section. A copy of the certificate must be served on the trial court administrator, the transcript coordinator and the parties.

(4) A transcriber may agree with a party or an attorney on the manner in which a transcript will be served. If there is no agreement, a transcriber shall serve a transcript in the following manner:

(a) Subject to paragraph (d) of this subsection, if an appellant is not represented by an attorney, the transcriber shall serve an electronic copy of the transcript on the appellant at the electronic mail address provided by the appellant unless the appellant specifically requests that a paper copy of the transcript be mailed to the appellant at the postal address indicated in the notice of appeal. If an electronic mail address for the appellant does not appear in the notice of appeal, the transcriber shall mail a paper copy of the transcript to the appellant at the postal address indicated in the notice of appeal.

(b) Subject to paragraph (d) of this subsection, if a respondent is not represented by an attorney, the transcriber shall mail a paper copy of the transcript to the respondent at the postal address indicated in the notice of appeal unless the respondent specifically requests that the transcriber serve an electronic copy of the transcript on the respondent at the electronic mail address provided by the respondent.

(c) If a party is represented by an attorney, the transcriber shall serve an electronic copy of the transcript on the attorney at the electronic mail address of the attorney identified in the notice of appeal.

(d) If two or more unrepresented appellants request paper copies of a transcript under paragraph (a) of this subsection, or two or more unrepresented respondents request paper copies of a transcript under paragraph (b) of this subsection, the transcriber shall deposit a copy of the transcript with the trial court administrator for the use of the unrepresented parties. The copy must be in the medium specified by the trial court administrator. The transcriber shall serve notice on the unrepresented parties that the transcript has been deposited with the trial court administrator, and file proof of that service with the trial court administrator and with the State Court Administrator. Deposit of a copy of a transcript with the trial court administrator under this paragraph constitutes service of the transcript on the unrepresented parties to the appeal.

(5) If two or more transcribers are preparing parts of the transcript, the certificate of preparation is considered filed under subsection (3) of this section when the final certificate of preparation is filed with the State Court Administrator.

(6)(a) Within 15 days after a certificate of preparation is filed under subsection (3) of this section, any party may file a motion with the trial court for correction of errors appearing in the transcript or to have additional parts of the proceedings included in the transcript. If a certificate of preparation is filed with the State Court Administrator during any period that the appeal is in abeyance by reason of the referral of the appeal to the appellate settlement program established by the Court of Appeals pursuant to ORS 2.560, a motion under this subsection must be filed within 15 days after the expiration of the abeyance.

(b) A copy of a motion to correct or add to the transcript made under this subsection must be served on the State Court Administrator. If the motion is denied, the trial court shall enter an order settling the transcript and transmit a copy of the order to the State Court Administrator.

(c) If a motion is granted under this subsection, the trial court shall direct the making of such corrections and the adding of such matter as may be appropriate and shall fix the time within which such corrections or additions must be made. Immediately after preparing the corrected or additional transcript, the transcriber shall serve a copy of the transcript on the parties in the manner required by subsection (4) of this section, and file proof of that service with the trial court administrator, the transcript coordinator and the State Court Administrator. Upon receiving proof of service from all transcribers of the proceedings, the State Court Administrator shall issue a notice to the parties indicating that the transcript has been settled.

(7) Unless a motion to correct or add to the transcript is made under subsection (6) of this section, a transcript is automatically settled 15 days after a certificate of preparation is filed under subsection (3) of this section. If a motion to correct or add to the transcript is made, the transcript is settled on the date that the State Court Administrator issues the notice to the parties under subsection (6) of this section.

(8) When a transcript is settled, the State Court Administrator shall notify each transcriber who filed a certificate of preparation. Upon receiving the notice, a transcriber shall file an electronic copy of the transcript with the State Court Administrator in the manner and format prescribed by rules of the appellate court. [Formerly 19.078; 1999 c.367 §13; 2001 c.341 §1; 2001 c.962 §62; 2012 c.48 §7; 2013 c.685 §6]

19.375 Cost of transcript. (1) Where more than one appeal is taken from the same judgment, only one original transcript shall be filed.

(2) The cost of preparing the transcript and copy shall be paid by the party designating it to be made, except that where a party has designated additional parts of the proceedings to be included in the transcript as provided in ORS 19.250 (2), the trial court on motion of such party may direct that the cost of preparing all or part of the additional parts of the transcript be paid by the appellant if it appears that such additional parts are necessary to the determination of the appeal. The cost of preparing the original and copy of the transcript shall be taxable as part of the costs on appeal. [Formerly 19.084]

19.380 Agreed narrative statement. In lieu of or in addition to a transcript, the parties may prepare an agreed narrative statement of the proceedings below or parts thereof. The narrative statement shall be signed by the parties or their attorneys and shall be filed with the trial court administrator within 30 days after the filing of the notice of appeal. When such a statement is filed, the appellant shall promptly notify the State Court Administrator, at Salem. [Formerly 19.088; 1999 c.367 §14]

19.385 Audio records. Where the trial proceedings are recorded on audio records, the court to which the appeal is made may waive transcription and provide for hearing of the appeal on the basis of the audio records alone under such rules as the court may prescribe. The reporter shall certify and file the audio recordings with the trial court administrator immediately upon receiving notice that the appeal is to be heard on the basis of the recordings alone. [Formerly 19.069; 1999 c.367 §15]

19.390 Bill of exceptions not required. A bill of exceptions is not required. For the purposes of section 3, Article VII (Amended) of the Oregon Constitution, the transcript, as defined in ORS 19.005, is the bill of exceptions. [Formerly 19.114]

19.395 Time extensions for preparation of record. Extensions of time for the performance of any act in connection with the preparation of the record may be granted only by the court to which the appeal is made and under such rules as that court may prescribe. [Formerly 19.095]

HEARINGS ON APPEALS

19.400 Where appeals heard. An appeal taken from any circuit court in any county lying east of the Cascade Mountains, except Klamath and Lake, shall be heard at Pendleton, unless otherwise ordered by the Court of Appeals if it has jurisdiction of the cause or if the cause is before the Supreme Court unless otherwise stipulated between the parties. All other appeals to the Supreme Court or to the Court of Appeals shall be heard at Salem, unless other locations are designated under ORS 1.085 (2). [Formerly 19.118]

DISPOSITION OF APPEALS

(Certification of Appeal to Supreme Court)

19.405 Certification of appeal to Supreme Court. (1) When the Court of Appeals has jurisdiction of an appeal, the court, through the Chief Judge and pursuant to appellate rules, may certify the appeal to the Supreme Court in lieu of disposition by the Court of Appeals. The Court of Appeals shall provide notice of certification to the parties to the appeal.
(2) The Supreme Court, by order entered within 20 days after the date of receiving certification of an appeal from the Court of Appeals under subsection (1) of this section, may accept or deny acceptance of the certified appeal. The Supreme Court, by order entered within that 20-day period, may extend by not more than 10 days the time for acceptance or denial of acceptance of the certified appeal. If the Supreme Court accepts a certified appeal, the Court of Appeals shall transmit the record of the case and the briefs of parties to the Supreme Court, the Supreme Court shall have jurisdiction of the cause, and the appeal shall be considered pending in the Supreme Court without additional notice of appeal, filing fee, undertaking or, except as the Supreme Court may require, briefs of parties. A certified appeal shall remain pending in the Court of Appeals before the Supreme Court accepts or denies acceptance, and if the Supreme Court denies acceptance or fails to accept or deny acceptance within the time provided for in this subsection. The Supreme Court shall provide notice of acceptance or denial of acceptance of certification to the parties to the appeal. [Formerly 19.210]

(Stipulated Dismissals and Settlements)

19.410 Stipulated dismissals; settlement; effect of settlement on pending appeal. (1) An appellate court may dismiss an appeal at any time if the parties to the appeal stipulate to the dismissal.
(2) Dismissal of an appeal shall operate as an affirmance of the judgment being appealed if the appellate court so directs in the order of dismissal.
(3) If the parties to an appeal settle all or part of the matter on appeal, the trial court has jurisdiction to enter any orders or judgments that may be necessary to implement the settlement. If the settlement disposes of all issues on appeal, the appellate court may dismiss the appeal. If the settlement disposes of part of the issues on appeal, the appellate court may limit the scope of the appeal to the issues not disposed of by the settlement. [Formerly 19.111]

(Disposition on Merits)

19.415 Scope of appellate review. (1) Except as provided in this section, upon an appeal in an action or proceeding, without regard to whether the action or proceeding was triable to the court or a jury, the scope of review shall be as provided in section 3, Article VII (Amended) of the Oregon Constitution.
(2) No judgment shall be reversed or modified except for error substantially affecting the rights of a party.
(3) Upon an appeal in an equitable action or proceeding, review by the Court of Appeals shall be as follows:
(a) Upon an appeal from a judgment in a proceeding for the termination of parental rights, the Court of Appeals shall try the cause anew upon the record; and
(b) Upon an appeal in an equitable action or proceeding other than an appeal from a judgment in a proceeding for the termination of parental rights, the Court of Appeals, acting in its sole discretion, may try the cause anew upon the record or make one or more factual findings anew upon the record.
(4) When the Court of Appeals has tried a cause anew upon the record or has made one or more factual findings anew upon the record, the Supreme Court may limit its review of the decision of the Court of Appeals to questions of law. [Formerly 19.125; 2003 c.576 §88; 2005 c.568 §27; 2009 c.231 §2]

19.420 Action by appellate court on appeal; review of order granting new trial or judgment notwithstanding verdict; reversal upon loss or destruction of reporter's notes or audio records. (1) Upon an appeal, the court to which the appeal is made may affirm, reverse or modify the judgment or part thereof appealed from as to any or all of the parties joining in the appeal, and may include in such decision any or all of the parties not joining in the appeal, except a codefendant of the appellant against whom a several judgment might have been given in the court below; and may, if necessary and proper, order a new trial.
(2) Where in the trial court a motion for judgment notwithstanding the verdict and a motion for a new trial were made in the alternative, and an appeal is taken from a judgment notwithstanding the verdict or an order granting a new trial, the court to which the appeal is made may consider the correctness of the ruling of the trial court on either or both motions if such ruling is assigned as erroneous in the brief of any party affected by the appeal, without the necessity of a cross-appeal.
(3) Whenever it appears that an appeal cannot be prosecuted, by reason of the loss or destruction, through no fault of the appellant, of the reporter's notes or audio records, or of the exhibits or other matter necessary to the prosecution of the appeal, the judgment appealed from may be reversed and a new trial ordered as justice may require. [Formerly 19.130]

19.425 Review of intermediate orders; directing restitution. Upon an appeal, the appellate court may review any intermediate order involving the merits or necessarily affecting the judgment appealed from; and when it reverses or modifies such judgment, may direct complete restitution of all property and rights lost thereby. [Formerly 19.140; 2003 c.576 §283]

19.430 Review of trial court order granting a new trial on court's own initiative. If an appeal is taken from an order of the trial court granting a new trial on its own initiative, the order shall be affirmed on appeal only on grounds set forth in the order or because of reversible error affirmatively appearing in the record. [Formerly 19.200]

19.435 Memorandum decisions. The Supreme Court or the Court of Appeals may decide cases before it by means of memorandum decisions and shall prepare full opinions only in such cases as it deems proper. [Formerly 19.180]

(Attorney Fees and Penalties)

19.440 Award of attorney fees authorized by statute. (1) If a statute of this state authorizes or requires an award of attorney fees to a party to a proceeding, but does not expressly authorize or require that award on appeal, judicial review or other appellate review of the decision in the proceeding, and does not expressly prohibit that award on an appeal, judicial review or other appellate review, the statute shall be construed as authorizing or requiring the award of attorney fees on appeal, judicial review or other appellate review of the decision in the proceeding, including any denial of a petition for review by the Supreme Court in the proceeding.
(2) If a statute of this state authorizes or requires an award of attorney fees to a party to a proceeding, but does not expressly authorize or require an award of attorney fees in a mandamus proceeding arising out of the original proceeding, the statute shall be construed as authorizing or requiring the award of attorney fees in the mandamus proceeding.

169

(3) The provisions of this section apply to statutes that authorize or require the award of attorney fees in administrative proceedings in addition to statutes that authorize or require the award of attorney fees in civil proceedings in courts. [Formerly 19.220; 2011 c.513 §1]

19.445 Damages upon affirmance of judgment. Whenever a judgment is affirmed on appeal, and it is for recovery of money, or personal property or the value thereof, the judgment shall be given for 10 percent of the amount thereof, for damages for the delay, unless it appears evident to the appellate court that there was probable cause for taking the appeal. [Formerly 19.160; 2003 c.576 §284]

(Appellate Judgment)

19.450 Appellate judgment; when effective; effect of entry in trial court register; effect on judgment lien. (1) As used in this section:
(a) "Decision" means a memorandum opinion, an opinion indicating the author or an order denying or dismissing an appeal issued by the Court of Appeals or the Supreme Court. The decision shall state the court's disposition of the judgment being appealed, and may provide for final disposition of the cause. The decision shall designate the prevailing party or parties, state whether a party or parties will be allowed costs and disbursements, and if so, by whom the costs and disbursements will be paid.
(b) "Appellate judgment" means the decision of the Court of Appeals or Supreme Court, or such portion of the decision as may be specified by the rule of the Supreme Court, together with an award of attorney fees or allowance of costs and disbursements, if any.
(2) As to appeals from circuit and tax courts, the appellate judgment is effective when a copy of the appellate judgment is entered in the court's register and mailed by the State Court Administrator to the court from which the appeal was taken. When the State Court Administrator mails a copy of the appellate judgment to the court from which the appeal was taken, the administrator also shall mail a copy to the parties to the appeal.
(3) If a new trial is ordered, upon the receipt of the appellate judgment by the trial court administrator for the court below, the trial court administrator shall enter the appellate court's decision in the register of the court below and thereafter the cause shall be deemed pending for trial in such court, according to the directions of the court which rendered the decision. If a new trial is not ordered, upon the receipt of the appellate judgment by the trial court administrator, a judgment shall be entered in the register according to the directions of the court which rendered the decision, in like manner and with like effect as if the same was given in the court below.
(4) A party entitled to enforce an undertaking may obtain judgment against a surety by filing a request with the State Court Administrator and serving a copy of the request on the other parties and the surety. The request must identify the surety against whom judgment is to be entered and the amount of the judgment sought to be imposed against the surety. Unless otherwise directed by the appellate court, upon receiving the request the State Court Administrator shall include in the appellate judgment a judgment against the surety in the amount specified.
(5) If the appellate judgment terminating an appeal contains a judgment against a surety for an undertaking, the trial court administrator shall enter the judgment against the surety in like manner and with like effect as if the judgment was given in the court below.
(6) Except as provided in ORS 18.154, an appeal does not discharge the lien of a judgment and unless the judgment is reversed, the lien of the judgment merges with and continues in the affirmed or modified judgment given on appeal, from the time of the entry of the judgment in the court below. The lien of any judgment created by recording a certified copy of the judgment or a lien record abstract continues in force in the same manner as the original judgment lien as provided in this subsection. [Formerly 19.190; 1999 c.367 §16; 2003 c.576 §89]

MISCELLANEOUS

19.500 Service of documents under provisions of chapter. Except as otherwise provided in this chapter, when any provision of this chapter requires that a document be served and filed, the document shall be served in the manner provided in ORCP 9 B on all other parties who have appeared in the action, suit or proceeding and who are not represented by the same counsel as the party serving the document, and shall be filed, with proof of service indorsed thereon, with the trial court administrator. [Formerly 19.104; 2007 c.129 §10]

19.510 Powers of successor trial judge with respect to appeals. In case of death, resignation, expiration of the term of office or vacancy in office for any other cause of the judge before whom the matter was tried, or in case illness or other cause prevents the judge from performing the duties of judge, a successor in office or any other judge assigned to perform the duties of the judge, may take any action with respect to the appeal which the judge who tried it could take. [Formerly 19.170]

_____

Chapter 20 — Attorney Fees; Costs and Disbursements

2017 EDITION

ATTORNEY FEES; COSTS AND DISBURSEMENTS

PROCEDURE IN CIVIL PROCEEDINGS

ATTORNEY FEES; EXPERT WITNESS FEES

20.075   Factors to be considered by court in awarding attorney fees; limitation on appellate review of attorney fee award

20.077   Determination of prevailing party; cases in which more than one claim made; prevailing party on appeal

20.080   Attorney fees for certain small tort claims

20.082   Attorney fees for small contract claims

20.083   Award of attorney fees under void contract, under unenforceable contract or to person who is not party to contract

20.085   Costs and attorney fees in inverse condemnation proceedings

20.094   Attorney fees in actions or suits in which discharge in bankruptcy asserted

20.096   Reciprocity of attorney fees and costs in proceedings to enforce contract

20.097   Attorney fees and costs where defendant prevails in certain proceedings to enforce contract

20.098   Attorney fees and compensation of expert witnesses in certain proceedings for breach of warranty

20.105   Attorney fees where party disobeys court order or asserts claim, defense or ground for appeal without objectively reasonable basis

20.107   Attorney and expert witness fees and other costs on claim of unlawful discrimination; defense

OTHER COSTS

20.115   Service expenses recoverable as costs and disbursements

20.120   Costs on review of decision of officer, tribunal, or court of inferior jurisdiction

20.125   Assessment of costs and attorney fees against attorney causing mistrial

20.130   Proceeding to which state or public corporation is party

20.140   State and certain public corporations not required to advance costs; payment of costs recovered

20.150   Recovery of costs and disbursements when party represented by another

20.180   Effect of tender as to costs

PREVAILING PARTY FEES

20.190   Prevailing party fees

APPEALS ON ATTORNEY FEES AND OTHER COSTS

20.220   Appeal on attorney fees and costs; effect of reversal or modification

COSTS AND DISBURSEMENTS IN APPELLATE COURTS

20.310   Costs and disbursements in Supreme Court or Court of Appeals

20.320   Statement of costs and disbursements; objections

20.330   Costs and disbursements in cases of original jurisdiction

CONTINGENT FEE AGREEMENTS

20.340   Contingent fee agreement

20.010 [Repealed by 1981 c.898 §53]

20.015 [1983 c.527 §3; repealed by 2001 c.417 §5]

20.020 [Repealed by 1981 c.898 §53]

20.030 [Repealed by 1979 c.284 §199]

20.040 [Amended by 1979 c.284 §59; repealed by 1981 c.898 §53]

20.050 [Repealed by 1981 c.898 §53]

20.055 [1967 c.359 §703a; repealed by 1981 c.898 §53]

20.060 [Repealed by 1981 c.898 §53]

20.070 [Amended by 1977 c.544 §1; repealed by 1981 c.898 §53]

ATTORNEY FEES; EXPERT WITNESS FEES

20.075 Factors to be considered by court in awarding attorney fees; limitation on appellate review of attorney fee award. (1) A court shall consider the following factors in determining whether to award attorney fees in any case in which an award of attorney fees is authorized by statute and in which the court has discretion to decide whether to award attorney fees:

(a) The conduct of the parties in the transactions or occurrences that gave rise to the litigation, including any conduct of a party that was reckless, willful, malicious, in bad faith or illegal.

(b) The objective reasonableness of the claims and defenses asserted by the parties.

(c) The extent to which an award of an attorney fee in the case would deter others from asserting good faith claims or defenses in similar cases.

(d) The extent to which an award of an attorney fee in the case would deter others from asserting meritless claims and defenses.

(e) The objective reasonableness of the parties and the diligence of the parties and their attorneys during the proceedings.

(f) The objective reasonableness of the parties and the diligence of the parties in pursuing settlement of the dispute.

(g) The amount that the court has awarded as a prevailing party fee under ORS 20.190.

(h) Such other factors as the court may consider appropriate under the circumstances of the case.

(2) A court shall consider the factors specified in subsection (1) of this section in determining the amount of an award of attorney fees in any case in which an award of attorney fees is authorized or required by statute. In addition, the court shall consider the following factors in determining the amount of an award of attorney fees in those cases:

(a) The time and labor required in the proceeding, the novelty and difficulty of the questions involved in the proceeding and the skill needed to properly perform the legal services.

(b) The likelihood, if apparent to the client, that the acceptance of the particular employment by the attorney would preclude the attorney from taking other cases.

(c) The fee customarily charged in the locality for similar legal services.

(d) The amount involved in the controversy and the results obtained.

(e) The time limitations imposed by the client or the circumstances of the case.

171

(f) The nature and length of the attorney's professional relationship with the client.
(g) The experience, reputation and ability of the attorney performing the services.
(h) Whether the fee of the attorney is fixed or contingent.
(3) In any appeal from the award or denial of an attorney fee subject to this section, the court reviewing the award may not modify the decision of the court in making or denying an award, or the decision of the court as to the amount of the award, except upon a finding of an abuse of discretion.
(4) Nothing in this section authorizes the award of an attorney fee in excess of a reasonable attorney fee. [1995 c.618 §6; 2001 c.417 §3]

20.077 Determination of prevailing party; cases in which more than one claim made; prevailing party on appeal. (1) In any action or suit in which one or more claims are asserted for which an award of attorney fees is either authorized or required, the prevailing party on each claim shall be determined as provided in this section. The provisions of this section apply to all proceedings in the action or suit, including arbitration, trial and appeal.
(2) For the purposes of making an award of attorney fees on a claim, the prevailing party is the party who receives a favorable judgment or arbitration award on the claim. If more than one claim is made in an action or suit for which an award of attorney fees is either authorized or required, the court or arbitrator shall:
(a) Identify each party that prevails on a claim for which attorney fees could be awarded;
(b) Decide whether to award attorney fees on claims for which the court or arbitrator is authorized to award attorney fees, and the amount of the award;
(c) Decide the amount of the award of attorney fees on claims for which the court or arbitrator is required to award attorney fees; and
(d) Enter a judgment that complies with the requirements of ORS 18.038 and 18.042.
(3) Notwithstanding subsection (2) of this section, upon appeal of a judgment in an action or suit in which one or more claims are asserted for which the prevailing party may receive an award of attorney fees, the appellate court in its discretion may designate as the prevailing party a party who obtains a substantial modification of the judgment.
(4) This section does not create a claim to an award of attorney fees in any action or suit in which the court or arbitrator is not otherwise authorized or required to make an award of attorney fees by contract or other law. [2001 c.417 §1; 2003 c.576 §167]

20.080 Attorney fees for certain small tort claims. (1) In any action for damages for an injury or wrong to the person or property, or both, of another where the amount pleaded is $10,000 or less, and the plaintiff prevails in the action, there shall be taxed and allowed to the plaintiff, at trial and on appeal, a reasonable amount to be fixed by the court as attorney fees for the prosecution of the action, if the court finds that written demand for the payment of such claim was made on the defendant, and on the defendant's insurer, if known to the plaintiff, not less than 30 days before the commencement of the action or the filing of a formal complaint under ORS 46.465, or not more than 30 days after the transfer of the action under ORS 46.461. However, no attorney fees shall be allowed to the plaintiff if the court finds that the defendant tendered to the plaintiff, prior to the commencement of the action or the filing of a formal complaint under ORS 46.465, or not more than 30 days after the transfer of the action under ORS 46.461, an amount not less than the damages awarded to the plaintiff.
(2) If the defendant pleads a counterclaim, not to exceed $10,000, and the defendant prevails in the action, there shall be taxed and allowed to the defendant, at trial and on appeal, a reasonable amount to be fixed by the court as attorney fees for the prosecution of the counterclaim.
(3) A written demand for the payment of damages under this section must include the following information, if the information is in the plaintiff's possession or reasonably available to the plaintiff at the time the demand is made:
(a) In an action for an injury or wrong to a person, a copy of medical records and bills for medical treatment adequate to reasonably inform the person receiving the written demand of the nature and scope of the injury claimed; or
(b) In an action for damage to property, documentation of the repair of the property, a written estimate for the repair of the property or a written estimate of the difference in the value of the property before the damage and the value of the property after the damage.
(4) If after making a demand under this section, and before commencing an action, a plaintiff acquires any additional information described in subsection (3) of this section that was not provided with the demand, the plaintiff must provide that information to the defendant, and to the defendant's insurer, if known to the plaintiff, as soon as possible after the information becomes available to the plaintiff.
(5) A plaintiff may not recover attorney fees under this section if the plaintiff does not comply with the requirements of subsections (3) and (4) of this section.
(6) The provisions of this section do not apply to any action based on contract. [Amended by 1955 c.554 §1; 1979 c.525 §1; 1981 c.897 §1; 1981 c.898 §19; 1985 c.342 §7; 1985 c.618 §15c; 1997 c.46 §2; 1999 c.947 §1; 2001 c.542 §2; 2009 c.487 §§1,3]

20.082 Attorney fees for small contract claims. (1) As used in this section, "contract" includes:
(a) Express contracts;
(b) Implied contracts; and
(c) Instruments or documents evidencing a debt.
(2) Except as provided in this section, a court shall allow reasonable attorney fees to the prevailing party on any claim based on contract if:
(a) The amount of the principal together with interest due on the contract at the time the claim is filed is $10,000 or less; and
(b) The contract does not contain a clause that authorizes or requires the award of attorney fees.
(3) Attorney fees may not be awarded to a plaintiff under the provisions of this section unless written demand for payment of the claim was made on the defendant not less than 20 days before the commencement of the action or the filing of a formal complaint under ORS 46.465, or not more than 20 days after the transfer of the action under ORS 46.461. The failure of a plaintiff to give notice under the provisions of this subsection does not affect the ability of a defendant to claim attorney fees under the provisions of this section.
(4) Attorney fees may not be awarded to a plaintiff under the provisions of this section if the court finds that the defendant tendered to the plaintiff, prior to the commencement of the action or the filing of a formal complaint under ORS 46.465, or not more than 20 days after the transfer of the action under ORS 46.461, an amount not less than the amount awarded to the plaintiff.
(5) The provisions of this section do not apply to:
(a) Contracts for insurance;
(b) Contracts for which another statute authorizes or requires an award of attorney fees;
(c) Any action for damages for breach of an express or implied warranty in a sale of consumer goods or services that is subject to ORS 20.098; or
(d) Any action against the maker of a dishonored check that is subject to ORS 30.701. [2001 c.542 §1; 2005 c.22 §10; 2009 c.487 §5]

20.083 Award of attorney fees under void contract, under unenforceable contract or to person who is not party to contract. A prevailing party in a civil action relating to an express or implied contract is entitled to an award of attorney fees that is authorized by the terms of the contract or by statute, even though the party prevails by reason of a claim or defense asserting that the contract is in whole or part void, a claim or defense asserting that the contract is unenforceable or a claim or defense asserting that the prevailing party was not a party to the contract. [2003 c.393 §1; 2009 c.285 §1]

20.085 Costs and attorney fees in inverse condemnation proceedings. In a proceeding brought under section 18, Article I or section 4, Article XI of the Oregon Constitution by an owner of property or by a person claiming an interest in property, if the owner or other person prevails, the owner or other person shall be entitled to costs and disbursements and reasonable attorney fees at trial and on appeal. [1965 c.484 §1; 1981 c.897 §2; 1995 c.79 §8]

20.090 [Amended by 1963 c.247 §1; 1973 c.553 §1; 1981 c.897 §3; repealed by 1997 c.182 §7]

20.094 Attorney fees in actions or suits in which discharge in bankruptcy asserted. In any action or suit on a debt in which the defendant asserts a discharge in bankruptcy as a defense, the court shall award a reasonable attorney fee at trial and on appeal to the prevailing party. [1971 c.167 §2; 1973 c.216 §1; 1981 c.897 §4; 1995 c.618 §18]

20.095 [1953 c.213 §1; repealed by 1965 c.611 §18]

20.096 Reciprocity of attorney fees and costs in proceedings to enforce contract. (1) In any action or suit in which a claim is made based on a contract that specifically provides that attorney fees and costs incurred to enforce the provisions of the contract shall be awarded to one of the parties, the party that prevails on the claim shall be entitled to reasonable attorney fees in addition to costs and disbursements, without regard to whether the prevailing party is the party specified in the contract and without regard to whether the prevailing party is a party to the contract.

(2) Attorney fees provided for in a contract described in subsection (1) of this section shall not be subject to waiver by the parties to any such contract that is entered into after September 9, 1971. Any provision in such a contract that provides for a waiver of attorney fees is void.

(3) As used in this section and ORS 20.097, "contract" includes any instrument or document evidencing a debt. [1971 c.202 §1; 1975 c.623 §3; 1979 c.735 §1; 1981 c.898 §20; 1983 c.527 §1; 2001 c.542 §§3,3a; 2009 c.285 §2]

20.097 Attorney fees and costs where defendant prevails in certain proceedings to enforce contract. (1) In any action or suit on a contract by an assignee of any right under that contract, the maker of that contract and the plaintiff in the action or suit on that contract shall be severally liable for any attorney fees and costs that may be awarded to the defendant in the action.

(2) As used in this section, "maker" means the original party to the contract which is the subject of the action or suit who is the predecessor in interest of the plaintiff under the contract.

(3) A maker shall be liable under this section only if the defense successfully asserted by the defendant existed at the time of the assignment of the contract. [1975 c.623 §2; 1989 c.1065 §1; 2001 c.542 §4]

20.098 Attorney fees and compensation of expert witnesses in certain proceedings for breach of warranty. (1) In any action for damages for breach of an express or implied warranty in a sale of consumer goods or services where the amount pleaded is $2,500 or less and the plaintiff prevails in the action, there shall be taxed and allowed to the plaintiff, at trial and on appeal, a reasonable amount to be fixed by the court as attorney fees for the prosecution of the action, and as part of the disbursements of the action, a reasonable amount to be fixed by the court as compensation of expert witnesses, if the court finds that written demand for the payment of such claim was made on the defendant not less than 30 days before commencement of the action and that the defendant was allowed within that 30 days reasonable opportunity to inspect any property pertaining to the claim; provided, that no attorney fees at trial and on appeal or compensation of expert witnesses shall be allowed to the plaintiff if the court finds that the defendant tendered to the plaintiff, prior to the commencement of the action, an amount not less than the damages awarded to the plaintiff.

(2) If the defendant prevails in an action in which the plaintiff requests attorney fees or compensation of expert witnesses under subsection (1) of this section, the court may in its discretion allow reasonable attorney fees at trial and on appeal or a reasonable amount as compensation of expert witnesses to the defendant if it finds the action to have been frivolous. [1971 c.744 §23; 1975 c.586 §1; 1981 c.897 §5; 1981 c.898 §21]

20.100 [Repealed by 1981 c.898 §53]

20.105 Attorney fees where party disobeys court order or asserts claim, defense or ground for appeal without objectively reasonable basis. (1) In any civil action, suit or other proceeding in a circuit court or the Oregon Tax Court, or in any civil appeal to or review by the Court of Appeals or Supreme Court, the court shall award reasonable attorney fees to a party against whom a claim, defense or ground for appeal or review is asserted, if that party is a prevailing party in the proceeding and to be paid by the party asserting the claim, defense or ground, upon a finding by the court that the party willfully disobeyed a court order or that there was no objectively reasonable basis for asserting the claim, defense or ground for appeal.

(2) All attorney fees paid to any agency of the state under this section shall be deposited to the credit of the agency's appropriation or cash account from which the costs and expenses of the proceeding were paid or incurred. If the agency obtained an Emergency Board allocation to pay costs and expenses of the proceeding, to that extent the attorney fees shall be deposited in the General Fund available for general governmental expenses. [1983 c.763 §57; 1995 c.618 §2]

20.107 Attorney and expert witness fees and other costs on claim of unlawful discrimination; defense. (1) In any civil judicial proceeding, including judicial review of an administrative proceeding based on a claim of unlawful discrimination, the court shall award to the prevailing plaintiff attorney and expert witness fees reasonably and necessarily incurred in connection with the discrimination claim, at the trial court or agency level and on appeal. The court may award reasonable attorney fees and expert witness fees incurred by a defendant who prevails in the action if the court determines that the plaintiff had no objectively reasonable basis for asserting a claim or no reasonable basis for appealing an adverse decision of a trial court or agency.

(2) In making an award under this section, the court shall calculate attorney and expert witness fees on the basis of a reasonable hourly rate at the time the award is made, multiplied by the amount of time actually and reasonably spent in connection with the discrimination claim.

(3) When an award under this section is made against a state agency or an officer or employee of a state agency, the award shall be paid by the agency directly from funds available to it.

(4) As used in this section, "unlawful discrimination" means discrimination based upon personal characteristics including, but not limited to, race, religion, sex, sexual orientation, national origin, alienage, marital status or age. [1985 c.768 §1; 1995 c.618 §20; 2007 c.100 §14]

20.110 [Repealed by 1981 c.898 §53]

OTHER COSTS

20.115 Service expenses recoverable as costs and disbursements. (1) A person who is otherwise entitled to recover costs and disbursements may recover the following amounts as part of costs and disbursements:

(a) An amount paid to a sheriff for service of process or other documents under ORS 21.300.

(b) An amount paid to a person other than a sheriff for service of process or other documents. Except as provided in subsection (2) of this section, the amount that may be recovered as costs and disbursements under this paragraph may not exceed the maximum amount payable to a sheriff for service of the same process or document under ORS 21.300.

(2) In addition to amounts recoverable under subsection (1) of this section, a person who is otherwise entitled to recover costs and disbursements may recover the following amounts paid to a person other than a sheriff for service of process or other documents:

(a) The reasonable cost of service outside this state.

(b) The reasonable rate for mileage.

(c) The reasonable cost of locating and serving a party when routine service methods are unsuccessful.

(d) The reasonable cost of expedited service if expedited service is necessary.

(3) In addition to amounts recoverable under subsections (1) and (2) of this section, a person who is otherwise entitled to recover costs and disbursements may recover amounts paid for an attempt at service made in good faith if the amounts paid would be recoverable under subsections (1) and (2) of this section had service of process or other documents been accomplished.

(4) The provisions of this section do not limit the ability of a party to recover any reasonable costs of service if the party has a contract right to recover those costs. [1997 c.202 §1]

20.120 Costs on review of decision of officer, tribunal, or court of inferior jurisdiction. When the decision of an officer, tribunal, or court of inferior jurisdiction is brought before a court for review, such review shall, for all the purposes of costs or disbursements, be deemed an appeal to such court upon errors in law, and costs therein shall be allowed and recovered accordingly.

20.125 Assessment of costs and attorney fees against attorney causing mistrial. In the case of a mistrial in a civil or criminal action, if the court determines that the mistrial was caused by the deliberate misconduct of an attorney, the court, upon motion by the opposing party or upon motion of the court, shall assess against the attorney causing the mistrial costs and disbursements, as defined in ORCP 68, and reasonable attorney fees incurred by the opposing party as a result of the misconduct. [1985 c.556 §1; 1995 c.618 §3]

20.130 Proceeding to which state or public corporation is party. In all actions or suits prosecuted or defended in the name and for the use of the state, or any county or other public corporation therein, the state or public corporation is liable for and may recover costs and disbursements in like manner and with like effect as in the case of natural persons. When a natural person is joined with the state as plaintiff, or the action is upon the information of such natural person, the natural person shall be liable in the first instance for the defendant's costs and disbursements; and such costs and disbursements shall not be recovered from the state until after execution is issued therefor against such person and returned unsatisfied in whole or in part.

20.140 State and certain public corporations not required to advance costs; payment of costs recovered. When the state or any county, city or school district in this state, or an officer, employee or agent thereof appearing in a representative or other official capacity, is a party in an action or proceeding in any court in this state, that party is not required to pay in advance to a state or county officer any fee taxable as costs and disbursements in the action or proceeding. If that party is entitled to recover costs and disbursements in the action or proceeding, the amount of the fee not paid in advance shall be included in the statement of costs and disbursements claimed by the party, shall be entered as part of the judgment and, if recovered by the party, shall be paid by the party to the state or county officer entitled to receive the fee. The party shall employ reasonable effort to recover the amount of the fee. [Amended by 1983 c.763 §19; 1987 c.405 §1]

20.150 Recovery of costs and disbursements when party represented by another. In an action, suit or proceeding prosecuted or defended by an executor, administrator, trustee of an express trust or person expressly authorized by statute to prosecute or defend therein, or in which a party appears by general guardian, conservator or guardian ad litem, costs and disbursements shall be recovered or not as in ordinary cases, but if recovered shall be chargeable only upon or collected from the estate, trust fund or party represented or for whom appearance is made, unless the court or judge thereof shall order such costs and disbursements to be recovered from the executor, administrator, trustee, person, guardian or conservator personally for mismanagement or bad faith in the commencement, prosecution or defense of the action, suit or proceeding. [Amended by 1961 c.344 §99]

20.160 [Amended by 1991 c.331 §5; 1997 c.631 §367; 2003 c.576 §285; 2005 c.22 §11; repealed by 2009 c.427 §1]

20.170 [Amended by 1991 c.331 §6; repealed by 2009 c.427 §1]

20.180 Effect of tender as to costs. When in any action or suit for the recovery of money or damages only, the defendant shall allege in answer that before the commencement thereof the defendant tendered to the plaintiff a certain amount of money in full payment or satisfaction of the cause, and now brings the same into court and deposits it with the clerk for the plaintiff, if such allegation of tender is found true, and the plaintiff does not recover a greater sum than the amount so tendered, the plaintiff shall not recover costs from the defendant, but the defendant shall recover costs from the plaintiff. [Amended by 2005 c.22 §12]

PREVAILING PARTY FEES

20.190 Prevailing party fees. (1) Except as provided in subsections (2) to (5) of this section, a prevailing party in a civil action or proceeding who has a right to recover costs and disbursements in the following cases also has a right to recover, as a part of the costs and disbursements, the following additional amounts:
    (a) In the Supreme Court or Court of Appeals, on an appeal, $100.
    (b) In a circuit court:
    (A) When judgment is given without trial of an issue of law or fact or on an appeal, $85; or
    (B) When judgment is given after trial of an issue of law or fact, $105.
    (c) In a small claims department, a county court or justice court:
    (A) When judgment is given without trial of an issue of law or fact or on an appeal, $50; or
    (B) When judgment is given after trial of an issue of law or fact, $60.
    (2) In lieu of the prevailing party fee provided for in subsection (1) of this section, in any civil action or proceeding in which recovery of money or damages is sought, a prevailing party who has a right to recover costs and disbursements also has a right to recover, as a part of the costs and disbursements, the following additional amounts:
    (a) In a circuit court:
    (A) When judgment is given without trial of an issue of law or fact, $325; or
    (B) When judgment is given after trial of an issue of law or fact, $600.
    (b) In a small claims department, a county court or justice court:
    (A) When judgment is given without trial of an issue of law or fact, $110; or
    (B) When judgment is given after trial of an issue of law or fact, $125.
    (3) In addition to the amounts provided for in subsection (2) of this section, in any civil action or proceeding in a circuit court in which recovery of money or damages is sought, the court may award to the prevailing party up to an additional $5,000 as a prevailing party fee. The court shall consider the following factors in making an award under the provisions of this subsection:
    (a) The conduct of the parties in the transactions or occurrences that gave rise to the litigation, including any conduct of a party that was reckless, willful, malicious, in bad faith or illegal.
    (b) The objective reasonableness of the claims and defenses asserted by the parties.
    (c) The extent to which an award of a larger prevailing party fee in the case would deter others from asserting good faith claims or defenses in similar cases.
    (d) The extent to which an award of a larger prevailing party fee in the case would deter others from asserting meritless claims and defenses.
    (e) The objective reasonableness of the parties and the diligence of the parties and their attorneys during the proceedings.
    (f) The objective reasonableness of the parties and the diligence of the parties in pursuing settlement of the dispute.
    (g) Any award of attorney fees made to the prevailing party as part of the judgment.
    (h) Such other factors as the court may consider appropriate under the circumstances of the case.
    (4) Nonprevailing parties are jointly liable for the prevailing party fees provided for in this section. A court may not award more than one prevailing party fee to a prevailing party under this section, or more than one prevailing party fee against a nonprevailing party regardless of the number of parties in the action, and, upon being paid the amount of the award, the prevailing party may not seek recovery of any additional amounts under the provisions of this section from any other nonprevailing party.
    (5) In any appeal from the award or denial of a prevailing party fee under subsection (2) of this section, the court reviewing the award may not modify the decision of the court in making or denying an award, or the decision of the court as to the amount of the award, except upon a finding of an abuse of discretion.

174

(6) The prevailing party fees provided for in this section may not be awarded in the following proceedings:

(a) A class action proceeding under ORCP 32.

(b) A condemnation proceeding.

(c) Proceedings under the provisions of ORS chapters 25, 107, 108, 109 and 110.

(7) Mandatory arbitration under ORS 36.400 to 36.425 does not constitute a trial of an issue of law or fact for the purposes of this section. [1981 c.898 §18a; 1987 c.725 §6; 1989 c.1007 §1; 1995 c.618 §7; 1997 c.249 §13; 1997 c.801 §§56,56a; 2005 c.702 §93; 2007 c.860 §16; 2011 c.595 §170a; 2013 c.685 §44; 2017 c.663 §25]

20.210 [Amended by 1959 c.638 §7; 1979 c.284 §60; repealed by 1981 c.898 §53]

APPEALS ON ATTORNEY FEES AND OTHER COSTS

20.220 Appeal on attorney fees and costs; effect of reversal or modification. (1) An appeal may be taken from a judgment under ORCP 68 C(4) allowing or denying attorney fees or costs and disbursements on questions of law only, as in other cases. On such appeal the statement of attorney fees or costs and disbursements, the objections thereto and the judgment rendered thereon shall constitute the trial court file, as defined in ORS 19.005.

(2) If an appeal is taken from a judgment under ORS 19.205 before the trial court enters a judgment under ORCP 68 C(4), any necessary modification of the appeal shall be pursuant to rules of the appellate court.

(3) When an appeal is taken from a judgment under ORS 19.205 to which an award of attorney fees or costs and disbursements relates:

(a) If the appellate court reverses the judgment, the award of attorney fees or costs and disbursements shall be deemed reversed; or

(b) If the appellate court modifies the judgment such that the party who was awarded attorney fees or costs and disbursements is no longer entitled to the award, the party against whom attorney fees or costs and disbursements were awarded may move for relief under ORCP 71 B(1)(e). [Amended by 1967 c.471 §2; 1981 c.898 §22; 1989 c.768 §7]

20.230 [Repealed by 1981 c.898 §53]

COSTS AND DISBURSEMENTS IN APPELLATE COURTS

20.310 Costs and disbursements in Supreme Court or Court of Appeals. (1) In any appeal to the Court of Appeals or review by the Supreme Court, the court shall allow costs and disbursements to the prevailing party, unless a statute provides that in the particular case costs and disbursements shall not be allowed to the prevailing party or shall be allowed to some other party, or unless the court directs otherwise. If, under a special provision of any statute, a party has a right to recover costs, such party shall also have a right to recover disbursements. On the same terms and conditions, when the Supreme Court denies a petition for review, the respondent on review is entitled to costs and disbursements reasonably incurred in connection with the petition for review.

(2) Costs and disbursements on appeal to the Court of Appeals or Supreme Court or on petition for review by the Supreme Court are the filing or appearance fee, the reasonable cost for any bond or irrevocable letter of credit, the prevailing party fee provided for under ORS 20.190, the printing, including the excerpt of record, required by rule of the court, postage for the filing or service of items that are required to be filed or served by law or court rule, and the transcript of testimony or other proceedings, when necessarily forming part of the record on appeal. [Amended by 1971 c.99 §1; 1977 c.290 §2; 1985 c.734 §13; 1987 c.314 §1; 1991 c.331 §7; 1997 c.389 §11; 2007 c.547 §6]

20.320 Statement of costs and disbursements; objections. Costs or disbursements shall not be allowed in the Supreme Court or Court of Appeals to a party unless the party serves on the adverse party or the adverse party's attorney, and files with the State Court Administrator, a statement certified under ORCP 17 showing with reasonable certainty all costs and disbursements claimed by the party. The statement must be accompanied by proof of service on all adverse parties, and must be filed within 21 days from the date of the court's decision, or within such further time as may be allowed by the court. The total of the items included in the statement of costs and disbursements thus filed, with the exception of items or amounts not allowed by law or by rules of the Supreme Court or Court of Appeals, shall be entered by the administrator as a part of the appellate judgment, in favor of the party entitled to the costs and disbursements, unless an adverse party within 14 days from date of service of the statement serves and files objections to the statement. The filing or appearance fee and the prevailing party fee under ORS 20.190 (1) shall be awarded by the court without the filing of a statement of costs and disbursements. [Amended by 1971 c.99 §2; 1983 c.774 §4; 1985 c.734 §14; 2003 c.518 §3]

20.330 Costs and disbursements in cases of original jurisdiction. Litigants shall recover their costs and disbursements in cases of original jurisdiction in the Supreme Court, the same as provided in cases on appeal.

CONTINGENT FEE AGREEMENTS

20.340 Contingent fee agreement. (1) In any civil action arising out of bodily injury, death or property damage, including claims for emotional injury or distress, loss of care, comfort, companionship and society, and loss of consortium, if an attorney for a plaintiff in respect to any civil action enters into an agreement with the plaintiff whereby the attorney receives as a fee a percentage of the amount of any settlement or judgment awarded to the plaintiff:

(a) The contingent fee agreement shall be written in plain and simple language reasonably believed to be understandable by the plaintiff.

(b) The attorney shall explain the terms and conditions of the agreement in compliance with a model explanation in plain and simple language prepared by the Oregon State Bar a reasonable time before the agreement is signed.

(c) The contingent fee agreements must contain a provision allowing the plaintiff to rescind the agreement within 24 hours after signing upon written notice to the attorney.

(2) Any contingent fee agreement entered into on or after September 26, 1987, that does not comply with the requirements of subsection (1) of this section is voidable. [Formerly 9.400]

Chapter 21 — State Court Fees

2017 EDITION

STATE COURT FEES

PROCEDURE IN CIVIL PROCEEDINGS

GENERALLY

21.005   Transfers to General Fund

21.006   Transfers to State Court Technology Fund

21.007   Legislative intent relating to funding certain programs, services and activities

APPELLATE COURT FEES

21.010   Appellate court filing fees

21.020   Seal of court; copies of appellate court and administrative records

21.025   Motion fees in appellate courts; exceptions

CIRCUIT COURT FEES

(Filing Fees)

21.100   Filing fees payable in advance

21.105   Caption of pleading; amended pleadings

21.135   Standard filing fee

21.145   Simple proceeding filing fee

21.155   Domestic relations filing fee

21.160   Filing fee for tort and contract actions

21.165   Third-party complaints

21.170   Probate filing fees and accounting fees

21.175   Guardianship filing fees

21.180   Conservatorship filing fees and accounting fees

21.185   Child support cases exempt from certain filing fees

(Motion Fees)

21.200   Motion fees generally

21.205   Motion fees in domestic relations cases

(Fees for Settlement Conferences)

21.215   Fees for settlement conferences

(Trial Fees)

21.225   Trial fees

(Fees for Documents and Forms)

21.235   Document fee

21.245   Form fees

21.255   Court Forms Revolving Fund

(Fees for Other Services)

21.258   Fees for other court services

(Fees Not Collectible From Public Bodies)

21.259   Fees not collectible from public bodies

(Appeals From Justice Courts and Municipal Courts)

21.285   Fees payable in appeals from justice courts and municipal courts

SHERIFF AND PROCESS SERVER FEES

21.300   Sheriff and process server fees

TRANSCRIPT FEES

21.345   Transcript fees

REFEREE FEES

21.400   Referee fees

WAIVER AND DEFERRAL OF FEES

21.680   Definitions for ORS 21.680 to 21.698

21.682   Authority to waive or defer fees and court costs; delegation

21.685   Application for waiver or deferral of fees or court costs

21.690   Waived fees; recovery

21.692   Judgment for deferred fees and court costs

21.695   Waiver or deferral of costs of transcript on appeal

21.698   Confidentiality of information related to waiver or deferral

21.700   Interest on judgments for deferred fees and costs; satisfaction; compromise prohibited

GENERALLY

21.005 Transfers to General Fund. Except as otherwise provided by law, all amounts collected as fees and charges in the Supreme Court, the Court of Appeals, the Oregon Tax Court and the circuit courts shall be transferred to the State Court Administrator for deposit in the General Fund. [2011 c.595 §1]

21.006 Transfers to State Court Technology Fund. Notwithstanding ORS 21.005, each month the State Court Administrator shall transfer to the State Court Technology Fund 8.85 percent of the fees collected by the State Court Administrator under ORS 21.010, 21.135, 21.145, 21.155, 21.160, 21.170, 21.180, 21.235, 46.570, 105.130 and 106.120. [2013 c.685 §47; 2017 c.663 §27]

21.007 Legislative intent relating to funding certain programs, services and activities. It is the intent of the Legislative Assembly that funding be provided to the following entities by appropriations each biennium to fund programs, services and activities that were funded through court fees before the 2011-2013 biennium:
(1) To the counties of this state for the purposes of funding mediation services, conciliation services and other services in domestic relations cases.
(2) To the counties of this state for the purposes of funding the operation of law libraries or of providing law library services.
(3) To Portland State University and the University of Oregon to fund the programs and expenses of the Mark O. Hatfield School of Government and the University of Oregon School of Law under ORS 36.100 to 36.238 and 183.502.
(4) To the Housing and Community Services Department for the purpose of funding programs that defray the cost of rent for dwelling units for very low income households.
(5) To the Higher Education Coordinating Commission to fund clinical legal education programs at accredited institutions of higher education that provide civil legal services to victims of domestic violence, stalking or sexual assault.
(6) To the State Department of Agriculture for the purpose of funding mediation programs established by the department, other than individual farm credit mediations.
(7) To the Judicial Department for the purposes of funding the appellate settlement program established under ORS 2.560.
(8) To the Department of Human Services for the funding of the Office of Children's Advocate. [2011 c.595 §3; 2012 c.48 §8; 2013 c.768 §100; 2015 c.767 §44]

APPELLATE COURT FEES

21.010 Appellate court filing fees. (1) Except as provided in this section, the appellant in an appeal or the petitioner in a judicial review in the Supreme Court or the Court of Appeals shall pay a filing fee of $391 in the manner prescribed by ORS 19.265. The respondent in such case and any other person appearing in the appeal, upon entering first appearance or filing first brief in the court, shall pay to the State Court Administrator a filing fee of $391. The party entitled to costs and disbursements on such appeal shall recover from the opponent the amount so paid.
(2) Filing and appearance fees may not be assessed in appeals from habeas corpus proceedings under ORS 34.710, post-conviction relief proceedings under ORS 138.650, juvenile court under ORS 419A.200, the involuntary commitment of persons determined to be persons with mental illness under ORS 426.135 or persons determined to have an intellectual disability under ORS 427.295 or orders of the State Board of Parole and Post-Prison Supervision or on judicial review of orders entered under ORS 161.315 to 161.351 by the Psychiatric Security Review Board.
(3) Filing and appearance fees shall be assessed in an appeal from an appeal to a circuit court from a justice court or municipal court in an action alleging commission of a state offense designated as a violation or an action alleging violation of a city charter or ordinance, but not in an action alleging commission of a state crime.
(4) Filing and appearance fees shall only be assessed in an appeal in a contempt proceeding seeking imposition of remedial sanctions under the provisions of ORS 33.055.
(5) The filing and appearance fees established by this section apply to cases of original jurisdiction in the Supreme Court. [Amended by 1963 c.556 §1; 1967 c.398 §3; 1969 c.198 §50; 1981 s.s. c.3 §§66,67; 1985 c.734 §15; 1987 c.852 §4; 1991 c.724 §17; 1993 c.33 §276; 1997 c.801 §27; 1999 c.1051 §118; 2003 c.737 §§1,3; 2005 c.702 §§1,2,3; 2005 c.843 §33; 2007 c.70 §7; 2007 c.860 §1; 2009 c.659 §§28,30; 2009 c.885 §§37e,37f; 2011 c.595 §66; 2011 c.658 §§28,29; 2011 c.708 §§17,18; 2013 c.360 §3; 2013 c.685 §§29,29a; 2014 c.76 §3; 2017 c.442 §14; 2017 c.663 §1]

Note: The amendments to 21.010 by section 14, chapter 442, Oregon Laws 2017, become operative July 1, 2018. See section 36, chapter 442, Oregon Laws 2017. The text that is operative until July 1, 2018, including amendments by section 1, chapter 663, Oregon Laws 2017, is set forth for the user's convenience.
21.010. (1) Except as provided in this section, the appellant in an appeal or the petitioner in a judicial review in the Supreme Court or the Court of Appeals shall pay a filing fee of $391 in the manner prescribed by ORS 19.265. The respondent in such case and any other person appearing in the appeal, upon entering first appearance or filing first brief in the court, shall pay to the State Court Administrator a filing fee of $391. The party entitled to costs and disbursements on such appeal shall recover from the opponent the amount so paid.
(2) Filing and appearance fees may not be assessed in appeals from habeas corpus proceedings under ORS 34.710, post-conviction relief proceedings under ORS 138.650, juvenile court under ORS 419A.200, the involuntary commitment of persons determined to be persons with mental illness under ORS 426.135 or persons determined to have an intellectual disability under ORS 427.295 or orders of the State Board of Parole and Post-Prison Supervision or on judicial review of orders entered under ORS 161.315 to 161.351 by the Psychiatric Security Review Board or the Oregon Health Authority.
(3) Filing and appearance fees shall be assessed in an appeal from an appeal to a circuit court from a justice court or municipal court in an action alleging commission of a state offense designated as a violation or an action alleging violation of a city charter or ordinance, but not in an action alleging commission of a state crime.
(4) Filing and appearance fees shall only be assessed in an appeal in a contempt proceeding seeking imposition of remedial sanctions under the provisions of ORS 33.055.

(5) The filing and appearance fees established by this section apply to cases of original jurisdiction in the Supreme Court.

21.020 Seal of court; copies of appellate court and administrative records. (1) The State Court Administrator shall collect a fee of $1 for affixing the seal of the court to a document.

(2) The Chief Justice of the Supreme Court by order may establish or authorize fees for copies of records of the appellate courts and the administrative offices of the State Court Administrator, for services relating to those records and for other services that the appellate courts or administrative offices of the State Court Administrator are authorized or required to perform for which no fees are specifically provided by law. The fee established by the Chief Justice for paper copies of records may not exceed 25 cents per page, except for records for which additional services are required. If additional services are required, fees for providing the records are subject to ORS 192.324. [Amended by 1967 c.398 §4; 1969 c.198 §51; 1971 c.193 §25; 1997 c.801 §47; 2003 c.576 §286; 2005 c.385 §1]

21.025 Motion fees in appellate courts; exceptions. (1) In any appeal or petition for review subject to a fee under ORS 21.010, a $53 fee must be paid by the party filing one of the following motions and by the party responding to the motion:
(a) A motion to dismiss filed by a respondent.
(b) A motion to determine jurisdiction.
(c) A motion for continuance.
(d) A motion for an extension of time for the filing of a brief or other document in the proceeding.
(2) The fees provided for in this section may not be collected from the state, a county, a city or a school district. [2011 c.595 §76; 2013 c.685 §28a; 2017 c.663 §11]

21.030 [Repealed by 1967 c.398 §10]

21.040 [Amended by 1967 c.398 §5; 1997 c.801 §48; 2003 c.737 §§5,6; 2005 c.702 §§5,6,7; 2007 c.129 §11; repealed by 2011 c.595 §68]

21.050 [Amended by 1969 c.198 §52; 1971 c.193 §26; repealed by 1981 s.s. c.1 §25]

21.060 [1981 s.s. c.3 §81; 1983 c.308 §1; 1985 c.496 §16; 1995 c.658 §23; 1997 c.801 §§49,49a; 1997 c.872 §1; renumbered 21.325 in 1997]

21.070 [1981 s.s. c.3 §82; 1983 c.763 §40; renumbered 21.335 in 1997]

CIRCUIT COURT FEES

(Filing Fees)

21.100 Filing fees payable in advance. A pleading or other document may be filed by the circuit court only if the filing fee required by law is paid by the person filing the document or a request for a fee waiver or deferral is granted by the court. Filing fees are not refundable under any circumstances. Unless otherwise specifically provided by statute, the filing fee for an action or proceeding is the only fee or charge that may be collected for the filing, whether by the court or any other public body, as defined by ORS 174.109. [2011 c.595 §4]

21.105 Caption of pleading; amended pleadings. (1) The caption of any complaint or other document filed in a circuit court for the purpose of commencing an action or other civil proceeding must include a reference to the statute that establishes the filing fee for the proceeding. If the proceeding is subject to a filing fee established under ORS 21.160, the caption must indicate the amount in controversy. If the proceeding is subject to a filing fee established under ORS 21.170 or 21.180, the caption must indicate the value of the estate.

(2) If at any time a party files an amended pleading in a proceeding that is subject to a filing fee established under ORS 21.160, 21.170 or 21.180, and the pleading increases the amount in controversy or the value of the estate in the proceeding, the caption of the pleading must note that increased amount. The court shall collect an additional filing fee from the party filing the pleading that is equal to the difference between the filing fee that was paid by the party when the original pleading was filed and the filing fee that would have been collected if the amount had been pleaded in the original pleading.

(3) If at any time the court determines that a party has failed to comply with the requirements of this section, the court may require that the party pay all fees that should have been paid at the time the document was filed. [2011 c.595 §5]

21.110 [Amended by 1955 c.458 §1; 1959 c.563 §2; 1965 c.619 §8; 1971 c.621 §1; 1975 c.607 §1; 1979 c.833 §3; 1981 s.s. c.3 §§68,69; 1983 c.581 §2; 1983 c.763 §20; 1985 c.496 §1; 1995 c.273 §8; 1995 c.658 §140; 1995 c.664 §69; 1997 c.801 §§25,25a; 2003 c.530 §4; 2003 c.737 §§8a,10a; 2005 c.702 §§9,10,11; 2007 c.129 §12; 2007 c.860 §2; 2009 c.659 §§14,16; 2009 c.885 §§37b,37c; 2010 c.107 §§28,29,31; 2011 c.271 §§5,6; 2011 c.398 §§5,6; repealed by 2011 c.595 §7]

21.111 [1997 c.801 §26; 2003 c.737 §§12,14a,14c; 2005 c.702 §§13,14,15; 2007 c.129 §13; 2007 c.666 §1; 2007 c.860 §3; repealed by 2011 c.595 §10]

21.112 [1963 c.434 §11; 1971 c.280 §20; 1975 c.607 §2; 1979 c.833 §4; 1981 c.835 §1; 1981 s.s. c.3 §70; 1983 c.671 §6; 1983 c.763 §38; 1985 c.412 §1; 1995 c.273 §9; 1997 c.475 §§5,5a; 1999 c.59 §11; 2001 c.394 §1; 2003 c.737 §107; repealed by 2011 c.595 §108]

21.114 [Formerly 21.320; 2003 c.737 §§16,17; 2005 c.702 §§17,18,19; 2007 c.129 §14; 2007 c.860 §4; repealed by 2011 c.595 §17]

21.115 [Formerly 21.210; 1965 c.619 §9; renumbered 21.375]

21.120 [Amended by 1959 c.453 §1; 1963 c.519 §6; 1965 c.619 §10; 1967 c.111 §2; 1971 c.621 §2; 1981 c.571 §1; 1981 s.s. c.3 §71; repealed by 1981 s.s. c.3 §141]

21.125 [2007 c.860 §29; 2009 c.484 §4; 2011 c.398 §2; 2011 c.595 §73; renumbered 21.200 in 2011]

21.130 [Amended by 1959 c.678 §1; 1963 c.519 §7; 1965 c.619 §11; 1967 c.111 §3; 1971 c.61 §1; 1979 c.631 §1; repealed by 1981 s.s. c.3 §141]

21.135 Standard filing fee. (1) Unless a specific fee is provided by subsection (3) of this section or other law for a proceeding, a circuit court shall collect a filing fee of $265 when a complaint or other document is filed for the purpose of commencing an action or other civil proceeding and when an answer or other first appearance is filed in the proceeding.
(2) The filing fee established by subsection (1) of this section applies to:
(a) Proceedings in which only equitable remedies are sought.
(b) Appeals from a conviction of a violation in justice or municipal courts as provided in ORS 21.285.
(c) Interpleader actions.
(d) Actions relating to a trust.

(e) Proceedings for judicial review of an agency order.

(f) Declaratory judgment actions.

(g) Any other action or proceeding that is statutorily made subject to the fee established by this section and any other civil proceeding for which a specific filing fee is not provided.

(3)(a) The circuit court shall collect a filing fee of $255 in adoption cases under ORS chapter 109, excluding readoptions under ORS 109.385, when a petition is filed for the purpose of commencing an adoption proceeding or when any other document or other first appearance is filed in the proceeding. The fee shall include the cost of issuing one or more certificates of adoption under ORS 109.410.

(b) When separate petitions for adoption of multiple minor children are concurrently filed under ORS 109.309 by the same petitioner, one filing fee shall be charged for the first petition filed and the filing fees for concurrently filed petitions shall not be charged. [2011 c.595 §8; 2013 c.685 §§30,30a; 2014 c.76 §4; 2015 c.511 §8; 2015 c.512 §1a; 2017 c.663 §2]

21.140 [Amended by 1961 c.563 §1; 1963 c.519 §8; 1965 c.619 §12; renumbered 21.350]

21.145 Simple proceeding filing fee. In the following proceedings, a circuit court shall collect a filing fee of $117 when a complaint or other document is filed for the purpose of commencing an action or other proceeding and at the time of filing an answer or other first appearance in the proceeding:

(1) Applications for change of name under ORS 33.410.

(2) Applications for a legal change of sex under ORS 33.460.

(3) Guardianship proceedings under ORS chapter 125.

(4) Any other action or proceeding that is statutorily made subject to the fee established by this section. [2011 c.595 §13; 2013 c.685 §§31,31a; 2014 c.76 §5; 2017 c.663 §3]

21.150 [Amended by 1963 c.519 §9; repealed by 1965 c.619 §39]

21.155 Domestic relations filing fee. A circuit court shall collect a filing fee of $287 when a complaint or other document is filed for the purpose of commencing one of the following proceedings and when an answer or other first appearance is filed in the proceeding:

(1) Proceedings for dissolution of marriage, annulment of marriage or separation.

(2) Filiation proceedings under ORS 109.124 to 109.230.

(3) Proceedings under ORS 108.110, 109.100 and 109.103. [2011 c.595 §11; 2013 c.685 §§32,32a; 2014 c.76 §6; 2017 c.663 §4]

21.160 Filing fee for tort and contract actions. (1) A circuit court shall collect the following filing fees when a complaint or other document is filed for the purpose of commencing an action or other civil proceeding based on a tort or contract and when an answer or other first appearance is filed in the proceeding:

(a) If the amount claimed is $10,000 or less, the court shall collect a filing fee of $165.

(b) If the amount claimed is more than $10,000 and less than $50,000, the court shall collect a filing fee of $267.

(c) If the amount claimed is $50,000 or more, and less than $1 million, the court shall collect a filing fee of $560.

(d) If the amount claimed is $1 million or more and less than $10 million, the court shall collect a fee of $834.

(e) If the amount claimed is $10 million or more, the court shall collect a filing fee of $1,111.

(2) The filing fees provided by this section apply to proceedings for the foreclosure of a mortgage, lien or other security interest. For the purposes of such proceedings, the amount claimed is the amount of the debt secured by the mortgage, lien or other security interest that is owing as of the date that the proceeding is filed.

(3) The filing fees provided by this section apply to proceedings for specific performance of a contract. For the purposes of such proceedings, the amount claimed is the amount owing under the contract on the date that the proceeding is filed.

(4) A court shall collect the filing fees provided by this section when an appeal from a justice court is filed under ORS 53.005 to 53.125 or a case is transferred from a justice court under ORS 52.320.

(5) For purposes of this section, the amount claimed in a proceeding does not include any amount claimed as attorney fees or as costs and disbursements.

(6) For purposes of this section, the amount claimed in a proceeding includes any penalty or forfeiture provided by statute or arising out of contract. [2011 c.595 §15; 2012 c.48 §2; 2013 c.685 §§33,33a; 2014 c.76 §7; 2017 c.663 §5]

21.165 Third-party complaints. (1) When a person files a third-party complaint in a civil action or proceeding in circuit court and the complaint names a defendant who has not already appeared in the proceeding, the clerk of the court shall collect from the third-party plaintiff the same filing fee that would be required of a plaintiff filing the same complaint in an original action.

(2) When a third-party defendant files an appearance in a civil action or proceeding in circuit court, and defendant has not already appeared in the action or proceeding, the clerk of the court shall collect the same filing fee that would be required of a defendant filing the same appearance in an original action. [2009 c.659 §13; 2010 c.107 §27; 2011 c.271 §§25,26; 2011 c.595 §§81,81a; 2012 c.48 §4]

21.170 Probate filing fees and accounting fees. (1) Except as provided in ORS 114.515, a probate court shall collect the following filing fees for the filing of a petition for the appointment of personal representative:

(a) If the value of the estate is less than $50,000, $265.

(b) If the value of the estate is $50,000 or more, but less than $1 million, $558.

(c) If the value of the estate is $1 million or more, but less than $10 million, $832.

(d) If the value of the estate is $10 million or more, $1,109.

(2) A probate court shall collect the following fees for an annual or final accounting filed in a probate proceeding:

(a) If the value of the estate is less than $50,000, $33.

(b) If the value of the estate is $50,000 or more, but less than $1 million, $281.

(c) If the value of the estate is $1 million or more, but less than $10 million, $558.

(d) If the value of the estate is $10 million or more, $1,109.

(3) For the purpose of determining the value of the estate under this section, the amount of a settlement in a wrongful death action brought for the benefit of the decedent's surviving spouse or dependents is not part of the estate.

(4) A person filing an appearance in a probate proceeding must pay the fee established under ORS 21.135.

(5) The fees established under this section apply to county courts exercising probate jurisdiction. [2011 c.595 §21; 2013 c.685 §§34,34a; 2014 c.76 §8; 2017 c.663 §6]

21.175 Guardianship filing fees. (1) A circuit court shall collect the filing fee established under ORS 21.145 for the filing of the initial documents in a guardianship proceeding and for filing an appearance in a guardianship proceeding.

(2) The fees established under this section apply to county courts exercising probate jurisdiction. [2011 c.595 §27]

21.180 Conservatorship filing fees and accounting fees. (1) The court shall collect the following filing fees for the filing of the initial documents in a conservatorship proceeding:

(a) If the value of the estate is less than $50,000, $265.

(b) If the value of the estate is $50,000 or more, but less than $1 million, $558.

(c) If the value of the estate is $1 million or more, but less than $10 million, $832.
(d) If the value of the estate is $10 million or more, $1,109.
(2) The court shall collect the following fees for an annual or final accounting filed in a conservatorship proceeding:
(a) If the value of the estate is less than $50,000, $33.
(b) If the value of the estate is $50,000 or more, but less than $1 million, $281.
(c) If the value of the estate is $1 million or more, but less than $10 million, $558.
(d) If the value of the estate is $10 million or more, $1,109.
(3) For the purpose of determining the value of the estate under this section, the amount of a settlement in a wrongful death action brought for the benefit of the decedent's surviving spouse or dependents is not part of the estate.
(4) Except as provided in subsection (1) of this section, at the time of filing an appearance in a conservatorship proceeding the party filing the appearance must pay the filing fee established under ORS 21.135.
(5) The fees established by this section apply to county courts exercising probate jurisdiction. [2011 c.595 §28; 2013 c.685 §§35,35a; 2014 c.76 §9; 2017 c.663 §7]

21.185 Child support cases exempt from certain filing fees. The filing fees described in ORS 21.135, 21.145, 21.155 and 21.160 may not be charged to a district attorney or to the Division of Child Support of the Department of Justice for the filing of any proceeding related to the provision of support enforcement services as described in ORS 25.080. [2011 c.595 §16a]

(Motion Fees)

21.200 Motion fees generally. (1) In any action or other proceeding subject to a fee under ORS 21.135, 21.145 or 21.160, a $105 fee must be paid by the party filing one of the following motions and by the party responding to the motion:
(a) A motion for summary judgment under ORCP 47.
(b) A motion for judgment notwithstanding the verdict under ORCP 63.
(c) A motion for new trial under ORCP 64.
(d) A motion for relief from judgment under ORCP 71.
(e) A motion for preliminary injunction under ORCP 79.
(f) A motion seeking remedies for contempt of court.
(2) The fees provided for in this section may not be collected from the state, a county, a city or a school district.
(3) The fees provided for in this section may not be collected for motions made to an arbitrator or mediator in an arbitration or mediation required or offered by a court, or to any motion relating to an arbitration or mediation required or offered by a court.
(4) The clerk shall file a motion or response that is subject to a fee under this section only if the fee required by this section is paid when the motion or response is submitted for filing. [Formerly 21.125; 2017 c.663 §12]

21.205 Motion fees in domestic relations cases. (1) In any action or other proceeding subject to a fee under ORS 21.155, a $158 fee must be paid by the party filing a motion that seeks entry of a supplemental judgment and by a party responding to the motion.
(2) The fee provided for in subsection (1) of this section does not apply to any motion under ORCP 68, 69 or 71.
(3) In any action or other proceeding subject to a fee under ORS 21.155, a $53 fee must be paid by the party filing one of the following motions and by a party responding to the motion:
(a) A motion filed under ORS 107.434; and
(b) A motion seeking remedies for contempt of court.
(4) Only the fees specified by subsection (1) of this section may be collected if a party concurrently files a motion that seeks entry of a supplemental judgment and a motion seeking remedies for contempt of court. [2011 c.595 §74; 2017 c.663 §13]

21.210 [Amended by 1955 c.458 §2; renumbered 21.115 and then 21.375]

(Fees for Settlement Conferences)

21.215 Fees for settlement conferences. (1) In any civil proceeding subject to a fee under ORS 21.155 in which the parties request a settlement conference before a judge, or in which a settlement conference before a judge is required by law or by the court, each party participating in the conference shall pay a $105 fee to the court for each day or partial day during which the conference is conducted.
(2) Notwithstanding ORS 3.428 (3), the fee required under subsection (1) of this section must be paid when parties request a settlement conference through a family law facilitation program.
(3) In civil proceedings other than those described in subsection (1) of this section, if the parties request a settlement conference before a judge, or a settlement conference before a judge is required by law or by the court, each party participating in the conference shall pay a $210 fee to the court for each day or partial day during which the conference is conducted.
(4) The fees required by this section shall be collected in advance, and are due and payable on the first day of the settlement conference. [2009 c.659 §32; 2011 c.595 §§83,83a; 2017 c.663 §15]

21.220 [Amended by 1963 c.519 §10; repealed by 1965 c.619 §39]

(Trial Fees)

21.225 Trial fees. (1) In any civil action, suit or proceeding in the circuit court, other than a protective proceeding under ORS chapter 125 or a probate, adoption or change of name proceeding, trial fees shall be collected as provided in this section.
(2) The clerk of the circuit court shall collect from the plaintiff, appellant or moving party, for a trial on the merits without a jury, a trial fee of $131 for each full or partial day of the trial. The amount of the fee for the first day of trial shall be collected in advance and is due and payable when the action, suit or proceeding is set for trial. The amount of the fee for subsequent days of trial shall be collected on the day the trial concludes.
(3)(a) The clerk shall collect from the plaintiff or appellant, for a trial by a jury of more than six persons, a jury trial fee of $236 for each full or partial day of the trial. The clerk shall collect from the plaintiff or appellant, for a trial by a jury of six persons, a jury trial fee of $158 for each full or partial day of the trial. The amount of the fee for the first day of trial shall be collected in advance and is due and payable when the action, suit or proceeding is set for trial by jury. The amount of the fee for subsequent days of trial shall be collected on the day the trial concludes.
(b) If the plaintiff or appellant waives a trial by jury, and the defendant or respondent desires a trial by jury, the clerk shall collect the jury trial fee from the defendant or respondent, and not from the plaintiff or appellant.
(c) A case in which the jury trial fee for the first day of trial has not been paid shall be tried by the court without a jury, unless the court otherwise orders. If a case in which the jury trial fee for the first day of trial has not been paid is tried by a jury, the clerk shall tax against the losing party the total amount of the jury trial fee. The jury trial fee constitutes a monetary obligation payable to the court, and may be made part of the judgment in the case by the clerk without further notice to the debtor or further order of the court.
(4) If a counterclaim, cross-claim or third party claim is tried on any day other than a day on which the claim of the plaintiff is tried, the clerk shall collect from the party asserting the counterclaim, cross-claim or third party claim the trial fee or jury trial fee, whichever is applicable, for that day, and shall not collect the applicable fee for that day from the plaintiff. If the party asserting a counterclaim, cross-claim or third party claim waives a trial by jury on the

claim, and the party defending against the claim desires a trial by jury on the claim, the clerk shall collect the jury trial fee from the defending party and not from the asserting party.

(5) The fees provided for in this section include any reporting of the trial proceedings, but not the preparation of transcripts of a report.

(6) Except as otherwise provided in subsection (3)(c) of this section, the fees provided for in this section that are paid by a party shall be considered costs and disbursements and may be taxed and collected as other costs and disbursements by the prevailing party.

(7) A court shall order that a trial fee paid under the provisions of this section be refunded to the party that paid the fee if all claims in the action or proceeding are decided without the commencement of a trial and the party that paid the fee files a motion and affidavit requesting refund of the fee not more than 15 days after entry of judgment disposing of the action or proceeding. [Formerly 21.270; 2017 c.663 §17]

21.230 [Amended by 1963 c.519 §11; repealed by 1965 c.619 §39]

(Fees for Documents and Forms)

21.235 Document fee. (1) A circuit court shall collect a fee of $17 for:
(a) Making or entering a transcript of a judgment.
(b) Preparing a certified copy of a satisfaction document under ORS 18.225 (5).
(c) Issuing notices of restitution as provided in ORS 105.151.
(d) Any other service that is statutorily made subject to the fee established in this section.
(2) A circuit court shall collect a fee of $45 for issuing a writ of execution or a writ of garnishment. [2011 c.595 §70; 2013 c.685 §§40,40a; 2014 c.76 §12; 2017 c.663 §20]

21.240 [Amended by 1959 c.563 §3; 1963 c.519 §12; repealed by 1965 c.619 §39]

21.245 Form fees. (1) The State Court Administrator may prescribe and charge a reasonable price, covering the costs of labor and material, for any forms provided by the courts of this state. The sums so collected shall be paid over to the State Treasurer and credited to the Court Forms Revolving Fund.
(2) Notwithstanding subsection (1) of this section, no charge shall be made for forms made available under the provisions of ORS 107.700 to 107.735 or 124.005 to 124.040 or ORS 163.760 to 163.777. [Formerly 21.361; 2013 c.687 §11]

21.250 [Amended by 1963 c.519 §13; repealed by 1965 c.619 §39]

21.255 Court Forms Revolving Fund. There is established in the General Fund of the State Treasury the Court Forms Revolving Fund. Moneys in the revolving fund are continuously appropriated to the Judicial Department for the purpose of paying the costs of labor and materials incurred by the courts of this state in providing forms as provided in ORS 21.245. [Formerly 21.363]

(Fees for Other Services)

21.258 Fees for other court services. (1) A circuit court may collect such fees as the Chief Justice of the Supreme Court may establish or authorize for any service the court may be required or authorized to perform and for which no fee is provided by law.
(2) A fee may not be established under this section for location or inspection of court records. [2011 c.595 §72]

(Fees Not Collectible From Public Bodies)

21.259 Fees not collectible from public bodies. The fees prescribed in ORS 21.235, and the fees established or authorized by the Chief Justice of the Supreme Court under ORS 21.258, may not be collected from the state, from the county in which the court is located or from a city in the county in which the court is located. [2012 c.48 §11]

21.260 [Amended by 1959 c.563 §4; 1963 c.519 §14; repealed by 1965 c.619 §39]

21.270 [Amended by 1963 c.519 §15; 1965 c.619 §13; 1971 c.621 §4; 1975 c.607 §4; 1979 c.833 §5; 1981 s.s. c.3 §§72,73; 1983 c.763 §21; 1985 c.496 §2; 1995 c.664 §70; 1997 c.801 §51; 2003 c.737 §§19,21; 2005 c.702 §§21,22,23; 2011 c.595 §79; renumbered 21.225 in 2011]

21.275 [1985 c.496 §4; 1995 c.664 §71; 1997 c.801 §52; 2003 c.737 §§23,24; 2005 c.702 §§25,26,27; 2007 c.129 §15; repealed by 2011 c.595 §78]

21.280 [1959 c.563 §1; 1963 c.519 §16; repealed by 1965 c.619 §39]

(Appeals From Justice Courts and Municipal Courts)

21.285 Fees payable in appeals from justice courts and municipal courts. (1) In an appeal to a circuit court from a justice court or municipal court in an action for commission of a state violation or an action for violation of a city charter or ordinance, but not in an action for commission of a state crime, the filing and trial fees required by ORS 21.135 and 21.225 are required of the appellant and respondent.
(2) Payment of fees required by subsection (1) of this section is subject to ORS 20.140.
(3) Fees required by subsection (1) of this section may be waived or deferred by a judge of the circuit court for the reason and in the manner provided in ORS 21.680 to 21.698. [Formerly 21.615]

SHERIFF AND PROCESS SERVER FEES

21.300 Sheriff and process server fees. (1) The sheriff of a county shall collect the following fees in civil actions, suits and proceedings for each case delivered to the office of the sheriff:
(a) $45 for serving a summons, a subpoena, a citation, an order, a notice, including notice of seizure and sale of personal or real property, a notice of restitution and notice of seizure under writ of attachment or execution or a similar document, including small claims or writ of execution, directed to not more than two parties at the same address. If service is requested for more than two parties at the same address, the fee is $25 for each party at the same address. The fee authorized by this paragraph shall not be charged to the state in civil actions, suits and proceedings where one party is a person who has been appointed counsel at state expense.
(b) For seizure and sale of personal or real property, enforcement of writ of execution of judgment of restitution, or other enforcement or seizure under writ of attachment or execution, or other process or proceeding, $80, and, in addition, such sums as may be reasonable and necessary for the costs of standing by in anticipation of securing custody of the property, the expense of securing each keeper or custodian of property, the expense of inventory of property and the expense incurred in advertising required by law in the sale of the property.
(c) For making a sheriff's deed, certificate of redemption or conveyance of real property sold on any process, $50, to be paid by, or for, the grantee.
(d) For making a copy of any process, order, notice or other instrument in writing, when necessary to complete the service thereof, for each folio, $3; but no charge shall be made for copy of complaint or other document not actually made by the sheriff.

(2) Persons other than a sheriff serving process and other documents may charge any fee agreed to between the server and the person requesting service.

(3) The county may retain fees collected for service by the sheriff if the party to be served cannot be found.

(4) A sheriff may not collect mileage or commission for service of any document or process but in any service involving travel in excess of 75 miles round trip a sheriff may bill and collect an additional fee not to exceed $45. Mileage shall be measured from the location at which the service is made to the circuit court in that county.

(5) Amounts paid for service of process and other documents may be recovered as costs and disbursements to the extent provided by ORS 20.115.

(6) A sheriff may not collect a fee under this section for serving a foreign restraining order or an order that only grants relief under ORS 107.095 (1)(c).

(7) As used in this section:

(a) "Folio" means 100 words, counting two figures as one word. Any portion of a folio, when the whole paper contains less than a folio, or when such portion is an excess over the last folio, shall be deemed a folio.

(b) "Foreign restraining order" means a restraining order that is a foreign judgment as defined by ORS 24.105. [Formerly 21.410; 2017 c.390 §1]

Note: Section 3, chapter 390, Oregon Laws 2017, provides:

Sec. 3. (1) On January 1, 2021, the Oregon Department of Administrative Services shall determine the cumulative percentage increase or decrease in the cost of living for the previous four years, based on changes in the Portland-Salem, OR-WA, Consumer Price Index for All Urban Consumers for All Items as published by the Bureau of Labor Statistics of the United States Department of Labor. The Oregon Department of Administrative Services shall adjust the fees under ORS 21.300 (1) and (4) as follows:

(a) If the cost of living has increased, the department shall adjust the fees by multiplying the fee amounts by the percentage amount determined under this subsection. The department shall round the adjusted fees up to the nearest $1. The adjusted fees become effective on July 1, 2021, and apply to all fees incurred on or after July 1, 2021.

(b) If the cost of living has not increased, the department may not change the fees.

(2) After the department adjusts the fees under ORS 21.300 (1) and (4) as provided in subsection (1) of this section, the department shall promptly notify the Oregon State Sheriffs' Association of the adjusted fees. [2017 c.390 §3]

21.310 [Amended by 1955 c.458 §3; 1965 c.619 §14; 1971 c.621 §5; 1973 c.506 §1; 1975 c.607 §5; 1979 c.833 §6; 1981 s.s. c.3 §74; 1985 c.496 §5; 1995 c.664 §72; 1997 c.801 §28; 2003 c.737 §§26,27; 2005 c.702 §§29,30,31; 2007 c.129 §16; repealed by 2011 c.595 §20]

21.313 [1959 c.452 §2; 1967 c.111 §4; repealed by 1969 c.591 §305]

21.315 [Formerly 21.360; repealed by 1965 c.619 §39]

21.320 [Amended by 1963 c.519 §17; 1965 c.619 §15; 1967 c.534 §10; 1971 c.621 §6; 1975 c.607 §6; 1979 c.833 §7; 1981 s.s. c.3 §§75,76; 1985 c.496 §7; 1997 c.801 §29; renumbered 21.114 in 1997]

21.325 [Formerly 21.060; 1999 c.649 §43; 2001 c.596 §42; 2003 c.737 §§29,30a,30c; 2005 c.702 §§33,34,35; 2007 c.860 §10; repealed by 2011 c.595 §69]

21.330 [Amended by 1961 c.563 §2; 1963 c.519 §18; repealed by 1965 c.619 §39]

21.335 [Formerly 21.070; repealed by 2011 c.595 §114]

21.340 [Amended by 1963 c.519 §19; repealed by 1965 c.619 §39]

TRANSCRIPT FEES

21.345 Transcript fees. (1)(a) A transcriber may not charge more than $3 per page for preparation of a transcript.

(b) A transcriber may not charge a fee in addition to the fee established under this subsection for:

(A) An electronic copy required to be served on a party;

(B) A paper copy required to be served on an unrepresented party under ORS 19.370 (4)(a) or (b); or

(C) A paper copy required to be filed with the trial court under ORS 19.370 (4)(d).

(2) Except as provided in subsection (3) of this section, a reporter employed by one of the parties may charge fees as agreed to between the reporter and all of the parties to the proceeding for preparing transcripts on appeal. The reporter and the parties must agree to the fees to be charged before the commencement of the proceeding to be recorded. A share of any fees agreed upon shall be charged to parties joining the proceeding after the commencement of the proceeding.

(3) A reporter employed by one of the parties may not charge a public body, as defined by ORS 174.109, fees for preparing transcripts on appeal that exceed the fees established by subsection (1) of this section.

(4) Each page of the original transcript on appeal prepared under this section must be prepared as specified by rules for transcripts on appeal adopted by the Supreme Court and the Court of Appeals.

(5) Except as otherwise provided by law, the fees for preparing a transcript requested by a party shall be paid forthwith by the party, and when paid shall be taxable as disbursements in the case. The fees for preparing a transcript requested by the court, and not by a party, shall be paid by the state from funds available for the purpose.

(6) When the court provides personnel to prepare transcripts from audio records of court proceedings, the fees provided in subsection (1) of this section to be paid by a party shall be paid to the clerk of the court.

(7) For purposes of this section, "transcript" has the meaning given that term in ORS 19.005. [Formerly 21.470; 2013 c.685 §7]

21.350 [Formerly 21.140; 1973 c.381 §6; 1981 s.s. c.3 §77; 1997 c.801 §46; 2007 c.860 §13; 2011 c.224 §4; repealed by 2011 c.595 §104]

21.360 [Amended by 1955 c.458 §4; renumbered 21.315]

21.361 [1991 c.790 §21; 1995 c.666 §11; renumbered 21.245 in 2011]

21.363 [1991 c.790 §22; 2005 c.22 §13; renumbered 21.255 in 2011]

21.370 [Amended by 1963 c.519 §20; repealed by 1965 c.619 §39]

21.375 [Formerly 21.210 and then 21.115; 1971 c.621 §7; 1975 c.607 §8; 1979 c.833 §8; 1981 c.883 §30; 1981 c.898 §23; 1981 s.s. c.3 §83; 1985 c.496 §17; 1995 c.559 §56; 1997 c.872 §3; renumbered 5.125 in 1997]

21.380 [Amended by 1963 c.519 §21; repealed by 1965 c.619 §39]

21.385 [Formerly 46.223; repealed by 1999 c.59 §12]

REFEREE FEES

21.400 Referee fees. The fees of referees shall be fixed by the court, but the parties may agree in writing upon any other rate of compensation and thereupon such rate shall be allowed. [Formerly 21.510]

21.410 [Amended by 1959 c.620 §1; 1965 c.619 §16; 1969 c.252 §1; 1973 c.393 §1; 1975 c.607 §9; 1977 c.547 §1; 1979 c.833 §9; 1981 c.835 §2; 1981 c.883 §31; 1989 c.910 §1; 1989 c.1053 §1; 1991 c.594 §1; 1995 c.559 §53; 1995 c.583 §1; 1997 c.202 §2; 1997 c.249 §14; 1999 c.1052 §8; 2001 c.104 §4; 2001 c.962 §86; 2003 c.304 §§6,7; 2007 c.129 §17; 2009 c.835 §1; renumbered 21.300 in 2011]

21.420 [Repealed by 2011 c.595 §114]

21.460 [Amended by 1961 c.446 §1; 1975 c.607 §10; 1979 c.833 §10; 1981 s.s. c.3 §§84,85; repealed by 1985 c.496 §32]

21.470 [Amended by 1959 c.446 §1; 1971 c.565 §15; 1973 c.195 §1; 1979 c.833 §11; 1981 s.s. c.3 §86; 1987 c.796 §1; 2005 c.164 §1; renumbered 21.345 in 2011]

21.480 [1977 c.112 §1; 1981 c.664 §1; 1983 c.114 §1; 1985 c.342 §5; 1989 c.385 §1; 1997 c.801 §§45,45a; 2003 c.737 §§92,94,96; 2003 c.791 §§8,8a; 2005 c.817 §2; 2007 c.129 §18; 2007 c.860 §24; 2010 c.107 §§33,34; repealed by 2011 c.595 §97a]

21.485 [1977 c.112 §2; 1981 c.664 §2; 1983 c.114 §2; 1985 c.342 §6; 1989 c.385 §2; repealed by 1995 c.658 §127]

21.490 [1977 c.112 §3; 1983 c.763 §39; repealed by 1997 c.801 §77]

21.510 [Renumbered 21.400 in 2011]

21.520 [1979 c.429 §1; renumbered 205.245]

21.530 [1979 c.429 §2; renumbered 205.255]

21.560 [Repealed by 1983 c.763 §24]

21.570 [Amended by 1965 c.619 §17; 1967 c.398 §6; repealed by 1983 c.763 §24]

21.580 [Amended by 1965 c.619 §18; 1981 s.s. c.3 §87; 1983 c.763 §22; 1985 c.496 §26; 1991 c.790 §3; repealed by 2011 c.595 §69]

21.590 [Repealed by 1981 s.s. c.3 §141]

21.600 [Amended by 1965 c.619 §19; 1967 c.398 §7; repealed by 1985 c.496 §32]

21.605 [1969 c.288 §1; 1973 c.67 §1; 1977 c.416 §2; 1981 s.s. c.3 §88; 1983 c.673 §24; 1985 c.342 §24; 1985 c.496 §24; 1995 c.273 §11; 1995 c.658 §25; 1999 c.367 §4; 1999 c.657 §7a; 2003 c.518 §5; 2003 c.576 §178; 2003 c.737 §85; 2007 c.129 §19; repealed by 2007 c.493 §§18,18a]

21.607 [1995 c.273 §12; 1997 c.801 §129; 1999 c.367 §17; 2003 c.576 §179; 2007 c.493 §9; renumbered 21.700 in 2007]

21.610 [Amended by 1963 c.519 §22; repealed by 1965 c.619 §39]

21.615 [1985 c.342 §27; 1999 c.1051 §120; 2007 c.493 §10; 2011 c.595 §101; renumbered 21.285 in 2011]

21.620 [Amended by 1963 c.519 §23; 1965 c.619 §20; repealed by 1981 s.s. c.3 §141]

21.630 [Repealed by 1955 c.458 §5]

21.640 [Repealed by 1955 c.458 §5]

21.650 [Repealed by 1955 c.458 §5]

21.660 [Amended by 2003 c.576 §288; repealed by 2011 c.595 §114]

21.670 [Repealed by 2011 c.595 §114]

WAIVER AND DEFERRAL OF FEES

21.680 Definitions for ORS 21.680 to 21.698. As used in ORS 21.680 to 21.698:
(1) "Applicant" means a person who applies for waiver or deferral of fees or court costs under ORS 21.680 to 21.698.
(2) "Court administrator" means:
(a) The State Court Administrator for the Supreme Court, the Court of Appeals and the Oregon Tax Court;
(b) A trial court administrator in a circuit court that has a trial court administrator; and
(c) The clerk of the court in all other courts.
(3) "Judge" means the Chief Justice of the Supreme Court, the Chief Judge of the Court of Appeals, a judge of a circuit or county court, the judge of the Oregon Tax Court, a tax court magistrate or a justice of the peace.
(4) "Obligor" means a person who has had payment of all or part of fees or court costs deferred under ORS 21.680 to 21.698. [2007 c.493 §1]

21.682 Authority to waive or defer fees and court costs; delegation. (1) A judge may waive or defer all or part of the fees and court costs payable to the court by a party in a civil action or proceeding, including sheriff's fees under ORS 21.300 (1)(a), if the judge finds that the party is unable to pay all or any part of the fees and costs. Waiver or deferral under this section of the fees or court costs of an inmate, as defined in ORS 30.642, is subject to ORS 30.642 to 30.650.

(2) A presiding judge may delegate authority to waive or defer fees and court costs under this section to the court administrator for the court in which the judge serves. A delegation of authority under this subsection must be in writing and must be subject to clear standards. If a delegation is made under this subsection, an applicant may seek review of the court administrator's decision by a judge. If an applicant requests review of a court administrator's decision, the court administrator shall forward the application for waiver or deferral of the fees or court costs to the appropriate judge.

(3) A court may not delay or refuse to enter an order or judgment in an action or proceeding because deferred fees and court costs have not been paid.

(4) The Chief Justice of the Supreme Court by order may provide standards and practices for waiver or deferral of fees or court costs under ORS 21.680 to 21.698. [2007 c.493 §2; 2009 c.484 §5]

21.685 Application for waiver or deferral of fees or court costs. Upon request of a party, a court administrator shall provide a party with an application for waiver or deferral of fees or court costs. The form of the application must be consistent with the standards prescribed by the Chief Justice of the Supreme Court under ORS 21.682 (4). The application must contain a notice that the court may enter judgment against the applicant for any deferred fees or court costs. A fee may not be charged for providing the application or for the filing of an application. [2007 c.493 §3]

21.690 Waived fees; recovery. (1) If the fees and court costs of a person have been waived under ORS 21.680 to 21.698 and the person prevails in the action or proceeding for which fees and court costs were waived, the court may include in the judgment a money award, payable by any party who is liable to the person receiving the waiver for costs and disbursements in the action or proceeding, in an amount equal to the waived fees and court costs. The money award shall be in favor of the state in courts other than justice courts and county courts. In justice courts and county courts, the money award shall be in favor of the county in which the justice court or county court is located. The judgment debtor must pay the money award amount to the court administrator.

(2) The state is liable for the payment of fees and court costs waived by a court only if a money award as described in subsection (1) of this section is entered against the state. [2007 c.493 §4]

21.692 Judgment for deferred fees and court costs. (1) In courts other than justice courts and county courts, fees and court costs deferred under ORS 21.680 to 21.698 constitute a monetary obligation of the obligor that is payable to the state. In justice courts and county courts, fees and court costs deferred under ORS 21.680 to 21.698 constitute a monetary obligation of the obligor that is payable to the county in which the justice court or county court is located. The court may render a judgment in favor of the state or county for any unpaid part of the obligation. A limited or supplemental judgment may be rendered for the obligation, or the obligation may be included in the general judgment in an action or proceeding. If the court renders a limited judgment for the obligation, the money award may be only for unpaid fees and court costs and may not include any other financial obligation. A court administrator may sign a judgment for deferred fees and costs on behalf of the court.

(2) A court may render a limited or supplemental judgment for unpaid deferred fees or costs, or include a money award for the obligation in a general judgment, without further notice to the obligor or further order of the court.

(3) An obligor subject to a judgment for unpaid fees and court costs may move for relief from the judgment based on a showing that the obligor's financial circumstances have changed since the time of the entry of the judgment such that the obligor is no longer able to pay the judgment amount. A motion for relief under this subsection must be made in the manner provided by ORCP 71 and must be made within one year after the judgment containing the money award is entered. [2007 c.493 §5]

21.695 Waiver or deferral of costs of transcript on appeal. (1) In a civil action or proceeding, the Supreme Court or the Court of Appeals may waive in whole or in part, defer in whole or in part, or partially waive and partially defer, the expense of preparing a transcript on appeal if:

(a) The party requesting the transcript is unable to pay the expense of preparing the transcript; and

(b) The party requesting the transcript makes a prima facie showing that the transcript is necessary to prosecute the appeal and would reveal reversible error in the action or proceeding.

(2) If the Supreme Court or the Court of Appeals waives or defers any part of the expense of preparing a transcript on appeal, the court shall authorize preparation of only as much of the transcript as is necessary to prosecute the appeal. The State Court Administrator shall pay the unpaid costs of preparing the transcript out of funds appropriated for that purpose.

(3) If the Supreme Court or the Court of Appeals defers payment of any part of the expense of preparing a transcript on appeal and any part of the deferred expense remains unpaid at the conclusion of the appeal, a judgment may be entered for the unpaid amount in the manner provided by ORS 21.692.

(4) If the State Court Administrator pays any costs of preparing a transcript on appeal under subsection (2) of this section and costs on appeal are awarded to the obligor, a money award to the State Court Administrator shall be included in the judgment for all waived or deferred transcript costs paid by the State Court Administrator.

(5) Waiver or deferral under this section of the transcript costs of an inmate, as defined in ORS 30.642, is subject to ORS 30.642 to 30.650. [2007 c.493 §6]

21.698 Confidentiality of information related to waiver or deferral. (1) Except as provided in subsection (2) of this section, information supplied by a person filing an application for waiver or deferral of fees or court costs, and information collected by the courts for purposes of determining eligibility for waiver or deferral of fees or costs, is confidential and may not be used for any purpose other than determining eligibility for waiver or deferral.

(2) Information described in subsection (1) of this section may be:

(a) Introduced in an action or proceeding arising out of a determination that a person is not eligible for waiver or deferral of fees or court costs;

(b) Introduced in a proceeding arising as a result of an allegation that a person has supplied false information in seeking waiver or deferral of fees or court costs;

(c) Used by a court, the Department of Revenue and the assignees of a court or the Department of Revenue for the purpose of collecting delinquent amounts owed to this state by the person providing the information; and

(d) Released pursuant to a subpoena issued as a result of an allegation that a person has supplied false information in seeking waiver or deferral of fees or court costs. [2007 c.493 §7]

21.700 Interest on judgments for deferred fees and costs; satisfaction; compromise prohibited. (1) Notwithstanding ORS 82.010, judgments resulting from the deferral of fees and court costs under the provisions of ORS 21.680 to 21.698 bear no interest.

(2) If a judge of a circuit or county court defers payment of any fees or court costs under the provisions of ORS 21.680 to 21.698, and the amount of those deferred fees or court costs is subsequently paid in full, the trial court administrator for the court shall note in the register or docket that the deferred fees and costs have been paid in full. Notation in the register or docket that deferred fees and costs have been paid in full constitutes a satisfaction of the judgment for those fees and costs.

(3) If the Chief Justice of the Supreme Court, the Chief Judge of the Court of Appeals or the judge of the Oregon Tax Court defers payment of any fees or court costs under the provisions of ORS 21.680 to 21.698, including deferral of the cost of preparing the transcript on appeal, and the amount of those deferred fees or court costs is subsequently paid in full, the State Court Administrator shall note upon the register of the court that the deferred fees and costs have been paid in full. Notation in the register that deferred fees and costs have been paid in full constitutes a satisfaction of the judgment for those fees and costs.

(4) Upon notation in the register or docket that deferred fees and costs have been paid in full, a certified copy of the notation may be filed with any circuit court or County Clerk Lien Record in which the judgment was filed under the provisions of ORS 21.680 to 21.698. Upon filing of the certified copy, the trial court administrator for the court, or the county clerk if the judgment was filed in the County Clerk Lien Record, shall cause the certified copy to be entered in the register or docket of the court or recorded in the County Clerk Lien Record.

(5) Judgments resulting from the deferral of fees and court costs under the provisions of ORS 21.680 to 21.698 may not be compromised, settled or adjusted by a trial court administrator or the State Court Administrator. [Formerly 21.607]

21.710 [Repealed by 1997 c.249 §15]

21.720 [Repealed by 1981 s.s. c.3 §141]

21.730 [Repealed by 2011 c.595 §114]

21.990 [Repealed by 2011 c.595 §114]

———————————

Chapter 22 — Bonds and Other Security Deposits

2017 EDITION

BONDS AND OTHER SECURITY DEPOSITS

PROCEDURE IN CIVIL PROCEEDINGS

22.010   State, county or city not required to furnish any bond in any action

22.020   Deposit of money, letter of credit, checks or federal or municipal obligations, in lieu of security or bond

22.030   Officers with whom deposit is made; duplicate receipts

22.040   Filing duplicate receipt

22.050   Discharge or forfeiture of bond or security; garnishment

22.060   Deposit to be in special fund or depository; interest

22.070   Redemption of money or securities; exchange of securities

22.090   Qualifications and justification of surety

22.010 State, county or city not required to furnish any bond in any action. The state, or any county or incorporated city, shall not be required to furnish any bond or undertaking upon appeal or otherwise in any action or proceeding in any court in this state in which it is a party or interested.

22.020 Deposit of money, letter of credit, checks or federal or municipal obligations, in lieu of security or bond. (1) In any cause, action, proceeding or matter before any court, board or commission in this state or upon appeal from any action of any such court, board or commission, where bond or security deposit of any character is required or permitted for any purpose, it is lawful for the party required or permitted to furnish such security or bond to deposit, in lieu thereof, in the manner provided in ORS 22.020 to 22.070, money, an irrevocable letter of credit issued by an insured institution, as defined in ORS 706.008, a certified check or checks on any state or national bank within this country payable to the officer with whom such check is filed, satisfactory municipal bonds negotiable by delivery, or obligations of the United States Government negotiable by delivery, equal in amount to the amount of the bond or security deposit so required or permitted.

(2) Notwithstanding subsection (1) of this section, an irrevocable letter of credit may not be furnished to a court in lieu of other security or bond to be deposited in any criminal offense, action, proceeding or matter before any court, in a protective proceeding under ORS chapter 125, or in any cause, action, proceeding or matter before any court under ORS 105.395 or 125.715. In any other type of civil cause, action, proceeding or matter before any court, an irrevocable letter of credit may be furnished pursuant to subsection (1) of this section subject to approval of its terms by the parties and to its being in the form and amount prescribed by statute, rule or order of the court. [Amended by 1973 c.836 §316; 1991 c.331 §8; 1995 c.664 §73; 1997 c.631 §368; 1999 c.1051 §236; 2017 c.169 §41]

22.030 Officers with whom deposit is made; duplicate receipts. (1) Any party desiring to make use of the provisions of ORS 22.020 to 22.070 shall, except as provided in subsection (2) of this section, make or cause to be made, with the treasurer of the county or city within which the bond is to be furnished, or, in any case, with the State Treasurer, the deposit authorized by ORS 22.020. The treasurer, upon tender, must accept such money or securities and deliver to the depositor a duplicate receipt reciting the fact of such deposit; provided, that in case of bond or security deposit is required after the office hours of any such treasurer with whom it is desired to make the deposit, the deposit may be made with the chief clerk of such court, board or commission or with the sheriff of the county or the deputy in charge of the county jail or the sheriff's office, who shall accept the same, giving duplicate receipts therefor, and cause such money or securities to be delivered to the proper treasurer within 48 hours thereafter.

(2) In any criminal case or in any proceeding in any court the deposit may be made with the court or clerk thereof, with the same effect and result as though made with such treasurer, and it shall not be necessary for the money or securities to be delivered to the treasurer. [Amended by 1973 c.836 §317; 1999 c.1051 §237]

22.040 Filing duplicate receipt. The filing of one of such duplicate receipts with the court, board or commission with which such bond or security deposit is required or permitted to be filed shall have the same effect as the furnishing of such bond or security deposit and shall be taken and accepted by the court, board or commission or by the chief clerk in lieu of such bond or security deposit. [Amended by 1973 c.836 §318; 1999 c.1051 §238]

22.050 Discharge or forfeiture of bond or security; garnishment. If the bond or security deposit is discharged, an order to that effect shall be entered upon the records of the court, board or commission with a statement of the amount to be returned to the person making the deposit. Upon presentation to the treasurer of a copy of such order, duly certified by the clerk of the court, board or commission making the same, the treasurer shall pay to the person named therein or to the order of the person the amount specified or shall return the securities, as the case may be. If the bond or security deposit is forfeited, an order to that effect shall be entered upon the records of the court, board or commission, and upon presentation to the treasurer of a copy of such order, certified by the chief clerk of the court, board or commission making the same, the treasurer shall make such disposition of the money or securities as the order shall provide. In case the money or securities are in the hands of the clerk of the court, board or commission at the time the bond or security deposit is declared discharged or forfeited, the clerk shall make the same disposition of the money or securities as the treasurer would be required to make in similar circumstances. Whenever the order of the court, board or commission requires or contemplates the same, the treasurer or clerk shall indorse to the proper party any certified check deposited with the treasurer or clerk as security. Money or securities deposited under ORS 22.020 to 22.070 shall not be subject to garnishment. [Amended by 1973 c.836 §319; 1999 c.1051 §239]

22.060 Deposit to be in special fund or depository; interest. Any money or securities received by any treasurer under the provisions of ORS 22.030 shall be deposited in a special fund or place of deposit subject to the order of the proper court, board or commission. Any interest accumulating upon such fund shall be paid into the general fund or corresponding fund of the state, county or city, according to the nature of the case or in accordance with the order of the proper court, board or commission; provided, however, that when bonds or other securities are deposited the interest coupons shall not be detached therefrom but shall follow the disposition of the securities.

22.070 Redemption of money or securities; exchange of securities. Any party making use of the provisions of ORS 22.020 to 22.070 may, at any time before forfeiture of the same, redeem any money or securities so deposited by submitting the bond originally required or permitted, or may exchange such securities for others of equal value if satisfactory to the officer with whom the same have been deposited. [Amended by 1999 c.1051 §240]

22.090 Qualifications and justification of surety. References in the statute laws of this state to the qualifications of a surety in a bond or undertaking as in bail on arrest and the justification of that surety are intended to be and shall be considered, except where and to the extent that the context of a reference requires otherwise, references to the qualifications and justification of a surety as provided in ORCP 82 D through G. [1981 c.898 §14]

————————————

Chapter 23 (Former Provisions)

Enforcement of Judgments and Decrees;
Executions and Exemptions

ENFORCEMENT OF JUDGMENTS; EXECUTIONS

PROCEDURE IN CIVIL PROCEEDINGS

23.005 [1999 c.788 §28; repealed by 2003 c.576 §580]

23.010 [Repealed by 1979 c.284 §199]

23.020 [Amended by 1955 c.648 §3; 1979 c.284 §61; repealed by 1981 c.898 §53]

23.030 [Amended by 1987 c.586 §12; 1989 c.768 §9; 1997 c.340 §1; 1999 c.788 §29; repealed by 2003 c.576 §580]

23.040 [Amended by 1981 c.898 §24; repealed by 2003 c.576 §580]

23.050 [Amended by 1981 c.898 §25; 1989 c.229 §14; 1999 c.80 §33; 1999 c.788 §30a; 2003 c.73 §15; repealed by 2003 c.576 §580]

23.060 [Repealed by 2003 c.576 §580]

23.070 [Repealed by 2003 c.576 §580]

23.080 [Repealed by 1981 c.898 §53]

23.090 [Repealed by 1981 c.898 §53]

23.100 [Repealed by 1989 c.229 §15]

23.105 [1989 c.229 §13; renumbered 18.312 in 2003]

23.160 [Amended by 1957 c.687 §1; 1965 c.577 §1; 1975 c.208 §1; 1981 c.903 §2; 1993 c.439 §5; 1995 c.289 §1; 1999 c.745 §1; 2001 c.249 §68; 2001 c.538 §1; 2003 c.79 §1; 2003 c.572 §1; 2003 c.576 §83; renumbered 18.345 in 2003]

23.164 [1957 c.687 §2; 1971 c.765 §1; 1975 c.208 §2; 1981 c.840 §3; 1981 c.903 §3a; 1983 c.454 §1; 1993 c.439 §1; 1999 c.135 §2; 1999 c.788 §11a; 2001 c.596 §43; 2003 c.378 §6a; renumbered 18.428 in 2003]

23.166 [1977 c.623 §4; 1979 c.814 §4; 1980 c.19 §1; 1983 c.586 §42; 1987 c.490 §48; 1989 c.356 §2; 1991 c.845 §2; 1999 c.130 §2; 2001 c.12 §9; 2001 c.249 §69; renumbered 18.348 in 2003]

23.168 [1957 c.687 §3; 1977 c.623 §5; 1981 c.840 §4; 1987 c.873 §22; 1997 c.340 §2; renumbered 18.322 in 2003]

23.170 [Amended by 1979 c.85 §1; 1985 c.671 §1; 1987 c.688 §1; 1989 c.356 §1; 1989 c.726 §1a; 1993 c.33 §277; 1993 c.798 §23; 1995 c.608 §21; 1999 c.80 §85; 1999 c.162 §1; 1999 c.745 §2; renumbered 18.358 in 2003]

23.175 [1969 c.403 §2; 1985 c.671 §2; 1989 c.726 §2; 1993 c.33 §278; 1993 c.798 §24; 1995 c.608 §22; renumbered 18.375 in 2003]

23.180 [Amended by 1957 c.550 §1; repealed by 1965 c.486 §1 (23.181 enacted in lieu of 23.180)]

23.181 [1965 c.486 §2 (enacted in lieu of 23.180); repealed by 1969 c.403 §4]

23.185 [1969 c.403 §3; 1971 c.498 §1; 1973 c.273 §1; 1973 c.519 §1; 1975 c.208 §3; 1975 c.458 §3; 1979 c.847 §1; 1981 c.883 §32; 1983 c.622 §1; 1989 c.726 §3; 1989 c.810 §11; 1991 c.845 §1; 1993 c.33 §279; 1993 c.798 §25; 1995 c.608 §23; repealed by 2001 c.249 §69a (23.186 enacted in lieu of 23.185)]

23.186 [2001 c.249 §69b (enacted in lieu of 23.185); renumbered 18.385 in 2003]

23.190 [Amended by 1959 c.671 §1; renumbered 18.318 in 2003]

23.200 [Amended by 1961 c.599 §1; 1993 c.439 §6; renumbered 18.362 in 2003]

23.210 [Renumbered 18.364 in 2003]

23.220 [Amended by 1975 c.208 §4; renumbered 18.305 in 2003]

23.230 [Renumbered 18.352 in 2003]

23.240 [Amended by 1959 c.561 §1; 1969 c.525 §1; 1975 c.208 §5; 1981 c.840 §5; 1981 c.903 §4a; 1993 c.439 §2; 1999 c.135 §1; 1999 c.788 §12a; renumbered 18.395 in 2003]

23.242 [1989 c.1007 §3; 1993 c.33 §280; 1995 c.608 §24; 1995 c.664 §74; 2003 c.576 §289; renumbered 18.398 in 2003]

23.250 [Amended by 1959 c.561 §2; 1975 c.208 §6; 1981 c.903 §5; 1993 c.439 §3; renumbered 18.402 in 2003]

23.260 [Amended by 1969 c.591 §270; 1981 c.840 §6; 1981 c.903 §6; renumbered 18.406 in 2003]

23.270 [Amended by 1959 c.561 §3; 1975 c.208 §7; repealed by 1981 c.840 §13 and 1981 c.903 §7a]

23.280 [1975 c.742 §2; 1981 c.840 §7; 1981 c.903 §8a; 1993 c.439 §4; 2003 c.576 §226; renumbered 18.412 in 2003]

23.290 [1975 c.742 §4; 1981 c.840 §8; 2003 c.576 §227; renumbered 18.415 in 2003]

23.300 [1975 c.742 §3; 1987 c.586 §13; 1999 c.788 §32a; 2003 c.576 §228; renumbered 18.422 in 2003]

23.305 [1981 c.903 §1; renumbered 18.300 in 2003]

23.310 [Amended by 1977 c.547 §2; 1981 c.898 §26; 1991 c.331 §9; renumbered 18.482 in 2003]

23.320 [Repealed by 2003 c.576 §580]

23.330 [Repealed by 2003 c.576 §580]

23.340 [Amended by 1981 c.898 §27; repealed by 2003 c.576 §580]

23.350 [Amended by 1991 c.331 §10; 1997 c.631 §369; repealed by 2003 c.576 §580]

23.410 [Amended by 2003 c.576 §79; renumbered 18.478 in 2003]

23.420 [Repealed by 1981 c.883 §1]

23.425 [1981 c.883 §35; 2001 c.249 §70; repealed by 2003 c.576 §580]

23.430 [Repealed by 1981 c.883 §1]

23.440 [Renumbered 18.486 in 2003]

23.445 [1981 c.840 §2; 1983 c.454 §2; 1983 c.463 §1; 1989 c.1007 §4; 1999 c.788 §13; 2001 c.596 §44; 2003 c.378 §7; 2003 c.576 §290; renumbered 18.536 in 2003]

23.450 [Amended by 1979 c.761 §1; 1981 c.840 §9; 1981 c.903 §9a; 1991 c.249 §3; renumbered 18.532 in 2003]

23.460 [Amended by 1971 c.120 §1; 1981 c.840 §10; renumbered 18.538 in 2003]

23.470 [Renumbered 18.542 in 2003]

23.480 [Renumbered 18.545 in 2003]

23.490 [Amended by 1959 c.638 §8; 2003 c.576 §80; renumbered 18.548 in 2003]

23.500 [Renumbered 18.555 in 2003]

23.510 [Renumbered 18.562 in 2003]

23.515 [1981 c.840 §12; renumbered 18.552 in 2003]

23.520 [Renumbered 18.565 in 2003]

23.530 [Amended by 2003 c.576 §291; renumbered 18.568 in 2003]

23.540 [Renumbered 18.572 in 2003]

23.550 [Renumbered 18.578 in 2003]

23.560 [Amended by 1979 c.562 §4; 1979 c.794 §2a; 1985 c.760 §2; 1999 c.788 §33; renumbered 18.582 in 2003]

23.570 [Amended by 1991 c.111 §2; 2003 c.576 §81; renumbered 18.585 in 2003]

23.580 [Renumbered 18.588 in 2003]

23.590 [Renumbered 18.594 in 2003]

23.600 [Renumbered 18.598 in 2003]

23.650 [1977 c.613 §1; repealed by 1981 c.883 §1]

23.655 [1977 c.613 §2; repealed by 1981 c.883 §1]

23.660 [1977 c.613 §3; repealed by 1981 c.883 §1]

23.665 [1977 c.613 §§4,5; 1979 c.761 §2; repealed by 1981 c.883 §1]

23.670 [1977 c.613 §6; 1979 c.833 §12a; repealed by 1981 c.883 §1]

23.710 [Amended by 1975 c.131 §1; 1983 c.747 §1; 1989 c.171 §3; 1995 c.38 §1; repealed by 2003 c.576 §580]

23.720 [Amended by 1975 c.131 §2; 1983 c.744 §1; 1983 c.747 §2; 1987 c.873 §23; 1991 c.724 §18; repealed by 2003 c.576 §580]

23.730 [Amended by 1987 c.873 §24; repealed by 2003 c.576 §580]

23.740 [Repealed by 1981 c.898 §53]

23.750 [Repealed by 1981 c.883 §1]

23.760 [1975 c.458 §1; 1985 c.671 §25; renumbered 25.010]

23.765 [1975 c.458 §10; 1980 c.20 §1; 1981 c.168 §1; 1981 c.596 §1; 1981 c.822 §1; 1985 c.671 §50; renumbered 25.020]

23.767 [1975 c.458 §19; 1977 c.216 §3; 1981 c.822 §2; 1981 s.s. c.3 §25; renumbered 25.030]

23.775 [1961 c.210 §1; 1963 c.497 §3; 1969 c.619 §9; 1971 c.280 §21; 1973 c.502 §12; 1981 c.822 §4; 1981 s.s. c.3 §28; renumbered 25.040]

23.777 [1975 c.458 §2; 1981 c.822 §5; renumbered 25.050]

23.778 [1979 c.343 §2; 1985 c.610 §3; renumbered 25.360]

23.780 [1961 c.210 §2; 1971 c.779 §2; renumbered 25.060]

23.783 [1975 c.458 §4; 1981 c.822 §6; renumbered 25.350]

23.785 [1961 c.210 §3; repealed by 1975 c.458 §18]

23.787 [1975 c.458 §5; 1981 c.822 §9; renumbered 25.070]

23.789 [1975 c.458 §6; 1979 c.589 §1; 1983 c.761 §8; 1985 c.671 §51; renumbered 25.080]

23.790 [1961 c.210 §4; 1981 c.822 §7; renumbered 25.090]

23.795 [1963 c.498 §2; 1969 c.619 §10; 1971 c.280 §22; 1973 c.502 §15; subsection (2) compiled as 107.400; 1973 c.524 §3; 1979 c.245 §1; 1981 s.s. c.3 §29; 1985 c.610 §5; renumbered 25.100]

23.800 [1963 c.498 §3; 1973 c.524 §2; 1979 c.245 §2; renumbered 25.110]

23.805 [1963 c.498 §4; renumbered 25.120]

23.807 [1977 c.216 §1; 1981 c.822 §8; 1981 s.s. c.3 §30; renumbered 25.130]

23.808 [1981 c.822 §10; 1981 s.s. c.3 §27; renumbered 25.140]

23.809 [1977 c.216 §2; repealed by 1981 c.822 §12]

23.810 [Repealed by 1981 c.898 §53]

23.815 [1981 c.822 §3; 1981 s.s. c.3 §26; renumbered 25.150]

23.820 [Repealed by 1981 c.898 §53]

23.825 [1981 c.822 §11; renumbered 25.160]

23.830 [Repealed by 1981 c.898 §53]

23.835 [1983 c.761 §1; renumbered 25.170]

23.837 [1983 c.761 §2; renumbered 25.180]

23.840 [Repealed by 1981 c.898 §53]

23.842 [1983 c.761 §3; renumbered 25.190]

23.845 [1983 c.761 §4; renumbered 25.200]

23.847 [1983 c.761 §5; renumbered 25.210]

23.850 [Repealed by 1981 c.898 §53]

23.855 [1983 c.767 §3; renumbered 25.220]

23.860 [Repealed by 1981 c.898 §53]

23.865 [1983 c.761 §7; renumbered 25.230]

23.870 [Repealed by 1981 c.898 §53]

23.880 [Repealed by 1981 c.898 §53]

23.890 [Repealed by 1981 c.898 §53]

23.900 [Repealed by 1981 c.898 §53]

23.910 [Repealed by 1981 c.898 §53]

23.920 [Repealed by 1981 c.898 §53]

23.930 [Repealed by 1981 c.898 §53]

Chapter 24 —— Enforcement and Recognition of Foreign Judgments; Foreign-Money Claims

2017 EDITION

FOREIGN JUDGMENTS; FOREIGN-MONEY CLAIMS

PROCEDURE IN CIVIL PROCEEDINGS

UNIFORM ENFORCEMENT OF FOREIGN JUDGMENTS ACT

24.105   Definitions for ORS 24.105 to 24.125, 24.135 and 24.155 to 24.175

24.115   Filing of foreign judgment; effect

24.125   Notice of filing of judgment; delay in enforcement

24.129   Certification of filing in single court; filing of certified copy or lien record abstract for other counties

24.135   Grounds for staying enforcement of judgment; security for satisfaction of judgment

24.140   Interest and costs

24.150   Satisfaction of judgment; filing

24.155   Optional procedure

24.165   Construction of ORS 24.105 to 24.125, 24.135 and 24.155 to 24.175

24.175   Short title

FOREIGN RESTRAINING ORDERS

24.190   Foreign restraining orders

UNIFORM FOREIGN-MONEY CLAIMS ACT

24.260   Definitions for ORS 24.260 to 24.335

24.265   Scope of application of ORS 24.260 to 24.335

24.270   Variation of application by agreement

24.275   Determining proper money of the claim

24.280   Determining amount of money of certain contract claims

24.285   Asserting and defending foreign-money claim

24.290   Judgments and awards on foreign-money claims; times of money conversion; form of judgment; post-judgment enforcement

24.295   Conversions of foreign money in distribution proceeding

24.300   Prejudgment and judgment interest

24.305   Enforcement of foreign judgments

24.310   Determining United States dollar value of foreign-money claims for limited purposes

24.315   Effect of currency substitution

24.320   Supplementary general principles of law

24.325   Uniformity of application and construction

24.330   Severability

24.335   Short title

UNIFORM FOREIGN-COUNTRY MONEY JUDGMENTS RECOGNITION ACT

24.350   Definitions for ORS 24.350 to 24.400

24.355   Applicability to judgments

24.360   Standards for recognition of foreign-country judgment

24.365   Personal jurisdiction

24.370   Procedure for recognition of foreign-country judgment

24.375   Effect of recognition of foreign-country judgment

24.380   Stay of proceedings pending appeal of foreign-country judgment

24.385   Statute of limitations

24.390   Uniformity of interpretation

24.395   Saving clause

24.400   Short title

24.010 [1955 c.647 §1; repealed by 1979 c.577 §8]

24.020 [1955 c.647 §2; repealed by 1979 c.577 §8]

24.030 [1955 c.647 §3; repealed by 1979 c.577 §8]

24.040 [1955 c.647 §4; repealed by 1979 c.577 §8]

24.050 [1955 c.647 §5; repealed by 1979 c.577 §8]

24.060 [1955 c.647 §6; repealed by 1979 c.577 §8]

24.070 [1955 c.647 §7; repealed by 1979 c.577 §8]

24.080 [1955 c.647 §8; repealed by 1979 c.577 §8]

24.090 [1955 c.647 §9; repealed by 1979 c.577 §8]

24.100 [1955 c.647 §10; repealed by 1979 c.577 §8]

UNIFORM ENFORCEMENT OF FOREIGN JUDGMENTS ACT

24.105 Definitions for ORS 24.105 to 24.125, 24.135 and 24.155 to 24.175. In ORS 24.105 to 24.125, 24.135 and 24.155 to 24.175 "foreign judgment" means any judgment, decree or order of a court of the United States or of any other court which is entitled to full faith and credit in this state. [1979 c.577 §1]

24.110 [1955 c.647 §11; repealed by 1979 c.577 §8]

24.115 Filing of foreign judgment; effect. (1) A copy of any foreign judgment authenticated in accordance with the Act of Congress or the statutes of this state may be filed in the office of the clerk of any circuit court of any county of this state. Except as otherwise provided by law, the person filing the copy of the foreign judgment must pay the filing fee established under ORS 21.135. The clerk shall treat the foreign judgment in the same manner as a judgment of the circuit court.

(2) A certified copy of any foreign judgment authenticated in accordance with the Act of Congress or the statutes of this state shall be recorded in the County Clerk Lien Record of any county other than the county in which the judgment is originally filed, in order to become a lien upon the real property of the judgment debtor in that county as provided in ORS 18.152.

(3) A judgment so filed has the same effect and is subject to the same procedures, defenses and proceedings for reopening, vacating or staying as a judgment of the circuit court in which the foreign judgment is filed, and may be enforced or satisfied in like manner.

(4) A foreign judgment of a tribal court of a federally recognized Indian tribe that is filed in a circuit court under this section, and that otherwise complies with 26 U.S.C. 414(p) as a domestic relations order as defined in 26 U.S.C. 414(p), is a domestic relations order made pursuant to the domestic relations laws of this state for the purposes of 26 U.S.C. 414(p). [1979 c.577 §2; 1985 c.343 §5; 1987 c.586 §14; 1995 c.273 §13; 2003 c.576 §180; 2007 c.663 §1; 2011 c.595 §32]

24.120 [1955 c.647 §12; repealed by 1979 c.577 §8]

24.125 Notice of filing of judgment; delay in enforcement. (1) At the time of the filing of the foreign judgment, the judgment creditor or the creditor's lawyer shall make and file with the clerk of the court an affidavit setting forth the names and last-known post-office addresses of the judgment debtor and the judgment creditor, together with a separate statement containing the information required to be contained in a judgment under ORS 18.042.

(2) Promptly after filing the foreign judgment and the affidavit, the judgment creditor must mail notice of the filing of the foreign judgment to the judgment debtor. The notice shall include the name and post-office address of the judgment creditor and the judgment creditor's lawyer, if any, in this state. The judgment creditor must file with the court proof of mailing the notice.

(3) No execution or other process for enforcement of a foreign judgment filed pursuant to ORS 24.105 to 24.125, 24.135 and 24.155 to 24.175, except a judgment, decree or order of a court of the United States, shall issue until five days after the date the judgment, affidavit and separate statement required in subsection (1) of this section are filed. [1979 c.577 §3; 1985 c.343 §6; 1987 c.873 §25; 1989 c.768 §8; 1997 c.872 §7; 2003 c.576 §168]

24.129 Certification of filing in single court; filing of certified copy or lien record abstract for other counties. At the time of filing of any foreign judgment as provided in ORS 24.115, the judgment creditor shall certify that the judgment creditor is filing such judgment in only one court in Oregon. Thereafter, a certified copy of the judgment or a lien record abstract may be recorded in the County Clerk Lien Record of any other county in this state as provided in ORS 18.152. [1985 c.343 §9; 1987 c.586 §15; 2003 c.576 §574]

24.130 [1955 c.647 §13; repealed by 1979 c.577 §8]

24.135 Grounds for staying enforcement of judgment; security for satisfaction of judgment. (1) If the judgment debtor shows the court of any county that an appeal from the foreign judgment is pending or will be taken, or that a stay of execution has been granted, the court shall stay enforcement of the foreign judgment until the appeal is concluded, the time for appeal expires, or the stay of execution expires or is vacated, upon proof that the judgment debtor has furnished the security for the satisfaction of the judgment required by the state in which it was rendered.

(2) If the judgment debtor shows the court of any county any ground upon which enforcement of a judgment of any court of any county of this state would be stayed, the court shall stay enforcement of the foreign judgment for an appropriate period, upon requiring the same security for satisfaction of the judgment which is required in this state.

(3) Any person making an appearance in proceedings related to foreign judgments filed under ORS 24.115, including a judgment debtor filing a proceeding seeking a stay of judgment under this section or otherwise seeking relief from enforcement of the judgment, must pay the filing fee established under ORS 21.160 (1)(a). [1979 c.577 §4; 2011 c.595 §33; 2017 c.663 §7a]

24.140 Interest and costs. When a registered foreign judgment becomes a final judgment of this state, the court shall include as part of the judgment interest payable on the foreign judgment under the law of the state in which it was rendered, and the cost of obtaining the authenticated copy of the original judgment. The court shall include as part of its judgment court costs incidental to the proceeding in accordance with the law of this state and the costs of recording documents as permitted by statute. [1955 c.647 §14; 1987 c.586 §16]

24.150 Satisfaction of judgment; filing. Satisfaction, either partial or complete, of the original judgment or of a judgment entered thereupon in any other state shall operate to the same extent as satisfaction of the judgment in this state, except as to costs authorized by ORS 24.140. When such judgment in this state has been satisfied, including costs authorized by ORS 24.140, it shall be the responsibility of the judgment creditor to provide an executed satisfaction to this judgment debtor. The judgment debtor may file the satisfaction in the records of the court in which the judgment was originally filed in this state, and may record the satisfaction in every county in this state in which a certified copy of the judgment or a lien record abstract has been recorded. [1955 c.647 §15; 1985 c.343 §7; 1987 c.586 §17]

24.155 Optional procedure. The right of a judgment creditor to bring an action to enforce the judgment instead of proceeding under ORS 24.105 to 24.125, 24.135 and 24.155 to 24.175 remains unimpaired. [1979 c.577 §5]

24.160 [1955 c.647 §16; repealed by 1979 c.577 §8]

24.165 Construction of ORS 24.105 to 24.125, 24.135 and 24.155 to 24.175. ORS 24.105 to 24.125, 24.135 and 24.155 to 24.175 shall be interpreted and construed in order to effectuate its general purpose to make uniform the law of those states which enact it. [1979 c.577 §6]

24.170 [1955 c.647 §17; repealed by 1979 c.577 §8]

24.175 Short title. ORS 24.105 to 24.125, 24.135 and 24.155 to 24.175 may be cited as the Uniform Enforcement of Foreign Judgments Act. [1979 c.577 §7]

24.180 [1955 c.647 §18; repealed by 1979 c.577 §8]

24.185 [1991 c.222 §1; 1993 c.188 §9; 1997 c.863 §1; repealed by 1999 c.250 §5]

FOREIGN RESTRAINING ORDERS

24.190 Foreign restraining orders. (1) For the purposes of this section:
(a) "Foreign restraining order" means a restraining order that is a foreign judgment as defined by ORS 24.105.
(b)(A) "Restraining order" means an injunction or other order issued for the purpose of preventing:
(i) Violent or threatening acts or harassment against another person;
(ii) Contact or communication with another person; or
(iii) Physical proximity to another person.
(B) "Restraining order" includes temporary and final orders, other than support or child custody orders, issued by a civil or criminal court regardless of whether the order was obtained by filing an independent action or as a pendente lite order in another proceeding. However, for a civil order to be considered a restraining order, the civil order must have been issued in response to a complaint, petition or motion filed by or on behalf of a person seeking protection.
(2)(a) Except as otherwise provided in paragraph (b) of this subsection, immediately upon the arrival in this state of a person protected by a foreign restraining order, the foreign restraining order is enforceable as an Oregon order without the necessity of filing and continues to be enforceable as an Oregon order without any further action by the protected person.
(b) A foreign restraining order is not enforceable as an Oregon order if:
(A) The person restrained by the order shows that:
(i) The court that issued the order lacked jurisdiction over the subject matter or lacked personal jurisdiction over the person restrained by the order; or
(ii) The person restrained by the order was not given reasonable notice and an opportunity to be heard under the law of the jurisdiction in which the order was issued; or
(B) The foreign restraining order was issued against a person who had petitioned for a restraining order unless:
(i) The person protected by the foreign restraining order filed a separate petition seeking the restraining order; and
(ii) The court issuing the foreign restraining order made specific findings that the person was entitled to the order.
(3)(a) A person protected by a foreign restraining order may present a true copy of the order to a county sheriff for entry into the Law Enforcement Data System maintained by the Department of State Police. Subject to paragraph (b) of this subsection, the county sheriff shall enter the order into the Law Enforcement Data System if the person certifies that the order is the most recent order in effect between the parties and provides proof of service or other written certification that the person restrained by the order has been personally served with a copy of the order or has actual notice of the order. Entry into

the Law Enforcement Data System constitutes notice to all law enforcement agencies of the existence of the restraining order. Law enforcement agencies shall establish procedures adequate to ensure that an officer at the scene of an alleged violation of the order may be informed of the existence and terms of the order. The order is fully enforceable as an Oregon order in any county or tribal land in this state.

(b) The Department of State Police shall specify information that is required for a foreign restraining order to be entered into the Law Enforcement Data System.

(c) At the time a county sheriff enters an order into the Law Enforcement Data System under paragraph (a) of this subsection, the sheriff shall also enter the order into the databases of the National Crime Information Center of the United States Department of Justice.

(4) Pending a contempt hearing for alleged violation of a foreign restraining order, a person arrested and taken into custody pursuant to ORS 133.310 may be released as provided in ORS 135.230 to 135.290. Unless the order provides otherwise, the security amount for release is $5,000.

(5) ORS 24.115, 24.125, 24.129, 24.135, 24.140, 24.150 and 24.155 do not apply to a foreign restraining order.

(6) A person protected by a foreign restraining order may file a certified copy of the order and proof of service in the office of the clerk of any circuit court of any county of this state. A judgment so filed has the same effect and is subject to the same procedures, defenses and proceedings for reopening, vacating or staying as a judgment of the circuit court in which the foreign judgment is filed, and may be enforced or satisfied in like manner. The court may not collect a filing fee for a filing under this section. [1999 c.250 §1; 2003 c.737 §§74,75; 2011 c.595 §117]

24.200 [1977 c.61 §1; 1991 c.67 §3; repealed by 2009 c.48 §14]

24.210 [1977 c.61 §7; repealed by 2009 c.48 §14]

24.220 [1977 c.61 §§2,3,4; 2003 c.281 §2; repealed by 2009 c.48 §14]

24.230 [1977 c.61 §6; repealed by 2009 c.48 §14]

24.240 [1977 c.61 §5; repealed by 2009 c.48 §14]

24.250 [1977 c.61 §8; repealed by 2009 c.48 §14]

24.255 [1977 c.61 §9; repealed by 2009 c.48 §14]

UNIFORM FOREIGN-MONEY CLAIMS ACT

24.260 Definitions for ORS 24.260 to 24.335. For the purposes of ORS 24.260 to 24.335:

(1) "Action" means a judicial proceeding or arbitration in which a payment in money may be awarded or enforced with respect to a foreign-money claim.

(2) "Bank-offered spot rate" means the spot rate of exchange at which a bank will sell foreign money at a spot rate.

(3) "Conversion date" means the banking day next preceding the date on which money, in accordance with ORS 24.260 to 24.335, is:

(a) Paid to a claimant in an action or distribution proceeding;

(b) Paid to the official designated by law to enforce a judgment or award on behalf of a claimant; or

(c) Used to recoup, setoff or counterclaim in different moneys in an action or distribution proceeding.

(4) "Distribution proceeding" means a judicial or nonjudicial proceeding for the distribution of a fund in which one or more foreign-money claims is asserted and includes an accounting, an assignment for the benefit of creditors, a foreclosure, the liquidation or rehabilitation of a corporation or other entity, and the distribution of an estate, trust or other fund.

(5) "Foreign money" means money other than money of the United States of America.

(6) "Foreign-money claim" means a claim upon an obligation to pay, or a claim for recovery of a loss, expressed in or measured by a foreign money.

(7) "Money" means a medium of exchange for the payment of obligations or a store of value authorized or adopted by a government or by intergovernmental agreement.

(8) "Money of the claim" means the money determined as proper pursuant to ORS 24.275.

(9) "Person" means an individual, a corporation, government or governmental subdivision or agency, business trust, joint venture, partnership, association, two or more persons having a joint or common interest or any other legal or commercial entity.

(10) "Rate of exchange" means the rate at which money of one country may be converted into money of another country in a free financial market convenient to or reasonably usable by a person obligated to pay or to state a rate of conversion. If separate rates of exchange apply to different kinds of transactions, the term means the rate applicable to the particular transaction giving rise to the foreign-money claim.

(11) "Spot rate" means the rate of exchange at which foreign money is sold by a bank or other dealer in foreign exchange for immediate or next day availability or for settlement by immediate payment in cash or equivalent, by charge to an account, or by an agreed delayed settlement not exceeding two days.

(12) "State" means a state of the United States, the District of Columbia, the Commonwealth of Puerto Rico or a territory or insular possession subject to the jurisdiction of the United States. [1991 c.202 §2; 2009 c.294 §1]

24.265 Scope of application of ORS 24.260 to 24.335. (1) ORS 24.260 to 24.335 apply only to a foreign-money claim in an action or distribution proceeding.

(2) ORS 24.260 to 24.335 apply to foreign-money issues even if other law under the conflict of laws rules of this state applies to other issues in the action or distribution proceeding. [1991 c.202 §3]

24.270 Variation of application by agreement. (1) The effect of ORS 24.260 to 24.335 may be varied by agreement of the parties made before or after commencement of an action or distribution proceeding or the entry of judgment. The right of the parties to vary the effect of ORS 24.260 to 24.335 includes, but is not limited to, the selection of the date and time for conversion or of a specified rate of exchange to be applied to a particular transaction or a portion thereof and, after the entry of judgment, any agreement as to how the judgment is to be satisfied.

(2) Parties to a transaction may agree upon the money to be used in a transaction giving rise to a foreign-money claim and may agree to use different moneys for different aspects of the transaction. Stating the price in a foreign money for one aspect of a transaction does not alone require the use of that money for other aspects of the transaction. [1991 c.202 §4]

24.275 Determining proper money of the claim. (1) The money in which the parties to a transaction have agreed that payment is to be made is the proper money of the claim for payment.

(2) If the parties to a transaction have not otherwise agreed, the money of the claim, as in each case may be appropriate, is the money:

(a) Regularly used between the parties as a matter of usage or course of dealing;

(b) Used at the time of a transaction in international trade, by trade usage or common practice, for valuing or settling transactions in the particular commodity or service involved; or

(c) In which the loss was ultimately felt or will be incurred by the party claimant. [1991 c.202 §5]

24.280 Determining amount of money of certain contract claims. (1) If an amount contracted to be paid in a foreign money is measured by a specified amount of a different money, the amount to be paid is determined on the conversion date.

(2) If an amount contracted to be paid in a foreign money is to be measured by a different money at the rate of exchange prevailing on a date before default, that rate of exchange applies only to payments made within a reasonable time after default, not exceeding 30 days. Thereafter, conversion is made at the bank-offered spot rate on the conversion date.

(3) A monetary claim is neither usurious nor unconscionable because the agreement on which it is based provides that the amount of the debtor's obligation to be paid in the debtor's money, when received by the creditor, must equal a specified amount of the foreign money of the country of the creditor. If, because of unexcused delay in payment of a judgment or award, the amount received by the creditor does not equal the amount of the foreign money specified in the agreement, the court or arbitrator shall, upon the motion of any party, amend the judgment or award accordingly. [1991 c.202 §6]

24.285 Asserting and defending foreign-money claim. (1) A person may assert a claim in a specified foreign money. If a foreign-money claim is not asserted, the claimant makes the claim in United States dollars.

(2) An opposing party may allege and prove that a claim, in whole or in part, is in a different money than that asserted by the claimant.

(3) A person may assert a defense, setoff, recoupment or counterclaim in any money without regard to the money of other claims.

(4) The determination of the proper money of the claim is a question of law. [1991 c.202 §7]

24.290 Judgments and awards on foreign-money claims; times of money conversion; form of judgment; post-judgment enforcement. (1) Except as provided in subsection (3) of this section, a judgment or award on a foreign-money claim must be stated in an amount of the money of the claim.

(2) A judgment or award on a foreign-money claim is payable in that foreign money or, at the option of the debtor, in the amount of United States dollars which will purchase that foreign money on the conversion date at a bank-offered spot rate, except that any payment made through a court pursuant to ORS 18.235 must be made in United States dollars. When a payment is made to the court, the judgment debtor shall simultaneously file with the court an affidavit or certificate executed in good faith by its counsel or a bank officer stating the rate of exchange used and how it was obtained and setting forth the calculation and the amount of the money of the claim that will be satisfied by the payment. Affected court officials incur no liability, after a filing of the affidavit or certificate, for acting as if the judgment were in the amount of United States dollars stated in the affidavit or certificate.

(3) Assessed costs, disbursements and attorney fees must be entered in United States dollars.

(4) Each payment in United States dollars must be accepted and credited on a judgment or award on a foreign-money claim in the amount of the foreign money that could be purchased by the dollars at a bank-offered spot rate of exchange at or near the close of business on the conversion date for that payment.

(5) A judgment or award made in an action or distribution proceeding on both a defense, setoff, recoupment or counterclaim and the adverse party's claim, must be netted by converting the money of the smaller into the money of the larger, and by subtracting the smaller from the larger, and specify the rates of exchange used.

(6) A judgment or award substantially complies with subsection (1) of this section when it is plainly titled as a judgment, it complies with the requirements of ORS 18.038 and it includes all of the following:

(a) The names of the judgment creditor, the judgment creditor's attorney and the judgment debtor.

(b) The amount of the judgment in the foreign money of the claim, the type of foreign money and the foreign country, as defined in ORS 24.350, utilizing the money that the claim is denominated in.

(c) The interest owed to the date of the judgment, either as a specific amount in the foreign money or as accrual information, including the rate or rates of interest as determined by ORS 24.300, the balance or balances upon which the interest accrues, the date or dates from which interest at each rate on each balance runs, and whether interest is simple or compounded and, if compounded, at what intervals.

(d) Post-judgment interest accrual information, including the rate or rates of interest as determined by ORS 24.300, the balance or balances upon which interest accrues, the date or dates from which interest at each rate on each balance runs, and whether interest is simple or compounded and, if compounded, at what intervals.

(e) For judgments that accrued on a periodic basis, any accrued arrearages, required further payments per period in the foreign money and accrual dates.

(f) A statement that the judgment debtor has the option to pay the judgment or award, including the interest owed on the date of judgment and the post-judgment interest, unless the parties have agreed otherwise as according to ORS 24.270, in the amount of United States dollars that will purchase that foreign money on the conversion date at a bank-offered spot rate at or near the close of business on the banking day before the day of payment.

(g) A statement that, if the judgment debtor pays the judgment through a court under ORS 18.235, the payment must be in United States dollars as provided in subsection (2) of this section.

(h) The amount of assessed costs, disbursements and attorney fees in United States dollars, if they are awarded, and any specific amounts awarded. This paragraph does not require inclusion of specific amounts where such will be determined later under ORCP 68 C.

(i) The terms of any agreement made by the parties, before the entry of the judgment, to vary the effect of ORS 24.260 to 24.335.

(7) If a contract claim is of the type covered by ORS 24.280 (1) or (2), the judgment or award must be entered for the amount of money stated to measure the obligation to be paid in the money specified for payment or, at the option of the debtor, the number of United States dollars which will purchase the computed amount of the money of payment on the conversion date at a bank-offered spot rate.

(8) When a judgment is given on a foreign-money claim in circuit court, the clerk shall enter the judgment in the register and shall note that the judgment creates a judgment lien. The judgment shall have the same force and effect as any other judgment obtained in the circuit court.

(9) A judgment or award may be discharged by payment.

(10) A party seeking enforcement of a judgment entered as provided in this section shall file with each request or application an affidavit or certificate executed in good faith by its counsel or a bank officer, stating the rate of exchange used and how it was obtained and setting forth the calculation and the amount of United States dollars that would satisfy the judgment on the date of the affidavit or certificate by applying said rate of exchange. Affected court officials incur no liability, after a filing of the affidavit or certificate, for acting as if the judgment were in the amount of United States dollars stated in the affidavit or certificate. The computation contained in the affidavit or certificate shall remain in effect for 60 days following the filing of the affidavit or certificate and may be recomputed before the expiration of 60 days by the filing of additional affidavits or certificates provided that recomputation shall not affect any payment obtained before the filing of the recomputation. [1991 c.202 §8; 1993 c.545 §114; 1995 c.658 §26; 2003 c.576 §181; 2009 c.48 §13]

24.295 Conversions of foreign money in distribution proceeding. The rate of exchange prevailing at or near the close of business on the day the distribution proceeding is initiated governs all exchanges of foreign money in a distribution proceeding. A foreign-money claimant in a distribution proceeding shall assert its claim in the named foreign money and show the amount of United States dollars resulting from a conversion as of the date the proceeding was initiated. [1991 c.202 §9]

24.300 Prejudgment and judgment interest. (1) With respect to a foreign-money claim, recovery of prejudgment or preaward interest and the rate of interest to be applied in the action or distribution proceeding, except as provided in subsection (2) of this section, are matters of the substantive law governing the right to recovery under the conflict of laws rules of this state.

(2) The court or arbitrator shall increase or decrease the amount of prejudgment or preaward interest otherwise payable in a judgment or award in foreign money to the extent required by the law of this state governing a failure to make or accept an offer of settlement or offer of judgment, or conduct by a party or its attorney causing undue delay or expense.

(3) A judgment or award on a foreign-money claim bears interest at the rate applicable to judgments of this state. [1991 c.202 §10]

24.305 Enforcement of foreign judgments. (1) If an action is brought to enforce a judgment of another jurisdiction expressed in a foreign money and the judgment is recognized in this state as enforceable, the enforcing judgment must be entered as provided in ORS 24.290, whether or not the foreign judgment confers an option to pay in an equivalent amount of United States dollars.

(2) A foreign judgment may be entered in the register in accordance with any rule or statute of this state providing a procedure for its recognition and enforcement.

(3) A satisfaction or partial payment made upon the foreign judgment, on proof thereof, shall operate to the same extent as a satisfaction of the judgment in this state, except as to costs authorized by ORS 24.140, notwithstanding the entry of judgment in this state.

(4) A judgment entered on a foreign-money claim only in United States dollars in another state must be enforced in this state in United States dollars only. [1991 c.202 §11; 2003 c.576 §182]

24.310 Determining United States dollar value of foreign-money claims for limited purposes. (1) Computations under this section are for the limited purposes of the section and do not affect computation of the United States dollar equivalent of the money of the judgment for the purpose of payment.

(2) For the limited purpose of facilitating the enforcement of provisional remedies in an action, the value in United States dollars of assets to be seized or restrained pursuant to a writ of attachment, garnishment, execution or other legal process, the amount of the United States dollars at issue for assessing costs or the amount of United States dollars involved for a surety bond or other court-required undertaking, must be ascertained as provided in subsections (3) and (4) of this section.

(3) A party seeking process, costs, bond or other undertaking under subsection (2) of this section shall compute in United States dollars the amount of the foreign money claimed from a bank-offered spot rate prevailing at or near the close of business on the banking day next preceding the filing of a request or application for the issuance of process or for the determination of costs, or an application for a bond or other court-required undertaking.

(4) A party seeking the process, costs, bond or other undertaking under subsection (2) of this section shall file with each request or application an affidavit or certificate executed in good faith by its counsel or a bank officer, stating the market quotation used and how it was obtained and setting forth the calculation. Affected court officials incur no liability, after a filing of the affidavit or certificate, for acting as if the judgment were in the amount of United States dollars stated in the affidavit or certificate. [1991 c.202 §12]

24.315 Effect of currency substitution. (1) If, after an obligation is expressed or a loss is incurred in a foreign money, the country issuing or adopting that money substitutes a new money in place of that money, the obligation or the loss is treated as if expressed or incurred in the new money at the rate of conversion the issuing country establishes for the payment of like obligations or losses denominated in the former money.

(2) If substitution under subsection (1) of this section occurs after a judgment or award is entered on a foreign-money claim, the court or arbitrator shall amend, upon the motion of any party, the judgment or award by a like conversion of the former money. [1991 c.202 §13]

24.320 Supplementary general principles of law. Unless displaced by particular provisions of ORS 24.260 to 24.335, the principles of law and equity, including the law merchant, and the law relative to capacity to contract, principal and agent, estoppel, fraud, misrepresentation, duress, coercion, mistake, bankruptcy or other validating or invalidating causes supplement its provisions. [1991 c.202 §14]

24.325 Uniformity of application and construction. ORS 24.260 to 24.335 shall be applied and construed to effectuate its general purpose to make uniform the law with respect to the subject of ORS 24.260 to 24.335 among states enacting it. [1991 c.202 §15]

24.330 Severability. If any provision of ORS 24.260 to 24.335 or its application to any person or circumstance is held invalid, the invalidity does not affect other provisions or applications of ORS 24.260 to 24.335 which can be given effect without the invalid provision or application, and to this end the provisions of ORS 24.260 to 24.335 are severable. [1991 c.202 §17]

24.335 Short title. ORS 24.260 to 24.335 may be cited as the Uniform Foreign-Money Claims Act. [1991 c.202 §16]

UNIFORM FOREIGN-COUNTRY MONEY JUDGMENTS RECOGNITION ACT

24.350 Definitions for ORS 24.350 to 24.400. As used in ORS 24.350 to 24.400:
(1) "Foreign country" means a government other than:
(a) The United States;
(b) A state, district, commonwealth, territory or insular possession of the United States; or
(c) Any other government with regard to which the decision in this state as to whether to recognize a judgment of that government's courts is initially subject to determination under the Full Faith and Credit Clause of the United States Constitution.
(2) "Foreign-country judgment" means a judgment of a court of a foreign country. [2009 c.48 §1]

24.355 Applicability to judgments. (1) Except as provided in subsection (2) of this section, ORS 24.350 to 24.400 apply to a foreign-country judgment to the extent that the judgment:
(a) Grants or denies recovery of a sum of money; and
(b) Under the law of the foreign country where rendered, is final, conclusive and enforceable.
(2) ORS 24.350 to 24.400 do not apply to a foreign-country judgment, even if the judgment grants or denies recovery of a sum of money, to the extent that the judgment is:
(a) A judgment for taxes;
(b) A fine or other penalty; or
(c) A judgment for divorce, support or maintenance, or other judgment rendered in connection with domestic relations.
(3) A party seeking recognition of a foreign-country judgment has the burden of establishing that ORS 24.350 to 24.400 apply to the foreign-country judgment. [2009 c.48 §2]

Note: Section 12, chapter 48, Oregon Laws 2009, provides:
Sec. 12. Sections 1 to 11 of this 2009 Act [24.350 to 24.400] apply only to actions commenced on or after the effective date of this 2009 Act [January 1, 2010] in which the issue of recognition of a foreign-country judgment is raised. Any action commenced before the effective date of this 2009 Act in which the issue of recognition of a foreign-country judgment is raised shall continue to be governed by the provisions of ORS 24.200 to 24.255, as those statutes were in effect immediately before the effective date of this 2009 Act. [2009 c.48 §12]

24.360 Standards for recognition of foreign-country judgment. (1) Except as provided in subsections (2) and (3) of this section, a court of this state shall recognize a foreign-country judgment to which ORS 24.350 to 24.400 apply.
(2) A court of this state may not recognize a foreign-country judgment if:
(a) The judgment was rendered under a judicial system that does not provide impartial tribunals or procedures compatible with the requirements of due process of law;
(b) The foreign court did not have personal jurisdiction over the defendant; or
(c) The foreign court did not have jurisdiction over the subject matter.
(3) A court of this state need not recognize a foreign-country judgment if:
(a) The defendant in the proceeding in the foreign court did not receive notice of the proceeding in sufficient time to enable the defendant to defend;
(b) The judgment was obtained by fraud that deprived the losing party of an adequate opportunity to present the party's case;
(c) The judgment or the claim for relief on which the judgment is based is repugnant to the public policy of this state or of the United States;
(d) The judgment conflicts with another final and conclusive judgment;

(e) The proceeding in the foreign court was contrary to an agreement between the parties under which the dispute in question was to be determined other than by proceedings in that foreign court;

(f) In the case of jurisdiction based only on personal service, the foreign court was a seriously inconvenient forum for the trial of the action;

(g) The judgment was rendered in circumstances that raise substantial doubt about the integrity of the rendering court with respect to the judgment; or

(h) The specific proceeding in the foreign court leading to the judgment was not compatible with the requirements of due process of law.

(4) A party resisting recognition of a foreign-country judgment has the burden of establishing that a ground for nonrecognition stated in subsection (2) or (3) of this section exists. [2009 c.48 §3]

24.365 Personal jurisdiction. (1) A foreign-country judgment may not be refused recognition for lack of personal jurisdiction if:

(a) The defendant was served with process personally in the foreign country;

(b) The defendant voluntarily appeared in the proceeding other than for the purpose of protecting property seized or threatened with seizure in the proceeding or for the purpose of contesting the jurisdiction of the court over the defendant;

(c) The defendant, before the commencement of the proceeding, had agreed to submit to the jurisdiction of the foreign court with respect to the subject matter involved;

(d) The defendant was domiciled in the foreign country when the proceeding was instituted or was a corporation or other form of business organization that had its principal place of business in, or was organized under the laws of, the foreign country;

(e) The defendant had a business office in the foreign country and the proceeding in the foreign court involved a claim for relief arising out of business done by the defendant through that office in the foreign country; or

(f) The defendant operated a motor vehicle or airplane in the foreign country and the proceeding involved a claim for relief arising out of that operation.

(2) The list of bases for personal jurisdiction in subsection (1) of this section is not exclusive. The courts of this state may recognize bases for personal jurisdiction other than those listed in subsection (1) of this section as sufficient to support a foreign-country judgment. [2009 c.48 §4]

24.370 Procedure for recognition of foreign-country judgment. (1) If recognition of a foreign-country judgment is sought as an original matter, the issue of recognition shall be raised by filing an action seeking recognition of the foreign-country judgment.

(2) If recognition of a foreign-country judgment is sought in a pending action, the issue of recognition may be raised by counterclaim, cross-claim or affirmative defense. [2009 c.48 §5]

24.375 Effect of recognition of foreign-country judgment. If the court in a proceeding under ORS 24.370 finds that the foreign-country judgment is entitled to recognition under ORS 24.350 to 24.400, then, to the extent that the foreign-country judgment grants or denies recovery of a sum of money, the foreign-country judgment is:

(1) Conclusive between the parties to the same extent as the judgment of another state entitled to full faith and credit in this state is conclusive; and

(2) Enforceable in the same manner and to the same extent as a judgment rendered in this state. [2009 c.48 §6]

24.380 Stay of proceedings pending appeal of foreign-country judgment. If a party establishes that an appeal from a foreign-country judgment is pending or that an appeal will be taken, the court may stay any proceedings with regard to the foreign-country judgment until the appeal is concluded, the time for appeal expires or the appellant has had sufficient time to prosecute the appeal and has failed to do so. [2009 c.48 §7]

24.385 Statute of limitations. An action to recognize a foreign-country judgment must be commenced within the earlier of the time during which the foreign-country judgment is effective in the foreign country or 15 years from the date that the foreign-country judgment became effective in the foreign country. [2009 c.48 §8]

24.390 Uniformity of interpretation. In applying and construing ORS 24.350 to 24.400, consideration must be given to the need to promote uniformity of the law with respect to its subject matter among states that enact it. [2009 c.48 §9]

24.395 Saving clause. ORS 24.350 to 24.400 do not prevent the recognition under principles of comity or otherwise of a foreign-country judgment not within the scope of ORS 24.350 to 24.400. [2009 c.48 §10]

24.400 Short title. ORS 24.350 to 24.400 may be cited as the Uniform Foreign-Country Money Judgments Recognition Act. [2009 c.48 §11]

Chapter 25 — Support Enforcement

2017 EDITION

SUPPORT ENFORCEMENT

PROCEDURE IN CIVIL PROCEEDINGS

GENERAL PROVISIONS

25.010   Definitions for support enforcement laws

25.011   "Address" defined

25.015   When payment on support order begins; determining; notification of date

25.020   When support payment to be made to Department of Justice; collection agency services; duties of department; credit for payments not made to department; rules

25.025   Annual notice to parties receiving services under ORS 25.020

25.030   When payment payable to bank account or escrow agent

25.070   Order may include payment of support enforcement fees; limitation

25.075   Cooperative agreements with Indian tribes or tribal organizations

25.080   Entity primarily responsible for support enforcement services; duties; application fees; rules

25.081   Access to records with Social Security number

25.082   Administrative subpoenas; civil penalty; rules

25.083   High-volume automated administrative enforcement services

25.084   Assignment of rights or written application required for services; incorporation in judgment

25.085   Service on obligee; methods

25.088   Effect of dismissal of judicial proceeding on existing administrative order of support

25.089   Enforcement and modification of child support judgments

25.091   Multiple child support judgments

25.095   Later-issued child support judgment

25.100   Designation of auxiliary court in county where party resides or property located

25.110   Jurisdiction of designated auxiliary court

25.125   Disposition of support obligation overpayments; liquidated debts in favor of state; rules

25.130   Election of alternative support payment method; termination of election

25.140   Copies of new or modified support orders to department

25.150   Department to collect fees for services

25.160   Referral of support cases to department; duration of collection services

25.164   Payment of support through Department of Justice; application

25.165   Application of support payments; rules

25.166   Support payment due dates

25.167   Procedure for determining arrearages

25.170   Proceedings to require delinquent obligor to appear for examination of financial circumstances

25.180   Examination of obligor's financial circumstances

25.190   Continuance of proceedings; certification of matter to court; service of notice to obligor and obligee

25.200   Arrest of obligor for failure to appear

25.210   Use of obligor's property for delinquent support payments

25.213   Assignment of proceeds of insurance policy to secure support obligation

25.220   Computer printouts of administrator; evidence of authenticity not required in support proceedings; evidentiary effect

25.230   Court authorized to require security for support payments

25.240   Order to pay support by parent with legal custody of minor

25.243   Grievance procedure; rules

25.245   Rebuttable presumption of inability to pay child support when parent receiving certain assistance payments; rules

25.247   Rebuttable presumption of inability to pay child support when obligor incarcerated

25.260   Confidentiality of records; rules

25.265   Access to information in Federal Parent Locator Service; rules

FORMULA FOR DETERMINING AMOUNT OF CHILD SUPPORT

25.270   Legislative findings

25.275   Formula for determining child support awards; criteria to be considered; mandated standards; reduction; rules

25.280   Formula amount presumed correct; rebuttal of presumption; criteria

25.287   Proceedings to modify orders to comply with formula; when proceeding may be initiated; issues considered

25.290   Determining disposable income of obligor; offsets; rules

MEDICAL SUPPORT

25.321   Definitions for ORS 25.321 to 25.343

25.323   Medical support

25.325   Enforcing medical support; form of notice; rules

25.327   Service of medical support notice

25.329   Actions required after service of medical support notice; rules

25.331   Obligation to withhold

25.333   Contesting medical support notice

25.335   Termination of support order

25.337   Liability

25.339   Priority of medical support notice

25.341   Notice of termination of employer's relationship with providing party

25.342   Rules

25.343   Authorization for reimbursement payments

INCOME WITHHOLDING AND PAYMENT RECORDS

25.372   Applicability

25.375   Priority of withholding

25.378   Payment of support by income withholding; initiation of income withholding

25.381   Establishing income withholding as method of paying support; records

25.384   Statement on withholding in support order

25.387   Withholding more than amount authorized by law

25.390   Amendment of support order not required for withholding

25.393   Remedy additional to other remedies

25.396   Exception to withholding; termination of withholding; rules

25.399   Notice of order to withhold; contents of notice

25.402   Service of order on withholder; contents

25.405   Contesting order to withhold; basis

25.408   Withholding is continuing obligation

25.411   When withholding begins; payment to Department of Justice or obligee

25.414   Standard amount to be withheld; processing fee; rules

25.417   Amount to be withheld when obligor paid more frequently than monthly

25.421   Procedure if withholder does not withhold support

25.424   Liability of withholder; action against withholder; penalty; attorney fees; unlawful employment practice

25.427   Rules

INCOME TAX INTERCEPT

25.610   Procedure to collect support orders from state tax refunds; voluntary withholding; rules

25.620   Procedures to collect past due support from state tax refunds; fees

25.625   Federal tax offset; passport denial; rules

DISCLOSURES OF INFORMATION BY FINANCIAL INSTITUTIONS

25.640   Definitions for ORS 25.643 and 25.646

25.643   Disclosure of information on obligors by financial institutions; fees; liability; rules

25.646   Disclosure of financial records of customers by financial institutions; liability

CONSUMER REPORTING AGENCIES

25.650   Information on past due support to consumer reporting agencies; rules

LIENS ON PERSONAL PROPERTY

25.670   Judgment lien on personal property

25.680   Effect of lien; priority

25.690   Foreclosure of lien

MISCELLANEOUS

25.710   Duty of district attorney

25.715   Child support paid from security deposit

25.720   When support assignable

25.725   Child Support Deposit Fund

25.727   Garnishing income of person required to provide health insurance for child eligible under Medicaid

25.729   Application of laws to effectuate purposes of ORS chapter 110

SUSPENSION OF OCCUPATIONAL AND DRIVER LICENSES

25.750   Suspension of licenses, certificates, permits and registrations; when authorized; rules

25.752   Memberships in professional organizations that are required by state law

25.756   Identifying persons holding licenses, certificates, permits and registrations

25.759   Notice to persons subject to suspension; contents

25.762   Agreement between obligor and administrator; effect of failure to contest suspension or to enter into agreement

25.765   Procedure if obligor contacts administrator within time limits; hearing

25.768   Judicial review of order

25.771   Obligor holding more than one license, certificate, permit or registration

25.774   Reinstatement

25.777   Reimbursing issuing entities for costs incurred

25.780   Other licenses, certificates, permits and registrations subject to suspension

25.783   Confidentiality of information

25.785   Issuing entities to require Social Security number

EMPLOYER REPORTING PROGRAM

25.790   Hiring or rehiring individual; report required; contents

25.792   Confidentiality

25.793   Disclosure of employer-reported information

25.794   Verification of employment; information about compensation and benefits; rules

PENALTIES

25.990   Penalties

GENERAL PROVISIONS

25.010 Definitions for support enforcement laws. As used in ORS chapters 25, 107, 109 and 416 and any other statutes providing for support payments or support enforcement procedures, unless the context requires otherwise:
    (1) "Administrator" means either the Administrator of the Division of Child Support of the Department of Justice or a district attorney, or the administrator's or a district attorney's authorized representative.
    (2) "Child" has the meaning given that term in ORS 110.503.
    (3) "Child support rights" means the right to establish or enforce an obligation imposed or imposable by law to provide support, including but not limited to medical support as defined in ORS 25.321 and an unsatisfied obligation to provide support.
    (4) "Department" means the Department of Justice.

(5) "Disposable income" means that part of the income of an individual remaining after the deduction from the income of any amounts required to be withheld by law except laws enforcing spousal or child support and any amounts withheld to pay medical or dental insurance premiums.

(6) "Employer" means any entity or individual who engages an individual to perform work or services for which compensation is given in periodic payments or otherwise.

(7) "Income" is any monetary obligation in excess of $4.99 after the fee described in ORS 25.414 (6) has been deducted that is in the possession of a third party owed to an obligor and includes but is not limited to:

(a) Compensation paid or payable for personal services whether denominated as wages, salary, commission, bonus or otherwise;

(b) Periodic payments pursuant to a pension or retirement program;

(c) Cash dividends arising from stocks, bonds or mutual funds;

(d) Interest payments;

(e) Periodic payments from a trust account;

(f) Any program or contract to provide substitute wages during times of unemployment or disability;

(g) Any payment pursuant to ORS chapter 657; or

(h) Amounts payable to independent contractors.

(8) "Obligee" has the meaning given that term in ORS 110.503.

(9) "Obligor" has the meaning given that term in ORS 110.503.

(10) "Order to withhold" means an order or other legal process that requires a withholder to withhold support from the income of an obligor.

(11) "Public assistance" has the meaning given that term in ORS 416.400.

(12) "Withholder" means any person who disburses income and includes but is not limited to an employer, conservator, trustee or insurer of the obligor. [Formerly 23.760; 1991 c.362 §1; 1993 c.798 §4; 1995 c.608 §1; 1997 c.704 §13; 1999 c.80 §1; 2001 c.334 §2; 2001 c.455 §1; 2003 c.572 §2; 2005 c.560 §1; 2009 c.351 §4; 2015 c.298 §85]

25.011 "Address" defined. As used in ORS chapters 25, 106, 107, 108, 109, 110 and 416, when a person is required to provide an address, "address" means a residence, mailing or contact address in the same state as the person's home. [1993 c.448 §1; 1995 c.608 §25]

Note: 25.011 was enacted into law by the Legislative Assembly but was not added to or made a part of ORS chapter 25 or any series therein by legislative action. See Preface to Oregon Revised Statutes for further explanation.

25.015 When payment on support order begins; determining; notification of date. (1) The Department of Justice shall notify the parties to a support order that payment is to commence on the first due date following the date of the notice when:

(a) The department receives a copy of a support order of a court that requires payments to be made through the department or for which there is an application for support enforcement services;

(b) The department commences accounting services; and

(c) The order has been entered within the previous 180 days.

(2) The department shall include in the notice under subsection (1) of this section a statement that the department will adjust the account to reflect an accrued arrearage for the period of time between the effective date of the order and the period for which there is an notice, a party requests that the department establish the arrearage on the account as provided in ORS 25.167 or 416.429.

(3) If, within 30 days after the date of the notice under subsection (1) of this section, a party requests the department to establish the arrearage as provided in ORS 25.167 or 416.429, the department may not reflect an accrued arrearage on the account until the arrearage has been established.

(4) If a party does not request the department to establish the arrearage as provided in subsection (3) of this section, the department shall adjust the account to reflect the arrearage for the period of time between the effective date of the order and the date of the notice. [1997 c.500 §2; 1999 c.18 §4; 2011 c.318 §15]

25.020 When support payment to be made to Department of Justice; collection agency services; duties of department; credit for payments not made to department; rules. (1) Support payments for or on behalf of any person that are ordered, registered or filed under this chapter or ORS chapter 107, 108, 109, 110, 416, 419B or 419C, unless otherwise authorized by ORS 25.030, shall be made to the Department of Justice as the state disbursement unit:

(a) During periods for which support is assigned under ORS 412.024, 418.032, 419B.406 or 419C.597;

(b) As provided by rules adopted under ORS 180.345, when public assistance is provided to a person who receives or has a right to receive support payments on the person's own behalf or on behalf of another person;

(c) After the assignment of support terminates for as long as amounts assigned remain owing;

(d) For any period during which support enforcement services are provided under ORS 25.080;

(e) When ordered by the court under ORS 419B.400;

(f) When a support order that is entered or modified on or after January 1, 1994, includes a provision requiring the obligor to pay support by income withholding; or

(g) When ordered by the court under any other applicable provision of law.

(2)(a) The Department of Justice shall disburse payments, after lawful deduction of fees and in accordance with applicable statutes and rules, to those persons and entities that are lawfully entitled to receive such payments.

(b) During a period for which support is assigned under ORS 412.024, for an obligee described in subsection (1)(b) of this section, the department shall disburse to the obligee, from child support collected each month, $50 for each child up to a maximum of $200 per family.

(3)(a) When the administrator is providing support enforcement services under ORS 25.080, the obligee may enter into an agreement with a collection agency, as defined in ORS 697.005, for assistance in collecting child support payments.

(b) The collection agency:

(A) May provide investigative and location services to the obligee and disclose relevant information from those services to the administrator for purposes of providing support enforcement services under ORS 25.080;

(B) May not charge interest or a fee for its services exceeding 29 percent of each support payment received unless the collection agency, if allowed by the terms of the agreement between the collection agency and the obligee, hires an attorney to perform legal services on behalf of the obligee;

(C) May not initiate, without written authorization from the administrator, any enforcement action relating to support payments on which support enforcement services are provided by the administrator under ORS 25.080; and

(D) Shall include in the agreement with the obligee a notice printed in type size equal to at least 12-point type that provides information on the fees, penalties, termination and duration of the agreement.

(c) The administrator may use information disclosed by the collection agency to provide support enforcement services under ORS 25.080.

(4) The Department of Justice may immediately transmit to the obligee payments received from any obligor without waiting for payment or clearance of the check or instrument received if the obligor has not previously tendered any payment by a check or instrument that was not paid or was dishonored.

(5) The Department of Justice shall notify each obligor and obligee by mail when support payments shall be made to the department and when the obligation to make payments in this manner shall cease.

(6)(a) The administrator shall provide information about a child support account directly to a party to the support order regardless of whether the party is represented by an attorney. As used in this subsection, "information about a child support account" means the:

(A) Date of issuance of the support order.

(B) Amount of the support order.

(C) Dates and amounts of payments.

(D) Dates and amounts of disbursements.

(E) Payee of any disbursements.

(F) Amount of any arrearage.

(G) Source of any collection, to the extent allowed by federal law.

(b) Nothing in this subsection limits the information the administrator may provide by law to a party who is not represented by an attorney.

(7) Any pleading for the entry or modification of a support order must contain a statement that payment of support under a new or modified order will be by income withholding unless an exception to payment by income withholding is granted under ORS 25.396.

(8)(a) Except as provided in paragraphs (d) and (e) of this subsection, a judgment or order establishing parentage or including a provision concerning support must contain:

(A) The residence, mailing or contact address, final four digits of the Social Security number, telephone number and final four digits of the driver license number of each party;

(B) The name, address and telephone number of all employers of each party;

(C) The names and dates of birth of the joint children of the parties; and

(D) Any other information required by rule adopted by the Chief Justice of the Supreme Court under ORS 1.002.

(b) The judgment or order shall also include notice that the obligor and obligee:

(A) Must inform the court and the administrator in writing of any change in the information required by this subsection within 10 days after the change; and

(B) May request that the administrator review the amount of support ordered after three years, or such shorter cycle as determined by rule of the Department of Justice, or at any time upon a substantial change of circumstances.

(c) The administrator may require of the parties any additional information that is necessary for the provision of support enforcement services under ORS 25.080.

(d)(A) Upon a finding, which may be made ex parte, that the health, safety or liberty of a party or child would unreasonably be put at risk by the disclosure of information specified in this subsection or by the disclosure of other information concerning a child or party to a parentage or support proceeding or if an existing order so requires, a court or administrator or administrative law judge, when the proceeding is administrative, shall order that the information not be contained in any document provided to another party or otherwise disclosed to a party other than the state.

(B) The Department of Justice shall adopt rules providing for similar confidentiality for information described in subparagraph (A) of this paragraph that is maintained by an entity providing support enforcement services under ORS 25.080.

(e) The Chief Justice of the Supreme Court may, in consultation with the Department of Justice, adopt rules under ORS 1.002 to designate information specified in this subsection as confidential and require that the information be submitted through an alternate procedure to ensure that the information is exempt from public disclosure under ORS 192.355.

(9)(a) Except as otherwise provided in paragraph (b) of this subsection, in any subsequent child support enforcement action, the court or administrator, upon a showing of diligent effort made to locate the obligor or obligee, may deem due process requirements to be met by mailing notice to the last-known residential, mailing or employer address or contact address as provided in ORS 25.085.

(b) Service of an order directing an obligor to appear in a contempt proceeding is subject to ORS 33.015 to 33.155.

(10) Subject to ORS 25.030, this section, to the extent it imposes any duty or function upon the Department of Justice, shall be deemed to supersede any provisions of ORS chapters 107, 108, 109, 110, 416, 419A, 419B and 419C that would otherwise impose the same duties or functions upon the county clerk or the Department of Human Services.

(11) Except as provided for in subsections (12), (13) and (14) of this section, credit may not be given for payments not made to the Department of Justice as required under subsection (1) of this section.

(12) The Department of Justice shall give credit for payments not made to the department:

(a) When payments are not assigned to this or another state and the obligee and obligor agree in writing that specific payments were made and should be credited, limited to the current balance owed to the obligee;

(b) When payments are assigned to another state and that state verifies that payments not paid to the department were received by the other state; or

(c) As provided by rule adopted under ORS 180.345.

(13) An obligor may apply to the Department of Justice for credit for payments made other than to the Department of Justice. If the obligee or other state does not provide the agreement or verification required by subsection (12) of this section, credit may be given pursuant to order of an administrative law judge assigned from the Office of Administrative Hearings after notice and opportunity to object and be heard are given to both obligor and obligee. Notice shall be served upon the obligee as provided by ORS 25.085. Notice to the obligor may be by regular mail at the address provided in the application for credit. A hearing conducted under this subsection is a contested case hearing and ORS 183.413 to 183.470 apply. Any party may seek a hearing de novo in the circuit court.

(14) Nothing in this section precludes the Department of Justice from giving credit for payments not made to the department when there has been a judicially determined credit or satisfaction or when there has been a satisfaction of support executed by the person to whom support is owed.

(15) The Department of Justice shall adopt rules that:

(a) Direct how support payments that are made through or credited by the department are to be applied and, if applicable, disbursed; and

(b) Are consistent with federal regulations. [Formerly 23.765; 1991 c.724 §19; 1993 c.33 §366; 1993 c.448 §2; 1993 c.596 §1; 1995 c.608 §2; 1997 c.704 §14; 1999 c.18 §1; 1999 c.80 §42; 1999 c.798 §1; 2001 c.322 §1; 2001 c.455 §§2,3; 2001 c.961 §1; 2003 c.73 §17a; 2003 c.75 §23; 2003 c.380 §§6,7; 2003 c.421 §§1,2; 2003 c.572 §3; 2003 c.576 §§292,293a; 2005 c.561 §2; 2007 c.861 §10; 2007 c.878 §1; 2009 c.352 §3; 2015 c.197 §4; 2017 c.463 §1; 2017 c.467 §3; 2017 c.651 §8]

25.025 Annual notice to parties receiving services under ORS 25.020. Once each year, the Department of Justice shall notify the parties in child support cases receiving services under ORS 25.020 of all the following:

(1) When physical custody of a child changes from the obligee to the obligor, the obligation to pay child support for the child is not automatically terminated.

(2) When a physical change of custody of a child occurs, either party may request a modification of the support order to terminate support based on a substantial change of circumstances.

(3) At the request of either party, child support may be established for the parent with current physical custody of the child.

(4) If a change in the physical custody of a child is temporary, the obligee may satisfy support accruing for the child for periods that the child is in the physical custody of the obligor as provided in ORS 18.225, 18.228, 18.232 and 18.235. [1997 c.385 §4; 2003 c.73 §18; 2003 c.576 §575]

Note: 25.025 was enacted into law by the Legislative Assembly but was not added to or made a part of ORS chapter 25 or any series therein by legislative action. See Preface to Oregon Revised Statutes for further explanation.

25.030 When payment payable to bank account or escrow agent. (1) Support orders in respect of obligees not subject to ORS 25.020 may provide for payment under the order to a checking or savings account or by electronic transfer to an account maintained by an escrow agent, licensed under ORS 696.511, for distribution to the obligee, if the obligor and obligee have so elected or if the court in its discretion believes that payment to a checking or savings account or payment by electronic transfer to an account maintained by a licensed escrow agent will be in the best interest of the parties.

(2) Subsection (1) of this section applies only if an election has been made as provided in ORS 25.130. [Formerly 23.767; 1989 c.976 §36; 1991 c.230 §32; 1997 c.872 §4; 1999 c.80 §78; 2003 c.210 §1]

25.040 [Formerly 23.775; 1993 c.33 §281; 1993 c.448 §3; repealed by 1999 c.80 §95]

25.050 [Formerly 23.777; 1989 c.633 §4; 1989 c.726 §4; 1991 c.519 §1; repealed by 1993 c.798 §21]

25.060 [Formerly 23.780; repealed by 1999 c.80 §95]

25.070 Order may include payment of support enforcement fees; limitation. Any judgment or order entered in a proceeding for the enforcement of any delinquent support obligation, including an order entered under ORS 25.378, shall include, on the motion of the Division of Child Support of the Department of Justice or the district attorney, if either has appeared in the case, an order for payment of any support enforcement fees required by law in addition to any other costs chargeable to the obligor, and in addition to the support obligation. The Department of Justice shall deduct the amount of any previously imposed support enforcement fees from any payment subsequently made by the obligor but the amount of the deduction shall not exceed 25 percent of any payment. The support enforcement fee, when collected, shall be paid to the Division of Child Support of the Department of Justice or the district attorney, whichever appeared in the case. [Formerly 23.787; 1993 c.798 §34; 1997 c.704 §15; 1999 c.80 §79; 2003 c.576 §294]

25.075 Cooperative agreements with Indian tribes or tribal organizations. (1) Notwithstanding the provisions of ORS 25.080, the Department of Justice may enter into cooperative agreements with Indian tribes or tribal organizations within the borders of this state, if the Indian tribe or tribal organization demonstrates that the tribe or organization has an established tribal court system or a Court of Indian Offenses with the authority to:
(a) Establish parentage;
(b) Establish, modify and enforce support orders; and
(c) Enter support orders in accordance with child support guidelines established by the tribe or organization.
(2) The agreements must provide for the cooperative delivery of child support enforcement services and for the forwarding of all child support collections pursuant to the functions performed by the tribe or organization to the department, or conversely, by the department to the tribe or organization, which shall distribute the child support collections in accordance with the agreement. [1997 c.746 §131; 1999 c.735 §5; 2003 c.73 §19; 2017 c.651 §9]

Note: 25.075 was enacted into law by the Legislative Assembly but was not added to or made a part of ORS chapter 25 or any series therein by legislative action. See Preface to Oregon Revised Statutes for further explanation.

25.080 Entity primarily responsible for support enforcement services; duties; application fees; rules. (1) The following entity is primarily responsible for providing the support enforcement services described in subsection (4) of this section when an application as described in ORS 25.084 is made, or when an assignment of support rights is made to the state:
(a) The Division of Child Support of the Department of Justice:
(A) If support rights are, or were within the past five months, assigned to this or another state; or
(B) In any case where arrearage under a support order is assigned or owed to or the right to recover back support or state debt is held by this state or another state.
(b) Except as provided in subsection (6) of this section, the district attorney in cases other than those described in paragraph (a) of this subsection if an application as described in ORS 25.084 is made by the obligee, by the obligor, by a person having physical custody of a minor child or by a child attending school, as defined in ORS 107.108.
(2) The provisions of this section apply to support enforcement services for any order or judgment that is or could be entered under ORS 419B.400 or 419C.590 or ORS chapter 107, 108, 109, 110 or 416. The entity specified in subsection (1) of this section shall provide the support enforcement services on behalf of the State of Oregon and not on behalf of any other party or on behalf of a parent. The Department of Justice shall adopt rules addressing the provision of support enforcement services when the purposes of the state in providing those services may be contradictory in individual cases.
(3) Notwithstanding the division of responsibility for providing support enforcement services between the Division of Child Support and the district attorney as described in subsection (1) of this section, provision of support enforcement services may not be challenged on the basis that the entity providing the services in a particular case is not the entity responsible for the case under subsection (1) of this section.
(4) When responsible for providing support enforcement services and there is sufficient evidence available to support the action to be taken, the entity described in subsection (1) of this section:
(a) Shall establish and enforce any child support obligation;
(b) Shall establish paternity;
(c) Shall enforce spousal support when the obligee is living with the obligor's child for whom support enforcement services are being provided and those services are funded in part by federal moneys;
(d) May enforce any other order or judgment for spousal support;
(e) Shall, on behalf of the state, initiate and respond to child support modification proceedings based upon a substantial change of circumstances;
(f) Shall, on behalf of the state, initiate and respond to child support modification proceedings based upon a modification conducted under ORS 25.287 concerning existing child support orders;
(g) Shall establish and enforce obligations to provide medical insurance coverage for dependent children;
(h) Shall ensure compliance with the provisions of 42 U.S.C. 651 to 669 and 45 C.F.R. Chapter III as authorized by state law;
(i) Shall carry out the policy of the State of Oregon regarding child support obligations as expressed in ORS 416.405; and
(j) Shall ensure that child support orders are in compliance with the formula established by this chapter.
(5) In any proceeding under subsection (4) of this section, the parties are those described in ORS 416.407.
(6) The district attorney of any county and the department may provide by agreement for assumption by the Division of Child Support of the functions of the district attorney under subsection (1) of this section or for redistribution between the district attorney and the Division of Child Support of all or any portion of the duties, responsibilities and functions set forth in subsections (1) and (4) of this section.
(7) All county governing bodies and all district attorneys shall enter into child support cooperative agreements with the department. The following apply to this subsection:
(a) The agreements shall contain appropriate terms and conditions sufficient for the state to comply with all child support enforcement service requirements under federal law; and
(b) If this state loses any federal funds due to the failure of a county governing body or district attorney to either enter into an agreement under this subsection or to provide sufficient support enforcement service, the county shall be liable to the department for, and the liability shall be limited to, the amount of money the state determines it lost because of the failure. The state shall offset the loss from any moneys the state is holding for or owes the county or from any moneys the state would pay to the county for any purpose.
(8) The Department of Justice shall enter into an agreement with the Oregon District Attorneys Association to establish a position or positions to act as a liaison between the Division of Child Support and those district attorneys who provide support enforcement services under this section. The department shall fund the position or positions. The Oregon District Attorneys Association shall administer the liaison position or positions under the agreement. The liaison shall work to:
(a) Enhance the participation and interaction of the district attorneys in the development and implementation of Child Support Program policies and services; and
(b) Increase the effectiveness of child support enforcement services provided by the district attorneys.
(9) The district attorney or the Division of Child Support, whichever is appropriate, shall provide the services specified in subsections (1) and (4) of this section to any applicant, but may in their discretion, upon a determination and notice to the applicant that the prospect of successful recovery from the obligor of a portion of the delinquency or future payments is remote, require payment to the district attorney or the Division of Child Support of an application fee, in accordance with an application fee schedule established by rule by the department. If service performed results in the district attorney or the Division of Child Support recovering any support enforcement fees, the fees shall be paid to the applicant in an amount equal to the amount of the application fee.

(10) An obligee may request the Division of Child Support or a district attorney to cease all collection efforts if it is anticipated that physical or emotional harm will be caused to the parent or caretaker relative or the child for whom support was to have been paid. The department, by rule, shall set out the circumstances under which such requests shall be honored. [Formerly 23.790; 1991 c.758 §1; 1993 c.33 §367; 1995 c.608 §9; 1997 c.704 §16; 2001 c.900 §236; 2003 c.73 §20; 2003 c.576 §295; 2005 c.560 §2; 2009 c.352 §4]

25.081 Access to records with Social Security number. (1) Notwithstanding any other provision of law, an entity providing support enforcement services under ORS 25.080 shall have access, using a Social Security number as an identifier, to any record required by law to contain the Social Security number of an individual.

(2) To the maximum extent feasible, a public body maintaining records described in ORS 25.785, including automated records, shall make the records accessible by Social Security number for purposes of support enforcement.

(3) For purposes of this section, "public body" has the meaning given that term in ORS 192.311. [1997 c.746 §118]

Note: 25.081 was enacted into law by the Legislative Assembly but was not added to or made a part of ORS chapter 25 or any series therein by legislative action. See Preface to Oregon Revised Statutes for further explanation.

25.082 Administrative subpoenas; civil penalty; rules. (1) When services are being provided under Title IV-D of the Social Security Act, the enforcing agency of this or any other state may subpoena financial records and other information needed to establish parentage or to establish, modify or enforce a support order. The subpoena may be served on a party or on a public or private entity. Service of the subpoena may be by certified mail.

(2) A party or public or private entity that discloses information to the enforcing agency in compliance with a subpoena served under subsection (1) of this section is not liable to any person for any loss, damage or injury arising out of the disclosure.

(3) Upon request of an enforcing agency of another state, only a court or enforcing agency of Oregon may enforce a subpoena issued by the enforcing agency of the other state.

(4) Notwithstanding ORS 192.600, a party or public or private entity that fails without good cause to comply with a subpoena issued under this section is subject to a civil penalty not to exceed $250. A civil penalty under this section must be imposed in the manner provided by ORS 183.745.

(5) The Department of Justice shall adopt rules to implement the provisions of this section. [1997 c.746 §33; 2003 c.73 §21; 2017 c.651 §10]

Note: 25.082 was enacted into law by the Legislative Assembly but was not added to or made a part of ORS chapter 25 or any series therein by legislative action. See Preface to Oregon Revised Statutes for further explanation.

25.083 High-volume automated administrative enforcement services. (1) As necessary to meet the requirements of 42 U.S.C. 666(a)(14), the Division of Child Support of the Department of Justice, when requested by another state, shall provide high-volume automated administrative enforcement services. In providing services to another state under this section, the division may:

(a) Through automated data matches with financial institutions and other entities where assets may be found, identify assets owned by persons who owe child support in other states; and

(b) Seize such assets by execution as defined in ORS 18.005 or by such other processes to seize property as the division is authorized by law to use.

(2) A request by another state for services provided under subsection (1) of this section:

(a) Must include information, as required by rule, that will enable the department to compare the information about the case with information in databases within Oregon; and

(b) Constitutes a certification by the state requesting the services:

(A) Of the amount of periodic support under an order, the payment of which is in arrears; and

(B) That it has complied with all procedural due process requirements applicable to the case.

(3) The administrator is authorized to request from other states services of the type provided under subsection (1) of this section. [1999 c.930 §2; 2001 c.249 §71; 2003 c.576 §576]

25.084 Assignment of rights or written application required for services; incorporation in judgment. (1) The administrator may provide support enforcement services as described in ORS 25.080 only if support rights have been assigned to the state or if a person has provided a written application to the administrator that:

(a) Is signed by the person;

(b) Includes the last-known addresses of the obligor and the obligee; and

(c) Indicates that the person is applying for child support services.

(2) Any support judgment that provides for payment to the Department of Justice under ORS 25.020 may have an application incorporated in the judgment. [2009 c.352 §2; 2011 c.318 §5]

Note: 25.084 was added to and made a part of ORS chapter 25 by legislative action but was not added to any smaller series therein. See Preface to Oregon Revised Statutes for further explanation.

25.085 Service on obligee; methods. (1) In any proceeding under ORS 25.080, service of legal documents upon an obligee may be by regular mail to the address at which the obligee receives public assistance, to an address provided by the obligee on the obligee's application for child support enforcement services or to any other address given by the obligee. When service is authorized by regular mail under this section, proof of service may be by notation upon the computerized case record made by the person making the mailing. The notation must set forth the address to which the documents were mailed, the date they were mailed, the description of the documents mailed and the name of the person making the notation. If the documents are returned by the postal service as undeliverable as addressed, that fact must be noted on the computerized case record. If no new address for service by regular mail can be obtained, service must be by certified mail, return receipt requested, by personal service upon the obligee, or by any other mail service with delivery confirmation.

(2) Notwithstanding any other provision of this chapter or ORS chapter 110 or 416, when a case is referred to this state by a public child support agency of another state for action in this state, there is no requirement that an obligee, present in the initiating state and receiving child support enforcement services from that state, be served in any action taken in this state as a consequence of the interstate referral. In such cases the requirement to serve the obligee that would otherwise apply is satisfied by sending to the initiating agency in the other state, by regular mail, any documents that would otherwise be served upon the obligee.

(3) The appropriate child support agency of the state shall make any mailings to or service upon the obligee that is required by this section. [1993 c.596 §17; 1995 c.608 §26; 1997 c.249 §16; 1999 c.87 §1; 2003 c.572 §4; 2011 c.318 §8]

Note: 25.085 was added to and made a part of ORS chapter 25 by legislative action but was not added to any smaller series therein. See Preface to Oregon Revised Statutes for further explanation.

25.088 Effect of dismissal of judicial proceeding on existing administrative order of support. Unless otherwise provided, a general judgment of dismissal of a judicial proceeding under ORS chapter 107, 108 or 109 for want of prosecution under ORCP 54 B(3) does not dismiss an administrative support order that was entered under ORS 416.400 to 416.465 before the date of the dismissal where the parental parties involved in the judicial proceeding are the same as those affected by the administrative order of support. [2013 c.185 §2]

Note: 25.088 was added to and made a part of ORS chapter 25 by legislative action but was not added to any smaller series therein. See Preface to Oregon Revised Statutes for further explanation.

25.089 Enforcement and modification of child support judgments. (1) As used in this section, "child support judgment" means the terms of a judgment or order of a court, or an order that has been filed under ORS 416.440, that provide for past or current child support, including medical support as defined in ORS 25.321. "Child support judgment" does not include any term of a judgment or order that deals with matters other than child support.

(2)(a) A child support judgment originating under ORS 416.440 has all the force, effect and attributes of a circuit court judgment. The judgment lien created by a child support judgment originating under ORS 416.440 applies to all arrearages owed under the underlying order from the date the administrator or administrative law judge entered, filed or registered the underlying order under ORS 416.400 to 416.465 or ORS chapter 110.

(b) Until the underlying order is filed under ORS 416.440, the order may not be enforced against and has no lien effect on real property.

(c) No action to enforce a child support judgment originating under ORS 416.440 may be taken while the child support judgment is stayed under ORS 416.427, except as permitted in the order granting the stay.

(3) In any judicial or administrative proceeding in which child support may be awarded under this chapter or ORS chapter 107, 108, 109, 110 or 416 or ORS 125.025, 419B.400 or 419C.590, if a child support judgment already exists with regard to the same obligor and child:

(a) A court may only enforce the existing child support judgment, modify the existing child support judgment as specifically authorized by law or set aside the existing child support judgment under subsection (6) of this section or under the provisions of ORCP 71. If the court sets aside the existing child support judgment, the court may issue a new child support judgment.

(b) The administrator or administrative law judge may only enforce the existing child support judgment, modify the existing child support judgment as specifically authorized by law or, with regard to an existing child support judgment originating under ORS 416.400, move to set aside the existing child support judgment under subsection (6) of this section or for the reasons set out in ORCP 71.

(4) If the administrator or administrative law judge finds that there exist two or more child support judgments involving the same obligor and child and the same period of time, the administrator or administrative law judge shall apply the provisions of ORS 416.448.

(5)(a) If the court finds that there exist two or more child support judgments involving the same obligor and child and the same period of time, and each judgment was issued in this state, the court shall apply the provisions of ORS 25.091 to determine the controlling terms of the child support judgments and to issue a governing child support judgment as defined in ORS 25.091.

(b) If the court finds that there exist two or more child support judgments involving the same obligor and child and the same period of time, and one or more of the judgments was issued by a tribunal of another state, the court shall apply the provisions of ORS chapter 110 to determine which judgment is the controlling child support order.

(6) Subject to the provisions of subsection (3) of this section, a court may modify or set aside a child support judgment issued in this state when:

(a) The child support judgment was issued without prior notice to the issuing court, administrator or administrative law judge that:

(A) There was pending in this state or any other jurisdiction any type of support proceeding involving the child; or

(B) There existed in this state or any other jurisdiction another child support judgment involving the child; or

(b) The child support judgment was issued after another child support judgment, and the later judgment did not enforce, modify or set aside the earlier judgment in accordance with this section.

(7) When modifying a child support judgment, the court, administrator or administrative law judge shall specify in the modification judgment the effects of the modification on the child support judgment being modified. [2003 c.146 §2; 2003 c.576 §298a; 2005 c.22 §14; 2009 c.351 §5]

Note: 25.089 and 25.091 were added to and made a part of ORS chapter 25 by legislative action but were not added to any smaller series therein. See Preface to Oregon Revised Statutes for further explanation.

25.090 [Formerly 23.790; repealed by 1999 c.80 §95]

25.091 Multiple child support judgments. (1) As used in this section:

(a) "Child support judgment" has the meaning given that term in ORS 25.089.

(b) "Governing child support judgment" means a child support judgment issued in this state that addresses child support, including medical support as defined in ORS 25.321, and is entitled to exclusive prospective enforcement or modification with respect to any earlier child support judgment issued in this state.

(2) Notwithstanding any other provision of this section or ORS 25.089, when two or more child support judgments exist involving the same obligor and child and one or more of the judgments was issued by a tribunal of another state, the court shall apply the provisions of ORS chapter 110 before enforcing or modifying a judgment under this section or ORS 25.089.

(3) When two or more child support judgments exist involving the same obligor and child and the same period, any party to one or more of the child support judgments or the administrator, under ORS 416.448, may file a petition with the court for a governing child support judgment under this section. When a matter involving a child is before the court and the court finds that two or more child support judgments exist involving the same obligor and child and the same period, the court on its own motion, and after notice to all affected parties, may determine the controlling terms of the child support judgments and issue a governing child support judgment under this section.

(4)(a) Except as provided in paragraph (b) of this subsection, when two or more child support judgments exist involving the same obligor and child and the same period, and each judgment was issued in this state, there is a presumption that the terms of the last-issued child support judgment are the controlling terms and terminate contrary terms of each earlier-issued child support judgment.

(b) If the earlier-issued child support judgment requires provision of a specific type of child support and the last-issued child support judgment is silent with respect to that type of child support, the requirement of the earlier-issued child support judgment continues in effect.

(5) A party may rebut the presumption in subsection (4) of this section by showing that:

(a) The last-issued child support judgment should be set aside under the provisions of ORCP 71;

(b) The last-issued child support judgment was issued without prior notice to the issuing court, administrator or administrative law judge that:

(A) There was pending in this state or any other jurisdiction any type of support proceeding involving the child; or

(B) There existed in this state or any other jurisdiction another child support judgment involving the child; or

(c) The last-issued child support judgment was issued after an earlier child support judgment and did not enforce, modify or set aside the earlier child support judgment in accordance with ORS 25.089.

(6) When a court finds that two or more child support judgments exist involving the same obligor and child and the same period, and each child support judgment was issued in this state, the court shall set the matter for hearing to determine the controlling terms of the child support judgments. When the child support judgments were issued in different counties of this state, the court may designate an auxiliary court under ORS 25.100.

(7) Following a review of each child support judgment and any other evidence admitted by the court:

(a) The court shall apply the presumption in subsection (4) of this section, unless the presumption is rebutted, and shall determine the controlling terms of the child support judgments; and

(b) Notwithstanding ORS 25.089 (3), the court shall issue a governing child support judgment addressing child support, including medical support as defined in ORS 25.321, for the benefit of the child.

(8) The governing child support judgment must include:

(a) A reference to each child support judgment considered and a copy of the judgment;

(b) A determination of which terms regarding child support, including medical support as defined in ORS 25.321, are controlling and which child support judgment or judgments contain those terms;

(c) An affirmation, termination or modification of the terms regarding child support, including medical support as defined in ORS 25.321, in each of the child support judgments;

(d) Except as provided in subsection (9) of this section, a reconciliation of any child support arrears or credits under all of the child support judgments; and

(e) The effective date of each controlling term and the termination date of each noncontrolling term in each of the child support judgments. In determining these dates, the court may apply the following:

(A) A controlling term is effective on the date specified in the child support judgment containing that term or, if no date is specified, on the date the child support judgment was entered as described in ORS 18.075.

(B) A noncontrolling term is terminated on the date the governing child support judgment is entered as described in ORS 18.075.

(9) The court may order the parties, in a separate proceeding under ORS 25.167 or 416.429, to reconcile any child support arrears or credits under all of the child support judgments.

(10) When the governing child support judgment is entered as described in ORS 18.075, the noncontrolling terms of each earlier child support judgment are terminated. However, subject to subsection (11) of this section, the entry of the governing child support judgment does not affect any child support payment arrearage or any liability related to medical support, as defined in ORS 25.321, that has accrued under a child support judgment before the governing child support judgment is entered.

(11) For purposes of reconciling any child support arrears or credits under all of the child support judgments, amounts collected and credited for a particular period under one child support judgment must be credited against the amounts accruing or accrued for the same period under any other child support judgment.

(12) Not sooner than 30 days and not later than 60 days after entry of the governing child support judgment, a party named by the court, or the petitioner if the court names no other party, shall file a copy of the governing child support judgment with each court or the administrator that issued an earlier child support judgment. A party who fails to file a copy of the governing child support judgment as required by this subsection is subject to monetary sanctions, including but not limited to attorney fees, costs and disbursements. A failure to file does not affect the validity or enforceability of the governing child support judgment.

(13) This section applies to any judicial proceeding in which child support may be awarded or modified under this chapter or ORS chapter 107, 108, 109 or 416 or ORS 125.025, 419B.400, 419B.923, 419C.590 or 419C.610. [2003 c.146 §3; 2005 c.22 §15; 2005 c.83 §2; 2009 c.351 §6; 2017 c.252 §4]

Note: See note under 25.089.

25.095 Later-issued child support judgment. (1) As used in this section:

(a) "Administrator" has the meaning given that term in ORS 25.010.

(b) "Child support judgment" has the meaning given that term in ORS 25.089.

(2) Notwithstanding the provisions of ORS 25.089, 25.091 and 416.448 to the contrary, the terms of a child support judgment originating under ORS 416.440 are terminated by the terms of a later-issued child support judgment of a court if:

(a) The two child support judgments involve the same obligor and child and the same period;

(b) The administrator is providing services under ORS 25.080;

(c) The administrator or a court gives the later-issued child support judgment precedence over the earlier-issued child support judgment originating under ORS 416.440; and

(d) All parties had an opportunity to challenge the amount of child support ordered in the later-issued child support judgment.

(3) Notwithstanding the provisions of ORS 25.091 (11) and 416.448 (7), for purposes of reconciling any support payment records under the two child support judgments described in subsection (2) of this section:

(a) The terms of the child support judgment originating under ORS 416.440 are deemed terminated on the effective date of the later-issued child support judgment; and

(b) Entry of the later-issued child support judgment does not affect any support payment arrearage or credit that has accrued under the earlier-issued child support judgment originating under ORS 416.440. [2005 c.83 §1; 2007 c.356 §2; 2015 c.73 §1]

Note: 25.095 was enacted into law by the Legislative Assembly but was not added to or made a part of ORS chapter 25 or any series therein by legislative action. See Preface to Oregon Revised Statutes for further explanation.

25.100 Designation of auxiliary court in county where party resides or property located. (1) With respect to any order or judgment entered pursuant to ORS 107.095, 107.105, 108.120, 109.155, 416.400 to 416.465, 419B.400 or 419C.590 or ORS chapter 110, if a party seeking modification or enforcement of an order or judgment for the payment of money files a certificate to the effect that a party is presently in another county of this state, the court may, upon motion of the party, enter an order designating the circuit court of any county in this state in which the obligee or obligor resides, or in which property of the obligor is located, as an auxiliary court for purposes of the order or judgment.

(2) The clerk of the circuit court in which the original order or judgment was entered shall notify the auxiliary court of the order designating the auxiliary court. [Formerly 23.795; 1993 c.33 §283; 1995 c.608 §27; 1995 c.609 §4; 1997 c.704 §18; 1999 c.80 §43; 2003 c.576 §296; 2017 c.252 §3]

25.110 Jurisdiction of designated auxiliary court. (1) Upon entry of an order designating an auxiliary court under ORS 25.100, the auxiliary court has jurisdiction to compel compliance with an order or judgment for payment of support the same as if it were the court that made and entered the original order or judgment.

(2) The only courts that have jurisdiction to modify any provision of the original order or judgment are:

(a) The court having original jurisdiction of the cause in which the order or judgment was entered; and

(b) An auxiliary court designated under ORS 25.100.

(3) When an auxiliary court enters an order or judgment under this section, the clerk of the auxiliary court shall forward the order or judgment to the clerk of the court in which the original order or judgment was entered. The clerk of the court in which the original order or judgment was entered shall file the auxiliary court's order or judgment in the original court file. [Formerly 23.800; 2003 c.576 §297; 2017 c.252 §6]

25.120 [Formerly 23.805; 1993 c.33 §284; repealed by 1999 c.80 §95]

25.125 Disposition of support obligation overpayments; liquidated debts in favor of state; rules. (1) The Department of Justice may return moneys to an obligor when the department determines that the obligor has paid more moneys than are due under a support obligation. However, when the obligor has an ongoing support obligation, the department may give the obligor credit for the excess amount paid and apply the credit to the future support obligation until the credit is fully used. When the department applies a credit to offset a future support obligation, the department shall so notify the obligee. The notice must inform the obligee that, if the obligee requests, the department will conduct an administrative review to determine if the record keeping and accounting related to the calculation of the credit balance is correct. The department shall conduct the administrative review within 30 days after receiving the request.

(2) An overpayment in favor of the state is created when the Department of Justice, under ORS 25.020, has transmitted moneys received from, or on behalf of, any person or entity, including but not limited to an obligor, an obligee or a collection agency, a child support agency of another state or an agency of this state, and:

(a) The amount transmitted is more than the support obligation requires and the Department of Justice has returned the excess to the obligor under subsection (1) of this section;

(b) The Department of Justice has misapplied moneys received; or

(c) The amount transmitted is attributable in whole or in part to a tax refund offset collection all or part of which has been taken back by the Internal Revenue Service or the Department of Revenue.

(3)(a) The person or entity to which the moneys were transmitted owes the amount of the overpayment to the state. The Department of Justice shall:

(A) Attempt to recover the overpayment if it is cost-effective to do so;

(B) Notify the person or entity to whom the overpayment was made that the person or entity owes money to the state and specify the amount of the overpayment to be returned to the department; and

(C) Give the person or entity opportunity to object.

(b) If the person or entity does not file a timely written objection, the overpayment amount determined by the department becomes a liquidated debt and creates an account receivable owed to the department, and the provisions of subsection (4) of this section apply. If the department does not resolve an objection to the person's or entity's satisfaction, an administrative law judge assigned from the Office of Administrative Hearings shall hear the objection. An order by the administrative law judge becomes a liquidated debt and creates an account receivable owed to the department. The person or entity may appeal the decision of an administrative law judge to the circuit court for a hearing de novo.

(c) Notwithstanding paragraph (a) of this subsection, if an agency of this or another state owes the overpayment, the agency shall return the amount of the overpayment to the department without notice and opportunity to object.

(4)(a) The amount of the overpayment specified in subsection (3)(a) of this section is a liquidated debt owed to the state and an associated account receivable. The Department of Justice may recover the debt by obtaining from the obligee a voluntary assignment of a portion of future support payments to be applied to the account receivable or in any other way permitted by law.

(b) Accounts receivable are considered delinquent for purposes of this subsection and are subject to the provisions of ORS chapter 293 if:

(A) The person or entity fails to make full payment within 90 days of liquidation; or

(B) A period of 90 days elapses without a payment as required by a payment agreement between the department and the obligated person or entity.

(5)(a) In addition to the account receivable created under subsection (2) of this section, a debt in favor of the state and an associated account receivable are created when:

(A) The Department of Justice receives payment for support amounts due from an obligor, a withholder subject to an order to withhold under this chapter or another issuer on behalf of an obligor;

(B) The Department of Justice transmits the amount to any other person or entity; and

(C) The payment is dishonored or reversed.

(b) When a debt is created under paragraph (a) of this subsection, the amount of money specified in the payment is owed to the state, and the department may collect the debt from one of the following:

(A) The obligor, regardless of who presented the check.

(B) The withholder, if the withholder presented the check.

(C) The other issuer, if another issuer presented the check.

(D) The person or entity to which the amount was transmitted by the department.

(c) The Department of Justice shall:

(A) Attempt to recover the debt if it is cost-effective to do so;

(B) Notify the obligor, withholder or other issuer who made the payment that the person or entity owes the money to the state; and

(C) Specify the amount of the debt to be paid to the department.

(d) The amount of the debt specified in paragraph (c) of this subsection is a liquidated debt owed to the state and an account receivable. The Department of Justice may recover the debt and collect on the account receivable in any way permitted under law.

(e) Accounts receivable are considered delinquent for purposes of this subsection and are subject to the provisions of ORS chapter 293 when:

(A) The person or entity fails to make full payment within 90 days of liquidation; or

(B) A period of 90 days elapses without a payment as required by a payment agreement between the department and the obligated person or entity.

(6)(a) When an action is pending to terminate, vacate or set aside a support order or to modify a support order because of a change in physical custody of the child, the administrator may suspend enforcement of the support order if:

(A) Collection of support would result in a credit balance if the motion were granted; or

(B) Collection of child support would impair the ability of the obligor with physical custody of all of the parties' children to provide direct support to the children.

(b) The obligee may object, within 14 days after the date of the notice of intent to suspend enforcement of the support order, only on the grounds that:

(A) The child is not in the physical custody of the obligor;

(B) The child is in the physical custody of the obligor without the consent of the obligee; or

(C) The basis for the suspension of enforcement is factually incorrect.

(c) A party may appeal the administrator's decision to suspend or not to suspend enforcement of the support order under ORS 183.484.

(d) As used in this subsection, "credit balance" means that payments have been made in excess of all amounts owed by an obligor for ongoing and past due child support.

(7) The Department of Justice shall adopt rules to carry out the provisions of this section. [1997 c.385 §2; 2001 c.961 §2; 2003 c.73 §22a; 2003 c.75 §72; 2003 c.572 §5; 2005 c.560 §3; 2015 c.72 §1; 2015 c.74 §1; 2017 c.459 §1]

25.130 Election of alternative support payment method; termination of election. (1) The parties may elect to make support payments as provided in ORS 25.030 unless the provisions of ORS 25.020 (1) apply. The election terminates when the provisions of ORS 25.020 (1) apply subsequent to the election.

(2) The election must be in writing and filed with the court that entered the support order. The election must be signed by both the obligor and the obligee and must specify the amount of the support payment, the date payment is due, the court order number and:

(a) The account number of the checking or savings account that is to be used; or

(b) The name of an escrow agent, licensed under ORS 696.511, to whom, and the account number into which, the payments are to be electronically transferred.

(3) Notice of termination of the bank or escrow agent option and payment requirements pursuant to ORS 25.020 or 25.030 shall be sent by the Department of Justice to the obligor's and to the obligee's last-known address. [Formerly 23.807; 1993 c.596 §3; 1995 c.608 §8; 1997 c.704 §19; 1999 c.80 §80; 2003 c.210 §2]

25.140 Copies of new or modified support orders to department. Counties that have heretofore transferred the collection, accounting and disbursement responsibilities to the Department of Justice, or that have elected not to maintain support collections, accounting and disbursement services, and clerks of courts not maintaining support collection services, shall forward to the department copies of all new and modified support orders, satisfactions or other pertinent documents in a timely manner. [Formerly 23.808; 1997 c.704 §20]

25.150 Department to collect fees for services. The Department of Justice shall assess and collect any fees for establishment, enforcement, collection, accounting and disbursement services required by state law or administrative rule or by federal law or regulation, including the annual fee required under Title IV-D of the Social Security Act. [Formerly 23.815; 1997 c.704 §21; 1999 c.80 §81; 2007 c.878 §2]

25.160 Referral of support cases to department; duration of collection services. (1) For the purposes of ORS 25.020, 25.030, 25.070, 25.080, 25.085 and 25.130 to 25.160, a child support case shall be referred to the Department of Justice for provision of collection, accounting and disbursement services if an application as described in ORS 25.084 is made to the district attorney or to the Division of Child Support and the case qualifies for support enforcement services under federal regulations and state law.

(2) The Department of Justice shall continue collection, accounting and disbursement services for a case referred to the department under subsection (1) of this section until notified by the district attorney or the Division of Child Support that enforcement action has been discontinued. [Formerly 23.825; 1997 c.704 §22; 1999 c.80 §82; 2009 c.352 §5]

25.164 Payment of support through Department of Justice; application. (1) If the payment method for support payments set forth in the support judgment does not require that payments be made through the Department of Justice, an application may be made to the department for support enforcement services under this chapter and under federal laws and regulations relating to support payments and enforcement of judgments. An application under this section may be made by an obligee, by an obligor, by a person having physical custody of a minor child or by a child attending school, as defined in ORS 107.108.

(2) An application under subsection (1) of this section must be in the form prescribed by ORS 25.084.

(3) If an application is made under subsection (1) of this section, the administrator shall give notice to all parties that the application has been made. All support payments under the judgment that are due after the notice is given must be made through the department.

(4) When an application is made under this section, the method of support accounting previously used for the support judgment terminates on the first day of the month following the month the application is made, and the department shall thereafter provide support accounting for the support judgment and disburse amounts paid under the judgment.

(5) If an application is made under this section and a complete record of support payments does not exist, the department may establish a record of arrearage under ORS 25.167. [Formerly 25.320; 2003 c.146 §6; 2009 c.352 §6]

25.165 Application of support payments; rules. The Division of Child Support of the Department of Justice shall adopt rules that:

(1) Require distribution of payments to child, medical or spousal support obligations and arrears in any sequence that is consistent with federal law;

(2) Permit the division to develop criteria for when the division may override the debtor's designation of the particular support debt to which the payment of child support or spousal support is applied; and

(3) Provide the manner in which payments of child, medical or spousal support shall be applied to principal and interest that is due and owing on such obligations and arrears, irrespective of any contrary law. [2017 c.458 §2]

Note: 25.165 was added to and made a part of ORS chapter 25 by legislative action but was not added to any smaller series therein. See Preface to Oregon Revised Statutes for further explanation.

25.166 Support payment due dates. (1) Any court order or administrative order issued or modified in a proceeding under ORS chapter 107, 108, 109, 110, 416, 419B or 419C that contains an order for the payment of child support or spousal support must specify an initial due date and year for the payment of support that is on the first day of a calendar month, with subsequent payments due on the first day of each subsequent month for which the support is payable.

(2) For purposes of support enforcement, any support payment that becomes due and payable on a day other than the first day of the month in which the payment is due shall be enforceable by income withholding as of the first day of that month.

(3) Any court order or administrative order that contains an award of child, medical or spousal support that accrues on other than a monthly basis may, for income withholding and administrative support billing purposes only, be converted to a monthly amount.

(4) Support payments become delinquent only if not paid in full within one month of the payment due date. A monthly child support obligation that is to be paid in two or more installments does not become delinquent until the obligation is not paid in full by the due date for the first installment in the next month.

(5) Subsections (2) and (3) of this section do not apply to the determination or issuance of support arrearage liens, installment arrearage liens, judgment liens, writs of garnishment or any other action or proceeding that affects property rights under ORS chapter 18. [2017 c.462 §1]

Note: 25.166 was enacted into law by the Legislative Assembly but was not added to or made a part of ORS chapter 25 or any series therein by legislative action. See Preface to Oregon Revised Statutes for further explanation.

25.167 Procedure for determining arrearages. This section establishes procedures for determining the amount of arrearage and for making a record of arrearage of support payments. All of the following apply to this section:

(1) A record of support payment arrearage may be established by:

(a) Court order;

(b) A governing child support judgment issued under ORS 25.091 or 416.448;

(c) Administrative order issued under ORS 416.427 or 416.429;

(d) Stipulation of the parties; or

(e) The procedures under subsection (2) of this section whenever an existing child or spousal support case enters the Department of Justice records system without a current payment record maintained by any court clerk.

(2) When allowed under subsection (1) of this section, arrearage amounts may be established under this subsection. All of the following apply to this subsection:

(a) The obligee or obligor may execute a certificate in a form acceptable to the Department of Justice that states the total amount owed or the payment history in as much detail as is necessary to demonstrate the periods and amounts of any arrearage.

(b) The person making the certificate shall file the original certificate with the court in which the support judgment was entered. When a governing child support judgment has been issued, the person making the certificate shall file the original certificate with the court that issued the governing child support judgment.

(c) The person making the certificate shall serve a true copy of the certificate upon the other party together with a notice that the certificate will be the basis of a permanent record unless the other party files objections.

(d) For objections to be valid under paragraph (c) of this subsection, the other party must file the objection with the court within 30 days from the date of service of the certificate and must mail or serve true copies of the objections on both the party who filed the certificate and either:

(A) The district attorney; or

(B) If support rights are or have been assigned to the State of Oregon at any time within the last five months or if arrears under the support judgment are so assigned, the Division of Child Support of the Department of Justice.

(e) If objections are filed within the time allowed, the party filing the certificate must file a supplemental certificate that is in a form acceptable to the department and that provides any information concerning the payment history that the department determines necessary.

(f) If objections are filed within the time allowed, the district attorney or the Division of Child Support shall cause the case to be set for a court hearing. At the hearing, the court shall consider the correctness of the certificate but may not consider objections to the merits of the support judgment. The parties may settle the case by written agreement anytime before the court hearing. Notice of the court hearing shall be served upon the party filing the objections as authorized in ORCP 9 B.

(g) If no objections are filed under this subsection within the time allowed, the amount of arrearage stated in the certificate is the amount owed for purposes of any subsequent action. The district attorney or the Division of Child Support shall file with the court a certificate stating the arrearage established under this paragraph.

(3) When an application for support enforcement services is made under ORS 25.164, an agency or court may not take or allow any ex parte enforcement action on amounts owed as arrearage from before the time that the Department of Justice commences support accounting and disbursement until the amount is established under this section. This subsection does not prohibit or limit any enforcement action on support payments that become due subsequent to the department's commencement of support accounting and disbursement under ORS 25.164.

(4) In any determination under this section, a canceled check, payable to the obligee, indorsed by the obligee or deposited to an account of the obligee, drawn on the account of the obligor and marked as child support shall be prima facie evidence that child support was paid to the obligee in the amount shown on the face of the check. It is immaterial that the check was signed by a person other than the obligor, provided that the person who signed the check was an authorized signatory of checks drawn on the account. [Formerly 25.330; 2003 c.146 §7; 2003 c.576 §298; 2009 c.352 §7; 2011 c.318 §1]

25.170 Proceedings to require delinquent obligor to appear for examination of financial circumstances. When a support obligation is more than one month in arrears, the Attorney General or a district attorney may upon motion obtain an order requiring the obligor to appear for the purpose of examination regarding the obligor's financial circumstances. The court shall require the obligor to appear at a time and date certain at such place as may be appropriate. The order to appear shall inform the obligor that the obligor's answers may be used in subsequent enforcement and possible criminal proceedings, and that the obligor has a right to be represented by an attorney at the examination. The order shall be served upon the obligor in the same manner as service of summons. The order to appear shall also be served upon the obligee by regular mail. The obligee shall have the right to attend any such examination. [Formerly 23.835; 1989 c.599 §1; 1993 c.596 §4]

25.180 Examination of obligor's financial circumstances. (1) The examination shall be conducted under oath by an employee of the Department of Justice or district attorney. The employee shall inform the obligor that the obligor's answers may be used in subsequent enforcement and possible criminal proceedings, and that the obligor has a right to be represented by an attorney at the examination. A record of the examination may be made by either stenographic or electronic means. The obligor may be examined in regard to the obligor's income and property, and to any matter relevant to the obligor's ability to pay support.
(2) An obligee or the obligee's attorney may examine the obligor in a proceeding conducted under this section. [Formerly 23.837; 1989 c.599 §2; 1993 c.596 §5]

25.190 Continuance of proceedings; certification of matter to court; service of notice to obligor and obligee. (1) The examination may be continued for further review of the obligor's financial circumstances and employment, or the matter may be certified to the court for a contempt hearing on the issue of failure to pay support as ordered. If the examination is to be continued for further review or is to be certified to the court for a contempt hearing, the obligor shall be served at the examination with a notice stating the time, date and place for further examination or hearing before the court. Service may be made by an employee of the Department of Justice or district attorney.
(2) Any notice served upon the obligor regarding a continuation of the examination or regarding the certification of the matter to the court for a contempt hearing must also be served upon the obligee. Such service upon the obligee may be by regular mail. [Formerly 23.842; 1989 c.599 §3; 1993 c.596 §6]

25.200 Arrest of obligor for failure to appear. (1) If the obligor fails to appear for examination or further examination, the Attorney General or a district attorney may apply to the court which issued the order to appear for an order directing the issuance of a warrant for the arrest of the obligor. The motion shall be accompanied by an affidavit which shall state the relevant facts and whether the obligor contacted the Department of Justice or district attorney, as appropriate. If the court finds that the obligor had notice and failed to appear, the court shall order the issuance of a warrant for the arrest of the obligor in order to bring the obligor before the court to show cause why the obligor should not be held in contempt for a failure to appear as ordered.
(2) If the matter has been certified to the court for a contempt hearing and the obligor, having been properly served, fails to appear, the court shall order the issuance of a warrant for the arrest of the obligor. Upon arrest, the obligor shall be brought before the court to show cause why the obligor should not be held in contempt for a failure to appear as ordered. [Formerly 23.845; 1989 c.599 §4]

25.210 Use of obligor's property for delinquent support payments. If by examination of the obligor it appears that the obligor has any property liable to execution, the court, upon motion of the Attorney General or a district attorney, shall order that the obligor apply the same in satisfaction of the arrears or that the property be levied on by execution, or both. [Formerly 23.847; 1989 c.599 §5]

25.213 Assignment of proceeds of insurance policy to secure support obligation. If by examination of the obligor under ORS 25.170, it appears that the obligor is the beneficiary and owner of an insurance policy on the life of the child, the court, upon motion of the Attorney General or a district attorney, may order that the obligor assign to the obligee the rights to as much of the proceeds of the insurance policy as necessary to secure the obligation to make support payments, if assignment is permitted in the policy. This assignment shall be in addition to any other security ordered by the court. [1997 c.54 §2]

25.220 Computer printouts of administrator; evidence of authenticity not required in support proceedings; evidentiary effect. (1) In any proceeding to establish, enforce or modify a support obligation, extrinsic evidence of authenticity is not required as a condition precedent to the admission of a computer printout of the administrator that may reflect the employment records of a parent, the support payment record of an obligor, the payment of public assistance, the amounts paid, the period during which public assistance was paid, the persons receiving or having received assistance and any other pertinent information, if the printout bears a seal purporting to be that of the administrator and is certified as a true copy by original or facsimile signature of a person purporting to be an officer or employee of the administrator. Printouts certified in accordance with this section constitute prima facie evidence of the existence of the facts stated therein.
(2) To the extent permitted under federal and state law, obligors and obligees, and their attorneys, may obtain copies of such printouts upon request made to the administrator. [Formerly 23.855; 1989 c.519 §1; 1997 c.704 §23; 1999 c.735 §19]

25.230 Court authorized to require security for support payments. Whenever a court has entered an order for the payment of support, the court may provide for such security, bond or other guarantee satisfactory to the court to secure the obligation to make support payments. [Formerly 23.865]

25.240 Order to pay support by parent with legal custody of minor. Notwithstanding any other law, where a court or the administrator has the authority under ORS chapter 107, 108, 109, 110 or 416 or ORS 419B.400 to 419B.406 or 419C.590, 419C.592 and 419C.597 to require a parent without legal custody to pay support for a minor child, then the court or administrator may require a parent with legal custody to pay support for such a child as long as that parent does not have physical custody of such child or is not providing the child with the necessities of life, including but not limited to lodging, food and clothing. [1985 c.610 §11; 1993 c.33 §368; 1995 c.608 §28; 2001 c.455 §5]

25.243 Grievance procedure; rules. In addition to any other hearing rights authorized by law, an applicant for services provided under ORS 25.080 and any party to a child support order for which services are provided under ORS 25.080 may file a grievance with the Department of Justice concerning any service provided under ORS 25.080. The department shall adopt rules establishing a process for handling grievances under this section. The process must provide that grievances not involving a public child support agency in another state be addressed no later than 90 days after the grievance is submitted to the department. [1995 c.608 §45; 2003 c.73 §23]

25.245 Rebuttable presumption of inability to pay child support when parent receiving certain assistance payments; rules. (1) Notwithstanding any other provision of Oregon law, a parent who is eligible for and receiving cash payments under ORS 412.001 to 412.069, Title IV-A of the Social Security Act, the general assistance program as provided in ORS chapter 411 or a general assistance program of another state or tribe, the Oregon Supplemental Income Program or the federal Supplemental Security Income Program shall be rebuttably presumed unable to pay child support and a child support obligation does not accrue unless the presumption is rebutted.
(2) Each month, the Department of Human Services shall identify those persons receiving cash payments under the programs listed in subsection (1) of this section that are administered by the State of Oregon and provide that information to the administrator. If benefits are received from programs listed in

subsection (1) of this section that are administered by other states, tribes or federal agencies, the obligor shall provide the administrator with written documentation of the benefits. The Department of Human Services shall adopt rules to implement this subsection.

(3) The administrator shall refer to the information provided in subsection (2) of this section prior to establishing any child support obligation. Within 30 days following identification of persons under subsection (2) of this section, the entity responsible for support enforcement services under ORS 25.080 shall provide notice of the presumption to the obligee and obligor and shall inform all parties to the support order that, unless a party objects as provided in subsection (4) of this section, child support shall cease accruing beginning with the support payment due on or after the date the obligor first begins receiving the cash payments and continuing through the support payment due in the last month in which the obligor received the cash payments. The entity responsible for support enforcement services shall serve the notice on the obligee in the manner provided for the service of summons in a civil action, by certified mail, return receipt requested, or by any other mail service with delivery confirmation and shall serve the notice on the obligor by first class mail to the obligor's last-known address. The notice shall specify the month in which cash payments are first made and shall contain a statement that the administrator represents the state and that low cost legal counsel may be available.

(4) A party may object to the presumption by sending an objection to the entity responsible for support enforcement services under ORS 25.080 within 30 days after the date of service of the notice. The objection must describe the resources of the obligor or other evidence that might rebut the presumption of inability to pay child support. The entity receiving the objection shall cause the case to be set for a hearing before a court or an administrative law judge. The court or administrative law judge may consider only whether the presumption has been rebutted.

(5) If no objection is made, or if the court or administrative law judge finds that the presumption has not been rebutted, the Department of Justice shall discontinue billing the obligor for the period of time described in subsection (3) of this section and no arrearage shall accrue for the period during which the obligor is not billed. In addition, the entity providing support enforcement services shall file with the circuit court in which the support order or judgment has been entered a copy of the notice described in subsection (3) of this section or, if an objection is made and the presumption is not rebutted, a copy of the administrative law judge's order.

(6)(a) Within 30 days after the date the obligor ceases receiving cash payments under a program listed in subsection (1) of this section, the Department of Justice shall provide notice to all parties to the support order:

(A) Specifying the last month in which a cash payment was made;

(B) Stating that the payment of those benefits has terminated and that by operation of law billing and accrual of support resumes; and

(C) Informing the parties of their rights to request a review and modification of the support order based on a substantial change in circumstance or pursuant to ORS 25.287 or any other provision of law.

(b) The notice shall include a statement that the administrator represents the state and that low cost legal counsel may be available.

(c) The entity providing enforcement services shall file a copy of the notice required by paragraph (a) of this subsection with the circuit court in which the support order or judgment has been entered.

(7) Receipt by a child support obligor of cash payments under any of the programs listed in subsection (1) of this section shall be sufficient cause for a court or administrative law judge to allow a credit and satisfaction against child support arrearage for months that the obligor received the cash payments.

(8) The notice and finding of financial responsibility required by ORS 416.415 shall include notice of the presumption, nonaccrual and arrearage credit rights provided for in this section.

(9) The presumption, nonaccrual and arrearage credit rights created by this section shall apply whether or not child support enforcement services are being provided under Title IV-D of the Social Security Act.

(10) Application of the presumption, nonaccrual and arrearage credit rights created by this section does not constitute a modification but does not limit the right of any party to seek a modification of a support order based upon a change of circumstances or pursuant to ORS 25.287 or any other provision of law. In determining whether a change in circumstances has occurred or whether three years have elapsed, or such shorter cycle as determined by rule of the Department of Justice, since entry of a support order, the court or administrative law judge may not consider any action taken under this section as entry of a support order. The presumption stated in subsection (1) of this section applies in any modification proceeding. [1991 c.520 §3; 1993 c.799 §1; 1997 c.704 §24; 2001 c.104 §5; 2001 c.455 §6; 2003 c.75 §73; 2003 c.576 §299; 2007 c.861 §11; 2007 c.878 §3; 2009 c.80 §1; 2011 c.318 §2]

25.247 Rebuttable presumption of inability to pay child support when obligor incarcerated. (1) An obligor who is incarcerated for a period of 180 or more consecutive days shall be rebuttably presumed unable to pay child support and a child support obligation does not accrue for the duration of the incarceration unless the presumption is rebutted as provided in this section.

(2) The Department of Justice and the Department of Corrections shall enter into an agreement to conduct data matches to identify the obligors described in subsection (1) of this section or as determined by the court.

(3) Within 30 days following identification of an obligor described in subsection (1) of this section whose child support obligation has not already been modified due to incarceration, the entity responsible for support enforcement services under ORS 25.080 shall provide notice of the presumption to the obligee and obligor and shall inform all parties to the support order that, unless a party objects as provided in subsection (4) of this section, child support shall cease accruing beginning with the first day of the first month that follows the obligor becoming incarcerated for a period of at least 180 consecutive days and continuing through the support payment due in the last month prior to the reinstatement of the support order as provided in subsection (6) of this section. The entity shall serve the notice on the obligee in the manner provided for the service of summons in a civil action, by certified mail, return receipt requested, or by any other mail service with delivery confirmation and shall serve the notice on the obligor by first class mail to the obligor's last-known address. The notice shall specify the month in which the obligor became incarcerated and shall contain a statement that the administrator represents the state and that low-cost legal counsel may be available.

(4) A party may object to the presumption by sending an objection to the entity that served the notice under subsection (3) of this section within 30 days after the date of service of the notice. The objection must describe the resources of the obligor or other evidence that rebuts the presumption of inability to pay child support. The entity receiving the objection shall cause the case to be set for a hearing before a court or an administrative law judge. The court or administrative law judge may consider only whether the presumption has been rebutted.

(5) If no objection is made, or if the court or administrative law judge finds that the presumption has not been rebutted, the Department of Justice shall discontinue billing the obligor for the period of time described in subsection (3) of this section and no arrearage shall accrue for the period during which the obligor is not billed. In addition, the entity providing support enforcement services shall file with the circuit court in which the support order or judgment has been entered a copy of the notice described in subsection (3) of this section or, if an objection is made and the presumption is not rebutted, a copy of the court's or administrative law judge's order.

(6) An order that has been suspended as provided in this section will automatically be reinstated at 50 percent of the previously ordered support amount on the first day of the first month that follows the 120th day after the obligor's release from incarceration.

(7)(a) Within 30 days following reinstatement of the order pursuant to subsection (6) of this section, the Department of Justice shall provide notice to all parties to the support order:

(A) Specifying the last date on which the obligor was incarcerated;

(B) Stating that by operation of law, billing and accrual of support resumed on the first day of the first month that follows the 120th day after the obligor's release from incarceration; and

(C) Informing the parties that the administrator will review the support order for purposes of modification of the support order as provided in subsection (8) of this section within 60 days following reinstatement of the order.

(b) The notice shall include a statement that the administrator represents the state and that low-cost legal counsel may be available.

(c) The entity providing support enforcement services shall file a copy of the notice required by paragraph (a) of this subsection with the circuit court in which the support order or judgment has been entered.

(8) Within 60 days of the reinstatement under subsection (6) of this section, the administrator shall review the support order for purposes of modifying the support order.

(9) An obligor's incarceration for at least 180 consecutive days or an obligor's release from incarceration is considered a substantial change of circumstances for purposes of child support modification proceedings.

208

(10) Proof of incarceration for at least 180 consecutive days is sufficient cause for the administrator, court or administrative law judge to allow a credit and satisfaction against child support arrearages for each month that the obligor was incarcerated or that is within 120 days following the obligor's release from incarceration unless the presumption of inability to pay has been rebutted.

(11) Orders modified to zero prior to January 1, 2018, remain in force with reinstatement at the full amount ordered by the court occurring 61 days after release. Such orders are not subject to suspension and reinstatement as provided in this section.

(12) The provisions of subsections (1), (9) and (10) of this section apply regardless of whether child support enforcement services are being provided under Title IV-D of the Social Security Act.

(13) The Department of Justice shall adopt rules to implement this section.

(14) As used in this section, "support order" means a judgment or administrative order that creates child support rights and that is entered or issued under ORS 416.400 to 416.465, 419B.400 or 419C.590 or this chapter or ORS chapter 107, 108, 109 or 110. [2017 c.464 §2]

25.250 [1987 c.427 §1; repealed by 1993 c.798 §21]

25.255 [1989 c.812 §2; 1991 c.67 §4; 1991 c.519 §2; 1993 c.33 §286; 1993 c.800 §1; 1995 c.506 §§12,12a; 1999 c.80 §10; 2003 c.73 §24a; 2003 c.75 §74; repealed by 2003 c.637 §14]

25.260 Confidentiality of records; rules. (1) As used in this section, "Child Support Program" means:

(a) The program described in ORS 180.345;

(b) The Administrator of the Division of Child Support of the Department of Justice;

(c) A district attorney; and

(d) The administrator's or district attorney's authorized representative.

(2) Unless otherwise authorized by law, child support records, including data contained in the Child Support Program's automated system, are confidential and may be disclosed or used only as necessary for the administration of the program.

(3) In administering the Child Support Program, the program may:

(a) In accordance with rules adopted under subsection (7) of this section, report abuse as defined in ORS 419B.005 if the abuse is discovered while providing program services.

(b) Extract and receive information from other databases as necessary to carry out the program's responsibilities under state and federal law.

(4) The Child Support Program may compare and share information with public and private entities as necessary to perform the program's responsibilities under state and federal law.

(5) The Child Support Program may exchange information with state agencies administering programs funded under Title XIX and Part A of Title IV of the Social Security Act as necessary for the Child Support Program and the state agencies to perform their responsibilities under state and federal law.

(6) In addition to any penalty to which an individual may be subject under ORS 25.990, an employee of the Department of Justice, of a district attorney or of the Department of Human Services who discloses or uses the contents of any records in violation of subsection (2) of this section is subject to discipline, up to and including dismissal from employment.

(7) The Department of Justice shall adopt rules consistent with federal regulations governing confidentiality of Child Support Program information. [1989 c.812 §3(1); 1991 c.758 §2; 1995 c.609 §7; 1999 c.80 §72; 2003 c.450 §1; 2005 c.22 §16]

25.265 Access to information in Federal Parent Locator Service; rules. The Department of Justice shall adopt rules establishing a procedure by which a person authorized under federal law may access information in the Federal Parent Locator Service. [1997 c.746 §22a; 2003 c.73 §25]

Note: 25.265 was enacted into law by the Legislative Assembly but was not added to or made a part of ORS chapter 25 or any series therein by legislative action. See Preface to Oregon Revised Statutes for further explanation.

FORMULA FOR DETERMINING AMOUNT OF CHILD SUPPORT

25.270 Legislative findings. The Legislative Assembly finds that:

(1) The federal Family Support Act of 1988 mandates that the state must establish a formula for child support award amounts that is applicable in any judicial or administrative proceeding for the award of child support.

(2) It is further mandated that the amount of child support determined by the formula must be presumed to be the correct amount unless rebutted by a specific finding on the record that the application of the formula would be unjust or inappropriate in the particular case as determined under criteria established by the state.

(3) It is also mandated that the formula is to be reviewed at least once every four years to insure that the application of the formula results in appropriate child support awards.

(4) There is a need for uniformity in child support awards, and child support awards often are based upon noneconomic factors and are inadequate in terms of the needs of the child.

(5) The Division of Child Support of the Department of Justice is the appropriate agency to establish the required formula. [1989 c.811 §2]

25.275 Formula for determining child support awards; criteria to be considered; mandated standards; reduction; rules. (1) The Division of Child Support of the Department of Justice shall establish by rule a formula for determining child support awards in any judicial or administrative proceeding. In establishing the formula, the division shall take into consideration the following criteria:

(a) All earnings, income and resources of each parent, including real and personal property;

(b) The earnings history and potential of each parent;

(c) The reasonable necessities of each parent;

(d) The ability of each parent to borrow;

(e) The educational, physical and emotional needs of the child for whom the support is sought;

(f) The amount of assistance that would be paid to the child under the full standard of need of the state's IV-A plan;

(g) Preexisting support orders and current dependents; and

(h) Other reasonable criteria that the division may find to be appropriate.

(2) The formula described in subsection (1) of this section must also comply with the following standards:

(a) The child is entitled to benefit from the income of both parents to the same extent that the child would have benefited had the family unit remained intact or if there had been an intact family unit consisting of both parents and the child.

(b) Both parents should share in the costs of supporting the child in the same proportion as each parent's income bears to the combined income of both parents.

(3) The formula described in subsection (1) of this section must be designed to ensure, as a minimum, that the child for whom support is sought benefits from the income and resources of the absent parent on an equitable basis in comparison with any other minor children of the absent parent.

(4) The child support obligation to be paid by the obligor and determined under the formula described in subsection (1) of this section:

(a) May be reduced or increased in consideration of medical support, as provided in ORS 25.321 to 25.343.

(b) May be reduced dollar for dollar in consideration of any Social Security or apportioned Veterans' benefits paid to the child, or to a representative payee administering the funds for the child's use and benefit, as a result of the obligor's disability or retirement.

(c) Shall be reduced dollar for dollar in consideration of any Survivors' and Dependents' Educational Assistance under 38 U.S.C. chapter 35 paid to the child, or to a representative payee administering the funds for the child's use and benefit, as a result of the obligor's disability or retirement. [1989 c.811 §3; 1993 c.800 §2; 1999 c.1030 §1; 2003 c.73 §26a; 2003 c.75 §75; 2003 c.572 §6; 2003 c.637 §15; 2009 c.351 §7]

25.280 Formula amount presumed correct; rebuttal of presumption; criteria. In any judicial or administrative proceeding for the establishment or modification of a child support obligation under ORS chapter 107, 108, 109, 110 or 416 or ORS 419B.400, 419B.923, 419C.590 or 419C.610, the amount of support determined by the formula established under ORS 25.275 is presumed to be the correct amount of the obligation. This is a rebuttable presumption and a written finding or a specific finding on the record that the application of the formula would be unjust or inappropriate in a particular case is sufficient to rebut the presumption. The following criteria shall be considered in making the finding:
(1) Evidence of the other available resources of a parent;
(2) The reasonable necessities of a parent;
(3) The net income of a parent remaining after withholdings required by law or as a condition of employment;
(4) A parent's ability to borrow;
(5) The number and needs of other dependents of a parent;
(6) The special hardships of a parent including, but not limited to, any medical circumstances of a parent affecting the parent's ability to pay child support;
(7) The needs of the child;
(8) The desirability of the custodial parent remaining in the home as a full-time parent and homemaker;
(9) The tax consequences, if any, to both parents resulting from spousal support awarded and determination of which parent will name the child as a dependent; and
(10) The financial advantage afforded a parent's household by the income of a spouse or another person with whom the parent lives in a relationship similar to that of a spouse. [1989 c.811 §4; 1993 c.33 §287; 1993 c.354 §1; 1995 c.608 §30; 2001 c.622 §42; 2007 c.71 §8; 2007 c.356 §3; 2015 c.629 §1]

25.285 [1989 c.811 §5; repealed by 1991 c.519 §8 (25.287 enacted in lieu of 25.285 in 1993)]

25.287 Proceedings to modify orders to comply with formula; when proceeding may be initiated; issues considered. (1)(a) The entity providing support enforcement services under ORS 25.080 may initiate proceedings to modify a support obligation to ensure that the support obligation is in accordance with the formula established under ORS 25.275.
(b) Proceedings under this subsection may occur only after three years have elapsed, or such shorter cycle as determined by rule of the Department of Justice, from the later of the following:
(A) The date the original support obligation took effect;
(B) The date any previous modification of the support obligation took effect; or
(C) The date of any previous review and determination under this subsection that resulted in no modification of the support obligation.
(c) For purposes of paragraph (b) of this subsection, a support obligation or modification takes effect on the first date on which the obligor is to pay the established or modified support amount.
(d) The only issues at proceedings under this subsection are whether three years have elapsed, or such shorter cycle as determined by rule of the department, and whether the support obligation is in substantial compliance with the formula established under ORS 25.275.
(e) Upon review, if the administrator determines that a support obligation does not qualify for modification under this section, a party may object to the determination within 30 days after the date of the determination. A hearing on the objection shall be conducted by an administrative law judge assigned from the Office of Administrative Hearings. Appeal of the order of the administrative law judge may be taken to the circuit court of the county in which the support obligation has been entered or registered for a hearing de novo. The appeal to the court shall be by petition for review filed within 60 days after entry of the order of the administrative law judge.
(f) If the court, the administrator or the administrative law judge finds that more than three years have elapsed, or such shorter cycle as determined by rule of the department, the court, the administrator or the administrative law judge shall modify the support order to bring the support obligation into substantial compliance with the formula established under ORS 25.275, regardless of whether there has been a substantial change in circumstances since the support obligation was last established, modified or reviewed. Proceedings by the administrator or administrative law judge under this subsection shall be conducted according to the provisions of ORS 416.425 and 416.427.
(g) The provisions of this subsection apply to any support obligation established by a support order under this chapter or ORS chapter 107, 108, 109, 110 or 416 or ORS 419B.400 or 419C.590.
(2) The entity providing support enforcement services shall state in the document initiating the proceeding, to the extent known:
(a) Whether there is pending in this state or any other jurisdiction any type of support proceeding involving the child, including a proceeding brought under ORS 107.085, 107.135, 107.431, 108.110, 109.100, 109.103, 109.165, 125.025, 416.400 to 416.465, 419B.400 or 419C.590 or ORS chapter 110; and
(b) Whether there exists in this state or any other jurisdiction a support order, as defined in ORS 110.503, involving the child, other than the support obligation the entity seeks to modify.
(3) The entity providing support enforcement services shall include with the document initiating the proceeding a certificate regarding any pending support proceeding and any existing support order other than the support obligation the entity seeks to modify. The entity providing support enforcement services shall use a certificate that is in a form prescribed by the administrator and shall include information required by the administrator and subsection (2) of this section.
(4) The administrator, court or administrative law judge may use the provisions of subsection (1) of this section when a support order was entered in another state and registered in Oregon, the provisions of ORS chapter 110 apply and more than three years have elapsed, or such shorter cycle as determined by rule of the department.
(5) Notwithstanding the provisions of this section, proceedings may be initiated at any time to modify a support obligation based upon a substantial change of circumstances under any other provision of law.
(6) The obligee is a party to any action to modify a support obligation under this section. [1991 c.519 §3; 1993 c.33 §369; 1993 c.596 §7 (enacted in lieu of 25.285 in 1993); 1995 c.608 §31; 1999 c.80 §64; 1999 c.735 §1; 2001 c.455 §§7,8; 2003 c.75 §24; 2003 c.116 §§1,2; 2003 c.576 §§183,184; 2005 c.560 §4; 2007 c.71 §9; 2007 c.878 §4; 2015 c.298 §86]

25.290 Determining disposable income of obligor; offsets; rules. (1) In determining the disposable income of an obligor, the obligor may claim offsets against gross receipts for ordinary and necessary business expenses and taxes directly related to the income withheld. The obligor has the burden of proof and must furnish documentation to support any offsets claimed.
(2) The Department of Justice may adopt rules governing the determination of the income subject to withholding that remains after application of offsets. Withholding actions in a case that is not receiving support enforcement services under ORS 25.080 may be appealed to the circuit court. [1995 c.608 §1b; 2003 c.73 §27]

25.310 [1985 c.671 §4; 1989 c.812 §4; 1991 c.362 §2; repealed by 1993 c.798 §21]

25.311 [1993 c.798 §5; 1995 c.608 §32; 1999 c.80 §2; 1999 c.735 §8; 1999 c.849 §§38,39; renumbered 25.378 in 1999]

25.313 [1993 c.798 §3; renumbered 25.393 in 1999]

210

25.314 [1993 c.798 §6; 1995 c.272 §6; 1997 c.704 §26; 1999 c.80 §3; renumbered 25.402 in 1999]

25.315 [1993 c.798 §7; 1999 c.80 §4; renumbered 25.399 in 1999]

25.316 [1993 c.798 §8; 1999 c.80 §5; 1999 c.735 §12; renumbered 25.405 in 1999]

25.317 [1993 c.798 §9; 1999 c.735 §11; renumbered 25.396 in 1999]

25.318 [1993 c.798 §10; renumbered 25.390 in 1999]

25.320 [1985 c.671 §5; 1997 c.704 §27; renumbered 25.164 in 1999]

MEDICAL SUPPORT

25.321 Definitions for ORS 25.321 to 25.343. As used in ORS 25.321 to 25.343:
(1) "Cash medical support" means an amount that a parent is ordered to pay to defray the cost of health care coverage provided for a child by the other parent or a public body, or to defray uninsured medical expenses of the child.
(2) "Child support order" means a judgment or administrative order that creates child support rights and that is entered or issued under ORS 416.400 to 416.465, 419B.400 or 419C.590 or this chapter or ORS chapter 107, 108, 109 or 110.
(3) "Employee health benefit plan" means a health benefit plan that is available to a providing party by reason of the providing party's employment.
(4) "Enforcing agency" means the administrator.
(5) "Health benefit plan" means any policy or contract of insurance, indemnity, subscription or membership issued by an insurer, including health care coverage provided by a public body, and any self-insured employee benefit plan that provides coverage for medical expenses.
(6) "Health care coverage" means providing and paying for the medical needs of a child through a policy or contract of insurance, indemnity, subscription or membership issued by an insurer, including medical assistance provided by a public body, and any self-insured employee benefit plan that provides coverage for medical expenses.
(7) "Medical support" means cash medical support and health care coverage.
(8) "Medical support clause" means a provision in a child support order that requires one or both of the parents to provide medical support for the child.
(9) "Medical support notice" means a notice in the form prescribed under ORS 25.325 (5).
(10) "Plan administrator" means:
(a) The employer, union or other provider that offers a health benefit plan; or
(b) The person to whom, under a written agreement of the parties, the duty of plan administrator is delegated by the employer, union or other provider that offers a health benefit plan.
(11) "Providing party" means a party to a child support order who has been ordered by the court or the enforcing agency to provide medical support.
(12) "Public body" has the meaning given that term in ORS 174.109. [2003 c.637 §2; 2007 c.878 §5; 2009 c.351 §1; 2011 c.318 §13; 2017 c.467 §2]

25.323 Medical support. (1) Every child support order must include a medical support clause.
(2) Whenever a child support order that does not include a medical support clause is modified the modification must include a medical support clause.
(3) A medical support clause may require that medical support be provided in more than one form, and may make the requirement that medical support be provided in a particular form contingent on the availability of another form of medical support.
(4) A medical support clause must require that one or both parents provide health care coverage for a child that is appropriate and available at the time the order is entered. If health care coverage for a child is not appropriate and available at the time the order is entered, the order must:
(a) Require that one or both parents provide health care coverage for the child at any time thereafter when such coverage becomes available; and
(b) Either require the payment of cash medical support, or include findings on why cash medical support has not been required.
(5) For the purposes of subsection (4) of this section, health care coverage is appropriate and available for a child if the coverage:
(a) Is accessible, as described in subsection (6) of this section;
(b) Is reasonable in cost and does not require the payment of unreasonable deductibles or copayments; and
(c) Provides coverage, at a minimum, for medical expenses, hospital expenses, preventive care, emergency care, acute care and chronic care.
(6) Health care coverage is accessible for the purposes of subsection (5)(a) of this section if:
(a) The coverage will be available for at least one year, based on the work history of the parent providing the coverage; and
(b) The coverage either does not have service area limitations or the child lives within 30 miles or 30 minutes of a primary care provider who is eligible for payment under the coverage.
(7) A medical support clause may not order a providing party to pay cash medical support or to pay to provide health care coverage if the providing party's income is equal to or less than the Oregon minimum wage for full-time employment.
(8) Cash medical support and the cost of other medical support ordered under a medical support clause constitute a child support obligation and must be included in the child support calculation made under ORS 25.275. [2003 c.637 §3; 2007 c.878 §6; 2009 c.351 §2; 2009 c.595 §55; 2011 c.318 §6; 2017 c.467 §1]

25.325 Enforcing medical support; form of notice; rules. (1) When a child support order with a medical support clause is entered, the court or the enforcing agency may issue a qualified medical child support order as provided in section 609 of the Employee Retirement Income Security Act of 1974 (29 U.S.C. 1169). The qualified medical child support order shall direct the providing party's employer, or the plan administrator for the providing party's employee health care coverage, to enroll the providing party's child in the employee health benefit plan and direct the providing party's employer to withhold any required premium from the providing party's compensation.
(2) When a child support order with a medical support clause is entered and support enforcement services are being provided under ORS 25.080, the enforcing agency shall, when appropriate, issue a medical support notice to the providing party's employer within two business days after receiving information under ORS 25.790 that the employer has hired or rehired the providing party.
(3) If a child support order with a medical support clause is in effect or is being sought:
(a) The providing party's employer or the plan administrator for the providing party's employee health care coverage shall release to the enforcing agency, upon request, the name and address of the health benefit plan that provides the coverage and the plan administrator; and
(b) The plan administrator shall release to the obligee or the enforcing agency, upon request, information about health care coverage for dependents under the employee health benefit plan.
(4) If a qualified medical child support order or a medical support notice has been served on the providing party's employer, the order or notice is binding on the employer and the plan administrator for the providing party's employee health benefit plan to the extent that the child is eligible to be enrolled in the health benefit plan under the applicable terms and conditions of the plan and the standard enrollment guidelines as described in ORS 743B.470. Enrollment of the child shall be allowed at any time, notwithstanding any enrollment season restrictions.
(5) The Department of Justice, by rule, shall prescribe the form of a medical support notice for the purposes of ORS 25.321 to 25.343. In prescribing the form, the department shall consider all relevant federal law relating to medical support notices. [2003 c.637 §4; 2007 c.878 §7; 2009 c.351 §3]

25.327 Service of medical support notice. (1) The enforcing agency shall serve the medical support notice on the providing party's employer as a withholder. The notice may be served upon the withholder or the withholder's registered agent, corporate officer, bookkeeper, accountant, person responsible for payroll or local office manager by:

(a) Personal service;

(b) Any type of mail that is calculated to give actual notice and is addressed to one of the persons listed in this subsection; or

(c) Electronic means if the employer has the ability to receive the medical support notice in that manner.

(2) Service of a medical support notice constitutes receipt of a medical child support order.

(3) The enforcing agency shall, as provided in ORS 25.333, notify the parties that the medical support notice has been served on the providing party's employer. [2003 c.637 §5; 2007 c.878 §8]

25.329 Actions required after service of medical support notice; rules. When the enforcing agency serves a medical support notice on an employer:

(1) The employer shall comply with the provisions in the medical support notice;

(2) The plan administrator and the employer shall treat the medical support notice as an application by the enforcing agency for health care coverage for the named child under the health benefit plan to the extent an application is required by the plan;

(3) If the providing party named in the medical support notice is not an employee of the employer, or if a health benefit plan is not offered or available to the providing party, the employer shall notify the enforcing agency within 20 business days after the date of the medical support notice;

(4) If a health benefit plan is offered or available to the providing party, the employer shall send the plan administrator's portion of the notice to each appropriate plan administrator within 20 business days after the date of the medical support notice;

(5) Within 40 business days after the date of the medical support notice, the plan administrator shall do all of the following as directed by the notice:

(a) Complete the appropriate portion of the notice and return the portion to the enforcing agency;

(b) If the child is or will be enrolled, notify the parties and furnish the obligee with the information necessary to effectuate coverage and submit claims for benefits;

(c) If the child has been or will be enrolled, provide the enforcing agency with the type of health benefit plan under which the child has been or will be enrolled, including whether dental, optical, office visits and prescription drugs are covered services;

(d) If more than one health benefit plan is available to the providing party and the providing party is not enrolled, forward the health benefit plan descriptions and documents to the enforcing agency;

(e) If the providing party is subject to a waiting period that expires more than 90 days after the date of receipt of the medical support notice by the plan administrator or if the providing party has not completed a waiting period that is measured in a manner other than the passage of time, notify the employer, the enforcing agency and the parties; and

(f) Upon completion of the enrollment, notify the employer of the enrollment;

(6) If the plan administrator notifies the employer that the providing party is subject to a waiting period that expires more than 90 days after the date of receipt of the medical support notice by the plan administrator or that the providing party is subject to a waiting period that is measured in a manner other than the passage of time, the employer shall, when the providing party becomes eligible to enroll in the plan, notify the plan administrator that the medical support notice requires that the child named in the notice be enrolled in the plan; and

(7) The plan administrator shall enroll the child and, if necessary to the enrollment of the child, enroll the providing party in the plan as provided by rules adopted by the Department of Justice. [2003 c.637 §6; 2007 c.878 §9]

25.330 [1985 c.671 §6; 1991 c.588 §1; 1995 c.609 §5; 1997 c.704 §28; renumbered 25.167 in 1999]

25.331 Obligation to withhold. (1) Upon notification from the plan administrator that the child is enrolled in the health benefit plan, the employer shall withhold from the providing party's compensation the providing party's share, if any, of premiums for the health benefit plan. The employer shall forward the amount withheld as required by the health benefit plan.

(2) The withholding required by a qualified medical child support order or a medical support notice is a continuing obligation. The qualified medical child support order or medical support notice and the withholding remain in effect and are binding upon the employer until further notice from the court or the enforcing agency.

(3)(a) An amount withheld by an employer in compliance with a withholding order issued for monetary support and a qualified medical child support order or medical support notice may not exceed 50 percent of the providing party's net disposable income.

(b) Notwithstanding paragraph (a) of this subsection, upon the motion of a party and after a hearing, the court may order the withholding of more than 50 percent of the providing party's net disposable income. However, the amount withheld may not exceed the amount allowed under section 303(b) of the federal Consumer Credit Protection Act (15 U.S.C. 1673(b)).

(4) If a providing party's compensation drops to a level at which withholding under this section exceeds the amount allowed under subsection (3) of this section, the employer shall stop the withholding and send the court or the enforcing agency, as the case may be, a written notice within 15 days of stopping the withholding. The notice shall include the providing party's name, address and Social Security number and the date the employer stopped withholding under this section.

(5) An employer is not subject to civil liability to an individual or agency for conduct or actions in compliance with a medical support notice if the employer:

(a) Is served with a medical support notice under ORS 25.327 that is regular on its face; and

(b) Complies with the provisions of the medical support notice if the notice appears to be in conformance with section 609 of the Employee Retirement Income Security Act of 1974 (29 U.S.C. 1169). [2003 c.637 §7; 2007 c.878 §10]

25.333 Contesting medical support notice. (1) When the enforcing agency issues a medical support notice under ORS 25.325, the enforcing agency shall notify the parties by regular mail to the last known addresses of the parties:

(a) That the notice has been sent to the providing party's employer; and

(b) Of the providing party's rights and duties under the notice.

(2) A providing party may contest a medical support notice within 30 days after the date the premium is first withheld pursuant to the notice or, if the health benefit plan is provided at no cost to the providing party, the date the first premium is paid by the employer.

(3) The only basis for contesting a medical support notice is a mistake of fact. A "mistake of fact" means any of the following:

(a) No order to provide health care coverage under a health benefit plan has been issued in regard to the providing party's child;

(b) The amount to be withheld for premiums is greater than is permissible under ORS 25.331;

(c) The alleged providing party is not the party from whom health care coverage is required; or

(d) The providing party's income is equal to or less than Oregon minimum wage for full-time employment.

(4) The providing party may contest the medical support notice by requesting an administrative review. After receiving a request for review and within 45 days after the date the premium is first withheld pursuant to the medical support notice, the enforcing agency shall determine, based on an evaluation of the facts, whether the withholding for premiums may continue. The enforcing agency shall inform the parties of the determination in writing and include information regarding the right to appeal the determination.

(5) Any appeal of the enforcing agency's determination under subsection (4) of this section is to the circuit court for a hearing under ORS 183.484.

(6) The initiation of proceedings to contest a medical support notice or an appeal of the enforcing agency's determination under this section does not stay the withholding of premiums. [2003 c.637 §8; 2007 c.878 §11; 2009 c.351 §10; 2011 c.318 §9]

25.335 Termination of support order. When support enforcement services are being provided under ORS 25.080, the enforcing agency shall notify the employer when there is no longer in effect a support order requiring health care coverage for which the enforcing agency is responsible. However, termination of the health care coverage is governed by the health benefit plan's provisions for termination and by applicable federal law. [2003 c.637 §9]

25.337 Liability. (1) If the plan administrator or the employer fails to comply with the requirements described in ORS 25.329 or 25.331, the enforcing agency or obligee may bring a civil action against the plan administrator or employer for medical expenses, the providing party's share of the premiums, attorney fees and costs.

(2) An employer commits an unlawful employment practice if the employer discharges a providing party, refuses to hire a providing party or in any other manner discriminates, retaliates or takes disciplinary action against a providing party because of the entry of a medical support notice or qualified medical child support order or because of the obligations imposed upon the plan administrator by the order. An employee may bring a civil action under ORS 659A.885 or may file a complaint with the Commissioner of the Bureau of Labor and Industries in the manner provided by ORS 659A.820.

(3) A providing party who fails to maintain health care coverage for a child as ordered is liable, from the date of the order, for any medical expenses resulting from the failure to maintain coverage.

(4) The remedies described in this section are not exclusive. Nothing in this section precludes action by the court to enforce a judicial or administrative order requiring health care coverage or payment of medical support by imposition of remedial or punitive sanctions for contempt or otherwise. [2003 c.637 §10; 2007 c.878 §12]

25.339 Priority of medical support notice. A medical support notice issued under ORS 25.325 has priority over any previously filed attachment, execution, garnishment or assignment of income other than a withholding order issued for monetary support, unless otherwise requested by the obligee. [2003 c.637 §11]

25.340 [1985 c.671 §7; 1993 c.798 §35; renumbered 25.381 in 1999]

25.341 Notice of termination of employer's relationship with providing party. When an employer is unable to continue withholding from a providing party's compensation because the relationship between the employer and the providing party ends, the employer shall send the enforcing agency a written notice within 15 days of the termination of the relationship. The notice must include the providing party's name, the providing party's last known address, the providing party's Social Security number, the date the relationship terminated and, if known, the name and address of a new employer of or other provider of a health benefit plan to the providing party. [2003 c.637 §12; 2007 c.878 §13]

25.342 Rules. The Department of Justice may adopt all rules necessary for implementation of ORS 25.321 to 25.343. [2009 c.351 §12]

25.343 Authorization for reimbursement payments. The signature of the obligee or guardian of a child covered by a health benefit plan is a valid authorization for purposes of processing an insurance reimbursement payment to the provider of the health services as provided in ORS 743B.470. [2003 c.637 §13]

25.350 [Formerly 23.783; repealed by 1993 c.798 §21]

25.351 [1993 c.798 §12; 1995 c.272 §1; 1997 c.704 §29; 1999 c.80 §6; renumbered 25.414 in 1999]

25.353 [1993 c.798 §14; 1995 c.272 §7; 1997 c.704 §30; 1999 c.80 §7; renumbered 25.417 in 1999]

25.354 [1995 c.272 §4; 1999 c.735 §15; renumbered 25.387 in 1999]

25.355 [1993 c.798 §15; 1997 c.704 §31; 1999 c.80 §8; renumbered 25.411 in 1999]

25.357 [1993 c.798 §16; renumbered 25.421 in 1999]

25.359 [1993 c.798 §17; renumbered 25.408 in 1999]

25.360 [Formerly 23.778; repealed by 1993 c.798 §21]

25.361 [1993 c.798 §18; repealed by 1999 c.735 §23]

25.363 [1993 c.798 §19; 1999 c.80 §9; renumbered 25.424 in 1999]

25.365 [1993 c.798 §20; renumbered 25.427 in 1999]

25.367 [1993 c.798 §2; 1995 c.608 §33; 1999 c.130 §3; renumbered 25.372 in 1999]

25.370 [1985 c.671 §8; 1989 c.812 §5; 1993 c.798 §26; 1997 c.704 §32; renumbered 25.384 in 1999]

INCOME WITHHOLDING AND PAYMENT RECORDS

25.372 Applicability. ORS 25.372 to 25.427 apply to current support, arrears and interest on arrears, independently or combined, whether arrears are owed to an obligee, the state or a foreign jurisdiction. [Formerly 25.367; 2001 c.249 §73; 2003 c.73 §28; 2003 c.572 §7]

25.375 Priority of withholding. Except as provided in ORS 25.339, withholding under ORS 25.378 has priority over any other legal process under Oregon law against the same income. [Formerly 25.722; 2003 c.637 §16]

25.378 Payment of support by income withholding; initiation of income withholding. (1) Except as otherwise provided in ORS 25.396, when a support order is entered or modified by the Division of Child Support, a district attorney, an administrative law judge or a circuit court, including a juvenile court, the order shall include a provision requiring the obligor to pay support by income withholding regardless of whether support enforcement services are being provided under ORS 25.080. In addition to the income withholding provided for in this subsection, income withholding may be initiated in accordance with subsections (2) to (6) of this section.

(2) When an obligor is subject to a support order issued or registered in this state and fails to make payments at least equal to the amount of support payable for one month, a court or the administrator, whichever is appropriate, shall initiate income withholding without the need for a judicial or administrative hearing and without the need for advance notice to the obligor of the withholding.

(3) When an arrearage exists and notice of the delinquent amount has been given to the obligor, a court, upon application, shall issue a withholding order upon the ex parte request of a person holding support rights or the administrator.

(4) If an obligor is not otherwise subject to income withholding a court or the administrator may issue an order to withhold upon the ex parte motion of the obligor.

(5) Upon the request of the holder of support rights, a court or the administrator, as appropriate, may issue a withholding order at any time if:

(a) The obligor is not otherwise subject to withholding; and

(b) After notice and an opportunity to object has been given to the obligor, a finding is made that it would be in the best interests of the child to issue a withholding order.

(6) A court or the administrator shall issue an order to withhold when a support order or an arrearage from another jurisdiction is entered in Oregon in accordance with interstate income withholding under ORS chapter 110. [Formerly 25.311; 2001 c.104 §§6,7; 2003 c.73 §§29,30; 2003 c.75 §25; 2013 c.184 §2]

25.381 Establishing income withholding as method of paying support; records. (1) Whenever services are being provided under ORS 25.080, support rights are not and have not at any time during the past five months been assigned to this or another state, and no arrearages under a support order are so assigned, the administrator shall provide, upon request of an obligor or obligee, services sufficient to permit establishment of income withholding under ORS 25.378, including services necessary to establish a support payment record under ORS 25.164 and 25.167.

(2) Regardless of whether services are being provided under ORS 25.080, the administrator shall provide, upon request of an obligor or obligee, services sufficient to permit establishment of income withholding under ORS 25.378:

(a) For the payment of child support without the necessity of an application for support enforcement services under Title IV-D of the Social Security Act (42 U.S.C. 651 et seq.); and

(b) For the payment of spousal support if the obligee is receiving supplemental nutrition assistance or any other form of public assistance, as defined in ORS 411.010, from the Department of Human Services or medical assistance, as defined in ORS 414.025, from the department or the Oregon Health Authority. [Formerly 25.340; 2001 c.900 §8; 2003 c.73 §31; 2005 c.265 §1; 2009 c.599 §15; 2013 c.688 §7]

25.384 Statement on withholding in support order. (1) Any child support order issued or modified after October 1, 1989, shall include a statement in substantially the following form:

NOTICE OF INCOME WITHHOLDING

The support order is enforceable by income withholding under ORS 25.372 to 25.427. Withholding shall occur immediately, whenever there are arrears at least equal to the support payment for one month, whenever the obligated parent requests such withholding or whenever the obligee requests withholding for good cause. The district attorney or, as appropriate, the Division of Child Support of the Department of Justice will assist in securing such withholding. Exceptions may apply in some circumstances.

---

(2) The Department of Justice shall provide annual notice to each obligor and obligee on support orders being enforced by the district attorney or Division of Child Support of the availability of and requirements for exceptions to withholding. [Formerly 25.370]

25.387 Withholding more than amount authorized by law. Notwithstanding ORS 25.414 and 656.234, the court upon motion of a party holding the support rights, the Division of Child Support or the district attorney, and after a hearing, may order the withholding of more than the amount otherwise authorized by law. In no case may an order require payment of an amount that exceeds the limits imposed by the Consumer Credit Protection Act (15 U.S.C. 1673(b)). [Formerly 25.354]

25.390 Amendment of support order not required for withholding. Disposable income is subject to an order to withhold to satisfy a support obligation without the need for any amendment to the support order involved or for any further action, other than those actions required or permitted under ORS 25.378. [Formerly 25.318]

25.393 Remedy additional to other remedies. Collection of support by withholding income pursuant to ORS chapter 25 is in addition to any other remedy provided by law for the enforcement of support. [Formerly 25.313]

25.396 Exception to withholding; termination of withholding; rules. (1) When a court or the administrator enters or modifies a support order, the court or administrator may grant an exception to income withholding required under ORS 25.378 if the court or administrator makes a written finding that there is good cause not to require income withholding. Good cause exists when there is proof of timely payment of previously ordered support and when initiating or continuing income withholding would not be in the best interests of the child.

(2) The court or administrator may grant an exception to income withholding required under ORS 25.378 if:

(a) The obligor and obligee at any time agree in writing to an alternative payment method;

(b) When money is owed to the state under the support order, the state agrees in writing to the alternative payment method;

(c) The obligor has paid in full all arrears accrued under the support order;

(d) The obligor has complied with the terms of any previous exception granted under this section; and

(e) The court or administrator accepts the alternative payment method.

(3) Notwithstanding subsection (1) of this section, when child support is currently assigned to the state and the child is in the custody of the Oregon Youth Authority or the Department of Human Services, the state or the obligor may request and the court or administrator may grant an exception from income withholding if:

(a) The order to withhold is a barrier to reunification of the family or rehabilitation of the youth or is prejudicial to the obligor's ability to provide for another child to whom a duty of support is owed; and

(b) The state and the obligor agree in writing to an alternative payment method.

(4) Exceptions to income withholding described in this section may be granted by the administrator or the court, except that when support enforcement services are being provided under ORS 25.080 the only permissible alternative payment methods are an electronic funds transfer to the Department of Justice or another method permitted under rules adopted under this section.

(5) A party may appeal the administrator's decision granting or denying an exception under this section to the circuit court in accordance with ORS 183.484.

(6) Income withholding may be terminated only if the conditions set forth in this section are met.

(7) The Department of Justice shall adopt rules and establish procedures to implement this section. [Formerly 25.317; 2001 c.171 §1; 2003 c.73 §32; 2003 c.572 §8]

25.399 Notice of order to withhold; contents of notice. (1) When an order to withhold is issued under ORS 25.378, the party or entity initiating the action shall send notice of the order to withhold to the obligor by regular mail to the last-known addresses of the obligor. The notice must state:

(a) That withholding has commenced;

(b) The amount to be withheld and the amount of arrears, if any;

(c) That the order to withhold applies to any current or subsequent withholder or period of employment;

(d) The procedures available for contesting the withholding and that the only basis for contesting the withholding is a mistake of fact, which means an error in the amount of current support or arrearages, or an error in the identity of the obligor;

(e) The availability of and requirements for exceptions to withholding;

(f) That the obligor has 30 days from the date that the income is first withheld pursuant to the order to withhold to contest the withholding; and

(g) The actions that will be taken if the obligor contests the withholding.

(2) The notice requirement of subsection (1) of this section may be met by mailing a copy of the order to withhold, by regular mail, to the obligor. [Formerly 25.315; 2011 c.318 §10; 2017 c.461 §1]

25.402 Service of order on withholder; contents. (1)(a) The party initiating the support action shall serve the order to withhold on the withholder. The order may be personally served upon the withholder or the withholder's registered agent, an officer of the corporation, bookkeeper, accountant, person responsible for payroll or local office manager or may be served by any type of mail which is calculated to give actual notice and is addressed to one of the persons listed above.

(b) Notwithstanding paragraph (a) of this subsection and unless the Department of Justice, prior to initiating service, receives written notice of completion of service by another party, the department shall serve the order to withhold in all cases affecting a support order for which the department or the district attorney has responsibility under ORS 25.080 for providing support enforcement services regardless of whether the department or another party initiated the support action.

(2) The order to withhold shall inform the withholder of all of the following:

(a) The amount of the obligor's continuing support obligation.

(b) That the withholder is required to withhold from the obligor's disposable income due or becoming due to the obligor at each pay period an amount as determined by ORS 25.414.

(c) The appropriate person to whom to make the withholding payment.

(d) The information contained in ORS 25.375, 25.387, 25.411, 25.414, 25.417, 25.421 and 25.424. [Formerly 25.314]

25.405 Contesting order to withhold; basis. (1) An obligor contesting an order to withhold issued under ORS 25.378 must do so within 30 days from the date income is first withheld pursuant to the order to withhold. The obligor may not contest an order to withhold issued under ORS 25.378 (5).

(2) The only basis for contesting the order to withhold is a mistake of fact. "Mistake of fact" means an error in the amount of current support or arrearages, or an error in the identity of the obligor. Payment of all arrearages shall not be the sole basis for not implementing withholding.

(3) If the order to withhold was issued by a court of this state, the obligor must contest the order to withhold in the court that issued the order.

(4) If the order to withhold was issued by a court or administrative agency of another state and was received directly by an employer in this state under ORS 110.594, the obligor may contest the order to withhold by:

(a) Seeking relief from enforcement of the order in the appropriate tribunal of the state that issued the order;

(b) Contesting the validity and enforcement of the order under ORS 110.601; or

(c) Registering the underlying withholding order in Oregon in the manner provided by ORS 110.605 to 110.611 and seeking relief from enforcement of the order as provided in ORS 110.617 and 110.620.

(5) If the order to withhold was issued pursuant to a request for enforcement under ORS 25.080, the obligor may contest the order to withhold to the district attorney or the Division of Child Support. The district attorney or the Division of Child Support need not provide an opportunity for a contested case administrative hearing under ORS chapter 183 or a hearing in circuit court. Within 45 days after the date income is first withheld pursuant to the order to withhold, the district attorney or the Division of Child Support shall determine, based on an evaluation of the facts, if the withholding shall continue and notify the obligor of the determination and of the obligor's right to appeal the determination.

(6) Any appeal of the decision of the district attorney or the Division of Child Support made under subsection (5) of this section is to the circuit court for a hearing under ORS 183.484.

(7) The initiation of proceedings to contest an order to withhold under subsection (4) of this section, a motion or request to contest an order to withhold or an appeal of the decision of the district attorney or the Division of Child Support made under subsection (5) of this section does not act to stay withholding unless otherwise ordered by a court. [Formerly 25.316; 2009 c.80 §2; 2011 c.318 §11; 2015 c.298 §87]

25.408 Withholding is continuing obligation. The withholding required by the order is a continuing obligation. The notice and the withholding required by the order remain in effect and are binding upon the withholder until further notice from the court or the entity issuing the notice. [Formerly 25.359]

25.410 [1985 c.671 §13a; 1993 c.798 §27; 1993 c.800 §3; repealed by 1995 c.608 §46]

25.411 When withholding begins; payment to Department of Justice or obligee. (1) The withholder shall start withholding not later than the first pay period occurring five days after the date of the order to withhold. However, if on the date the employer receives the order the employer has already calculated the payroll for that pay period and has prepared the paycheck or submitted a deposit for that payroll, the employer shall start withholding no later than the second pay period occurring after the date of the order to withhold.

(2) Within seven business days after the date the obligor receives income, the withholder shall pay amounts withheld to the Department of Justice or to the obligee by deposit into the obligee's bank account, whichever is specified in the order to withhold. The withholder shall include, with the payment, the obligor's name and case number and the date upon which the income was withheld.

(3) When payments are made to the Department of Justice, the withholder may combine amounts withheld from different obligors' incomes in a single payment as long as such payment is accompanied by a list that separately identifies which portion of the payment is attributable to each obligor, the obligor's name and case number, if any.

(4) As used in this section, "business day" means a day on which the Department of Justice is open for regular business. [Formerly 25.355; 2007 c.356 §4]

25.414 Standard amount to be withheld; processing fee; rules. (1) The withholder shall withhold from the obligor's disposable monthly income, other than workers' compensation under ORS chapter 656 or unemployment compensation under ORS chapter 657, the amount stated in the order to withhold. The entity issuing the order to withhold shall compute this amount subject to the following:

(a) If withholding is for current support only, the amount to be withheld is the amount specified as current support in the support order.

(b) If withholding is for current support and there is an arrearage, the amount to be withheld is 120 percent of the amount specified as current support in the support order.

(c) If withholding is only for arrearage, the amount to be withheld is one of the following:

(A) The amount of the last ordered monthly support.

(B) If there is no last ordered monthly support amount, the monthly support amount used to calculate the arrearage amount specified in the order or judgment for arrearage.

(C) If there is no last ordered monthly support amount and if there was no monthly support amount, an amount calculated under the formula established under ORS 25.275. For purposes of this subparagraph, this calculation shall be based on the obligor's current monthly gross income or, if the obligor's current monthly gross income is not known, the Oregon hourly minimum wage converted to a monthly amount based upon a 40-hour workweek, zero income for the obligee, and one joint child, regardless of how many children the parties may actually have. No rebuttals to this calculation may be allowed.

(d) Notwithstanding the amount determined to be withheld under paragraph (c) of this subsection, the obligor must retain disposable monthly income of at least 160 times the applicable federal minimum hourly wage prescribed by section 6 (a)(1) of the Fair Labor Standards Act of 1938 (29 U.S.C. 206) or any future minimum hourly wages prescribed in that section, if the order to withhold is issued for:

(A) Disability benefits payments from the United States Social Security Administration;

(B) Black lung benefits payments from the United States Department of Labor; or

(C) Disability benefits payments from the United States Department of Veterans Affairs.

(2) The amount to be withheld from unemployment compensation under ORS chapter 657 is calculated as follows:

(a) If withholding is for a current support order, regardless of the existence of arrearage, the amount to be withheld is the lesser of:

(A) Twenty-five percent of the benefits paid; or

(B) The current monthly support obligation. The entity issuing the order to withhold may convert the monthly support obligation amount to a percentage to be withheld from each benefits payment.

(b) If withholding is for arrearage only, the amount to be withheld is the lesser of:

(A) Fifteen percent of the benefits paid; or

(B) The amount of the last ordered monthly support obligation. The entity issuing the order to withhold may convert the last ordered monthly support obligation amount to a percentage to be withheld from each benefits payment.

(c) The withholder may not charge or collect a processing fee when withholding from unemployment compensation.

(3) The amount to be withheld from workers' compensation under ORS chapter 656 is set forth in ORS 656.234.

(4) Notwithstanding any other provision of this section, when withholding is from a lump sum payment or benefit, including but not limited to retroactive workers' compensation benefits, lump sum retirement plan disbursements or withdrawals, insurance payments or settlements, severance pay, bonus payments or any other similar payments or benefits that are not periodic recurring income, the amount subject to withholding for payment of a support obligation may not exceed one-half of the amount of the lump sum payment or benefit.

(5)(a) Notwithstanding any other provision of this section, when the withholding is only for arrearage, the administrator shall set a lesser amount to be withheld if the obligor demonstrates the withholding is prejudicial to the obligor's ability to provide for a child the obligor has a duty to support or the obligor's ability to provide for the obligor's basic needs. The factors to be considered by the administrator in determining whether the obligor can provide for the obligor's basic needs include but are not limited to:

(A) The health expenses of the obligor;

(B) A verified disability affecting the obligor's ability to work;

(C) Whether the obligor's income remaining after withholding would be less than the self-support reserve established by rule of the Department of Justice under paragraph (c) of this subsection;

(D) The available resources of the obligor; and

(E) The number and basic needs of other persons in the obligor's household.

(b) The administrator shall establish a procedure to give advance and periodic notice to the obligor of the provisions of paragraph (a) of this subsection and of the means to reduce the amount stated in the order to withhold.

(c) The Department of Justice shall adopt rules to implement this subsection.

(6) Except as provided in subsection (2) of this section, the withholder may deduct from the obligor's disposable income a monthly processing fee not to exceed $5. The processing fee is in addition to the amount calculated to be withheld for support, unless the amount to be withheld for support is the maximum allowed under subsection (8) of this section, in which case the fee is deducted from the amount withheld as support.

(7) If there are multiple withholding orders against the same obligor, the amount to be withheld is the sum of each support order calculated independently.

(8) No withholding as calculated under this section, including the processing fee permitted in subsection (6) of this section, shall exceed 50 percent of the obligor's net disposable income. The limit established in this subsection applies whenever withholding is implemented under this section, whether by a single order or by multiple orders against the same obligor.

(9) When the obligor's income is not sufficient for the withholder to fully comply with each withholding order, the withholder shall withhold the maximum amount allowed under this section. If all withholding orders for a particular obligor are payable to or through the department, the withholder shall pay to the department the income withheld and the department shall determine priorities for allocating income withheld to multiple child support cases relative to that obligor. If one or more of the withholding orders for a particular obligor require payment other than to or through the department, the withholder shall use the following to determine priorities for withholding and allocating income withheld to multiple child support cases:

(a) If the amount withheld from the obligor's income is sufficient to pay the current support due to each case but is not enough to fully comply with the withholding order for each case where past due support is owed, the withholder shall:

(A) Pay to each case the amount of support due for the current month; and

(B) Pay the remainder of the amount withheld in equal amounts to each case where past due support is owed. However, no case shall receive more than the total amount of current support and past due support owed to that case at the time the payment is made.

(b) If the amount withheld is not sufficient to pay the current support due to each case, each case shall be paid a proportionate share of the amount withheld. The withholder shall determine this for each case by dividing the monthly amount ordered as current support for that case by the combined monthly amount ordered as current support for all cases relative to the same obligor, and multiplying this percentage by the total amount withheld.

(10) An order to withhold income is not subject to the limitations of ORS 18.385.

(11) A withholder shall withhold funds as directed in the order to withhold, except that when a withholder receives an income-withholding order issued by another state, the withholder shall apply the income-withholding law of the state of the obligor's principal place of employment in determining:

(a) The withholder's fee for processing an income-withholding order;

(b) The maximum amount permitted to be withheld from the obligor's income;

(c) The time periods within which the withholder must implement the income-withholding order and forward the child support payment;

(d) The priorities for withholding and allocating income withheld for multiple child support obligees; and

(e) Any withholding terms or conditions not specified in the order. [Formerly 25.351; 2001 c.455 §10; 2003 c.73 §33; 2003 c.572 §9; 2011 c.317 §1]

25.417 Amount to be withheld when obligor paid more frequently than monthly. When an obligor is required to pay support by income withholding and is paid more often than monthly, the withholder shall withhold up to the full amount specified in the order to withhold, based on the obligor's pay period as specified in the order to withhold. The amount withheld may not exceed the maximum amount allowed under ORS 25.414 (8). [Formerly 25.353; 2001 c.455 §11]

25.420 [1985 c.671 §13; 1993 c.800 §4; repealed by 1995 c.608 §46]

25.421 Procedure if withholder does not withhold support. If for any reason a withholder does not withhold support in any month, the withholder shall explain the reason for not withholding. The withholder shall send the explanation for not withholding to the person or entity to whom the withholder sends payments and shall send the explanation on the date that the withholder would normally send a payment. If the withholder does not send a payment because the obligor is no longer employed by the withholder, the withholder may include in the explanation the name and address of the obligor's new employer, if known. A withholder is not liable to the obligor for disclosure of this information. [Formerly 25.357]

25.424 Liability of withholder; action against withholder; penalty; attorney fees; unlawful employment practice. (1) A person who is served with an order to withhold is not subject to civil liability to an individual or agency for conduct or actions in compliance with the order if:

(a) The order is served on the person in the manner provided by ORS 25.402 (1);

(b) The order is regular on its face; and

(c) The order complies with ORS 25.402 (2).

(2) A person who is served with an order to withhold is liable to the obligee for:

(a) All amounts that the person fails to withhold or pay as required by the order;

(b) Any damages suffered by the obligee by reason of the failure of the person to withhold or pay as required by the order; and

(c) Any damages suffered by the obligee by reason of the failure of the person to pay withheld amounts within the time specified by ORS 25.411.

(3) A person who is served with an order to withhold is liable to the obligor for:

(a) All amounts withheld in excess of the amount required by the terms of the order;

(b) Any damages suffered by the obligor by reason of withholding that is in excess of the amount required by the terms of the order;

(c) Any damages suffered by the obligor by reason of the failure of the person to pay withheld amounts within the time specified by ORS 25.411; and

(d) Any other damages suffered by the obligor by reason of the failure of the person to withhold or pay as required by the order.

(4) An obligee or obligor may bring an action to recover amounts under this section, or the Division of Child Support or a district attorney may bring an action on behalf of the obligee or obligor to recover amounts under this section.

(5) If the plaintiff in an action under this section establishes that the conduct of the defendant was willful or grossly negligent, the court shall:

(a) Enter judgment against the defendant for a penalty, payable to the court, not to exceed $250 for each time the defendant failed to withhold or pay the amount required by the terms of the order to withhold, withheld an amount exceeding the amount required by the terms of the order, or failed to pay withheld amounts within the time specified by ORS 25.411; and

(b) Enter judgment against the defendant, payable to the plaintiff, for reasonable attorney fees incurred by the plaintiff.

(6)(a) An employer commits an unlawful employment practice if the employer discharges an employee, refuses to hire an individual or in any other manner discriminates, retaliates or takes disciplinary action against an obligor because of the entry or service of an order to withhold under ORS 25.378 and 25.402 or because of the obligations or additional obligations that the order imposes upon the employer. An obligor may bring an action under ORS 659A.885 or may file a complaint with the Commissioner of the Bureau of Labor and Industries in the manner provided by ORS 659A.820. These remedies are in addition to any other remedy available in law or equity.

(b) Paragraph (a) of this subsection does not apply to actions taken by an employer pursuant to any condition of employment required by law.

(7) Nothing in ORS 25.372 to 25.427 precludes an action for contempt for disobedience of a judicial order to withhold. [Formerly 25.363; 2001 c.621 §67; 2003 c.572 §10; 2009 c.445 §1]

25.427 Rules. The Department of Justice shall make rules and take action as is necessary to carry out the purposes of ORS 25.372 to 25.427. [Formerly 25.365; 2003 c.73 §34]

25.430 [1985 c.671 §13b; repealed by 1995 c.608 §46]

25.440 [1985 c.671 §14; repealed by 1995 c.608 §46]

25.450 [1985 c.671 §15; 1989 c.520 §1; 1993 c.596 §9; 1993 c.798 §28; 1993 c.800 §5; repealed by 1995 c.608 §46]

25.460 [1985 c.671 §16; 1993 c.596 §10; 1993 c.798 §29; repealed by 1995 c.608 §46]

25.470 [1985 c.671 §17; 1993 c.798 §30; repealed by 1995 c.608 §46]

25.480 [1985 c.671 §18; 1993 c.596 §11; 1993 c.798 §36; repealed by 1995 c.608 §46]

25.490 [1985 c.671 §19; 1993 c.798 §37; repealed by 1995 c.608 §46]

25.500 [1985 c.671 §20; 1993 c.798 §38; repealed by 1995 c.608 §46]

25.510 [1985 c.671 §21; 1993 c.798 §39; repealed by 1995 c.608 §46]

25.520 [1985 c.671 §22; 1993 c.798 §40; repealed by 1995 c.608 §46]

25.530 [1985 c.671 §23; repealed by 1995 c.608 §46]

INCOME TAX INTERCEPT

25.610 Procedure to collect support orders from state tax refunds; voluntary withholding; rules. (1) Whenever support enforcement services are being provided, the administrator may request the Department of Revenue, through the Department of Justice or its designee, to collect past due child and spousal support from income tax refunds due to the obligor. The request shall be based upon the payment record maintained under ORS 25.020.

(2) If support payment records have not been maintained as provided in ORS 25.020, then a support payment record may be established under ORS 25.164, 25.167 and 416.429.

(3) The Department of Justice shall adopt rules:

(a) Setting out additional criteria for requests under subsection (1) of this section; and

(b) Directing how any support obligation collected by the Department of Revenue shall be distributed, consistent with federal regulations.

(4) Before a request is made to the Department of Revenue under subsection (1) of this section, the Department of Justice shall provide advance written notice to the obligor, and may send advance written notice to the obligee, of its intent to refer the case to the Department of Revenue. The notice shall inform the parties:

(a) Of the proposed action;

(b) Of the obligor's right to request an administrative review of the proposed action;

(c) That an administrative review, if desired, must be requested by the obligor within 30 days after the date of the notice; and

(d) That the only issues that may be considered in the administrative review are:

(A) Whether the obligor is the person who owes the support obligation; and

(B) Whether the amount shown as the past due support is correct.

(5) An administrative review must be requested within 30 days after the date of the notice described in subsection (4) of this section. At the administrative review, an issue may not be considered if it was previously litigated or if the obligor failed to exercise rights to appear and be heard or to appeal a decision that resulted in the accrual of the arrearage being used as a basis for a request under subsection (1) of this section. A party may appeal a decision from the administrative review under ORS 183.484.

(6) When the Department of Revenue has been requested to collect past due child and spousal support from income tax refunds due to the obligor, the Department of Revenue may not allow the obligor to apply any income tax refund to future taxes of the obligor.

(7) Notwithstanding any other provision of this section, an obligor who is not delinquent in payment of child or spousal support may authorize the Department of Revenue, through the Department of Justice or its designee, to withhold any income tax refund owing to that obligor for the purpose of applying the moneys as a credit to the support account maintained by the Department of Justice. [1985 c.671 §§27,28; 1989 c.519 §6; 1991 c.588 §2; 1993 c.596 §12; 1997 c.170 §12; 1997 c.704 §33; 2001 c.455 §12; 2003 c.73 §35; 2003 c.572 §11; 2005 c.560 §5; 2009 c.210 §1; 2017 c.461 §2]

25.620 Procedures to collect past due support from state tax refunds; fees. (1) The Department of Revenue shall establish procedures consistent with ORS 25.610 to collect past due child and spousal support from income tax refunds due to the obligor in the same manner that other delinquent accounts are collected under ORS 293.250.

(2) The Department of Revenue shall establish procedures to ensure that when an obligor has filed a joint income tax return, the obligor's spouse may apply for a share of the refund, if any. The procedures shall provide for notice to the obligee regarding any application by the obligor's spouse for a share of the refund.

(3) No collection shall be made by the Department of Revenue unless the debt is in a liquidated amount.

217

(4) Notwithstanding the provisions of ORS 293.250, the Department of Revenue shall designate a single fee to retain from moneys collected for child support as a reasonable fee to cover only the actual cost.

(5) The Department of Revenue shall forward the net proceeds of collections made under subsection (1) of this section to the Department of Justice. Such proceeds shall be applied pursuant to ORS 25.610 (3).

(6) Notwithstanding any other law relating to the confidentiality of tax records, the Department of Revenue shall send the Department of Justice the obligor's home address and Social Security number or numbers on each case submitted for collection pursuant to ORS 25.610. [1985 c.671 §29; 1993 c.596 §13; 1997 c.170 §13; 1997 c.704 §34; 2001 c.455 §27]

25.625 Federal tax offset; passport denial; rules.

(1) The Department of Justice may furnish to the United States Secretary of Health and Human Services certifications appropriate to and required for action by the secretary to offset federal income tax returns and to deny, revoke or limit passports of individuals owing child support arrearages.

(2) The department shall adopt rules to carry out the purposes of subsection (1) of this section. [1997 c.746 §13; 2003 c.73 §36]

Note: 25.625 was enacted into law by the Legislative Assembly but was not added to or made a part of ORS chapter 25 or any series therein by legislative action. See Preface to Oregon Revised Statutes for further explanation.

DISCLOSURES OF INFORMATION
BY FINANCIAL INSTITUTIONS

25.640 Definitions for ORS 25.643 and 25.646. For purposes of ORS 25.643 and 25.646:

(1) "Account" means a demand deposit account, checking or negotiable withdrawal order account, savings account, share draft account, time deposit account, money-market mutual fund account or a claim for insurance benefits or payments of at least $500, not including a claim for property damage, under a liability insurance policy or uninsured motorist insurance policy issued by an insurance company authorized to do business in this state.

(2) "Claimant" means an obligor who is asserting a claim of at least $500, not including a claim for property damage, under a liability insurance policy or uninsured motorist policy issued by an insurer that is authorized to do business in this state.

(3) "Customer" has the meaning given that term in ORS 192.583.

(4) "Financial institution" means:

(a) A depository institution, as defined in section 3(c) of the Federal Deposit Insurance Act (12 U.S.C. 1813(c));

(b) Any federal credit union or state credit union, as defined in section 101 of the Federal Credit Union Act (12 U.S.C. 1752), including an institution-affiliated party of such a credit union, as defined in section 206(r) of the Federal Credit Union Act (12 U.S.C. 1786(r)); and

(c) Any benefit association, insurance company, safe deposit company, money-market mutual fund or similar entity authorized to do business in this state.

(5) "Financial records" means any original written or electronic document or copy of the document, or any information contained in the document, held by or in the custody of a financial institution, when the document, copy or information is identifiable as pertaining to one or more customers or claimants of the financial institution. [1997 c.746 §120; 2017 c.486 §1]

Note: 25.640 to 25.646 were enacted into law by the Legislative Assembly but were not added to or made a part of ORS chapter 25 or any series therein by legislative action. See Preface to Oregon Revised Statutes for further explanation.

25.643 Disclosure of information on obligors by financial institutions; fees; liability; rules. (1) The Department of Justice and financial institutions doing business in this state shall enter into agreements to develop and operate a data match system using automated data exchanges to the maximum extent feasible.

(2) Pursuant to the agreements, financial institutions shall provide, for each calendar quarter, the name, address, Social Security number or other taxpayer identification number and other identifying information for each obligor who:

(a) Maintains an account at, or has a claim for insurance benefits or payments with, the institution; and

(b) Owes past due support, as identified by the administrator by name and Social Security number or other taxpayer identification number.

(3) Notwithstanding subsection (2) of this section, a financial institution can satisfy its obligation to conduct a data match and provide information to the administrator under this section as provided in rules adopted by the department.

(4) If a financial institution at which an obligor has a claim for insurance benefits or payments has not previously provided the administrator with the information required by this section, the financial institution must provide the administrator with at least three business days' advance written notice before disbursing any payment to the obligor pursuant to the claim.

(5) The administrator shall pay a reasonable fee to a financial institution for conducting the data match provided for in this section. The fee may not exceed the actual costs incurred by the financial institution.

(6) A financial institution, including an institution-affiliated party as defined in section 3(u) of the Federal Deposit Insurance Act (12 U.S.C. 1813(u)), is not liable under any state law to any person and, except as provided in this section, shall not be in violation of any other law regulating the handling of an account because the financial institution:

(a) Discloses information to the administrator under this section;

(b) Encumbers or surrenders any assets held by the financial institution in response to a notice of lien or levy issued by the administrator; or

(c) Takes any other action in good faith to comply with the requirements of this section.

(7) The department may adopt rules to implement and direct the provision of information pursuant to the agreements entered into for automated data exchanges performed by the data match system developed and operated under this section. [1997 c.746 §121; 2003 c.73 §37; 2009 c.80 §3; 2017 c.486 §2]

Note: See note under 25.640.

25.646 Disclosure of financial records of customers by financial institutions; liability. (1) Upon request of the administrator and the receipt of the certification required under subsection (2) of this section, a financial institution shall provide financial records of a customer or claimant.

(2) In requesting information under subsection (1) of this section, the administrator shall provide the name and Social Security number of the person whose financial records are sought and shall state with reasonable specificity the financial records requested. The administrator shall provide to the financial institution a signed document in a form established by the Department of Justice certifying that:

(a) The person whose financial records are sought is a party to a proceeding to establish, modify or enforce the child support obligation of the person; and

(b) The administrator has authorization from the person for release of the financial records, has given the person written notice of its request for financial records or will give the notice within five days after the financial institution responds to the request.

(3) The administrator shall reimburse a financial institution supplying financial records under this section for actual costs incurred.

(4) A financial institution, including an institution-affiliated party as defined in section 3(u) of the Federal Deposit Insurance Act (12 U.S.C. 1813(u)), that supplies financial records to the administrator under this section is not liable to any person for any loss, damage or injury arising out of or in any way pertaining to the disclosure of the financial records.

(5) A financial institution that is requested to supply financial records under this section may enter into an agreement with the administrator concerning the method by which requests for financial records and responses from the financial institution shall be made.

(6) The administrator shall provide a reasonable time to the financial institution for responding to a request for financial records.

(7) The administrator shall seek financial records under this section only:

(a) With respect to a person who is a party to a proceeding to establish, modify or enforce the child support obligation of the person; or

(b) According to the provisions of ORS 25.083. [1997 c.746 §122; 1999 c.930 §4; 2001 c.455 §13; 2009 c.80 §4; 2017 c.486 §3]

Note: See note under 25.640.

CONSUMER REPORTING AGENCIES

25.650 Information on past due support to consumer reporting agencies; rules. (1) As used in this section, "consumer reporting agency" means any person that, for monetary fees or dues or on a cooperative nonprofit basis, regularly engages in whole or in part in the practice of assembling or evaluating consumer credit information or other information on consumers for the purpose of furnishing consumer reports to third parties, and that uses any means or facility of interstate commerce for the purpose of preparing or furnishing consumer reports.

(2)(a) Notwithstanding any other law, and subject to rules established by the Department of Justice, for cases in which there is past due support, the department shall:

(A) Report periodically to consumer reporting agencies the name of any obligor who is delinquent in the payment of support and the amount owed by the obligor; and

(B) Otherwise make available to a consumer reporting agency upon its request information regarding the amount of past due support owed by an obligor.

(b) The department shall provide advance notice to the obligor concerning the proposed reporting of information to the consumer reporting agencies. The notice must inform the obligor:

(A) Of the amount of the past due support the department will report to the consumer reporting agencies;

(B) That the department will continue to report the past due support amount owed without sending additional notice to the obligor;

(C) Of the obligor's right to request an administrative review within 30 days after the date of the notice; and

(D) Of the issues that may be considered on review.

(c) If an obligor requests an administrative review, the department may not report the past due support amount until the review is complete.

(d) A party may appeal a decision from the administrative review under ORS 183.484. An appeal of the decision does not stay the department from making reports to consumer reporting agencies.

(3) The administrator may request that a consumer reporting agency provide a consumer report when needed for one or more of the following purposes:

(a) To establish or modify a support order.

(b) When parentage has been established with respect to an individual, to establish the individual's capacity to make child support payments or the appropriate amount of child support that may be ordered.

(c) To enforce a support order.

(4) The department shall report information under subsection (2) of this section only to a person that has furnished evidence satisfactory to the department that the person is a consumer reporting agency.

(5) When the department has made a report to a consumer reporting agency under subsection (2) of this section, the department shall promptly notify the consumer reporting agency when the department's records show that the obligor no longer owes past due support. [1985 c.671 §§45,46; 1993 c.596 §14; 1997 c.704 §35; 1999 c.80 §66; 2003 c.73 §38; 2005 c.560 §6; 2017 c.460 §1; 2017 c.461 §3]

LIENS ON PERSONAL PROPERTY

25.670 Judgment lien on personal property. (1) Whenever there is a judgment for unpaid child or spousal support, a lien arises by operation of law on any personal property owned by the obligor, and the lien continues until the liability for the unpaid support is satisfied or the judgment or renewal thereof has expired. For purposes of this section and ORS 25.680 and 25.690, liability for the unpaid support includes the amount of unpaid support, with interest, and any costs that may be associated with lawful execution on the lien including, but not limited to, attorney fees, costs of notice and sale, storage and handling.

(2)(a) A lien arising under subsection (1) of this section may be recorded by filing a written notice of claim of lien with the county clerk of the county in which the obligor resides or the property is located. The notice of claim of lien required under this subsection shall be a written statement and must include:

(A) A statement of the total amount due, as of the date of the filing of the notice of claim of lien;

(B) The name and address of the obligor and obligee;

(C) The name and address of the office of the district attorney, Division of Child Support or other person or entity filing the notice;

(D) A statement identifying the county where the underlying support order was entered and its case number;

(E) A description of the personal property to be charged with the lien sufficient for identification; and

(F) A statement of the date the lien expires under the laws of the issuing state. If no expiration date is provided, the lien expires in Oregon five years from the date of recording.

(b) The county clerk shall record the notice of claim of lien filed under paragraph (a) of this subsection in the County Clerk Lien Record.

(3) When a notice of claim of lien is recorded pursuant to subsection (2) of this section, the person or entity filing the notice of claim of lien shall send forthwith a copy of the notice to the owner of the personal property to be charged with the lien by registered or certified mail, or by any other mail service with delivery confirmation, sent to the owner's last-known address.

(4) Liens described in subsection (1) of this section that arise by operation of law in another state must be accorded full faith and credit if the state agency, party or other entity seeking to enforce the lien follows the applicable procedures for recording and service of notice of claim of lien set forth in this section. A state agency, party or other entity may not file an action to enforce a lien described in this section until the underlying judgment has been filed in Oregon as provided in ORS chapter 110. [1985 c.671 §47; 1993 c.223 §3; 1993 c.596 §15; 1999 c.80 §34; 2003 c.576 §577; 2011 c.318 §12; 2017 c.461 §4]

25.680 Effect of lien; priority. (1) Whenever a notice of claim of lien has been recorded under ORS 25.670 (2), the owner of the personal property may not release, sell, transfer, pay over, encumber or convey the personal property that is the subject of the lien until the Department of Justice or person to whom the support is or was owed or, if services are being provided under ORS 25.080, the enforcing agency of this or any other state releases the lien, the lien has been satisfied or a court has ordered release of the lien on the basis that no debt exists or that the debt has been satisfied. The limitations of this subsection do not apply to transfers or conveyances of the property by the owner to the holder of a security interest that was in existence at the time the notice of claim of lien was filed.

(2) The rights of bona fide purchasers for value or persons with a security interest in the personal property are not affected by the creation or the existence of the lien.

(3) Liens filed under ORS 25.670 do not have priority over previously perfected security interests. [1985 c.671 §48; 1999 c.80 §35; 2003 c.73 §39]

25.690 Foreclosure of lien. A lien arising pursuant to ORS 25.670 may be foreclosed in the manner set out in ORS 87.262 or ORS chapter 18 or in any other manner permitted under law. [1985 c.671 §49; 1999 c.80 §36; 2003 c.576 §577a]

25.700 [1993 c.763 §§2,4; repealed by 2003 c.576 §580]

25.710 Duty of district attorney. (1) Notwithstanding ORS 25.080, the district attorney, except as provided in subsection (2) of this section, shall continue to enforce support enforcement cases until the Department of Justice otherwise directs if:
(a) The case was being enforced by the district attorney on October 1, 1985; and
(b) The case involves any arrearages assigned to the state or any other state.
(2) This section does not apply when the obligor or beneficiary of the support judgment or order is receiving any of the following:
(a) Public assistance; or
(b) Care, support or services under ORS 418.015. [1985 c.671 §51a; 2003 c.73 §40; 2003 c.572 §12; 2003 c.576 §301]

25.715 Child support paid from security deposit. (1) The court may order that the portion of a security deposit made under ORS 135.265 that would otherwise be returned to the person who made the deposit or the amount of child support arrearages, whichever is less, be paid to an obligee or the Division of Child Support of the Department of Justice if:
(a) The defendant is an obligor who owes child support arrearages;
(b) The obligee or the administrator has filed a motion requesting the court to make such an order;
(c) The obligee or the administrator has served the defendant with a copy of the motion;
(d) The defendant has an opportunity to respond and request a hearing; and
(e) The court has determined that such an order is appropriate.
(2) The court may order that a portion of a security deposit that is forfeited under ORS 135.280 be paid to the division and be applied to any unsatisfied child support judgment and to provide security for child support payments in accordance with ORS 25.230 if:
(a) The defendant is an obligor who owes child support;
(b) The administrator has filed a motion requesting the court to make such an order;
(c) The motion specifies the amount to be applied to the child support judgment under ORS 135.280; and
(d) The court has determined that such an order is appropriate. [1999 c.1030 §5; 2001 c.705 §1; 2011 c.597 §40]

25.720 When support assignable. (1) Except as provided in ORS 25.125, 412.024, 418.032, 419B.406 or 419C.597 or subsection (2) of this section, the right to receive child or spousal support payments under ORS chapters 107, 108, 109, 110, 416, 419B and 419C is not assignable, and any transaction in violation of this section is void.
(2) Notwithstanding the provisions of subsection (1) of this section, the right to receive support payments is assignable as may be appropriate for the protection of a minor or other person for whom a fiduciary has been appointed under ORS chapter 125 or for whom a trust has been established.
(3) A person may not solicit or accept the assignment of support rights under subsection (1) of this section. [1985 c.671 §52(1),(2),(3); 1993 c.33 §288; 1995 c.514 §12; 1995 c.608 §34; 1995 c.664 §75; 1997 c.385 §3; 2003 c.131 §1]

25.722 [1993 c.798 §11; renumbered 25.375 in 1999]

25.725 Child Support Deposit Fund. (1) The Child Support Deposit Fund is established in the State Treasury separate and distinct from the General Fund. Interest earned by the Child Support Deposit Fund shall be credited to the fund. All moneys in the Child Support Deposit Fund are appropriated continuously for use by the Department of Justice as the state disbursement unit.
(2) All moneys received by the department under ORS 25.020 and 25.620 and any other state or federal law authorizing the department to collect or receive child support payments shall be deposited in the Child Support Deposit Fund. The Child Support Deposit Fund is not subject to the provisions of ORS 291.234 to 291.260. [1995 c.262 §2; 1997 c.704 §36; 2003 c.73 §41]

25.727 Garnishing income of person required to provide health insurance for child eligible under Medicaid. (1) The Department of Justice, or its designee, may garnish the wages, salary or other employment income of, and withhold amounts from state tax refunds to, any person who:
(a) Is required by court or administrative order to provide coverage of the cost of health services to a child eligible for medical assistance under Medicaid; and
(b) Has received payment from a third party for the costs of such services but has not used the payments to reimburse either the other parent or guardian of the child or the provider of the services.
(2) The department, or its designee, may take this action to the extent necessary to reimburse the state Medicaid agency for its costs, but claims for current and past due child support shall take priority over these claims. [1995 c.506 §9; 2003 c.73 §42]

25.729 Application of laws to effectuate purposes of ORS chapter 110. Any provision in the laws of this state relating to establishment, modification and enforcement of support may be applied to effectuate the purposes of ORS chapter 110 to the extent that such application is not inconsistent with ORS chapter 110. [1995 c.608 §11]

SUSPENSION OF OCCUPATIONAL
AND DRIVER LICENSES

25.750 Suspension of licenses, certificates, permits and registrations; when authorized; rules. (1) All licenses, certificates, permits or registrations that a person is required by state law to possess in order to engage in an occupation or profession or to use a particular occupational or professional title, all annual licenses issued to individuals by the Oregon Liquor Control Commission, all driver licenses or permits issued by the Department of Transportation and recreational hunting and fishing licenses, as defined by rule of the Department of Justice, are subject to suspension by the respective issuing entities upon certification to the issuing entity by the administrator that a child support case record is being maintained by the Department of Justice, that the case is being enforced by the administrator under the provisions of ORS 25.080 and that one or both of the following conditions apply:
(a) That the party holding the license, certificate, permit or registration is in arrears under any child support judgment or order, in an amount equal to the greater of three months of support or $2,500, and:
(A) Has not entered into an agreement with the administrator with respect to the child support obligation; or
(B) Is not in compliance with an agreement entered into with the administrator; or
(b) That the party holding the license, certificate, permit or registration has failed, after receiving appropriate notice, to comply with a subpoena or other procedural order relating to a parentage or child support proceeding and:
(A) Has not entered into an agreement with the administrator with respect to compliance; or
(B) Is not in compliance with such an agreement.
(2) The Department of Justice by rule shall specify the conditions and terms of agreements, compliance with which precludes the suspension of the license, certificate, permit or registration. [1993 c.365 §2; 1995 c.620 §1; 1995 c.750 §7; 1997 c.704 §37; 1999 c.80 §11; 2001 c.323 §1; 2001 c.455 §14; 2003 c.73 §43; 2009 c.209 §1; 2017 c.651 §12]

25.752 Memberships in professional organizations that are required by state law. As used in ORS 25.750 to 25.783, "licenses, certificates, permits or registrations" includes, but is not limited to, memberships in professional organizations that are required by state law in order to engage in a profession. [1995 c.620 §12]

25.753 [1993 c.365 §3; repealed by 1995 c.620 §13]

25.756 Identifying persons holding licenses, certificates, permits and registrations. The Department of Justice shall enter into agreements regarding the identification of persons who are subject to the provisions of ORS 25.750 to 25.783 and who hold licenses, certificates, permits or registrations with:

(1) The Oregon Liquor Control Commission;

(2) All entities that issue licenses, certificates, permits or registrations that a person is required by state law to possess to engage in an occupation, profession or recreational hunting or fishing or to use a particular occupational or professional title; and

(3) The Department of Transportation. [1993 c.365 §4; 1995 c.620 §2; 1995 c.750 §8; 1997 c.704 §38; 1999 c.80 §12]

25.759 Notice to persons subject to suspension; contents. Upon identification of a person subject to suspension under ORS 25.750 to 25.783, the administrator may issue a notice, sent by regular mail to both the address of record as shown in the records of the issuing entity and the address of record as shown on the administrator's child support file. Such notice shall contain the following information:

(1) That certain licenses, certificates, permits and registrations, which shall be specified in the notice, are subject to suspension as provided for by ORS 25.750 to 25.783.

(2) The name, final four digits of the Social Security number, if available, year of birth, if known, and child support case number or numbers of the person subject to the action.

(3) The amount of arrears and the amount of the monthly child support obligation, if any, or, if suspension is based on ORS 25.750 (1)(b), a description of the subpoena or other procedural order with which the person subject to the action has failed to comply.

(4) The procedures available for contesting the suspension of a license, certificate, permit or registration.

(5) That the only bases for contesting the suspension are:

(a) That the arrears are not greater than three months of support or $2,500;

(b) That there is a mistake in the identity of the obligor;

(c) That the person subject to the suspension has complied with the subpoena or other procedural order identified in subsection (3) of this section; or

(d) That the person subject to the suspension is in compliance with a previous agreement as provided for by ORS 25.750 to 25.783.

(6) That the obligor may enter into an agreement, prescribed by rule by the Department of Justice, compliance with which shall preclude the suspension under ORS 25.750 to 25.783.

(7) That the obligor has 30 days from the date of the notice to contact the administrator in order to:

(a) Contest the action in writing on a form prescribed by the administrator;

(b) Comply with the subpoena or procedural order identified in subsection (3) of this section; or

(c) Enter into an agreement authorized by ORS 25.750 and 25.762. The notice shall state that any agreement must be in writing and must be entered into within 30 days of making contact with the administrator.

(8) That failure to contact the administrator within 30 days of the date of the notice shall result in notification to the issuing entity to suspend the license, certificate, permit or registration. [1993 c.365 §5; 1995 c.620 §3; 1997 c.704 §39; 1999 c.80 §13; 2001 c.323 §2; 2001 c.455 §15; 2003 c.73 §44; 2011 c.318 §14; 2013 c.184 §3]

25.762 Agreement between obligor and administrator; effect of failure to contest suspension or to enter into agreement. (1) If the administrator is contacted within 30 days of the date of the notice specified in ORS 25.759, the administrator and the obligor may enter into an agreement as provided for by rule of the Department of Justice. If no contest is filed or if no agreement is entered into within the time prescribed by ORS 25.750 to 25.783, or if the obligor fails to comply with the terms of an agreement previously entered into, the administrator shall advise the issuing entity to suspend the license, certificate, permit or registration forthwith.

(2) After receipt of notice to suspend from the administrator, no further administrative review or contested case proceeding within or by the issuing entity is required. [1993 c.365 §6; 1995 c.620 §4; 1999 c.80 §14; 2001 c.323 §3; 2003 c.73 §45]

25.765 Procedure if obligor contacts administrator within time limits; hearing. (1) If the obligor makes the contact within 30 days of the date of the notice as provided for in ORS 25.759, the administrator shall provide the obligor with the opportunity to contest the suspension on the bases set forth in ORS 25.759 (5). The administrator shall determine whether suspension should occur. If the administrator determines that suspension should occur, the administrator shall make a written determination of such finding.

(2) The obligor may object to the determination described in subsection (1) of this section within 30 days after the date of the determination. Any hearing on the objection shall be conducted by an administrative law judge assigned from the Office of Administrative Hearings. Any suspension is stayed pending the decision of the administrative law judge. Any order of the administrative law judge that supports a suspension shall result in the notification to the issuing entity by the administrator to suspend the license, certificate, permit or registration forthwith.

(3) After receipt of notice to suspend from the administrator, no further administrative review or contested case proceeding within or by the issuing entity is required. [1993 c.365 §7; 1995 c.620 §5; 1999 c.80 §15; 1999 c.849 §§43,44; 2001 c.323 §§4,5; 2003 c.75 §26; 2005 c.560 §7]

25.768 Judicial review of order. The order of the administrative law judge is final and is subject to judicial review as provided in ORS 183.482. Any suspension under ORS 25.750 to 25.783 is not stayed pending judicial review. [1993 c.365 §8; 2003 c.75 §76]

25.771 Obligor holding more than one license, certificate, permit or registration. In the event that an obligor holds more than one license, certificate, permit or registration described in ORS 25.750, any determination regarding suspension of one license, certificate, permit or registration is sufficient to suspend any other license, certificate, permit or registration described in ORS 25.750. [1993 c.365 §9; 1995 c.620 §6]

25.774 Reinstatement. When, at any time after suspension under ORS 25.750 to 25.783, the conditions resulting in the suspension no longer exist, the administrator shall so notify the issuing entity and shall confirm that the license, certificate, permit or registration may be reinstated contingent upon the requirements of the issuing entity. Until the issuing entity receives notice under this section, the issuing entity may not reinstate, reissue, renew or otherwise make the license, certificate, permit or registration available to the holder of the suspended license, certificate, permit or registration. [1993 c.365 §10; 1995 c.620 §7; 1999 c.80 §16; 2001 c.323 §6]

25.777 Reimbursing issuing entities for costs incurred. The Department of Justice shall enter into agreements to reimburse issuing entities for their costs of compliance with ORS 25.750 to 25.783 to the extent that those costs are eligible for Federal Financial Participation under Title IV-D of the Social Security Act. [1993 c.365 §11; 1995 c.620 §8; 2001 c.323 §7]

25.780 Other licenses, certificates, permits and registrations subject to suspension. In addition to any other grounds for suspension provided by law:

(1) The Oregon Liquor Control Commission and any entity that issues licenses, certificates, permits or registrations that a person is required by state law to possess to engage in an occupation, profession or recreational hunting or fishing or to use a particular occupational or professional title shall suspend without further hearing the licenses, certificates, permits or registrations of a person upon certification by the administrator that the person is subject to an order suspending the license, certificate, permit or registration. The certification must include the information specified in ORS 25.750 (1).

(2) The Department of Transportation shall suspend without further hearing the driver license or driver permit of a person upon certification by the administrator that the person is subject to an order suspending the license or permit. The certification must include the information specified in ORS 25.750 (1). [1993 c.365 §13; 1995 c.620 §9; 1995 c.750 §5; 1999 c.80 §17; 2001 c.323 §8]

25.783 Confidentiality of information. Any entity described in ORS 25.756 that receives an inquiry as to the status of a person who has had a license, certificate, permit or registration suspended under ORS 25.750 to 25.783 shall respond only that the license, certificate, permit or registration was suspended pursuant to ORS 25.750 to 25.783. The entity shall not release or make other use of information that it receives pursuant to ORS 25.750 to 25.783. [1993 c.365 §14; 1995 c.620 §10]

25.785 Issuing entities to require Social Security number. (1) Any state agency, board or commission that is authorized to issue an occupational, professional, recreational or driver license, certificate, permit or registration subject to suspension under ORS 25.750 to 25.783 shall require that an individual's Social Security number be recorded on an application for, or form for renewal of, a license, certificate, permit or registration and to the maximum extent feasible shall include the Social Security number in automated databases containing information about the individual.

(2) A state agency, board or commission described in subsection (1) of this section may accept a written statement from an individual who has not been issued a Social Security number by the United States Social Security Administration to fulfill the requirement in subsection (1) of this section.

(3) An individual may not submit to a state agency, board or commission a written statement described in subsection (2) of this section knowing the statement to be false. [1997 c.746 §117; 1999 c.80 §93; 2003 c.610 §1; 2005 c.22 §17]

Note: 25.785 was enacted into law by the Legislative Assembly but was not added to or made a part of ORS chapter 25 or any series therein by legislative action. See Preface to Oregon Revised Statutes for further explanation.

EMPLOYER REPORTING PROGRAM

25.790 Hiring or rehiring individual; report required; contents. (1)(a) An employer shall report to the Division of Child Support of the Department of Justice the hiring or rehiring of an individual who resides or works in the state and to whom the employer anticipates paying earnings if the employer:

(A) Has employees working only in this state; or

(B) Is a multistate employer and has designated to the United States Secretary of Health and Human Services that Oregon is the employer's reporting state.

(b) The employer shall submit the report by mail or other means in accordance with rules adopted by the Department of Justice.

(2)(a) An employer shall make the report required by subsection (1) of this section with respect to an employee:

(A) Not later than 20 days after the date the employer hires or rehires the employee; or

(B) In the case of an employer transmitting reports magnetically or electronically, by transmissions each month not less than 12 days nor more than 16 days apart.

(b) An employer may submit a cumulative report for all individuals hired or rehired during the previous reporting period.

(3) The report required under subsection (1) of this section may be made on a W-4 form or, at the option of the employer, an equivalent form approved by the Division of Child Support of the Department of Justice, but must contain the employer's name, address and federal tax identification number and the employee's name, address and Social Security number.

(4) As used in this section:

(a) "Employee" means an individual who must file a federal withholding form W-4 under the Internal Revenue Code.

(b) "Rehire" means to re-employ any individual who was laid off, separated, furloughed, granted a leave without pay or terminated from employment for more than 60 days. [1993 c.753 §1; 1995 c.381 §2; 1999 c.80 §18; 2003 c.73 §46; 2013 c.184 §4]

25.792 Confidentiality. Information received under ORS 25.790 is confidential and exempt from public disclosure, except that the Division of Child Support of the Department of Justice shall provide information to other public agencies, upon request, as required by law. [1993 c.753 §2; 1999 c.80 §19]

25.793 Disclosure of employer-reported information. (1) Subject to the limitations provided in subsection (2) of this section, the Division of Child Support of the Department of Justice may enter into agreements with other divisions of the Department of Justice or with the Department of Revenue for the provision of information reported to the Division of Child Support by an employer pursuant to ORS 25.790 regarding hiring or rehiring of individuals in this state. The information may be used for purposes other than paternity establishment or child support enforcement, including but not limited to debt collection.

(2) Information provided by the division under this section is limited to information reported pursuant to ORS 25.790 that has not yet been entered into either:

(a) The statewide automated data processing and information retrieval system required to be established and operated by the division under 42 U.S.C. 654a; or

(b) The automated state directory of new hires required to be established by the division under 42 U.S.C. 653a.

(3) An agreement entered into under this section must include, but is not limited to, provisions describing:

(a) How the information is to be reported or transferred from the division;

(b) Fees, reimbursements and other financial responsibilities of the recipient in exchange for receipt of the information from the division, not to exceed actual expenses;

(c) Coordination of data systems to facilitate the sharing of the information; and

(d) Such other terms and requirements as are necessary to accomplish the objectives of the agreement.

(4) An agreement entered into under this section is subject to the approval of the Department of Justice. [2017 c.644 §11]

25.794 Verification of employment; information about compensation and benefits; rules. (1) Upon the request of the administrator or an equivalent agency providing child support services in another state, all persons or entities in the state, including but not limited to for-profit, nonprofit and government employers, shall verify the employment of individuals and provide, in addition and if requested, information about compensation and benefits paid to the individual whether as an employee or a contractor.

(2) Upon request of an enforcing agency of another state, only a court or enforcing agency of Oregon may enforce a request for information made by the enforcing agency of the other state under this section.

(3) The Department of Justice shall adopt rules to implement the provisions of this section. [1993 c.753 §3; 1999 c.80 §29; 2003 c.73 §47]

PENALTIES

25.990 Penalties. (1) Violation of ORS 25.720 (3) is a Class A violation.

(2) Violation of ORS 25.260 is a Class C misdemeanor.

(3) Violation of ORS 25.785 (3) is a Class A misdemeanor. [1985 c.671 §52(4); 1989 c.812 §3(2); 1999 c.1051 §147; 2003 c.610 §4; 2011 c.597 §151]

_____

Chapter 26 (Former Provisions)

Judgments and Decrees by Confession

JUDGMENTS AND DECREES BY CONFESSION

PROCEDURE IN CIVIL PROCEEDINGS

26.010 [Repealed by 1981 c.898 §53]

26.020 [Amended by 1961 c.344 §100; repealed by 1981 c.898 §53]

26.030 [Repealed by 1981 c.898 §53]

26.040 [Repealed by 1981 c.898 §53]

26.110 [Repealed by 1981 c.898 §53]

26.120 [Repealed by 1981 c.898 §53]

26.130 [Repealed by 1981 c.898 §53]

_____

Chapter 27 (Former Provisions)

Submitting Controversy Without Action or Suit

SUBMITTING CONTROVERSY WITHOUT ACTION OR SUIT

PROCEDURE IN CIVIL PROCEEDINGS

Note: 27.010, 27.020 and 27.030 repealed by 1981 c.898 §53.

_____

TITLE 3 REMEDIES AND SPECIAL ACTIONS AND PROCEEDINGS

Chapter 28.   Declaratory Judgments; Certification of Questions of Law
30.   Actions and Suits in Particular Cases
31.   Tort Actions
33.   Special Proceedings and Procedures
34.   Writs
35.   Eminent Domain; Public Acquisition of Property
36.   Mediation and Arbitration
37.   Receivership

_____

Chapter 28 — Declaratory Judgments; Certification of Questions of Law

2017 EDITION

DECLARATORY JUDGMENTS; QUESTIONS OF LAW

SPECIAL ACTIONS AND PROCEEDINGS

DECLARATORY JUDGMENTS

28.010   Power of courts; form of declaration

28.020   Declarations as to writings and laws

28.030   Construction of contract before or after breach

28.040   Declaratory judgments on trusts or estates

28.050   Enumeration not exclusive

28.060   Discretion of court to refuse judgment

28.070   Appeal or review

28.080   Supplemental relief

28.090   Trial of issues of fact

28.100   Costs

28.110   Parties; service on Attorney General when constitutional question involved

28.120   Construction and administration

28.130   "Person" defined

28.140   Provisions severable

28.150   Uniformity of interpretation

28.160   Short title

CERTIFICATION OF QUESTIONS OF LAW

28.200   Supreme Court authorized to answer questions of law certified by other courts

28.205   Procedure to invoke ORS 28.200 to 28.255

28.210   Certification order

28.215   Form of certification order; submission of record

28.220   Fees; apportionment between parties

28.225   Procedure in certification matters

28.230   Opinion on certified question

28.235   Certification to another state

28.240   Procedure for certification to another state

28.245   Severability

28.250   Construction

28.255   Short title

DECLARATORY JUDGMENTS

28.010 Power of courts; form of declaration. Courts of record within their respective jurisdictions shall have power to declare rights, status, and other legal relations, whether or not further relief is or could be claimed. No action or proceeding shall be open to objection on the ground that a declaratory judgment is prayed for. The declaration may be either affirmative or negative in form and effect, and such declarations shall have the force and effect of a judgment. [Amended by 2003 c.576 §302]

28.020 Declarations as to writings and laws. Any person interested under a deed, will, written contract or other writing constituting a contract, or whose rights, status or other legal relations are affected by a constitution, statute, municipal charter, ordinance, contract or franchise may have determined any question of construction or validity arising under any such instrument, constitution, statute, municipal charter, ordinance, contract or franchise and obtain a declaration of rights, status or other legal relations thereunder.

28.030 Construction of contract before or after breach. A contract may be construed either before or after there has been a breach thereof.

28.040 Declaratory judgments on trusts or estates. Any person interested as or through an executor, administrator, trustee, guardian or other fiduciary, creditor, devisee, legatee, heir, next of kin, or cestui que trust, in the administration of a trust, or of the estate of a decedent, ward or insolvent, may have a declaration of rights or legal relations in respect thereto:
(1) To ascertain any class of creditors, devisees, legatees, heirs, next of kin or other; or
(2) To direct the executors, administrators, trustees, guardians or conservators to do or abstain from doing any particular act in their fiduciary capacity; or
(3) To determine any question arising in the administration of the estate or trust, including questions of construction of wills and other writings. [Amended by 1961 c.344 §101]

28.050 Enumeration not exclusive. The enumeration in ORS 28.010 to 28.040 does not limit or restrict the exercise of the general powers conferred in ORS 28.010, in any proceedings where declaratory relief is sought, in which a judgment will terminate the controversy or remove an uncertainty. [Amended by 2003 c.576 §303]

28.060 Discretion of court to refuse judgment. The court may refuse to render or enter a declaratory judgment where such judgment, if rendered or entered, would not terminate the uncertainty or controversy giving rise to the proceeding. [Amended by 2003 c.576 §304]

28.070 Appeal or review. All orders and judgments under this chapter may be appealed from or reviewed as other orders and judgments. [Amended by 2003 c.576 §305]

28.080 Supplemental relief. Further relief based on a declaratory judgment may be granted whenever necessary or proper. The application thereof shall be by petition to a court having jurisdiction to grant the relief. If the application be deemed sufficient, the court shall, on reasonable notice, require any adverse party whose rights have been adjudicated by the declaratory judgment to show cause why further relief should not be granted forthwith. [Amended by 2003 c.576 §306]

28.090 Trial of issues of fact. When a proceeding under this chapter involves the determination of an issue of fact, such issue may be tried and determined in the same manner as issues of fact are tried and determined in other actions at law or suits in equity in the court in which the proceeding is pending.

28.100 Costs. In any proceeding under this chapter the court may make such award of costs as may seem equitable and just.

28.110 Parties; service on Attorney General when constitutional question involved. When declaratory relief is sought, all persons shall be made parties who have or claim any interest which would be affected by the declaration, and no declaration shall prejudice the rights of persons not parties to the proceeding. In any proceeding which involves the validity of a municipal charter, ordinance or franchise, the municipality affected shall be made a party, and shall be entitled to be heard, and if the constitution, statute, charter, ordinance or franchise is alleged to be unconstitutional, the Attorney General of the state shall also be served with a copy of the proceeding and be entitled to be heard.

28.120 Construction and administration. This chapter is declared to be remedial. The purpose of this chapter is to settle and to afford relief from uncertainty and insecurity with respect to rights, status and other legal relations, and is to be liberally construed and administered. [Amended by 2005 c.22 §18]

28.130 "Person" defined. The word "person," wherever used in this chapter, shall be construed to mean any person, partnership, joint stock company, unincorporated association or society, or municipal or other corporation of any character whatsoever.

28.140 Provisions severable. The several sections and provisions of this chapter, except ORS 28.010 and 28.020, are hereby declared independent and severable, and the invalidity, if any, of any part or feature thereof shall not affect or render the remainder of the chapter invalid or inoperative.

28.150 Uniformity of interpretation. This chapter shall be so interpreted and construed as to effectuate its general purpose to make uniform the law of those states which enact it, and to harmonize, as far as possible, with federal laws and regulations on the subject of declaratory judgments. [Amended by 2003 c.576 §307]

28.160 Short title. This chapter may be cited as the "Uniform Declaratory Judgments Act."

CERTIFICATION OF QUESTIONS OF LAW

28.200 Supreme Court authorized to answer questions of law certified by other courts. The Supreme Court may answer questions of law certified to it by the Supreme Court of the United States, a Court of Appeals of the United States, a United States District Court, a panel of the Bankruptcy Appellate Panel Service or the highest appellate court or the intermediate appellate court of any other state, when requested by the certifying court if there are involved in any proceedings before it questions of law of this state which may be determinative of the cause then pending in the certifying court and as to which it appears to the certifying court there is no controlling precedent in the decisions of the Supreme Court and the intermediate appellate courts of this state. [1983 c.103 §1; 1995 c.197 §1]

Note: 28.200 to 28.255 were enacted into law by the Legislative Assembly but were not added to or made a part of ORS chapter 28 or any series therein by legislative action. See Preface to Oregon Revised Statutes for further explanation.

28.205 Procedure to invoke ORS 28.200 to 28.255. ORS 28.200 to 28.255 may be invoked by an order of any of the courts referred to in ORS 28.200 upon the court's own motion or upon the motion of any party to the cause. [1983 c.103 §2]

Note: See note under 28.200.

28.210 Certification order. A certification order shall set forth:
(1) The questions of law to be answered; and
(2) A statement of all facts relevant to the questions certified and showing fully the nature of the controversy in which the questions arose. [1983 c.103 §3]

Note: See note under 28.200.

28.215 Form of certification order; submission of record. The certification order shall be prepared by the certifying court, signed by the judge presiding at the hearing, and forwarded to the Supreme Court by the clerk of the certifying court under its official seal. The Supreme Court may require the original or copies of all or of any portion of the record before the certifying court to be filed with the certification order, if, in the opinion of the Supreme Court, the record or portion thereof may be necessary in answering the questions. [1983 c.103 §4]

Note: See note under 28.200.

28.220 Fees; apportionment between parties. Fees and costs shall be the same as in civil appeals docketed before the Supreme Court and shall be equally divided between the parties unless otherwise ordered by the certifying court in its order of certification. [1983 c.103 §5]

Note: See note under 28.200.

28.225 Procedure in certification matters. Proceedings in the Supreme Court shall be those provided in rules of appellate procedure and statutes governing briefs and arguments. [1983 c.103 §6]

Note: See note under 28.200.

28.230 Opinion on certified question. The written opinion of the Supreme Court stating the law governing the questions certified shall be sent by the clerk under the seal of the Supreme Court to the certifying court and to the parties. [1983 c.103 §7]

Note: See note under 28.200.

28.235 Certification to another state. The Supreme Court or the Court of Appeals of this state, on their own motion or the motion of any party, may order certification of questions of law to the highest court of any state when it appears to the certifying court that there are involved in any proceeding before the court questions of law of the receiving state which may be determinative of the cause then pending in the certifying court and it appears to the certifying court that there are no controlling precedents in the decisions of the highest court or intermediate appellate courts of the receiving state. [1983 c.103 §8]

Note: See note under 28.200.

28.240 Procedure for certification to another state. The procedures for certification from this state to the receiving state shall be those provided in the laws of the receiving state. [1983 c.103 §9]

Note: See note under 28.200.

28.245 Severability. If any provision of ORS 28.200 to 28.255 or the application thereof to any person, court, or circumstance is held invalid the invalidity does not affect other provisions or applications of ORS 28.200 to 28.255 which can be given effect without the invalid provision or application, and to this end the provisions of ORS 28.200 to 28.255 are severable. [1983 c.103 §10]

Note: See note under 28.200.

28.250 Construction. ORS 28.200 to 28.255 shall be so construed as to effectuate its general purpose to make uniform the law of those states which enact it. [1983 c.103 §11]

Note: See note under 28.200.

28.255 Short title. ORS 28.200 to 28.255 may be cited as the Uniform Certification of Questions of Law Act. [1983 c.103 §12]

Note: See note under 28.200.

―――――――――――

Chapter 29 (Former Provisions)

Provisional Process; Attachment and Garnishment

ATTACHMENT & GARNISHMENT

SPECIAL ACTIONS AND PROCEEDINGS

29.010 [Repealed by 1981 c.898 §53]

29.020 [1973 c.741 §1; repealed by 1981 c.898 §53]

29.025 [1973 c.741 §2; repealed by 1981 c.898 §53]

29.030 [1973 c.741 §3; 1979 c.284 §62; repealed by 1981 c.898 §53]

29.035 [1973 c.741 §4; repealed by 1981 c.898 §53]

29.040 [1973 c.741 §5; repealed by 1979 c.284 §199]

29.045 [1973 c.741 §6; repealed by 1981 c.898 §53]

29.050 [1973 c.741 §7; repealed by 1981 c.898 §53]

29.055 [1973 c.741 §8; repealed by 1981 c.898 §53]

29.060 [1973 c.741 §9; repealed by 1981 c.898 §53]

29.065 [1973 c.741 §10; repealed by 1981 c.898 §53]

29.070 [1973 c.741 §11; repealed by 1981 c.898 §53]

29.075 [1973 c.741 §12; repealed by 1981 c.898 §53]

29.080 [Formerly 29.810; repealed by 1981 c.898 §53]

29.085 [Formerly 29.830; repealed by 1981 c.898 §53]

29.087 [Formerly 29.890; 1981 c.898 §33; repealed by 2001 c.249 §84]

29.090 [Formerly 29.900; repealed by 1981 c.898 §53]

29.095 [Formerly 29.910; repealed by 1981 c.898 §53]

29.110 [Repealed by 1981 c.898 §53]

29.115 [Formerly 29.178; repealed by 2001 c.249 §84]

29.120 [Repealed by 1981 c.898 §53]

29.125 [1981 c.883 §2; 1989 c.726 §5; 1989 c.876 §8; 1997 c.704 §40; 1999 c.80 §37; 1999 c.930 §3; repealed by 2001 c.249 §84]

29.130 [Repealed by 1981 c.898 §53]

29.135 [1981 c.883 §3; repealed by 2001 c.249 §84]

29.137 [1987 c.873 §2; 1991 c.734 §2a; 1997 c.340 §3; 1997 c.387 §4; 1999 c.80 §38; 1999 c.153 §2; 1999 c.788 §36; repealed by 2001 c.249 §84]

29.138 [1987 c.873 §3; 1991 c.104 §1; 1997 c.439 §3; repealed by 2001 c.249 §84]

29.139 [1987 c.873 §4; 1991 c.104 §2; 1993 c.18 §7; 1997 c.69 §1; 1997 c.439 §4; 1999 c.80 §39; repealed by 2001 c.249 §84]

29.140 [Repealed by 1981 c.898 §53]

29.142 [1987 c.873 §6; 1989 c.412 §1; 1993 c.439 §7; 1995 c.322 §1; 1997 c.340 §4; 1999 c.303 §1; repealed by 2001 c.249 §84]

29.145 [1981 c.883 §4; 1987 c.873 §7; 1989 c.810 §3; 1989 c.876 §§9,11; 1991 c.845 §5; 1993 c.261 §1; 1993 c.798 §41; 1995 c.79 §9; 1997 c.338 §2; 1997 c.439 §5; 1999 c.5 §3; 1999 c.80 §83; repealed by 2001 c.249 §84]

29.147 [1987 c.873 §8; 1989 c.810 §4; 1989 c.876 §12; 1991 c.845 §6; 1993 c. 261 §2; 1993 c.798 §42; 1995 c.79 §10; 1997 c.69 §2; 1997 c.338 §§3,4; 1997 c.439 §6; 1999 c.5 §6; 1999 c.80 §84; repealed by 2001 c.249 §84]

29.150 [Repealed by 1981 c.898 §53]

29.155 [1981 c.883 §5; 1987 c.873 §9; 1989 c.171 §4; 1989 c.810 §5; 1997 c.439 §1; repealed by 2001 c.249 §84]

29.160 [Repealed by 1981 c.898 §53]

29.165 [1981 c.883 §6; 1987 c.873 §10; 1993 c.98 §1; 1995 c.583 §2; repealed by 2001 c.249 §84]

29.170 [Amended by 1961 c.726 §398; 1965 c.108 §1; 1969 c.95 §1; 1969 c.576 §1; 1977 c.786 §1; repealed by 1981 c.883 §1 and 1981 c.898 §53]

29.175 [Repealed by 1981 c.883 §1]

29.178 [1977 c.623 §2; 1981 c.883 §33; renumbered 29.115]

29.180 [Repealed by 1981 c.898 §53]

29.185 [1981 c.883 §7; 1985 c.676 §58; 1991 c.104 §3; 1993 c.261 §3; 1993 c.545 §115; 1995 c.328 §69; 1997 c.631 §370; repealed by 2001 c.249 §84]

29.190 [Repealed by 1981 c.898 §53]

29.195 [1981 c.883 §8; 1987 c.873 §11; 1989 c.876 §6; repealed by 2001 c.249 §84]

29.200 [Repealed by 1981 c.898 §53]

29.205 [1981 c.883 §9; 1989 c.810 §6; 1991 c.104 §4; 1993 c.261 §4; 1993 c.593 §1; 1997 c.338 §1; 1997 c.631 §371; 1999 c.80 §40; repealed by 2001 c.249 §84]

29.210 [Repealed by 1981 c.898 §53]

29.215 [1981 c.883 §10; 1987 c.873 §12; repealed by 2001 c.249 §84]

29.220 [Repealed by 1981 c.898 §53]

29.225 [1981 c.883 §11a; 1987 c.399 §1; 1987 c.873 §13; 1991 c.845 §4; 1993 c.18 §8; 1993 c.439 §8; 1995 c.322 §2; 1997 c.80 §1; 1997 c.170 §14; 1997 c.249 §17; 1999 c.80 §41; 1999 c.745 §7; repealed by 2001 c.249 §84]

29.230 [Repealed by 1981 c.898 §53]

29.235 [1981 c.883 §12; 1983 c.622 §3; 1987 c.873 §14; 1989 c.810 §7; 1989 c.876 §7; 1993 c.18 §9; 1993 c.261 §5; repealed by 2001 c.249 §84]

29.237 [1987 c.873 §15; repealed by 2001 c.249 §84]

29.240 [Repealed by 1981 c.898 §53]

29.245 [1981 c.883 §13; repealed by 2001 c.249 §84]

29.250 [Repealed by 1981 c.898 §53]

29.255 [1981 c.883 §14; 1987 c.873 §16; 1989 c.810 §8; repealed by 2001 c.249 §84]

29.260 [Repealed by 1981 c.898 §53]

29.265 [1981 c.883 §15; 1987 c.873 §17; repealed by 2001 c.249 §84]

29.270 [Repealed by 1981 c.883 §1 and 1981 c.898 §53]

29.275 [1981 c.883 §16; repealed by 2001 c.249 §84]

29.280 [Repealed by 1981 c.883 §1 and 1981 c.898 §53]

29.282 [1999 c.5 §2; repealed by 2001 c.249 §84]

29.285 [1981 c.883 §17; repealed by 2001 c.249 §84]

29.290 [Repealed by 1981 c.883 §1 and 1981 c.898 §53]

29.295 [1981 c.883 §18; repealed by 2001 c.249 §84]

29.300 [Repealed by 1981 c.883 §1 and 1981 c.898 §53]

29.305 [1981 c.883 §19; repealed by 2001 c.249 §84]

29.310 [Repealed by 1981 c.883 §1 and 1981 c.898 §53]

29.315 [1981 c.883 §20; repealed by 2001 c.249 §84]

29.320 [Repealed by 1981 c.883 §1 and 1981 c.898 §53]

29.325 [1981 c.883 §§21,22; repealed by 2001 c.249 §84]

29.330 [Repealed by 1981 c.883 §1 and 1981 c.898 §53]

29.335 [1981 c.883 §23; repealed by 2001 c.249 §84]

29.340 [Repealed by 1981 c.883 §1 and 1981 c.898 §53]

29.343 [1981 c.883 §24; repealed by 2001 c.249 §84]

29.345 [1981 c.883 §25; repealed by 2001 c.249 §84]

29.350 [Repealed by 1981 c.883 §1 and 1981 c.898 §53]

29.355 [1981 c.883 §26; repealed by 2001 c.249 §84]

29.357 [1991 c.734 §2c; 1997 c.387 §5; repealed by 2001 c.249 §84]

29.360 [Repealed by 1981 c.883 §1 and 1981 c.898 §53]

29.365 [1981 c.883 §27; 1987 c.873 §18; repealed by 2001 c.249 §84]

29.367 [1989 c.810 §13; 1989 c.910 §4; 1991 c.67 §5; 1995 c.321 §1; 2001 c.249 §72; renumbered 18.910 in 2001]

29.369 [1999 c.788 §35; repealed by 2001 c.249 §84]

29.370 [Repealed by 1981 c.883 §1 and 1981 c.898 §53]

29.371 [1999 c.930 §6; repealed by 2001 c.249 §84]

29.373 [1989 c.1081 §2; repealed by 2001 c.249 §84]

29.375 [1981 c.883 §28; 1983 c.622 §2; 1989 c.810 §9; 1991 c.567 §1; 1993 c.593 §2; repealed by 2001 c.249 §84]

29.377 [1989 c.810 §2; 1991 c.567 §2; 1993 c.261 §6; 1997 c.439 §2; 1997 c.631 §372; repealed by 2001 c.249 §84]

29.380 [Repealed by 1981 c.898 §53]

29.390 [Repealed by 1981 c.898 §53]

29.395 [1981 c.883 §40; repealed by 2001 c.249 §84]

29.400 [Repealed by 1981 c.883 §1 and 1981 c.898 §53]

29.401 [1989 c.876 §2; 1991 c.845 §9; repealed by 2001 c.249 §84]

29.405 [1989 c.876 §3; repealed by 2001 c.249 §84]

29.410 [1973 c.797 §422; repealed by 1981 c.898 §53]

29.411 [1989 c.876 §4; 1991 c.67 §6; 1991 c.845 §7; 1993 c.18 §10; 1993 c.261 §7; 1993 c.798 §43; 1995 c.79 §11; 1997 c.439 §7; 1999 c.5 §9; repealed by 2001 c.249 §84]

29.415 [1989 c.876 §5; 1991 c.845 §8; 1993 c.18 §11; 1993 c.261 §8; 1993 c.798 §44; 1997 c.69 §3; 1997 c.249 §18; 1997 c.439 §8; 1999 c.5 §10; repealed by 2001 c.249 §84]

29.510 [Repealed by 1979 c.284 §199]

29.520 [Repealed by 1981 c.898 §53]

29.530 [Repealed by 1981 c.898 §53]

29.540 [Repealed by 1981 c.898 §53]

29.550 [Repealed by 1981 c.898 §53]

29.560 [Amended by 1977 c.415 §5; repealed by 1981 c.898 §53]

29.570 [Repealed by 1981 c.898 §53]

29.580 [Repealed by 1981 c.898 §53]

29.590 [Repealed by 1981 c.898 §53]

29.600 [Repealed by 1981 c.898 §53]

29.610 [Repealed by 1981 c.898 §53]

29.620 [Amended by 1977 c.415 §6; repealed by 1981 c.898 §53]

29.630 [Repealed by 1981 c.898 §53]

29.640 [Repealed by 1981 c.898 §53]

29.650 [Repealed by 1981 c.898 §53]

29.660 [Repealed by 1981 c.898 §53]

29.670 [Repealed by 1981 c.898 §53]

29.680 [Repealed by 1981 c.898 §53]

29.690 [Repealed by 1981 c.898 §53]

29.700 [Repealed by 1981 c.898 §53]

29.710 [Repealed by 1981 c.898 §53]

29.720 [Repealed by 1981 c.898 §53]

29.730 [Repealed by 1981 c.898 §53]

29.740 [Repealed by 1981 c.898 §53]

29.810 [Amended by 1977 c.415 §1; renumbered 29.080]

29.820 [Repealed by 1977 c.415 §7]

29.830 [Amended by 1977 c.415 §2; renumbered 29.085]

29.840 [Repealed by 1977 c.415 §7]

29.850 [Repealed by 1977 c.415 §7]

29.860 [Repealed by 1977 c.415 §7]

29.870 [Repealed by 1977 c.415 §7]

29.880 [Repealed by 1977 c.415 §7]

29.890 [Renumbered 29.087]

29.900 [Amended by 1977 c.415 §3; renumbered 29.090]

29.910 [Amended by 1977 c.415 §4; renumbered 29.095]

Chapter 30 — Actions and Suits in Particular Cases

2017 EDITION

ACTIONS AND SUITS IN PARTICULAR CASES

SPECIAL ACTIONS AND PROCEEDINGS

ACTIONS FOR INJURY OR DEATH

30.010   Who may maintain action for injury or death of child

30.020   Action for wrongful death; when commenced; damages

30.030   Distribution of damages

30.040   Apportionment among dependents upon settlement

30.050   Apportionment among dependents after judgment

30.060   Appeal from order of distribution or apportionment

30.070   Settlement; discharge of claim

30.075   Procedure upon death of injured person

30.080   Effect of death of wrongdoer

30.090   Appointment of administrator of estate of wrongdoer

30.100   Substitution of personal representative as party defendant

ACTIONS BY GUEST PASSENGERS

30.115   Aircraft and watercraft guest passengers; definitions

30.130   Public carriers by aircraft and prospective aircraft purchasers

LIABILITY OF CERTAIN PERSONS PROVIDING MOTOR VEHICLES

30.135   Liability of certain persons that lend, rent, donate use of, make available for test drive or otherwise provide motor vehicle

ENFORCEMENT OF RIGHTS UNDER SERVICEMEMBERS CIVIL RELIEF ACT

30.136   Action to enforce right or remedy under Servicemembers Civil Relief Act

30.138   Remedies for violation of Servicemembers Civil Relief Act

ACTIONS ON CERTAIN CONSTRUCTION AGREEMENTS

30.140   Certain indemnification provisions in construction agreement void

30.145   Certain provisions relating to waivers in construction agreements void

ACTIONS AGAINST FORMER EMPLOYER FOR DISCLOSURE OF INFORMATION

30.178   Liability of employer for disclosing information about employee to new employer; no action based on compelled self-publication

ACTIONS ARISING OUT OF PROVISION OF UTILITY SERVICES

30.180   Definitions for ORS 30.180 to 30.186

30.182   Civil action for taking of or tampering with utility services

30.184   Amount recoverable; attorney fees

30.186   Remedies not exclusive

ACTIONS ARISING OUT OF PROVISION OF CABLE SERVICES

30.192   Definitions for ORS 30.192 to 30.196

30.194   Prohibitions relating to cable services

30.195   Civil action for violation of prohibitions relating to cable services

30.196   Amount recoverable; attorney fees

ACTIONS FOR INTIMIDATION

30.198   Civil action for intimidation; remedies; attorney fees; liability of parents

30.200   Action by district attorney; effect on others

ACTIONS ON OFFICIAL BONDS

30.210   To whom official bonds are security

30.220   Parties

30.230   Leave to begin action

30.240   Subsequent delinquencies on same bond

30.250   Amount of judgment

TORT ACTIONS AGAINST PUBLIC BODIES

(Generally)

30.260   Definitions for ORS 30.260 to 30.300

30.261   Limitation on applicability of ORS 30.260 to 30.300 to certain private, nonprofit organizations

30.262   Certain nonprofit facilities and homes public bodies for purposes of ORS 30.260 to 30.300

30.265   Scope of liability of public body, officers, employees and agents; liability in nuclear incident

230

30.267   Liability for certain medical treatment at Oregon Health and Science University facilities

30.268   Liability for certain medical treatment at facilities other than Oregon Health and Science University

30.269   Limitations on awards under Oregon Tort Claims Act generally

30.271   Limitations on liability of state for personal injury and death

30.272   Limitations on liability of local public bodies for personal injury and death

30.273   Limitations on liability of public bodies for property damage or destruction

30.274   Direct appeal of constitutionality of limitations

30.275   Notice of claim; time of notice; time of action

30.278   Reporting notice of claim of professional negligence to licensing board

30.282   Local public body insurance; self-insurance program; action against program

30.285   Public body shall indemnify public officers; procedure for requesting counsel; extent of duty of state; obligation for judgment and attorney fees

30.287   Counsel for public officer; when public funds not to be paid in settlement; effect on liability limit; defense by insurer

30.290   Settlement of claims by local public body

30.295   Payment of judgment or settlement; remedies for nonpayment; tax levy for payment; installment payments

30.297   Liability of certain state agencies for damages caused by foster child or youth offender; conditions; exceptions

30.298   Liability of certain state agencies to foster parents for injury or damage caused by foster child or youth offender; conditions; limitations

30.300   ORS 30.260 to 30.300 exclusive

(Certain Retired Health Care Providers)

30.302   Certain retired health care providers to be considered agents of public bodies

ACTIONS AND SUITS BY AND AGAINST GOVERNMENTAL UNITS AND OFFICIALS

30.310   Actions and suits by governmental units

30.312   Actions by governmental units under federal antitrust laws

30.315   Proceedings by cities and counties to enforce ordinances and resolutions

30.320   Contract and other actions and suits against governmental units

30.330   Contracts of Department of Transportation providing for arbitration

30.340   Title of proceedings by or against county; control of proceedings by county court

30.360   Governmental unit as defendant in actions involving liens on realty

30.370   Service of summons on Attorney General; content

30.380   Action by assignee of claim for money illegally charged or exacted

30.390   Satisfaction of judgment against public corporation

30.395   Settlement of certain claims against municipal corporations; manner of payment

30.400   Actions by and against public officers in official capacity

INJUNCTIONS BY PUBLIC SERVANT OR PUBLIC SERVANT'S EMPLOYER

30.405   Injunction for criminal conduct related to employment or status of public servant

30.407   Request for hearing following issuance of order under ORS 30.405

RECOVERY OF FINES AND FORFEITURES

30.410   In whose name action brought

30.420   Venue of action for forfeiture

30.430   Amount of penalty

30.440   Judgment by collusion not a bar

30.460   Payment of fines or costs in proceeding to enforce county ordinance or resolution; defendant personally liable

VOLUNTEERS TRANSPORTING OLDER PERSONS AND PERSONS WITH DISABILITIES

30.475 Legislative policy

30.480 Limitation on liability of volunteers; conditions

30.485 Apportionment of damages; insurance issues excluded from jury consideration

VOLUNTEERS PROVIDING ASSISTANCE OR ADVICE IN RESPONSE TO DISCHARGE OF HAZARDOUS MATERIAL OR RELATING TO COMPLIANCE WITH DISPOSAL LAWS

30.490 Definitions for ORS 30.490 to 30.497

30.492 Limitation on liability of volunteer providing assistance or advice related to mitigation or cleanup of discharge of hazardous material

30.495 Exceptions to limitation

30.497 When limitation on liability not applicable

30.500 Definitions for ORS 30.500 and 30.505

30.505 Limitation on liability of volunteer providing assistance relating to compliance with hazardous waste disposal laws; exceptions

ACTIONS FOR USURPATION OF OFFICE OR FRANCHISE; TO ANNUL CORPORATE EXISTENCE; TO ANNUL LETTERS PATENT

30.510 Action for usurpation of office or franchise, forfeiture of office or failure to incorporate

30.520 Joinder of defendants

30.530 Determining right of person claiming an office or franchise

30.540 Rights of person adjudged entitled to office or franchise

30.550 Action for damages

30.560 Judgment against usurper; imposition of fine

30.570 Action to annul corporate existence on direction of Governor

30.580 Action to annul corporate existence on leave of court

30.590 Judgment against corporation

30.600 Action to annul letters patent

30.610 Prosecutor; verification of pleadings; affidavit for leave of court; relator as coplaintiff

30.620 Duty of district attorney

30.630 Filing copy of judgment with Secretary of State

30.640 Enforcement of judgment

ACTIONS AGAINST PUBLIC BODY BY INMATES

30.642 Definitions for ORS 30.642 to 30.650

30.643 Waiver or deferral of fees and costs in action against public body by inmate

30.645 Waiver or deferral of fees after three dismissals of action

30.646 Payment of costs under judgment against inmate

30.647 Dismissal of inmate action during proceedings

30.648 Small claims actions by inmates against public bodies

30.650 Award of noneconomic damages in inmate action

ACTIONS ARISING OUT OF AGRI-TOURISM ACTIVITIES

30.671 Definitions for ORS 30.671 to 30.677

30.673 Limitations on liability of agri-tourism professional; exceptions

30.677 Notice

ACTIONS ARISING OUT OF EQUINE ACTIVITIES

30.687 Definitions for ORS 30.687 to 30.697

30.689　　Policy

30.691　　Limitations on liability; exceptions

30.693　　Additional exceptions to limitations on liability; effect of written release

30.695　　Effect of written release on liability of veterinarian or farrier

30.697　　Effect on workers' compensation benefits

MISCELLANEOUS ACTIONS

30.701　　Actions against maker of dishonored check; statutory damages and attorney fees; handling fee

30.715　　Successive actions or suits

30.740　　Right of gambling loser to recover double losses

30.750　　Liability of abstractors

30.765　　Liability of parents for tort by child; effect on foster parents

30.772　　Liability of landowner arising out of aviation activity; exceptions

30.774　　Indemnification of property owner that allows nonprofit organization or educational provider to use property

30.780　　Liability for damages caused by gambling

30.785　　Liability of construction design professional for injuries resulting from failure of employer to comply with safety standards

30.788　　Liability of architect, engineer, inspector or building evaluator for emergency relief services

30.792　　Liability of health care provider or health clinic for volunteer services to charitable organization

30.794　　Liability of physician or hospital arising out of care provided by direct entry midwife

30.800　　Liability for emergency medical assistance

30.802　　Liability for use of automated external defibrillator

30.803　　Liability of licensed emergency medical services provider acting as volunteer

30.805　　Liability for emergency medical assistance by government personnel

30.807　　Liability for emergency transportation assistance

30.809　　Liability of fraternal organization that provides used eyeglasses or hearing aids

30.811　　Liability of person providing outreach services to homeless individual or individual at risk of becoming homeless individual

30.813　　Liability of person who enters motor vehicle to remove unattended child or domestic animal; exceptions

30.815　　Liability of seller or lessor of law enforcement dog

30.820　　Action against seller of drugged horse; attorney fees

30.822　　Action for theft of or injury to search and rescue animal or therapy animal; attorney fees

30.825　　Action for unlawful tree spiking; attorney fees

30.860　　Action for trade discrimination; treble damages; attorney fees

30.862　　Action for public investment fraud; attorney fees

30.863　　Action for impersonation; attorney fees

30.864　　Action for disclosure of certain education records; limitation of action; attorney fees

30.865　　Action for invasion of personal privacy; attorney fees

30.866　　Action for issuance or violation of stalking protective order; attorney fees

30.867　　Action for violation of criminal laws relating to involuntary servitude or trafficking in persons; attorney fees

30.868　　Civil damages for custodial interference; attorney fees

30.870　　Definitions for ORS 30.870 and 30.875

30.875　　Civil damages for shoplifting or taking of agricultural produce

30.876   Treble damages and costs in actions arising out of interference with agricultural research

30.877   Treble damages and costs in actions arising out of research and animal interference and arising out of interference with livestock production

30.882   Award of liquidated damages to sports official subjected to offensive physical contact; attorney fees

30.890   Liability of food gleaners, donors and distributors

30.892   Liability of donors and distributors of general merchandise and household items

PRODUCT LIABILITY ACTIONS

30.900   "Product liability civil action" defined

30.902   Products provided by physicians

30.905   Time limitation for commencement of action

30.907   Action for damages from asbestos-related disease; limitations

30.908   Action arising out of injury from breast implants; limitations

30.910   Product disputably presumed not unreasonably dangerous

30.915   Defenses

30.920   When seller or lessor of product liable; effect of liability rule

30.925   Punitive damages

30.927   When manufacturer of drug not liable for punitive damages; exceptions

30.928   Time limitation for actions for damages caused by certain light bulbs

FARMING AND FOREST PRACTICES

30.930   Definitions for ORS 30.930 to 30.947

30.931   Transport or movement of equipment, device, vehicle or livestock as farming or forest practice

30.932   Definition of "nuisance" or "trespass"

30.933   Legislative findings; policy

30.934   Prohibition on local laws that make forest practice a nuisance or trespass; exceptions

30.935   Prohibition on local laws that make farm practice a nuisance or trespass

30.936   Immunity from private action based on farming or forest practice on certain lands; exceptions

30.937   Immunity from private action based on farming or forest practice allowed as preexisting nonconforming use; exceptions

30.938   Attorney fees and costs

30.939   When use of pesticide considered farming or forest practice

30.940   Effect on other remedies

30.942   Rules

30.943   Certain agencies not required to investigate complaints based on farming or forest practice

30.947   Effect of siting of destination resorts or other nonfarm or nonforest uses

30.949   Action for hindering, impairment or obstruction of forest practice on state forestland

ACTIONS ARISING OUT OF FOOD-RELATED CONDITION

30.961   Actions against sellers of food for food-related condition

30.963   Claim requirements for actions involving food-related conditions

SKIING ACTIVITIES

30.970   Definitions for ORS 30.970 to 30.990

30.975   Skiers assume certain risks

30.980   Notice to ski area operator of injury to skier; injuries resulting in death; statute of limitations; informing skiers of notice requirements

30.985   Duties of skiers; effect of failure to comply

ACTIONS FOR INJURY OR DEATH

30.010 Who may maintain action for injury or death of child. (1) A parent having custody of a child of the parent may maintain an action for the injury of the child.

(2) A parent may recover damages for the death of a child of the parent only under ORS 30.020. [Amended by 1961 c.344 §102; 1973 c.718 §1; 2003 c.14 §16]

30.020 Action for wrongful death; when commenced; damages. (1) When the death of a person is caused by the wrongful act or omission of another, the personal representative of the decedent, for the benefit of the decedent's surviving spouse, surviving children, surviving parents and other individuals, if any, who under the law of intestate succession of the state of the decedent's domicile would be entitled to inherit the personal property of the decedent, and for the benefit of any stepchild or stepparent whether that stepchild or stepparent would be entitled to inherit the personal property of the decedent or not, may maintain an action against the wrongdoer, if the decedent might have maintained an action, had the decedent lived, against the wrongdoer for an injury done by the same act or omission. The action shall be commenced within three years after the injury causing the death of the decedent is discovered or reasonably should have been discovered by the decedent, by the personal representative or by a person for whose benefit the action may be brought under this section if that person is not the wrongdoer. In no case may an action be commenced later than the earliest of:

(a) Three years after the death of the decedent; or

(b) The longest of any other period for commencing an action under a statute of ultimate repose that applies to the act or omission causing the injury, including but not limited to the statutes of ultimate repose provided for in ORS 12.110 (4), 12.115, 12.135, 12.137 and 30.905.

(2) In an action under this section damages may be awarded in an amount which:

(a) Includes reasonable charges necessarily incurred for doctors' services, hospital services, nursing services, other medical services, burial services and memorial services rendered for the decedent;

(b) Would justly, fairly and reasonably have compensated the decedent for disability, pain, suffering and loss of income during the period between injury to the decedent and the decedent's death;

(c) Justly, fairly and reasonably compensates for pecuniary loss to the decedent's estate;

(d) Justly, fairly and reasonably compensates the decedent's spouse, children, stepchildren, stepparents and parents for pecuniary loss and for loss of the society, companionship and services of the decedent; and

(e) Separately stated in finding or verdict, the punitive damages, if any, which the decedent would have been entitled to recover from the wrongdoer if the decedent had lived.

(3) For the purposes of this section:

(a) Two persons shall be considered to have a stepchild-stepparent relationship if one of the biological parents of the stepchild, while the stepchild is a minor and in the custody of this first biological parent, marries the stepparent who is not the second biological parent or the adoptive parent of the stepchild;

(b) The stepchild-stepparent relationship shall remain in effect even though the stepchild is older than the age of majority or has been emancipated;

(c) The stepchild-stepparent relationship shall remain in effect even though one or both of the biological parents of the stepchild die; and

(d) The stepchild-stepparent relationship shall end upon the divorce of the biological parent and the stepparent. [Amended by 1953 c.600 §3; 1961 c.437 §1; 1967 c.544 §1; 1973 c.718 §2; 1991 c.471 §1; 1991 c.608 §1; 1995 c.618 §19]

30.030 Distribution of damages. (1) Upon settlement of a claim, or recovery of judgment in an action, for damages for wrongful death, by the personal representative of a decedent under ORS 30.020, the amount of damages so accepted or recovered shall be distributed in the manner prescribed in this section.

(2) The personal representative shall make payment or reimbursement for costs, expenses and fees incurred in prosecution or enforcement of the claim, action or judgment.

(3) The personal representative shall make payment or reimbursement for reasonable charges necessarily incurred for doctors' services, hospital services, nursing services or other medical services, burial services and memorial services rendered for the decedent.

(4) If under ORS 30.040 or 30.050 or by agreement of the beneficiaries a portion of the damages so accepted or recovered is apportioned to a beneficiary as recovery for loss described in ORS 30.020 (2)(d), the personal representative shall distribute that portion to the beneficiary.

(5) The remainder of damages accepted or recovered shall be distributed to the beneficiaries in the proportions prescribed under the laws of intestate succession of the state of decedent's domicile, or as agreed by the beneficiaries, but no such damages shall be subject to payment of taxes or claims against the decedent's estate. [Amended by 1973 c.718 §3; 2009 c.51 §1]

30.040 Apportionment among dependents upon settlement. Except when all beneficiaries otherwise agree, if settlement, with or without action, is effected and there is more than one beneficiary, the amount to be distributed to each beneficiary as recovery for loss described in ORS 30.020 (2)(d) shall be apportioned by the probate court to each beneficiary in accordance with the beneficiary's loss. [Amended by 1973 c.718 §4]

30.050 Apportionment among dependents after judgment. Except when all beneficiaries otherwise agree, if the action described in ORS 30.020 is brought, and a judgment for the plaintiff is given, and there is more than one beneficiary, the amount to be distributed to each beneficiary as recovery for loss described in ORS 30.020 (2)(d) shall be apportioned by the trial court to each beneficiary in accordance with the beneficiary's loss. [Amended by 1973 c.718 §5]

30.060 Appeal from order of distribution or apportionment. In the case of an order of distribution under ORS 30.030 (5) or an order of apportionment made under either ORS 30.040 or 30.050, any individual who in the probate court or trial court claims to be a beneficiary may appeal therefrom, or from any part thereof, to the Court of Appeals, within the time, in the manner and with like effect as though such order was a judgment of the circuit court. [Amended by 1973 c.718 §6]

30.070 Settlement; discharge of claim. The personal representative of the decedent, with the approval of the court of appointment, shall have full power to compromise and settle any claim of the class described in ORS 30.030, whether the claim is reduced to judgment or not, and to execute such releases and other instruments as may be necessary to satisfy and discharge the claim. The party paying any such claim or judgment, whether in full or in part, or in an amount agreed upon in compromise, shall not be required to see that the amount paid is applied or apportioned as provided in ORS 30.030 to 30.060, but shall be fully discharged from all liability on payment to the personal representative.

30.075 Procedure upon death of injured person. (1) Causes of action arising out of injuries to a person, caused by the wrongful act or omission of another, shall not abate upon the death of the injured person, and the personal representatives of the decedent may maintain an action against the wrongdoer, if the decedent might have maintained an action, had the decedent lived, against the wrongdoer for an injury done by the same act or omission. The action shall be commenced within the limitations established in ORS 12.110 by the injured person and continued by the personal representatives under this section, or within three years by the personal representatives if not commenced prior to death.

(2) In any such action the court may award to the prevailing party, at trial and on appeal, a reasonable amount to be fixed by the court as attorney fees.

(3) Subsection (2) of this section does not apply to an action for damages arising out of injuries that result in death. If an action for wrongful death under ORS 30.020 is brought, recovery of damages for disability, pain, suffering and loss of income during the period between injury to the decedent and the resulting death of the decedent may only be recovered in the wrongful death action, and the provisions of subsection (2) of this section are not applicable to the recovery. [1965 c.620 §4; 1971 c.473 §2; 1981 c.810 §1; 1981 c.897 §6; 1995 c.618 §21]

30.080 Effect of death of wrongdoer. Claims for relief arising out of injury to or death of a person, caused by the wrongful act or negligence of another, shall not abate upon the death of the wrongdoer, and the injured person or the personal representatives of the one meeting death, as above stated, shall have a claim for relief against the personal representatives of the wrongdoer as if the wrongdoer had survived, except for those damages provided for in ORS 30.020 (2)(e). [Amended by 1953 c.600 §3; 1961 c.437 §2; 1967 c.544 §2; 1973 c.742 §1; 1983 c.662 §1]

30.085 [1987 c.774 §10; 1997 c.734 §1; renumbered 30.698 in 1997]

30.090 Appointment of administrator of estate of wrongdoer. If no probate of the estate of the wrongdoer has been instituted within 60 days from the death of the wrongdoer, the court, upon motion of the injured person, or of the personal representatives of one meeting death, as stated in ORS 30.080, shall appoint an administrator of the estate of the wrongdoer.

30.100 Substitution of personal representative as party defendant. In the event of the death of a wrongdoer, as designated in ORS 30.080, while an action is pending, the court, upon motion of the plaintiff, shall cause to be substituted as defendant the personal representative of the wrongdoer, and the action shall continue against such personal representative.

30.110 [Repealed by 1961 c.578 §1 (30.115 enacted in lieu of 30.110 and 30.120)]

ACTIONS BY GUEST PASSENGERS

30.115 Aircraft and watercraft guest passengers; definitions. No person transported by the owner or operator of an aircraft or a watercraft as a guest without payment for such transportation, shall have a cause of action for damages against the owner or operator for injury, death or loss, in case of accident, unless the accident was intentional on the part of the owner or operator or caused by the gross negligence or intoxication of the owner or operator. As used in this section:
(1) "Payment" means a substantial benefit in a material or business sense conferred upon the owner or operator of the conveyance and which is a substantial motivating factor for the transportation, and it does not include a mere gratuity or social amenity.
(2) "Gross negligence" refers to negligence which is materially greater than the mere absence of reasonable care under the circumstances, and which is characterized by conscious indifference to or reckless disregard of the rights of others. [1961 c.578 §2 (30.115 enacted in lieu of 30.110 and 30.120); 1979 c.866 §7]

30.120 [Repealed by 1961 c.578 §1 (30.115 enacted in lieu of 30.110 and 30.120)]

30.130 Public carriers by aircraft and prospective aircraft purchasers. ORS 30.115 shall not relieve a public carrier by aircraft, or any owner or operator of aircraft while the same is being demonstrated to a prospective purchaser, of responsibility for any injuries sustained by a passenger.

LIABILITY OF CERTAIN PERSONS PROVIDING MOTOR VEHICLES

30.135 Liability of certain persons that lend, rent, donate use of, make available for test drive or otherwise provide motor vehicle. (1) Subject to the provisions of this section, a person that lends, rents, donates use of, makes available for test drive or otherwise provides a motor vehicle, as defined in ORS 801.360, to another person is not liable for any injury, death or damage that arises out of the use of that motor vehicle by the other person, unless the person providing the motor vehicle is negligent in maintaining the motor vehicle or in providing the motor vehicle and the injury, death or damage results from that negligence.
(2) The limitation on liability provided by this section applies only if the person providing the motor vehicle is engaged in the business of selling, renting, leasing or repairing motor vehicles and the motor vehicle is provided to another person in the course of that business.
(3) The limitation on liability provided by this section applies only if there is a written agreement between the person providing the motor vehicle and the person receiving the motor vehicle, and the agreement specifically indicates that the person receiving the motor vehicle is liable for any injury, death or damage arising out of the use of the motor vehicle. The limitation on liability provided by this section applies to injury, death or damage suffered during the period specified in the written agreement, or until the return of the motor vehicle, whichever is later.
(4) The limitation on liability provided by this section applies without regard to whether the motor vehicle is provided for consideration or is provided without charge.
(5) Nothing in this section affects the liability of a manufacturer, distributor, seller or lessor of a product under the provisions of ORS 30.900 to 30.920.
(6) Nothing in this section increases, reduces or relates to those obligations that a self-insurer may choose to undertake pursuant to ORS 806.130. Nothing in ORS 806.130 increases, reduces or relates to the limitations of this section. [1999 c.438 §1; 2001 c.291 §1; 2003 c.331 §1; 2007 c.287 §4]

ENFORCEMENT OF RIGHTS UNDER SERVICEMEMBERS CIVIL RELIEF ACT

30.136 Action to enforce right or remedy under Servicemembers Civil Relief Act. (1) As used in this section and ORS 30.138, "servicemember" has the meaning given that term in 50 U.S.C. App. 511 as in effect on May 8, 2009.
(2) An action brought by a servicemember to enforce a right or remedy under 50 U.S.C. App. 501 et seq. is not subject to court-ordered arbitration under ORS 36.400 to 36.425 unless the parties to the action stipulate in writing to arbitration after the action is commenced.
(3) In addition to the counties specified in ORS 14.080, an action brought by a servicemember to enforce a right or remedy under 50 U.S.C. App. 501 et seq. may be brought in the Oregon county where the servicemember resides or where the servicemember was a resident at the time of bringing the action.
(4) Any contract term or provision providing for a choice of forum other than Oregon in an agreement entered into by a servicemember who resides in Oregon or is a resident of Oregon is voidable at the election of the servicemember. [2009 c.83 §1]

Note: Section 4, chapter 83, Oregon Laws 2009, provides:
Sec. 4. Sections 1 and 2 of this 2009 Act [30.136 and 30.138] apply only to conduct that violates 50 U.S.C. App. 501 et seq. that occurs on or after the effective date of this 2009 Act [May 8, 2009]. [2009 c.83 §4]

30.138 Remedies for violation of Servicemembers Civil Relief Act. (1) In addition to any other remedy payable to a servicemember for the enforcement of a right under 50 U.S.C. App. 501 et seq., a court shall award a servicemember reasonable attorney fees and the amounts specified in subsection (2) of this section if the court finds that written demand as described in subsection (3) of this section was mailed to the opposing party demanding relief under 50 U.S.C. App. 501 et seq., and the opposing party failed to remedy the violation of 50 U.S.C. App. 501 et seq. within 30 days after the mailing of the demand.

(2) If a court finds that notice was mailed as required by this section, and the opposing party failed to remedy the violation of 50 U.S.C. App. 501 et seq. within the time allowed, the court shall award the servicemember:

(a) The greater of $1,000 or actual damages, including damages for emotional distress; or

(b) If the court finds that the opposing party's conduct was willful, as described in ORS 646.605, the court shall award the servicemember the greater of $5,000, or three times the amount of actual damages, including damages for emotional distress.

(3) A written demand under subsection (1) of this section must be sent by certified mail, return receipt requested. The demand must include the servicemember's name and address, the date on which the servicemember went on active duty and a description of the alleged violation of 50 U.S.C. App. 501 et seq. [2009 c.83 §2]

Note: See note under 30.136.

ACTIONS ON CERTAIN CONSTRUCTION AGREEMENTS

30.140 Certain indemnification provisions in construction agreement void. (1) Except to the extent provided under subsection (2) of this section, any provision in a construction agreement that requires a person or that person's surety or insurer to indemnify another against liability for damage arising out of death or bodily injury to persons or damage to property caused in whole or in part by the negligence of the indemnitee is void.

(2) This section does not affect any provision in a construction agreement that requires a person or that person's surety or insurer to indemnify another against liability for damage arising out of death or bodily injury to persons or damage to property to the extent that the death or bodily injury to persons or damage to property arises out of the fault of the indemnitor, or the fault of the indemnitor's agents, representatives or subcontractors.

(3) As used in this section, "construction agreement" means any written agreement for the planning, design, construction, alteration, repair, improvement or maintenance of any building, highway, road excavation or other structure, project, development or improvement attached to real estate including moving, demolition or tunneling in connection therewith.

(4) This section does not apply to:

(a) Any real property lease or rental agreement between a landlord and tenant whether or not any provision of the lease or rental agreement relates to or involves planning, design, construction, alteration, repair, improvement or maintenance as long as the predominant purpose of the lease or rental agreement is not planning, design, construction, alteration, repair, improvement or maintenance of real property; or

(b) Any personal property lease or rental agreement.

(5) No provision of this section shall be construed to apply to a "railroad" as defined in ORS 824.200. [1973 c.570 §§1,2; 1987 c.774 §25; 1995 c.704 §1; 1997 c.858 §1; 2007 c.413 §1]

30.142 [2001 c.616 §1; renumbered 31.150 in 2003]

30.144 [2001 c.616 §2; renumbered 31.152 in 2003]

30.145 Certain provisions relating to waivers in construction agreements void. (1) Except as provided in this section, a provision in a construction agreement is void to the extent that the provision requires a party or the party's surety or insurer to waive a right of subrogation, indemnity or contribution for amounts paid by reason of death or bodily injury, or damage to property, caused in whole or in part by the negligence of another person.

(2) This section does not apply to a provision for waiver of subrogation, indemnity or contribution in an insurance policy issued pursuant to ORS 737.602 or to a provision for waiver of subrogation, indemnity or contribution that applies to proceeds of a property insurance policy.

(3) This section does not apply to a provision for waiver of subrogation, indemnity or contribution in a real property lease or rental agreement between a landlord and tenant, whether or not any provision of the lease or rental agreement relates to or involves planning, designing, constructing, altering, repairing, improving or maintaining, as long as the predominant purpose of the lease or rental agreement is not planning, designing, constructing, altering, repairing, improving or maintaining real property.

(4) This section does not apply to a provision for waiver of subrogation, indemnity or contribution in a personal property lease or rental agreement.

(5) This section does not apply to a provision for waiver of subrogation, indemnity or contribution in a construction agreement in which one of the parties is a railroad as defined in ORS 824.200.

(6) As used in this section, "construction agreement" has the meaning given that term in ORS 30.140. [2011 c.518 §1]

30.146 [2001 c.616 §3; renumbered 31.155 in 2003]

30.150 [Formerly 30.760; renumbered 31.200 in 2003]

30.155 [1955 c.365 §1; renumbered 31.205 in 2003]

30.160 [1955 c.365 §2; renumbered 31.210 in 2003]

30.165 [1955 c.365 §3; 1991 c.249 §4; renumbered 31.215 in 2003]

30.170 [1955 c.365 §4; renumbered 31.220 in 2003]

30.175 [1955 c.365 §5; renumbered 31.225 in 2003]

ACTIONS AGAINST FORMER EMPLOYER FOR DISCLOSURE OF INFORMATION

30.178 Liability of employer for disclosing information about employee to new employer; no action based on compelled self-publication. (1) An employer who discloses information about a former employee's job performance to a prospective employer of the former employee upon request of the prospective employer or of the former employee is presumed to be acting in good faith and, unless lack of good faith is shown by a preponderance of the evidence, is immune from civil liability for such disclosure or its consequences. For purposes of this section, the presumption of good faith is rebutted upon a showing that the information disclosed by the employer was knowingly false or deliberately misleading, was rendered with malicious purpose or violated any civil right of the former employee protected under ORS chapter 659 or 659A.

(2) A civil action for defamation may not be maintained against an employer by an employee who is terminated by the employer based on a claim that in seeking subsequent employment the former employee will be forced to reveal the reasons given by the employer for the termination. [1995 c.330 §1; 1997 c.754 §1; 2001 c.621 §68]

ACTIONS ARISING OUT OF PROVISION OF UTILITY SERVICES

30.180 Definitions for ORS 30.180 to 30.186. As used in ORS 30.180 to 30.186:

(1) "Customer" means the person in whose name a utility service is provided.

(2) "Divert" means to change the intended course or path of the utility service without the authorization or consent of the utility.

(3) "Person" means any individual, partnership, firm, association, corporation or government agency.

(4) "Reconnection" means the commencement of utility service to a customer or other person after service has been lawfully disconnected by the utility.

(5) "Tamper" means to rearrange, injure, alter, interfere with or otherwise prevent from performing the normal or customary function.

(6) "Utility" means a private corporation, a municipal corporation or an agency thereof, any other public corporation or any district that provides electricity, gas, water, telephone or cable television to customers on a retail or wholesale basis.

(7) "Utility service" means the provision of electricity, gas, water, telephone, cable television, electronic communications, steam or any other service or commodity furnished by the utility for compensation. [1989 c.670 §3]

30.182 Civil action for taking of or tampering with utility services. A utility may bring a civil action for damages against any person who knowingly and willfully commits, authorizes, solicits, aids, abets or attempts to:

(1) Divert, or cause to be diverted, utility services by any means whatsoever;

(2) Make, or cause to be made, any connection or reconnection with property owned or used by the utility to provide utility service without the authorization or consent of the utility;

(3) Prevent any utility meter or other device used in determining the charge for utility services from accurately performing its measuring function by tampering or by any other means;

(4) Tamper with any property owned or used by the utility to provide utility services; or

(5) Use or receive the direct benefit of all or a portion of the utility service with knowledge of, or reason to believe that, the diversion, tampering or unauthorized connection existed at the time of the use or that the use or receipt was without the authorization or consent of the utility. [1989 c.670 §1]

30.184 Amount recoverable; attorney fees. In any civil action brought under this section, the utility shall recover from the defendant the greater of actual damages, if any, or $100. Actual damages include the costs incurred on account of the bypassing, tampering or unauthorized reconnection, including but not limited to costs and expenses for investigation, disconnection, reconnection and service calls. The utility may recover punitive damages in addition to actual damages. The court may award reasonable attorney fees and expert witness fees to the prevailing party in an action under this section. [1989 c.670 §2; 1993 c.217 §1; 1995 c.618 §22]

30.186 Remedies not exclusive. The remedies provided in ORS 30.180 to 30.186 are in addition to, and not in lieu of, any and all other remedies, both civil and criminal, provided by law. [1989 c.670 §4]

30.190 [1981 c.785 §3; 1983 c.521 §3; 1995 c.618 §23; renumbered 30.198 in 1999]

ACTIONS ARISING OUT OF PROVISION OF CABLE SERVICES

30.192 Definitions for ORS 30.192 to 30.196. As used in ORS 30.192 to 30.196:

(1) "Cable operator" means a person who:

(a) Lawfully provides cable service over a cable system in which the person, directly or through one or more affiliates, owns a significant interest; or

(b) Lawfully controls or is responsible for the management and operation of a cable system through an arrangement.

(2) "Cable service" means:

(a) One-way transmission to subscribers of a video programming service;

(b) Two-way interactive services delivered over a cable system; or

(c) Any communication with subscribers necessary for the use of video programming or interactive service.

(3) "Cable system" means a facility consisting of closed transmission paths and associated signal operation, reception and control equipment that is designed to provide cable service. [1999 c.705 §1]

30.194 Prohibitions relating to cable services. A person shall not knowingly:

(1) Obtain cable service from a cable operator by trick, artifice, deception, use of an unauthorized device or decoder, or other means without authorization or with the intent to deprive the cable operator of lawful compensation for services rendered;

(2) Make or maintain, without authorization from or payment to a cable operator, a connection or connections, whether physical, electrical, mechanical, acoustical or otherwise with any cable, wire, component or other device used for the distribution of cable services, except that nothing in this subsection is intended to make unlawful circumstances in which the person has attached a wire or cable to extend authorized or paid cable services to an additional outlet or in which the cable operator has failed to disconnect previously authorized or paid cable service;

(3) Modify, alter or maintain a modification or alteration to a device installed by a cable operator if the modification or alteration is for the purpose of intercepting or otherwise receiving cable service without authorization from or payment to the cable operator;

(4) Possess, with intent to receive cable services without authorization from or payment to a cable operator, a printed circuit board or other device designed in whole or in part to facilitate:

(a) Receiving cable services offered for sale over a cable system; or

(b) Performing or facilitating any act described in subsections (1) to (3) of this section;

(5) Manufacture, import into this state, distribute, sell, lease or offer for sale or lease, with intent to promote the receipt of cable services without authorization from or payment to a cable operator, any printed circuit board, plan or other device, or a kit for such a device, designed in whole or in part to facilitate:

(a) Receiving cable services offered for sale over a cable system; or

(b) Performing or facilitating any act described in subsections (1) to (3) of this section; or

(6) Fail to return or surrender, upon demand and after service has been terminated, equipment provided by a cable operator to receive cable service. [1999 c.705 §2]

30.195 Civil action for violation of prohibitions relating to cable services. (1) A cable operator may bring a civil action for damages against any person who violates any provision of ORS 30.194.

(2) A cable operator who alleges a violation of ORS 30.194 may file for injunctive relief in the circuit court for the county where the alleged violation occurred or is occurring.

(3) A cable operator who files an action under this section is not required to plead damages with particularity as a condition of filing or maintaining the action.

(4) In any action brought under this section, there shall be a rebuttable presumption that a person has violated ORS 30.194 (1) if the person is in actual possession of a device that permits the reception of unauthorized cable services for which payment has not been made and for which no legitimate purpose exists.

(5) In any action brought under this section, there shall be a rebuttable presumption that a person has violated ORS 30.194 (2) if cable service to the person's business or residence was disconnected by a cable operator, notice of the disconnection was provided to the person by certified mail, and a connection exists at the person's business or residence after the date of the notice.

(6) In any action brought under this section, there shall be a rebuttable presumption that a person has violated ORS 30.194 (3) if the cable operator as standard procedure:

(a) Places written warning labels on its converters or decoders indicating that tampering with the devices is a violation of law and a converter or decoder is found to have been tampered with, altered or modified to allow the reception of cable services without authorization from or payment to the cable operator; or

(b) Seals its converters or decoders with a label or mechanical device and the label or device has been removed or broken.

(7) In any action brought under this section, there shall be a rebuttable presumption that a person has violated ORS 30.194 (4) if a person possesses 10 or more printed circuit boards or other devices designed to receive cable services. A person who is found to have violated ORS 30.194 (4) shall be subject to penalties described in ORS 30.196 (2).

(8) In any action brought under this section, there shall be a rebuttable presumption that a person has violated ORS 30.194 (5) if the person made representations to a buyer that the device offered for sale would allow the purchaser to obtain cable service without authorization from or payment to a cable operator. A person who is found to have violated ORS 30.194 (5) shall be subject to penalties described in ORS 30.196 (2).

(9) In any action brought under this section, there shall be a rebuttable presumption that a person has violated ORS 30.194 (6) if a cable operator sent to the person by certified mail, at the most recent address for the person shown in the records of the cable operator, a written demand for the return of converters, decoders or other equipment owned by the cable operator. The demand shall allow the person to make reasonable arrangements to return the equipment within 15 days of receiving the notice. Reasonable arrangements may include a request that the cable operator pick up the equipment, subject to the cable operators written policies.

(10) Statements from a manufacturer or retailer regarding the intended use or uses of a product shall not constitute a defense to an alleged violation of ORS 30.194 (5). [1999 c.705 §3]

30.196 Amount recoverable; attorney fees. (1) In addition to any other penalty provided by law, a cable operator who prevails on a claim under ORS 30.195 may recover the amount of $3,000.

(2)(a) A court may increase an award under subsection (1) of this section to an amount not to exceed $50,000 if the court determines that the violation was committed for purposes of commercial advantage.

(b) As used in this subsection, "commercial advantage" does not include any monetary gain realized by a person's private use of unauthorized cable services.

(3) The prevailing party in an action brought under ORS 30.195 shall be awarded reasonable court costs and attorney fees and all costs including but not limited to the cost of investigation, disconnection or reconnection, service calls, labor, equipment and expert testimony. [1999 c.705 §4]

ACTIONS FOR INTIMIDATION

30.198 Civil action for intimidation; remedies; attorney fees; liability of parents. (1) Irrespective of any criminal prosecution or the result thereof, any person injured by a violation of ORS 166.155 or 166.165 shall have a civil action to secure an injunction, damages or other appropriate relief against any and all persons whose actions are unlawful under ORS 166.155 and 166.165.

(2) Upon prevailing in such action, the plaintiff may recover:

(a) Both special and general damages, including damages for emotional distress; and

(b) Punitive damages.

(3) The court shall award reasonable attorney fees to the prevailing plaintiff in an action under this section. The court may award reasonable attorney fees and expert witness fees incurred by a defendant who prevails in the action if the court determines that the plaintiff had no objectively reasonable basis for asserting a claim or no reasonable basis for appealing an adverse decision of a trial court.

(4) The parent, parents or legal guardian of an unemancipated minor shall be liable for any judgment recovered against such minor under this section, in an amount not to exceed $5,000. [Formerly 30.190]

30.200 Action by district attorney; effect on others. If any district attorney has reasonable cause to believe that any person or group of persons is engaged in violation of ORS 166.155 or 166.165, the district attorney may bring a civil claim for relief in the appropriate court, setting forth facts pertaining to such violation, and request such relief as may be necessary to restrain or prevent such violation. Any claim for relief under this section does not prevent any person from seeking any other remedy otherwise available under law. [1981 c.785 §4]

ACTIONS ON OFFICIAL BONDS

30.210 To whom official bonds are security. The official undertaking or other security of a public officer to the state, or to any county, city or other public corporation of like character therein, is a security to the state, county, city or public corporation, as the case may be, and also, to all persons severally for the official delinquencies against which it is intended to provide.

30.220 Parties. When a public officer by official misconduct or neglect of duty forfeits an official undertaking or other security of the public officer, or renders the sureties of the public officer liable thereon, any person injured by the misconduct or neglect, or who is by law entitled to the benefit of the security, may maintain an action thereon in the name of the person, against the officer and the sureties of the officer, to recover the amount to which the person may by reason thereof be entitled.

30.230 Leave to begin action. Before an action can be commenced by a plaintiff other than the state, or the public corporation named in the undertaking or security, leave shall be obtained of the court or judge thereof where the action is triable. Such leave shall be granted upon the production of a certified copy of the undertaking or security, and an affidavit of the plaintiff or some person on behalf of the plaintiff showing the delinquency; but if the matters set forth in the affidavit are such that, if true, the party applying would clearly not be entitled to recover in the action, the leave shall not be granted. If it does not appear from the complaint that leave has been granted, the defendant on motion shall be entitled to judgment of dismissal without prejudice; if it does, the defendant may controvert the allegation, and if the issue be found in favor of the defendant, judgment shall be given accordingly. [Amended by 1979 c.284 §63]

30.240 Subsequent delinquencies on same bond. A judgment in favor of a party for one delinquency shall not preclude the same or another party from maintaining another action on the same undertaking or security for another delinquency.

30.250 Amount of judgment. In an action upon an official undertaking or security, if judgments have already been recovered on the same undertaking or security against the surety therein, other than by confession, and if such recovery is established on the trial, judgment shall not be given against the surety for an amount exceeding the difference between the amount of the penalty and the amount that already has been recovered against the surety.

TORT ACTIONS AGAINST PUBLIC BODIES

(Generally)

30.260 Definitions for ORS 30.260 to 30.300. As used in ORS 30.260 to 30.300, unless the context requires otherwise:

(1) "Department" means the Oregon Department of Administrative Services.

(2) "Director" means the Director of the Oregon Department of Administrative Services.

(3) "Governing body" means the group or officer in which the controlling authority of any public body is vested.

(4) "Public body" means:

(a) A public body as defined in ORS 174.109;

(b) Any nonprofit corporation that is organized and existing under ORS chapter 65 and that has only political subdivisions or municipal, quasi-municipal or public corporations in this state as members;

(c) A child-caring agency, as defined in ORS 418.205, that meets the criteria specified in ORS 278.322 (1)(a) and that receives more than 50 percent of its funding from the state for the purpose of providing residential treatment to children who have been placed in the care and custody of the state or that provides residential treatment to children more than half of whom have been placed in the care and custody of the state; or

(d) A private, nonprofit organization that provides public transportation services if more than 50 percent of the organization's funding for the purpose of providing public transportation services is received from governmental bodies.

(5) "State" means:

(a) State government as defined in ORS 174.111;

(b) The State Accident Insurance Fund Corporation; and

(c) The Oregon Utility Notification Center.

(6) "Local public body" means any public body other than the state.

(7) "Nuclear incident" has the meaning given that term in 42 U.S.C. 2014(q).

(8) "Tort" means the breach of a legal duty that is imposed by law, other than a duty arising from contract or quasi-contract, the breach of which results in injury to a specific person or persons for which the law provides a civil right of action for damages or for a protective remedy. [1967 c.627 §1; 1975 c.609 §11; 1977 c.823 §1; 1981 c.109 §1; 1987 c.915 §9; subsections (7) and (8) enacted as 1987 c.705 §6; 1989 c.905 §1; 1989 c.1004 §2; 1993 c.500 §3; 1997 c.215 §4; 2005 c.684 §1; 2005 c.798 §2; 2009 c.67 §9; 2016 c.106 §41]

30.261 Limitation on applicability of ORS 30.260 to 30.300 to certain private, nonprofit organizations. A private, nonprofit organization described under ORS 30.260 (4)(d) is subject to ORS 30.260 to 30.300 only for the purposes of providing public transportation services. [2005 c.684 §4; 2009 c.67 §17]

Note: 30.261 was added to and made a part of 30.260 to 30.300 by legislative action but was not added to any smaller series therein. See Preface to Oregon Revised Statutes for further explanation.

30.262 Certain nonprofit facilities and homes public bodies for purposes of ORS 30.260 to 30.300. (1) The following facilities and training homes are public bodies for the purposes of ORS 30.260 to 30.300:

(a) A nonprofit residential training facility as defined in ORS 443.400, nonprofit residential training home as defined in ORS 443.400 or nonprofit facility as defined in ORS 427.005, organized and existing under ORS chapter 65, that receives more than 50 percent of its funding from the state or a political subdivision of the state for the purpose of providing residential or vocational services to individuals with intellectual or other developmental disabilities.

(b) A nonprofit residential training facility as defined in ORS 443.400, nonprofit residential training home as defined in ORS 443.400 or nonprofit facility as defined in ORS 427.005, organized and existing under ORS chapter 65, that receives less than 50 percent of its funding from the state or a political subdivision of the state but that provides residential or vocational services to individuals with intellectual or other developmental disabilities, more than half of whom are eligible for funding for services by the Department of Human Services under criteria established by the department.

(2) The provisions of this section apply only to a nonprofit residential training facility, nonprofit residential training home or nonprofit facility that provides services to individuals with intellectual or other developmental disabilities under a contract with:

(a) The Department of Human Services; or

(b) A community mental health program or community developmental disabilities program established pursuant to ORS 430.620. [1997 c.579 §2; 2001 c.900 §9; 2007 c.70 §8; 2011 c.658 §30; 2011 c.720 §52]

Note: 30.262 was added to and made a part of 30.260 to 30.300 by legislative action but was not added to any smaller series therein. See Preface to Oregon Revised Statutes for further explanation.

30.264 [2001 c.370 §2; 2011 c.637 §60; repealed by 2013 c.301 §1]

30.265 Scope of liability of public body, officers, employees and agents; liability in nuclear incident. (1) Subject to the limitations of ORS 30.260 to 30.300, every public body is subject to civil action for its torts and those of its officers, employees and agents acting within the scope of their employment or duties, whether arising out of a governmental or proprietary function or while operating a motor vehicle in a ridesharing arrangement authorized under ORS 276.598.

(2) The sole cause of action for a tort committed by officers, employees or agents of a public body acting within the scope of their employment or duties and eligible for representation and indemnification under ORS 30.285 or 30.287 is an action under ORS 30.260 to 30.300. The remedy provided by ORS 30.260 to 30.300 is exclusive of any other action against any such officer, employee or agent of a public body whose act or omission within the scope of the officer's, employee's or agent's employment or duties gives rise to the action. No other form of civil action is permitted.

(3) If an action under ORS 30.260 to 30.300 alleges damages in an amount equal to or less than the damages allowed under ORS 30.271, 30.272 or 30.273, the sole cause of action for a tort committed by officers, employees or agents of a public body acting within the scope of their employment or duties and eligible for representation and indemnification under ORS 30.285 or 30.287 is an action against the public body. If an action is filed against an officer, employee or agent of a public body, and the plaintiff alleges damages in an amount equal to or less than the damages allowed under ORS 30.271, 30.272 or 30.273, the court upon motion shall substitute the public body as the defendant. Substitution of the public body as the defendant does not exempt the public body from making any report required under ORS 742.400.

(4) If an action under ORS 30.260 to 30.300 alleges damages in an amount greater than the damages allowed under ORS 30.271, 30.272 or 30.273, the action may be brought and maintained against an officer, employee or agent of a public body, whether or not the public body is also named as a defendant. An action brought under this subsection is subject to the limitations on damages imposed under ORS 30.271, 30.272 or 30.273, and the total combined amount recovered in the action may not exceed those limitations for a single accident or occurrence without regard to the number or types of defendants named in the action.

(5) Every public body is immune from liability for any claim for injury to or death of any person or injury to property resulting from an act or omission of an officer, employee or agent of a public body when such officer, employee or agent is immune from liability.

(6) Every public body and its officers, employees and agents acting within the scope of their employment or duties, or while operating a motor vehicle in a ridesharing arrangement authorized under ORS 276.598, are immune from liability for:

(a) Any claim for injury to or death of any person covered by any workers' compensation law.

(b) Any claim in connection with the assessment and collection of taxes.

(c) Any claim based upon the performance of or the failure to exercise or perform a discretionary function or duty, whether or not the discretion is abused.

(d) Any claim that is limited or barred by the provisions of any other statute, including but not limited to any statute of ultimate repose.

(e) Any claim arising out of riot, civil commotion or mob action or out of any act or omission in connection with the prevention of any of the foregoing.

(f) Any claim arising out of an act done or omitted under apparent authority of a law, resolution, rule or regulation that is unconstitutional, invalid or inapplicable except to the extent that they would have been liable had the law, resolution, rule or regulation been constitutional, valid and applicable, unless such act was done or omitted in bad faith or with malice.

(7) This section applies to any action of any officer, employee or agent of the state relating to a nuclear incident, whether or not the officer, employee or agent is acting within the scope of employment, and provided the nuclear incident is covered by an insurance or indemnity agreement under 42 U.S.C. 2210.

(8) Subsection (6)(c) of this section does not apply to any discretionary act that is found to be the cause or partial cause of a nuclear incident covered by an insurance or indemnity agreement under the provisions of 42 U.S.C. 2210, including but not limited to road design and route selection. [1967 c.627

§§2,3,10; 1969 c.429 §1; 1975 c.609 §12; 1977 c.823 §2; 1981 c.490 §4; 1985 c.731 §31; 1987 c.705 §7; 1991 c.861 §1; 2005 c.22 §19; 2007 c.803 §4; 2011 c.270 §1]

30.266 [1977 c.781 §2; 1981 c.109 §2; 1985 c.731 §20; 1989 c.873 §1; repealed by 1991 c.756 §5]

30.267 Liability for certain medical treatment at Oregon Health and Science University facilities. (1) For the purposes of ORS 30.260 to 30.300, all services constituting patient care, including, but not limited to, inpatient care, outpatient care and all forms of consultation, that are provided on the Oregon Health and Science University campus or in any Oregon Health and Science University clinic are within the scope of their state employment or duties when performed by:
(a) Salaried physicians, naturopathic physicians or dentists employed at any full-time equivalent by the Oregon Health and Science University;
(b) Nonsalaried or courtesy physicians, naturopathic physicians or dentists affiliated with the Oregon Health and Science University;
(c) Medical, dental or nursing students or trainees affiliated with the Oregon Health and Science University;
(d) Volunteer physicians, naturopathic physicians or dentists affiliated with the Oregon Health and Science University; or
(e) Any nurses, students, orderlies, volunteers, aides or employees of the Oregon Health and Science University.
(2) As used in this section:
(a) "Nonsalaried or courtesy physician, naturopathic physician or dentist" means a physician, naturopathic physician or dentist who receives a fee or other compensation for those services constituting patient care which are within the scope of state employment or duties under this section. The term does not include a physician, naturopathic physician or dentist described under subsection (1)(a) of this section.
(b) "Volunteer physician, naturopathic physician or dentist" means a physician, naturopathic physician or dentist who does not receive a salary, fee or other compensation for those services constituting patient care which are within the scope of state employment or duties under this section. [1977 c.851 §2; 2017 c.356 §1]

30.268 Liability for certain medical treatment at facilities other than Oregon Health and Science University. (1) For the purposes of ORS 30.260 to 30.300, all services constituting patient care, including, but not limited to, inpatient care, outpatient care and all forms of consultation that are provided at a location other than the Oregon Health and Science University campus or one of the Oregon Health and Science University clinics are within the scope of state employment or duties when:
(a) Provided by members of the Oregon Health and Science University faculty or staff, Oregon Health and Science University students under prior written express authorization from the president of the Oregon Health and Science University or a representative of the president to provide those services at that location;
(b) The services provided are within the scope of the express authorization; and
(c) The Oregon Health and Science University:
(A) Derives revenue in a similar amount or percentage as it would for care rendered on the Oregon Health and Science University campus or at an Oregon Health and Science University clinic; or
(B) Is performing a salaried, nonfee-generating or volunteer public community or nonfee-generating educational service by providing the services.
(2) For the purposes of ORS 30.260 to 30.300, services constituting patient care that are provided at a location other than the Oregon Health and Science University campus or one of the Oregon Health and Science University clinics are not within the scope of state employment or duties when:
(a) Such services constitute an exclusively private relationship between the patient and a person described in subsection (1)(a) of this section; and
(b) The requirements of subsection (1)(b) and (c) of this section are not met. [1977 c.851 §3; 1995 c.84 §1]

30.269 Limitations on awards under Oregon Tort Claims Act generally. (1) Punitive damages may not be awarded on any claim subject to ORS 30.260 to 30.300.
(2) Claims subject to ORS 30.260 to 30.300 are not subject to the limitation imposed by ORS 31.710.
(3) A court may not apply the limitations imposed on recovery under ORS 30.271, 30.272 and 30.273 until after the entry of a verdict or a stipulation by the parties to the amount of the damages.
(4) The limitations imposed under ORS 30.271 (2) and 30.272 (2) on single claimants include damages claimed for loss of services or loss of support arising out of the same tort.
(5) If two or more claimants recover on a claim that arises out of a single accident or occurrence, and the recovery is subject to a limitation imposed by ORS 30.271 (3), 30.272 (3) or 30.273 (2)(b), any party to the action in which the claim is made may apply to the court to apportion to each claimant the proper share of the amount allowed by ORS 30.271 (3), 30.272 (3) or 30.273 (2)(b). The share apportioned to each claimant shall be in the proportion that the ratio of the award or settlement made to the claimant bears to the aggregate awards and settlements for all claims arising out of the accident or occurrence.
(6) Liability of any public body and one or more of its officers, employees or agents, or two or more officers, employees or agents of a public body, on claims arising out of a single accident or occurrence, may not exceed in the aggregate the amounts allowed by ORS 30.271, 30.272 and 30.273.
(7) ORS 30.271, 30.272 and 30.273 do not apply to a claim arising in connection with a nuclear incident covered by an insurance or indemnity agreement under 42 U.S.C. 2210.
(8) For the purposes of the limitations imposed by ORS 30.271, 30.272 and 30.273, events giving rise to a proclamation of a state of emergency under ORS 401.165, or a proclamation of a public health emergency under ORS 433.441, do not constitute a single accident or occurrence. [2009 c.67 §2; 2009 c.718 §15]

Note: 30.269 to 30.274 were added to and made a part of 30.260 to 30.300 by legislative action but were not added to any smaller series therein. See Preface to Oregon Revised Statutes for further explanation.

30.270 [1967 c.627 §4; 1969 c.429 §2; 1975 c.609 §13; 1987 c.705 §8; 1987 c.915 §13; repealed by 2009 c.67 §20]

30.271 Limitations on liability of state for personal injury and death. (1) The limitations imposed by this section apply to claims that:
(a) Are subject to ORS 30.260 to 30.300;
(b) Are made against the state, or against an officer, employee or agent of the state acting within the person's scope of employment or duties;
(c) Arise out of a single accident or occurrence; and
(d) Are not claims for damage to or destruction of property.
(2) The liability of the state, and the liability of the state's officers, employees and agents acting within the scope of their employment or duties, to any single claimant for claims described in subsection (1) of this section may not exceed:
(a) $1.5 million, for causes of action arising on or after December 28, 2007, and before July 1, 2010.
(b) $1.6 million, for causes of action arising on or after July 1, 2010, and before July 1, 2011.
(c) $1.7 million, for causes of action arising on or after July 1, 2011, and before July 1, 2012.
(d) $1.8 million, for causes of action arising on or after July 1, 2012, and before July 1, 2013.
(e) $1.9 million, for causes of action arising on or after July 1, 2013, and before July 1, 2014.
(f) $2 million, for causes of action arising on or after July 1, 2014, and before July 1, 2015.
(g) The adjusted limitation provided by subsection (4) of this section, for causes of action arising on or after July 1, 2015.
(3) The liability of the state, and the liability of the state's officers, employees and agents acting within the scope of their employment or duties, to all claimants for claims described in subsection (1) of this section may not exceed:
(a) $3 million, for causes of action arising on or after December 28, 2007, and before July 1, 2010.

(b) $3.2 million, for causes of action arising on or after July 1, 2010, and before July 1, 2011.
(c) $3.4 million, for causes of action arising on or after July 1, 2011, and before July 1, 2012.
(d) $3.6 million, for causes of action arising on or after July 1, 2012, and before July 1, 2013.
(e) $3.8 million, for causes of action arising on or after July 1, 2013, and before July 1, 2014.
(f) $4 million, for causes of action arising on or after July 1, 2014, and before July 1, 2015.
(g) The adjusted limitation provided by subsection (4) of this section, for causes of action arising on or after July 1, 2015.
(4) Beginning in 2015, and every year thereafter, the State Court Administrator shall determine the percentage increase or decrease in the cost of living for the previous calendar year, based on changes in the Portland-Salem, OR-WA Consumer Price Index for All Urban Consumers for All Items as published by the Bureau of Labor Statistics of the United States Department of Labor. On or before July 1 of the year in which the State Court Administrator makes the determination required by this subsection, the State Court Administrator shall adjust the limitations imposed under subsections (2) and (3) of this section for the following calendar year by multiplying the limitation amounts applicable to the calendar year in which the adjustment is made by the percentage amount determined under this subsection. The adjustment may not exceed three percent for any year. The State Court Administrator shall round the adjusted limitation amount to the nearest $100, but the unrounded amount shall be used to calculate the adjustments to the limitations in subsequent calendar years. The adjusted limitation becomes effective on July 1 of the year in which the adjustment is made, and applies to all causes of action arising on or after July 1 of that year and before July 1 of the subsequent year.
(5) The limitations imposed by this section apply to claims against Oregon Health and Science University.
(6) The limitations imposed by this section apply to claims against the State Fair Council. [2009 c.67 §3; 2015 c.589 §1]

Note: See note under 30.269.

30.272 Limitations on liability of local public bodies for personal injury and death. (1) The limitations imposed by this section apply to claims that:
(a) Are subject to ORS 30.260 to 30.300;
(b) Are made against a local public body, or against an officer, employee or agent of a local public body acting within the person's scope of employment or duties;
(c) Arise out of a single accident or occurrence; and
(d) Are not claims for damage to or destruction of property.
(2) The liability of a local public body, and the liability of the public body's officers, employees and agents acting within the scope of their employment or duties, to any single claimant for claims described in subsection (1) of this section may not exceed:
(a) $500,000, for causes of action arising on or after July 1, 2009, and before July 1, 2010.
(b) $533,300, for causes of action arising on or after July 1, 2010, and before July 1, 2011.
(c) $566,700, for causes of action arising on or after July 1, 2011, and before July 1, 2012.
(d) $600,000, for causes of action arising on or after July 1, 2012, and before July 1, 2013.
(e) $633,300, for causes of action arising on or after July 1, 2013, and before July 1, 2014.
(f) $666,700, for causes of action arising on or after July 1, 2014, and before July 1, 2015.
(g) The adjusted limitation provided by subsection (4) of this section, for causes of action arising on or after July 1, 2015.
(3) The liability of a local public body, and the liability of the public body's officers, employees and agents acting within the scope of their employment or duties, to all claimants for claims described in subsection (1) of this section may not exceed:
(a) $1 million, for causes of action arising on or after July 1, 2009, and before July 1, 2010.
(b) $1,066,700, for causes of action arising on or after July 1, 2010, and before July 1, 2011.
(c) $1,133,300, for causes of action arising on or after July 1, 2011, and before July 1, 2012.
(d) $1,200,000, for causes of action arising on or after July 1, 2012, and before July 1, 2013.
(e) $1,266,700, for causes of action arising on or after July 1, 2013, and before July 1, 2014.
(f) $1,333,300, for causes of action arising on or after July 1, 2014, and before July 1, 2015.
(g) The adjusted limitation provided by subsection (4) of this section, for causes of action arising on or after July 1, 2015.
(4) Beginning in 2015, and every year thereafter, the State Court Administrator shall determine the percentage increase or decrease in the cost of living for the previous calendar year, based on changes in the Portland-Salem, OR-WA Consumer Price Index for All Urban Consumers for All Items as published by the Bureau of Labor Statistics of the United States Department of Labor. On or before July 1 of the year in which the State Court Administrator makes the determination required by this subsection, the State Court Administrator shall adjust the limitations imposed under subsections (2) and (3) of this section for the following calendar year by multiplying the limitation amounts applicable to the calendar year in which the adjustment is made by the percentage amount determined under this subsection. The adjustment may not exceed three percent for any year. The State Court Administrator shall round the adjusted limitation amount to the nearest $100, but the unrounded amount shall be used to calculate the adjustments to the limitations in subsequent calendar years. The adjusted limitation becomes effective on July 1 of the year in which the adjustment is made, and applies to all causes of action arising on or after July 1 of that year and before July 1 of the subsequent year.
(5) The limitations imposed by this section do not apply to claims against Oregon Health and Science University. [2009 c.67 §4]

Note: See note under 30.269.

30.273 Limitations on liability of public bodies for property damage or destruction. (1) The limitations imposed by this section apply to claims that:
(a) Are subject to ORS 30.260 to 30.300;
(b) Are made against a public body, or against a public body's officers, employees and agents acting within the scope of their employment or duties;
(c) Arise out of a single accident or occurrence; and
(d) Are claims for damage to or destruction of property, including consequential damages.
(2) The liability of a public body, and the liability of the public body's officers, employees and agents acting within the scope of their employment or duties, for claims described in subsection (1) of this section may not exceed:
(a) $100,000, or the adjusted limitation provided by subsection (3) of this section, to any single claimant.
(b) $500,000, or the adjusted limitation provided by subsection (3) of this section, to all claimants.
(3) Beginning in 2010, and every year thereafter, the State Court Administrator shall determine the percentage increase or decrease in the cost of living for the previous calendar year, based on changes in the Portland-Salem, OR-WA Consumer Price Index for All Urban Consumers for All Items as published by the Bureau of Labor Statistics of the United States Department of Labor. On or before July 1 of the year in which the State Court Administrator makes the determination required by this subsection, the State Court Administrator shall adjust the limitations imposed under subsection (2) of this section for the following calendar year by multiplying the limitation amounts applicable to the calendar year in which the adjustment is made by the percentage amount determined under this subsection. The adjustment may not exceed three percent for any year. The State Court Administrator shall round the adjusted limitation amount to the nearest $100, but the unrounded amount shall be used to calculate the adjustments to the limitations in subsequent calendar years. The adjusted limitation becomes effective on July 1 of the year in which the adjustment is made, and applies to all causes of action arising on or after July 1 of that year and before July 1 of the subsequent year. [2009 c.67 §5]

Note: See note under 30.269.

30.274 Direct appeal of constitutionality of limitations. (1) At the request of any party to an action under ORS 30.260 to 30.300, the court shall enter a limited judgment that is limited to the issue of the application of the limitations imposed by ORS 30.271, 30.272 or 30.273. A limited judgment may be entered under this section only after:

(a) The parties have stipulated to the total damages in the action; or

(b) The finder of fact has decided the total damages in the action.

(2) If a limited judgment is entered under this section, the court may not enter a general judgment until an appellate judgment on any appeal of the limited judgment has been entered.

(3) A limited judgment entered under this section may be appealed only by filing a notice of appeal directly with the Supreme Court within the time and in the manner specified in ORS chapter 19 for civil appeals to the Court of Appeals. Any party filing a notice of appeal under this subsection must note in the notice of appeal that the case is subject to this subsection.

(4) An appeal filed under this section may not raise any issue relating to the case other than the application of a limitation imposed under ORS 30.271, 30.272 or 30.273.

(5) If a limited judgment is not requested under this section, a party may seek judicial review of the imposition of any of the limitations under ORS 30.271, 30.272 or 30.273 in an appeal from the general judgment in the action. [2009 c.67 §6]

Note: See note under 30.269.

30.275 Notice of claim; time of notice; time of action. (1) No action arising from any act or omission of a public body or an officer, employee or agent of a public body within the scope of ORS 30.260 to 30.300 shall be maintained unless notice of claim is given as required by this section.

(2) Notice of claim shall be given within the following applicable period of time, not including the period, not exceeding 90 days, during which the person injured is unable to give the notice because of the injury or because of minority, incompetency or other incapacity:

(a) For wrongful death, within one year after the alleged loss or injury.

(b) For all other claims, within 180 days after the alleged loss or injury.

(3) Notice of claim required by this section is satisfied by:

(a) Formal notice of claim as provided in subsections (4) and (5) of this section;

(b) Actual notice of claim as provided in subsection (6) of this section;

(c) Commencement of an action on the claim by or on behalf of the claimant within the applicable period of time provided in subsection (2) of this section; or

(d) Payment of all or any part of the claim by or on behalf of the public body at any time.

(4) Formal notice of claim is a written communication from a claimant or representative of a claimant containing:

(a) A statement that a claim for damages is or will be asserted against the public body or an officer, employee or agent of the public body;

(b) A description of the time, place and circumstances giving rise to the claim, so far as known to the claimant; and

(c) The name of the claimant and the mailing address to which correspondence concerning the claim may be sent.

(5) Formal notice of claim shall be given by mail or personal delivery:

(a) If the claim is against the state or an officer, employee or agent thereof, to the office of the Director of the Oregon Department of Administrative Services.

(b) If the claim is against a local public body or an officer, employee or agent thereof, to the public body at its principal administrative office, to any member of the governing body of the public body, or to an attorney designated by the governing body as its general counsel.

(6) Actual notice of claim is any communication by which any individual to whom notice may be given as provided in subsection (5) of this section or any person responsible for administering tort claims on behalf of the public body acquires actual knowledge of the time, place and circumstances giving rise to the claim, where the communication is such that a reasonable person would conclude that a particular person intends to assert a claim against the public body or an officer, employee or agent of the public body. A person responsible for administering tort claims on behalf of a public body is a person who, acting within the scope of the person's responsibility, as an officer, employee or agent of a public body or as an employee or agent of an insurance carrier insuring the public body for risks within the scope of ORS 30.260 to 30.300, engages in investigation, negotiation, adjustment or defense of claims within the scope of ORS 30.260 to 30.300, or in furnishing or accepting forms for claimants to provide claim information, or in supervising any of those activities.

(7) In an action arising from any act or omission of a public body or an officer, employee or agent of a public body within the scope of ORS 30.260 to 30.300, the plaintiff has the burden of proving that notice of claim was given as required by this section.

(8) The requirement that a notice of claim be given under subsections (1) to (7) of this section does not apply if:

(a)(A) The claimant was under the age of 18 years when the acts or omissions giving rise to a claim occurred;

(B) The claim is against the Department of Human Services or the Oregon Youth Authority; and

(C) The claimant was in the custody of the Department of Human Services pursuant to an order of a juvenile court under ORS 419B.150, 419B.185, 419B.337 or 419B.527, or was in the custody of the Oregon Youth Authority under the provisions of ORS 419C.478, 420.011 or 420A.040, when the acts or omissions giving rise to a claim occurred.

(b) The claim is against a private, nonprofit organization that provides public transportation services described under ORS 30.260 (4)(d).

(9) Except as provided in ORS 12.120, 12.135 and 659A.875, but notwithstanding any other provision of ORS chapter 12 or other statute providing a limitation on the commencement of an action, an action arising from any act or omission of a public body or an officer, employee or agent of a public body within the scope of ORS 30.260 to 30.300 shall be commenced within two years after the alleged loss or injury. [1967 c.627 §5; 1969 c.429 §3; 1975 c.604 §1a; 1975 c.609 §14; 1977 c.823 §3; 1979 c.284 §64; 1981 c.350 §1; 1993 c.500 §4; 1993 c.515 §1; 2001 c.601 §1; 2001 c.621 §89; 2005 c.684 §2; 2009 c.67 §18]

30.278 Reporting notice of claim of professional negligence to licensing board. (1) When notice is received under ORS 30.275 of a claim of professional negligence against a physician, optometrist, dentist, dental hygienist or naturopath who is acting within the scope of employment by a public body or within the scope of duties as defined by ORS 30.267, the person receiving the notice shall report to the appropriate licensing board, in the same manner as required by ORS 742.400, the information required by ORS 742.400 to be reported by insurers or self-insured associations.

(2) This section does not apply to a notice of adverse health care incident received under section 2, chapter 5, Oregon Laws 2013. [1987 c.774 §64; 2013 c.5 §11]

Note: The amendments to 30.278 by section 12, chapter 5, Oregon Laws 2013, become operative December 31, 2023. See section 22, chapter 5, Oregon Laws 2013. The text that is operative on and after December 31, 2023, is set forth for the user's convenience.

30.278. When notice is received under ORS 30.275 of a claim of professional negligence against a physician, optometrist, dentist, dental hygienist or naturopath who is acting within the scope of employment by a public body or within the scope of duties as defined by ORS 30.267, the person receiving the notice shall report to the appropriate licensing board, in the same manner as required by ORS 742.400, the information required by ORS 742.400 to be reported by insurers or self-insured associations.

Note: 30.278 was enacted into law by the Legislative Assembly but was not added to or made a part of ORS chapter 30 or any series therein by legislative action. See Preface to Oregon Revised Statutes for further explanation.

30.280 [1967 c.627 §6; repealed by 1975 c.609 §25]

30.282 Local public body insurance; self-insurance program; action against program. (1) The governing body of any local public body may procure insurance against:

(a) Tort liability of the public body and its officers, employees and agents acting within the scope of their employment or duties; or

(b) Property damage.

(2) In addition to, or in lieu of procuring insurance, the governing body may establish a self-insurance program against the tort liability of the public body and its officers, employees and agents or against property damage. If the public body has authority to levy taxes, it may include in its levy an amount sufficient to establish and maintain a self-insurance program on an actuarially sound basis.

(3) Notwithstanding any other provision of law, two or more local public bodies may jointly provide by intergovernmental agreement for anything that subsections (1) and (2) of this section authorize individually.

(4) As an alternative or in addition to establishment of a self-insurance program or purchase of insurance or both, the governing body of any local public body and the Oregon Department of Administrative Services may contract for payment by the public body to the department of assessments determined by the department to be sufficient, on an actuarially sound basis, to cover the potential liability of the public body and its officers, employees or agents acting within the scope of their employment or duties under ORS 30.260 to 30.300, and costs of administration, or to cover any portion of potential liability, and for payment by the department of valid claims against the public body and its officers, employees and agents acting within the scope of their employment or duties. The department may provide the public body evidence of insurance by issuance of a certificate or policy.

(5) Assessments paid to the department under subsection (4) of this section shall be paid into the Insurance Fund created under ORS 278.425, and claims paid and administrative costs incurred under subsection (4) of this section shall be paid out of the Insurance Fund, and moneys in the Insurance Fund are continuously appropriated for those purposes. When notice of any claim is furnished as provided in the agreement, the claim shall be handled and paid, if appropriate, in the same manner as a claim against a state agency, officer, employee or agent, without regard to the amount the local public body has been assessed.

(6) A self-insurance program established by three or more public bodies under subsections (2) and (3) of this section is subject to the following requirements:

(a) The annual contributions to the program must amount in the aggregate to at least $1 million.

(b) The program must provide documentation that defines program benefits and administration.

(c) Program contributions and reserves must be held in separate accounts and used for the exclusive benefit of the program.

(d) The program must maintain adequate reserves. Reserve adequacy shall be calculated annually with proper actuarial calculations including the following:

(A) Known claims, paid and outstanding;

(B) Estimate of incurred but not reported claims;

(C) Claims handling expenses;

(D) Unearned contributions; and

(E) A claims trend factor.

(e) The program must maintain an unallocated reserve account equal to 25 percent of annual contributions, or $250,000, whichever is greater. As used in this paragraph, "unallocated reserves" means the amount of funds determined by a licensed independent actuary to be greater than what is required to fund outstanding claim liabilities, including an estimate of claims incurred but not reported.

(f) The program must make an annual independently audited financial statement available to the participants of the program.

(g) The program must maintain adequate excess or reinsurance against the risk of economic loss.

(h) The program, a third party administrator or an owner of a third party administrator may not collect commissions or fees from an insurer.

(7) A program operated under subsection (6) of this section that fails to meet any of the listed requirements for a period longer than 30 consecutive days shall be dissolved and any unallocated reserves returned in proportional amounts based on the contributions of the public body to the public bodies that established the program within 90 days of the failure.

(8) A local public body may bring an action against a program operated under subsection (6) of this section if the program fails to comply with the requirements listed in subsection (6) of this section. [1975 c.609 §19; 1977 c.428 §1; 1981 c.109 §4; 1985 c.731 §21; 2005 c.175 §2; 2009 c.67 §19]

30.285 Public body shall indemnify public officers; procedure for requesting counsel; extent of duty of state; obligation for judgment and attorney fees. (1) The governing body of any public body shall defend, save harmless and indemnify any of its officers, employees and agents, whether elective or appointive, against any tort claim or demand, whether groundless or otherwise, arising out of an alleged act or omission occurring in the performance of duty.

(2) The provisions of subsection (1) of this section do not apply in case of malfeasance in office or willful or wanton neglect of duty.

(3) If any civil action, suit or proceeding is brought against any state officer, employee or agent which on its face falls within the provisions of subsection (1) of this section, or which the state officer, employee or agent asserts to be based in fact upon an alleged act or omission in the performance of duty, the state officer, employee or agent may, after consulting with the Oregon Department of Administrative Services file a written request for counsel with the Attorney General. The Attorney General shall thereupon appear and defend the officer, employee or agent unless after investigation the Attorney General finds that the claim or demand does not arise out of an alleged act or omission occurring in the performance of duty, or that the act or omission complained of amounted to malfeasance in office or willful or wanton neglect of duty, in which case the Attorney General shall reject defense of the claim.

(4) Any officer, employee or agent of the state against whom a claim within the scope of this section is made shall cooperate fully with the Attorney General and the department in the defense of such claim. If the Attorney General after consulting with the department determines that such officer, employee or agent has not so cooperated or has otherwise acted to prejudice defense of the claim, the Attorney General may at any time reject the defense of the claim.

(5) If the Attorney General rejects defense of a claim under subsection (3) of this section or this subsection, no public funds shall be paid in settlement of said claim or in payment of any judgment against such officer, employee or agent. Such action by the Attorney General shall not prejudice the right of the officer, employee or agent to assert and establish an appropriate proceedings that the claim or demand in fact arose out of an alleged act or omission occurring in the performance of duty, or that the act or omission complained of did not amount to malfeasance in office or willful or wanton neglect of duty, in which case the officer, employee or agent shall be indemnified against liability and reasonable costs of defending the claim, cost of such indemnification to be a charge against the Insurance Fund established by ORS 278.425.

(6) Nothing in subsection (3), (4) or (5) of this section shall be deemed to increase the limits of liability of any public officer, agent or employee under ORS 30.260 to 30.300, or obviate the necessity of compliance with ORS 30.275 by any claimant, nor to affect the liability of the state itself or of any other public officer, agent or employee on any claim arising out of the same accident or occurrence.

(7) As used in this section, "state officer, employee or agent" includes district attorneys and deputy district attorneys, special prosecutors and law clerks of the office of district attorney who act in a prosecutorial capacity, but does not include any other employee of the office of district attorney or any employee of the justice or circuit courts whose salary is paid wholly or in part by the county. [1967 c.627 §7; 1975 c.609 §16; 1981 c.109 §5; 1981 c.913 §2; 1985 c.731 §22; 1987 c.763 §1; 2009 c.67 §11]

30.287 Counsel for public officer; when public funds not to be paid in settlement; effect on liability limit; defense by insurer. (1) If any civil action, suit or proceeding is brought against any officer, employee or agent of a local public body which on its face falls within the provisions of ORS 30.285 (1), or which the officer, employee or agent asserts to be based in fact upon an alleged act or omission in the performance of duty, the officer, employee or agent may file a written request for counsel with the governing body of the public body. The governing body shall thereupon engage counsel to appear and defend the officer, employee or agent unless after investigation it is determined that the claim or demand does not arise out of an alleged act or omission occurring in the performance of duty, or that the act or omission complained of amounted to malfeasance in office or willful or wanton neglect of duty, in which case the governing body shall reject defense of the claim.

(2) Any officer, employee or agent of a local public body against whom a claim within the scope of this section is made shall cooperate fully with the governing body and counsel in the defense of such claim. If the counsel determines and certifies to the governing body that such officer, employee or agent has not so cooperated or has otherwise acted in prejudice of the defense of the claim, the governing body may at any time reject the defense of the claim.

(3) If the governing body rejects defense of a claim under subsection (1) of this section, no public funds shall be paid in settlement of the claim or in payment of any judgment against such officer, employee or agent. Such action by the governing body shall not prejudice the right of the officer, employee or agent to assert and establish in an appropriate proceedings that the claim or demand in fact arose out of an alleged act or omission occurring in the performance of duty, or that the act or omission complained of did not amount to malfeasance in office or willful or wanton neglect of duty, in which case the officer, employee or agent shall be indemnified by the public body against liability and reasonable costs of defending the claim.

(4) Nothing in subsection (1), (2) or (3) of this section shall be deemed to increase the limits of liability of any public officer, agent or employee under ORS 30.260 to 30.300, or relieve any claimant of the necessity of compliance with ORS 30.275, nor to affect the liability of the local public body itself or of any other public officer, agent or employee on any claim arising out of the same accident or occurrence.

(5) The provisions of this section may be superseded to the extent that the claim against the public officer, employee or agent may be defended by any insurer, or may be subject under ORS 30.282 to agreement with the Oregon Department of Administrative Services, in which case the provisions of the policy of insurance or other agreement are applicable. [1975 c.609 §20; 1985 c.565 §3; 1989 c.1004 §1; 2009 c.67 §12]

30.290 Settlement of claims by local public body. The governing body of any local public body may, subject to the provisions of any contract of liability insurance existing, compromise, adjust and settle tort claims against the public body or its officers, employees or agents acting within the scope of their employment for damages under ORS 30.260 to 30.300 and may, subject to procedural requirements imposed by law or other charter, appropriate money for the payment of amounts agreed upon. [1967 c.627 §8; 1975 c.609 §17; 1989 c.655 §1]

30.295 Payment of judgment or settlement; remedies for nonpayment; tax levy for payment; installment payments. (1) When a judgment is entered against or a settlement is made by a public body for a claim within the scope of ORS 30.260 to 30.300, including claims against officers, employees or agents required to be indemnified under ORS 30.285, payment shall be made and the same remedies shall apply in case of nonpayment as in the case of other judgments or settlements against the public body except as otherwise provided in this section.

(2) If the public body is authorized to levy taxes that could be used to satisfy a judgment or settlement within the scope of ORS 30.260 to 30.300, and it has, by resolution, declared that the following conditions exist, interest shall accrue on the judgment or settlement, but the same shall not be due and payable until after the canvass and certification of an election upon a special tax levy for purposes of satisfying the judgment or settlement:

(a) The amount of the judgment or settlement would exceed amounts budgeted for contingencies, tort claims and projected surplus in the current budget;

(b) The amount of the judgment or settlement would exceed 10 percent of the total of the next fiscal year's projected revenues that are not restricted as to use, including the maximum amount of general property tax that could be levied without election but excluding any levy for debt service;

(c) Payment of the judgment or settlement within less than a certain number of years would seriously impair the ability of the public body to carry out its responsibilities as a unit of government; and

(d) The public body has passed an appropriate ordinance or resolution calling a special election to submit to its electors a special levy in an amount sufficient to satisfy the judgment or settlement.

(3) A certified copy of the resolution provided for in subsection (2) of this section shall be filed with the clerk of the court in which an order permitting installment payments could be entered.

(4) If the public body is not authorized to levy taxes as provided in subsection (2) of this section, and it has, by resolution, declared that the applicable conditions specified in subsection (2)(a) to (c) of this section exist, it may petition for an order permitting installment payments as provided in subsection (6) of this section.

(5)(a) The provisions of subsections (2) and (4) of this section do not apply to the State of Oregon.

(b) Notwithstanding paragraph (a) of this subsection, if the conditions specified in subsection (4) of this section exist, the Secretary of State may, under Seal of the State of Oregon, attest thereto in lieu of a resolution, and the State of Oregon may thereafter petition for an order permitting installment payments as provided in subsection (6) of this section.

(6) If the procedure specified in subsections (2) to (5) of this section has been followed, and, with respect to public bodies subject to subsection (2) of this section, the tax levy failed, the public body may petition for an order permitting installment payments. The petition shall be filed in the court in which judgment was entered or, if no judgment has been entered, it shall be filed in the circuit court of the judicial district in which the public body has its legal situs. Petitions by the State of Oregon when no judgment has been entered shall be filed in Marion County Circuit Court.

(7) The court in which a petition is filed shall order that the judgment or settlement be paid in quarterly, semiannual or annual installments over a period of time not to exceed 10 years. The court shall determine the term of years based upon the ability of the public body to effectively carry out its governmental responsibilities, and shall not allow a longer term than appears reasonably necessary to meet that need. The order permitting installment payments shall provide for annual interest at the judgment rate. [1967 c.627 §9; 1977 c.823 §4; 2005 c.22 §20]

30.297 Liability of certain state agencies for damages caused by foster child or youth offender; conditions; exceptions. (1) Notwithstanding ORS 125.235, the Department of Human Services is liable for damages resulting from the intentional torts of a foster child who is residing in:

(a) A foster home that has been certified by the department under the provisions of ORS 418.625 to 418.645, even though the child is temporarily absent from that home;

(b) An approved home that is receiving payment from the department under the provisions of ORS 418.027 or under the provisions of ORS 420.810 and 420.815, even though the child is temporarily absent from that home; or

(c) A developmental disability child foster home that has been certified by the department under the provisions of ORS 443.830 and 443.835, even though the foster child is temporarily absent from that home.

(2) Notwithstanding ORS 125.235, the Oregon Youth Authority is liable for damages resulting from the intentional torts of a youth offender who is residing in a youth offender foster home that has been certified by the authority under the provisions of ORS 420.888 to 420.892, even though the youth offender is temporarily absent from that home.

(3) Except as otherwise provided in this section, the liability of the department and the authority under this section is subject to the same requirements and limitations provided in ORS 30.260 to 30.300, and a claim under this section shall be treated as a claim for damages within the scope of ORS 30.260 to 30.300 for the purposes of ORS 278.120.

(4) Notwithstanding subsections (1) and (2) of this section:

(a) The department and the authority are not liable for any damages arising out of the operation of a motor vehicle by a foster child or youth offender; and

(b) The department and the authority are only liable for theft by a foster child or youth offender upon a showing by clear and convincing evidence that the foster child or youth offender committed the theft.

(5) For the purposes of this section:

(a) "Authority" means the Oregon Youth Authority.

(b) "Department" means the Department of Human Services.

(c) "Foster child" means:

(A) A minor child under the custody or guardianship of the department by reason of appointment pursuant to ORS chapter 125, 419A, 419B or 419C;

(B) A minor child under the physical custody of the department pursuant to a voluntary agreement with the parent under ORS 418.015 (1);

(C) A minor child placed in a certified foster home, pending hearing, by any person authorized by the department to make that placement;

(D) A person under 21 years of age who has been placed in an approved home that is receiving payment from the department under the provisions of ORS 418.027 or under the provisions of ORS 420.810 and 420.815; or

(E) A child residing in a developmental disability child foster home certified under ORS 443.830 and 443.835.

(d) "Youth offender" has the meaning given in ORS 419A.004. [1991 c.756 §2; 1993 c.33 §370; 1995 c.664 §76; 1997 c.130 §1; 1999 c.316 §6; 2001 c.900 §10; 2003 c.232 §1; 2005 c.374 §4]

Note: 30.297 and 30.298 were added to and made a part of 30.260 to 30.300 by legislative action but were not added to any smaller series therein. See Preface to Oregon Revised Statutes for further explanation.

30.298 Liability of certain state agencies to foster parents for injury or damage caused by foster child or youth offender; conditions; limitations. (1) Except as otherwise provided in this section, the Department of Human Services is liable, without regard to fault, for injury to the person of foster parents or damage to the property of foster parents caused by a foster child if the foster child is residing in:

(a) A foster home that is maintained by the foster parents and that has been certified by the department under the provisions of ORS 418.625 to 418.645;

(b) An approved home that is maintained by the foster parents and that is receiving payment from the department under the provisions of ORS 418.027 or under the provisions of ORS 420.810 and 420.815; or

(c) A developmental disability child foster home that has been certified by the department under the provisions of ORS 443.830 and 443.835.

(2) Except as otherwise provided in this section, the Oregon Youth Authority is liable, without regard to fault, for injury to the person of foster parents or damage to the property of foster parents caused by a youth offender if the youth offender resides in a youth offender foster home that is maintained by the foster parents and that has been certified by the authority under the provisions of ORS 420.888 to 420.892.

(3) Except as otherwise provided in this section, the liability of the department and of the authority under this section is subject to the same requirements and limitations provided in ORS 30.260 to 30.300, and a claim under this section shall be treated as a claim for damages within the scope of ORS 30.260 to 30.300 for the purposes of ORS 278.120.

(4) Notwithstanding ORS 30.260 to 30.300:

(a) In no event shall the liability of the department or the authority under this section exceed $5,000 for any number of claims arising out of a single occurrence;

(b) The liability of the department and the authority under this section is limited to economic damages, and in no event shall the department or the authority be liable for noneconomic damages;

(c) The department and the authority are liable under this section only to the extent the loss is not covered by other insurance; and

(d) No claim shall be allowed under this section unless written notice of the claim is delivered to the Oregon Department of Administrative Services within 90 days after the alleged loss or injury.

(5) The department and the authority are not liable under this section for:

(a) Damage to or destruction of currency, securities or any other intangible property;

(b) The unexplained disappearance of any property; or

(c) Loss or damage that is due to wear and tear, inherent vice or gradual deterioration.

(6) In no event does the liability of the department or the authority under this section for damage to property exceed the difference between the fair market value of the property immediately before its damage or destruction and its fair market value immediately thereafter. The department and the authority are not liable for the costs of any betterments to the property that may be required by code, statute or other law as a condition of repair, replacement or reconstruction.

(7) The liability imposed under this section is in addition to that imposed for the intentional torts of a foster child or youth offender under ORS 30.297, but any amounts paid under this section shall reduce any recovery that may be made under ORS 30.297.

(8) For the purposes of this section:

(a) "Authority" means the Oregon Youth Authority.

(b) "Department" means the Department of Human Services.

(c) "Economic damages" and "noneconomic damages" have those meanings given in ORS 31.710.

(d) "Foster child" has that meaning given in ORS 30.297.

(e) "Youth offender" has the meaning given in ORS 419A.004. [1991 c.756 §3; 1997 c.130 §2; 1999 c.316 §11; 2001 c.900 §11; 2003 c.232 §2; 2005 c.374 §5]

Note: See note under 30.297.

30.300 ORS 30.260 to 30.300 exclusive. ORS 30.260 to 30.300 are exclusive and supersede all home rule charter provisions and conflicting laws and ordinances on the same subject. [1967 c.627 §11]

(Certain Retired Health Care Providers)

30.302 Certain retired health care providers to be considered agents of public bodies. (1) As used in this section, "retired provider" means any person:

(a) Who holds a degree of Doctor of Medicine, Doctor of Osteopathic Medicine or Doctor of Podiatric Medicine, or who has met the minimum educational requirements for licensure to practice naturopathic medicine or as a physician assistant under ORS 677.505 to 677.525 or a nurse practitioner under ORS 678.375 to 678.390;

(b) Who has been licensed and is currently retired in accordance with the provisions of ORS chapter 677, 678 or 685;

(c) Who is registered with the Oregon Medical Board as a retired emeritus physician or who complies with the requirements of the Oregon Medical Board as a retired physician assistant, the Oregon State Board of Nursing as a retired nurse practitioner or the Oregon Board of Naturopathic Medicine as a retired naturopath;

(d) Who registers with the local health officer of the local public health authority, as defined in ORS 431.003, in which the physician, physician assistant, nurse practitioner or naturopath practices; and

(e) Who provides medical care as a volunteer without compensation solely through referrals from the local health officer specified in paragraph (d) of this subsection.

(2) Any retired provider who treats patients pursuant to this section shall be considered to be an agent of a public body for the purposes of ORS 30.260 to 30.300. [1991 c.952 §1; 2009 c.43 §2; 2013 c.129 §2; 2014 c.45 §2; 2015 c.736 §47; 2017 c.409 §1]

ACTIONS AND SUITS BY AND AGAINST GOVERNMENTAL UNITS AND OFFICIALS

30.310 Actions and suits by governmental units. A suit or action may be maintained by the State of Oregon or any county, incorporated city, school district or other public corporation of like character in this state, in its corporate name, upon a cause of suit or action accruing to it in its corporate character, and not otherwise, in the following cases:

(1) Upon a contract made with the public corporation.

(2) Upon a liability prescribed by law in favor of the public corporation.

(3) To recover a penalty or forfeiture given to the public corporation.

(4) To recover damages for injury to the corporate rights or property of the public corporation.

30.312 Actions by governmental units under federal antitrust laws. The State of Oregon, any city, county, school district, municipal or public corporation, political subdivision of the State of Oregon or any instrumentality thereof, or any agency created by two or more political subdivisions to provide themselves governmental services may bring an action in behalf of itself and others similarly situated for damages under section 4 of the Act of October 15, 1914, ch. 323, as amended prior to January 1, 1965 (38 Stat. 731, 15 U.S.C. 15). [1965 c.465 §1; 2005 c.22 §21]

30.315 Proceedings by cities and counties to enforce ordinances and resolutions. (1) An incorporated city or any county may maintain civil proceedings in courts of this state against any person or property to enforce requirements or prohibitions of its ordinances or resolutions when it seeks:

(a) To collect a fee or charge;

(b) To enforce a forfeiture;

(c) To require or enjoin the performance of an act affecting real property;

(d) To enjoin continuance of a violation that has existed for 10 days or more; or

(e) To enjoin further commission of a violation that otherwise may result in additional violations of the same or related penal provisions affecting the public morals, health or safety.

(2) The remedies provided by this section are supplementary and in addition to those described in ORS 30.310.

(3) Nothing in this section shall affect the limitations imposed on cities and counties by ORS 131A.010 (3) and (4). [1961 c.313 §2; 1963 c.338 §1; 1985 c.626 §1; 1989 c.882 §§1,2; 2009 c.78 §53]

30.320 Contract and other actions and suits against governmental units. A suit or action may be maintained against any county and against the State of Oregon by and through and in the name of the appropriate state agency upon a contract made by the county in its corporate character, or made by such agency and within the scope of its authority; provided, however, that no suit or action may be maintained against any county or the State of Oregon upon a contract relating to the care and maintenance of an inmate or patient of any county or state institution. An action or suit may be maintained against any other public corporation mentioned in ORS 30.310 for an injury to the rights of the plaintiff arising from some act or omission of such other public corporation within the scope of its authority. An action may be maintained against any governmental unit mentioned in ORS 30.310 for liability in tort only as provided in ORS 30.260 to 30.300. An action or suit to quiet title may be maintained against any governmental unit mentioned in ORS 30.310. [Amended by 1959 c.614 §1; 1969 c.429 §4; 1993 c.289 §1]

30.330 Contracts of Department of Transportation providing for arbitration. The provisions of ORS 30.310 and 30.320 do not apply to contracts made by the Department of Transportation that provide for arbitration under the provisions of ORS 36.600 to 36.740. [Amended by 2003 c.598 §32]

30.340 Title of proceedings by or against county; control of proceedings by county court. All actions, suits or proceedings by or against a county shall be in the name of the county, but the county is represented by the county court, which has the power to control the proceeding as if it were plaintiff or defendant, as the case may be.

30.350 [Repealed by 1979 c.284 §199]

30.360 Governmental unit as defendant in actions involving liens on realty. (1) In any suit, action or proceeding brought in any circuit court of this state, affecting the title to real property on which a governmental unit has, or claims to have, a lien, other than a suit, action or proceeding to foreclose tax liens or special improvement liens, the governmental unit may be made a party defendant, and its rights or interests adjudicated. When property has been or is acquired in the name of a governmental unit upon which there are valid, unpaid special improvement liens at the time of the acquisition, the governmental unit may be made a party defendant in a suit to foreclose the lien.

(2) In any suit, action or proceeding brought in any circuit court of this state involving the title to real property where a governmental unit has record title to contested real property, the governmental unit may be made a party defendant, and its rights or interests adjudicated.

(3) In no event shall any money judgment be rendered or recovery made against a governmental unit in any suit, action or proceeding brought under the provisions of this section.

(4) For the purposes of this section, "governmental unit" means the State of Oregon or any county, incorporated city, school district or other public corporation of like character in this state. [Amended by 1959 c.586 §1; 1993 c.289 §2]

30.370 Service of summons on Attorney General; content. In any suit, action or proceeding commenced under the provisions of ORS 30.360 to which the state is made a party, service of summons upon the state shall be made upon the Attorney General. In addition to other required content, any summons served pursuant to this section shall state the state agency involved in the suit, action or proceeding. [Amended by 1959 c.586 §2; 1979 c.284 §65]

30.380 Action by assignee of claim for money illegally charged or exacted. No assignee of any claim against any county, city or municipal corporation of this state or any county, city or municipal officer in this state, for money claimed to have been illegally charged or exacted by such county, city or municipal corporation or such officer, except money collected as taxes or license, or money due on contract, shall have the right to institute or maintain any action or suit for the recovery thereof in any court in this state.

30.390 Satisfaction of judgment against public corporation. If judgment is given for the recovery of money or damages against a public corporation mentioned in ORS 30.310, no execution shall issue thereon for the collection of such money or damages, but the judgment shall be satisfied as follows:

(1) The party in whose favor the judgment is given may, at any time thereafter, when an execution might issue on a like judgment against a private person, present a certified copy of the judgment document, to the officer of the public corporation who is authorized to draw orders on the treasurer thereof.

(2) On the presentation of the copy, the officer shall draw an order on the treasurer for the amount of the judgment, in favor of the party for whom the judgment was given. Thereafter, the order shall be presented for payment, and paid, with like effect and in like manner as other orders upon the treasurer of the public corporation.

(3) The certified copy provided for in subsection (1) of this section shall not be furnished by the clerk, unless at the time an execution might issue on the judgment if the same was against a private person, nor until satisfaction of the judgment in respect to such money or damages is acknowledged as in ordinary cases. The clerk shall provide with the copy a memorandum of such acknowledgment of satisfaction and the entry thereof. Unless the memorandum is provided, no order upon the treasurer shall issue thereon. [Amended by 2003 c.576 §185]

30.395 Settlement of certain claims against municipal corporations; manner of payment. (1) The governing body of any municipal corporation, as defined in ORS 297.405, may compromise, adjust and settle claims other than tort claims against the municipal corporation, its officers, employees or agents acting within the scope of their employment, and may, subject to procedural requirements imposed by law or charter, appropriate money for the payment of amounts agreed upon.

(2) When a judgment is entered or a settlement is made pursuant to subsection (1) of this section, payment therefor may be made in the same manner as payment for tort claims under ORS 30.295. [1979 c.630 §2; 1987 c.396 §1]

30.400 Actions by and against public officers in official capacity. An action may be maintained by or against any public officer in this state in an official character, when, as to such cause of action, the officer does not represent any of the public corporations mentioned in ORS 30.310, for any of the causes specified in such section and ORS 30.320. If judgment is given against the officer in such action, it may be enforced against the officer personally, and the amount thereof shall be allowed to the officer in the official accounts of the officer.

30.402 [1991 c.847 §1; renumbered 17.095 in 2003]

INJUNCTIONS BY PUBLIC SERVANT

30.405 Injunction for criminal conduct related to employment or status of public servant. (1) A public servant or the public servant's employer may petition a circuit court for an order enjoining a person who engages in conduct that:
(a) Is directed at the public servant;
(b) Relates to the public servant's employment or the public servant's status as an elected or appointed public servant; and
(c) Constitutes any of the following crimes:
(A) Obstructing governmental or judicial administration under ORS 162.235.
(B) Assault under ORS 163.160, 163.165, 163.175 or 163.185.
(C) Menacing under ORS 163.190.
(D) Criminal trespass in the first degree under ORS 164.255.
(E) Disorderly conduct under ORS 166.025.
(F) Harassment under ORS 166.065.
(G) Telephonic harassment under ORS 166.090.
(2) The petitioner has the burden of proof by a preponderance of the evidence under subsection (1) of this section. An order issued under this section is valid for one year after entry in the register of the court or until vacated by the court, whichever occurs first.
(3) Contempt proceedings against a person who violates an order issued by a circuit court under subsection (1) of this section shall be as provided in ORS 33.055 or 33.065.
(4) As used in this section, "public servant" has the meaning given that term in ORS 162.005. [2005 c.158 §1]

Note: 30.405 and 30.407 were enacted into law by the Legislative Assembly but were not added to or made a part of ORS chapter 30 or any series therein by legislative action. See Preface to Oregon Revised Statutes for further explanation.

30.407 Request for hearing following issuance of order under ORS 30.405. (1) A person against whom an order is issued under ORS 30.405 may file a request for hearing with the court that issued the order within 30 days after the order is served on the person. A request under this section shall be in writing, shall be signed by the person and shall include the printed name, telephone number and mailing address of the person.
(2) Upon the filing of a request under this section, the clerk of the court shall mail a copy of the request to the petitioner in the matter and shall notify the petitioner and the person filing the request of the date and time set for the hearing. [2005 c.158 §2]

Note: See note under 30.405.

RECOVERY OF FINES AND FORFEITURES

30.410 In whose name action brought. Fines and forfeitures may be recovered by an action at law in the name of the officer or person to whom they are by law given, or in the name of the officer or person who by law is authorized to prosecute for them.

30.420 Venue of action for forfeiture. Whenever, by law, any property is forfeited to the state, or to any officer for its use, the action for the recovery of such property may be commenced in any county where the defendant may be found, or where such property may be.

30.430 Amount of penalty. When an action is commenced for a penalty, which by law is not to exceed a certain amount, the action may be commenced for that amount, and if judgment is given for the plaintiff, it may be for such amount or less, in the discretion of the court, in proportion to the offense.

30.440 Judgment by collusion not a bar. A recovery of a judgment for a penalty or forfeiture by collusion between the plaintiff and defendant, with intent to save the defendant, wholly or partially, from the consequences contemplated by law, in case where the penalty or forfeiture is given wholly or partly to the person who prosecutes, shall not bar the recovery of the same by another person.

30.450 [Amended by 1981 s.s. c.3 §110; 1995 c.658 §27; repealed by 2011 c.597 §118]

30.460 Payment of fines or costs in proceeding to enforce county ordinance or resolution; defendant personally liable. When proceedings are conducted by county hearings officers to enforce requirements or prohibitions of county ordinances or resolutions, if fines or costs are not paid by a defendant within 60 days after payment is ordered, the defendant is personally liable to the county for the amount of the unpaid fines or costs. The county may file and record the order for payment in the County Clerk Lien Record. [1985 c.626 §3; 1999 c.1051 §241]

VOLUNTEERS TRANSPORTING OLDER PERSONS AND PERSONS WITH DISABILITIES

30.475 Legislative policy. In enacting ORS 30.480 and 30.485, the Legislative Assembly of the State of Oregon declares:
(1) That many persons with disabilities and older persons, due to disability or age, cannot obtain medical, educational, recreational or other important services or benefits, or pursue daily life activities outside the home, such as shopping or socializing, without transportation and other necessary assistance;
(2) That public resources are not adequate to provide dependable transportation to persons with disabilities and older persons, and that it is in the best interest of this state to encourage volunteers to provide transportation services to Oregon's people with disabilities and older people;
(3) That the threat or fear of personal liability arising from the provision of transportation services to persons with disabilities and older persons seriously discourages individuals from providing services on a volunteer basis;
(4) That the policy of this state is to encourage volunteers to provide such transportation services; and
(5) That, therefore, persons who qualify under ORS 30.480 must be protected from the threat of unlimited personal liability arising from the provision of volunteer transportation services, and that ORS 30.475 to 30.485 shall be liberally construed in favor of such persons in order to promote fully the foregoing policies. [1983 c.468 §1; 1989 c.224 §5; 2007 c.70 §9]

30.480 Limitation on liability of volunteers; conditions. (1) When a provider of volunteer transportation services who is qualified under subsection (3) of this section provides the services under the conditions described in subsection (4) of this section to a person with a disability or a person who is 55 years of age or older, the liability of the provider to the person for injury, death or loss arising out of the volunteer transportation services shall be limited as provided in this section. When volunteer transportation services are provided to five or fewer persons at one time, the liability of the provider of the volunteer transportation services shall not exceed the greater of the amount of coverage under the terms of the provider's motor vehicle liability insurance policy, as described in ORS 806.080, or the amounts specified in ORS 806.070 for future responsibility payments for:
(a) Bodily injury to or death of any one person to whom the transportation services are provided, in any one accident.
(b) Bodily injury to or death of two or more persons to whom the transportation services are provided, in any one accident.
(c) Injury to or destruction of the property of one or more persons to whom the transportation services are provided, in any one accident.
(2) Notwithstanding the amount specified in subsection (1)(b) of this section by reference to ORS 806.070, if a qualified provider of transportation services provides the services to more than five persons, but not more than 16, at one time who have disabilities or who are 55 years of age or older, under the conditions described in subsection (4) of this section, the liability under subsection (1)(b) of this section shall not exceed the greater of the amount of coverage under the terms of the provider's motor vehicle liability insurance policy or $300,000. The limitations on liability provided by ORS

30.475, 30.480 and 30.485 do not apply when volunteer transportation services are provided to 17 or more persons at one time who have disabilities or who are 55 years of age or older.

(3) The following persons qualify for the limitation on liability under subsections (1) and (2) of this section:

(a) The person who provides or sponsors transportation services.

(b) The owner of the vehicle in which transportation services are provided.

(c) The person who operates the vehicle in which transportation services are provided.

(4) The limitation on liability under subsections (1) and (2) of this section applies to a person qualified under subsection (3) of this section only under the following conditions:

(a) If the person is an individual, the individual must hold a valid Oregon driver's license.

(b) The person must provide the transportation services on a nonprofit and voluntary basis. However, this paragraph does not prohibit a sponsor of transportation services from reimbursing an operator of a private motor vehicle providing the services for actual expenses incurred by the operator. If an operator is paid, that operator is qualified only if operating as an emergency operator.

(c) The person providing the transportation services must not receive from the persons using the services any substantial benefit in a material or business sense that is a substantial motivating factor for the transportation. A contribution or donation to the provider of the transportation services other than the operator of the motor vehicle or any mere gratuity or social amenity shall not be a substantial benefit under this paragraph.

(d) Except as provided in paragraph (c) of this subsection, the transportation services must be provided without charge to the person using the services.

(5) The amounts received by a person with a disability or a person 55 years of age or older under the personal injury protection provisions of the insurance coverage of a person who qualifies for the limitation on liability under this section shall not reduce the amount that the person may recover under subsection (1) or (2) of this section.

(6) The liability of two or more persons whose liability is limited under this section, on claims arising out of a single accident, shall not exceed in the aggregate the amounts limited by subsection (1) or (2) of this section.

(7) This section does not apply in the case of an accident or injury if the accident or injury was intentional on the part of any person who provided the transportation services or if the accident or injury was caused by the person's gross negligence or intoxication. For purposes of this subsection, gross negligence is negligence which is materially greater than the mere absence of reasonable care under the circumstances, and which is characterized by conscious indifference to or reckless disregard of the rights of others.

(8) For purposes of this section, a person has a disability if the person has a physical or mental disability that for the person constitutes or results in a functional limitation to one or more of the following activities: Self-care, ambulation, communication, transportation, education, socialization or employment. [1983 c.468 §2; 1985 c.16 §443; 1987 c.915 §7; 1989 c.224 §6; 2007 c.70 §10]

30.485 Apportionment of damages; insurance issues excluded from jury consideration. (1) If the amount awarded by a court to multiple claimants exceeds the total amount limited under ORS 30.480 (1) or (2), the court shall apportion a proper share of that total amount to each claimant to whom ORS 30.480 (1) or (2) applies.

(2) If the amount settled upon by multiple claimants exceeds the total amount limited under ORS 30.480 (1) or (2), any party may apply to any circuit court to apportion a proper share of that total amount to each claimant to whom ORS 30.480 (1) or (2) applies.

(3) The share apportioned under subsection (1) or (2) of this section to each claimant to whom ORS 30.480 (1) or (2) applies shall be in the proportion that the ratio of the award or settlement made to the claimant bears to the aggregate awards and settlements for all claims arising out of the occurrence that are made by all claimants to whom ORS 30.480 (1) or (2) applies.

(4) Nothing in this section or ORS 30.480 authorizes the issues of insurance coverage or the amount of insurance coverage to be presented to a jury. [1983 c.468 §3]

VOLUNTEERS PROVIDING ASSISTANCE OR ADVICE IN RESPONSE TO DISCHARGE OF HAZARDOUS MATERIAL OR RELATING TO COMPLIANCE WITH DISPOSAL LAWS

30.490 Definitions for ORS 30.490 to 30.497. As used in ORS 30.490 to 30.497:

(1) "Discharge" means any leakage, seepage or any other release of hazardous material.

(2) "Hazardous material" means:

(a) Hazardous waste as defined in ORS 466.005;

(b) Hazardous substances as defined in ORS 453.005;

(c) Radioactive waste as defined in ORS 469.300;

(d) Uranium mine overburden or uranium mill tailings, mill wastes or mill by-product materials;

(e) Radioactive substance as defined in ORS 453.005;

(f) Any substance designated by the United States Department of Transportation as hazardous pursuant to the Hazardous Materials Transportation Act, 49 U.S.C. 5101 et seq., P.L. 93-633, as amended; and

(g) Any substance that the Environmental Protection Agency designates as hazardous pursuant to:

(A) The federal Toxic Substances Control Act, 15 U.S.C. 2601 to 2671; or

(B) The federal Resource Conservation and Recovery Act, 42 U.S.C. 6901 to 6992, P.L. 94-580, as amended.

(3) "Person" means an individual, corporation, association, firm, partnership, joint stock company or state or local government agency. [1985 c.376 §1; 1991 c.480 §9; 2005 c.22 §22]

30.492 Limitation on liability of volunteer providing assistance or advice related to mitigation or cleanup of discharge of hazardous material. (1) Except as provided in ORS 30.495 and 30.497, no person may maintain an action for damages against a person for voluntarily providing assistance or advice directly related to:

(a) Mitigating or attempting to mitigate the effects of an actual or threatened discharge of hazardous material; or

(b) Preventing, cleaning up or disposing of or in attempting to prevent, clean up or dispose of any discharge of hazardous material.

(2) Except as provided in ORS 30.495 and 30.497, no state or local agency may assess a civil or criminal penalty against a person for voluntarily providing assistance or advice directly related to:

(a) Mitigating or attempting to mitigate the effects of an actual or threatened discharge of hazardous material; or

(b) Preventing, cleaning up or disposing of or in attempting to prevent, clean up or dispose of any discharge of hazardous material. [1985 c.376 §2]

30.495 Exceptions to limitation. The immunity provided in ORS 30.492 shall not apply to any person:

(1) Whose act or omission caused in whole or in part the actual or threatened discharge and who would otherwise be liable for the damages; or

(2) Who receives compensation other than reimbursement for expenses for the person's service in rendering such assistance or advice. [1985 c.376 §3]

30.497 When limitation on liability not applicable. Nothing in ORS 30.492 shall be construed to limit or otherwise affect the liability of any person for damages resulting from the person's gross negligence or from the person's reckless, wanton or intentional misconduct. [1985 c.376 §4]

30.500 Definitions for ORS 30.500 and 30.505. As used in this section and ORS 30.505:

(1) "Generator" has the meaning given that term in ORS 466.005.

(2) "Person" means an individual, corporation, association, firm, partnership, joint stock company or state or local government agency. [1987 c.332 §1]

30.505 Limitation on liability of volunteer providing assistance relating to compliance with hazardous waste disposal laws; exceptions. (1) Except as provided in subsection (2) of this section, no person may maintain an action for damages against a person who voluntarily provides assistance, training or advice to a generator directly related to procedures or actions the generator must take to comply with the requirements of state or federal hazardous waste disposal laws.

(2) The immunity provided in subsection (1) of this section shall not apply to:

(a) Any person whose act or omission caused in whole or in part the occurrence resulting in the damages for which the action is brought and who would otherwise be liable for the damages.

(b) Any person who receives compensation other than reimbursement for expenses for the person's service in providing such assistance, training or advice.

(c) The liability of any person for damages resulting from the person's gross negligence or from the person's reckless, wanton or intentional misconduct.

(d) Any activity for which a person is otherwise strictly liable without regard to fault. [1987 c.332 §2]

ACTIONS FOR USURPATION OF OFFICE OR FRANCHISE; TO ANNUL CORPORATE EXISTENCE; TO ANNUL LETTERS PATENT

30.510 Action for usurpation of office or franchise, forfeiture of office or failure to incorporate. An action at law may be maintained in the name of the state, upon the information of the district attorney, or upon the relation of a private party against the person offending, in the following cases:

(1) When any person usurps, intrudes into, or unlawfully holds or exercises any public office, civil or military, or any franchise within this state, or any office in a corporation either public or private, created or formed by or under the authority of this state; or,

(2) When any public officer, civil or military, does or suffers an act which, by the provisions of law, makes a forfeiture of the office of the public officer; or,

(3) When any association or number of persons acts within this state, as a corporation, without being duly incorporated.

30.520 Joinder of defendants. Several persons may be joined as defendants in an action for the causes specified in ORS 30.510 (1), and in such action their respective rights to such office or franchise may be determined.

30.530 Determining right of person claiming an office or franchise. Whenever an action is brought against a person for any of the causes specified in ORS 30.510 (1), the district attorney, in addition to the statement of the cause of action, may separately set forth in the complaint the name of the person rightfully entitled to the office or franchise, with a statement of the facts constituting the right of the person thereto. In such case, judgment may be given upon the right of the defendant, and also upon the right of the person so alleged to be entitled, or only upon the right of the defendant, as justice may require.

30.540 Rights of person adjudged entitled to office or franchise. If judgment is given upon the right of and in favor of the person alleged in the complaint to be entitled to the office or franchise, the person shall be entitled to the possession and enjoyment of the franchise, or to take upon the person the execution of the office, after qualifying the person therefor as required by law, and to demand and receive the possession of all the books, papers and property belonging thereto.

30.550 Action for damages. If judgment is given upon the right of and in favor of the person alleged in the complaint to be entitled to the office or franchise, the person may afterwards maintain an action to recover the damages which the person has sustained by reason of the premises. [Amended by 1973 c.836 §320; 1981 c.898 §35]

30.560 Judgment against usurper; imposition of fine. When a defendant, whether a natural person or a corporation, against whom an action has been commenced for any of the causes specified in ORS 30.510 (1), is determined to be guilty of usurping, or intruding into, or unlawfully holding or exercising any office or franchise, judgment shall be given that such defendant be excluded therefrom. The court may also impose a fine upon the defendant not exceeding $2,000.

30.570 Action to annul corporate existence on direction of Governor. An action may be maintained in the name of the state, whenever the Governor shall so direct, against a corporation either public or private, for the purpose of avoiding the Act of incorporation, or an Act renewing or modifying its corporate existence, on the ground that such Act was procured upon some fraudulent suggestion or concealment of a material fact by the persons incorporated, or some of them, or with their knowledge and consent; or for annulling the existence of a corporation formed under any general law of this state, on the ground that such incorporation, or any renewal or modification thereof, was procured in like manner.

30.580 Action to annul corporate existence on leave of court. An action may be maintained in the name of the state against a corporation, other than a public one, on leave granted by the court or judge thereof where the action is triable, for the purpose of avoiding the charter or annulling the existence of such corporation, whenever it shall:

(1) Offend against any of the provisions of an Act creating, renewing, or modifying such corporation, or the provisions of any general law under which it became incorporated;

(2) Violate the provisions of any law, by which such corporation forfeits its charter, by abuse of its powers;

(3) Whenever it has forfeited its privileges or franchises, by failure to exercise its powers;

(4) Whenever it has done or omitted any act, which amounts to a surrender of its corporate rights, privileges and franchises; or,

(5) Whenever it exercises a franchise or privilege not conferred upon it by law.

30.590 Judgment against corporation. If it is determined that a corporation, against which an action has been commenced pursuant to ORS 30.570 or 30.580, has forfeited its corporate rights, privileges and franchises, judgment shall be given that the corporation be excluded therefrom, and that the corporation be dissolved.

30.600 Action to annul letters patent. An action may be maintained in the name of the state for the purpose of vacating or annulling letters patent, issued by the state, against the person to whom the letters were issued, or those claiming under the person, as to the subject matter thereof, in the following cases:

(1) When the letters patent were issued by means of some fraudulent suggestion or concealment of a material fact by the person to whom the letters were issued, or with the knowledge and consent of the person;

(2) When the letters patent were issued through mistake or in ignorance of a material fact; or

(3) When the patentee, or those claiming under the patentee, have done or omitted an act, in violation of the terms and conditions on which the letters patent were issued, or have by any other means forfeited the interest acquired under the letters. [Amended by 2001 c.104 §8]

30.610 Prosecutor; verification of pleadings; affidavit for leave of court; relator as coplaintiff. The actions provided for in ORS 30.510 to 30.640 shall be commenced and prosecuted by the district attorney of the district where the same are triable. When the action is upon the relation of a private party, as allowed in ORS 30.510, the pleadings on behalf of the state shall be signed by the relator as if the relator were the plaintiff, or otherwise as provided in

ORCP 17; in all other cases the pleadings shall be signed by the district attorney in like manner or otherwise as provided in ORCP 17. When an action can only be commenced by leave, as provided in ORS 30.580, the leave shall be granted when it appears by affidavit that the acts or omissions specified in that section have been done or suffered by the corporation. When an action is commenced on the information of a private person, as allowed in ORS 30.510, having an interest in the question, such person, for all the purposes of the action, and as to the effect of any judgment that may be given therein, shall be deemed a coplaintiff with the state. [Amended by 1979 c.284 §66]

30.620 Duty of district attorney. When directed by the Governor, as prescribed in ORS 30.570, it shall be the duty of the district attorney to commence the action therein provided for accordingly. In all other actions provided for in ORS 30.510 to 30.640 it shall be the duty of the proper district attorney to commence such action, upon leave given where leave is required, in every case of public interest, whenever the district attorney has reason to believe that a cause of action exists and can be proven, and also for like reasons in every case of private interest only in which satisfactory security is given to the state to indemnify it against the costs and expenses that may be incurred thereby.

30.630 Filing copy of judgment with Secretary of State. If judgment is given against a corporation, the effect of which is that the corporation ceases to exist, or whereby any letters patent are determined to be vacated or annulled, it shall be the duty of the district attorney to cause a copy of the judgment to be filed with the Secretary of State. [Amended by 1991 c.111 §3]

30.640 Enforcement of judgment. A judgment given in any action provided for in ORS 30.510 to 30.640, in respect to costs and disbursements, may be enforced by execution as a judgment which requires the payment of money. [Amended by 1981 c.898 §36]

ACTIONS AGAINST PUBLIC BODY BY INMATES

30.642 Definitions for ORS 30.642 to 30.650. As used in ORS 30.642 to 30.650:
 (1) "Action against a public body" means a civil action, including an action brought in a small claims department, an appeal or a petition for review, that names as a defendant a public body as defined in ORS 30.260 or an officer, employee or agent of a public body. "Action against a public body" does not mean petitions for writs of habeas corpus, petitions for writs of mandamus and petitions for post-conviction relief under ORS 138.510 to 138.680.
 (2) "Correctional facility" means a Department of Corrections institution or a jail.
 (3) "Inmate" means a person incarcerated or detained in a correctional facility who is accused of, convicted of or sentenced for a violation of criminal law or for the violation of the terms and conditions of pretrial release, probation, parole, post-prison supervision or a diversion program. [1999 c.657 §1; 2011 c.262 §3]

30.643 Waiver or deferral of fees and costs in action against public body by inmate. (1) If an inmate seeks to file an action against a public body, the fees and court costs of the inmate may be waived or deferred only in the manner provided by this section.
 (2) Any inmate seeking waiver or deferral of fees or court costs must submit with the application for waiver or deferral a certified copy of the inmate's trust account statement for the six-month period immediately preceding the filing of the complaint, petition, notice of appeal or petition for review. The statement must be certified as correct by an official of each correctional facility in which the inmate was confined within the six-month period or by an employee of the Department of Corrections charged with the responsibility of overseeing inmate trust accounts.
 (3) Upon the filing of a statement under subsection (2) of this section, the court shall review the information in the statement relating to deposits in the inmate's trust account and any other resources available to the inmate. The court may only waive the inmate's fees and court costs if the court determines that the inmate has no funds and will not have funds.
 (4) If the court makes a determination that an inmate has or will have funds to pay fees and court costs, the court shall require full payment of the filing fees and court costs, or, if funds are not immediately available in the inmate's trust account, shall assess and collect filing fees and court costs as funds become available in the inmate's trust account.
 (5) On its own motion or on the motion of the public body, the court may review the pleadings of the inmate in an action against a public body at the time a request for waiver or deferral of filing fees or court costs is made. If the court finds that the pleadings fail to state a claim for which relief may be granted, the court may decline to waive or defer filing fees or court costs. The court shall enter a denial of waiver or deferral of fees and costs under this subsection as a limited judgment. Notwithstanding the time established by statute for the commencement of an action, if a limited judgment is entered under this subsection within 30 days of the expiration of the time allowed for commencing the action, the inmate may commence the action not later than 45 days after the judgment is entered. Only one extension of the time allowed for commencing an action may be granted by the court under this section.
 (6) Nothing in this section shall be construed as preventing an inmate from bringing an action against a public body because the inmate has no assets or means by which to pay the initial partial filing fee as provided under this section. [1999 c.657 §2; 2005 c.530 §1; 2007 c.493 §11]

30.645 Waiver or deferral of fees after three dismissals of action. (1) Except as provided in subsection (2) of this section, the court may not waive or defer an inmate's fees or court costs under ORS 30.643 if the inmate has, on three or more prior occasions while incarcerated or detained in any correctional facility, filed an action against a public body in a court of this state that was dismissed on the grounds that the action:
 (a) Was frivolous or malicious;
 (b) Failed to state a claim upon which relief could be granted; or
 (c) Sought monetary relief from a defendant who is immune from a claim for monetary relief.
 (2) The court may waive or defer fees or court costs of an inmate who would not otherwise be eligible for waiver or deferral under subsection (1) of this section if the inmate establishes in the application for waiver or deferral that the inmate is in imminent danger of serious physical injury and the action against a public body is needed to seek relief from that danger. [1999 c.657 §3; 2007 c.493 §12]

30.646 Payment of costs under judgment against inmate. (1) If an inmate files an action against a public body and a judgment is entered that requires the inmate to pay costs to the public body, the inmate must pay the full amount of the costs ordered.
 (2) Payment for costs under this section shall be made by deductions from the income credited to the inmate's trust account. [1999 c.657 §4]

30.647 Dismissal of inmate action during proceedings. (1) If fees or court costs of an inmate have been waived or deferred under ORS 30.643, a court shall dismiss the case if at any time the court determines that the inmate was in fact able to pay fees and court costs at the time the application for waiver or deferral was made under ORS 21.680 to 21.698.
 (2) If an inmate's fees or court costs have been waived or deferred under ORS 30.643, a court shall dismiss the case if at any time the court determines that each claim in the action, petition or appeal:
 (a) Is frivolous or malicious;
 (b) Fails to state a claim upon which relief may be granted, and the court denies leave to amend; or
 (c) Seeks monetary relief against a defendant who is immune from a claim for monetary relief.
 (3) Upon appeal of any dismissal under this section, the Court of Appeals on its own motion, or on the motion of the respondent, may summarily affirm the judgment of the trial court, with or without submission of briefs and without oral argument, if the Court of Appeals determines that the appeal does not present a substantial question of law. Notwithstanding ORS 2.570, the Chief Judge of the Court of Appeals may deny a respondent's motion for summary affirmance under this subsection or may grant the motion if the petitioner does not oppose the motion. A dismissal of an appeal under this subsection constitutes a decision on the merits of the case. [1999 c.657 §5; 2007 c.493 §13]

30.648 Small claims actions by inmates against public bodies. (1)(a) An inmate who brings an action against a public body in a small claims department must serve the notice and claim and all subsequent filings on the public body. If the public body is the Department of Corrections or another state agency, the inmate must also serve the notice and claim and all subsequent filings on the Attorney General.

(b) Notice and claim served under paragraph (a) of this subsection must be served in the manner provided in ORS 46.445 except that the statement required under ORS 46.445 (4) must read "30 DAYS" instead of "14 DAYS."

(2) The public body or Attorney General served under subsection (1) of this section must take action as required under ORS 46.455 except that the public body or Attorney General must admit or deny the claim within 30 days after the date of service.

(3) Notwithstanding ORS 46.405, in an action against a public body brought under this section, the court shall transfer the action to the regular department of the circuit court upon request of the public body or, if the public body is the Department of Corrections or another state agency, or an officer, employee or agent of the Department of Corrections or the state agency, upon request of the public body or the Attorney General.

(4) Notwithstanding ORS 46.415, in an action against a public body brought under this section, if the public body is the Department of Corrections or another state agency, or an officer, employee or agent of the Department of Corrections or the state agency, an attorney or paralegal employed by the Department of Justice may appear and represent the public body.

(5)(a) Notwithstanding ORS 46.475, in an action against a public body brought under this section, notice of intent to apply for an order of default, in the form prescribed by Uniform Trial Court Rule 2.010, must be filed and served on the public body against which an order of default is sought at least 10 days before a court may enter an order of default. If the public body is the Department of Corrections or another state agency, or an officer, employee or agent of the Department of Corrections or the state agency, notice must also be served on the Attorney General.

(b) The court may not enter a default judgment in favor of the inmate unless the inmate submits to the court proof of service by affidavit of the notice and claim required under subsection (1) of this section and the notice of intent to apply for an order of default required under paragraph (a) of this subsection. [2011 c.262 §2]

30.650 Award of noneconomic damages in inmate action. Noneconomic damages, as defined in ORS 31.710, may not be awarded to an inmate in an action against a public body unless the inmate has established that the inmate suffered economic damages, as defined in ORS 31.710. [1999 c.657 §6]

30.655 [1999 c.810 §1; repealed by 2015 c.212 §18]

30.656 [1999 c.810 §2; repealed by 2015 c.212 §18]

30.658 [1999 c.810 §3; repealed by 2015 c.212 §18]

30.660 [1999 c.810 §4; repealed by 2015 c.212 §18]

30.661 [1999 c.810 §5; repealed by 2015 c.212 §18]

30.662 [1999 c.810 §6; repealed by 2015 c.212 §18]

30.664 [1999 c.810 §8; repealed by 2015 c.212 §18]

30.665 [1999 c.810 §9; repealed by 2015 c.212 §18]

30.670 [1953 c.495 §1; 1973 c.714 §1; 2001 c.621 §16; renumbered 659A.403 in 2001]

ACTIONS ARISING OUT OF AGRI-TOURISM ACTIVITIES

30.671 Definitions for ORS 30.671 to 30.677. As used in ORS 30.671 to 30.677:

(1) "Agri-tourism activity" means an activity carried out on a farm or ranch that allows members of the general public, for recreational, entertainment or educational purposes, to view or enjoy rural activities, including farming, wineries, ranching and historical, cultural or harvest-your-own activities or natural activities and attractions. An activity is an agri-tourism activity whether or not the participant paid to participate in the activity.

(2) "Agri-tourism professional" means a person who is engaged in the business of providing one or more agri-tourism activities, whether or not for compensation.

(3) "Farm or ranch" means an area of land used for the production, cultivation, growing, harvesting or processing of agricultural products.

(4) "Inherent risks of agri-tourism activity" means those dangers or conditions that are an integral part of an agri-tourism activity, including:

(a) Surface and subsurface conditions;

(b) Natural conditions of land, vegetation and waters;

(c) The behavior of wild or domestic animals;

(d) Ordinary dangers of structures or equipment ordinarily used in farming and ranching operations; and

(e) The potential of a participant to act in a negligent manner that may contribute to injury to the participant or others, including failing to follow instructions given by the agri-tourism professional or failing to exercise reasonable caution while engaging in the agri-tourism activity.

(5) "Participant" means an individual other than an agri-tourism professional who engages in an agri-tourism activity. [2015 c.535 §1]

30.673 Limitations on liability of agri-tourism professional; exceptions. (1) Except as provided in subsections (2) and (3) of this section, an agri-tourism professional that posts the notices required under ORS 30.677 is not liable for an injury to or the death of a participant arising from the inherent risks of an agri-tourism activity.

(2) Subsection (1) of this section does not limit the liability of an agri-tourism professional if the agri-tourism professional:

(a) Commits an act or omission that constitutes negligence or willful or wanton disregard for the safety of the participant, and that act or omission is a cause of injury to the participant;

(b) Intentionally injures the participant;

(c) Provides equipment to the participant and fails to make reasonable inspection of the equipment, and that failure is a cause of the injury to the participant;

(d) Fails to make reasonable inspection of the property on which the agri-tourism activity occurs, and that failure is a cause of the injury to the participant;

(e) Has actual knowledge or reasonably should have known of a dangerous condition on the land or in the facilities or equipment used in the activity, or of the dangerous propensity of a particular animal used in the activity, and does not make the danger known to the participant, and the danger causes injury, damage or death to the participant; or

(f) Fails to obtain necessary authorization for the agri-tourism activity under ORS 215.213 or 215.283.

(3) Subsection (1) of this section does not limit the liability of an agri-tourism professional under the product liability provisions of ORS 30.900 to 30.920. [2015 c.535 §2]

30.675 [1953 c.495 §2; 1957 c.724 §1; 1961 c.247 §1; 1973 c.714 §2; renumbered 659A.400 in 2001]

30.677 Notice. (1) An agri-tourism professional shall conspicuously post the notice specified in subsection (2) of this section:

(a) At the entrance to the agri-tourism site, in black letters at least one inch in height;
(b) At any location where an agri-tourism activity takes place, in black letters at least one inch in height; and
(c) In every written contract entered into between the agri-tourism professional and a participant.
(2) The notice required by subsection (1) of this section must read as follows:

WARNING

Under Oregon law, there is no liability for an injury to or the death of a participant in an agri-tourism activity conducted at this agri-tourism location if the injury or death results from the inherent risks of the agri-tourism activity. Inherent risks of agri-tourism activities are risks of injury inherent to land, equipment and animals, as well as the potential for you to act in a negligent manner that may contribute to your injury or death. You are assuming the risk of participating in this agri-tourism activity.

_____ [2015 c.535 §3]

30.680 [Amended by 1953 c.495 §3; 1957 c.724 §2; 1973 c.714 §3; 1981 c.897 §7; 1995 c.618 §24; repealed by 2001 c.621 §90]

30.685 [1973 c.714 §14; 2001 c.621 §17; renumbered 659A.406 in 2001]

ACTIONS ARISING OUT OF
EQUINE ACTIVITIES

30.687 Definitions for ORS 30.687 to 30.697. For the purposes of ORS 30.687 to 30.697:
(1) "Equine" means a horse, pony, mule, donkey or hinny.
(2) "Equine activity" means:
(a) Equine shows, fairs, competitions, performances or parades that involve any or all breeds of equines and any of the equine disciplines including, but not limited to, dressage, hunter and jumper horse shows, grand prix jumping, three-day events, combined training, rodeos, driving, pulling, cutting, polo, steeplechasing, endurance trail riding and western games and hunting;
(b) Equine training, grooming, breeding and teaching activities;
(c) Boarding equines;
(d) Riding, inspecting or evaluating an equine belonging to another whether or not the owner has received some monetary consideration or other thing of value for the use of the equine or is permitting a prospective purchaser of the equine to ride, inspect or evaluate the equine; and
(e) Rides, trips, hunts or other equine activities of any type however informal or impromptu that are sponsored by an equine activity sponsor.
(3) "Equine activity sponsor" means an individual, group or club, partnership or corporation, whether or not the sponsor is operating for profit or nonprofit, that sponsors, organizes or provides the facilities for an equine activity, including but not limited to pony clubs, 4-H clubs, hunt clubs, riding clubs, school and college sponsored classes and programs, therapeutic riding programs and operators, instructors, and promoters of equine facilities, including but not limited to stables, clubhouses, pony ride strings, fairs and arenas at which the activity is held.
(4) "Equine professional" means a person engaged for compensation:
(a) In instructing a participant or renting to a participant an equine for the purpose of riding, training, driving, grooming or being a passenger upon the equine; or
(b) In renting equipment or tack to a participant.
(5) "Participant" means any person, whether amateur or professional, who directly engages in an equine activity, whether or not a fee is paid to participate in the equine activity. "Participant" does not include a spectator at an equine activity or a person who participates in the equine activity but does not ride, train, drive, groom or ride as a passenger upon an equine. [1991 c.864 §2; 1995 c.211 §2]

30.689 Policy. (1) It is the purpose of ORS 30.687 to 30.697 to assist courts and juries to define the circumstances under which those persons responsible for equines may and may not be liable for damages to other persons harmed in the course of equine activities.
(2) It is the policy of the State of Oregon that no person shall be liable for damages sustained by another solely as a result of risks inherent in equine activity, insofar as those risks are, or should be, reasonably obvious, expected or necessary to the person injured.
(3) It is the policy of the State of Oregon that persons responsible for equines, or responsible for the safety of those persons engaged in equine activities, who are negligent and cause foreseeable injury to a person engaged in those activities, bear responsibility for that injury in accordance with other applicable law. [1991 c.864 §1]

30.691 Limitations on liability; exceptions. (1) Except as provided in subsection (2) of this section and in ORS 30.693, an equine activity sponsor or an equine professional shall not be liable for an injury to or the death of a participant arising out of riding, training, driving, grooming or riding as a passenger upon an equine, and, except as provided in subsection (2) of this section and ORS 30.693, no participant or participant's representative may maintain an action against or recover from an equine activity sponsor or an equine professional for an injury to or the death of a participant arising out of riding, training, driving, grooming or riding as a passenger upon an equine.
(2)(a) The provisions of ORS 30.687 to 30.697 do not apply to any injury or death arising out of a race as defined in ORS 462.010.
(b) Nothing in subsection (1) of this section shall limit the liability of an equine activity sponsor or an equine professional:
(A) If the equine activity sponsor or the equine professional commits an act or omission that constitutes willful or wanton disregard for the safety of the participant and that act or omission caused the injury;
(B) If the equine activity sponsor or the equine professional intentionally injures the participant;
(C) Under the products liability provisions of ORS 30.900 to 30.920; or
(D) Under ORS 30.820 or 608.015. [1991 c.864 §3]

30.693 Additional exceptions to limitations on liability; effect of written release. (1) Except as provided in subsection (2) of this section, nothing in ORS 30.691 shall limit the liability of an equine activity sponsor or an equine professional if the equine activity sponsor or the equine professional:
(a) Provided the equipment or tack, failed to make reasonable and prudent inspection of the equipment or tack, and that failure was a cause of the injury to the participant;
(b) Provided the equine and failed to make reasonable and prudent efforts to determine the ability of the participant to safely ride, train, drive, groom or ride as a passenger upon an equine, to determine the ability of the equine to behave safely with the participant and to determine the ability of the participant to safely manage the particular equine; or
(c) Owns, leases, rents or otherwise is in lawful possession and control of the land or facilities upon which the participant sustained injuries because of a dangerous latent condition which was known to or should have been known to the equine activity sponsor or the equine professional and for which warning signs have not been conspicuously posted.
(2) The limitations on liability provided in ORS 30.691 shall apply to an adult participant in the circumstances listed in subsection (1)(b) of this section if the participant, prior to riding, training, driving, grooming or riding as a passenger upon an equine, knowingly executes a release stating that as a condition of participation, the participant waives the right to bring an action against the equine professional or equine activity sponsor for any injury or death arising out of riding, training, driving, grooming or riding as a passenger upon the equine. A release so executed shall be binding upon the adult participant, and no equine professional or equine activity sponsor shall be liable in the circumstances described in subsection (1)(b) of this section except as provided in ORS 30.691 (2). [1991 c.864 §4]

253

30.695 Effect of written release on liability of veterinarian or farrier. (1) No veterinarian or farrier shall be liable to any person who assists the veterinarian or farrier in rendering veterinarian or farrier services to an equine if the person, prior to assisting the veterinarian or farrier, executes a release stating that the person rendering assistance waives the right to bring an action against the veterinarian or farrier for any injury or death arising out of assisting in the provision of veterinarian or farrier services. A release so executed shall be enforceable regardless of lack of consideration.

(2) A release executed pursuant to this section shall not limit the liability of a veterinarian or farrier for gross negligence or intentional misconduct. [1991 c.864 §5]

30.697 Effect on workers' compensation benefits. Nothing in ORS 30.687 to 30.695 shall affect the right of any person to any workers' compensation benefits that may be payable by reason of death, injury or other loss. [1991 c.864 §6]

30.698 [Formerly 30.085; renumbered 31.180 in 2003]

30.700 [1981 c.670 §§1,2; repealed by 1997 c.182 §1 (30.701 enacted in lieu of 30.700)]

MISCELLANEOUS ACTIONS

30.701 Actions against maker of dishonored check; statutory damages and attorney fees; handling fee. (1) In any action against a maker of a dishonored check, a payee may recover from the maker statutory damages in an amount equal to $100 or triple the amount for which the check is drawn, whichever is greater. Statutory damages awarded under this subsection are in addition to the amount for which the check was drawn and may not exceed by more than $500 the amount for which the check was drawn. The court shall allow reasonable attorney fees at trial and on appeal to the prevailing party in an action on a dishonored check and in any action on a check that is not paid because payment has been stopped.

(2) Statutory damages and attorney fees under subsection (1) of this section may be awarded only if the payee made written demand of the maker of the check not less than 30 days before commencing the action and the maker failed to tender to the payee before the commencement of the action an amount of money not less than the amount for which the check was drawn, all interest that has accrued on the check under ORS 82.010 as of the date of demand and any charges imposed under subsection (5) of this section.

(3) Statutory damages under subsection (1) of this section shall not be awarded by the court if after the commencement of the action but before trial the defendant tenders to the plaintiff an amount of money equal to the amount for which the check was drawn, all interest that has accrued on the check under ORS 82.010 as of the date of payment, any charges imposed under subsection (5) of this section, costs and disbursements and the plaintiff's reasonable attorney fees incurred as of the date of the tender.

(4) If the court or jury determines that the failure of the defendant to satisfy the dishonored check at the time demand was made under subsection (2) of this section was due to economic hardship, the court or jury has the discretion to waive all or part of the statutory damages provided for in subsection (1) of this section. If all or part of the statutory damages are waived under this subsection, judgment shall be entered in favor of the plaintiff for the amount of the dishonored check, all interest that has accrued on the check under ORS 82.010, any charges imposed under subsection (5) of this section, the plaintiff's reasonable attorney fees and costs and disbursements.

(5) If a check is dishonored, the payee may collect from the maker a fee not to exceed $35. Any award of statutory damages under subsection (1) of this section must be reduced by the amount of any charges imposed under this subsection that have been paid by the maker or that are entered as part of the judgment.

(6) The provisions of this section apply only to a check that has been dishonored because of a lack of funds or credit to pay the check, because the maker has no account with the drawee or because the maker has stopped payment on the check without good cause. A plaintiff is entitled to the remedies provided by this section without regard to the reasons given by the drawee for dishonoring the check.

(7) For the purposes of this section:
(a) "Check" means a check, draft or order for the payment of money.
(b) "Drawee" has that meaning given in ORS 73.0103.
(c) "Payee" means a payee, holder or assignee of a check. [1997 c.182 §2 (enacted in lieu of 30.700); 1999 c.707 §1; 2011 c.449 §1]

30.710 [Amended by 1961 c.344 §103; repealed by 1973 c.640 §1]

30.715 Successive actions or suits. Successive actions or suits may be maintained upon the same contract or transaction, whenever, after the former action or suit, a new cause of action or suit arises therefrom. [Formerly 11.030]

30.720 [Repealed by 1973 c.640 §1; amended by 1973 c.823 §§88,155]

30.725 [Repealed by 1974 c.36 §28]

30.730 [Repealed by 1979 c.801 §4]

30.740 Right of gambling loser to recover double losses. All persons losing money or anything of value at or on any unlawful game described in ORS 167.117, 167.122 and 167.127 shall have a cause of action to recover from the dealer winning the same, or proprietor for whose benefit such game was played or dealt, or such money or thing of value won, twice the amount of the money or double the value of the thing so lost. [Amended by 1971 c.743 §308; 1977 c.850 §4]

30.750 Liability of abstractors. Any person who, after May 24, 1923, certifies to any abstract of title to any land in Oregon, shall be liable for all damages sustained by any person who, in reliance on the correctness thereof, acts thereon with reference to the title of such land, and is damaged in consequence of any errors, omissions or defects therein, regardless of whether the abstract of title was ordered by the person so damaged. Nothing in this section shall be construed to prevent the maker of any abstract of title to land from limiting in the certificate to the abstract the liability of the maker thereunder to any person named in such certificate, but such limitation of liability must be expressly set forth in the certificate.

30.760 [Amended by 1953 c.565 §2; renumbered 30.150]

30.765 Liability of parents for tort by child; effect on foster parents. (1) In addition to any other remedy provided by law, the parent or parents of an unemancipated minor child shall be liable for actual damages to person or property caused by any tort intentionally or recklessly committed by such child. However, a parent who is not entitled to legal custody of the minor child at the time of the intentional or reckless tort shall not be liable for such damages.

(2) The legal obligation of the parent or parents of an unemancipated minor child to pay damages under this section shall be limited to not more than $7,500, payable to the same claimant, for one or more acts.

(3) When an action is brought under this section on parental responsibility for acts of their children, the parents shall be named as defendants therein and, in addition, the minor child shall be named as a defendant. The filing of an answer by the parents shall remove any requirement that a guardian ad litem be required.

(4) Nothing in subsections (1) to (3) of this section applies to foster parents. [1975 c.712 §§1,4; 1977 c.419 §1; 1991 c.968 §5]

30.770 [1959 c.310 §1; 1965 c.587 §1; 1973 c.827 §8; repealed by 1975 c.712 §5]

30.772 Liability of landowner arising out of aviation activity; exceptions. (1) As used in this section:

(a) "Airstrip" means land that contains a runway or heliport operated and maintained for the takeoff and landing of motorized aircraft and that is registered with the Oregon Department of Aviation or the Federal Aviation Administration at the time of the flight at issue.

(b) "Aviation activity" includes but is not limited to hang gliding, parachuting, paragliding and operating airplanes or ultralight aircraft.

(c) "Charge" has the meaning given that term in ORS 105.672.

(d) "Land" has the meaning given that term in ORS 105.672.

(e) "Nonpublic airstrip" means an airstrip that is registered as a private use airport with the Oregon Department of Aviation or the Federal Aviation Administration at the time of the flight at issue.

(f) "Owner" has the meaning given that term in ORS 105.672.

(g) "Public airstrip" means an airstrip that is not a nonpublic airstrip.

(2) An owner of land is not liable for any personal injury, death or property damage arising from the use of land for purposes of aviation activity, unless the owner intentionally causes the injury, death or property damage.

(3) Subsection (2) of this section does not apply to any of the following:

(a) An owner of a public airstrip.

(b) An owner of a nonpublic airstrip if:

(A) The owner is contacted by the operator of a motorized aircraft prior to the beginning of the aircraft's flight;

(B) The owner provides permission to the operator to use the owner's land for activities related to the aircraft's flight; and

(C) Gross negligence of the owner causes injury, death or property damage related to the aircraft's flight.

(c) An owner of land who imposes a charge for the use of the land for aviation purposes. [2015 c.308 §1]

30.774 Indemnification of property owner that allows nonprofit organization or educational provider to use property. (1) As used in this section, "educational provider" means a public or private elementary or secondary school or an education service district.

(2) A property owner that enters into a contract to allow a nonprofit organization or an educational provider to use the property owner's property or facilities may not require in any separate agreement any individual to indemnify the property owner for damages not caused by the individual while the nonprofit organization or educational provider and the individual use the property or facilities.

(3) This section does not prohibit a property owner from requiring a nonprofit organization or educational provider to indemnify the property owner for damages caused by the organization's or provider's use of the property or facilities. [2015 c.749 §1]

30.780 Liability for damages caused by gambling. Any person violating ORS 167.108 to 167.164 shall be liable in a civil suit for all damages occasioned thereby. [1959 c.681 §3; 1971 c.743 §309]

30.785 Liability of construction design professional for injuries resulting from failure of employer to comply with safety standards. (1) A construction design professional who is retained to perform professional services on a construction project, or an employee of the construction design professional in the performance of professional services on the construction project, shall not be liable for any injury to a worker on the construction project that is a compensable injury under ORS chapter 656 and that results from the failure of the employer of the worker to comply with safety standards on the construction project unless the construction design professional by contract specifically assumes responsibility for compliance with those safety standards. The immunity provided by this section to a construction design professional shall not apply to the negligent preparation of design plans or specifications.

(2) As used in this section, "construction design professional" means an architect, registered landscape architect, professional engineer or professional land surveyor. [1987 c.915 §12]

30.788 Liability of architect, engineer, inspector or building evaluator for emergency relief services. (1) An action for damages arising out of the practice of architecture, as defined in ORS 671.010, may not be maintained by any person against an architect for services rendered by the architect under the provisions of this section.

(2) An action for damages arising out of the practice of engineering, as described in ORS 672.007, may not be maintained by any person against an engineer for structural engineering services rendered by the engineer under the provisions of this section.

(3) An action for damages arising out of the provision of building code inspections, plan reviews or post-disaster building evaluations may not be maintained by any person against a certified inspector or certified building evaluator if the inspector or building evaluator is providing building code inspections, plan reviews or post-disaster building evaluations under the provisions of this section and the inspector or building evaluator is operating within the scope of the certification.

(4) The immunity provided by this section applies only to services that meet all of the following requirements:

(a) The services are rendered without compensation.

(b) The services are rendered within 60 days after the Governor declares a state of emergency under the provisions of ORS 401.165.

(c) The services are rendered to assist in relief efforts arising out of the emergency giving rise to the declaration of emergency.

(5) This section does not affect the liability of any architect, engineer, inspector or building evaluator for gross negligence or intentional torts.

(6) The immunity provided by this section applies only to:

(a) Inspectors certified under ORS 455.715 to 455.740;

(b) Building evaluators certified for post-disaster building evaluation by the Department of Consumer and Business Services;

(c) Architects who are registered under ORS 671.010 to 671.220;

(d) Engineers who are registered under ORS 672.002 to 672.325; and

(e) Architects and engineers who are licensed or registered under the laws of another state. [1995 c.616 §1; 2009 c.259 §19; 2013 c.196 §15]

30.790 [1963 c.524 §§1,2; repealed by 1971 c.780 §7]

30.792 Liability of health care provider or health clinic for volunteer services to charitable organization. (1) As used in this section:

(a)(A) "Charitable organization" means a charitable organization, as defined in ORS 128.620, that:

(i) Spends at least 65 percent of its revenues on charitable programs; and

(ii) Has a financially secure source of recovery for individuals who suffer harm as a result of actions taken by a volunteer on behalf of the organization.

(B) "Charitable organization" does not include hospitals, intermediate care facilities or long term care facilities, as those terms are defined in ORS 442.015.

(b) "Health care provider" means an individual licensed in this state as a practitioner of one or more healing arts as described in ORS 31.740.

(c) "Health clinic" means a public health clinic or a health clinic operated by a charitable organization that provides primarily primary physical health, dental or mental health services to low-income patients without charge or using a sliding fee scale based on the income of the patient.

(2) Except as provided in subsection (3) of this section, a person may not maintain an action for damages against:

(a) A health care provider who voluntarily provides assistance, services or advice through a charitable organization if:

(A) The assistance, services or advice that caused the damages are within the scope of the license of the health care provider; and

(B) The health care provider was acting within the course and scope of the provider's volunteer duties when the damages occurred; or

(b) A health clinic for the assistance, services or advice provided by a health care provider described in paragraph (a) of this subsection.

(3) The immunity provided in this section does not apply to:

(a) Any person who receives compensation other than reimbursement for expenses incurred by the person providing the assistance, services or advice described in subsection (2) of this section.

(b) A person operating a motor vehicle, vessel, aircraft or other vehicle for which the person or owner of the vehicle, vessel, aircraft or other vehicle is required to possess an operator's license or to maintain insurance.

(c) The liability of any person for damages resulting from the person's gross negligence or from the person's reckless, wanton or intentional misconduct.

(d) Any activity for which a person is otherwise strictly liable without regard to fault. [1995 c.616 §2; 2005 c.362 §2; 2012 c.41 §1]

30.794 Liability of physician or hospital arising out of care provided by direct entry midwife. (1) As used in this section:

(a) "Direct entry midwife" means a person practicing direct entry midwifery as defined in ORS 687.405.

(b) "Hospital" has the meaning given that term in ORS 442.015.

(2) A person may not bring a cause of action against a physician licensed under ORS chapter 677 or against a hospital for injury to a patient if:

(a) The injury occurred as a result of care provided by a direct entry midwife in a setting outside the hospital; and

(b) The direct entry midwife requested that the patient be transported to the hospital because the direct entry midwife could not provide appropriate care to the patient.

(3) This section does not apply to the extent the physician or hospital contributed to the injury or to a claim of vicarious liability for care provided by a direct entry midwife.

(4) This section does not limit the liability of a physician or a hospital for gross negligence or reckless, wanton or intentional misconduct. [2011 c.650 §3]

30.795 [1981 c.690 §2; 1985 c.530 §4; repealed by 1993 c.196 §12]

30.800 Liability for emergency medical assistance. (1) As used in this section and ORS 30.805, "emergency medical assistance" means:

(a) Medical or dental care not provided in a place where emergency medical or dental care is regularly available, including but not limited to a hospital, industrial first-aid station or the office of a physician, naturopathic physician, physician assistant or dentist, given voluntarily and without the expectation of compensation to an injured person who is in need of immediate medical or dental care and under emergency circumstances that suggest that the giving of assistance is the only alternative to death or serious physical aftereffects; or

(b) Medical care provided voluntarily in good faith and without expectation of compensation by a physician licensed under ORS chapter 677, a physician assistant licensed under ORS 677.505 to 677.525, a nurse practitioner licensed under ORS 678.375 to 678.390 or a naturopathic physician licensed under ORS chapter 685 and in the person's professional capacity as a provider of health care for an athletic team at a public or private school or college athletic event or as a volunteer provider of health care at other athletic events.

(2) No person may maintain an action for damages for injury, death or loss that results from acts or omissions of a person while rendering emergency medical assistance unless it is alleged and proved by the complaining party that the person was grossly negligent in rendering the emergency medical assistance.

(3) The giving of emergency medical assistance by a person does not, of itself, establish a professional relationship between the person giving the assistance and the person receiving the assistance insofar as the relationship carries with it any duty to provide or arrange for further medical care for the injured person after the giving of emergency medical assistance. [1967 c.266 §§1,2; 1973 c.635 §1; 1979 c.576 §1; 1979 c.731 §1; 1983 c.771 §1; 1983 c.779 §1; 1985 c.428 §1; 1989 c.782 §35; 1997 c.242 §1; 1997 c.751 §11; 2013 c.688 §8; 2014 c.45 §3; 2017 c.356 §2]

30.801 [1999 c.220 §1; repealed by 2005 c.551 §8]

30.802 Liability for use of automated external defibrillator. (1) As used in this section:

(a) "Automated external defibrillator" means an automated external defibrillator approved for sale by the federal Food and Drug Administration.

(b) "Public setting" means a location that is:

(A) Accessible to members of the general public, employees, visitors and guests, but that is not a private residence;

(B) A public school facility as defined in ORS 327.365;

(C) A health club as defined in ORS 431A.450; or

(D) A place of public assembly as defined in ORS 431A.455.

(2) A person may not bring a cause of action against another person for damages for injury, death or loss that result from acts or omissions involving the use, attempted use or nonuse of an automated external defibrillator when the other person:

(a) Used or attempted to use an automated external defibrillator;

(b) Was present when an automated external defibrillator was used or should have been used;

(c) Provided training in the use of an automated external defibrillator;

(d) Is a physician, physician assistant licensed under ORS 677.505 to 677.525, nurse practitioner licensed under ORS 678.375 to 678.390 or a naturopathic physician licensed under ORS chapter 685 and provided services related to the placement or use of an automated external defibrillator; or

(e) Possesses or controls one or more automated external defibrillators placed in a public setting.

(3) The immunity provided by this section does not apply if:

(a) The person against whom the action is brought acted with gross negligence or with reckless, wanton or intentional misconduct; or

(b) The use, attempted use or nonuse of an automated external defibrillator occurred at a location where emergency medical care is regularly available.

(4) Nothing in this section affects the liability of a manufacturer, designer, developer, distributor or supplier of an automated external defibrillator, or an accessory for an automated external defibrillator, under the provisions of ORS 30.900 to 30.920 or any other applicable state or federal law. [2005 c.551 §1; 2010 c.27 §3; 2014 c.45 §4; 2017 c.356 §3]

30.803 Liability of licensed emergency medical services provider acting as volunteer. A person may not maintain a cause of action for injury, death or loss against a licensed emergency medical services provider who acts as a volunteer without expectation of compensation, based on a claim of negligence unless the person shows that the injury, death or loss resulted from willful and wanton misconduct or intentional act or omission of the emergency medical services provider. [1987 c.915 §11; 2011 c.703 §19]

30.805 Liability for emergency medical assistance by government personnel. (1) No person may maintain an action for damages for injury, death or loss that results from acts or omissions in rendering emergency medical assistance unless it is alleged and proved by the complaining party that the acts or omissions violate the standards of reasonable care under the circumstances in which the emergency medical assistance was rendered, if the action is against:

(a) The staff person of a governmental agency or other entity if the staff person and the agency or entity are authorized within the scope of their official duties or licenses to provide emergency medical care; or

(b) A governmental agency or other entity that employs, trains, supervises or sponsors the staff person.

(2) As used in this section, "emergency medical care" means medical care to an injured or ill person who is in need of immediate medical care:

(a) Under emergency circumstances that suggest that the giving of assistance is the only alternative to serious physical aftereffects or death;

(b) In a place where emergency medical care is not regularly available;

(c) In the absence of a personal refusal of such medical care by the injured or ill person or the responsible relative of such person; and

(d) Which may include medical care provided through means of radio or telecommunication by a medically trained person, who practices in a hospital as defined in ORS 442.015 and licensed under ORS 441.015 to 441.087, and who is not at the location of the injured or ill person. [1979 c.782 §8; 1981 c.693 §27; 1985 c.747 §48]

30.807 Liability for emergency transportation assistance. (1) No person shall maintain an action for damages for injury, death or loss that results from acts or omissions in rendering emergency transportation assistance unless it is alleged and proved by the complaining party that the person rendering emergency transportation assistance was grossly negligent. The provisions of this section apply only to a person who provides emergency transportation assistance without compensation.

(2) As used in this section, "emergency transportation assistance" means transportation provided to an injured or ill person who is in need of immediate medical care:

(a) Under emergency circumstances that suggest that the giving of assistance is the only alternative to serious physical aftereffect or death;

(b) From a place where emergency medical care is not regularly available;

(c) In the absence of a personal refusal of such assistance by the injured or ill person or the responsible relative of the person; and

(d) Which may include directions on the transportation provided through means of radio or telecommunications by a medically trained person who practices in a hospital, as defined in ORS 442.015 and who is not at the location of the injured or ill person. [1987 c.915 §10; 1997 c.242 §2]

30.809 Liability of fraternal organization that provides used eyeglasses or hearing aids. (1) A fraternal organization, as defined in ORS 307.134, that is also a charitable corporation, as defined in ORS 128.620, and any other charitable corporation, as defined in ORS 128.620, that is affiliated with the fraternal organization are not liable for any damages arising out of providing previously owned eyeglasses or hearing aids to a person if:

(a) The person is at least 14 years of age; and

(b) The eyeglasses or hearing aids are provided to the person without charge.

(2) The immunity provided by subsection (1) of this section applies to eyeglasses only if the eyeglasses are provided by a licensed optometrist or ophthalmologist who has:

(a) Personally examined the person who will receive the eyeglasses and issued a prescription for the eyeglasses; or

(b) Personally consulted with the licensed optometrist or ophthalmologist who issued the prescription for the eyeglasses. [2011 c.59 §1]

30.810 [1969 c.387 §1; 1973 c.823 §89; renumbered 31.700 in 2003]

30.811 Liability of person providing outreach services to homeless individual or individual at risk of becoming homeless individual. (1) As used in this section:

(a) "Homeless individual" has the meaning given that term in 42 U.S.C. 11302, as in effect on March 16, 2012.

(b) "Outreach services" includes, but is not limited to:

(A) Case management services such as assessment and referral for alcohol or other drug-related services and for housing, financial, educational and related services; and

(B) Medical or dental services provided by a health practitioner who complies with ORS 676.340 and 676.345.

(2) Except as provided in subsection (3) of this section, a person providing outreach services to homeless individuals or individuals at risk of becoming homeless individuals is immune from civil liability for all acts or omissions in providing the care if:

(a) The person has registered as a volunteer with a nonprofit corporation organized under the laws of this state that has as one of its principal missions the provision of services to homeless individuals or individuals at risk of becoming homeless individuals; and

(b) The services are provided without compensation from the nonprofit corporation, the individual to whom services are rendered or any other person.

(3) This section does not apply to intentional torts or to acts or omissions that constitute gross negligence. [2012 c.41 §2]

30.813 Liability of person who enters motor vehicle to remove unattended child or domestic animal; exceptions. (1) As used in this section, "motor vehicle" has the meaning given that term in ORS 801.360.

(2) A person who enters a motor vehicle, by force or otherwise, to remove a child or domestic animal left unattended in the motor vehicle is not subject to criminal or civil liability if the person:

(a) Before entering the motor vehicle, determines that the motor vehicle is locked or there is no reasonable method for the child or animal to exit the motor vehicle without assistance;

(b) Has a good faith and reasonable belief, based upon the circumstances, that entry into the motor vehicle is necessary because the child or animal is in imminent danger of suffering harm;

(c) Before or as soon as is reasonably practicable after entering the motor vehicle, notifies law enforcement or emergency services;

(d) Uses no more force than is necessary to enter the motor vehicle and remove the child or animal; and

(e) Remains with the child or animal in a safe location, in reasonable proximity to the motor vehicle, until law enforcement, emergency services or the owner or operator of the motor vehicle arrives.

(3) This section does not limit the liability of a person for gross negligence or for reckless, wanton or intentional misconduct.

(4) This section does not limit the liability of a peace officer as defined in ORS 161.015. [2017 c.424 §1]

30.815 Liability of seller or lessor of law enforcement dog. (1) As used in this section, "law enforcement dog" means a dog that is sold or leased to a law enforcement agency and intended to be a law enforcement animal as defined in ORS 167.310.

(2) A seller or lessor of a law enforcement dog is not liable under ORS 30.920 for physical harm or damage to property caused by the law enforcement dog if the law enforcement agency to which the dog was sold or leased has begun or completed training the dog using a training program approved by the law enforcement agency or an accredited and recognized animal handling organization. [2017 c.258 §1]

30.820 Action against seller of drugged horse; attorney fees. In addition to and not in lieu of the penalty provided in ORS 165.825 (2), any person who buys a horse sold in violation of ORS 165.825 (1) may bring an action against the seller for any damages the buyer incurs as a result of the sale. The court may award reasonable attorney fees to the prevailing party in an action under this section. [1971 c.175 §3; 1981 c.897 §8; 1995 c.618 §25]

30.822 Action for theft of or injury to search and rescue animal or therapy animal; attorney fees. (1) In addition to and not in lieu of any other penalty provided by state law, the owner of a search and rescue animal or a therapy animal, as defined in ORS 167.352, may bring an action for economic and noneconomic damages against any person who steals or, without provocation, attacks the search and rescue animal or therapy animal. The owner may also bring an action for such damages against the owner of any animal that, without provocation, attacks a search and rescue animal or therapy animal. The action authorized by this subsection may be brought by the owner even if the search and rescue or therapy animal was in the custody or under the supervision of another person when the theft or attack occurred.

(2) If the theft of or unprovoked attack on a search and rescue animal or therapy animal described in subsection (1) of this section results in the death of the animal or the animal is not returned or if injuries sustained in the theft or attack prevent the animal from returning to service as a search and rescue animal or therapy animal, the measure of economic damages shall include, but need not be limited to, the replacement value of an equally trained animal, without any differentiation for the age or the experience of the animal.

(3) If the theft of or unprovoked attack on a search and rescue animal or therapy animal described in subsection (1) of this section results in injuries from which the animal recovers and returns to service, or if the animal is stolen and is recovered and returns to service, the measure of economic damages shall include, but need not be limited to, the costs of temporary replacement services, veterinary medical expenses and any other costs and expenses incurred by the owner as a result of the theft of or injury to the animal.

(4) No cause of action arises under this section if the owner or the person having custody or supervision of the search and rescue animal or therapy animal was committing a criminal or civil trespass at the time of the attack on the animal.

(5) The court may award reasonable attorney fees to the prevailing party in an action under this section. [1993 c.312 §4; 1995 c.618 §26]

30.825 Action for unlawful tree spiking; attorney fees. Any person who is damaged by an act prohibited in ORS 164.886 (1) to (3) may bring a civil action to recover damages sustained. A party seeking civil damages under this section may recover upon proof by a preponderance of the evidence of a violation of the provisions of ORS 164.886 (1) to (3). The court may award reasonable attorney fees to the prevailing party in an action under this section. [1989 c.1003 §4; 1995 c.618 §27]

30.830 [1971 c.186 §7; 1981 s.s. c.3 §111; 1983 c.763 §52; 1987 c.905 §3a; repealed by 2011 c.597 §118]

30.840 [1975 c.562 §1; renumbered 31.980 in 2003]

30.850 [1975 c.562 §2; renumbered 31.982 in 2003]

30.860 Action for trade discrimination; treble damages; attorney fees. (1) A person or governmental entity may not discriminate against, boycott, blacklist or refuse to buy from, sell to or trade with any person because of foreign government imposed or sanctioned discrimination based upon the race, religion, sex, sexual orientation or national origin of the person or of the person's partners, members, directors, stockholders, agents, employees, business associates, suppliers or customers.

(2) Any person directly injured in business or property by a violation of subsection (1) of this section may sue whoever knowingly practices, or conspires to practice, activities prohibited by subsection (1) of this section, and shall recover threefold the damages sustained. The court shall award reasonable attorney fees to the prevailing plaintiff in an action under this section. The court may award reasonable attorney fees and expert witness fees incurred by a defendant who prevails in the action if the court determines that the plaintiff had no objectively reasonable basis for asserting a claim or no objectively reasonable basis for appealing an adverse decision of a trial court. [1977 c.395 §§1,2; 1981 c.897 §9; 1995 c.618 §28; 2007 c.100 §15]

30.862 Action for public investment fraud; attorney fees. (1) Conduct constituting a violation of ORS 30.862 and 162.117 to 162.121 shall give rise to a civil cause of action by the state. The court may award reasonable attorney fees to the prevailing party in an action under this section.

(2) The application of one civil remedy under any provision of ORS 30.862 and 162.117 to 162.121 shall not preclude the application of any other remedy, civil or criminal, under ORS 30.862 and 162.117 to 162.121 or under any other provision of law. Civil remedies under ORS 30.862 and 162.117 to 162.121 are supplemental and not mutually exclusive. [1993 c.768 §4; 1995 c.618 §29]

30.863 Action for impersonation; attorney fees. (1) A plaintiff has a cause of action for the recovery of compensatory damages from any person who violates ORS 165.815.

(2) In an action brought under subsection (1) of this section, the court may award the prevailing party costs and reasonable attorney fees. [2016 c.22 §2]

30.864 Action for disclosure of certain education records; limitation of action; attorney fees. (1) Any person claiming to be aggrieved by the reckless disclosure of personally identifiable information from a student's education records as prohibited by standards issued by the State Board of Education or the governing board of a public university listed in ORS 352.002 may file a civil action in circuit court for equitable relief or, subject to the terms and conditions of ORS 30.265 to 30.300, for damages, or both. The court may order such other relief as may be appropriate.

(2) The action authorized by this section shall be filed within two years of the alleged unlawful disclosure.

(3) In an action brought under this section, the court may allow the prevailing party costs, disbursements and reasonable attorney fees. [1993 c.806 §8; 1995 c.618 §30; 2013 c.768 §102; 2015 c.767 §45]

30.865 Action for invasion of personal privacy; attorney fees. (1) A plaintiff has a cause of action for invasion of personal privacy if the plaintiff establishes any of the following:

(a) The defendant knowingly made or recorded a photograph, motion picture, videotape or other visual recording of the plaintiff in a state of nudity without the consent of the plaintiff, and at the time the visual recording was made or recorded the plaintiff was in a place and circumstances where the plaintiff had a reasonable expectation of personal privacy.

(b) For the purpose of arousing or gratifying the sexual desire of the defendant, the defendant was in a location to observe the plaintiff in a state of nudity without the consent of the plaintiff, and the plaintiff was in a place and circumstances where the plaintiff had a reasonable expectation of personal privacy.

(c) For the purpose of arousing or gratifying the sexual desire of any person, the defendant knowingly:

(A) Made or recorded a photograph, motion picture, videotape or other visual recording of an intimate area of the plaintiff without the consent of the plaintiff; or

(B) Viewed an intimate area of the plaintiff without the consent of the plaintiff.

(d) Without the consent of the plaintiff, the defendant disseminated a photograph, motion picture, videotape or other visual recording of the plaintiff in a state of nudity, and the defendant knew that at the time the visual recording was made or recorded the plaintiff was in a place and circumstances where the plaintiff had a reasonable expectation of personal privacy.

(2) A plaintiff who prevails in a cause of action for invasion of personal privacy under this section is entitled to receive:

(a) Compensatory damages; and

(b) Reasonable attorney fees.

(3) An action under this section must be commenced not later than two years after the conduct that gives rise to a claim for relief occurred.

(4) The remedy provided by this section is in addition to, and not in lieu of, any other claim for relief that may be available to a plaintiff by reason of conduct of a defendant described in subsection (1) of this section.

(5) The provisions of subsection (1)(a) and (d) of this section do not apply to a photograph, motion picture, videotape or other visual recording of a person under 12 years of age if:

(a) The person who makes, records or disseminates the visual recording is the father, mother, sibling, grandparent, aunt, uncle or first cousin, by blood, adoption or marriage, of the person under 12 years of age; and

(b) The visual recording is made, recorded or disseminated for a purpose other than arousing or gratifying the sexual desire of the person or another person.

(6) As used in this section:

(a) "Intimate area" means:

(A) Undergarments that are being worn by a person, are covered by clothing and are intended to be protected from being seen; and

(B) Any of the following that are covered by clothing and are intended to be protected from being seen:

(i) Genitals;

(ii) Pubic areas; or

(iii) Female breasts below the point immediately above the top of the areola.

(b) "Made or recorded a photograph, motion picture, videotape or other visual recording" includes, but is not limited to, making or recording or employing, authorizing, permitting, compelling or inducing another person to make or record a photograph, motion picture, videotape or other visual recording.

(c) "Nudity" means any part of the uncovered or less than opaquely covered:

(A) Genitals;

(B) Pubic area; or

(C) Female breast below a point immediately above the top of the areola.

(d) "Places and circumstances where the plaintiff has a reasonable expectation of personal privacy" includes, but is not limited to, a bathroom, dressing room, locker room that includes an enclosed area for dressing or showering, tanning booth and any area where a person undresses in an enclosed space that is not open to public view.

(e) "Public view" means that an area can be readily seen and that a person within the area can be distinguished by normal unaided vision when viewed from a public place as defined in ORS 161.015. [2005 c.544 §1; 2009 c.877 §3; 2013 c.1 §3]

30.866 Action for issuance or violation of stalking protective order; attorney fees. (1) A person may bring a civil action in a circuit court for a court's stalking protective order or for damages, or both, against a person if:

(a) The person intentionally, knowingly or recklessly engages in repeated and unwanted contact with the other person or a member of that person's immediate family or household thereby alarming or coercing the other person;

(b) It is objectively reasonable for a person in the victim's situation to have been alarmed or coerced by the contact; and

(c) The repeated and unwanted contact causes the victim reasonable apprehension regarding the personal safety of the victim or a member of the victim's immediate family or household.

(2) At the time the petition is filed, the court, upon a finding of probable cause based on the allegations in the petition, shall enter a temporary court's stalking protective order that may include, but is not limited to, all contact listed in ORS 163.730. The petition and the temporary order shall be served upon the respondent with an order requiring the respondent to personally appear before the court to show cause why the temporary order should not be continued for an indefinite period.

(3)(a) At the hearing, whether or not the respondent appears, the court may continue the hearing for up to 30 days or may proceed to enter a court's stalking protective order and take other action as provided in ORS 163.738.

(b) If respondent fails to appear after being served as required by subsection (2) of this section, the court may issue a warrant of arrest as provided in ORS 133.110 in order to ensure the appearance of the respondent in court.

(4) The plaintiff may recover:

(a) Both special and general damages, including damages for emotional distress;

(b) Punitive damages; and

(c) Reasonable attorney fees and costs.

(5) The court may enter an order under this section against a minor respondent without appointment of a guardian ad litem.

(6) An action under this section must be commenced within two years of the conduct giving rise to the claim.

(7) Proof of the claim shall be by a preponderance of the evidence.

(8) The remedy provided by this section is in addition to any other remedy, civil or criminal, provided by law for the conduct giving rise to the claim.

(9) No filing fee, service fee or hearing fee may be charged for a proceeding under this section.

(10) If the respondent was provided notice and an opportunity to be heard, the court shall also include in the order, when appropriate, terms and findings sufficient under 18 U.S.C. 922 (d)(8) and (g)(8) to affect the respondent's ability to possess firearms and ammunition or engage in activities involving firearms.

(11) ORS 163.741 applies to protective orders issued under this section.

(12) Except for purposes of impeachment, a statement made by the respondent at a hearing under this section may not be used as evidence in a prosecution for stalking as defined in ORS 163.732 or for violating a court's stalking protective order as defined in ORS 163.750. [1993 c.626 §9; 1995 c.353 §6; 1999 c.1052 §4; 2003 c.292 §3; 2015 c.89 §1]

Note: Definitions for 30.866 are found in 163.730.

30.867 Action for violation of criminal laws relating to involuntary servitude or trafficking in persons; attorney fees. (1) Irrespective of any criminal prosecution or the result of a criminal prosecution, a person injured by a violation of ORS 163.263, 163.264 or 163.266 may bring a civil action for damages against a person whose actions are unlawful under ORS 163.263, 163.264 or 163.266.

(2) Upon prevailing in an action under this section, the plaintiff may recover:

(a) Both special and general damages, including damages for emotional distress; and

(b) Punitive damages.

(3) The court shall award reasonable attorney fees to the prevailing plaintiff in an action under this section. The court may award reasonable attorney fees and expert witness fees incurred by a defendant who prevails in the action if the court determines that the plaintiff had no objectively reasonable basis for asserting a claim or no reasonable basis for appealing an adverse decision of a circuit court.

(4) An action under this section must be commenced within six years of the conduct giving rise to the claim. [2007 c.811 §9]

30.868 Civil damages for custodial interference; attorney fees. (1) Any of the following persons may bring a civil action to secure damages against any and all persons whose actions are unlawful under ORS 163.257 (1)(a):

(a) A person who is 18 years of age or older and who has been taken, enticed or kept in violation of ORS 163.257 (1)(a); or

(b) A person whose custodial rights have been interfered with if, by reason of the interference:

(A) The person has reasonably and in good faith reported a person missing to any city, county or state police agency; or

(B) A defendant in the action has been charged with a violation of ORS 163.257 (1)(a).

(2) An entry of judgment or a certified copy of a judgment against the defendant for a violation of ORS 163.257 (1)(a) is prima facie evidence of liability if the plaintiff was injured by the defendant's unlawful action under the conviction.

(3)(a) For purposes of this section, a public or private entity that provides counseling and shelter services to victims of domestic violence is not considered to have violated ORS 163.257 (1)(a) if the entity provides counseling or shelter services to a person who violates ORS 163.257 (1)(a).

(b) As used in this subsection, "victim of domestic violence" means an individual against whom domestic violence, as defined in ORS 135.230, 181A.355 or 411.117, has been committed.

(4) Bringing an action under this section does not prevent the prosecution of any criminal action under ORS 163.257.

(5) A person bringing an action under this section must establish by a preponderance of the evidence that a violation of ORS 163.257 (1)(a) has occurred.

(6) It is an affirmative defense to civil liability for an action under this section that the defendant reasonably and in good faith believed that the defendant's violation of ORS 163.257 (1)(a) was necessary to preserve the physical safety of:

(a) The defendant;

(b) The person who was taken, enticed or kept in violation of ORS 163.257 (1)(a); or

(c) The parent or guardian of the person who was taken, enticed or kept in violation of ORS 163.257 (1)(a).

(7)(a) If the person taken, enticed or kept in violation of ORS 163.257 (1)(a) is under 18 years of age at the time an action is brought under this section, the court may:

(A) Appoint an attorney who is licensed to practice law in Oregon to act as guardian ad litem for the person; and

(B) Appoint one of the following persons to provide counseling services to the person:

(i) A psychiatrist.

(ii) A psychologist licensed under ORS 675.010 to 675.150.

(iii) A clinical social worker licensed under ORS 675.530.

(iv) A professional counselor or marriage and family therapist licensed under ORS 675.715.

(b) The court may assess against the parties all costs of the attorney or person providing counseling services appointed under this subsection.

(8) If an action is brought under this section by a person described under subsection (1)(b) of this section and a party shows good cause that it is appropriate to do so, the court may order the parties to obtain counseling directed toward educating the parties on the impact that the parties' conflict has on the person taken, enticed or kept in violation of ORS 163.257 (1)(a). The court may assess against the parties all costs of obtaining counseling ordered under this subsection.

(9) Upon prevailing in an action under this section, the plaintiff may recover:

(a) Special and general damages, including damages for emotional distress; and

(b) Punitive damages.

(10) The court may award reasonable attorney fees to the prevailing party in an action under this section.

(11)(a) Notwithstanding ORS 12.110, 12.115, 12.117 or 12.160, an action under this section must be commenced within six years after the violation of ORS 163.257 (1)(a). An action under this section accruing while the person who is entitled to bring the action is under 18 years of age must be commenced not more than six years after that person attains 18 years of age.

(b) The period of limitation does not run during any time when the person taken, enticed or kept in violation of ORS 163.257 (1)(a) is removed from this state as a result of the defendant's actions in violation of ORS 163.257 (1)(a). [2005 c.841 §1; 2009 c.11 §5; 2009 c.442 §26]

30.870 Definitions for ORS 30.870 and 30.875. As used in this section and ORS 30.875:

(1) "Agricultural produce" means any plant including, but not limited to, trees, or animals, kept, grown or raised upon real property, and the products of those plants and animals.

(2) "Mercantile establishment" means any place where merchandise is displayed, held or offered for sale, either at retail or wholesale.

(3) "Merchandise" means all things movable and capable of manual delivery.

(4) "Owner" means any person who owns or operates a mercantile establishment or farm, or the agents or employees of that person. [1979 c.592 §1; 1981 c.716 §5]

30.875 Civil damages for shoplifting or taking of agricultural produce. (1) An adult or an emancipated minor who takes possession of any merchandise displayed or offered for sale by any mercantile establishment, or who takes from any real property any agricultural produce kept, grown or raised on the property for purposes of sale, without the consent of the owner and with the intention of converting such merchandise or produce to the individual's own use without having paid the purchase price thereof, or who alters the price indicia of such merchandise, shall be civilly liable to the owner for actual damages, for a penalty to the owner in the amount of the retail value of the merchandise or produce not to exceed $500, and for an additional penalty to the owner of not less than $100 nor more than $250.

(2) The parents having custody of an unemancipated minor who takes possession of any merchandise displayed or offered for sale by any mercantile establishment, or who takes from any real property any agricultural produce kept, grown or raised on the property for purposes of sale, without the consent of the owner, and with the intention of converting such merchandise or produce to the minor's own use without having paid the purchase price thereof, or who alters the price indicia of such merchandise or who engages in conduct described in ORS 164.125, 164.132 or 164.373, shall be civilly liable to the owner for actual damages, for a penalty to the owner in the amount of the retail value of the merchandise or produce not to exceed $250, plus an additional penalty to the owner of not less than $100 nor more than $250. Persons operating a foster home certified under ORS 418.625 to 418.645 are not liable under this subsection for the acts of children not related to them by blood or marriage and under their care.

(3) A conviction for theft is not a condition precedent to the maintenance of a civil action under this section.

(4) A civil liability under this section is not limited by any other law that limits liability of parents of minor children.

(5) An action for recovery of damages under this section may be brought in any court of competent jurisdiction, including the small claims department of a circuit court if the total damages do not exceed the jurisdictional limit of the small claims department.

(6) The fact that an owner or seller of merchandise or agricultural produce may bring an action against an individual for damages as provided in this section shall not limit the right of the owner or seller to demand, in writing, that a person who is liable for damages under this section remit said damages prior to the commencement of any legal action.

(7) Judgments, but not claims, arising under this section may be assigned.

(8) An action under this section may not be brought based on a dishonored check, draft or order for payment of money if an action can be brought on the dishonored check, draft or order under ORS 30.701.

(9) An action under this section must be commenced within three years after the merchandise or agricultural produce is taken. [1979 c.592 §2; 1981 c.716 §6; 1985 c.537 §6; 1987 c.907 §16; 1995 c.658 §28; 1997 c.182 §§3,4; 1999 c.705 §5; 2003 c.324 §1]

30.876 Treble damages and costs in actions arising out of interference with agricultural research. In any civil action arising out of conduct that would constitute interference with agricultural research under ORS 164.889, the court shall award:

(1) Treble the amount of damages claimed to real and personal property; and

(2) The costs of repeating experiments including, but not limited to, the costs of replacing records, data, equipment, specimens, labor and materials, if the conduct causes the failure of an experiment in progress or irreparable damage to completed research or experimentation. [2001 c.147 §4]

30.877 Treble damages and costs in actions arising out of research and animal interference and arising out of interference with livestock production. In any civil action arising out of conduct that would constitute a violation of ORS 167.312 or 167.388, the court shall award treble the amount of damages caused to real or personal property by the violation. In addition, in any civil action arising out of conduct that would constitute a violation of ORS 167.312, the court shall award the costs of repeating experiments, including but not limited to the costs of replacing records, data, equipment, specimens, labor and materials, if the conduct causes the failure of an experiment in progress or irreparable damage to completed research or experimentation. [2001 c.843 §1]

30.880 [1979 c.842 §5a; 1987 c.774 §148; 1987 c.915 §8; renumbered 278.322 in 2003]

30.882 Award of liquidated damages to sports official subjected to offensive physical contact; attorney fees. (1) In addition to, and not in lieu of any other damages that may be claimed, a plaintiff who is a sports official shall receive liquidated damages in an amount not less than $500 but not more than $1,000 in any action in which the plaintiff establishes that:

(a) The defendant intentionally subjected the plaintiff to offensive physical contact;

(b) The defendant knew that the plaintiff was a sports official at the time the offensive physical contact was made;

(c) The offensive physical contact is made while the plaintiff is within, or in the immediate vicinity of, a facility at which the plaintiff serves as a sports official for a sports event; and

(d) The offensive physical contact is made while the plaintiff is serving as a sports official or within a brief period of time thereafter.

(2) The court shall award reasonable attorney fees to a prevailing plaintiff in an action in which liquidated damages are awarded under this section.

(3) An award of liquidated damages under this section is not subject to ORS 31.725, 31.730 or 31.735.

(4) As used in this section, "sports official" means a person who:

(a) Serves as a referee, umpire, linesman or judge or performs similar functions under a different title; and

(b) Is a member of, or registered by, a local, state, regional or national organization that engages in providing education and training in sports officiating. [1999 c.786 §1]

30.890 Liability of food gleaners, donors and distributors. (1)(a) Notwithstanding any other provision of law, a gleaner or the good-faith donor of any food, apparently fit for human consumption, to a bona fide charitable or nonprofit organization, including but not limited to a food bank, for distribution without charge or on a scale reflecting ability to pay or only requiring a shared maintenance contribution, shall not be subject to criminal penalty or civil damages arising from the condition of the food, unless an injury is caused by the gross negligence, recklessness or intentional conduct of the donor or gleaner.

(b) The immunity from civil liability and criminal penalty provided by this section applies regardless of compliance with any laws, rules or ordinances regulating the packaging or labeling of food, and regardless of compliance with any laws, rules or ordinances regulating the storage or handling of the food by the donee after the donation of the food.

(2) Notwithstanding any other provision of law, a bona fide charitable or nonprofit organization which in good faith receives food, apparently fit for human consumption, and while apparently fit for human consumption distributes it at no charge or on a fee scale reflecting ability to pay or only requiring a shared maintenance contribution, shall not be subject to criminal penalty or civil damages resulting from the condition of the food unless an injury results from the gross negligence, recklessness or intentional conduct of the organization.

(3) This section applies to the good-faith donation of food not readily marketable due to appearance, freshness, grade, surplus or other considerations but does not restrict the authority of any appropriate agency to regulate or ban the use of such food for human consumption.

(4) As used in this section:

(a) "Donor" includes any person who operates a restaurant or other food establishment licensed or regulated by law.

(b) "Food" means any food whether or not it may spoil or otherwise become unfit for human consumption because of its nature, type or physical condition, including but not limited to fresh or processed meats, poultry, seafood, dairy products, bakery products, eggs in the shell, fresh fruits or vegetables, and foods that have been packaged, canned, refrigerated, freeze-dried or frozen.

(c) "Food bank" means a surplus food collection and distribution system operated and established to assist in bringing donated food to nonprofit charitable organizations and individuals for the purpose of reducing hunger and meeting nutritional needs.

(d) "Gleaner" means a person that harvests for free distribution an agricultural crop that has been donated by the owner. [1979 c.265 §1; 1989 c.808 §1]

30.892 Liability of donors and distributors of general merchandise and household items. (1) Notwithstanding any other provision of law, the good-faith donor of any general merchandise or household item, apparently fit for use to a bona fide charitable or nonprofit organization for distribution without charge or on a fee scale reflecting ability to pay, or only requiring a shared maintenance contribution, shall not be subject to criminal penalty or civil damages arising from the condition of the general merchandise or household item, unless an injury is caused by the gross negligence, recklessness or intentional conduct of the donor.

(2) The immunity from civil liability and criminal penalty provided by this section applies regardless of compliance with any laws, rules or ordinances regulating the packaging or labeling of general merchandise or household items, and regardless of compliance with any laws, rules or ordinances regulating the storage or handling of the general merchandise or household items by the donee after the donation.

(3) Notwithstanding any other provision of law, a bona fide charitable or nonprofit organization which in good faith receives general merchandise or household items, apparently fit for use, and while apparently still fit for use, distributes the merchandise or items at no charge or on a fee scale reflecting ability to pay or only requiring a shared maintenance contribution, shall not be subject to criminal penalty or civil damages resulting from the condition of the general merchandise or household items, unless an injury results from the gross negligence, recklessness or intentional conduct of the organization.

(4) This section applies to the good-faith donation of general merchandise or household items not readily marketable due to appearance, grade, surplus or considerations other than safety but does not restrict the authority of any appropriate agency to regulate or ban the use of such general merchandise or household items. The immunity from civil liability and criminal penalty provided by this section shall not apply if the general merchandise or household item is resold by either the donee or any other person. This section does not affect the liability of a manufacturer for products that are subject to a current or future safety recall whether such recall is initiated by the manufacturer or at the request of the state or federal government, nor shall this section affect the liability of a manufacturer under ORS 30.900 to 30.920.

(5) As used in this section:

(a) "Donor" includes all of the following, without regard to who is the owner of the general merchandise or household item at the time of the donation:

(A) A general merchandiser;

(B) A retail establishment;

(C) A wholesaler; and

(D) A manufacturer.

(b) "General merchandise or household item" means any item sold as general merchandise for household use, including but not limited to items sold in the following categories: Toiletries, cosmetics, domestics, electronics, sporting goods, clothing, toys, small appliances, personal care appliances, housewares, household chemicals, hardware, paint, sundries, plumbing, garden supplies, automotive, school supplies, pet food, pet supplies, over-the-counter drugs or vitamins, or other items of merchandise commonly sold in a retail or general merchandising establishment. [1989 c.1012 §2]

30.895 [1987 c.774 §11; renumbered 31.230 in 2003]

PRODUCT LIABILITY ACTIONS

30.900 "Product liability civil action" defined. As used in ORS 30.900 to 30.920, "product liability civil action" means a civil action brought against a manufacturer, distributor, seller or lessor of a product for damages for personal injury, death or property damage arising out of:

(1) Any design, inspection, testing, manufacturing or other defect in a product;

(2) Any failure to warn regarding a product; or

(3) Any failure to properly instruct in the use of a product. [1977 c.843 §1]

30.902 Products provided by physicians. A physician licensed pursuant to ORS chapter 677 is not a manufacturer, distributor, seller or lessor of a product for the purposes of ORS 30.900 to 30.920 if the product is provided by the physician to a patient as part of a medical procedure and the physician was not involved in the design or manufacture of the product. [2009 c.485 §9]

30.905 Time limitation for commencement of action. (1) Subject to the limitation imposed by subsection (2) of this section, a product liability civil action for personal injury or property damage must be commenced not later than two years after the plaintiff discovers, or reasonably should have discovered, the personal injury or property damage and the causal relationship between the injury or damage and the product, or the causal relationship between the injury or damage and the conduct of the defendant.

(2) A product liability civil action for personal injury or property damage must be commenced before the later of:

(a) Ten years after the date on which the product was first purchased for use or consumption; or

(b) The expiration of any statute of repose for an equivalent civil action in the state in which the product was manufactured, or, if the product was manufactured in a foreign country, the expiration of any statute of repose for an equivalent civil action in the state into which the product was imported.

(3) Subject to the limitation imposed by subsection (4) of this section, a product liability civil action for death must be commenced not later than three years after the decedent, the personal representative for the decedent or a person for whose benefit an action could be brought under ORS 30.020 discovers, or reasonably should have discovered, the causal relationship between the death and the product, or the causal relationship between the death and the conduct of the defendant.

(4) A product liability civil action for death must be commenced before the earlier of:

(a) Three years after the death of the decedent;

(b) Ten years after the date on which the product was first purchased for use or consumption; or

(c) The expiration of any statute of repose for an equivalent civil action in the state in which the product was manufactured, or, if the product was manufactured in a foreign country, the expiration of any statute of repose for an equivalent civil action in the state into which the product was imported.

(5) This section does not apply to a civil action brought against a manufacturer, distributor, seller or lessor of a manufactured dwelling, as defined in ORS 446.003, or of a prefabricated structure, as defined in ORS 455.010. Actions described in this subsection are subject to the statute of limitations provided by ORS 12.135. [1977 c.843 §3; 1983 c.143 §1; 1987 c.4 §1; 1993 c.259 §6; 2003 c.768 §1; 2009 c.485 §1]

Note: Section 2, chapter 485, Oregon Laws 2009, provides:
Sec. 2. The amendments to ORS 30.905 by section 1 of this 2009 Act apply only to causes of action that arise on or after the effective date of this 2009 Act [January 1, 2010]. [2009 c.485 §2]

30.907 Action for damages from asbestos-related disease; limitations. (1) A product liability civil action for damages resulting from asbestos-related disease must be commenced not later than two years after the date on which the plaintiff first discovered, or in the exercise of reasonable care should have discovered, the disease and the cause thereof.

(2) A product liability civil action for damages resulting from asbestos-related disease is not subject to ORS 30.905 or any other statute of limitation or statute of ultimate repose in Oregon Revised Statutes.

(3) A product liability civil action may not be brought against a contractor, as defined in ORS 701.005, for damages resulting from asbestos-related disease if the contractor:

(a) Used or installed products containing asbestos pursuant to plans, specifications or directions prepared for a project by or on behalf of the owner of the project;

(b) Is not the manufacturer or distributor of the products containing asbestos; and

(c) Did not furnish the products containing asbestos independent of the provision of labor.

(4) Subsection (3) of this section does not affect a plaintiff's ability to bring a product liability civil action against a contractor if:

(a) The contractor substituted a product containing asbestos on a project when the plans, specifications or directions for the project prepared by or on behalf of the owner did not specify the use or installation of a product containing asbestos; and

(b) The owner or the owner's representative did not expressly direct or consent to the substitution of the product containing asbestos. [1987 c.4 §3; 2005 c.740 §1; 2009 c.485 §7]

30.908 Action arising out of injury from breast implants; limitations. (1) Notwithstanding ORS 30.020, a product liability civil action for death, injury or damage resulting from breast implants containing silicone, silica or silicon as a component must be commenced not later than two years after the date on which the plaintiff first discovered, or in the exercise of reasonable care should have discovered:

(a) The death or specific injury, disease or damage for which the plaintiff seeks recovery;

(b) The tortious nature of the act or omission of the defendant that gives rise to a claim for relief against the defendant; and

(c) All other elements required to establish plaintiff's claim for relief.

(2) A product liability civil action for death, injury or damage resulting from breast implants containing silicone, silica or silicon as a component is not subject to ORS 30.905 or any other statute of limitation or statute of ultimate repose in Oregon Revised Statutes.

(3) For the purposes of subsection (1) of this section, an action for wrongful death must be commenced not later than two years after the earliest date that the discoveries required by subsection (1) of this section are made by any of the following persons:

(a) The decedent;

(b) The personal representative for the decedent; or

(c) Any person for whose benefit the action could be brought.

(4) Subsections (1) to (3) of this section do not apply to a person that supplied component parts or raw materials to manufacturers of breast implants containing silicone, silica or silicon as a component, and the person shall remain subject to the limitations on actions imposed by ORS 30.020 and 30.905, if:

(a) The person did not manufacture breast implants containing silicone, silica or silicon as a component at any time; and

(b) The person was not owned by and did not own a business that manufactured breast implants containing silicone, silica or silicon as a component at any time.

(5) A health care facility licensed under ORS chapter 441 is not a manufacturer, distributor, seller or lessor of a breast implant for the purposes of ORS 30.900 to 30.920 if the implant is provided by the facility to a patient as part of a medical implant procedure. [1993 c.259 §§4,5; 2007 c.71 §10; 2009 c.485 §10; 2011 c.9 §3]

30.910 Product disputably presumed not unreasonably dangerous. It is a disputable presumption in a products liability civil action that a product as manufactured and sold or leased is not unreasonably dangerous for its intended use. [1977 c.843 §2]

30.915 Defenses. It shall be a defense to a product liability civil action that an alteration or modification of a product occurred under the following circumstances:

(1) The alteration or modification was made without the consent of or was made not in accordance with the instructions or specifications of the manufacturer, distributor, seller or lessor;

(2) The alteration or modification was a substantial contributing factor to the personal injury, death or property damage; and

(3) If the alteration or modification was reasonably foreseeable, the manufacturer, distributor, seller or lessor gave adequate warning. [1977 c.843 §4]

30.920 When seller or lessor of product liable; effect of liability rule. (1) One who sells or leases any product in a defective condition unreasonably dangerous to the user or consumer or to the property of the user or consumer is subject to liability for physical harm or damage to property caused by that condition, if:

(a) The seller or lessor is engaged in the business of selling or leasing such a product; and

(b) The product is expected to and does reach the user or consumer without substantial change in the condition in which it is sold or leased.

(2) The rule stated in subsection (1) of this section shall apply, even though:

(a) The seller or lessor has exercised all possible care in the preparation and sale or lease of the product; and

(b) The user, consumer or injured party has not purchased or leased the product from or entered into any contractual relations with the seller or lessor.

(3) It is the intent of the Legislative Assembly that the rule stated in subsections (1) and (2) of this section shall be construed in accordance with the Restatement (Second) of Torts sec. 402A, Comments a to m (1965). All references in these comments to sale, sell, selling or seller shall be construed to include lease, leases, leasing and lessor.

(4) Nothing in this section shall be construed to limit the rights and liabilities of sellers and lessors under principles of common law negligence or under ORS chapter 72. [1979 c.866 §2]

30.925 Punitive damages. (1) In a product liability civil action, punitive damages shall not be recoverable except as provided in ORS 31.730.

(2) Punitive damages, if any, shall be determined and awarded based upon the following criteria:

(a) The likelihood at the time that serious harm would arise from the defendant's misconduct;

(b) The degree of the defendant's awareness of that likelihood;

(c) The profitability of the defendant's misconduct;

(d) The duration of the misconduct and any concealment of it;

(e) The attitude and conduct of the defendant upon discovery of the misconduct;

(f) The financial condition of the defendant; and

(g) The total deterrent effect of other punishment imposed upon the defendant as a result of the misconduct, including, but not limited to, punitive damage awards to persons in situations similar to the claimant's and the severity of criminal penalties to which the defendant has been or may be subjected. [1979 c.866 §3; 1995 c.688 §4]

30.927 When manufacturer of drug not liable for punitive damages; exceptions. (1) Where a drug allegedly caused the plaintiff harm, the manufacturer of the drug shall not be liable for punitive damages if the drug product alleged to have caused the harm:

(a) Was manufactured and labeled in relevant and material respects in accordance with the terms of an approval or license issued by the federal Food and Drug Administration under the Federal Food, Drug and Cosmetic Act or the Public Health Service Act; or

(b) Is generally recognized as safe and effective pursuant to conditions established by the federal Food and Drug Administration and applicable regulations, including packaging and labeling regulations.

(2) Subsection (1) of this section does not apply if the plaintiff proves, in accordance with the standard of proof set forth in ORS 30.925 (1), that the defendant, either before or after making the drug available for public use, knowingly in violation of applicable federal Food and Drug Administration regulations withheld from or misrepresented to the agency or prescribing physician information known to be material and relevant to the harm which the plaintiff allegedly suffered.

(3) Nothing contained in this section bars an award of punitive damages where a manufacturer of a drug intentionally fails to conduct a recall required by a valid order of a federal or state agency authorized by statute to require such a recall.

(4) For the purposes of this section, the term "drug" has the meaning given to the term in section 1201 (g)(1) of the Federal Food, Drug and Cosmetic Act, 21 U.S.C. 321 (g)(1). [1987 c.774 §5]

Note: Sections 1 and 2, chapter 536, Oregon Laws 2007, provide:

Sec. 1. (1) As used in this section, "COX-2 inhibitor" means a medication that is intended to inhibit the enzyme known as cyclooxygenase-2.

(2) A civil action for injury, including any product liability action under ORS 30.900 to 30.920 and any action based on negligence, resulting from the use of a COX-2 inhibitor must be commenced not later than four years after the date on which the plaintiff first discovered, or in the exercise of reasonable care should have discovered, the injury and the causal relationship between the injury and the product, or the causal relationship between the injury and the conduct of the defendant.

(3) A civil action for death, including any product liability action under ORS 30.900 to 30.920 and any action based on negligence, resulting from the use of a COX-2 inhibitor must be commenced not later than six years after the date on which the plaintiff first discovered, or in the exercise of reasonable care should have discovered, the causal relationship between the death and the product, or the causal relationship between the death and the conduct of the defendant. [2007 c.536 §1]

Sec. 2. (1) Except as provided in subsection (2) of this section, section 1 of this 2007 Act applies only to causes of action arising on or before January 1, 2007.

(2) Section 1 of this 2007 Act does not apply to any causes of action for which a judgment was entered in the register of a court before the effective date of this 2007 Act [January 1, 2008]. [2007 c.536 §2]

30.928 Time limitation for actions for damages caused by certain light bulbs. (1) As used in this section, "R type metal halide or mercury vapor light bulb" means a metal halide or mercury vapor light bulb that does not have an internal mechanism that shuts off the light automatically within 15 minutes after the bulb is broken.

(2) A product liability civil action for damages caused by R type metal halide or mercury vapor light bulbs may not be commenced more than two years after the date on which the plaintiff first discovered, or in the exercise of reasonable care should have discovered, the injury and the causal relationship between the injury and the conduct of the defendant.

(3) A product liability civil action for damages caused by R type metal halide or mercury vapor light bulbs is subject only to the limitation imposed by this section and is not subject to ORS 30.905 or any other statute of limitation or statute of ultimate repose. [2009 c.485 §11]

FARMING AND FOREST PRACTICES

30.930 Definitions for ORS 30.930 to 30.947. As used in ORS 30.930 to 30.947:

(1) "Farm" means any facility, including the land, buildings, watercourses and appurtenances thereto, used in the commercial production of crops, nursery stock, livestock, poultry, livestock products, poultry products, vermiculture products or the propagation and raising of nursery stock.

(2) "Farming practice" means a mode of operation on a farm that:

(a) Is or may be used on a farm of a similar nature;

(b) Is a generally accepted, reasonable and prudent method for the operation of the farm to obtain a profit in money;

(c) Is or may become a generally accepted, reasonable and prudent method in conjunction with farm use;

(d) Complies with applicable laws; and

(e) Is done in a reasonable and prudent manner.

(3) "Forestland" means land that is used for the growing and harvesting of forest tree species.

(4) "Forest practice" means a mode of operation on forestland that:

(a) Is or may be used on forestland of similar nature;

(b) Is a generally accepted, reasonable and prudent method of complying with ORS 527.610 to 527.770 and the rules adopted pursuant thereto;

(c) Is or may become a generally accepted, reasonable and prudent method in conjunction with forestland;

(d) Complies with applicable laws;

(e) Is done in a reasonable and prudent manner; and

(f) May include, but is not limited to, site preparation, timber harvest, slash disposal, road construction and maintenance, tree planting, precommercial thinning, release, fertilization, animal damage control and insect and disease control.

(5) "Pesticide" has the meaning given that term in ORS 634.006. [1981 c.716 §1; 1983 c.730 §1; 1993 c.792 §32; 1995 c.703 §1; 2005 c.657 §2]

30.931 Transport or movement of equipment, device, vehicle or livestock as farming or forest practice. Notwithstanding ORS 30.930, if the activities are conducted in a reasonable and prudent manner, the transport or movement of any equipment, device or vehicle used in conjunction with a farming practice or a forest practice on a public road or movement of livestock on a public road is a farming or forest practice under ORS 30.930 to 30.947. [1995 c.703 §9]

30.932 Definition of "nuisance" or "trespass." As used in ORS 30.930 to 30.947, "nuisance" or "trespass" includes but is not limited to actions or claims based on noise, vibration, odors, smoke, dust, mist from irrigation, use of pesticides and use of crop production substances. [1993 c.792 §33; 1995 c.703 §2]

30.933 Legislative findings; policy. (1) The Legislative Assembly finds that:

(a) Farming and forest practices are critical to the economic welfare of this state.

(b) The expansion of residential and urban uses on and near lands zoned or used for agriculture or production of forest products may give rise to conflicts between resource and nonresource activities.

(c) In the interest of the continued welfare of the state, farming and forest practices must be protected from legal actions that may be intended to limit, or have the effect of limiting, farming and forest practices.

(2) The Legislative Assembly declares that it is the policy of this state that:
(a) Farming practices on lands zoned for farm use must be protected.
(b) Forest practices on lands zoned for the production of forest products must be protected.
(c) Persons who locate on or near an area zoned for farm or forest use must accept the conditions commonly associated with living in that particular setting.
(d) Certain private rights of action and the authority of local governments and special districts to declare farming and forest practices to be nuisances or trespass must be limited because such claims for relief and local government ordinances are inconsistent with land use policies, including policies set forth in ORS 215.243, and have adverse effects on the continuation of farming and forest practices and the full use of the resource base of this state. [1993 c.792 §31]

30.934 Prohibition on local laws that make forest practice a nuisance or trespass; exceptions. (1) Any local government or special district ordinance or regulation now in effect or subsequently adopted that makes a forest practice a nuisance or trespass or provides for its abatement as a nuisance or trespass is invalid with respect to forest practices for which no claim or action is allowed under ORS 30.936 or 30.937.
(2) Subsection (1) of this section does not apply to:
(a) City rules, regulations or ordinances adopted in accordance with ORS 527.722; or
(b) Any forest practice conducted in violation of a solar energy easement that complies with ORS 105.880 to 105.890. [1993 c.792 §38]

30.935 Prohibition on local laws that make farm practice a nuisance or trespass. Any local government or special district ordinance or regulation now in effect or subsequently adopted that makes a farm practice a nuisance or trespass or provides for its abatement as a nuisance or trespass is invalid with respect to that farm practice for which no action or claim is allowed under ORS 30.936 or 30.937. [1981 c.716 §2; 1985 c.565 §4; 1993 c.792 §37]

30.936 Immunity from private action based on farming or forest practice on certain lands; exceptions. (1) No farming or forest practice on lands zoned for farm or forest use shall give rise to any private right of action or claim for relief based on nuisance or trespass.
(2) Subsection (1) of this section shall not apply to a right of action or claim for relief for:
(a) Damage to commercial agricultural products; or
(b) Death or serious physical injury as defined in ORS 161.015.
(3) Subsection (1) of this section applies regardless of whether the farming or forest practice has undergone any change or interruption. [1993 c.792 §34; 1995 c.547 §8; 1995 c.703 §3; 2001 c.401 §1]

30.937 Immunity from private action based on farming or forest practice allowed as preexisting nonconforming use; exceptions. (1) No farming or forest practice allowed as a preexisting nonconforming use shall give rise to any private right of action or claim for relief based on nuisance or trespass.
(2) Subsection (1) of this section shall not apply to a right of action or claim for relief for:
(a) Damage to commercial agricultural products; or
(b) Death or serious physical injury as defined in ORS 161.015.
(3) Subsection (1) of this section applies only where a farming or forest practice existed before the conflicting nonfarm or nonforest use of real property that gave rise to the right of action or claim for relief.
(4) Subsection (1) of this section applies only where a farming or forest practice has not significantly increased in size or intensity from November 4, 1993, or the date on which the applicable urban growth boundary is changed to include the subject farming or forest practice within its limits, whichever is later. [1993 c.792 §35; 1995 c.703 §4]

30.938 Attorney fees and costs. In any action or claim for relief alleging nuisance or trespass and arising from a practice that is alleged by either party to be a farming or forest practice, the prevailing party shall be entitled to judgment for reasonable attorney fees and costs incurred at trial and on appeal. [1993 c.792 §36]

30.939 When use of pesticide considered farming or forest practice. (1) Notwithstanding ORS 30.930 (2), the use of a pesticide shall be considered to be a farming practice for purposes of ORS 30.930 to 30.947, if the use of the pesticide:
(a) Is or may be used on a farm of a similar nature;
(b) Is a reasonable and prudent method for the operation of the farm to obtain a profit in money;
(c) Is or may become customarily utilized in conjunction with farm use;
(d) Complies with applicable laws; and
(e) Is done in a reasonable and prudent manner.
(2) Notwithstanding ORS 30.930 (4), the use of a pesticide shall be considered to be a forest practice for purposes of ORS 30.930 to 30.947, if the use of the pesticide:
(a) Is or may be used on forestland of a similar nature;
(b) Is a reasonable and prudent method of complying with ORS 527.610 to 527.770;
(c) Is or may become customarily utilized in conjunction with forestland;
(d) Complies with applicable laws;
(e) Is done in a reasonable and prudent manner; and
(f) Includes, but is not limited to, site preparation, timber harvest, slash disposal, road construction and maintenance, tree planting, precommercial thinning, release, fertilization, animal damage control and insect and disease control. [1993 c.792 §32a; 1995 c.703 §5]

30.940 Effect on other remedies. The provisions of ORS 30.930 to 30.947 shall not impair the right of any person or governmental body to pursue any remedy authorized by law that concerns matters other than a nuisance or trespass. [1981 c.716 §3; 1985 c.565 §5; 1993 c.792 §39]

30.942 Rules. (1) The State Department of Agriculture may adopt rules to implement the provisions of ORS 30.930 to 30.947.
(2) The State Forestry Department may adopt rules to implement the provisions of ORS 30.930 to 30.947. [1993 c.792 §41]

30.943 Certain agencies not required to investigate complaints based on farming or forest practice. The Department of Environmental Quality, Department of State Lands, State Department of Agriculture or State Forestry Department is not required to investigate complaints if the agency has reason to believe that the complaint is based on practices protected by ORS 30.930 or 30.947. [1995 c.703 §8]

30.945 [1981 c.716 §4; repealed by 1995 c.703 §12]

30.947 Effect of siting of destination resorts or other nonfarm or nonforest uses. The fact that a comprehensive plan and implementing ordinances allow the siting of destination resorts or other nonfarm or nonforest uses as provided in ORS 30.947, 197.435 to 197.467, 215.213, 215.283 and 215.284, does not in any way affect the provisions of ORS 30.930 to 30.947. [1987 c.886 §13; 1995 c.703 §6]

30.949 Action for hindering, impairment or obstruction of forest practice on state forestland. (1) As used in this section:
(a) "Access road" means a road owned or maintained by the State Forestry Department.
(b) "Forest practice" has the meaning given that term in ORS 527.620.
(c) "State forestland" means:

(A) Forestland acquired under ORS 530.010 to 530.040; and

(B) Common School Forest Lands and Elliott State Forest Lands managed under ORS 530.490.

(2) A private entity that contracts with the State Forestry Department to perform a forest practice has a right of action for the amount of actual damages against any person that, while on state forestland or an access road on state forestland, intentionally commits an act that hinders, impairs or obstructs or is an attempt to hinder, impair or obstruct, the performance of the forest practice by the private entity. A court shall award a plaintiff prevailing under this section reasonable attorney fees and costs.

(3) If the contract between the private entity and the department provides for the private entity to perform forest practices in a defined area of state forestland that lies in more than one county, venue for a cause of action under this section is proper in any county containing part of the area of state forestland defined by the contract terms in effect on the date the cause of action arose.

(4) An action under this section must be commenced within two years after the date of the act giving rise to the cause of action. [2013 c.461 §1]

30.950 [1979 c.801 §1; 1987 c.774 §13; 1997 c.249 §19; 1997 c.841 §1; 2001 c.534 §1; renumbered 471.565 in 2001]

30.955 [1979 c.801 §2; repealed by 1987 c.774 §14]

30.960 [1979 c.801 §3; 1991 c.860 §5; 1995 c.618 §31; 2001 c.791 §5; renumbered 471.567 in 2001]

ACTIONS ARISING OUT OF
FOOD-RELATED CONDITION

30.961 Actions against sellers of food for food-related condition. (1) As used in this section:

(a) "Food" has the meaning given that term in 21 U.S.C. 321, as in effect on January 1, 2006.

(b) "Food-related condition" means:

(A) Weight gain;

(B) Obesity;

(C) A health condition associated with weight gain or obesity; or

(D) A generally recognized health condition alleged to be caused by, or alleged to likely result from, long-term consumption of food rather than a single instance of consumption of food.

(2) A person may not maintain an action for a claim of injury or death caused by a food-related condition against a person involved in the selling of food, as described in ORS 616.210.

(3) This section does not apply to a claim that includes as an element of the cause of action that a food-related condition was caused by:

(a) Adulterated food, as described in ORS 616.235;

(b) Reliance on information about food that has been misbranded, as described in ORS 616.250;

(c) Violation of a provision of the Federal Food, Drug, and Cosmetic Act, 21 U.S.C. 301 et seq., as in effect on January 1, 2006, prohibiting adulterated or misbranded food; or

(d) Knowing and willful violation of any other state or federal law related to the manufacturing, marketing, distribution, advertisement, labeling or sale of food.

(4) A violation of law is knowing and willful for the purposes of subsection (3)(d) of this section if the person engaged in the conduct that constituted the violation with the intent to deceive or injure or with actual knowledge that the conduct was deceptive or injurious.

(5) This section does not create any claim, right of action or civil liability. This section does not affect any government agency's statutory authority to enforce laws relating to adulteration or misbranding of food. [2005 c.658 §1]

30.963 Claim requirements for actions involving food-related conditions. (1) As used in this section:

(a) "Food" has the meaning given that term in 21 U.S.C. 321, as in effect on January 1, 2006.

(b) "Food-related condition" means:

(A) Weight gain;

(B) Obesity;

(C) A health condition associated with weight gain or obesity; or

(D) A generally recognized health condition alleged to be caused by, or alleged to likely result from, long-term consumption of food rather than a single instance of consumption of food.

(2) A complaint, cross-claim, counterclaim or third-party complaint asserting a claim described in ORS 30.961 (3) must plead with particularity each element of the cause of action, including a description of all of the following:

(a) The law that allegedly was violated.

(b) The facts that are alleged to constitute a violation of the law identified in paragraph (a) of this subsection.

(c) The facts that are alleged to demonstrate that the food-related condition was caused by the violation.

(d) If the violation was of a law described in ORS 30.961 (3)(d), facts sufficient to support a reasonable inference that the violation was committed with the intent to deceive or injure or with actual knowledge that the conduct was deceptive or injurious.

(3) In any action for a claim of injury or death caused by a food-related condition, a court shall stay all discovery and other proceedings during the pendency of any motion to dismiss. The court, on motion and for good cause shown, shall order that specified discovery be conducted notwithstanding the stay imposed under this subsection. [2005 c.658 §3]

SKIING ACTIVITIES

30.970 Definitions for ORS 30.970 to 30.990. As used in ORS 30.970 to 30.990:

(1) "Inherent risks of skiing" includes, but is not limited to, those dangers or conditions which are an integral part of the sport, such as changing weather conditions, variations or steepness in terrain, snow or ice conditions, surface or subsurface conditions, bare spots, creeks and gullies, forest growth, rocks, stumps, lift towers and other structures and their components, collisions with other skiers and a skier's failure to ski within the skier's own ability.

(2) "Injury" means any personal injury or property damage or loss.

(3) "Skier" means any person who is in a ski area for the purpose of engaging in the sport of skiing or who rides as a passenger on any ski lift device.

(4) "Ski area" means any area designated and maintained by a ski area operator for skiing.

(5) "Ski area operator" means those persons, and their agents, officers, employees or representatives, who operate a ski area. [1979 c.665 §1]

30.975 Skiers assume certain risks. In accordance with ORS 31.600 and notwithstanding ORS 31.620 (2), an individual who engages in the sport of skiing, alpine or nordic, accepts and assumes the inherent risks of skiing insofar as they are reasonably obvious, expected or necessary. [1979 c.665 §2]

30.980 Notice to ski area operator of injury to skier; injuries resulting in death; statute of limitations; informing skiers of notice requirements. (1) A ski area operator shall be notified of any injury to a skier by registered or certified mail within 180 days after the injury or within 180 days after the skier discovers, or reasonably should have discovered, such injury.

(2) When an injury results in a skier's death, the required notice of the injury may be presented to the ski area operator by or on behalf of the personal representative of the deceased, or any person who may, under ORS 30.020, maintain an action for the wrongful death of the skier, within 180 days after

265

the date of the death which resulted from the injury. However, if the skier whose injury resulted in death presented a notice to the ski area operator that would have been sufficient under this section had the skier lived, notice of the death to the ski area operator is not necessary.

(3) An action against a ski area operator to recover damages for injuries to a skier shall be commenced within two years of the date of the injuries. However, ORS 12.160 and 12.190 apply to such actions.

(4) Failure to give notice as required by this section bars a claim for injuries or wrongful death unless:

(a) The ski area operator had knowledge of the injury or death within the 180-day period after its occurrence;

(b) The skier or skier's beneficiaries had good cause for failure to give notice as required by this section; or

(c) The ski area operator failed to comply with subsection (5) of this section.

(5) Ski area operators shall give to skiers, in a manner reasonably calculated to inform, notice of the requirements for notifying a ski area operator of injury and the effect of a failure to provide such notice under this section. [1979 c.665 §3]

30.985 Duties of skiers; effect of failure to comply. (1) Skiers shall have duties which include but are not limited to the following:

(a) Skiers who ski in any area not designated for skiing within the permit area assume the inherent risks thereof.

(b) Skiers shall be the sole judges of the limits of their skills and their ability to meet and overcome the inherent risks of skiing and shall maintain reasonable control of speed and course.

(c) Skiers shall abide by the directions and instructions of the ski area operator.

(d) Skiers shall familiarize themselves with posted information on location and degree of difficulty of trails and slopes to the extent reasonably possible before skiing on any slope or trail.

(e) Skiers shall not cross the uphill track of any surface lift except at points clearly designated by the ski area operator.

(f) Skiers shall not overtake any other skier except in such a manner as to avoid contact and shall grant the right of way to the overtaken skier.

(g) Skiers shall yield to other skiers when entering a trail or starting downhill.

(h) Skiers must wear retention straps or other devices to prevent runaway skis.

(i) Skiers shall not board rope tows, wire rope tows, j-bars, t-bars, ski lifts or other similar devices unless they have sufficient ability to use the devices, and skiers shall follow any written or verbal instructions that are given regarding the devices.

(j) Skiers, when involved in a skiing accident, shall not depart from the ski area without leaving their names and addresses if reasonably possible.

(k) A skier who is injured should, if reasonably possible, give notice of the injury to the ski area operator before leaving the ski area.

(L) Skiers shall not embark or disembark from a ski lift except at designated areas or by the authority of the ski area operator.

(2) Violation of any of the duties of skiers set forth in subsection (1) of this section entitles the ski area operator to withdraw the violator's privilege of skiing. [1979 c.665 §4]

30.990 Operators required to give skiers notice of duties. Ski area operators shall give notice to skiers of their duties under ORS 30.985 in a manner reasonably calculated to inform skiers of those duties. [1979 c.665 §5]_____

Chapter 31 — Tort Actions

New sections of law were enacted by the Legislative Assembly during its 2018 regular session and pertain to or are likely to be compiled in this ORS chapter. See sections in the following 2018 Oregon Laws chapters: 2018 Session Laws 0011

2017 EDITION

TORT ACTIONS

SPECIAL ACTIONS AND PROCEEDINGS

SPECIAL MOTION TO STRIKE

31.150   Special motion to strike; when available; burden of proof

31.152   Time for filing special motion to strike; discovery; attorney fees

31.155   Exempt actions; substantive law not affected

DEFENSES GENERALLY

31.180   Certain felonious conduct of plaintiff complete defense in tort actions; proof; exceptions

RULES GOVERNING PARTICULAR CLAIMS FOR RELIEF

(Defamation)

31.200   Liability of radio or television station personnel for defamation

31.205   Damages recoverable for defamation by radio, television, motion pictures, newspaper or printed periodical

31.210   When general damages allowed

31.215   Publication of correction or retraction upon demand

31.220   Effect of publication of correction or retraction prior to demand

31.225   Publisher's defenses and privileges not affected

(Wrongful Use of Civil Proceeding)

31.230   Wrongful use of civil proceeding; pleading; procedure

(Actions Against Health Practitioners and Health Care Facilities)

31.250   Mandatory dispute resolution for certain actions against health practitioners and health care facilities

(Resolution of Adverse Health Care Incidents)

(Temporary provisions relating to resolution of adverse health care incidents are compiled as notes following ORS 31.250)

(Actions Against Design Professionals)

31.300   Pleading requirements for actions against design professionals

(Actions Against Real Estate Licensees)

31.350   Pleading requirements for actions against real estate licensees

(Actions Arising From Injuries Caused by Dogs)

31.360   Proof required for claim of economic damages in action arising from injury caused by dog

ADVANCE PAYMENTS

31.550   "Advance payment" defined

31.555   Effect of advance payment; payment as satisfaction of judgment

31.560   Advance payment for death or personal injury not admission of liability; when advance payment made

31.565   Advance payment for property damage not admission of liability

COLLATERAL BENEFITS

31.580   Effect of collateral benefits

COMPARATIVE NEGLIGENCE

31.600   Contributory negligence not bar to recovery; comparative negligence standard; third party complaints

31.605   Special questions to trier of fact; jury not to be informed of settlement

31.610   Liability of defendants several only; determination of defendants' shares of monetary obligation; reallocation of uncollectible obligation; parties exempt from reallocation

31.615   Setoff of damages not allowed

31.620   Doctrines of last clear chance and implied assumption of risk abolished

DAMAGES

(Economic Damages)

31.700   Right to include medical expenses paid by parent or conservator in action to recover for damages to child; effect of consent to inclusion

(Verdict Form)

31.705   Economic and noneconomic damages separately set forth in verdict

(Noneconomic Damages)

31.710   Noneconomic damages; award; limit; "economic damages" and "noneconomic damages" defined

31.715   Limitation on recovery of noneconomic damages arising out of operation of motor vehicle; uninsured plaintiff; plaintiff driving under influence of intoxicants

(Punitive Damages)

31.725   Pleading punitive damages; motion to amend pleading to assert claim for punitive damages; hearing

31.730   Standards for award of punitive damages; required review of award by court; additional reduction of award for remedial measures

31.735   Distribution of punitive damages; notice to Department of Justice; order of application

31.740   When award of punitive damages against health practitioner prohibited

(Mitigation of Damages)

31.760   Evidence of nonuse of safety belt or harness to mitigate damages

CONTRIBUTION

31.800   Right of contribution among joint tortfeasors; limitations; subrogation of insurer; effect on indemnity right

31.805   Basis for proportional shares of tortfeasors

31.810   Enforcement of right of contribution; commencement of separate action; barring right of contribution; effect of satisfaction of judgment

31.815   Covenant not to sue; effect; notice

31.820   Severability

ASSIGNMENT OF CAUSE OF ACTION AGAINST INSURER

31.825   Assignment of cause of action against insurer

ABOLISHED COMMON LAW ACTIONS

31.980   Action for alienation of affections abolished

31.982   Action for criminal conversation abolished

31.010 [Repealed by 1981 c.898 §53]

31.020 [Repealed by 1981 c.898 §53]

31.030 [Repealed by 1981 c.898 §53]

31.040 [Repealed by 1981 c.898 §53]

31.050 [Renumbered 652.500]

SPECIAL MOTION TO STRIKE

31.150 Special motion to strike; when available; burden of proof. (1) A defendant may make a special motion to strike against a claim in a civil action described in subsection (2) of this section. The court shall grant the motion unless the plaintiff establishes in the manner provided by subsection (3) of this section that there is a probability that the plaintiff will prevail on the claim. The special motion to strike shall be treated as a motion to dismiss under ORCP 21 A but shall not be subject to ORCP 21 F. Upon granting the special motion to strike, the court shall enter a judgment of dismissal without prejudice. If the court denies a special motion to strike, the court shall enter a limited judgment denying the motion.
(2) A special motion to strike may be made under this section against any claim in a civil action that arises out of:
(a) Any oral statement made, or written statement or other document submitted, in a legislative, executive or judicial proceeding or other proceeding authorized by law;
(b) Any oral statement made, or written statement or other document submitted, in connection with an issue under consideration or review by a legislative, executive or judicial body or other proceeding authorized by law;
(c) Any oral statement made, or written statement or other document presented, in a place open to the public or a public forum in connection with an issue of public interest; or
(d) Any other conduct in furtherance of the exercise of the constitutional right of petition or the constitutional right of free speech in connection with a public issue or an issue of public interest.
(3) A defendant making a special motion to strike under the provisions of this section has the initial burden of making a prima facie showing that the claim against which the motion is made arises out of a statement, document or conduct described in subsection (2) of this section. If the defendant meets this burden, the burden shifts to the plaintiff in the action to establish that there is a probability that the plaintiff will prevail on the claim by presenting substantial evidence to support a prima facie case. If the plaintiff meets this burden, the court shall deny the motion.
(4) In making a determination under subsection (1) of this section, the court shall consider pleadings and supporting and opposing affidavits stating the facts upon which the liability or defense is based.
(5) If the court determines that the plaintiff has established a probability that the plaintiff will prevail on the claim:
(a) The fact that the determination has been made and the substance of the determination may not be admitted in evidence at any later stage of the case; and
(b) The determination does not affect the burden of proof or standard of proof that is applied in the proceeding. [Formerly 30.142; 2009 c.449 §1]

31.152 Time for filing special motion to strike; discovery; attorney fees. (1) A special motion to strike under ORS 31.150 must be filed within 60 days after the service of the complaint or, in the court's discretion, at any later time. A hearing shall be held on the motion not more than 30 days after the filing of the motion unless the docket conditions of the court require a later hearing.
(2) All discovery in the proceeding shall be stayed upon the filing of a special motion to strike under ORS 31.150. The stay of discovery shall remain in effect until entry of the judgment. The court, on motion and for good cause shown, may order that specified discovery be conducted notwithstanding the stay imposed by this subsection.
(3) A defendant who prevails on a special motion to strike made under ORS 31.150 shall be awarded reasonable attorney fees and costs. If the court finds that a special motion to strike is frivolous or is solely intended to cause unnecessary delay, the court shall award costs and reasonable attorney fees to a plaintiff who prevails on a special motion to strike.
(4) The purpose of the procedure established by this section and ORS 31.150 and 31.155 is to provide a defendant with the right to not proceed to trial in cases in which the plaintiff does not meet the burden specified in ORS 31.150 (3). This section and ORS 31.150 and 31.155 are to be liberally construed in favor of the exercise of the rights of expression described in ORS 31.150 (2). [Formerly 30.144; 2009 c.449 §3]

31.155 Exempt actions; substantive law not affected. (1) ORS 31.150 and 31.152 do not apply to an action brought by the Attorney General, a district attorney, a county counsel or a city attorney acting in an official capacity.
(2) ORS 31.150 and 31.152 create a procedure for seeking dismissal of claims described in ORS 31.150 (2) and do not affect the substantive law governing those claims. [Formerly 30.146]

DEFENSES GENERALLY

31.180 Certain felonious conduct of plaintiff complete defense in tort actions; proof; exceptions. (1) It is a complete defense in any civil action for personal injury or wrongful death that:
(a) The person damaged was engaged in conduct at the time that would constitute aggravated murder, murder or a Class A or a Class B felony; and
(b) The felonious conduct was a substantial factor contributing to the injury or death.
(2) To establish the defense described in this section, the defendant must prove by a preponderance of the evidence the fact that the person damaged was engaged in conduct that would constitute aggravated murder, murder or a Class A or a Class B felony.
(3) Nothing in this section affects any right of action under 42 U.S.C. 1983.

(4) The defense established by this section is not available if the injury or death resulted from a springgun or other device described in ORS 166.320 and the plaintiff establishes by a preponderance of the evidence that the use of the springgun or other device constituted a violation of ORS 166.320.

(5) The defense established by this section is not available if the injury or death resulted from the use of physical force that was not justifiable under the standards established by ORS 161.195 to 161.275. [Formerly 30.698]

RULES GOVERNING PARTICULAR CLAIMS FOR RELIEF

(Defamation)

31.200 Liability of radio or television station personnel for defamation. (1) The owner, licensee or operator of a radio or television broadcasting station, and the agents or employees of the owner, licensee or operator, shall not be liable for any damages for any defamatory statement published or uttered in a radio or television broadcast, by one other than the owner, licensee or operator, or agent or employee thereof, unless it is alleged and proved by the complaining party that the owner, licensee, operator, agent or employee failed to exercise due care to prevent the publication or utterance of such statement in such broadcast.

(2) In no event shall any owner, licensee or operator of a radio or television broadcasting station, or any agent or employee thereof, be liable for any damages for any defamatory statement published or uttered by one other than such owner, licensee, operator, agent or employee, in or as part of a radio or television broadcast by any candidate for public office, which broadcast cannot be censored by reason of federal statute or regulations of the Federal Communications Commission. [Formerly 30.150]

31.205 Damages recoverable for defamation by radio, television, motion pictures, newspaper or printed periodical. Except as provided in ORS 31.210, in an action for damages on account of a defamatory statement published or broadcast in a newspaper, magazine, other printed periodical, or by radio, television or motion pictures, the plaintiff may recover any general and special damages which, by competent evidence, the plaintiff can prove to have suffered as a direct and proximate result of the publication of the defamatory statement. [Formerly 30.155]

31.210 When general damages allowed. (1) In an action for damages on account of a defamatory statement published or broadcast in a newspaper, magazine, other printed periodical, or by radio, television or motion pictures, the plaintiff shall not recover general damages unless:

(a) A correction or retraction is demanded but not published as provided in ORS 31.215; or

(b) The plaintiff proves by a preponderance of the evidence that the defendant actually intended to defame the plaintiff.

(2) Where the plaintiff is entitled to recover general damages, the publication of a correction or retraction may be considered in mitigation of damages. [Formerly 30.160]

31.215 Publication of correction or retraction upon demand. (1) The demand for correction or retraction shall be in writing, signed by the defamed person or the attorney of the person and be delivered to the publisher of the defamatory statement, either personally, by registered mail or by certified mail with return receipt at the publisher's place of business or residence within 20 days after the defamed person receives actual knowledge of the defamatory statement. The demand shall specify which statements are false and defamatory and request that they be corrected or retracted. The demand may also refer to the sources from which the true facts may be ascertained with accuracy.

(2) The publisher of the defamatory statement shall have not more than two weeks after receipt of the demand for correction or retraction in which to investigate the demand; and, after making such investigation, the publisher shall publish the correction or retraction in:

(a) The first issue thereafter published, in the case of newspapers, magazines or other printed periodicals.

(b) The first broadcast or telecast thereafter made, in the case of radio or television stations.

(c) The first public exhibition thereafter made, in the case of motion picture theaters.

(3) The correction or retraction shall consist of a statement by the publisher substantially to the effect that the defamatory statements previously made are not factually supported and that the publisher regrets the original publication thereof.

(4) The correction or retraction shall be published in substantially as conspicuous a manner as the defamatory statement. [Formerly 30.165]

31.220 Effect of publication of correction or retraction prior to demand. A correction or retraction published prior to notice of demand therefor shall have the same effect as a correction or retraction after demand, if the requirements of ORS 31.215 (2), (3) and (4) are substantially complied with. [Formerly 30.170]

31.225 Publisher's defenses and privileges not affected. Nothing in ORS 31.205 to 31.220 shall be deemed to affect any defense or privilege which the publisher may possess by virtue of existing law. [Formerly 30.175]

(Wrongful Use of Civil Proceeding)

31.230 Wrongful use of civil proceeding; pleading; procedure. (1) In order to bring a claim for wrongful use of a civil proceeding against another, a person shall not be required to plead or prove special injury beyond the expense and other consequences normally associated with defending against unfounded legal claims.

(2) The filing of a civil action within 60 days of the running of the statute of limitations for the purpose of preserving and evaluating the claim when the action is dismissed within 120 days after the date of filing shall not constitute grounds for a claim for wrongful use of a civil proceeding under subsection (1) of this section.

(3) A claim for damages for wrongful use of a civil proceeding shall be brought in an original action after the proceeding which is the subject matter of the claim is concluded. [Formerly 30.895]

(Actions Against Health Practitioners and Health Care Facilities)

31.250 Mandatory dispute resolution for certain actions against health practitioners and health care facilities.

(1) In any action described in subsection (6) of this section, all parties to the action and their attorneys must participate in some form of dispute resolution within 270 days after the action is filed unless:

(a) The action is settled or otherwise resolved within 270 days after the action is filed; or

(b) All parties to the action agree in writing to waive dispute resolution under this section.

(2) Dispute resolution under this section may consist of arbitration, mediation or a judicial settlement conference.

(3) Within 270 days after filing an action described in subsection (6) of this section, the parties or their attorneys must file a certificate indicating that the parties and attorneys have complied with the requirements of this section.

(4) The court may impose appropriate sanctions against any party or attorney who:

(a) Fails to attend an arbitration hearing, mediation session or judicial settlement conference conducted for the purposes of the requirements of this section;

(b) Fails to act in good faith in any arbitration, mediation or judicial settlement conference conducted for the purposes of the requirements of this section;

(c) Fails to timely submit any documents required for an arbitration, mediation or judicial settlement conference conducted for the purposes of the requirements of this section; or

(d) Fails to have a person with authority to approve a resolution of the action available at the time of any arbitration hearing, mediation session or judicial settlement conference conducted for the purposes of the requirements of this section, unless the party or attorney receives from the court, before the hearing, session or conference commences, an exemption from the requirements of this paragraph.

(5) This section does not apply to parties to an action described in subsection (6) of this section that have participated in a discussion and mediation under sections 3 and 5, chapter 5, Oregon Laws 2013.

(6) The provisions of this section apply to any action in which a claim for damages is made against a health practitioner, as described in ORS 31.740, or against a health care facility, as defined in ORS 442.015, based on negligence, unauthorized rendering of health care or product liability under ORS 30.900 to 30.920. [2003 c.598 §54; 2013 c.5 §13]

Note: The amendments to 31.250 by section 14, chapter 5, Oregon Laws 2013, become operative December 31, 2023. See section 22, chapter 5, Oregon Laws 2013. The text that is operative on and after December 31, 2023, is set forth for the user's convenience.

31.250. (1) In any action described in subsection (5) of this section, all parties to the action and their attorneys must participate in some form of dispute resolution within 270 days after the action is filed unless:

(a) The action is settled or otherwise resolved within 270 days after the action is filed; or

(b) All parties to the action agree in writing to waive dispute resolution under this section.

(2) Dispute resolution under this section may consist of arbitration, mediation or a judicial settlement conference.

(3) Within 270 days after filing an action described in subsection (5) of this section, the parties or their attorneys must file a certificate indicating that the parties and attorneys have complied with the requirements of this section.

(4) The court may impose appropriate sanctions against any party or attorney who:

(a) Fails to attend an arbitration hearing, mediation session or judicial settlement conference conducted for the purposes of the requirements of this section;

(b) Fails to act in good faith in any arbitration, mediation or judicial settlement conference conducted for the purposes of the requirements of this section;

(c) Fails to timely submit any documents required for an arbitration, mediation or judicial settlement conference conducted for the purposes of the requirements of this section; or

(d) Fails to have a person with authority to approve a resolution of the action available at the time of any arbitration hearing, mediation session or judicial settlement conference conducted for the purposes of the requirements of this section, unless the party or attorney receives from the court, before the hearing, session or conference commences, an exemption from the requirements of this paragraph.

(5) The provisions of this section apply to any action in which a claim for damages is made against a health practitioner, as described in ORS 31.740, or against a health care facility, as defined in ORS 442.015, based on negligence, unauthorized rendering of health care or product liability under ORS 30.900 to 30.920.

(Resolution of Adverse Health Care Incidents)

Note: Sections 1 to 10, 17 to 19 and 23, chapter 5, Oregon Laws 2013, provide:

Sec. 1. Definitions. As used in sections 1 to 10 of this 2013 Act:

(1) "Adverse health care incident" means an objective, definable and unanticipated consequence of patient care that is usually preventable and results in the death of or serious physical injury to the patient.

(2) "Health care facility" has the meaning given that term in ORS 442.015.

(3) "Health care provider" means a person practicing within the scope of the person's license, registration or certification to practice as:

(a) A psychologist under ORS 675.030 to 675.070, 675.085 and 675.090;

(b) An occupational therapist under ORS 675.230 to 675.300;

(c) A physician under ORS 677.100 to 677.228;

(d) An emergency medical services provider under ORS chapter 682;

(e) A podiatric physician and surgeon under ORS 677.820 to 677.840;

(f) A registered nurse under ORS 678.010 to 678.410;

(g) A dentist under ORS 679.060 to 679.180;

(h) A dental hygienist under ORS 680.040 to 680.100;

(i) A denturist under ORS 680.515 to 680.535;

(j) An audiologist or speech-language pathologist under ORS 681.250 to 681.350;

(k) An optometrist under ORS 683.040 to 683.155 and 683.170 to 683.220;

(L) A chiropractor under ORS 684.040 to 684.105;

(m) A naturopath under ORS 685.060 to 685.110, 685.125 and 685.135;

(n) A massage therapist under ORS 687.011 to 687.250;

(o) A direct entry midwife under ORS 687.405 to 687.495;

(p) A physical therapist under ORS 688.040 to 688.145;

(q) A medical imaging licensee under ORS 688.445 to 688.525;

(r) A pharmacist under ORS 689.151 and 689.225 to 689.285;

(s) A physician assistant under ORS 677.505 to 677.525; or

(t) A professional counselor or marriage and family therapist under ORS 675.715 to 675.835.

(4) "Patient" means the patient or, if the patient is a minor, is deceased or has been medically confirmed by the patient's treating physician to be incapable of making decisions for purposes of sections 1 to 10 of this 2013 Act, the patient's representative as provided in section 8 of this 2013 Act. [2013 c.5 §1]

Sec. 2. Notice of adverse health care incident. (1)(a) When an adverse health care incident occurs in a health care facility or a location operated by a health care facility, the health care facility may file a notice of adverse health care incident with the Oregon Patient Safety Commission in the form and manner provided by the commission by rule.

(b) If a health care facility files a notice of adverse health care incident under this subsection, the health care facility shall provide a copy of the notice to the patient.

(c) A notice filed under this subsection may not include the name of a health care provider, but the health care facility filing the notice shall notify any health care providers involved in the adverse health care incident of the notice.

(2)(a) When an adverse health care incident occurs outside of a health care facility or a location operated by a health care facility, the health care provider treating the patient or the employer of the health care provider may file a notice of adverse health care incident with the commission in the form and manner provided by the commission by rule.

(b) If a health care provider or employer files a notice of adverse health care incident under this subsection, the health care provider or employer shall provide a copy of the notice to the patient.

(c) If an employer files the notice under this subsection, the notice may not include the name of the health care provider, but the employer shall notify each health care provider involved in the adverse health care incident of the notice.

(3) A patient may file a notice of adverse health care incident with the commission in the form and manner provided by the commission by rule. When the commission receives a notice of adverse health care incident from a patient under this subsection, the commission shall notify all health care facilities and health care providers named in the notice within seven days after receiving the notice.

(4) A notice of adverse health care incident filed under this section is not:

(a) A written claim or demand for payment.

(b) A claim for purposes of ORS 742.400.

(5) The filing of a notice of adverse health care incident as provided in this section satisfies the notice requirements of ORS 30.275.

(6) An inmate as defined in ORS 30.642 may not file a notice of adverse health care incident under this section. [2013 c.5 §2]

Sec. 3. Discussion of adverse health care incident. (1) A health care facility or health care provider who files or is named in a notice of adverse health care incident filed under section 2 of this 2013 Act and the patient involved in the incident may engage in a discussion regarding the incident within the time established by the Oregon Patient Safety Commission by rule.

(2) The health care facility or health care provider who files or is named in the notice shall notify the patient and all health care facilities and health care providers involved in the adverse health care incident of the date, time and location of the discussion and shall reasonably accommodate all persons that wish to attend.

(3) The patient and the health care facility or health care provider who files or is named in the notice may include other persons in the discussion.

(4) Within the time established by the commission by rule, the health care facility or health care provider who files or is named in the notice may:

(a) Communicate to the patient the steps the health care facility or health care provider will take to prevent future occurrences of the adverse health care incident; and

(b)(A) Determine that no offer of compensation for the adverse health care incident is warranted and communicate that determination to the patient orally or in writing; or

(B) Determine that an offer of compensation for the adverse health care incident is warranted and extend that offer in writing to the patient.

(5) If a health care facility or health care provider makes an offer of compensation under subsection (4) of this section, the facility or provider shall advise the patient of the patient's right to seek legal advice before accepting the offer.

(6) Except for offers of compensation extended under subsection (4) of this section, discussions between the health care facility or health care provider and the patient about the amount of compensation offered under subsection (4) of this section must remain oral.

(7) The health care facility or health care provider and the patient may agree to extend the time limit established by rule of the commission under this section, but a time limit may not be extended to more than 180 days after the notice of adverse health care incident is filed under section 2 of this 2013 Act unless the health care facility or health care provider and the patient also agree to extend the statute of limitations applicable to a negligence claim.

(8) If the patient accepts an offer of compensation made under subsection (4) of this section, the health care facility or health care provider who made the offer shall notify the commission.

(9) The commission shall request a report indicating the status of the matter from the person that filed the notice of adverse health care incident under section 2 of this 2013 Act within 180 days after the date the notice was filed. If the matter is not resolved 180 days after the notice was filed, the commission may request additional reports from the person that filed the notice as necessary. [2013 c.5 §3]

Sec. 4. Discussion communications. (1) As used in this section, "discussion communication" means:

(a) All communications, written and oral, that are made in the course of a discussion under section 3 of this 2013 Act; and

(b) All memoranda, work products, documents and other materials that are prepared for or submitted in the course of or in connection with a discussion under section 3 of this 2013 Act.

(2) Discussion communications and offers of compensation made under section 3 of this 2013 Act:

(a) Do not constitute an admission of liability.

(b) Are confidential and may not be disclosed.

(c) Except as provided in subsection (3) of this section, are not admissible as evidence in any subsequent adjudicatory proceeding and may not be disclosed by the parties in any subsequent adjudicatory proceeding.

(3)(a) A party may move the court or other decision maker to admit as evidence in a subsequent adjudicatory proceeding a discussion communication that contradicts a statement made during the subsequent adjudicatory proceeding. The court or other decision maker shall allow a discussion communication that contradicts a statement made at a subsequent adjudicatory proceeding into evidence only if the discussion communication is material to the claims presented in the subsequent adjudicatory proceeding.

(b) A party may not move to admit expressions of regret or apology that are inadmissible under ORS 677.082.

(4) Communications, memoranda, work products, documents and other materials, otherwise subject to discovery, that were not prepared specifically for use in a discussion under section 3 of this 2013 Act, are not confidential.

(5) Any communication, memorandum, work product or document that, before its use in a discussion under section 3 of this 2013 Act, was a public record as defined in ORS 192.410 [renumbered 192.311] remains subject to disclosure to the extent provided by ORS 192.410 to 192.505 [series became 192.311 to 192.478].

(6) The limitations on admissibility and disclosure in subsequent adjudicatory proceedings imposed by this section apply to any subsequent judicial proceeding, administrative proceeding or arbitration proceeding. The limitations on disclosure imposed by this section include disclosure during any discovery conducted as part of a subsequent adjudicatory proceeding, and a person that is prohibited from disclosing information under the provisions of this section may not be compelled to reveal confidential communications or agreements in any discovery conducted as part of a subsequent adjudicatory proceeding. [2013 c.5 §4]

Sec. 5. Mediation. (1) If a discussion under section 3 of this 2013 Act does not result in the resolution of an adverse health care incident, the patient and the health care facility or health care provider who files or is named in a notice of adverse health care incident filed under section 2 of this 2013 Act may enter into mediation.

(2) The Oregon Patient Safety Commission shall develop and maintain a panel of qualified individuals to serve as mediators. The parties, by mutual agreement, may choose any mediator from within or outside the panel.

(3) The parties shall bear the cost of mediation equally unless otherwise mutually agreed.

(4) Other persons that may participate in the mediation include, but are not limited to:

(a) Members of the patient's family, at the discretion of the patient;

(b) Attorneys for the patient, the health care facility and the health care provider;

(c) Professional liability insurance carriers;

(d) Risk management personnel; and

(e) Any lien holder with an interest in the dispute.

(5) If a health care facility or health care provider makes an offer of compensation as part of a mediation under this section, the facility or provider shall advise the patient of the patient's right to seek legal advice before accepting the offer.

(6) Mediation under this section is subject to ORS 36.210, 36.220, 36.222, 36.224, 36.226, 36.232, 36.234, 36.236 and 36.238. [2013 c.5 §5]

Sec. 6. Payment and resolution. (1) A payment made to a patient under section 3 of this 2013 Act or as a result of a mediation under section 5 of this 2013 Act is not a payment resulting from a written claim or demand for payment.

(2) A health care provider or health care facility may require the patient to execute all documents and obtain any necessary court approval to resolve an adverse health care incident. The parties shall negotiate the form of such documents or court approval as necessary. [2013 c.5 §6]

Sec. 7. Statute of limitations; evidence of offers and payments. (1) The provisions of sections 3 and 5 of this 2013 Act relating to discussion and mediation do not prevent a patient from bringing a civil action for negligence unless the patient signed a release of the claim.

(2) The statute of limitations applicable to a negligence claim is tolled for 180 days, or another period agreed upon by the patient and the health care facility or health care provider who files or is named in the notice of adverse health care incident filed under section 2 of this 2013 Act, from the date the notice is filed.

(3) If a civil action based on an adverse health care incident is commenced, the court shall inform the parties of the opportunity to participate in the notice, discussion and mediation process under sections 2, 3 and 5 of this 2013 Act.

(4) Except as provided in section 4 of this 2013 Act, evidence that a party participated or did not participate in the notice, discussion and mediation process under sections 2, 3 and 5 of this 2013 Act is inadmissible in any adjudicatory proceeding.

271

(5) Evidence of an offer of compensation, and the amount, payment or acceptance of any compensation, under section 3 or 5 of this 2013 Act is inadmissible in any adjudicatory proceeding. However, any judgment in favor of the patient must be reduced by the amount of any compensation paid under sections 3 and 5 of this 2013 Act. [2013 c.5 §7]

Sec. 8. Patient representatives. (1) A patient who is a minor, is deceased or has been medically confirmed by the patient's treating physician to be incapable of making decisions for purposes of sections 1 to 10 of this 2013 Act may be represented for purposes of sections 1 to 10 of this 2013 Act by the first of the persons, in the following order of priority, who can be located upon reasonable effort by the health care facility or health care provider and who is willing to serve as the patient's representative:

(a) A guardian of the patient who is authorized to make health care decisions for the patient.

(b) The spouse of the patient.

(c) A parent of the patient.

(d) A majority of the adult children of the patient who can be located.

(e) A majority of the adult siblings of the patient who can be located.

(f) An adult friend of the patient.

(g) A person, other than a health care provider who files or is named in a notice of adverse health care incident under section 2 of this 2013 Act, appointed by a hospital under ORS 127.760.

(2) The conservator of the patient appointed under ORS chapter 125 may serve as a patient's representative with the patient's representative designated under subsection (1) of this section if the conservator's representation is necessary to consider an offer of compensation under section 3 or 5 of this 2013 Act. [2013 c.5 §8]

Sec. 9. Duties of Oregon Patient Safety Commission. (1) The Oregon Patient Safety Commission shall make rules establishing requirements and procedures as necessary to implement sections 1 to 10 of this 2013 Act, including, but not limited to:

(a) Procedures for filing a notice of adverse health care incident under section 2 of this 2013 Act and for conducting discussions and mediations under sections 3 and 5 of this 2013 Act.

(b) The form of the notice of adverse health care incident under section 2 of this 2013 Act.

(2) The commission shall use notices of adverse health care incidents filed under section 2 of this 2013 Act to:

(a) Establish quality improvement techniques to reduce patient care errors that contribute to adverse health care incidents.

(b) Develop evidence-based prevention practices to improve patient outcomes and disseminate information about those practices.

(c) Upon the request of a health care facility or health care provider, assist the facility or provider in reducing the frequency of a particular adverse health care incident, including, but not limited to, determining the underlying cause of the incident and providing advice regarding preventing reoccurrence of the incident. [2013 c.5 §9]

Sec. 10. Use of information by Oregon Patient Safety Commission. (1) The Oregon Patient Safety Commission may disseminate information relating to a notice of adverse health care incident filed under section 2 of this 2013 Act to the public and to health care providers and health care facilities not involved in the adverse health care incident as necessary to meet the goals described in section 9 of this 2013 Act. Information disclosed under this subsection may not identify a health care facility, health care provider or patient involved in the adverse health care incident.

(2) The commission may not disclose any information provided pursuant to a discussion under section 3 of this 2013 Act to a regulatory agency or licensing board.

(3) The commission may use and disclose information provided pursuant to a discussion under section 3 of this 2013 Act as necessary to assist a health care facility or health care provider involved in an adverse health care incident in determining the cause of and potential mitigation of the incident. If the commission discloses information under this subsection to a person not involved in the incident, the information may not identify a health care facility, health care provider or patient involved in the incident.

(4) A regulatory agency, licensing board, health care facility, health insurer or credentialing entity may not ask the commission, a health care facility, a health care provider or other person whether a facility or provider has filed a notice of adverse health care incident or use the fact that a notice of adverse health care incident was filed as the basis of disciplinary, regulatory, licensure or credentialing action. This subsection does not prevent a person from using information, if the information is otherwise available, to engage in quality review of patient care or as the basis of imposing a restriction, limitation, loss or denial of privileges on a health care provider or other action against a health care provider based on a finding of medical incompetence, unprofessional conduct, physical incapacity or impairment. [2013 c.5 §10]

Sec. 17. Task Force on Resolution of Adverse Health Care Incidents. (1) The Task Force on Resolution of Adverse Health Care Incidents is established, consisting of 14 members appointed as follows:

(a) The President of the Senate shall appoint two members from among members of the Senate as follows:

(A) One member from the Democratic party.

(B) One member from the Republican party.

(b) The Speaker of the House of Representatives shall appoint two members from among members of the House of Representatives as follows:

(A) One member from the Democratic party.

(B) One member from the Republican party.

(c) The Governor shall appoint 10 members, including:

(A) At least three members who are physicians licensed under ORS chapter 677 and in active practice;

(B) At least three members who are trial lawyers;

(C) One member who is a representative of the hospital industry; and

(D) One member who is an advocate for patient safety.

(2) The task force shall:

(a) Evaluate the implementation and effects of sections 1 to 10 of this 2013 Act; and

(b) Before December 31 of each year, report to an appropriate committee or interim committee of the Legislative Assembly on the implementation and effects of sections 1 to 10 of this 2013 Act.

(3) The task force may recommend legislation to be introduced to improve the resolution of adverse health care incidents.

(4) A majority of the voting members of the task force constitutes a quorum for the transaction of business.

(5) Official action by the task force requires the approval of a majority of the voting members of the task force.

(6) The Governor shall select one member of the task force to serve as chairperson and another to serve as vice chairperson, for the terms and with the duties and powers necessary for the performance of the functions of such offices as the Governor determines.

(7) The term of a member of the task force is four years, but a member serves at the pleasure of the appointing authority. A member may be reappointed. Before the expiration of the term of a member, the appointing authority shall appoint a successor or reappoint the member. If there is a vacancy for any cause, the appointing authority shall make an appointment to become immediately effective.

(8) Members of the Legislative Assembly appointed to the task force are nonvoting members of the task force and may act in an advisory capacity only.

(9) The task force shall meet at times and places specified by the call of the chairperson or of a majority of the voting members of the task force.

(10) The task force may adopt rules necessary for the operation of the task force.

(11) The Oregon Patient Safety Commission shall provide staff support to the task force.

(12) Members of the task force who are not members of the Legislative Assembly are not entitled to compensation, but may be reimbursed for actual and necessary travel and other expenses incurred by them in the performance of their official duties in the manner and amounts provided for in ORS 292.495. Claims for expenses incurred in performing functions of the task force shall be paid out of funds appropriated to the commission for purposes of the task force.

(13) All agencies of state government, as defined in ORS 174.111, are directed to assist the task force in the performance of its duties and, to the extent permitted by laws relating to confidentiality, to furnish such information and advice as the members of the task force consider necessary to perform their duties. [2013 c.5 §17]

Sec. 18. Report. On or before October 1, 2018, the Task Force on Resolution of Adverse Health Care Incidents shall report to an appropriate committee or interim committee of the Legislative Assembly. The report must evaluate whether any improvements to the process are necessary. [2013 c.5 §18]

Sec. 19. Notwithstanding the terms of office specified in section 17 of this 2013 Act, of the members first appointed by the Governor to the Task Force on Resolution of Adverse Health Care Incidents:

(1) Three shall serve for a term ending June 30, 2014.

(2) Four shall serve for a term ending June 30, 2015.

(3) Three shall serve for a term ending June 30, 2016. [2013 c.5 §19]

Sec. 23. Sections 1 to 10 of this 2013 Act and the amendments to ORS 30.278, 31.250 and 743.056 [renumbered 742.407] by sections 11, 13 and 15 of this 2013 Act apply only to adverse health care incidents that occur on or after the operative date specified in section 21 of this 2013 Act [July 1, 2014]. [2013 c.5 §23]

Note: Section 20, chapter 5, Oregon Laws 2013, provides:

Sec. 20. Sections 1 to 10 and 17 to 19 of this 2013 Act are repealed on December 31, 2023. [2013 c.5 §20]

(Actions Against Design Professionals)

31.300 Pleading requirements for actions against design professionals. (1) As used in this section, "design professional" means an architect, landscape architect, professional engineer or professional land surveyor registered under ORS chapter 671 or 672 or licensed to practice as an architect, landscape architect, professional engineer or professional land surveyor in another state.

(2) A complaint, cross-claim, counterclaim or third-party complaint asserting a claim against a design professional that arises out of the provision of services within the course and scope of the activities for which the person is registered or licensed may not be filed unless the claimant's attorney certifies that the attorney has consulted a design professional with similar credentials who is qualified, available and willing to testify to admissible facts and opinions sufficient to create a question of fact as to the liability of the design professional. The certification must contain a statement that a design professional with similar credentials who is qualified to testify as to the standard of professional skill and care applicable to the alleged facts, is available and willing to testify that:

(a) The alleged conduct of the design professional failed to meet the standard of professional skill and care ordinarily provided by other design professionals with similar credentials, experience and expertise and practicing under the same or similar circumstances; and

(b) The alleged conduct was a cause of the claimed damages, losses or other harm.

(3) In lieu of providing the certification described in subsection (2) of this section, the claimant's attorney may file with the court at the time of filing a complaint, cross-claim, counterclaim or third-party complaint an affidavit that states:

(a) The applicable statute of limitations is about to expire;

(b) The certification required under subsection (2) of this section will be filed within 30 days after filing the complaint, cross-claim, counterclaim or third-party complaint or such longer time as the court may allow for good cause shown; and

(c) The attorney has made such inquiry as is reasonable under the circumstances and has made a good faith attempt to consult with at least one registered or licensed design professional who is qualified to testify as to the standard of professional skill and care applicable to the alleged facts, as required by subsection (2) of this section.

(4) Upon motion of the design professional, the court shall enter judgment dismissing any complaint, cross-claim, counterclaim or third-party complaint against any design professional that fails to comply with the requirements of this section.

(5) This section applies only to a complaint, cross-claim, counterclaim or third-party complaint against a design professional by any plaintiff who:

(a) Is a design professional, contractor, subcontractor or other person providing labor, materials or services for the real property improvement that is the subject of the claim;

(b) Is the owner, lessor, lessee, renter or occupier of the real property improvement that is the subject of the claim;

(c) Is involved in the operation or management of the real property improvement that is the subject of the claim;

(d) Has contracted with or otherwise employed the design professional; or

(e) Is a person for whose benefit the design professional performed services. [2003 c.418 §1; 2015 c.610 §1]

(Actions Against Real Estate Licensees)

31.350 Pleading requirements for actions against real estate licensees. (1) As used in this section, "real estate licensee" has the meaning given that term in ORS 696.010.

(2) A complaint, cross-claim, counterclaim or third-party complaint asserting a claim of professional negligence against a real estate licensee for conduct occurring within the course and scope of the professional real estate activity for which the individual is licensed may not be filed unless the claimant's attorney certifies that the attorney has consulted a real estate licensee who is qualified, available and willing to testify to admissible facts and opinions sufficient to create a question of fact as to the liability of the real estate licensee. The certification required by this section must be filed with or be made part of the original complaint, cross-claim, counterclaim or third-party complaint. The certification must contain a statement that a real estate licensee who is qualified to testify as to the standard of care applicable to the alleged facts, is available and willing to testify that:

(a) The alleged conduct of the real estate licensee failed to meet the standard of professional care applicable to the real estate licensee in the circumstances alleged; and

(b) The alleged conduct was a cause of the claimed damages, losses or other harm.

(3) In lieu of providing the certification described in subsection (2) of this section, the claimant's attorney may file with the court at the time of filing a complaint, cross-claim, counterclaim or third-party complaint an affidavit that states:

(a) The applicable statute of limitations is about to expire;

(b) The certification required under subsection (2) of this section will be filed within 30 days after filing the complaint, cross-claim, counterclaim or third-party complaint or such longer time as the court may allow for good cause shown; and

(c) The attorney has made such inquiry as is reasonable under the circumstances and has made a good faith attempt to consult with at least one real estate licensee who is qualified to testify as to the standard of care applicable to the alleged facts, as required by subsection (2) of this section.

(4) Upon motion of the real estate licensee, the court shall enter judgment dismissing any complaint, cross-claim, counterclaim or third-party complaint against any real estate licensee who fails to comply with the requirements of this section.

(5) This section applies only to a complaint, cross-claim, counterclaim or third-party complaint against a real estate licensee by any plaintiff who:

(a) Has contracted with or otherwise employed the real estate licensee; or

(b) Is a person for whose benefit the real estate licensee performed services. [2005 c.277 §1; 2007 c.319 §25]

(Actions Arising From Injuries Caused by Dogs)

31.360 Proof required for claim of economic damages in action arising from injury caused by dog. (1) For the purpose of establishing a claim for economic damages, as defined in ORS 31.710, in an action arising from an injury caused by a dog:

(a) The plaintiff need not prove that the owner of the dog could foresee that the dog would cause the injury; and

(b) The owner of the dog may not assert as a defense that the owner could not foresee that the dog would cause the injury.

(2) This section does not prevent the owner of a dog that caused an injury from asserting that the dog was provoked, or from asserting any other defense that may be available to the owner.

(3) This section does not affect the requirements for an award of punitive damages provided in ORS 31.730 (1). [2007 c.402 §1]

ADVANCE PAYMENTS

31.550 "Advance payment" defined. As used in ORS 12.155 and 31.550 to 31.565, "advance payment" means compensation for the injury or death of a person or the injury or destruction of property prior to the determination of legal liability therefor. [Formerly 18.500]

31.555 Effect of advance payment; payment as satisfaction of judgment. (1) If judgment is entered against a party on whose behalf an advance payment referred to in ORS 31.560 or 31.565 has been made and in favor of a party for whose benefit any such advance payment has been received, the amount of the judgment shall be reduced by the amount of any such payments in the manner provided in subsection (3) of this section. However, nothing in ORS 12.155, 31.560 and 31.565 and this section authorizes the person making such payments to recover such advance payment if no damages are awarded or to recover any amount by which the advance payment exceeds the award of damages.

(2) If judgment is entered against a party who is insured under a policy of liability insurance against such judgment and in favor of a party who has received benefits that have been the basis for a reimbursement payment by such insurer under ORS 742.534, the amount of the judgment shall be reduced by reason of such benefits in the manner provided in subsection (3) of this section.

(3)(a) The amount of any advance payment referred to in subsection (1) of this section may be submitted by the party making the payment, in the manner provided in ORCP 68 C(4) for the submission of disbursements.

(b) The amount of any benefits referred to in subsection (2) of this section, diminished in proportion to the amount of negligence attributable to the party in favor of whom the judgment was entered and diminished to an amount no greater than the reimbursement payment made by the insurer under ORS 742.534, may be submitted by the insurer which has made the reimbursement payment, in the manner provided in ORCP 68 C(4) for the submission of disbursements.

(c) Unless timely objections are filed as provided in ORCP 68 C(4), the court clerk shall apply the amounts claimed pursuant to this subsection in partial satisfaction of the judgment. Such partial satisfaction shall be allowed without regard to whether the party claiming the reduction is otherwise entitled to costs and disbursements in the action. [Formerly 18.510]

31.560 Advance payment for death or personal injury not admission of liability; when advance payment made. (1) Advance payment made for damages arising from the death or injury of a person is not an admission of liability for the death or injury by the person making the payment unless the parties to the payment agree to the contrary in writing.

(2) For the purpose of subsection (1) of this section, advance payment is made when payment is made with or to:

(a) The injured person;

(b) A person acting on behalf of the injured person with the consent of the injured person; or

(c) Any other person entitled to recover damages on account of the injury or death of the injured or deceased person. [Formerly 18.520]

31.565 Advance payment for property damage not admission of liability. Any advance payment made for damages arising from injury or destruction of property is not an admission of liability for the injury or destruction by the person making the payment unless the parties to the payment agree to the contrary in writing. [Formerly 18.530]

COLLATERAL BENEFITS

31.580 Effect of collateral benefits. (1) In a civil action, when a party is awarded damages for bodily injury or death of a person which are to be paid by another party to the action, and the party awarded damages or person injured or deceased received benefits for the injury or death other than from the party who is to pay the damages, the court may deduct from the amount of damages awarded, before the entry of a judgment, the total amount of those collateral benefits other than:

(a) Benefits which the party awarded damages, the person injured or that person's estate is obligated to repay;

(b) Life insurance or other death benefits;

(c) Insurance benefits for which the person injured or deceased or members of that person's family paid premiums; and

(d) Retirement, disability and pension plan benefits, and federal Social Security benefits.

(2) Evidence of the benefit described in subsection (1) of this section and the cost of obtaining it is not admissible at trial, but shall be received by the court by affidavit submitted after the verdict by any party to the action. [Formerly 18.580]

COMPARATIVE NEGLIGENCE

31.600 Contributory negligence not bar to recovery; comparative negligence standard; third party complaints. (1) Contributory negligence shall not bar recovery in an action by any person or the legal representative of the person to recover damages for death or injury to person or property if the fault attributable to the claimant was not greater than the combined fault of all persons specified in subsection (2) of this section, but any damages allowed shall be diminished in the proportion to the percentage of fault attributable to the claimant. This section is not intended to create or abolish any defense.

(2) The trier of fact shall compare the fault of the claimant with the fault of any party against whom recovery is sought, the fault of third party defendants who are liable in tort to the claimant, and the fault of any person with whom the claimant has settled. The failure of a claimant to make a direct claim against a third party defendant does not affect the requirement that the fault of the third party defendant be considered by the trier of fact under this subsection. Except for persons who have settled with the claimant, there shall be no comparison of fault with any person:

(a) Who is immune from liability to the claimant;

(b) Who is not subject to the jurisdiction of the court; or

(c) Who is not subject to action because the claim is barred by a statute of limitation or statute of ultimate repose.

(3) A defendant who files a third party complaint against a person alleged to be at fault in the matter, or who alleges that a person who has settled with the claimant is at fault in the matter, has the burden of proof in establishing:

(a) The fault of the third party defendant or the fault of the person who settled with the claimant; and

(b) That the fault of the third party defendant or the person who settled with the claimant was a contributing cause to the injury or death under the law applicable in the matter.

(4) Any party to an action may seek to establish that the fault of a person should not be considered by the trier of fact by reason that the person does not meet the criteria established by subsection (2) of this section for the consideration of fault by the trier of fact.

(5) This section does not prevent a party from alleging that the party was not at fault in the matter because the injury or death was the sole and exclusive fault of a person who is not a party in the matter. [Formerly 18.470]

31.605 Special questions to trier of fact; jury not to be informed of settlement. (1) When requested by any party the trier of fact shall answer special questions indicating:

(a) The amount of damages to which a party seeking recovery would be entitled, assuming that party not to be at fault.

(b) The degree of fault of each person specified in ORS 31.600 (2). The degree of each person's fault so determined shall be expressed as a percentage of the total fault attributable to all persons considered by the trier of fact pursuant to ORS 31.600.

(2) A jury shall be informed of the legal effect of its answer to the questions listed in subsection (1) of this section.

(3) The jury shall not be informed of any settlement made by the claimant for damages arising out of the injury or death that is the subject of the action.

(4) For the purposes of subsection (1) of this section, the court may order that two or more persons be considered a single person for the purpose of determining the degree of fault of the persons specified in ORS 31.600 (2). [Formerly 18.480]

31.610 Liability of defendants several only; determination of defendants' shares of monetary obligation; reallocation of uncollectible obligation; parties exempt from reallocation. (1) Except as otherwise provided in this section, in any civil action arising out of bodily injury, death or property damage, including claims for emotional injury or distress, loss of care, comfort, companionship and society, and loss of consortium, the liability of each defendant for damages awarded to plaintiff shall be several only and shall not be joint.

(2) In any action described in subsection (1) of this section, the court shall determine the award of damages to each claimant in accordance with the percentages of fault determined by the trier of fact under ORS 31.605 and shall enter judgment against each party determined to be liable. The court shall enter a judgment in favor of the plaintiff against any third party defendant who is found to be liable in any degree, even if the plaintiff did not make a direct claim against the third party defendant. The several liability of each defendant and third party defendant shall be set out separately in the judgment, based on the percentages of fault determined by the trier of fact under ORS 31.605. The court shall calculate and state in the judgment a monetary amount reflecting the share of the obligation of each person specified in ORS 31.600 (2). Each person's share of the obligation shall be equal to the total amount of the damages found by the trier of fact, with no reduction for amounts paid in settlement of the claim or by way of contribution, multiplied by the percentage of fault determined for the person by the trier of fact under ORS 31.605.

(3) Upon motion made not later than one year after judgment has become final by lapse of time for appeal or after appellate review, the court shall determine whether all or part of a party's share of the obligation determined under subsection (2) of this section is uncollectible. If the court determines that all or part of any party's share of the obligation is uncollectible, the court shall reallocate any uncollectible share among the other parties. The reallocation shall be made on the basis of each party's respective percentage of fault determined by the trier of fact under ORS 31.605. The claimant's share of the reallocation shall be based on any percentage of fault determined to be attributable to the claimant by the trier of fact under ORS 31.605, plus any percentage of fault attributable to a person who has settled with the claimant. Reallocation of obligations under this subsection does not affect any right to contribution from the party whose share of the obligation is determined to be uncollectible. Unless the party has entered into a covenant not to sue or not to enforce a judgment with the claimant, reallocation under this subsection does not affect continuing liability on the judgment to the claimant by the party whose share of the obligation is determined to be uncollectible.

(4) Notwithstanding subsection (3) of this section, a party's share of the obligation to a claimant may not be increased by reason of reallocation under subsection (3) of this section if:

(a) The percentage of fault of the claimant is equal to or greater than the percentage of fault of the party as determined by the trier of fact under ORS 31.605; or

(b) The percentage of fault of the party is 25 percent or less as determined by the trier of fact under ORS 31.605.

(5) If any party's share of the obligation to a claimant is not increased by reason of the application of subsection (4) of this section, the amount of that party's share of the reallocation shall be considered uncollectible and shall be reallocated among all other parties who are not subject to subsection (4) of this section, including the claimant, in the same manner as otherwise provided for reallocation under subsection (3) of this section.

(6) This section does not apply to:

(a) A civil action resulting from the violation of a standard established by Oregon or federal statute, rule or regulation for the spill, release or disposal of any hazardous waste, as defined in ORS 466.005, hazardous substance, as defined in ORS 453.005 or radioactive waste, as defined in ORS 469.300.

(b) A civil action resulting from the violation of Oregon or federal standards for air pollution, as defined in ORS 468A.005 or water pollution, as defined in ORS 468B.005. [Formerly 18.485]

31.615 Setoff of damages not allowed. Setoff of damages shall not be granted in actions subject to ORS 31.600 to 31.620. [Formerly 18.490]

31.620 Doctrines of last clear chance and implied assumption of risk abolished. (1) The doctrine of last clear chance is abolished.

(2) The doctrine of implied assumption of the risk is abolished. [Formerly 18.475]

DAMAGES

(Economic Damages)

31.700 Right to include medical expenses paid by parent or conservator in action to recover for damages to child; effect of consent to inclusion. (1) When the guardian ad litem or conservator of the estate of a child maintains a cause of action for recovery of damages to the child caused by a wrongful act, the parent, parents, or conservator of the estate of the child may file a consent accompanying the complaint of the guardian ad litem or conservator to include in the cause of action the damages as, in all the circumstances of the case, may be just, and will reasonably and fairly compensate for the doctor, hospital and medical expenses caused by the injury.

(2)(a) If the consent is filed as provided in subsection (1) of this section and the court allows the filing by a guardian ad litem, no court shall entertain a cause of action by the parent, parents or conservator for doctor, hospital or medical expenses caused by the injury.

(b) If the consent is filed as provided in subsection (1) of this section and the filing is by a conservator, no court shall entertain a cause of action by the parent or parents for doctor, hospital or medical expenses caused by the injury. [Formerly 30.810; 2015 c.213 §1]

(Verdict Form)

31.705 Economic and noneconomic damages separately set forth in verdict. A verdict shall set forth separately economic damages and noneconomic damages, if any, as defined in ORS 31.710. [Formerly 18.570]

(Noneconomic Damages)

31.710 Noneconomic damages; award; limit; "economic damages" and "noneconomic damages" defined. (1) Except for claims subject to ORS 30.260 to 30.300 and ORS chapter 656, in any civil action seeking damages arising out of bodily injury, including emotional injury or distress, death or property damage of any one person including claims for loss of care, comfort, companionship and society and loss of consortium, the amount awarded for noneconomic damages shall not exceed $500,000.

(2) As used in this section:

(a) "Economic damages" means objectively verifiable monetary losses including but not limited to reasonable charges necessarily incurred for medical, hospital, nursing and rehabilitative services and other health care services, burial and memorial expenses, loss of income and past and future impairment of earning capacity, reasonable and necessary expenses incurred for substitute domestic services, recurring loss to an estate, damage to reputation that is economically verifiable, reasonable and necessarily incurred costs due to loss of use of property and reasonable costs incurred for repair or for replacement of damaged property, whichever is less.

(b) "Noneconomic damages" means subjective, nonmonetary losses, including but not limited to pain, mental suffering, emotional distress, humiliation, injury to reputation, loss of care, comfort, companionship and society, loss of consortium, inconvenience and interference with normal and usual activities apart from gainful employment.

(3) This section does not apply to punitive damages.

(4) The jury shall not be advised of the limitation set forth in this section. [Formerly 18.560]

31.715 Limitation on recovery of noneconomic damages arising out of operation of motor vehicle; uninsured plaintiff; plaintiff driving under influence of intoxicants. (1) Except as provided in this section, a plaintiff may not recover noneconomic damages, as defined in ORS 31.710, in any action for injury or death arising out of the operation of a motor vehicle if the plaintiff was in violation of ORS 806.010 or 813.010 at the time the act or omission causing the death or injury occurred. A claim for noneconomic damages shall not be considered by the jury if the jury determines that the limitation on liability established by this section applies to the claim for noneconomic damages.

(2) For the purpose of the limitation on liability established by this section, a person is conclusively presumed to have been in violation of ORS 806.010 or 813.010 if the person is convicted in a criminal proceeding of one or both of those offenses. If the person has not been convicted of violating ORS 806.010 or 813.010, the defendant in the civil action may establish in the civil action, by a preponderance of the evidence, that the plaintiff was in violation of ORS 806.010 or 813.010 at the time the act or omission causing the death or injury occurred.

(3) The court shall abate a civil action upon the motion of any defendant in the civil action against whom a plaintiff has asserted a claim for noneconomic damages if the defendant alleges that the claim of the plaintiff is subject to the limitation on liability established by this section and:

(a) A criminal proceeding for a violation of ORS 813.010 has been commenced against the plaintiff in the civil action at the time the motion is made; or

(b) The district attorney for the county in which the conduct occurred informs the court at the time the motion is made that criminal proceedings for a violation of ORS 813.010 will be commenced against the plaintiff in the civil action.

(4) The court may order that only the claim that is subject to the limitation on liability established by this section be abated under subsection (3) of this section. An abatement under subsection (3) of this section shall remain in effect until the conclusion of the criminal proceedings.

(5) The limitation on liability established by this section does not apply if:

(a) The defendant in the civil action was also in violation of ORS 806.010 or 813.010 at the time the act or omission causing the death or injury occurred;

(b) The death or injury resulted from acts or omissions of the defendant that constituted an intentional tort;

(c) The defendant was engaged in conduct that would constitute a violation of ORS 811.140 at the time the act or omission causing the death or injury occurred; or

(d) The defendant was engaged in conduct that would constitute a felony at the time the act or omission causing the death or injury occurred.

(6) The limitation on liability established by this section based on a violation of ORS 806.010 does not apply if the plaintiff in the civil action was insured under a motor vehicle liability insurance policy within 180 days before the act or omission occurred, and the plaintiff has not operated a motor vehicle in violation of ORS 806.010 within the one-year period immediately preceding the date on which coverage under the motor vehicle liability insurance policy lapsed. [Formerly 18.592]

(Punitive Damages)

31.725 Pleading punitive damages; motion to amend pleading to assert claim for punitive damages; hearing. (1) A pleading in a civil action may not contain a request for an award of punitive damages except as provided in this section.

(2) At the time of filing a pleading with the court, the pleading may not contain a request for an award of punitive damages. At any time after the pleading is filed, a party may move the court to allow the party to amend the pleading to assert a claim for punitive damages. The party making the motion may submit affidavits and documentation supporting the claim for punitive damages. The party or parties opposing the motion may submit opposing affidavits and documentation.

(3) The court shall deny a motion to amend a pleading made under the provisions of this section if:

(a) The court determines that the affidavits and supporting documentation submitted by the party seeking punitive damages fail to set forth specific facts supported by admissible evidence adequate to avoid the granting of a motion for a directed verdict to the party opposing the motion on the issue of punitive damages in a trial of the matter; or

(b) The party opposing the motion establishes that the timing of the motion to amend prejudices the party's ability to defend against the claim for punitive damages.

(4) The court may grant a continuance on a motion under this section to allow a party opposing the motion to conduct such discovery as is necessary to establish one of the grounds for denial of the motion specified in subsection (3) of this section. If the court grants the motion, the court may continue the action to allow such discovery as the defendant may require to defend against the claim for punitive damages.

(5) Subject to subsection (4) of this section, the court shall conduct a hearing on a motion filed under this section not more than 30 days after the motion is filed and served. The court shall issue a decision within 10 days after the hearing. If no decision is issued within 10 days, the motion shall be considered denied.

(6) Discovery of evidence of a defendant's ability to pay shall not be allowed by a court unless and until the court grants a motion to amend a pleading under this section. [Formerly 18.535]

31.730 Standards for award of punitive damages; required review of award by court; additional reduction of award for remedial measures. (1) Punitive damages are not recoverable in a civil action unless it is proven by clear and convincing evidence that the party against whom punitive damages are sought has acted with malice or has shown a reckless and outrageous indifference to a highly unreasonable risk of harm and has acted with a conscious indifference to the health, safety and welfare of others.

(2) If an award of punitive damages is made by a jury, the court shall review the award to determine whether the award is within the range of damages that a rational juror would be entitled to award based on the record as a whole, viewing the statutory and common-law factors that allow an award of punitive damages for the specific type of claim at issue in the proceeding.

(3) In addition to any reduction that may be made under subsection (2) of this section, upon the motion of a defendant the court may reduce the amount of any judgment requiring the payment of punitive damages entered against the defendant if the defendant establishes that the defendant has taken remedial measures that are reasonable under the circumstances to prevent reoccurrence of the conduct that gave rise to the claim for punitive damages. In reducing awards of punitive damages under the provisions of this subsection, the court shall consider the amount of any previous judgment for punitive damages entered against the same defendant for the same conduct giving rise to a claim for punitive damages. [Formerly 18.537]

31.735 Distribution of punitive damages; notice to Department of Justice; order of application. (1) Upon the entry of a verdict including an award of punitive damages, the Department of Justice becomes a judgment creditor as to the amounts payable under paragraphs (b) and (c) of this section, and the punitive damage portion of an award shall be allocated as follows:

(a) Thirty percent is payable to the prevailing party. The attorney for the prevailing party shall be paid out of the amount allocated under this paragraph, in the amount agreed upon between the attorney and the prevailing party. However, in no event may more than 20 percent of the amount awarded as punitive damages be paid to the attorney for the prevailing party.

(b) Sixty percent is payable to the Attorney General for deposit in the Criminal Injuries Compensation Account of the Department of Justice Crime Victims' Assistance Section, and may be used only for the purposes set forth in ORS chapter 147. However, if the prevailing party is a public entity, the amount otherwise payable to the Criminal Injuries Compensation Account shall be paid to the general fund of the public entity.

(c) Ten percent is payable to the Attorney General for deposit in the State Court Facilities and Security Account established under ORS 1.178, and may be used only for the purposes specified in ORS 1.178 (2)(d).

(2) The party preparing the proposed judgment shall assure that the judgment identifies the judgment creditors specified in subsection (1) of this section.

(3) Upon the entry of a verdict including an award of punitive damages, the prevailing party shall provide notice of the verdict to the Department of Justice. In addition, upon entry of a judgment based on a verdict that includes an award of punitive damages, the prevailing party shall provide notice of the

judgment to the Department of Justice. The notices required under this subsection must be in writing and must be delivered to the Department of Justice Crime Victims' Assistance Section in Salem, Oregon within five days after the entry of the verdict or judgment.

(4) Whenever a judgment includes both compensatory and punitive damages, any payment on the judgment by or on behalf of any defendant, whether voluntary or by execution or otherwise, shall be applied first to compensatory damages, costs and court-awarded attorney fees awarded against that defendant and then to punitive damages awarded against that defendant unless all affected parties, including the Department of Justice, expressly agree otherwise, or unless that application is contrary to the express terms of the judgment.

(5) Whenever any judgment creditor of a judgment which includes punitive damages governed by this section receives any payment on the judgment by or on behalf of any defendant, the judgment creditor receiving the payment shall notify the attorney for the other judgment creditors and all sums collected shall be applied as required by subsections (1) and (4) of this section, unless all affected parties, including the Department of Justice, expressly agree otherwise, or unless that application is contrary to the express terms of the judgment. [Formerly 18.540; 2011 c.597 §311; 2011 c.689 §1]

Note: Section 3, chapter 689, Oregon Laws 2011, provides:
Sec. 3. The amendments to ORS 31.735 by section 1 of this 2011 Act apply only to causes of action that arise on or after the effective date of this 2011 Act [August 2, 2011]. [2011 c.689 §3]

31.740 When award of punitive damages against health practitioner prohibited. Punitive damages may not be awarded against a health practitioner if:
(1) The health practitioner is licensed, registered or certified as:
(a) A psychologist under ORS 675.030 to 675.070, 675.085 and 675.090;
(b) An occupational therapist under ORS 675.230 to 675.300;
(c) A regulated social worker under ORS 675.510 to 675.600;
(d) A physician under ORS 677.100 to 677.228 or 677.805 to 677.840;
(e) An emergency medical services provider under ORS chapter 682;
(f) A nurse under ORS 678.040 to 678.101;
(g) A nurse practitioner under ORS 678.375 to 678.390;
(h) A dentist under ORS 679.060 to 679.180;
(i) A dental hygienist under ORS 680.040 to 680.100;
(j) A denturist under ORS 680.515 to 680.535;
(k) An audiologist or speech-language pathologist under ORS 681.250 to 681.350;
(L) An optometrist under ORS 683.040 to 683.155 and 683.170 to 683.220;
(m) A chiropractor under ORS 684.040 to 684.105;
(n) A naturopath under ORS 685.060 to 685.110, 685.125 and 685.135;
(o) A massage therapist under ORS 687.011 to 687.250;
(p) A physical therapist under ORS 688.040 to 688.145;
(q) A medical imaging licensee under ORS 688.445 to 688.525;
(r) A pharmacist under ORS 689.151 and 689.225 to 689.285;
(s) A physician assistant as provided by ORS 677.505 to 677.525; or
(t) A professional counselor or marriage and family therapist under ORS 675.715 to 675.835; and
(2) The health practitioner was engaged in conduct regulated by the license, registration or certificate issued by the appropriate governing body and was acting within the scope of practice for which the license, registration or certificate was issued and without malice. [Formerly 18.550; 2005 c.366 §4; 2009 c.442 §27; 2009 c.833 §26; 2011 c.396 §1; 2011 c.703 §20; 2013 c.129 §20]

Note: Section 2, chapter 396, Oregon Laws 2011, provides:
Sec. 2. The amendments to ORS 31.740 by section 1 of this 2011 Act apply only to causes of action that arise on or after the effective date of this 2011 Act [January 1, 2012]. [2011 c.396 §2]

(Mitigation of Damages)

31.760 Evidence of nonuse of safety belt or harness to mitigate damages. (1) In an action brought to recover damages for personal injuries arising out of a motor vehicle accident, evidence of the nonuse of a safety belt or harness may be admitted only to mitigate the injured party's damages. The mitigation shall not exceed five percent of the amount to which the injured party would otherwise be entitled.
(2) Subsection (1) of this section shall not apply to:
(a) Actions brought under ORS 30.900 to 30.920; or
(b) Actions to recover damages for personal injuries arising out of a motor vehicle accident when nonuse of a safety belt or harness is a substantial contributing cause of the accident itself. [Formerly 18.590]

CONTRIBUTION

31.800 Right of contribution among joint tortfeasors; limitations; subrogation of insurer; effect on indemnity right. (1) Except as otherwise provided in this section, where two or more persons become jointly or severally liable in tort for the same injury to person or property or for the same wrongful death, there is a right of contribution among them even though judgment has not been recovered against all or any of them. There is no right of contribution from a person who is not liable in tort to the claimant.
(2) The right of contribution exists only in favor of a tortfeasor who has paid more than a proportional share of the common liability, and the total recovery of the tortfeasor is limited to the amount paid by the tortfeasor in excess of the proportional share. No tortfeasor is compelled to make contribution beyond the proportional share of the tortfeasor of the entire liability.
(3) A tortfeasor who enters into a settlement with a claimant is not entitled to recover contribution from another tortfeasor whose liability for the injury or wrongful death is not extinguished by the settlement nor in respect to any amount paid in a settlement which is in excess of what is reasonable.
(4) A liability insurer, who by payment has discharged in full or in part the liability of a tortfeasor and has thereby discharged in full its obligation as insurer, is subrogated to the tortfeasor's right of contribution to the extent of the amount it has paid in excess of the tortfeasor's proportional share of the common liability. This subsection does not limit or impair any right of subrogation arising from any other relationship.
(5) This section does not impair any right of indemnity under existing law. Where one tortfeasor is entitled to indemnity from another, the right of the indemnity obligee is for indemnity and not contribution, and the indemnity obligor is not entitled to contribution from the obligee for any portion of the indemnity obligation.
(6) This section shall not apply to breaches of trust or of other fiduciary obligation. [Formerly 18.440]

31.805 Basis for proportional shares of tortfeasors. (1) The proportional shares of tortfeasors in the entire liability shall be based upon their relative degrees of fault or responsibility. In contribution actions arising out of liability under ORS 31.600, the proportional share of a tortfeasor in the entire liability shall be based upon the tortfeasor's percentage of the common negligence of all tortfeasors.
(2) If equity requires, the collective liability of some as a group shall constitute a single share. Principles of equity applicable to contribution generally shall apply. [Formerly 18.445]

31.810 Enforcement of right of contribution; commencement of separate action; barring right of contribution; effect of satisfaction of judgment. (1) Whether or not judgment has been entered in an action against two or more tortfeasors for the same injury or wrongful death, contribution may be enforced by separate action.

(2) Where a judgment has been entered in an action against two or more tortfeasors for the same injury or wrongful death, contribution may be enforced in that action by judgment in favor of one against other judgment defendants by motion upon notice to all parties to the action.

(3) If there is a judgment for the injury or wrongful death against the tortfeasor seeking contribution, any separate action by the tortfeasor to enforce contribution must be commenced within two years after the judgment has become final by lapse of time for appeal or after appellate review.

(4) If there is no judgment for the injury or wrongful death against the tortfeasor seeking contribution, the right of contribution of that tortfeasor is barred unless the tortfeasor has either:

(a) Discharged by payment the common liability within the statute of limitations period applicable to claimant's right of action against the tortfeasor and has commenced action for contribution within two years after payment; or

(b) Agreed while action is pending against the tortfeasor to discharge the common liability and has within two years after the agreement paid the liability and commenced action for contribution.

(5) The running of the statute of limitations applicable to a claimant's right of recovery against a tortfeasor shall not operate to bar recovery of contribution against the tortfeasor or the claimant's right of recovery against a tortfeasor specified in ORS 31.600 (2) who has been made a party by another tortfeasor.

(6) The recovery of a judgment for an injury or wrongful death against one tortfeasor does not of itself discharge the other tortfeasors from liability for the injury or wrongful death unless the judgment is satisfied. The satisfaction of the judgment does not impair any right of contribution.

(7) The judgment of the court in determining the liability of the several defendants to the claimant for an injury or wrongful death shall be binding as among such defendants in determining their right to contribution. [Formerly 18.450]

31.815 Covenant not to sue; effect; notice. (1) When a covenant not to sue or not to enforce judgment is given in good faith to one of two or more persons liable in tort for the same injury to person or property or the same wrongful death or claimed to be liable in tort for the same injury or the same wrongful death:

(a) It does not discharge any of the other tortfeasors from liability for the injury or wrongful death unless its terms so provide; but the claimant's claim against all other persons specified in ORS 31.600 (2) for the injury or wrongful death is reduced by the share of the obligation of the tortfeasor who is given the covenant, as determined under ORS 31.605 and 31.610; and

(b) It discharges the tortfeasor to whom it is given from all liability for contribution to any other tortfeasor.

(2) When a covenant described in subsection (1) of this section is given, the claimant shall give notice of all of the terms of the covenant to all persons against whom the claimant makes claims. [Formerly 18.455]

31.820 Severability. If any provision of ORS 31.800 to 31.820 or the application thereof to any person is held invalid, the invalidity shall not affect other provisions or applications of ORS 31.800 to 31.820 which can be given effect without the invalid provision or application and to this end the provisions of ORS 31.800 to 31.820 are severable. [Formerly 18.460]

ASSIGNMENT OF CAUSE OF ACTION AGAINST INSURER

31.825 Assignment of cause of action against insurer. A defendant in a tort action against whom a judgment has been rendered may assign any cause of action that defendant has against the defendant's insurer as a result of the judgment to the plaintiff in whose favor the judgment has been entered. That assignment and any release or covenant given for the assignment shall not extinguish the cause of action against the insurer unless the assignment specifically so provides. [Formerly 17.100]

31.850 [2009 c.451 §1; renumbered 15.400 in 2011]

31.855 [2009 c.451 §2; renumbered 15.405 in 2011]

31.860 [2009 c.451 §3; renumbered 15.410 in 2011]

31.862 [2009 c.451 §4; renumbered 15.415 in 2011]

31.865 [2009 c.451 §5; renumbered 15.420 in 2011]

31.870 [2009 c.451 §6; renumbered 15.430 in 2011]

31.872 [2009 c.451 §7; renumbered 15.435 in 2011]

31.875 [2009 c.451 §8; renumbered 15.440 in 2011]

31.878 [2009 c.451 §9; renumbered 15.445 in 2011]

31.880 [2009 c.451 §10; renumbered 15.450 in 2011]

31.885 [2009 c.451 §11; renumbered 15.455 in 2011]

31.890 [2009 c.451 §12; renumbered 15.460 in 2011]

ABOLISHED COMMON LAW ACTIONS

31.980 Action for alienation of affections abolished. There shall be no civil cause of action for alienation of affections. [Formerly 30.840]
31.982 Action for criminal conversation abolished. There shall be no civil cause of action for criminal conversation. [Formerly 30.850]

―――――――――

Chapter 32 (Former Provisions)

Injunctions

INJUNCTIONS

SPECIAL ACTIONS AND PROCEEDINGS

32.010 [Repealed by 1981 c. 898 §53]

32.020 [Amended by 1977 c.416 §3; repealed by 1981 c.898 §53]

32.030 [Repealed by 1981 c. 898 §53]

32.040 [Repealed by 1981 c. 898 §53]

32.050 [Repealed by 1981 c. 898 §53]

32.060 [Repealed by 1981 c. 898 §53]

Chapter 33 — Special Proceedings and Procedures

2017 EDITION

SPECIAL PROCEEDINGS AND PROCEDURES

SPECIAL ACTIONS AND PROCEEDINGS

CONTEMPT PROCEEDINGS

33.015   Definitions for ORS 33.015 to 33.155

33.025   Nature of contempt power; entity defendants

33.035   Appointed counsel

33.045   Types of sanctions

33.055   Procedure for imposition of remedial sanctions

33.065   Procedure for imposition of punitive sanctions

33.075   Compelling attendance of defendant

33.085   Compelling testimony of witness

33.096   Summary imposition of sanction

33.105   Sanctions authorized

33.115   Referral to another judge

33.125   Appeal

33.135   Limitations of actions

33.145   Rules

33.155   Applicability

CHANGE OF NAME

33.410   Jurisdiction; grounds

33.420   Notice of application in case of minor child; exception; sealing of record in certain cases

33.430   Change of name on record of live birth; court conference with child

33.440   Application by minor child; court conference

CHANGE OF SEX

33.460   Jurisdiction; grounds; procedure

SURETIES

33.510   Discharge of surety or letter of credit issuer on application of surety or issuer

33.520   Discharge of surety or letter of credit issuer on application of principal

33.530   Liability of sureties or letter of credit issuer after termination of bond or letter of credit

EVALUATING SECURITIES OF SECURED CREDITOR

33.610   Evaluating securities of secured creditor

DETERMINATION OF LEGALITY OF MUNICIPAL CORPORATION'S ORGANIZATION AND ACTIONS

33.710   Definitions; judicial examination to determine legality of any municipal corporation's organization and actions

33.720   Proceeding in rem; practice and procedure as in action not triable by right to jury; service by publication; appeal; costs

TRANSFER OF STRUCTURED SETTLEMENT PAYMENT RIGHTS

33.850   Definitions for ORS 33.850 to 33.875

33.855   Transfer of payment rights; petition; notice

33.857   Contents of petition

33.860   Disclosure statement

33.862   Information that may be requested at hearing

33.865   Required findings by court or responsible administrative authority

33.870   Liability of parties after transfer

33.875   Limitations on transfers

33.010 [Amended by 1981 c.898 §37; repealed by 1991 c.724 §32]

CONTEMPT PROCEEDINGS

33.015 Definitions for ORS 33.015 to 33.155. For the purposes of ORS 33.015 to 33.155:
(1) "Confinement" means custody or incarceration, whether actual or constructive.
(2) "Contempt of court" means the following acts, done willfully:
(a) Misconduct in the presence of the court that interferes with a court proceeding or with the administration of justice, or that impairs the respect due the court.
(b) Disobedience of, resistance to or obstruction of the court's authority, process, orders or judgments.
(c) Refusal as a witness to appear, be sworn or answer a question contrary to an order of the court.
(d) Refusal to produce a record, document or other object contrary to an order of the court.
(e) Violation of a statutory provision that specifically subjects the person to the contempt power of the court.
(3) "Punitive sanction" means a sanction imposed to punish a past contempt of court.
(4) "Remedial sanction" means a sanction imposed to terminate a continuing contempt of court or to compensate for injury, damage or costs resulting from a past or continuing contempt of court. [1991 c.724 §1; 2005 c.22 §23]

33.020 [Repealed by 1991 c.724 §32]

33.025 Nature of contempt power; entity defendants. (1) The power of a court to impose a remedial or punitive sanction for contempt of court is an inherent judicial power. ORS 33.015 to 33.155 establish procedures to govern the exercise of that power.
(2) An entity is liable for contempt if:
(a) The conduct constituting contempt is engaged in by an agent of the entity while acting within the scope of employment and on behalf of the entity;
(b) The conduct constituting contempt consists of an omission to discharge a specific duty of affirmative performance imposed on an entity by a court; or
(c) The conduct constituting contempt is engaged in, authorized, solicited, requested, commanded or knowingly tolerated by a high managerial agent of an entity, the board of directors of a corporation, a manager or member of a limited liability company or a partner in a partnership, acting within the scope of employment and on behalf of the entity.
(3) The high managerial agents of an entity, the board of directors of a corporation, the managers and members of a limited liability company and the partners in a partnership are subject to the contempt powers of a court for contempt by an entity if those persons engage in, authorize, solicit, request, command or knowingly tolerate the conduct constituting contempt.
(4) As used in this section:
(a) "Agent" means a person who is authorized to act on behalf of an entity.
(b) "Entity" has the meaning given that term in ORS 63.001.
(c) "High managerial agent" means an officer of an entity who exercises authority with respect to the formulation of policy or the supervision in a managerial capacity of subordinate employees, or any other agent in a position of comparable authority.
(d) "Manager" and "member" have the meaning given those terms in ORS 63.001.
(e) "Partnership" has the meaning given that term in ORS 67.005. [1991 c.724 §2; 2017 c.153 §1]

33.030 [Repealed by 1991 c.724 §32]

33.035 Appointed counsel. Whenever ORS 33.015 to 33.155 provide for appointed counsel, appointment of counsel and payment of counsel and related expenses shall be made as follows:
(1) For contempt of a circuit court, the Oregon Tax Court, the Court of Appeals or the Supreme Court, appointment and payment of counsel shall be made as provided in ORS 135.055, 151.216 and 151.219.
(2) For contempt of a justice court, municipal court or other public body not described in subsection (1) of this section, payment for and appointment of counsel shall be made as otherwise provided by law for the court or public body. [1991 c.724 §3; 2001 c.962 §63]

33.040 [Amended by 1955 c.648 §2; 1961 c.210 §5; repealed by 1991 c.724 §32]

33.045 Types of sanctions. (1) A court may impose either remedial or punitive sanctions for contempt.
(2) Confinement may be remedial or punitive. The sanction is:
(a) Remedial if it continues or accumulates until the defendant complies with the court's order or judgment.
(b) Punitive if it is for a definite period that will not be reduced even if the defendant complies with the court's order or judgment.
(3) A fine may be remedial or punitive. A fine is:
(a) Punitive if it is for a past contempt.

(b) Remedial if it is for continuing contempt and the fine accumulates until the defendant complies with the court's judgment or order or if the fine may be partially or entirely forgiven when the defendant complies with the court's judgment or order.

(4) Any sanction requiring payment of amounts to one of the parties to a proceeding is remedial.

(5) Any sanction imposed by a court for contempt is in addition to any civil remedy or criminal sanction that may be available as a result of the conduct constituting contempt. In any civil or criminal proceedings arising out of the conduct constituting contempt, the court shall take into consideration any contempt sanctions previously imposed for the same act. [1991 c.724 §4]

33.050 [Repealed by 1991 c.724 §32]

33.055 Procedure for imposition of remedial sanctions. (1) Except as otherwise provided in ORS 161.685, proceedings to impose remedial sanctions for contempt shall be conducted as provided in this section.

(2) The following persons may initiate the proceeding or, with leave of the court, participate in the proceeding, by filing a motion requesting that defendant be ordered to appear:

(a) A party aggrieved by an alleged contempt of court.

(b) A district attorney.

(c) A city attorney.

(d) The Attorney General.

(e) Any other person specifically authorized by statute to seek imposition of sanctions for contempt.

(3) If the alleged contempt is related to another proceeding, a motion to initiate a proceeding to impose remedial sanctions must be filed in accordance with rules adopted under ORS 33.145.

(4) The person initiating a proceeding under this section shall file supporting documentation or affidavits sufficient to give defendant notice of the specific acts alleged to constitute contempt.

(5)(a) The court may issue an order directing the defendant to appear. Except as otherwise provided in paragraph (b) of this subsection, the defendant shall be personally served with the order to appear in the manner provided in ORCP 7 and 9. The court may order service by a method other than personal service or issue an arrest warrant if, based upon motion and supporting affidavit, the court finds that the defendant cannot be personally served.

(b) The defendant shall be served by substituted service if personal service is waived under ORS 107.835. If personal service is waived under ORS 107.835, the defendant shall be served by the method specified in the waiver.

(6) The court may impose a remedial sanction only after affording the defendant opportunity for a hearing tried to the court. The defendant may waive the opportunity for a hearing by stipulated order filed with the court.

(7) A defendant has no right to a jury trial and, except as provided in this section, has only those rights accorded to a defendant in a civil action.

(8) A defendant is entitled to be represented by counsel. A court shall not impose on a defendant a remedial sanction of confinement unless, before the hearing is held, the defendant is:

(a) Informed that such sanction may be imposed; and

(b) Afforded the same right to appointed counsel required in proceedings for the imposition of an equivalent punitive sanction of confinement.

(9) If the defendant is not represented by counsel when coming before the court, the court shall inform the defendant of the right to counsel, and of the right to appointed counsel if the defendant is entitled to, and financially eligible for, appointed counsel under subsection (8) of this section.

(10) Inability to comply with an order of the court is an affirmative defense.

(11) In any proceeding for imposition of a remedial sanction other than confinement, proof of contempt shall be by clear and convincing evidence. In any proceeding for imposition of a remedial sanction of confinement, proof of contempt shall be beyond a reasonable doubt.

(12) Proceedings under this section are subject to rules adopted under ORS 33.145. Proceedings under this section are not subject to the Oregon Rules of Civil Procedure except as provided in subsection (5) of this section or as may be provided in rules adopted under ORS 33.145. [1991 c.724 §5; 1993 c.448 §7; 2001 c.962 §77; 2005 c.22 §24; 2017 c.252 §1]

33.060 [Amended by 1981 c.781 §1; 1983 c.561 §1; repealed by 1991 c.724 §32]

33.065 Procedure for imposition of punitive sanctions. (1) Except as otherwise provided in ORS 161.685, proceedings to impose punitive sanctions for contempt shall be conducted as provided in this section.

(2) The following persons may initiate the proceeding by an accusatory instrument charging a person with contempt of court and seeking a punitive sanction:

(a) A city attorney.

(b) A district attorney.

(c) The Attorney General.

(3) If a city attorney, district attorney or Attorney General who regularly appears before the court declines to prosecute a contempt, and the court determines that remedial sanctions would not provide an effective alternative remedy, the court may appoint an attorney who is authorized to practice law in this state, and who is not counsel for an interested party, to prosecute the contempt. The court shall allow reasonable compensation for the appointed attorney's attendance, to be paid by:

(a) The Oregon Department of Administrative Services, if the attorney is appointed by the Supreme Court, the Court of Appeals or the Oregon Tax Court;

(b) The city where the court is located, if the attorney is appointed by a municipal court; and

(c) The county where the prosecution is initiated, in all other cases.

(4) The prosecutor may initiate proceedings on the prosecutor's own initiative, on the request of a party to an action or proceeding or on the request of the court. After the prosecutor files an accusatory instrument, the court may issue any order or warrant necessary to compel the appearance of the defendant.

(5) Except as otherwise provided by this section, the accusatory instrument is subject to the same requirements and laws applicable to an accusatory instrument in a criminal proceeding, and all proceedings on the accusatory instrument shall be in the manner prescribed for criminal proceedings.

(6) Except for the right to a jury trial, the defendant is entitled to the constitutional and statutory protections, including the right to appointed counsel, that a defendant would be entitled to in a criminal proceeding in which the fine or term of imprisonment that could be imposed is equivalent to the punitive sanctions sought in the contempt proceeding. This subsection does not affect any right to a jury that may otherwise be created by statute.

(7) Inability to comply with an order of the court is an affirmative defense. If the defendant proposes to rely in any way on evidence of inability to comply with an order of the court, the defendant shall, not less than five days before the trial of the cause, file and serve upon the city attorney, district attorney or Attorney General prosecuting the contempt a written notice of intent to offer that evidence. If the defendant fails to file and serve the notice, the defendant shall not be permitted to introduce evidence of inability to comply with an order of the court at the trial of the cause unless the court, in its discretion, permits such evidence to be introduced where just cause for failure to file the notice, or to file the notice within the time allowed, is made to appear.

(8) The court may impose a remedial sanction in addition to or in lieu of a punitive sanction.

(9) In any proceeding for imposition of a punitive sanction, proof of contempt shall be beyond a reasonable doubt. [1991 c.724 §6; 2001 c.962 §78]

33.070 [Amended by 1973 c.836 §321; repealed by 1991 c.724 §32]

33.075 Compelling attendance of defendant. (1) If a person served with an order to appear under ORS 33.055 fails to appear at the time and place specified in the order, the court may issue any order or warrant necessary to compel the appearance of the defendant.

(2) A person against whom a complaint has been issued under ORS 33.065 may be cited to appear in lieu of custody as provided in ORS 133.055. If the person fails to appear at the time and place specified in the citation, the court may issue any order or warrant necessary to compel the appearance of the defendant.

(3) When the court issues a warrant for contempt, the court shall specify a security amount. Unless the defendant pays the security amount upon arrest, the sheriff shall keep the defendant in custody until either a release decision is made by the court or until disposition of the contempt proceedings.

(4) The defendant shall be discharged from the arrest upon executing and delivering to the sheriff, at any time before the return day of the warrant, a security release or a release agreement as provided in ORS 135.230 to 135.290, to the effect that the defendant will appear on the return day and abide by the order or judgment of the court or officer or pay, as may be directed, the sum specified in the warrant.

(5) The sheriff shall return the warrant and the security deposit, if any, given to the sheriff by the defendant by the return day specified in the warrant.

(6) When a warrant for contempt issued under subsection (2) of this section has been returned after having been served and the defendant does not appear on the return day, the court may do either or both of the following:

(a) Issue another warrant.

(b) Proceed against the security deposited upon the arrest.

(7) If the court proceeds against the security under subsection (6) of this section and the sum specified is recovered, the court may award to any party to the action any or all of the money recovered as remedial damages. [1991 c.724 §7; 1993 c.196 §3; 2011 c.597 §119]

33.080 [Amended by 1973 c.836 §322; repealed by 1991 c.724 §32]

33.085 Compelling testimony of witness. (1) Upon the motion of the person initiating the proceeding, the court may compel the testimony of a witness as provided under ORS 136.617 in a contempt proceeding under ORS 33.055 or 33.065.

(2) In any case where the person initiating the proceeding is not represented by the district attorney, county counsel or Attorney General, the person initiating the proceeding shall serve a notice of intent to compel testimony on the district attorney of the county where the contempt proceeding is pending and on the Attorney General. The notice shall be served not less than 14 calendar days before any hearing on the motion to compel testimony.

(3) The notice required by this section shall identify the witness whose testimony the person initiating the proceeding intends to compel and include, if known, the witness' name, date of birth, residence address and Social Security number, and other pending proceedings or criminal charges involving the witness. The notice shall also include the case name and number of the contempt proceeding and the date, time and place set for any hearing scheduled as provided in ORS 136.617.

(4) If the person initiating the proceeding fails to serve the required advance notice or fails to serve the notice within the time required, the court shall grant a continuance for not less than 14 calendar days from the date the notice is served to allow the district attorney and Attorney General opportunity to be heard on the matter of compelling testimony. The court may compel testimony under this subsection only after the full notice period and opportunity to be heard, unless before that time the district attorney and Attorney General waive in writing any objection to the motion to compel.

(5) In any hearing on a motion to compel testimony under this section, the district attorney of the county in which the contempt proceeding is pending and the Attorney General each may appear to present evidence or arguments to support or oppose the motion.

(6) In lieu of compelling testimony under this section, the court may continue the contempt proceeding until disposition of any criminal action that is pending against the witness whose testimony is sought and that charges the witness with a crime. [1991 c.724 §7a]

33.090 [Amended by 1973 c.836 §323; repealed by 1991 c.724 §32]

33.095 [1975 c.516 §2; 1981 c.898 §38; 1987 c.803 §15; 1989 c.171 §5; repealed by 1991 c.724 §32]

33.096 Summary imposition of sanction. A court may summarily impose a sanction upon a person who commits a contempt of court in the immediate view and presence of the court. The sanction may be imposed for the purpose of preserving order in the court or protecting the authority and dignity of the court. The provisions of ORS 33.055 and 33.065 do not apply to summary imposition of sanctions under this section. [1991 c.724 §8]

33.100 [Repealed by 1991 c.724 §32]

33.105 Sanctions authorized. (1) Unless otherwise provided by statute, a court may impose one or more of the following remedial sanctions:

(a) Payment of a sum of money sufficient to compensate a party for loss, injury or costs suffered by the party as the result of a contempt of court.

(b) Confinement for so long as the contempt continues, or six months, whichever is the shorter period.

(c) An amount not to exceed $500 or one percent of the defendant's annual gross income, whichever is greater, for each day the contempt of court continues. The sanction imposed under this paragraph may be imposed as a fine or to compensate a party for the effects of the continuing contempt.

(d) An order designed to insure compliance with a prior order of the court, including probation.

(e) Payment of all or part of any attorney fees incurred by a party as the result of a contempt of court.

(f) A sanction other than the sanctions specified in paragraphs (a) to (e) of this subsection if the court determines that the sanction would be an effective remedy for the contempt.

(2) Unless otherwise provided by statute, a court may impose one or more of the following punitive sanctions for each separate contempt of court:

(a) A fine of not more than $500 or one percent of the defendant's annual gross income, whichever is greater.

(b) Forfeiture of any proceeds or profits obtained through the contempt.

(c) Confinement for not more than six months.

(d) Probation or community service.

(3) In a summary proceeding under ORS 33.096, a court may impose one or more of the following sanctions for each separate contempt of court:

(a) A punitive fine of not more than $500;

(b) Confinement as a punitive sanction for not more than 30 days; or

(c) Probation or community service.

(4) The court may impose a punitive sanction for past conduct constituting contempt of court even though similar present conduct is a continuing contempt of court. [1991 c.724 §9]

33.110 [Repealed by 1991 c.724 §32]

33.115 Referral to another judge. A judge may be disqualified from a contempt proceeding as provided for in other cases under ORS 14.210 to 14.270. ORS 14.260 (3) shall not apply to a motion to disqualify a judge in a contempt proceeding. The judge to whom the contempt is referred shall assume authority over and conduct any further proceedings relating to the contempt. [1991 c.724 §10; 1995 c.658 §121]

33.125 Appeal. (1) The imposition of a sanction for contempt shall be by a judgment.

(2) A judgment in a proceeding for imposition of a remedial sanction may be appealed in the same manner as from a judgment in an action at law. An appeal from a judgment imposing a punitive sanction shall be in the manner provided for appeals in ORS chapter 138. Appeals from judgments imposing sanctions for contempt in municipal courts and justice courts shall be in the manner provided by law for appeals from those courts.

(3) If a proceeding to impose remedial sanctions is related to another proceeding as described in ORS 33.055 (3) and the court determines, before entry of judgment in the related proceeding, that the defendant is in contempt, the court may suspend impositions of sanctions and entry of judgment on the contempt until entry of judgment in the related proceeding.

(4) An appeal from a contempt judgment shall not stay any action or proceeding to which the contempt is related. [1991 c.724 §11; 2003 c.576 §233; 2005 c.568 §28; 2017 c.252 §2]

33.130 [Repealed by 1991 c.724 §32]

33.135 Limitations of actions. (1) Except as provided in subsection (5) of this section, proceedings under ORS 33.055 to impose remedial sanctions for contempt and under ORS 33.065 to impose punitive sanctions for contempt shall be commenced within two years of the act or omission constituting the contempt.

(2) For the purposes of this section, a proceeding to impose remedial sanctions shall be deemed commenced as to each defendant when the motion provided for in ORS 33.055 is filed.

(3) Proceedings to impose punitive sanctions are subject to ORS 131.135, 131.145 and 131.155.

(4) The time limitations imposed by subsection (1) of this section shall not act to bar proceedings to impose sanctions for an act or omission that constitutes a continuing contempt at the time contempt proceedings are commenced. The willful failure of an obligor, as that term is defined in ORS 110.503, to pay a support obligation after that obligation becomes a judgment is a contempt without regard to when the obligation became a judgment.

(5) Proceedings to impose remedial or punitive sanctions for failure to pay a support obligation by an obligor, as defined in ORS 110.503, shall be commenced within 10 years of the act or omission constituting contempt. [1991 c.724 §12; 2005 c.560 §15; 2015 c.298 §88]

33.140 [Repealed by 1991 c.724 §32]

33.145 Rules. The Supreme Court may adopt rules to carry out the purposes of ORS 33.015 to 33.155. [1991 c.724 §13]

33.150 [Repealed by 1991 c.724 §32]

33.155 Applicability. ORS 33.015 to 33.145 apply to every court and judicial officer of this state, including municipal, county and justice courts. Rules adopted by the Supreme Court apply to those courts, but the application of such rules to municipal, county and justice courts does not confer any supervisory or administrative authority on the Supreme Court or the State Court Administrator with respect to those courts. [1991 c.724 §14]

33.210 [Amended by 1979 c.284 §67; 1989 c.955 §1; renumbered 36.300 in 1989]

33.220 [Renumbered 36.305 in 1989]

33.230 [Amended by 1979 c.284 §68; renumbered 36.310 in 1989]

33.240 [Renumbered 36.315 in 1989]

33.250 [Renumbered 36.320 in 1989]

33.260 [Renumbered 36.325 in 1989]

33.270 [Renumbered 36.330 in 1989]

33.280 [Renumbered 36.335 in 1989]

33.290 [Renumbered 36.340 in 1989]

33.300 [Amended by 1985 c.496 §19; renumbered 36.345 in 1989]

33.310 [Amended by 1985 c.496 §20; renumbered 36.350 in 1989]

33.320 [Amended by 1985 c.496 §21; renumbered 36.355 in 1989]

33.330 [Renumbered 36.360 in 1989]

33.340 [Amended by 1985 c.496 §22; renumbered 36.365 in 1989]

33.350 [1983 c.670 §1; 1985 c.342 §3; renumbered 36.400 in 1989]

33.360 [1983 c.670 §2; 1987 c.116 §1; 1987 c.125 §1; renumbered 36.405 in 1989]

33.370 [1983 c.670 §3; 1987 c.116 §2; renumbered 36.410 in 1989]

33.380 [1983 c.670 §4; 1985 c.342 §4; 1987 c.116 §3; renumbered 36.415 in 1989]

33.390 [1983 c.670 §5; renumbered 36.420 in 1989]

33.400 [1983 c.670 §6; renumbered 36.425 in 1989]

CHANGE OF NAME

33.410 Jurisdiction; grounds. Application for change of name of a person may be heard and determined by the probate court or, if the circuit court is not the probate court, the circuit court if its jurisdiction has been extended to include this section pursuant to ORS 3.275 of the county in which the person resides. The change of name shall be granted by the court unless the court finds that the change is not consistent with the public interest. [Amended by 1967 c.534 §11; 1975 c.733 §1]

33.420 Notice of application in case of minor child; exception; sealing of record in certain cases. (1) Except as provided in ORS 109.360, before entering a judgment for a change of name in the case of a minor child, the court shall require that written notice be given to the parents of the child, both custodial and noncustodial, and to any legal guardian of the child.

(2) Notwithstanding subsection (1) of this section, notice of an application for the change of name of a minor child does not need to be given to a parent of the child if the other parent of the child files a verified statement in the change of name proceeding that asserts that the minor child has not resided with the other parent and that the other parent has not contributed or has not tried to contribute to the support of the child.

(3)(a) In a case to determine an application for change of name of a person under ORS 33.410, if an applicant who is a certified adult program participant in the Address Confidentiality Program under ORS 192.826 requests the court to seal the record of the case, the court shall seal the record of the case unless the court issues an order pursuant to a finding of good cause under ORS 192.848.

(b) This subsection does not apply to an adult applicant appearing as a guardian ad litem for a minor child.

(4) In a case to determine an application for legal change of sex of a person under ORS 33.460, if an applicant requests the court to seal the record of the case, the court shall seal the record of the case. [Amended by 1983 c.369 §6; 1997 c.872 §22; 2001 c.779 §12; 2003 c.576 §308; 2013 c.316 §1; 2017 c.100 §4]

33.430 Change of name on record of live birth; court conference with child. (1) In the case of a change, by court order, of the name of the parents of any minor child, if the child's record of live birth is on file in this state, the State Registrar of the Center for Health Statistics, upon receipt of a certified copy of the court order changing the name, together with the information required to locate the original record of live birth, shall prepare a new record of live birth for the child in the new name of the parents of the child. The name of the parents as so changed shall be set forth in a new certified copy of the record of live birth, in place of their original name.

(2) The evidence upon which the new record of live birth was made, and the original record of live birth, shall be sealed and filed by the State Registrar of the Center for Health Statistics, and may be opened only upon demand of the person whose name was changed, if of legal age, or by an order of a court of competent jurisdiction.

(3) When a change of name by parents will affect the name of their child under subsection (1) of this section, the court, on its own motion or on request of a child of the parents, may take testimony from or confer with the child and may exclude from the conference the parents and other persons if the court finds that such action would be in the best interests of the child. However, the court shall permit an attorney for the parents to attend the conference, and the conference shall be reported. If the court finds that a change of name would not be in the best interests of the child, the court may provide in the order changing the name of the parents that such change of name shall not affect the child, and a new record of live birth shall not be prepared for the child. [Amended by 1983 c.369 §7; 2005 c.22 §25; 2013 c.366 §51]

33.440 Application by minor child; court conference. When a minor child applies for a change of name under ORS 33.410, the court may, upon its own motion, confer with the child and may exclude from the conference the parents and other persons if the court finds that such action would be in the best interests of the child. However, the court shall permit an attorney for the child to attend the conference, and the conference shall be reported. [1983 c.369 §5]

CHANGE OF SEX

33.460 Jurisdiction; grounds; procedure. (1) Application for legal change of sex of a person may be heard and determined by any circuit court in this state. A circuit court may order a legal change of sex and enter a judgment indicating the change of sex if the individual attests that the individual has undergone surgical, hormonal or other treatment appropriate for the individual for the purpose of affirming gender identity.

(2) The court may order a legal change of sex and enter the judgment in the same manner as that provided for change of name of a person under ORS 33.410.

(3) If a person applies for a change of name under ORS 33.410 at the time the person applies for a legal change of sex under this section, the court may order change of name and legal change of sex at the same time and in the same proceeding. [1981 c.221 §1; 1997 c.872 §23; 2003 c.576 §309; 2013 c.366 §52; 2017 c.100 §3]

SURETIES

33.510 Discharge of surety or letter of credit issuer on application of surety or issuer. The surety or the representatives of any surety upon the bond of any trustee, committee, guardian, assignee, receiver, executor, administrator or other fiduciary, and any irrevocable letter of credit issuer for any trustee, committee, guardian, assignee, receiver, executor, administrator or other fiduciary is entitled as a matter of right to be discharged from liability as provided in this section, and to that end may, on notice to the principal named in the bond or irrevocable letter of credit, apply to the court that accepted the bond or irrevocable letter of credit or to the court of which the judge who accepted the bond or irrevocable letter of credit was a member or to any judge thereof, praying to be relieved from liability for the act or omission of the principal occurring after the date of the order relieving such person, and that the principal be required to account and give new sureties or cause to be issued new letters of credit. Notice of the application shall be served on the principal personally not less than five days prior to the date on which the application is to be made, unless it satisfactorily appears to the court or judge that personal service cannot be had with due diligence within the state, in which case notice may be given by personal service without the state or in such manner as the court or judge directs. Pending the hearing of the application the court or judge may restrain the principal from acting except to preserve the trust estate until further order. If upon the return of the application the principal fails to file a new bond or irrevocable letter of credit to the satisfaction of the court or judge, the court or judge must make an order requiring the principal to file a new bond or irrevocable letter of credit within a period not exceeding five days. If the new bond or irrevocable letter of credit is filed upon the return of the application, or within the time fixed by the order, the court or judge must make a judgment or order requiring the principal to account for all acts and proceedings to and including the date of the judgment or order, and to file such account within a time fixed, not exceeding 20 days, and discharge the surety or letter of credit issuer making application from liability for any act or default of the principal subsequent to the date of the judgment or order. If the principal fails to file a new bond or irrevocable letter of credit within the time specified, a judgment or order must be made revoking the appointment of the principal or removing and requiring the principal to file an account within not more than 20 days. If the principal fails to file the account, the surety or letter of credit issuer may make and file an account with like force and effect as though filed by the principal, and upon settlement thereof and upon the trust fund or estate being found or made good and paid over or properly secured, credit shall be given for all commissions, costs, disbursements and allowances to which the principal would be entitled were the principal accounting, and allowance shall be made to the surety or letter of credit issuer for the expense incurred in filing the account and procuring the settlement thereof. After the filing of the account, either by the principal or the surety or the letter of credit issuer, the court or judge must, upon the petition of the principal or surety or the letter of credit issuer, issue an order requiring all persons interested in the estate or trust to attend a settlement of the account at a time and place therein specified, and upon the trust fund or estate being found or made good and paid over or properly secured, the surety or the letter of credit issuer shall be discharged from all liability. Upon demand in writing by the principal, the surety or the letter of credit issuer shall return any compensation that has been paid for the unexpired period of the bond or the letter of credit. [Amended by 1991 c.331 §11; 2003 c.576 §310]

33.520 Discharge of surety or letter of credit issuer on application of principal. Any trustee, committee, guardian, assignee, receiver, executor, administrator or other fiduciary shall be entitled to have any surety on the bond of the fiduciary or of any irrevocable letter of credit issuer discharged from liability thereon, and the fiduciary may file a new bond or irrevocable letter of credit as provided in this section. The fiduciary may, on written notice to the surety or letter of credit issuer and to all other interested persons, apply to the court that accepted the bond or irrevocable letter of credit, or to a judge thereof, praying that the surety or irrevocable letter of credit be discharged from liability thereon, and that the principal be allowed to file a new bond or irrevocable letter of credit and to account. Notice of the application shall be served on the surety or letter of credit issuer and on each of the persons interested, within the state, not less than 10 days prior to the date on which the application is to be made, unless it satisfactorily appears to the court or judge that the notice cannot with due diligence be served within the state, in which case notice may be given in such manner as the court or judge shall direct. Upon the return of the application, the principal may file a new bond or irrevocable letter of credit satisfactory to the court or judge, and therewith file an account of all proceedings, whereupon the court or judge shall proceed, upon due notice to all persons interested, to judicially settle the account and duly credit and charge the principal; and upon the trust fund or estate being found or made good and paid over or properly secured, the surety or letter of credit issuer shall be discharged from all liability. [Amended by 1991 c.331 §12]

33.530 Liability of sureties or letter of credit issuer after termination of bond or letter of credit. (1) When a bond or an irrevocable letter of credit of any personal representative, guardian or conservator is terminated upon the issuance of a new bond or irrevocable letter of credit to the personal representative, guardian or conservator by a new surety or letter of credit issuer, the former surety or letter of credit issuer shall not be liable on the old bond or irrevocable letter of credit for any acts or omissions of the personal representative, guardian or conservator which occur after the issuance of the new bond or irrevocable letter of credit.

(2) A new surety for a personal representative, guardian or conservator who issues a new bond or irrevocable letter of credit after the termination of a previous bond or irrevocable letter of credit written by another surety or letter of credit issuer for a personal representative, guardian or conservator shall not be liable for any acts or omissions of the personal representative, guardian or conservator which occurred prior to the issuance of the new bond or irrevocable letter of credit. [1983 c.613 §§2,3; 1991 c.331 §13]

EVALUATING SECURITIES OF SECURED CREDITOR

33.610 Evaluating securities of secured creditor. In the administration of a decedent's estate, or whenever the assets of any person, partnership or corporation are being administered in receivership or any liquidation proceedings, or under an assignment for the benefit of creditors, the value of securities held by secured creditors shall be determined by converting the same into money according to the terms of the agreement pursuant to which the securities were delivered to the creditors, or by the creditors and the person or official liquidating the assets by agreement, arbitration, compromise or litigation. Where the proceedings are in court, the determination shall be subject to the control or decision of the court. If, under an assignment for the benefit of creditors, the secured creditor and the assignee cannot, by agreement, arbitration or compromise, determine the value, either the assignee or the creditor may apply to a court of competent jurisdiction in the place of residence of the assignee for determination of the value by declaratory judgment, or otherwise. In all cases, the amount of the determined value shall be credited upon the secured claim and a general or unsecured creditor's dividend shall be paid only on the uncredited balance, if any, of the claim. Nothing contained in this section shall be construed to compel any creditor holding security to file a claim for participation in any such estate or proceeding, or to compel the creditor, if the creditor does not file a claim, to foreclose or realize upon the security of the creditor.

DETERMINATION OF LEGALITY OF MUNICIPAL CORPORATION'S ORGANIZATION AND ACTIONS

33.710 Definitions; judicial examination to determine legality of any municipal corporation's organization and actions. (1) As used in this section and ORS 33.720, unless the context requires otherwise:

(a) "Governing body" means the city council, board of commissioners, board of directors, county court or other managing board of a municipal corporation, including a board managing a municipally owned public utility or a dock commission and the governing board of a public university listed in ORS 352.002.

(b) "Municipal corporation" means any county, city, port, school district, union high school district, community college district or public university listed in ORS 352.002 with a governing board and all other public or quasi-public corporations, including a municipal utility or dock commission operated by a separate board or commission.

(2) The governing body may commence a proceeding in the circuit court of the county in which the municipal corporation or the greater part thereof is located, for the purpose of having a judicial examination and judgment of the court as to the regularity and legality of:

(a) The proceedings in connection with the establishment or creation of the municipal corporation, including any action or proceedings proclaiming the creation of the municipal corporation or declaring the result of any election therein.

(b) The proceedings of the governing body and of the municipal corporation providing for and authorizing the issue and sale of bonds of the municipal corporation, whether the bonds or any of them have or have not been sold or disposed of.

(c) Any order of the governing body levying a tax.

(d) The authorization of any contract and as to the validity of the contract, whether or not it has been executed.

(e) Any decision of the governing body that raises novel or important legal issues that would be efficiently and effectively resolved by a proceeding before the decision becomes effective, when the decision will:

(A) Require a significant expenditure of public funds;

(B) Significantly affect the lives or businesses of a significant number of persons within the boundaries of the governing body; or

(C) Indirectly impose a significant financial burden on the cost of conducting business within the boundaries of the governing body.

(f) The authority of the governing body to enact any ordinance, resolution or regulation.

(g) Any ordinance, resolution or regulation enacted by the governing body, including the constitutionality of the ordinance, resolution or regulation.

(3) All proceedings of the municipal corporation may be judicially examined and determined in one special proceeding, or any part thereof may be separately examined and determined by the court.

(4) Nothing in this section allows a governing body to have a judicial examination and judgment of the court without a justiciable controversy. [Amended by 1975 c.133 §1; 2003 c.548 §1; 2013 c.768 §124; 2015 c.767 §46]

33.720 Proceeding in rem; practice and procedure as in action not triable by right to jury; service by publication; appeal; costs. (1) The determination authorized by ORS 33.710 shall be in the nature of a proceeding in rem; and the practice and procedure therein shall follow the practice and procedure of an action not triable by right to a jury, as far as the same is consistent with the determination sought to be obtained, except as provided in this section.

(2) Jurisdiction of the municipal corporation shall be obtained by the publication of notice directed to the municipal corporation; and jurisdiction of the electors of the municipal corporation shall be obtained by publication of notice directed to all electors, freeholders, taxpayers and other interested persons, without naming such electors, freeholders, taxpayers and other interested persons individually. The notice shall be served on all parties in interest by publication thereof for at least once a week for three successive weeks in a newspaper of general circulation published in the county where the proceeding is pending, or if no such newspaper is published therein, then in a contiguous county. Jurisdiction shall be complete within 10 days after the date of completing publication of the notice as provided in this section.

(3) Any person interested may at any time before the expiration of the 10 days appear and contest the validity of such proceeding, or of any of the acts or things therein enumerated. Such proceeding shall be tried forthwith and judgment rendered as expeditiously as possible declaring the matter so contested to be either valid or invalid. Any order or judgment in the course of such proceeding may be made and rendered by the judge in vacation or otherwise; and for that purpose, the court shall be deemed at all times to be in session and the act of the judge in making the order or judgment shall be the act of the court.

(4) Any party may appeal to the Court of Appeals from a judgment rendered in such proceeding. The court, in inquiring into the regularity, legality or correctness of any proceeding of the municipal corporation or its governing body shall disregard any error, irregularity or omission which does not affect the substantial rights of the parties to the special proceeding, and may approve the proceedings in part and may disapprove and declare illegal or invalid in part other or subsequent proceedings, or may approve or disapprove the proceedings, or may approve the proceedings in part and disapprove the remainder thereof.

(5) Costs of the proceeding may be allowed and apportioned between the parties in the discretion of the court.

(6) Upon conclusion of a proceeding authorized by ORS 33.710 (2)(b), including any appeal of a judgment, the judgment entered in the proceeding is binding upon the parties and all other persons. Claim preclusion and issue preclusion apply to all matters adjudicated in the proceeding. Except for an action to enforce a judgment, the courts of this state do not have jurisdiction over an action by or against the governing body or municipal corporation

named in the judgment if the purpose of the action is to seek judicial review or judicial examination, directly or indirectly, of a matter adjudicated in the proceeding. [Amended by 1975 c.133 §2; 1979 c.284 §69; 2001 c.537 §1; 2003 c.576 §234]

33.810 [1955 c.522 §1; repealed by 1967 c.460 §8]

33.820 [1955 c.522 §2; repealed by 1967 c.460 §8]

33.830 [1955 c.522 §3; repealed by 1967 c.460 §8]

TRANSFER OF STRUCTURED SETTLEMENT PAYMENT RIGHTS

33.850 Definitions for ORS 33.850 to 33.875. As used in ORS 33.850 to 33.875:
(1) "Annuity issuer" means an insurer that has entered into a contract to fund periodic payments under a structured settlement agreement.
(2) "Independent professional advice" means advice of an attorney, certified public accountant, actuary, financial advisor or other professional advisor:
(a) Who is engaged by a payee to render advice concerning the legal, tax or financial implications of a transfer;
(b) Who is not affiliated with or compensated by the transferee; and
(c) Whose compensation for providing the advice is not affected by whether a transfer occurs or does not occur.
(3) "Obligor" means a party that has a continuing obligation to make periodic payments to a payee under a structured settlement agreement or an agreement that provides for a qualified assignment as defined in section 130 of the Internal Revenue Code, as of January 1, 2006.
(4) "Payee" means an individual who is receiving tax-free payments under a structured settlement agreement and proposes to make a transfer of payment rights.
(5) "Payment rights" means rights to receive periodic payments under a structured settlement agreement, whether from the obligor or the annuity issuer.
(6) "Periodic payments" includes both recurring payments and scheduled future lump sum payments.
(7) "Responsible administrative authority" means a government authority vested by law with exclusive jurisdiction over the original tort claim or workers' compensation claim that was resolved in a structured settlement agreement.
(8) "Structured settlement agreement" means an agreement, judgment, stipulation or release embodying the terms of an arrangement for periodic payment of damages from an obligor or an annuity issuer for:
(a) Personal injuries or sickness established by settlement or judgment in resolution of a tort claim; or
(b) Periodic payments in settlement of a workers' compensation claim.
(9) "Terms of the structured settlement agreement" includes the terms of:
(a) A structured settlement agreement;
(b) An annuity contract;
(c) An agreement that provides for a qualified assignment as defined in section 130 of the Internal Revenue Code, as of January 1, 2006; and
(d) Any order or other approval of any court, responsible administrative authority or other government authority that authorized or approved the structured settlement agreement.
(10) "Transfer" means any sale, assignment, pledge or other alienation or encumbrance of payment rights made by a payee for consideration. "Transfer" does not include the creation or perfection of an unspecified security interest in all of the payee's payment rights entered into with an insured depository institution, or an agent or successor in interests of the insured depository institution, in the absence of any action to redirect the payments under the structured settlement agreement to the insured depository institution or otherwise to enforce a security interest against the payment rights.
(11) "Transfer agreement" means an agreement providing for a transfer of payment rights.
(12) "Transferee" means a party acquiring or proposing to acquire payment rights through a transfer agreement. [2005 c.173 §1; 2013 c.736 §1]

33.855 Transfer of payment rights; petition; notice. (1) A payee may transfer payment rights under ORS 33.850 to 33.875 if:
(a) The payee is domiciled in this state;
(b) The domicile or principal place of business of the obligor or the annuity issuer is located in this state;
(c) The structured settlement agreement was approved by a court or responsible administrative authority in this state; or
(d) The structured settlement agreement is expressly governed by the laws of this state.
(2) Prior to transferring payment rights under ORS 33.850 to 33.875, the transferee shall file a petition for approval of the transfer:
(a) In the county in which the payee resides; or
(b) In any court or before any responsible administrative authority in this state that approved the structured settlement agreement.
(3) Not less than 20 days prior to the scheduled hearing on a petition for approval of a transfer of payment rights, the transferee shall send notice of the proposed transfer to:
(a) The payee;
(b) Any beneficiary irrevocably designated under the annuity contract to receive payments following the payee's death;
(c) The annuity issuer;
(d) The obligor; and
(e) Any other party that has continuing rights or obligations under the structured settlement agreement that is the subject of the hearing.
(4) The notice sent under subsection (3) of this section shall include:
(a) A copy of the transferee's petition.
(b) A copy of the transfer agreement.
(c) A copy of the disclosure statement provided to the payee as required under ORS 33.860.
(d) A listing of each person for whom the payee is legally obligated to provide support, including the age of each of those persons.
(e) Notification that any person receiving notice under subsection (3) of this section is entitled to support, oppose or otherwise respond to the transferee's petition, either in person or by counsel, by submitting written comments to the court or responsible administrative authority or by participating in the hearing.
(f) Notification of the time and place of the hearing.
(g) Notification of the manner in which and the time by which written responses to the petition must be filed, which shall not be less than 15 days after service of the transferee's notice, in order to be considered by the court or responsible administrative authority. [2005 c.173 §2; 2013 c.736 §2]

33.857 Contents of petition. (1) A petition for approval of a transfer of payment rights filed under ORS 33.855 must:
(a) Include the payee's name, age and county of residence.
(b) Describe the financial terms of the proposed transfer, including the payment rights to be transferred by the payee and the amount to be received by the payee in return for the transfer.
(c) Be accompanied by a copy of the transfer agreement.
(d) Be accompanied by a copy of the disclosure statement required under ORS 33.860, and the signature of the payee acknowledging the payee's receipt of the disclosure statement.
(e) Generally describe the reasons why the payee seeks to transfer the payment rights.
(f) Be accompanied by a declaration under penalty of perjury by the payee:
(A) Stating whether the payee depends on structured settlement payments or government benefits for the payee's necessary living expenses or required medical care and treatment.

(B) Stating whether the payee personally sustained physical injuries or sickness in connection with the incident from which the structured settlement arose and whether the injuries or sickness currently prevents the payee from working or substantially limits the work that the payee can perform.

(C) Providing a summary of:

(i) Any prior transfers of structured settlement payments by the payee to the transferee within the five years preceding the date of the pending transfer agreement.

(ii) Any prior transfers of structured settlement payments by the payee to a person other than the transferee within the five years preceding the date of the pending transfer agreement.

(iii) Any attempted prior transfers of structured settlement payments by the payee to the transferee or to a person other than the transferee within the year preceding the date of the pending transfer agreement, including any prior attempted transfers that were denied or that were dismissed or withdrawn prior to a decision on the merits of the transfer.

(D) If the payee has minor children, stating whether the payee is currently obligated to pay child support under any child support order, and whether the payee is current or in arrears under any child support order.

(2)(a) If the summaries required under subsection (1)(f) of this section describe any prior transfers or attempted transfers of structured settlement payments, the transferee shall, at or before the hearing on the petition:

(A) Provide to the court or responsible administrative authority a copy of the court orders approving, denying or otherwise relating to the transfers or attempted transfers involving the transferee; and

(B) Request from the payee or the annuity issuer or obligor under the structured settlement agreement copies of any court orders relating to any transfer or attempted transfer involving the payee and any other party and, if any orders are provided to the transferee, provide a copy of the orders to the court or responsible administrative authority at or before the hearing on the petition.

(b) The inability of the transferee or payee to provide copies of court orders under this subsection does not preclude the court or responsible administrative authority from approving the proposed transfer, if the court or authority determines that the court orders are not available to the transferee or payee after the transferee and payee have made reasonable requests to obtain the court orders. [2013 c.736 §4]

33.860 Disclosure statement. Not less than 14 days before a payee signs a transfer agreement, a transferee shall provide the payee with a disclosure statement in not less than 14-point type that sets forth:

(1) The amounts and due dates of the structured settlement payments to be transferred.

(2) The aggregate amount of the payments to be transferred.

(3) The discounted present value of the payments and the rate used in calculating the discounted present value. The discounted present value shall be calculated by using the most recently published applicable federal rate for determining the present value of an annuity, as issued by the Internal Revenue Service.

(4) The amount payable to a payee as the result of a transfer. The amount set forth in this subsection shall be calculated before any reductions are made for transfer expenses required to be listed under subsection (5) of this section or any related disbursements.

(5) An itemized listing of all applicable transfer expenses and the transferee's best estimate of the amount of any attorney fees and disbursements. For the purposes of this subsection, "transfer expenses":

(a) Includes all fees, costs and expenses of a transfer that are required under the transfer agreement to be paid by the payee to the transferee or deducted from the amount payable to a payee as the result of a transfer.

(b) Does not include preexisting obligations of the payee payable for the payee's account from the proceeds of a transfer.

(6) The amount calculated by subtracting the aggregate amount of the actual and estimated transfer expenses required to be listed under subsection (5) of this section from the amount identified in subsection (4) of this section.

(7) The amount of any penalties or liquidated damages payable by the payee in the event of a breach of the transfer agreement by the payee.

(8) A statement that the payee has the right to cancel the transfer agreement, without penalty or further obligation, before the approval of the transfer by the court or responsible administrative authority.

(9) A statement that the payee is entitled to, and should, seek independent professional advice regarding the proposed transfer.

(10) A statement that transferring payment rights may or may not be financially appropriate for the payee and the payee should not proceed without first weighing and considering other offers and alternate means of obtaining funds through borrowing or the sale of other assets.

(11) A statement that the transferee's attorney does not represent the payee in connection with the proposed transfer.

(12) A statement that the court or responsible administrative authority may require the payee to seek independent professional advice and that the expenses for the independent professional advice may be paid out of the amount paid by the transferee to the payee. [2005 c.173 §3; 2013 c.736 §6]

33.862 Information that may be requested at hearing. At the hearing on a petition to transfer payment rights filed under ORS 33.855, the court or responsible administrative authority may ask the payee to provide testimony on or other evidence related to the following matters and any other relevant evidence that the court or authority deems appropriate to make the findings required by ORS 33.865:

(1) The payee's marital status and, if married or separated, the name of the payee's spouse.

(2) The names, ages and place or places of residence of any minor children or other dependents of the payee.

(3) The amounts and sources of the payee's monthly income and, if the payee is married, the amounts and sources of the payee's spouse's monthly income.

(4) If the payee has minor children, whether the payee is currently obligated to pay child support under any child support order, whether the payee is current or in arrears under any child support order and the names, addresses and telephone numbers of any persons or agencies receiving child support from the payee under the order.

(5) Whether the payee depends on the structured settlement payments that the payee proposes to transfer for the payee's necessary living expenses or required medical care and treatment. [2013 c.736 §5]

33.865 Required findings by court or responsible administrative authority. (1) A transfer of payment rights under ORS 33.850 to 33.875 is not effective and an obligor or annuity issuer is not required to make any payments directly or indirectly to a transferee unless the transferee has filed a petition under ORS 33.857 and the transfer is approved by the court or responsible administrative authority based on express findings by the court or authority that:

(a) The transfer is in the best interest of the payee, taking into account the welfare and support of all persons for whom the payee is legally obligated to provide support.

(b) The payee has been advised in writing by the transferee to seek independent professional advice and the payee has either received independent professional advice regarding the transfer or knowingly waived independent professional advice in writing.

(c) The transfer does not contravene any applicable statute or order of any court or other government authority.

(d) The payee understands the transfer agreement, the disclosure statement required under ORS 33.860 and the financial terms of the transfer.

(e) The payee understands the payee's right to cancel the transfer agreement as set forth in the disclosure statement required by ORS 33.860 and knowingly elected not to cancel the transfer agreement.

(f) The payee confirmed to the court or responsible administrative authority at the hearing that the payee wanted the court or authority to approve the proposed transfer and understood that the court or authority would not approve the transfer if the payee did not want the court or authority to do so.

(2) When determining whether the proposed transfer should be approved, including whether the transfer agreement is fair, reasonable and in the payee's best interest, the court or responsible administrative authority may consider all relevant information, including information contained in the petition and any other document that is filed with the court or authority and provided at the hearing. Relevant information that may be considered under this subsection includes, but is not limited to:

(a) The reasonable preference and desire of the payee to complete the proposed transfer, taking into account the payee's age and apparent maturity level.

(b) The purpose of the transfer and the intended use of the proceeds by the payee.

(c) The payee's financial situation.

(d) Whether the payee depends on the structured settlement payments that the payee proposes to transfer for the payee's necessary living expenses or required medical care and treatment.

(e) Whether the payee is employed or employable.

(f) The terms of the transfer agreement, including whether the payee is transferring monthly or lump sum payments or all or a portion of the payee's future payments, the size of the transaction and the financial alternatives available to the payee to achieve the payee's stated objectives.

(g) Whether the payee has experienced a change in personal, family or financial circumstances.

(h) Whether the payee has income or support other than the future periodic payments sufficient to meet the payee's future financial obligations for support of the payee's dependents, including child support obligations.

(i) Whether the terms of the proposed transfer agreement, including the amount to be paid to the payee and the expenses and costs of the transfer for the payee and the transferee are fair and reasonable.

(j) Whether the payee has completed or attempted previous transfers of payment rights.

(k) Whether the payee, or the payee's family or dependents, may suffer personal, family or financial hardship if the transfer is not approved.

(L) Whether the payee received independent professional advice regarding the transaction. [2005 c.173 §4; 2013 c.736 §7]

33.870 Liability of parties after transfer. Following a transfer of payment rights under ORS 33.850 to 33.875:

(1) The obligor and the annuity issuer shall, as to all parties except the transferee, be discharged and released from all liability for the transferred payments.

(2) The transferee shall be liable to the obligor and the annuity issuer:

(a) If the transfer contravenes the terms of the structured settlement agreement, for any taxes incurred by the parties as a consequence of the transfer; and

(b) For any other liabilities or costs, including reasonable costs and attorney fees, arising from compliance by the parties with the order of the court or responsible administrative authority or arising as a consequence of the transferee's failure to comply with ORS 33.850 to 33.875.

(3) An annuity issuer or an obligor may not be required to divide any periodic payments between the payee and any transferee or assignee or between two or more transferees or assignees.

(4) Any further transfer of payment rights by the payee may be made only after compliance with all of the requirements of ORS 33.850 to 33.875. [2005 c.173 §5]

33.875 Limitations on transfers. (1) The provisions of ORS 33.850 to 33.875 may not be waived by any payee.

(2) A transfer agreement entered into on or after January 1, 2006, by a payee who resides in this state shall provide that disputes under the transfer agreement, including any claim that the payee has breached the agreement, shall be determined under the laws of this state. A transfer agreement may not authorize the transferee or any other party to confess judgment or consent to entry to judgment against the payee.

(3) A transfer of payment rights may not extend to any payments that are life contingent unless, prior to the date on which the payee signs the transfer agreement, the transferee has established and has agreed to maintain procedures reasonably satisfactory to the annuity issuer and the obligor for:

(a) Periodically confirming the payee's survival.

(b) Giving the annuity issuer and the obligor prompt written notice in the event of the payee's death.

(4) A payee who proposes to make a transfer of payment rights does not incur any penalty, forfeit any application fee or other payment, or otherwise incur any liability to the proposed transferee or a assignee based on any failure of the transfer to satisfy the conditions of ORS 33.850 to 33.875.

(5) Nothing in ORS 33.850 to 33.875 shall be construed to authorize a transfer of payment rights in contravention of any law or to imply that any transfer under a transfer agreement entered into prior to January 1, 2006, is valid or invalid.

(6) Compliance with the requirements of ORS 33.850 to 33.875 is solely the responsibility of the transferee in any transfer of payment rights, and neither the obligor nor the annuity issuer shall bear any responsibility for, or any liability arising from, noncompliance with the requirements or failure to fulfill the conditions. [2005 c.173 §6; 2013 c.736 §8]

————————————

Chapter 34 — Writs

WRITS

SPECIAL ACTIONS AND PROCEEDINGS

WRIT OF REVIEW

34.010   Former writ of certiorari as writ of review

34.020   Who may obtain review; intermediate orders reviewable

34.030   Jurisdiction to grant writ; petition for writ; time limit

34.040   When allowed

34.050   Plaintiff's undertaking

34.060   To whom directed; return

34.070   Stay of proceedings

34.080   Issuance and service of writ

34.090   Order for further return

34.100   Power of court on review; appeal

34.102   Review of decisions of municipal corporations; transfers between circuit court and Land Use Board of Appeals; limitations

WRIT OF MANDAMUS

(Generally)

34.105   Definitions for ORS 34.105 to 34.240

34.110   When and to whom writ issued

34.120   Courts having jurisdiction

34.130   Petition for writ; service; order of allowance; intervention

34.140   Direction and service of writ; proof of service; enforcing obedience to writ

34.150   Peremptory and alternative writs; form

34.160   Allowance of peremptory writ in first instance

34.170   Answer or motion to dismiss by defendant

34.180   Failure to answer or move for dismissal; additional pleadings

34.190   Other pleadings; construction and amendment of pleadings; motions; manner of trial

34.200   Allowance and trial in Supreme Court

34.210   Recovery of damages; attorney fees, costs and disbursements

34.220   Recovery as a bar

34.230   Imposition of fine; payment as bar

34.240   Appeal

(Mandamus Under Supreme Court's Original Jurisdiction)

34.250   Certain mandamus proceedings under Supreme Court's original jurisdiction

WRIT OF HABEAS CORPUS

34.310   Purpose of writ; who may prosecute

34.320   Courts having jurisdiction; transfer of proceedings

34.330   Who may not prosecute writ

34.340   Petition; who may apply; fee

34.350   Application by district attorney

34.355   Appointment of counsel; compensation and costs

34.360   Contents of petition when person challenges authority for confinement

34.362   Contents of petition when person challenges conditions of confinement or deprivation of rights while confined

34.365   Filing petition of prisoner without payment of filing fees; fee as charge against trust account

34.370   Order to show cause; time for ruling on show cause order; attorney fees; entry of judgment or issuance of writ; effect

34.380   Warrant in lieu of writ; when issued

34.390   Order for arrest of person having custody

34.400   Execution of warrant; return and proceedings thereon

34.410   Criminal offense by person having custody

34.421   Contents of writ

34.430   Defect of form; designation of persons

34.440   Who may serve writ; tender of fees and undertaking when service is on sheriff or other officer

34.450   Payment of charges when service is on person other than sheriff or other officer

34.460   Manner of service

34.470   Service when officer or other person hides or refuses admittance

34.480   Proof of service

34.490   Duty to obey writ

34.500   When return must be made

34.520   Sickness of person

34.530   Requiring return and production of party by order

34.540   Contents of return

34.550   Warrant in case of refusal or neglect to obey writ

34.560   Failure of sheriff to return writ

34.570   Precept commanding bringing of prisoner

34.580   Inquiry into cause of imprisonment

34.590   Discharge when no legal cause for restraint is shown

34.600   When party to be remanded

34.610   Grounds for discharge of prisoner in custody under order or civil process

34.620   Inquiry into legality of certain judgments and process not permitted

34.630   Proceedings where commitment for criminal offense is legal, or party probably is guilty

34.640   Custody of party pending proceedings

34.650   Notice to third persons

34.660   Notice to district attorney

34.670   Replication following return; hearing

34.680   Motion to deny petition; motion to strike; controverting replication; time to plead; construction and effect of pleadings

34.690   Requiring production of person after writ issued

34.695   Conduct of hearing

34.700   Judgment; liability for obedience to judgment; payment of attorney fees

34.710   Appeal; conclusiveness of judgment

34.712   Summary affirmation of judgment on appeal
34.720   Imprisonment after discharge

34.730   Forfeiture for refusing copy of order or process

AMENDMENT OF PETITION OR ACTION TO SEEK PROPER REMEDY

34.740   Amendment of petition or action against public body when wrong remedy sought; effect of amendment on time limitations; attorney fees

CERTAIN WRITS ABOLISHED

34.810   Scire facias and quo warranto

WRIT OF REVIEW

34.010 Former writ of certiorari as writ of review. The writ heretofore known as the writ of certiorari is known in these statutes as the writ of review.

34.020 Who may obtain review; intermediate orders reviewable. Except for a proceeding resulting in a land use decision or limited land use decision as defined in ORS 197.015, for which review is provided in ORS 197.830 to 197.845, or an expedited land division as described in ORS 197.360, for which review is provided in ORS 197.375 (8), any party to any process or proceeding before or by any inferior court, officer, or tribunal may have the decision or determination thereof reviewed for errors, as provided in ORS 34.010 to 34.100, and not otherwise. Upon a review, the court may review any intermediate order involving the merits and necessarily affecting the decision or determination sought to be reviewed. [Amended by 1979 c.772 §8; 1981 c.748 §38; 1983 c.827 §42; 1991 c.817 §18; 1995 c.595 §21]

34.030 Jurisdiction to grant writ; petition for writ; time limit. The writ shall be allowed by the circuit court, or, in counties where the county court has judicial functions, by the county court wherein the decision or determination sought to be reviewed was made, upon the petition of the plaintiff, describing the decision or determination with convenient certainty, and setting forth the errors alleged to have been committed therein. The petition shall be signed by the plaintiff or the attorney of the plaintiff, and verified by the certificate of an attorney to the effect that the attorney has examined the process or proceeding, and the decision or determination therein, and that it is erroneous as alleged in the petition. A writ shall not be allowed unless the petition therefor is made within 60 days from the date of the decision or determination sought to be reviewed. [Amended by 1979 c.772 §9a]

34.040 When allowed. (1) The writ shall be allowed in all cases in which a substantial interest of a plaintiff has been injured and an inferior court including an officer or tribunal other than an agency as defined in ORS 183.310 (1) in the exercise of judicial or quasi-judicial functions appears to have:

(a) Exceeded its jurisdiction;
(b) Failed to follow the procedure applicable to the matter before it;
(c) Made a finding or order not supported by substantial evidence in the whole record;
(d) Improperly construed the applicable law; or
(e) Rendered a decision that is unconstitutional.
(2) The fact that the right of appeal exists is no bar to the issuance of the writ. [Amended by 1965 c.292 §1; 1973 c.561 §1; 1979 c.772 §13; 1995 c.79 §12; 1995 c.658 §29]

34.050 Plaintiff's undertaking. Before allowing the writ, the court shall require the plaintiff to give an undertaking to its approval, with one or more sureties, in the sum of $100, to the effect that the plaintiff will pay all costs and disbursements that may be adjudged to the defendant on the review. [Amended by 1977 c.515 §3; 1979 c.772 §9]

34.055 [1977 c.515 §2; repealed by 1979 c.772 §26]

34.060 To whom directed; return. The writ shall be directed to the court, officer, or tribunal whose decision or determination is sought to be reviewed, or to the clerk or other person having the custody of its records or proceedings, requiring return of the writ to the circuit court, with a certified copy of the record or proceedings in question annexed thereto, so that the same may be reviewed by the circuit court. The court allowing the writ shall fix the date on which it is to be returned, and such date shall be specified in the writ. [Amended by 1959 c.638 §9]

34.070 Stay of proceedings. In the discretion of the court issuing the writ, the writ may contain a requirement that the defendant desist from further proceedings in the matter to be reviewed, whereupon the proceedings shall be stayed accordingly. [Amended by 1977 c.515 §4; 1979 c.772 §10]

34.080 Issuance and service of writ. Upon the filing of the order allowing the writ, and the petition and undertaking of the plaintiff, the clerk shall issue the writ, as ordered. The writ shall be served by delivering the original, according to the direction thereof, and may be served by any person authorized to serve a summons. A certified copy of the writ shall be served by delivery to the opposite party in the suit or proceeding sought to be reviewed, at least 10 days before the return of the original writ.

34.090 Order for further return. If the return to the writ is incomplete, the court may order a further return to be made.

34.100 Power of court on review; appeal. Upon the review, the court shall have power to affirm, modify, reverse or annul the decision or determination reviewed, and if necessary, to award restitution to the plaintiff, or to direct the inferior court, officer, or tribunal to proceed in the matter reviewed according to its decision. From the judgment of the circuit court on review, an appeal may be taken in like manner and with like effect as from a judgment of a circuit court in an action. [Amended by 1973 c.197 §2; 1981 c.178 §2]

34.102 Review of decisions of municipal corporations; transfers between circuit court and Land Use Board of Appeals; limitations. (1) As used in this section, "municipal corporation" means a county, city, district or other municipal corporation or public corporation organized for a public purpose, including a cooperative body formed between municipal corporations.
(2) Except for a proceeding resulting in a land use decision or limited land use decision as defined in ORS 197.015, for which review is provided in ORS 197.830 to 197.845, or an expedited land division as described in ORS 197.360, for which review is provided in ORS 197.375 (8), the decisions of the governing body of a municipal corporation acting in a judicial or quasi-judicial capacity and made in the transaction of municipal corporation business shall be reviewed only as provided in ORS 34.010 to 34.100, and not otherwise.
(3) A petition for writ of review filed in the circuit court and requesting review of a land use decision or limited land use decision as defined in ORS 197.015 of a municipal corporation shall be transferred to the Land Use Board of Appeals and treated as a notice of intent to appeal if the petition was filed within the time allowed for filing a notice of intent to appeal pursuant to ORS 197.830. If the petition was not filed within the time allowed by ORS 197.830, the court shall dismiss the petition.
(4) A notice of intent to appeal filed with the Land Use Board of Appeals pursuant to ORS 197.830 and requesting review of a decision of a municipal corporation made in the transaction of municipal corporation business that is not reviewable as a land use decision or limited land use decision as defined in ORS 197.015 shall be transferred to the circuit court and treated as a petition for writ of review. If the notice was not filed with the board within the time allowed for filing a petition for writ of review pursuant to ORS 34.010 to 34.100, the court shall dismiss the petition.
(5) In any case in which the Land Use Board of Appeals or circuit court to which a petition or notice is transferred under subsection (3) or (4) of this section disputes whether it has authority to review the decision with which the petition or notice is concerned, the board or court before which the matter is pending shall refer the question of whether the board or court has authority to review to the Court of Appeals, which shall decide the question in a summary manner. [Formerly 19.230]

Note: 34.102 was enacted into law by the Legislative Assembly but was not added to or made a part of ORS chapter 34 or any series therein by legislative action. See Preface to Oregon Revised Statutes for further explanation.

WRIT OF MANDAMUS

(Generally)

34.105 Definitions for ORS 34.105 to 34.240. As used in ORS 34.105 to 34.240:
(1) "Adverse party" means a beneficially interested party to a judicial or administrative proceeding from which a mandamus proceeding arises, whose interests are adverse to the relator.
(2) "Counsel for defendant" means the attorney who appears on behalf of the defendant in a mandamus proceeding as provided in ORS 34.130 (4).
(3) "Defendant" means the court, corporation, board, officer or person against whom relief is sought in a mandamus proceeding.
(4) "Relator" means the beneficially interested party on whose relation a mandamus proceeding is brought. [1989 c.702 §2]

34.110 When and to whom writ issued. A writ of mandamus may be issued to any inferior court, corporation, board, officer or person, to compel the performance of an act which the law specially enjoins, as a duty resulting from an office, trust or station; but though the writ may require such court, corporation, board, officer or person to exercise judgment, or proceed to the discharge of any functions, it shall not control judicial discretion. The writ shall not be issued in any case where there is a plain, speedy and adequate remedy in the ordinary course of the law.

34.120 Courts having jurisdiction. (1) Except as provided in subsection (2) of this section, the circuit court or judge thereof of the county wherein the defendant, if a public officer or body, exercises functions, or if a private person or corporation, wherein such person resides or may be found, or such private corporation might be sued in an action, shall have exclusive jurisdiction of mandamus proceedings, including proceedings under ORS 215.429 and 227.179.
(2) The regular division of the Oregon Tax Court or judge thereof shall have jurisdiction in mandamus proceedings in all cases involving tax laws as described in ORS 305.410, and the Supreme Court may take original jurisdiction in mandamus proceedings as provided in section 2 of amended Article VII of the Oregon Constitution. [Amended by 1965 c.6 §10; 1999 c.340 §6; 1999 c.533 §1]

34.130 Petition for writ; service; order of allowance; intervention. (1) The relator shall file a petition for a writ of mandamus with the clerk of the court or court administrator.

(2) The relator shall serve a copy of the petition on the defendant and, if the mandamus proceeding arises from a judicial or administrative proceeding, on all parties to such proceeding. Service of the petition on the defendant and adverse parties is sufficient if it complies with ORCP 9 B. The court in its discretion may act on a petition regardless of defects in the service of the petition on any adverse party, and the petition may be allowed with or without notice to the adverse party, as in a writ of review proceeding.

(3) Except as to a petition filed in the Supreme Court, the writ shall be allowed by the court or judge thereof on the petition. On the filing of the order of allowance, the clerk or court administrator forthwith shall issue the writ in accordance with the petition. The clerk or court administrator may require the relator to provide a form of writ in accordance with the petition.

(4)(a) Except as provided in paragraph (b) of this subsection, at any time in the course of a mandamus action until the return date of the alternative writ, any adverse party may intervene in the mandamus proceeding as matter of right. At any time subsequent to the return date of the alternative writ, the court in its discretion may allow an adverse party to intervene. With the consent of the defendant and, if the defendant is a judge of the Supreme Court, Court of Appeals, Oregon Tax Court or circuit court, subject to ORS 1.550 and 1.560, the attorney for an adverse party may appear on behalf of the defendant.

(b) For a petition filed pursuant to ORS 215.429 or 227.179, a motion to intervene must be filed with the court within 21 days of the date the petition was filed under subsection (1) of this section.

(5) The filing or allowance of a petition for a writ of mandamus does not stay any judicial or administrative proceeding from which the mandamus proceeding may arise, but the court in its discretion may stay such proceeding. [Amended by 1971 c.193 §27; 1989 c.702 §3; 1999 c.533 §2]

34.140 Direction and service of writ; proof of service; enforcing obedience to writ. (1) The writ shall be directed to the court, corporation, board, officer or person designated in the order of allowance, and may be served thereon, by any person authorized to serve a summons, by delivery of the original to such officer or person, or to any member of such court, or to any officer of such corporation upon whom a summons lawfully may be served. A certified copy of the writ shall be served on all intervenors, adverse parties and counsel for the defendant. Such service is sufficient if it complies with ORCP 9. The relator shall file with the court proof of service of the writ on the defendant, and intervenors, adverse parties and counsel for the defendant, if any.

(2) Obedience to the writ may be enforced in such manner as the court or judge thereof shall direct. [Amended by 1989 c.702 §4]

34.150 Peremptory and alternative writs; form. (1) The writ shall be either alternative or peremptory.

(2) When in the alternative, the writ shall:

(a) State concisely the facts, according to the petition, showing:

(A) The obligation of the defendant to perform the act; and

(B) The omission of the defendant to perform the act;

(b) Command that the defendant, immediately after the receipt of the writ, or at some other specified time:

(A) Perform the act required to be performed; or

(B) Show cause before the court or judge thereof, by whom the writ was allowed, at a time and place therein specified, why the defendant has not done so; and

(c) Command that the defendant then and there return the writ, with the certificate of the defendant annexed, of having done as the defendant is commanded, or the cause of omission thereof.

(3) When peremptory, the writ shall be in a form similar to that described in subsection (2) of this section, except that the words requiring the defendant to show cause why the defendant has not done as commanded, and to return the cause therefor, shall be omitted. [Amended by 2005 c.22 §26]

34.160 Allowance of peremptory writ in first instance. When the right to require the performance of the act is clear, and it is apparent that no valid excuse can be given for not performing it, a peremptory mandamus shall be allowed in the first instance; in all other cases, the alternative writ shall be first issued.

34.170 Answer or motion to dismiss by defendant. On the return day of the alternative writ, or such further day as the court or judge thereof may allow, the defendant on whom the writ was served may show cause by motion to dismiss or answer to the writ, in the same manner as to a complaint in an action. [Amended by 1979 c.284 §70]

34.180 Failure to answer or move for dismissal; additional pleadings. If the defendant does not show cause by motion to dismiss or answer, a peremptory mandamus shall be allowed against the defendant. If the answer contains new matter, the same may be moved against or replied to by the plaintiff, within such time as the court or judge may prescribe. If the replication contains new matter, the same may be moved against by the defendant within such time as the court or judge may prescribe, or the defendant may countervail such matter on the trial or other proceedings by proof, either in direct denial or by way of avoidance. [Amended by 1979 c.284 §71]

34.190 Other pleadings; construction and amendment of pleadings; motions; manner of trial. The pleadings in the proceeding by mandamus are those mentioned in ORS 34.170 and 34.180, and none other are allowed. They are to have the same effect and construction, and may be amended in the same manner, as pleadings in an action. Either party may move to strike out, or be allowed to plead over after motion; and the issues joined shall be tried, and the further proceedings thereon had in like manner and with like effect as in an action. [Amended by 1979 c.284 §72]

34.200 Allowance and trial in Supreme Court. In the Supreme Court the writ may be allowed by the court or any judge thereof, but shall only be tried and determined by the court. All issues therein shall be tried by the court. [Amended by 1965 c.6 §11; 2005 c.22 §27; 2015 c.212 §14]

34.210 Recovery of damages; attorney fees, costs and disbursements. (1) If the court orders issuance of a peremptory writ of mandamus, the relator shall recover from the defendant damages which the relator has sustained from a false return, to be ascertained in the same manner as in an action.

(2) The court in its discretion may designate a prevailing party and award attorney fees, costs and disbursements to the prevailing party, but no attorney fees, costs and disbursements shall be awarded against a judge as a defendant in a mandamus action for any action taken in the judge's official capacity. Attorney fees, costs and disbursements may only be awarded against adverse parties who have been served with the petition and writ. [Amended by 1989 c.702 §5]

34.220 Recovery as a bar. A recovery of damages by virtue of ORS 34.210 against a party who has made a return to a writ of mandamus is a bar to any other action or suit against the same party for the same cause.

34.230 Imposition of fine; payment as bar. Whenever a peremptory mandamus is directed to a public officer or body commanding the performance of any public duty specially enjoined by law, if it appears to the court or judge thereof that the officer or any member of the body has without just excuse refused or neglected to perform the duty so enjoined, the court or judge may impose a fine, not exceeding $500, upon every such officer or member of such body; and the payment thereof is a bar to any action for any penalty incurred by the officer or member by reason of the refusal or neglect of the officer or member to perform the duty so enjoined.

34.240 Appeal. From the judgment of the circuit court or Oregon Tax Court, or judge thereof, refusing to allow a mandamus, or directing a peremptory mandamus, an appeal may be taken in like manner and with like effect as in an action. [Amended by 1965 c.6 §12; 1973 c.197 §3]

34.250 Certain mandamus proceedings under Supreme Court's original jurisdiction. (1) The provisions of this section apply only to the exercise of the Supreme Court's original jurisdiction in mandamus proceedings that challenge the actions of judges in particular cases in the circuit courts, the Oregon Tax Court or the Court of Appeals. The provisions of this section do not apply to the exercise of the Supreme Court's original jurisdiction in mandamus proceedings that challenge the administrative action of a judge or court, or that challenge other action of a judge or court that is of an institutional nature. To the extent that any provision of ORS 34.105 to 34.240 is inconsistent with the provisions of this section, the provisions of this section govern in mandamus proceedings subject to this section.

(2) The case title of a petition in a mandamus proceeding that is subject to this section must be the same as the case title of the proceeding in the lower court, except that the relator must be designated as "relator" in addition to the relator's designation in the lower court, and any party who is adverse to the relator must be designated as "adverse party" in addition to that party's designation in the lower court. The petition must not name as a party to the mandamus proceeding the lower court or the judge whose action is challenged.

(3) The relator must serve a copy of the petition on all parties who have appeared in the lower court case and on the judge or court whose action is being challenged.

(4) The judge or court whose action is challenged in the mandamus proceeding may seek to intervene in the mandamus proceeding if the judge or court wishes to assert an interest separate from the parties. If the Supreme Court allows the judge or court to intervene, the judge or court shall be designated as "intervenor" in the mandamus proceeding.

(5) If the Supreme Court elects to issue an alternative writ of mandamus, the Supreme Court shall issue an order allowing the petition. The order may be issued in combination with the alternative writ of mandamus. The State Court Administrator shall mail copies of the Supreme Court's order and alternative writ of mandamus to the relator, to the adverse party, to any intervenor, and to the judge or court whose action is challenged in the petition. Proof of service of an alternative writ need not be filed with the Supreme Court, and the judge or court to which the writ is issued need not file a return unless the alternative writ specifically requires a return.

(6) At any time after the filing of the petition for writ of mandamus or issuance of the alternative writ of mandamus, if the judge or court whose action is being challenged performs the act sought in the petition or required by the alternative writ, the relator shall notify the Supreme Court that the judge or court has complied. The judge, the court, or any other party to the lower court case may also give notice to the Supreme Court of the compliance. On motion of any party or on its own motion, the Supreme Court may dismiss a mandamus proceeding after receiving the notice provided for in this subsection.

(7) If the judge or court to whom the alternative writ of mandamus is directed does not perform the act required by the writ, the mandamus proceeding will proceed to briefing and oral argument as provided in the rules of the Supreme Court or as directed by the Supreme Court. An answer or other responsive pleading need not be filed by any party to the proceeding unless the alternative writ specifically requires the filing of an answer or other responsive pleading.

(8) If the Supreme Court has determined that the relator is entitled to a peremptory writ of mandamus, the court shall direct the State Court Administrator to issue a peremptory writ of mandamus. The peremptory writ of mandamus may be combined with the appellate judgment. If a combined peremptory writ of mandamus and an appellate judgment issue, the relator need not file proof of service of the writ with the court, and the judge or court to which the writ is issued need not file a return showing compliance with the writ.

(9) The State Court Administrator shall issue an appellate judgment showing the Supreme Court's disposition of the matter, as provided in the rules of the Supreme Court, if:

(a) The court has issued an alternative or peremptory writ of mandamus, the mandamus proceeding is concluded and all issues in the proceeding have been decided; or

(b) The court has not issued a writ of mandamus, but the court has awarded costs and disbursements or attorney fees in the proceeding. [1997 c.388 §2]

WRIT OF HABEAS CORPUS

34.310 Purpose of writ; who may prosecute. The writ of habeas corpus ad subjiciendum is the writ designated in ORS 34.310 to 34.730, and every other writ of habeas corpus is abolished. Every person imprisoned or otherwise restrained of liberty, within this state, except in the cases specified in ORS 34.330, may prosecute a writ of habeas corpus to inquire into the cause of such imprisonment or restraint, and if illegal, to be delivered therefrom.

34.320 Courts having jurisdiction; transfer of proceedings. The circuit court of the judicial district wherein the party is imprisoned or restrained, and, if vested with power to exercise judicial functions, the county court and county judge of the county wherein the party is imprisoned or restrained, shall have concurrent jurisdiction of proceedings by habeas corpus, and said courts and judges may issue, hear and decide all questions arising upon habeas corpus. If a plaintiff has filed a petition in a court with jurisdiction over the proceedings, and the plaintiff is thereafter transferred to a place that is outside of the jurisdiction of that court, the court shall transfer the proceedings to the circuit court for the judicial district in which the party is imprisoned or restrained. If the court in which the petition was filed determines that by reason of the plaintiff's transfer the claims of the plaintiff do not require immediate judicial scrutiny, or are otherwise subject to dismissal, the court shall dismiss the petition. [Amended by 1999 c.114 §1]

34.330 Who may not prosecute writ. A person may not prosecute a writ of habeas corpus if:

(1) The person is imprisoned or restrained by virtue of process issued by a court of the United States, or a judge, commissioner or other officer thereof, in cases where such courts, or judges or officers thereof, have exclusive jurisdiction under the laws of the United States, or have acquired exclusive jurisdiction by the commencement of actions, suits or other proceedings in such court, or before such commissioner or other officer.

(2) The person is imprisoned or restrained by virtue of the judgment of a competent tribunal of civil or criminal jurisdiction, or by virtue of an execution issued upon such judgment.

(3) Except as provided in ORS 138.530, the person is eligible to obtain post-conviction relief pursuant to ORS 138.510 to 138.680.

(4) The person is eligible to seek judicial review of a final order of the State Board of Parole and Post-Prison Supervision under ORS 144.335 but the person fails to seek judicial review of the order in a timely manner.

(5) The person seeks judicial review of a final order of the board under ORS 144.335 but the Court of Appeals:

(a) Summarily affirms the order of the board on the grounds that the person failed to present a substantial question of law;

(b) Otherwise disposes of the judicial review on the merits of the petitioner's issues on judicial review; or

(c) Dismisses the judicial review because of a procedural defect. [Amended by 1959 c.636 §22; 2001 c.661 §2; 2003 c.576 §311; 2007 c.411 §2]

34.340 Petition; who may apply; fee. The writ shall be allowed by the court or judge thereof upon the petition of the party for whose relief it is intended, or of some other person in behalf of the party, signed and verified by the oath of the plaintiff, to the effect that the plaintiff believes it to be true. The petition must be accompanied by the filing fee established under ORS 21.135. [Amended by 1995 c.657 §6; 1999 c.114 §2; 2003 c.737 §§32,33; 2005 c.702 §§37,38,39; 2011 c.595 §39]

34.350 Application by district attorney. Whenever a writ of habeas corpus is required in any action, suit or proceeding, civil or criminal, to which the state is a party, the application therefor may be made by the district attorney having charge thereof, and whenever so issued the court or judge shall state in the order of allowance that it was issued on such application.

34.355 Appointment of counsel; compensation and costs. If counsel is appointed by a court to represent, in an initial proceeding by habeas corpus or on appeal as provided in ORS 34.710, a person who is imprisoned or otherwise restrained of liberty by virtue of a charge or conviction of crime and who is determined to be financially eligible for appointed counsel at state expense, the public defense services executive director shall determine compensation for counsel and costs and expenses of the person in the proceeding or on appeal. Compensation for counsel and expenses of the person in an initial proceeding or in a circuit court on appeal shall be determined and paid as provided in ORS 135.055. Compensation for counsel and costs and expenses of the person on appeal to the Court of Appeals or on review by the Supreme Court shall be determined and paid as provided in ORS 138.500. The compensation and expenses so allowed in an initial proceeding in a county court shall be paid by the county in which the person was charged or convicted of crime. [1979 c.867 §17; 1981 s.s. c.3 §128; 1985 c.502 §21; 2001 c.962 §64]

34.360 Contents of petition when person challenges authority for confinement. If the challenge is to the authority for confinement, the petition shall state, in substance:
(1) That the party in whose behalf the writ is petitioned is imprisoned or restrained of liberty, the place where, and officer or person by whom the party is imprisoned or restrained, naming both parties if their names are known, or describing them if not known.
(2) That such person is not imprisoned or restrained by virtue of any order, judgment or process specified in ORS 34.330.
(3) The cause or pretense of the imprisonment or restraint, according to the best knowledge or belief of the plaintiff.
(4) If the original imprisonment or restraint is by virtue of any order, warrant or process, a copy thereof shall be annexed to the petition, or it must be alleged that, by reason of the removal or concealment of the party before the application, a demand of such copy could not be made, or that the demand was made, and the legal fees therefor tendered to the person having the party in custody, and that a copy was refused.
(5) That the claim has not already been adjudged upon a prior writ of habeas corpus, to the knowledge or belief of the plaintiff. [Amended by 1991 c.884 §3; 1999 c.114 §3; 2003 c.576 §312]

34.362 Contents of petition when person challenges conditions of confinement or deprivation of rights while confined. If the person is imprisoned or restrained by virtue of any order, judgment or process specified in ORS 34.330 and the person challenges the conditions of confinement or complains of a deprivation of rights while confined, the petition shall:
(1) Comply with requirements of ORS 34.360 (1), (3), (4) and (5); and
(2) State facts in support of a claim that the person is deprived of a constitutional right that requires immediate judicial attention and for which no other timely remedy is practicably available to the plaintiff. [1991 c.884 §5; 2003 c.576 §313]

34.365 Filing petition of prisoner without payment of filing fees; fee as charge against trust account. (1) Any court of the State of Oregon may authorize the filing of a petition for a writ of habeas corpus by or on behalf of any person imprisoned or otherwise restrained of liberty by virtue of a charge or conviction of crime without payment of the filing fees therefor, if such person presents to the court or judge thereof satisfactory proof, by affidavit and as otherwise required by such judge, that the person is unable to pay such fees.
(2) Notwithstanding the fact that a court has authorized the filing of a petition without payment of the filing fee required by ORS 34.340, the fee may be drawn from, or charged against, the plaintiff's trust account if the plaintiff is an inmate in a correctional facility. [1955 c.493 §1; 1995 c.657 §7; 1999 c.114 §4]

34.370 Order to show cause; time for ruling on show cause order; attorney fees; entry of judgment or issuance of writ; effect. (1) Except as provided in subsection (6) of this section, the judge to whom the petition for a writ of habeas corpus is presented shall, without delay, issue an order directing the defendant to show cause why the writ should not be allowed.
(2) Upon the issuance of a show cause order under subsection (1) of this section, the following shall apply:
(a) The judge shall order that the defendant appear in writing in opposition to the issuance of the writ as soon as is practicable and not more than 14 days from the date that the show cause order issues.
(b) The judge shall rule on the show cause order within seven days after either the defendant files a written appearance in opposition or the appearance period expires, whichever comes first. Upon making a ruling, the judge shall do one of the following, as appropriate:
(A) If the petition is a meritless petition, issue a judgment denying the petition and ordering the plaintiff to pay the cost of attorney fees incurred by the defendant. In no case shall the award of attorney fees exceed $100. The fees may be drawn from, or charged against, the inmate's trust account.
(B) Issue a judgment granting appropriate habeas corpus relief.
(C) Issue a writ of habeas corpus requiring that a return be made.
(3) Entry of a judgment under subsection (2)(b)(A) or subsection (6) of this section shall be without prejudice. The judgment shall explain to the parties the reason for the denial.
(4) If the court has issued a writ of habeas corpus requiring a return under subsection (2)(b)(C) of this section, the parties may stipulate to a hearing as described in ORS 34.670 without the necessity of a return or a replication. If the court accepts the stipulation, it shall set the matter for hearing in an expedited manner.
(5) Issuance of the writ under subsection (2) of this section shall not bind the court with respect to any subsequent rulings related to the pleadings of the parties or the ultimate disposition of the proceeding.
(6) The court may, on its own motion, enter a judgment denying a meritless petition brought under ORS 34.310 to 34.730.
(7) As used in this section, "meritless petition" means one which, when liberally construed, fails to state a claim upon which habeas corpus relief may be granted. [Amended by 1963 c.322 §1; 1991 c.884 §6; 1995 c.294 §1; 1995 c.657 §8; 1999 c.114 §5]

34.380 Warrant in lieu of writ; when issued. Whenever it appears by satisfactory evidence that any person is illegally imprisoned or restrained and there is good reason to believe that the person will be carried out of the state or suffer irreparable injury before the person can be relieved by the issuing of a habeas corpus, any court or judge authorized to issue such writ may issue a warrant reciting the facts, directed to any sheriff or other person therein designated, commanding the sheriff or other person to take such illegally imprisoned or restrained person and forthwith bring the person before such court or judge, to be dealt with according to law.

34.390 Order for arrest of person having custody. When the proof mentioned in ORS 34.380 is also sufficient to justify an arrest of the person having the party in custody, as for a criminal offense committed in the taking or detaining of such party, the warrant may also contain an order for the arrest of such person for such offense.

34.400 Execution of warrant; return and proceedings thereon. Any officer or person to whom a warrant issued under ORS 34.380 is directed shall execute the same by bringing the party therein named and the person who detains the party, if so commanded by the warrant, before the court or judge issuing the warrant; and thereupon the person detaining such party shall make a return in like manner, and the like proceedings shall be had thereon, as if a writ of habeas corpus had been issued in the first instance.

34.410 Criminal offense by person having custody. If the person having such party in custody is brought before the court or judge as for a criminal offense, the person shall be examined, committed, released or discharged by the court or judge in like manner as in other criminal cases of like nature. [Amended by 1973 c.836 §324]

34.420 [Repealed by 1991 c.884 §1 (34.421 enacted in lieu of 34.420)]

34.421 Contents of writ. The writ shall require the defendant to file a return, at a specified time and place, that states the time and cause of plaintiff's imprisonment or restraint. The writ shall not command the defendant to produce the plaintiff before the court or judge issuing the writ, unless the court, in its discretion, so orders. The court shall consider an allegation of lack of authority, brought only under ORS 34.360, as a factor weighing in favor of requiring the defendant to produce the plaintiff at the time of the return. [1991 c.884 §2 (enacted in lieu of 34.420)]

34.430 Defect of form; designation of persons. The writ shall not be disobeyed for any defect of form. It is sufficient:

(1) If the officer or person having the custody of the person imprisoned or restrained is designated either by name of office, if the officer or person has any, or by the own name of the officer or person, or if both such names are unknown or uncertain, the officer or person may be described by an assumed appellation; and anyone who may be served with the writ is to be deemed the officer or person to whom it was directed, although it may be directed to the officer or person by a wrong name or description, or to another person.

(2) If the person who is directed to be produced is designated by name, or if the name of the person is uncertain or unknown, the person may be described in any other way, so as to designate the person intended.

34.440 Who may serve writ; tender of fees and undertaking when service is on sheriff or other officer. (1) A writ of habeas corpus may be served by any sheriff within the county of the sheriff, or by any other person designated in the writ in any county within the state. The service of the writ shall be deemed complete, so as to require the prisoner to be brought up before the court or judge issuing the writ under the provisions of ORS 34.370, only if:

(a) The party serving the writ tenders to the person in whose custody the prisoner may be, if such person is a sheriff or other officer, the fees allowed by law for bringing up such prisoner; and

(b) The party also enters into an undertaking to such sheriff or other officer, in a penalty double the sum for which the prisoner is detained, if the prisoner is detained for any specific sum of money, and if not, then in such a sum as the judge granting the writ directs, not exceeding $1,000, to the effect that such person shall pay the charges for carrying back the prisoner if the prisoner is remanded, and that the prisoner will not escape, either in going to or returning from the place to which the prisoner is to be taken.

(2) If such fees are not paid, or such security is not tendered, the officer to whom the writ is directed shall make a return, in the manner required by ORS 34.540, and shall state in the return the reason why the prisoner is not produced, and thereupon the court or judge granting the writ may proceed as if the prisoner was produced. This section, except for the first sentence, does not apply to a case wherein the writ is issued on the application of the district attorney. [Amended by 1991 c.884 §7]

34.450 Payment of charges when service is on person other than sheriff or other officer. Every court or judge allowing a writ of habeas corpus, directed to a person other than a sheriff or other officer, may require, in order to render the service effectual, that the charges of producing the party be paid by the applicant; and in such case the court or judge shall, in the order allowing the writ, specify the amount of such charges, which shall not exceed the fees allowed by law to sheriffs for similar services.

34.460 Manner of service. The writ of habeas corpus may be served by delivery of the original to the officer or person to whom it is directed, or if the officer or person cannot be found, by leaving it at the jail or other place in which the party is imprisoned or restrained, with any under officer or other person having charge for the time of such party.

34.470 Service when officer or other person hides or refuses admittance. If the officer or person on whom the writ ought to be served hides from the person attempting to make service, or refuses admittance to the person attempting to make service, it may be served by affixing it in some conspicuous place on the outside, either of the dwelling house of the officer or person or the jail or other place where the party is confined. [Amended by 1987 c.158 §5]

34.480 Proof of service. The proof of service of the writ shall be the same as in the service of a summons, except that the same shall be indorsed upon a copy of the writ made by the officer or person serving it, and returned to the clerk who issued the writ.

34.490 Duty to obey writ. It is the duty of every sheriff or other officer upon whom a writ of habeas corpus is served, whether such writ is directed to the sheriff or officer or not, upon payment or tender of the fees allowed by law, and the delivery or tender of the undertaking described in ORS 34.440, to obey and return the writ according to the exigency thereof; and it is the duty of every other person upon whom the writ is served, having the custody of the person for whose benefit it is issued, to obey and return it in like manner, without requiring the payment of any fees, unless the payment of such fees has been required by the court or judge allowing such writ.

34.500 When return must be made. If the writ is returnable at a certain time, the return shall be made at the time and place specified therein; if it is returnable forthwith, and the place of return is within 20 miles of the place of service, the return must be made within 24 hours, and the same time is allowed for every additional 20 miles.

34.510 [Repealed by 1991 c.884 §10]

34.520 Sickness of person. Whenever, from the sickness or infirmity of the party, the party cannot, without danger, be produced, the officer or person in whose custody the party is may state that fact in the return to the writ, and if satisfied of the truth of the allegation, and the return is otherwise sufficient, the court or judge shall proceed to decide on the return, and to dispose of the matter, the same as if the party had been produced.

34.530 Requiring return and production of party by order. At any time after the allowance of a writ of habeas corpus, the plaintiff therein, or the person applying therefor on behalf of the plaintiff, may give notice to the judge issuing the writ, and thereupon, if necessary to avoid delay, the judge shall by order require that the return be made and the party produced before the judge at such time and place, within the county or district, as may be convenient.

34.540 Contents of return. (1) The officer or person upon whom the writ was duly served shall state in the return, plainly and unequivocally:

(a) Whether the officer or person has the party in custody or power or under restraint, and if the officer or person has not, whether the officer or person has had the party in custody or under power or restraint at any and what time prior or subsequent to the date of the writ.

(b) If the officer or person has the party in custody or power or under restraint, the authority and true cause of such imprisonment or restraint, setting forth the same at large.

(2) If the party is detained by virtue of any writ, warrant or other written authority, a copy thereof shall be annexed to the return, and the original shall be produced, and exhibited on the return of the writ, to the court or judge before whom the writ is returnable.

(3) If the person upon whom the writ was served has had the party in power or custody or under restraint at any time prior or subsequent to the date of the writ, but has transferred such custody or restraint to another, the return shall state particularly to whom, at what time, for what cause, and by what authority the transfer took place.

(4) The return shall be signed by the person making the same, and except where the person is a sworn public officer, and makes the return in official capacity, it shall be verified by oath.

34.550 Warrant in case of refusal or neglect to obey writ. If the person upon whom the writ was duly served refuses or neglects to obey the same by producing the party named in the writ and making a full and explicit return thereto within the time required, and no sufficient excuse is shown therefor, the court or judge before whom the writ was made returnable shall, upon due proof of the service thereof, forthwith issue a warrant against such person, directed to any sheriff in this state, commanding the sheriff forthwith to apprehend such person and bring the person immediately before such court or judge; and on the person being so brought, the person shall be committed to close custody in the jail of the county in which such judge shall be until the person makes return to the writ and complies with any order made in relation to the party for whose relief the writ was issued.

34.560 Failure of sheriff to return writ. If a sheriff neglects to return the writ, the warrant may be directed to any other person to be designated therein, who shall have full power to execute the same, and such sheriff, upon being brought up, may be committed to the jail of any county other than the county over which the sheriff has jurisdiction. [Amended by 1965 c.221 §12; 1987 c.158 §6]

34.570 Precept commanding bringing of prisoner. The court or judge issuing the warrant may also, at the same time or afterwards, issue a precept to the person to whom the warrant is directed, commanding the person to bring forthwith before such court or judge the party for whose benefit the writ was allowed, who shall thereafter remain in the custody of such person until discharged or remanded.

34.580 Inquiry into cause of imprisonment. The court or judge before whom the party is brought on the writ shall, immediately after the return thereof, proceed to examine into the facts contained in the return, and into the cause of the imprisonment or restraint of such party.

34.590 Discharge when no legal cause for restraint is shown. If no legal cause is shown for the imprisonment or restraint, or for the continuation thereof, the court or judge shall discharge such party from the custody or restraint under which the person is held.

34.600 When party to be remanded. It shall be the duty of the court or judge forthwith to remand such party if it appears that the party is legally detained in custody, either:
(1) By virtue of process issued by any court, or judge or commissioner or any other officer thereof, of the United States, in a case where such court, or judge or officer thereof, has exclusive jurisdiction; or,
(2) By virtue of the judgment of any court, or of any execution issued upon such judgment; or,
(3) For any contempt, specially and plainly charged in the commitment, by some court, officer or body having authority to commit for the contempt so charged; and,
(4) That the time during which such party may legally be detained has not expired. [Amended by 2003 c.576 §314]

34.610 Grounds for discharge of prisoner in custody under order or civil process. If it appears on the return that the prisoner is in custody by virtue of an order or civil process of any court legally constituted, or issued by an officer in the course of judicial proceedings before the officer, authorized by law, such prisoner shall be discharged only if one of the following cases exists:
(1) The jurisdiction of the court or officer has been exceeded, either as to matter, place, sum or person.
(2) The original imprisonment was lawful, yet by some act, omission or event which has taken place afterwards, the party has become entitled to be discharged.
(3) The order or process is defective in some matter of substance required by law, rendering the same void.
(4) The order or process, though in proper form, has been issued in a case not allowed by law.
(5) The person having the custody of the prisoner under such order or process is not the person empowered by law to detain the prisoner.
(6) The order or process is not authorized by any judgment of any court, nor by any provision of law. [Amended by 2003 c.576 §315]

34.620 Inquiry into legality of certain judgments and process not permitted. No court or judge, on the return of a writ of habeas corpus, has power to inquire into the legality or justice of any order, judgment or process specified in ORS 34.330, nor into the justice, propriety or legality of any commitment for a contempt made by a court, officer or body, according to law, and charged in such commitment, as provided by law.

34.630 Proceedings where commitment for criminal offense is legal, or party probably is guilty. If it appears that the party has legally been committed for a criminal offense, or if the party appears by the testimony offered with the return, or upon the hearing thereof, probably to be guilty of such offense, although the commitment is irregular, the party shall forthwith be remanded to the custody or placed under the restraint from which the party was taken, if the officer or person under whose custody or restraint the party was, is legally entitled thereto; if not so entitled, the party shall be committed to the custody of the officer or person so entitled.

34.640 Custody of party pending proceedings. Until judgment is given upon the return, the party may either be committed to the custody of the sheriff of the county, or placed in such care or custody as age and other circumstances may require.

34.650 Notice to third persons. When it appears from the return that the party named therein is in custody on an order or process under which another person has an interest in continuing imprisonment or restraint of the party, no order shall be made for discharge of the party until it shall appear that the party so interested, or the attorney of the party so interested has had notice of the time and place at which the writ has been made returnable.

34.660 Notice to district attorney. When it appears from the return that the party is imprisoned or restrained on a criminal accusation, the court or judge shall make no order for the discharge of the party until notice of the return is given to the district attorney of the county where the party is imprisoned or restrained.

34.670 Replication following return; hearing. The plaintiff in the proceeding, on the return of the writ, may, by replication, signed as in an action, controvert any of the material facts set forth in the return, or the plaintiff may allege therein any fact to show, either that imprisonment or restraint of the plaintiff is unlawful, or that the plaintiff is entitled to discharge. Thereupon the court or judge shall proceed in a summary way to hear such evidence as may be produced in support of or against the imprisonment or restraint, and to dispose of the party as the law and justice of the case may require. [Amended by 1979 c.284 §73; 2005 c.22 §28]

34.680 Motion to deny petition; motion to strike; controverting replication; time to plead; construction and effect of pleadings. (1) The defendant may, before the writ issues, move to deny the petition on the grounds that the petition fails to state a claim for habeas corpus relief. The defendant may, at any time after the writ issues, move to dismiss the writ on the grounds that the pleadings, including the petition, the return, the replication, if any, and any supporting evidence, demonstrate that plaintiff has failed to state or establish a claim for habeas corpus relief.
(2) The plaintiff may move to strike the return or any allegation or defense in the return. The defendant may move to strike the replication or any new matter in the replication, or by proof controvert the same, as upon a direct denial or avoidance.
(3) The return and replication shall be made within such time as the court or judge shall direct, and the petition, return and replication shall be construed and have the same effect as in an action. [Amended by 1979 c.284 §74; 1991 c.884 §8]

34.690 Requiring production of person after writ issued. The court or judge before whom the writ is returnable may, before final decision, issue a precept to the officer or other person to whom the writ is directed, requiring the production of the person. [Amended by 1991 c.884 §9]

34.695 Conduct of hearing. If the matter proceeds to an evidentiary hearing, as described in ORS 34.670, the court shall decide the issues raised in the pleadings and may receive proof by affidavits, depositions, oral testimony or other competent evidence. [1991 c.884 §12]

34.700 Judgment; liability for obedience to judgment; payment of attorney fees. (1) If it appears that the party detained is imprisoned or restrained illegally, judgment shall be given that the party be discharged forthwith; otherwise, judgment shall be given that the proceeding be dismissed and the party remanded. No officer or other person is liable to any action or proceeding for obeying such judgment of discharge.

(2) The court shall include in the judgment an order that the defendant pay the attorney fees incurred by the petition, not to exceed $100, if:

(a) The court enters a judgment requiring that the plaintiff be discharged; and

(b) The court finds that the allegations or defenses in the return were frivolous. [Amended by 1995 c.657 §9; 1999 c.114 §6]

34.710 Appeal; conclusiveness of judgment. Any party to a proceeding by habeas corpus, including the state when the district attorney appears therein, may appeal from the judgment of the court refusing to allow such writ or any judgment therein, in like manner and with like effect as in an action. No question once finally determined upon a proceeding by habeas corpus shall be reexamined upon another proceeding of the same kind. [Amended by 2003 c.576 §235; 2015 c.212 §15]

34.712 Summary affirmation of judgment on appeal. In reviewing the judgment of any court under ORS 34.310 to 34.730, the Court of Appeals, on its own motion or on the motion of the defendant, may summarily affirm, without oral argument, the judgment after submission of the appellant's brief and without submission of the defendant's brief if the court finds that no substantial question of law is presented by the appeal. Notwithstanding ORS 2.570, the Chief Judge of the Court of Appeals may deny or, if the plaintiff does not oppose the motion, grant a defendant's motion for summary affirmation. A dismissal of appeal under this section constitutes a decision upon the merits of the appeal. [1995 c.294 §3; 1999 c.114 §7]

34.720 Imprisonment after discharge. A person who has been finally discharged upon a proceeding by habeas corpus may not again be imprisoned, restrained or kept in custody for the same cause. A person is not deemed to be imprisoned, restrained or kept in custody for the same cause if:

(1) The person has been discharged from a commitment on a criminal charge, and afterwards is committed for the same offense by the legal order or process of the court wherein the person is bound by a release agreement or has deposited security, or in which the person is indicted or convicted for the same offense;

(2) After a judgment of discharge for a defect of evidence or for a material defect in the commitment, in a criminal case, the party again is arrested on sufficient evidence, and committed by legal process for the same offense;

(3) In a civil action or suit, the party has been discharged for illegality in the judgment or process, and afterwards is imprisoned for the same cause of action or suit; or

(4) In a civil action or suit, the person has been discharged from commitment on a writ of arrest, and afterwards is committed on execution, in the same action or suit, or on a writ of arrest in another action or suit, after the dismissal of the first one. [Amended by 1973 c.836 §325; 2003 c.14 §17; 2003 c.576 §316]

34.730 Forfeiture for refusing copy of order or process. Any officer or other person refusing to deliver a copy of any order, warrant, process or other authority by which the officer or person detains any person, to anyone who demands a copy, and tenders the fees therefor, shall forfeit $200 to the person so detained.

AMENDMENT OF PETITION OR ACTION TO SEEK PROPER REMEDY

34.740 Amendment of petition or action against public body when wrong remedy sought; effect of amendment on time limitations; attorney fees. (1) A circuit court shall allow a person to amend a petition or action in the manner provided by this section if:

(a) The person seeks relief against a public body, as defined in ORS 192.311;

(b) The person incorrectly filed a petition for a writ of review, a petition for a writ of mandamus or an action for declaratory judgment; and

(c) The correct remedy of the person is a petition for a writ of review, a petition for a writ of mandamus or an action for declaratory judgment.

(2) If a petition or action is amended under this section, the petition or action is not subject to dismissal by reason of not having been commenced within the time otherwise allowed by law if the reason that the person filed the wrong petition or action was either:

(a) The person relied on a reasonable interpretation of the law relating to the correct remedy; or

(b) The public body that is the respondent or defendant in the proceeding gave misleading information to the person about the proper remedy, the person relied in good faith on the information provided by the public body and by reason of that reliance the person sought the wrong remedy.

(3) A circuit court shall order a public body, as defined in ORS 192.311, to pay reasonable attorney fees incurred by any person in filing a petition for a writ of review, a petition for a writ of mandamus or an action for declaratory judgment seeking relief from the public body if:

(a) The court determines that the person has filed the wrong petition or action, and the person subsequently amends the pleading in the manner provided by subsection (1) of this section;

(b) The public body that is the respondent or defendant in the proceeding gave information to the person with the intent to mislead the person as to the proper remedy or gave information to the person, with a reckless disregard for the truth or falsity of the information, about the proper remedy; and

(c) The person relied in good faith on the information provided by the public body, and by reason of that reliance the person sought the wrong remedy. [2001 c.561 §2]

Note: 34.740 was enacted into law by the Legislative Assembly but was not added to or made a part of ORS chapter 34 or any series therein by legislative action. See Preface to Oregon Revised Statutes for further explanation.

CERTAIN WRITS ABOLISHED

34.810 Scire facias and quo warranto. The writ of scire facias, the writ of quo warranto, and proceedings by information in the nature of quo warranto are abolished, and the remedies heretofore obtainable under those forms may be obtained by action in the mode prescribed in ORS 30.510 to 30.640.

34.820 [Repealed 1981 c.898 §53]

————————

Chapter 35 — Eminent Domain; Public Acquisition of Property

2017 EDITION

EMINENT DOMAIN; PUBLIC ACQUISITION OF PROPERTY

SPECIAL ACTIONS AND PROCEEDINGS

LIMITATION OF CONDEMNATION POWER

35.015   Prohibition on condemnation of certain properties with intent to convey property to private party; exceptions

35.018   Severability

PROCEDURE

35.205   Short title

35.215   Definitions for chapter

35.220   Precondemnation entry on real property

35.235   Agreement for compensation; status of resolution or ordinance of public condemner; status of action of private condemner; agreement effort not prerequisite

35.245   Commencement of action; jurisdiction; parties

35.255   Content of complaint

35.265   Advance deposit by public condemner requiring immediate possession; effect on interest otherwise allowable

35.275   Advance occupancy by private condemner; hearing; deposit or bond; effect of size of bond or deposit on amount of just compensation

35.285   Distribution of deposits; effect of withdrawal on appeal

35.295   Defendant's answer

35.300   Offer of compromise

35.305   Conduct of trial; defendant's option; jury argument; neither side has burden of proof of just compensation

35.315   View of property by order of court

35.325   Effect of judgment; effect of payment under judgment

35.335   Effect of condemner's abandonment of action

35.346   Offer to purchase required before filing action for condemnation; appraisal; arbitration; when costs and disbursements allowed

35.348   Immediate possession of property

35.350   Immediate possession of property by public body

35.352   Notice of immediate possession of property by public condemner; objection

35.355   Appeal

35.365   Effect of withdrawal of award; disposition of award

35.375   Chapter as exclusive condemnation proceeding; exception

35.385   Public purpose use required of condemner; right of repurchase; specification of duration of public purpose use; effect

35.390   Effect of failure of condemner to use property as required; price of repurchase; form of offer of repurchase

35.395   Change in period of use; notice; effect of failure to agree on change; review by court

35.400   Designation of person to exercise right of repurchase; effect of failure to designate; offer to repurchase; acceptance; notice; determination of price

35.405   Designation of person to exercise right of repurchase by multiple owners

35.410   Right to contest change in public purpose use; notice of proposed change

35.415   Application of ORS 35.385 to 35.415

RELOCATION OF DISPLACED PERSONS

35.500   Definitions for ORS 35.500 to 35.530

35.505   Relocation within neighborhood; notice prior to move; costs and allowances

35.510   Duties of public entities acquiring real property

35.515   Required disclosures for business and farm operations

35.520   Decision on benefits; hearing; review

35.525   Construction

35.530   Federal law controls

CONDEMNATION BY STATE

35.550   Definitions for ORS 35.550 to 35.575

35.555   Determination of necessity; suit by Attorney General

35.560   Action by district attorney

35.565   Procedure for condemnation

35.570   Payment of expenses of proceeding, value and damages

35.575   Precondemnation compensation not required

CONDEMNATION OF PROPERTY ADJOINING PROPOSED ROADWAYS

35.600   Application

35.605   Authorization to acquire adjoining property for roadways

35.610   Ordinance or resolution required

35.615   Restrictions on future use of property acquired adjacent to roadway

35.620   Acquisition of land adjoining road boundaries declared necessary

35.625   Procedure to ascertain compensation and damages

35.010 [Repealed by 1971 c.741 §38]

LIMITATION OF CONDEMNATION POWER

35.015 Prohibition on condemnation of certain properties with intent to convey property to private party; exceptions. (1) Except as otherwise provided in this section, a public body as defined in ORS 174.109 may not condemn private real property used as a residence, business establishment, farm or forest operation if at the time of the condemnation the public body intends to convey fee title to all or a portion of the real property, or a lesser interest than fee title, to another private party.
(2) Subsection (1) of this section does not apply to condemnation of:
(a) Improved or unimproved real property that constitutes a danger to the health or safety of the community by reason of contamination, dilapidated structures, improper or insufficient water or sanitary facilities, or any combination of these factors;
(b) Any timber, crops, topsoil, gravel or fixtures to be removed from the real property being condemned; or
(c) Real property condemned for maintenance, improvement, or construction of transportation facilities, transportation systems, utility facilities or utility transmission systems.
(3) Subsection (1) of this section does not prohibit a public body from leasing a portion of a public facility to a privately owned business for the provision of retail services designed primarily to serve the patrons of the public facility.
(4) A public body as defined in ORS 174.109 may at any time publish notice that the public body intends to consider condemnation of a lot or parcel. If the public body publishes notice under this subsection, subsection (1) of this section does not apply for such time necessary to provide the public body reasonable opportunity to condemn the property, if the lot or parcel is conveyed by the owner of the lot or parcel to another private party after the notice is published, but prior to the time the property is condemned.
(5) Subsection (1) of this section does not affect the ability of a public body as defined in ORS 174.109 to make a conveyance of a nonpossessory interest in condemned property for the purpose of financing acquisition of the property.
(6) A court shall independently determine whether a taking of property complies with the requirements of this section, without deference to any determination made by the public body. If a court determines that a taking of property does not comply with the requirements of this section, the owner of the lot or parcel that is the subject of the condemnation proceeding shall be entitled to reasonable attorney fees, expenses, costs and other disbursements reasonably incurred to defend against the proposed condemnation. [2007 c.1 §2; 2009 c.11 §6]

35.018 Severability. If any portion or portions of chapter 1, Oregon Laws 2007, are declared invalid by a court of competent jurisdiction, the remaining portions of chapter 1, Oregon Laws 2007, shall remain in full force and effect. [2007 c.1 §3]

Note: 35.018 was enacted into law but was not added to or made a part of ORS chapter 35 or any series therein by law. See Preface to Oregon Revised Statutes for further explanation.

Note: Legislative Counsel has substituted "chapter 1, Oregon Laws 2007," for the words "this 2006 Act" in section 3, chapter 1, Oregon Laws 2007, compiled as 35.018. Specific ORS references have not been substituted, pursuant to 173.160. The sections for which substitution otherwise would be made may be determined by referring to the 2007 Comparative Section Table located in Volume 20 of ORS.

35.020 [Repealed by 1971 c.741 §38]

35.030 [Repealed by 1971 c.741 §38]

35.040 [Amended by 1967 c.479 §1; repealed by 1971 c.741 §38]

35.050 [Repealed by 1971 c.741 §38]

35.060 [Repealed by 1971 c.741 §38]

35.070 [Amended by 1967 c.479 §2; repealed by 1971 c.741 §38]

35.080 [Repealed by 1971 c.741 §38]

35.085 [1967 c.479 §§4,5; repealed by 1971 c.741 §38]

35.090 [Repealed by 1971 c.741 §38]

35.100 [Repealed by 1971 c.741 §38]

35.105 [1967 c.479 §6; repealed by 1971 c.741 §38]

35.110 [Repealed by 1971 c.741 §38]

35.120 [Repealed by 1971 c.741 §38]

35.130 [Repealed by 1971 c.741 §38]

35.140 [Repealed by 1971 c.741 §38]

PROCEDURE

35.205 Short title. This chapter may be cited as the General Condemnation Procedure Act. [1971 c.741 §2]

35.215 Definitions for chapter. As used in this chapter, unless the context otherwise requires:
(1) "Condemner" means the state, any city, county, school district, municipal or public corporation, political subdivision or any instrumentality or any agency thereof or a private corporation that has the power to exercise the right of eminent domain.
(2) "Owner" or "owner of the property" means the owner of property.
(3) "Person" means person as defined by ORS 174.100 and also includes the state, any city, county, school district, municipal or public corporation, political subdivision or any instrumentality or any agency thereof.
(4) "Private condemner" means a private corporation that has the power to exercise the right of eminent domain.
(5) "Property" means real or personal property or any interest therein of any kind or nature that is subject to condemnation.
(6) "Public condemner" means condemner other than private condemner. [1971 c.741 §4; 1983 c.327 §10; 2003 c.14 §18]

35.220 Precondemnation entry on real property. (1) Subject to the requirements of this section, a condemner may enter upon, examine, survey, conduct tests upon and take samples from any real property that is subject to condemnation by the condemner. A condemner may not enter upon any land under the provisions of this section without first attempting to provide actual notice to the owner or occupant of the property. If the condemner has not provided actual notice, written notice must be posted in a conspicuous place where the notice is most likely to be seen. The posted notice must give the condemner's name, address and telephone number and the purpose of the entry. A condemner may conduct tests upon or take samples from real property only with the consent of the owner or pursuant to an order entered under subsection (2) of this section. All testing and sampling must be done in conformity with applicable laws and regulations. Testing and sampling results shall be provided to the owner upon request.
(2) If the owner of property objects to examination or survey of the property under this section, or does not consent to the terms and conditions for testing or sampling of the property, the condemner may file a petition with the court seeking an order providing for entry upon the property and allowing such examination, survey, testing or sampling as may be requested by the condemner. The court may enter an order establishing reasonable terms and conditions for entry and for any examination, survey, testing or sampling of the property requested by the condemner. Reasonable compensation for damage or interference under subsection (3) of this section may be established in the proceeding either before or after entry is made upon the property by the condemner.
(3) An owner is entitled to reasonable compensation for:
(a) Any physical damage caused to the property by the entry upon or examination, survey, testing or sampling of the property, including any damage attributable to the diffusion of hazardous substances found on the property; and
(b) Any substantial interference with the property's possession or use caused by the entry upon or examination, survey, testing or sampling of the property.
(4) If a condemner is required to pay compensation to an owner in a proceeding under subsection (2) of this section, and the condemner thereafter seeks condemnation of the same property, the owner is not entitled to any payment of compensation in the condemnation action that would result in the owner receiving a second recovery for the same damage or interference.
(5) Nothing in this section affects any liability under any other provision of law that a condemner may have to an owner or occupant of property by reason of entry upon or examination, survey, testing or sampling of property. [2003 c.477 §2]

35.225 [1971 c.741 §5; repealed by 1979 c.284 §199]

35.235 Agreement for compensation; status of resolution or ordinance of public condemner; status of action of private condemner; agreement effort not prerequisite. (1) Subject to ORS 758.015 and 836.050, whenever in the judgment of the condemner it is necessary to acquire property for a purpose for which the condemner is authorized by law to acquire property, the condemner shall, after first declaring by resolution or ordinance such necessity and the purpose for which it is required, attempt to agree with the owner with respect to the compensation to be paid therefor, and the damages, if any, for the taking thereof.
(2) The resolution or ordinance of a public condemner is presumptive evidence of the public necessity of the proposed use, that the property is necessary therefor and that the proposed use, improvement or project is planned or located in a manner which will be most compatible with the greatest public good and the least private injury.
(3) The commencement of an action to condemn property by a private condemner creates a disputable presumption of the necessity of the proposed use, that the property is necessary therefor and that the proposed use, improvement or project is planned or located in a manner which will be most compatible with the greatest public good and the least private injury.
(4) The question of the validity of the disputable presumptions created in subsection (3) of this section, if raised, shall be determined by the court in a summary proceeding prior to trial.
(5) It is not a prerequisite to the exercise of the right of eminent domain by the condemner to attempt first to agree with an owner or to allege or prove any effort to agree with such owner as to reasonable value, when such owner is at the time concealed within the state or, after reasonable effort by condemner, cannot be found within the state. [1971 c.741 §6; 1973 c.579 §1]

35.245 Commencement of action; jurisdiction; parties. (1) If the condemner is unable to agree with or locate the owner of the property under ORS 35.235, then an action to condemn property may be commenced in the circuit court of the county in which the property proposed to be condemned, or the greater portion thereof, is located.
(2) An action may be commenced against the person in whose name the record title appears. There may be included as defendants any lessee or other person in possession and all other persons having or claiming an interest in the property. [1971 c.741 §7]

35.255 Content of complaint. The complaint shall describe the property sought to be condemned and shall allege the true value of the property sought and the damage, if any, resulting from the appropriation thereof. [1971 c.741 §8; 1979 c.284 §75]

35.265 Advance deposit by public condemner requiring immediate possession; effect on interest otherwise allowable. (1) When a public condemner commences an action for the condemnation of property and immediate possession of the property is considered necessary by the public condemner, a fund shall be created in the amount estimated to be the just compensation for the property and placed in the hands of the treasurer of the public condemner for deposit with the clerk of the court wherein the action was commenced, for the use of the defendants in the action.

(2) When the public condemner is a state agency and immediate possession of property is considered necessary by the agency, the agency shall certify to such facts and authorize an advancement out of funds available to the agency of the amount estimated by the agency to be just compensation for the property. Upon such certification and authorization, a warrant shall be drawn in favor of the clerk of the court in the amount authorized.

(3) Upon the deposit in court by the public condemner of the estimated amount of just compensation as provided by subsections (1) and (2) of this section, no interest shall be allowed thereon in the judgment. [1971 c.741 §10; 2003 c.576 §236]

35.275 Advance occupancy by private condemner; hearing; deposit or bond; effect of size of bond or deposit on amount of just compensation. (1) At any time after an action is commenced to acquire any property, a private condemner may apply to the court for an order to occupy the property to be condemned and to make use of the property for the purposes for which it is being appropriated.

(2) At the hearing on the motion, the court shall determine the reasons for requiring a speedy occupation. The court shall grant the motion if, giving consideration to the public interest involved, it finds that the interests of the owners will be adequately protected. The court may make such provisions or orders as necessary, so that the advance taking or an advance payment, as provided by subsection (3) of this section, will not be prejudicial to either party.

(3)(a) If an order to occupy the property is granted, it may also require the private condemner to deposit with the court either such sum as the court finds reasonable on account of just compensation to be awarded or to deposit a surety bond in an amount and with such surety as the court may approve. The surety bond shall be conditioned to the effect that the private condemner shall pay to the owners of the property just compensation for the property taken or restitution, if any, and costs, disbursements and reasonable attorney fees as finally determined.

(b) After an order to occupy is entered, if it appears necessary in order to protect the interests of the owners of the property, the court at any time may require the private condemner to deposit with the court an additional bond or sum on account of just compensation to be awarded.

(c) Evidence as to the finding of the court regarding the amount of such bond or deposit shall not be admissible at the trial of just compensation. [1971 c.741 §11]

35.285 Distribution of deposits; effect of withdrawal on appeal. (1) The court may distribute all or any part of the funds deposited by a condemner to the persons entitled thereto for or on account of the just compensation to be awarded in the action, upon such terms and conditions as may appear just and reasonable.

(2) Any persons entitled to withdraw any or all of the deposit, as provided by subsection (1) of this section, may do so at any time without waiving rights of appeal provided by ORS 35.355. [1971 c.741 §12]

35.295 Defendant's answer. The defendant in answer may set forth any legal defense the defendant may have to the condemnation. The defendant shall also allege the true value of the property and the damage, if any, resulting from the appropriation thereof. [1971 c.741 §13]

35.300 Offer of compromise. (1) After the filing of a condemnation action, a condemner may serve an offer of compromise on the defendant in the action. An offer of compromise must be served on the defendant not later than 10 days before the trial of the action. The offer of compromise must identify the amount offered as just compensation for the property and as compensable damages to remaining property of the defendant. The offer of compromise must also indicate whether the offer includes any amount for costs and disbursements, attorney fees and expenses and, if so, the amounts included for costs and disbursements, attorney fees and expenses. If the defendant accepts the amount offered as just compensation for the property and as compensable damages to remaining property of the defendant, the defendant shall file with the court an acceptance signed by the defendant or the defendant's attorney. The acceptance must be filed not more than three days after the time the offer was served on the defendant. A copy of the offer must be attached to the acceptance.

(2) If an offer of compromise under this section does not specifically include amounts for costs and disbursements, attorney fees and expenses, upon acceptance of the offer the court shall give judgment to the defendant for the amount offered as just compensation for the property and as compensable damages to remaining property of the defendant and, in addition, for costs and disbursements, attorney fees and expenses that are determined by the court to have been incurred before service of the offer on the defendant.

(3) If an offer of compromise under this section specifically includes amounts for costs and disbursements, attorney fees and expenses, the defendant may accept all amounts offered, or may accept only that portion of the offer identified as just compensation for the property and as compensable damages to remaining property of the defendant. If the defendant accepts only that portion of the offer identified as just compensation for the property and as compensable damages to remaining property of the defendant, the defendant is entitled to an award for costs and disbursements, attorney fees and expenses incurred by the defendant before service of the offer on the defendant. The court shall determine the amount of costs and disbursements, attorney fees and expenses to be awarded to the defendant after acceptance of the offer is filed under subsection (1) of this section.

(4) If an offer of compromise is not accepted within the time allowed under subsection (1) of this section, the offer is withdrawn and may not be given in evidence at trial. If the defendant fails to obtain a judgment more favorable than the offer:

(a) The defendant may not recover prevailing party fees or costs and disbursements, attorney fees and expenses that were incurred on and after service of the offer;

(b) Unless the parties agree otherwise, the court shall give judgment to the defendant for costs and disbursements, attorney fees and expenses that were incurred by the defendant before service of the offer; and

(c) The court shall give judgment to the condemner for the condemner's costs and disbursements, other than prevailing party fees, incurred by the condemner on and after service of the offer.

(5) For the purpose of determining whether the defendant has failed to obtain a judgment more favorable than an offer of compromise that specifically includes amounts for costs and disbursements, attorney fees and expenses, the court shall first determine the amount of costs and disbursements, attorney fees and expenses incurred by the defendant before service of the offer on the defendant. The court shall add that amount to the amounts awarded under the judgment as just compensation for the property and as compensable damages to remaining property of the defendant. If the sum of those amounts is equal to or less than the total amount specified in the offer of compromise, the defendant has not obtained a judgment more favorable than the offer of compromise.

(6) For the purposes of this section, "expenses" has the meaning given that term in ORS 35.335. [2009 c.530 §5]

35.305 Conduct of trial; defendant's option; jury argument; neither side has burden of proof of just compensation. (1) Evidence shall be received and the trial conducted in the order and manner prescribed for a civil action in the circuit court, except that the defendant shall have the option of proceeding first or last in the presentation of evidence, if notice of such election is filed with the court and served on the condemner at least seven days prior to the date set for trial. If no notice of election is filed, the condemner shall proceed first in the presentation of evidence. Unless the case is submitted by both sides to the jury without argument, the party who presents evidence first shall also open and close the argument to the jury.

(2) Condemner and defendant may offer evidence of just compensation, but neither party shall have the burden of proof of just compensation. [1971 c.741 §14; 1979 c.284 §76]

35.315 View of property by order of court. If motion is made by either party before the formation of the jury, the court shall order a view of the property in question. Upon the return of the jury, the evidence of the parties may be heard and the verdict of the jury given. [1971 c.741 §15; 2007 c.71 §11]

35.325 Effect of judgment; effect of payment under judgment. Upon the assessment of the compensation by the jury, the court shall give judgment appropriating the property in question to the condemner, conditioned upon the condemner's paying into court the compensation assessed by the jury; and, after the making of such payment, the judgment shall become effective to convey the property, and the right of possession thereof to the condemner if not previously acquired. [1971 c.741 §16]

35.335 Effect of condemner's abandonment of action. (1) If an action is abandoned by the condemner, the court shall enter judgment in favor of the defendant for costs and disbursements in the action and for reasonable attorney fees and reasonable expenses as determined by the court.

(2) Expenses mean costs of appraisals and fees for experts incurred in preparing and conducting the defense to the action.

(3) An action is considered abandoned if, at any time after filing a complaint, the case is dismissed or terminated or the condemner files an election not to take the property. If an election is not filed within 60 days after the verdict, the condemner is considered to have elected to take the property. [1971 c.741 §17]

35.345 [1971 c.741 §18; repealed by 1973 c.617 §1 (35.346 enacted in lieu of 35.345)]

35.346 Offer to purchase required before filing action for condemnation; appraisal; arbitration; when costs and disbursements allowed. (1) At least 40 days before the filing of any action for condemnation of property or any interest in property, the condemner shall make a written offer to the owner or party having an interest to purchase the property or interest, and to pay just compensation therefor and for any compensable damages to remaining property.

(2) The offer shall be accompanied by any written appraisal upon which the condemner relied in establishing the amount of compensation offered. If the condemner determines that the amount of just compensation due is less than $20,000, the condemner, in lieu of a written appraisal, may provide to the owner or other person having an interest in the property a written explanation of the bases and method by which the condemner arrived at the specific valuation of the property. The amount of just compensation offered shall not be reduced by amendment or otherwise before or during trial except on order of the court entered not less than 60 days prior to trial. An order for reduction of just compensation offered, pleaded by the condemner in the complaint or deposited with the court for the use and benefit of the owner pending outcome of the condemnation action, may be entered only upon motion of the condemner and a finding by clear and convincing evidence that the appraisal upon which the original offer is based was the result of a mistake of material fact that was not known and could not reasonably have been known at the time of the original appraisal or was based on a mistake of law.

(3) Unless otherwise agreed to by the condemner and the owner, prior to appraising the property the condemner shall provide not less than 15 days' written notice to the owner of the planned appraisal inspection. The property owner and designated representative, if any, shall be invited to accompany the condemner's appraiser on any inspection of the property for appraisal purposes.

(4) The owner has not less than 40 days from the date the owner receives the written offer required by subsection (1) of this section, accompanied by the appraisal or written explanation required by subsection (2) of this section, to accept or reject the offer. If the owner rejects the condemner's offer and obtains a separate appraisal, the owner shall provide the condemner with a copy of the owner's appraisal not less than 60 days prior to trial or arbitration.

(5)(a) Failure to provide the opposing party with a copy of the appropriate appraisal as provided in subsections (2) and (4) of this section shall prohibit the use of the appraisal in arbitration or at trial.

(b) In the event the owner and condemner are unable to reach agreement and proceed to trial or arbitration as provided in subsection (6) of this section, each party to the proceeding shall provide to every other party a copy of every appraisal obtained by the party as part of the condemnation action.

(6)(a) If an action based on the condemnation is filed, the owner may elect to have compensation determined by binding arbitration if the total amount of compensation claimed by any party does not exceed $20,000. Notice of an election of binding arbitration must be given to the condemner at least 90 days prior to the date on which an arbitration hearing is scheduled under ORS 36.420.

(b) Notwithstanding the amount established under ORS 36.400, if the owner elects to proceed with binding arbitration, the arbitration shall be conducted according to the mandatory arbitration program established under ORS 36.400 to 36.425. Notwithstanding ORS 36.425, no party may request a trial de novo after the filing of the decision and award of the arbitrator. Within 20 days after the filing of the decision and award of the arbitrator under ORS 36.425, any party may file a motion with the court for the vacation, modification or correction of the award. The court may vacate an award only if there is a basis to vacate the award described in ORS 36.705 (1)(a) to (d). The court may modify or correct an award only for the grounds given in ORS 36.710. Except as provided in this subsection, no party may appeal from the decision and award of an arbitrator if the owner elects binding arbitration in lieu of trial.

(c) If the total amount of compensation claimed exceeds $20,000 but is less than $50,000, the owner may elect to have compensation determined by nonbinding arbitration under the applicable provisions of ORS 36.400 to 36.425.

(7) If a trial is held or arbitration conducted for the fixing of the amount of compensation to be awarded to the defendant owner or party having an interest in the property being condemned, the court or arbitrator shall award the defendant costs and disbursements including reasonable attorney fees and reasonable expenses as defined in ORS 35.335 (2) in the following cases, and no other:

(a) If the amount of just compensation assessed by the verdict in the trial exceeds the highest written offer in settlement submitted by condemner before the filing of the action to those defendants appearing in the action pursuant to subsection (1) of this section; or

(b) If the court finds that the first written offer made by condemner to defendant in settlement before the filing of the action did not constitute a good faith offer of an amount reasonably believed by condemner to be just compensation.

(8) If any appraisal provided to a party under this section relies on a written report, opinion or estimate of a person who is not an appraiser, a copy of the written report, opinion or estimate must be provided with the appraisal. If any appraisal provided under this section relies on an unwritten report, opinion or estimate of a person who is not an appraiser, the party providing the appraisal must also provide the name and address of the person who provided the unwritten report, opinion or estimate.

(9) Costs and disbursements other than reasonable attorney fees and expenses as defined in ORS 35.335 (2) shall be awarded to condemner in all cases other than those in which defendant is entitled to costs and disbursements under subsection (7) of this section. [1973 c.617 §2 (enacted in lieu of 35.345); 1997 c.797 §1; 2003 c.476 §1; 2003 c.598 §33; 2005 c.274 §5; 2005 c.433 §1; 2007 c.1 §4; 2009 c.530 §1]

35.348 Immediate possession of property. Notwithstanding ORS 35.346, if a condemner determines that an emergency that poses a threat to persons or property exists and that immediate possession of the property is necessary, the condemner may immediately file a condemnation action after making the written offer required under ORS 35.346 (1) accompanied by the appraisal or explanation required by ORS 35.346 (2). [1997 c.797 §3; 2003 c.476 §3; 2009 c.530 §2]

35.350 Immediate possession of property by public body. This chapter does not affect the ability of a public body, as defined in ORS 174.109, to take immediate possession of property in an emergency that poses a threat to persons or property. [2005 c.565 §2]

35.352 Notice of immediate possession of property by public condemner; objection. (1) At any time after a condemnation action is commenced, a public condemner may serve notice that the public condemner will take immediate possession of the property that is the subject of the action. The notice must be served in the manner provided by ORCP 9 on all defendants in the action.

(2) If notice is served under this section, a defendant in a condemnation action may object to immediate possession of property by a public condemner by filing a written objection with the court within 10 days after notice is served on the defendant under this section and serving a copy of the objection on the public condemner in the manner provided by ORCP 9. The objection must request that the court schedule a hearing on the objection at the earliest possible time. The only issues that a court may consider upon objection are:

(a) Whether the condemnation is legal; and

(b) Subject to the presumption established by ORS 35.235 (2), whether the public condemner has acted in bad faith, engaged in fraud or engaged in an abuse of discretion under a delegation of authority.

(3) If notice is served under this section and an objection is not filed with the court within the time allowed under subsection (2) of this section, the public condemner may at any time thereafter file with the court a form of order confirming the public condemner's possession of the property as of the date specified in the notice. The form of order must be accompanied by an affidavit attesting to service of the notice as required by subsection (1) of this

section, and a statement that an objection was not filed within 10 days after notice was served on the defendants in the action. Upon filing of the affidavit, the clerk of the court shall affix the seal of the court to the form of order. The order may thereafter be enforced in the same manner as any other order of the court.

(4) A notice under this section must be in substantially the following form:

CIRCUIT COURT FOR THE
COUNTY OF _____

```
                 )
_____          )
Plaintiff,       )        NOTICE OF
        )        IMMEDIATE
        )        POSSESSION
        )
vs.     )          Case No. _____
        )
_____          )
Defendant.       )
```

TO THE DEFENDANTS:
By service of this notice, you are advised that the plaintiff will take possession of the property described in the complaint on:
(1) _____, 2____, if the deposit required by ORS 35.265 has been made by that date; or
(2) The date on which the deposit required by ORS 35.265 is made if that date is later than the date specified above.
You may file an objection with the court within 10 days after this notice is served on you. An objection may be made only to determine:
(1) Whether the condemnation is legal; and
(2) Subject to the presumption established by ORS 35.235 (2), whether the public condemner has acted in bad faith, engaged in fraud or engaged in an abuse of discretion under a delegation of authority.

_____
Attorney for Plaintiff

_____
Address

_____
Telephone Number

(5) The court shall expeditiously consider any objection filed under this section to prevent prejudice to the public condemner's need for immediate possession.
(6) The ability of the defendant in a condemnation action to assert legal defenses in the answer of the defendant under ORS 35.295 is not affected solely by reason of the filing of an objection to a notice served under this section, or by reason of the failure to file an objection.
(7) This section does not impose a requirement that a public condemner use the procedure described in this section, and the procedure described in this section is not the exclusive method by which a public condemner may obtain possession of property. [2005 c.565 §3]

35.355 Appeal. Either party to the action may appeal from the judgment in like manner and with like effect as in ordinary cases, but the appeal shall not stay the proceedings so as to prevent the condemner from taking possession of the property and using it for the purposes for which it is being appropriated. In the event the defendant prevails on an appeal, the costs and disbursements of the defendant, including a reasonable attorney fee to be fixed by the court, shall be taxed by the clerk and recovered from the condemner. [1971 c.741 §19]

35.365 Effect of withdrawal of award; disposition of award. If the defendant withdraws the compensation awarded by the court or jury, the defendant waives the right of appeal; and, if the defendant does not, such sum shall remain in the control of the court, to abide the event of the appeal. If an unknown owner of the property or other defendant does not appear and claim the sum, it shall be invested for the benefit of whom it may concern, as in case of unclaimed moneys in the sale and partition of lands. [1971 c.741 §20]

35.375 Chapter as exclusive condemnation proceeding; exception. Except for procedures provided in ORS chapter 368, any action for the condemnation of property under the power of eminent domain shall be conducted according to this chapter. [1971 c.741 §3; 1979 c.873 §3; 1981 c.153 §52]

35.385 Public purpose use required of condemner; right of repurchase; specification of duration of public purpose use; effect. (1) If real property is acquired by a condemner by agreement with the owner of such property after the adoption of a resolution or ordinance under ORS 35.235 (1) for the acquisition of the property but before entry of a judgment in a condemnation action under ORS 35.245, the condemner and the owner shall:
(a) Specify in such agreement for the real property a reasonable period within which the real property must be used by the condemner for a public purpose or specify a 10-year period for such use and provide that the right of repurchase of the real property or any portion thereof may be exercised as provided in ORS 35.385 to 35.415; or
(b) Specify that the right of repurchase of the real property has been waived by the owner and, in such case, not specify a period within which the real property must be used by the condemner for a public purpose.
(2) If real property is acquired by a condemner under this chapter by judgment given in a condemnation action under ORS 35.325, the court shall:
(a) Specify in the judgment a reasonable period within which the real property must be used by the condemner for a public purpose or specify a 10-year period, and provide that the right of repurchase may be exercised with respect to the real property as provided in ORS 35.385 to 35.415; or
(b) Specify that the right of repurchase of the real property has been waived by the owner and, in such case, not specify a period within which the real property must be used by the condemner for a public purpose.
(3) For the purposes of subsection (2)(a) of this section, the resolution or ordinance of the condemner is presumptive evidence that the period of time that is proposed by the condemner is a reasonable period in which the real property must be used by the condemner for a public purpose; provided, however, that if the resolution or ordinance specifies a 10-year period or less, neither the owner nor a designated beneficiary of the owner can contest the reasonableness of the period specified.

(4) If real property is acquired by a condemner by agreement with the owner as described in subsection (1) of this section, and the agreement does not contain one of the provisions required by subsection (1)(a) or (b) of this section, the owner may repurchase the property, or any portion of the property, in the manner provided by ORS 35.385 to 35.415 if:

(a) Ten years have expired since the date of the transfer of the property; and

(b) The condemner has not used the property for a public purpose.

(5) Subsection (4) of this section does not apply to real property acquired by a condemner for the purpose of constructing, improving or maintaining a transportation facility or system. [1973 c.720 §2; 2011 c.426 §1]

Note: Section 2, chapter 426, Oregon Laws 2011, provides:

Sec. 2. The amendments to ORS 35.385 by section 1 of this 2011 Act apply only to agreements for acquisition by a condemner as described in ORS 35.385 (1) that are entered into on or after the effective date of this 2011 Act [June 17, 2011]. [2011 c.426 §2]

35.390 Effect of failure of condemner to use property as required; price of repurchase; form of offer of repurchase. (1) If a condemner fails to use the real property or any portion thereof acquired under this chapter within the time specified in an agreement entered into under ORS 35.385 (1) or with the terms of a judgment given under ORS 35.325 and 35.385 (2), whichever applies, and the prior owner of the real property has not waived the right to repurchase the real property, the condemner shall offer such property or any portion thereof, that has not been used for a public purpose within the specified period, to the prior owner or the beneficiary of the prior owner designated as provided in ORS 35.400. The condemner shall, at its expense, insure the title to any property or portion thereof conveyed or vested in the owner or beneficiary under any provision of ORS 35.385 to 35.415, free and clear of any and all encumbrances except those subject to which the condemner originally took such property.

(2) The prior owner or beneficiary described in subsection (1) of this section may repurchase from the condemner the real property that is subject to the right of repurchase for a price equal to the sum of the compensation and damages paid by the condemner for the real property plus interest at the rate of seven percent per year from the date of the conveyance of the real property by the prior owner to the condemner.

(3) If only a portion of the real property acquired by a condemner is subject to the right of repurchase under ORS 35.385 to 35.415, the prior owner or beneficiary may acquire such portion for a price equal to the sum of:

(a) The fair cash market value of the portion subject to the right of repurchase, as of the date of the commencement of any action subject to ORS 35.385;

(b) The damages for diminution in value of the remainder, if any, of the former owner's property not so acquired, as of the date of the commencement of any action subject to ORS 35.385; and

(c) Interest at the rate of seven percent per year from the date of the conveyance of the real property by the prior owner to the condemner.

(4) The offer to repurchase only a portion of real property as provided in subsection (1) of this section and ORS 35.400 (3), shall be in writing and shall include the price for repurchase as determined by the condemner, including an itemization of the components thereof, pursuant to subsection (3) of this section. [1973 c.720 §3; 2003 c.14 §19]

35.395 Change in period of use; notice; effect of failure to agree on change; review by court. (1) The period specified in an agreement or judgment as provided in ORS 35.385 may be changed as provided in this section, if the prior owner of the real property has not waived the right of repurchase and the condemner finds that it will be unable to use all or a portion of the real property for such purpose within the specified period and requires a reasonable extension of such period for the completion of its project on the real property.

(2) Upon a finding under subsection (1) of this section, a condemner shall notify the prior owner or designated beneficiary of the requested change in period. The condemner shall negotiate with the prior owner or beneficiary on the requested change.

(a) Notification under this subsection shall consist of mailing a letter by certified mail to the last address of the prior owner or the designated beneficiary of the owner as shown in the agreement or judgment whereby the real property was acquired or the address subsequently supplied by such owner or beneficiary. If no response has been received by the condemner within 60 days after receipt of notice by the owner or designated beneficiary, all the rights of the owner or designated beneficiary under ORS 35.385 to 35.415 shall be considered waived.

(b) If the condemner cannot locate the prior owner or the designated beneficiary of the owner at the last-known address of the owner or the designated beneficiary, notice may be effected by publication. The publication shall be made in a newspaper published in the county where the property is located, or if no newspaper is published in the county, then in a newspaper designated as being most likely to give notice to the prior owner or the beneficiary of the prior owner. The newspaper utilized shall meet the requirements of ORS 193.020. The notice shall contain the name of the public project, a general description of the location of the property, the change in purpose or extension of time desired by the condemner and a time within which the owner or the beneficiary of the owner must respond to the notice. The notice shall be published not less than once each week for four weeks. The publication of notice may be directed to one or more owners or beneficiaries affected by the same project. If no response is received by the condemner within 10 days after the date of the last publication of notice, all rights of the prior owner or designated beneficiary shall be considered waived.

(3) If, after negotiation, the prior owner or beneficiary and the condemner agree on the proposed change in period, the period as changed shall, for the purposes of ORS 35.385 to 35.415, be considered the period as specified in the agreement or judgment under ORS 35.385. In the case of real property acquired by a condemner by judgment under ORS 35.325, the condemner shall notify the court by which the judgment was given of the agreed upon change in period and the court shall modify such judgment accordingly.

(4) If the prior owner or beneficiary and the condemner cannot, after negotiation, agree on the proposed change in period, the condemner may:

(a) In the case of real property acquired by an agreement under ORS 35.235 (1), petition the circuit court for the county within which such real property is situated for a hearing to determine whether the proposed change in period is reasonable and necessary in the public interest; or

(b) In the case of real property acquired by a judgment given under ORS 35.325, petition the court by which such judgment was given for a hearing to determine whether it is reasonable and necessary in the public interest to modify such judgment to permit the proposed change in period. The condemner in its petition may include as parties and serve all or any owners and designated beneficiaries whose property is affected by the same project.

(5) If, after a hearing under subsection (4) of this section, the court finds that the proposed change in period is reasonable and necessary in the public interest, the court shall grant such change. For the purposes of ORS 35.385 to 35.415, a period as changed by the court shall be considered the period specified in the agreement or judgment described in ORS 35.385. For the purposes of this subsection, the resolution or ordinance of the condemner is presumptive evidence that the change in period proposed by the condemner is reasonable and necessary in the public interest.

(6) If, after a hearing under subsection (4) of this section, the court finds that the proposed change in period is unreasonable or not necessary in the public interest, the court shall deny the requested change. In such case, the terms of the original agreement or judgment shall control for the purpose of the exercise of the right of repurchase under ORS 35.385 to 35.415. [1973 c.720 §4]

35.400 Designation of person to exercise right of repurchase; effect of failure to designate; offer to repurchase; acceptance; notice; determination of price. (1) At the time of entering into an agreement pursuant to ORS 35.385 (1) for the acquisition of real property by a condemner or prior to the time of giving judgment for the acquisition of real property by a condemner under ORS 35.325, the owner of the real property to be acquired may, if such owner has not waived the right of repurchase under ORS 35.385 to 35.415, designate a person to exercise such right of repurchase. Such designation shall constitute an assignment of the right of the owner of such property to exercise the right of repurchase otherwise available under ORS 35.385 to 35.415. The name and address of the person so designated shall be included in such agreement or judgment. Such owners and designated beneficiaries shall also notify the condemner in writing of any change of address so that their respective current addresses shall be of record with the condemner. The person so designated may not assign or transfer the right of repurchase.

(2) If an owner of real property to be acquired by a condemner does not designate a person to exercise the right of repurchase under ORS 35.385 to 35.415 and such owner has not waived such right of repurchase, only the owner may exercise the right of repurchase under ORS 35.385 to 35.415. If such owner dies while real property is still subject to a right of repurchase by the owner, the personal representative of such owner's estate may act as the

owner to exercise the right of repurchase with respect to such property on behalf of the estate of the owner at any time prior to the discharge of the personal representative under ORS 116.213.

(3) Upon receipt from a condemner of an offer to repurchase any real property or portion thereof in accordance with ORS 35.385 to 35.415:

(a) In the case of an offer to repurchase the entire parcel of real property to which ORS 35.385 applies, if the owner or beneficiary of such right of repurchase does not accept such offer within 30 days, the right of repurchase is terminated and the condemner may use and dispose of such property or portion as otherwise provided by law.

(b) In the case of an offer to repurchase only a portion of a parcel of real property to which ORS 35.385 applies, the owner or beneficiary of such right of repurchase may:

(A) Accept such offer within 30 days; or

(B) Notify the condemner within 30 days of the desire of the owner or beneficiary to exercise such right, but refuse to accept the price established by the condemner in the offer to repurchase made pursuant to ORS 35.390 (4).

(c) If the owner or beneficiary of the right of repurchase fails to timely notify the condemner pursuant to either paragraph (b)(A) or (B) of this subsection, the right of repurchase is terminated and the condemner may use or dispose of such portion of property as otherwise provided by law.

(d) If timely notice of intent to exercise the right of repurchase is given by the owner or beneficiary as provided by paragraph (b)(B) of this subsection, the owner or beneficiary must within 60 days thereafter commence an action, in the court in which the original action by the condemner to acquire such real property was commenced, to determine the sole issue of the price to be paid upon such repurchase, pursuant to the provisions of ORS 35.390 (3). Failure to commence such an action within such 60-day period shall void such notice of intention to exercise repurchase for the purposes of paragraph (c) of this subsection.

(A) Upon the determination of the price for repurchase by the court or jury, the court shall give judgment vesting title to the property in the owner or the beneficiary, conditioned upon payment into court of the assessed price by the owner or beneficiary within 90 days after the date of the judgment; and upon the making of such payment, the judgment shall become effective to convey the property and the right of possession thereof to the owner or beneficiary. Failure to make such payment into court within 90 days of the date of the judgment shall void the notice of intent to exercise the right of repurchase for the purposes of paragraph (c) of this subsection, and the judgment shall be withdrawn by the court.

(B) If the price determined pursuant to the provisions of this paragraph is less than the price established by the condemner in its written offer to repurchase, the costs and disbursements of the owner or beneficiary, as specified in ORS 35.335 and 35.346, shall be taxed by the clerk; and the judgment rendered shall reflect such costs and disbursements only as an offset against the price to be paid into court by the owner or beneficiary. [1973 c.720 §5]

35.405 Designation of person to exercise right of repurchase by multiple owners. Notwithstanding any other provision of ORS 35.385 to 35.415, in any instance in which ORS 35.385 applies, where the agreement by which the condemner acquired the property is executed by more than one person exclusive of the condemner, or where the judgment given in a condemnation action by which the condemner acquired the property includes more than one named defendant, all such persons executing such agreement, or all such named defendants must designate one person to act as beneficiary in the exercise of the right of repurchase, unless all such persons executing such agreement, or all such named defendants, waive such right of repurchase as provided in ORS 35.385 to 35.415. Such designated beneficiary thereafter shall exclusively have and exclusively may exercise all rights, remedies and obligations provided in ORS 35.385 to 35.415. [1973 c.720 §6]

35.410 Right to contest change in public purpose use; notice of proposed change. A prior owner of real property acquired pursuant to an agreement entered into under ORS 35.385 (1) or a judgment given under ORS 35.235 and 35.385 (2), whichever applies, or the designated beneficiary of such owner, may contest any proposed change by the condemner in the public purpose for which such real property was acquired in the manner provided for contesting a change in the period specified for the use of such real property by the condemner under ORS 35.395 (4). The resolution or ordinance of the condemner is presumptive evidence that a proposed change of use proposed by the condemner is reasonable and necessary in the public interest. Each condemner proposing any such change in public purpose shall notify each such owner or designated beneficiary of such proposed change and the reasons therefor in the manner provided in ORS 35.395 (2) for notification of a proposed change in the period specified for use of such real property by the condemner. Each such notice shall be mailed to the most recent address of the owner or designated beneficiary of record with the condemner. [1973 c.720 §7]

35.415 Application of ORS 35.385 to 35.415. (1) ORS 35.385 to 35.415 apply only to property acquired after the filing of a complaint pursuant to a resolution or ordinance adopted as provided in ORS 35.235 (1) on or after October 5, 1973, and for which a condemnation action is commenced on or after October 5, 1973.

(2) Notwithstanding ORS 35.375, ORS 35.385 to 35.415 apply to real property acquired by a county pursuant to ORS chapter 368.

(3) ORS 35.385 to 35.415 shall not apply to any real property acquired under ORS 35.385 (1) and (2) after the date the real property is used for the purpose for which it was acquired nor shall ORS 35.385 to 35.415 apply to any tract of real property where the compensation and damages paid to the owner is less than $1,000. [1973 c.720 §8; 1981 c.153 §53]

RELOCATION OF DISPLACED PERSONS

35.500 Definitions for ORS 35.500 to 35.530. As used in ORS 35.500 to 35.530:

(1) "Displaced person" means any person who moves, or is required to move the person's residence and personal property incident thereto, or the person's business or farm operation as a result of:

(a) Acquisition of the real property, in whole or in part, by a public entity; or

(b) Receipt of a written order by such person from a public entity to vacate the property for public use.

(2) "Federal Act" means the Uniform Relocation Assistance and Real Property Acquisition Policies Act of 1970 (P.L. 91-646, 42 U.S.C. 4601 et seq.) as in effect on January 1, 2003.

(3) "Public entity" includes the state, a county, a city, a consolidated city-county as defined in ORS 199.705 (1), a district, public authority, public agency and any other political subdivision or public corporation in the state when acquiring real property or any interest therein for public use. "Public entity" also includes a private corporation that has the power to exercise the right of eminent domain.

(4) "Public use" means a use for which real property may be acquired by a public entity as provided by law.

(5) "Real property" or any interest therein includes tenements and hereditaments, and includes every interest, freehold and chattel, legal and equitable, present and future, vested and contingent, in such tenements and hereditaments. [Formerly 281.045]

35.505 Relocation within neighborhood; notice prior to move; costs and allowances. (1) A public entity undertaking urban renewal or neighborhood development shall make all reasonable efforts to insure that all displaced persons shall have the option to relocate within their urban renewal or development neighborhood or area and shall not be displaced, except temporarily as required by emergency, until appropriate residential units shall become available to them within their neighborhood or area and within their financial means.

(2) Except as required by emergency, no displaced person shall be required to move from any real property without first having written notice from the public entity at least 90 days prior to the date by which the move is required. In no case shall any displaced person be required to move until the public entity notifies the person in writing of all costs and allowances to which such person may become entitled under federal, state or local law. [Formerly 281.055]

35.510 Duties of public entities acquiring real property. Whenever any program or project is undertaken by a public entity which program or project will result in the acquisition of real property, notwithstanding any other statute, charter, ordinance, or rule or regulation, the public entity shall:

(1) Provide fair and reasonable relocation payments and assistance to or for displaced persons as provided under sections 202, 203, 204 and 206 of the Federal Act;

(2) Provide relocation assistance programs offering to displaced persons and others occupying property immediately adjacent to the real property acquired the services described in section 205 of the Federal Act on the conditions prescribed therein;

(3) In acquiring the real property, be guided by the land acquisition policies in sections 301 and 302 of the Federal Act;

(4) Pay or reimburse property owners for necessary expenses as specified in sections 303 and 304 of the Federal Act;

(5) Share costs of providing payments and assistance with the federal government in the manner and to the extent required by sections 211 (a) and (b) of the Federal Act; and

(6) Appoint such officers, enter into such contracts, utilize federal funds for planning and providing comparable replacement housing and take such other actions as may be necessary to comply with the conditions and requirements of the Federal Act. [Formerly 281.060]

35.515 Required disclosures for business and farm operations. To be eligible for the payment authorized by ORS 35.510, a business or farm operation must make its state income tax returns and its financial statements and accounting records available for audit for confidential use to determine the payment authorized. [Formerly 281.070]

35.520 Decision on benefits; hearing; review. Any person who applies for relocation benefits or assistance under ORS 35.510 shall receive the public entity's written decision on the application, which shall include the statement of any amount awarded, the statutory basis for the award and the statement of any finding of fact that the public entity made in arriving at its decision. A person aggrieved by the decision shall be entitled to a hearing substantially of the character required by ORS 183.413 to 183.470, unless federal, state or local law provides otherwise. Notice required by ORS 183.415 must be served within 180 days of the receipt of the written decision by the aggrieved party. The decision of the public entity shall be reviewable pursuant to ORS 183.480. [Formerly 281.085; 2007 c.288 §5]

35.525 Construction. Nothing in ORS 35.510, 35.515 or 35.520 shall be construed as creating in any condemnation proceedings brought under the power of eminent domain, any element of value or of damage not in existence immediately prior to May 7, 1971. [Formerly 281.090]

35.530 Federal law controls. If a public entity is receiving federal financial assistance and is thereby required to comply with applicable federal laws and regulations relating to relocation assistance, such federal laws and regulations shall control should there be any conflict with ORS 35.500 to 35.530. [Formerly 281.105]

CONDEMNATION BY STATE

35.550 Definitions for ORS 35.550 to 35.575. As used in ORS 35.550 to 35.575:

(1) "Property" means real property, water, watercourses, and water and riparian rights, or any right or interest therein.

(2) "Board" means:

(a) The state board of commissioners, trustees, or other state board, having direction of the state department or institution for which the property is desired; or

(b) The Department of State Lands, if there is no other state board for the department or institution for which the property is sought to be acquired. [Formerly 281.210]

35.555 Determination of necessity; suit by Attorney General. Whenever the state requires property for any public use, the necessity for the acquisition to be decided and declared in the first instance by the board, if the board and the owner of such property cannot agree upon the price to be paid for the amount of or interest in the property required for such public use, and the damages for the taking thereof, the board may request the Attorney General to, and the Attorney General shall when so requested, commence and prosecute in any court of competent jurisdiction in the name of the State of Oregon any necessary or appropriate suit, action or proceeding for the condemnation of the amount of or interest in the property required for such purposes and for the assessment of the damages for the taking thereof. [Formerly 281.220]

35.560 Action by district attorney. The district attorney of the judicial district in which the property to be condemned lies shall:

(1) Commence and prosecute the suit, action or proceeding in the circuit court of such district, when requested by the board; or

(2) Aid the Attorney General in so doing in any manner requested by the Attorney General. [Formerly 281.230]

35.565 Procedure for condemnation. The procedure in the suit, action or proceeding referred to in ORS 35.555 or 35.560 shall be, as far as applicable, the procedure prescribed by law for the condemnation of lands or rights of way by public corporations or quasi-public corporations for public use or for corporate purposes. [Formerly 281.240]

35.570 Payment of expenses of proceeding, value and damages. The expenses of the condemnation proceeding, the value of the property, and the damages for the taking thereof, shall be paid out of the funds provided for the department or institution for which the property is acquired in the same manner as other expenses for like purposes of such department or institution are paid. If no funds have been provided out of which the same can be paid, payment shall be made out of any funds in the treasury not otherwise appropriated, and the Oregon Department of Administrative Services is authorized to draw a warrant on the treasurer therefor. [Formerly 281.250]

35.575 Precondemnation compensation not required. ORS 35.550 to 35.575 do not require the state to make or tender compensation prior to condemning and taking possession of the lands or property. [Formerly 281.260]

CONDEMNATION OF PROPERTY ADJOINING PROPOSED ROADWAYS

35.600 Application. ORS 35.600 to 35.625 apply to all condemners other than the state. [Formerly 281.505]

35.605 Authorization to acquire adjoining property for roadways. (1) Every condemner having the right to purchase, acquire, enter upon and appropriate land and property for establishing, laying out, widening, enlarging or extending roads, streets or highways, may purchase, acquire, enter upon and appropriate, in or in connection with establishing, laying out, widening, enlarging or extending roads, streets or highways, land and property immediately adjoining the proposed boundaries of such roads, streets or highways.

(2) The authority conferred by subsection (1) of this section does not extend to the purchase, acquisition, entering upon or appropriation of any adjoining land or property situate more than 100 feet distant from or beyond the proposed boundaries of any such road, street or highway, or of any such adjoining land or property that constitutes the whole or any part of a platted lot or tract of rectangular shape and having an area of 5,000 square feet or more and its shorter dimension not less than 50 feet in length, or that constitutes the whole or any part of any tract of land in common ownership of like shape and having like minimum area and dimensions. [Formerly 281.510]

35.610 Ordinance or resolution required. Before the right to purchase, acquire, enter upon and appropriate any adjoining land or property under ORS 35.605 is exercised by any condemner, the governing body shall by appropriate ordinance or resolution describe the land to be purchased, acquired, entered upon or appropriated, and shall further determine that the appropriation of such land is reasonably necessary to protect the full use and enjoyment by the public of the road, street or highway. [Formerly 281.520]

35.615 Restrictions on future use of property acquired adjacent to roadway. After an appropriation of land and property authorized by ORS 35.605 has been made, the land and property so appropriated adjoining the boundaries of any road, street or highway and not actually occupied by the road, street or highway, may, by appropriate ordinance or resolution, be declared subject to and burdened with the restrictions upon the future use and occupation thereof that are considered necessary for protecting the full use and enjoyment by the public of the road, street or highway. Such land and property may thereafter be sold by the condemner subject to the declared restrictions and the proceeds of the sale applied and accounted for as may be provided by the charter, charter ordinances or ordinances of, or law governing the condemner. The deed or other conveyance of such land and property shall contain the restrictions and all such land and property shall be sold, burdened with and subject to the restrictions. [Formerly 281.530]

35.620 Acquisition of land adjoining road boundaries declared necessary. The purchase, acquisition, entering upon and appropriation of lands and property immediately adjoining the boundaries of roads, streets or highways, as defined and limited in, and to the extent authorized by, ORS 35.600 to 35.625 is declared to be necessary for the development and welfare of the state and its inhabitants and to be a public use. [Formerly 281.540]

35.625 Procedure to ascertain compensation and damages. If private property is appropriated for the public use as authorized by ORS 35.605, and the compensation and damages arising from the appropriation cannot be agreed upon, the appropriation shall be made and the compensation and damages shall be considered, ascertained, determined, awarded and paid in the manner provided by this chapter. [Formerly 281.550]

Chapter 36 —— Mediation and Arbitration

2017 EDITION

MEDIATION AND ARBITRATION

SPECIAL ACTIONS AND PROCEEDINGS

DISPUTE RESOLUTION

(Generally)

36.100   Policy for ORS 36.100 to 36.238

36.105   Declaration of purpose of ORS 36.100 to 36.238

36.110   Definitions for ORS 36.100 to 36.238

(Dispute Resolution Programs)

36.135   Review of dispute resolution programs; suspension or termination of funding

36.145   Dispute Resolution Account

36.150   Additional funding

36.155   Grants for dispute resolution services in counties; rules

36.160   Participation by counties; notice; contents; effect of failure to give notice

36.165   Termination of county participation

(Program Standards)

36.175   Rules for administration of dispute resolution programs

(Dispute Resolution for Public Bodies)

36.179   Mediation and other alternative dispute resolution services for public bodies

(Mediation in Civil Cases)

36.185   Referral of civil dispute to mediation; objection; information to parties

36.190   Stipulation to mediation; selection of mediator; stay of proceedings

36.195   Presence of attorney; authority and duties of mediator; notice to court at completion of mediation

36.200   Mediation panels; qualification; procedure for selecting mediator

(Liability of Mediators and Programs)

36.210   Liability of mediators and programs

(Confidentiality of Mediation Communications and Agreements)

36.220   Confidentiality of mediation communications and agreements; exceptions

36.222   Admissibility and disclosure of mediation communications and agreements in subsequent adjudicatory proceedings

36.224   State agencies; confidentiality of mediation communications; rules

36.226   Public bodies other than state agencies; confidentiality of mediation communications

36.228   Mediations in which two or more public bodies are parties

36.230   Public bodies; confidentiality of mediation agreements

36.232   Disclosures allowed for reporting, research, training and educational purposes

36.234   Parties to mediation

36.236   Effect on other laws

36.238   Application of ORS 36.210 and 36.220 to 36.238

MEDIATION OF DISPUTES RELATED TO AGRICULTURE

(Agricultural Mediation Services)

36.252   Agricultural mediation services coordinated by State Department of Agriculture; rules

36.254   Contracts for mediation services

36.256   Request for mediation services

36.258   Duties of mediator

36.260   Mediation agreement

36.262   Confidentiality of mediation materials

36.264   Civil immunity for mediators and mediation service providers

36.266   Suspension of court proceedings during mediation; dismissal of action

36.268   Provision of mediation services contingent on funding

(Mediation of Disputes Related to Farming Practices)

36.280   Mediation of disputes related to interference with farming practices

36.283   Confidentiality of mediation communications and agreement

COURT ARBITRATION PROGRAM

36.400   Mandatory arbitration programs
36.405   Referral to mandatory arbitration; exemptions

36.410   Stipulation for arbitration; conditions; relief

36.415   Arbitration after waiver of amount of claim exceeding $50,000; motion for referral to arbitration

36.420   Notice of arbitration hearing; open proceeding; compensation and expenses

36.425   Filing of decision and award; notice of appeal; trial de novo; attorney fees and costs; effect of arbitration decision and award

OREGON INTERNATIONAL COMMERCIAL ARBITRATION AND CONCILIATION ACT

36.450   Definitions for ORS 36.450 to 36.558

36.452   Policy

36.454   Application of ORS 36.450 to 36.558; when arbitration or conciliation agreement is international; validity of written agreements

36.456   Construction of ORS 36.450 to 36.558

36.458   When written communication considered to have been received

36.460   Waiver of objection to arbitration

36.462   Prohibition on intervention by court

36.464   Venue

36.466   Arbitration agreements to be in writing

36.468   Application to stay judicial proceedings and compel arbitration

36.470   Interim judicial relief; factors considered by court; determination of arbitral tribunal's jurisdiction

36.472   Number of arbitrators

36.474   Procedure for appointment of arbitrators; appointment by circuit court

36.476   Disclosure by proposed arbitrators and conciliators; waiver of disclosure; grounds for challenge

36.478   Procedure for challenging arbitrator

36.480   Withdrawal of arbitrator; termination of mandate

36.482   Substitute arbitrator; effect of substitution

36.484   Arbitral tribunal may rule on own jurisdiction; time for raising issue of jurisdiction; review by circuit court

36.486   Interim measures of protection ordered by arbitral tribunal; security

36.488   Fairness in proceedings

36.490   Procedures subject to agreement by parties; procedure in absence of agreement

36.492   Place of arbitration

36.494   Commencement of arbitral proceedings

36.496   Language used in proceedings

36.498   Contents of statements by claimant and respondent; amendment or supplement

36.500   Oral hearing; notice; discovery

36.502   Effect of failure to make required statement or to appear at oral hearing

36.504   Appointment of experts

36.506   Circuit court assistance in taking evidence; circuit court authorized to enter certain orders upon application

36.508   Choice of laws

36.510   Decision of arbitral tribunal

36.512   Settlement

36.514   Arbitral award; contents; interim award; award for costs of arbitration

36.516   Termination of arbitral proceedings

36.518   Correction of errors in award; interpretation of award; additional award

36.520   Setting aside award; grounds; time for application; circuit court fees

36.522   Enforcement of award; procedure; fee; entry of judgment

36.524   Grounds for refusal to enforce award; fee

36.526   Provisions to be interpreted in good faith

36.528   Policy to encourage conciliation

36.530   Guiding principles of conciliators

36.532   Manner of conducting conciliation proceedings

36.534   Draft conciliation settlement

36.536   Prohibition on use of statements, admissions or documents arising out of conciliation proceedings

36.538   Conciliation to act as stay of other proceedings; tolling of limitation periods during conciliation

36.540   Termination of conciliation proceedings

36.542   Conciliator not to be arbitrator or take part in arbitral or judicial proceedings

36.544   Submission to conciliation not waiver

36.546   Conciliation agreement to be treated as arbitral award

36.548   Costs of conciliation proceedings

36.550   Payment of costs

36.552   Effect of conciliation on jurisdiction of courts

36.554   Immunities

36.556   Severability

36.558   Short title

UNIFORM ARBITRATION ACT

36.600   Definitions

36.605   Notice

36.610   Effect of agreement to arbitrate; nonwaivable provisions

36.615   Application for judicial relief; fees

36.620   Validity of agreement to arbitrate; form of acknowledgment of agreement

36.625   Petition to compel or stay arbitration

36.630   Provisional remedies

36.635   Initiation of arbitration

36.640   Consolidation of separate arbitration proceedings

36.645   Appointment of arbitrator; service as neutral arbitrator

36.650   Disclosure by arbitrator

36.655   Action by majority

36.660   Immunity of arbitrator; competency to testify; attorney fees and costs

36.665   Arbitration process

36.670   Representation by a lawyer; representation of legal or commercial entities

36.675   Witnesses; subpoenas; depositions; discovery

36.680   Judicial enforcement of preaward ruling by arbitrator

36.685   Award

36.690   Change of award by arbitrator

36.695   Remedies; fees and expenses of arbitration proceeding

36.700   Confirmation of award

36.705   Vacating award

36.710   Modification or correction of award

36.715   Judgment on award; attorney fees and litigation expenses

36.720   Jurisdiction

36.725   Venue

36.730   Appeals

36.735   Uniformity of application and construction

36.740   Relationship to electronic signatures in Global and National Commerce Act

DISPUTE RESOLUTION

(Generally)

36.100 Policy for ORS 36.100 to 36.238. It is the policy and purpose of ORS 36.100 to 36.238 that, when two or more persons cannot settle a dispute directly between themselves, it is preferable that the disputants be encouraged and assisted to resolve their dispute with the assistance of a trusted and competent third party mediator, whenever possible, rather than the dispute remaining unresolved or resulting in litigation. [1989 c.718 §1; 2003 c.791 §9]

36.105 Declaration of purpose of ORS 36.100 to 36.238. The Legislative Assembly declares that it is the purpose of ORS 36.100 to 36.238 to:
(1) Foster the development of community-based programs that will assist citizens in resolving disputes and developing skills in conflict resolution;
(2) Allow flexible and diverse programs to be developed in this state, to meet specific needs in local areas and to benefit this state as a whole through experiments using a variety of models of peaceful dispute resolution;
(3) Find alternative methods for addressing the needs of crime victims in criminal cases when those cases are either not prosecuted for lack of funds or can be more efficiently handled outside the courts;

(4) Provide a method to evaluate the effect of dispute resolution programs on communities, local governments, the justice system and state agencies;

(5) Encourage the development and use of mediation panels for resolution of civil litigation disputes;

(6) Foster the development or expansion of integrated, flexible and diverse state agency programs that involve state and local agencies and the public and that provide for use of alternative means of dispute resolution pursuant to ORS 183.502; and

(7) Foster efforts to integrate community, judicial and state agency dispute resolution programs. [1989 c.718 §2; 1997 c.706 §3; 2003 c.791 §10]

36.110 Definitions for ORS 36.100 to 36.238. As used in ORS 36.100 to 36.238:

(1) "Arbitration" means any arbitration whether or not administered by a permanent arbitral institution.

(2) "Dean" means the Dean of the University of Oregon School of Law.

(3) "Dispute resolution program" means an entity that receives a grant under ORS 36.155 to provide dispute resolution services.

(4) "Dispute resolution services" includes but is not limited to mediation, conciliation and arbitration.

(5) "Mediation" means a process in which a mediator assists and facilitates two or more parties to a controversy in reaching a mutually acceptable resolution of the controversy and includes all contacts between a mediator and any party or agent of a party, until such time as a resolution is agreed to by the parties or the mediation process is terminated.

(6) "Mediation agreement" means an agreement arising out of a mediation, including any term or condition of the agreement.

(7) "Mediation communications" means:

(a) All communications that are made, in the course of or in connection with a mediation, to a mediator, a mediation program or a party to, or any other person present at, the mediation proceedings; and

(b) All memoranda, work products, documents and other materials, including any draft mediation agreement, that are prepared for or submitted in the course of or in connection with a mediation or by a mediator, a mediation program or a party to, or any other person present at, mediation proceedings.

(8) "Mediation program" means a program through which mediation is made available and includes the director, agents and employees of the program.

(9) "Mediator" means a third party who performs mediation. "Mediator" includes agents and employees of the mediator or mediation program and any judge conducting a case settlement conference.

(10) "Public body" has the meaning given that term in ORS 174.109.

(11) "State agency" means any state officer, board, commission, bureau, department, or division thereof, in the executive branch of state government. [1989 c.718 §3; 1997 c.670 §11; 2003 c.791 §§11,11a; 2005 c.817 §3]

36.115 [1989 c.718 §4; 1991 c.538 §1; repealed by 2003 c.791 §33]

36.120 [1989 c.718 §5; repealed by 2003 c.791 §33]

36.125 [1989 c.718 §6; repealed by 2003 c.791 §33]

36.130 [1989 c.718 §7; repealed by 2003 c.791 §33]

(Dispute Resolution Programs)

36.135 Review of dispute resolution programs; suspension or termination of funding. The Dean of the University of Oregon School of Law shall periodically review dispute resolution programs in this state. If the dean determines that there are reasonable grounds to believe that a program is not in substantial compliance with the standards and guidelines adopted under ORS 36.175, the dean may suspend or terminate the funding of the program under ORS 36.155 and recover any unexpended funds or improperly expended funds from the program. [1989 c.718 §8; 1995 c.781 §31; 2003 c.791 §12; 2005 c.817 §4]

36.140 [1989 c.718 §9; repealed by 2003 c.791 §33]

36.145 Dispute Resolution Account. The Dispute Resolution Account is established in the State Treasury, separate and distinct from the General Fund. All moneys received under ORS 36.150 shall be deposited to the credit of the account. Notwithstanding the provisions of ORS 291.238, all moneys in the account are continuously appropriated to the University of Oregon or Portland State University for the purposes for which the moneys were made available and shall be expended in accordance with the terms and conditions upon which the moneys were made available. [1989 c.718 §10; 1997 c.801 §44; 2003 c.791 §§13,13a; 2005 c.817 §4a; 2009 c.762 §42; 2013 c.768 §103]

36.150 Additional funding. Portland State University, on behalf of the Mark O. Hatfield School of Government and the University of Oregon, on behalf of the University of Oregon School of Law, may accept and expend moneys from any public or private source, including the federal government, made available for the purpose of encouraging, promoting or establishing dispute resolution programs in Oregon or to facilitate and assist the schools in carrying out the responsibilities of the schools under ORS 36.100 to 36.238 and 183.502. All moneys received by the University of Oregon and Portland State University under this section shall be deposited in the Dispute Resolution Account. [1989 c.718 §11; 2003 c.791 §15; 2005 c.817 §4b; 2009 c.762 §43; 2013 c.768 §104]

36.155 Grants for dispute resolution services in counties; rules. The Dean of the University of Oregon School of Law shall award grants for the purpose of providing dispute resolution services in counties. Grants under this section shall be made from funds allocated to the University of Oregon on behalf of the University of Oregon School of Law for distribution under this section. The Board of Trustees of the University of Oregon may adopt standards for the operation of the grant program. [1989 c.718 §12; 1991 c.538 §2; 1997 c.801 §41; 2001 c.581 §1; 2003 c.791 §16; 2005 c.817 §4c; 2009 c.762 §44; 2013 c.768 §105]

36.160 Participation by counties; notice; contents; effect of failure to give notice. (1) To qualify for a grant under ORS 36.155, a county shall notify the Dean of the University of Oregon School of Law in accordance with the schedule established by rule by the dean. Such notification shall be by resolution of the appropriate board of county commissioners or, if the programs are to serve more than one county, by joint resolution. A county providing notice may select the dispute resolution programs to receive grants under ORS 36.155 for providing dispute resolution services within the county from among qualified dispute resolution programs.

(2) The county's notification to the dean must include a statement of agreement by the county to engage in a selection process and to select as the recipient of funding an entity capable of and willing to provide dispute resolution services according to the rules of the dean. The award of a grant is contingent upon the selection by the county of a qualified entity. The dean may provide consultation and technical assistance to a county to identify, develop and implement dispute resolution programs that meet the standards and guidelines adopted by the dean under ORS 36.175.

(3) If a county does not issue a notification according to the schedule established by the dean, the dean may notify a county board of commissioners that the dean intends to make a grant to a dispute resolution program in the county. The dean may, after such notification, assume the county's role under subsection (1) of this section unless the county gives the notice required by subsection (1) of this section. If the dean assumes the county's role, the dean may contract with a qualified program for a two-year period. The county may, 90 days before the expiration of an agreement between a qualified program and the dean, notify the dean under subsection (1) of this section that the county intends to assume its role under subsection (1) of this section.

(4) All dispute resolution programs identified for funding shall comply with the rules adopted under ORS 36.175.

(5) All funded dispute resolution programs shall submit informational reports and statistics as required by the dean. [1989 c.718 §13; 1991 c.538 §3; 1995 c.515 §1; 1997 c.801 §43; 2003 c.791 §17; 2005 c.817 §4d]

36.165 Termination of county participation. (1) Any county that receives a grant under ORS 36.155 may terminate its participation at the end of any month by delivering a resolution of its board of commissioners to the Dean of the University of Oregon School of Law not less than 180 days before the termination date.

(2) If a county terminates its participation under ORS 36.160, the remaining portion of the grant made to the county under ORS 36.160 shall revert to the University of Oregon School of Law to be used as specified in ORS 36.155. [1989 c.718 §14; 2003 c.791 §18; 2005 c.817 §4e]

36.170 [1989 c.718 §15; 1991 c.538 §4; 1991 c.790 §4; 1995 c.664 §77; 1995 c.666 §12; 1997 c.801 §§38,39; 2003 c.791 §18a; 2005 c.817 §4f; 2007 c.860 §26; 2009 c.659 §§18,19; 2010 c.107 §§36,37,38; repealed by 2011 c.595 §107]

(Program Standards)

36.175 Rules for administration of dispute resolution programs. (1) The Dean of the University of Oregon School of Law shall adopt by rule:
(a) Standards and guidelines for dispute resolution programs receiving grants under ORS 36.155;
(b) Minimum reporting requirements for dispute resolution programs receiving grants under ORS 36.155;
(c) Methods for evaluating dispute resolution programs receiving grants under ORS 36.155;
(d) Minimum qualifications and training for persons conducting dispute resolution services in dispute resolution programs receiving grants under ORS 36.155;
(e) Participating funds requirements, if any, for entities receiving grants under ORS 36.155;
(f) Requirements, if any, for the payment by participants for services provided by a program receiving grants under ORS 36.155; and
(g) Any other provisions or procedures for the administration of ORS 36.100 to 36.175.
(2) This section does not apply to state agency dispute resolution programs. [1989 c.718 §16; 1997 c.706 §4; 2003 c.791 §19; 2005 c.817 §4g]

(Dispute Resolution for Public Bodies)

36.179 Mediation and other alternative dispute resolution services for public bodies. The Mark O. Hatfield School of Government shall establish and operate a program to provide mediation and other alternative dispute resolution services to public bodies, as defined by ORS 174.109, and to persons who have disputes with public bodies, as defined by ORS 174.109. [2005 c.817 §11]

36.180 [1989 c.718 §18; repealed by 2003 c.791 §33]

(Mediation in Civil Cases)

36.185 Referral of civil dispute to mediation; objection; information to parties. After the appearance by all parties in any civil action, except proceedings under ORS 107.700 to 107.735, 124.005 to 124.040 or 163.760 to 163.777, a judge of any circuit court may refer a civil dispute to mediation under the terms and conditions set forth in ORS 36.185 to 36.210. When a party to a case files a written objection to mediation with the court, the action shall be removed from mediation and proceed in a normal fashion. All civil disputants shall be provided with written information describing the mediation process, as provided or approved by the State Court Administrator, along with information on established court mediation opportunities. Filing parties shall be provided with this information at the time of filing a civil action. Responding parties shall be provided with this information by the filing party along with the initial service of filing documents upon the responding party. [1989 c.718 §19; 1993 c.327 §1; 1995 c.666 §13; 2003 c.791 §20; 2013 c.687 §12]

36.190 Stipulation to mediation; selection of mediator; stay of proceedings. (1) On written stipulation of all parties at any time prior to trial, the parties may elect to mediate their civil dispute under the terms and conditions of ORS 36.185 to 36.210.

(2) Upon referral or election to mediate, the parties shall select a mediator by written stipulation or shall follow procedures for assignment of a mediator from the court's panel of mediators.

(3) During the period of any referred or elected mediation under ORS 36.185 to 36.210, all trial and discovery timelines and requirements shall be tolled and stayed as to the participants. Such tolling shall commence on the date of the referral or election to mediate and shall end on the date the court is notified in writing of the termination of the mediation by the mediator or one party requests the case be put back on the docket. All time limits and schedules shall be tolled, except that a judge shall have discretion to adhere to preexisting pretrial order dates, trial dates or dates relating to temporary relief. [1989 c.718 §20]

36.195 Presence of attorney; authority and duties of mediator; notice to court at completion of mediation. (1) Unless otherwise agreed to in writing by the parties, the parties' legal counsel shall not be present at any scheduled mediation sessions conducted under the provisions of ORS 36.100 to 36.175.

(2) Attorneys and other persons who are not parties to a mediation may be included in mediation discussions at the mediator's discretion, with the consent of the parties, for mediation held under the provisions of ORS 36.185 to 36.210.

(3) The mediator, with the consent of the parties, may adopt appropriate rules to facilitate the resolution of the dispute and shall have discretion, with the consent of the parties, to suspend or continue mediation. The mediator may propose settlement terms either orally or in writing.

(4) All court mediators shall encourage disputing parties to obtain individual legal advice and individual legal review of any mediated agreement prior to signing the agreement.

(5) Within 10 judicial days of the completion of the mediation, the mediator shall notify the court whether an agreement has been reached by the parties. If the parties do not reach agreement, the mediator shall report that fact only to the court, but shall not make a recommendation as to resolution of the dispute without written consent of all parties or their legal counsel. The action shall then proceed in the normal fashion on either an expedited or regular pretrial list.

(6) The court shall retain jurisdiction over a case selected for mediation and shall issue orders as it deems appropriate. [1989 c.718 §21]

36.200 Mediation panels; qualification; procedure for selecting mediator. (1) A circuit court providing mediation referral under ORS 36.185 to 36.210 shall establish mediation panels. The mediators on such panels shall have such qualifications as established by rules adopted under ORS 1.002. Formal education in any particular field shall not be a prerequisite to serving as a mediator.

(2) Unless instructed otherwise by the court, upon referral by the court to mediation, the clerk of the court shall select at least three individuals from the court's panel of mediators and shall send their names to legal counsel for the parties, or to a party directly if not represented, with a request that each party state preferences within five judicial days. If timely objection is made to all of the individuals named, the court shall select some other individual from the mediator panel. Otherwise, the clerk, under the direction of the court, shall select as mediator one of the three individuals about whom no timely objection was made.

(3) Upon the court's or the parties' own selection of a mediator, the clerk shall:
(a) Notify the designated person of the assignment as mediator.
(b) Provide the mediator with the names and addresses of the parties and their representatives and with copies of the order of assignment.

(4) The parties to a dispute that is referred by the court to mediation may choose, at their option and expense, mediation services other than those suggested by the court, and entering into such private mediation services shall be subject to the same provisions of ORS 36.185 to 36.210.

(5) Disputing parties in mediation shall be free, at their own expense, to retain jointly or individually, experts, attorneys, fact finders, arbitrators and other persons to assist the mediation, and all such dispute resolution efforts shall be subject to the protection of ORS 36.185 to 36.210. [1989 c.718 §22; 1993 c.327 §2; 2003 c.791 §21]

36.205 [1989 c.718 §23; 1995 c.678 §1; repealed by 1997 c.670 §15]

(Liability of Mediators and Programs)

36.210 Liability of mediators and programs. (1) Mediators, mediation programs and dispute resolution programs are not civilly liable for any act or omission done or made while engaged in efforts to assist or facilitate a mediation or in providing other dispute resolution services, unless the act or omission was made or done in bad faith, with malicious intent or in a manner exhibiting a willful, wanton disregard of the rights, safety or property of another.

(2) Mediators, mediation programs and dispute resolution programs are not civilly liable for the disclosure of a confidential mediation communication unless the disclosure was made in bad faith, with malicious intent or in a manner exhibiting a willful, wanton disregard of the rights, safety or property of another.

(3) The limitations on liability provided by this section apply to the officers, directors, employees and agents of mediation programs and dispute resolution programs. [1989 c.718 §24; 1995 c.678 §2; 1997 c.670 §12; 2001 c.72 §1; 2003 c.791 §§22,22a]

(Confidentiality of Mediation Communications and Agreements)

36.220 Confidentiality of mediation communications and agreements; exceptions. (1) Except as provided in ORS 36.220 to 36.238:
(a) Mediation communications are confidential and may not be disclosed to any other person.
(b) The parties to a mediation may agree in writing that all or part of the mediation communications are not confidential.
(2) Except as provided in ORS 36.220 to 36.238:
(a) The terms of any mediation agreement are not confidential.
(b) The parties to a mediation may agree that all or part of the terms of a mediation agreement are confidential.
(3) Statements, memoranda, work products, documents and other materials, otherwise subject to discovery, that were not prepared specifically for use in a mediation, are not confidential.
(4) Any document that, before its use in a mediation, was a public record as defined in ORS 192.311 remains subject to disclosure to the extent provided by ORS 192.311 to 192.478.
(5) Any mediation communication relating to child abuse that is made to a person who is required to report child abuse under the provisions of ORS 419B.010 is not confidential to the extent that the person is required to report the communication under the provisions of ORS 419B.010. Any mediation communication relating to elder abuse that is made to a person who is required to report elder abuse under the provisions of ORS 124.050 to 124.095 is not confidential to the extent that the person is required to report the communication under the provisions of ORS 124.050 to 124.095.
(6) A mediation communication is not confidential if the mediator or a party to the mediation reasonably believes that disclosing the communication is necessary to prevent a party from committing a crime that is likely to result in death or substantial bodily injury to a specific person.
(7) A party to a mediation may disclose confidential mediation communications to a person if the party's communication with that person is privileged under ORS 40.010 to 40.585 or other provision of law. A party may disclose confidential mediation communications to any other person for the purpose of obtaining advice concerning the subject matter of the mediation, if all parties to the mediation so agree.
(8) The confidentiality of mediation communications and agreements in a mediation in which a public body is a party, or in which a state agency is mediating a dispute as to which the state agency has regulatory authority, is subject to ORS 36.224, 36.226 and 36.230. [1997 c.670 §1]

36.222 Admissibility and disclosure of mediation communications and agreements in subsequent adjudicatory proceedings. (1) Except as provided in ORS 36.220 to 36.238, mediation communications and mediation agreements that are confidential under ORS 36.220 to 36.238 are not admissible as evidence in any subsequent adjudicatory proceeding, and may not be disclosed by the parties or the mediator in any subsequent adjudicatory proceeding.

(2) A party may disclose confidential mediation communications or agreements in any subsequent adjudicative proceeding if all parties to the mediation agree in writing to the disclosure.

(3) A mediator may disclose confidential mediation communications or confidential mediation agreements in a subsequent adjudicatory proceeding if all parties to the mediation, the mediator, and the mediation program, if any, agree in writing to the disclosure.

(4) In any proceeding to enforce, modify or set aside a mediation agreement, confidential mediation communications and confidential mediation agreements may be disclosed to the extent necessary to prosecute or defend the matter. At the request of a party, the court may seal any part of the record of the proceeding to prevent further disclosure of mediation communications or agreements to persons other than the parties to the agreement.

(5) In an action for damages or other relief between a party to a mediation and a mediator or mediation program, confidential mediation communications or confidential mediation agreements may be disclosed to the extent necessary to prosecute or defend the matter. At the request of a party, the court may seal any part of the record of the proceeding to prevent further disclosure of the mediation communications or agreements.

(6) A mediator may disclose confidential mediation communications directly related to child abuse or elder abuse if the mediator is a person who has a duty to report child abuse under ORS 419B.010 or elder abuse under ORS 124.050 to 124.095.

(7) The limitations on admissibility and disclosure in subsequent adjudicatory proceedings imposed by this section apply to any subsequent judicial proceeding, administrative proceeding or arbitration proceeding. The limitations on disclosure imposed by this section include disclosure during any discovery conducted as part of a subsequent adjudicatory proceeding, and no person who is prohibited from disclosing information under the provisions of this section may be compelled to reveal confidential communications or agreements in any discovery proceeding conducted as part of a subsequent adjudicatory proceeding. Any confidential mediation communication or agreement that may be disclosed in a subsequent adjudicatory proceeding under the provisions of this section may be introduced into evidence in the subsequent adjudicatory proceeding. [1997 c.670 §2]

36.224 State agencies; confidentiality of mediation communications; rules. (1) Except as provided in this section, mediation communications in mediations in which a state agency is a party, or in which a state agency is mediating a dispute as to which the state agency has regulatory authority, are not confidential and may be disclosed or admitted as evidence in subsequent adjudicatory proceedings, as described in ORS 36.222 (7).

(2) The Attorney General shall develop model rules that provide for the confidentiality of mediation communications in mediations described in subsection (1) of this section. The rules shall also provide for limitations on admissibility and disclosure in subsequent adjudicatory proceedings, as described in ORS 36.222 (7). The rules shall contain provisions governing mediations of workplace interpersonal disputes. The rules may be amended by the Attorney General after notice and opportunity for hearing as required by rulemaking procedures under ORS chapter 183.

(3) Model rules developed by the Attorney General under this section must include a provision for notice to the parties to a mediation regarding the extent to which the mediation communications are confidential or subject to disclosure or introduction as evidence in subsequent adjudicatory proceedings.

(4) A state agency may adopt the model rules developed by the Attorney General under this section in their entirety without complying with the rulemaking procedures under ORS 183.335. The agency shall file notice of adoption of rules under this subsection with the Secretary of State in the manner provided by ORS 183.355 for the filing of rules.

(5) Except as provided in ORS 36.222, mediation communications in any mediation regarding a claim for workers' compensation benefits conducted pursuant to rules adopted by the Workers' Compensation Board are confidential, are not subject to disclosure under ORS 192.311 to 192.478 and may not be disclosed or admitted as evidence in subsequent adjudicatory proceedings, as described in ORS 36.222 (7), without regard to whether a state agency or other public body is a party to the mediation or is the mediator in the mediation.

(6) Mediation communications made confidential by a rule adopted by a state agency are not subject to disclosure under ORS 192.311 to 192.478. [1997 c.670 §3; 2003 c.791 §23; 2005 c.333 §1; 2015 c.114 §1]

36.226 Public bodies other than state agencies; confidentiality of mediation communications. (1) Except as provided in subsection (2) of this section, mediation communications in mediations in which a public body other than a state agency is a party are confidential and may not be disclosed or admitted as evidence in subsequent adjudicatory proceedings, as described in ORS 36.222 (7).

(2) A public body other than a state agency may adopt a policy that provides that all or part of mediation communications in mediations in which the public body is a party will not be confidential. If a public body adopts a policy under this subsection, notice of the policy must be provided to all other parties in mediations that are subject to the policy. [1997 c.670 §4]

36.228 Mediations in which two or more public bodies are parties. (1) Notwithstanding any other provision of ORS 36.220 to 36.238, if the only parties to a mediation are public bodies, mediation communications and mediation agreements in the mediation are not confidential except to the extent those communications or agreements are exempt from disclosure under ORS 192.311 to 192.478. Mediation of workplace interpersonal disputes between employees of a public body is not subject to this subsection.

(2) Notwithstanding any other provision of ORS 36.220 to 36.238, if two or more public bodies are parties to a mediation in which a private person is also a party, mediation communications in the mediation are not confidential if the laws, rules or policies governing confidentiality of mediation communications for at least one of the public bodies provide that mediation communications in the mediation are not confidential.

(3) Notwithstanding any other provision of ORS 36.220 to 36.238, if two or more public bodies are parties to a mediation in which a private person is also a party, mediation agreements in the mediation are not confidential if the laws, rules or policies governing confidentiality of mediation agreements for at least one of the public bodies provide that mediation agreements in the mediation are not confidential. [1997 c.670 §4a; 2007 c.12 §1]

36.230 Public bodies; confidentiality of mediation agreements. (1) Except as provided in this section, mediation agreements are not confidential if a public body is a party to the mediation or if the mediation is one in which a state agency is mediating a dispute as to which the state agency has regulatory authority.

(2) If a public body is a party to a mediation agreement, any provisions of the agreement that are exempt from disclosure as a public record under ORS 192.311 to 192.478 are confidential.

(3) If a public body is a party to a mediation agreement, and the agreement is subject to the provisions of ORS 17.095, the terms of the agreement are confidential to the extent that those terms are confidential under ORS 17.095 (2).

(4) If a public body is a party to a mediation agreement arising out of a workplace interpersonal dispute:

(a) The agreement is confidential if the public body is not a state agency, unless the public body adopts a policy that provides otherwise;

(b) The agreement is confidential if the public body is a state agency only to the extent that the state agency has adopted a rule under ORS 36.224 that so provides; and

(c) Any term of an agreement that requires an expenditure of public funds, other than expenditures of $1,000 or less for employee training, employee counseling or purchases of equipment that remain the property of the public body, may not be made confidential by a rule or policy of a public body. [1997 c.670 §5; 2005 c.352 §2]

36.232 Disclosures allowed for reporting, research, training and educational purposes. (1) If a public body conducts or makes available a mediation, ORS 36.220 to 36.238 do not limit the ability of the mediator to report the disposition of the mediation to that public body at the conclusion of the mediation proceeding. The report made by a mediator to a public body under this subsection may not disclose specific confidential mediation communications made in the mediation.

(2) If a public body conducts or makes available a mediation, ORS 36.220 to 36.238 do not limit the ability of the public body to compile and disclose general statistical information concerning matters that have gone to mediation if the information does not identify specific cases.

(3) In any mediation in a case that has been filed in court, ORS 36.220 to 36.238 do not limit the ability of the court to:

(a) Require the parties or the mediator to report to the court the disposition of the mediation at the conclusion of the mediation proceeding;

(b) Disclose records reflecting which matters have been referred for mediation; or

(c) Disclose the disposition of the matter as reported to the court.

(4) ORS 36.220 to 36.238 do not limit the ability of a mediator or mediation program to use or disclose confidential mediation communications, the disposition of matters referred for mediation and the terms of mediation agreements to another person for use in research, training or educational purposes, subject to the following:

(a) A mediator or mediation program may only use or disclose confidential mediation communications if the communications are used or disclosed in a manner that does not identify individual mediations or parties.

(b) A mediator or mediation program may use or disclose confidential mediation communications that identify individual mediations or parties only if and to the extent allowed by a written agreement with, or written waiver of confidentiality by, the parties. [1997 c.670 §6]

36.234 Parties to mediation. For the purposes of ORS 36.220 to 36.238, a person, state agency or other public body is a party to a mediation if the person or public body participates in a mediation and has a direct interest in the controversy that is the subject of the mediation. A person or public body is not a party to a mediation solely because the person or public body is conducting the mediation, is making the mediation available or is serving as an information resource at the mediation. [1997 c.670 §7]

36.236 Effect on other laws. (1) Nothing in ORS 36.220 to 36.238 affects any confidentiality created by other law, including but not limited to confidentiality created by ORS 107.755 to 107.795.

(2) Nothing in ORS 36.220 to 36.238 relieves a public body from complying with ORS 192.610 to 192.690. [1997 c.670 §9]

36.238 Application of ORS 36.210 and 36.220 to 36.238. The provisions of ORS 36.210 and 36.220 to 36.238 apply to:

(1) All mediations, whether conducted by a publicly funded program or by a private mediation provider; and

(2) Facilitated dispute resolution services conducted by the Public Records Advocate under ORS 192.464. Solely for purposes of ORS 36.210 and 36.220 to 36.238, a facilitated dispute resolution shall be deemed a mediation. [1997 c.670 §8; 2017 c.728 §7]

36.245 [1997 c.706 §2; repealed by 2003 c.791 §33]

36.250 [1989 c.967 §2; 2001 c.104 §9; 2005 c.657 §3; 2009 c.294 §2; repealed by 2015 c.202 §1]

MEDIATION OF DISPUTES RELATED TO AGRICULTURE

(Agricultural Mediation Services)

36.252 Agricultural mediation services coordinated by State Department of Agriculture; rules. (1) The State Department of Agriculture shall coordinate agricultural mediation services for disputes directly related to activities of the department and agricultural issues under the jurisdiction of the department.

(2) The Director of Agriculture or a designee of the director shall serve as the agricultural mediation service coordinator. The coordinator shall establish rules necessary to implement ORS 36.252 to 36.268. The rules must include, but need not be limited to:

(a) Reasonable mediator training guidelines for persons providing agricultural mediation services under ORS 36.252 to 36.268.

(b) Fees to be charged for agricultural mediation services.
(c) Methods for advertising the availability of agricultural mediation services.
(d) Procedures for accepting applications for agricultural mediation services and for notifying any other person who is identified in the request for mediation as a party to the dispute. [1989 c.967 §3; 2015 c.202 §2]

Note: 36.252 to 36.268 were enacted into law by the Legislative Assembly but were not added to or made a part of ORS chapter 36 or any series therein by legislative action. See Preface to Oregon Revised Statutes for further explanation.

36.254 Contracts for mediation services. (1) The agricultural mediation service coordinator serving under ORS 36.252 shall contract with one or more providers of agricultural mediation services to provide impartial mediators who are knowledgeable in agriculture and financial matters.
(2) The coordinator may contract with, or use the services of, a private mediation organization, a community-based program, a state agency or a combination of organizations and agencies.
(3) A contract entered into under this section may be terminated by the coordinator only upon 30 days' written notice and for good cause.
(4) An agricultural mediation service provider other than a state agency is an independent contractor and is not a state agency for any purpose. [1989 c.967 §4; 2015 c.202 §3]

Note: See note under 36.252.

36.256 Request for mediation services. (1) The State Department of Agriculture may accept a request for mediation under ORS 36.252 to 36.268 of a dispute directly related to activities of the department or agricultural issues under the jurisdiction of the department from:
(a) A person engaged in the production of livestock, poultry, field crops, fruit, dairy, fur-bearing animals, Christmas trees, vermiculture products, food fish or other animal and vegetable matter; or
(b) Any other person at the discretion of the department.
(2) A person may request mediation by submitting the request to the department on a form provided by the department. A mediation request must include:
(a) The name and address of each party to the dispute;
(b) The name of each party's legal representative, if applicable; and
(c) Any additional information the department may require.
(3) ORS 36.252 to 36.268 do not require a person to engage or continue in the mediation of any dispute. Mediation under ORS 36.252 to 36.268 is voluntary for all parties to the dispute, and if the parties agree to engage in mediation, any party may at any time withdraw from mediation.
(4) The submission of a request for mediation does not operate to stay, impede or delay in any manner the commencement, prosecution or defense of any action or proceeding by any person. [1989 c.967 §5; 1995 c.277 §6; 1997 c.631 §566; 2005 c.22 §29; 2015 c.27 §2; 2015 c.202 §4]

Note: See note under 36.252.

36.258 Duties of mediator. In carrying out mediation under ORS 36.252 to 36.268, a mediator shall:
(1) Listen to the parties that are desiring to be heard.
(2) Attempt to facilitate a negotiated agreement that provides for mutual satisfaction.
(3) Seek assistance as necessary from any public or private agency to effect the goals of ORS 36.252 to 36.268.
(4) Permit any person who is a party to the mediation to be represented in all mediation proceedings by any person selected by the party. [1989 c.967 §6; 2001 c.104 §10; 2015 c.202 §5]

Note: See note under 36.252.

36.260 Mediation agreement. (1) If an agreement is reached between the parties in a mediation under ORS 36.252 to 36.268, the parties shall sign a written mediation agreement.
(2) The parties to a mediation agreement:
(a) Are bound by the terms of the agreement;
(b) May enforce the mediation agreement as a legal contract; and
(c) May use the mediation agreement as a defense against an action contrary to the mediation agreement.
(3) If the mediator drafts the agreement, the mediator shall encourage the parties to have the agreement reviewed by independent legal counsel before signing the agreement. [1989 c.967 §7; 2015 c.202 §6]

Note: See note under 36.252.

36.262 Confidentiality of mediation materials. (1) For purposes of a mediation under ORS 36.252 to 36.268, all memoranda, work products and other materials contained in the case files of a mediator, an agricultural mediation service provider or the State Department of Agriculture are confidential. Any communication made in, or in connection with, the mediation that relates to the dispute being mediated, whether made to the mediator or a party, or to any other person if made at a mediation session, is confidential. However, a mediation agreement entered into under ORS 36.260 is not confidential unless the parties otherwise agree in writing.
(2) Confidential materials and communications are not subject to disclosure in any judicial or administrative proceeding except:
(a) When all parties to the mediation agree, in writing, to waive the confidentiality;
(b) In a subsequent action between the mediator and a party to the mediation for damages arising out of the mediation; or
(c) When the material or communications are statements, memoranda, materials and other tangible evidence, otherwise subject to discovery, that were not prepared specifically for use in and not actually used in the mediation.
(3) Notwithstanding subsection (2) of this section, a mediator may not be compelled to testify in any proceeding, unless all parties to the mediation and the mediator agree, in writing, to waive the confidentiality. [1989 c.967 §8; 2015 c.202 §7]

Note: See note under 36.252.

36.264 Civil immunity for mediators and mediation service providers. Mediators and agricultural mediation service providers are immune from civil liability for, or resulting from, any act or omission done or made while engaged in efforts to assist or facilitate a mediation under ORS 36.252 to 36.268, unless the act or omission was made or done in bad faith, with malicious intent or in a manner exhibiting a willful, wanton disregard of the rights, safety or property of another. [1989 c.967 §9; 2015 c.202 §8]

Note: See note under 36.252.

36.266 Suspension of court proceedings during mediation; dismissal of action. (1) During the pendency of any action between parties to a mediation under ORS 36.252 to 36.268, the court may, upon stipulation by all parties, enter an order suspending the action.
(2) A suspension order under subsection (1) of this section suspends all orders and proceedings in the action for the time period specified in the suspension order. In specifying the time period, the court shall exercise its discretion for the purpose of permitting the parties to engage in mediation

without prejudice to the rights of any person. The suspension order may include other terms and conditions as the court may consider appropriate. The suspension order may be revoked upon motion of any party or upon motion of the court.

(3) If all parties to the action agree, by written stipulation, that all issues before the court are resolved by mediation under ORS 36.252 to 36.268, the court shall dismiss the action. If the parties do not agree that the issues are resolved or if the court revokes the suspension order under subsection (2) of this section, the action shall proceed as if mediation had not been attempted. [1989 c.967 §10; 2015 c.202 §9]

Note: See note under 36.252.

36.268 Provision of mediation services contingent on funding. The duty of the State Department of Agriculture and the Director of Agriculture to provide mediation services under ORS 36.252 to 36.268 is contingent upon the existence and the level of funding specifically made available to carry out that duty. Should continuation of mediation services be threatened for lack of funding, the department shall proceed with all diligence to secure additional funds, including but not limited to requesting an additional allocation of funds from the Emergency Board. [1993 c.163 §2]

Note: See note under 36.252.

36.270 [1995 c.277 §5; repealed by 2015 c.202 §1]

(Mediation of Disputes Related to Farming Practices)

36.280 Mediation of disputes related to interference with farming practices. (1) If a person that is engaged in a farming practice, as defined in ORS 30.930, has a reasonable belief that the planting, growing or harvesting of an agricultural or horticultural commodity on nearby land might interfere with or is interfering with the farming practice, and the person responsible for the planting, growing or harvesting disputes that it might interfere with or is interfering with the farming practice, the State Department of Agriculture shall, if requested by either party to the dispute:

(a) Provide mediation program services under ORS 36.252 to assist the parties in attempting to reach a voluntary resolution of the dispute; or

(b) Refer the parties to the United States Department of Agriculture for the purpose of participating in a certified state agricultural mediation program.

(2) A person that is requested to participate in a mediation proceeding under this section may elect to have the proceeding conducted through the use of mediation program services described in subsection (1)(a) of this section or under a mediation program described in subsection (1)(b) of this section. However, if the State Department of Agriculture has referred the parties under subsection (1)(b) of this section, a person electing to instead use mediation services described in subsection (1)(a) of this section must pay any additional costs and fees resulting from that election.

(3) If the State Department of Agriculture provides mediation program services under subsection (1)(a) of this section, the total amount that the department may require of the parties as costs and fees for services provided in connection with the mediation of the dispute may not exceed $2,500. The party requesting the mediation services is responsible for paying the costs and fees unless both parties agree to divide the costs and fees. Unless the parties agree to a shorter time, the department shall conduct at least four hours of mediation proceedings to attempt to reach resolution of the dispute.

(4) If a party is offered dispute mediation under subsection (1) of this section and is unwilling to participate in a mediation proceeding, a court may consider that unwillingness when determining whether to grant or deny a preliminary injunction.

(5) If a court action arises out of an alleged interference with the use of land for a farming practice due to the planting, growing or harvesting of an agricultural or horticultural commodity on nearby land, and the parties to the action have not previously attempted to have the dispute mediated, the parties must participate in a mediation proceeding under a program described under subsection (1) of this section beginning no later than 270 days after the action is filed. This subsection does not require participation in a mediation proceeding if the action settles or is otherwise resolved within 270 days after filing or if all parties to the action agree to waive mediation. A court may impose sanctions against a party that is unwilling to participate for at least four hours, or for a shorter time that was agreed to by the parties, in a mediation proceeding required under this subsection.

(6) This section does not create any new cause of action or supersede any requirement, condition or prohibition otherwise established by law regarding the bringing of an action. [2015 c.630 §1; 2017 c.72 §1]

Note: Section 3, chapter 630, Oregon Laws 2015, provides:

Sec. 3. Section 1 of this 2015 Act [36.280] does not apply to any dispute regarding the planting, growing or harvesting of a genetically engineered agricultural or horticultural commodity in a county that has in effect a valid ordinance lawfully adopted on or before the effective date of this 2015 Act [January 1, 2016] that regulates the planting, growing or harvesting of genetically engineered agricultural or horticultural commodities. [2015 c.630 §3]

Note: 36.280 and 36.283 were enacted into law by the Legislative Assembly but were not added to or made a part of ORS chapter 36 or any series therein by legislative action. See Preface to Oregon Revised Statutes for further explanation.

36.283 Confidentiality of mediation communications and agreement. (1) A mediation described in ORS 36.280 (1) is subject to ORS 36.220.

(2) Except as provided under ORS 36.220 to 36.238, if the parties to a mediation described in ORS 36.280 have agreed in writing that all or part of the mediation communications or all or part of the terms of a mediation agreement are confidential, a cause of action exists against a party that discloses the confidential communications or terms for damages resulting from the disclosure.

(3) ORS 36.280 does not require a party to a mediation proceeding to disclose confidential business information or to disclose other confidential information that may be adverse to the legal interests of the party. [2015 c.630 §2]

Note: See second note under 36.280.

36.300 [Formerly 33.210; repealed by 2003 c.598 §57]

36.305 [Formerly 33.220; repealed by 2003 c.598 §57]

36.310 [Formerly 33.230; repealed by 2003 c.598 §57]

36.315 [Formerly 33.240; repealed by 2003 c.598 §57]

36.320 [Formerly 33.250; repealed by 2003 c.598 §57]

36.325 [Formerly 33.260; repealed by 2003 c.598 §57]

36.330 [Formerly 33.270; repealed by 2003 c.598 §57]

36.335 [Formerly 33.280; repealed by 2003 c.598 §57]

36.340 [Formerly 33.290; repealed by 2003 c.598 §57]

36.345 [Formerly 33.300; repealed by 2003 c.598 §57]

36.350 [Formerly 33.310; 1997 c.801 §53; 1999 c.63 §1; 2003 c.737 §35; repealed by 2003 c.598 §57]

36.355 [Formerly 33.320; 1997 c.801 §54; 2003 c.737 §38; repealed by 2003 c.598 §57]

36.360 [Formerly 33.330; repealed by 2003 c.598 §57]

36.365 [Formerly 33.340; repealed by 2003 c.598 §57]

COURT ARBITRATION PROGRAM

36.400 Mandatory arbitration programs. (1) A mandatory arbitration program is established in each circuit court.
(2) Rules consistent with ORS 36.400 to 36.425 to govern the operation and procedure of an arbitration program established under this section may be made in the same manner as other rules applicable to the court and are subject to the approval of the Chief Justice of the Supreme Court.
(3) Each circuit court shall require arbitration under ORS 36.400 to 36.425 in matters involving $50,000 or less.
(4) ORS 36.400 to 36.425 do not apply to appeals from a county, justice or municipal court or actions in the small claims department of a circuit court. Actions transferred from the small claims department of a circuit court by reason of a request for a jury trial under ORS 46.455, by reason of the filing of a counterclaim in excess of the jurisdiction of the small claims department under ORS 46.461, or for any other reason, shall be subject to ORS 36.400 to 36.425 to the same extent and subject to the same conditions as a case initially filed in circuit court. The arbitrator shall not allow any party to appear or participate in the arbitration proceeding after the transfer unless the party pays the arbitrator fee established by court rule or the party obtains a waiver or deferral of the fee from the court and provides a copy of the waiver or deferral to the arbitrator. The failure of a party to appear or participate in the arbitration proceeding by reason of failing to pay the arbitrator fee or obtain a waiver or deferral of the fee does not affect the ability of the party to appeal the arbitrator's decision and award in the manner provided by ORS 36.425. [Formerly 33.350; 1993 c.482 §1; 1995 c.618 §10; 1995 c.658 §30a; 1997 c.46 §§3,4; 2005 c.274 §1]

36.405 Referral to mandatory arbitration; exemptions. (1) Except as provided in ORS 30.136, in a civil action in a circuit court where all parties have appeared, the court shall refer the action to arbitration under ORS 36.400 to 36.425 if either of the following applies:
(a) The only relief claimed is recovery of money or damages, and no party asserts a claim for money or general and special damages in an amount exceeding $50,000, exclusive of attorney fees, costs and disbursements and interest on judgment.
(b) The action is a domestic relations suit, as defined in ORS 107.510, in which the only contested issue is the division or other disposition of property between the parties.
(2) The presiding judge for a judicial district may do either of the following:
(a) Exempt from arbitration under ORS 36.400 to 36.425 a civil action that otherwise would be referred to arbitration under this section.
(b) Remove from further arbitration proceedings a civil action that has been referred to arbitration under this section, when, in the opinion of the judge, good cause exists for that exemption or removal.
(3) If a court has established a mediation program that is available for a civil action that would otherwise be subject to arbitration under ORS 36.400 to 36.425, the court shall not assign the proceeding to arbitration if the proceeding is assigned to mediation pursuant to the agreement of the parties. Notwithstanding any other provision of ORS 36.400 to 36.425, a party who completes a mediation program offered by a court shall not be required to participate in arbitration under ORS 36.400 to 36.425. [Formerly 33.360; 1995 c.455 §2a; 1995 c.618 §11; 1995 c.658 §31a; 1995 c.781 §32; 2005 c.274 §2; 2009 c.83 §3]

36.410 Stipulation for arbitration; conditions; relief. (1) In a civil action in a circuit court where all parties have appeared and agreed to arbitration by stipulation, the court shall refer the action to arbitration under ORS 36.400 to 36.425 if:
(a) The relief claimed is more than or other than recovery of money or damages.
(b) The only relief claimed is recovery of money or damages and a party asserts a claim for money or general and special damages in an amount exceeding $50,000, exclusive of attorney fees, costs and disbursements and interest on judgment.
(2) If a civil action is referred to arbitration under this section, the arbitrator may grant any relief that could have been granted if the action were determined by a judge of the court. [Formerly 33.370; 1995 c.618 §12; 1995 c.658 §32; 2005 c.274 §3]

36.415 Arbitration after waiver of amount of claim exceeding $50,000; motion for referral to arbitration. (1) In a civil action in a circuit court where all parties have appeared, where the only relief claimed is recovery of money or damages, where a party asserts a claim for money or general and special damages in an amount exceeding $50,000, exclusive of attorney fees, costs and disbursements and interest on judgment, and where all parties asserting those claims waive the amounts of those claims that exceed $50,000, the court shall refer the action to arbitration under ORS 36.400 to 36.425. A waiver of an amount of a claim under this section shall be for the purpose of arbitration under ORS 36.400 to 36.425 only and shall not restrict assertion of a larger claim in a trial de novo under ORS 36.425.
(2) In a civil action in a circuit court where all parties have appeared, where the only relief claimed is recovery of money or damages and where a party asserts a claim for money or general and special damages in an amount exceeding $50,000, exclusive of attorney fees, costs and disbursements and interest on judgment, any party against whom the claim is made may file a motion with the court requesting that the matter be referred to arbitration. After hearing upon the motion, the court shall refer the matter to arbitration under ORS 36.400 to 36.425 if the defendant establishes by affidavits and other documentation that no objectively reasonable juror could return a verdict in favor of the claimant in excess of $50,000, exclusive of attorney fees, costs and disbursements and interest on judgment. [Formerly 33.380; 1995 c.618 §13; 1995 c.658 §33; 2005 c.274 §4]

36.420 Notice of arbitration hearing; open proceeding; compensation and expenses. (1) At least five days before the date set for an arbitration hearing, the arbitrator shall notify the clerk of the court of the time and place of the hearing. The clerk shall post a notice of the time and place of the hearing in a conspicuous place for trial notices at the principal location for the sitting of the court in the county in which the action was commenced.
(2) The arbitration proceeding and the records thereof shall be open to the public to the same extent as would a trial of the action in the court and the records thereof.
(3) The compensation of the arbitrator and other expenses of the arbitration proceeding shall be the obligation of the parties or any of them as provided by rules made under ORS 36.400. However, if those rules require the parties or any of them to pay any of those expenses in advance, in the form of fees or otherwise, as a condition of arbitration, the rules shall also provide for the waiver in whole or in part, deferral in whole or in part, or both, of that payment by a party whom the court finds is then unable to pay all or any part of those advance expenses. Expenses so waived shall be paid by the state from funds available for the purpose. Expenses so deferred shall be paid, if necessary, by the state from funds available for the purpose, and the state shall be reimbursed according to the terms of the deferral. [Formerly 33.390; 1993 c.482 §2]

36.425 Filing of decision and award; notice of appeal; trial de novo; attorney fees and costs; effect of arbitration decision and award. (1) At the conclusion of arbitration under ORS 36.400 to 36.425 of a civil action, the arbitrator shall file the decision and award with the clerk of the court that referred the action to arbitration, together with proof of service of a copy of the decision and award upon each party. If the decision and award require the payment of money, including payment of costs or attorney fees, the decision and award must be substantially in the form prescribed by ORS 18.042.
(2)(a) Within 20 days after the filing of a decision and award with the clerk of the court under subsection (1) of this section, a party against whom relief is granted by the decision and award or a party whose claim for relief was greater than the relief granted to the party by the decision and award, but no other party, may file with the clerk a written notice of appeal and request for a trial de novo of the action in the court on all issues of law and fact. A copy of the notice of appeal and request for a trial de novo must be served on all other parties to the proceeding. After the filing of the written notice a trial

317

de novo of the action shall be held. If the action is triable by right to a jury and a jury is demanded by a party having the right of trial by jury, the trial de novo shall include a jury.

(b) If a party files a written notice under paragraph (a) of this subsection, a trial fee or jury trial fee, as applicable, shall be collected as provided in ORS 21.225.

(c) A party filing a written notice under paragraph (a) of this subsection shall deposit with the clerk of the court the sum of $150. If the position under the arbitration decision and award of the party filing the written notice is not improved as a result of a judgment in the action on the trial de novo, the clerk shall dispose of the sum deposited in the same manner as a fee collected by the clerk. If the position of the party is improved as a result of a judgment, the clerk shall return the sum deposited to the party. If the court finds that the party filing the written notice is then unable to pay all or any part of the sum to be deposited, the court may waive in whole or in part, defer in whole or in part, or both, the sum. If the sum or any part thereof is so deferred and the position of the party is not improved as a result of a judgment, the deferred amount shall be paid by the party according to the terms of the deferral.

(3) If a written notice is not filed under subsection (2)(a) of this section within the 20 days prescribed, the court shall cause to be prepared and entered a judgment based on the arbitration decision and award. A judgment entered under this subsection may not be appealed.

(4) Notwithstanding any other provision of law or the Oregon Rules of Civil Procedure:

(a) If a party requests a trial de novo under the provisions of this section, the action is subject to arbitration under the provisions of ORS 36.405 (1)(a), the party is entitled to attorney fees by law or contract, and the position of the party is not improved after judgment on the trial de novo, the party shall not be entitled to an award of attorney fees or costs and disbursements incurred by the party before the filing of the decision and award of the arbitrator, and shall be taxed the reasonable attorney fees and costs and disbursements incurred by the other parties to the action on the trial de novo after the filing of the decision and award of the arbitrator.

(b) If a party requests a trial de novo under the provisions of this section, the action is subject to arbitration under ORS 36.405 (1)(a), the party is not entitled to attorney fees by law or contract, and the position of the party is not improved after judgment on the trial de novo, pursuant to subsection (5) of this section the party shall be taxed the reasonable attorney fees and costs and disbursements of the other parties to the action on the trial de novo incurred by the other parties after the filing of the decision and award of the arbitrator.

(c) If a party requests a trial de novo under the provisions of this section, the action is subject to arbitration under ORS 36.405 (1)(b), and the position of the party is not improved after judgment on the trial de novo, the party shall not be entitled to an award of attorney fees or costs or costs and disbursements and shall be taxed the costs and disbursements incurred by the other parties after the filing of the decision and award of the arbitrator.

(5) If a party is entitled to an award of attorney fees under subsection (4) of this section, but is also entitled to an award of attorney fees under contract or another provision of law, the court shall award reasonable attorney fees pursuant to the contract or other provision of law. If a party is entitled to an award of attorney fees solely by reason of subsection (4) of this section, the court shall award reasonable attorney fees not to exceed the following amounts:

(a) Twenty percent of the judgment, if the defendant requests the trial de novo but the position of the defendant is not improved after the trial de novo; or

(b) Ten percent of the amount claimed in the complaint, if the plaintiff requests the trial de novo but the position of the plaintiff is not improved after the trial de novo.

(6) Within seven days after the filing of a decision and award under subsection (1) of this section, a party may file with the court and serve on the other parties to the arbitration written exceptions directed solely to the award or denial of attorney fees or costs. Exceptions under this subsection may be directed to the legal grounds for an award or denial of attorney fees or costs, or to the amount of the award. Any party opposing the exceptions must file a written response with the court and serve a copy of the response on the party filing the exceptions. Filing and service of the response must be made within seven days after the service of the exceptions on the responding party. A judge of the court shall decide the issue and enter a decision on the award of attorney fees and costs. If the judge fails to enter a decision on the award within 20 days after the filing of the exceptions, the award of attorney fees and costs shall be considered affirmed. The filing of exceptions under this subsection does not constitute an appeal under subsection (2) of this section and does not affect the finality of the award in any way other than as specifically provided in this subsection.

(7) For the purpose of determining whether the position of a party has improved after a trial de novo under the provisions of this section, the court shall not consider any money award or other relief granted on claims asserted by amendments to the pleadings made after the filing of the decision and award of the arbitrator. [Formerly 33.400; 1993 c.482 §3; 1995 c.455 §3; 1995 c.618 §14a; 1995 c.658 §34; 1997 c.756 §§1,2; 2003 c.576 §170]

OREGON INTERNATIONAL COMMERCIAL ARBITRATION AND CONCILIATION ACT

36.450 Definitions for ORS 36.450 to 36.558. For the purposes of ORS 36.450 to 36.558:

(1) "Arbitral award" means any decision of the arbitral tribunal on the substance of the dispute submitted to it and includes any interim, interlocutory or partial arbitral award.

(2) "Arbitral tribunal" means a sole arbitrator or a panel of arbitrators.

(3) "Arbitration" means any arbitration whether or not administered by a permanent arbitral institution.

(4) "Arbitration agreement" means an agreement by the parties to submit to arbitration all or certain disputes which may arise between them in respect to a defined legal relationship, whether contractual or not. An arbitration agreement may be in the form of an arbitration clause in a contract or in the form of a separate agreement.

(5) "Commercial" means matters arising from all relationships of a commercial nature including, but not limited to, any of the following transactions:

(a) A transaction for the supply or exchange of goods or services.

(b) A distribution agreement.

(c) A commercial representation or agency.

(d) An exploitation agreement or concession.

(e) A joint venture or other forms of industrial or business cooperation.

(f) The carriage of goods or passengers by air, sea, rail or road.

(g) Construction.

(h) Insurance.

(i) Licensing.

(j) Factoring.

(k) Leasing.

(L) Consulting.

(m) Engineering.

(n) Financing.

(o) Banking.

(p) The transfer of data or technology.

(q) Intellectual or industrial property, including trademarks, patents, copyrights and software programs.

(r) Professional services.

(6) "Conciliation" means any conciliation whether or not administered by a permanent conciliation institution.

(7) "Chief Justice" means the Chief Justice of the Supreme Court of Oregon or designee.

(8) "Circuit court" means the circuit court in the county in this state selected as pursuant to ORS 36.464.

(9) "Court" means a body or an organ of the judicial system of a state or country.

(10) "Party" means a party to an arbitration or conciliation agreement.

(11) "Supreme Court" means the Supreme Court of Oregon. [1991 c.405 §4]

36.452 Policy. (1) It is the policy of the Legislative Assembly to encourage the use of arbitration and conciliation to resolve disputes arising out of international relationships and to assure access to the courts of this state for legal proceedings ancillary to or otherwise in aid of such arbitration and conciliation and to encourage the participation and use of Oregon facilities and resources to carry out the purposes of ORS 36.450 to 36.558.

(2) Any person may enter into a written agreement to arbitrate or conciliate any existing dispute or any dispute arising thereafter between that person and another. If the dispute is within the scope of ORS 36.450 to 36.558, the agreement shall be enforced by the courts of this state in accordance with ORS 36.450 to 36.558 without regard to the justiciable character of the dispute. In addition, if the agreement is governed by the law of this state, it shall be valid and enforceable in accordance with ordinary principles of contract law. [1991 c.405 §2; 1993 c.18 §12]

36.454 Application of ORS 36.450 to 36.558; when arbitration or conciliation agreement is international; validity of written agreements. (1) ORS 36.450 to 36.558 apply to international commercial arbitration and conciliation, subject to any agreement in force between the United States of America and any other country or countries.

(2) The provisions of ORS 36.450 to 36.558, except ORS 36.468, 36.470, 36.522 and 36.524, apply only if the place of arbitration or conciliation is within the territory of the State of Oregon.

(3) An arbitration or conciliation agreement is international if any of the following applies:

(a) The parties to an arbitration or conciliation agreement have, at the time of the conclusion of that agreement, their places of business in different countries.

(b) One of the following places is situated outside the country in which the parties have their places of business:

(A) The place of arbitration or conciliation if determined in, or pursuant to, the arbitration or conciliation agreement.

(B) Any place where a substantial part of the obligations of the commercial relationship is to be performed.

(C) The place with which the subject matter of the dispute is most closely connected.

(c) The parties have expressly agreed that the subject matter of the arbitration or conciliation agreement relates to commercial interests in more than one country.

(d) The subject matter of the arbitration or conciliation agreement is otherwise related to commercial interests in more than one country.

(4) For the purposes of subsection (3) of this section:

(a) If a party has more than one place of business, the place of business is that which has the closest relationship to the arbitration or conciliation agreement; or

(b) If a party does not have a place of business, reference is to be made to the habitual residence of the party.

(5) If a written agreement to submit an existing controversy to arbitration or a provision in a written contract to submit to arbitration a controversy thereafter arising between the parties qualifies for arbitration pursuant to this section, that written agreement or provision shall be valid, enforceable and irrevocable, save on such grounds as exist at law or in equity for the revocation of any contract.

(6) Except as provided in this subsection, ORS 36.450 to 36.558 shall not affect any other law of the State of Oregon by virtue of which certain disputes may not be submitted to arbitration or conciliation or may be submitted to arbitration or conciliation only according to provisions other than those of ORS 36.450 to 36.558. ORS 36.450 to 36.558 supersede ORS 36.100 to 36.425 with respect to international commercial arbitration and conciliation. [1991 c.405 §3]

36.456 Construction of ORS 36.450 to 36.558. (1) Except as specified in ORS 36.508, where a provision of ORS 36.450 to 36.558 leaves the parties free to determine a certain issue, such freedom includes the right of the parties to authorize a third party, including an institution, to make that determination.

(2) Where a provision of ORS 36.450 to 36.558 refers to the fact that the parties have agreed or that they may agree or in any other way refers to an agreement of the parties, such agreement includes any arbitration or conciliation rules referred to in that agreement.

(3) Except as provided in ORS 36.502 (1) and 36.516 (2)(a), where a provision of ORS 36.450 to 36.558 refers to a claim, it also applies to a counterclaim, and where it refers to a defense, it also applies to a defense of a counterclaim. [1991 c.405 §5]

36.458 When written communication considered to have been received. (1) Unless otherwise agreed by the parties:

(a) Any written communication is considered to have been received if it is delivered to the addressee personally or if it is delivered at the place of business, habitual residence or mailing address of the addressee. If none of these can be found after making a reasonable inquiry, a written communication is considered to have been received if it is sent to the addressee's last-known place of business, habitual residence or mailing address by registered letter or by any other means which provides a record of the attempt to deliver it; and

(b) The communication is considered to have been received on the day it is so delivered.

(2) The provisions of this section do not apply to communications in court proceedings. [1991 c.405 §6]

36.460 Waiver of objection to arbitration. (1) A party who knows that any provision of ORS 36.450 to 36.558 or of any requirement under the arbitration agreement that has not been complied with and yet proceeds with the arbitration without stating an objection to such noncompliance without undue delay or, if a time limit is provided for stating that objection, within that period of time, shall be deemed to have waived the right to object.

(2) For purposes of subsection (1) of this section, "any provision of ORS 36.450 to 36.558" means any provision of ORS 36.450 to 36.558 in respect of which the parties may otherwise agree. [1991 c.405 §7]

36.462 Prohibition on intervention by court. In matters governed by ORS 36.450 to 36.558, no court shall intervene except where so provided in ORS 36.450 to 36.558 or in applicable federal law. [1991 c.405 §8]

36.464 Venue. (1) The functions referred to in ORS 36.468 and 36.470 shall be performed by the circuit court in:

(a) The county where the arbitration agreement is to be performed or was made.

(b) If the arbitration agreement does not specify a county where the agreement is to be performed and the agreement was not made in any county in the State of Oregon, the county where any party to the court proceeding resides or has a place of business.

(c) In any case not covered by paragraph (a) or (b) of this subsection, in any county in the State of Oregon.

(2) All other functions assigned by ORS 36.450 to 36.558 to the circuit court shall be performed by the circuit court of the county in which the place of arbitration is located. [1991 c.405 §9]

36.466 Arbitration agreements to be in writing. The arbitration agreement shall be in writing. An agreement is in writing if it is contained in a document signed by the parties or in an exchange of letters, telex, telegrams or other means of telecommunication which provides a record of the agreement, or in an exchange of statements of claim and defense in which the existence of an agreement is alleged by one party and not denied by another. The reference in a contract to a document containing an arbitration clause constitutes an arbitration agreement provided that the contract is in writing and the reference is such as to make that clause a part of the contract. [1991 c.405 §10]

36.468 Application to stay judicial proceedings and compel arbitration. (1) When a party to an international commercial arbitration agreement commences judicial proceedings seeking relief with respect to a matter covered by the agreement to arbitrate, the court shall, if a party so requests not later than when submitting the party's first statement on the substance of the dispute, stay the proceedings and refer the parties to arbitration unless it finds that the agreement is null and void, inoperative or incapable of being performed.

(2) Arbitral proceedings may begin or continue, and an award may be made, while a judicial proceeding described in subsection (1) of this section is pending before the court.

(3) A court may not, without a request from a party made pursuant to subsection (1) of this section, refer the parties to arbitration. [1991 c.405 §11; 1993 c.244 §1]

36.470 Interim judicial relief; factors considered by court; determination of arbitral tribunal's jurisdiction. (1) It is not incompatible with an arbitration agreement for a party to request from a court, before or during arbitral proceedings, an interim measure of protection or for the court to grant such a measure.

(2) Any party to an arbitration governed by ORS 36.450 to 36.558 may request from the circuit court the enforcement of an order of an arbitral tribunal granting an interim measure of protection pursuant to ORS 36.486. Enforcement shall be granted pursuant to the law applicable to the granting of the type of interim relief requested.

(3) Measures which the circuit court may grant in connection with a pending arbitration include, but are not limited to:

(a) An order of attachment issued to assure that the award to which the applicant may be entitled is not rendered ineffectual by the dissipation of party assets.

(b) A preliminary injunction granted in order to protect trade secrets or to conserve goods which are the subject matter of the arbitral dispute.

(4) In considering a request for interim relief, the court, subject to subsection (5) of this section, shall give preclusive effect to any and all findings of fact of the arbitral tribunal, including the probable validity of the claim which is the subject of the award for interim relief that the arbitral tribunal has previously granted in the proceeding in question, provided that such interim award is consistent with public policy.

(5) Where the arbitral tribunal has not ruled on an objection to its jurisdiction, the court shall not grant preclusive effect to the tribunal's findings until the court has made an independent finding as to the jurisdiction of the arbitral tribunal. If the court rules that the arbitral tribunal did not have jurisdiction, the application for interim measures of relief shall be denied. Such a ruling by the court that the arbitral tribunal lacks jurisdiction is not binding on the arbitral tribunal or subsequent judicial proceedings. [1991 c.405 §12; 1993 c.244 §2]

36.472 Number of arbitrators. The parties may agree on the number of arbitrators. If the parties do not agree, the number of arbitrators shall be one. [1991 c.405 §13]

36.474 Procedure for appointment of arbitrators; appointment by circuit court. (1) No person shall be precluded by reason of nationality from acting as an arbitrator unless otherwise agreed by the parties.

(2) The parties may agree on a procedure for appointing the arbitrator or arbitrators, subject to the provisions of subsections (4), (5) and (6) of this section.

(3) If the parties do not agree on a procedure for appointing the arbitrator or arbitrators:

(a) In an arbitration with two parties and involving three or more arbitrators, each party shall appoint one arbitrator and the appointed arbitrators shall appoint the remaining arbitrators. If a party fails to appoint an arbitrator within 30 days of receipt of a request to do so from the other party or parties, or if the two appointed arbitrators fail to agree on the remaining arbitrators within 30 days of their appointment, then, upon the request of any party, the circuit court shall make the appointment.

(b) In an arbitration with more than two parties or in an arbitration with two parties involving fewer than three arbitrators, then, upon the request of any party, the arbitrator or arbitrators shall be appointed by the circuit court.

(4) Unless the parties' agreement on the appointment procedure provides other means for securing the appointment, any party may request the circuit court to make the appointment if there is an appointment procedure agreed upon by the parties and if:

(a) A party fails to act as required under such procedure;

(b) The parties, or the appointed arbitrators, are unable to reach an agreement as expected of them under such procedure; or

(c) A third party, including an institution, fails to perform any function entrusted to it under such procedure.

(5) A decision by the circuit court on a matter entrusted to it by subsection (3) or (4) of this section shall be final and not subject to appeal.

(6) The circuit court, in appointing an arbitrator, shall have due regard to all of the following:

(a) Any qualifications required of the arbitrator by the agreement of the parties;

(b) Other considerations as are likely to secure the appointment of an independent and impartial arbitrator; and

(c) The advisability of appointing an arbitrator of a nationality other than those of the parties. [1991 c.405 §14; 1993 c.244 §3]

36.476 Disclosure by proposed arbitrators and conciliators; waiver of disclosure; grounds for challenge. (1) Except as otherwise provided in ORS 36.450 to 36.558, all persons whose names have been submitted for consideration for appointment or designation as arbitrators or conciliators, or who have been appointed or designated as such, shall, within 15 days, make a disclosure to the parties of any information which might cause their impartiality to be questioned including, but not limited to, any of the following instances:

(a) The person has a personal bias or prejudice concerning a party or personal knowledge of the disputed evidentiary facts concerning the proceeding.

(b) The person served as a lawyer in the matter in controversy, or the person is or has been associated with another who has participated in the matter during such association, or the person has been a material witness concerning it.

(c) The person served as an arbitrator or conciliator in another proceeding involving one or more of the parties to the proceeding.

(d) The person, individually or as a fiduciary, or the person's spouse or minor child, or anyone residing in the person's household, has a financial interest in the subject matter in controversy or in a party to the proceeding, or any other interest that could be substantially affected by the outcome of the proceeding.

(e) The person, the person's spouse or minor child, anyone residing in the person's household, any individual within the third degree of relationship to any of them, or the spouse of any of them, meets any of the following conditions:

(A) The person is or has been a party to the proceeding, or an officer, director or trustee of a party.

(B) The person is acting or has acted as a lawyer in the proceeding.

(C) The person is known to have an interest that could be substantially affected by the outcome of the proceeding.

(D) The person is likely to be a material witness in the proceeding.

(f) The person has a close personal or professional relationship with a person who meets any of the following conditions:

(A) The person is or has been a party to the proceeding, or an officer, director or trustee of a party.

(B) The person is acting or has acted as a lawyer or representative in the proceeding.

(C) The person is or expects to be nominated as an arbitrator or conciliator in the proceedings.

(D) The person is known to have an interest that could be substantially affected by the outcome of the proceeding.

(E) The person is likely to be a material witness in the proceeding.

(2) The obligation to disclose information set forth in subsection (1) of this section is mandatory and cannot be waived by the parties with respect to persons serving either as the sole arbitrator or sole conciliator or as one of two arbitrators or conciliators or as the chief or prevailing arbitrator or conciliator. The parties may otherwise agree to waive such disclosure.

(3) From the time of appointment and throughout the arbitral proceedings, an arbitrator shall, without delay, disclose to the parties any circumstances referred to in subsection (1) of this section which were not previously disclosed.

(4) Unless otherwise agreed by the parties or allowed by the rules governing the arbitration, an arbitrator may be challenged only if circumstances exist that give rise to justifiable doubts as to the independence or impartiality of the arbitrator, or as to possession of the qualifications upon which the parties have agreed.

(5) A party may challenge an arbitrator appointed by it, or in whose appointment it has participated, only for reasons of which it becomes aware after the appointment has been made. [1991 c.405 §15]

36.478 Procedure for challenging arbitrator. (1) Subject to subsection (4)(a) of this section, the parties may agree on a procedure for challenging an arbitrator.

(2) Failing any agreement referred to in subsection (1) of this section, a party which intends to challenge an arbitrator shall, within 15 days after becoming aware of the constitution of the arbitral tribunal or after becoming aware of any circumstances referred to in ORS 36.476 (4) and (5), whichever shall be later, send a written statement of the reasons for the challenge to the arbitral tribunal.

(3) Unless the arbitrator challenged under subsection (2) of this section withdraws from office or the other party agrees to the challenge, the arbitral tribunal shall decide the challenge.

(4)(a) If a challenge under any procedure agreed upon by the parties or under the procedure under subsections (2) and (3) of this section is not successful, the challenging party may request the circuit court, within 30 days after having received notice of the decision rejecting the challenge, to decide on the challenge.

(b) When the request is made, the circuit court may refuse to decide on the challenge if it is satisfied that, under the procedure agreed upon by the parties, the party making the request had an opportunity to have the challenge decided upon by other than the arbitral tribunal.

(c) Notwithstanding paragraph (b) of this subsection, whether the challenge is under any procedure agreed upon by the parties or under the procedure under subsections (2) and (3) of this section, if a challenge is based upon the grounds set forth in ORS 36.476 (1), the circuit court shall hear the challenge and, if it determines that the facts support a finding that such ground or grounds fairly exist, then the challenge shall be sustained.

(5) The decision of the circuit court under subsection (4) of this section is final and not subject to appeal.

(6) While a request under subsection (4) of this section is pending, the arbitral tribunal, including the challenged arbitrator, may continue with the arbitral proceedings and make an arbitral award. [1991 c.405 §16; 1993 c.244 §4]

36.480 Withdrawal of arbitrator; termination of mandate. (1) If an arbitrator withdraws from the case or if the parties agree on termination because the arbitrator becomes unable, de facto or de jure, to perform the functions of the arbitrator or for other reasons fails to act without undue delay, then the arbitrator's mandate terminates.

(2) If a controversy remains concerning any of the grounds referred to in subsection (1) of this section, a party may request the circuit court to decide on the termination of the mandate.

(3) The decision of the circuit court under subsection (2) of this section is not subject to appeal.

(4) If, under this section or ORS 36.478 (3), an arbitrator withdraws from office or a party agrees to the termination of the mandate of an arbitrator, this does not imply acceptance of the validity of any ground referred to under this section or under ORS 36.476 (4) and (5). [1991 c.405 §17]

36.482 Substitute arbitrator; effect of substitution. (1) In addition to the circumstances referred to under ORS 36.478 and 36.480, the mandate of an arbitrator terminates upon withdrawal from office for any reason, or by or pursuant to the agreement of the parties.

(2) Where the mandate of an arbitrator terminates, a substitute arbitrator shall be appointed according to the rules that were applicable to the appointment of the arbitrator being replaced.

(3) Unless otherwise agreed by the parties:

(a) Where the number of arbitrators is less than three and an arbitrator is replaced, any hearings previously held shall be repeated.

(b) Where the presiding arbitrator is replaced, any hearings previously held shall be repeated.

(c) Where the number of arbitrators is three or more and an arbitrator other than the presiding arbitrator is replaced, any hearings previously held may be repeated at the discretion of the arbitral tribunal.

(4) Unless otherwise agreed by the parties, an order or ruling of the arbitral tribunal made prior to the replacement of an arbitrator under this section is not invalid because there has been a change in the composition of the tribunal. [1991 c.405 §18]

36.484 Arbitral tribunal may rule on own jurisdiction; time for raising issue of jurisdiction; review by circuit court. (1) The arbitral tribunal may rule on its own jurisdiction, including any objections with respect to the existence or validity of the arbitration agreement and, for that purpose, an arbitration clause which forms part of a contract shall be treated as an agreement independent of the other terms of the contract. A decision by the arbitral tribunal that the contract is null and void shall not entail ipso jure the invalidity of the arbitration clause.

(2) A plea that the arbitral tribunal does not have jurisdiction shall be raised no later than the submission of the statement of defense. However, a party is not precluded from raising such a plea by the fact that the party has appointed, or participated in the appointment of, an arbitrator. A plea that the arbitral tribunal is exceeding the scope of its authority shall be raised as soon as the matter alleged to be beyond the scope of its authority is raised during the arbitral proceedings. In either case, the arbitral tribunal may admit a later plea if it considers the delay justified.

(3) The arbitral tribunal may rule on a plea referred to in subsection (2) of this section either as a preliminary question or in an award on the merits. If the arbitral tribunal rules as a preliminary question that it has jurisdiction, any party shall request the circuit court, within 30 days after having received notice of that ruling, to decide the matter or shall be deemed to have waived objection to such finding.

(4) The decision of the circuit court under subsection (3) of this section is not subject to appeal.

(5) While a request under subsection (3) of this section is pending, the arbitral tribunal may continue with the arbitral proceedings and make an arbitral award. [1991 c.405 §19; 1993 c.244 §5]

36.486 Interim measures of protection ordered by arbitral tribunal; security. Unless otherwise agreed by the parties, at the request of a party, the arbitral tribunal may order any party to take such interim measure of protection as the arbitral tribunal may consider necessary in respect to the subject matter of the dispute. The arbitral tribunal may require any party to provide appropriate security in connection with such measure. [1991 c.405 §20]

36.488 Fairness in proceedings. The parties shall be treated with equality and each party shall be given a full opportunity to present the case of the party. [1991 c.405 §21]

36.490 Procedures subject to agreement by parties; procedure in absence of agreement. (1) Subject to the provisions of ORS 36.450 to 36.558, the parties are free to agree on the procedure to be followed by the arbitral tribunal in conducting the proceedings.

(2) If the parties fail to agree, subject to the provisions of ORS 36.450 to 36.558, the arbitral tribunal may conduct the arbitration in such a manner as it considers appropriate.

(3) The power of the arbitral tribunal under subsection (2) of this section includes the power to determine the admissibility, relevance, materiality and weight of any evidence. [1991 c.405 §22]

36.492 Place of arbitration. (1) The parties are free to agree on the place of arbitration. If the parties do not agree, the place of arbitration shall be determined by the arbitral tribunal or, if any members of the arbitral tribunal are not yet appointed and are to be appointed by the circuit court as pursuant to ORS 36.474 (4), by the Chief Justice, taking into account the circumstances of the case, including the convenience of the parties.

(2) Notwithstanding the provisions of subsection (1) of this section, unless otherwise agreed by the parties, the arbitral tribunal may meet at any place it considers appropriate for consultation among its members, for hearing witnesses, experts or the parties, or for the inspection of documents, goods or other property. [1991 c.405 §23]

36.494 Commencement of arbitral proceedings. Unless otherwise agreed by the parties, the arbitral proceedings in respect to a particular dispute commence on the date which a request for referral of that dispute to arbitration is received by the respondent. [1991 c.405 §24]

36.496 Language used in proceedings. (1) The parties are free to agree on the language or languages to be used in the arbitral proceedings. If the parties do not agree, the arbitral tribunal shall determine the language or languages to be used in the proceedings. Unless otherwise specified therein, this agreement or determination shall apply to any written statement by a party, any hearing and any award, decision or other communication by the arbitral tribunal.

(2) The arbitral tribunal may order that any documentary evidence shall be accompanied by a translation into the language or languages agreed upon by the parties or determined by the arbitral tribunal. [1991 c.405 §25]

36.498 Contents of statements by claimant and respondent; amendment or supplement. (1) Within the period of time agreed upon by the parties or determined by the arbitral tribunal, the claimant shall state the facts supporting the claim of the claimant, the points at issue, and the relief or remedy sought, and the respondent shall state the defense of the respondent in respect of these particulars, unless the parties have otherwise agreed as to the required elements of those statements.

(2) The parties may submit with their statements all documents they consider to be relevant or may add a reference to the documents or other evidence they will submit.

(3) Unless otherwise agreed by the parties, either party may amend or supplement the claim or defense of the party during the course of the arbitral proceedings, unless the arbitral tribunal considers it inappropriate to allow the amendment or supplement having regard to the delay in making it. [1991 c.405 §26]

36.500 Oral hearing; notice; discovery. (1) Unless otherwise agreed by the parties, the arbitral tribunal shall decide whether to hold oral hearings for the presentation of evidence or for oral argument or whether the proceedings shall be conducted on the basis of documents and other materials.

(2) Unless the parties have agreed that no oral hearings shall be held, the arbitral tribunal shall hold oral hearings at an appropriate stage of the proceedings, if so requested by a party.

(3) The parties shall be given sufficient advance notice of any hearing and of any meeting of the arbitral tribunal for the purpose of the inspection of documents, goods or other property.

(4) All statements, documents or other information supplied to, or applications made to, the arbitral tribunal by one party shall be communicated to the other party. Any expert report or evidentiary document on which the arbitral tribunal may rely in making its decision shall be communicated to the parties.

(5) Unless otherwise agreed by the parties, all oral hearings and meetings in arbitral proceedings shall be held in camera. [1991 c.405 §27; 1993 c.244 §6]

36.502 Effect of failure to make required statement or to appear at oral hearing. (1) Unless otherwise agreed by the parties, where, without showing sufficient cause, the claimant fails to communicate the statement of claim of the claimant in accordance with ORS 36.498 (1) and (2), the arbitral tribunal shall terminate the proceedings.

(2) Unless otherwise agreed by the parties, where, without showing sufficient cause, the respondent fails to communicate the statement of defense of the respondent in accordance with ORS 36.498 (1) and (2), the arbitral tribunal shall continue the proceedings without treating that failure in itself as an admission of the claimant's allegations.

(3) Unless otherwise agreed by the parties, where, without showing sufficient cause, a party fails to appear at an oral hearing or to produce documentary evidence, the arbitral tribunal may continue with the proceedings and make the arbitral award on the evidence before it. [1991 c.405 §28]

36.504 Appointment of experts. (1) Unless otherwise agreed by the parties, the arbitral tribunal may appoint one or more experts to report to it on specific issues to be determined by the arbitral tribunal and require a party to give the expert any relevant information or to produce, or to provide access to, any relevant documents, goods or other property for the expert's inspection.

(2) Unless otherwise agreed by the parties, if a party so requests or if the arbitral tribunal considers it necessary, the expert shall, after delivery of the expert's written or oral report, participate in an oral hearing where the parties have the opportunity to question the expert and to present expert witnesses on the points at issue. [1991 c.405 §29; 1993 c.244 §7]

36.506 Circuit court assistance in taking evidence; circuit court authorized to enter certain orders upon application. (1) The arbitral tribunal, or a party with the approval of the arbitral tribunal, may request from the circuit court assistance in taking evidence and the court may execute the request within its competence and according to its rules on taking evidence. In addition, a subpoena may be issued as provided in ORCP 55, in which case the witness compensation provisions of ORS chapter 44 shall apply.

(2) When the parties to two or more arbitration agreements have agreed in their respective arbitration agreements or otherwise, the circuit court may, on application by one party with the consent of all other parties to those arbitration agreements, do one or more of the following:

(a) Order the arbitration proceedings arising out of those arbitration agreements to be consolidated on terms the court considers just and necessary.

(b) Where all the parties cannot agree on an arbitral tribunal for the consolidated arbitration, appoint an arbitral tribunal in accordance with ORS 36.474 (6).

(c) Where the parties cannot agree on any other matter necessary to conduct the consolidated arbitration, make any other order it considers necessary.

(d) Order the arbitration proceedings arising out of those arbitration agreements to be held at the same time or one immediately after another.

(e) Order any of the arbitration proceedings arising out of those arbitration agreements to be stayed until the determination of any other of them.

(3) Nothing in this section shall be construed to prevent the parties to two or more arbitrations from agreeing to consolidate those arbitrations and taking any steps that are necessary to effect that consolidation. [1991 c.405 §30; 1993 c.244 §8]

36.508 Choice of laws. (1) The arbitral tribunal shall decide the dispute in accordance with the rules of law designated by the parties as applicable to the substance of the dispute.

(2) Any designation by the parties of the law or legal system of a given country or political subdivision thereof shall be construed, unless otherwise expressed, as directly referring to the substantive law of that state and not to its conflict of laws rules.

(3) Failing any designation of the law under subsection (1) of this section by the parties, the arbitral tribunal shall apply the rules of law it considers to be appropriate given all the circumstances surrounding the dispute.

(4) The arbitral tribunal shall decide ex aequo et bono or as amiable compositeur if the parties have expressly authorized it to do so.

(5) In all cases, the arbitral tribunal shall decide in accordance with the terms of the contract and shall take into account the usages of the trade applicable to the transaction. [1991 c.405 §31]

36.510 Decision of arbitral tribunal. Unless otherwise agreed by the parties, any decision of the arbitral tribunal in arbitral proceedings with more than one arbitrator shall be made by a majority of all its members. However, the parties or all members of the arbitral tribunal may authorize a presiding arbitrator to decide questions of procedure. [1991 c.405 §32; 1993 c.244 §9]

36.512 Settlement. (1) It is not incompatible with an arbitration agreement for an arbitral tribunal to encourage settlement of the dispute and, with the agreement of the parties, the arbitral tribunal may use mediation, conciliation or other procedures at any time during the arbitral proceedings to encourage settlement. If agreed by the parties, the members of the arbitral tribunal are not disqualified from resuming their roles as arbitrators by reason of the mediation, conciliation or other procedure.

(2) If, during the arbitral proceedings, the parties settle the dispute, the arbitral tribunal shall terminate the proceedings and, if requested by the parties and not objected to by the arbitral tribunal, record the settlement in the form of an arbitral award on agreed terms.

(3) An arbitral award on agreed terms shall be made in accordance with ORS 36.514 and shall state that it is an arbitral award.

(4) An arbitral award on agreed terms has the same status and effect as any other arbitral award on the substance of the dispute. [1991 c.405 §33; 1993 c.244 §10]

36.514 Arbitral award; contents; interim award; award for costs of arbitration. (1) The arbitral award shall be made in writing and shall be signed by the arbitrator or arbitrators. In arbitral proceedings with more than one arbitrator, the signatures of the majority of all the members of the arbitral tribunal shall suffice so long as the reason for any omitted signature is stated.

(2) The arbitral award shall state the reasons upon which it is based, unless the parties have agreed that no reasons are to be given or the award is an arbitral award on agreed terms under ORS 36.512.

(3) The arbitral award shall state its date and the place of arbitration as determined in accordance with ORS 36.492 (1) and the award shall be considered to have been made at that place.

(4) After the arbitral award is made, a copy signed by the arbitrators in accordance with subsection (1) of this section shall be delivered to each party.

(5) The arbitral tribunal may, at any time during the arbitral proceedings, make an interim arbitral award on any matter with respect to which it may make a final arbitral award. The interim award may be enforced in the same manner as a final arbitral award.

(6) Unless otherwise agreed by the parties, the arbitral tribunal may award interest.

(7)(a) Unless otherwise agreed by the parties, the costs of an arbitration shall be at the discretion of the arbitral tribunal.

(b) In making an order for costs, the arbitral tribunal may include as costs any of the following:

(A) The fees and expenses of the arbitrators and expert witnesses.

(B) Legal fees and expenses.

(C) Any administration fees of the institution supervising the arbitration, if any.

(D) Any other expenses incurred in connection with the arbitral proceedings.

(c) In making an order for costs, the arbitral tribunal may specify any of the following:

(A) The party entitled to costs.

(B) The party who shall pay the costs.

(C) The amount of costs or the method of determining that amount.

(D) The manner in which the costs shall be paid. [1991 c.405 §34]

36.516 Termination of arbitral proceedings. (1) The arbitral proceedings are terminated by the final arbitral award or by an order of the arbitral tribunal in accordance with subsection (2) of this section. The award shall be final upon the expiration of the applicable periods in ORS 36.518.

(2) The arbitral tribunal shall issue an order for the termination of the arbitral proceedings when:

(a) The claimant withdraws the claim, unless the respondent objects thereto and the arbitral tribunal recognizes a legitimate interest on the part of the respondent in obtaining a final settlement of the dispute;

(b) The parties agree on the termination of the proceedings; or

(c) The arbitral tribunal finds that the continuation of the proceedings has for any other reason become unnecessary or impossible.

(3) Subject to ORS 36.518 and 36.520 (4), the mandate of the arbitral tribunal terminates with the termination of the arbitral proceeding. [1991 c.405 §35; 1993 c.244 §11]

36.518 Correction of errors in award; interpretation of award; additional award. (1) Within 30 days of receipt of the arbitral award, unless another period of time has been agreed upon by the parties:

(a) A party, with notice to the other party, may request the arbitral tribunal to correct in the award any errors in computation, clerical or typographical errors, or errors of similar nature; and

(b) A party may, if agreed by the parties, request the arbitral tribunal to give an interpretation of a specific point or part of the arbitral award.

(2) If the arbitral tribunal considers any request made under subsection (1) of this section to be justified, it shall make the correction or give the interpretation within 30 days of the receipt of the request. The interpretation shall form part of the arbitral award.

(3) The arbitral tribunal may correct any error of the type referred to in subsection (1)(a) of this section on its own initiative within 30 days of the date of the award.

(4) Unless otherwise agreed by the parties, a party, with notice to the other party, may request, within 30 days of receipt of the award, the arbitral tribunal to make an additional award as to claims presented in the arbitral proceedings but omitted from the award. If the arbitral tribunal considers the request to be justified, it shall make the additional award within 60 days.

(5) If necessary, the arbitral tribunal may extend the period of time within which it shall make a correction, interpretation or an additional award under subsection (1) or (4) of this section.

(6) The provisions of ORS 36.514 shall apply to a correction or interpretation of the award or to an additional award. [1991 c.405 §36; 1993 c.244 §12]

36.520 Setting aside award; grounds; time for application; circuit court fees. (1) Recourse to a court against an arbitral award may only be by an application for setting aside in accordance with subsections (2) and (3) of this section.

(2) An arbitral award may be set aside by the circuit court only if:

(a) The party making application furnishes proof that:

(A) A party to the arbitration agreement referred to in ORS 36.466 was under some incapacity or that the agreement is not valid under the law to which the parties have subjected it or, failing any indication thereon, under the laws of the State of Oregon or the United States;

(B) The party making the application was not given proper notice of the appointment of an arbitrator or of the arbitral proceedings or was otherwise unable to present the party's case;

(C) The award deals with a dispute not contemplated by or not falling within the terms of the submission to arbitration or contains decisions on matters beyond the scope of the submission to arbitration, provided that, if the decisions on matters not submitted to arbitration can be separated from those not so submitted, only that part of the award which contains decisions on matters not submitted to arbitration may be set aside; or

(D) The composition of the arbitral tribunal or the arbitral procedure was not in accordance with the agreement of the parties, unless such agreement was in conflict with a provision of ORS 36.450 to 36.558 from which the parties cannot derogate, or, failing such agreement, was not in accordance with ORS 36.450 to 36.558; or

(b) The circuit court finds that:

(A) The subject matter of the dispute is not capable of settlement by arbitration under the laws of the State of Oregon or of the United States; or

(B) The award is in conflict with the public policy of the State of Oregon or of the United States.

(3) An application for setting aside may not be made after three months have elapsed from the date on which the party making that application had received the award or, if a request had been made under ORS 36.518, from the date on which that request had been disposed of by the arbitral tribunal.

(4) The circuit court, when asked to set aside an arbitral award, may, where appropriate and so requested by a party, suspend the setting aside proceedings for a period of time determined by it in order to give the arbitral tribunal an opportunity to resume the arbitral proceedings or to take such other action as in the arbitral tribunal's opinion will eliminate the grounds for setting aside.

(5) The clerk of the circuit court shall collect the filing fees established under ORS 21.135 from the party making application for setting aside under subsection (1) of this section and from a party filing an appearance in opposition to the application. [1991 c.405 §37; 1993 c.244 §13; 1997 c.801 §55; 2003 c.737 §§41,42; 2005 c.702 §§41,42,43; 2007 c.860 §5; 2011 c.595 §41]

36.522 Enforcement of award; procedure; fee; entry of judgment. (1) An arbitral award, irrespective of the country in which it was made, shall be recognized as binding and, upon application in writing to the circuit court, shall be enforced subject to the provisions of this section and ORS 36.524.

(2) The party relying on an award or applying for its enforcement shall supply the authenticated original or a certified copy of the award and the original or certified copy of the arbitration agreement referred to in ORS 36.466. If the award or agreement is not made in the English language, then the party relying on the award or applying for its enforcement shall supply a duly certified translation thereof into the English language.

(3) The party relying on an arbitral award or applying for its enforcement shall deliver to the clerk of the circuit court the documents specified in subsection (2) of this section along with proof of the delivery of a copy of the arbitral award as required by ORS 36.514 (4). The relying party shall pay to the clerk the filing fee established under ORS 21.135, after which the clerk shall enter the arbitral award of record in the office of the clerk. If no application to set aside is filed against the arbitral award as provided in ORS 36.520 within the time specified in ORS 36.520 (3) or, if such an application is filed, the relying party after the disposition of the application indicates the intention to still rely on the award or to apply for its enforcement, judgment shall be entered as upon the verdict of a jury, and execution may issue thereon, and the same proceedings may be had upon the award with like effect as upon a verdict in a civil action. [1991 c.405 §38; 2011 c.595 §42]

36.524 Grounds for refusal to enforce award; fee. (1) Recognition or enforcement of an arbitral award, irrespective of the country in which it was made, may be refused only:

(a) At the request of the party against whom it is invoked, if that party pays the clerk of the circuit court the filing fee established under ORS 21.135 and furnishes to the court where recognition or enforcement is sought proof that:

(A) A party to the arbitration agreement referred to in ORS 36.466 was under some incapacity or that the agreement is not valid under the law to which the parties have subjected it or under the law of the country where the award was made;

(B) The party against whom the award is invoked was not given proper notice of the appointment of an arbitrator or of the arbitral proceedings or was otherwise unable to present the party's case;

(C) The arbitral award deals with a dispute not contemplated by or not falling within the terms of the submission to arbitration or the award contains decisions on matters beyond the scope of the submission to arbitration, provided that, if the decisions on matters submitted to arbitration can be separated from those not so submitted, that part of the award which contains decisions on matters submitted to arbitration may be recognized and enforced;

(D) The composition of the arbitral tribunal or the arbitral procedure was not in accordance with the agreement of the parties or, failing such agreement, was not in accordance with the law of the country where the arbitration took place; or

(E) The award has not yet become binding on the parties or has been set aside or suspended by a court of the country in which, or under the law of which, that award was made; or

(b) If the court finds that:

(A) The subject matter of the dispute is not capable of settlement by arbitration under the laws of the State of Oregon or of the United States; or

(B) The recognition or enforcement of the arbitral award would be contrary to the public policy of the State of Oregon or of the United States.

(2) If an application for setting aside or suspension of an award has been made to the court referred to in subsection (1)(a)(E) of this section, and if it considers it proper, the court where recognition or enforcement is sought may adjourn its decision on application of the party claiming recognition or enforcement of the award. The court may also order the other party to provide appropriate security. [1991 c.405 §39; 2011 c.595 §43]

36.526 Provisions to be interpreted in good faith. In construing ORS 36.454 to 36.524, a court or arbitral tribunal shall interpret those sections in good faith, in accordance with the ordinary meaning to be given to their terms in their context, and in light of their objects and purposes. Recourse may be had for these purposes, in addition to aids in interpretation ordinarily available under the laws of this state, to the documents of the United Nations Commission on International Trade Law and its working group respecting the preparation of the UNCITRAL Model Law on International Commercial Arbitration and shall give those documents the weight that is appropriate in the circumstances. [1991 c.405 §40]

36.528 Policy to encourage conciliation. It is the policy of the State of Oregon to encourage parties to an international commercial agreement or transaction which qualifies for arbitration or conciliation pursuant to ORS 36.454 (3) to resolve disputes arising from such agreements or transactions through conciliation. The parties may select or permit an arbitral tribunal or other third party to select one or more persons to service as the conciliator or conciliators who shall assist the parties in an independent and impartial manner in their attempt to reach an amicable settlement of their dispute. [1991 c.405 §41]

36.530 Guiding principles of conciliators. The conciliator or conciliators shall be guided by principles of objectivity, fairness and justice, giving consideration to, among other things, the rights and obligations of the parties, the usages of the trade concerned and the circumstances surrounding the dispute, including any previous practices between the parties. [1991 c.405 §42]

36.532 Manner of conducting conciliation proceedings. The conciliator or conciliators may conduct the conciliation proceedings in such a manner as they consider appropriate, taking into account the circumstances of the case, the wishes of the parties and the desirability of a speedy settlement of the dispute. Except as otherwise provided in ORS 36.450 to 36.558, no provision of the Oregon Rules of Civil Procedure nor any other provision of the Oregon Revised Statutes governing procedural matters shall apply to any conciliation proceeding brought under ORS 36.450 to 36.558. [1991 c.405 §43]

36.534 Draft conciliation settlement. (1) At any time during the proceedings, the conciliator or conciliators may prepare a draft conciliation settlement which may include the assessment and apportionment of costs between the parties and send copies to the parties, specifying the time within which the parties must signify their approval.

(2) No party may be required to accept any settlement proposed by the conciliator or conciliators. [1991 c.405 §44]

36.536 Prohibition on use of statements, admissions or documents arising out of conciliation proceedings. When the parties agree to participate in conciliation under ORS 36.450 to 36.558:

(1) Evidence of anything said or of any admission made in the course of the conciliation is not admissible in evidence and disclosure of any such evidence shall not be compelled in any civil action in which, pursuant to law, testimony may be compelled to be given. However, this subsection does not limit the admissibility of evidence if all parties participating in conciliation consent, in writing, to its disclosure, provided that such consent is given after the statement or admission is made in the conciliation proceeding.

(2) In the event that any such evidence is offered in contravention of this section, the arbitration tribunal or the court shall make any order which it considers to be appropriate to deal with the matter, including, without limitation, orders restricting the introduction of evidence, or dismissing the case without prejudice.

(3) Unless the document otherwise provides, no document prepared for the purpose of, or in the course of, or pursuant to, the conciliation, or any copy thereof, is admissible in evidence and disclosure of any such document shall not be compelled in any arbitration or civil action in which, pursuant to law, testimony may be compelled to be given. [1991 c.405 §45; 1993 c.244 §14]

36.538 Conciliation to act as stay of other proceedings; tolling of limitation periods during conciliation. (1) The agreement of the parties to submit a dispute to conciliation shall be deemed an agreement between or among those parties to stay all judicial or arbitral proceedings from the commencement of conciliation until the termination of conciliation proceedings.

(2) All applicable limitation periods, including periods of prescription, shall be tolled or extended upon the commencement of conciliation proceedings to conciliate a dispute under ORS 36.450 to 36.558 and all limitation periods shall remain tolled and periods of prescription extended as to all parties to the conciliation proceedings until the 10th day following the termination of conciliation proceedings.

(3) For purposes of this section, conciliation proceedings are deemed to have commenced as soon as:

(a) A party has requested conciliation of a particular dispute or disputes; and

(b) The other party or parties agree to participate in the conciliation proceeding. [1991 c.405 §46]

36.540 Termination of conciliation proceedings. (1) The conciliation proceedings may be terminated as to all parties by any of the following:
(a) A written declaration of the conciliator or conciliators, after consultation with the parties, to the effect that further efforts at conciliation are no longer justified, on the date of the declaration.
(b) A written declaration of the parties addressed to the conciliator or conciliators to the effect that the conciliation proceedings are terminated, on the date of the declaration.
(c) The signing of a settlement agreement by all of the parties, on the date of the agreement.
(2) The conciliation proceedings may be terminated as to particular parties by either of the following:
(a) A written declaration of a party to the other party or parties and the conciliator or conciliators, if appointed, to the effect that the conciliation proceedings shall be terminated as to that particular party, on the date of the declaration.
(b) The signing of a settlement agreement by some of the parties, on the date of the agreement. [1991 c.405 §47; 1993 c.244 §15]

36.542 Conciliator not to be arbitrator or take part in arbitral or judicial proceedings. No person who has served as conciliator may be appointed as an arbitrator for, or take part in, any arbitral or judicial proceedings in the same dispute unless all parties manifest their consent to such participation or the rules adopted for conciliation or arbitration otherwise provide. [1991 c.405 §48]

36.544 Submission to conciliation not waiver. By submitting to conciliation, no party shall be deemed to have waived any rights or remedies which that party would have had if conciliation had not been initiated, other than those set forth in any settlement agreement which results from the conciliation. [1991 c.405 §49]

36.546 Conciliation agreement to be treated as arbitral award. If the conciliation succeeds in settling the dispute and the result of the conciliation is reduced to writing and signed by the conciliator or conciliators and the parties or their representatives, the written agreement shall be treated as an arbitral award rendered by an arbitral tribunal duly constituted in and pursuant to the laws of this state and shall have the same force and effect as a final award in arbitration. [1991 c.405 §50]

36.548 Costs of conciliation proceedings. Upon termination of the conciliation proceedings, the conciliator or conciliators shall fix the costs of the conciliation and give written notice thereof to the parties. As used in this section and in ORS 36.550, "costs" includes only the following:
(1) A reasonable fee to be paid to the conciliator or conciliators.
(2) The travel and other reasonable expenses of the conciliator or conciliators.
(3) The travel and other reasonable expenses of witnesses requested by the conciliator or conciliators with the consent of the parties.
(4) The cost of any expert advice requested by the conciliator or conciliators with the consent of the parties.
(5) The cost of any court. [1991 c.405 §51]

36.550 Payment of costs. The costs fixed by the conciliator or conciliators as pursuant to ORS 36.548 shall be borne equally by the parties unless the settlement agreement provides for a different apportionment. All other expenses incurred by a party shall be borne by that party. [1991 c.405 §52]

36.552 Effect of conciliation on jurisdiction of courts. Neither the request for conciliation, the consent to participate in the conciliation proceeding, the participation in such proceedings, nor the entering into a conciliation agreement or settlement, shall be deemed as consent to the jurisdiction of any court in this state in the event conciliation fails. [1991 c.405 §53]

36.554 Immunities. (1) Neither the arbitrator or arbitrators, the conciliator or conciliators, the parties, nor their representatives, shall be subject to service of process on any civil matter while they are present in this state for the purpose of arranging for or participating in any arbitration or conciliation proceedings subject to ORS 36.450 to 36.558.
(2) No person who serves as an arbitrator or as a conciliator shall be held liable in an action for damages resulting from any act or omission in the performance of their role as an arbitrator or as a conciliator in any proceeding subject to ORS 36.450 to 36.558. [1991 c.405 §54; 1993 c.244 §16]

36.556 Severability. If any provision of ORS 36.450 to 36.558 or its application to any person or circumstance is held to be invalid, the invalidity does not affect the other provisions or applications of ORS 36.450 to 36.558 which can be given effect without the invalid provision or application and to this end the provisions of ORS 36.450 to 36.558 are severable. [1991 c.405 §55]

36.558 Short title. ORS 36.450 to 36.558 shall be known and may be cited as the "Oregon International Commercial Arbitration and Conciliation Act." [1991 c.405 §1]

UNIFORM ARBITRATION ACT

36.600 Definitions. As used in ORS 36.600 to 36.740:
(1) "Arbitration organization" means an association, agency, board, commission or other entity that is neutral and initiates, sponsors or administers an arbitration proceeding or is involved in the appointment of an arbitrator.
(2) "Arbitrator" means an individual appointed to render an award, alone or with others, in a controversy that is subject to an agreement to arbitrate.
(3) "Court" means a circuit court.
(4) "Knowledge" means actual knowledge.
(5) "Person" means an individual, corporation, business trust, partnership, limited liability company, association, joint venture, government, governmental subdivision, agency or instrumentality, public corporation or any other legal or commercial entity.
(6) "Record" means information that is inscribed on a tangible medium or that is stored in an electronic or other medium and is retrievable in perceivable form. [2003 c.598 §1; 2009 c.294 §3]

Note: 36.600 to 36.740 were enacted into law by the Legislative Assembly but were not added to or made a part of ORS chapter 36 or any series therein by legislative action. See Preface to Oregon Revised Statutes for further explanation.

36.605 Notice. (1) Except as otherwise provided in ORS 36.600 to 36.740, a person gives notice to another person by taking action that is reasonably necessary to inform the other person in ordinary course, whether or not the other person acquires knowledge of the notice.
(2) A person has notice if the person has knowledge of the notice or has received notice.
(3) A person receives notice when it comes to the person's attention or the notice is delivered at the person's place of residence or place of business, or at another location held out by the person as a place of delivery of such communications. [2003 c.598 §2]

Note: See note under 36.600.

36.610 Effect of agreement to arbitrate; nonwaivable provisions. (1) Except as otherwise provided in this section, a party to an agreement to arbitrate or to an arbitration proceeding may waive, or the parties may vary the effect of, the requirements of ORS 36.600 to 36.740 to the extent permitted by law.
(2) Before a controversy arises that is subject to an agreement to arbitrate, a party to the agreement may not:

(a) Waive or agree to vary the effect of the requirements of this section or ORS 36.615, 36.620 (1), 36.630, 36.675 (1) or (2), 36.720 or 36.730;

(b) Agree to unreasonably restrict the right under ORS 36.635 to notice of the initiation of an arbitration proceeding;

(c) Agree to unreasonably restrict the right under ORS 36.650 to disclosure of any facts by a neutral arbitrator; or

(d) Waive the right under ORS 36.670 of a party to an agreement to arbitrate to be represented by a lawyer at any proceeding or hearing under ORS 36.600 to 36.740, but an employer and a labor organization may waive the right to representation by a lawyer in a labor arbitration.

(3) A party to an agreement to arbitrate or arbitration proceeding may not waive, or the parties may not vary the effect of, the requirements of this section or ORS 36.625, 36.660, 36.680, 36.690 (4) or (5), 36.700, 36.705, 36.710, 36.715 (1) or (2), 36.735 or 36.740 or section 3 (1) or (3) or 31, chapter 598, Oregon Laws 2003.

(4) Subsections (2) and (3) of this section do not apply to agreements to arbitrate entered into by two or more insurers, as defined by ORS 731.106, or self-insured persons for the purpose of arbitration of disputes arising out of the provision of insurance. [2003 c.598 §4; 2011 c.595 §118]

Note: See note under 36.600.

36.615 Application for judicial relief; fees. (1) Except as otherwise provided in ORS 36.730, an application for judicial relief under ORS 36.600 to 36.740 must be made by petition to the court. The petitioner and the respondent must pay the filing fees established under ORS 21.135.

(2) Unless a civil action involving the agreement to arbitrate is pending, notice of a first petition to the court under ORS 36.600 to 36.740 must be served in the manner provided by ORCP 7 D. Otherwise, notice of the petition must be given in the manner provided by ORCP 9. [2003 c.598 §5; 2003 c.737 §§40a,40c; 2005 c.702 §§45,46,47; 2007 c.860 §6; 2010 c.107 §§40,41; 2011 c.595 §44]

Note: See note under 36.600.

36.620 Validity of agreement to arbitrate; form of acknowledgment of agreement. (1) An agreement contained in a record to submit to arbitration any existing or subsequent controversy arising between the parties to the agreement is valid, enforceable and irrevocable except upon a ground that exists at law or in equity for the revocation of a contract.

(2) Subject to ORS 36.625 (8), the court shall decide whether an agreement to arbitrate exists or a controversy is subject to an agreement to arbitrate.

(3) An arbitrator shall decide whether a condition precedent to arbitrability has been fulfilled.

(4) If a party to a judicial proceeding challenges the existence of, or claims that a controversy is not subject to, an agreement to arbitrate, the arbitration proceeding may continue pending final resolution of the issue by the court, unless the court otherwise orders.

(5) A written arbitration agreement entered into between an employer and employee and otherwise valid under subsection (1) of this section is voidable and may not be enforced by a court unless:

(a) At least 72 hours before the first day of the employee's employment, the employee has received notice in a written employment offer from the employer that an arbitration agreement is required as a condition of employment, and the employee has been provided with the required arbitration agreement that meets the requirements of, and includes the acknowledgment set forth in, subsection (6) of this section; or

(b) The arbitration agreement is entered into upon a subsequent bona fide advancement of the employee by the employer.

(6) The acknowledgment required by subsection (5) of this section must be signed by the employee and must include the following language in boldfaced type:

_____

I acknowledge that I have received and read or have had the opportunity to read this arbitration agreement. I understand that this arbitration agreement requires that disputes that involve the matters subject to the agreement be submitted to mediation or arbitration pursuant to the arbitration agreement rather than to a judge and jury in court.

_____ [2003 c.598 §6; 2007 c.902 §1; 2011 c.489 §1]

Note: Section 4, chapter 902, Oregon Laws 2007, provides:

Sec. 4. The amendments to ORS 36.620 by section 1 of this 2007 Act apply to arbitration agreements entered into on or after the effective date of this 2007 Act [January 1, 2008]. [2007 c.902 §4]

Note: Section 2, chapter 489, Oregon Laws 2011, provides:

Sec. 2. The amendments to ORS 36.620 by section 1 of this 2011 Act apply to arbitration agreements entered into on or after the effective date of this 2011 Act [January 1, 2012]. [2011 c.489 §2]

Note: See note under 36.600.

36.625 Petition to compel or stay arbitration. (1) On petition of a person showing an agreement to arbitrate and alleging another person's refusal to arbitrate pursuant to the agreement:

(a) If the refusing party does not appear or does not oppose the petition, the court shall order the parties to arbitrate; and

(b) If the refusing party opposes the petition, the court shall proceed summarily to decide the issue as provided in subsection (8) of this section and order the parties to arbitrate unless it finds that there is no enforceable agreement to arbitrate.

(2) On petition of a person alleging that an arbitration proceeding has been initiated or threatened but that there is no agreement to arbitrate, the court shall proceed summarily to decide the issue as provided in subsection (8) of this section. If the court finds that there is an enforceable agreement to arbitrate, it shall order the parties to arbitrate.

(3) If the court finds that there is no enforceable agreement to arbitrate, it may not order the parties to arbitrate pursuant to subsection (1) or (2) of this section.

(4) The court may not refuse to order arbitration because the claim subject to arbitration lacks merit or grounds for the claim have not been established.

(5) If a proceeding involving a claim referable to arbitration under an alleged agreement to arbitrate is pending in court, a petition under this section must be made in that court. Otherwise, a petition under this section may be made in any court as provided in ORS 36.725.

(6) If a party makes a petition to the court to order arbitration, the court on just terms shall stay any judicial proceeding that involves a claim alleged to be subject to the arbitration until the court renders a final decision under this section.

(7) If the court orders arbitration, the court on just terms shall stay any judicial proceeding that involves a claim subject to the arbitration. If a claim subject to the arbitration is severable, the court may limit the stay to that claim.

(8) A judge shall decide all issues raised under a petition filed under ORS 36.600 to 36.740 unless there is a constitutional right to jury trial on the issue. If there is a constitutional right to jury trial on an issue, the issue shall be tried to a jury upon the request of any party to the proceeding. [2003 c.598 §7]

Note: See note under 36.600.

36.630 Provisional remedies. (1) Before an arbitrator is appointed and is authorized and able to act, the court, upon petition of a party to an arbitration proceeding and for good cause shown, may enter an order for provisional remedies to protect the effectiveness of the arbitration proceeding to the same extent and under the same conditions as if the controversy were the subject of a civil action.

326

(2) After an arbitrator is appointed and is authorized and able to act:

(a) The arbitrator may issue such orders for provisional remedies, including interim awards, as the arbitrator finds necessary to protect the effectiveness of the arbitration proceeding and to promote the fair and expeditious resolution of the controversy, to the same extent and under the same conditions as if the controversy were the subject of a civil action; and

(b) A party to an arbitration proceeding may move the court for a provisional remedy only if the matter is urgent and the arbitrator is not able to act timely or the arbitrator cannot provide an adequate remedy.

(3) A party does not waive a right of arbitration by making a petition under subsection (1) or (2) of this section. [2003 c.598 §8]

Note: See note under 36.600.

36.635 Initiation of arbitration. (1) A person initiates an arbitration proceeding by giving notice in a record to the other parties to the agreement to arbitrate in the agreed manner between the parties or, in the absence of agreement, by certified mail, return receipt requested and obtained, or by service as authorized for summons under ORCP 7 D. The notice must describe the nature of the controversy and the remedy sought.

(2) Unless a person objects for lack or insufficiency of notice under ORS 36.665 (3) not later than the beginning of the arbitration hearing, the person by appearing at the hearing waives any objection to lack or insufficiency of notice. [2003 c.598 §9]

Note: See note under 36.600.

36.640 Consolidation of separate arbitration proceedings. (1) Except as otherwise provided in subsection (3) of this section, upon petition of a party to an agreement to arbitrate or to an arbitration proceeding, the court may order consolidation of separate arbitration proceedings as to all or some of the claims if:

(a) There are separate agreements to arbitrate or separate arbitration proceedings between the same persons or one of them is a party to a separate agreement to arbitrate or a separate arbitration proceeding with a third person;

(b) The claims subject to the agreements to arbitrate arise in substantial part from the same transaction or series of related transactions;

(c) The existence of a common issue of law or fact creates the possibility of conflicting decisions in the separate arbitration proceedings; and

(d) Prejudice resulting from a failure to consolidate is not outweighed by the risk of undue delay or prejudice to the rights of or hardship to parties opposing consolidation.

(2) The court may order consolidation of separate arbitration proceedings as to some claims and allow other claims to be resolved in separate arbitration proceedings.

(3) The court may not order consolidation of the claims of a party to an agreement to arbitrate if the agreement prohibits consolidation. [2003 c.598 §10]

Note: See note under 36.600.

36.645 Appointment of arbitrator; service as neutral arbitrator. (1) If the parties to an agreement to arbitrate agree on a method for appointing an arbitrator, that method must be followed, unless the method fails. If the parties have not agreed on a method, the agreed method fails, or an arbitrator designated or appointed fails or is unable to act and a successor has not been appointed, the court, on petition of a party to the arbitration proceeding, shall appoint the arbitrator. An arbitrator so appointed has all the powers of an arbitrator designated in the agreement to arbitrate or appointed pursuant to the agreed method.

(2) An individual who has a known, direct and material interest in the outcome of the arbitration proceeding or a known, existing and substantial relationship with a party may not serve as an arbitrator required by an agreement to be neutral. [2003 c.598 §11]

Note: See note under 36.600.

36.650 Disclosure by arbitrator. (1) Before accepting appointment, an individual who is requested to serve as an arbitrator, after making a reasonable inquiry, shall disclose to all parties to the agreement to arbitrate and arbitration proceeding and to any other arbitrators in the arbitration proceeding any known facts that a reasonable person would consider likely to affect the impartiality of the arbitrator in the arbitration proceeding, including:

(a) A financial or personal interest in the outcome of the arbitration proceeding; and

(b) An existing or past relationship with any of the parties to the agreement to arbitrate or the arbitration proceeding, their counsel or representatives, a witness or another arbitrator in the proceeding.

(2) An arbitrator has a continuing obligation to disclose to all parties to the agreement to arbitrate and arbitration proceeding and to any other arbitrators in the proceeding any facts that the arbitrator learns after accepting appointment that a reasonable person would consider likely to affect the impartiality of the arbitrator.

(3) If an arbitrator discloses a fact required by subsection (1) or (2) of this section to be disclosed and a party timely objects to the appointment or continued service of the arbitrator based upon the fact disclosed, the objection may be a ground under ORS 36.705 (1)(b) for vacating an award made by the arbitrator.

(4) If the arbitrator did not disclose a fact as required by subsection (1) or (2) of this section, upon timely objection by a party, the court under ORS 36.705 (1)(b) may vacate an award.

(5) An arbitrator appointed as a neutral arbitrator who does not disclose a known, direct and material interest in the outcome of the arbitration proceeding or a known, existing and substantial relationship with a party, the party's counsel or representatives, a witness or another arbitrator in the proceeding is presumed to act with evident partiality under ORS 36.705 (1)(b).

(6) If the parties to an arbitration proceeding agree to the procedures of an arbitration organization or any other procedures for challenges to arbitrators before an award is made, substantial compliance with those procedures is a condition precedent to a petition to vacate an award on that ground under ORS 36.705 (1)(b). [2003 c.598 §12]

Note: See note under 36.600.

36.655 Action by majority. If there is more than one arbitrator, the powers of an arbitrator must be exercised by a majority of the arbitrators, but all of them shall conduct the hearing under ORS 36.665 (3). [2003 c.598 §13]

Note: See note under 36.600.

36.660 Immunity of arbitrator; competency to testify; attorney fees and costs. (1) An arbitrator or an arbitration organization acting in that capacity is immune from civil liability to the same extent as a judge of a court of this state acting in a judicial capacity.

(2) The immunity afforded by this section supplements any immunity under other law.

(3) The failure of an arbitrator to make a disclosure required by ORS 36.650 does not cause any loss of immunity under this section.

(4) In a judicial, administrative or similar proceeding, an arbitrator or representative of an arbitration organization is not competent to testify, and may not be required to produce records as to any statement, conduct, decision or ruling occurring during the arbitration proceeding, to the same extent as a judge of a court of this state acting in a judicial capacity. This subsection does not apply:

(a) To the extent necessary to determine the claim of an arbitrator, arbitration organization or representative of the arbitration organization against a party to the arbitration proceeding; or

(b) To a hearing on a petition to vacate an award under ORS 36.705 (1)(a) or (b) if the petitioner establishes prima facie that a ground for vacating the award exists.

(5) If a person commences a civil action against an arbitrator, arbitration organization or representative of an arbitration organization arising from the services of the arbitrator, organization or representative, or if a person seeks to compel an arbitrator or a representative of an arbitration organization to testify or produce records in violation of subsection (4) of this section, and the court decides that the arbitrator, arbitration organization or representative of an arbitration organization is immune from civil liability or that the arbitrator or representative of the organization is not competent to testify, the court shall award to the arbitrator, organization or representative reasonable attorney fees. [2003 c.598 §14]

Note: See note under 36.600.

36.665 Arbitration process. (1) An arbitrator may conduct an arbitration in such manner as the arbitrator considers appropriate for a fair and expeditious disposition of the proceeding. The authority conferred upon the arbitrator includes the power to hold conferences with the parties to the arbitration proceeding before the hearing and, among other matters, determine the admissibility, relevance, materiality and weight of any evidence.

(2) An arbitrator may decide a request for summary disposition of a claim or particular issue:

(a) If all interested parties agree; or

(b) Upon request of one party to the arbitration proceeding, if that party gives notice to all other parties to the proceeding and the other parties have a reasonable opportunity to respond.

(3) If an arbitrator orders a hearing, the arbitrator shall set a time and place and give notice of the hearing not less than five days before the hearing begins. Unless a party to the arbitration proceeding makes an objection to lack or insufficiency of notice not later than the beginning of the hearing, the party's appearance at the hearing waives any objection based on lack or insufficiency of notice. Upon request of a party to the arbitration proceeding and for good cause shown, or upon the arbitrator's own initiative, the arbitrator may adjourn the hearing from time to time as necessary but may not postpone the hearing to a time later than that fixed by the agreement to arbitrate for making the award unless the parties to the arbitration proceeding consent to a later date. The arbitrator may hear and decide the controversy upon the evidence produced although a party who was duly notified of the arbitration proceeding did not appear. The court, on request, may direct the arbitrator to conduct the hearing promptly and render a timely decision.

(4) At a hearing under subsection (3) of this section, a party to the arbitration proceeding has a right to be heard, to present evidence material to the controversy and to cross-examine witnesses appearing at the hearing.

(5) If an arbitrator ceases or is unable to act during the arbitration proceeding, a replacement arbitrator must be appointed in accordance with ORS 36.645 to continue the proceeding and to resolve the controversy. [2003 c.598 §15]

Note: See note under 36.600.

36.670 Representation by a lawyer; representation of legal or commercial entities. A party to an arbitration proceeding may be represented by a lawyer admitted to practice in this state or any other state. A corporation, business trust, partnership, limited liability company, association, joint venture or other legal or commercial entity may be represented by a lawyer admitted to practice in this state or any other state, by an officer of the entity, or by an employee or other agent authorized by the entity to represent the entity in the proceeding. [2003 c.598 §16]

Note: See note under 36.600.

36.675 Witnesses; subpoenas; depositions; discovery. (1) An arbitrator may administer oaths. An arbitrator or an attorney for any party to the arbitration proceeding may issue a subpoena for the attendance of a witness and for the production of records and other evidence at any hearing. A subpoena must be served in the manner for service of subpoenas under ORCP 55 D and, upon petition to the court by a party to the arbitration proceeding or the arbitrator, enforced in the manner provided by ORCP 55 G.

(2) In order to make the proceedings fair, expeditious and cost-effective, upon request of a party to or a witness in an arbitration proceeding, an arbitrator may permit a deposition of any witness to be taken for use as evidence at the hearing, including a witness who cannot be subpoenaed for or is unable to attend a hearing. The arbitrator shall determine the conditions under which the deposition is taken.

(3) An arbitrator may permit such discovery as the arbitrator decides is appropriate in the circumstances, taking into account the needs of the parties to the arbitration proceeding and other affected persons and the desirability of making the proceeding fair, expeditious and cost-effective.

(4) If an arbitrator permits discovery under subsection (3) of this section, the arbitrator may order a party to the arbitration proceeding to comply with the arbitrator's discovery-related orders, issue subpoenas for the attendance of a witness and for the production of records and other evidence at a discovery proceeding, and take action against a noncomplying party to the extent a court could if the controversy were the subject of a civil action in this state.

(5) An arbitrator may issue a protective order to prevent the disclosure of privileged information, confidential information, trade secrets and other information protected from disclosure to the extent a court could if the controversy were the subject of a civil action in this state.

(6) All laws compelling a person under subpoena to testify and all fees for attending a judicial proceeding, a deposition or a discovery proceeding as a witness apply to an arbitration proceeding as if the controversy were the subject of a civil action in this state.

(7) The court may enforce a subpoena or discovery-related order for the attendance of a witness within this state, and for the production of records and other evidence issued by an arbitrator or by an attorney for any party to the proceeding in connection with an arbitration proceeding in another state, upon conditions determined by the court so as to make the arbitration proceeding fair, expeditious and cost-effective. A subpoena or discovery-related order issued by an arbitrator or by an attorney for any party to the proceeding in another state must be served in the manner provided by ORCP 55 D for service of subpoenas in a civil action in this state and, upon petition to the court by a party to the arbitration proceeding or the arbitrator, enforced in the manner provided by ORCP 55 G for enforcement of subpoenas in a civil action in this state. [2003 c.598 §17]

Note: See note under 36.600.

36.680 Judicial enforcement of preaward ruling by arbitrator. If an arbitrator makes a preaward ruling in favor of a party to the arbitration proceeding, the party may request the arbitrator to incorporate the ruling into an award under ORS 36.685. A prevailing party may make a petition to the court for an expedited order to confirm the award under ORS 36.700, in which case the court shall summarily decide the petition. The court shall issue an order to confirm the award unless the court vacates, modifies, or corrects the award under ORS 36.705 or 36.710. [2003 c.598 §18]

Note: See note under 36.600.

36.685 Award. (1) An arbitrator shall make a record of an award. The record must be signed or otherwise authenticated by any arbitrator who concurs with the award. If the award requires the payment of money, including but not limited to payment of costs or attorney fees, the award must be accompanied by a separate statement that contains the information required by ORS 18.042 for judgments that include money awards. The arbitrator or the arbitration organization shall give notice of the award, including a copy of the award, to each party to the arbitration proceeding.

(2) An award must be made within the time specified by the agreement to arbitrate or, if not specified therein, within the time ordered by the court. The court may extend or the parties to the arbitration proceeding may agree in a record to extend the time. The court or the parties may extend the time within or after the time specified or ordered. A party waives any objection that an award was not timely made unless the party gives notice of the objection to the arbitrator before receiving notice of the award. [2003 c.598 §19; 2003 c.576 §169a]

Note: See note under 36.600.

328

36.690 Change of award by arbitrator. (1) Upon request by a party to an arbitration proceeding, an arbitrator may modify or correct an award:

(a) Upon a ground stated in ORS 36.710 (1)(a) or (c);

(b) Because the arbitrator has not made a final and definite award upon a claim submitted by the parties to the arbitration proceeding; or

(c) To clarify the award.

(2) A request under subsection (1) of this section must be made and notice given to all parties within 20 days after the requesting party receives notice of the award.

(3) A party to the arbitration proceeding must give notice of any objection to the request within 10 days after receipt of the notice under subsection (2) of this section.

(4) If a petition to the court is pending under ORS 36.700, 36.705 or 36.710, the court may submit the claim to the arbitrator to consider whether to modify or correct the award:

(a) Upon a ground stated in ORS 36.710 (1)(a) or (c);

(b) Because the arbitrator has not made a final and definite award upon a claim submitted by the parties to the arbitration proceeding; or

(c) To clarify the award.

(5) An award modified or corrected pursuant to this section is subject to ORS 36.685 (1), 36.700, 36.705 and 36.710. [2003 c.598 §20]

Note: See note under 36.600.

36.695 Remedies; fees and expenses of arbitration proceeding. (1) An arbitrator may award punitive damages or other exemplary relief if such an award is authorized by law in a civil action involving the same claim and the evidence produced at the hearing justifies the award under the legal standards otherwise applicable to the claim.

(2) An arbitrator may award reasonable attorney fees and other reasonable expenses of arbitration as may be specified in the arbitration agreement if such an award is authorized by law in a civil action involving the same claim or by the agreement of the parties to the arbitration proceeding.

(3) As to all remedies other than those authorized by subsections (1) and (2) of this section, an arbitrator may order such remedies as the arbitrator considers just and appropriate under the circumstances of the arbitration proceeding. The fact that such a remedy could not or would not be granted by the court is not a ground for refusing to confirm an award under ORS 36.700 or for vacating an award under ORS 36.705.

(4) An arbitrator's expenses and fees, together with other expenses, must be paid as provided in the award.

(5) If an arbitrator awards punitive damages or other exemplary relief under subsection (1) of this section, the arbitrator shall specify in the award the basis in fact justifying and the basis in law authorizing the award and state separately the amount of the punitive damages or other exemplary relief. [2003 c.598 §21]

Note: See note under 36.600.

36.700 Confirmation of award. (1) After a party to an arbitration proceeding receives notice of an award, the party may make a petition to the court for an order confirming the award. The party filing the petition must serve a copy of the petition on all other parties to the proceedings. The court shall issue a confirming order unless within 20 days after the petition is served on the other parties:

(a) A party requests that the arbitrator modify or correct the award under ORS 36.690; or

(b) A party petitions the court to vacate, modify or correct the award under ORS 36.705 or 36.710.

(2) If a party requests that the arbitrator modify or correct the award under ORS 36.690, or petitions the court to vacate, modify or correct the award under ORS 36.705 or 36.710, the court may stay entry of an order on a petition filed under this section until a final decision is made on the request or petition. [2003 c.598 §22]

Note: See note under 36.600.

36.705 Vacating award. (1) Upon petition to the court by a party to an arbitration proceeding, the court shall vacate an award made in the arbitration proceeding if:

(a) The award was procured by corruption, fraud or other undue means;

(b) There was:

(A) Evident partiality by an arbitrator appointed as a neutral arbitrator;

(B) Corruption by an arbitrator; or

(C) Misconduct by an arbitrator prejudicing the rights of a party to the arbitration proceeding;

(c) An arbitrator refused to postpone the hearing upon showing of sufficient cause for postponement, refused to consider evidence material to the controversy or otherwise conducted the hearing contrary to ORS 36.665 so as to prejudice substantially the rights of a party to the arbitration proceeding;

(d) An arbitrator exceeded the arbitrator's powers;

(e) There was no agreement to arbitrate, unless the person participated in the arbitration proceeding without raising an objection under ORS 36.665 (3) not later than the beginning of the arbitration hearing; or

(f) The arbitration was conducted without proper notice of the initiation of an arbitration as required in ORS 36.635 so as to prejudice substantially the rights of a party to the arbitration proceeding.

(2) A petition under this section must be filed within 20 days after the petitioner is served with a petition for confirmation of an award under ORS 36.700, unless the petitioner alleges that the award was procured by corruption, fraud or other undue means. If the petitioner alleges that the award was procured by corruption, fraud or other undue means, a petition under this section must be filed within 90 days after the grounds for challenging the award are known or, by the exercise of reasonable care, would have been known by the petitioner. A party filing a petition under this section must serve a copy of the petition on all other parties to the proceedings.

(3) If the court vacates an award on a ground other than that set forth in subsection (1)(e) of this section, it may order a rehearing. If the award is vacated on a ground stated in subsection (1)(a) or (b) of this section, the rehearing must be before a new arbitrator. If the award is vacated on a ground stated in subsection (1)(c), (d) or (f) of this section, the rehearing may be before the arbitrator who made the award or before any successor appointed for that arbitrator. The arbitrator must render the decision in the rehearing within the same time as that provided for an award in ORS 36.685 (2).

(4) If the court denies a petition to vacate an award, it shall confirm the award unless a petition to modify or correct the award is pending. [2003 c.598 §23]

Note: See note under 36.600.

36.710 Modification or correction of award. (1) Upon petition filed within 20 days after the petitioner is served with a petition for confirmation of an award under ORS 36.700, the court shall modify or correct the award if:

(a) There was an evident mathematical miscalculation or an evident mistake in the description of a person, thing or property referred to in the award;

(b) The arbitrator has made an award on a claim not submitted to the arbitrator and the award may be corrected without affecting the merits of the decision upon the claims submitted; or

(c) The award is imperfect in a matter of form not affecting the merits of the decision on the claims submitted.

(2) If a petition made under subsection (1) of this section is granted, the court shall modify or correct and confirm the award as modified or corrected. Otherwise, unless a petition to vacate is pending, the court shall confirm the award.

(3) A petition to modify or correct an award pursuant to this section may be joined with a petition to vacate the award.

(4) A party filing a petition under this section must serve a copy of the petition on all other parties to the proceedings. [2003 c.598 §24]

Note: See note under 36.600.

36.715 Judgment on award; attorney fees and litigation expenses. (1) Upon granting an order confirming, vacating without directing a rehearing, modifying or correcting an award, the court shall enter a judgment in conformity with the order. The judgment may be entered in the register and enforced as any other judgment in a civil action.

(2) A court may allow reasonable costs of the petition and subsequent judicial proceedings.

(3) On application of a prevailing party to a contested judicial proceeding under ORS 36.700, 36.705 or 36.710, the court may add reasonable attorney fees incurred in a judicial proceeding after the award is made to a judgment confirming, vacating without directing a rehearing, modifying or correcting an award. [2003 c.598 §25]

Note: See note under 36.600.

36.720 Jurisdiction. (1) A court having jurisdiction over the controversy and the parties may enforce an agreement to arbitrate.

(2) An agreement to arbitrate providing for arbitration in this state confers exclusive jurisdiction on the court to enter judgment on an award under ORS 36.600 to 36.740. [2003 c.598 §26]

Note: See note under 36.600.

36.725 Venue. A petition pursuant to ORS 36.615 must be made in the court for the county in which the agreement to arbitrate specifies the arbitration hearing is to be held or, if the hearing has been held, in the court for the county in which it was held. Otherwise, the petition may be made in the court for any county in which an adverse party resides or has a place of business or, if no adverse party has a residence or place of business in this state, in the court of any county in this state. All subsequent petitions must be made in the court hearing the initial petition unless the court otherwise directs. [2003 c.598 §27]

Note: See note under 36.600.

36.730 Appeals. (1) An appeal may be taken from:

(a) An order denying a petition to compel arbitration.

(b) An order granting a petition to stay arbitration.

(c) A judgment entered pursuant to ORS 36.600 to 36.740, including but not limited to a judgment:

(A) Confirming or denying confirmation of an award.

(B) Modifying or correcting an award.

(C) Vacating an award without directing a rehearing.

(2) An appeal under this section must be taken as provided in ORS chapter 19. [2003 c.598 §28]

Note: See note under 36.600.

36.735 Uniformity of application and construction. In applying and construing ORS 36.600 to 36.740, consideration must be given to the need to promote uniformity of the law with respect to its subject matter among states that enact it. [2003 c.598 §29]

Note: See note under 36.600.

36.740 Relationship to electronic signatures in Global and National Commerce Act. The provisions of ORS 36.600 to 36.740 governing the legal effect, validity and enforceability of electronic records or electronic signatures, and of contracts performed with the use of such records or signatures, conform to the requirements of Section 102 of the Electronic Signatures in Global and National Commerce Act, 15 U.S.C. 7001 and 7002, as in effect on January 1, 2004. [2003 c.598 §30]

Note: See note under 36.600.

———————————

Chapter 37 — Receivership

2017 EDITION

RECEIVERSHIP

SPECIAL ACTIONS AND PROCEEDINGS

37.010   Short title

37.020   Receivership described

37.030   Definitions

37.040   Applicability

37.050   Property not subject to receivership; exception

37.060   Appointment of receiver

37.070   Eligibility to serve as receiver

37.080   Required disclosures relating to conflicts of interest

37.090   Receiver's bond, alternative security or insurance

37.100   Exclusive jurisdiction of appointing court

37.110   Powers of receiver

37.120   Duties of receiver

37.130   Turnover of property

37.140   Collection by receiver of debts owed to owner

37.150   Duties of owner

37.160   Mailing and special notice lists to be maintained by receiver

37.170   Notices

37.180   When court order required

37.190   Creditor list and inventory

37.200   Receiver's periodic reports

37.210   Claims bar date

37.220   Automatic stay of certain proceedings

37.230   Utility service

37.240   Executory contracts

37.250   Use or transfer of estate property outside ordinary course of business; transfer of co-owned property; limitation on disposition of residential property

37.260   Receivership financing

37.270   Recovery of costs related to secured property

37.280   Abandonment of property

37.290   Actions by or against receiver or affecting estate property

37.300   Personal liability of receiver

37.310   Employment and compensation of professionals

37.320   Participation of creditors and other interested persons in receivership; effect of receivership on nonparties

37.330   Initial notice to creditors and other interested persons

37.340   Claims process

37.350   Submission of claims by creditors

37.360   Objection to and allowance of claims

37.370   Priorities

37.380   Secured claims against after-acquired property

37.390   Ancillary receiverships

37.400   Removal of receiver

37.410   Termination of receivership

37.010 Short title. ORS 37.020 to 37.410 may be cited as the Oregon Receivership Code. [2017 c.358 §1]

37.020 Receivership described. Receivership is the process by which a court appoints a person to take charge of property during the pendency of an action or upon a judgment or order entered therein and to manage or dispose of the property as the court may direct. [2017 c.358 §2]

37.030 Definitions. As used in the Oregon Receivership Code:
(1) "Affiliate" means:
(a) With respect to an individual:
(A) A companion of the individual;
(B) A lineal ancestor or descendant, whether by blood or adoption, of the individual or a companion of the individual;
(C) A companion of an ancestor or descendant described in subparagraph (B) of this paragraph;
(D) A sibling, aunt, uncle, great-aunt, great-uncle, first cousin, niece, nephew, grandniece or grandnephew of the individual, whether related by the whole or the half blood or adoption, or a companion of any of them; or
(E) Any other individual occupying the residence of the individual; and
(b) With respect to any person:
(A) Another person that directly or indirectly controls, is controlled by or is under common control with the person;
(B) An officer, director, manager, member, partner, employee or trustee or other fiduciary of the person; or

(C) A companion of, or an individual occupying the residence of, an individual described in subparagraph (A) or (B) of this paragraph.

(2) "Companion" means spouse or domestic partner.

(3) "Domestic relations suit" has the meaning given that term in ORS 107.510.

(4) "Entity" means a person other than a natural person.

(5) "Estate" means the entirety of the property over which a receiver is appointed.

(6) "Executory contract" means:

(a) A contract, including an unexpired lease, under which the obligations of both parties are so far unperformed that the failure of either to complete performance would constitute a material breach excusing the performance of the other; or

(b) A contract, including an unexpired lease, under which a party has an unexercised option to require its counterparty to perform.

(7) "Foreign action" means an action in a federal or state court outside of this state.

(8) "Insolvency" means a financial condition of a person such that:

(a) The sum of the person's debts and other obligations is greater than a fair valuation of all of the person's property, excluding:

(A) Property transferred, concealed or removed with intent to hinder, delay or defraud any creditors of the person; and

(B) Any property exempt from execution under any law of this state; or

(b) The person is generally not paying debts as they become due.

(9) "Interested person" means any person having a claim against the owner or a claim or interest in any estate property.

(10) "Lien" means a charge against or interest in property to secure payment of a debt or the performance of an obligation.

(11) "Owner" means the person over whose property a receiver is appointed.

(12) "Party" means:

(a) When used in relation to an action, a person named in the caption of the action; or

(b) When used in relation to a contract, a signatory to the contract.

(13) "Person" means an individual, corporation, limited liability company, general partnership, limited partnership, limited liability partnership, cooperative, business trust, governmental entity or other entity, of any kind or nature.

(14) "Property" includes all right, title and interests, both legal and equitable, in or with respect to any property with respect to which a receiver is appointed, including any proceeds, products, offspring, rents or profits, regardless of the manner by which the property has been or is acquired.

(15) "Receiver" means a person appointed by the court as the court's agent, and subject to the court's direction, to take possession of, manage or dispose of property.

(16) "Receivership" means an action in which a receiver is appointed.

(17) "Residential property" means real property:

(a) Upon which are situated four or fewer residential units, one of which is occupied as a principal residence by the owner, the owner's spouse or a dependent of the owner; and

(b) Where residential use is the primary activity occurring on the real property.

(18) "Security interest" means a lien created by agreement.

(19) "Special notice list" means a special notice list maintained by a receiver as required under ORS 37.160.

(20) "State agency" has the meaning given that term in ORS 36.110.

(21) "Utility" means a person providing any service regulated by the Public Utility Commission. [2017 c.358 §3]

37.040 Applicability. (1) Except as otherwise provided by law, the Oregon Receivership Code applies to all receiverships initiated in a court of this state, except for:

(a) Actions in which a state agency or officer is expressly authorized by statute to seek or obtain the appointment of a receiver; and

(b) Actions authorized by or commenced under federal law.

(2) In cases in which a state agency or officer is expressly authorized by statute to seek or obtain the appointment of a receiver, the state agency or officer may elect, when seeking appointment, for the receivership to be governed by the provisions of the Oregon Receivership Code.

(3) Except as otherwise provided by law, the provisions of the Oregon Receivership Code control over conflicting provisions of state law, including ORCP 80, with respect to receiverships governed by the Oregon Receivership Code. [2017 c.358 §4]

Note: Section 42, chapter 358, Oregon Laws 2017, provides:

Sec. 42. Sections 2 to 41 of this 2017 Act [37.020 to 37.410] apply to receiverships in which the receiver is appointed on or after the effective date of this 2017 Act [January 1, 2018]. [2017 c.358 §42]

37.050 Property not subject to receivership; exception. (1) A court may not appoint a receiver with respect to the following:

(a) Personal property of an individual that is used primarily for personal, family or household purposes.

(b) Property of an individual exempt from execution under the laws of this state.

(c) Any power or interest that a person may exercise solely for the benefit of another person.

(d) Property held in trust for another person.

(2) Notwithstanding subsection (1) of this section, a court may appoint a receiver with respect to property described in subsection (1)(a) of this section in a domestic relations suit.

(3) A court may appoint a receiver with respect to any nonexempt interest in property that is partially exempt from execution, including fee title to real property subject to a homestead exemption. [2017 c.358 §5]

37.060 Appointment of receiver. (1) A court may appoint a receiver in the following cases, upon motion by any person or upon its own motion:

(a) Before judgment, if the property that is the subject of the action, or rents or profits deriving from the property, are in danger of being lost or materially injured or impaired.

(b) After judgment, if reasonably necessary to carry the judgment into effect.

(c) After judgment, to dispose of property according to the judgment, to preserve the property during the pendency of an appeal or when an execution has been returned unsatisfied and the debtor refuses to apply the property in satisfaction of the judgment.

(d) In an action under ORS 95.200 to 95.310.

(e) When property is attached by a creditor, if:

(A) The property is of a perishable nature or is otherwise in danger of waste, impairment or destruction; or

(B) The debtor has abandoned the property and receivership is reasonably necessary to conserve, protect or dispose of the property.

(f) After judgment, either before or after the issuance of an execution, to preserve, protect or prevent the transfer of property subject to execution and sale thereunder.

(g) When an entity has been dissolved or is insolvent or in imminent danger of insolvency, if receivership is reasonably necessary to protect the property of the entity or to conserve or protect the interests of the entity's stockholders, members, partners or creditors.

(h) In any situation in which the appointment of a receiver is expressly required or permitted by statute.

(i) In any situation in which, in the discretion of the court, appointment of a receiver is reasonably necessary to secure justice to the parties.

(2) In determining whether to appoint a receiver, a court may consider the existence of a contract provision providing for the appointment of a receiver, but the court is not bound by such a provision.

(3) If a court in a foreign action has appointed a person as receiver with respect to property in this state, whether with respect to the property specifically or the owner's property generally, a court in this state shall:

(a) Upon motion by the receiver or by any party to the foreign action, appoint the person as receiver of the property in this state, if the person is eligible under ORS 37.070 and fulfills such other requirements as are required by statute or imposed by the court.

(b) Following the appointment, give effect to orders, judgments and decrees of the foreign court affecting the property in this state held by the receiver, unless the court determines that to do so would be manifestly unjust or inequitable.

(4) The venue of an action described in subsection (3) of this section may be any county in which the receiver appointed in the foreign action resides or maintains an office, or any county in which any property over which the receiver is to be appointed is located at the time the action is commenced.

(5)(a) An order appointing a receiver must reasonably describe the property over which the receiver is to take charge, by category, individual items or any combination thereof, if the receiver is appointed over less than all of a person's property.

(b) An order appointing a receiver may appoint the receiver over all of a person's property, wherever located.

(c) An order that appoints a receiver over a person and does not describe the property over which the receiver is to take charge is construed to appoint the receiver over all of the person's property, except for property not subject to receivership under ORS 37.050.

(6) A court may condition the appointment of a receiver upon the giving of security by the person seeking the receiver's appointment, in such amount as the court may specify, for the payment of costs incurred or damages suffered by any person if a receivership is determined to be wrongfully obtained. [2017 c.358 §6]

37.070 Eligibility to serve as receiver. (1) Any person, whether or not a resident of this state, may serve as a receiver, except for:

(a) An entity that is not authorized to conduct business in this state;

(b) A person who has been convicted of a crime involving moral turpitude, or is controlled by a person who has been convicted of a crime involving moral turpitude; and

(c) The sheriff of any county, except as expressly permitted by statute.

(2) If a court appoints an entity as a receiver, the court may require a specific individual to appear in the receivership on behalf of the entity. [2017 c.358 §7]

37.080 Required disclosures relating to conflicts of interest. A court may not appoint a person as a receiver unless the person first:

(1) Discloses whether the person:

(a) Is an affiliate of a party to the receivership;

(b) Has an interest materially adverse to an interest of a party to the receivership;

(c) Has a material financial interest in the outcome of the action, other than compensation approved by the court;

(d) Has a debtor-creditor relationship with the owner; or

(e) Holds an equity interest in a party to the receivership, other than a noncontrolling interest in a publicly traded company; and

(2) Affirms under oath that the person's disclosure under subsection (1) of this section is true and complete. [2017 c.358 §8]

37.090 Receiver's bond, alternative security or insurance. (1) Except as otherwise provided by law, a court may, at any time before or during the service of a receiver, require a receiver or person nominated as a receiver to post a bond that:

(a) Is conditioned on the faithful discharge of the receiver's duties;

(b) Is in an amount that is determined by the court to be adequate to secure payment of any costs, damages and attorney fees that may be sustained or suffered by any person due to a wrongful act of the receiver; and

(c) Has one or more sureties that meet the qualifications set forth in ORCP 82 D or that are approved by the court.

(2) Except as otherwise provided by law, the court may require the posting of alternative security in lieu of a bond, such as a letter of credit or a deposit of funds with the clerk of the court, to be held to secure the receiver's faithful performance of the receiver's duties until the court authorizes the release or return of the alternative security. The court shall remit any interest that may accrue on a deposit under this subsection to the receiver upon the receiver's discharge.

(3) Except as otherwise provided by law, the court may require the receiver or person nominated as receiver to carry an insurance policy with coverage and limits determined by the court in lieu of a bond.

(4) A receiver may charge the cost of a bond, alternative security or insurance policy required by the court under this section against the estate.

(5) The court may authorize a receiver to act before the receiver posts a required bond or alternative security or acquires a required insurance policy. [2017 c.358 §9]

37.100 Exclusive jurisdiction of appointing court. (1) The court appointing a receiver has:

(a) Exclusive authority over the receiver;

(b) Exclusive jurisdiction over and right to control all real property and all tangible and intangible personal property constituting the estate, wherever located, to the full extent of the court's jurisdiction; and

(c) Exclusive jurisdiction to determine all controversies relating to the collection, preservation, application and distribution of the estate and all claims against the receiver arising out of the exercise of the receiver's powers or the performance of the receiver's duties.

(2) Notwithstanding subsection (1) of this section, if any part of the estate is subject to the jurisdiction of another court under ORS 107.105, the court appointing the receiver may not exercise authority over such part of the estate unless expressly permitted by order of the other court. [2017 c.358 §10]

37.110 Powers of receiver. (1) The court appointing a receiver may confer upon the receiver the power to perform any of the following actions, in any combination:

(a) Collect, control, manage, conserve and protect estate property;

(b) Operate a business constituting estate property, including preservation, use, sale, lease, license, exchange, collection or disposition of property in the ordinary course of business;

(c) In the ordinary course of business, incur unsecured debt and pay expenses incidental to the receiver's preservation, use, sale, lease, license, exchange, collection or disposition of estate property;

(d) Assert a right, claim, cause of action or defense of the owner that relates to estate property;

(e) Assert in the name of the receiver any claim under ORS 95.200 to 95.310 assertible by any creditor of the owner;

(f) Seek and obtain instruction from the court concerning estate property, exercise of the receiver's powers and performance of the receiver's duties;

(g) On subpoena, compel a person to submit to examination under oath in the manner of a deposition in a civil case, or to produce and permit inspection and copying of designated records or tangible things, with respect to estate property or any other matter that may affect administration of the receivership;

(h) Engage and pay compensation to one or more professionals under ORS 37.310;

(i) Apply to a court of another state for appointment as ancillary receiver with respect to estate property in that state under ORS 37.390;

(j) Incur debt for the use or benefit of estate property other than in the ordinary course of business under ORS 37.260;

(k) Make improvements to estate property;

(L) Use or transfer estate property other than in the ordinary course of business under ORS 37.250;

(m) Assume an executory contract of the owner under ORS 37.240;

(n) Pay compensation to the receiver;

(o) Determine whether or not to establish a claims procedure under ORS 37.340;

(p) Allow or disallow a claim of a creditor under ORS 37.360;

(q) Make a distribution of estate property under ORS 37.370;

(r) Take any other action authorized under the Oregon Receivership Code; and

(s) Take any other actions that the court deems reasonably necessary to avoid injustice.

(2) The court may limit, expand or modify the powers conferred by the court on the receiver at any time.

(3) A receiver has powers conferred by the court under this section in addition to the powers conferred on the receiver by statute. [2017 c.358 §11]

37.120 Duties of receiver. (1) A receiver shall notify all federal and state taxing and applicable regulatory agencies of the receiver's appointment in accordance with any applicable laws imposing this duty, including 26 U.S.C. 6036.

(2) A receiver shall comply with applicable law.

(3) If appointed with respect to any real property, a receiver shall file with the recorder of the county in which the real property is located a certified copy of the order of appointment, together with a legal description of the real property if one is not included in the order.

(4) The court appointing a receiver may impose additional duties on the receiver at any time. The court may limit, expand or modify duties imposed by the court on a receiver at any time. [2017 c.358 §12]

37.130 Turnover of property. (1) Upon demand by a receiver, a person shall turn over to the receiver any estate property within the possession, custody or control of the person.

(2) If a bona fide dispute exists over whether property is estate property, the court in which the receivership is pending shall resolve the dispute.

(3) A receiver may not demand a turnover of residential property without specific judicial approval, which the court may grant only in case of waste, destruction, obstruction of marketing of the property, enforcement of an order in a domestic relations suit or other good cause shown.

(4) If a creditor has possession or control of estate property and the validity, perfection or priority of the creditor's lien depends on the creditor's possession or control, the creditor may retain possession or control of the property until the court orders adequate protection of the creditor's lien. [2017 c.358 §13]

37.140 Collection by receiver of debts owed to owner. (1) Upon demand by a receiver, a person that owes a debt that is estate property and is matured or payable on demand shall pay the debt to the receiver, except to the extent that the debt is subject to setoff or recoupment.

(2) A person who has notice of the appointment of a receiver and owes a debt that is estate property may not satisfy the debt by payment to the owner. [2017 c.358 §14]

37.150 Duties of owner. (1) An owner shall:

(a) Assist and cooperate fully with the receiver in the administration of the estate and the discharge of the receiver's duties, and comply with all orders of the court;

(b) Supply to the receiver information necessary to enable the receiver to complete any schedules that the receiver is required to file under ORS 37.190, and otherwise assist the receiver in the completion of the schedules;

(c) Upon the receiver's appointment, deliver to the receiver all of the estate property in the person's possession, custody or control, including accounts, books, papers, records and other documents; and

(d) After the receiver's appointment, submit to examination under oath by the receiver, or by any other person upon order of the court, concerning the acts, conduct, property, liabilities and financial condition of the owner or any matter relating to the receiver's administration of the estate.

(2) When the owner is an entity, each officer, director, manager, member, partner or other individual exercising or having the power to exercise control over the affairs of the entity are subject to the requirements of this section. [2017 c.358 §15]

37.160 Mailing and special notice lists to be maintained by receiver. (1) A receiver shall maintain a master mailing list of the names and addresses of all parties to the receivership, all known creditors of the owner and interested persons who have filed notices of appearance in the receivership. The receiver shall make a copy of the current master mailing list available to any person on the list upon the person's request.

(2)(a) A receiver shall maintain a special notice list of the names and addresses of all parties to the receivership and any other person who requests to be placed on the list. The receiver shall make a copy of the current special notice list available to any person on the list upon the person's request.

(b) Any person on the special notice list may notify the receiver of the person's preferred means of receiving notices and other communications. If the receiver is so notified, the receiver shall add the information to the special notice list. [2017 c.358 §16]

37.170 Notices. (1)(a) Whenever a person is required to give notice under a provision of the Oregon Receivership Code, the person must:

(A) Serve notice on all persons specified by the provision;

(B) Serve notice on all persons on the special notice list;

(C) File notice with the court; and

(D) File proof of service with the court.

(b) If the provision does not specify to whom notice must be given, the person must give notice to all known persons whose property interests will or may be directly affected by the proposed action, as well as comply with paragraph (a)(B) to (D) of this subsection.

(2) Whenever a person is required to give notice under a provision of the Oregon Receivership Code, the person must give at least as much time notice as specified by the relevant provision, or 14 days if no time is specified.

(3)(a) Except as otherwise provided, notice to any person not on the special notice list must be served by first class mail or as otherwise directed by the court.

(b) Notice to any person on the special notice list who has specified a preferred means of receiving notice must be served by those means, except as otherwise ordered by the court.

(4)(a) Except as provided in ORS 37.180, whenever a provision of the Oregon Receivership Code authorizes a person to take an action after giving notice, the person may take the action without specific authorization from the court if:

(A) The person gives notice that describes the action that the person will take unless an objection is filed and describes a procedure for objecting to the proposed action; and

(B) No objections are filed.

(b) If an objection is filed, the court shall hear the objection and issue an order allowing, disallowing or allowing a modified form of the action.

(c) The court may, on its own motion, require a hearing on any proposed action.

(d) If a person is allowed under this subsection to take an action without specific authorization from the court, the person may nonetheless move the court for an order authorizing the action.

(5) The court may extend or shorten any notice periods for good cause shown.

(6) The court may order that notice of any proposed action be given to any person, regardless of whether such notice is otherwise required under the Oregon Receivership Code.

(7) In all circumstances, the court may consider motions and grant or deny relief without notice or hearing, if it appears to the court that no party to the receivership or interested person would be prejudiced or harmed by the relief requested. [2017 c.358 §17]

37.180 When court order required. (1) A receiver may not take any of the following actions unless the receiver, after giving notice, obtains a court order specifically authorizing the action, except as provided in subsection (2) of this section:

(a) Sale or other disposition of real property;

(b) Use or transfer of property outside the ordinary course of business;

(c) Sale of a co-owner's interest in jointly owned property;

(d) Assumption of an executory contract;

(e) Obtaining credit or incurring debt outside the ordinary course of business;

(f) Compromise or settlement of a controversy that might affect the distribution to creditors from the estate;

(g) Disallowance of all or part of a claim against the estate; and

(h) Termination of the receivership.

(2) For any action described in subsection (1)(a) to (f) of this section, a court may establish conditions under which a receiver may take the action without first obtaining an order specifically authorizing the action, if the court finds that the burden of seeking a court order is likely to outweigh the materiality of the actions under those conditions. The court may establish such conditions in the order appointing the receiver or in any other order. [2017 c.358 §18]

37.190 Creditor list and inventory. (1) Within 60 days after appointment, or within such other time as the court may specify, a receiver shall file with the court a schedule of all known creditors of the owner, their last known mailing addresses, the amount and nature of their claims and whether their claims are disputed.

(2) If the court concludes that the estate is unlikely to be sufficient to make material distributions to unsecured creditors, the court may order that the receiver need not file a schedule as described in subsection (1) of this section. The court may order the receiver to file a schedule of any appropriate subset of creditors.

(3) Within 60 days after appointment, or within such other time as the court may specify, a receiver shall file with the court a true inventory of all estate property of which the receiver has taken possession, custody or control, except that the inventory need not include legal claims that are estate property. [2017 c.358 §19]

37.200 Receiver's periodic reports. (1) A receiver shall file with the court a monthly report of the receiver's operations and financial affairs, unless the court orders a different reporting period. The receiver shall file each report no later than 30 days after the end of a reporting period. The initial report under this section must be filed no later than 60 days after the receiver is appointed, unless the court orders a different deadline.

(2) Each periodic report must include:

(a) A concise narrative summary of the receiver's activities during the period and a description of any major upcoming events;

(b) Beginning and ending cash balances;

(c) A statement of cash receipts and disbursements;

(d) A statement of noncash receipts and payments;

(e) A statement of receipts and dispositions of estate property outside the ordinary course of business, including a description of the property, the value of the property and the amounts received from any disposition of the property;

(f) A statement of accounts receivable;

(g) A statement of fees and expenses of the receiver;

(h) A tax disclosure statement listing taxes due or tax deposits required, the name of the taxing agency, the date due and an explanation for any failure to make payments or deposits; and

(i) Any other information required by the court. [2017 c.358 §20]

37.210 Claims bar date. A receiver may, after providing notice to all known creditors of the owner, set a deadline for the submission of claims by creditors. The receiver, upon court order, may disallow any claims submitted after the deadline. [2017 c.358 §21]

37.220 Automatic stay of certain proceedings. (1) Except as otherwise ordered by the court, the entry of an order appointing a receiver operates as a stay, applicable to all persons, of:

(a) The commencement or continuation, including the issuance or employment of process, of a judicial, administrative or other action or proceeding against the owner that was or could have been commenced before the entry of the order of appointment, or to recover a claim against the owner that arose before the entry of the order of appointment;

(b) The enforcement, against the owner or any estate property, of a judgment entered before the entry of the order of appointment;

(c) Any act to obtain possession of estate property from the receiver, or to interfere with, or exercise control over, estate property;

(d) Any act to create, perfect or enforce any lien or claim against estate property, to the extent that the lien secures a claim against the owner that arose before the entry of the order of appointment;

(e) Any act to collect, assess or recover a claim against the owner that arose before the entry of the order of appointment; or

(f) The exercise of a right of setoff against the owner.

(2) The stay automatically expires as to the acts specified in subsection (1)(a), (b) and (e) of this section six months after the entry of the order of appointment, unless the stay is extended by court order.

(3) A person whose action or proceeding is stayed may move the court for relief from the stay, and the court shall grant such relief for good cause shown. A motion for relief from stay under this subsection is deemed granted if the court does not act on the motion within 60 days after the motion is filed. A person may move the court ex parte for an expedited hearing on a motion for relief from stay.

(4) Any judgment obtained against the owner or estate property after entry of the order of appointment is not a lien against estate property unless the receivership is terminated before a conveyance of the property against which the judgment would otherwise constitute a lien.

(5) The entry of an order appointing a receiver does not operate as a stay of:

(a) The continuation of a judicial or nonjudicial foreclosure action that was initiated by the party seeking the receiver's appointment, unless otherwise ordered by the court;

(b) The commencement or continuation of a criminal action against the owner;

(c) The commencement or continuation of an action or proceeding to establish paternity, to establish or modify an order for spousal or child support or to collect spousal or child support under any order of a court;

(d) Any act to perfect, or to maintain or continue the perfection of, an interest in estate property if the interest perfected would be effective against a creditor of the owner holding at the time of the entry of the order of appointment either a perfected nonpurchase money security interest under ORS chapter 79 against the property, or a lien by attachment, levy or the like, including liens under ORS chapter 87, whether or not such a creditor exists, except that if perfection of an interest would require seizure of the property involved or the commencement of an action, the perfection may and must instead be accomplished by filing and serving on the receiver notice of the interest within the time fixed by law for seizure or commencement;

(e) The commencement or continuation of an action or proceeding by a governmental unit to enforce its police or regulatory power;

(f) The enforcement of a judgment, other than a money judgment, obtained in an action or proceeding by a governmental unit to enforce its police or regulatory power, or with respect to any licensure of the owner; or

(g) The establishment by a governmental unit of any tax liability and any appeal thereof.

(6) The court may void an act that violates the stay imposed by this section.

(7) If a person knowingly violates the stay imposed by this section, the court may:

(a) Award actual damages caused by the violation, reasonable attorney fees and costs; and

(b) Sanction the violation as civil contempt.

(8) The stay described in this section expires upon the termination of the receivership. [2017 c.358 §22]

37.230 Utility service. (1) A utility providing service to estate property may not alter, refuse or discontinue service to the property without first giving the receiver 14 days' notice of any default or intention to alter, refuse or discontinue service to estate property.

(2) Nothing in this section precludes the court from prohibiting the alteration or cessation of utility service if the receiver can furnish adequate assurance of payment, in the form of deposit or other security, for service to be provided after entry of the order appointing the receiver. [2017 c.358 §23]

37.240 Executory contracts. (1) A receiver may, upon order of the court, assume any executory contract of the owner. A receiver may, after giving notice, reject any executory contract of the owner. The court may condition assumption or rejection of any executory contract on terms and conditions that the court deems just and proper. A receiver's performance of an executory contract does not constitute an assumption of the contract or an agreement by the receiver to assume it, nor otherwise preclude the receiver from rejecting it.

(2) If a receiver assumes an executory contract, the receiver must assume the contract in its entirety.

(3) Any obligation or liability incurred by a receiver due to the receiver's assumption of an executory contract is an expense of the receivership. A receiver's rejection of an executory contract is treated as a breach of the contract occurring immediately before the receiver's appointment, and the receiver's right to possess or use property pursuant to an executory contract terminates upon rejection of the contract. The other party to an executory contract that is rejected by a receiver may take any necessary steps to terminate or cancel the contract. Any claims resulting from a receiver's rejection of an executory contract must be submitted to the receiver in the manner provided for by ORS 37.350 within 30 days after the rejection.

(4) A receiver's power under this section to assume an executory contract is not affected by any provision in the contract that would effect or permit a forfeiture, modification or termination of the contract on account of the receiver's appointment, the financial condition of the owner or an assignment for the benefit of creditors by the owner.

(5) A receiver may not assume an executory contract of the owner without the consent of the other party to the contract if:

(a) Applicable law would excuse the other party from accepting performance from or rendering performance to anyone other than the owner even in the absence of any provisions in the contract expressly restricting or prohibiting an assignment of rights or duties;

(b) The contract is a contract to make a loan or extend credit or financial accommodations to or for the benefit of the owner, or to issue a security of the owner; or

(c) The contract expires by its own terms, or under applicable law, prior to the receiver's assumption thereof.

(6) A receiver may not assign an executory contract lease without assuming it, unless the receiver obtains consent from all other parties to the contract.

(7) If the receiver rejects an executory contract for the sale of real property under which the owner is the seller and the purchaser is in possession of the real property, the sale of a real property timeshare interest under which the owner is the seller, the license of intellectual property rights under which the owner is the licensor or the lease of real property under which the owner is the lessor, then:

(a) The purchaser, licensee or lessee may:

(A) Treat the rejection as a termination of the contract, license agreement or lease; or

(B) Remain in possession and continue to perform all obligations arising under the contract, but offset against any payments any damages occurring on account of the rejection after it occurs.

(b) A purchaser of real property is entitled to receive from the receiver any deed or any other instrument of conveyance that the owner is obligated to deliver under the contract when the purchaser becomes entitled to receive it, and the deed or instrument has the same force and effect as if given by the owner.

(c) A purchaser, licensee or lessee who elects to remain in possession under the terms of this subsection has no claim or rights against the receiver on account of any damages arising from the receiver's rejection except as expressly permitted by this subsection.

(d) A purchaser of real property who elects to treat rejection of an executory contract as a termination has a lien against the real property for the portion of the purchase price that the purchaser has paid.

(8)(a) If a receiver does not seek authorization from the court to assume an executory contract within 180 days after the receiver's appointment, the receiver is deemed to have rejected the contract.

(b) The court may shorten or extend the time period described in paragraph (a) of this subsection for good cause shown.

(9) Nothing in this section affects the enforceability of prohibitions against assignment that exist under contract or applicable law. [2017 c.358 §24]

37.250 Use or transfer of estate property outside ordinary course of business; transfer of co-owned property; limitation on disposition of residential property. (1) Upon court order, a receiver may use estate property outside the ordinary course of business.

(2) Upon court order, a receiver may transfer estate property other than in the ordinary course of business by sale, lease, license, exchange or other disposition. Unless the transfer agreement provides otherwise, a transfer under this section is free and clear of a lien of the person that obtained appointment of the receiver, any subordinate liens and any right of redemption, but is subject to any senior liens. A transfer under this section may occur by means other than a public auction sale. On motion by any party or interested person, the court may prescribe standards or procedures calculated to maximize the proceeds of the transfer.

(3) If a lien on estate property is extinguished by a transfer under this section, the lien attaches to the proceeds of the transfer with the same validity, perfection and priority that the extinguished lien had on the transferred property immediately before the transfer, regardless of whether the proceeds are sufficient to satisfy all obligations secured by the lien.

(4) A creditor holding a valid lien on the property to be transferred may purchase the property and offset against the purchase price all or part of the allowed amount secured by the lien, if the creditor tenders sufficient funds to satisfy the reasonable expenses of transfer and any obligation secured by any senior lien extinguished by the transfer.

(5) A reversal or modification of an order authorizing a transfer under this section does not affect the validity of the transfer to a person that acquired the property in good faith or revive against any person any lien extinguished by the transfer, regardless of whether the transferee knew of the request for reversal or modification before the transfer, unless the court stayed the order before the transfer.

(6) If estate property includes an interest as a co-owner of property, the receiver has all rights and powers of a co-owner afforded by applicable law, including any rights of partition.

(7) If at the time of appointment of a receiver an owner holds an undivided interest in property as a tenant in common, joint tenant or tenant by the entirety, the receiver may sell both the interest that is estate property and the interest of any co-owner upon court order if the court determines that:

(a) Partition in kind of the property is impracticable;

(b) Sale of the estate's undivided interest in the property would realize significantly less for the estate than sale of the property free and clear of the interests of the co-owner; and

(c) The benefit to the estate of the sale outweighs the detriment, if any, to the co-owner.

(8) A receiver may not sell, transfer or otherwise dispose of residential property, or an undivided interest therein, without specific judicial approval, which a court may grant only in case of waste, destruction, obstruction of marketing of the property, enforcement of an order in a domestic relations suit or other good cause shown.

(9) As used in this section, "good faith" means honesty in fact and the observance of reasonable commercial standards of fair dealing. [2017 c.358 §25]

37.260 Receivership financing. (1) If a receiver is authorized to operate the business of a person or manage a person's property, the receiver may obtain credit and incur debt in the ordinary course of business. Expenses related to such credit and debt are allowable under ORS 37.370 as an administrative expense of the receiver.

(2) Upon court order, a receiver may obtain credit or incur debt other than in the ordinary course of business. The court may allow the receiver to mortgage, pledge, hypothecate or otherwise encumber estate property as security for repayment of any debt incurred under this subsection. A creditor's security interest may be in the form of a receiver's certificate. [2017 c.358 §26]

37.270 Recovery of costs related to secured property. A receiver may recover from property securing a secured claim the necessary costs and expenses of preserving, or disposing of, the property to the extent of any benefit to the holder of such claim, including the payment of all ad valorem property taxes with respect to the property. [2017 c.358 §27]

37.280 Abandonment of property. (1) A receiver, after giving notice, may abandon estate property that is burdensome to the receiver or is of inconsequential value or benefit. Property that is abandoned no longer constitutes estate property.

(2) A receiver may not abandon property in contravention of a state statute or rule that is reasonably designed to protect the public health or safety from identified hazards, including ORS chapters 465 and 466. [2017 c.358 §28]

37.290 Actions by or against receiver or affecting estate property. (1) A person may not sue a receiver personally for an act or omission in administering estate property unless permitted by the court that appointed the receiver.

(2) A person may not initiate or continue an action seeking to dispossess the receiver of any estate property or to otherwise interfere with the receiver's management or control of any estate property unless permitted by the court that appointed the receiver.

(3) Actions by or against a receiver are adjunct to the receivership. All pleadings in adjunct actions must include the case number of the receivership. All adjunct actions shall be referred to the judge assigned to the receivership action, unless:

(a) The court does not have jurisdiction over the adjunct action; or

(b) The assignment would not promote judicial efficiency.

(4) If an action is filed against a receiver in a court in this state other than the court in which the receivership is pending, the court in which the action is filed shall transfer the action to the court in which the receivership is pending upon the receiver's motion if the receiver files the motion within 30 days after service of original process upon the receiver. However, if a state agency is a party to the action, the action may not be transferred under this subsection unless the agency consents to the transfer.

(5) The receiver may be joined or substituted as a party in any action that was pending at the time of the receiver's appointment and in which the owner is a party, upon motion by the receiver to the court or agency in which the action is pending.

(6) In case of the death, removal or resignation of the receiver, an action by or against a receiver continues by or against the successor receiver or, if a successor receiver is not appointed, by or against the owner.

(7) Whenever the assets of any domestic or foreign entity that has been doing business in this state have been placed in the hands of a receiver, service of all process upon the entity may be made upon the receiver.

(8) A judgment against a receiver is not a lien on the property or funds of the receivership, and no execution may issue thereon. Upon entry of the judgment in the court in which the receivership is pending, or upon filing in the receivership of a certified copy of a judgment from another jurisdiction, the judgment is treated as an allowed claim in the receivership.

(9) No person other than a successor receiver duly appointed by the court has a right of action against a former receiver to recover property or the value thereof for or on behalf of the estate. [2017 c.358 §29]

37.300 Personal liability of receiver. (1) A receiver may be personally liable to the owner, or a record or beneficial owner of estate property, for loss or diminution in value of or damage to estate property only if the loss, diminution or damage is caused by:

(a) Failure of the receiver to comply with an order of the court; or

(b) An act or omission for which liability could not be limited under ORS 60.047 if the receiver were an Oregon corporation.

(2) A receiver may be personally liable to a person other than the owner, or the record or beneficial owner of estate property, for any loss, diminution or damage caused by the receiver's performance of the receiver's duties, or the receiver's authorized operation of a business, only if the loss, diminution or damage is caused by:

(a) Fraud by the receiver;

(b) An act intended by the receiver to cause loss, diminution or damage to the specific claimant; or

(c) An act or omission for which an officer or director of an Oregon corporation would be liable to the claimant under the same circumstances.

(3) Notwithstanding subsections (1) and (2) of this section, a receiver has no personal liability to any person for acts or omissions of the receiver permitted by any order of the court.

(4) A receiver is entitled to all defenses and immunities provided by law for an act or omission within the scope of the receiver's appointment.

(5) Nothing in this section may be construed to expand any obligation or liability of a receiver under state law, common law or federal law for remediation of environmental damages or hazards. [2017 c.358 §30]

37.310 Employment and compensation of professionals. (1) After giving notice, a receiver may employ attorneys, accountants, appraisers, brokers, real estate licensees, auctioneers or other professionals to represent or assist the receiver in carrying out the receiver's duties.

(2) The notice given by the receiver before employing a professional must disclose:

(a) The identity and qualifications of the professional;

(b) The scope and nature of the proposed engagement;

(c) Any potential conflict of interest; and

(d) The proposed compensation.

(3) If an objection is filed after the receiver provides notice of the professional's employment, the professional may continue to perform the professional's duties while the objection is pending.

(4)(a) A receiver may not employ a professional who holds or represents an interest adverse to the estate, except by order of the court.

(b) A professional is not disqualified for employment under this subsection solely because of the professional's employment by, representation of or other relationship with a creditor or other interested person, if the relationship is disclosed in the notice of the professional's employment.

(5) Nothing in this section precludes the receiver from acting as attorney or accountant if doing so is in the best interests of the estate.

(6) After giving notice, the receiver may make payments to professionals for services rendered to the receiver. The notice must include an itemized billing statement indicating the time spent, billing rates of all persons who performed work to be compensated and a detailed list of expenses. [2017 c.358 §31]

37.320 Participation of creditors and other interested persons in receivership; effect of receivership on nonparties. (1) Any interested person may appear in a receivership, either in person or by an attorney. Before appearing in the receivership, an interested person who is not party to the receivership must file with the court a written notice of appearance, including the name and mailing address of the interested person, and the name and address of the person's attorney, if any, and serve a copy of the notice upon the receiver. A creditor or other interested person may be heard with respect to all matters affecting the person, whether or not the person is joined as a party to the receivership.

(2) Persons who receive notice of the pendency of a receivership, whether actual or constructive, and creditors or other persons submitting written claims in the receivership or otherwise appearing and participating in the receivership, are bound by the acts of the receiver with respect to management and disposition of estate property, regardless of whether they are formally joined as parties to the receivership.

(3) Any person having a claim against or interest in estate property and having actual or constructive knowledge of the receivership is bound by acts of the receiver or orders of the court with respect to the treatment of claims and disposition of estate property, including sales of property free and clear of liens, regardless of whether the person receives written notice from the receiver and regardless of whether the person appears in the receivership.

(4) A person duly notified by the receiver of a proposed act by the receiver is bound with respect to the act, regardless of whether the person objected to the act or is joined formally as a party in the receivership.

(5) As used in this section, "bound" means barred from bringing a motion or proceeding to contest an act or order, either within or outside of the receivership. [2017 c.358 §32]

37.330 Initial notice to creditors and other interested persons. (1) A receiver shall, within 30 days after the receiver's appointment, provide notice of the receivership to all known creditors of the owner and any other known interested persons that includes:

(a) The date of appointment of the receiver;
(b) The name of the court and the case number of the receivership;
(c) The deadline for the submission of claims by creditors, if known;
(d) The name and address of the owner;
(e) The name and address of the receiver and receiver's attorney, if any;
(f) A procedure for notifying the receiver if the recipient is represented by an attorney;
(g) A procedure for being placed on the special notice list; and
(h) A statement that the person may not receive notice of all further proceedings in the receivership unless the person requests to be placed on the special notice list.

(2) The notice required under this section must be given by first class mail or by such other methods as the court may approve or require.

(3) In addition to the methods described in subsection (2) of this section, the notice required under this section must be published at least once per week for two consecutive weeks in a newspaper of general circulation in all counties in which estate property is known to be located. [2017 c.358 §33]

37.340 Claims process. (1) If a receiver determines that the estate is sufficient to provide distributions to creditors, the receiver shall, upon notice, establish a claims process by sending a written document describing a claims process, including relevant dates and deadlines, to all known creditors of the owner. The receiver may prescribe forms or otherwise specify information required to be included in a claim.

(2) If the receiver determines that the estate is insufficient to provide distributions to creditors, the receiver may give notice that no claims process will take place in the receivership. [2017 c.358 §34]

37.350 Submission of claims by creditors. (1) Claims may not be submitted until a claims process is established under ORS 37.340.

(2) All claims that arose before the receiver's appointment, whether contingent, liquidated, unliquidated or disputed, other than claims of creditors with security interests in or other liens against estate property, must be submitted in accordance with this section. Any claim not so submitted is barred from participating in any distribution to creditors.

(3) Claims must be submitted by delivering the claim to the receiver or an agent designated by the receiver within 30 days after the claims process is established, except that a claim arising from the rejection of an executory contract of the owner must be submitted within 30 days after the rejection. Claims by state agencies must be submitted within 180 days after the claims process is established. The court may shorten or extend any time period set forth in this subsection.

(4) Claims must be submitted in a form prescribed by the receiver. If no form is prescribed, claims must be in written form and must:
(a) Include the name and address of the claimant;
(b) Set forth the nature and amount of the claim;
(c) Be executed by the claimant or the claimant's agent; and
(d) Include any other information required by the receiver.

(5) Claims may not be filed with the court. If a claim is incorrectly filed with the court, the court shall forward the claim to the receiver or an agent designated by the receiver.

(6) A claim executed and submitted in accordance with this section constitutes prima facie evidence of the validity and amount of the claim. [2017 c.358 §35]

37.360 Objection to and allowance of claims. (1)(a) At any time before the entry of an order approving the receiver's final report, a receiver may, upon court order and after at least 21 days' notice, disallow a claim. The notice must set forth the grounds for the disallowance.

(b) At any time before the entry of an order approving the receiver's final report, any interested person may object to a claim. The objector must mail a copy of the objection, together with a notice of hearing, to the receiver and claimant at least 21 days before the hearing. The court shall hear the objection and enter an order allowing or disallowing the claim.

(2) Upon request of a creditor, the receiver or a person objecting to a creditor's claim, or upon order of the court, an objection is subject to mediation before adjudication of the objection, under the rules or orders adopted or issued with respect to mediations. However, claims by the state are not subject to mediation unless the state consents to mediation.

(3) Upon motion of the receiver or an interested person, the following claims may be estimated for purpose of allowance under this section under the rules or orders applicable to the estimation of claims under this subsection:
(a) Any contingent or unliquidated claim, the fixing or liquidation of which, as the case may be, would unduly delay the administration of the receivership; or
(b) Any right to payment arising from a right to an equitable remedy for breach of performance.

(4) Claims estimated under subsection (3) of this section are allowed in the estimated amount thereof. [2017 c.358 §36]

37.370 Priorities. (1) Allowed claims in a receivership receive distribution under the Oregon Receivership Code in the order of priority set forth in this subsection.
(a) The first priority is unpaid costs and expenses allowable under ORS 37.270.
(b) The second priority is claims of creditors with liens on estate property that are duly perfected under applicable law. Such creditors receive the proceeds from the disposition of their collateral. Secured claims must be paid from the proceeds in accordance with their respective priorities under otherwise applicable law.
(c) The third priority is actual, necessary costs and expenses incurred during the administration of the estate, other than those expenses allowable under subsection (2) of this section, including allowed fees and reimbursement of reasonable charges and expenses of the receiver and professional persons employed by the receiver under ORS 37.310. Notwithstanding paragraph (b) of this subsection, expenses incurred during the administration of the estate have priority over the secured claim of any creditor obtaining the appointment of the receiver.
(d) The fourth priority is claims to which 31 U.S.C. 3713 applies.
(e) The fifth priority is claims of creditors with liens on estate property that are not required to be perfected under applicable law. Such creditors receive the proceeds of the disposition of their collateral.
(f) The sixth priority is claims of creditors with liens on estate property that have not been duly perfected under applicable law. Such creditors receive the proceeds from the disposition of their collateral if and to the extent that unsecured claims are made subject to those liens under applicable law.
(g) The seventh priority is claims for wages, salaries or commissions, including vacation, severance and sick leave pay, or contributions to an employee benefit plan, earned by the claimant within 180 days of the earlier of the date of appointment of the receiver and the cessation of the estate's business, but only to the extent of $12,850 in aggregate for each claimant.
(h) The eighth priority is unsecured claims of individuals, to the extent of $2,850 for each claimant, arising from the deposit with the owner before the date of appointment of the receiver of moneys in connection with the purchase, lease or rental of property or the purchase of services for personal, family or household use that were not delivered or provided.
(i) The ninth priority is claims for a spousal support debt or child support debt, except to the extent that the debt:
(A) Is assigned to another entity, voluntarily, by operation of law, or otherwise; or
(B) Includes a liability designated as a support obligation, unless that liability is actually in the nature of a support obligation.
(j) The tenth priority is unsecured claims of state governmental units for taxes that accrued before the appointment of the receiver.
(k) The eleventh priority is other unsecured claims.
(L) The last priority is interests of the owner.

(2) If the proceeds from the disposition of collateral securing an allowed secured claim are less than the amount of the claim or a creditor's lien is avoided on any basis, the creditor has an unsecured claim in the amount of the deficiency.

338

(3) Except for claimants described in subsection (1)(b) and (d) of this section, claimants receive distributions on a pro rata basis.

(4) If all of the claims under subsection (1) of this section have been paid in full, the receiver shall pay any residue to the owner. [2017 c.358 §37]

37.380 Secured claims against after-acquired property. Property acquired by the estate or by the owner after the date of appointment of the receiver is subject to an allowed secured claim to the same extent as would be the case in the absence of a receivership. [2017 c.358 §38]

37.390 Ancillary receiverships. (1) A receiver appointed in any action pending in the courts of this state may, upon court order, apply to any court outside of this state for appointment as receiver with respect to any estate property that is located in any other jurisdiction, if the appointment is necessary to the receiver's possession, control, management or disposition of property in accordance with orders of the court. The receiver may move the court ex parte for an expedited hearing on a motion for leave to apply for an ancillary receivership.

(2) A receiver appointed in a foreign action, or any party to the foreign action, may move a court of this state for appointment of that same receiver with respect to any property of the foreign receivership that is located in this state. The court shall act on the motion as provided in ORS 37.060 (3). A receiver appointed in an ancillary receivership in this state is subject to the requirements imposed on receivers by statutes of this state, except as expressly exempted by the court. [2017 c.358 §39]

37.400 Removal of receiver. (1) On motion of the owner, the receiver or any creditor, or on the court's own motion, the court shall remove a receiver if the receiver resigns or refuses or fails to serve for any reason, or for other good cause.

(2) Upon removal of the receiver, the court shall appoint a successor receiver if the court determines that further administration of the estate is required. Upon appointment, the successor receiver immediately takes possession of the estate and assumes the duties of receiver.

(3) If the court is satisfied that a replaced receiver has fully accounted for and turned over to the successor receiver all of the property of the estate and has filed a report of all receipts and disbursements during the person's tenure as receiver, the court shall, after notice to all persons on the special notice list and hearing, enter an order discharging the replaced receiver from all further duties and responsibilities as receiver. [2017 c.358 §40]

37.410 Termination of receivership. (1) Upon distribution or disposition of all property of the estate or the completion of the receiver's duties with respect to estate property, or for other good cause, the receiver shall move the court for an order discharging the receiver.

(2) The receiver shall attach to the motion for discharge a final report and accounting setting forth:

(a) A list of estate property received during the receivership;

(b) A list of disbursements, including payments to professionals engaged by the receiver;

(c) A list of dispositions of estate property;

(d) A list of distributions made or proposed to be made from the estate for creditor claims;

(e) If not filed separately, a request for approval of the payment of fees and expenses of the receiver; and

(f) Any other information required by the court.

(3) If the court approves the final report and accounting, the court shall discharge the receiver. The court may issue an order exonerating the receiver's bond or alternative security.

(4) The receiver's discharge:

(a) Releases the receiver from any further duties and responsibilities under the Oregon Receivership Code; and

(b) Releases the receiver and any persons acting on behalf of the receiver from all further liability in connection with the administration of estate property or the receivership.

(5) Upon motion of any interested person, or upon the court's own motion, the court may discharge the receiver and terminate the court's administration of the property over which the receiver was appointed.

(6) Upon termination of the receivership under any circumstances, if the court determines that the appointment of the receiver was wrongfully procured or procured in bad faith, the court may assess against the person who procured the receiver's appointment all of the receiver's fees and other costs of the receivership, and any other sanctions the court deems appropriate. [2017 c.358 §41]

CHAPTERS 38 AND 39 [Reserved for expansion]_____

TITLE 4 EVIDENCE AND WITNESSES

Chapter   40.   Evidence Code
           41.   Evidence Generally
           42.   Execution, Formalities and Interpretation of Writings
           43.   Public Writings
           44.   Witnesses
           45.   Testimony Generally

_____

Chapter 40 — Evidence Code

ORS sections in this chapter were amended or repealed by the Legislative Assembly during its 2018 regular session. See the table of ORS sections amended or repealed during the 2018 regular session: 2018 A&R Tables

New sections of law were enacted by the Legislative Assembly during its 2018 regular session and pertain to or are likely to be compiled in this ORS chapter. See sections in the following 2018 Oregon Laws chapters: 2018 Session Laws 0002

2017 EDITION

EVIDENCE CODE

EVIDENCE AND WITNESSES

GENERAL PROVISIONS

40.010   Rule 100. Short title

40.015   Rule 101. Applicability of Oregon Evidence Code

40.020   Rule 102. Purpose and construction

40.025   Rule 103. Rulings on evidence

40.030   Rule 104. Preliminary questions

40.035   Rule 105. Limited admissibility

40.040   Rule 106. When part of transaction proved, whole admissible

JUDICIAL NOTICE

40.060   Rule 201(a). Scope

40.065   Rule 201(b). Kinds of facts

40.070   Rules 201(c) and 201(d). When mandatory or discretionary

40.075   Rule 201(e). Opportunity to be heard

40.080   Rule 201(f). Time of taking notice

40.085   Rule 201(g). Instructing the jury

40.090   Rule 202. Law that is judicially noticed

BURDEN OF PERSUASION; BURDEN OF PRODUCING EVIDENCE; PRESUMPTIONS

40.105   Rule 305. Allocation of the burden of persuasion

40.110   Rule 306. Instructions on the burden of persuasion

40.115   Rule 307. Allocation of the burden of producing evidence

40.120   Rule 308. Presumptions in civil proceedings

40.125   Rule 309. Presumptions in criminal proceedings

40.130   Rule 310. Conflicting presumptions

40.135   Rule 311. Presumptions

RELEVANCY

40.150   Rule 401. Definition of "relevant evidence"

40.155   Rule 402. Relevant evidence generally admissible

40.160   Rule 403. Exclusion of relevant evidence on grounds of prejudice, confusion or undue delay

40.170   Rule 404. Character evidence; evidence of other crimes, wrongs or acts

40.172   Rule 404-1. Pattern, practice or history of abuse; expert testimony

40.175   Rule 405. Methods of proving character

40.180   Rule 406. Habit; routine practice

40.185   Rule 407. Subsequent remedial measures

40.190   Rule 408. Compromise and offers to compromise

40.195   Rule 409. Payment of medical and similar expenses

40.200   Rule 410. Withdrawn plea or statement not admissible

40.205   Rule 411. Liability insurance

40.210   Rule 412. Sex offense cases; relevance of victim's past behavior or manner of dress

40.211   Rule 412-1. Evidence not admissible in civil proceeding involving sexual misconduct

40.215   Rule 413. Measures and assessments intended to minimize impact of or plan for natural disaster

PRIVILEGES

40.225   Rule 503. Lawyer-client privilege

40.230   Rule 504. Psychotherapist-patient privilege

40.235   Rule 504-1. Physician-patient privilege

40.240   Rule 504-2. Nurse-patient privilege

40.245   Rule 504-3. School employee-student privilege

40.250   Rule 504-4. Regulated social worker-client privilege

40.252   Rule 504-5. Communications revealing intent to commit certain crimes

40.255   Rule 505. Spousal privilege

40.260   Rule 506. Member of clergy-penitent privilege

40.262   Rule 507. Counselor-client privilege

40.264   Rule 507-1. Certified advocate-victim privilege

40.265   Rule 508a. Stenographer-employer privilege

40.270   Rule 509. Public officer privilege

40.272   Rule 509-1. Sign language interpreter privilege

40.273   Rule 509-2. Non-English-speaking person-interpreter privilege

40.275   Rule 510. Identity of informer

40.280   Rule 511. Waiver of privilege by voluntary disclosure

40.285   Rule 512. Privileged matter disclosed under compulsion or without opportunity to claim privilege

40.290   Rule 513. Comment upon or inference from claim of privilege

40.295   Rule 514. Effect on existing privileges

WITNESSES

40.310   Rule 601. General rule of competency

40.315   Rule 602. Lack of personal knowledge

40.320   Rule 603. Oath or affirmation

40.325   Rule 604. Interpreters

40.330   Rule 605. Competency of judge as witness

40.335   Rule 606. Competency of juror as witness

40.345   Rule 607. Who may impeach

40.350   Rule 608. Evidence of character and conduct of witness

40.355   Rule 609. Impeachment by evidence of conviction of crime; exceptions

40.360   Rule 609-1. Impeachment for bias or interest

40.365   Rule 610. Religious beliefs or opinions

40.370   Rule 611. Mode and order of interrogation and presentation

40.375   Rule 612. Writing used to refresh memory

40.380   Rule 613. Prior statements of witnesses

40.385   Rule 615. Exclusion of witnesses

OPINIONS AND EXPERT TESTIMONY

40.405   Rule 701. Opinion testimony by lay witnesses

40.410   Rule 702. Testimony by experts

40.415   Rule 703. Bases of opinion testimony by experts

40.420   Rule 704. Opinion on ultimate issue

40.425   Rule 705. Disclosure of fact or data underlying expert opinion

40.430   Rule 706. Impeachment of expert witness by learned treatise

HEARSAY

40.450   Rule 801. Definitions for ORS 40.450 to 40.475

40.455   Rule 802. Hearsay rule

40.460   Rule 803. Hearsay exceptions; availability of declarant immaterial

40.465   Rule 804. Hearsay exceptions when the declarant is unavailable

40.470   Rule 805. Hearsay within hearsay

40.475   Rule 806. Attacking and supporting credibility of declarant

AUTHENTICATION AND IDENTIFICATION

40.505   Rule 901. Requirement of authentication or identification

40.510   Rule 902. Self-authentication

40.515   Rule 903. Subscribing witness' testimony unnecessary

CONTENTS OF WRITINGS, RECORDINGS AND PHOTOGRAPHS

40.550   Rule 1001. Definitions for ORS 40.550 to 40.585

40.555   Rule 1002. Requirement of original

40.560   Rule 1003. Admissibility of duplicates

40.562   Rule 1003-1. Admissibility of reproduction

40.565   Rule 1004. Admissibility of other evidence of contents

40.570   Rule 1005. Public records

40.575   Rule 1006. Summaries

40.580   Rule 1007. Testimony or written admission of party

40.585   Rule 1008. Functions of court and jury

GENERAL PROVISIONS

40.010 Rule 100. Short title. ORS 40.010 to 40.585 and 41.415 shall be known and may be cited as the Oregon Evidence Code. [1981 c.892 §1]

40.015 Rule 101. Applicability of Oregon Evidence Code. (1) The Oregon Evidence Code applies to all courts in this state except for:
(a) A hearing or mediation before a magistrate of the Oregon Tax Court as provided by ORS 305.501;
(b) The small claims department of a circuit court as provided by ORS 46.415; and
(c) The small claims department of a justice court as provided by ORS 55.080.
(2) The Oregon Evidence Code applies generally to civil actions, suits and proceedings, criminal actions and proceedings and to contempt proceedings except those in which the court may act summarily.
(3) ORS 40.225 to 40.295 relating to privileges apply at all stages of all actions, suits and proceedings.
(4) ORS 40.010 to 40.210 and 40.310 to 40.585 do not apply in the following situations:
(a) The determination of questions of fact preliminary to admissibility of evidence when the issue is to be determined by the court under ORS 40.030.
(b) Proceedings before grand juries, except as required by ORS 132.320.
(c) Proceedings for extradition, except as required by ORS 133.743 to 133.857.
(d) Sentencing proceedings, except proceedings under ORS 138.052 and 163.150, as required by ORS 137.090 or proceedings under ORS 136.765 to 136.785.
(e) Proceedings to revoke probation, except as required by ORS 137.090.
(f) Proceedings conducted in a reentry court under section 29, chapter 649, Oregon Laws 2013.
(g) Issuance of warrants of arrest, bench warrants or search warrants.
(h) Proceedings under ORS chapter 135 relating to conditional release, security release, release on personal recognizance, or preliminary hearings, subject to ORS 135.173.
(i) Proceedings to determine proper disposition of a child in accordance with ORS 419B.325 (2) and 419C.400 (4).
(j) Proceedings under ORS 813.210, 813.215, 813.220, 813.230, 813.250 and 813.255 to determine whether a driving while under the influence of intoxicants diversion agreement should be allowed or terminated.
(k) Proceedings under ORS 147.530 relating to victims' rights, except for the provisions of ORS 40.105 and 40.115. [1981 c.892 §2; 1983 c.784 §1; 1985 c.16 §444; 1987 c.441 §10; 1993 c.18 §13; 1993 c.33 §289; 1995 c.531 §1; 1995 c.650 §22; 1995 c.657 §22; 1995 c.658 §35; 1999 c.1055 §11; 2005 c.345 §2; 2005 c.463 §8; 2005 c.463 §13; 2005 c.843 §25; 2007 c.16 §2; 2009 c.178 §23; 2013 c.649 §32]

Note: The amendments to 40.015 by section 37, chapter 649, Oregon Laws 2013, become operative July 1, 2023. See section 38, chapter 649, Oregon Laws 2013. The text that is operative on and after July 1, 2023, is set forth for the user's convenience.
40.015. (1) The Oregon Evidence Code applies to all courts in this state except for:
(a) A hearing or mediation before a magistrate of the Oregon Tax Court as provided by ORS 305.501;
(b) The small claims department of a circuit court as provided by ORS 46.415; and
(c) The small claims department of a justice court as provided by ORS 55.080.
(2) The Oregon Evidence Code applies generally to civil actions, suits and proceedings, criminal actions and proceedings and to contempt proceedings except those in which the court may act summarily.
(3) ORS 40.225 to 40.295 relating to privileges apply at all stages of all actions, suits and proceedings.
(4) ORS 40.010 to 40.210 and 40.310 to 40.585 do not apply in the following situations:

(a) The determination of questions of fact preliminary to admissibility of evidence when the issue is to be determined by the court under ORS 40.030.

(b) Proceedings before grand juries, except as required by ORS 132.320.

(c) Proceedings for extradition, except as required by ORS 133.743 to 133.857.

(d) Sentencing proceedings, except proceedings under ORS 138.052 and 163.150, as required by ORS 137.090 or proceedings under ORS 136.765 to 136.785.

(e) Proceedings to revoke probation, except as required by ORS 137.090.

(f) Issuance of warrants of arrest, bench warrants or search warrants.

(g) Proceedings under ORS chapter 135 relating to conditional release, security release, release on personal recognizance, or preliminary hearings, subject to ORS 135.173.

(h) Proceedings to determine proper disposition of a child in accordance with ORS 419B.325 (2) and 419C.400 (4).

(i) Proceedings under ORS 813.210, 813.215, 813.220, 813.230, 813.250 and 813.255 to determine whether a driving while under the influence of intoxicants diversion agreement should be allowed or terminated.

(j) Proceedings under ORS 147.530 relating to victims' rights, except for the provisions of ORS 40.105 and 40.115.

40.020 Rule 102. Purpose and construction. The Oregon Evidence Code shall be construed to secure fairness in administration, elimination of unjustifiable expense and delay, and promotion of growth and development of the law of evidence to the end that the truth may be ascertained and proceedings justly determined. [1981 c.892 §3]

40.025 Rule 103. Rulings on evidence. (1) Evidential error is not presumed to be prejudicial. Error may not be predicated upon a ruling which admits or excludes evidence unless a substantial right of the party is affected, and:

(a) In case the ruling is one admitting evidence, a timely objection or motion to strike appears of record, stating the specific ground of objection, if the specific ground was not apparent from the context; or

(b) In case the ruling is one excluding evidence, the substance of the evidence was made known to the court by offer or was apparent from the context within which questions were asked.

(2) The court may add any other or further statement which shows the character of the evidence, the form in which it was offered, the objection made and the ruling thereon. It may direct the making of an offer in question and answer form.

(3) In jury cases, proceedings shall be conducted, to the extent practicable, so as to prevent inadmissible evidence from being suggested to the jury by any means, such as making statements or offers of proof or asking questions in the hearing of the jury.

(4) Nothing in this rule precludes taking notice of plain errors affecting substantial rights although they were not brought to the attention of the court. [1981 c.892 §4]

40.030 Rule 104. Preliminary questions. (1) Preliminary questions concerning the qualification of a person to be a witness, the existence of a privilege or the admissibility of evidence shall be determined by the court, subject to the provisions of subsection (2) of this section. In making its determination the court is not bound by the rules of evidence except those with respect to privileges.

(2) When the relevancy of evidence depends upon the fulfillment of a condition of fact, the court shall admit it upon, or subject to, the introduction of evidence sufficient to support a finding of the fulfillment of the condition.

(3) Hearings on the admissibility of confessions shall in all cases be conducted out of the hearing of the jury. Hearings on other preliminary matters shall be so conducted when the interests of justice require or, when an accused is a witness, if the accused so requests.

(4) The accused does not, by testifying upon a preliminary matter, become subject to cross-examination as to other issues in the case.

(5) This section does not limit the right of a party to introduce before the jury evidence relevant to weight or credibility. [1981 c.892 §5]

40.035 Rule 105. Limited admissibility. When evidence which is admissible as to one party or for one purpose but not admissible as to another party or for another purpose is admitted, the court, upon request, shall restrict the evidence to its proper scope and instruct the jury accordingly. [1981 c.892 §6]

40.040 Rule 106. When part of transaction proved, whole admissible. When part of an act, declaration, conversation or writing is given in evidence by one party, the whole on the same subject, where otherwise admissible, may at that time be inquired into by the other; when a letter is read, the answer may at that time be given; and when a detached act, declaration, conversation or writing is given in evidence, any other act, declaration, conversation or writing which is necessary to make it understood may at that time also be given in evidence. [1981 c.892 §6a]

JUDICIAL NOTICE

40.060 Rule 201(a). Scope. ORS 40.060 to 40.085 govern judicial notice of adjudicative facts. ORS 40.090 governs judicial notice of law. [1981 c.892 §7]

40.065 Rule 201(b). Kinds of facts. A judicially noticed fact must be one not subject to reasonable dispute in that it is either:

(1) Generally known within the territorial jurisdiction of the trial court; or

(2) Capable of accurate and ready determination by resort to sources whose accuracy cannot reasonably be questioned. [1981 c.892 §8]

40.070 Rules 201(c) and 201(d). When mandatory or discretionary. (1) A court may take judicial notice, whether requested or not.

(2) A court shall take judicial notice if requested by a party and supplied with the necessary information. [1981 c.892 §9]

40.075 Rule 201(e). Opportunity to be heard. A party is entitled upon timely request to an opportunity to be heard as to the propriety of taking judicial notice and the tenor of the matter noticed. In the absence of prior notification, the request may be made after judicial notice has been taken. [1981 c.892 §10]

40.080 Rule 201(f). Time of taking notice. Judicial notice may be taken at any stage of the proceeding. [1981 c.892 §11]

40.085 Rule 201(g). Instructing the jury. (1) In a civil action or proceeding, the court shall instruct the jury to accept as conclusive any fact or law judicially noticed.

(2) In a criminal case, the court shall instruct the jury that it may, but is not required to, accept as conclusive any fact judicially noticed in favor of the prosecution. [1981 c.892 §12]

40.090 Rule 202. Law that is judicially noticed. Law judicially noticed is defined as:

(1) The decisional, constitutional and public statutory law of Oregon, the United States, any federally recognized American Indian tribal government and any state, territory or other jurisdiction of the United States.

(2) Public and private official acts of the legislative, executive and judicial departments of this state, the United States, any federally recognized American Indian tribal government and any other state, territory or other jurisdiction of the United States.

(3) Rules of professional conduct for members of the Oregon State Bar.

(4) Regulations, ordinances and similar legislative enactments issued by or under the authority of the United States, any federally recognized American Indian tribal government or any state, territory or possession of the United States.

(5) Rules of court of any court of this state or any court of record of the United States, of any federally recognized American Indian tribal government or of any state, territory or other jurisdiction of the United States.

(6) The law of an organization of nations and of foreign nations and public entities in foreign nations.

(7) An ordinance, comprehensive plan or enactment of any county or incorporated city in this state, or a right derived therefrom. As used in this subsection, "comprehensive plan" has the meaning given that term by ORS 197.015. [1981 c.892 §13; 2007 c.63 §1]

BURDEN OF PERSUASION; BURDEN OF PRODUCING EVIDENCE; PRESUMPTIONS

40.105 Rule 305. Allocation of the burden of persuasion. A party has the burden of persuasion as to each fact the existence or nonexistence of which the law declares essential to the claim for relief or defense the party is asserting. [1981 c.892 §14]

40.110 Rule 306. Instructions on the burden of persuasion. The court shall instruct the jury as to which party bears the applicable burden of persuasion on each issue only after all of the evidence in the case has been received. [1981 c.892 §15]

40.115 Rule 307. Allocation of the burden of producing evidence. (1) The burden of producing evidence as to a particular issue is on the party against whom a finding on the issue would be required in the absence of further evidence.

(2) The burden of producing evidence as to a particular issue is initially on the party with the burden of persuasion as to that issue. [1981 c.892 §16]

40.120 Rule 308. Presumptions in civil proceedings. In civil actions and proceedings, a presumption imposes on the party against whom it is directed the burden of proving that the nonexistence of the presumed fact is more probable than its existence. [1981 c.892 §17]

40.125 Rule 309. Presumptions in criminal proceedings. (1) The judge is not authorized to direct the jury to find a presumed fact against the accused.

(2) When the presumed fact establishes guilt or is an element of the offense or negates a defense, the judge may submit the question of guilt or the existence of the presumed fact to the jury only if:

(a) A reasonable juror on the evidence as a whole could find that the facts giving rise to the presumed fact have been established beyond a reasonable doubt; and

(b) The presumed fact follows more likely than not from the facts giving rise to the presumed fact. [1981 c.892 §18]

40.130 Rule 310. Conflicting presumptions. If presumptions are conflicting, the presumption applies that is founded upon weightier considerations of policy and logic. If considerations of policy and logic are of equal weight, neither presumption applies. [1981 c.892 §19]

40.135 Rule 311. Presumptions. (1) The following are presumptions:

(a) A person intends the ordinary consequences of a voluntary act.

(b) A person takes ordinary care of the person's own concerns.

(c) Evidence willfully suppressed would be adverse to the party suppressing it.

(d) Money paid by one to another was due to the latter.

(e) A thing delivered by one to another belonged to the latter.

(f) An obligation delivered to the debtor has been paid.

(g) A person is the owner of property from exercising acts of ownership over it or from common reputation of the ownership of the person.

(h) A person in possession of an order on that person, for the payment of money or the delivery of a thing, has paid the money or delivered the thing accordingly.

(i) A person acting in a public office was regularly appointed to it.

(j) Official duty has been regularly performed.

(k) A court, or judge acting as such, whether in this state or any other state or country, was acting in the lawful exercise of the jurisdiction of the court.

(L) Private transactions have been fair and regular.

(m) The ordinary course of business has been followed.

(n) A promissory note or bill of exchange was given or indorsed for a sufficient consideration.

(o) An indorsement of a negotiable promissory note, or bill of exchange, was made at the time and place of making the note or bill.

(p) A writing is truly dated.

(q) A letter duly directed and mailed was received in the regular course of the mail.

(r) A person is the same person if the name is identical.

(s) A person not heard from in seven years is dead.

(t) Persons acting as copartners have entered into a contract of copartnership.

(u) Two individuals deporting themselves as legally married to each other have entered into a lawful contract of marriage.

(v) A child born in lawful wedlock is legitimate.

(w) A thing once proved to exist continues as long as is usual with things of that nature.

(x) The law has been obeyed.

(y) An uninterrupted adverse possession of real property for 20 years or more has been held pursuant to a written conveyance.

(z) A trustee or other person whose duty it was to convey real property to a particular person has actually conveyed it to the person, when such presumption is necessary to perfect the title of the person or the person's successor in interest.

(2) A statute providing that a fact or a group of facts is prima facie evidence of another fact establishes a presumption within the meaning of this section. [1981 c.892 §20; 2016 c.46 §2]

RELEVANCY

40.150 Rule 401. Definition of "relevant evidence." "Relevant evidence" means evidence having any tendency to make the existence of any fact that is of consequence to the determination of the action more probable or less probable than it would be without the evidence. [1981 c.892 §21]

40.155 Rule 402. Relevant evidence generally admissible. All relevant evidence is admissible, except as otherwise provided by the Oregon Evidence Code, by the Constitutions of the United States and Oregon, or by Oregon statutory and decisional law. Evidence which is not relevant is not admissible. [1981 c.892 §22]

40.160 Rule 403. Exclusion of relevant evidence on grounds of prejudice, confusion or undue delay. Although relevant, evidence may be excluded if its probative value is substantially outweighed by the danger of unfair prejudice, confusion of the issues, or misleading the jury, or by considerations of undue delay or needless presentation of cumulative evidence. [1981 c.892 §23]

40.170 Rule 404. Character evidence; evidence of other crimes, wrongs or acts. (1) Evidence of a person's character or trait of character is admissible when it is an essential element of a charge, claim or defense.

(2) Evidence of a person's character is not admissible for the purpose of proving that the person acted in conformity therewith on a particular occasion, except:

(a) Evidence of a pertinent trait of character offered by an accused, or by the prosecution to rebut the same;

(b) Evidence of a pertinent trait of character of the victim of the crime offered by an accused, or by the prosecution to rebut the same or evidence of a character trait of peacefulness of the victim offered by the prosecution to rebut evidence that the victim was the first aggressor;

(c) Evidence of the character of a witness, as provided in ORS 40.345 to 40.355; or

(d) Evidence of the character of a party for violent behavior offered in a civil assault and battery case when self-defense is pleaded and there is evidence to support such defense.

(3) Evidence of other crimes, wrongs or acts is not admissible to prove the character of a person in order to show that the person acted in conformity therewith. It may, however, be admissible for other purposes, such as proof of motive, opportunity, intent, preparation, plan, knowledge, identity, or absence of mistake or accident.

(4) In criminal actions, evidence of other crimes, wrongs or acts by the defendant is admissible if relevant except as otherwise provided by:

(a) ORS 40.180, 40.185, 40.190, 40.195, 40.200, 40.205, 40.210 and, to the extent required by the United States Constitution or the Oregon Constitution, ORS 40.160;

(b) The rules of evidence relating to privilege and hearsay;

(c) The Oregon Constitution; and

(d) The United States Constitution. [1981 c.892 §24; 1997 c.313 §29]

40.172 Rule 404-1. Pattern, practice or history of abuse; expert testimony. (1) In any proceeding, any party may introduce evidence establishing a pattern, practice or history of abuse of a person and may introduce expert testimony to assist the fact finder in understanding the significance of such evidence if the evidence:

(a) Is relevant to any material issue in the proceeding; and

(b) Is not inadmissible under any other provision of law including, but not limited to, rules regarding relevance, privilege, hearsay, competency and authentication.

(2) This section may not be construed to limit any evidence that would otherwise be admissible under the Oregon Evidence Code or any other provision of law.

(3) As used in this section, "abuse" has the meaning given that term in ORS 107.705. [1997 c.397 §2]

Note: 40.172 was added to and made a part of 40.010 to 40.585 by legislative action but was not added to any smaller series therein. See Preface to Oregon Revised Statutes for further explanation.

40.175 Rule 405. Methods of proving character. (1) In all cases in which evidence of character or a trait of character of a person is admissible, proof may be made by testimony as to reputation or by testimony in the form of an opinion. On cross-examination, inquiry is allowable into relevant specific instances of conduct.

(2)(a) In cases in which character or a trait of character of a person is admissible under ORS 40.170 (1), proof may also be made of specific instances of the conduct of the person.

(b) When evidence is admissible under ORS 40.170 (3) or (4), proof may be made of specific instances of the conduct of the person. [1981 c.892 §25; 1997 c.313 §34]

40.180 Rule 406. Habit; routine practice. (1) Evidence of the habit of a person or of the routine practice of an organization, whether corroborated or not and regardless of the presence of eyewitnesses, is relevant to prove that the conduct of the person or organization on a particular occasion was in conformity with the habit or routine practice.

(2) As used in this section, "habit" means a person's regular practice of meeting a particular kind of situation with a specific, distinctive type of conduct. [1981 c.892 §21]

40.185 Rule 407. Subsequent remedial measures. When, after an event, measures are taken which, if taken previously, would have made the event less likely to occur, evidence of the subsequent measures is not admissible to prove negligence or culpable conduct in connection with the event. This section does not require the exclusion of evidence of subsequent measures when offered for another purpose, such as proving ownership, control, or feasibility of precautionary measures, if controverted, or impeachment. [1981 c.892 §27]

40.190 Rule 408. Compromise and offers to compromise. (1)(a) Evidence of furnishing or offering or promising to furnish, or accepting or offering or promising to accept, a valuable consideration in compromising or attempting to compromise a claim which was disputed as to either validity or amount, is not admissible to prove liability for or invalidity of the claim or its amount.

(b) Evidence of conduct or statements made in compromise negotiations is likewise not admissible.

(2)(a) Subsection (1) of this section does not require the exclusion of any evidence otherwise discoverable merely because it is presented in the course of compromise negotiations.

(b) Subsection (1) of this section also does not require exclusion when the evidence is offered for another purpose, such as proving bias or prejudice of a witness, negating a contention of undue delay, or proving an effort to obstruct a criminal investigation or prosecution. [1981 c.892 §28]

40.195 Rule 409. Payment of medical and similar expenses. Evidence of furnishing or offering or promising to pay medical, hospital or similar expenses occasioned by an injury is not admissible to prove liability for the injury. Evidence of payment for damages arising from injury or destruction of property is not admissible to prove liability for the injury or destruction. [1981 c.892 §29]

40.200 Rule 410. Withdrawn plea or statement not admissible. (1) A plea of guilty or no contest which is not accepted or has been withdrawn shall not be received against the defendant in any criminal proceeding.

(2) No statement or admission made by a defendant or a defendant's attorney during any proceeding relating to a plea of guilty or no contest which is not accepted or has been withdrawn shall be received against the defendant in any criminal proceeding. [1981 c.892 §29a]

40.205 Rule 411. Liability insurance. (1) Except where lack of liability insurance is an element of an offense, evidence that a person was or was not insured against liability is not admissible upon the issue whether the person acted negligently or otherwise wrongfully.

(2) Subsection (1) of this section does not require the exclusion of evidence of insurance against liability when offered for another purpose, such as proving agency, ownership or control, or bias, prejudice or motive of a witness. [1981 c.892 §30]

40.210 Rule 412. Sex offense cases; relevance of victim's past behavior or manner of dress. (1) Notwithstanding any other provision of law, in a prosecution for a crime described in ORS 163.266 (1)(b) or (c), 163.355 to 163.427, 163.670 or 167.017, in a prosecution for an attempt to commit one of those crimes or in a proceeding conducted under ORS 163.760 to 163.777, the following evidence is not admissible:

(a) Reputation or opinion evidence of the past sexual behavior of an alleged victim or a corroborating witness; or

(b) Reputation or opinion evidence presented for the purpose of showing that the manner of dress of an alleged victim incited the crime or, in a proceeding under ORS 163.760 to 163.777, incited the sexual abuse, or indicated consent to the sexual acts that are alleged.

(2) Notwithstanding any other provision of law, in a prosecution for a crime or an attempt to commit a crime listed in subsection (1) of this section or in a proceeding conducted under ORS 163.760 to 163.777, evidence of an alleged victim's past sexual behavior other than reputation or opinion evidence is also not admissible, unless the evidence other than reputation or opinion evidence:

(a) Is admitted in accordance with subsection (4) of this section; and

(b) Is evidence that:

(A) Relates to the motive or bias of the alleged victim;

(B) Is necessary to rebut or explain scientific or medical evidence offered by the state; or

(C) Is otherwise constitutionally required to be admitted.

(3) Notwithstanding any other provision of law, in a prosecution for a crime or an attempt to commit a crime listed in subsection (1) of this section or in a proceeding conducted under ORS 163.760 to 163.777, evidence, other than reputation or opinion evidence, of the manner of dress of the alleged victim or a corroborating witness, presented by a person accused of committing the crime or, in a proceeding conducted under ORS 163.760 to 163.777, by the respondent, is also not admissible, unless the evidence is:

(a) Admitted in accordance with subsection (4) of this section; and

(b) Is evidence that:

(A) Relates to the motive or bias of the alleged victim;

(B) Is necessary to rebut or explain scientific, medical or testimonial evidence offered by the state;

(C) Is necessary to establish the identity of the alleged victim; or

(D) Is otherwise constitutionally required to be admitted.

(4)(a) If the person accused of a crime or an attempt to commit a crime listed in subsection (1) of this section, or the respondent in a proceeding conducted under ORS 163.760 to 163.777, intends to offer evidence under subsection (2) or (3) of this section, the accused or the respondent shall make a written motion to offer the evidence not later than 15 days before the date on which the trial in which the evidence is to be offered is scheduled to begin, except that the court may allow the motion to be made at a later date, including during trial, if the court determines either that the evidence is newly discovered and could not have been obtained earlier through the exercise of due diligence or that the issue to which the evidence relates has newly arisen in the case. Any motion made under this paragraph shall be served on all other parties and, in a criminal proceeding, on the alleged victim through the office of the prosecutor.

(b) The motion described in paragraph (a) of this subsection shall be accompanied by a written offer of proof. If the court determines that the offer of proof contains evidence described in subsection (2) or (3) of this section, the court shall order a hearing in camera to determine if the evidence is admissible. At the hearing the parties may call witnesses, including the alleged victim, and offer relevant evidence. Notwithstanding ORS 40.030 (2), if the relevancy of the evidence that the accused or the respondent seeks to offer in the trial depends upon the fulfillment of a condition of fact, the court, at the hearing in camera or at a subsequent hearing in camera scheduled for the same purpose, shall accept evidence on the issue of whether the condition of fact is fulfilled and shall determine the issue.

(c) If the court determines on the basis of the hearing described in paragraph (b) of this subsection that the evidence the accused or the respondent seeks to offer is relevant and that the probative value of the evidence outweighs the danger of unfair prejudice, the evidence shall be admissible in the trial to the extent an order made by the court specifies evidence that may be offered and areas with respect to which a witness may be examined or cross-examined.

(d) An order admitting evidence under this subsection in a criminal prosecution may be appealed by the state before trial.

(5) For purposes of this section:

(a) "Alleged victim" includes the petitioner in a proceeding conducted under ORS 163.760 to 163.777.

(b) "In camera" means out of the presence of the public and the jury.

(c) "Past sexual behavior" means sexual behavior other than:

(A) The sexual behavior with respect to which the crime or attempt to commit the crime listed in subsection (1) of this section is alleged; or

(B) In a proceeding conducted under ORS 163.760 to 163.777, the alleged sexual abuse.

(d) "Trial" includes a hearing conducted under ORS 163.760 to 163.777. [1981 c.892 §31; 1993 c.301 §1; 1993 c.776 §1; 1997 c.249 §20; 1999 c.949 §3; 2013 c.687 §21; 2013 c.720 §5]

40.211 Rule 412-1. Evidence not admissible in civil proceeding involving sexual misconduct. (1) Unless the alleged victim has placed the evidence in controversy and the court determines that the probative value of the evidence substantially outweighs the danger of harm to any victim and of unfair prejudice to any party, the following evidence is not admissible in a civil proceeding involving alleged sexual misconduct:

(a) Evidence offered to prove that an alleged victim engaged in other sexual behavior; or

(b) Evidence offered to prove an alleged victim's sexual predisposition.

(2) If a party intends to offer evidence under subsection (1) of this section, the party must:

(a) Make a written motion at least 15 days before the date on which the proceeding in which the evidence is to be offered is scheduled to begin unless the court, for good cause, sets a different time;

(b) In the motion, specifically describe the evidence and state the purpose for which it is to be offered;

(c) Serve the motion on all parties; and

(d) Notify the alleged victim or the alleged victim's representative.

(3) Before admitting evidence under this section, the court must conduct an in camera hearing and give the alleged victim and parties a right to attend and be heard. Unless the court orders otherwise, the motion, related materials and the record of the hearing are confidential. A party making a motion under this section shall state in the caption that the motion is confidential.

(4) As used in this section, "in camera" means out of the presence of the public and the jury. [2017 c.321 §2]

40.215 Rule 413. Measures and assessments intended to minimize impact of or plan for natural disaster. Evidence of measures taken or vulnerability assessments conducted before a natural disaster occurs that were intended to minimize the impact of or plan for the natural disaster is not admissible to prove negligence or culpable conduct in connection with damage, harm, injury or death resulting from the natural disaster. [2015 c.541 §2]

PRIVILEGES

40.225 Rule 503. Lawyer-client privilege. (1) As used in this section, unless the context requires otherwise:

(a) "Client" means a person, public officer, corporation, association or other organization or entity, either public or private, who is rendered professional legal services by a lawyer, or who consults a lawyer with a view to obtaining professional legal services from the lawyer.

(b) "Confidential communication" means a communication not intended to be disclosed to third persons other than those to whom disclosure is in furtherance of the rendition of professional legal services to the client or those reasonably necessary for the transmission of the communication.

(c) "Lawyer" means a person authorized, or reasonably believed by the client to be authorized, to practice law in any state or nation.

(d) "Representative of the client" means:

(A) A principal, an officer or a director of the client; or

(B) A person who has authority to obtain professional legal services, or to act on legal advice rendered, on behalf of the client, or a person who, for the purpose of effectuating legal representation for the client, makes or receives a confidential communication while acting in the person's scope of employment for the client.

(e) "Representative of the lawyer" means one employed to assist the lawyer in the rendition of professional legal services, but does not include a physician making a physical or mental examination under ORCP 44.

(2) A client has a privilege to refuse to disclose and to prevent any other person from disclosing confidential communications made for the purpose of facilitating the rendition of professional legal services to the client:

(a) Between the client or the client's representative and the client's lawyer or a representative of the lawyer;

(b) Between the client's lawyer and the lawyer's representative;

(c) By the client or the client's lawyer to a lawyer representing another in a matter of common interest;

(d) Between representatives of the client or between the client and a representative of the client; or

(e) Between lawyers representing the client.

(3) The privilege created by this section may be claimed by the client, a guardian or conservator of the client, the personal representative of a deceased client, or the successor, trustee, or similar representative of a corporation, association, or other organization, whether or not in existence. The person who was the lawyer or the lawyer's representative at the time of the communication is presumed to have authority to claim the privilege but only on behalf of the client.

(4) There is no privilege under this section:

(a) If the services of the lawyer were sought or obtained to enable or aid anyone to commit or plan to commit what the client knew or reasonably should have known to be a crime or fraud;

(b) As to a communication relevant to an issue between parties who claim through the same deceased client, regardless of whether the claims are by testate or intestate succession or by inter vivos transaction;

(c) As to a communication relevant to an issue of breach of duty by the lawyer to the client or by the client to the lawyer;

(d) As to a communication relevant to an issue concerning an attested document to which the lawyer is an attesting witness; or

(e) As to a communication relevant to a matter of common interest between two or more clients if the communication was made by any of them to a lawyer retained or consulted in common, when offered in an action between any of the clients.

(5) Notwithstanding ORS 40.280, a privilege is maintained under this section for a communication made to the office of public defense services established under ORS 151.216 for the purpose of seeking preauthorization for or payment of nonroutine fees or expenses under ORS 135.055.

(6) Notwithstanding subsection (4)(c) of this section and ORS 40.280, a privilege is maintained under this section for a communication that is made to the office of public defense services established under ORS 151.216 for the purpose of making, or providing information regarding, a complaint against a lawyer providing public defense services.

(7) Notwithstanding ORS 40.280, a privilege is maintained under this section for a communication ordered to be disclosed under ORS 192.311 to 192.478. [1981 c.892 §32; 1987 c.680 §1; 2005 c.356 §1; 2005 c.358 §1; 2007 c.513 §3; 2009 c.516 §1]

40.230 Rule 504. Psychotherapist-patient privilege. (1) As used in this section, unless the context requires otherwise:

(a) "Confidential communication" means a communication not intended to be disclosed to third persons except:

(A) Persons present to further the interest of the patient in the consultation, examination or interview;

(B) Persons reasonably necessary for the transmission of the communication; or

(C) Persons who are participating in the diagnosis and treatment under the direction of the psychotherapist, including members of the patient's family.

(b) "Patient" means a person who consults or is examined or interviewed by a psychotherapist.

(c) "Psychotherapist" means a person who is:

(A) Licensed, registered, certified or otherwise authorized under the laws of any state to engage in the diagnosis or treatment of a mental or emotional condition; or

(B) Reasonably believed by the patient so to be, while so engaged.

(2) A patient has a privilege to refuse to disclose and to prevent any other person from disclosing confidential communications made for the purposes of diagnosis or treatment of the patient's mental or emotional condition among the patient, the patient's psychotherapist or persons who are participating in the diagnosis or treatment under the direction of the psychotherapist, including members of the patient's family.

(3) The privilege created by this section may be claimed by:

(a) The patient.

(b) A guardian or conservator of the patient.

(c) The personal representative of a deceased patient.

(d) The person who was the psychotherapist, but only on behalf of the patient. The psychotherapist's authority so to do is presumed in the absence of evidence to the contrary.

(4) The following is a nonexclusive list of limits on the privilege granted by this section:

(a) If the judge orders an examination of the mental, physical or emotional condition of the patient, communications made in the course thereof are not privileged under this section with respect to the particular purpose for which the examination is ordered unless the judge orders otherwise.

(b) There is no privilege under this rule as to communications relevant to an issue of the mental or emotional condition of the patient:

(A) In any proceeding in which the patient relies upon the condition as an element of the patient's claim or defense; or

(B) After the patient's death, in any proceeding in which any party relies upon the condition as an element of the party's claim or defense.

(c) Except as provided in ORCP 44, there is no privilege under this section for communications made in the course of mental examination performed under ORCP 44.

(d) There is no privilege under this section with regard to any confidential communication or record of such confidential communication that would otherwise be privileged under this section when the use of the communication or record is allowed specifically under ORS 426.070, 426.074, 426.075, 426.095, 426.120 or 426.307. This paragraph only applies to the use of the communication or record to the extent and for the purposes set forth in the described statute sections. [1981 c.892 §33; 1987 c.903 §1]

40.235 Rule 504-1. Physician-patient privilege. (1) As used in this section, unless the context requires otherwise:

(a) "Confidential communication" means a communication not intended to be disclosed to third persons except:

(A) Persons present to further the interest of the patient in the consultation, examination or interview;

(B) Persons reasonably necessary for the transmission of the communication; or

(C) Persons who are participating in the diagnosis and treatment under the direction of the physician, including members of the patient's family.

(b) "Patient" means a person who consults or is examined or interviewed by a physician.

(c)(A) "Physician" means a person authorized or licensed and licensed or certified to practice medicine, podiatry or dentistry in any state or nation, or reasonably believed by the patient so to be, while engaged in the diagnosis or treatment of a physical condition.

(B) "Physician" includes licensed or certified naturopathic and chiropractic physicians and dentists.

(2) A patient has a privilege to refuse to disclose and to prevent any other person from disclosing confidential communications in a civil action, suit or proceeding, made for the purposes of diagnosis or treatment of the patient's physical condition, among the patient, the patient's physician or persons who are participating in the diagnosis or treatment under the direction of the physician, including members of the patient's family.

(3) The privilege created by this section may be claimed by:

(a) The patient;

(b) A guardian or conservator of the patient;

(c) The personal representative of a deceased patient; or

(d) The person who was the physician, but only on behalf of the patient. Such person's authority so to do is presumed in the absence of evidence to the contrary.

(4) The following is a nonexclusive list of limits on the privilege granted by this section:

(a) If the judge orders an examination of the physical condition of the patient, communications made in the course thereof are not privileged under this section with respect to the particular purpose for which the examination is ordered unless the judge orders otherwise.

(b) Except as provided in ORCP 44, there is no privilege under this section for communications made in the course of a physical examination performed under ORCP 44.

(c) There is no privilege under this section with regard to any confidential communication or record of such confidential communication that would otherwise be privileged under this section when the use of the communication or record is specifically allowed under ORS 426.070, 426.074, 426.075, 426.095, 426.120 or 426.307. This paragraph only applies to the use of the communication or record to the extent and for the purposes set forth in the described statute sections. [1981 c.892 §33a; 1987 c.903 §2; 2005 c.353 §1; 2013 c.129 §3]

40.240 Rule 504-2. Nurse-patient privilege. A licensed professional nurse shall not, without the consent of a patient who was cared for by such nurse, be examined in a civil action or proceeding, as to any information acquired in caring for the patient, which was necessary to enable the nurse to care for the patient. [1981 c.892 §33b]

40.245 Rule 504-3. School employee-student privilege. (1) A certificated staff member of an elementary or secondary school shall not be examined in any civil action or proceeding, as to any conversation between the certificated staff member and a student which relates to the personal affairs of the student or family of the student, and which if disclosed would tend to damage or incriminate the student or family. Any violation of the privilege provided by this subsection may result in the suspension of certification of the professional staff member as provided in ORS 342.175, 342.177 and 342.180.

(2) A certificated school counselor regularly employed and designated in such capacity by a public school shall not, without the consent of the student, be examined as to any communication made by the student to the counselor in the official capacity of the counselor in any civil action or proceeding or a criminal action or proceeding in which such student is a party concerning the past use, abuse or sale of drugs, controlled substances or alcoholic liquor. Any violation of the privilege provided by this subsection may result in the suspension of certification of the professional school counselor as provided in ORS 342.175, 342.177 and 342.180. However, in the event that the student's condition presents a clear and imminent danger to the student or to others, the counselor shall report this fact to an appropriate responsible authority or take such other emergency measures as the situation demands. [1981 c.892 §33c]

40.250 Rule 504-4. Regulated social worker-client privilege. A regulated social worker under ORS 675.510 to 675.600 may not be examined in a civil or criminal court proceeding as to any communication given the regulated social worker by a client in the course of noninvestigatory professional activity when the communication was given to enable the regulated social worker to aid the client, except when:

(1) The client or a person legally responsible for the client's affairs gives consent to the disclosure;

(2) The client initiates legal action or makes a complaint against the regulated social worker to the State Board of Licensed Social Workers;

(3) The communication reveals a clear intent to commit a crime that reasonably is expected to result in physical injury to a person;

(4) The communication reveals that a minor was the victim of a crime, abuse or neglect; or

(5) The regulated social worker is a public employee and the public employer has determined that examination in a civil or criminal court proceeding is necessary in the performance of the duty of the regulated social worker as a public employee. [1981 c.892 §33d; 1989 c.721 §46; 2009 c.442 §28]

40.252 Rule 504-5. Communications revealing intent to commit certain crimes. (1) In addition to any other limitations on privilege that may be imposed by law, there is no privilege under ORS 40.225, 40.230, 40.250 or 40.264 for communications if:

(a) In the professional judgment of the person receiving the communications, the communications reveal that the declarant has a clear and serious intent at the time the communications are made to subsequently commit a crime involving physical injury, a threat to the physical safety of any person, sexual abuse or death or involving an act described in ORS 167.322;

(b) In the professional judgment of the person receiving the communications, the declarant poses a danger of committing the crime; and

(c) The person receiving the communications makes a report to another person based on the communications.

(2) The provisions of this section do not create a duty to report any communication to any person.

(3) A person who discloses a communication described in subsection (1) of this section, or fails to disclose a communication described in subsection (1) of this section, is not liable to any other person in a civil action for any damage or injury arising out of the disclosure or failure to disclose. [2001 c.640 §2; 2007 c.731 §4; 2015 c.265 §3]

Note: 40.252 was added to and made a part of 40.225 to 40.295 by legislative action but was not added to any smaller series therein. See Preface to Oregon Revised Statutes for further explanation.

40.255 Rule 505. Spousal privilege. (1) As used in this section, unless the context requires otherwise:

(a) "Confidential communication" means a communication by a spouse to the other spouse and not intended to be disclosed to any other person.

(b) "Marriage" means a marital relationship between two individuals, legally recognized under the laws of this state.

(c) "Spouse" means an individual in a marriage with another individual.

(2) In any civil or criminal action, a spouse has a privilege to refuse to disclose and to prevent the other spouse from disclosing any confidential communication made by one spouse to the other during the marriage. The privilege created by this subsection may be claimed by either spouse. The authority of the spouse to claim the privilege and the claiming of the privilege is presumed in the absence of evidence to the contrary.

(3) In any criminal proceeding, neither spouse, during the marriage, shall be examined adversely against the other as to any other matter occurring during the marriage unless the spouse called as a witness consents to testify.

(4) There is no privilege under this section:

(a) In all criminal actions in which one spouse is charged with bigamy or with an offense or attempted offense against the person or property of the other spouse or of a child of either, or with an offense against the person or property of a third person committed in the course of committing or attempting to commit an offense against the other spouse;

(b) As to matters occurring prior to the marriage; or

(c) In any civil action where the spouses are adverse parties. [1981 c.892 §34; 1983 c.433 §1; 2016 c.46 §1]

40.260 Rule 506. Member of clergy-penitent privilege. (1) As used in this section, unless the context requires otherwise:

(a) "Confidential communication" means a communication made privately and not intended for further disclosure except to other persons present in furtherance of the purpose of the communication.

(b) "Member of the clergy" means a minister of any church, religious denomination or organization or accredited Christian Science practitioner who in the course of the discipline or practice of that church, denomination or organization is authorized or accustomed to hearing confidential communications and, under the discipline or tenets of that church, denomination or organization, has a duty to keep such communications secret.

(2) A member of the clergy may not be examined as to any confidential communication made to the member of the clergy in the member's professional character unless consent to the disclosure of the confidential communication is given by the person who made the communication.

(3) Even though the person who made the communication has given consent to the disclosure, a member of the clergy may not be examined as to any confidential communication made to the member in the member's professional character if, under the discipline or tenets of the member's church, denomination or organization, the member has an absolute duty to keep the communication confidential. [1981 c.892 §35; 1999 c.7 §1]

40.262 Rule 507. Counselor-client privilege. A professional counselor or a marriage and family therapist licensed by the Oregon Board of Licensed Professional Counselors and Therapists under ORS 675.715 shall not be examined in a civil or criminal court proceeding as to any communication given the counselor or therapist by a client in the course of a noninvestigatory professional activity when such communication was given to enable the counselor or the therapist to aid the client, except:

(1) When the client or those persons legally responsible for the affairs of the client give consent to the disclosure. If both parties to a marriage have obtained marital and family therapy by a licensed marital and family therapist or a licensed counselor, the therapist or counselor shall not be competent to testify in a domestic relations action other than child custody action concerning information acquired in the course of the therapeutic relationship unless both parties consent;

(2) When the client initiates legal action or makes a complaint against the licensed professional counselor or licensed marriage and family therapist to the board;

(3) When the communication reveals the intent to commit a crime or harmful act; or

(4) When the communication reveals that a minor is or is suspected to be the victim of crime, abuse or neglect. [1989 c.721 §20]

Note: 40.262 was added to and made a part of 40.010 to 40.585 by legislative action but was not added to any smaller series therein. See Preface to Oregon Revised Statutes for further explanation.

40.264 Rule 507-1. Certified advocate-victim privilege. (1) As used in this section:
(a) "Certified advocate" means a person who:
(A) Has completed at least 40 hours of training in advocacy for victims of domestic violence, sexual assault or stalking, approved by the Attorney General by rule; and
(B) Is an employee or a volunteer of a qualified victim services program.
(b) "Confidential communication" means a written or oral communication that is not intended for further disclosure, except to:
(A) Persons present at the time the communication is made who are present to further the interests of the victim in the course of seeking safety planning, counseling, support or advocacy services;
(B) Persons reasonably necessary for the transmission of the communication; or
(C) Other persons, in the context of group counseling.
(c) "Qualified victim services program" means:
(A) A nongovernmental, nonprofit, community-based program receiving moneys administered by the state Department of Human Services or the Oregon or United States Department of Justice, or a program administered by a tribal government, that offers safety planning, counseling, support or advocacy services to victims of domestic violence, sexual assault or stalking; or
(B) A sexual assault center, victim advocacy office, women's center, student affairs center, health center or other program providing safety planning, counseling, support or advocacy services to victims that is on the campus of or affiliated with a two- or four-year post-secondary institution that enrolls one or more students who receive an Oregon Opportunity Grant.
(d) "Victim" means a person seeking safety planning, counseling, support or advocacy services related to domestic violence, sexual assault or stalking at a qualified victim services program.
(2) Except as provided in subsection (3) of this section, a victim has a privilege to refuse to disclose and to prevent any other person from disclosing:
(a) Confidential communications made by the victim to a certified advocate in the course of safety planning, counseling, support or advocacy services.
(b) Records that are created or maintained in the course of providing services regarding the victim.
(3) The privilege established by this section does not apply to the disclosure of confidential communications, only to the extent disclosure is necessary for defense, in any civil, criminal or administrative action that is brought against the certified advocate, or against the qualified victim services program, by or on behalf of the victim.
(4) The privilege established in this section is not waived by disclosure of the communications by the certified advocate to another person if the disclosure is reasonably necessary to accomplish the purpose for which the certified advocate is consulted.
(5) This section does not prohibit the disclosure of aggregate, nonpersonally identifying data.
(6) This section applies to civil, criminal and administrative proceedings and to institutional disciplinary proceedings at a two-year or four-year post-secondary institution that enrolls one or more students who receive an Oregon Opportunity Grant. [2015 c.265 §2; 2017 c.256 §1]

Note: 40.264 was added to and made a part of 40.225 to 40.295 by legislative action but was not added to any smaller series therein. See Preface to Oregon Revised Statutes for further explanation.

40.265 Rule 508a. Stenographer-employer privilege. A stenographer shall not, without the consent of the stenographer's employer, be examined as to any communication or dictation made by the employer to the stenographer in the course of professional employment. [1981 c.892 §36]

40.270 Rule 509. Public officer privilege. A public officer shall not be examined as to public records determined to be exempt from disclosure under ORS 192.338, 192.345 and 192.355. [1981 c.892 §37]

40.272 Rule 509-1. Sign language interpreter privilege. (1) As used in this section:
(a) "Person with a disability" means a person who cannot readily understand or communicate the spoken English language, or cannot understand proceedings in which the person is involved, because of deafness or because of a physical hearing impairment or cannot communicate in the proceedings because of a physical speaking impairment.
(b) "Sign language interpreter" or "interpreter" means a person who translates conversations or other communications for a person with a disability or translates the statements of a person with a disability.
(2) A person with a disability has a privilege to refuse to disclose and to prevent a sign language interpreter from disclosing any communications to which the person with a disability was a party that were made while the interpreter was providing interpretation services for the person with a disability. The privilege created by this section extends only to those communications between a person with a disability and another, and translated by the interpreter, that would otherwise be privileged under ORS 40.225 to 40.295. [1993 c.179 §2; 2007 c.70 §11]

Note: 40.272 was added to and made a part of 40.225 to 40.295 by legislative action but was not added to any smaller series therein. See Preface to Oregon Revised Statutes for further explanation.

40.273 Rule 509-2. Non-English-speaking person-interpreter privilege. (1) As used in this section:
(a) "Interpreter" means a person who translates conversations or other communications for a non-English-speaking person or translates the statements of a non-English-speaking person.
(b) "Non-English-speaking person" means a person who, by reason of place of birth or culture, speaks a language other than English and does not speak English with adequate ability to communicate in the proceedings.
(2) A non-English-speaking person has a privilege to refuse to disclose and to prevent an interpreter from disclosing any communications to which the non-English-speaking person was a party that were made while the interpreter was providing interpretation services for the non-English-speaking person. The privilege created by this section extends only to those communications between a non-English-speaking person and another, and translated by the interpreter, that would otherwise be privileged under ORS 40.225 to 40.295. [1993 c.179 §3]

Note: 40.273 was enacted into law by the Legislative Assembly but was not added to or made a part of ORS chapter 40 or any series therein by legislative action. See Preface to Oregon Revised Statutes for further explanation.

40.275 Rule 510. Identity of informer. (1) As used in this section, "unit of government" means:
(a) The federal government or any state or political subdivision thereof;
(b) A university that has commissioned police officers under ORS 352.121 or 353.125; or
(c) A tribal government as defined in ORS 181A.680, if the information referred to in this section relates to or assists in an investigation conducted by an authorized tribal police officer as defined in ORS 181A.680.
(2) A unit of government has a privilege to refuse to disclose the identity of a person who has furnished information relating to or assisting in an investigation of a possible violation of law to a law enforcement officer or member of a legislative committee or its staff conducting an investigation.
(3) The privilege created by this section may be claimed by an appropriate representative of the unit of government if the information was furnished to an officer thereof.

(4) No privilege exists under this section:

(a) If the identity of the informer or the informer's interest in the subject matter of the communication has been disclosed to those who would have cause to resent the communication by a holder of the privilege or by the informer's own action, or if the informer appears as a witness for the unit of government.

(b) If it appears from the evidence in the case or from other showing by a party that an informer may be able to give testimony necessary to a fair determination of the issue of guilt or innocence in a criminal case or of a material issue on the merits in a civil case to which the unit of government is a party, and the unit of government invokes the privilege, and the judge gives the unit of government an opportunity to show in camera facts relevant to determining whether the informer can, in fact, supply that testimony. The showing will ordinarily be in the form of affidavits, but the judge may direct that testimony be taken if the judge finds that the matter cannot be resolved satisfactorily upon affidavit. If the judge finds that there is a reasonable probability that the informer can give the testimony, and the unit of government elects not to disclose identity of the informer, the judge on motion of the defendant in a criminal case shall dismiss the charges to which the testimony would relate, and the judge may do so on the judge's own motion. In civil cases, the judge may make any order that justice requires. Evidence submitted to the judge shall be sealed and preserved to be made available to the appellate court in the event of an appeal, and the contents shall not otherwise be revealed without consent of the unit of government. All counsel and parties shall be permitted to be present at every stage of proceedings under this paragraph except a showing in camera, at which no counsel or party shall be permitted to be present.

(c) If information from an informer is relied upon to establish the legality of the means by which evidence was obtained and the judge is not satisfied that the information was received from an informer reasonably believed to be reliable or credible. The judge may require the identity of the informer to be disclosed. The judge shall, on request of the unit of government, direct that the disclosure be made in camera. All counsel and parties concerned with the issue of legality shall be permitted to be present at every stage of proceedings under this paragraph except a disclosure in camera, at which no counsel or party shall be permitted to be present. If disclosure of the identity of the informer is made in camera, the record thereof shall be sealed and preserved to be made available to the appellate court in the event of an appeal, and the contents shall not otherwise be revealed without consent of the unit of government. [1981 c.892 §38; 2011 c.506 §2; 2011 c.644 §§10,37; 2013 c.180 §§2,3; 2015 c.174 §2]

40.280 Rule 511. Waiver of privilege by voluntary disclosure. A person upon whom ORS 40.225 to 40.295 confer a privilege against disclosure of the confidential matter or communication waives the privilege if the person or the person's predecessor while holder of the privilege voluntarily discloses or consents to disclosure of any significant part of the matter or communication. This section does not apply if the disclosure is itself a privileged communication. Voluntary disclosure does not occur with the mere commencement of litigation or, in the case of a deposition taken for the purpose of perpetuating testimony, until the offering of the deposition as evidence. Voluntary disclosure does not occur when representatives of the news media are allowed to attend executive sessions of the governing body of a public body as provided in ORS 192.660 (4), or when representatives of the news media disclose information after the governing body has prohibited disclosure of the information under ORS 192.660 (4). Voluntary disclosure does not occur when a public body, as defined in ORS 192.311, discloses information or records in response to a written request for public records made under ORS 192.311 to 192.478. Voluntary disclosure does occur, as to psychotherapists in the case of a mental or emotional condition and physicians in the case of a physical condition upon the holder's offering of any person as a witness who testifies as to the condition. [1981 c.892 §39; 2003 c.259 §1; 2017 c.456 §9]

40.285 Rule 512. Privileged matter disclosed under compulsion or without opportunity to claim privilege. Evidence of a statement or other disclosure of privileged matter is not admissible against the holder of the privilege if the disclosure was:

(1) Compelled erroneously; or

(2) Made without opportunity to claim the privilege. [1981 c.892 §40]

40.290 Rule 513. Comment upon or inference from claim of privilege. (1) The claim of a privilege, whether in the present proceeding or upon a prior occasion, is not a proper subject of comment by judge or counsel. No inference may be drawn from a claim of privilege.

(2) In jury cases, proceedings shall be conducted, to the extent practicable, so as to facilitate the making of claims of privilege without the knowledge of the jury.

(3) Upon request, any party against whom the jury might draw an adverse inference from a claim of privilege is entitled to an instruction that no inference may be drawn therefrom. [1981 c.892 §41]

40.295 Rule 514. Effect on existing privileges. Unless expressly repealed by section 98, chapter 892, Oregon Laws 1981, all existing privileges either created under the Constitution or statutes of the State of Oregon or developed by the courts of Oregon are recognized and shall continue to exist until changed or repealed according to law. [1981 c.892 §42]

WITNESSES

40.310 Rule 601. General rule of competency. Except as provided in ORS 40.310 to 40.335, any person who, having organs of sense can perceive, and perceiving can make known the perception to others, may be a witness. [1981 c.892 §43]

40.315 Rule 602. Lack of personal knowledge. Subject to the provisions of ORS 40.415, a witness may not testify to a matter unless evidence is introduced sufficient to support a finding that the witness has personal knowledge of the matter. Evidence to prove personal knowledge may, but need not, consist of the testimony of the witness. [1981 c.892 §44]

40.320 Rule 603. Oath or affirmation. (1) Before testifying, every witness shall be required to declare that the witness will testify truthfully, by oath or affirmation administered in a form calculated to awaken the conscience of the witness and impress the mind of the witness with the duty to do so.

(2) An oath may be administered as follows: The person who swears holds up one hand while the person administering the oath asks: "Under penalty of perjury, do you solemnly swear that the evidence you shall give in the issue (or matter) now pending between _____ and _____ shall be the truth, the whole truth and nothing but the truth, so help you God?" If the oath is administered to any other than a witness, the same form and manner may be used. The person swearing must answer in an affirmative manner.

(3) An affirmation may be administered as follows: The person who affirms holds up one hand while the person administering the affirmation asks: "Under penalty of perjury, do you promise that the evidence you shall give in the issue (or matter) now pending between _____ and _____ shall be the truth, the whole truth and nothing but the truth?" If the affirmation is administered to any other than a witness, the same form and manner may be used. The person affirming must answer in an affirmative manner. [1981 c.892 §45]

40.325 Rule 604. Interpreters. Except as provided in ORS 45.275 (7), an interpreter is subject to the provisions of the Oregon Evidence Code relating to qualification as an expert and the administration of an oath or affirmation that the interpreter will make a true and impartial interpretation of the proceedings in an understandable manner using the interpreter's best skills and judgment in accordance with the standards and ethics of the interpreter profession. [1981 c.892 §47; 1981 s.s. c.3 §138; 1989 c.224 §7; 1991 c.750 §7; 2001 c.242 §4; 2005 c.385 §3; 2015 c.155 §5]

40.330 Rule 605. Competency of judge as witness. The judge presiding at the trial may not testify in that trial as a witness. No objection need be made in order to preserve the point. [1981 c.892 §48]

40.335 Rule 606. Competency of juror as witness. A member of the jury may not testify as a witness before that jury in the trial of the case in which the member has been sworn to sit as a juror. If the juror is called so to testify, the opposing party shall be afforded an opportunity to object out of the presence of the jury. [1981 c.892 §49]

40.340 [1981 c.892 §50; repealed by 1987 c.352 §1]

40.345 Rule 607. Who may impeach. The credibility of a witness may be attacked by any party, including the party calling the witness. [1981 c.892 §51]

40.350 Rule 608. Evidence of character and conduct of witness. (1) The credibility of a witness may be attacked or supported by evidence in the form of opinion or reputation, but:
(a) The evidence may refer only to character for truthfulness or untruthfulness; and
(b) Evidence of truthful character is admissible only after the character of the witness for truthfulness has been attacked by opinion or reputation evidence or otherwise.
(2) Specific instances of the conduct of a witness, for the purpose of attacking or supporting the credibility of the witness, other than conviction of crime as provided in ORS 40.355, may not be proved by extrinsic evidence. Further, such specific instances of conduct may not, even if probative of truthfulness or untruthfulness, be inquired into on cross-examination of the witness. [1981 c.892 §52]

40.355 Rule 609. Impeachment by evidence of conviction of crime; exceptions. (1) For the purpose of attacking the credibility of a witness, evidence that the witness has been convicted of a crime shall be admitted if elicited from the witness or established by public record, but only if the crime:
(a) Was punishable by death or imprisonment in excess of one year under the law under which the witness was convicted; or
(b) Involved false statement or dishonesty.
(2)(a) If a defendant is charged with one or more of the crimes listed in paragraph (b) of this subsection, and the defendant is a witness, evidence that the defendant has been convicted of committing one or more of the following crimes against a family or household member, as defined in ORS 135.230, may be elicited from the defendant, or established by public record, and admitted into evidence for the purpose of attacking the credibility of the defendant:
(A) Assault in the fourth degree under ORS 163.160.
(B) Menacing under ORS 163.190.
(C) Harassment under ORS 166.065.
(D) Attempted assault in the fourth degree under ORS 163.160 (1).
(E) Attempted assault in the fourth degree under ORS 163.160 (3).
(F) Strangulation under ORS 163.187.
(G) The statutory counterpart in another jurisdiction to a crime listed in this paragraph.
(b) Evidence may be admitted into evidence for the purpose of attacking the credibility of a defendant under the provisions of this subsection only if the defendant is charged with committing one or more of the following crimes against a family or household member, as defined in ORS 135.230:
(A) Aggravated murder under ORS 163.095.
(B) Murder under ORS 163.115.
(C) Manslaughter in the first degree under ORS 163.118.
(D) Manslaughter in the second degree under ORS 163.125.
(E) Assault in the first degree under ORS 163.185.
(F) Assault in the second degree under ORS 163.175.
(G) Assault in the third degree under ORS 163.165.
(H) Assault in the fourth degree under ORS 163.160.
(I) Rape in the first degree under ORS 163.375 (1)(a).
(J) Sodomy in the first degree under ORS 163.405 (1)(a).
(K) Unlawful sexual penetration in the first degree under ORS 163.411 (1)(a).
(L) Sexual abuse in the first degree under ORS 163.427 (1)(a)(B).
(M) Kidnapping in the first degree under ORS 163.235.
(N) Kidnapping in the second degree under ORS 163.225.
(O) Burglary in the first degree under ORS 164.225.
(P) Coercion under ORS 163.275.
(Q) Stalking under ORS 163.732.
(R) Violating a court's stalking protective order under ORS 163.750.
(S) Menacing under ORS 163.190.
(T) Harassment under ORS 166.065.
(U) Strangulation under ORS 163.187.
(V) Attempting to commit a crime listed in this paragraph.
(3) Evidence of a conviction under this section is not admissible if:
(a) A period of more than 15 years has elapsed since the date of the conviction or of the release of the witness from the confinement imposed for that conviction, whichever is the later date; or
(b) The conviction has been expunged by pardon, reversed, set aside or otherwise rendered nugatory.
(4) When the credibility of a witness is attacked by evidence that the witness has been convicted of a crime, the witness shall be allowed to explain briefly the circumstances of the crime or former conviction; once the witness explains the circumstances, the opposing side shall have the opportunity to rebut the explanation.
(5) The pendency of an appeal therefrom does not render evidence of a conviction inadmissible. Evidence of the pendency of an appeal is admissible.
(6) An adjudication by a juvenile court that a child is within its jurisdiction is not a conviction of a crime.
(7) A conviction of any of the statutory counterparts of offenses designated as violations as described in ORS 153.008 may not be used to impeach the character of a witness in any criminal or civil action or proceeding. [1981 c.892 §53; 1987 c.2 §9; subsection (6) of 1993 Edition enacted as 1993 c.379 §4; 1999 c.1051 §121; 2001 c.714 §1; 2003 c.577 §3; 2009 c.56 §1]

Note: 40.355 (7) was enacted into law by the Legislative Assembly but was not added to or made a part of ORS chapter 40 or any series therein by legislative action. See Preface to Oregon Revised Statutes for further explanation.

40.360 Rule 609-1. Impeachment for bias or interest. (1) The credibility of a witness may be attacked by evidence that the witness engaged in conduct or made statements showing bias or interest. In examining a witness concerning a prior statement made by the witness, whether written or not, the statement need not be shown nor its contents disclosed to the witness at that time, but on request the statement shall be shown or disclosed to the opposing party.
(2) If a witness fully admits the facts claimed to show the bias or interest of the witness, additional evidence of that bias or interest shall not be admitted. If the witness denies or does not fully admit the facts claimed to show bias or interest, the party attacking the credibility of the witness may then offer evidence to prove those facts.

(3) Evidence to support or rehabilitate a witness whose credibility has been attacked by evidence of bias or interest shall be limited to evidence showing a lack of bias or interest. [1981 c.892 §54; 1999 c.100 §1]

40.365 Rule 610. Religious beliefs or opinions. Evidence of the beliefs or opinions of a witness on matters of religion is not admissible for the purpose of showing that by reason of their nature the credibility of the witness is impaired or enhanced. [1981 c.892 §54a]

40.370 Rule 611. Mode and order of interrogation and presentation. (1) The court shall exercise reasonable control over the mode and order of interrogating witnesses and presenting evidence so as to make the interrogation and presentation effective for the ascertainment of the truth, avoid needless consumption of time and protect witnesses from harassment or undue embarrassment.

(2) Cross-examination should be limited to the subject matter of the direct examination and matters affecting the credibility of the witness. The court may, in the exercise of discretion, permit inquiry into additional matters as if on direct examination.

(3) Leading questions should not be used on the direct examination of a witness except as may be necessary to develop the witness' testimony. Ordinarily leading questions should be permitted on cross-examination. When a party calls a hostile witness, an adverse party, or a witness identified with an adverse party, interrogation may be by leading questions. [1981 c.892 §54b]

40.375 Rule 612. Writing used to refresh memory. If a witness uses a writing to refresh memory for the purpose of testifying, either while testifying or before testifying if the court in its discretion determines it is necessary in the interests of justice, an adverse party is entitled to have the writing produced at the hearing, to inspect it, to cross-examine the witness thereon, and to introduce into evidence those portions which relate to the testimony of the witness. If it is claimed that the writing contains matters not related to the subject matter of the testimony, the court shall examine the writing in camera, excise any portions not so related, and order delivery of the remainder to the party entitled thereto. Any portion withheld over objections shall be preserved and made available to the appellate court in the event of an appeal. If a writing is not produced or delivered pursuant to order under this section, the court shall make any order justice requires, except that in criminal cases when the prosecution elects not to comply the order shall be one striking the testimony or, if the court in its discretion determines that the interests of justice so require, declaring a mistrial. [1981 c.892 §55]

40.380 Rule 613. Prior statements of witnesses. (1) In examining a witness concerning a prior statement made by the witness, whether written or not, the statement need not be shown nor its contents disclosed to the witness at that time, but on request the same shall be shown or disclosed to opposing counsel.

(2) Extrinsic evidence of a prior inconsistent statement by a witness is not admissible unless the witness is afforded an opportunity to explain or deny the same and the opposite party is afforded an opportunity to interrogate the witness thereon, or the interests of justice otherwise require. This provision does not apply to admissions of a party-opponent as defined in ORS 40.450. [1981 c.892 §55a; 1983 c.433 §2; 1983 c.740 §5]

40.385 Rule 615. Exclusion of witnesses. At the request of a party the court may order witnesses excluded until the time of final argument, and it may make the order of its own motion. This rule does not authorize exclusion of:
(1) A party who is a natural person;
(2) An officer or employee of a party which is not a natural person designated as its representative by its attorney;
(3) A person whose presence is shown by a party to be essential to the presentation of the party's cause; or
(4) The victim in a criminal case. [1981 c.892 §56; 1987 c.2 §5; 2003 c.14 §20]

OPINIONS AND EXPERT TESTIMONY

40.405 Rule 701. Opinion testimony by lay witnesses. If the witness is not testifying as an expert, testimony of the witness in the form of opinions or inferences is limited to those opinions or inferences which are:
(1) Rationally based on the perception of the witness; and
(2) Helpful to a clear understanding of testimony of the witness or the determination of a fact in issue. [1981 c.892 §57]

40.410 Rule 702. Testimony by experts. If scientific, technical or other specialized knowledge will assist the trier of fact to understand the evidence or to determine a fact in issue, a witness qualified as an expert by knowledge, skill, experience, training or education may testify thereto in the form of an opinion or otherwise. [1981 c.892 §58]

40.415 Rule 703. Bases of opinion testimony by experts. The facts or data in the particular case upon which an expert bases an opinion or inference may be those perceived by or made known to the expert at or before the hearing. If of a type reasonably relied upon by experts in the particular field in forming opinions or inferences upon the subject, the facts or data need not be admissible in evidence. [1981 c.892 §59]

40.420 Rule 704. Opinion on ultimate issue. Testimony in the form of an opinion or inference otherwise admissible is not objectionable because it embraces an ultimate issue to be decided by the trier of fact. [1981 c.892 §60]

40.425 Rule 705. Disclosure of fact or data underlying expert opinion. An expert may testify in terms of opinion or inference and give reasons therefor without prior disclosure of the underlying facts or data, unless the court requires otherwise. The expert may in any event be required to disclose the underlying facts or data on cross-examination. [1981 c.892 §61]

40.430 Rule 706. Impeachment of expert witness by learned treatise. Upon cross-examination, an expert witness may be questioned concerning statements contained in a published treatise, periodical or pamphlet on a subject of history, medicine or other science or art if the treatise, periodical or pamphlet is established as a reliable authority. A treatise, periodical or pamphlet may be established as a reliable authority by the testimony or admission of the witness, by other expert testimony or by judicial notice. Statements contained in a treatise, periodical or pamphlet established as a reliable authority may be used for purposes of impeachment but may not be introduced as substantive evidence. [1999 c.85 §2]

HEARSAY

40.450 Rule 801. Definitions for ORS 40.450 to 40.475. As used in ORS 40.450 to 40.475, unless the context requires otherwise:
(1) A "statement" is:
(a) An oral or written assertion; or
(b) Nonverbal conduct of a person, if intended as an assertion.
(2) A "declarant" is a person who makes a statement.
(3) "Hearsay" is a statement, other than one made by the declarant while testifying at the trial or hearing, offered in evidence to prove the truth of the matter asserted.
(4) A statement is not hearsay if:
(a) The declarant testifies at the trial or hearing and is subject to cross-examination concerning the statement, and the statement is:
(A) Inconsistent with the testimony of the witness and was given under oath subject to the penalty of perjury at a trial, hearing or other proceeding, or in a deposition;
(B) Consistent with the testimony of the witness and is offered to rebut an inconsistent statement or an express or implied charge against the witness of recent fabrication or improper influence or motive; or

(C) One of identification of a person made after perceiving the person.

(b) The statement is offered against a party and is:

(A) That party's own statement, in either an individual or a representative capacity;

(B) A statement of which the party has manifested the party's adoption or belief in its truth;

(C) A statement by a person authorized by the party to make a statement concerning the subject;

(D) A statement by the party's agent or servant concerning a matter within the scope of the agency or employment, made during the existence of the relationship; or

(E) A statement by a coconspirator of a party during the course and in furtherance of the conspiracy.

(c) The statement is made in a deposition taken in the same proceeding pursuant to ORCP 39 I. [1981 c.892 §62; 1987 c.275 §3]

40.455 Rule 802. Hearsay rule. Hearsay is not admissible except as provided in ORS 40.450 to 40.475 or as otherwise provided by law. [1981 c.892 §63]

40.460 Rule 803. Hearsay exceptions; availability of declarant immaterial. The following are not excluded by ORS 40.455, even though the declarant is available as a witness:

(1) (Reserved.)

(2) A statement relating to a startling event or condition made while the declarant was under the stress of excitement caused by the event or condition.

(3) A statement of the declarant's then existing state of mind, emotion, sensation or physical condition, such as intent, plan, motive, design, mental feeling, pain or bodily health, but not including a statement of memory or belief to prove the fact remembered or believed unless it relates to the execution, revocation, identification, or terms of the declarant's will.

(4) Statements made for purposes of medical diagnosis or treatment and describing medical history, or past or present symptoms, pain or sensations, or the inception or general character of the cause or external source thereof insofar as reasonably pertinent to diagnosis or treatment.

(5) A memorandum or record concerning a matter about which a witness once had knowledge but now has insufficient recollection to enable the witness to testify fully and accurately, shown to have been made or adopted by the witness when the matter was fresh in the memory of the witness and to reflect that knowledge correctly. If admitted, the memorandum or record may be read into evidence but may not itself be received as an exhibit unless offered by an adverse party.

(6) A memorandum, report, record, or data compilation, in any form, of acts, events, conditions, opinions, or diagnoses, made at or near the time by, or from information transmitted by, a person with knowledge, if kept in the course of a regularly conducted business activity, and if it was the regular practice of that business activity to make the memorandum, report, record, or data compilation, all as shown by the testimony of the custodian or other qualified witness, unless the source of information or the method of circumstances of preparation indicate lack of trustworthiness. The term "business" as used in this subsection includes business, institution, association, profession, occupation, and calling of every kind, whether or not conducted for profit.

(7) Evidence that a matter is not included in the memoranda, reports, records, or data compilations, and in any form, kept in accordance with the provisions of subsection (6) of this section, to prove the nonoccurrence or nonexistence of the matter, if the matter was of a kind of which a memorandum, report, record, or data compilation was regularly made and preserved, unless the sources of information or other circumstances indicate lack of trustworthiness.

(8) Records, reports, statements or data compilations, in any form, of public offices or agencies, including federally recognized American Indian tribal governments, setting forth:

(a) The activities of the office or agency;

(b) Matters observed pursuant to duty imposed by law as to which matters there was a duty to report, excluding, in criminal cases, matters observed by police officers and other law enforcement personnel;

(c) In civil actions and proceedings and against the government in criminal cases, factual findings, resulting from an investigation made pursuant to authority granted by law, unless the sources of information or other circumstances indicate lack of trustworthiness; or

(d) In civil actions and criminal proceedings, a sheriff's return of service.

(9) Records or data compilations, in any form, of births, fetal deaths, deaths or marriages, if the report thereof was made to a public office, including a federally recognized American Indian tribal government, pursuant to requirements of law.

(10) To prove the absence of a record, report, statement or data compilation, in any form, or the nonoccurrence or nonexistence of a matter of which a record, report, statement or data compilation, in any form, was regularly made and preserved by a public office or agency, including a federally recognized American Indian tribal government, evidence in the form of a certification in accordance with ORS 40.510, or testimony, that diligent search failed to disclose the record, report, statement or data compilation, or entry.

(11) Statements of births, marriages, divorces, deaths, legitimacy, ancestry, relationship by blood or marriage, or other similar facts of personal or family history, contained in a regularly kept record of a religious organization.

(12) A statement of fact contained in a certificate that the maker performed a marriage or other ceremony or administered a sacrament, made by a member of the clergy, a public official, an official of a federally recognized American Indian tribal government or any other person authorized by the rules or practices of a religious organization or by law to perform the act certified, and purporting to have been issued at the time of the act or within a reasonable time thereafter.

(13) Statements of facts concerning personal or family history contained in family bibles, genealogies, charts, engravings on rings, inscriptions on family portraits, engravings on urns, crypts, or tombstones, or the like.

(14) The record of a document purporting to establish or affect an interest in property, as proof of content of the original recorded document and its execution and delivery by each person by whom it purports to have been executed, if the record is a record of a public office, including a federally recognized American Indian tribal government, and an applicable statute authorizes the recording of documents of that kind in that office.

(15) A statement contained in a document purporting to establish or affect an interest in property if the matter stated was relevant to the purpose of the document, unless dealings with the property since the document was made have been inconsistent with the truth of the statement or the purport of the document.

(16) Statements in a document in existence 20 years or more the authenticity of which is established.

(17) Market quotations, tabulations, lists, directories, or other published compilations, generally used and relied upon by the public or by persons in particular occupations.

(18) (Reserved.)

(18a)(a) A complaint of sexual misconduct, complaint of abuse as defined in ORS 107.705 or 419B.005, complaint of abuse of an elderly person, as those terms are defined in ORS 124.050, or a complaint relating to a violation of ORS 163.205 or 164.015 in which a person 65 years of age or older is the victim, made by the witness after the commission of the alleged misconduct or abuse at issue. Except as provided in paragraph (b) of this subsection, such evidence must be confined to the fact that the complaint was made.

(b) A statement made by a person concerning an act of abuse as defined in ORS 107.705 or 419B.005, a statement made by a person concerning an act of abuse of an elderly person, as those terms are defined in ORS 124.050, or a statement made by a person concerning a violation of ORS 163.205 or 164.015 in which a person 65 years of age or older is the victim, is not excluded by ORS 40.455 if the declarant either testifies at the proceeding and is subject to cross-examination, or is unavailable as a witness but was chronologically or mentally under 12 years of age when the statement was made or was 65 years of age or older when the statement was made. However, if a declarant is unavailable, the statement may be admitted in evidence only if the proponent establishes that the time, content and circumstances of the statement provide indicia of reliability, and in a criminal trial that there is corroborative evidence of the act of abuse and of the alleged perpetrator's opportunity to participate in the conduct and that the statement possesses indicia of reliability as is constitutionally required to be admitted. No statement may be admitted under this paragraph unless the proponent of the statement makes known to the adverse party the proponent's intention to offer the statement and the particulars of the statement no later than 15 days before trial, except for good cause shown. For purposes of this paragraph, in addition to those situations described in ORS 40.465 (1), the declarant shall be considered "unavailable" if the declarant has a substantial lack of memory of the subject matter of the statement, is presently incompetent to testify, is unable to communicate about the abuse or sexual conduct because of fear or other similar reason or is substantially likely, as established by expert testimony, to suffer lasting severe emotional trauma from testifying. Unless otherwise agreed by the parties, the court shall examine the declarant in chambers and on the record or outside the presence of the jury and on the record. The examination shall be conducted immediately prior to the commencement of the trial in the presence of the attorney and the legal guardian or other suitable person as designated by the court. If the declarant is found to be unavailable, the court shall then determine the admissibility of the evidence. The determinations shall be appealable under ORS 138.045 (1)(d). The purpose of the examination shall be to aid the court in making its findings regarding the availability of the declarant as a witness and the reliability of the statement of the declarant. In determining whether a statement possesses indicia of reliability under this paragraph, the court may consider, but is not limited to, the following factors:

(A) The personal knowledge of the declarant of the event;

(B) The age and maturity of the declarant or extent of disability if the declarant is a person with a developmental disability;

(C) Certainty that the statement was made, including the credibility of the person testifying about the statement and any motive the person may have to falsify or distort the statement;

(D) Any apparent motive the declarant may have to falsify or distort the event, including bias, corruption or coercion;

(E) The timing of the statement of the declarant;

(F) Whether more than one person heard the statement;

(G) Whether the declarant was suffering pain or distress when making the statement;

(H) Whether the declarant's young age or disability makes it unlikely that the declarant fabricated a statement that represents a graphic, detailed account beyond the knowledge and experience of the declarant;

(I) Whether the statement has internal consistency or coherence and uses terminology appropriate to the declarant's age or to the extent of the declarant's disability if the declarant is a person with a developmental disability;

(J) Whether the statement is spontaneous or directly responsive to questions; and

(K) Whether the statement was elicited by leading questions.

(c) This subsection applies to all civil, criminal and juvenile proceedings.

(d) This subsection applies to a child declarant, a declarant who is an elderly person as defined in ORS 124.050 or an adult declarant with a developmental disability. For the purposes of this subsection, "developmental disability" means any disability attributable to mental retardation, autism, cerebral palsy, epilepsy or other disabling neurological condition that requires training or support similar to that required by persons with mental retardation, if either of the following apply:

(A) The disability originates before the person attains 22 years of age, or if the disability is attributable to mental retardation the condition is manifested before the person attains 18 years of age, the disability can be expected to continue indefinitely, and the disability constitutes a substantial handicap to the ability of the person to function in society.

(B) The disability results in a significant subaverage general intellectual functioning with concurrent deficits in adaptive behavior that are manifested during the developmental period.

(19) Reputation among members of a person's family by blood, adoption or marriage, or among a person's associates, or in the community, concerning a person's birth, adoption, marriage, divorce, death, legitimacy, relationship by blood or adoption or marriage, ancestry, or other similar fact of a person's personal or family history.

(20) Reputation in a community, arising before the controversy, as to boundaries of or customs affecting lands in the community, and reputation as to events of general history important to the community or state or nation in which located.

(21) Reputation of a person's character among associates of the person or in the community.

(22) Evidence of a final judgment, entered after a trial or upon a plea of guilty, but not upon a plea of no contest, adjudging a person guilty of a crime other than a traffic offense, to prove any fact essential to sustain the judgment, but not including, when offered by the government in a criminal prosecution for purposes other than impeachment, judgments against persons other than the accused. The pendency of an appeal may be shown but does not affect admissibility.

(23) Judgments as proof of matters of personal, family or general history, or boundaries, essential to the judgment, if the same would be provable by evidence of reputation.

(24) Notwithstanding the limits contained in subsection (18a) of this section, in any proceeding in which a child under 12 years of age at the time of trial, or a person with a developmental disability as described in subsection (18a)(d) of this section, may be called as a witness to testify concerning an act of abuse, as defined in ORS 419B.005, or sexual conduct performed with or on the child or person with a developmental disability by another, the testimony of the child or person with a developmental disability taken by contemporaneous examination and cross-examination in another place under the supervision of the trial judge and communicated to the courtroom by closed-circuit television or other audiovisual means. Testimony will be allowed as provided in this subsection only if the court finds that there is a substantial likelihood, established by expert testimony, that the child or person with a developmental disability will suffer severe emotional or psychological harm if required to testify in open court. If the court makes such a finding, the court, on motion of a party, the child, the person with a developmental disability or the court in a civil proceeding, or on motion of the district attorney, the child or the person with a developmental disability in a criminal or juvenile proceeding, may order that the testimony of the child or the person with a developmental disability be taken as described in this subsection. Only the judge, the attorneys for the parties, the parties, individuals necessary to operate the equipment and any individual the court finds would contribute to the welfare and well-being of the child or person with a developmental disability may be present during the testimony of the child or person with a developmental disability.

(25)(a) Any document containing data prepared or recorded by the Oregon State Police pursuant to ORS 813.160 (1)(b)(C) or (E), or pursuant to ORS 475.235 (4), if the document is produced by data retrieval from the Law Enforcement Data System or other computer system maintained and operated by the Oregon State Police, and the person retrieving the data attests that the information was retrieved directly from the system and that the document accurately reflects the data retrieved.

(b) Any document containing data prepared or recorded by the Oregon State Police that is produced by data retrieval from the Law Enforcement Data System or other computer system maintained and operated by the Oregon State Police and that is electronically transmitted through public or private computer networks under an electronic signature adopted by the Oregon State Police if the person receiving the data attests that the document accurately reflects the data received.

(c) Notwithstanding any statute or rule to the contrary, in any criminal case in which documents are introduced under the provisions of this subsection, the defendant may subpoena the analyst, as defined in ORS 475.235 (6), or other person that generated or keeps the original document for the purpose of testifying at the preliminary hearing and trial of the issue. Except as provided in ORS 44.550 to 44.566, no charge shall be made to the defendant for the appearance of the analyst or other person.

(26)(a) A statement that purports to narrate, describe, report or explain an incident of domestic violence, as defined in ORS 135.230, made by a victim of the domestic violence within 24 hours after the incident occurred, if the statement:

(A) Was recorded, either electronically or in writing, or was made to a peace officer as defined in ORS 161.015, corrections officer, youth correction officer, parole and probation officer, emergency medical services provider or firefighter; and

(B) Has sufficient indicia of reliability.

(b) In determining whether a statement has sufficient indicia of reliability under paragraph (a) of this subsection, the court shall consider all circumstances surrounding the statement. The court may consider, but is not limited to, the following factors in determining whether a statement has sufficient indicia of reliability:

(A) The personal knowledge of the declarant.

(B) Whether the statement is corroborated by evidence other than statements that are subject to admission only pursuant to this subsection.

(C) The timing of the statement.

(D) Whether the statement was elicited by leading questions.

(E) Subsequent statements made by the declarant. Recantation by a declarant is not sufficient reason for denying admission of a statement under this subsection in the absence of other factors indicating unreliability.

(27) A report prepared by a forensic scientist that contains the results of a presumptive test conducted by the forensic scientist as described in ORS 475.235, if the forensic scientist attests that the report accurately reflects the results of the presumptive test.

(28)(a) A statement not specifically covered by any of the foregoing exceptions but having equivalent circumstantial guarantees of trustworthiness, if the court determines that:

(A) The statement is relevant;

(B) The statement is more probative on the point for which it is offered than any other evidence that the proponent can procure through reasonable efforts; and

(C) The general purposes of the Oregon Evidence Code and the interests of justice will best be served by admission of the statement into evidence.

(b) A statement may not be admitted under this subsection unless the proponent of it makes known to the adverse party the intention to offer the statement and the particulars of it, including the name and address of the declarant, sufficiently in advance of the trial or hearing, or as soon as practicable after it becomes apparent that such statement is probative of the issues at hand, to provide the adverse party with a fair opportunity to prepare to meet it. [1981 c.892 §64; 1989 c.300 §1; 1989 c.881 §1; 1991 c.391 §1; 1995 c.200 §1; 1995 c.476 §1; 1995 c.804 §2; 1999 c.59 §13; 1999 c.674 §1; 1999 c.945 §1; 2001 c.104 §11; 2001 c.533 §1; 2001 c.870 §5; 2003 c.538 §2; 2005 c.118 §3; 2007 c.63 §2; 2007 c.70 §12; 2007 c.636 §3; 2009 c.610 §9; 2011 c.661 §14; 2011 c.703 §21; 2017 c.529 §21]

40.465 Rule 804. Hearsay exceptions when the declarant is unavailable. (1) "Unavailability as a witness" includes situations in which the declarant:

(a) Is exempted by ruling of the court on the ground of privilege from testifying concerning the subject matter of a statement;

(b) Persists in refusing to testify concerning the subject matter of a statement despite an order of the court to do so;

(c) Testifies to a lack of memory of the subject matter of a statement;

(d) Is unable to be present or to testify at the hearing because of death or then existing physical or mental illness or infirmity; or

(e) Is absent from the hearing and the proponent of the declarant's statement has been unable to procure the declarant's attendance (or in the case of an exception under subsection (3)(b), (c) or (d) of this section, the declarant's attendance or testimony) by process or other reasonable means.

(2) A declarant is not unavailable as a witness if the declarant's exemption, refusal, claim of lack of memory, inability, or absence is due to the procurement or wrongdoing of the proponent of the declarant's statement for the purpose of preventing the witness from attending or testifying.

(3) The following are not excluded by ORS 40.455 if the declarant is unavailable as a witness:

(a) Testimony given as a witness at another hearing of the same or a different proceeding, or in a deposition taken in compliance with law in the course of the same or another proceeding, if the party against whom the testimony is now offered, or, in a civil action or proceeding a predecessor in interest, had an opportunity and similar motive to develop the testimony by direct, cross, or redirect examination.

(b) A statement made by a declarant while believing that death was imminent, concerning the cause or circumstances of what the declarant believed to be impending death.

(c) A statement which was at the time of its making so far contrary to the declarant's pecuniary or proprietary interest, or so far tended to subject the declarant to civil or criminal liability, or to render invalid a claim by the declarant against another, that a reasonable person in the declarant's position would not have made the statement unless the person believed it to be true. A statement tending to expose the declarant to criminal liability and offered to exculpate the accused is not admissible unless corroborating circumstances clearly indicate the trustworthiness of the statement.

(d)(A) A statement concerning the declarant's own birth, adoption, marriage, divorce, legitimacy, relationship by blood or adoption or marriage, ancestry, or other similar fact of personal or family history, even though the declarant had no means of acquiring personal knowledge of the matter stated; or

(B) A statement concerning the foregoing matters, and death also, of another person, if the declarant was related to the other by blood, adoption, or marriage or was so intimately associated with the other's family as to be likely to have accurate information concerning the matter declared.

(e) A statement made at or near the time of the transaction by a person in a position to know the facts stated therein, acting in the person's professional capacity and in the ordinary course of professional conduct.

(f) A statement offered against a party who intentionally or knowingly engaged in criminal conduct that directly caused the death of the declarant, or directly caused the declarant to become unavailable as a witness because of incapacity or incompetence.

(g) A statement offered against a party who engaged in, directed or otherwise participated in wrongful conduct that was intended to cause the declarant to be unavailable as a witness, and did cause the declarant to be unavailable.

(h) A statement not specifically covered by any of the foregoing exceptions but having equivalent circumstantial guarantees of trustworthiness, if the court determines that (A) the statement is offered as evidence of a material fact; (B) the statement is more probative on the point for which it is offered than any other evidence which the proponent can procure through reasonable efforts; and (C) the general purposes of the Oregon Evidence Code and the interests of justice will best be served by admission of the statement into evidence. However, a statement may not be admitted under this paragraph unless the proponent of it makes known to the adverse party the intention to offer the statement and the particulars of it, including the name and address of the declarant, sufficiently in advance of the trial or hearing, or as soon as practicable after it becomes apparent that the statement is probative of the issues at hand, to provide the adverse party with a fair opportunity to prepare to meet it. [1981 c.892 §65; 2005 c.458 §1]

40.470 Rule 805. Hearsay within hearsay. Hearsay included within hearsay is not excluded under ORS 40.455 if each part of the combined statements conforms with an exception set forth in ORS 40.460 or 40.465. [1981 c.892 §66]

40.475 Rule 806. Attacking and supporting credibility of declarant. When a hearsay statement, or a statement defined in ORS 40.450 (4)(b)(C), (D) or (E), has been admitted in evidence, the credibility of the declarant may be attacked, and if attacked may be supported, by any evidence which would be admissible for those purposes if the declarant had testified as a witness. Evidence of a statement or conduct by the declarant at any time, inconsistent with the hearsay statement of the declarant, is not subject to any requirement under ORS 40.380 relating to impeachment by evidence of inconsistent statements. If the party against whom a hearsay statement has been admitted calls the declarant as a witness, the party is entitled to examine the declarant on the statement as if under cross-examination. [1981 c.892 §67]

AUTHENTICATION AND IDENTIFICATION

40.505 Rule 901. Requirement of authentication or identification. (1) The requirement of authentication or identification as a condition precedent to admissibility is satisfied by evidence sufficient to support a finding that the matter in question is what its proponent claims.

(2) By way of illustration only, and not by way of limitation, the following are examples of authentication or identification conforming with the requirements of subsection (1) of this section:

(a) Testimony by a witness with knowledge that a matter is what it is claimed to be.

(b) Nonexpert opinion as to the genuineness of handwriting, based upon familiarity not acquired for purposes of the litigation.

(c) Comparison by the trier of fact or by expert witnesses with specimens which have been authenticated.

(d) Appearance, contents, substance, internal patterns or other distinctive characteristics, taken in conjunction with circumstances.

(e) Identification of a voice, whether heard firsthand or through mechanical or electronic transmission or recording, by opinion based upon hearing the voice at any time under circumstances connecting it with the alleged speaker.

(f) Telephone conversations, by evidence that a call was made to the number assigned at the time by the telephone company to a particular person or business, if:

(A) In the case of a person, circumstances, including self-identification, show the person answering to be the one called; or

(B) In the case of a business, the call was made to a place of business and the conversation related to business reasonably transacted over the telephone.

(g) Evidence that a writing authorized by law to be recorded or filed and in fact recorded or filed in a public office, or a purported public record, report, statement, or data compilation, in any form, is from the public office where items of this nature are kept.

(h) Evidence that a document or data compilation, in any form:

(A) Is in such condition as to create no suspicion concerning its authenticity;

(B) Was in a place where it, if authentic, would likely be; and

(C) Has been in existence 20 years or more at the time it is offered.

(i) Evidence describing a process or system used to produce a result and showing that the process or system produces an accurate result.

(j) Any method of authentication or identification otherwise provided by law or by other rules prescribed by the Supreme Court. [1981 c.892 §68]

40.510 Rule 902. Self-authentication. (1) Extrinsic evidence of authenticity as a condition precedent to admissibility is not required with respect to the following:

(a) A document bearing a seal purporting to be that of the United States, or of any state, district, commonwealth, territory, or insular possession thereof, or the Panama Canal Zone, or the Trust Territory of the Pacific Islands, or of a political subdivision, department, officer, or agency thereof, and a signature purporting to be an attestation or execution.

(b) A document purporting to bear the signature, in an official capacity, of an officer or employee of any entity included in subsection (1)(a) of this section, having no seal, if a public officer having a seal and having official duties in the district or political subdivision of the officer or employee certifies under seal that the signer has the official capacity and that the signature is genuine.

(c) A document purporting to be:

(A) Executed or attested in an official capacity by a person authorized by the laws of a foreign country to make the execution or attestation; and

(B) Accompanied by a final certification as provided in subsection (3) of this section as to the genuineness of the signature and official position of:

(i) The executing or attesting person; or

(ii) Any foreign official whose certificate of genuineness of signature and official position relates to the execution or attestation or is in a chain of certificates of genuineness of signature and official position relating to the execution or attestation.

(d) A copy of an official record or report or entry therein, or of a document authorized by law to be recorded or filed and actually recorded or filed in a public office, including data compilations in any form, certified as correct by the custodian or other person authorized to make the certification, by certificate complying with subsection (1)(a), (b) or (c) of this section or otherwise complying with any law or rule prescribed by the Supreme Court.

(e) Books, pamphlets or other publications purporting to be issued by public authority.

(f) Printed materials purporting to be newspapers or periodicals.

(g) Inscriptions, signs, tags or labels purporting to have been affixed in the course of business and indicating ownership, control or origin.

(h) Documents accompanied by a certificate of acknowledgment executed in the manner provided by law by a notary public or other officer authorized by law to take acknowledgments.

(i) Commercial paper, signatures thereon and documents relating thereto to the extent provided by the Uniform Commercial Code or ORS chapter 83.

(j) Any signature, documents or other matter declared by law to be presumptively or prima facie genuine or authentic.

(k)(A) A document bearing a seal purporting to be that of a federally recognized Indian tribal government or of a political subdivision, department, officer, or agency thereof, and a signature purporting to be an attestation or execution.

(B) A document purporting to bear the signature, in an official capacity, of an officer or employee of any entity included in subparagraph (A) of this paragraph, having no seal, if a public officer having a seal and having official duties in the district or political subdivision or the officer or employee certifies under seal that the signer has the official capacity and that the signature is genuine.

(L)(A) Any document containing data prepared or recorded by the Oregon State Police pursuant to ORS 813.160 (1)(b)(C) or (E), or pursuant to ORS 475.235 (4), if the document is produced by data retrieval from the Law Enforcement Data System or other computer system maintained and operated by the Oregon State Police, and the person retrieving the data attests that the information was retrieved directly from the system and that the document accurately reflects the data retrieved.

(B) Any document containing data prepared or recorded by the Oregon State Police that is produced by data retrieval from the Law Enforcement Data System or other computer system maintained and operated by the Oregon State Police and that is electronically transmitted through public or private computer networks under an electronic signature adopted by the Oregon State Police if the person receiving the data attests that the document accurately reflects the data received.

(m) A report prepared by a forensic scientist that contains the results of a presumptive test conducted by the forensic scientist as described in ORS 475.235, if the forensic scientist attests that the report accurately reflects the results of the presumptive test.

(2) For the purposes of this section, "signature" includes any symbol executed or adopted by a party with present intention to authenticate a writing.

(3) A final certification for purposes of subsection (1)(c) of this section may be made by a secretary of embassy or legation, consul general, consul, vice consul, or consular agent of the United States, or a diplomatic or consular official of the foreign country assigned or accredited to the United States. If reasonable opportunity has been given to all parties to investigate the authenticity and accuracy of official documents, the court may, for good cause shown, order that they be treated as presumptively authentic without final certification or permit them to be evidenced by an attested summary with or without final certification. [1981 c.892 §69; 1995 c.200 §2; 1999 c.674 §2; 2001 c.104 §12; 2003 c.14 §21; 2003 c.538 §3; 2005 c.22 §31; 2005 c.118 §4; 2007 c.636 §4; 2009 c.610 §10]

40.515 Rule 903. Subscribing witness' testimony unnecessary. The testimony of a subscribing witness is not necessary to authenticate a writing unless required by the laws of the jurisdiction whose laws govern the validity of the writing. [1981 c.892 §70]

CONTENTS OF WRITINGS, RECORDINGS AND PHOTOGRAPHS

40.550 Rule 1001. Definitions for ORS 40.550 to 40.585. As used in ORS 40.550 to 40.585, unless the context requires otherwise:

(1) "Duplicate" means a counterpart produced by the same impression as the original, or from the same matrix, or by means of photography, including enlargements and miniatures, by mechanical or electronic re-recording, by chemical reproduction, by optical imaging or by other equivalent techniques that accurately reproduce the original, including reproduction by facsimile machines if the reproduction is identified as a facsimile and printed on nonthermal paper.

(2) "Original" of a writing or recording is the writing or recording itself or any counterpart intended to have the same effect by a person executing or issuing it. An "original" of a photograph includes the negative or any print therefrom. If data are stored in a computer or similar device, any printout or other output readable by sight, shown to reflect the data accurately, is an "original."

(3) "Photographs" includes still photographs, X-ray films, video tapes and motion pictures.

(4) "Writings" and "recordings" mean letters, words or numbers, or their equivalent, set down by handwriting, typewriting, printing, photostating, photographing, magnetic impulse, optical imaging, mechanical or electronic recording or other form of data compilation. [1981 c.892 §71; 1991 c.857 §1; 1995 c.760 §1]

40.555 Rule 1002. Requirement of original. To prove the content of a writing, recording or photograph, the original writing, recording or photograph is required, except as otherwise provided in ORS 40.550 to 40.585 or other law. [1981 c.892 §72]

40.560 Rule 1003. Admissibility of duplicates. A duplicate is admissible to the same extent as an original unless:

(1) A genuine question is raised as to the authenticity of the original; or

(2) In the circumstances it would be unfair to admit the duplicate in lieu of the original. [1981 c.892 §73]

40.562 Rule 1003-1. Admissibility of reproduction. (1) If any business, institution or member of a profession or calling, in the regular course of business or activity, has kept or recorded any memorandum, writing, entry, print, representation or a combination thereof, of any act, transaction, occurrence or event, and in the regular course of business has caused any or all of the same to be recorded, copied or reproduced by any photographic, photostatic, microfilm, micro-card, miniature photographic, optical imaging or other process that accurately reproduces or forms a durable medium for so reproducing the original, the original may be destroyed in the regular course of business unless held in a custodial or fiduciary capacity and the principal or true owner has not authorized destruction or unless its preservation is required by law. Such reproduction, when satisfactorily identified, is as admissible in evidence as the original itself in any judicial or administrative proceeding whether the original is in existence or not and an enlargement or facsimile of such reproduction is likewise admissible in evidence if the original reproduction is in existence and available for inspection under direction of the court. The introduction of a reproduced record, enlargement or facsimile does not preclude admission of the original.

(2) If any department or agency of government, in the regular course of business or activity, has kept or recorded any memorandum, writing, entry, print, representation or combination thereof, of any act, transaction, occurrence or event, and in the regular course of business, and in accordance with ORS 192.040 to 192.060 and 192.105, has caused any or all of the same to be recorded, copied or reproduced by any photographic, photostatic, microfilm, micro-card, miniature photographic, optical imaging or other process that accurately reproduces or forms a durable medium for so reproducing the original, the original may be destroyed in the regular course of business unless held in a custodial or fiduciary capacity and the principal or true owner has not authorized destruction or unless its preservation is required by law. Such reproduction, when satisfactorily identified, is as admissible in evidence as the original itself in any judicial or administrative proceeding whether the original is in existence or not and an enlargement or facsimile of such reproduction is likewise admissible in evidence if the original reproduction is in existence and available for inspection under direction of the court. The introduction of a reproduced record, enlargement or facsimile does not preclude admission of the original. [1995 c.760 §3]

40.565 Rule 1004. Admissibility of other evidence of contents. The original is not required, and other evidence of the contents of a writing, recording or photograph is admissible when:

(1) All originals are lost or have been destroyed, unless the proponent lost or destroyed them in bad faith;

(2) An original cannot be obtained by any available judicial process or procedure;

(3) At a time when an original was under the control of the party against whom offered, that party was put on notice, by the pleadings or otherwise, that the contents would be a subject of proof at the hearing, and the party does not produce the original at the hearing; or

(4) The writing, recording or photograph is not closely related to a controlling issue. [1981 c.892 §74]

40.570 Rule 1005. Public records. The contents of an official record or of a document authorized to be recorded or filed and actually recorded or filed, including data compilations in any form, if otherwise admissible, may be proved by copy, certified as correct in accordance with ORS 40.510 or testified to be correct by a witness who has compared it with the original. If such a copy cannot be obtained by the exercise of reasonable diligence, then other evidence of the contents may be given. [1981 c.892 §75; 1983 c.433 §3]

40.575 Rule 1006. Summaries. The contents of voluminous writings, recordings or photographs which cannot conveniently be examined in court may be presented in the form of a chart, summary or calculation. The originals, or duplicates, shall be made available for examination or copying, or both, by other parties at a reasonable time and place. The court may order that they be produced in court. [1981 c.892 §76]

40.580 Rule 1007. Testimony or written admission of party. Contents of writings, recordings or photographs may be proved by the testimony or deposition of the party against whom offered or by the party's written admission, without accounting for the nonproduction of the original. [1981 c.892 §77]

40.585 Rule 1008. Functions of court and jury. When the admissibility of other evidence of contents of writings, recordings or photographs under ORS 40.550 to 40.585 depends upon the fulfillment of a condition of fact, the question whether the condition has been fulfilled is ordinarily for the court to determine in accordance with ORS 40.030. However, the issue is for the trier of fact to determine as in the case of other issues of fact when the issue raised is:

(1) Whether the asserted writing ever existed;

(2) Whether another writing, recording or photograph produced at the trial is the original; or

(3) Whether the other evidence of contents correctly reflects the contents. [1981 c.892 §78]

Chapter 41 —— Evidence Generally

2017 EDITION

EVIDENCE GENERALLY

EVIDENCE AND WITNESSES

41.010   Judicial evidence; proof

41.110   Satisfactory evidence

41.270   Proof of usage

41.415   Photograph of victim in prosecution for criminal homicide

41.500   "Secondary evidence" defined for ORS 41.500 to 41.580

41.510   Indispensable evidence

41.520   Evidence to prove a will

41.530   Evidence of representations as to third persons

41.560   Grant or assignment of trust

41.570   Contracts and communications made by telegraph

41.580   Statute of frauds

357

41.660   Admissibility of objects cognizable by the senses

41.675   Inadmissibility of certain data provided to peer review body of health care providers and health care groups

41.685   Inadmissibility of certain data relating to emergency medical services system

41.740   Parol evidence rule

41.815   Evidence of compliance with or attempt to comply with ORCP 32 I; when admissible

41.905   Admissibility in subsequent civil action of procedures in traffic crimes

41.910   Certain intercepted communications inadmissible

41.930   Admissibility of copies of original records

41.945   Application of ORS 41.930 and ORCP 55 H

41.010 Judicial evidence; proof. Judicial evidence is the means, sanctioned by law, of ascertaining in a judicial proceeding the truth respecting a question of fact. Proof is the effect of evidence, the establishment of the fact by evidence.

41.020 [Repealed by 1981 c.892 §98]

41.030 [Repealed by 1981 c.892 §98]

41.040 [Repealed by 1981 c.892 §98]

41.050 [Repealed by 1981 c.892 §98]

41.060 [Repealed by 1981 c.892 §98]

41.070 [Repealed by 1981 c.892 §98]

41.080 [Repealed by 1981 c.892 §98]

41.090 [Repealed by 1981 c.892 §98]

41.100 [Repealed by 1981 c.892 §98]

41.110 Satisfactory evidence. Satisfactory evidence is that which ordinarily produces moral certainty or conviction in an unprejudiced mind. It alone will justify a verdict. Evidence less than this is insufficient evidence.

41.120 [Repealed by 1981 c.892 §98]

41.130 [Repealed by 1981 c.892 §98]

41.140 [Repealed by 1981 c.892 §98]

41.150 [Repealed by 1981 c.892 §98]

41.210 [Repealed by 1981 c.892 §98]

41.220 [Repealed by 1981 c.892 §98]

41.230 [Repealed by 1981 c.892 §98]

41.240 [Repealed by 1981 c.892 §98]

41.250 [Repealed by 1981 c.892 §98]

41.260 [Repealed by 1981 c.892 §98]

41.270 Proof of usage. (1) Usage shall be proved by the testimony of at least two witnesses.
(2) Evidence may be given of usage to explain the true character of an act, contract or instrument when such true character is not otherwise plain, but usage is never admissible except as a means of interpretation. [Amended by 1981 c.892 §86]

41.280 [Repealed by 1981 c.892 §98]

41.310 [Repealed by 1981 c.892 §98]

41.315 [1987 c.774 §§1,2; repealed by 1995 c.688 §6]

41.320 [Repealed by 1981 c.892 §98]

41.330 [Repealed by 1981 c.892 §98]

41.340 [Repealed by 1981 c.892 §98]

41.350 [Amended by 1971 c.127 §1; repealed by 1981 c.892 §98]

41.360 [Amended by 1957 c.679 §1; 1961 c.726 §399; repealed by 1981 c.892 §98]

41.410 [Repealed by 1981 c.892 §98]

41.415 Photograph of victim in prosecution for criminal homicide. In a prosecution for any criminal homicide, a photograph of the victim while alive shall be admissible evidence when offered by the district attorney to show the general appearance and condition of the victim while alive. [1987 c.2 §8]

41.420 [Repealed by 1981 c.892 §98]

41.430 [Repealed by 1981 c.892 §98]

41.440 [Repealed by 1981 c.892 §98]

41.450 [Repealed by 1981 c.892 §98]

41.460 [Repealed by 1981 c.892 §98]

41.470 [Repealed by 1981 c.892 §98]

41.480 [Repealed by 1981 c.892 §98]

41.500 "Secondary evidence" defined for ORS 41.500 to 41.580. As used in ORS 41.500 to 41.580, "secondary evidence" means a copy, or oral evidence, of an original writing or object. [1981 c.892 §81]

41.510 Indispensable evidence. Certain evidence is necessary to the validity of particular acts or the proof of particular facts.

41.520 Evidence to prove a will. Evidence of a will shall be the written instrument itself, or secondary evidence of the contents of the will, in the cases prescribed by law. [Amended by 1969 c.591 §271]

41.530 Evidence of representations as to third persons. No evidence is admissible to charge a person upon a representation as to the credit, skill or character of a third person, unless the representation, or some memorandum thereof, be in writing, and either subscribed by or in the handwriting of the party to be charged.

41.540 [Repealed by 1977 c.479 §1]

41.550 [Repealed by 1961 c.726 §427]

41.560 Grant or assignment of trust. Every grant or assignment of any existing trust in lands, tenements, hereditaments, goods or things in action is void, unless it is in writing and subscribed by the party making it or by the lawfully authorized agent of the party.

41.570 Contracts and communications made by telegraph. Contracts made by telegraph shall be held to be in writing; and all communications sent by telegraph, and signed by the sender, or by the authority of the sender, shall be held to be in writing.

41.580 Statute of frauds. (1) In the following cases the agreement is void unless it, or some note or memorandum thereof, expressing the consideration, is in writing and subscribed by the party to be charged, or by the lawfully authorized agent of the party; evidence, therefore, of the agreement shall not be received other than the writing, or secondary evidence of its contents in the cases prescribed by law:
    (a) An agreement that by its terms is not to be performed within a year from the making.
    (b) An agreement to answer for the debt, default or miscarriage of another.
    (c) An agreement by an executor or administrator to pay the debts of the testator or intestate out of the estate of the executor or administrator.
    (d) An agreement made upon consideration of marriage, other than a mutual promise to marry.
    (e) An agreement for the leasing for a longer period than one year, or for the sale of real property, or of any interest therein.
    (f) An agreement concerning real property made by an agent of the party sought to be charged unless the authority of the agent is in writing.
    (g) An agreement authorizing or employing an agent or broker to sell or purchase real estate for a compensation or commission; but if the note or memorandum of the agreement is in writing and subscribed by the party to be charged, or by the lawfully authorized agent of the party, and contains a description of the property sufficient for identification, and authorizes or employs the agent or broker to sell the property, and expresses with reasonable certainty the amount of the commission or compensation to be paid, the agreement shall not be void for failure to state a consideration.
    (h) An agreement, promise or commitment to lend money, to otherwise extend credit, to forbear with respect to the repayment of any debt payable in money, to modify or amend the terms under which the person has lent money or otherwise extended credit, to release any guarantor or cosigner or to make any other financial accommodation pertaining to an existing debt or other extension of credit. This paragraph does not apply:
    (A) If no party to the agreement, promise or commitment is a financial institution as defined in ORS 706.008, a consumer finance company licensed under ORS chapter 725 or a mortgage banker as defined in ORS 86A.100; or
    (B) To a loan of money or extension of credit to a natural person which is primarily for personal, family or household purposes and not for business or agricultural purposes or which is secured solely by residential property consisting of one to four dwelling units, one of which is the primary residence of the debtor.
    (2)(a) Except as provided in this subsection, defenses and exceptions created by provisions of the Oregon Revised Statutes or recognized by the courts of this state do not apply to subsection (1)(h) of this section.
    (b) An agreement, promise or commitment which does not satisfy the requirements of subsection (1)(h) of this section, but which is valid in other respects, is enforceable if the party against whom enforcement is sought admits in the party's pleading, testimony or otherwise in court that the agreement, promise or commitment was made. The agreement is not enforceable under this paragraph beyond the dollar amount admitted.
    (c) Nothing in subsection (1)(h) of this section precludes a party from seeking to prove the modification of any term relating to the time of repayment.
    (3)(a) If a financial institution as defined in ORS 706.008, a consumer finance company licensed under ORS chapter 725 or a mortgage banker as defined in ORS 86A.100 lends money or extends credit, and subsection (1)(h) of this section applies to the loan or extension of credit, the financial institution, consumer finance company or mortgage banker shall, not later than the time the loan or extension of credit is initially made, include within the loan or credit document, or within a separate document which identifies the loan or extension of credit, a statement which is underlined or in at least 10-point bold type and which is substantially to the following effect:

Under Oregon law, most agreements, promises and commitments made by us concerning loans and other credit extensions which are not for personal, family or household purposes or secured solely by the borrower's residence must be in writing, express consideration and be signed by us to be enforceable.

(b) The financial institution, consumer finance company or mortgage banker shall obtain the borrower's signature on the original document described in paragraph (a) of this subsection and shall give the borrower a copy. [Amended by 1989 c.967 §§1,19; 1993 c.508 §39; 1997 c.631 §373; 2003 c.386 §1]

41.590 [Repealed by 1961 c.726 §427]

41.610 [Repealed by 1981 c.892 §98]

41.615 [1959 c.353 §§1,3 (subsection (2) enacted in lieu of 41.630); 1973 c.231 §1; repealed by 1977 c.358 §1 (41.616 enacted in lieu of 41.615)]

41.616 [1977 c.358 §2 (enacted in lieu of 41.615); repealed by 1979 c.284 §199]

41.617 [1977 c.358 §3; repealed by 1979 c.284 §199]

41.618 [1977 c.358 §4; repealed by 1979 c.284 §199]

41.620 [Repealed by 1979 c.284 §199]

41.622 [1977 c.744 §2; repealed by 1979 c.284 §199]

41.625 [1959 c.349 §1; repealed by 1977 c.240 §1; (41.626 enacted in lieu of 41.625)]

41.626 [1977 c.240 §2 (enacted in lieu of 41.625); repealed by 1979 c.284 §199]

41.630 [Repealed by 1959 c.353 §2 (subsection (2) of 41.615 enacted in lieu of 41.630)]

41.631 [1977 c.240 §4; repealed by 1979 c.284 §199]

41.635 [1977 c.240 §3 and 1977 c.358 §5; repealed by 1979 c.284 §199]

41.640 [Repealed by 1981 c.892 §98]

41.650 [Repealed by 1981 c.892 §98]

41.660 Admissibility of objects cognizable by the senses. Whenever an object, cognizable by the senses, has such a relation to the fact in dispute as to afford reasonable grounds of belief respecting it, or to make an item in the sum of the evidence, the object may be exhibited to the jury, or its existence, situation and character may be proved by witnesses. The exhibition of the object to the jury shall be regulated by the sound discretion of the court.

41.670 [Repealed by 1981 c.892 §98]

41.675 Inadmissibility of certain data provided to peer review body of health care providers and health care groups. (1) As used in this section, "peer review body" includes tissue committees, governing bodies or committees including medical staff committees of a health care facility licensed under ORS chapter 441, medical staff committees of the Department of Corrections and similar committees of professional societies, a health care service contractor as defined in ORS 750.005, an emergency medical service provider as defined in ORS 41.685 or any other medical group or provider of medical services in connection with bona fide medical research, quality assurance, utilization review, credentialing, education, training, supervision or discipline of physicians or other health care providers or in connection with the grant, denial, restriction or termination of clinical privileges at a health care facility. "Peer review body" also includes utilization review and peer review organizations.

(2) As used in subsection (3) of this section, "data" means all oral communications or written reports to a peer review body, and all notes or records created by or at the direction of a peer review body, including the communications, reports, notes or records created in the course of an investigation undertaken at the direction of a peer review body.

(3) All data shall be privileged and shall not be admissible in evidence in any judicial, administrative, arbitration or mediation proceeding. This section shall not affect the admissibility in evidence of records dealing with a patient's care and treatment, other than data or information obtained through service on, or as an agent for, a peer review body.

(4) A person serving on or communicating information to any peer review body or person conducting an investigation described in subsection (1) of this section shall not be examined as to any communication to or from, or the findings of, that peer review body or person.

(5) A person serving on or communicating information to any peer review body or person conducting an investigation described in subsection (1) of this section shall not be subject to an action for civil damages for affirmative actions taken or statements made in good faith.

(6) Subsection (3) of this section shall not apply to proceedings in which a health care practitioner contests the denial, restriction or termination of clinical privileges by a health care facility or the denial, restriction or termination of membership in a professional society or any other health care group. However, any data disclosed in those proceedings shall not be admissible in any other judicial, administrative, arbitration or mediation proceeding. [1963 c.181 §1; 1971 c.412 §1; 1975 c.796 §11; 1977 c.448 §9; 1981 c.806 §1; 1991 c.225 §1; 1995 c.485 §1; 1997 c.791 §6; 1997 c.792 §§29,29a]

41.680 [Repealed by 1981 c.892 §98]

41.685 Inadmissibility of certain data relating to emergency medical services system. (1) All data shall be privileged and are not public records as defined in ORS 192.311 and shall not be admissible in evidence in any judicial proceeding except as provided under ORS 676.175. However, nothing in this section affects the admissibility in evidence of a party's medical records dealing with a party's medical care.

(2) On request, an emergency medical service provider shall submit data not subject to ORS 676.175 to any committee or governing body of the county, counties or state as provided for by state or county administrative rule.

(3) A person serving on or communicating information to any governing body or committee shall not be examined as to any communication to that body or committee or the findings thereof.

(4) A person serving on or communicating information to any governing body or committee shall not be subject to an action for civil damages for affirmative actions taken or statements made in good faith.

(5) As used in this section:

(a) "Committee or governing body" means any committee or governing body that has authority to undertake an evaluation of an emergency medical services system as part of a quality assurance program and includes any committee of an emergency medical service provider undertaking a quality assurance program.

(b) "Data" means all oral communications or written reports, notes or records provided to, or prepared by or for, a committee or governing body that are part of an evaluation of an emergency medical services system and includes any information submitted by any health care provider relating to training, supervision, performance evaluation or professional competency.

(c) "Emergency medical service provider" means any public, private or volunteer entity providing prehospital functions and services that are required to prepare for and respond to medical emergencies including rescue, ambulance, treatment, communication and evaluation.

(d) "Emergency medical services system" means those prehospital functions and services that are required to prepare for and respond to medical emergencies, including rescue, ambulance, treatment, communication and evaluation. [1989 c.1079 §1; 1997 c.791 §7; 1997 c.792 §30]

41.690 [Repealed by 1981 c.892 §98]

41.700 [Repealed by 1981 c.892 §98]

41.710 [Repealed by 1981 c.892 §98]

41.720 [Repealed by 1981 c.892 §98]

41.730 [Repealed by 1981 c.892 §98]

41.740 Parol evidence rule. When the terms of an agreement have been reduced to writing by the parties, it is to be considered as containing all those terms, and therefore there can be, between the parties and their representatives or successors in interest, no evidence of the terms of the agreement, other than the contents of the writing, except where a mistake or imperfection of the writing is put in issue by the pleadings or where the validity of the agreement is the fact in dispute. However this section does not exclude other evidence of the circumstances under which the agreement was made, or to which it relates, as defined in ORS 42.220, or to explain an ambiguity, intrinsic or extrinsic, or to establish illegality or fraud. The term "agreement" includes deeds and wills as well as contracts between parties.

41.810 [Repealed by 1981 c.892 §98]

41.815 Evidence of compliance with or attempt to comply with ORCP 32 I; when admissible. Attempts to comply with the provisions of ORCP 32 I by a person receiving a demand shall be construed to be an offer to compromise and shall be inadmissible as evidence. Such attempts to comply with a demand shall not be considered an admission of engaging in the act or practice alleged to be unlawful nor of the unlawfulness of that act. Evidence of compliance or attempts to comply with the provisions of ORCP 32 I may be introduced by a defendant for the purpose of establishing good faith or to show compliance with the provisions of ORCP 32 I. [Formerly 13.310; 1981 c.912 §3]

41.820 [Repealed by 1981 c.892 §98]

41.830 [Repealed by 1981 c.892 §98]

41.840 [Repealed by 1981 c.892 §98]

41.850 [Repealed by 1981 c.892 §98]

41.860 [Repealed by 1981 c.892 §98]

41.870 [Repealed by 1981 c.892 §98]

41.880 [Repealed by 1981 c.892 §98]

41.890 [Repealed by 1981 c.892 §98]

41.900 [Repealed by 1981 c.892 §98]

41.905 Admissibility in subsequent civil action of procedures in traffic crimes. A plea to a charge of a traffic crime, as defined in ORS 801.545, and any judgment of conviction or acquittal of a person charged with a traffic crime, as defined by ORS 801.545, are not admissible in the trial of a subsequent civil action arising out of the same accident or occurrence to prove or negate the facts upon which such judgment was rendered. [1975 c.542 §1; 1981 c.892 §87; 1999 c.1051 §242; 2007 c.784 §6; 2011 c.597 §30]

41.910 Certain intercepted communications inadmissible. Evidence of the contents of any wire or oral communication intercepted:

(1) In violation of ORS 165.540 shall not be admissible in any court of this state, except as evidence of unlawful interception or when the evidence was created by the use of a video camera worn upon a law enforcement officer's person and the officer either substantially complied with or attempted in good faith to comply with ORS 165.540 (5)(d)(B).

(2) Under ORS 165.540 (2)(a) shall not be admissible in any court of this state unless:

(a) The communication was intercepted by a public official in charge of and at a jail, police premises, sheriff's office, Department of Corrections institution or other penal or correctional institution; and

(b) The participant in the communication, against whom the evidence is being offered, had actual notice that the communication was being monitored or recorded. [1955 c.675 §6; 1959 c.681 §5; 1979 c.716 §12; 1983 c.824 §4; 1993 c.178 §1; 2001 c.385 §5; 2015 c.550 §3]

41.915 [1973 c.263 §1; repealed by 1979 c.284 §199]

41.920 [1973 c.263 §2; repealed by 1979 c.284 §199]

41.925 [1973 c.263 §3; repealed by 1979 c.284 §199]

41.930 Admissibility of copies of original records. The copy of the records described in ORCP 55 H or ORS 136.447 is admissible in evidence to the same extent as though the original thereof were offered and a custodian of hospital records had been present and testified to the matters stated in the affidavit. The affidavit is admissible as evidence of the matters stated therein. The matters stated therein are presumed to be true. The presumption established by this section is a presumption affecting the burden of producing evidence. [1973 c.263 §4; 1979 c.284 §77; 1995 c.196 §4]

41.935 [1973 c.263 §5; repealed by 1979 c.284 §199]

41.940 [1973 c.263 §§6,7; repealed by 1979 c.284 §199]

41.945 Application of ORS 41.930 and ORCP 55 H. ORS 41.930 and ORCP 55 H apply in any proceedings in which testimony may be compelled. [1973 c.263 §8; 1979 c.284 §78]

41.950 [1971 c.331 §1; renumbered 18.500]

41.960 [1971 c.331 §2; renumbered 18.520]

41.970 [1971 c.331 §3; renumbered 18.530]

41.980 [1971 c.331 §4; repealed by 1981 c.892 §98]

Chapter 42 — Execution, Formalities and Interpretation of Writings

2017 EDITION

WRITINGS

EVIDENCE AND WITNESSES

PRIVATE WRITINGS

42.010 Private writings

42.020 Execution of a writing

42.030 Subscribing witness

42.040 Proof of attested writing other than a will

SEALS

42.110 Seal defined

42.115 Effect of presence or absence of seal

42.125 Seal of state officer or state agency authorized

INTERPRETATION OF WRITINGS

42.210 Effect of the place of execution

42.220 Consideration of circumstances

42.230 Office of judge in construing instruments

42.240 Intention of the parties; general and particular provisions and intents

42.250 Terms construed as generally accepted; evidence of other signification

42.260 Ambiguous terms

42.270 Written words control printed form

42.280 Deciphering characters and translating languages

42.290 Construction of notices

42.300 Parties to written instrument not to deny facts recited therein

42.005 [1981 c.892 §79a; 1993 c.546 §96; repealed by 2001 c.104 §13]

PRIVATE WRITINGS

 42.010 Private writings. All writings, other than public writings, are private and may be sealed or unsealed.

 42.020 Execution of a writing. The execution of a writing is the subscribing and delivering it, with or without affixing a seal.

 42.030 Subscribing witness. A subscribing witness is one who sees a writing executed, or hears it acknowledged, and at the request of the party thereupon signs one's name as a witness.

 42.040 Proof of attested writing other than a will. Any attested writing other than a will may be proved in the same manner as though it had not been attested.

 42.050 [Repealed by 1981 c.892 §98]

 42.060 [Repealed by 1981 c.892 §98]

 42.070 [Repealed by 1981 c.892 §98]

 42.080 [Repealed by 1981 c.892 §98]

42.110 Seal defined. A seal is a particular sign made to attest in the most formal manner the execution of an instrument.

42.115 Effect of presence or absence of seal. The presence or absence of a seal, corporate or otherwise, shall have no effect upon the validity, enforceability or character of any written instrument except where specifically otherwise provided by statute. A writing under seal may be modified or discharged by writing not under seal or by a valid oral agreement. [1965 c.502 §2]

42.120 [Repealed by 1965 c.502 §6]

42.125 Seal of state officer or state agency authorized. (1) For the purposes of ORS 40.510 (1)(a) and (d), each state officer and state agency may have a seal which, unless specifically provided otherwise by law, shall consist of an impression, imprint or likeness of the state seal accompanied by the name of the state officer or state agency.
(2) As used in this section:
(a) "Seal" has the meaning given that term in ORS 42.110.
(b) "State agency" means every state officer, board, commission, department, institution, branch or agency of the state government, except:
(A) The Legislative Assembly and the courts and their officers and committees; and
(B) The Public Defense Services Commission.
(c) "State officer" includes any appointed state official who is authorized by the Oregon Department of Administrative Services to have a seal and any elected state official, except members of the Legislative Assembly. [1982 s.s.1 c.14 §1; 2003 c.449 §23; 2005 c.22 §32]

42.130 [Repealed by 1965 c.502 §6]

42.140 [Repealed by 1965 c.502 §6]

42.150 [Repealed by 1965 c.502 §6]

42.160 [Repealed by 1965 c.502 §6]

INTERPRETATION OF WRITINGS

42.210 Effect of the place of execution. The language of a writing is to be interpreted according to the meaning it bears in the place of execution, unless the parties have reference to a different place.

42.220 Consideration of circumstances. In construing an instrument, the circumstances under which it was made, including the situation of the subject and of the parties, may be shown so that the judge is placed in the position of those whose language the judge is interpreting.

42.230 Office of judge in construing instruments. In the construction of an instrument, the office of the judge is simply to ascertain and declare what is, in terms or in substance, contained therein, not to insert what has been omitted, or to omit what has been inserted; and where there are several provisions or particulars, such construction is, if possible, to be adopted as will give effect to all.

42.240 Intention of the parties; general and particular provisions and intents. In the construction of an instrument the intention of the parties is to be pursued if possible; and when a general and particular provision are inconsistent, the latter is paramount to the former. So a particular intent shall control a general one that is inconsistent with it.

42.250 Terms construed as generally accepted; evidence of other signification. The terms of a writing are presumed to have been used in their primary and general acceptation, but evidence is admissible that they have a technical, local, or otherwise peculiar signification and were used and understood in the particular instance, in which case the agreement shall be construed accordingly.

42.260 Ambiguous terms. When the terms of an agreement have been intended in a different sense by the parties, that sense is to prevail, against either party, in which the party supposed the other understood it. When different constructions of a provision are otherwise equally proper, that construction is to be taken which is most favorable to the party in whose favor the provision was made.

42.270 Written words control printed form. When an instrument consists partly of written words and partly of a printed form, and the two are inconsistent, the former controls.

42.280 Deciphering characters and translating languages. When the characters in which an instrument is written are difficult to be deciphered, or the language is not understood by the court, evidence of persons skilled in deciphering the characters, or who understand the language, is admissible to declare the characters or the meaning of the language.

42.290 Construction of notices. A written notice is to be construed according to the ordinary acceptation of its terms. Thus, a notice to the drawers or indorsers of a bill of exchange or promissory note, that it has been protested for want of acceptance or payment, shall be held to import that it has been duly presented for acceptance or payment and refused, and that the holder looks for payment to the person to whom the notice is given.

42.300 Parties to written instrument not to deny facts recited therein. Except for the recital of a consideration, the truth of the facts recited from the recital in a written instrument shall not be denied by the parties thereto, their representatives or successors in interest by a subsequent title. [1981 c.892 §83]

––––––––––––––––

Chapter 43 — Public Writings

2017 EDITION

PUBLIC WRITINGS

EVIDENCE AND WITNESSES

43.130   Judicial orders that are conclusive

43.140 Judicial orders that create a disputable presumption

43.150 When parties the same

43.160 What determined by former judgment

43.170 Effect on principal of judgment against surety

43.180 Effect of judicial record of other jurisdictions

43.200 Effect of judicial record of foreign admiralty court

43.220 Impeachment of judicial record

43.450 Official records and files of United States Army, Navy and Air Force

43.010 [Repealed by 1981 c.892 §98]

43.020 [Repealed by 1981 c.892 §98]

43.030 [Repealed by 1981 c.892 §98]

43.040 [Repealed by 1981 c.892 §98]

43.050 [Repealed by 1981 c.892 §98]

43.060 [Repealed by 1981 c.892 §98]

43.070 [Repealed by 1981 c.892 §98]

43.080 [Repealed by 1981 c.892 §98]

43.110 [Repealed by 1981 c.892 §98]

43.120 [Repealed by 1981 c.892 §98]

43.130 Judicial orders that are conclusive. The effect of a judgment, decree or final order in an action, suit or proceeding before a court or judge of this state or of the United States, having jurisdiction is as follows:
(1) In case of a judgment, decree or order against a specific thing or in respect to the probate of a will or the administration of the estate of a deceased person or in respect to the personal, political, or legal condition or relation of a particular person, the judgment, decree or order is conclusive upon the title to the thing, the will or administration, or the condition or relation of the person.
(2) In other cases, the judgment, decree or order is, in respect to the matter directly determined, conclusive between the parties, their representatives and their successors in interest by title subsequent to the commencement of the action, suit or proceeding, litigating for the same thing, under the same title and in the same capacity.

43.140 Judicial orders that create a disputable presumption. A judicial order, other than a judgment, decree or final order, in an action, suit or proceeding before a court or judge of this state or of the United States creates a disputable presumption concerning the matter directly determined between the same parties, their representatives and their successors in interest by title subsequent to the commencement of the action, suit or proceeding, litigating for the same thing, under the same title and in the same capacity.

43.150 When parties the same. The parties are the same when those between whom the evidence is offered were adverse in the former case, and a judgment, decree or other determination could have been made between them alone, though other parties were joined.

43.160 What determined by former judgment. That only is determined by a former judgment, decree or order which appears upon its face to have been so determined or which was actually and necessarily included therein or necessary thereto.

43.170 Effect on principal of judgment against surety. Whenever, pursuant to ORS 43.130 to 43.160, a party is bound by a record, and stands in the relation of surety for another, the latter is also bound from the time that the latter has notice of the action, suit or proceeding and a request from the surety to defend against it.

43.180 Effect of judicial record of other jurisdictions. The effect of a judicial record of a sister state, the District of Columbia or a territory of the United States is the same in this state as in the place where it was made, except:
(1) It can be enforced in this state only by an action, suit or proceeding; and
(2) The authority of a guardian, conservator, committee, executor or administrator does not extend beyond the jurisdiction of the government under which the guardian, conservator, committee, executor or administrator is invested with authority. [Amended by 1973 c.823 §90; 2005 c.22 §33]

43.190 [Repealed by 1975 c.542 §2]

43.200 Effect of judicial record of foreign admiralty court. The effect of a judicial record of a court of admiralty of a foreign country is the same as if it were the record of a court of admiralty of the United States.

43.210 [Repealed by 1981 c.892 §98]

43.220 Impeachment of judicial record. Any judicial record may be impeached and the presumption arising therefrom overcome by evidence of a want of jurisdiction, collusion between the parties, or fraud in the party offering the record. The jurisdiction sufficient to sustain a record is jurisdiction over the cause, over the parties and, when a specific thing is the subject of the determination, over the thing.

43.310 [Repealed by 1981 c.892 §98]

43.320 [Repealed by 1981 c.892 §98]

43.330 [Repealed by 1981 c.892 §98]

43.340 [Repealed by 1981 c.892 §98]

43.350 [Repealed by 1981 c.892 §98]

43.360 [Repealed by 1981 c.892 §98]

43.370 [Amended by 1967 c.489 §1; repealed by 1981 c.892 §98]

43.380 [Renumbered 432.175]

43.390 [Repealed by 1981 c.892 §98]

43.400 [Repealed by 1981 c.892 §98]

43.410 [Amended by 1961 c.150 §7; 1961 c.160 §3a; repealed by 1981 c.892 §98]

43.420 [Repealed by 1981 c.892 §98]

43.430 [Repealed by 1981 c.892 §98]

43.440 [Repealed by 1981 c.892 §98]

43.450 Official records and files of United States Army, Navy and Air Force. Relevant official records and files of the Departments of the Army, Navy and Air Force of the United States shall be accorded prima facie probative value in evidence before any court or agency in which there is an issue of fact as to the death or disappearance of any person while serving in or with the Armed Forces of the United States.

43.460 [Repealed by 1981 c.892 §98]

43.470 [Amended by 1967 c.489 §2; repealed by 1981 c.892 §98]

Chapter 44 — Witnesses

2017 EDITION

WITNESSES

EVIDENCE AND WITNESSES

GENERAL PROVISIONS

44.080   Protection of witness from improper questions and excessive detention

44.090   Protection of witness from arrest

44.150   Service of subpoena if witness concealed

44.240   Production of witness confined in Department of Corrections institution

44.320   Authority to take testimony and administer oath or affirmation

44.370   Witness presumed to speak truth; jury judges of credibility

FEES

44.415   Fees and mileage of witnesses

MEDIA PERSONS AS WITNESSES

44.510   Definitions for ORS 44.510 to 44.540

44.520   Limitation on compellable testimony from media persons; search of media persons' papers, effects or work premises prohibited; exception

44.530   Application of ORS 44.520

44.540   Effect of informant as witness

CHILDREN OR PERSONS WITH DEVELOPMENTAL DISABILITIES AS WITNESSES

44.545   Expediting proceedings

44.547   Notice to court; accommodations

LAW ENFORCEMENT PERSONNEL AS WITNESSES

44.550   Definitions for ORS 44.550 to 44.566

44.552   Method of subpoenaing law enforcement personnel; subpoena to reflect whether expert opinion to be asked

44.554   Payment of law enforcement personnel subpoenaed as expert witness; obligation of party to reimburse law enforcement agency; method of payment

44.556   Prepayment of expenses in certain cases required

44.558   Payment for additional attendance beyond first day required in advance

44.560   Application to subpoenas for depositions

44.562   Party and law enforcement personnel may agree to modify time of appearance

44.564   Right of action to recover payment due

44.566   Provisions not applicable if public body a party

44.010 [Repealed by 1981 c.892 §98]

44.020 [Repealed by 1981 c.892 §98]

44.030 [Repealed by 1981 c.892 §98]

44.040 [Amended by 1957 c.44 §1; 1963 c.396 §16; 1971 c.512 §4; 1973 c.136 §6; 1973 c.777 §19a; 1973 c.794 §13; 1975 c.694 §1; 1975 c.726 §1; 1977 c.656 §1; 1977 c.677 §12a; 1979 c.284 §79; 1979 c.731 §2; 1979 c.744 §1a; 1979 c.769 §12b; repealed by 1981 c.892 §98]

44.050 [Repealed by 1981 c.892 §98]

44.060 [Repealed by 1981 c.892 §98]

44.070 [Repealed by 1981 c.892 §98]

GENERAL PROVISIONS

44.080 Protection of witness from improper questions and excessive detention. It is the right of a witness to be protected from irrelevant, insulting or improper questions, and from harsh or insulting demeanor. The witness is to be detained only so long as the interests of justice require.

44.090 Protection of witness from arrest. (1) Every person who has been, in good faith, served with a subpoena to attend as a witness before a court, judge, commissioner, referee or other officer, is exonerated from arrest, in a civil case, while going to the place of attendance, necessarily remaining there and returning. The arrest of a witness contrary to this section is void, and when willfully made is a contempt of the court; and the officer making the arrest is responsible to the witness for double the amount of the damages which may be assessed against the officer, and is also liable in an action by the party serving the witness with the subpoena, for the damages sustained by that party in consequence of the arrest.
    (2) But the officer is not liable in any way, unless the person claiming the exemption makes, if required, an affidavit stating:
    (a) That the person has been served with a subpoena to attend as a witness before a court, judge or other officer, specifying the same, the place of attendance and the action, suit or proceeding in which the subpoena was issued; and
    (b) That the person has not been served by the procurement of the person with the intention of avoiding an arrest.
    (3) The affidavit may be taken by the officer and exonerates the officer from liability for not making the arrest, or for discharging the witness when arrested.
    (4) The court, judge or officer before whom the attendance of the witness is required may discharge the witness from an arrest made in violation of this section.

44.095 [1973 c.386 §1; repealed by 1981 c.892 §98]

44.110 [Repealed by 1979 c.284 §199]

44.120 [Amended by 1969 c.383 §1; repealed by 1979 c.284 §199]

44.130 [Amended by 1969 c.383 §2; repealed by 1979 c.284 §199]

44.140 [Amended by 1977 c.789 §2; repealed by 1979 c.284 §199]

44.150 Service of subpoena if witness concealed. A sheriff, deputy or some person specially appointed by the sheriff, but none other, is authorized and required to break into any building or vessel in which a witness may be concealed to prevent the service of a subpoena, and serve it on the witness.

44.160 [Repealed by 1979 c.284 §199]

44.170 [Repealed by 1961 c.413 §1 (44.171 enacted in lieu of 44.170)]

44.171 [1961 c.413 §2 (enacted in lieu of 44.170); repealed by 1979 c.284 §199]

44.180 [Repealed by 1979 c.284 §199]

44.190 [Repealed by 1979 c.284 §199]

44.200 [Repealed by 1979 c.284 §199]

44.210 [Repealed by 1979 c.284 §199]

44.220 [Repealed by 1979 c.284 §199]

44.230 [Amended by 1973 c.836 §326; repealed by 1979 c.284 §199]

44.240 Production of witness confined in Department of Corrections institution. (1) Whenever a court or judge makes an order for the temporary removal and production of a witness who is confined in a Department of Corrections institution within this state before a court or officer for the purpose of being orally examined this section applies. The superintendent of the institution shall, at the institution, deliver the witness to the sheriff of the county in which the court or judge making the order is located.

(2) The sheriff shall give the superintendent a signed receipt when taking custody of the witness under subsection (1) of this section. The sheriff shall be responsible for the custody of the witness until the sheriff returns the witness to the institution. Upon the return of the witness to the institution by the sheriff, the superintendent shall give a signed receipt therefor to the sheriff.

(3) When a witness is delivered to a sheriff under subsection (1) of this section, or at any time while the witness is in the custody of the sheriff as provided in subsection (2) of this section, the superintendent may give the sheriff a list of persons who may communicate with the witness or with whom the witness may communicate. Except as otherwise required by law, upon receipt of the list and while the witness is in the custody of the sheriff, the sheriff shall permit communication only between the witness and those persons designated by the list.

(4) The sheriff and neither the institution nor the Department of Corrections shall be liable for any expense incurred in connection with the witness while the witness is in the custody of the sheriff as provided in subsection (2) of this section. If the witness is a party plaintiff, the sheriff shall recover costs of the care of the witness from the plaintiff, and shall have a lien upon any judgment for the plaintiff. In all other cases, the sheriff and not the witness shall be entitled to the witness fees and mileage to which the witness would otherwise be entitled under ORS 44.415 (2), or other applicable law. [1955 c.523 §1; 1969 c.502 §2; 1973 c.836 §327; 1987 c.320 §13; 1987 c.606 §6; 1989 c.980 §3a]

44.310 [Repealed by 1981 c.892 §98]

44.320 Authority to take testimony and administer oath or affirmation. Every court, judge, clerk of a court, justice of the peace, certified shorthand reporter as defined in ORS 8.415 or notary public is authorized to take testimony in any action or proceeding, as are other persons in particular cases authorized by statute or the Oregon Rules of Civil Procedure and is authorized to administer oaths and affirmations generally, and every such other person in the particular case authorized. [Amended by 1979 c.284 §81; 1989 c.1055 §13; 1997 c.249 §21]

44.330 [Repealed by 1981 c.892 §98]

44.340 [Repealed by 1981 c.892 §98]

44.350 [Repealed by 1981 c.892 §98]

44.360 [Repealed by 1981 c.892 §98]

44.370 Witness presumed to speak truth; jury judges of credibility. A witness is presumed to speak the truth. This presumption, however, may be overcome by the manner in which the witness testifies, by the character of the testimony of the witness, or by evidence affecting the character or motives of the witness, or by contradictory evidence. Where the trial is by the jury, they are the exclusive judges of the credibility of the witness.

44.410 [Amended by 1959 c.158 §1; repealed by 1989 c.980 §24]

FEES

44.415 Fees and mileage of witnesses. (1) Except as provided in subsection (2) of this section, a person is entitled to receive $30 for each day's attendance as a witness and mileage reimbursement at the rate of 25 cents a mile if the person is required to travel from a place within or outside this state in order to perform duties as a witness. Total mileage reimbursement shall not exceed the necessary cost of transportation on reasonably available common carriers.

(2) In any criminal proceeding, any proceeding prosecuted by a public body or any proceeding where a public body is a party, a person is entitled to receive $5 for each day's attendance as a witness and mileage reimbursement at the rate of eight cents a mile if the person is required to travel from a place within or outside this state in order to perform duties as a witness. Total mileage reimbursement shall not exceed the necessary cost of transportation on reasonably available common carriers.

(3) As used in this section, "public body" means any state, city, county, school district, other political subdivision, municipal corporation, public corporation and any instrumentality thereof. [1989 c.980 §2]

44.420 [Repealed by 1959 c.158 §2]

44.430 [Repealed by 1989 c.980 §24]

44.440 [Amended by 1963 c.519 §24; 1977 c.408 §1; repealed by 1981 s.s. c.3 §141]

44.450 [Amended by 1977 c.593 §1; repealed by 1981 s.s. c.3 §141]

MEDIA PERSONS AS WITNESSES

44.510 Definitions for ORS 44.510 to 44.540. As used in ORS 44.510 to 44.540, unless the context requires otherwise:

(1) "Information" has its ordinary meaning and includes, but is not limited to, any written, oral, pictorial or electronically recorded news or other data.

(2) "Medium of communication" has its ordinary meaning and includes, but is not limited to, any newspaper, magazine or other periodical, book, pamphlet, news service, wire service, news or feature syndicate, broadcast station or network, or cable television system. Any information which is a portion of a governmental utterance made by an official or employee of government within the scope of the official's or employee's governmental function, or any political publication subject to ORS 260.532, is not included within the meaning of "medium of communication."

(3) "Processing" has its ordinary meaning and includes, but is not limited to, the compiling, storing and editing of information.

(4) "Published information" means any information disseminated to the public.

(5) "Unpublished information" means any information not disseminated to the public, whether or not related information has been disseminated. "Unpublished information" includes, but is not limited to, all notes, outtakes, photographs, tapes or other data of whatever sort not themselves disseminated to the public through a medium of communication, whether or not published information based upon or related to such material has been disseminated. [1973 c.22 §2; 1979 c.190 §398; 2001 c.965 §18; 2005 c.797 §50]

44.520 Limitation on compellable testimony from media persons; search of media persons' papers, effects or work premises prohibited; exception. (1) No person connected with, employed by or engaged in any medium of communication to the public shall be required by a legislative, executive or judicial officer or body, or any other authority having power to compel testimony or the production of evidence, to disclose, by subpoena or otherwise:

(a) The source of any published or unpublished information obtained by the person in the course of gathering, receiving or processing information for any medium of communication to the public; or

(b) Any unpublished information obtained or prepared by the person in the course of gathering, receiving or processing information for any medium of communication to the public.

(2) No papers, effects or work premises of a person connected with, employed by or engaged in any medium of communication to the public shall be subject to a search by a legislative, executive or judicial officer or body, or any other authority having power to compel the production of evidence, by search warrant or otherwise. The provisions of this subsection, however, shall not apply where probable cause exists to believe that the person has committed, is committing or is about to commit a crime. [1973 c.22 §3; 1979 c.820 §1]

44.530 Application of ORS 44.520. (1) ORS 44.520 applies regardless of whether a person has disclosed elsewhere any of the information or source thereof, or any of the related information.

(2) ORS 44.520 continues to apply in relation to any of the information, or source thereof, or any related information, even in the event of subsequent termination of a person's connection with, employment by or engagement in any medium of communication to the public.

(3) The provisions of ORS 44.520 (1) do not apply with respect to the content or source of allegedly defamatory information, in civil action for defamation wherein the defendant asserts a defense based on the content or source of such information. [1973 c.22 §§4,5; 1979 c.820 §2]

44.540 Effect of informant as witness. If the informant offers the informant as a witness, it is deemed a consent to the examination also of a person described in ORS 44.520 on the same subject. [1973 c.22 §6]

CHILDREN OR PERSONS WITH DEVELOPMENTAL DISABILITIES AS WITNESSES

44.545 Expediting proceedings. (1) Except as otherwise provided in subsection (2) of this section or except for good cause shown by either party, in any case where a child or a member of the family of the child is a victim of a crime and where a child under 18 years of age is called to give testimony, the court, consistent with the rules of civil or criminal procedure, shall expedite the action and insure that it takes precedence over any other. When determining whether or not to grant a continuance, the judge shall take into consideration the age of the child and the potential adverse impact the delay may have on the well-being of the child. The court shall make written findings of fact and conclusions of law when granting a continuance.

(2) The provisions of subsection (1) of this section do not apply to any juvenile proceeding other than the termination of parental rights. [1991 c.387 §1]

Note: 44.545 was enacted into law by the Legislative Assembly but was not added to or made a part of ORS chapter 44 or any series therein by legislative action. See Preface to Oregon Revised Statutes for further explanation.

44.547 Notice to court; accommodations. (1) In any case in which a child under 12 years of age or a person with a developmental disability described in subsection (2) of this section is called to give testimony, the attorney or party who plans to call the witness must notify the court at least seven days before the trial or proceeding of any special accommodations needed by the witness. Upon receiving the notice, the court shall order such accommodations as are appropriate under the circumstances considering the age or disability of the witness. Accommodations ordered by the court may include:

(a) Break periods during the proceedings for the benefit of the witness.

(b) Designation of a waiting area appropriate to the special needs of the witness.

(c) Conducting proceedings in clothing other than judicial robes.

(d) Relaxing the formalities of the proceedings.

(e) Adjusting the layout of the courtroom for the comfort of the witness.

(f) Conducting the proceedings outside of the normal courtroom.

(2) For the purposes of this section, "developmental disability" means a disability attributable to mental retardation, autism, cerebral palsy, epilepsy or other disabling neurological condition that requires training or support similar to that required by persons with mental retardation, if either of the following apply:

(a) The disability originates before the person attains 22 years of age, or if the disability is attributable to mental retardation the condition is manifested before the person attains 18 years of age, the disability can be expected to continue indefinitely, and the disability constitutes a substantial handicap to the ability of the person to function in society.

(b) The disability results in a significant subaverage general intellectual functioning with concurrent deficits in adaptive behavior that are manifested during the developmental period. [1995 c.804 §1]

Note: 44.547 was enacted into law by the Legislative Assembly but was not added to or made a part of ORS chapter 44 or any series therein by legislative action. See Preface to Oregon Revised Statutes for further explanation.

LAW ENFORCEMENT PERSONNEL AS WITNESSES

44.550 Definitions for ORS 44.550 to 44.566. As used in ORS 44.550 to 44.566:

(1) "Civil case" means any proceeding other than a criminal prosecution.

(2) "Law enforcement unit" means:

(a) The police department of a city;

(b) The sheriff's department or other police organization of a county; or

(c) A police department established by a university under ORS 352.121 or 353.125.

(3) "Police officer" means an officer or member of a law enforcement unit who is employed full-time as a peace officer by the city or county and who is responsible for enforcing the criminal laws of this state.

(4) "Tribunal" means any person or body before which attendance of witnesses may be required by subpoena, including an arbitrator in arbitration proceedings. [1991 c.550 §1; 2011 c.506 §3; 2013 c.180 §4]

Note: 44.550 to 44.566 were enacted into law by the Legislative Assembly but were not added to or made a part of ORS chapter 44 or any series therein by legislative action. See Preface to Oregon Revised Statutes for further explanation.

44.552 Method of subpoenaing law enforcement personnel; subpoena to reflect whether expert opinion to be asked. (1) Whenever a police officer or an employee of the Department of State Police is called as an expert witness in a civil case by a party by whom the officer or employee is not employed, a subpoena requiring attendance may be served by delivering a copy either to the officer or employee personally or to the officer's or employee's immediate superior.

(2)(a) A person causing a subpoena to be issued to compel the attendance of a police officer or an employee of the Department of State Police before a tribunal shall indicate on the face of the subpoena whether the person or the person's representative intends to ask the expert opinion of the officer or employee as to any aspect of the proceedings.

(b) A police officer or an employee of the Department of State Police may not be required by a tribunal to give the officer's or employee's expert opinion on any matter before the tribunal unless the subpoena compelling the officer's or employee's presence indicates that the officer's or employee's expert opinion will be asked. [1991 c.550 §2; 2011 c.547 §22]

Note: See note under 44.550.

44.554 Payment of law enforcement personnel subpoenaed as expert witness; obligation of party to reimburse law enforcement agency; method of payment. (1) A police officer or an employee of the Department of State Police who is obliged by a subpoena issued pursuant to ORS 44.552 (2) to attend as an expert witness shall receive from the law enforcement unit by which the officer is employed or the Department of State Police, respectively:

(a) The salary or other compensation to which the officer or employee is normally entitled during the time that the officer or employee travels to and from the place where the court or other tribunal is located and while the officer or employee is required to remain at that place pursuant to the subpoena; and

(b) The actual necessary and reasonable traveling expenses incurred in complying with the subpoena.

(2)(a) The party at whose request a subpoena is issued pursuant to ORS 44.552 (2) compelling the attendance of a police officer or employee of the Department of State Police as an expert witness shall reimburse the law enforcement unit by which the officer is employed or the Department of State Police, respectively, for the full cost to the law enforcement unit or the department incurred in reimbursing the officer or employee as provided in subsection (1) of this section for each day that the officer or employee is required to remain in attendance pursuant to the subpoena.

(b) The amount of $160 must be tendered with any subpoena issued under ORS 44.552 (2) to compel the attendance of a police officer or an employee of the Department of State Police as an expert witness for each day that the officer or employee is required to remain in attendance pursuant to the subpoena.

(c) Notwithstanding paragraph (b) of this subsection, if the person causing the issuance of a subpoena requiring the expert opinion of a police officer or an employee of the Department of State Police makes arrangements with the officer or the employee and with the tribunal prior to the issuance of the subpoena to take the testimony of the officer or employee by telephone, and testimony by telephone is otherwise allowed by the Oregon Rules of Civil Procedure, the amount of $80 shall be tendered with the subpoena for each day that the officer or employee is required to testify pursuant to the subpoena.

(3) If the actual expenses are less than the amount tendered, the excess of the amount tendered shall be refunded.

(4)(a) If the actual expenses are greater than the amount tendered, the difference shall be paid to the law enforcement unit by which the officer is employed or the Department of State Police, as appropriate, by the party at whose request the subpoena is issued.

(b) Notwithstanding paragraph (a) of this subsection, additional amounts are not payable unless, within seven days after the final day on which the officer or employee appears in the proceedings, the law enforcement unit or the Department of State Police, respectively, mails a statement to the party or to the party's attorney reflecting the additional amounts due.

(5) If a court or tribunal continues a proceeding on its own motion, no additional expert witness fee may be required prior to the issuance of a subpoena or the making of an order directing the officer or employee to appear on the date to which the proceeding is continued. [1991 c.550 §3; 2011 c.547 §23]

Note: See note under 44.550.

44.556 Prepayment of expenses in certain cases required. A police officer or an employee of the Department of State Police who is called as an expert witness in a civil case may demand the payment specified in ORS 44.554 (2) for one day, in advance, and when so demanded may not be compelled to attend until the payment is tendered. [1991 c.550 §4; 2011 c.547 §24]

Note: See note under 44.550.

44.558 Payment for additional attendance beyond first day required in advance. A police officer or an employee of the Department of State Police may not be ordered to return by the court or tribunal for subsequent proceedings beyond the day stated in the subpoena requiring the officer or employee to give the officer's or employee's expert opinion referred to in ORS 44.552 (2) or the day upon which the officer or employee appeared under ORS 44.562 (2), unless the party at whose request the subpoena was issued, or the party at whose request the officer or employee is ordered to return, shall first tender to the officer or employee the same sum required to be tendered with a subpoena in the first instance. [1991 c.550 §5; 2011 c.547 §25]

Note: See note under 44.550.

44.560 Application to subpoenas for depositions. ORS 44.552, 44.554 and 44.558 apply to subpoenas issued for the taking of depositions of police officers and employees of the Department of State Police. [1991 c.550 §6; 2011 c.547 §26]

Note: See note under 44.550.

44.562 Party and law enforcement personnel may agree to modify time of appearance. A police officer or an employee of the Department of State Police who has been subpoenaed under ORS 44.552 and 44.560 for the purpose of giving the officer's or employee's expert opinion, in lieu of attendance at the time specified in the subpoena, may agree with the party at whose request the subpoena was issued to appear at another time or pursuant to such notice as may be agreed upon. [1991 c.550 §7; 2011 c.547 §27]

Note: See note under 44.550.

44.564 Right of action to recover payment due. Whenever a police officer or an employee of the Department of State Police appears as an expert witness under ORS 44.550 to 44.566 and reimbursement is not made as provided for in ORS 44.550 to 44.566, the law enforcement unit by which the officer is employed or the Department of State Police, respectively, has standing to bring an action in order to recover the funds. [1991 c.550 §8; 2011 c.547 §28]

Note: See note under 44.550.

44.566 Provisions not applicable if public body a party. ORS 44.550 to 44.566 shall not apply to any proceeding in which a public body is a party. For the purposes of this section, "public body" has the meaning given in ORS 30.260. [1991 c.550 §9]

Note: See note under 44.550.

44.610 [1973 c.136 §1; repealed by 1979 c.284 §199]

44.620 [1973 c.136 §§2,3; repealed by 1979 c.284 §199]

44.630 [1973 c.136 §4; repealed by 1979 c.284 §199]

44.640 [1973 c.136 §5; repealed by 1979 c.284 §199]

Chapter 45 — Testimony Generally

TESTIMONY GENERALLY

EVIDENCE AND WITNESSES

MODES OF TAKING TESTIMONY

45.010   Modes of testimony

45.020   Affidavit described

45.040   Oral examination described

AFFIDAVITS AND DECLARATIONS IN SUPPORT OF PROVISIONAL REMEDIES

45.130   Production of affiant or declarant for cross-examination

DEPOSITIONS

(Taking of Deposition)

45.132   Definition for ORS 45.135, 45.138 and 45.142

45.135   Who may not report deposition in civil action

45.138   Duties of person recording or reporting deposition

45.142   Recording or reporting services provided under contract; required disclosures; objection to reporter

(Use of Deposition)

45.250   Use of deposition

45.260   Introduction, or exclusion, of part of deposition

45.270   Use of deposition in same or other proceedings

INTERPRETERS

45.272   Definitions for ORS 45.272 to 45.297

45.273   Policy

45.275   Appointment of interpreter for non-English-speaking party, witness or victim; substitution; payment of costs

45.285   Appointment of interpreter for party, witness or victim with disability; provision of assistive communication device

45.288   Appointment of certified interpreter required; exceptions; disqualifications; code of professional responsibility

45.291   Certification program; establishment by State Court Administrator; rules

45.292   Certification required for use of title or designation "certified court interpreter" or "court certified interpreter"

45.294   Court Interpreter and Shorthand Reporter Certification Account; sources; uses

45.297   Authority to enter into service contracts

REMOTE LOCATION TESTIMONY

45.400   Remote location testimony; when authorized; notice; payment of costs

PENALTIES

45.900   Penalty for violation of ORS 45.135 or 45.138

MODES OF TAKING TESTIMONY

45.010 Modes of testimony. The testimony of a witness is taken by six modes:
(1) Affidavit.
(2) Deposition.
(3) Oral examination.
(4) Remote location examination under ORS 45.400.
(5) Examination before a grand jury by means of simultaneous television transmission under ORS 132.320.
(6) Declaration under penalty of perjury, as described in ORCP 1 E, or unsworn declaration under ORS 194.800 to 194.835, if the declarant is physically outside the boundaries of the United States. [Amended by 1993 c.425 §2; 1995 c.126 §3; 2003 c.194 §2; 2013 c.218 §11; 2017 c.240 §2]

45.020 Affidavit described. An affidavit is a written declaration under oath, made without notice to the adverse party.

45.030 [Repealed by 1979 c.284 §199]

45.040 Oral examination described. An oral examination is an examination in the presence of the jury or tribunal which is to decide the fact, or act upon it, the testimony being heard by the jury or tribunal from the mouth of the witness.

45.050 [Amended by 1961 c.461 §1; 1979 c.284 §82; repealed by 1981 c.898 §53]

45.110 [Repealed by 1979 c.284 §199]

45.120 [Repealed by 1979 c.284 §199]

45.125 [Formerly 45.180; repealed by 1977 c.404 §2 (194.500 to 194.580 enacted in lieu of 45.125)]

AFFIDAVITS AND DECLARATIONS IN SUPPORT OF PROVISIONAL REMEDIES

45.130 Production of affiant or declarant for cross-examination. Whenever a provisional remedy has been allowed upon affidavit, a declaration under penalty of perjury as described in ORCP 1 E or an unsworn declaration under ORS 194.800 to 194.835, if the declarant is physically outside the boundaries of the United States, the party against whom it is allowed may serve upon the party by whom it was obtained a notice, requiring the affiant or declarant to be produced for cross-examination before a named officer authorized to administer oaths. Thereupon the party to whom the remedy was allowed shall lose the benefit of the affidavit or declaration and all proceedings founded thereon, unless within eight days, or such other time as the court or judge may direct, upon a previous notice to the adversary of at least three days, the party produces the affiant or declarant for examination before the officer mentioned in the notice, or some other of like authority, provided for in the order of the court or judge. Upon production, the affiant or declarant may be examined by either party, but a party is not obliged to make this production of an affiant or a declarant except within the county where the provisional remedy was allowed. [Amended by 2003 c.194 §3; 2013 c.218 §12]

DEPOSITIONS

(Taking of Deposition)

45.132 Definition for ORS 45.135, 45.138 and 45.142. As used in ORS 45.135, 45.138 and 45.142, "deposition" means the taking of testimony for discovery, the taking of testimony for perpetuation of the testimony and the taking of testimony in arbitration proceedings. [1999 c.942 §5]

45.135 Who may not report deposition in civil action. (1) A deposition in a civil action may not be stenographically reported by:
(a) A party in the action;
(b) A person with a financial interest in the outcome of the action;
(c) An attorney for a party in the action;
(d) An attorney for a person with a financial interest in the outcome of the action;
(e) An employee of a party in the action;
(f) An employee of an attorney for a party in the action;
(g) An employee of a person with a financial interest in the outcome of the action;
(h) An employee of an attorney for a person with a financial interest in the outcome of the action; or
(i) A person related, by affinity or consanguinity within the third degree, to a party in the action or to a person with a financial interest in the outcome of the action.
(2) Any deposition recorded or reported by a person in violation of this section may not be introduced in evidence or used for any other purpose in a civil action. [1999 c.942 §1]

45.138 Duties of person recording or reporting deposition. (1) A person recording or reporting a deposition is personally responsible for the accurate and complete recording or reporting of the deposition. No person who employs or otherwise engages a person to record or report a deposition may modify or attempt to modify the record or report of the deposition, except to the extent allowed for the correction of errors in the record or report.
(2) Any person employed or otherwise engaged to record or report a deposition must provide equal services, and charge equal fee rates, to all parties and attorneys in the proceeding. A person employed or otherwise engaged to record or report a deposition must distribute copies of the record or report at the same time to all parties and attorneys who are entitled to receive a copy. In addition, a person employed or otherwise engaged to record or report a deposition must:
(a) Disclose the fee rates of the person for services, transcripts and copies to the attorneys identified in the proceeding and to any party who is not represented by an attorney and who is identified in the proceeding; or
(b) Provide a complete, individual accounting of all appearance fees, transcript fees and any other fees charged for services rendered in the proceeding. [1999 c.942 §2]

45.140 [Repealed by 1979 c.284 §199]

45.142 Recording or reporting services provided under contract; required disclosures; objection to reporter. (1) Before recording or reporting a deposition, the person recording or reporting the deposition must disclose if the person has a contract to provide reporting services for depositions on a full-time or part-time basis for any of the following persons:
(a) A party in the action;
(b) A person with a financial interest in the outcome of the action;
(c) An attorney for a party in the action; or
(d) An attorney for a person with a financial interest in the outcome of the action.
(2) If the person recording or reporting a deposition has a contract to provide reporting services for depositions on a full-time or part-time basis for any of the persons specified in subsection (1) of this section, any party to the action may object to the person employed for the purpose of recording or reporting the deposition. Upon objection, the parties shall attempt to agree upon a different person who shall record or report the deposition. If the parties cannot reach agreement, any of the parties may move the court to appoint an independent person who shall record or report the deposition.
(3) A party that objects to a person employed for the purpose of recording or reporting a deposition in the manner provided by this section is not subject to any penalty or sanction for making the objection and is not required to pay any fee of the person objected to.
(4) This section does not apply to contracts for reporting services for a single deposition, case or incident.
(5) This section does not apply to a person who records or reports depositions for a public body, as defined in ORS 30.260, or for a federal agency or any instrumentality of the federal government. [1999 c.942 §4]

45.150 [Repealed by 1955 c.611 §13]

45.151 [1955 c.611 §1; repealed by 1979 c.284 §199]

45.160 [Repealed by 1955 c.611 §13]

45.161 [1955 c.611 §2; repealed by 1979 c.284 §199]

45.170 [Repealed by 1955 c.611 §13]

45.171 [1955 c.611 §3; repealed by 1979 c.284 §199]

45.180 [Renumbered 45.125]

45.181 [1955 c.611 §5; repealed by 1977 c.358 §12]

45.185 [1959 c.354 §1; 1977 c.358 §6; repealed by 1979 c.284 §199]

45.190 [1955 c.611 §6; 1977 c.358 §7; repealed by 1979 c.284 §199]

45.200 [1955 c.611 §7; repealed by 1979 c.284 §199]

45.210 [Repealed by 1955 c.611 §13]

45.220 [Repealed by 1955 c.611 §13]

45.230 [Repealed by 1979 c.284 §199]

45.240 [Repealed by 1979 c.284 §199]

(Use of Deposition)

45.250 Use of deposition. (1) At the trial or upon the hearing of a motion or an interlocutory proceeding, any part or all of a deposition, so far as admissible under the rules of evidence, may be used against any party who was present or represented at the taking of the deposition or who had due notice thereof, in accordance with any of the following provisions of this subsection:
(a) Any deposition may be used by any party for the purpose of contradicting or impeaching the testimony of a deponent as a witness.
(b) The deposition of a party, or of anyone who at the time of taking the deposition was an officer, director or managing agent of a public or private corporation, partnership or association that is a party, may be used by an adverse party for any purpose.
(2) At the trial or upon the hearing of a motion or an interlocutory proceeding, any part or all of a deposition, so far as admissible under the rules of evidence, may be used against any party for any purpose, if the party was present or represented at the taking of the deposition or had due notice thereof, and if the court finds that:
(a) The witness is dead;
(b) The witness is unable to attend or testify because of age, sickness, infirmity or imprisonment;
(c) The party offering the deposition has been unable to procure the attendance of the witness by subpoena;
(d) Upon application and notice, such exceptional circumstances exist as to make it desirable, in the interest of justice and with due regard to the importance of presenting the testimony of witnesses orally in open court, to allow the deposition to be used; or
(e) The deposition was taken in the same proceeding pursuant to ORCP 39 I.
(3) For the purpose of subsection (2)(c) of this section, the failure of a party to serve a witness at the time of deposition with a subpoena that requires the appearance of the witness at trial or other hearing does not constitute sufficient grounds to deny the use of the deposition of that witness at the trial or other hearing without further showing of a lack of diligence on the part of the party offering the deposition. [1955 c.611 §§8,9; 1979 c.284 §83; 1987 c.275 §1; 1989 c.980 §4; 2001 c.234 §1; 2007 c.71 §12]

45.260 Introduction, or exclusion, of part of deposition. If only part of a deposition is offered in evidence by a party, an adverse party may require the party to introduce all of it which is relevant to the part introduced and any party may introduce any other parts, so far as admissible under the rules of evidence. When any portion of a deposition is excluded from a case, so much of the adverse examination as relates thereto is excluded also. [1955 c.611 §10]

45.270 Use of deposition in same or other proceedings. Substitution of parties shall not affect the right to use the depositions previously taken; and when an action, suit or proceeding has been dismissed and another action, suit or proceeding involving the same subject matter is afterward brought between the same parties or their representatives or successors in interest, any deposition lawfully taken and duly filed in the former action, suit or proceeding may be used in the latter as if originally taken therefor, and is then to be deemed the evidence of the party reading it. [1955 c.611 §11]

INTERPRETERS

45.272 Definitions for ORS 45.272 to 45.297. As used in ORS 45.272 to 45.297:
(1) "Adjudicatory proceeding" means:
(a) Any contested case hearing conducted under ORS chapter 183; or
(b) Any hearing conducted by an agency in which the individual legal rights, duties or privileges of specific parties are determined if that determination is subject to judicial review by a circuit court or by the Court of Appeals.
(2) "Agency" has that meaning given in ORS 183.310.
(3) "Critical stage of the proceeding" has the meaning given that term in ORS 147.500.
(4) "Victim" has the meaning given that term in ORS 147.500. [1999 c.1041 §3; 2015 c.155 §1]

45.273 Policy. (1) It is declared to be the policy of this state to secure the constitutional rights and other rights of persons who are unable to readily understand or communicate in the English language because of a non-English-speaking cultural background or a disability, and who as a result cannot be fully protected in administrative and court proceedings unless qualified interpreters are available to provide assistance.
(2) It is the intent of the Legislative Assembly in passing ORS 45.272 to 45.297 to provide a procedure for the qualification and use of court interpreters. Nothing in ORS 45.272 to 45.297 abridges the rights or obligations of parties under other laws or court rules. [1993 c.687 §1; 1999 c.1041 §1]

45.275 Appointment of interpreter for non-English-speaking party, witness or victim; substitution; payment of costs. (1)(a) The court shall appoint a qualified interpreter in a civil or criminal proceeding, and a hearing officer or the designee of a hearing officer shall appoint a qualified interpreter in an adjudicatory proceeding, whenever it is necessary:
(A) To interpret the proceedings to a non-English-speaking party;
(B) To interpret the testimony of a non-English-speaking party or witness; or
(C) To assist the court, agency or hearing officer in performing the duties and responsibilities of the court, agency or hearing officer.

(b) The court shall appoint a qualified interpreter in a criminal proceeding whenever it is necessary to interpret the proceedings to a non-English-speaking victim who seeks to exercise in open court a right that is granted by Article I, section 42 or 43, of the Oregon Constitution, including the right to be present at a critical stage of the proceeding.

(2) A fee may not be charged to any person for the appointment of an interpreter to interpret testimony of a non-English-speaking party or witness, to interpret the proceedings to a non-English-speaking party or victim or to assist the court, agency or hearing officer in performing the duties and responsibilities of the court, agency or hearing officer. A fee may not be charged to any person for the appointment of an interpreter if appointment is made to determine whether the person is non-English-speaking for the purposes of this section.

(3) Fair compensation for the services of an interpreter appointed under this section shall be paid:

(a) By the county, subject to the approval of the terms of the contract by the governing body of the county, in a proceeding in a county or justice court.

(b) By the city, subject to the approval of the terms of the contract by the governing body of the city, in a proceeding in a municipal court.

(c) By the state in a proceeding in a circuit court. Amounts payable by the state are not payable from the Public Defense Services Account established by ORS 151.225 or from moneys appropriated to the Public Defense Services Commission. Fees of an interpreter necessary for the purpose of communication between appointed counsel and a client or witness in a criminal case are payable from the Public Defense Services Account or from moneys appropriated to the Public Defense Services Commission.

(d) By the agency in an adjudicatory proceeding.

(4) If a party, victim or witness is dissatisfied with the interpreter appointed by the court, the hearing officer or the designee of the hearing officer, the party, victim or witness may request the appointment of a different interpreter. A request under this subsection must be made in a manner consistent with the policies and notice requirements of the court or agency relating to the appointment and scheduling of interpreters. If the substitution of another interpreter will delay the proceeding, the person making the request must show good cause for the substitution. Any party may object to use of any interpreter for good cause. Unless the court, hearing officer or the designee of the hearing officer has appointed a different interpreter for cause, the party using any interpreter other than the interpreter originally appointed by the court, hearing officer or the designee of the hearing officer shall bear any additional costs beyond the amount required to pay the original interpreter.

(5) A judge or hearing officer, on the judge's or hearing officer's own motion, may substitute a different interpreter for the interpreter initially appointed in a proceeding. A judge or hearing officer may make a substitution under this subsection at any time and for any reason.

(6) A court may allow as costs reasonable expenses incurred by a party in employing the services of an interpreter in civil proceedings in the manner provided by ORCP 68.

(7) A court, a hearing officer or the designee of a hearing officer shall require any person serving as an interpreter for the court or agency to state the person's name on the record and whether the person is certified under ORS 45.291. If the person is certified under ORS 45.291, the interpreter need not make the oath or affirmation required by ORS 40.325 or submit the interpreter's qualifications on the record. If the person is not certified under ORS 45.291, the interpreter must make the oath or affirmation required by ORS 40.325 and submit the interpreter's qualifications on the record.

(8) For the purposes of this section:

(a) "Hearing officer" includes an administrative law judge.

(b) "Non-English-speaking person" means a person who, by reason of place of birth or culture, speaks a language other than English and does not speak English with adequate ability to communicate effectively in the proceedings.

(c) "Qualified interpreter" means a person who is readily able to communicate with the non-English-speaking person and who can orally transfer the meaning of statements to and from English and the language spoken by the non-English-speaking person. A qualified interpreter must be able to interpret in a manner that conserves the meaning, tone, level, style and register of the original statement, without additions or omissions. "Qualified interpreter" does not include any person who is unable to interpret the dialect, slang or specialized vocabulary used by the party, victim or witness. [1991 c.750 §2; 1993 c.687 §8; 1995 c.273 §16; 1997 c.872 §18; 1999 c.1041 §4; 2001 c.242 §1; 2001 c.962 §§65,66; 2003 c.75 §§77,78; 2005 c.385 §2; 2012 c.107 §39; 2015 c.155 §2]

45.280 [1955 c.611 §12; repealed by 1979 c.284 §199]

45.285 Appointment of interpreter for party, witness or victim with disability; provision of assistive communication device. (1) For the purposes of this section:

(a) "Assistive communication device" means any equipment designed to facilitate communication by a person with a disability.

(b) "Hearing officer" includes an administrative law judge.

(c) "Person with a disability" means a person who cannot readily understand the proceedings because of deafness or a physical hearing impairment, or cannot communicate in the proceedings because of a physical speaking impairment.

(d) "Qualified interpreter" means a person who is readily able to communicate with the person with a disability, interpret the proceedings and accurately repeat and interpret the statements of the person with a disability to the court.

(2) In any civil action, adjudicatory proceeding or criminal proceeding, including a court-ordered deposition if no other person is responsible for providing an interpreter, in which a person with a disability is a party or witness, the court, hearing officer or the designee of the hearing officer shall appoint a qualified interpreter and make available appropriate assistive communication devices whenever it is necessary to interpret the proceedings to the person with a disability, or to interpret the testimony of the person with a disability.

(3) In any criminal proceeding, the court shall appoint a qualified interpreter and make available appropriate assistive communication devices whenever it is necessary to interpret the proceedings to a victim who is a person with a disability and who seeks to exercise in open court a right that is granted by Article I, section 42 or 43, of the Oregon Constitution, including the right to be present at a critical stage of the proceeding.

(4) A fee may not be charged to the person with a disability for the appointment of an interpreter or use of an assistive communication device under this section. A fee may not be charged to any person for the appointment of an interpreter or the use of an assistive communication device if appointment or use is made to determine whether the person is a person with a disability for the purposes of this section.

(5) Fair compensation for the services of an interpreter or the cost of an assistive communication device under this section shall be paid:

(a) By the county, subject to the approval of the terms of the contract by the governing body of the county, in a proceeding in a county or justice court.

(b) By the city, subject to the approval of the terms of the contract by the governing body of the city, in a proceeding in a municipal court.

(c) By the state in a proceeding in a circuit court. Amounts payable by the state are not payable from the Public Defense Services Account established by ORS 151.225 or from moneys appropriated to the Public Defense Services Commission. Fees of an interpreter necessary for the purpose of communication between appointed counsel and a client or witness in a criminal case are payable from the Public Defense Services Account or from moneys appropriated to the Public Defense Services Commission.

(d) By the agency in an adjudicatory proceeding. [1991 c.750 §1; 1993 c.687 §6; 1999 c.1041 §5; 2001 c.962 §§67,68; 2003 c.75 §§79,80; 2007 c.70 §13; 2012 c.107 §40; 2015 c.155 §3]

45.288 Appointment of certified interpreter required; exceptions; disqualifications; code of professional responsibility. (1) For the purposes of this section:

(a) "Hearing officer" includes an administrative law judge.

(b) "Non-English-speaking person" has the meaning given that term in ORS 45.275.

(c) "Person with a disability" has the meaning given that term in ORS 45.285.

(d) "Qualified interpreter" means a person who meets the requirements of ORS 45.285 for an interpreter for a person with a disability, or a person who meets the requirements of ORS 45.275 for an interpreter for a non-English-speaking person.

(2) Except as provided by this section, whenever a court is required to appoint an interpreter for any person in a proceeding before the court, or whenever a hearing officer is required to appoint an interpreter in an adjudicatory proceeding, the court, hearing officer or the designee of the hearing officer shall appoint a qualified interpreter who has been certified under ORS 45.291. If no certified interpreter is available, able or willing to serve, the

court, hearing officer or the designee of the hearing officer shall appoint a qualified interpreter. Upon request of a party, victim or witness, the court, hearing officer or designee of the hearing officer, in the discretion of the court, hearing officer or the designee of the hearing officer, may appoint a qualified interpreter to act as an interpreter in lieu of a certified interpreter in any case or adjudicatory proceeding.

(3) The requirements of this section apply to appointments of interpreters for persons with disabilities and for non-English-speaking persons.

(4) The court, hearing officer or the designee of the hearing officer may not appoint any person under ORS 45.272 to 45.297, 132.090 or 419C.285 if:

(a) The person has a conflict of interest with any of the parties, victims or witnesses in the proceeding;

(b) The person is unable to understand the judge, hearing officer, party, victim or witness, or cannot be understood by the judge, hearing officer, party, victim or witness; or

(c) The person is unable to work cooperatively with the judge of the court, the hearing officer, the person in need of an interpreter or the counsel for that person.

(5) The Supreme Court shall adopt a code of professional responsibility for interpreters. The code is binding on all interpreters who provide interpreter services in the courts or in adjudicatory proceedings before agencies. [1993 c.687 §2; 1999 c.1041 §6; 2001 c.242 §2; 2001 c.243 §2; 2003 c.75 §81; 2007 c.70 §14; 2015 c.155 §4]

45.291 Certification program; establishment by State Court Administrator; rules. (1) Subject to the availability of funding, the State Court Administrator shall establish a program for the certification of court interpreters. The program shall be established by rules adopted pursuant to ORS 1.002 and shall include, but not be limited to, provisions for:

(a) Prescribing the form and content of applications for certification;

(b) Prescribing and collecting reasonable fees for the application, examination, certification and renewal of certification for court interpreters;

(c) Establishing categories of certificates based on the nature of the interpreter services to be provided, including categories for interpreters for persons with disabilities, as defined in ORS 45.285, and for interpreters for non-English-speaking persons, as defined in ORS 45.275;

(d) Establishing minimum competency requirements for court interpreters in the various categories of certification;

(e) Establishing teaching programs designed to educate court interpreters in ethical, substantive and procedural legal issues;

(f) Prescribing the form of and administering examinations for the purpose of testing court interpreters for competency and ethics;

(g) Establishing grounds for renewal, suspension or cancellation of certificates;

(h) Establishing a process for receiving comments and input into the policy and procedures of the certification program;

(i) Establishing a process for receiving comments and input on compliance with ORS 45.272 to 45.297;

(j) Establishing a process for receiving comments and input on compliance with the code of professional responsibility adopted under ORS 45.288; and

(k) Establishing a process by which an adversely affected interpreter may seek review of any decision made by the State Court Administrator on renewal, suspension or cancellation of a certificate.

(2) An interpreter may be certified in Oregon by the State Court Administrator upon satisfactory proof that the interpreter is certified in good standing by the federal courts or by a state having a certification program that is equivalent to the program established under this section. [1993 c.687 §3; 2001 c.242 §3; 2007 c.70 §15]

45.292 Certification required for use of title or designation "certified court interpreter" or "court certified interpreter." (1) Except as provided in this section, a person may not assume or use the title or designation "certified court interpreter" or "court certified interpreter," or any other title, designation, words, letters, abbreviation, sign or device tending to indicate that the person is certified for the purposes of providing interpreter services under ORS 45.272 to 45.297.

(2) Subsection (1) of this section does not apply to any person who:

(a) Is certified under the program established under ORS 45.291;

(b) Is certified as an interpreter by the federal courts; or

(c) Is certified as an interpreter in another state that has a certification program that is equivalent to the program established under ORS 45.291. [1999 c.1041 §8]

45.294 Court Interpreter and Shorthand Reporter Certification Account; sources; uses. (1) The Court Interpreter and Shorthand Reporter Certification Account is established as an account in the General Fund of the State Treasury. All moneys received by the State Court Administrator from fees imposed under ORS 8.445 and 45.291 shall be paid into the State Treasury and credited to the account. All moneys in the account are appropriated continuously to the State Court Administrator to carry out the provisions of ORS 8.415 to 8.455 and 45.291.

(2) The State Court Administrator may apply for and receive funds or grants from federal, state and private sources to be credited to the Court Interpreter and Shorthand Reporter Certification Account and used for the purposes specified in ORS 8.415 to 8.455 and 45.291. [1993 c.687 §4; 1995 c.386 §7]

45.297 Authority to enter into service contracts. The State Court Administrator may enter into service contracts and may establish uniform policies and procedures, subject to the approval of the Chief Justice of the Supreme Court, governing the appointment, provision and payment of interpreters in proceedings before the circuit courts of the state, including the provision of interpreter services utilizing telecommunications methods. [1993 c.687 §5]

45.310 [Repealed by 1955 c.611 §13]

45.320 [Repealed by 1979 c.284 §199]

45.325 [1955 c.611 §4; repealed by 1979 c.284 §199]

45.330 [Repealed by 1979 c.284 §199]

45.340 [Amended by 1959 c.96 §1; repealed by 1979 c.284 §199]

45.350 [Repealed by 1979 c.284 §199]

45.360 [Repealed by 1979 c.284 §199]

45.370 [Repealed by 1979 c.284 §199]

45.380 [Repealed by 1955 c.611 §13]

REMOTE LOCATION TESTIMONY

45.400 Remote location testimony; when authorized; notice; payment of costs. (1) A party to any civil proceeding or any proceeding under ORS chapter 419B may move that the party or any witness for the moving party may give remote location testimony.

(2) A party filing a motion under this section must give written notice to all other parties to the proceeding at least 30 days before the trial or hearing at which the remote location testimony will be offered. The court may allow written notice less than 30 days before the trial or hearing for good cause shown.

(3)(a) Except as provided under subsection (5) of this section, the court may allow remote location testimony under this section upon a showing of good cause by the moving party, unless the court determines that the use of remote location testimony would result in prejudice to the nonmoving party and that prejudice outweighs the good cause for allowing the remote location testimony.

(b) Factors that a court may consider that would support a finding of good cause for the purpose of a motion under this subsection include:

(A) Whether the witness or party might be unavailable because of age, infirmity or mental or physical illness.

(B) Whether the party filing the motion seeks to take the remote location testimony of a witness whose attendance the party has been unable to secure by process or other reasonable means.

(C) Whether a personal appearance by the witness or party would be an undue hardship on the witness or party.

(D) Whether a perpetuation deposition under ORCP 39 I, or another alternative, provides a more practical means of presenting the testimony.

(E) Any other circumstances that constitute good cause.

(c) Factors that a court may consider that would support a finding of prejudice under this subsection include:

(A) Whether the ability to evaluate the credibility and demeanor of a witness or party in person is critical to the outcome of the proceeding.

(B) Whether the nonmoving party demonstrates that face-to-face cross-examination is necessary because the issue or issues the witness or party will testify about may be determinative of the outcome.

(C) Whether the exhibits or documents the witness or party will testify about are too voluminous to make remote location testimony practical.

(D) The nature of the proceeding, with due consideration for a person's liberty or parental interests.

(E) Whether facilities that would permit the taking of remote location testimony are readily available.

(F) Whether the nonmoving party demonstrates that other circumstances exist that require the personal appearance of a witness or party.

(4) In exercising its discretion to allow remote location testimony under this section, a court may authorize telephone or other nonvisual transmission only upon finding that video transmission is not readily available.

(5) The court may not allow use of remote location testimony in a jury trial unless good cause is shown and there is a compelling need for the use of remote location testimony.

(6) A party filing a motion for remote location testimony under this section must pay all costs of the remote location testimony, including the costs of alternative procedures or technologies used for the taking of remote location testimony. No part of those costs may be recovered by the party filing the motions as costs and disbursements in the proceeding.

(7) This section does not apply to a workers' compensation hearing or to any other administrative proceeding.

(8) As used in this section:

(a) "Remote location testimony" means live testimony given by a witness or party from a physical location outside of the courtroom of record via simultaneous electronic transmission.

(b) "Simultaneous electronic transmission" means television, telephone or any other form of electronic communication transmission if the form of transmission allows:

(A) The court, the attorneys and the person testifying from a remote location to communicate with each other during the proceeding;

(B) A witness or party who is represented by counsel at the hearing to be able to consult privately with counsel during the proceeding; and

(C) The public to hear and, if the transmission includes a visual image, to see the witness or party if the public would otherwise have the right to hear and see the witness or party testifying in the courtroom of record. [1993 c.425 §1; 2001 c.398 §1; 2003 c.262 §1; 2017 c.240 §1]

45.410 [Repealed by 1979 c.284 §199]

45.420 [Repealed by 1979 c.284 §199]

45.430 [Repealed by 1979 c.284 §199]

45.440 [Repealed by 1979 c.284 §199]

45.450 [Repealed by 1979 c.284 §199]

45.460 [Repealed by 1979 c.284 §199]

45.470 [Repealed by 1979 c.284 §199]

45.510 [Repealed by 1981 c.892 §98]

45.520 [Repealed by 1981 c.892 §98]

45.530 [Repealed by 1981 c.892 §98]

45.540 [Repealed by 1981 c.892 §98]

45.550 [Repealed by 1981 c.892 §98]

45.560 [Repealed by 1981 c.892 §98]

45.570 [Repealed by 1981 c.892 §98]

45.580 [Repealed by 1981 c.892 §98]

45.590 [Repealed by 1981 c.892 §98]

45.600 [Repealed by 1981 c.892 §98]

45.610 [Repealed by 1981 c.892 §98]

45.620 [Repealed by 1981 c.892 §98]

45.630 [Repealed by 1981 c.892 §98]

PENALTIES

45.900 Penalty for violation of ORS 45.135 or 45.138. Violation of ORS 45.135 or 45.138 is a Class B violation. [1999 c.942 §3; 1999 c.1051 §322d; 2011 c.597 §152]

45.910 [1959 c.523 §§1,2,3; repealed by 1979 c.284 §199]

TITLE 5 SMALL CLAIMS DEPARTMENT OF CIRCUIT COURT

Chapter   46.   Small Claims Department of Circuit Court

Chapter 46 — Small Claims Department of Circuit Court

2017 EDITION

SMALL CLAIMS DEPARTMENT OF CIRCUIT COURT

SMALL CLAIMS DEPARTMENT OF CIRCUIT COURT

46.405   Small claims department; jurisdiction

46.415   Circuit judges to sit in department; procedure

46.425   Commencement of actions; contents of claim

46.441   Explanation to plaintiff of how notice may be served

46.445   Notice of claim; content; service

46.455   Admission or denial of claim; request for jury trial

46.461   Counterclaims; fee; transfer of case to circuit court

46.465   Time and place of hearing; notice; procedure if right to jury trial asserted; attorney fees

46.475   Additional time for appearances; default and dismissal

46.485   Extent and effect of small claims judgment

46.488   Lien effect of small claims judgments

46.560   Where action to be commenced and tried

46.570   Fees

46.010 [Amended by 1961 c.724 §16; 1965 c.510 §13; 1965 c.568 §1; 1967 c.575 §1; 1971 c.633 §4; 1973 c.645 §1; 1977 c.387 §1; 1981 c.759 §11; 1995 c.658 §36; renumbered 3.014 in 1997]

46.019 [1975 c.327 §§2,4; 1979 c.568 §1; 1983 c.763 §33; 1983 c.765 §1; 1987 c.762 §3; repealed by 1995 c.658 §127]

46.020 [Amended by 1957 c.405 §1; 1961 c.724 §17; repealed by 1965 c.510 §24]

46.025 [Amended by 1953 c.563 §7; 1957 c.726 §1; 1959 c.559 §3; 1961 c.724 §18; 1965 c.510 §14; 1965 c.568 §4; 1967 c.623 §1; 1969 c.333 §1; 1971 c.640 §3; 1975 c.327 §1; 1977 c.385 §1; 1979 c.568 §12; 1981 c.253 §1; 1981 c.759 §13; 1983 c.763 §34; 1989 c.1021 §5; 1991 c.458 §§3,7; repealed by 1995 c.658 §127]

46.026 [1961 c.724 §19; 1963 c.614 §1; 1995 c.712 §80; repealed by 1995 c.658 §127]

46.028 [1961 c.724 §20; repealed by 1965 c.510 §24]

46.030 [Amended by 1953 c.112 §2; 1979 c.568 §6; repealed by 1995 c.658 §127]

46.040 [Amended by 1963 c.513 §2; 1971 c.743 §311; 1973 c.645 §2; 1983 c.673 §1; 1995 c.16 §1; 1995 c.658 §38; renumbered 3.132 in 1997]

46.045 [1971 c.633 §2; 1985 c.750 §1; 1995 c.658 §39; renumbered 3.136 in 1997]

46.047 [1975 c.611 §15; 1995 c.658 §40; renumbered 3.134 in 1997]

46.050 [Amended by 1957 c.405 §3; 1961 c.724 §21; repealed by 1995 c.658 §127]

46.060 [Amended by 1957 c.661 §1; 1965 c.495 §1; 1975 c.611 §18; 1983 c.149 §1; 1985 c.342 §1; 1985 c.496 §28; 1985 c.588 §3a; 1987 c.714 §8; 1989 c.839 §33; repealed by 1995 c.658 §127]

46.063 [1975 c.611 §10; repealed by 1987 c.714 §10]

46.064 [1987 c.714 §2; 1995 c.664 §78; repealed by 1995 c.658 §127]

46.065 [1965 c.495 §3; repealed by 1975 c.611 §24]

46.070 [Amended by 1965 c.495 §2; 1975 c.611 §19; 1985 c.240 §1; 1985 c.342 §2; 1985 c.496 §29; repealed by 1987 c.714 §10]

46.075 [1965 c.495 §4; 1985 c.496 §30; 1985 c.540 §13; 1987 c.714 §3; 1991 c.790 §6; 1995 c.781 §33; repealed by 1995 c.658 §127]

46.080 [Amended by 1957 c.661 §2; 1981 c.898 §39; repealed by 1995 c.658 §127]

46.082 [1977 c.876 §5; repealed by 1995 c.658 §127]

46.084 [1977 c.876 §6; 1987 c.714 §7; repealed by 1995 c.658 §127]

46.090 [Amended by 1955 c.664 §1; 1957 c.661 §3; repealed by 1977 c.876 §12]

46.092 [1955 c.540 §1; 1957 c.403 §1; 1965 c.510 §15; 1967 c.534 §12; 1969 c.591 §272; repealed by 1995 c.658 §127]

46.093 [1963 c.512 §2; repealed by 1965 c.510 §24]

46.094 [1955 c.540 §2; 1957 c.403 §2; repealed by 1995 c.658 §127]

46.096 [1955 c.540 §3; 1957 c.403 §3; repealed by 1995 c.658 §127]

46.098 [1955 c.540 §4; 1957 c.403 §4; repealed by 1961 c.406 §2]

46.099 [1961 c.406 §1; 1969 c.96 §1; repealed by 1995 c.658 §127]

46.100 [Amended by 1957 c.661 §4; 1969 c.438 §1; repealed by 1995 c.658 §127]

46.110 [Amended by 1967 c.391 §1; repealed by 1979 c.284 §199]

46.120 [Amended by 1953 c.479 §4; 1973 c.827 §9; repealed by 1977 c.877 §17]

46.130 [Amended by 1957 c.405 §4; 1961 c.724 §22; 1995 c.781 §34; repealed by 1995 c.658 §127]

46.140 [Repealed by 1961 c.468 §1 (46.141 enacted in lieu of 46.140)]

46.141 [1961 c.468 §2 (enacted in lieu of 46.140); repealed by 1995 c.658 §127]

46.150 [Amended by 1969 c.96 §2; repealed by 1995 c.658 §127]

46.155 [1975 c.611 §§12,13,14; repealed by 1979 c.284 §199]

46.160 [Repealed by 1979 c.284 §199]

46.170 [Amended by 1953 c.398 §2; 1961 c.705 §1; repealed by 1965 c.510 §24]

46.175 [1961 c.705 §3; 1965 c.510 §16; 1971 c.628 §1; 1979 c.113 §1; repealed by 1981 s.s. c.3 §141]

46.180 [Amended by 1957 c.594 §3; 1961 c.705 §2; 1965 c.510 §17; 1971 c.628 §2; 1977 c.519 §3; 1981 s.s. c.3 §61; 1985 c.496 §12; 1985 c.703 §21a; repealed by 1995 c.658 §127]

46.190 [Repealed by 1995 c.658 §127]

46.200 [Amended by 1961 c.446 §2; 1969 c.96 §3; 1971 c.565 §16; repealed by 1975 c.611 §24]

46.210 [Amended by 1955 c.459 §1; repealed by 1995 c.658 §127]

46.220 [Repealed by 1953 c.393 §3]

46.221 [1953 c.393 §1; 1965 c.510 §18; 1965 c.619 §22; 1971 c.621 §8; 1973 c.381 §2; 1975 c.88 §6; 1975 c.327 §6; 1975 c.607 §11; 1977 c.875 §1; 1979 c.833 §12; 1981 c.898 §40; 1981 s.s. c.3 §92; 1981 s.s. c.3 §93; 1983 c.763 §41; 1985 c.342 §25; 1985 c.496 §8; 1987 c.725 §5; 1989 c.718 §17; 1991 c.538 §5; 1991 c.790 §5; 1995 c.273 §25; 1995 c.664 §79; 1997 c.801 §§30,30a; renumbered 46.570 in 1997]

46.223 [1985 c.342 §29; 1995 c.658 §42; renumbered 21.385 in 1997]

46.230 [Amended by 1965 c.510 §19; repealed by 1965 c.619 §39]

46.240 [Amended by 1961 c.563 §3; 1971 c.621 §9; repealed by 1973 c.381 §8]

46.250 [Amended by 1975 c.611 §20; 1977 c.416 §7; 1979 c.562 §34; 1985 c.734 §16; 1997 c.389 §7; repealed by 1995 c.658 §127]

46.253 [1975 c.611 §5; repealed by 1985 c.734 §20]

46.255 [1975 c.611 §6; 1981 c.178 §3; repealed by 1985 c.734 §20]

46.260 [Amended by 1969 c.96 §4; repealed by 1977 c.290 §5]

46.265 [1975 c.611 §7; repealed by 1995 c.658 §127]

46.270 [Amended by 1971 c.224 §2; repealed by 1995 c.658 §127]

46.274 [1955 c.664 §2; 1965 c.619 §23; 1971 c.621 §10; 1975 c.607 §12; 1979 c.833 §13; 1981 c.835 §3; 1981 s.s. c.3 §32; 1985 c.540 §15; 1995 c.273 §14; repealed by 1995 c.658 §127]

46.275 [1977 c.876 §7; repealed by 1983 c.405 §5]

46.276 [1955 c.664 §3; 1969 c.438 §2; 1987 c.586 §18; repealed by 1995 c.658 §127]

46.278 [1977 c.876 §8; 1987 c.586 §19; repealed by 1995 c.658 §127]

46.280 [Amended by 1973 c.484 §5; 1981 s.s. c.1 §11; 1983 c.763 §32; 1995 c.781 §35; repealed by 1995 c.658 §127]

46.290 [Repealed by 1981 s.s. c.3 §141]

46.300 [1959 c.552 §11; 1971 c.718 §3; 1979 c.568 §7; repealed by 1983 c.763 §9]

46.330 [1975 c.611 §2; repealed by 1995 c.658 §127]

46.335 [1975 c.611 §3; 1977 c.876 §2; 1995 c.244 §7; repealed by 1995 c.658 §127]

46.340 [1975 c.611 §4; 1985 c.540 §16; 1995 c.244 §8; repealed by 1995 c.658 §127]

46.345 [1975 c.611 §§8,9; 1981 s.s. c.3 §33; 1985 c.496 §11; repealed by 1995 c.658 §127]

46.350 [1975 c.611 §11; repealed by 1985 c.540 §47]

46.405 Small claims department; jurisdiction. (1) Except as provided in subsection (6) of this section, each circuit court shall have a small claims department.

(2) Except as provided in this section, all actions for the recovery of money, damages, specific personal property, or any penalty or forfeiture must be commenced and prosecuted in the small claims department if the amount or value claimed in the action does not exceed $750.

(3) Except as provided in this section, an action for the recovery of money, damages, specific personal property, or any penalty or forfeiture may be commenced and prosecuted in the small claims department if the amount or value claimed in the action does not exceed $10,000.

(4)(a) Class actions may not be commenced and prosecuted in the small claims department.

(b) An action by an inmate, as defined in ORS 30.642, against another inmate may not be commenced and prosecuted in the small claims department.

(5) Actions providing for statutory attorney fees in which the amount or value claimed does not exceed $750 may be commenced and prosecuted in the small claims department or may be commenced and prosecuted in the regular department of the circuit court. This subsection does not apply to an action based on contract for which attorney fees are authorized under ORS 20.082.

(6) If a circuit court is located in the same city as a justice court, the circuit court need not have a small claims department if the circuit court and the justice court enter into an intergovernmental agreement that provides that only the justice court will operate a small claims department. If an intergovernmental agreement is entered into under this subsection, the agreement must establish appropriate procedures for referring small claims cases to the justice court. [1971 c.760 §2; 1973 c.812 §2; 1975 c.592 §1; 1979 c.567 §1; 1983 c.242 §1; 1985 c.367 §1; 1987 c.725 §1; 1995 c.227 §1; 1995 c.658 §43; 1997 c.378 §1; amendments by 1997 c.378 §2 repealed by 1999 c.84 §9; 1997 c.801 §78; 1999 c.84 §1; 1999 c.673 §1; 2001 c.542 §5; 2007 c.125 §1; 2011 c.262 §4; 2011 c.595 §47]

46.410 [Amended by 1959 c.326 §1; 1965 c.569 §1; 1969 c.683 §1; repealed by 1971 c.760 §11]

46.415 Circuit judges to sit in department; procedure. (1) The judges of a circuit court shall sit as judges of the small claims department.

(2) No formal pleadings other than the claim shall be necessary.

(3) The hearing and disposition of all cases shall be informal, the sole object being to dispense justice promptly and economically between the litigants. The parties shall have the privilege of offering evidence and testimony of witnesses at the hearing. The judge may informally consult witnesses or otherwise investigate the controversy and give judgment or make such orders as the judge deems to be right, just and equitable for the disposition of the controversy.

(4) No attorney at law or person other than the plaintiff and defendant and their witnesses shall appear on behalf of any party in litigation in the small claims department without the consent of the judge of the court.

(5) Notwithstanding the provisions of ORS 9.320, a party that is not a natural person, the state or any city, county, district or other political subdivision or public corporation in this state, without appearance by attorney, may appear as a party to any action in the small claims department and in any supplementary proceeding in aid of execution after entry of a small claims judgment.

(6) Assigned claims may be prosecuted by an assignee in small claims department to the same extent they may be prosecuted in any other state court.

(7) When spouses are both parties to a case, one spouse may appear on behalf of both spouses in mediation or litigation in the small claims department:

(a) With the written consent of the other spouse; or

(b) If the appearing spouse declares under penalty of perjury that the other spouse consents. [1971 c.760 §3; 1973 c.484 §6; 1981 s.s. c.1 §22; 1987 c.811 §1; 1993 c.282 §2; 1995 c.658 §44; 1997 c.808 §§6,7; 2015 c.7 §3; 2017 c.268 §1]

46.420 [Repealed by 1971 c.760 §11]

46.425 Commencement of actions; contents of claim. (1) An action in the small claims department shall be commenced by the plaintiff's filing with the clerk of the court a claim in the form prescribed by the court.

(2) The claim shall:

(a) Contain the name and address of the plaintiff and of the defendant, followed by a plain and simple statement of the claim, including the amount and the date the claim allegedly accrued;

(b) State that the plaintiff made a good faith effort to collect the claim from the defendant before filing the claim with the clerk; and

(c) Include an affidavit attesting to the accuracy of the statements described in paragraphs (a) and (b) of this subsection or a declaration under penalty of perjury in the form required by ORCP 1 E.

(3) Except in actions arising under ORS chapter 90, the plaintiff must include in a claim all amounts claimed from the defendant arising out of a single transaction or occurrence. Any plaintiff alleging damages on a transaction requiring installment payments need only claim the installment payments due and owing as of the date of filing of the claim, and need not accelerate the remaining payments. The plaintiff may include in a claim all amounts claimed from a defendant on more than one transaction or occurrence if the total amount of the claim does not exceed $10,000.

(4) Notwithstanding subsection (3) of this section, a plaintiff bringing an action on assigned claims:

(a) Need bring an action only on those claims that have been assigned as of the date the action is filed; and

(b) May bring separate actions for each person assigning claims to the plaintiff. [1971 c.760 §4; 1977 c.875 §2; 1991 c.195 §1; 1995 c.658 §45; 1997 c.378 §4; amendments by 1997 c.378 §5 repealed by 1999 c.84 §9; 1997 c.801 §80; 1999 c.84 §2; 2007 c.125 §2; 2011 c.595 §48; 2015 c.121 §1]

46.430 [Repealed by 1971 c.760 §11]

46.435 [1971 c.760 §5; 1973 c.393 §2; 1977 c.875 §3; 1979 c.567 §2; repealed by 1979 c.833 §36]

46.440 [Repealed by 1971 c.760 §11]

46.441 Explanation to plaintiff of how notice may be served. The small claims department of a circuit court shall provide to each plaintiff who files a claim with the department a written explanation of how notice may be served in actions in the department. [1977 c.875 §9; 1995 c.658 §46]

46.445 Notice of claim; content; service. (1) Upon the filing of a claim in the small claims department of a circuit court, the clerk shall issue a notice in the form prescribed by the court.

(2) The notice shall be directed to the defendant, naming the defendant, and shall contain a copy of the claim.

(3) The notice and claim shall be served upon the defendant either in the manner provided for the service of summons and complaint in proceedings in the circuit courts or by certified mail, at the option of the plaintiff. If service by certified mail is attempted, the plaintiff shall mail the notice and claim by certified mail addressed to the defendant at the last-known mailing address of the defendant. The envelope shall be marked with the words "Deliver to Addressee Only" and "Return Receipt Requested." The date of delivery appearing on the return receipt shall be prima facie evidence of the date on which the notice and claim was served upon the defendant. If service by certified mail is not successfully accomplished, the notice and claim shall be served in the manner provided for the service of summons and complaint in proceedings in the circuit courts.

(4) The notice shall include a statement in substantially the following form:

NOTICE TO DEFENDANT:
READ THESE PAPERS CAREFULLY!!
Within 14 DAYS after receiving this notice you MUST do ONE of the following things:
Pay the claim plus filing fees and service expenses paid by plaintiff OR
Demand a hearing OR
Demand a jury trial
If you fail to do one of the above things within 14 DAYS after receiving this notice, then upon written request from the plaintiff the clerk of the court will enter a judgment against you for the amount claimed plus filing fees and service expenses paid by the plaintiff, plus a prevailing party fee.
If you have questions about the small claims court filing procedures after reading this notice, you may contact the clerk of the court; however, the clerk cannot give you legal advice on the claim.

_____ [1971 c.760 §6; 1977 c.875 §4;
1977 c.877 §9a; 1989 c.741 §1; 1991 c.111 §4; 1991 c.195 §2; 1995 c.658 §47; 1997 c.872 §§8,9]

46.450 [Repealed by 1971 c.760 §11]

46.455 Admission or denial of claim; request for jury trial. Within 14 days after the date of service of the notice and claim upon the defendant as provided in ORS 46.445:

(1) If the defendant admits the claim, the defendant may settle it by:

(a) Paying to the plaintiff the amount of the claim plus the amount of all filing fees and service expenses paid by the plaintiff and mailing proof of that payment to the court.

(b) If the claim is for recovery of specific personal property, delivering the property to the plaintiff and paying to the plaintiff the amount of all filing fees and service expenses paid by the plaintiff and mailing proof of that delivery and payment to the court.

(2) If the defendant denies the claim, the defendant:

(a) May demand a hearing in the small claims department in a written request to the clerk in the form prescribed by the court, accompanied by payment of the defendant's fee prescribed; and

(b) When demanding a hearing, may assert a counterclaim in the form provided by the court.

(3) If the amount or value claimed exceeds $750, the defendant has a constitutional right to a jury trial and may claim that right in a written request to the clerk in the form prescribed by the court, accompanied by payment of the appearance fee required from defendants under ORS 21.160. The request shall designate a mailing address to which a summons and copy of the complaint may be served by mail. Thereafter, the plaintiff's claim will not be limited to the amount stated in the claim, though it must involve the same controversy. [1971 c.760 §7; 1973 c.654 §1; 1973 c.812 §3a; 1977 c.875 §5; 1977 c.877 §10a; 1981 s.s. c.3 §94; 1983 c.673 §2; 1985 c.496 §13; 1991 c.111 §5; 1991 c.195 §3; 1995 c.227 §2; 1995 c.455 §4; 1995 c.658 §48; 1997 c.46 §§6,7; 2011 c.595 §49]

46.458 [1995 c.455 §2; 1995 c.618 §15b; repealed by 1997 c.46 §1]

46.460 [Amended by 1965 c.619 §24; 1969 c.683 §2; repealed by 1971 c.760 §11]

46.461 Counterclaims; fee; transfer of case to circuit court. (1) The defendant in an action in the small claims department may assert as a counterclaim any claim that, on the date of issuance of notice pursuant to ORS 46.445, the defendant may have against the plaintiff and that arises out of the same transaction or occurrence that is the subject matter of the claim filed by the plaintiff.

(2) If the amount or value of the counterclaim exceeds $10,000, the court shall strike the counterclaim and proceed to hear and dispose of the case as though the counterclaim had not been asserted unless the defendant files with the counterclaim a motion requesting that the case be transferred from the small claims department to the circuit court. After the transfer the plaintiff's claim will not be limited to the amount stated in the claim filed with the small claims department, though it must involve the same controversy.

(3)(a) If the amount or value of the counterclaim exceeds that specified in subsection (2) of this section, and the defendant files a motion requesting transfer as provided in subsection (2) of this section, the case shall be transferred to the circuit court. The clerk of the court shall notify the plaintiff and defendant, by mail, of the transfer. The notice to the plaintiff shall contain a copy of the counterclaim and shall instruct the plaintiff to file with the court and serve by mail on the defendant, within 20 days following the mailing of the notice, a reply to the counterclaim and, if the plaintiff proposes to increase the amount of the claim originally filed with the small claims department, an amended claim for the increased amount. Proof of service on the defendant of the plaintiff's reply and amended claim may be made by certificate of the plaintiff or plaintiff's attorney attached to the reply and amended claim filed with the court. The defendant is not required to answer an amended claim of the plaintiff.

(b) Upon filing the motion requesting transfer, the defendant shall pay to the clerk of the court an amount equal to the difference between the fee paid by the defendant as required by ORS 46.570 and the fee required of a defendant under ORS 21.160. Upon filing a reply to the counterclaim, the plaintiff shall pay to the clerk of the court an amount equal to the difference between the fee paid by the plaintiff as required by ORS 46.570 and the fee required of a plaintiff under ORS 21.160. [1977 c.875 §10; 1979 c.567 §3; 1983 c.242 §2; 1983 c.673 §5; 1985 c.367 §2; 1985 c.496 §31; 1987 c.714 §9;

1987 c.725 §2; 1991 c.790 §7; 1995 c.658 §49; 1997 c.378 §7; amendments by 1997 c.378 §8 repealed by 1999 c.84 §9; 1997 c.801 §82; 1999 c.84 §3; 2007 c.125 §3; 2011 c.595 §50]

46.465 Time and place of hearing; notice; procedure if right to jury trial asserted; attorney fees. (1) If the defendant demands a hearing in the small claims department, under the direction of the court the clerk shall fix a day and time for the hearing and shall mail to the parties a notice of the hearing time in the form prescribed by the court, instructing them to bring witnesses, documents and other evidence pertinent to the controversy.

(2) If the defendant asserts a counterclaim, the notice of the hearing time shall contain a copy of the counterclaim.

(3)(a) If the defendant claims the right to a jury trial, the clerk shall notify the plaintiff by mail of the requirements of this paragraph. Within 20 days after the mailing of the notice, the plaintiff must file a formal complaint with the court and serve by mail a summons and copy of the complaint on the defendant at the designated address of the defendant. Proof of service must be filed by the plaintiff with the court. Proof of service may be made by filing a certificate of the plaintiff or the plaintiff's attorney with the complaint.

(b) The plaintiff's claim in the formal complaint filed pursuant to this subsection is not limited to the amount stated in the claim filed in the small claims department, but the claim in the formal complaint must relate to the same controversy.

(c) The defendant must file an appearance in the matter within 10 days after the date on which the summons and copy of the complaint would be delivered to the defendant in due course of mail. Thereafter the cause shall proceed as other causes in the court, and costs and disbursements shall be allowed and taxed. Fees not previously paid shall be charged and collected as provided for other cases tried in the circuit court, except that the filing fee for the plaintiff shall be an amount equal to the difference between the filing fee paid by the plaintiff as required by ORS 46.570 and the filing fee required of the plaintiff under ORS 21.160.

(4)(a) If the defendant claims the right to a jury trial and does not prevail in the action, the court shall award to the plaintiff reasonable attorney fees incurred by the plaintiff in the action. Unless attorney fees are otherwise provided for in the action by contract or statutory provision, attorney fees awarded under this paragraph may not exceed $1,000.

(b) If the defendant asserts a counterclaim that requires transfer of the matter under the provisions of ORS 46.461, and the defendant does not prevail in the action, the court shall award to the plaintiff reasonable attorney fees incurred by the plaintiff in the action. [1971 c.760 §8; 1975 c.346 §1; 1983 c.673 §3; 1985 c.496 §14; 1991 c.790 §8; 1995 c.455 §5; 1995 c.618 §15a; 1997 c.46 §§9,10; 2011 c.595 §51]

46.470 [Amended by 1963 c.248 §1; repealed by 1971 c.760 §11]

46.475 Additional time for appearances; default and dismissal. (1) Upon written request, the court may extend to the parties additional time within which to make formal appearances required in the small claims department of a circuit court.

(2) If the defendant fails to pay the claim, demand a hearing, or demand a jury trial and comply with ORS 46.465 (3)(c), upon written request from the plaintiff the clerk shall enter a judgment against the defendant for the relief claimed plus the amount of the small claims filing fees and service expenses paid by the plaintiff and the prevailing party fee provided by ORS 20.190.

(3) If the plaintiff fails within the time provided to file a formal complaint pursuant to ORS 46.465 (3)(a), the clerk shall dismiss the case without prejudice.

(4) If the defendant appears at the time set for hearing but no appearance is made by the plaintiff, the claim shall be dismissed with prejudice. If neither party appears, the claim shall be dismissed without prejudice.

(5) Upon good cause shown within 60 days, the court may set aside a default judgment or dismissal and reset the claim for hearing. [1971 c.760 §9; 1977 c.875 §6; 1985 c.496 §15; 1991 c.111 §6; 1995 c.618 §§8,8a; 1995 c.658 §51; 1997 c.46 §§12,13; 1999 c.84 §10; 2011 c.595 §52]

46.480 [Amended by 1969 c.683 §3; repealed by 1971 c.760 §11]

46.485 Extent and effect of small claims judgment. (1) In addition to any other award, the prevailing party shall be entitled to a judgment for the small claims filing fees and service expenses paid by the party and the prevailing party fee provided for in ORS 20.190 (1)(c) or (2)(b). The prevailing party may also be awarded prevailing party fees under ORS 20.190 (3). The award shall be paid or the property delivered upon such terms and conditions as the judge may prescribe.

(2) The court may allow to the defendant a setoff not to exceed the amount of plaintiff's claim, but in such case the court shall cause to be entered in the record the amount of the setoff allowed.

(3) No attachment shall issue on any cause in the small claims department.

(4) A judgment in the small claims department is conclusive upon the parties and no appeal may be taken from the judgment.

(5) The clerk of the court shall keep a record of all actions, proceedings and judgments in the small claims department.

(6) A judgment in the small claims department is a judgment of the circuit court. The clerk shall enter such judgment in the register of the circuit court in the manner provided by ORS 18.075. A judgment in the small claims department may create a lien as provided by ORS 46.488. Judgments that include money awards, as defined by ORS 18.005, are subject to ORS 18.042. [1971 c.760 §10; 1977 c.875 §7; 1985 c.540 §17; 1991 c.111 §7; 1995 c.618 §9; 1995 c.658 §52; 1997 c.801 §60; 1999 c.84 §8; 2003 c.576 §91]

46.488 Lien effect of small claims judgments. (1) A judgment creditor may not create a judgment lien for a judgment entered in the small claims department of a circuit court if the money award is less than $10, exclusive of costs and disbursements. A judgment creditor may create a judgment lien for a judgment entered in the small claims department of a circuit court in an amount of $10 or more and less than $3,000, exclusive of costs and disbursements, only as provided in subsection (3) of this section.

(2) If a judgment is rendered in the small claims department in an amount of $3,000 or more, the clerk shall note in the register of the circuit court that the judgment creates a judgment lien if the judgment otherwise complies with the requirements of ORS chapter 18 for creating a judgment lien. A judgment creditor may create a lien for the judgment in other counties in the manner provided by ORS 18.152.

(3) When a judgment is entered in the small claims department in an amount of $10 or more and less than $3,000, exclusive of costs or disbursements, a judgment creditor may at any time before expiration of judgment remedies for the judgment under ORS 18.180 create a judgment lien for the judgment by paying to the clerk of the court that entered the judgment the fees established under ORS 21.235 (1)(a) and requesting that the clerk of the court note in the register and in the judgment lien record that the judgment creates a judgment lien. Upon receipt of the fees and request for creating a judgment lien, the clerk shall note in the register that the judgment creates a judgment lien. Upon entry of the notation in the register, the judgment creates a lien as described in ORS 18.150, and a judgment creditor may create a lien for the judgment in other counties in the manner provided by ORS 18.152. [1997 c.801 §57; 1997 c.801 §58; 1999 c.195 §3; 1999 c.1095 §12; 2003 c.576 §92; 2003 c.737 §§77,78; 2007 c.339 §11; 2011 c.595 §119]

Note: Section 8 (1) and (2), chapter 195, Oregon Laws 1999, provides:

Sec. 8. (1) The amendments to ORS 18.350 by section 1 of this 1999 Act, and the amendments to ORS 46.488 by section 58, chapter 801, Oregon Laws 1997, and by section 3 of this 1999 Act, do not affect any judgment docketed in the circuit court under the provisions of ORS 46.488 (1997 Edition) before the effective date of this 1999 Act [October 23, 1999]. Notwithstanding the amendments to ORS 46.488 by section 58, chapter 801, Oregon Laws 1997, and by section 3 of this 1999 Act, any judgment entered in the small claims department of a circuit court before the effective date of this 1999 Act that was not docketed in the circuit court under the provisions of ORS 46.488 (1997 Edition) before the effective date of this 1999 Act may become a lien on real property only in the manner provided by ORS 46.488 (1997 Edition).

(2) Any judgment docketed before the effective date of this 1999 Act, including judgments docketed under the provisions of ORS 46.488 (1997 Edition), that did not become a lien on real property by reason of failure of the judgment creditor to file a lien certificate with the court in the manner required by ORS 18.350 (4) to (9) (1997 Edition) shall automatically become a lien on real property to the extent described in ORS 18.350, as amended

by section 1 of this 1999 Act, on January 1, 2000, and shall be considered in all respects as though the judgment had been docketed on January 1, 2000. [1999 c.195 §8(1),(2); 1999 c.195 §8a(1),(2)]

46.490 [Repealed by 1971 c.760 §11]

46.495 [1979 c.567 §4; repealed by 1981 c.883 §1]

46.500 [Amended by 1969 c.683 §4; repealed by 1971 c.760 §11]

46.505 [1969 c.683 §6; repealed by 1971 c.760 §11]

46.510 [Repealed by 1971 c.760 §11]

46.520 [Amended by 1969 c.683 §7; repealed by 1971 c.760 §11]

46.530 [Repealed by 1971 c.760 §11]

46.540 [Amended by 1969 c.683 §8; repealed by 1971 c.760 §11]

46.550 [Repealed by 1981 s.s. c.3 §141]

46.560 Where action to be commenced and tried. (1) Except as provided in subsections (2) and (3) of this section, all actions in small claims department shall be commenced and tried in the county in which the defendants, or one of them, reside or may be found at the commencement of the action.
(2) When an action is founded on an alleged tort, it may be commenced either in the county where the cause of action arose or in the county where the defendants, or one of them, reside or may be found at the commencement of the action.
(3) When the defendant has contracted to perform an obligation in a particular county, action may be commenced either in that county or in the county where the defendants, or one of them, reside or may be found at the commencement of the action. [1973 c.446 §2; 2015 c.27 §3]

46.570 Fees. The small claims department of a circuit court shall collect the following filing fees from the plaintiff when a claim is filed in the court, and from the defendant when the defendant demands a hearing:
(1) $55, when the amount claimed is $2,500 or less; and
(2) $99, when the amount is more than $2,500. [Formerly 46.221; 2003 c.737 §§44,45a,45c; 2005 c.702 §§49,50,51; 2007 c.129 §20; 2007 c.860 §7; 2011 c.595 §46; 2013 c.685 §§36,36a; 2014 c.76 §10; 2017 c.663 §8]

46.610 [Amended by 1965 c.510 §20; 1971 c.633 §16; 1975 c.327 §7; 1979 c.568 §8; repealed by 1995 c.658 §127]

46.620 [Repealed by 1995 c.658 §127]

46.630 [Amended by 1957 c.726 §2; 1963 c.614 §2; 1969 c.96 §5; repealed by 1995 c.658 §127]

46.632 [1959 c.559 §5; 1961 c.628 §1; 1963 c.487 §1; 1965 c.171 §2; 1967 c.38 §2; 1969 c.365 §2; 1971 c.642 §2; repealed by 1995 c.658 §127]

46.635 [Amended by 1953 c.563 §7; 1955 c.562 §1; 1957 c.439 §1; repealed by 1959 c.559 §10]

46.638 [1959 c.552 §8; repealed by 1975 c.706 §10]

46.640 [Repealed by 1959 c.559 §10]

46.642 [1965 c.377 §1; 1969 c.269 §3; 1971 c.213 §3; repealed by 1975 c.706 §10]

46.648 [1959 c.552 §10; 1995 c.781 §36; repealed by 1995 c.658 §127]

46.650 [Repealed by 1961 c.724 §34]

46.655 [1961 c.724 §23; repealed by 1995 c.658 §127]

46.660 [Repealed by 1961 c.724 §34]

46.665 [1961 c.724 §24; 1981 s.s. c.1 §10; repealed by 1995 c.658 §127 and 1995 c.781 §51]

46.670 [Repealed by 1969 c.96 §6]

46.680 [Repealed by 1995 c.658 §127]

46.684 [1957 c.405 §5; repealed by 1961 c.724 §34]

46.686 [1957 c.405 §6; repealed by 1961 c.724 §34]

46.690 [Repealed by 1959 c.552 §16]

46.710 [Repealed by 1969 c.96 §6]

46.720 [Amended by 1953 c.306 §17; 1979 c.568 §9; repealed by 1981 s.s. c.3 §141]

46.725 [1975 c.327 §5; repealed by 1979 c.568 §17]

46.730 [Amended by 1955 c.664 §4; repealed by 1981 s.s. c.3 §141]

46.735 [1979 c.58 §4; repealed by 1985 c.540 §47]

46.740 [Amended by 1955 c.664 §5; 1963 c.427 §1; 1975 c.611 §21; repealed by 1985 c.540 §47]

46.750 [Amended by 1959 c.524 §1; 1963 c.474 §1; 1979 c.58 §2; repealed by 1985 c.540 §47]

46.760 [Repealed by 1985 c.540 §47]

46.770 [Amended by 1977 c.518 §1; repealed by 1981 s.s. c.3 §141]

46.780 [1965 c.203 §1; 1975 c.327 §8; 1979 c.568 §10; repealed by 1981 s.s. c.3 §141]

46.800 [1977 c.876 §10 (enacted in lieu of 156.610, 156.620, 156.640 and 156.650); 1981 s.s. c.3 §103; 1983 c.763 §43; 1985 c.565 §6; 1987 c.905 §4; repealed by 1995 c.658 §127]

46.810 [Formerly 157.081; repealed by 1995 c.658 §127]

CHAPTERS 47 TO 50 [Reserved for expansion]_____

TITLE 6 JUSTICE COURTS

Chapter 51.   Justice Courts; Jurisdiction
        52.   Civil Actions
        53.   Appeals in Civil Actions
        54.   Juries
        55.   Small Claims

_____

Chapter 51 — Justice Courts; Jurisdiction

2017 EDITION

JUSTICE COURTS; JURISDICTION

JUSTICE COURTS

ORGANIZATION AND JURISDICTION

51.010   Justice court defined; no terms of court; court always open for business

51.020   Justice of the peace districts; establishing and modifying boundaries; maximum number of districts

51.025   Justice court as court of record

51.028   Justice court ceasing operation as court of record

51.035   Justice of peace as municipal judge

51.037   Agreement between city and county for provision of judicial services

51.050   Criminal jurisdiction; transfer to circuit court

51.055   Notice to Department of State Police of conviction; rules

51.070   Crimes triable in justice court

51.080   Civil jurisdiction of justice court

51.090   Civil jurisdiction not to extend to certain actions

51.100   Where action may be commenced in civil cases

51.105   Recording and reporting of proceedings

51.110   Records and files of a justice court

51.120   Justice court docket

51.130   Disposition of docket and files; docket and files are public writings

51.140   Office, courtroom and clerical assistance; books, office equipment and supplies

JUSTICES OF THE PEACE

51.210   Each district to elect one justice

51.230   At what election justice to be elected

51.240   Qualifications for office

51.245   Continuing education

51.250   Time when term begins; filing certificate of election, oath of office and undertaking

51.260   Filling vacancy; temporary appointment; appointment during justice's vacation

51.270   Form of justice's undertaking

51.280   Qualifications of sureties; filing justification

51.300   Temporary service by circuit court judge or other justice of the peace

FEES AND FINES

51.310   Schedule of fees; payment of fees to county treasurer

51.340   Monthly report of fines collected

ORGANIZATION AND JURISDICTION

51.010 Justice court defined; no terms of court; court always open for business. A justice court is a court held by a justice of the peace within the justice of the peace district for which the justice of the peace may be chosen. There are no particular terms of such court, but the same is always open for the transaction of business, according to the mode of proceeding prescribed for it.

51.020 Justice of the peace districts; establishing and modifying boundaries; maximum number of districts. (1) The county court or board of county commissioners of every county may set off and establish, or modify the boundaries of, justice of the peace districts within the county. No more than six justice of the peace districts shall be set off or established or permitted to remain in existence within any county. Except in the counties of Baker, Gilliam, Grant, Harney, Morrow, Sherman, Tillamook and Wheeler, a justice of the peace district may not include any portion of the city that is the county seat for the county or any portion of a city in which a circuit court regularly holds court. In the counties of Baker, Gilliam, Grant, Harney, Morrow, Sherman, Tillamook and Wheeler, a justice of the peace district in existence on January 15, 1998, may include any portion of the city that is the county seat for the county, or any portion of a city in which a circuit court regularly holds court, until such time as the justice court ceases to provide judicial services within the county seat or city. If the justice court ceases to provide judicial services within the county seat or city, the district that includes portions of the county seat or city shall cease to exist and may not thereafter be reestablished.

(2) At the time that the county court or board of county commissioners of a county sets off and establishes the boundaries of a justice of the peace district, the county court or board of county commissioners may require as a qualification for the office that a person serving as justice of the peace in the district be a member of the Oregon State Bar.

(3) The prohibition of subsection (1) of this section on a justice of the peace district that includes any portion of the city that is the county seat for the county, or any portion of a city in which a circuit court regularly holds court, does not prevent a justice of the peace from conducting an arraignment for a person in custody in the city that is the county seat for the county, or in a city in which a circuit court regularly holds court, if the accusatory instrument for the offense was filed in the justice court and the offense was committed within the boundaries of the justice of the peace district. [Amended by 1965 c.568 §5; 1995 c.658 §53; 1997 c.801 §105; 1999 c.449 §1; 2011 c.420 §1]

51.025 Justice court as court of record. (1) Except as provided in subsection (7) of this section, any justice court may become a court of record by:
(a) The passage of an ordinance by the governing body of the county in which the court is located; and
(b) The entry of an order by the Supreme Court acknowledging the filing of the declaration required under subsection (2) of this section.
(2) Before a justice court may become a court of record, the governing body of the county in which the court is located must file a declaration with the Supreme Court that includes:
(a) A statement that the justice court satisfies the requirements of this section for becoming a court of record;
(b) The address and telephone number of the clerk of the justice court; and
(c) The date on which the justice court will commence operations as a court of record.
(3) The Supreme Court may not charge a fee for filing a declaration under subsection (2) of this section. Not later than 30 days after a declaration is filed under subsection (2) of this section, the Supreme Court shall enter an order acknowledging the filing of the declaration and give notice of the order of acknowledgment to the county and the public.
(4) The county shall provide a court reporter or an audio recording device for each justice court made a court of record under this section.
(5) The appeal from a judgment entered in a justice court that becomes a court of record under this section shall be as provided in ORS chapters 19 and 138 for appeals from judgments of circuit courts.
(6) As a qualification for the office, the justice of the peace for any justice court that becomes a court of record must be a member of the Oregon State Bar.
(7) A justice court may not become a court of record under the provisions of this section if the court is located within 50 driving miles of the circuit court for the county in which the justice court is located, measured by the shortest distance by public roads between the justice court and the circuit court. [1999 c.682 §1; 2007 c.330 §1]

Note: Section 4, chapter 682, Oregon Laws 1999, provides:
Sec. 4. Sections 1 (3) and 3 (3) of this 1999 Act [51.025 (3) and 221.342 (3)] do not affect the term of office of any justice of the peace or municipal judge serving on the effective date of an ordinance passed for the purpose of making a justice court or municipal court a court of record. Any justice of the peace or municipal judge elected or appointed after the effective date of the ordinance must, as a qualification for the office, be a member of the Oregon State Bar. [1999 c.682 §4]

51.028 Justice court ceasing operation as court of record. (1) Any justice court that has become a court of record under ORS 51.025 may cease to operate as a court of record only if the governing body of the county in which the court is located files a declaration with the Supreme Court identifying the date on which the justice court will cease operation as a court of record. The date identified in the declaration may not be less than 31 days after the date the declaration is filed.
(2) The Supreme Court may not charge a fee for filing a declaration under subsection (1) of this section. Not later than 30 days after a declaration is filed under subsection (1) of this section, the Supreme Court shall enter an order acknowledging the filing of the declaration and give notice of the order of acknowledgment to the county and the public.
(3) The appeal from a judgment entered in a justice court after the date identified in a declaration filed under this section shall be as provided in ORS 53.005 to 53.125 and ORS chapter 157. [2007 c.330 §2]

51.030 [Amended by 1963 c.614 §3; repealed by 1997 c.487 §2 and 1997 c.801 §106]

51.035 Justice of peace as municipal judge. Except as provided in ORS 3.136, any city situated wholly or in largest part within the boundaries of a justice of the peace district may enter into an agreement pursuant to ORS 190.010 with the county in which the justice of the peace district is located providing that the justice court for the district shall have all judicial jurisdiction, authority, powers, functions and duties of the municipal court of the city and the judges thereof with respect to all or any violations of the charter or ordinances of the city. [1975 c.713 §1]

51.037 Agreement between city and county for provision of judicial services. Any city may enter into an agreement pursuant to ORS 190.010 with the county in which a justice of the peace district is located for the provision of judicial services. A justice of the peace providing services to a city pursuant to such an agreement shall have all judicial jurisdiction, authority, powers, functions and duties of the municipal court of the city and the judges thereof with respect to all and any violations of the charter or ordinances of the city. Unless the agreement provides otherwise, and subject to the provisions of ORS 153.640 to 153.680, all fines, costs and forfeited security deposits collected shall be paid to the prosecuting city, and the city shall reimburse the county providing judicial services for expenses incurred under the agreement. The exercise of jurisdiction under such an agreement by a justice of the peace shall not constitute the holding of more than one office. [1989 c.679 §2; 1999 c.1051 §243; 2011 c.597 §120]

51.040 [Amended by 1971 c.743 §312; 1979 c.777 §43; 1987 c.907 §13; repealed by 1999 c.605 §8 and 1999 c.1051 §42]

51.050 Criminal jurisdiction; transfer to circuit court. (1) Except as otherwise provided in this section, in addition to the criminal jurisdiction of justice courts already conferred upon and exercised by them, justice courts have jurisdiction of all offenses committed or triable in their respective counties. The jurisdiction conveyed by this section is concurrent with any jurisdiction that may be exercised by a circuit court or municipal court.
(2) In any justice court that has not become a court of record under ORS 51.025, a defendant charged with a misdemeanor shall be notified immediately after entering a plea of not guilty of the right of the defendant to have the matter transferred to the circuit court for the county where the justice court is located. The election shall be made within 10 days after the plea of not guilty is entered, and the justice shall immediately transfer the case to the appropriate court.
(3) A justice court does not have jurisdiction over the trial of any felony or a designated drug-related misdemeanor as defined in ORS 423.478. Except as provided in ORS 51.037, a justice court does not have jurisdiction over offenses created by the charter or ordinance of any city. [Amended by 1963 c.513 §3; 1969 c.180 §1; 1971 c.743 §313; 1973 c.625 §1; 1995 c.658 §55; 1999 c.605 §1; 1999 c.682 §10; 1999 c.1051 §41; 2017 c.706 §20]

51.055 Notice to Department of State Police of conviction; rules. (1) A justice or municipal court shall notify the Department of State Police when the justice or municipal court enters a judgment of conviction for a Class A misdemeanor.
(2) The department shall make rules establishing:
(a) Requirements for notification under this section.
(b) Procedures for entry of convictions described in subsection (1) of this section into the Law Enforcement Data System the department maintains. The rules must provide that it is not necessary to enter a conviction into the Law Enforcement Data System if a record of the conviction already exists in the system. [2013 c.141 §1]

51.060 [Amended by 1957 c.644 §27; 1971 c.743 §314; repealed by 1999 c.605 §8 and 1999 c.1051 §42]

51.070 Crimes triable in justice court. A crime is triable in a justice court when, by the provisions of ORS 131.205 to 131.325, an action may be commenced therefor in the county where such court is held. [Amended by 1973 c.836 §328]

51.080 Civil jurisdiction of justice court. (1) A justice court has jurisdiction, but not exclusive, of the following actions:
(a) For the recovery of money or damages only, when the amount claimed does not exceed $10,000.
(b) For the recovery of specific personal property, when the value of the property claimed and the damages for the detention do not exceed $10,000.
(c) For the recovery of any penalty or forfeiture, whether given by statute or arising out of contract, not exceeding $10,000.
(d) To give judgment without action, upon the confession of the defendant for any of the causes specified in this section, except for a penalty or forfeiture imposed by statute.
(2) For purposes of this section, the amount claimed, value of property, damages or any amount in controversy does not include any amount claimed as costs and disbursements or attorney fees as defined by ORCP 68 A. [Amended by 1973 c.625 §2; 1979 c.447 §1; 1983 c.149 §2; 1989 c.839 §34; 1993 c.735 §10; 1997 c.801 §107; 1999 c.84 §4; 2007 c.71 §13; 2007 c.125 §4; 2011 c.595 §52a]

51.090 Civil jurisdiction not to extend to certain actions. The jurisdiction conferred by ORS 51.080 does not extend to:
(1) An action in which the title to real property shall come in question.
(2) An action for false imprisonment, libel, slander or malicious prosecution.
(3) An action brought by an inmate as defined in ORS 30.642. [Amended by 1983 c.673 §9; 2003 c.14 §22; 2011 c.262 §5]

51.100 Where action may be commenced in civil cases. (1) Except as provided in this section, a civil action subject to the jurisdiction of a justice court must be commenced in the county where one of the parties resides.
(2) If a defendant in a civil action subject to the jurisdiction of a justice court does not reside in this state, the action may be commenced in any justice district of this state.
(3) If all parties reside in the same justice district, a civil action may be brought only in the justice court for that justice district.
(4) Motions for change of venue in justice courts are subject to the same laws governing change of venue in circuit court. [Amended by 1999 c.605 §2]

51.105 Recording and reporting of proceedings. (1) In any proceeding conducted in open court in a justice court, any party may arrange for audio recording or reporting of the proceeding by stenographic or other means. The court may not prohibit recording or reporting of the proceeding under this section.
(2) A reporter providing stenographic reporting services under this section must be certified in shorthand reporting under ORS 8.415 to 8.455 or by a nationally recognized certification program. A party arranging for reporting of the proceeding by stenographic means must provide the court with the name of the reporter and an address and telephone number where the reporter may be contacted.
(3) If all parties to the proceeding and the court agree, the audio recording or stenographic or other reporting of the proceeding arranged under this section may be used by the parties during the proceeding.
(4) If all parties to the proceeding and the court agree, the audio recording or stenographic or other reporting of the proceeding arranged under this section is the official record of the proceeding.
(5) Unless other parties agree to pay all or part of the cost of the audio recording or stenographic or other reporting of the proceeding, the party arranging for the recording or reporting must pay all costs of the recording or reporting. [2015 c.623 §8]

51.110 Records and files of a justice court. The records and files of a justice court are the docket and all papers and process filed in or returned to such court, concerning or belonging to any proceeding authorized to be had or taken therein, or before the justice of the peace who holds such court.

51.120 Justice court docket. (1) The docket of a justice of the peace is a record in which the justice of the peace must enter:

(a) The title of every action or proceeding commenced in the court of the justice of the peace or before the justice of the peace, with the names of the parties thereto and the time of the commencement thereof.

(b) The date of making or filing any pleading.

(c) An order allowing a provisional remedy, and the date of issuing and returning the summons or other process.

(d) The time when the parties or either of them appears, or their failure to do so.

(e) Every postponement of a trial or proceeding, and upon whose application, and to what time.

(f) The demand for a jury, if any, and by whom made; the order for a jury, and the time appointed for trial.

(g) The return of an order for a jury, the names of the persons impaneled and sworn as a jury, and the names of all witnesses sworn, and at whose request.

(h) The verdict of the jury, and when given; and if the jury disagree and are discharged without giving a verdict, a statement of such disagreement and discharge.

(i) The judgment of the court, and when given.

(j) The date on which any judgment is docketed in the docket.

(k) The fact of an appeal having been made and allowed, and the date thereof, with a memorandum of the undertaking, and the justification of the sureties.

(L) Satisfaction of the judgment or any part thereof.

(m) A memorandum of all orders relating to security release.

(n) All other matters which may be material or specially required by any statute.

(2) The docket of a justice court may be maintained in electronic form. [Amended by 1999 c.788 §43; 1999 c.1051 §244]

51.130 Disposition of docket and files; docket and files are public writings. The docket and files of a justice court are to be safely and securely kept by the justice of the peace, and by the justice of the peace forthwith delivered to a successor in office. When any justice court is abolished, the docket and files of that court shall be turned over to the clerk of the circuit court for the county in which the justice court was located. Such docket and files are public writings. [Amended by 1995 c.658 §56]

51.140 Office, courtroom and clerical assistance; books, office equipment and supplies. The county court or board of county commissioners of the county in which the justice of the peace has been elected or appointed:

(1) May provide for the office of the justice of the peace the office and courtroom and clerical assistance necessary to enable the justice of the peace to effectuate the prompt, efficient and dignified administration of justice.

(2) Shall provide for the office of the justice of the peace:

(a) The books, records, forms, papers, stationery, postage and office equipment and supplies necessary in the proper keeping of the records and files of the judicial office and the transaction of the business thereof.

(b) The latest edition of the Oregon Revised Statutes and all official materials published from time to time to supplement such edition. [Amended by 1955 c.448 §1; 1957 c.180 §1]

JUSTICES OF THE PEACE

51.210 Each district to elect one justice. Each justice of the peace district shall elect one justice of the peace, who shall hold office for six years and until a successor is elected and qualified.

51.220 [Amended by 1961 c.724 §25; 1965 c.510 §21; repealed by 1997 c.487 §2 and 1997 c.801 §106]

51.230 At what election justice to be elected. The election at which a justice of the peace shall be elected shall be the general election or, if applicable, the election specified in ORS 249.088 next preceding the expiration of the term of the incumbent of the office. [Amended by 1991 c.719 §3]

51.240 Qualifications for office. (1) As a qualification for the office:

(a) A justice of the peace must be a citizen of the United States and a resident of this state.

(b) A justice of the peace must be a resident of or have a principal office in the justice of the peace district in which the justice court is located. For purposes of this paragraph, a "principal office" is the primary location from which a person conducts the person's business or profession.

(c) A justice of the peace must have maintained the residence within this state required by paragraph (b) of this subsection for at least three years immediately prior to appointment or becoming a candidate for election to the office of justice of the peace.

(d) A justice of the peace must have maintained the residence or principal office required by paragraph (b) of this subsection for at least one year immediately prior to appointment or becoming a candidate for election to the office of justice of the peace.

(e) A justice of the peace must:

(A) Be a member of the Oregon State Bar;

(B) Have completed a course on courts of special jurisdiction offered by the National Judicial College, or complete the course within 12 months after appointment or election to the office of justice of the peace; or

(C) Have completed, or complete within 12 months after appointment or election to the office of justice of the peace, a course that is equivalent to the course described in subparagraph (B) of this paragraph, proposed by the justice of the peace and approved by the Chief Justice of the Supreme Court.

(2) If exigent circumstances prevent a justice of the peace from completing the course required under subsection (1)(e)(B) of this section within 12 months after appointment or election to the office of justice of the peace, the presiding judge of the judicial district in which the justice court is located may grant the justice of the peace one extension of time to complete the course. The extension may not exceed 12 months. The presiding judge may require the justice of the peace to complete additional educational requirements during an extension granted under this subsection.

(3) Notwithstanding subsection (1)(e) of this section, a justice of the peace in a justice court that is a court of record under ORS 51.025 must be a member of the Oregon State Bar. [1991 c.458 §10; 1993 c.493 §88; 2015 c.570 §6]

51.245 Continuing education. (1) Each justice of the peace who is not a member of the Oregon State Bar shall attend or participate in a minimum of 30 hours of educational programs every two calendar years. The programs shall be those conducted and supervised or approved by the Chief Justice of the Supreme Court or designee.

(2) Each justice of the peace who is not a member of the Oregon State Bar shall submit a written annual report of the hours of educational programs referred to in subsection (1) of this section that are attended or participated in by the justice during each calendar year to the Oregon Justices of the Peace Association and shall submit a copy of that report to the governing body of the county in which the justice has been elected or appointed. The report and copy shall be submitted not later than March 1 of the year following the calendar year for which the report is applicable. [1989 c.1005 §1; 1993 c.742 §39]

51.250 Time when term begins; filing certificate of election, oath of office and undertaking. The term of office of a justice of the peace shall commence on the first Monday in January next following election. Before entering upon the duties of office, the person elected thereto shall qualify by filing with the county clerk of the county wherein the person is elected:

(1) The certificate of election of the person.

(2) An oath of office, by the person subscribed, to the effect that the person will support the Constitution of the United States and the Constitution of Oregon and will faithfully and honestly perform the duties of the office.

(3) Also an official undertaking, duly approved by the county court or board of county commissioners in the penal sum of $2,500; provided, that the official undertaking of a justice of the peace in any district in which is located the county seat, or any part thereof, shall be in such greater penal sum, not exceeding $10,000, as the court or board shall designate. [Amended by 1987 c.158 §7]

51.260 Filling vacancy; temporary appointment; appointment during justice's vacation. (1) If a vacancy occurs in the office of justice of the peace, the Governor immediately shall appoint some person possessing the qualifications for election to that office to fill the vacancy until the next general election and until such appointee's successor is elected and qualified. The person appointed to fill the vacancy shall qualify in the same manner as a person elected to the office.

(2) In the event of a temporary absence or other incapacity of a justice of the peace, the county court, if it deems it in the public interest, may appoint a sitting justice of the peace from any county justice of the peace district within the State of Oregon, or may appoint a person possessing the qualifications for election as justice of the peace, to serve as justice of the peace pro tempore during the period of absence or incapacity. An appointment under this subsection may not be for a period exceeding one year.

(3) In the event of a temporary absence of a justice of the peace for a period of more than 60 consecutive days, or in the event of inability for a like period to act by reason of illness or other cause, the Governor, if the Governor deems it necessary in the public interest that a person be appointed to fill such temporary vacancy, shall appoint some person possessing the qualifications for election to such office to fill the temporary vacancy.

(4) The person appointed by the county court or Governor pursuant to subsection (2) or (3) of this section immediately shall qualify in the same manner as a person elected to the office, and thereupon shall perform the duties of justice of the peace for the district during the temporary absence or inability. During the temporary tenure, the person shall receive the salary that the absent justice of the peace otherwise would have received during the period. When any such appointee has qualified and entered upon the duties of office, the appointment thereto shall not be revoked or rescinded during the actual trial or hearing of any action or proceeding before the appointee; but the temporary appointment may be terminated at any other time by written notice to that effect given by the appointing authority and filed with the county clerk of the county.

(5) Every justice of the peace is entitled to two weeks paid vacation every year and during such absence the county court may appoint a justice of the peace pro tempore pursuant to the provisions of subsections (2) and (4) of this section. [Amended by 1961 c.724 §26; 1995 c.329 §1; 1995 c.658 §58]

51.270 Form of justice's undertaking. The official undertaking of a justice of the peace shall be in substantially the following form:

___

Whereas A B has been duly elected justice of the peace in and for the District of_____, in the County of_____, at an election held on the ___ day of_____, 2__, we, C D and E F, hereby undertake that if A B shall not faithfully pay over according to law all moneys that shall come into the hands of A B by virtue of such office, then we, or either of us, will pay to the State of Oregon the sum of $___.

C D.

E F.

___

51.280 Qualifications of sureties; filing justification. The sureties in the undertaking provided for in ORS 51.250 shall have the qualifications of bail and shall be residents of the county, and their justification must be filed with the undertaking.

51.290 [Repealed by 1953 c.306 §18]

51.300 Temporary service by circuit court judge or other justice of the peace. A judge of the circuit court for a county, or any justice of the peace for a justice court district located within the county, may exercise the powers and duties of justice of the peace of any justice court in the county:
(1) At the request of the justice of the peace of the justice court;
(2) In the event of a vacancy in the office of the justice of the peace, until the vacancy is filled as provided by law; or
(3) In the event of the absence, incapacity or disqualification of the justice of the peace, during the period of such absence, incapacity or disqualification. [1965 c.377 §2; 1979 c.69 §1; 1999 c.605 §3]

FEES AND FINES

51.310 Schedule of fees; payment of fees to county treasurer. (1) Except as provided in ORS 105.130, the justice of the peace shall collect, in advance except in criminal cases, and issue receipts for, the following fees:
(a) For the first appearance of the plaintiff, $90.
(b) For the first appearance of the defendant, $90.
(c) In the small claims department, for a plaintiff filing a claim, $37; and for a defendant requesting a hearing, $37.
(d) For transcript of judgment, $9.
(e) For transcript of judgment from the small claims department, $9.
(f) For certified copy of judgment, $9.
(g) For issuing writs of execution or writs of garnishment, $20 for each writ.
(h) For issuing notices of restitution as provided in ORS 105.151, $10 for each notice.
(i) For filing a motion described in ORS 21.200 in an action not in the small claims department, $30.
(j) For supplying to private parties copies of records and files, the same fees as provided or established for the county clerk under ORS 205.320.
(k) For each official certificate, $10.
(L) For taking and certifying for a private party an acknowledgment of proof of any instrument, $10.
(m) Costs in criminal cases, where there has been a conviction, or upon forfeiture of security, $5.
(2) Not later than the last day of the month immediately following the month in which fees set forth in subsection (1) of this section are collected, the justice of the peace shall pay all such fees, other than those for performing marriage ceremonies, over to the county treasurer of the county wherein the justice of the peace was elected or appointed, for crediting to the general fund of the county, and shall take the receipt of the treasurer therefor. [Amended by 1965 c.619 §25; 1979 c.447 §2; 1987 c.829 §1; 1989 c.583 §10; 1991 c.458 §2; 1997 c.801 §132; 1999 c.1051 §245; 2003 c.687 §1; 2011 c.595 §52b; 2015 c.623 §§1,2]

51.340 Monthly report of fines collected. Justices of the peace in each county shall report to the county treasurer once in each month the amount of all fines collected by them, from whom collected, and what the fine was for, and at the same time pay to the county treasurer in money the full amount of the fines collected. If the justices of the peace have collected no fines, they shall report that fact to the county treasurer.

51.350 [Repealed by 1983 c.77 §1 and 1983 c.310 §21]

51.360 [Repealed by 1983 c.77 §1 and 1983 c.310 §21]

51.410 [Repealed by 1965 c.624 §12]

51.440 [Amended by 1965 c.624 §1; 1971 c.136 §1; 1995 c.658 §59; repealed by 2015 c.212 §19]

51.450 [Amended by 1965 c.624 §3; 1983 c.83 §3; 1995 c.658 §60; repealed by 2015 c.212 §19]

51.460 [Amended by 1965 c.624 §4; 1995 c.658 §61; repealed by 2015 c.212 §19]

51.470 [Amended by 1965 c.624 §5; 1995 c.658 §62; repealed by 2015 c.212 §19]

51.480 [Repealed by 2015 c.212 §19]

51.490 [Amended by 1965 c.624 §6; repealed by 2015 c.212 §19]

51.500 [Amended by 1965 c.624 §7; repealed by 2015 c.212 §19]

51.520 [Repealed by 1953 c.306 §18]

51.530 [Amended by 1965 c.624 §8; repealed by 1973 c.393 §4]

51.540 [Amended by 1965 c.624 §9; repealed by 2015 c.212 §19]

51.550 [Amended by 1965 c.624 §10; repealed by 2015 c.212 §19]

51.610 [Amended by 1965 c.134 §1; 1965 c.624 §11; repealed by 1971 c.136 §3]

51.620 [Repealed by 1971 c.136 §3]

51.630 [Amended by 1959 c.621 §1; repealed by 1971 c.136 §3]

51.640 [Amended by 1965 c.613 §26; repealed by 1971 c.136 §3]

51.650 [Repealed by 1953 c.306 §18]

51.660 [Repealed by 1965 c.510 §24]

51.670 [Amended by 1965 c.510 §22; repealed by 1965 c.624 §12]

51.680 [Repealed by 1953 c.306 §18]

51.690 [Repealed by 1953 c.306 §18]

51.700 [1965 c.624 §2; repealed by 1971 c.136 §3]

Chapter 52 —— Civil Actions

CIVIL ACTIONS

JUSTICE COURTS

GENERAL PROVISIONS

52.010   Actions commenced and prosecuted, and judgments enforced, as in circuit court; prevailing party entitled to disbursements

52.020   Mode of proceeding and rules of evidence

52.030   Court rules and procedures

52.035   Dismissal of civil cases for want of prosecution

52.040   Contempt in justice court

52.060   Persons entitled to act as attorneys in justice court

SUMMONS

52.110   Service; form, contents and requisites of summons

52.120   Persons authorized to serve summons; compensation; manner of service

52.130   Appointment of persons to serve process or order

52.170   Security for disbursements

52.180   Form of undertaking; qualifications and justification of sureties; deposit in lieu of undertaking

ATTACHMENT

52.210   Plaintiff entitled to attachment as in circuit court

52.220   Attachment proceedings conducted as in circuit court

52.250   Attachment of real property prohibited

PLEADINGS

52.310   Pleadings governed by rules applicable to pleadings in circuit court

52.320   Counterclaim exceeding jurisdiction; transfer to circuit court; time allowed plaintiff to plead; costs; effect of failure to tender costs

TRIAL FEES

52.410   Trial fee

52.420   Trial fee payable in advance; effect of failure to pay; recovery of fee as disbursement

52.430   State or county exempted from prepaying trial fee; recovery of trial fee

52.440   Accounting for and disposition of trial fee

TRIAL AND JUDGMENT

52.510   Postponement of trial

52.520   Depositions of witnesses as condition to postponement

52.530   Change of place of trial

52.540   Payment of disbursements for change of venue; subpoenaed witnesses

52.550   When change of venue deemed complete

52.560   Jurisdiction to cease when title to real property in question; further proceedings in circuit court

52.570   Right to jury trial

52.580   Judgment

52.590   Judgment may not determine or affect title to real property

ENFORCEMENT AND SETOFF OF JUDGMENTS; EXECUTIONS

52.600   Enforcement of justice court judgments generally

52.610   Enforcement of judgment given by other justice

52.620   Filing transcript of judgment in another county; issuance of execution

52.635   Liens based on justice court judgment

52.640   Setoff of judgment; application and notice

52.650   Right of appeal precludes setoff; procedure to set off judgment of another court

52.660   Enforcement of setoff judgment stayed

52.670   Setoff of mutual judgments

52.680   Setoff of judgments in different amounts; disallowance of setoff

52.700   Return on execution; to whom directed; duty of officer to execute writ

52.710   Renewal of execution; indorsement and entry of renewal

GENERAL PROVISIONS

52.010 Actions commenced and prosecuted, and judgments enforced, as in circuit court; prevailing party entitled to disbursements. (1) Actions at law in justice courts shall be commenced and prosecuted to final determination and judgment enforced therein, in the manner provided for similar actions in the circuit courts, except as in this chapter otherwise provided.

(2) All disbursements shall in all cases be allowed the prevailing party.

52.020 Mode of proceeding and rules of evidence. The mode of proceeding and the rules of evidence are the same in a justice court as in a like action or proceeding in the circuit courts, except where otherwise specially provided.

52.030 Court rules and procedures. The rules in justice courts governing mistakes in pleadings and amendments thereof, vacating defaults and judgments for mistake, inadvertence, surprise or excusable neglect, the formation of issues of both law and fact, the postponing of trials for cause shown, the mode of trial, the formation of the jury, the conduct and manner of trial by jury or by the justice without a jury, the procedure regarding the verdict and judgment and the enforcement thereof by execution shall be as prescribed for civil actions in the circuit courts, except as otherwise provided.

52.035 Dismissal of civil cases for want of prosecution. The justice of the peace of every justice court shall mail a notice to each of the attorneys of record, or, to the plaintiff where there is no licensed attorney representing the plaintiff, in every pending civil action, suit or proceeding in their respective courts in which no proceedings have been had or papers filed for a period of more than one year. The notice shall state that each such case will be dismissed by the court for want of prosecution 60 days from the date of mailing the notice, unless, on or before the expiration of the 60 days, application, either oral or written, be made to the court and good cause shown why it should be continued as a pending case. If such application is not made or good cause is not shown, the court shall dismiss each such case. Nothing contained herein shall be construed to prevent the dismissing at any time, for want of prosecution, of any suit, action or proceeding upon motion of any party thereto. [1953 c.360 §1]

52.040 Contempt in justice court. ORS 33.015 to 33.155, defining acts that constitute contempt and the proceedings for imposing sanctions for contempt, apply to justice courts. [Amended by 1991 c.724 §20; 1999 c.605 §4; 2005 c.22 §34]

52.050 [Repealed by 1999 c.605 §8]

52.060 Persons entitled to act as attorneys in justice court. Any person may act as attorney for another in a justice court, except a person or officer serving any process in the action or proceeding, other than a subpoena.

SUMMONS

52.110 Service; form, contents and requisites of summons. (1) At any time after the action is commenced by the filing of a complaint with the justice of the peace, the plaintiff may cause a summons to be served on the defendant. It shall be subscribed by the plaintiff or plaintiff's attorney or the justice of the peace. It shall specify the name of the court in which the complaint is filed and shall contain the title of the cause specifying the names of the parties to the action, plaintiff and defendant. It shall be directed to the defendant and shall require the defendant to appear and defend within the time required by ORCP 7 C(2) or, in case of failure to so appear and defend, the plaintiff will take judgment against the defendant for the money, property or other relief demanded in the complaint, with costs and disbursements of the action.
(2) A summons shall contain a notice printed in type size equal to at least 8-point type which may be substantially in the following form:

NOTICE TO DEFENDANT:
READ THESE PAPERS
CAREFULLY!
You must "appear" in this case or the other side will win automatically. To "appear" you must file with the court a legal paper called a "motion" or "answer." The "motion" or "answer" must be given to the justice of the peace within 30 days along with the required filing fee. It must be in proper form and have proof of service on the plaintiff's attorney or, if the plaintiff does not have an attorney, proof of service on the plaintiff.
If you have questions, you should see an attorney immediately.

_____ [Amended by 1983 c.673 §10]

52.120 Persons authorized to serve summons; compensation; manner of service. (1) The summons in an action in a justice court shall be served by a person authorized to serve summons, who shall be compensated for service of the summons, as provided for the service of summons in civil action in a circuit court.
(2) The summons shall be served in the manner provided for the service of summons in a civil action in a circuit court. The summons shall be returned to the justice by whom it was issued by the person serving it, with proof of service or that the defendant cannot be found. [Amended by 1953 c.749 §4; 1973 c.827 §10; 1977 c.877 §11; 1979 c.284 §84]

52.130 Appointment of persons to serve process or order. Whenever it appears to the justice that any process or order authorized to be issued or made will not be served for want of an officer, the justice may appoint any other person authorized by ORS 52.120, to serve it. Such an appointment may be made by an indorsement on the process or order, in substantially the following form and signed by the justice with the name of the office of the justice:

I hereby appoint A B to serve the within process or order.

_____ [Amended by 1977 c.877 §12; 1979 c.284 §85; 1995 c.79 §13]

52.140 [Amended by 1953 c.479 §4; 1977 c.877 §13; repealed by 1979 c.284 §199]

52.150 [Repealed by 1979 c.284 §199]

52.160 [Repealed by 1979 c.284 §199]

52.170 Security for disbursements. If the plaintiff is a nonresident of this state, the justice may require the plaintiff to give an undertaking with one or more sureties, or an irrevocable letter of credit issued by an insured institution, as defined in ORS 706.008, for the disbursements of the action before issuing the summons; and if at any time before the commencement of the trial the defendant applies therefor, the justice must require such plaintiff to give the undertaking or irrevocable letter of credit. If the plaintiff is a resident of this state, the justice may, in the discretion of the justice, upon a like application on the part of the defendant, require the plaintiff to give such undertaking or irrevocable letter of credit. However, if the plaintiff is a resident of Oregon and makes the affidavit that the plaintiff is unable to furnish the undertaking or irrevocable letter of credit as required by this section, the giving of such undertaking or irrevocable letter of credit shall be waived. [Amended by 1991 c.331 §14; 1997 c.631 §374]

52.180 Form of undertaking; qualifications and justification of sureties; deposit in lieu of undertaking. (1) The undertaking may be substantially in the following form:

"I, A B," or "We, A B and C D, undertake to pay E F, the defendant in this action, all disbursements that may be adjudged to E F in this action."

---

(2) The sureties must possess the qualifications of bail upon arrest, and, if required by the defendant, must justify in a sum not less than $50. A deposit with the justice of such sum as the justice may deem sufficient shall be equivalent to giving the required undertaking. If the undertaking or deposit in lieu thereof is not given or made by the time the action is at issue and ready for trial on a question of fact, the justice must dismiss the action as for want of prosecution. [Amended by 1995 c.79 §14]

ATTACHMENT

52.210 Plaintiff entitled to attachment as in circuit court. In a civil action in a justice court the plaintiff is entitled to the benefit of the provisional remedies of attachment and delivery of personal property claimed in the action, as in like cases in the circuit courts. All affidavits, orders and undertakings for these remedies are to be taken or made and filed with the justice, and the process is to be issued by and made returnable before the justice. A writ of attachment or an order for the delivery of personal property claimed in the action may be served and executed by any person authorized to serve a summons. [Amended by 1981 c.898 §41]

52.220 Attachment proceedings conducted as in circuit court. The provisions for proceedings in the circuit courts on attachment and delivery of personal property shall govern in like cases in justice courts, except as otherwise provided. [Amended by 1981 c.898 §42]

52.230 [Repealed by 1981 c.898 §53]

52.240 [Repealed by 1981 c.898 §53]

52.250 Attachment of real property prohibited. Real property or any interest therein cannot be attached upon a writ of attachment in a civil action in a justice court.

52.260 [Repealed by 1981 c.898 §53]

PLEADINGS

52.310 Pleadings governed by rules applicable to pleadings in circuit court. The pleadings in actions in justice courts, the forms thereof and the rules by which the sufficiency of the pleadings are to be determined, shall be those prescribed for civil actions in the circuit courts.

52.320 Counterclaim exceeding jurisdiction; transfer to circuit court; time allowed plaintiff to plead; costs; effect of failure to tender costs. In all actions instituted in a justice court a defendant shall have the right to plead a counterclaim in excess of the jurisdiction of the court, whereupon the justice of the peace shall, within 10 days following the filing of the answer, file with the clerk of the circuit court for the county in which the justice court is located, a transcript of the cause containing a copy of all the material entries in the justice's docket, together with all the original papers relating to the cause. Upon the filing of the transcript with the clerk of the circuit court, the justice of the peace shall proceed no further in the cause, but the cause shall thenceforth be considered as transferred to the circuit court and be deemed pending and for trial therein as if originally commenced in the court. The circuit court shall have jurisdiction of the cause and shall proceed to hear, determine and try the same. In the event of the justice's failure to file the transcript in the circuit court within the time specified, the judge of the circuit court may make an order upon the justice to comply within a specified time with the provisions of this section. The plaintiff in the action shall have 10 days after the filing of the transcript in the circuit court in which to move against or reply to defendant's answer. All costs incurred in the transfer of the case, including the fee for filing the same in the circuit court, shall be borne by the defendant and must be tendered by the defendant to the justice of the peace at the time of filing with the justice the counterclaim, and the costs may be recovered by the defendant in the event the defendant prevails. On failure of the defendant to pay to the justice of the peace the required fee at the time of filing the counterclaim, or within two days thereafter, the justice of the peace shall disregard the counterclaim of the defendant and proceed to try the cause as though the counterclaim had never been filed. [Amended by 1979 c.284 §86]

TRIAL FEES

52.410 Trial fee. (1) Parties to judicial proceedings in justice courts are required to contribute toward the expense of maintaining justice courts, or a particular action or proceeding therein, by the payment of a trial fee, except that a trial fee may not be required for a hearing or trial in the small claims department of a justice court.
(2) The trial fee in a justice court for a trial by jury is $125 for each full or partial day of trial, payable by the party demanding the jury trial at the time the demand is made.
(3) The trial fee in a justice court for a trial without a jury is $75 for each full or partial day of trial, payable by the plaintiff when the action or proceeding is set for trial.
(4) If a trial continues beyond the number of days originally paid for under subsection (2) or (3) of this section, the fee for subsequent days of trial must be paid in advance of each day the trial continues by the party responsible for the fee under subsection (2) or (3) of this section. [Amended by 1979 c.447 §3; 1997 c.801 §133; 2015 c.623 §4]

52.420 Trial fee payable in advance; effect of failure to pay; recovery of fee as disbursement. (1) The trial fee in a justice court shall be paid to the justice upon the demand for a jury, and unless so paid the demand shall be disregarded and the trial proceed as if no demand had been made.
(2) If the party paying the fee prevails in the action or proceeding so as to be entitled to recover costs therein, the fee shall be allowed and taxed as a disbursement and collected from the adverse party. [Amended by 2005 c.22 §35]

52.430 State or county exempted from prepaying trial fee; recovery of trial fee. When the state or any county is a party to a judicial proceeding in a justice court, the state or county need not pay the trial fee upon demanding a jury, and if the state or county is entitled to recover costs therein, the trial fee shall be allowed and taxed in the state's or county's favor as a disbursement, and collected from the adverse party as in ordinary cases. [Amended by 2005 c.22 §36]

52.440 Accounting for and disposition of trial fee. In a justice court, the trial fee is paid to the justice. The justice shall keep an account of such fees, and by whom paid, and distribute the amount among the jury in the particular case, in partial payment of their legal fees.

TRIAL AND JUDGMENT

52.510 Postponement of trial. When a cause is at issue upon a question of fact, the justice must, upon sufficient cause shown on the application of either party, postpone the trial for a period not exceeding 60 days.

52.520 Depositions of witnesses as condition to postponement. An application for the postponement of the trial shall not be granted unless the party applying therefor, if required by the adverse party, consents to take the deposition of any witness of the adverse party then in attendance upon the court. If the consent is given, the justice shall take the deposition, and it may be read on the trial, subject to the same objection as if the witness were present and gave the testimony orally.

52.530 Change of place of trial. (1) The justice shall change the place of trial, on motion of either party to the action, when it appears from a supporting affidavit of the party that:
(a) The justice is a party to or directly interested in the event of the action, or connected by consanguinity or affinity within the third degree with the adverse party or those for whom the justice prosecutes or defends; or
(b) The justice is so prejudiced against the party making the motion that the party cannot expect an impartial trial before the justice.
(2) The justice may change the place of trial, on motion of either party to the action, when it appears from a supporting affidavit of the party that the convenience of parties and witnesses would be promoted by the change, and that the motion is not made for the purpose of delay.
(3) The motion for change of place of trial cannot be made or allowed in any action until after the cause is at issue on a question of fact. The change shall be made to the nearest justice court in the county. If there is only one justice court in the county the change shall be made to the circuit court for the county in which the justice court is located. Neither party shall be entitled to more than one change in the place of trial, except for causes not in existence when the first change was allowed. When the place of trial has been changed, the justice shall forthwith transmit to the justice court or circuit court to whom the case is transferred a transcript of the proceedings had in the case with all the original papers filed thereon. All costs incurred in the transfer of such

case, including the fee for filing the same in the court to which the case is transferred shall be borne by the party requesting the change and must be tendered by the party to the justice at the time of filing the motion for the change. Such costs may be recovered by such party in the event the party prevails in the trial of the action. On the failure of the party to tender or pay the required fee at the time the motion is filed the justice shall disregard the motion and proceed to try the action as though no motion had been filed. [Amended by 1959 c.159 §1; 1995 c.658 §63; 2005 c.22 §37]

52.540 Payment of disbursements for change of venue; subpoenaed witnesses. (1) The disbursements of the change of venue shall be paid by the party applying therefor, and not taxed as a part of the costs in the case.

(2) It shall not be necessary to issue new subpoenas to witnesses, but the witnesses shall appear before the justice before whom the cause has been transferred without the issue of any other notice than the allowance of the motion for the change of venue.

52.550 When change of venue deemed complete. Upon the filing of the transcript and papers with the justice to whom the cause has been transferred, the change of venue shall be deemed complete, and thereafter the action shall proceed as though it had been commenced before such justice.

52.560 Jurisdiction to cease when title to real property in question; further proceedings in circuit court. If it appears on the trial of any cause before a justice of the peace from the evidence of either party, or from the pleadings, that the title to real property is in question, which title is disputed by the other party, the justice shall immediately make an entry thereof in the docket of the justice and cease all further proceedings in the cause. The justice shall certify and return to the circuit court of the county a transcript of all the entries made in the docket of the justice relating to the case, together with all the process and other papers relating to the action, in the same manner and within the same time as upon an appeal. Thereupon the circuit court shall proceed in the cause to final judgment and execution in the same manner as if the action had been originally commenced therein, and disbursements shall abide the event of the action.

52.570 Right to jury trial. When a cause is at issue upon a question of fact, if either party then demands a jury trial and deposits with the justice such trial fee as is required to be paid in advance by ORS 52.420 and 52.430, the issue must be tried by a jury and not the justice; but otherwise it must be tried by the justice.

52.580 Judgment. When an issue of fact is tried by the justice, it is not necessary that there be any special statement of the facts found or law determined on the trial. It is sufficient for the justice to give judgment generally, as the law and evidence may require, for the plaintiff or the defendant, stating therein for what amount or what relief or to what effect the same is given.

52.590 Judgment may not determine or affect title to real property. Although the title to real property may be controverted or questioned in an action in a justice court, the judgment in the action shall in no way affect or determine the title as between the parties, or otherwise.

ENFORCEMENT AND SETOFF OF JUDGMENTS; EXECUTIONS

52.600 Enforcement of justice court judgments generally. (1) Upon the docketing of a judgment by a justice court, the judgment may be enforced by the justice court in the manner provided in this section.

(2) Enforcement proceedings on a judgment docketed by a justice court may include:

(a) Writ of execution proceedings for personal property under ORS 18.252 to 18.993.

(b) Proceedings in support of execution under ORS 18.265, 18.268 and 18.270.

(c) Garnishment proceedings under ORS 18.600 to 18.850.

(3) In addition to the enforcement proceedings specified in subsection (2) of this section, a docketed justice court judgment may be enforced by the court that rendered the judgment through the issuance of a writ of execution on real property under ORS 18.252 to 18.993. A writ of execution on real property may be issued by a justice court only after the judgment has been transcribed or recorded in the manner provided by ORS 52.635.

(4) ORS 18.038, 18.042, 18.048 and 137.071 apply to judgments rendered in justice courts.

(5) Except as provided in subsection (6) of this section, the provisions of this section apply to all judgments docketed by justice courts, including judgments imposed in violation proceedings and other criminal proceedings.

(6) The provisions of this section and ORS 52.635 do not apply to proceedings for enforcement of ordinances governing the parking of vehicles. Ordinances governing the parking of vehicles shall be enforced as provided by other law. [1999 c.788 §2; 2001 c.249 §74; 2003 c.576 §95]

52.610 Enforcement of judgment given by other justice. A justice of the peace has authority and power to enforce a judgment given by the predecessor in office, or by a justice whose docket has been transferred to the justice of the peace, and to complete any unfinished business begun before such predecessor, or entered in such docket, as if the same had been given or begun before the justice of the peace.

52.620 Filing transcript of judgment in another county; issuance of execution. The party entitled to the benefit of a judgment in a justice court may at any time have a certified transcript of the judgment and file it with any justice in any other county. Upon the filing of the transcript, the justice with whom it is filed must make an entry thereof in the docket of the justice, giving the title of the cause, the names of the parties and the substance of the judgment. Thereafter execution may issue to enforce the judgment, or any part thereof remaining unsatisfied, as if it had been given by the justice with whom the transcript is filed.

52.630 [Amended by 1965 c.619 §27; 1971 c.621 §11; 1975 c.607 §13; 1979 c.833 §14; 1981 c.835 §4; 1983 c.696 §6; 1987 c.586 §20; 1995 c.273 §15; repealed by 1999 c.788 §3 (52.635 enacted in lieu of 52.630)]

52.635 Liens based on justice court judgment. (1) After a judgment that includes a money award is docketed in a justice court, a certified copy of the judgment or a lien record abstract for the judgment may be recorded in the County Clerk Lien Record for the county that contains the justice court that rendered the judgment. The certified copy or lien record abstract may be recorded by the judgment creditor or by the agent of the judgment creditor at any time after the judgment is rendered and before the judgment expires under ORS 18.194 or is fully satisfied. From the time the certified copy of the judgment or the lien record abstract is recorded in the County Clerk Lien Record, the judgment is a lien upon the real property of the defendant in the county.

(2) In lieu of recording a certified copy of a judgment or a lien record abstract for a judgment under subsection (1) of this section, a judgment that includes a money award rendered by a justice court in a civil action may be transcribed to the circuit court for the county that contains the justice court that rendered the judgment. The judgment may be transcribed by the filing of a certified transcript of the judgment with the clerk of the circuit court. The transcript must contain a copy of all the docket entries made in the case and the judgment as rendered by the justice court, certified to be a true and correct transcript from the original entries by the justice court. Upon filing of the certified transcript, the clerk shall enter the transcribed judgment in the register of the circuit court and in the judgment lien record. The clerk shall note in the register that the transcribed judgment creates a judgment lien. A judgment in a criminal action may not be transcribed to circuit court under the provisions of this subsection.

(3) A certified copy of a judgment docketed in a justice court, or a lien record abstract for the judgment, may be recorded in any County Clerk Lien Record. The judgment or lien record abstract may be recorded in a county other than the county that contains the justice court that rendered the judgment without transcribing the justice court judgment to the circuit court for the county that contains the justice court that rendered the judgment, or recording a certified copy of the judgment or a lien record abstract for the judgment in the County Clerk Lien Record for the county that contains the justice court. If the judgment has been transcribed to circuit court, or a certified copy of the judgment or a lien record abstract for the judgment has been recorded in any County Clerk Lien Record, a lien record abstract for the judgment in the form provided by ORS 18.170 may be recorded in the County Clerk Lien Record for

any other county. From the time the certified copy of the judgment or lien record abstract for the judgment is recorded in the County Clerk Lien Record of another county, the judgment is a lien upon the real property of the defendant in that county.

(4) A certified copy of a certificate of extension filed under ORS 18.194, or a lien record abstract for the certificate of extension, may be transcribed to circuit court or recorded in a County Clerk Lien Record in the same manner as provided for judgments under this section and with like effect.

(5) The transcribing of a justice court judgment to circuit court under this section, or the recording of a certified copy of a justice court judgment or a lien record abstract under this section, does not extend the lien of the judgment more than 10 years from the original entry of the judgment in the justice court.

(6) The fee for filing a transcript with the clerk of the circuit court under subsection (2) of this section shall be as provided in ORS 21.235 (1). The fee for recording a certified copy of a justice court judgment or a lien record abstract under this section shall be as provided in ORS 205.320.

(7) A justice court and circuit court may enter into an agreement to allow for electronic transcription of justice court judgments under this section. A justice court and county clerk may enter into an agreement to allow for electronic recording of judgments and lien record abstracts under this section. [1999 c.788 §4 (enacted in lieu of 52.630); 2003 c.576 §96; 2003 c.737 §§80,81; 2007 c.339 §12; 2011 c.595 §120]

Note: Section 62 (1) and (2), chapter 788, Oregon Laws 1999, provides:
Sec. 62. (1) The repeal of ORS 52.630 by section 3 of this 1999 Act does not affect any judgment docketed in a circuit court under the provisions of ORS 52.630 (1997 Edition) before the effective date of this 1999 Act [October 23, 1999].

(2) Any judgment rendered by a justice court before the effective date of this 1999 Act that was not docketed in the circuit court under the provisions of ORS 52.630 (1997 Edition) before the effective date of this 1999 Act may become a lien on real property only in the manner provided by section 4 of this 1999 Act [52.635]. Any judgment rendered in a justice court on or after the effective date of this 1999 Act may become a lien on real property only in the manner provided by section 4 of this 1999 Act. [1999 c.788 §62(1),(2)]

52.640 Setoff of judgment; application and notice. A party against whom a judgment is given in a justice court may, upon three days' notice to the adverse party, apply to the justice of the court to have another judgment given in a justice court, between the same parties and against the adverse party, set off against the first mentioned judgment.

52.650 Right of appeal precludes setoff; procedure to set off judgment of another court. A judgment proposed as a setoff under ORS 52.640 must be final and no longer subject to appeal. If the judgment was given in another court than the one where the application is made, the party proposing the setoff must produce the transcript of the judgment, certified by the proper justice, which certificate shall also state how much of the judgment remains unsatisfied and that the transcript is given for the purpose of being a setoff against the judgment to which it is proposed as a setoff. [Amended by 2003 c.14 §23]

52.660 Enforcement of setoff judgment stayed. The justice making the transcript and certificate shall make an entry thereof in the docket of the justice and thereafter all proceedings to enforce the judgment shall be stayed, unless the transcript is returned with the certificate of the proper justice indorsed thereon, to the effect that it has not been allowed to be set off.

52.670 Setoff of mutual judgments. If upon the hearing of the application the justice finds that the judgments are mutual, the justice shall give judgment allowing the proposed setoff.

52.680 Setoff of judgments in different amounts; disallowance of setoff. If there is any difference in the amount of the two judgments, judgment for the difference must be given in favor of the party owning the larger judgment. If the justice refuses to allow the setoff, the justice shall so certify on the transcript and return it to the party.

52.690 [Repealed by 1999 c.788 §5]

52.700 Return on execution; to whom directed; duty of officer to execute writ. An execution issued by a justice must be made returnable within 30 days from the date thereof, and may be directed to the sheriff of the county, or any constable or marshal or police officer authorized to act as a constable therein, and must be executed by any one of such officers when delivered to the officer. [Amended by 1991 c.67 §8]

52.710 Renewal of execution; indorsement and entry of renewal. At any time before the expiration of the return day of the execution, it may be renewed for another period of 30 days, at the request of the plaintiff, by an indorsement to that effect made thereon by the justice. The indorsement must be dated and, if any part of the execution has been satisfied, must state the amount then due thereon. An entry of the renewal must also be made in the docket of the justice.

Chapter 53 — Appeals in Civil Actions

2017 EDITION

APPEALS IN CIVIL ACTIONS

JUSTICE COURTS

53.005   Application of ORS 53.005 to 53.125

53.010   Appeal from justice courts

53.020   Court to which appeal lies; designation of parties

53.030   Manner of taking appeal; notice; undertaking for costs and disbursements

53.040   Requisites of undertaking for costs and disbursements and stay of proceedings

53.050   Stay of proceedings without undertaking

53.060   Allowance of appeal; recall of execution when stay granted

53.070   Qualification of sureties

53.080   Enforcement of judgment notwithstanding appeal and undertaking for stay of proceedings

53.090   Transcript to be filed; proceedings on appeal

53.100   Amendment of pleadings in appellate court

53.110   Dismissal of appeal; judgment on dismissal or after trial; judgment against sureties

53.120   Insufficiency of undertaking as ground for dismissal of appeal

53.125   Judgment or order of appellate court

53.130   Writ of review in civil cases

53.005 Application of ORS 53.005 to 53.125. ORS 53.005 to 53.125 apply only to justice courts that have not become courts of record under ORS 51.025. Appeals of civil judgments in justice courts that have become courts of record under ORS 51.025 shall be as provided in ORS chapter 19 for appeals from judgments of circuit courts. [1999 c.682 §6]

53.010 Appeal from justice courts. Any party to a judgment in a civil action in a justice court, other than a judgment by confession or for want of an answer, may appeal therefrom when the sum in controversy is not less than $30, or when the action is for the recovery of personal property of the value of not less than $30, exclusive of disbursements in either case, also when the action is for the recovery of the possession of real property under ORS 105.110. [Amended by 1977 c.365 §4; 1977 c.416 §4]

53.020 Court to which appeal lies; designation of parties. An appeal is taken to the circuit court for the county wherein the judgment is given. The party appealing is known as the appellant and the adverse party as the respondent, but the title of the action is not thereby changed. [Amended by 1985 c.342 §8; 1995 c.658 §64]

53.030 Manner of taking appeal; notice; undertaking for costs and disbursements. An appeal is taken by serving, within 30 days after rendition of judgment, a written notice thereof on the adverse party, or the attorney of the adverse party, and filing the original with the proof of service indorsed thereon with the justice, and by giving the undertaking for the costs and disbursements on the appeal, as provided in ORS 53.040. A written acknowledgment of service by the respondent or the attorney of the respondent, indorsed on the notice of appeal, shall be sufficient proof of service. When the notice of appeal has been served and filed, the appellate court shall have jurisdiction of the cause. [Amended by 1973 c.477 §1]

53.040 Requisites of undertaking for costs and disbursements and stay of proceedings. The undertaking of the appellant must be given with one or more sureties, to the effect that the appellant will pay all costs and disbursements that may be awarded against the appellant on the appeal. The undertaking does not stay the proceedings unless the undertaking further provides that the appellant will satisfy any judgment that may be given against the appellant in the appellate court on the appeal. The undertaking must be filed with the justice within five days after the notice of appeal is given or filed. The justice may waive, reduce or limit the undertaking upon a showing of good cause, including indigency, and on such terms as shall be just and equitable. The justice or the appellate court may waive a failure to file the undertaking within the time required upon a showing of good cause for that failure. [Amended by 1983 c.673 §12]

53.050 Stay of proceedings without undertaking. If the judgment appealed from is in favor of the appellant, the proceedings thereon are stayed by the notice of appeal and the undertaking for the costs of the appeal.

53.060 Allowance of appeal; recall of execution when stay granted. When an appeal is taken, the justice must allow the same and make an entry thereof in the docket of the justice, stating whether the proceedings are thereby stayed or not. When the proceedings are stayed, if an execution has been issued to enforce judgment, the justice must recall the execution by written notice to the officer holding it. Thereupon it must be returned and all property taken thereon and not sold released. [Amended by 1981 c.898 §43]

53.070 Qualification of sureties. All sureties on an undertaking on appeal must have the qualifications established by ORCP 82. Challenges to the qualifications of sureties may be made as provided by ORCP 82. [Amended by 1997 c.71 §17]

53.080 Enforcement of judgment notwithstanding appeal and undertaking for stay of proceedings. When a judgment has been given for money in an action upon a contract to pay money, notwithstanding an appeal and undertaking for the stay of proceedings, the respondent may enforce the judgment, if within five days from the allowance of the appeal the respondent files with the justice an undertaking, with one or more sureties, to the effect that if the judgment is changed or modified on the appeal the respondent will make such restitution as the appellate court may direct. This undertaking must be taken by the justice on not less than two days' notice to the other party.

53.090 Transcript to be filed; proceedings on appeal. Within 30 days next following the allowance of the appeal, the appellant must cause to be filed with the clerk of the appellate court a transcript of the cause. The transcript must contain a copy of all the material entries in the justice docket relating to the cause or the appeal and any transcript or audio record made under ORS 51.105, and must have annexed thereto all the original papers relating to the cause or the appeal and filed with the justice. Upon the filing of the transcript with the clerk of the appellate court, the appeal is perfected. Thenceforth the action shall be deemed pending and for trial therein as if originally commenced in such court, and the court shall have jurisdiction of the cause and shall proceed to hear, determine and try it anew, disregarding any irregularity or imperfection in matters of form which may have occurred in the proceedings in the justice court. If the transcript and papers are not filed with the clerk of the appellate court within the time provided, the appellate court, or the judge thereof, may by order extend the time for filing the same upon such terms as the court or judge may deem just. However, such order shall be made within the time allowed to file the transcript. [Amended by 1985 c.342 §9; 2015 c.623 §9]

53.100 Amendment of pleadings in appellate court. The appellate court may, in furtherance of justice and upon such terms as may be just, allow the pleadings in the action to be amended so as not to change substantially the issue tried in the justice court or to introduce any new cause of action or defense.

53.110 Dismissal of appeal; judgment on dismissal or after trial; judgment against sureties. The appellate court may dismiss an appeal from a justice court if it is not properly taken and perfected. When an appeal is dismissed the appellate court must give judgment as it was given in the court below, and against the appellant for the costs and disbursements of the appeal. When judgment is given in the appellate court against the appellant, either with or without the trial of the action, it must also be given against the sureties in the undertaking of the appellant, according to its nature and effect.

53.120 Insufficiency of undertaking as ground for dismissal of appeal. An appeal cannot be dismissed on the motion of the respondent on account of the undertaking therefor being defective, if the appellant before the determination of the motion to dismiss will execute a sufficient undertaking and file it in the appellate court, upon such terms as may be deemed just.

53.125 Judgment or order of appellate court. The appellate court may give a final judgment in the cause, to be enforced as a judgment of such court; or the appellate court may give such other judgment or order as may be proper, and direct that the cause be remitted to the court below for further proceedings in accordance with the decision of the appellate court. [1959 c.558 §47; 1981 c.178 §4]

53.130 Writ of review in civil cases. No provision of ORS 53.005 to 53.125, in relation to appeals or the right of appeal in civil cases, shall be construed to prevent either party to a judgment given in a justice court from having it reviewed in the circuit court for errors in law appearing upon the face of the judgment or the proceedings connected therewith, as provided in ORS 34.010 to 34.100.

———————————

Chapter 54 — Juries

2017 EDITION

JURIES

JUSTICE COURTS

54.010   Trial jury defined

54.020   Jury not selected from jury list

54.030   Service and return of order; persons to be summoned

54.040   Insufficient number of jurors; summoning others; challenges

54.050   Qualifications of jurors

54.060   Making of jury lists

54.070   Number of names on list; certifying and filing list

54.090   Justice not in office or present when list was made must procure and file copy thereof

54.100   Drawing jury list; jury box; depositing ballots

54.110   Selection of jury from jury list

54.120   Manner of drawing jury panel; making and signing list of names for panel

54.130   Names drawn which are not entered on list of panel

54.140   Selection of jury by striking names from the panel

54.150   Order for jury selected from jury list; manner of summoning and forming jury; challenges

54.160   Punishment of jurors

54.010 Trial jury defined. A trial jury is a body of persons, six in number in the justice courts, sworn to try and determine a question of fact and drawn according to the mode provided for in this chapter.

54.020 Jury not selected from jury list. When a jury has been demanded by a party to an action in the justice court, and neither party requires that the jury be drawn from the jury list, the justice must make an order in writing, directed to the sheriff of the county, or to any constable of the district or to any marshal or police officer authorized to act as constable therein, commanding the sheriff, constable, marshal or police officer to summon six persons to serve as jurors in the action between the parties, naming the parties, at a time and place to be named in the order. The order shall require the jurors to appear before the justice forthwith, or at some future time to which the trial of the issue may be postponed. [Amended by 1991 c.67 §9]

54.030 Service and return of order; persons to be summoned. The officer serving the order for a jury must do so impartially by selecting only such persons as the officer knows, or has good reason to believe, are qualified according to law to serve as jurors in the court to which they are summoned and in the particular action for which they are selected. The officer must serve the order, by giving notice to each person selected of the time and place the person is required to appear and for what purpose, and return the same, according to the direction therein, with the names of the persons summoned, verified by the certificate of the officer.

54.040 Insufficient number of jurors; summoning others; challenges. If a sufficient number of jurors does not appear at the time and place required, or if any of those appearing are peremptorily challenged, or upon a challenge for cause are found disqualified, the justice must order the proper officer to summon a sufficient number of other qualified persons until the jury is complete. Each party is entitled to three peremptory challenges, and no more.

54.050 Qualifications of jurors. A person competent to act as a juror in a justice court, in addition to the qualifications prescribed in ORS 10.030, must be an inhabitant of the district in which the court is being held at the time the person is summoned, and must have been an inhabitant of that district for three months next preceding such time. [Amended by 1983 c.673 §13]

54.060 Making of jury lists. (1) The justice of the peace in each district shall, in January of each year, or in case of an omission or neglect so to do then as soon as possible thereafter, make a jury list for the district.

(2) A preliminary jury list shall be made by selecting names of inhabitants of the district by lot from the latest jury list sources. The jury list sources are the elector registration list for the district, copies of the Department of Transportation records for the county referred to in ORS 802.260 (2) furnished to the justice at county expense by the clerk of court, as defined in ORS 10.010, for the county and any other source that the justice determines will furnish a fair cross section of the inhabitants of the district.

(3) Jury list sources may not contain and the justice of the peace is not required to obtain information about individuals who are participants in the Address Confidentiality Program under ORS 192.820 to 192.868.

(4) From the preliminary jury list the names of those persons known not to be qualified by law to serve as jurors shall be deleted. The remaining names shall constitute the jury list. The preliminary jury list and jury list may be made by means of electronic equipment. [Amended by 1983 c.673 §14; 1987 c.681 §4; 2007 c.542 §15]

54.070 Number of names on list; certifying and filing list. The jury list shall:
(1) Contain the names of at least 50 persons, if there are that number of persons in the district who are qualified as provided in ORS 54.050.
(2) Contain the first name, the surname and the place of residence of each person named therein.
(3) Be certified by the justice of the peace and placed on file in the office of the justice. [Amended by 1975 c.233 §1; 1983 c.673 §15]

54.080 [Repealed by 1983 c.673 §26]

54.090 Justice not in office or present when list was made must procure and file copy thereof. A justice of the peace not in office or attendance when a jury list is made must procure, and file in the office of the justice of the peace, a certified copy thereof.

54.100 Drawing jury list; jury box; depositing ballots. Unless juries are drawn and selected from the jury list of the district by means of electronic equipment, the justice of the peace shall keep in the office of the justice a jury box. After the jury list is filed, the justice shall destroy all ballots remaining in the box and shall prepare and deposit in such box separate ballots, containing the name and place of residence of each person named in the list, and folded as nearly alike as practicable so that the name cannot be seen. [Amended by 1983 c.673 §16]

54.110 Selection of jury from jury list. When a jury is demanded in a justice court, instead of being selected by the officers, as provided in ORS 54.020 to 54.040, the jury must be drawn and selected from the jury list of the district, if either party requires it.

54.120 Manner of drawing jury panel; making and signing list of names for panel. When a jury is to be selected from the jury list of the district, the justice shall draw from the box in the presence of the parties, or select by means of electronic equipment, 12 ballots or names, or any greater number, if necessary, until the names of 12 persons, who are deemed able to attend at the time and place required, are obtained. The justice must make and sign a list of the 12 names thus drawn. [Amended by 1983 c.673 §17]

54.130 Names drawn which are not entered on list of panel. If it appears to the justice that a person whose name is drawn is dead or resides out of the district, the ballot must be destroyed or the name deleted. If it appears to the justice, or the justice has good reason to believe, that a person whose name is drawn is temporarily absent from the district, or is unwell, or so engaged as to be unable to attend at the time and place required without great inconvenience, the ballot or name must be laid aside, without the name being entered on the list drawn, and returned to the box or restored to the list from which selected by means of electronic equipment when the drawing is completed. A person whose name is drawn is deemed able to attend within the meaning of ORS 54.120, and the name of the person is deemed to be entered on the list drawn, except as provided in this section. [Amended by 1983 c.673 §18]

54.140 Selection of jury by striking names from the panel. When the drawing is completed, from the 12 names drawn the parties must select a jury by each striking from the list three names, alternately, commencing with the defendant. The remaining six must be summoned as jurors in the action.

54.150 Order for jury selected from jury list; manner of summoning and forming jury; challenges. The names of the six jurors so selected must be inserted in the order to summon a jury, and thereafter the proceedings in the summoning and formation of the jury must be conducted in the manner provided in ORS 54.020 to 54.040; but neither party is entitled to a peremptory challenge as to any of the six jurors.

54.160 Punishment of jurors. A person duly summoned to attend a justice court as a juror may be punished by the justice of the peace as provided for contempt of court if:
(1) The person fails to attend the justice court as required or fails to give a valid excuse for not attending;
(2) The person fails to give attention to matters before the jury;
(3) The person leaves the court without permission while the court is in session; or
(4) The person without valid excuse otherwise fails to complete required jury service. [Amended by 1999 c.605 §5]

———————————

Chapter 55 — Small Claims

SMALL CLAIMS

JUSTICE COURTS

55.011	Small claims department; jurisdiction
55.020	Commencement of action
55.030	Contents of claim
55.040	Verification and prosecution of claim
55.045	Notice of claim; content; service
55.055	Explanation to plaintiff of how notice may be served
55.065	Admission or denial of claim; request for jury trial
55.075	Time and place of hearing; procedure if right to jury trial asserted; fees
55.077	Additional time for appearances; default and dismissal
55.080	Formal pleadings unnecessary; issuance of attachment, garnishment or execution; costs of execution taxable
55.090	Appearance by parties and attorneys; witnesses

55.095   Counterclaim; procedure; fee; transfer of jurisdiction

55.100   Payment of judgment

55.110   Conclusiveness of judgment; appeal; costs and fees on appeal

55.120   Form of appeal; bond; proceedings in circuit court; no further appeal

55.130   Enforcement of judgment when no appeal is taken; fees

55.140   Separate docket for small claims department

55.010 [Amended by 1955 c.44 §1; 1959 c.326 §2; repealed by 1963 c.404 §1 (55.011 enacted in lieu of 55.010)]

55.011 Small claims department; jurisdiction. (1) Except as provided in subsection (8) of this section, in each justice court created under any law of this state there shall be a small claims department.
(2) Except as provided in this section, all actions for the recovery of money, damages, specific personal property, or any penalty or forfeiture must be commenced and prosecuted in the small claims department if the amount or value claimed in the action does not exceed $750.
(3) Except as provided in this section, an action for the recovery of money, damages, specific personal property, or any penalty or forfeiture may be commenced and prosecuted in the small claims department if the amount or value claimed in the action does not exceed $10,000.
(4) Class actions may not be commenced and prosecuted in the small claims department.
(5) Actions providing for statutory attorney fees in which the amount or value claimed does not exceed $750 may be commenced and prosecuted in the small claims department or may be commenced and prosecuted in the regular department of the justice court. This subsection does not apply to an action based on contract for which attorney fees are authorized under ORS 20.082.
(6) Jurisdiction of the person of the defendant in an action commenced in the small claims department shall be deemed acquired as of the time of service of the notice and claim.
(7) Except as provided in ORS 55.065 (2)(c), the provisions of ORS 55.020 to 55.140 shall apply with regard to proceedings in the small claims department of any justice court.
(8) If a justice court is located in the same city as a circuit court, the justice court need not have a small claims department if the justice court and the circuit court enter into an intergovernmental agreement that provides that only the circuit court will operate a small claims department. If an intergovernmental agreement is entered into under this subsection, the agreement must establish appropriate procedures for referring small claims cases to the circuit court. [1963 c.404 §2 (enacted in lieu of 55.010); 1965 c.569 §2; 1973 c.625 §3; 1973 c.812 §7; 1975 c.346 §2a; 1975 c.592 §2; 1983 c.673 §6; 1985 c.367 §3; 1987 c.725 §3; 1989 c.583 §1; 1995 c.227 §4; 1997 c.801 §108; 1999 c.84 §5; 1999 c.673 §4; 2001 c.542 §6; 2007 c.125 §5; 2011 c.595 §53]

55.020 Commencement of action. An action in the small claims department shall be commenced by the plaintiff appearing in person or by agent or assignee before the court and filing a verified claim in the form prescribed by the justice of the peace along with the fee prescribed by ORS 51.310 (1)(c). [Amended by 1989 c.583 §2]

55.030 Contents of claim. The claim shall contain the name and address of the plaintiff and of the defendant, followed by a plain and simple statement of the claim, including the amount and date the claim allegedly accrued. The claim shall include an affidavit signed by the plaintiff and stating that the plaintiff made a bona fide effort to collect the claim from the defendant before filing the claim with the justice court. [Amended by 1977 c.875 §11; 1989 c.583 §3]

55.040 Verification and prosecution of claim. All claims shall be verified by the real party in interest, the agent or assignee of the party. Any claim may be filed and prosecuted in the small claims department by such agent or the assignee of the cause of action upon which recovery is sought.

55.045 Notice of claim; content; service. (1) Upon the filing of a claim, the court shall issue a notice in the form prescribed by the court.
(2) The notice shall be directed to the defendant, naming the defendant, and shall contain a copy of the claim.
(3) If the amount or value claimed is $50 or more, the notice and claim shall be served upon the defendant in the manner provided for the service of summons and complaint in proceedings in the circuit courts.
(4) If the amount or value claimed is less than $50, the notice and claim shall be served upon the defendant either in the manner provided for the service of summons and complaint in proceedings in the circuit courts or by certified mail, at the option of the plaintiff. If service by certified mail is attempted, the court shall mail the notice and claim by certified mail addressed to the defendant at the last-known mailing address of the defendant within the territorial jurisdiction of the court. The envelope shall be marked with the words "Deliver to Addressee Only" and "Return Receipt Requested." The date of delivery appearing on the return receipt shall be prima facie evidence of the date on which the notice and claim was served upon the defendant. If service by certified mail is not successfully accomplished, the notice and claim shall be served in the manner provided for the service of summons and complaint in proceedings in the circuit courts.
(5) The notice shall include a statement in substantially the following form:

NOTICE TO DEFENDANT:
READ THESE PAPERS CAREFULLY!
    Within 14 DAYS after receiving this notice you MUST do ONE of the following things:
    Pay the claim plus fees and service expenses paid by plaintiff OR
    Demand a hearing OR
    Demand a jury trial
    If you fail to do one of the above things within 14 DAYS after receiving this notice, then upon written request from the plaintiff, the court will enter a judgment against you for the amount claimed plus fees and service expenses paid by the plaintiff.
    If you have questions about this notice, you should contact the court immediately.
_____ [1989 c.583 §5]

55.050 [Amended by 1965 c.619 §28; 1977 c.875 §12; 1981 s.s. c.3 §95; 1987 c.829 §2; repealed by 1989 c.583 §11]

55.055 Explanation to plaintiff of how notice may be served. The justice of the peace shall provide to each plaintiff who files a claim with the small claims department of the court of the justice of the peace a written explanation of how notice may be served in actions in the department. [1977 c.875 §21]

55.060 [Amended by 1977 c.875 §13; repealed by 1989 c.583 §11]

55.065 Admission or denial of claim; request for jury trial. Within 14 days after the date of service of the notice and claim upon the defendant as provided in ORS 55.045:

(1) If the defendant admits the claim, the defendant may settle it by:

(a) Paying to the court the amount of the claim plus the amount of the small claims fee and service expenses paid by the plaintiff. The court shall pay to the plaintiff the amounts paid by the defendant.

(b) If the claim is for recovery of specific personal property, delivering the property to the plaintiff and paying to the plaintiff the amount of the small claims fee and service expenses paid by the plaintiff.

(2) If the defendant denies the claim, the defendant:

(a) May demand a hearing in the small claims department in a written request to the court in the form prescribed by the court, accompanied by payment of the defendant's fee prescribed; and

(b) When demanding a hearing, may assert a counterclaim in the form provided by the court; or

(c) If the amount or value claimed exceeds $750, may demand a jury trial in a written request to the court in the form prescribed by the court, accompanied by payment of the appearance fee prescribed by ORS 51.310 (1)(b) together with the trial fee prescribed by ORS 52.410. The request shall designate a mailing address to which a summons and copy of the complaint may be served by mail. Thereafter, the plaintiff's claim will not be limited to the amount stated in the claim, though it must involve the same controversy. [1989 c.583 §6; 1995 c.227 §3]

55.070 [Amended by 1957 c.6 §1; 1965 c.619 §29; 1973 c.393 §3; 1977 c.875 §14; 1977 c.877 §14a; 1979 c.284 §87; repealed by 1989 c.583 §11]

55.075 Time and place of hearing; procedure if right to jury trial asserted; fees. (1) If the defendant demands a hearing in the small claims department of the court, the court shall fix a day and time for the hearing and shall mail to the parties a notice of the hearing time in the form prescribed by the court, instructing them to bring witnesses, documents and other evidence pertinent to the controversy.

(2) If the defendant asserts a counterclaim, the notice of the hearing time shall contain a copy of the counterclaim.

(3) If the defendant claims the right to a jury trial, the court shall notify the plaintiff to file a formal complaint within 20 days following the mailing of such notice. The notice shall instruct the plaintiff to serve a summons and copy of the complaint by mail on the defendant at the designated address of the defendant. Proof of service of the summons and complaint copy may be made by certificate of the plaintiff or plaintiff's attorney attached to the complaint prior to its filing. The plaintiff's claim in such formal complaint is not limited to the amount stated in the claim filed in the small claims department but it must involve the same controversy. The defendant shall have 10 days in which to move, plead or otherwise appear following the day on which the summons and copy of the complaint would be delivered to the defendant in due course of mail. Thereafter, the cause shall proceed as other causes in the justice court, and costs and disbursements shall be allowed and taxed and fees not previously paid shall be charged and collected as provided in ORS 51.310 and 52.410 for other cases tried in justice court, except that the appearance fee for plaintiff shall be an amount equal to the difference between the fee paid by the plaintiff as required by ORS 51.310 (1)(c) and the fee required of a plaintiff by ORS 51.310 (1)(a). [1989 c.583 §8]

55.077 Additional time for appearances; default and dismissal. (1) Upon written request, the court may extend to the parties additional time within which to make formal appearances required in the small claims department.

(2) If the defendant fails to pay the claim, demand a hearing or demand a jury trial, upon written request from the plaintiff, the court shall enter a judgment against the defendant for the relief claimed plus the amount of the small claims fee and service expenses paid by the plaintiff.

(3) If the plaintiff fails within the time provided to file a formal complaint pursuant to ORS 55.075 (3), the court shall:

(a) Dismiss the case without prejudice; and

(b) If the defendant applies therefor in writing to the court not later than 30 days after the expiration of the time provided for the plaintiff to file a formal complaint, refund to the defendant the amount of the jury trial fee paid by the defendant under ORS 55.065 (2)(c).

(4) If the defendant appears at the time set for hearing but no appearance is made by the plaintiff, the claim shall be dismissed with prejudice. If neither party appears, the claim shall be dismissed without prejudice.

(5) Upon good cause shown within 60 days, the court may set aside a default judgment or dismissal and reset the claim for hearing. [1989 c.583 §9]

55.080 Formal pleadings unnecessary; issuance of attachment, garnishment or execution; costs of execution taxable. No formal pleading, other than the claim and notice, shall be necessary. The hearing and disposition of all actions shall be informal, the sole object being to dispense justice between the litigants promptly. No attachment, garnishment or execution shall issue from the small claims department on any claim except as provided in this chapter. A prevailing party's costs in securing and service of such execution shall be taxed against the other party and recoverable as part of the judgment. [Amended by 1971 c.179 §1; 1977 c.875 §15]

55.090 Appearance by parties and attorneys; witnesses. (1) Except as may otherwise be provided by ORS 55.040, no attorney at law nor any person other than the plaintiff and defendant shall become involved in or in any manner interfere with the prosecution or defense of the litigation in the department without the consent of the justice of the justice court, nor shall it be necessary to summon witnesses. But the plaintiff and defendant may offer evidence in their behalf by witnesses appearing at the hearing, and the justice may informally consult witnesses or otherwise investigate the controversy and give judgment or make such orders as the justice deems right, just and equitable for the disposition of the controversy.

(2) Notwithstanding ORS 9.320, a party that is not a natural person, state or any city, county, district or other political subdivision or public corporation in this state may appear as a party to any action in the department without appearance by attorney.

(3) When spouses are both parties to an action, one spouse may appear on behalf of both spouses in mediation or litigation in the small claims department:

(a) With the written consent of the other spouse; or

(b) If the appearing spouse declares under penalty of perjury that the other spouse consents. [Amended by 1973 c.625 §4; 1987 c.158 §8; 1993 c.282 §3; 1997 c.808 §9; 2015 c.7 §4; 2017 c.268 §2]

55.095 Counterclaim; procedure; fee; transfer of jurisdiction. (1) The defendant in an action in the small claims department may assert as a counterclaim any claim that, on the date of issuance of notice pursuant to ORS 55.045, the defendant may have against the plaintiff and that arises out of the same transaction or occurrence that is the subject matter of the claim filed by the plaintiff.

(2) If the amount of the counterclaim asserted by the defendant exceeds $10,000, the justice of the peace shall strike the counterclaim and proceed to hear and dispose of the case as though the counterclaim had not been asserted unless the defendant files with the counterclaim a motion requesting that the case be transferred from the small claims department to a court of appropriate jurisdiction and an amount to pay the costs of the transfer. After the transfer the plaintiff's claim will not be limited to the amount stated in the claim filed with the justice of the peace, though it must involve the same controversy.

(3)(a) If the amount or value of the counterclaim exceeds the jurisdictional limit of the justice court for a counterclaim and the defendant files a motion requesting transfer and an amount to pay the costs of transfer as provided in subsection (2) of this section, the case shall be transferred to the circuit court for the county in which the justice court is located and be governed as provided in ORS 52.320 for transfers to the circuit court. The justice court shall notify the plaintiff and defendant, by mail within 10 days following the order of transfer, of the transfer. The notice to the plaintiff shall contain a copy of the counterclaim and shall inform the plaintiff as to further pleading by the plaintiff in the court of appropriate jurisdiction.

(b) Upon filing the motion requesting transfer, the defendant shall pay to the court of appropriate jurisdiction an amount equal to the difference between the fee paid by the defendant as required by ORS 51.310 (1)(c) and the appearance fee for a defendant in the court of appropriate jurisdiction. [1977 c.875 §22; 1981 s.s. c.3 §96; 1983 c.673 §8; 1985 c.367 §4; 1987 c.725 §4; 1987 c.829 §3; 1989 c.583 §7; 1995 c.658 §65; 1997 c.801 §109; 1999 c.84 §6; 2007 c.125 §6; 2011 c.595 §53a]

55.100 Payment of judgment. If the judgment is against a party to make payment, the party shall pay the same forthwith upon the terms and conditions prescribed by the justice of the peace. [Amended by 1977 c.875 §16]

55.110 Conclusiveness of judgment; appeal; costs and fees on appeal. The judgment of the court shall be conclusive upon the plaintiff in respect to the claim filed by the plaintiff and upon the defendant in respect to a counterclaim asserted by the defendant. The defendant may appeal if dissatisfied in respect to the claim filed by the plaintiff. The plaintiff may appeal if dissatisfied in respect to a counterclaim asserted by the defendant. A party entitled to appeal may, within 10 days after the entry of the judgment against the party, appeal to the circuit court for the county in which the justice court is located. If final judgment is rendered against the party appealing in the appellate court, that party shall pay, in addition to the judgment, an attorney's fee to the other party in the sum of $10. Appeals from the small claims department shall only be allowed in cases in which appeals would be allowed if the action were instituted and the judgment rendered in the justice courts, as is provided by law. [Amended by 1977 c.875 §17; 1985 c.342 §10; 1995 c.658 §66]

55.120 Form of appeal; bond; proceedings in circuit court; no further appeal. (1) The appeal from the small claims department may be in the following form:

In the Circuit Court for _____ County, Oregon.

Plaintiff,
vs.

Defendant.

Comes now_____, a resident of _____ County, Oregon, and appeals from the decision of the small claims department of the justice court for _____ District, _____County, Oregon, wherein a judgment for _____ dollars was awarded against the appellant on the _____ day of_____, 2__.

_____, Appellant.

(2) All appeals shall be filed with the justice of the peace and accompanied by a bond, with satisfactory surety, to secure the payment of the judgment, costs and attorney's fees, as provided in ORS 55.110. The appeal shall be tried in the circuit court without any other pleadings than those required in the justice court originally trying the cause. All papers in the cause shall be certified to the circuit court as is provided by law in other cases of appeals in civil actions in justice courts. The circuit court may require any other or further statements or information it may deem necessary for a proper consideration of the controversy. The appeal shall be tried in the circuit court without a jury. There shall be no appeal from any judgment of the circuit court rendered upon the appeal, but such judgment shall be final and conclusive. [Amended by 1977 c.875 §18; 1985 c.342 §11; 2005 c.22 §38]

55.130 Enforcement of judgment when no appeal is taken; fees. (1) If no appeal is taken by a party against whom a judgment to make payment is rendered and the party fails to pay the judgment according to the terms and conditions thereof, the justice of the peace before whom the hearing was had, may, on application of the prevailing party, certify the judgment in substantially the following form:

In the Justice Court for _____ District, _____County, Oregon.

Plaintiff,
vs.

Defendant.

In the Small Claims Department
This is to certify that in a certain action before me, the undersigned, had on this, the _____ day of_____, 2__, wherein _____ was plaintiff and _____ was defendant, jurisdiction of the defendant having been had by personal service (or otherwise), as provided by law, I then and there entered judgment against the (defendant or plaintiff) in the sum of ____ dollars, which judgment has not been paid.
Witness my hand this ____ day of_____, 2__.

_____

Justice of the Peace

Sitting in the Small

Claims Department.

(2) Upon the payment of a fee of $9, the justice of the peace shall forthwith enter the judgment transcript on the docket of the justice court. Thereafter execution and other process on execution provided by law may issue thereon as in other cases of judgments of justice courts, and transcripts of the judgments may be filed and entered in judgment dockets in circuit courts with like effect as in other cases. [Amended by 1965 c.619 §30; 1977 c.875 §19; 1987 c.829 §4; 1997 c.801 §134; 2015 c.623 §5]

55.140 Separate docket for small claims department. Each justice of the peace shall keep a separate docket for the small claims department of the court of the justice of the peace, in which the justice of the peace shall make a permanent record of all proceedings, orders and judgments had and made in the small claims department.

Made in United States
Troutdale, OR
10/16/2023

13777482R00224